Cisco CCNA Exam #640-607 Certification Guide

Wendell Odom, CCIE #1624

Cisco Press

201 West 103rd Street

Indianapolis, IN 46290 USA

Cisco CCNA Exam #640-607 Certification Guide

Wendell Odom

Published by:
Cisco Press
201 West 103rd Street
Indianapolis, IN 46290 USA

Printed in the United States of America 2 3 4 5 6 7 8 9 0

Second Printing April 2002

Library of Congress Cataloging-in-Publication Number: 2001098200

ISBN: 1-58720-055-4

Warning and Disclaimer

This book is designed to provide information about CCNA Exam #640-607. Every effort has been made to make this book as complete and accurate as possible, but no warranty or fitness is implied.

The information is provided on an "as is" basis. The authors, Cisco Press, and Cisco Systems, Inc. shall have neither liability nor responsibility to any person or entity with respect to any loss or damages arising from the information contained in this book or from the use of the discs or programs that may accompany it.

The opinions expressed in this book belong to the author and are not necessarily those of Cisco Systems, Inc.

Trademark Acknowledgments

All terms mentioned in this book that are known to be trademarks or service marks have been appropriately capitalized. Cisco Press or Cisco Systems, Inc. cannot attest to the accuracy of this information. Use of a term in this book should not be regarded as affecting the validity of any trademark or service mark.

Feedback Information

At Cisco Press, our goal is to create in-depth technical books of the highest quality and value. Each book is crafted with care and precision, undergoing rigorous development that involves the unique expertise of members of the professional technical community.

Reader feedback is a natural continuation of this process. If you have any comments regarding how we could improve the quality of this book, or otherwise alter it to better suit your needs, you can contact us through e-mail at feedback@ciscopress.com. Please be sure to include the book title and ISBN in your message.

We greatly appreciate your assistance.

Publisher	John Wait
Editor-In-Chief	John Kane
Cisco Systems Program Manager	Michael Hakkert
Executive Editor	Brett Bartow
Production Manager	Patrick Kanouse
Development Editor	Christopher Cleveland
Project Editor	Marc Fowler
Copy Editors	Gayle Johnson
	Krista Hansing
Technical Editors	David Barnes
	Tim Faulk
	Steven Kalman
	Barb Nolley
Team Coordinator	Tammi Ross
Book Designer	Gina Rexrode
Cover Designer	Louisa Klucznik
Composition	Scan Communications Group, Inc.
Indexer	Tim Wright

CISCO SYSTEMS

Corporate Headquarters
Cisco Systems, Inc.
170 West Tasman Drive
San Jose, CA 95134-1706
USA
http://www.cisco.com
Tel: 408 526-4000
800 553-NETS (6387)
Fax: 408 526-4100

European Headquarters
Cisco Systems Europe
11 Rue Camille Desmoulins
92782 Issy-les-Moulineaux
Cedex 9
France
http://www-europe.cisco.com
Tel: 33 1 58 04 60 00
Fax: 33 1 58 04 61 00

Americas Headquarters
Cisco Systems, Inc.
170 West Tasman Drive
San Jose, CA 95134-1706
USA
http://www.cisco.com
Tel: 408 526-7660
Fax: 408 527-0883

Asia Pacific Headquarters
Cisco Systems Australia,
Pty., Ltd
Level 17, 99 Walker Street
North Sydney
NSW 2059 Australia
http://www.cisco.com
Tel: +61 2 8448 7100
Fax: +61 2 9957 4350

Cisco Systems has more than 200 offices in the following countries. Addresses, phone numbers, and fax numbers are listed on the Cisco Web site at www.cisco.com/go/offices

Argentina • Australia • Austria • Belgium • Brazil • Bulgaria • Canada • Chile • China • Colombia • Costa Rica • Croatia • Czech Republic • Denmark • Dubai, UAE • Finland • France • Germany • Greece • Hong Kong • Hungary • India • Indonesia • Ireland Israel • Italy • Japan • Korea • Luxembourg • Malaysia • Mexico • The Netherlands • New Zealand • Norway • Peru • Philippines Poland • Portugal • Puerto Rico • Romania • Russia • Saudi Arabia • Scotland • Singapore • Slovakia • Slovenia • South Africa • Spain Sweden • Switzerland • Taiwan • Thailand • Turkey • Ukraine • United Kingdom • United States • Venezuela • Vietnam • Zimbabwe

About the Author

Wendell Odom, CCIE #1624, is a senior instructor with Skyline Computer. Currently, he is project leader for Skylabs, a service offering access to lab gear and exercises for Cisco Certification Exam practice (http://www.skylinecomputer.com/skylabs.htm). Wendell has worked in the networking arena for 19 years, working in pre- and post-sales technical consulting, teaching, and course development. He has authored portions of over 12 courses, including topics such as IP routing, MPLS, Cisco WAN switches, SNA protocols, and LAN troubleshooting.

About the Technical Reviewers

David Barnes manages Cisco's Advanced Services Team in Richardson, Texas. He is CCIE #6563, CCDP, MCSE+I, Master CNE, and a Certified Technical Trainer. The organization he manages specializes in network consulting for many of Cisco's largest customers. He designed, implemented, and managed networks for numerous Fortune 500 companies in the 10 years before he joined Cisco Systems, Inc. in 1999.

Tim Faulk is a professor and curriculum developer in the networks department of American Intercontinental University in Atlanta, GA. He holds a master's degree in education and a Cisco Certified Network Professional certification. He teaches Cisco technology, TCP/IP-related courses, and security courses. He is presently developing a master's program in network security.

Steven Kalman is the principal officer at Esquire Micro Consultants, which performs lecturing, writing, and consulting. He has more than 30 years of experience in data processing, with strengths in network design and implementation. He is an instructor and author for Learning Tree International and has written and reviewed many networking-related titles. He holds CCNA, CCDA, ECNE, CNE, CISSP, and CNI certifications.

Barb Nolley is the president and principal consultant for BJ Consulting, Inc., a small consulting firm that specializes in networking education. Since starting BJ Consulting, she has developed and taught training courses for Novell's Master CNE certification, as well as several courses for Cisco Systems' Engineering Education group and a CCNA track for the University of California-Riverside Extension. Her certifications include CCNA, CNE, and CNI. She lives in and works out of an RV with her husband, Joe.

Dedications

To the little boys and girls of our Cisco Press team who missed seeing their daddies for the final month it took to plow through the updates for this edition: I pray a blessing of more time with your daddies the next time we change the book! For my precious Hannah Grace, and for Matthew Christopher Cleveland, I thank you for your sacrifices!

Acknowledgments

I can write a 1000-page book, but I can't find enough words to describe the credit Chris Cleveland deserves for what is good about this book. Michael Jordan, Wayne Gretsky, Chris Cleveland—a list of the absolutely best at what they do! Chris, thanks for putting up with the hand-drawn figures, for meeting my schedule requirements, and for working hard during the holidays. Your ability to edit my style of writing and revising makes my job a breeze. I still refuse to write a book unless you develop it!

Brett Bartow steered the project as executive editor. In his usual unflappable way, he dealt with all the planning and changes with content issues, business issues, and the flow of information to us from Cisco—without ever getting rattled. In the process of hurry up and wait, and then really hurry up, Brett provided calm. Thanks for that, Brett!

For Tammi Ross, who handles a lot of the administrative tasks, thanks for handling things quickly and correctly. It's great to ask for something at a moment's notice, and things happen, no problems!

Behind the scenes at Cisco Press is a vast array of talented people—all of whom are shielded from us authors by the development editor, who was Chris Cleveland again in my case. These are people who take figure changes with scribbled notes and make something meaningful and nice-looking out of them. People who fix my English—I never made an A in an English class in high school or college! People who do the meticulous tasks that make the whole book come together—making sure figures fit on the same page as the text that refers to them, making sure the index is complete and accurate, and the like. I have the easy job in this arrangement. Many thanks to you all for the hard and good work!

The technical editors deserve most of the credit for making the content of this book robust and complete. Even with this third edition of the book, I am constantly amazed at what happens when talented technical editors take the time to really read through the material. Brett lined up the "first team" again, with three editors returning from the last edition—David Barnes, Steve Kalman, and Barb Nolley. Tim Faulk joined us for the first time, bringing his perspective from teaching CCNA classes at a university. All the credit for technical errors in this book lies with me, and all credit for the reduction of technical errors lies with these technical editors. But more importantly, they get credit for their input on improving sections, rewording phrases to clarify information, for finding better ways to describe how the technical pieces fit together, for fixing errors when there was a disconnection between my brain and what I wrote, and yes, even for finding errors in subnetting examples—and so much more. Without you, this book simply wouldn't be nearly as good or as accurate. Many thanks to you for that.

Finally, my boss at Skyline Computer, Mike Zanotto (a.k.a. Mike Z), Managing Director, helped this project by letting me schedule the new CCIE Skylabs remote lab offering to go live the same day I had to have this book's manuscript completed! Seriously, Z always helped by finding a way to give me the time I needed to work on this book and by making sure the job was fun. Thanks, Mike!

Finally, no acknowledgments section could be complete without acknowledging my wife, Kris, who took on all the duties at home with our 7-month-old child during the last month of getting this edition written. She was a trouper, sacrificing without being asked. Thank you so much, my love! Finally, to Jesus Christ, who gives us strength when things are tough, and peace beyond belief—thank you.

Contents at a Glance

Table of Contents

Foreword

Cisco CCNA Exam #640-607 Certification Guide is a complete study tool for the Cisco Certified Network Associate exam. It helps you to assess your knowledge, identify areas to concentrate your study, and master key concepts to help you succeed on the exam and in your daily job. The book is filled with features that help you master the skills to install, configure, and operate LAN, WAN, and dial-access services for small networks—skills you must master to become an effective CCNA professional. This book was developed in cooperation with the Cisco Internet Learning Solutions Group. Cisco Press books are the only self-study books authorized by Cisco for CCNA exam preparation.

Cisco Systems and Cisco Press present this material in a text-based format to provide another learning vehicle for our customers and the broader user community in general. Although a publication does not duplicate the instructor-led or e-learning environment, we acknowledge that not everyone responds in the same way to the same delivery mechanism. It is our intent that presenting this material through a Cisco Press publication will enhance the transfer of knowledge to a broad audience of networking professionals.

Cisco Press will present study guides on existing and future exams through these Exam Certification Guides to help achieve Cisco Internet Learning Solutions Group's principle objectives: to educate the Cisco community of networking professionals and to enable that community to build and maintain reliable, scalable networks. The Cisco Career Certifications and classes that support these certifications are directed at meeting these objectives through a disciplined approach to progressive learning. In order to succeed on the Cisco Career Certifications exams, as well as in your daily job as a Cisco certified professional, we recommend a blended learning solution that combines instructor-led, e-learning, and self-study training with hands-on experience. Cisco Systems has created an authorized Cisco Learning Partner program to provide you with the most highly qualified instruction and invaluable hands-on experience in lab and simulation environments. To learn more about Cisco Learning Partner programs that are available in your area, please go to www.cisco.com/go/training.

The books that Cisco Press creates, in partnership with Cisco Systems, meet the same standards for content quality demanded of the courses and certifications. Our intent is that you will find this and subsequent Cisco Press certification and training publications of value as you build your networking knowledge base.

Thomas M. Kelly
Vice President, Internet Learning Solutions Group
Cisco Systems, Inc.
March 2002

Icons Used in This Book

Throughout this book, you will see the following icons used for networking devices:

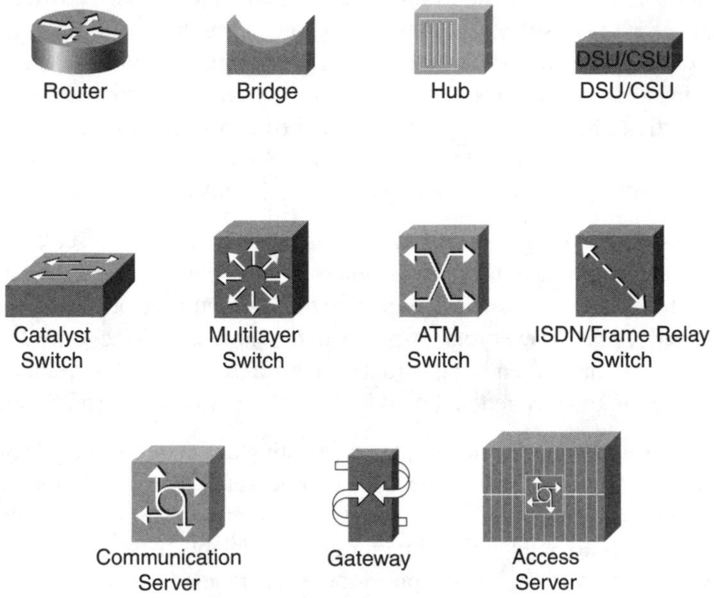

The following icons are used for peripherals and other devices:

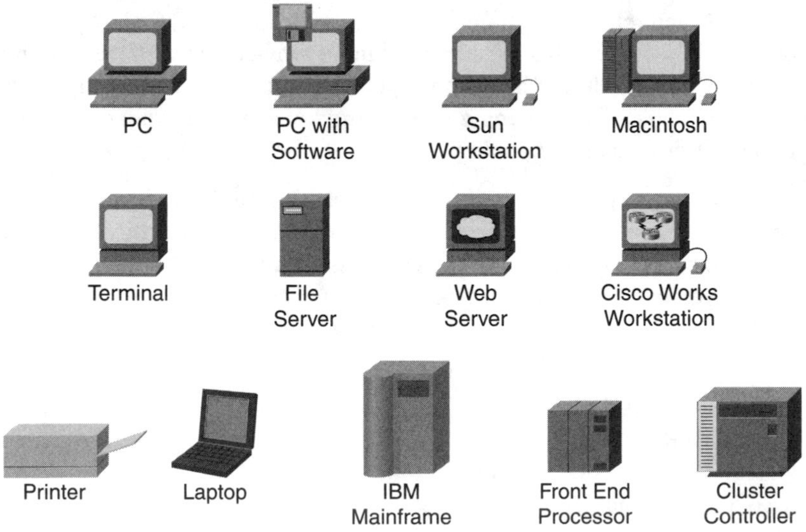

The following icons are used for networks and network connections:

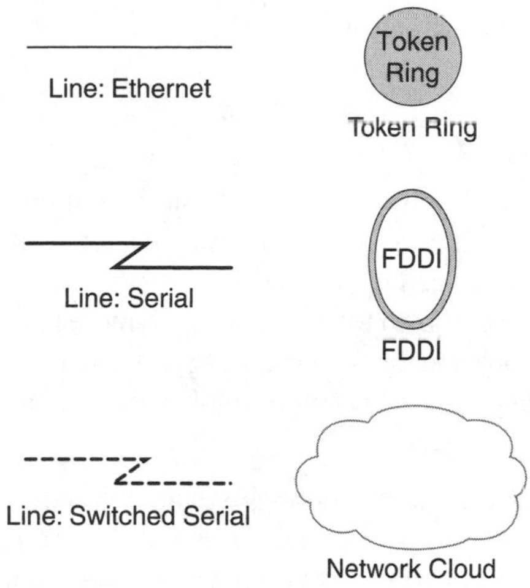

Command Syntax Conventions

The conventions used to present command syntax in this book are the same conventions used in the IOS Command Reference. The Command Reference describes these conventions as follows:

- Vertical bars (|) separate alternative, mutually exclusive elements.
- Square brackets ([ ]) indicate optional elements.
- Braces ({ }) indicate a required choice.
- Braces within brackets ([{ }]) indicate a required choice within an optional element.
- **Boldface** indicates commands and keywords that are entered exactly as shown. In configuration examples and output (not general command syntax), boldface indicates commands that are manually input by the user (such as a **show** command).
- *Italic* indicates arguments for which you supply values.

Introduction: Overview of Certification and How to Succeed

Professional certifications have been an important part of the computing industry for many years and will continue to become more important. Many reasons exist for these certifications, but the most popularly cited reason is that of credibility. All other considerations held equal, the certified employee/consultant/job candidate is considered more valuable than one who is not.

Objectives and Methods

The most important and somewhat obvious objective of this book is to help you pass the CCNA exam (#640-607). In fact, if the primary objective of this book were different, the book's title would be misleading. However, the methods used in this book to help you pass the CCNA exam are also designed to make you much more knowledgeable about how to do your job. Although this book and the accompanying CD together have more than 500 questions, the method in which they are used is not to simply make you memorize as many questions and answers as you possibly can.

Key methodologies used in this book are to help you discover the exam topics on which you need more review, to help you fully understand and remember those details, and to help you prove to yourself that you have retained your knowledge of those topics. So, this book does not try to help you pass by memorization, but by truly learning and understanding the topics. The CCNA exam is the foundation for many of the Cisco professional certifications, and it would be a disservice to you if this book did not help you truly learn the material. Therefore, this book helps you pass the CCNA exam by using the following methods:

- Helping you discover which test topics you have not mastered
- Providing explanations and information to fill in your knowledge gaps
- Supplying exercises and scenarios that enhance your ability to recall and deduce the answers to test questions
- Providing practice exercises on the topics and the testing process via test questions on the CD

Who Should Read This Book?

This book is not designed to be a general networking topics book, although it can be used for that purpose. This book is intended to tremendously increase your chances of passing the CCNA exam. Although other objectives can be achieved from using this book, it was written with one goal in mind: to help you pass the exam.

So why should you want to pass the CCNA exam? To get a raise. To show your manager you are working hard to increase your skills. To fulfill a requirement from your manager before he or she will spend money on another course. To enhance your resume. To please your reseller-employer, who needs more certified employees for a higher discount from

Cisco. To prove that you know the topic, if you learned through on-the-job training (OJT) rather than from taking the prerequisite classes. Or one of many other reasons.

Others who might want to read this book are those considering skipping Cisco's Interconnecting Cisco Network Devices (ICND) course to take Cisco's Building Scalable Cisco Networks (BSCN) or Building Cisco Multilayer Switched Networks (BCMSN) courses. If you can answer a high percentage of the questions in this book, you should be ready for those courses.

Strategies for Exam Preparation

The strategy you use for CCNA preparation might vary from strategies used by other readers, mainly based on the skills, knowledge, and experience you already have obtained. For instance, if you have attended Cisco's ICND course, you need to take a slightly different approach compared to someone who has gained Cisco knowledge through on-the-job training. Chapter 1, "All About the Cisco Certified Network Associate Certification," includes a strategy that should closely match your background. Regardless of the strategy you use or your background, this book is designed to help you get to the point where you can pass the exam with the least amount of time required. For instance, there is no need for you to practice or read about IP addressing and subnetting if you fully understand it. However, many people like to make sure that they truly know a topic and thus read over material they already know. Several of this book's features help you gain the confidence you need to be convinced that you know some material already. The features also help you know which topics you need to study more.

How This Book Is Organized

This book contains 10 core chapters—Chapters 2 through 11. Each chapter covers a subset of the topics on the exam. Along with these core chapters, three other chapters help you succeed on the CCNA exam. Chapter 1 helps you understand how to use this book to efficiently and effectively study for the CCNA exam. Chapter 12 is full of lab scenarios that force you to think about all the topics in the book, which helps you with final preparation. And, if you can get access to some lab gear, read Chapter 13—it's full of topical lab exercises.

The core chapters cover the following topics:

- **Chapter 2, "Cisco IOS Software Fundamentals"**

The Cisco IOS™ Software runs on a variety of Cisco products, particularly in routers and in some LAN switches. This chapter covers many of the features and functions of the Cisco IOS Software, as well as its command-line interface (CLI). Also included in this chapter are details about router hardware.

- **Chapter 3, "OSI Reference Model and Layered Communication"**

  The OSI reference model is mainly used today for comparison to other protocol architectures. This chapter discusses the purposes and meanings behind the use of a layered model. The features typically implemented at the various layers are covered, and sample protocols for each layer are given. Much of this information is conceptual and is not necessarily needed in order to implement networks, but it is covered on the exam. Also covered in Chapter 3 are the concepts involved in the typical operation of the OSI network and data link layers. This conceptual discussion is vital to a complete understanding of OSI Layer 2 and Layer 3 operation.

- **Chapter 4, "LANs, Bridges, and Switches"**

  LANs, particularly the various forms of Ethernet, are covered in this chapter. It also covers the concepts behind LAN segmentation using bridges, switches, and routers—a popular set of exam topics, according to the list of exam topics posted on Cisco's Web site. Basic bridge and switch operation is also covered, along with the concepts of collision domains and broadcast domains. The chapter ends with coverage of the Cisco 1900 series LAN switch CLI.

- **Chapter 5, "Intermediate LANs: Spanning Tree, VLANs, and Trunking"**

  Most LANs with multiple interconnected switches have redundant Ethernets between the switches. For such a LAN to be usable, Spanning-Tree Protocol (STP) must be used. The first topic in this chapter describes how STP prevents loops while allowing the redundancy to be used for backup purposes. EtherChannel, a feature that helps optimize STP, is also covered.

  The second section in this chapter covers virtual LANs (VLANs). VLANs allow the engineer to create multiple broadcast domains in a single switch, or spanning multiple interconnected switches. When you use VLANs, interconnected switches need to use VLAN trunking, which is also covered in this chapter. The chapter ends with coverage of configuration details for all these features.

- **Chapter 6, "TCP/IP and IP Routing"**

  This chapter begins by describing TCP and UDP, the two main options for OSI Layer 4 protocols in TCP/IP. After TCP and UDP, a couple other short topics, ARP and ICMP, are covered. The TCP/IP protocols require ARP and ICMP in order to work.

You also need solid skills with IP addressing and subnetting to succeed as a network engineer, or on the CCNA exam. The second section of this chapter details IP addressing and subnetting, including some tricks that make the math required to answer test questions a bit easier.

Finally, you need to be able to configure TCP/IP in a Cisco router. Actually, that part of the chapter is a bit anticlimactic, because configuring IP is pretty easy. Included in that section are some additional features about how to troubleshoot and manage an IP network.

- **Chapter 7, "Routing and Routing Protocols"**

  This chapter deals with the concepts and configuration required to fill a router's routing table. Cisco expects CCNAs to demonstrate a comfortable understanding of the logic behind the routing of packets and the different-but-related logic behind a routing protocol. This chapter focuses on *routing protocols*—the protocols used to discover routes.

  The CCNA exam covers the details of distance vector logic, so this topic is covered in the first section of this chapter. This is the logic used by the Routing Information Protocol (RIP) and Interior Gateway Routing Protocol (IGRP), as well as IP RIP. Along the way, alternative routing protocol algorithms (link-state and Diffusing Update Algorithm [DUAL]) are mentioned briefly. Implementation details of RIP (Version 1 and Version 2) and IGRP are covered next. Because EIGRP configuration is similar to IGRP, it is also covered briefly.

- **Chapter 8, "Understanding Access List Security"**

  Cisco expects CCNAs to understand security from the perspective of filtering traffic using access lists. Access lists are important to CCNA candidates because practically every network uses them. If you do more than basic filtering, access lists can become very tricky. Access lists are likely to remain a core competency issue for router support personnel for a long time. Also, several other IOS features call on access list logic to perform packet-matching features.

  This chapter covers standard and extended IP access lists, as well as named IP access lists.

- **Chapter 9, "WAN Protocols and Design"**

  This chapter covers the two popular data link protocols used on point-to-point links—HDLC and PPP. HDLC is pretty simple, but PPP has a few more interesting features. ISDN concepts and configuration are also covered, with a fair number of samples covering dial-on-demand routing, which is one way of causing a dialed ISDN connection to be established between routers.

- **Chapter 10, "Frame Relay Concepts and Configuration"**

Engineers deploy Frame Relay more than any other WAN protocol today, so it is no surprise that Frame Relay is an important topic for the CCNA exam. This chapter reviews the details of how Frame Relay accomplishes its goal of delivering frames to multiple WAN-connected sites. This chapter covers all the terminology and concepts of Frame Relay that are covered on the exam. This chapter also describes Frame Relay configuration, with its many options.

- **Chapter 11, "Novell IPX"**

  Routing for IP and IPX is similar, so if you understand IP routing, you probably will find IPX routing easy to grasp. Routing protocols for IP and IPX are also similar. However, unlike TCP/IP, Novell relies on the ability for clients to find their servers, so Novell uses protocols such as Service Advertisement Protocol (SAP) to advertise information about servers. This chapter briefly reviews the concepts that are similar to TCP/IP, details the concepts that are specific to Novell, and helps you refine your retention and recall of the configuration with questions and scenarios. This chapter also describes Novell access lists.

When you are finished with the core chapters, you have several options as to how to finish your exam preparation. Additional scenarios in Chapter 12 provide a method of final preparation with more questions and exercises. If you have access to lab equipment, Chapter 13 provides some lab exercises that can guide you through the hands-on learning experience. You can review the questions at the end of each chapter, and you can use the CD's testing software to practice the exam.

The core chapters have several features that help you make the best use of your time:

- **"Do I Know This Already?" Quiz and Quizlets**—Each chapter begins with a quiz that helps you determine the amount of time you need to spend studying that chapter. The quiz is broken into smaller sections called "quizlets," which correspond to a section of the chapter. If you follow the directions at the beginning of the chapter, the "Do I Know This Already?" quiz directs you to study all or particular parts of the chapter.

- **Foundation Topics**—These are the core sections of each chapter. They explain the protocols, concepts, and configuration for the topics in that chapter.

- **Foundation Summary**—Near the end of each chapter, a summary collects the most important tables and figures from the chapter. The "Foundation Summary" section is designed to help you review the key concepts in the chapter if you scored well on the "Do I Know This Already?" quiz. This section is an excellent tool for last-minute review.

- **Q&A**—Each chapter ends with a Q&A section that forces you to exercise your recall of the facts and processes described inside that chapter. The questions are generally harder than the actual exam, partly because the questions are in "short answer" format, instead of multiple choice. These questions are a great way to increase the accuracy of your recollection of the facts.
- **Extra Credit**—Network engineers need to know more than the CCNA exam covers to build networks. Most chapters contain a few more advanced topics that are not on the CCNA exam, but that are very important when building networks with the technologies described in that chapter. The book denotes these short sections as "extra credit"—ignore them if you are focusing only on the exam, but read them if you are preparing to use this knowledge in your job soon.
- **Scenarios**—Located at the end of most chapters, the scenarios allow a much more in-depth examination of a network implementation. Rather than posing a simple question asking for a single fact, the scenarios let you design and build networks (at least on paper) without the clues inherent in a multiple-choice quiz format.
- **CD-based practice exam**—The companion CD contains a large number of questions not included in the book. You can answer these questions by using the simulated exam feature or the topical review feature. This is the best tool for helping you prepare for the test-taking process.

Approach

Retention and recall are the two features of human memory most closely related to performance on tests. This exam preparation guide focuses on increasing both retention and recall of the exam topics. The other human characteristic involved in successfully passing the exam is intelligence, but this book does not address that issue!

Adults' retention is typically less than that of children. For example, it is common for 4-year-olds to pick up basic language skills in a new country faster than their parents. Children retain facts as an end unto itself; adults typically either need a stronger reason to remember a fact or must have a reason to think about that fact several times to retain it in memory. For these reasons, a student who attends a typical Cisco course and retains 50 percent of the material is actually quite an amazing student.

Memory recall is based on connectors to the information that needs to be recalled. The greater the number of connectors to a piece of information, the better the chance and speed of recall. For example, if the exam asks what ARP stands for, you automatically add information to the question. You know the topic is networking because of the nature of the test. You might recall the term "ARP broadcast," which implies that ARP is the name of something that flows in a network. Maybe you do not recall all three words in the acronym, but you recall that it has something to do with addressing. Of course, because the test is multiple-choice, if only one answer begins with "address," you have a pretty good guess. Having read the answer "Address Resolution Protocol," you might even have the infamous "aha" experience, in which you are then sure that your answer is correct (and possibly a brightly lit lightbulb is hovering over your head). All these added facts and assumptions are the connectors that eventually lead your brain to the fact that needs to be recalled. Of course, recall and retention work together. If you do not retain the knowledge, it will be difficult to recall it.

This book is designed with features to help you increase retention and recall. It does this in the following ways:

- By providing succinct and complete methods of helping you decide what you recall easily and what you do not recall at all.
- By giving references to the exact passages in the book that review the concepts you did not recall so that you can quickly be reminded of a fact or concept. Repeating information that connects to another concept helps retention, and describing the same concept in several ways throughout a chapter increases the number of connectors to the same piece of information.
- By including exercise questions that supply fewer connectors than multiple-choice questions. This helps you exercise recall and avoids giving you a false sense of confidence, as an exercise with only multiple-choice questions might do. For example, fill-in-the-blank questions require you to have better recall than a multiple-choice question.

- By pulling the entire breadth of subject matter together. Chapter 12 contains scenarios and several related questions that cover every topic on the exam. It gives you a chance to prove that you have mastered the subject matter. This reduces the connectors implied by questions residing in a particular chapter and requires you to exercise other connectors to remember the details.
- Finally, accompanying this book is a CD-ROM that has exam-like multiple-choice questions. These help you practice taking the exam and let you get accustomed to the time restrictions imposed during the exam.

CHAPTER 1

All About the Cisco Certified Network Associate Certification

Congratulations! You have taken your first step toward becoming a member of the group of network professionals who are Cisco Career Certified. The credibility you gain by becoming a Cisco Certified Network Associate (CCNA) is the first important key step to opening doors for career advancement in networking.

In case you have already heard some things about the exam, be forewarned—the exam format has changed, as compared with the other Cisco exams, including the old CCNA exam. The latest CCNA exam (test number 640-607) includes the usual types of questions—multiple-choice, single-answer; multiple-choice, multiple-answer; fill-in-the-blank; and drag-and-drop questions. However, for the first time, *Cisco is including router and switch simulations on the exam.* So, your ability to not just remember command syntax but also know what commands to use will be very important. This book is filled with lots of extensive examples as well as complete topical lab scenarios at the end of the chapters designed to help you prepare for the hands-on portions of the exam, even if you do not have lab equipment. If you can get access to some equipment, this book includes a specific lab exercise chapter in addition to more than 20 lab scenarios throughout Chapters 2 through 11. So, you have lots of different scenarios and lab exercises that you can perform on your own gear or using a lab rental service.

You can take the exam either from Vue (www.vue.com) or from Sylvan Prometric (www.2test.com). In the past, Cisco has changed the number of questions and passing score without notice, so, over time, the duration and number of questions per exam will vary. The older version of the test, 640-507, used a point-scoring system in which your score was between 300 and 1000, with a passing score being 849 or better.

Cisco generally succeeds in making the exam truly prove that you know the topic. The exam questions are painstakingly formulated to reduce the number of clues to giving away the correct answer. The test adapts to you—if you answer a question wrong, you will get more questions on that topic. Currently, there are 65 questions and 75 minutes in which to answer them—not a lot of time. And you cannot go back and change earlier answers—when you click on the Next button, you're done with that question!

Be aware that when you register for the exam, you might be notified of a specific length of time; when you actually log in to the testing software at the testing center, you might find that the testing time is 15 minutes shorter. That's because the testing company expects some time to be required for getting settled and taking the tutorial on the testing engine or for taking a survey.

The "read the book and pass the test" method of certification does not typically work with CCNA. So much of networking relates to how the concepts, protocols, and configurations interact, so it is easy for Cisco to create questions that test your understanding more than just asking for a simple fact. Every vendor, including Cisco, hopes to create certification tests that do not become too easy and, therefore, meaningless. Cisco's philosophy is that, by passing the exam, you fully understand the concepts. More important, Cisco wants to be sure that passing the exam proves that you have the skills to actually implement the features, not just talk about them—that's why simulations are included. From a statistical perspective, those of you who use routers and switches every day have a better chance of passing because more of you will easily remember the commands needed for the simulation questions. But do not despair—CCNA certification can be achieved through study, plus some hands-on experience. In the end, if Cisco succeeds in maintaining the difficulty of the CCNA exam, your CCNA certification will remain valuable.

Overview of Cisco Certifications

Cisco measures the technical readiness of channel partners (resellers) and professional services partners partially by requiring specific numbers of certified employees. For instance, Premier, Silver, and Gold Channel Partners are required to have either two or four CCNAs on staff, along with Cisco professional- and expert-level certified individuals. (see http://www.cisco.com/warp/public/765/partner_programs/certification/requirements.shtml for details). Cisco fulfills only a small portion of its orders through direct sale from Cisco; most often, a Cisco reseller is involved. Also, Cisco has not attempted to become the primary source for consulting and implementation services for network deployment using Cisco products; instead, the company prefers to use partners as much as possible. With that business model, a great need arose to certify the skill levels of the partner companies.

The Cisco Certified Internetworking Expert (CCIE) program was Cisco's first foray into certifications. Introduced in 1994, the CCIE was designed to be one of the most respected, difficult-to-achieve certifications. To certify, a person must pass a written test (also given at Sylvan Prometric centers) and then pass a one-day, hands-on lab test administered by Cisco. Cisco does not publish numbers on pass/fail rates for CCIE or the other certifications, but rumors have it that the failure rate on all lab test takers is more than 50 percent, with failure rate for first-time lab takers at more than 80 percent; a typical CCIE reportedly takes the lab test three times before passing.

Cisco requires a partner to accumulate points, based on the number of employees with certain certifications, to become a Premier, Silver, or Gold Channel Partner. The status, in turn, dictates the discount received by the reseller when buying from Cisco. This practice continues to be a good way for Cisco to judge the commitment of resellers to hire people with proven Cisco skills, which then improves customer satisfaction—and customer satisfaction is tied to every Cisco executive's bonus plan.

Historically, CCIE was the first and only Cisco certification for about four years (1994 to 1998). As Cisco's base of channel partners grew, The CCIE certification did not provide enough flexibility toward the goal of certifying resellers. For instance, there are around 6,909 CCIEs worldwide (as of January 2002) and about 3,000 resellers—and not all the CCIEs work for resellers, of course. More important, some resellers did not need a CCIE on staff, except to get a better discount. Thus, Cisco needed certifications that were less rigorous than CCIE, which would allow Cisco more granularity in judging the skills of the staff at a partner company. So, Cisco created several additional certifications, with CCNA included. Figure 1-1 shows the CCIE and career certifications for routing and switching.

Figure 1-1 *Cisco Routing and Switching Certifications*

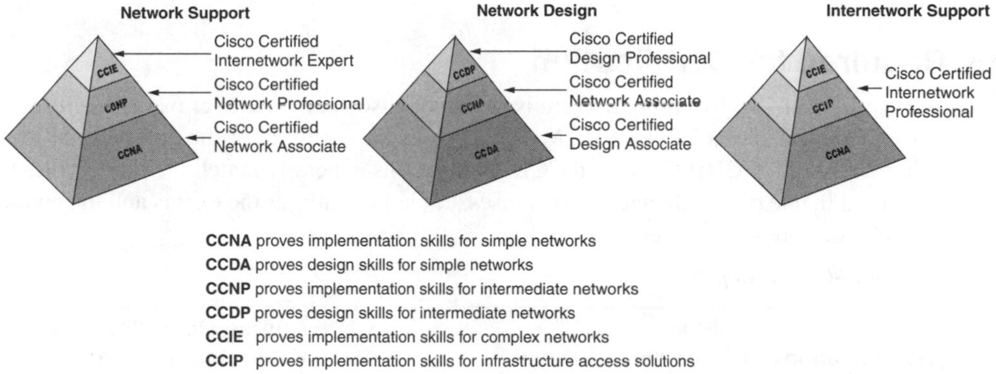

Instead of instituting just one level of certification besides CCIE, Cisco created two additional levels: an associate level and a professional level. CCNA is the more basic, and CCNP is the intermediate level between CCNA and CCIE. CCDA, CCDP, and CCIP are a few of the more closely related certifications. You can view these details at Cisco's Web site:

www.cisco.com/warp/public/10/wwtraining/certprog/lan/course.html
www.cisco.com/warp/customer/10/wwtraining/certprog/c_and_s/ccip/
www.cisco.com/warp/customer/10/wwtraining/certprog/lan2/course.html.

Cisco created two categories of certifications: one to certify implementation skills and the other to certify design skills. Resellers working in a presale environment need more design skills, whereas services companies need more implementation skills. So, the CCNA and CCNP certifications provide implementation-oriented certifications, whereas the CCDA and CCDP certifications provide design-oriented certifications.

Several of the certifications require other certifications as a prerequisite. For instance, CCNP certification requires CCNA as a prerequisite. Also, CCDP requires both CCDA and CCNA certification. CCIE, however, does not require any other certification before the written and lab tests, mainly for historical reasons.

The Cisco Certified Internetworking Professional (CCIP) is a more recent addition to the Cisco series of certifications. Cisco's customers fall into several categories, the largest two being what Cisco terms "enterprise" and "service provider." The CCIP certification is a professional-level certification, like CCNP, that is more oriented toward service provider personnel. Although CCIP does not require CCNA certification first, it is strongly recommended.

Cisco certifications have taken on a much larger role in the networking industry. From a career standpoint, Cisco certification certainly can be used to help you get a new job. Or, you can add certification to your performance-evaluation plan and justify a raise based on passing an exam. If you are looking for a new job, not only might certification help you land the job, but it actually might help you make more money!

Exams Required for Certification

To certify for CCNA, a single exam is required: Cisco exam number 640-607. For CCDA, a single exam is required as well. Multiple exams are required for the professional-level certifications—CCNP, CCIP, and CCDP. The exams generally match the same topics that are covered in one of the official Cisco courses. Table 1-1 outlines the exams and the courses with which they are most closely matched.

Table 1-1 *Exam-to-Course Mappings*

Certification	Exam Number	Name	Course Most Closely Matching Exam Requirements
CCNA	640-607	CCNA Exam	Interconnecting Cisco Network Devices (ICND).
CCDA	640-441	DCN Exam	Designing Cisco Networks.
CCNP	640-503	Routing Exam	Building Scalable Cisco Networks (BSCN).
	640-504	Switching Exam	Building Cisco Multilayer Switched Networks (BCMSN).
	640-505	Remote Access Exam	Building Cisco Remote Access Networks (BCRAN).
	640-509*	Foundation Exam	BSCN, BCMSN, and BCRAN.
	640-506	Support Exam	Cisco Internetwork Troubleshooting (CIT).
CCDP	640-503	Routing Exam	Building Scalable Cisco Networks (BSCN).
	640-504	Switching Exam	Building Cisco Multilayer Switched Networks (BCMSN).
	640-505	Remote Access Exam	Building Cisco Remote Access Networks (BCRAN).

Table 1-1 *Exam-to-Course Mappings (Continued)*

Certification	Exam Number	Name	Course Most Closely Matching Exam Requirements
	640-509*	Foundation Exam	BSCN, BCMSN, and BCRAN.
	640-025	CID Exam	Cisco Internetwork Design (CID).
CCIP	640-900	BSCI	Building Scalable Cisco Internetworks.
	640-905	Mcast+Qos Exam	Implementing Cisco Multicast.
			Implementing Cisco QoS.
		Various	Elective exam(s). Topics include MPLS, CDN, cable, DSL, metro, packet telephony, and security.

*Exam 640-509 meets the same requirements as passing these three exams: 640-503, 640-504, and 640-505.

Other Cisco Certifications

Cisco has many other certifications as well, as summarized in Table 1-2. Refer to Cisco's Web site at www.cisco.com/warp/public/10/wwtraining/certprog for the latest information.

Table 1-2 *Additional Cisco Certifications*

Certification	Purpose, Prerequisites
CCIE Routing & Switching	The granddaddy of them all! CCIE focused on routing and switching, and is the logical conclusion after getting CCNA and then CCNP.
CCIP	Cisco Certified Internetworking Professional is in concept like CCNP, with a focus on service provider–oriented technologies.
CCIE Communications and Services	CCIE, with a focus on service provider–oriented technologies. Replaces the old CCIE WAN.
CCIE Security	CCIE, requiring IP and IP routing knowledge as well as security.
CCNA WAN	CCNA-level coverage of Cisco WAN switches.
CCNP-WAN	Intermediate certification for Cisco WAN switches. Requires CCNA-WAN.
CCDP-WAN	Design certification for Cisco WAN switches. Requires CCNP-WAN.
Cisco Qualified Specialists	Several specialized certifications are available; these are used as part of the points calculation for channel partners. See http://www.cisco.com/warp/public/10/wwtraining/certprog/ for more details.

What's on the CCNA Exam

Every test taker would like to know exactly what is on the CCNA exam as well as the other Cisco certification exams. Well, to be honest, *exactly* what is on the exam is a very closely guarded secret. Only those who write the questions for Cisco and who have access to the entire question database truly know what is really on the exam.

Cisco makes fairly general CCNA exam content available to the public at the Web site www.cisco.com/warp/public/10/wwtraining/certprog/testing/current_exams/640-507.html.

In fact, this direct quote from the Cisco Web site summarizes the exam:

> CCNA certified professionals can install, configure, and operate LAN, WAN, and dial access services for small networks (100 nodes or fewer), including but not limited to use of these protocols: IP, IGRP, IPX, Serial, AppleTalk, Frame Relay, IP RIP, VLANs, RIP, Ethernet, Access Lists.

Well, a lawyer might have been involved in crafting that message. "Including but not limited to" is a telling phrase—technically, anything is fair game. All of us would like to study and understand exactly the topics that are on the test. I strive to meet that goal, but keep the following perspective in mind—the exam that you take will not include questions on every topic in Cisco's CCNA question database. Someone else may get topics that you will not. Many topics are covered on each exam, but with far fewer than 100 questions, it would be impossible to cover all the topics.

So what did we do to help? Well, in this book, we err on the side of covering everything that is fair game on the exam. So, we operate under the following self-imposed rules:

- If we at Cisco Press believe that a topic is definitely on the exam, it is covered in Chapters 2 through 11. If it's in the exam question database, even though you might not get it on your individual test, it's covered in these chapters!
- If we at Cisco Press believe that a topic is simply not in the Cisco CCNA question database, it is not covered in this book.
- If the topic is in the exam question database, but it has a low likelihood of being on the exam, the book notes the corresponding section with an "extra credit" icon.

Start Extra Credit

Studying these sections might help, but spend time on these topics only after you have mastered the most important topics.

End Extra Credit

Cisco posts the list of exam topics on its Web site, www.cisco.com/warp/public/10/wwtraining/certprog/testing/current_exams/640-507.html.

These topics provide the greatest insight into what is covered on the exam. The topics are listed in bullet format on the Cisco Web site. To refer to the topics more easily in the book, I have numbered the exam topics. Table 1-3 lists the exam topics, their respective numbers, and an interpretation.

Table 1-3 *CCNA Exam Topics and Comments*

Exam Topic Reference Number	Exam Topic	Comments
1	Name and describe two switching methods.	Cut-through and store-and-forward are the two types referred to, with a third type being FragmentFree. Chapter 4, "LANs, Bridges, and Switches," covers the details.
2	Distinguish between cut-through and store-and-forward LAN switching.	Deal with differences in internal processing by a LAN switch. Details are found in Chapter 4.
3	Describe the operation of the Spanning Tree Protocol and its benefits.	STP prevents frames from looping around LANs when physically redundant links exist. Chapter 5, "Intermediate LANs: Spanning Tree, VLANs, and Trunking," covers the details.
4	Describe the benefits of virtual LANs.	Also in Chapter 5, VLANs allow one switch to create multiple broadcast domains instead of requiring a different switch for each different broadcast domain.
5	Describe data link and network addresses and identify key differences between them.	This topic relates more to the concepts behind addressing, as defined in the OSI reference model. Network addresses are (typically) not correlated to a particular type of physical network, whereas data-link addresses are. Details appear in Chapter 3, "OSI Reference Model & Layered Communication."
6	Define and describe the function of a MAC address.	Media Access Control (MAC) addresses are used to address LAN network interface cards. These addresses include unicast (addressing a single card), broadcast, and multicast.
7	List the key internetworking functions of the OSI Network layer.	Too much to list here—see Chapter 3 for a complete long list and another shorter, easy-to-memorize list.

continues

Table 1-3 *CCNA Exam Topics and Comments (Continued)*

Exam Topic Reference Number	Exam Topic	Comments
8	Identify at least three reasons why the industry uses a layered model.	Chapter 3 once again covers most of the pure conceptual materials on networking protocols, including layering. Making the software easier to write, making it easier for different vendors to interface with other products, and ensuring that two computers can communicate with each other are just some of the reasons.
9	Describe the two parts of network addressing, then identify the parts in specific protocol address examples.	The first part of several network layer addresses identifies a group, with the second part identifying a single member of the group. For instance, IP has a network or subnet part, followed by the host part of an address. Chapter 3 covers the basics for IP, IPX, and AppleTalk. Chapter 6, "TCP/IP and IP Routing," and Chapter 11, "Novell IPX," cover the details for IP and IPX, respectively.
10	Define and explain the five conversion steps of data encapsulation.	Using the TCP/IP protocol stack as an example, Cisco has described the process of data encapsulation. This explanation has been a part of Cisco's intro courses for many years. The full explanation is in Chapter 3.
11	Describe connection-oriented network service and connectionless network service, and identify their key differences.	Chapter 3 defines and contrasts these two terms. Briefly, *connection-oriented* means that the protocol communicates between the endpoints before any data is passed, and *connectionless* protocols do not.
12	Identify the parts in specific protocol address examples.	IP, IPX, and AppleTalk examples are included in Chapter 3. The formats are actually pretty easy, and IP and IPX are covered in more detail in later chapters, so address formats for IP and IPX will become second nature.
13	Describe the advantages of LAN segmentation.	Segmentation deals with the concept of separating devices that were previously on a single LAN into multiple LANs. Chapter 4 covers the details and benefits.
14	Describe LAN segmentation using bridges.	Segmentation using bridges is the same as segmentation using switches. The main advantage is to split the LANs into different collision domains.

Table 1-3 *CCNA Exam Topics and Comments (Continued)*

Exam Topic Reference Number	Exam Topic	Comments
15	Describe LAN segmentation using routers.	The main advantage is to split the LANs into different collision and different broadcast domains.
16	Describe LAN segmentation using switches.	Segmentation using switches is the same as segmentation using bridges. The main advantage is to split the LANs into different collision domains.
17	Describe the benefits of network segmentation with bridges.	This exam topic and the next two are really simply reworded versions of the previous three topics. All are covered in Chapter 4.
18	Describe the benefits of network segmentation with routers.	This exam topic, like the one before and after it, is really a simply reworded version of the previous three topics. All are covered in Chapter 4.
19	Describe the benefits of network segmentation with switches.	This exam topic, like the two before it, is really simply a reworded version of the previous three topics. All are covered in Chapter 4.
20	Describe the different classes of IP addresses [and subnetting].	This topic covers all details of IP addressing. If you want to work in networking, you need to know this well. Chapter 6 describes the details.
21	Identify the functions of the TCP/IP network-layer protocols.	There are many parts of the TCP/IP protocol suite, including IP. This topic implies that you need to know the various components and their functions—such as TCP, UDP, ICMP, and ARP. Chapter 6 discusses all these protocols.
22	Identify the functions performed by ICMP.	ICMP has many functions, including the ICMP echo and echo reply messages sent when the **ping** command is used. Chapter 6 covers the details.
23	Configure IP addresses.	Configuration of IP addresses is straightforward when you know the format of IP addresses. Configuration is covered in Chapter 6.
24	Verify IP addresses.	Several **show** commands list information about the configured IP addresses and whether the corresponding interfaces are up and working. Chapter 6 lists the commands.

continues

Table 1-3 *CCNA Exam Topics and Comments (Continued)*

Exam Topic Reference Number	Exam Topic	Comments
25	List the required IPX address and encapsulation type.	Chapter 11 covers all the details of IPX, including encapsulation types. When a router forwards a packet, it creates a new data-link header. On LANs, there are several alternative types of headers or encapsulation types. Be sure to memorize these types.
26	Define flow control and describe the three basic methods used in networking.	Flow control is normally performed by OSI Layer 4 protocols, but, in some cases, it is performed by protocols from other layers. The basic methods are all covered in Chapter 3.
27	Add the RIP routing protocol to your configuration.	RIP configuration and the concepts behind this distance vector protocol are covered in Chapter 7, "Routing and Routing Protocols." RIP is a routing protocol that fills the IP routing table with routes.
28	Add the IGRP routing protocol to your configuration.	Likewise, IGRP configuration and concepts are covered in Chapter 7. IGRP is an alternative routing protocol.
29	Recognize key Frame Relay terms and features.	Chapter 10, "Frame Relay Concepts and Configuration," is devoted to all Frame Relay concepts and configuration. The terms and features are covered in the first section of the chapter.
30	List commands to configure Frame Relay LMIs, maps, and subinterfaces.	Frame Relay can be configured in several different ways, depending on the network design and the Frame Relay provider. Cisco expects CCNAs to be able to configure all the options.
31	List commands to monitor Frame Relay operation in the router.	The commands are listed, with examples, in Chapter 10. Cisco will test you on these commands with multiple-choice questions as well as with the simulations on the exam.
32	State a relevant use and context for ISDN networking.	Chapter 9, "WAN Protocols and Design," covers the details of ISDN concepts and configuration. ISDN is used as a dial technology, both for occasional access and for dial backup.
33	Identify ISDN protocols, function groups, reference points, and channels.	ISDN includes many options, all defined by a myriad of ITU specifications. Chapter 9 lists the specifications and explains the core concepts.

Table 1-3 *CCNA Exam Topics and Comments (Continued)*

Exam Topic Reference Number	Exam Topic	Comments
34	Identify PPP operations to encapsulate WAN data on Cisco routers.	Also in Chapter 9, PPP is a serial data-link protocol used on point-to-point serial links.
35	Configure standard access lists to figure IP traffic.	Chapter 8, "Understanding Access List Security," covers the details of all IP access lists. Access lists are used to filter packets as well as filter routing updates and classify traffic for QoS features.
36	Configure extended access lists to filter IP traffic.	Extended IP access lists do the same thing as standard access lists, but with many more options for matching the packets.
37	Monitor and verify selected access list operations on the router.	Regardless of whether standard or extended access lists are used, the same commands, covered in Chapter 8, list the details of what is configured.
38	Describe full- and half-duplex Ethernet operation.	Covered in Chapter 4, Ethernet can operate at full duplex as long as only two devices exist in the same collision domain. This is typical when a single device is cabled to a LAN switch.
39	Describe network congestion problem in Ethernet networks.	Ironically, I first heard of the "Ethernet congestion problem" graphed when researching my senior project in college 18 years ago. Covered in Chapter 4, the problem is that Ethernet collisions and wait times increase as load increases, reducing performance.
40	Describe the features and benefits of Fast Ethernet.	Also covered in Chapter 4, Fast Ethernet is—faster. And it uses the same framing as 10-Mbps Ethernet, which allows for easy migration.
41	Describe the guidelines and distance limitations of Fast Ethernet.	The details are listed in tables in Chapter 4.
42	Examine router elements (RAM, ROM, CDP, **show**).	Cisco IOS Software and configuration files are stored in routers, and you will need to know the commands used to examine them. Also, CDP reveals details about neighboring routers, and you will need to be able to display CDP information as well. Chapter 2, "Cisco IOS Software Fundamentals," covers the router memory, and Chapter 6 covers CDP.

continues

Table 1-3 *CCNA Exam Topics and Comments (Continued)*

Exam Topic Reference Number	Exam Topic	Comments
43	Manage configuration files from the privileged exec mode.	Managing configuration files includes manipulating the configuration, as well as manipulating and choosing which IOS version to use in the router. Chapter 2 covers the details.
44	Control router passwords, identification, and banner.	Again, in Chapter 2, there are many basic commands that are both useful and covered on the exam. If you see a command in Chapter 2 specifically, you should memorize it—it is surely in the exam question database.
45	Identify the main Cisco IOS software commands for router startup.	All basic commands, router configuration details, and Cisco IOS Software commands are covered in Chapter 2.
46	Log in to a router in both user and privileged modes.	The Cisco IOS Software command-line interface (CLI) allows you to log in using user and privileged modes. Look to Chapter 2 for details.
47	Check an initial configuration using the **setup** command.	If you turn on or reboot your router when there is no configuration stored in NVRAM, the router allows you to enter setup mode. You can also enter setup mode using the **setup** command. Regardless, setup is a way to easily configure the basic information needed for a router configuration, without knowing the syntax of router commands.

Table 1-3 *CCNA Exam Topics and Comments (Continued)*

Exam Topic Reference Number	Exam Topic	Comments
48	Use the context-sensitive help facility.	You can always get help by simply typing a **?**. There are a few variations on what you get, depending on when you type the **?**. See Chapter 2 for details.
49	Use the command history and editing features.	Chapter 2 lists the picky details, which you should memorize!
50	List the commands to load Cisco IOS software from: flash memory, a TFTP server, or ROM.	These commands are very important to network engineers because the commands let you migrate from one IOS to another.
51	Prepare to backup, upgrade, and load a backup Cisco IOS software image.	The process of upgrading the IOS is as important as the commands used to perform the upgrade, as mentioned in the previous exam topic. The process and the configuration are covered in Chapter 2.
52	List problems that each routing type encounters when dealing with topology changes, and describe techniques to reduce the number of these problems.	Chapter 7 covers IP routing protocols, including the theory and concepts behind routing protocols. Distance vector and link-state routing protocols are the two main categories.
53	Prepare the initial configuration of your router and enable IP.	You should be able to use setup mode, as well as configure the router using configuration mode. Both are covered in detail in Chapter 2.

Cross-Reference Between Exam Topics and Book Chapters

Table 1-4 lists each exam topic, along with the chapter of the book in which the topic's concepts are covered.

Table 1-4 *CCNA Exam Topics Cross-Reference to Chapters*

Exam Topic	Chapter
1	4
2	4
3	5
4	5
5	3
6	3
7	3
8	3
9	3
10	3
11	3
12	3
13	4
14	4
15	4
16	4
17	4
18	4
19	4
20	6
21	6
22	6
23	6
24	11
25	6
26	3
27	7
28	7
29	10
30	10
31	10
32	9
33	9
34	9
35	8
36	8
37	8
38	4
39	4
40	4
41	4
42	2
43	2
44	2
45	2
46	2
47	2
48	2
49	2
50	2
51	2
52	7
53	2

Cross-Reference Between Chapter and Exam Topics

Table 1-5 lists each chapter, along with the exam topics covered in that chapter.

Table 1-5 *CCNA Chapters Cross-Reference to Exam Topics*

Chapter	Exam Topics
2	42–51, 53
3	5–12, 26
4	1–2, 13–19, 38–41
5	3–4
6	20–24
7	27–28, 52
8	35–37
9	32–34
10	29–31
11	25

Recommended Training Paths for CCNA

Cisco recommends that you take two courses before you take the CCNA exam. The first, CCNA Basics (CCNAB), is a Web-based introductory course that you can order directly from most any learning partner, my company included. This course covers the basic protocol information needed for CCNA, with an emphasis on the OSI reference model.

The other suggested course is the instructor-led Interconnecting Cisco Network Devices (ICND) course, which is available from almost every Cisco training partner (for a list of training partners, go to www.cisco.com/warp/public/10/wwtraining/listAllTP.html).

So, if you have taken or will take the ICND, that's the best way to prepare for the CCNA exam. But what if you took the Cisco Networking Academy curriculum? Or what if you simply choose not to spend the money on an introductory course? The final section of this chapter suggests a strategy for people from each background.

First, an outline of the ICND course, shown in Table 1-6, should be helpful. Remember, although the CCNA exam is not a test on the ICND course, the ICND is the course that most closely matches the CCNA topics.

Table 1-6 *ICND Course Summary*

Module Title	Topics in This Module
Interconnecting Cisco Networking Devices Introduction	Typical administrative details.
Internetworking Concepts Overview	OSI model details; common physical and data-link specifications; MAC address definition; description of Ethernet, Token Ring, and FDDI operation; a brief explanation of WAN data links.
Assembling and Cabling Cisco Devices	Basic physical setup and cabling.
Operating and Configuring a Cisco IOS Device	Logging in, initialization, modes of operation, passwords, help, command editing, and various **show** commands.
Managing Your Network Environment	Telnet, CDP, and managing the IOS and config files.
Catalyst 1900 Switch Operations	LAN switching concepts, spanning tree, and 1900 switch configuration.
Extending Switched Networks with Virtual LANs	Virtual LANs, VLAN trunking, and VLAN configuration on 1900 switches.
Interconnecting Networks with TCP/IP	Protocol stack versus OSI; application layer examples; TCP error recovery; TCP and UDP ports; TCP, UDP, and IP headers; and ICMP. For Class A, B, and C networks: IP addresses, mask subnetting, and planning; configuring IP addresses; configuring host names; configuring DNS; and verifying operation with **ping**, **trace**, and **show** commands.
Determining IP Routes	Configuring static routes, configuring default routes, interior versus exterior routing protocols, configuring RIP, debugging RIP, IGRP configuration, and IGRP **debug** and **show** commands.
Basic IP Traffic Management with Access Lists	The purpose of using access lists, logic diagrams, standard and extended access lists, and TCP/IP access lists; wildcard masks; configuring standard IP access lists; configuring extended access lists; monitoring IP access lists.
Configuring Novell IPX	Protocol versus OSI, IPX addresses, Novell encapsulation options, RIP, SAP, GNS, configuring IPX, displaying IPX, debugging IPX, and IPX access lists.
Establishing Serial Point-to-Point Connections	Telephone company service basics, survey of data-link protocols for WANs, SDLC/HDLC/PPP/LAPB framing, PPP functions, PAP and CHAP authentication, and PAP and CHAP configuration.
Completing an ISDN BRI Call	ISDN protocol basics and dial-on-demand routing (DDR).
Establishing a Frame Relay PVC Connection	Terminology, LMI messages, Inverse ARP, addressing, configuration, monitoring, configuration using subinterfaces, NBMA, and full and partial mesh issues.

How to Use This Book to Pass the Exam

You can choose between two approaches to using this book. In some respects, the *CCNA Exam #640-607 Certification Guide* is really two books—one book for each of two recommended ways to approach reading the book. "Book 1" guides the reader who is new to CCNA networking topics. If you use this approach, you know that you need to learn about all the topics covered on the exam. "Book 2" guides the reader who has already been to a CCNA-oriented class or who is experienced in these same topics. If you take this approach, you study more quickly, taking advantage of the fact that you already know parts of the knowledge that you need, so you just need to fill in the rest of your knowledge.

So, which method is right for you? Well, I recommend the Book 1 approach if you fall into the following categories:

- You already know that you want to read the book cover to cover.
- You have never been, or you have not recently been, to Cisco's official Interconnecting Cisco Network Devices (ICND) course.
- You have never been, or you have not recently been, to some other CCNA-oriented course or through the Cisco Networking Academy CCNA curriculum.
- You do not have much experience using Cisco routers and switches.

In short, if you need to learn, for the first time, most of the CCNA materials, then Book 1 is where you should start! Figure 1-2 outlines the Book 1 approach.

Figure 1-2 *How to Use This Book: Book 1*

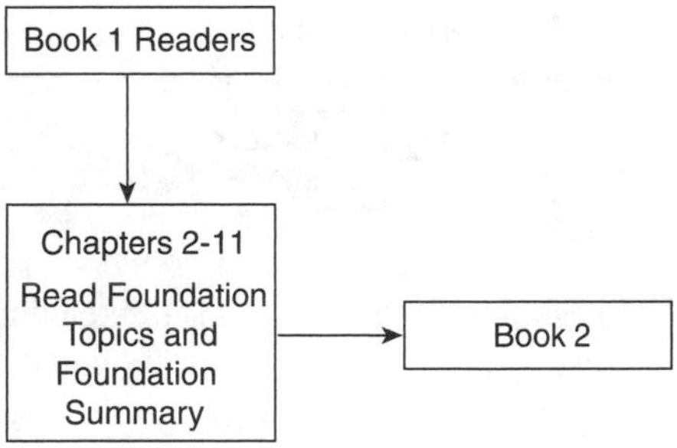

You will notice that you read the core parts of each chapter, ignoring each chapter's quizzes and scenarios. The quizzes and scenarios are most useful to fill in the final gaps in your learning—you will use these sections, but just not yet! You will also notice that, after reading the core parts of all the chapters, it is suggested that you move on to Book 2—the approach that helps you fill in the gaps of your memory.

Book 2 helps you fill in the gaps in your knowledge and skills. Using the Book 2 approach, you will discover what you know and what you do not know, to focus your study on the topics that you have not mastered. Whether you read Book 1 first, or whether you already knew something about networking when you bought this book, Book 2 will help you with the final steps of preparation. You might not realize which topics you need to study and which topics you really already know, but Book 2 guides you through the process. Figure 1-3 outlines the process that I call Book 2.

Figure 1-3 *How to Use This Book: Book 2*

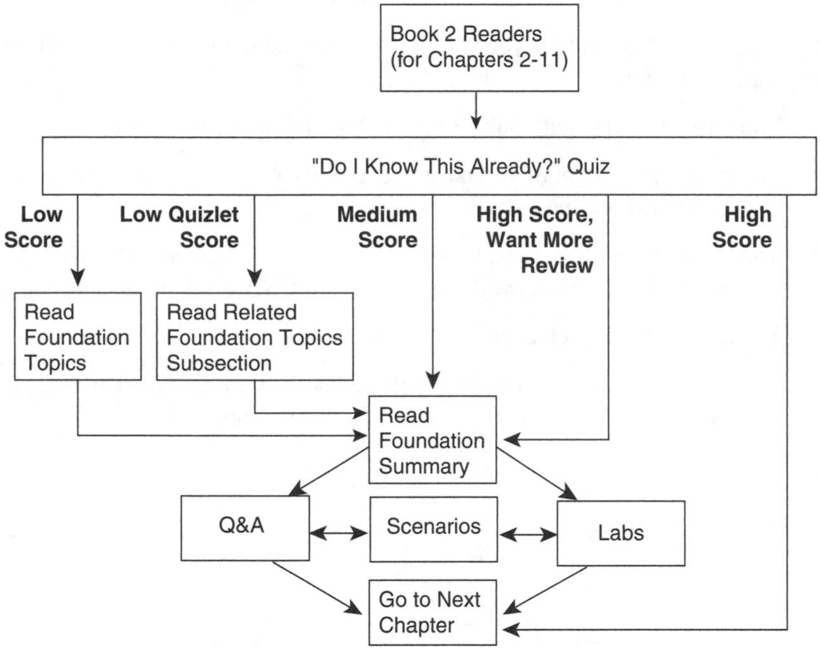

Chapters 2 through 11 begin with a quiz, which is broken into subdivisions called "quizlets." If you get a high score, you might simply review the "Foundation Summary" section at the end of the chapter because you already remember a lot. If you score well on one quizlet but low on another, you are directed to the section of the chapter corresponding to the quizlet on which your score was low. If you score less than 50 percent on the overall quiz, you should read the whole chapter. Of course, these are simply guidelines—if you score well but want more review on that topic, read away!

After completing the core chapters (Chapters 2 through 11), you have several options for your next study activity. Because Chapter 12, "Scenarios for Final Preparation," is the next chapter in succession, it outlines the directions on what to do at the end of your study, right before the test. These same directions are repeated here as well. Figure 1-4 outlines your options for final study for the exam.

Figure 1-4 *How to Use This Book: Final CCNA Exam Preparation Strategy*

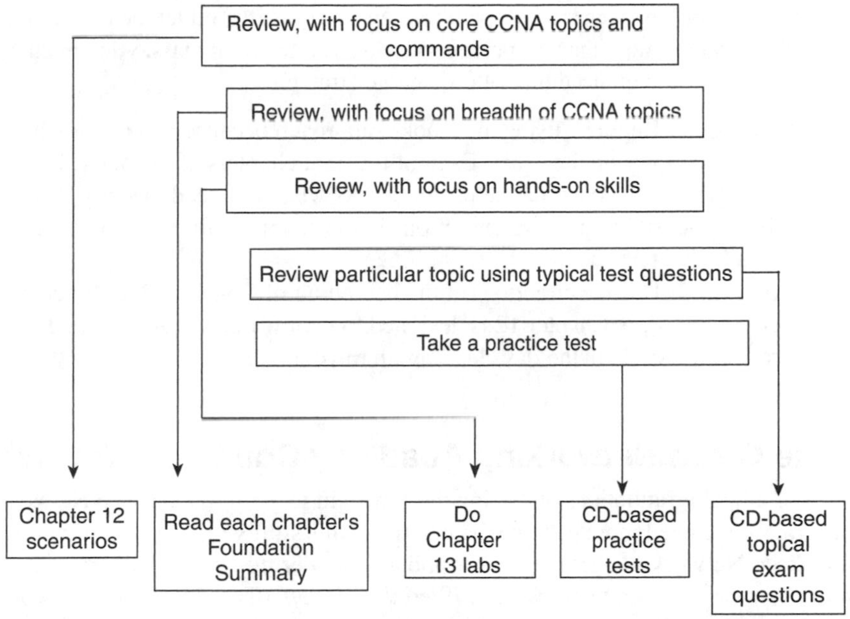

As shown, if you want even more final preparation, you can go over the many practice questions located in each chapter and on the CD. All prechapter quiz and chapter-ending questions, with answers, are in Appendix A, "Answers to the 'Do I Know This Already?' Quizzes and Q&A Sections." You can read and review these conveniently located questions and explanations quickly. The CD includes testing software as well as many additional questions in the format of the CCNA exam. These questions should be a valuable resource when performing final preparations.

You should also strongly consider getting some hands-on experience with real routers and switches. I imagine that most of you will want to do that, and those of you who have access to equipment at work can easily do that. For the rest of you, you might have to buy your own gear, use simulators, or rent lab time from companies such as my company, Skyline Computer. Although this book gives a large number of examples, lab scenarios, and lab exercises, there is no substitute for exercising your memory by actually doing real commands on real devices.

Anyone preparing for the CCNA exam can use the guidelines at the beginning of each chapter as a study aid. However, for some additional guidance, the final parts of this chapter give a few strategies for study, based on how you have prepared before buying this book. So, find the section that most closely matches your background in the next few pages, and read about some additional ideas to help you prepare. There is a section for people who have taken ICND, one for those from the Cisco Networking Academies, one for those who will not be taking any classes and have not had much experience, and a final set of strategies for those who will not be taking any classes but who have some experience.

I've Taken ICND—Now What?

For starters, you've taken the best path to prepare yourself. But let me temper that with the fact that, if you retain more than 50 percent of what you heard in class, you are an extraordinary person! That said, you need the following two strategies:

Strategy 1: Begin by using the Book 2 approach because you already have learned a lot about the topics on the exam. Each of the core chapters of the book, Chapters 2 through 11, begins with a quiz that helps you assess what you need to study. The chapter then directs you to the appropriate sections in the chapter rather than requiring you to read all of each chapter.

Strategy 2: Use the directions at the beginning of Chapter 12 to direct your final study before the exam. Chapter 12 is designed to review many concepts, and it outlines a good process for study in the days leading up to your exam.

I've Taken the Cisco Networking Academy Courses—Now What?

First of all, congratulations on having the foresight to get into the Cisco Networking Academy program—we need more people who can make this stuff work! (Those of you who didn't take the Cisco Networking Academy track and are wondering what it's all about can check out http://www.cisco.com/warp/public/779/edu/academy/.) Thankfully, the Networking Academy curriculum actually does a great job of preparing you with the skills and knowledge you need to pass the exam. Unfortunately, your study was probably spread over several semesters, and possibly over a couple of years. So, the details that you do not use frequently might have been forgotten. Now, on to the strategies for success on CCNA:

Strategy 1: Pull out your Networking Academy curriculum and notes, and reread them. Most people's memory is exercised better by seeing familiar material—even more so when you wrote it down yourself. If you have ever taken a test and pictured in your mind where the answer was on your page of notes, you can relate.

Strategy 2: Use the Book 2 approach exactly as described here in Chapter 1. Each of the core chapters of the book, Chapters 2 through 11, begins with a quiz that helps you assess what you need to study. It then directs you to the appropriate sections in the chapter rather than requiring you to read all of each chapter.

Strategy 3: Make it a point to read the sections of this book that cover some of the theory behind networking and some of the standards. The biggest reason for that is that the Networking Academy is oriented more toward building practical skills than using theoretical knowledge. The suggested sections are listed here:

— Chapter 5—"Spanning-Tree Protocol"

— Chapter 7—"Distance Vector Routing Protocols"

Strategy 4: Use the directions at the beginning of Chapter 12 to direct your final study before the exam. Chapter 12 is designed to review many concepts, and it outlines a good process for study in the days leading up to your exam.

This book should help you sift through the topics and choose the right areas for study, and it also should help you to not waste your time. Congratulations on your Networking Academy work—now add the CCNA certification to take away any doubt in the minds of prospective employers that you know Cisco!

I'm New to Internetworking with Cisco, I Will Not Be Taking the ICND Course, and This Book Is My Only Reference—Now What?

You can pass the CCNA exam without taking any courses. Of course, Cisco wants you to take the recommended courses for all the exams. Its motivation is not to make more money because Cisco does not actually deliver the training; the training partners do. Instead, Cisco truly believes that the more people understand its products, ultimately the happier its customers will be and the more products Cisco will sell. Cisco also believes that the official training is the right way to teach people about Cisco products, so you're encouraged to take the classes.

Of course, if you use only one reference and it is this one, thank you! However, no single book or course will provide every reader with everything they need, so a second source is usually very beneficial. If you are looking to save money but can afford one more book, the Cisco Press *Interconnecting Cisco Network Devices* (*ICND*) book is definitely the best companion. The CCNA exam lists ICND as the main prerequisite course before taking the exam. The Cisco Press ICND book contains the actual ICND course materials, which were given to Cisco Press by Cisco and then converted into book format. The same figures used in the presentations by ICND instructors are used as the figures in the ICND book, with explanations matching what a senior instructor might say when teaching the course. So, if you use one other reference, this is the one!

But, under the assumptions that you are new to Cisco and have only this book, here's what you should do:

Strategy 1: Start with the Book 1 approach to this book. Resist the temptation to read the quiz questions—they will actually help you more if you wait until later.

Strategy 2: After reading Book 1, use the Book 2 approach. Each of the core chapters of the book, Chapters 2 through 11, begins with a quiz that helps you assess what you need to study. It then directs you to the appropriate sections in the chapter rather than requiring you to read all of each chapter.

Strategy 3: Use the directions at the beginning of Chapter 12 to direct your final study before the exam. Chapter 12 is designed to review many concepts, and it outlines a good process for study in the days leading up to your exam.

Strategy 4: Find any and every opportunity to get your hands on some Cisco routers and switches. You will learn the user interface and command structures much more easily by doing rather than by reading!

I'm New to Internetworking with Cisco, I Will Not Be Taking the ICND Course, and I Bought the *Interconnecting Cisco Network Devices* Book as Well—Now What?

If you have no networking experience at all, start with the ICND book. The CCNA exam lists ICND as the main prerequisite course before taking the exam. The Cisco Press ICND book contains the actual ICND course materials, handed over by Cisco to Cisco Press, and then converted into book format. The same figures used in the presentations by instructors are used as the figures in the book, with explanations matching what a senior instructor might say when teaching the course. So, if you use one other reference, this is the one!

Use the Cisco Press book, *Internetworking Technologies Handbook,* Third Edition, as a reference—it's got great 4–5 page synopses of what a particular technology is all about. If you want some quick review, and want to get a different perspective on it, use ITH.

After using ICND, you should take the Book 2 approach to using this book.

I've Learned a Lot About CCNA Topics Through Experience, but I Will Not Be Taking the ICND Course—Now What?

If you feel that you know a fair amount about CCNA topics already, but you are worried about the topics you simply just have not worked with, this strategy is for you. This book is designed to help you figure out what CCNA topics you need some help with and then help you learn about them. Here's the simple strategy for you:

Strategy 1: Use the Book 2 approach exactly as described in this chapter. Each of the core chapters of the book, Chapters 2 through 11, begins with a quiz that helps you assess what you need to study. It then directs you to the appropriate sections in the chapter rather than requiring you to read all of each chapter.

Strategy 2: Use the directions at the beginning of Chapter 12 to direct your final study before the exam. Chapter 12 is designed to review many concepts, and it outlines a good process for study in the days leading up to your exam.

You should be able to fill in the gaps in your knowledge this way and not risk being bored in the ICND class when it covers the topics you already know.

Conclusion

The CCNA certification is arguably the most important Cisco certification. It certainly is the most popular, is required for several other certifications, and is the first step in distinguishing yourself as someone who has proven knowledge of Cisco.

The *CCNA Exam #640-607 Certification Guide* is designed to help you attain CCNA certification. This is the CCNA certification book from the only Cisco-authorized publisher. We at Cisco Press believe that this book certainly can help you achieve CCNA certification—but the real work is up to you! I trust that your time will be well spent.

Exam Topics in This Chapter

42 Examine router elements (RAM, ROM, CDP, **show**).

43 Manage configuration files from the privileged exec mode.

44 Control router passwords, identification, and banner.

45 Identify the main Cisco IOS Software commands for router startup.

46 Log in to a router in both user and privileged modes.

47 Check an initial configuration using the **setup** command.

48 Use the context-sensitive help facility.

49 Use the command history and editing features.

50 List the commands to load Cisco IOS Software from: Flash memory, a TFTP server, or ROM.

51 Prepare to back up, upgrade, and load a backup Cisco IOS Software image.

52 Prepare the initial configuration of your router and enable IP.

CHAPTER 2

Cisco IOS Software Fundamentals

Cisco routers run the Cisco Internetworking Operating System (IOS). So, as you would probably guess, all the questions about implementing something on a router require you to know all about the IOS. Although many topics on the CCNA exam do not relate to the actual implementation on Cisco gear, you probably will not pass the test if you do not know the details of how IOS works.

But do not despair! You need to know about the three main topics of the IOS, and most of this is basic. First, you must know about the IOS command-line interface (CLI)—how to access the interface and how to use it. Next, you need to know how configure the router, even though you might not know what you want to configure yet! Finally, you need to know about upgrading IOS Software; this requires a reboot of the router, so you also need to know what happens during the boot process. By the time you are finished with your CCNA study, the CLI and configuration topics in this chapter will be second nature, for the most part.

The IOS also runs on some Cisco switch models, and it uses CLI. However, in some cases, the IOS CLI on a switch is slightly different than on a router. In fact, the IOS on the 1900 series switches, on which the exam questions are based, is slightly different than on some other Cisco IOS-based switches. This chapter covers the IOS CLI on a router, and Chapter 4, "LANs, Bridges, and Switches," covers some details of the IOS CLI on LAN switches. Chapter 4 outlines the key differences between the IOS on routers and the IOS on 1900 series switches.

How to Best Use This Chapter

You can choose from two main approaches for using this book, which are described in Chapter 1, "All About the Cisco Certified Network Associate Certification," and are called "Book 1" and "Book 2." Book 1 is for readers who need a through background before their final study time; Book 2 is intended for readers who are reviewing and filling in the missing parts of their CCNA knowledge. Using Figure 2-1 as a guide, you should either read the Foundation sections of this chapter or begin with the "Do I Know This Already?" quiz.

Figure 2-1 *How to Use This Chapter*

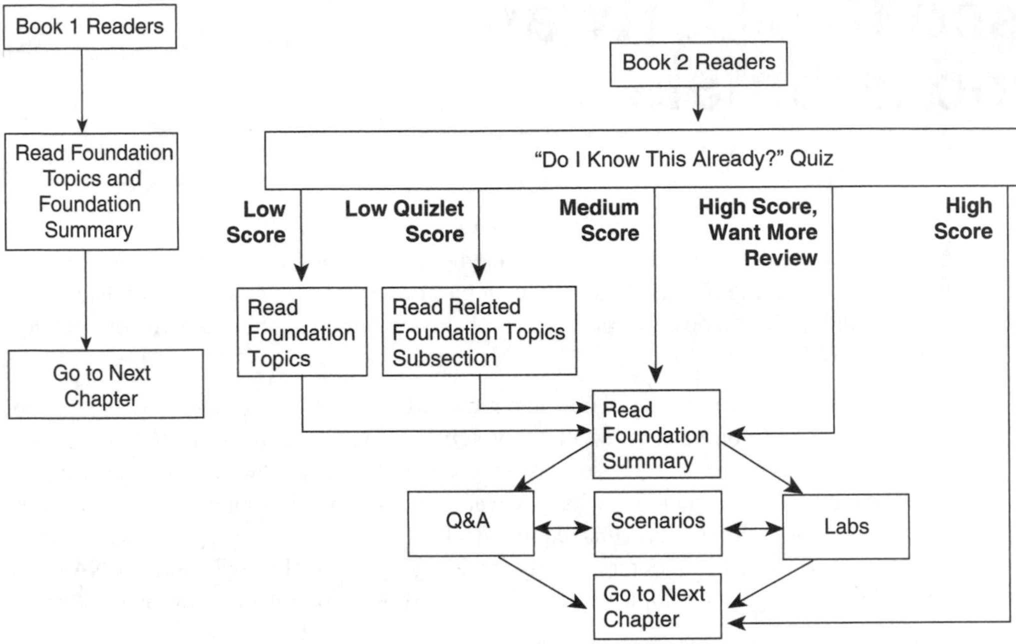

"Do I Know This Already?" Quiz

The purpose of the "Do I Know This Already?" quiz is to help you decide what parts of this chapter to use. If you already intend to read the entire chapter, you do not necessarily need to answer these questions now.

This 12-question quiz helps you determine how to spend your limited study time. The quiz is sectioned into three smaller four-question "quizlets," which correspond to the three major topic headings in the chapter. Figure 2-1 outlines suggestions on how to spend your time in this chapter based on your quiz score. Use Table 2-1 to record your scores.

Table 2-1 *Scoresheet for Quiz and Quizlets*

Quizlet Number	Foundation Topics Section Covering These Questions	Questions	Score
1	Cisco IOS Software and Its User Interface	1 to 4	
2	Configuration Processes and the Configuration File	5 to 8	
3	Managing Cisco IOS Software Images	9 to 12	
All questions		1 to 12	

1 What are the two different names for the router's mode of operation that, when accessed, enables you to issue commands that could be disruptive to router operations?

____

____

____

2 What command would you use to receive command help if you knew that a **show** command option begins with a *c* but you could not recall the option?

____

____

____

3 After typing **show ip route,** which is the only command that you issued since logging in to the router, you now want to issue the **show ip arp** command. What steps would you take to execute this command by using command-recall keystrokes?

____

____

____

4 What is the name of the user interface mode of operation used when you cannot issue disruptive commands?

____

____

____

5 What configuration command causes the router to require a password from a user at the console? What configuration mode context must you be in? (That is, what command(s) must be typed before this command after entering configuration mode?) List the commands in the order in which they must be typed while in config mode.

____

____

____

6 What does the "NV" stand for in NVRAM?

____

____

____

7 Name two commands used to view the configuration that is currently used in a router. Which one is a more recent addition to the IOS?

____

____

____

8 Name two commands used to view the configuration to be used at the next reload of the router. Which one is a more recent addition to the IOS?

____

____

____

9 What two methods could a router administrator use to cause a router to load the IOS stored in ROM?

____

____

____

10 What is the process used to update the contents of Flash memory so that a new IOS in a file called c4500-d-mz.120-5.bin, on TFTP server 128.1.1.1, is copied into Flash memory?

____

____

____

11 Two different IOS files are in a router's Flash memory: one called c2500-j-l.111-3.bin and one called c2500-j-l.112-14.bin. Which one does the router use when it boots up? How could you force the other IOS file to be used? Without looking at the router configuration, what command could be used to discover which file was used for the latest boot of the router?

____

____

____

12 What are the primary purposes of Flash memory in a Cisco router?

____

____

____

The answers to the "Do I Know This Already?" quiz are found in Appendix A, "Answers to the 'Do I Know This Already?' Quizzes and Q&A Sections." The suggested choices for your next step are as follows:

- **6 or less overall score**—Read the entire chapter. This includes the "Foundation Topics" and "Foundation Summary" sections, the Q&A section, and the scenarios at the end of the chapter.
- **2 or less on any quizlet**—Review the subsection(s) of the "Foundation Topics" part of this chapter, based on Table 2-1. Then move on to the "Foundation Summary" section, the Q&A section, and the scenarios at the end of the chapter.
- **7, 8, or 9 overall score**—Begin with the "Foundation Summary" section and then go to the Q&A section and the scenarios at the end of the chapter.
- **10 or more overall score**—If you want more review on these topics, skip to the "Foundation Summary" section and then go to the Q&A section and the scenarios at the end of the chapter. Otherwise, move to the next chapter.

Foundation Topics

The Cisco IOS Software Command-Line Interface

42 Examine router elements (RAM, ROM, CDP, **show**).

44 Control router passwords, identification, and banner.

45 Identify the main Cisco IOS Software commands for router startup.

46 Log in to a router in both user and privileged modes.

48 Use the context-sensitive help facility.

49 Use the command history and editing features.

The majority of Cisco routers run Cisco IOS Software, with its familiar command-line interface (CLI). Some routing cards in other devices also run Cisco IOS Software. For example, the Multilayer Switch Feature Card (MSFC) daughter card for the Catalyst 6000 series LAN switches performs routing functions and executes IOS. Understanding the Cisco IOS Software CLI is as fundamental to supporting routers as understanding addition is to being able to do math problems!

The exam topics covered in this section will become second nature to you as you work with Cisco routers and switches more often. In fact, because this book purposefully was written for an audience that already has some training and experience with Cisco routers, several of the details in this chapter might already be ingrained in your memory. If you would like more review, or if you are still new to the IOS, read on—the details in this section are important to using Cisco routers and switches. This chapter reviews such topics as the CLI and how to navigate the IOS command set using help and key sequences for command editing and recall.

Access to the CLI

Cisco uses the acronym CLI to refer to the terminal user command-line interface to the IOS. The term *CLI* implies that the user is typing commands at a terminal, a terminal emulator, or a Telnet connection. Although you can pass the CCNA exam without ever having used the CLI, actually using the CLI will greatly enhance your chances.

To access the CLI, use one of three methods, as illustrated in Figure 2-2.

Figure 2-2 *CLI Access*

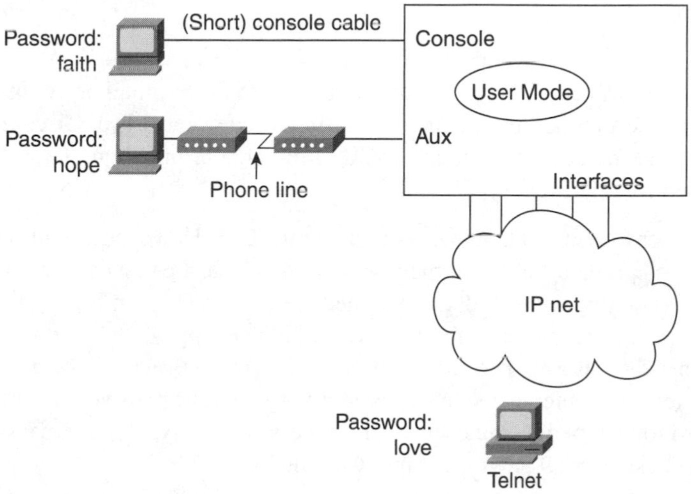

You access the router through the console, through a dialup device through a modem attached to the auxiliary port, or by using Telnet. In any case, you enter *user exec mode* first. User exec mode, also sometimes called user mode, allows you to look but not break anything. The passwords shown in Figure 2-2 are not defaults—those passwords would be required if the configuration used in Table 2-2 were used. The console, auxiliary, and Telnet passwords are all set separately.

Table 2-2 *CLI Password Configuration*

Access from . . .	Password Type	Configuration
Console	Console password	**line console** *0* **login** **password** *faith*
Auxiliary	Auxiliary password	**line aux** *0* **login** **password** *hope*
Telnet	vty password	**line vty** *0 4* **login** **password** *love*

Passwords are required for Telnet and auxiliary access as of Cisco IOS Software Release 12.*x*, and the exam is based on Cisco IOS Software Release 12.2. However, there are no preconfigured passwords—therefore, you must configure passwords for Telnet and auxiliary access from the console first.

All Cisco routers have a console port, and most have an auxiliary port. The console port is intended for local administrative access from an ASCII terminal or a computer using a terminal emulator. The auxiliary port, which is missing on a few models of Cisco routers, is intended for asynchronous dial access from an ASCII terminal or terminal emulator; the auxiliary port is often used for dial backup.

This chapter focuses on the process of using the CLI. However, if you see a command in this chapter, you probably should remember it. In this case, the first command in each configuration is a context-setting command, as described later in this chapter. But, as you see, the second and third commands would be ambiguous if we did not supply some additional information, such as whether the **password** command was for the console, aux, or Telnet. The **login** command actually tells the router to display a password prompt. The **password** commands specify the text password to be typed by the user to gain access. Typically, all three passwords have the same value because they all let you get into user mode.

Several concurrent Telnet connections to a router are allowed. The **line vty** *0 4* command signifies that this configuration applies to vtys (virtual teletypes/terminals) 0 through 4. Only these five vtys are allowed by the IOS, unless it is an IOS for a dial access server, such as a Cisco AS5300. All five vtys typically have the same password, which is handy because users connecting to the router through Telnet cannot choose which vty they get.

User exec mode is one of two command exec modes in the IOS user interface. *Enable* mode (also known as *privileged* mode or *privileged* exec mode) is the other. Enable mode is so named because the **enable** command is used to reach this mode, as shown in Figure 2-3; privileged mode earns its name because powerful, or privileged, commands can be executed there.

Figure 2-3 *User and Privileged Modes*

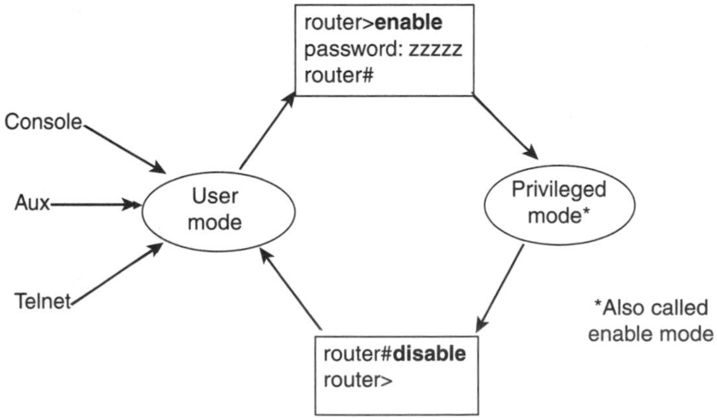

CLI Help Features

If you printed the IOS Command Reference documents, you would end up with a stack of paper several feet tall. No one should expect to memorize all the commands—and no one does in real life, either. Several very easy, convenient tools can be used to help you remember commands and then also save you time typing. As you progress through your Cisco certifications, the exam will cover progressively more commands. However, the only Cisco exam that covers the methods of getting command help is the CCNA exam. So, the following details are important in real life as well as for cramming for the exam.

Table 2-3 summarizes command-recall help options available at the CLI. Note that in the first column, "Command" represents any command. Likewise, "parm" represents a command's parameter. For instance, the third row lists "command ?," which means that commands such as **show ?** and **copy ?** would list help for the **show** and **copy** commands, respectively.

Table 2-3 *Cisco IOS Software Command Help*

What You Type	The Help You Get
?	Help for all commands available in this mode.
Help	Text describing how to get help. No actual command help is given.
Command ?	Text help describing all the first parameter options for the command.
com?	A list of commands that start with "com."
Command parm?	This style of help lists all parameters beginning with "parm." (Notice that no spaces exist between "parm" and the ?.)
command parm<Tab>	If you press the Tab key midword, the CLI will either spell the rest of this parameter at the command line or do nothing. If the CLI does nothing, it means that this string of characters represents more than one possible next parameter, so the CLI does not know which to spell out.
command parm1 ?	If a space is inserted before the question mark, the CLI lists all the next parameters and gives a brief explanation of each.

When you type the **?**, IOS's CLI reacts immediately; that is, you don't need to press the Enter key or any other keys. The router also redisplays what you typed before the **?**, to save you some keystrokes. If you press Enter immediately after the **?**, IOS tries to execute the command with only the parameters that you have typed so far.

"Command" represents any command, not the word *command*. Likewise, "parm" represents a command's parameter, not the word *parameter*.

The information supplied by using help depends on the CLI mode. For example, when **?** is typed in user mode, the commands allowed only in privileged exec mode are not displayed. Also, help is available in configuration mode; only configuration commands are displayed in that mode of operation.

IOS stores the commands that you type in a history buffer, storing ten commands by default. You can change the history size with the **terminal history size** *x* command, where *x* is the number of commands for the CLI to recall; this can be set to a value between 0 and 256. You can then retrieve commands so that you do not have to retype the commands. Table 2-4 lists the commands used to manipulate previously typed commands.

Table 2-4 *Key Sequences for Command Edit and Recall*

Keyboard Command	What You Get
Up arrow or Ctrl-p	This displays the most recently used command. If it is pressed again, the next most recent command appears until the history buffer is exhausted. (The *p* stands for *previous*.)
Down arrow or Ctrl-n	If you have gone too far back into the history buffer, these keys will go forward, in order, to the more recently typed commands. (The *n* is for *next*.)
Left arrow or Ctrl-b	This moves the cursor backward in the currently displayed command without deleting characters. (The *b* stands for *back*.)
Right arrow or Ctrl-f	This moves the cursor forward in the currently displayed command without deleting characters. (The *f* stands for *forward*.)
Backspace	This moves the cursor backward in the currently displayed command, deleting characters.
Ctrl-a	This moves the cursor directly to the first character of the currently displayed command.
Ctrl-e	This moves the cursor directly to the end of the currently displayed command.
Esc-b	This moves the cursor back one word in the currently displayed command.
Esc-f	This moves the cursor forward one word in the currently displayed command.
Ctrl-r	This creates a new command prompt, followed by all the characters typed since the last command prompt was written. This is particularly useful if system messages confuse the screen and it is unclear what you have typed so far.

Syslog and debug

Start Extra Credit

IOS creates messages when different events occur and, by default, sends them to the console. These messages are called *syslog* messages. If you have used the console of a router for any length of time, you likely have noticed these messages—and when they are frequent, you probably became a little frustrated.

The router also generates messages that are treated like syslog messages in response to some troubleshooting tasks that you might perform. The **debug** command is one of the key diagnostic tools for troubleshooting difficult problems on a router. **debug** enables monitoring points in the IOS and generates messages that describe what the IOS is doing and seeing. When any **debug** command option is enabled, the router processes the messages with the same logic as other syslog messages. Beware: Some **debug** options create so many messages that the IOS cannot process them all, possibly crashing the IOS.

End Extra Credit

NOTE The **no debug all** command disables all debugs. Before enabling an unfamiliar **debug** command option, issue a **no debug all** and then issue the **debug** that you want to use; then quickly retrieve the **no debug all** command. If the messages are voluminous, press Enter immediately, executing the **no debug all** command to try to prevent the router from crashing by immediately disabling all debugs.

You might or might not be interested in seeing the messages as they occur. The console port always receives syslog messages. When you Telnet to the router, however, no syslog messages are seen unless you issue the **terminal monitor** command. This command simply means that this terminal is monitoring syslog messages. Another alternative for viewing syslog messages is to have the IOS record the syslog messages in a buffer in RAM and then use the **show logging** command to display the messages. For Telnet users, having the messages buffered using the global config command **logging buffered** is particularly useful. Because Telnet users do not get syslog messages by default anyway, these users can wait and look at syslog messages when desired. Finally, the **logging synchronous** line-configuration subcommand can be used for the console and vtys to tell the router to wait until the last command output is displayed before showing any syslog messages onscreen. That provides a little less interruption.

Syslog messages also can be sent to another device. Two alternatives exist: sending the messages to a syslog server, and sending the messages as SNMP traps to a management station. The **logging** *host* command, where *host* is the IP address or host name of the syslog server, is used to enable sending messages to the external server. After SNMP is configured, the **snmp-server enable traps** tells the IOS to forward traps, including syslog messages.

Figure 2-4 summarizes the flow of syslog messages, including debug messages. For a more detailed view of syslog messages, including restricting messages based on message severity, refer to the Cisco IOS Software documentation CD manual called "Troubleshooting Commands."

Figure 2-4 *Syslog Message Flows*

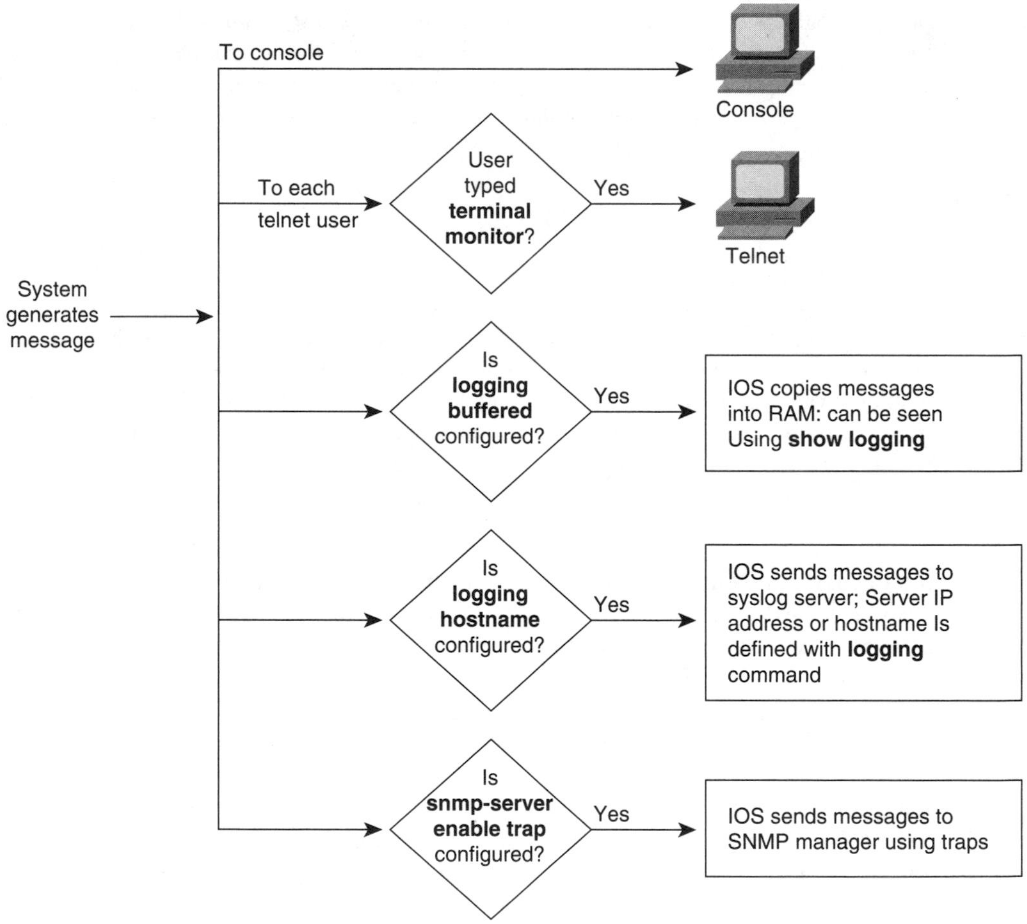

Configuring Cisco IOS Software

43 Manage configuration files from the privileged exec mode.

47 Check an initial configuration using the **setup** command.

53 Prepare the initial configuration of your router and enable IP.

You must understand how to configure a Cisco router to succeed on the exam—or to succeed in supporting Cisco routers. This section covers the basic configuration processes, including the concept of a configuration file and the locations in which the configuration files can be stored.

As mentioned in Chapter 1, *configuration mode* is another mode for the Cisco CLI, similar to user mode and privileged mode. User mode allows commands that are not disruptive to be issued, with some information being displayed to the user. Privileged mode supports a superset of commands compared to user mode, including commands that might harm the router. However, none of the commands in user or privileged mode changes the configuration of the router. Configuration mode is another mode in which configuration commands are typed. Figure 2-5 illustrates the relationships among configuration mode, user exec mode, and privileged exec mode.

Figure 2-5 *CLI Configuration Mode versus Exec Modes*

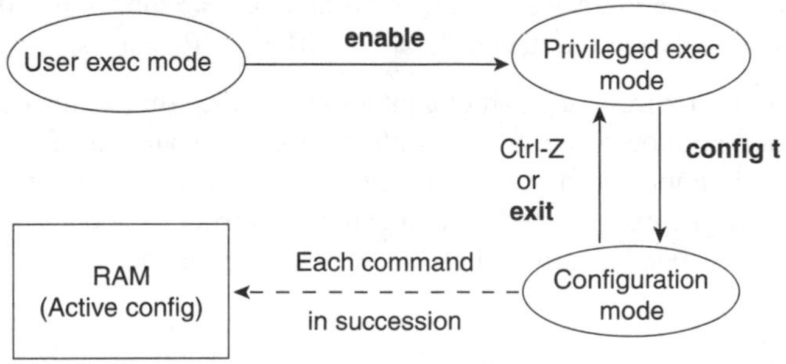

Commands typed in configuration mode update the active configuration file. *These changes to the configuration occur immediately each time you press the Enter key at the end of a command.* Be careful when you type in a configuration command!

Configuration mode itself contains a multitude of *subcommand modes*. Context-setting commands move you from one configuration subcommand mode to another. These context-setting commands tell the router the topic about which you will type the next few configuration commands. More importantly, they tell the router what commands to list when you ask for help.

After all, the whole reason for these contexts is to make online help more convenient and clear for you. So, if you are confused now, hang on—the next sample will clarify what I mean.

NOTE *Context setting* is not a Cisco term—it's just a term used here to help make sense of configuration mode.

The **interface** command is the most commonly used context-setting configuration command. As an example, the CLI user could enter interface configuration mode after typing the **interface ethernet 0** configuration command. Command help in Ethernet interface configuration mode displays only commands that are useful when configuring Ethernet interfaces. Commands used in this context are called *subcommands*—or, in this specific case, *interface subcommands*. If you have significant experience using the CLI in configuration mode, much of this will be second nature. From a CCNA exam perspective, recalling whether popular commands are global commands or subcommands will be useful, but you should really focus on the particular commands covered here. As a side effect, you will learn whether the commands are global configuration commands or subcommands.

No set rules exist for what commands are global commands or subcommands. Generally, however, when multiple instances of a parameter can be set in a single router, the command used to set the parameter is likely a configuration subcommand. Items that are set once for the entire router are likely global commands. For instance, the **hostname** command is a global command because there is only one host name per router. The **interface ethernet 0** command is a global configuration command because there is only one such interface in this router. Finally, the **ip address** command is an interface subcommand that sets the IP address on the interface; each interface will have a different IP address.

Use Ctrl-z from any part of configuration mode (or use the **exit** command from global configuration mode) to exit configuration mode and return to privileged exec mode. The configuration mode **end** command also exits from any point in the configuration mode back to privileged exec mode. The **exit** commands from submodes or contexts of configuration mode back up one level toward global configuration mode.

Example Configuration Process

Example 2-1 illustrates how the console password is defined; provides banner, host name, prompt, and interface descriptions; and shows the finished configuration. The lines beginning with "!" are comment lines that highlight significant processes or command lines within the example. The **show running-config** command output also includes comment lines with just a "!" to make the output more readable—many comment lines in the examples in this book were added to explain the meaning of the configuration. You should remember the process as well as these particular commands for the CCNA exam.

Example 2-1 *Configuration Process Example*

```
User Access Verification

Password:
Router>enable
Password:
Router #configure terminal
Router(config)#enable password lu
Router(config)#line console 0
Router(config-line)#login
Router(config-line)#password cisco
Router(config-line)#hostname Critter
Critter(config)#prompt Emma
Emma(config)#interface serial 1
Emma(config-if)#description this is the link to Albuquerque
Emma(config-if)#exit
Emma(config)#exit
Emma#
Emma#show running-config
Building configuration...

Current configuration:
!
version 12.2  934 bytes
! Version of IOS on router, automatic command


service timestamps debug uptime
service timestamps log uptime
no service password-encryption
!
hostname Critter
prompt Emma
!
enable password lu
!
ip subnet-zero
no ip domain-lookup
!
interface Serial0
!
interface Serial1
 description this is the link to Albuquerque
!
interface Ethernet0
!
ip classless
no ip http server
line con 0
 password cisco
```

continues

Example 2-1 *Configuration Process Example (Continued)*

```
 login
!
line aux 0
line vty 0 4
!
end
```

Several differences exist between user and privileged mode, compared to configuration mode. The **configure terminal** command is used to move into configuration mode. The command prompt changes based on the configuration subcommand mode that you are in. Plus, typing a **?** in configuration mode gives you help just on configuration commands.

When you change from one configuration mode to another, the prompt changes. Example 2-2 repeats the same example as in Example 2-1, but with annotations for what is happening.

Example 2-2 *Configuration Process with Annotations*

```
User Access Verification

Password:
Router>enable
!In user mode, then you type the enable command
Password:
Router #configure terminal
!In privileged mode, using the configure terminal command to enter global
Router(config)#enable password lu
!The enable password command is a global command - so the prompt stays as a global
  command prompt
Router(config)#line console 0
!line console changes the context to console line configuration mode
Router(config-line)#login
!login is a console subcommand, so the prompt remains the same
Router(config-line)#password cisco
!password is also a console sub-command
Router(config-line)#hostname Critter
!hostname is a global command, so it is used, and the mode changes back to global
  config mode
Critter(config)#prompt Emma
!prompt is a global command, so the prompt stays as a global command mode prompt
Emma(config)#interface serial 1
!interface changes contexts to interface subcommand mode
Emma(config-if)#description link to Albuquerque
!description is a sub-command in interface config mode, so prompt stays the same
Emma(config-if)#exit
!exit backs up one mode towards global
Emma(config)#exit
!exit in global mode exits back to privileged mode
```

Router Memory, Processors, and Interfaces

The configuration file contains the configuration commands that you have typed, as well as some configuration commands entered by default by the router. The configuration file can be stored in a variety of places, including two inside a router. The router has a couple of other types of memory as well:

- **RAM**—Sometimes called DRAM for dynamic random-access memory, RAM is used by the router just as it is used by any other computer: for working storage. The *running* or *active configuration* file is stored here.
- **ROM**—This type of memory (read-only memory) stores a bootable IOS image, which is not typically used for normal operation. ROM contains the code that is used to boot the router until the router knows where to get the full IOS image, or as a backup bootable image in case there are problems.
- **Flash memory**—Either an EEPROM or a PCMCIA card, Flash memory stores fully functional IOS images and is the default location where the router gets its IOS at boot time. Flash memory also can be used to store configuration files on some Cisco routers.
- **NVRAM**—Nonvolatile RAM stores the initial or *startup* configuration file.

All these types of memory, except RAM, are permanent memory. No hard disk or diskette storage exists on Cisco routers. Figure 2-6 summarizes the use of memory in Cisco routers.

Figure 2-6 *Cisco Router Memory Types*

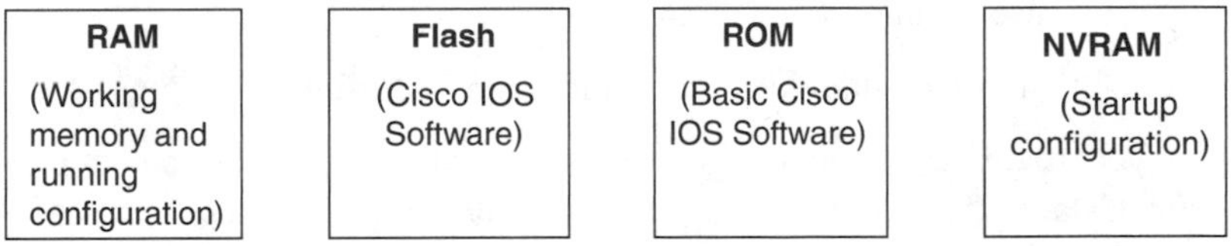

The processors in the routers vary from model to model. Although knowledge of them is not specifically listed as a requirement for the CCNA exam, some reference to terminology is useful. In most routers, only one processor option is available; thus, you would not order a specific processor type or card. The exception to this is the 7200 and 7500 families of routers. For instance, on the 7500 series, you choose either a Route Switch Processor 1 (RSP-1), RSP-2, or RSP-4 processor. In any case, all 7200 and 7500 routers, as well as most of the other Cisco router families, run IOS. This commonality enables Cisco to formulate exams, such as CCNA, that cover the IOS features without having to cover many hardware details.

The terminology used to describe the physical interfaces used for routing packets and bridging frames varies based on the model of router. Also, the types of interfaces available change over time because of new technology. For example, Packet over SONET and voice interfaces are relatively recent additions to the product line. However, some confusion exists about what to call the actual cards that house the physical interfaces. Table 2-5 summarizes the terminology that might be referred to on the test.

Table 2-5 *Samples of Router Interface Terminology*

Model Series	What Cisco IOS Software Calls Interfaces	What the Product Catalog Calls the Cards with the Interfaces on Them
2500	Interface	Modules and WAN interface cards
2600/3600	Interface	Network modules and WAN interface cards
4500	Interface	Network processor modules
7200	Interface	Port adapters and service adapters
7500	Interface	Interface processors and versatile interface processors with port adapters

But there is hope! Cisco IOS Software always uses the term *interfaces* rather than any of the other terms, so IOS commands familiar on one platform will be familiar on another. Some nuances are involved in numbering the interfaces, however. In some smaller routers, the interface number is a single number. However, with some other families of routers, the interface is numbered first with the slot in which the card resides, followed by a slash and then the port number on that card. For example, port 3 on the card in slot 2 would be interface 2/3. Numbering starts with 0 for card slots and 0 for ports on any card. In some cases, the interface is defined by three numbers: first the card slot, then the daughter card (typically called a port adapter), and then a number for the physical interface on the port adapter. The 2600 and 3600 families also use a slot/port numbering scheme.

In this book, the single-digit interface numbers are used simply for consistency and readability.

If you want to dig deeper, you might want to read about processors and interfaces in the Cisco Product Catalog (http://www.cisco.com/univercd/cc/td/doc/pcat/).

Managing Configuration Files

The CCNA exam requires that you be able to distinguish between the configuration file used at startup and the active, running configuration file. The startup configuration file is in NVRAM; the other file, which is in RAM, is the one that the router uses during operation. When the router first comes up, the router copies the stored configuration file from NVRAM into RAM, so the running and startup configuration files are identical at that point. Also, exterior to the router, configuration files can be stored as ASCII text files anywhere using TFTP or FTP.

Example 2-3 demonstrates the basic interaction between the two files. In this example, the **show running-config** and **show startup-config** commands are used. These commands display the currently used, active, *running* configuration, and the stored, *startup* configuration used when the router boots, respectively. The full command output is not shown; instead, you can see only a brief excerpt including the **host** command, which will be changed several times. (Notes are included inside the example that would not appear if doing these commands on a real router.)

Example 2-3 *Configuration Process Example*

```
hannah#show running-config
… (lines omitted)
hostname hannah
… (rest of lines omitted)

hannah#show startup-config
… (lines omitted)
hostname hannah
… (rest of lines omitted)
hannah#configure terminal
hannah(config)#hostname jessie
jessie(config)#exit
jessie#show running-config
… (lines omitted)
hostname jessie
… (rest of lines omitted - notice that the running configuration reflects the
  changed hostname)
jessie# show startup-config
… (lines omitted)
hostname hannah
… (rest of lines omitted - notice that the changed configuration is not shown
  in the startup config)
```

If you reload the router now, the host name would revert back to hannah. However, if you want to keep the changed host name of jessie, you would use the command **copy running-config startup-config**, which overwrites the current startup-config file with what is currently in the running configuration file.

The **copy** command can be used to copy files in a router, most typically a configuration file, or a new version of the IOS Software. The most basic method for moving configuration files in and out of a router is by using a TFTP server. The **copy** command is used to move configuration files among RAM, NVRAM, and a TFTP server. The files can be copied between any pair, as Figure 2-7 illustrates.

Figure 2-7 *Locations for Copying and Results from Copy Operations*

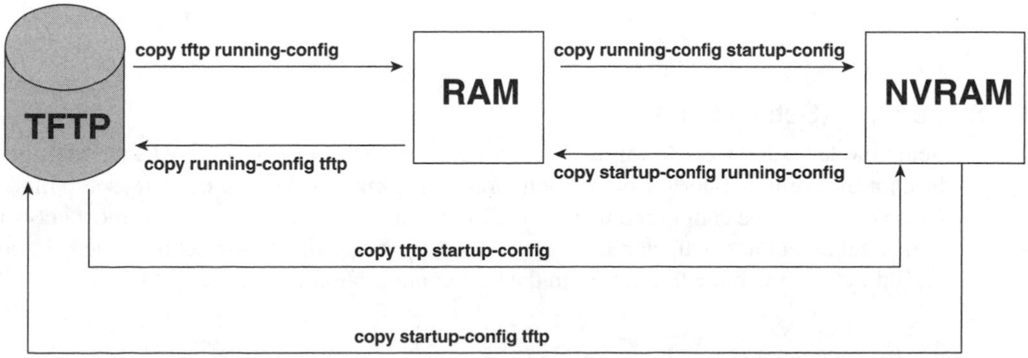

The commands can be summarized as follows:

```
copy {tftp | running-config | startup-config} {tftp | running-config | startup-config}
```

The first parameter is the "from" location; the next one is the "to" location. (Of course, choosing the same option for both parameters is not allowed.)

The **copy** command does not always replace the existing file that it is copying. Any **copy** command option moving a file into NVRAM or a TFTP server replaces the existing file—that's the easy, straightforward action. Effectively, any **copy** into RAM works just as if you typed the commands in the "from" configuration file in the order listed in the config file.

So, who cares? Well, we do. If you change the running config and then decide that you want to revert to what's in the startup-config file, the only way to guarantee that is to issue the **reload** command, which reloads, or reboots, the router.

Two key commands can be used to erase the contents of NVRAM. The **write erase** command is the older command, and the **erase startup-config** command is the newer command. Both simply erase the contents of the NVRAM configuration file. Of course, if the router is reloaded at this point, there will be no initial configuration.

Viewing the Configuration and Old-Style Configuration Commands

Once upon a time, commands that were used to display and move configuration files among RAM, NVRAM, and TFTP did not use easy-to-recall parameters such as **startup-config** and **running-config**. In fact, most people could not remember the commands or got the different ones confused. Figure 2-8 shows both the old and the new commands used to view configurations.

Figure 2-8 *Configuration* **show** *Commands*

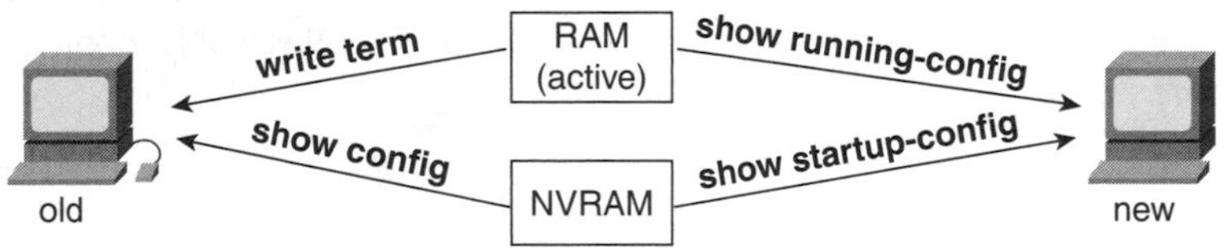

Initial Configuration (Setup Mode)

Setup mode leads a router administrator to a basic router configuration by using questions that prompt the administrator for basic configuration parameters. Instead of using setup mode, a Cisco router can be configured using the CLI in configuration mode. In fact, most networking personnel do not use setup at all, but new users sometimes like to use setup mode, particularly until they become more familiar with the CLI configuration mode.

NOTE If you plan to work with Cisco routers much, you should become accustomed with the CLI configuration mode discussed earlier. Setup mode allows only basic configuration. Both topics are covered on the CCNA exam.

Figure 2-9 and Example 2-4 describe the process used by setup mode. Setup mode is most frequently used when the router boots, and it has no configuration in NVRAM. Setup mode also can be entered by using the **setup** command from privileged mode.

Figure 2-9 *Getting into Setup Mode*

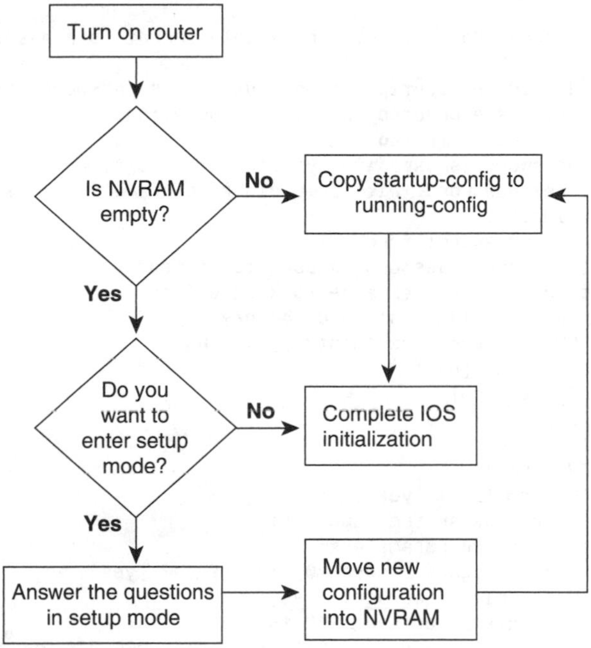

Example 2-4 shows a screen capture of using setup mode after booting a router with no configuration in NVRAM.

Example 2-4 *Router Setup Configuration Mode*

```
         --- System Configuration Dialog ---

Would you like to enter the initial configuration dialog? [yes/no]: yes
At any point you may enter a question mark '?' for help.
Use ctrl-c to abort configuration dialog at any prompt.
Default settings are in square brackets '[]'.Basic management setup configures
  only enough connectivity
```

continues

Example 2-4 *Router Setup Configuration Mode (Continued)*

```
for management of the system, extended setup will ask you
to configure each interface on the system

Would you like to enter basic management setup? [yes/no]: no
First, would you like to see the current interface summary? [yes]:
Any interface listed with OK? value "NO" does not have a valid configuration

Interface              IP-Address      OK? Method Status                Protocol
Ethernet0              unassigned      NO  unset  up                    down
Serial0                unassigned      NO  unset  down                  down
Serial1                unassigned      NO  unset  down                  down

Configuring global parameters:

  Enter host name [Router]: R1  The enable secret is a password used to protect
    access to
  privileged EXEC and configuration modes. This password, after
  entered, becomes encrypted in the configuration.
  Enter enable secret: cisco
The enable password is used when you do not specify an
  enable secret password, with some older software versions, and
  some boot images.
  Enter enable password: fred
The virtual terminal password is used to protect
  access to the router over a network interface.
  Enter virtual terminal password: barney
Configure SNMP Network Management? [yes]: no
Configure bridging? [no]:
Configure DECnet? [no]:
Configure AppleTalk? [no]:
Configure IPX? [no]:
Configure IP? [yes]:
Configure IGRP routing? [yes]:
Your IGRP autonomous system number [1]:
Configuring interface parameters:
Do you want to configure Ethernet0  interface? [yes]:
Configure IP on this interface? [yes]:
IP address for this interface: 172.16.1.1
Subnet mask for this interface [255.255.0.0] : 255.255.255.0
Class B network is 172.16.0.0, 24 subnet bits; mask is /24
Do you want to configure Serial0  interface? [yes]:
  Configure IP on this interface? [yes]:
Configure IP unnumbered on this interface? [no]:
IP address for this interface: 172.16.12.1
Subnet mask for this interface [255.255.0.0] : 255.255.255.0
Class B network is 172.16.0.0, 24 subnet bits; mask is /24
Do you want to configure Serial1  interface? [yes]:
Configure IP on this interface? [yes]:
Configure IP unnumbered on this interface? [no]:
IP address for this interface: 172.16.13.1
Subnet mask for this interface [255.255.0.0] : 255.255.255.0
Class B network is 172.16.0.0, 24 subnet bits; mask is /24
```

Example 2-4 *Router Setup Configuration Mode (Continued)*

```
The following configuration command script was created:

hostname R1
enable secret 5 $1$VOLh$pkIe0Xjx2sgjgZ/Y6Gt1s.
enable password fred
line vty 0 4
password barney
no snmp-server
!
no bridge 1
no decnet routing
no appletalk routing
no ipx routing
ip routing
!
interface Ethernet0
ip address 172.16.1.1 255.255.255.0
no mop enabled
!
interface Serial0
ip address 172.16.12.1 255.255.255.0
no mop enabled
!
interface Serial1
ip address 172.16.13.1 255.255.255.0
no mop enabled
dialer-list 1 protocol ip permit
dialer-list 1 protocol ipx permit
!
router igrp 1
redistribute connected
network 172.16.0.0
!
end

[0] Go to the IOS command prompt without saving this config.
[1] Return back to the setup without saving this config.
[2] Save this configuration to nvram and exit.

Enter your selection [2]: 2
Building configuration...
[OK]Use the enabled mode 'configure' command to modify this configuration.
Press RETURN to get started!
```

Setup behaves like Example 2-2 illustrates, whether setup was reached by booting with an empty NVRAM or whether the **setup** privileged exec command was used. First, the router asks whether you want to enter the "initial configuration dialog." Answering **y** or **yes** puts you in setup mode.

When you are finished with setup, you select one of three options for what to do next. Option 2 tells the router to save the configuration to NVRAM and exit; this option is used in Example 2-4. The router places the config in both NVRAM and RAM. This is the only operation in the IOS that changes both configuration files to include the same contents based on a single action by the user. Options 0 and 1 tell the router to ignore the configuration that you just entered and to either exit to the command prompt (option 1) or start over gain with setup (option 1).

Upgrading Cisco IOS Software and the Cisco IOS Software Boot Process

50 List the commands to load Cisco IOS Software from: Flash memory, a TFTP server, or ROM.

51 Prepare to back up, upgrade, and load a backup Cisco IOS Software image.

Engineers need to know how to upgrade the IOS to move to a later release. Typically, a router has one IOS image in Flash memory, and that is the IOS that is used. (The term *IOS image* simply refers to a file containing the IOS.) The upgrade process might include steps such as copying a newer IOS image into Flash memory, configuring the router to tell it which IOS image to use, and deleting the old one when you are confident that the new release works well.

A router decides what IOS image to use when the router boots. Also, to upgrade to a new IOS or back out to an older IOS, you must reload the router. So, it's a convenient time to cover the boot sequence and some of the related issues.

Finally, password recovery is covered in this section. Password recovery is less likely to be on the CCNA exam than some other topics, but, guess what—it requires a reboot of the router, so now is a good time to cover it.

Upgrading an IOS Image into Flash Memory

IOS files typically are stored in Flash memory. Flash memory is rewriteable, permanent storage, which is ideal for storing files that need to be retained when the router loses power. Also, because there are no moving parts, there is a smaller chance of failure as compared with disk drives, which provides better availability. As you will read soon, IOS can be placed on an external TFTP server, but using an external server typically is done for testing—in production, practically every Cisco router loads an IOS stored in the only type of large, permanent memory, and that is Flash memory.

As Figure 2-10 illustrates, to upgrade an IOS image into Flash memory, you first must obtain the IOS image from Cisco. Then you must place the IOS image into the default directory of a TFTP server. Finally, you must issue the **copy** command from the router, copying the file into Flash memory.

NOTE You also can copy the IOS image directly from the FTP server. However, because the TFTP server function has been around a long time, I show it here. There could be plenty of exam questions left in the question database that cover TFTP.

Figure 2-10 *Complete Cisco IOS Software Upgrade Process*

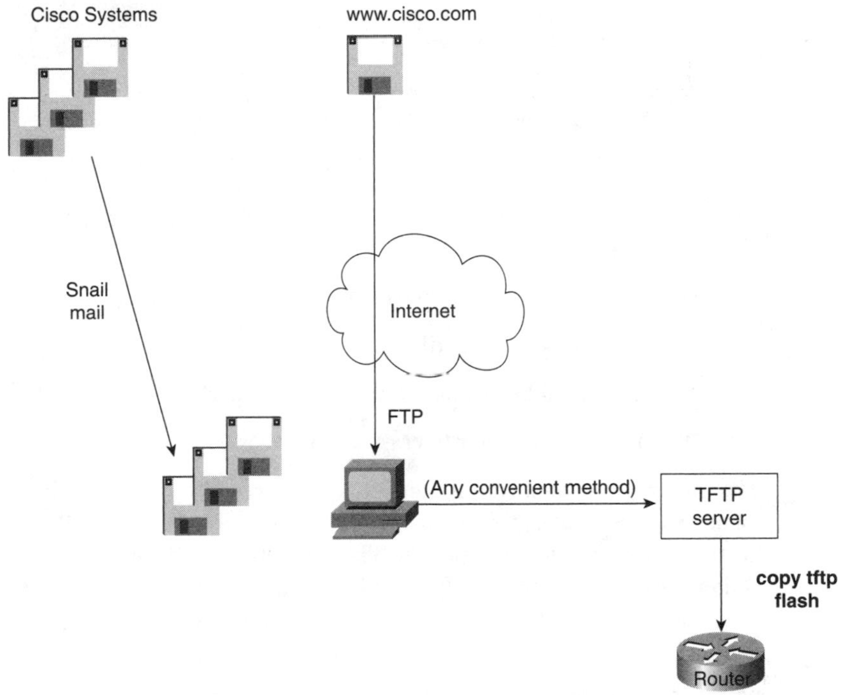

Example 2-5 provides an example of the final step, copying the IOS image into Flash memory.

Example 2-5 **copy tftp flash** *Command Copies the IOS Image to Flash Memory*

```
R1#copy tftp flash

System flash directory:
File  Length   Name/status
  1   7530760   c4500-d-mz.120-2.bin
[7530824 bytes used, 857784 available, 8388608 total]
```

continues

Example 2-5 **copy tftp flash** *Command Copies the IOS Image to Flash Memory (Continued)*

```
Address or name of remote host [255.255.255.255]? 134.141.3.33
Source file name? c4500-d-mz.120-5.bin
Destination file name [c4500-d-mz.120-5.bin]?
Accessing file c4500-d-mz.120-5.bin ' on 134.141.3.33...
Loading c4500-d-mz.120-5.bin from 134.141.3.33 (via TokenRing0): ! [OK]

Erase flash device before writing? [confirm]
Flash contains files. Are you sure you want to erase? [confirm]

Copy 'c4500-d-mz.120-5.bin ' from server
  as 'c4500-d-mz.120-5.bin ' into Flash WITH erase? [yes/no]y
Erasing device... eeeeeeeeeeeeeeeeeeeeeeeeeeeeeeee ...erased
Loading c4500-d-mz.120-5.bin  from 134.141.3.33 (via TokenRing0):
!!!!!!!!!!!!!!!!!!!!!!!!!!!!!!!!!!!!!!!!!!!!!!!!!!!!!!!!!!!!!!!!!!!!!!!!!!!!!!!
!!!!!!!!!!!!!!!!!!!!!!!!!!!!!!!!!!!!!!!!!!!!!!!!!!!!!!!!!!!!!!!!!!!! (leaving out
lots of exclamation points…)
[OK - 7530760/8388608 bytes]

Verifying checksum...  OK (0xA93E)
Flash copy took 0:04:26 [hh:mm:ss]
R1#
```

During this process of copying the IOS image into Flash memory, the router will need to discover several important facts:

1. What is the IP address or host name of the TFTP server?
2. What is the name of the file?
3. Is space available for this file in Flash memory?
4. Do you want the router to erase the old files?

The router will prompt you for answers, as necessary. Afterward, the router erases Flash memory as needed, copies the file, and then verifies that the checksum for the file shows that no errors occurred in transmission. The **show flash** command then can be used to verify the contents of Flash memory (see Example 2-6). (The **show flash** output can vary among router families.) Before the new IOS is used, however, the router must be reloaded.

Example 2-6 *Verifying Flash Memory Contents with the* **show flash** *Command*

```
fred#show flash

System flash directory:
File  Length   Name/status
  1   6181132 c4500-d-mz.120-5.bin
[4181196 bytes used, 4207412 available, 8388608 total]
8192K bytes of processor board System flash (Read ONLY)
```

In some cases, Flash memory could be in read-only mode. That is the case when a router loads only part of the IOS into RAM, to conserve RAM. Other parts of the IOS file are kept in Flash memory (Flash memory access time is much slower than RAM's). In this case, if Flash memory must be erased to make room for a new image, the IOS could not continue to run. So, if the router is running from a portion of IOS in Flash memory, the router first must be booted using IOS in ROM. Then the Flash memory will be in read/write mode and the erase and copy processes can be accomplished. The **copy tftp flash** command in later releases of the IOS actually performs the entire process for you. In earlier releases, you had to boot the router from ROM and then issue the **copy tftp flash** command.

The Cisco IOS Software Boot Sequence

Cisco routers perform the same types of tasks that a typical computer performs when you power it on or reboot (reload) it. Of course, most of us do not think about these details very often. The router performs some somewhat obvious steps, with one of those being tricky—namely, the process of choosing the location of the software to load and use in the router. And that software might not be IOS!

The boot process follows this basic litany:

1. The router performs a power-on self-test (POST) to discover and verify the hardware.
2. The router loads and runs bootstrap code from ROM.
3. The router finds the IOS or other software and loads it.
4. The router finds the configuration file and loads it into running config.

All routers attempt all four steps each time that the router is powered on or reloaded. The POST code and functions cannot be changed by the router administrator. The location of the bootstrap code, the IOS to load, and the configuration file can be changed by the administrator—but you almost always use the default location for the bootstrap code (ROM) and for the initial configuration (NVRAM). So, the location of IOS or other software is the only part that typically is changed.

Three categories of operating systems can be loaded into the router:

- The full-function IOS image that you have been introduced to in this chapter.
- A limited-function IOS that resides in ROM.
- A different non-IOS operating system that is also stored in ROM, and this can be loaded. This operating system, called ROM Monitor, is used for two purposes—for low-level debugging and for password recovery. Unless you are performing password recovery, you would seldom use ROMMON mode.

Table 2-6 lists the three operating system categories and their main functions.

Table 2-6 *Three OS Categories for Routers*

Operating System	Location Where It Is Stored	Purpose
Full-featured IOS	Typically in Flash memory; can be on TFTP server	Full-featured, normal IOS used in production.
Limited-function IOS	ROM	Basic IP connectivity, used when Flash memory is broken and you need IP connectivity to copy a new IOS into Flash memory. Called RXBOOT mode.
ROMMON	ROM	Low-level debugging, usually by the Cisco TAC and for password recovery. Called ROM Monitor mode.

So, you need to tell the router whether to use ROMMON, the limited-function IOS, or the full-featured IOS. Of course, most of the time you use the full-featured IOS in Flash memory. However, you might want to use IOS that resides on a TFTP server, or there could be multiple IOS images in Flash memory—and all of these options are configurable.

Two configuration tools tell the router what OS to load. First, the configuration register tells the router whether to use a full-featured IOS, ROMMON, or the limited-feature IOS, which is also called RXBOOT mode. The *configuration register* is a 16-bit software register in the router, and its value is set using the **config-register** global configuration command. (Some older routers had a hardware configuration register with jumpers on the processor card, to set bits to a value of 0 or 1.) Figure 2-11 shows an example binary breakdown of the default value for the configuration register, which is hexadecimal 2102.

Figure 2-11 *Binary Version of Configuration Register, Value Hex 2102*

15	14	13	12	11	10	9	8	7	6	5	4	3	2	1	0
0	0	1	0	0	0	0	1	0	0	0	0	0	0	1	0

The *boot field* is the name of the low-order 4 bits of the configuration register. This field can be considered a 4-bit value, represented as a single hexadecimal digit. (Cisco represents hexadecimal values by preceding the hex digit(s) with 0x—for example, 0xA would mean a single hex digit *A*.) If the boot field is hex 0, ROMMON is loaded. If the boot field is hex 1, RXBOOT mode is used. For anything else, it loads a full-featured IOS. But which one?

The second method used to determine where the router tries to obtain an IOS image is through the use of the **boot system** configuration command. If the configuration register calls for a full-featured IOS (boot field 2-F), the router reads the configuration file for boot system commands. If there are no boot system commands, the router takes the default action, which is to load the first file in Flash memory. Table 2-7 summarizes the use of the configuration register and the **boot system** command at initialization time.

Table 2-7 **boot system** *Command*

Value of Boot Field	Boot System Commands	Result
0x0	Ignored if present	ROMMON is loaded.
0x1	Ignored if present	IOS from ROM is loaded, also known as RXBOOT mode.
0x2-0xF	No **boot** command	The first IOS file in Flash memory is loaded; if that fails, the router broadcasts looking for an IOS on a TFTP server. If that fails, IOS from ROM is loaded.
0x2-0xF	**boot system ROM**	IOS from ROM is loaded.
0x2-0xF	**boot system flash**	The first file from Flash memory is loaded.
0x2-0xF	**boot system flash** *filename*	IOS with the name *filename* is loaded from Flash memory.
0x2-0xF	**boot system tftp** *filename* **10.1.1.1**	IOS with the name *filename* is loaded from the TFTP server.
0x2-0xF	Multiple boot system commands, any variety	An attempt occurs to load IOS based on the first boot command in configuration. If that fails, the second boot command is used, and so on, until one is successful.

Password Recovery

Start Extra Credit

The password-recovery process relies on the fact that the configuration register can be used to make the router ignore the NVRAM configuration when the router is reloaded. The router will be up, but with a default configuration; this allows a console user to log in, enter privileged mode, and change any encrypted passwords or view any unencrypted passwords. However, there is a "chicken and the egg" problem—to cause the router to ignore NVRAM at boot time, the configuration register must be changed. To do that, you must be in privileged mode—and if you were already there, you could reset any encrypted passwords or view any unencrypted ones. It seems to be a vicious circle.

ROMMON will allow you to change the configuration register without knowing any passwords or even booting the IOS. To enter ROMMON mode, press the Break key during the first 60 seconds after power-on of the router. Then you must set bit 6 in the configuration register to binary 1, which is done by setting the entire config register with a four-digit hexadecimal value. For example, hex 2142 is identical to hex 2102, except that bit 6 is binary 1. Knowing how to reset the config register enables you to boot the router (ignoring NVRAM), allowing the console user to see or change the unencrypted or encrypted passwords, respectively.

The process is slightly different for different models of routers, although the concepts are identical. Table 2-8 outlines the process for each type of router. For more information, see http://www.cisco.com/warp/public/474/.

End Extra Credit

Table 2-8 *Password Recovery*

Step	Function	How to Do This for 1600, 2600, 3600, 4500, 7200, 7500	How to Do This for 2000, 2500, 3000, 4000, 7000
1	Turn the router off and then back on again.	Use the power switch.	Same as other routers.
2	Press the Break key within the first 60 seconds.	Find the Break key on your console device's keyboard.	Same as other routers.
3	Change the configuration register so that bit 6 is 1.	Use the ROMMON command **confreg**, and answer the prompts.	Use the ROMMON command **o/r 0x2142**.
4	Cause the router to load IOS.	Use the ROMMON **reload** command or, if unavailable, power off and on.	Use the ROMMON command **initialize**.

Table 2-8 *Password Recovery (Continued)*

Step	Function	How to Do This for 1600, 2600, 3600, 4500, 7200, 7500	How to Do This for 2000, 2500, 3000, 4000, 7000
5	Avoid using setup mode, which will be prompted for at the console.	Just say no.	Same as other routers.
6	Enter privileged mode at console.	Press Enter and use the **enable** command (no password required).	Same as other routers.
7	Assuming that you still want to use the configuration in NVRAM, copy it to the running config.	**copy startup-config running-config**	**copy startup-config running-config**
8	View startup config to see unencrypted passwords.	Use the exec command **show startup-config**.	Same as other routers.
9	Use the appropriate config commands to reset encrypted commands.	For example, use **enable secret xyz123** command to set the enable secret password.	Same as other routers.
10	Change the config register back to its original value.	Use the config command **config-reg 0x2102**.	Same as other routers.
11	Reload the router after saving the configuration.	Use the **copy running-config startup-config** and **reload** commands.	Same as other routers.

A few nuances need further explanation. First, the **confreg** ROMMON command prompts you with questions that correspond to the functions of the bits in the configuration register. When the prompt asks, "Ignore system config info[y/n]?", it is asking you about bit 6. Entering **yes** sets the bit to 1. The rest of the questions can be defaulted. The last **confreg** question asks, "Change boot characteristics[y/n]?", which asks whether you want to change the boot field of the config register. You don't really need to change it, but the published password-recovery algorithm lists that step, which is the only reason that it is mentioned here. Just changing bit 6 to 1 is enough to get the router booted and you into privileged mode to find or change the passwords.

Foundation Summary

The "Foundation Summary" is a collection of tables and figures that provide a convenient review of many key concepts in this chapter. For those of you already comfortable with the topics in this chapter, this summary could help you recall a few details. For those of you who just read this chapter, this review should help solidify some key facts. For any of you doing your final preparation before the exam, these tables and figures will be a convenient way to review the day before the exam.

The console, auxiliary, and Telnet passwords are all set separately, as shown in Table 2-9.

Table 2-9 *CLI Password Configuration*

Access from . . .	Password Type	Configuration
Console	Console password	**line console** *0* **login** **password** *faith*
Auxiliary	Auxiliary password	**line aux** *0* **login** **password** *hope*
Telnet	vty password	**line vty** *0 4* **login** **password** *love*

Table 2-10 lists the commands used to manipulate previously typed commands.

Table 2-10 *Key Sequences for Command Edit and Recall*

Keyboard Command	What the User Gets
Up arrow or Ctrl-p	This displays the most recently used command. If it is pressed again, the next most recent command appears until the history buffer is exhausted. (The *p* stands for *previous.*)
Down arrow or Ctrl-n	If you have gone too far back into the history buffer, these keys will go forward, in order, to the more recently typed commands. (The *n* is for *next.*)
Left arrow or Ctrl-b	This moves the cursor backward in the currently displayed command without deleting characters. (The *b* stands for *back.*)
Right arrow or Ctrl-f	This moves the cursor forward in the currently displayed command without deleting characters. (The *f* stands for *forward.*)

Table 2-10 *Key Sequences for Command Edit and Recall (Continued)*

Keyboard Command	What the User Gets
Backspace	This moves the cursor backward in the currently displayed command, deleting characters.
Ctrl-a	This moves the cursor directly to the first character of the currently displayed command.
Ctrl-e	This moves the cursor directly to the end of the currently displayed command.
Esc-b	This moves the cursor back one word in the currently displayed command.
Esc-f	This moves the cursor forward one word in the currently displayed command.
Ctrl-r	This creates a new command prompt, followed by all the characters typed since the last command prompt was written. This is particularly useful if system messages confuse the screen and it is unclear what you have typed so far.

Figure 2-12 illustrates the relationships among configuration mode, user exec mode, and privileged exec mode.

Figure 2-12 *CLI Configuration Mode versus Exec Modes*

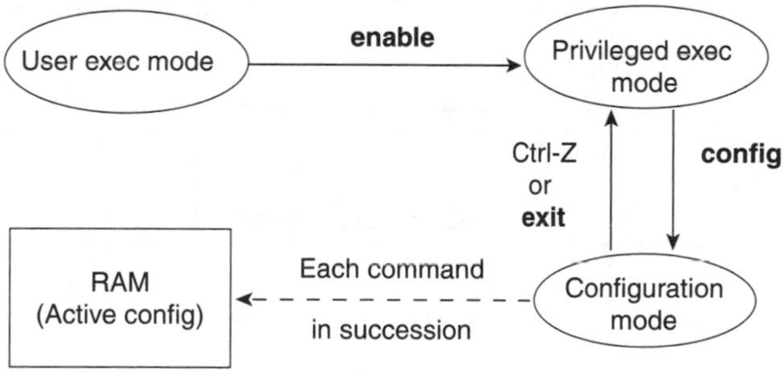

Routers have four types of memory:

- **RAM**—Sometimes called DRAM for *dynamic* random-access memory, RAM is used by the router just as it is used by any other computer: for working storage. The *running* or *active configuration* file is stored here.
- **ROM**—This type of memory (read-only memory) stores a bootable IOS image, which is not typically used for normal operation. ROM contains the code that is used to boot the router until the router knows where to get the full IOS image, or as a backup bootable image in case there are problems.

- **Flash memory**—Either an EEPROM or a PCMCIA card, Flash memory stores fully functional IOS images and is the default location where the router gets its IOS at boot time. Flash memory also can be used to store configuration files on some Cisco routers.
- **NVRAM**—Nonvolatile RAM stores the initial or startup configuration file.

All these types of memory, except RAM, are permanent memory. No hard disk or diskette storage exists on Cisco routers. Figure 2-13 summarizes the use of memory in Cisco routers.

Figure 2-13 *Cisco Router Memory Types*

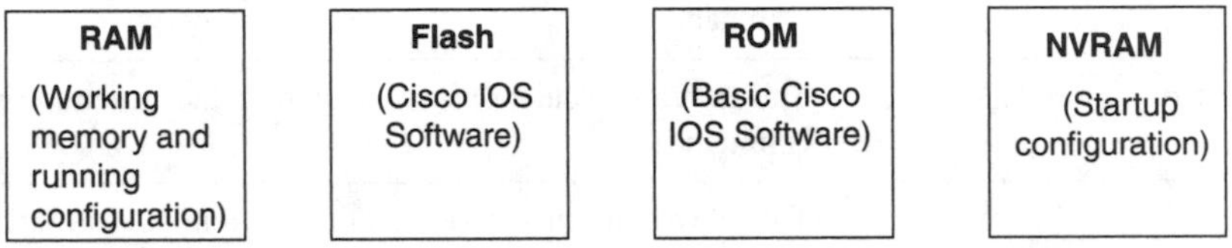

The **copy** command is used to move configuration files among RAM, NVRAM, and a TFTP server. The files can be copied between any pair, as Figure 2-14 illustrates.

Figure 2-14 *Locations for Copying and Results from Copy Operations*

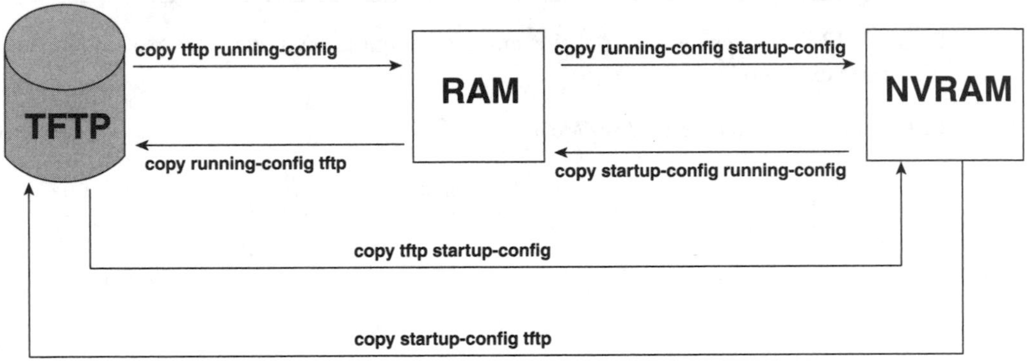

The commands can be summarized as follows:

```
copy {tftp | running-config | startup-config} {tftp | running-config | startup-config}
```

The first parameter is the "from" location; the next one is the "to" location. (Of course, choosing the same option for both parameters is not allowed.)

Figure 2-15 shows both the old and the new commands used to view configurations.

Figure 2-15 *Configuration* **show** *Commands*

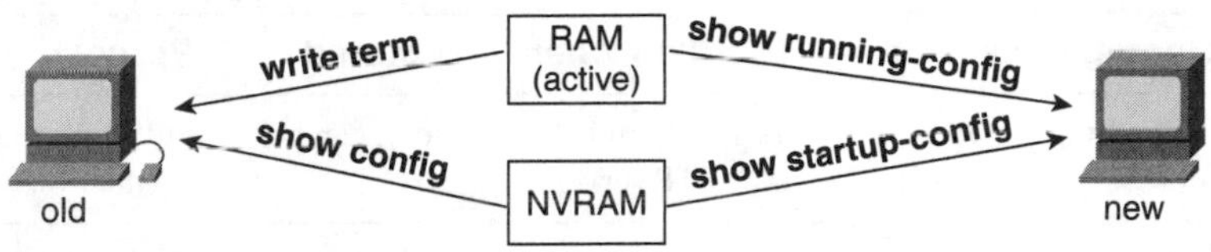

Figure 2-16 illustrates the process of upgrading Cisco IOS Software.

Figure 2-16 *Complete Cisco IOS Software Upgrade Process*

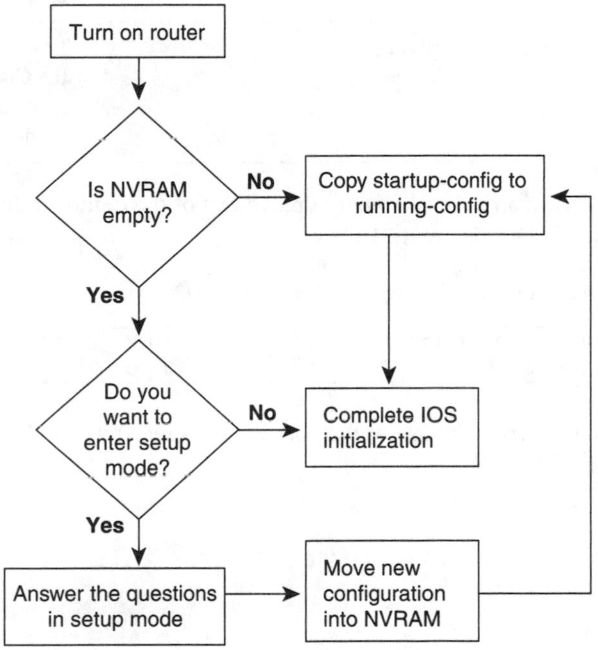

The boot process follows this basic litany:

1. The router performs a power-on self-test (POST) to discover and verify the hardware.
2. The router loads and runs the bootstrap code from ROM.
3. The router finds the IOS or other software and loads it.
4. The router finds the configuration file and loads it into the running config.

Table 2-11 lists the three operating system categories and their main functions.

Table 2-11 *Three OS Categories for Routers*

Operating System	Location Where It Is Stored	Purpose
Full-featured IOS	Typically in Flash memory, can be on TFTP server	Full-featured, normal IOS used in production
Limited-function IOS	ROM	Basic IP connectivity, used when Flash memory is broken and you need IP connectivity to copy a new IOS into Flash memory. Called RXBOOT mode.
ROMMON	ROM	Low-level debugging, usually by the Cisco TAC and for password recovery. Called ROM Monitor mode.

Figure 2-17 shows an example binary breakdown of the default value for the configuration register, which is hexadecimal 2102.

Figure 2-17 *Binary Version of Configuration Register, Value Hex 2102*

15	14	13	12	11	10	9	8	7	6	5	4	3	2	1	0
0	0	1	0	0	0	0	1	0	0	0	0	0	0	1	0

Table 2-12 summarizes the use of the configuration register and the **boot system** command at initialization time.

Table 2-12 **boot system** *Command*

Value of Boot Field	Boot System Commands	Result
0x0	Ignored if present	ROMMON is loaded.
0x1	Ignored if present	IOS from ROM is loaded, also known as RXBOOT mode.
0x2-0xF	No **boot** command	The first IOS file in Flash memory is loaded; if that fails, the router broadcasts looking for an IOS on a TFTP server. If that fails, IOS from ROM is loaded.
0x2-0xF	**boot system ROM**	IOS from ROM is loaded.
0x2-0xF	**boot system flash**	The first file from Flash memory is loaded.
0x2-0xF	**boot system flash** *filename*	IOS with the name *filename* is loaded from Flash memory.
0x2-0xF	**boot system tftp** *filename* **10.1.1.1**	IOS with the name *filename* is loaded from the TFTP server.
0x2-0xF	Multiple boot system commands, any variety	An attempt occurs to load the IOS based on the first boot command in configuration. If that fails, the second boot command is used, and so on, until one is successful.

Q&A

As mentioned in Chapter 1, the questions and scenarios in this book are more difficult than what you should experience on the actual exam. The questions do not attempt to cover more breadth or depth than the exam; however, they are designed to make sure that you know the answer. Rather than allowing you to derive the answer from clues hidden inside the question itself, the questions challenge your understanding and recall of the subject. Questions from the "Do I Know This Already?" quiz from the beginning of the chapter are repeated here to ensure that you have mastered the chapter's topic areas. Hopefully, these questions will help limit the number of exam questions on which you narrow your choices to two options and then guess. Make sure to use the CD and take the simulated exams.

The answers to these questions can be found in Appendix A.

1 What are the two names for the router's mode of operation that, when accessed, enables you to issue commands that could be disruptive to router operations?

____

____

____

2 What are three methods of logging on to a router?

____

____

____

3 What is the name of the user interface mode of operation used when you cannot issue disruptive commands?

____

____

____

4 Can the auxiliary port be used for anything besides remote modem user access to a router? If so, what other purpose can it serve?

____

____

____

5 How many console ports can be installed on a Cisco 7500 router?

6 What command would you use to receive command help if you knew that a **show** command option *begins with a c but you cannot recall the option?*

7 While you are logged in to a router, you issue the command **copy ?** and get a response of "Unknown command, computer name, or host." Offer an explanation for why this error message appears.

8 Is the number of retrievable commands based on the number of characters in each command, or is it simply a number of commands, regardless of their size?

9 How can you retrieve a previously used command? (Name two ways.)

10 After typing **show ip route,** which is the only command that you typed since logging in to the router, you now want to issue the **show ip arp** command. What steps would you take to execute this command by using command-recall keystrokes?

11 After typing **show ip route 128.1.1.0,** you now want to issue the command **show ip route 128.1.4.0.** What steps would you take to do so, using command-recall and command-editing keystrokes?

____

____

____

12 What configuration command causes the router to require a password from a user at the console? What configuration mode context must you be in? (That is, what command(s) must be typed before this command after entering configuration mode?) List the commands in the order in which they must be typed while in config mode.

____

____

____

13 What configuration command is used to tell the router the password that is required at the console? What configuration mode context must you be in? (That is, what command(s) must you type before this command after entering configuration mode?) List the commands in the order in which they must be typed while in config mode.

____

____

____

14 What are the primary purposes of Flash memory in a Cisco router?

____

____

____

15 What is the intended purpose of NVRAM memory in a Cisco router?

____

____

____

16 What does the "NV" stand for in NVRAM?

____

____

____

17 What is the intended purpose of RAM in a Cisco router?

______

______

______

18 What is the main purpose of ROM in a Cisco router?

______

______

______

19 What configuration command would be needed to cause a router to use an IOS image named c2500-j-l.112-14.bin on TFTP server 128.1.1.1 when the router is reloaded? If you forgot the first parameter of this command, what steps must you take to learn the correct parameters and add the command to the configuration? (Assume that you are not logged in to the router when you start.)

______

______

______

20 What command sets the password that would be required after typing the **enable** command? Is that password encrypted by default?

______

______

______

21 To have the correct syntax, what must you add to the following configuration command:

______

______

______

22 Name two commands that affect the text used as the command prompt.

______

______

______

23 When using setup mode, you are prompted at the end of the process for whether you want to use the configuration parameters that you just typed in. Which type of memory is this configuration stored in if you type **yes**?

____

____

____

24 What two methods could a router administrator use to cause a router to load IOS stored in ROM?

____

____

____

25 What could a router administrator do to cause a router to load file xyz123.bin from TFTP server 128.1.1.1 upon the next reload? Is there more than one way to accomplish this?

____

____

____

26 What is the process used to update the contents of Flash memory so that a new IOS in a file called c4500-d-mz.120-5.bin on TFTP server 128.1.1.1 is copied into Flash memory?

____

____

____

27 Name three possible problems that could prevent the command **boot system tftp c2500-j-l.112- 14.bin 128.1.1.1** from succeeding.

____

____

____

28 Two different IOS files are in a router's Flash memory: one called c2500-j-l.111-3.bin and one called c2500-j-l.112-14.bin. Which one does the router use when it boots up? How could you force the other IOS file to be used? Without looking at the router configuration, what command could be used to discover which file was used for the latest boot of the router?

29 Is the password required at the console the same one that is required when Telnet is used to access a router?

30 Which IP routing protocols could be enabled using setup?

31 Name two commands used to view the configuration to be used at the next reload of the router. Which one is a more recent addition to the IOS?

32 Name two commands used to view the configuration that is currently used in a router. Which one is a more recent addition to IOS?

33 True or false: The **copy startup-config running-config** command always changes the currently used configuration for this router to exactly match what is in the startup configuration file. Explain.\

Scenarios

Scenario 2-1

Compare the following output in Example 2-7 and Example 2-8. Example 2-7 was gathered at 11:00 a.m., 30 minutes earlier than in Example 2-8. What can you definitively say happened to this router during the intervening half hour?

Example 2-7 *1:00 a.m.* **show running-config**

```
hostname Gorno
!
enable password cisco
!
interface Serial0
 ip address 134.141.12.1 255.255.255.0
!
interface Serial1
 ip address 134.141.13.1 255.255.255.0
!
interface Ethernet0
 ip address 134.141.1.1 255.255.255.0
!
router rip
 network 134.141.0.0
!
line con 0
 password cisco
 login
line aux 0
line vty 0 4
 password cisco
 login
```

Example 2-8 *11:30 a.m.* **show running-config**

```
hostname SouthernSiberia
prompt Gorno
!
enable secret $8df003j56ske92
enable password cisco
!
interface Serial0
 ip address 134.141.12.1 255.255.255.0
!
interface Serial1
 ip address 134.141.13.1 255.255.255.0
!
interface Ethernet0
 ip address 134.141.1.1 255.255.255.0
```

Example 2-8 *11:30 a.m.* **show running-config** *(Continued)*

```
 no cdp enable
!
router rip
 network 134.141.0.0
!
line con 0
 password cisco
 login
line aux 0
line vty 0 4
 password cisco
 login
```

Questions on Scenario 2-1

1 During the process of changing the configuration in Scenario 2-1, the command prompt temporarily was **SouthernSiberia(config)#.** What configuration commands, and in what order, could have changed the configuration as shown and allowed the prompt to temporarily be **SouthernSiberia(config)#**?

2 Assuming that Figure 2-18 is complete, what effect does the **no cdp enable** command have?

Figure 2- 18 *Siberian Enterprises' Sample Network*

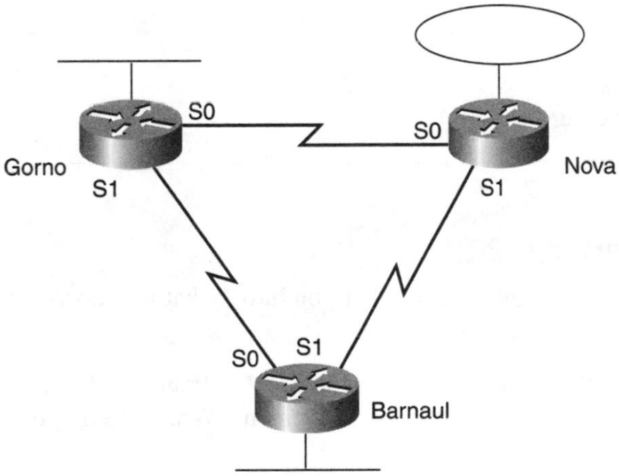

3 What effect would the **no enable password cisco** command have at this point?

Scenario 2-2

Example 2-9 shows that the **running-config** command was executed on the Nova router.

Example 2-9 *Configuration of Router Nova*

```
hostname Nova
banner # This is the router in Nova Sibiersk; Dress warmly before entering! #
!
boot system tftp c2500-js-113.bin 134.141.88.3
boot system flash c2500-j-l.111-9.bin
boot system rom
!
enable password cisco
!
interface Serial0
 ip address 134.141.12.2 255.255.255.0
!
interface Serial1
 ip address 134.141.23.2 255.255.255.0
!
interface TokenRing0
 ip address 134.141.2.2 255.255.255.0
!
router rip
 network 134.141.0.0
!
line con 0
 password cisco
 login
line aux 0
line vty 0 4
 password cisco
 login
```

Questions on Scenario 2-2

1 If this is all the information that you have, what IOS do you expect will be loaded when the user reloads Nova?

2 Examine the following command output in Example 2-10, taken immediately before the user is going to type the **reload** command. What IOS do you expect will be loaded?

Example 2-10 show ip route *Command Output for Nova*

```
Nova#show ip route
Codes: C - connected, S - static, I - IGRP, R - RIP, M - mobile, B - BGP
       D - EIGRP, EX - EIGRP external, O - OSPF, IA - OSPF inter area
       N1 - OSPF NSSA external type 1, N2 - OSPF NSSA external type 2
       E1 - OSPF external type 1, E2 - OSPF external type 2, E - EGP
       i - IS-IS, L1 - IS-IS level-1, L2 - IS-IS level-2, ia - IS-IS inter area
       * - candidate default, U - per-user static route, o - ODR
       P - periodic downloaded static route


Gateway of last resort is not set

     134.141.0.0/24 is subnetted, 6 subnets
C       134.141.2.0 is directly connected, TokenRing0
R       134.141.3.0 [120/1] via 134.141.23.3, 00:00:15, Serial1
R       134.141.1.0 [120/1] via 134.141.12.1, 00:00:20, Serial0
C       134.141.12.0 is directly connected, Serial0
R       134.141.13.0 [120/1] via 134.141.12.1, 00:00:20, Serial0
                     [120/1] via 134.141.23.3, 00:00:15, Serial1
C       134.141.23.0 is directly connected, Serial1
```

3 Now examine the following **show flash** command in Example 2-11, which was issued immediately after the **show ip route** command in Example 2-10 but before the user issued the **reload** command. What IOS do you think would be loaded in this case?

Example 2-11 show flash *Command Output for Nova*

```
Nova#show flash
4096K bytes of flash memory sized on embedded flash.
File   name/status
 0 c2500-j-l.111-3.bin
[682680/4194304 bytes free/total]
```

4 Now examine the configuration in Example 2-12. Assume that there is now a route to 134.141.88.0 and that the file c2500-j-l.111-9.bin is an IOS image in Flash memory. What IOS do you expect will be loaded now?

Example 2-12 show running-config *Command Output for Router Nova*

```
hostname Nova
banner # This is the router in Nova Sibiersk; Dress warmly before entering! #
!
boot system tftp c2500-js-113.bin 134.141.88.3
boot system flash c2500-j-l.111-9.bin
!
enable password cisco
!
interface Serial0
 ip address 134.141.12.2 255.255.255.0
!
interface Serial1
 ip address 134.141.23.2 255.255.255.0
!
interface Ethernet0
 ip address 134.141.2.2 255.255.255.0
!
router rip
 network 134.141.0.0
!
line con 0
 password cisco
 login
line aux 0
line vty 0 4
 password cisco
 login
!
config-register 0x2101
```

Answers to Scenarios

Scenario 2-1 Answers

In Scenario 2-1, the following commands were added to the configuration:

- **enable secret** as a global command.
- **prompt** as a global command.
- **no cdp enable** as an Ethernet0 subcommand.
- The **hostname** command also was changed.

The scenario questions' answers are as follows:

1. If the host name was changed to SouthSiberia first and the **prompt** command was added next, the prompt would have temporarily been SouthSiberia. Configuration commands are added to the RAM configuration file immediately and are used. In this case, when the **prompt** command was added, it caused the router to use Gorno, not the then-current host name SouthernSiberia, as the prompt.
2. No practical effect takes place. Because no other Cisco CDP–enabled devices are on that Ethernet, CDP messages from Gorno are useless. So, the only effect is to lessen the overhead on that Ethernet in a very small way.
3. No effect takes place, other than cleaning up the configuration file. The **enable password** is not used if an **enable secret** is configured.

Scenario 2-2 Answers

The answers to the questions in Scenario 2-2 are as follows:

1 The first boot system statement would be used: **boot system tftp c2500-js-113.bin 134.141.88.3**.

2 The **boot system flash** command would be used. The TFTP boot presumably would fail because there is not currently a route to the subnet of which the TFTP server is a part. It is reasonable to assume that a route would not be learned 2 minutes later when the router had reloaded. So, the next **boot system** command (**flash**) would be used.

3 The **boot system ROM** command would be used. Because there is no file in Flash memory called c2500-j- l.111-9.bin, the boot from Flash memory would fail as well, leaving only one **boot** command.

4 IOS from ROM would be loaded because of the configuration register. If the configuration register boot field is set to 0x1, **boot system** commands are ignored. So, having a route to the 134.141.88.0/ 24 subnet and having c2500-j-l.111-9.bin in Flash memory does not help.

Exam Topics in This Chapter

5 Describe data-link and network addresses, and identify key differences between them.

6 Define and describe the function of a MAC address.

7 List the key internetworking functions of the OSI network layer.

8 Identify at least three reasons why the industry uses a layered model.

9 Describe the two parts of network addressing, and then identify the parts in specific protocol address examples.

10 Define and explain the five conversion steps of data encapsulation.

11 Describe connection-oriented network service and connectionless network service, and identify their key differences.

12 Identify the parts in specific protocol address examples.

CHAPTER 3

OSI Reference Model and Layered Communication

In years past, the need to understand the Open System Interconnection (OSI) reference model for networking grew rapidly. The U.S. government passed laws requiring vendors to support OSI software on their systems; if vendors did not offer this support, the government would no longer buy the systems. Several vendors even predicted that the global Internet would evolve toward using the OSI protocols instead of TCP/IP. As the century turns, however, OSI has been implemented on a much smaller scale than predicted. Today, no one even sells a full-complement OSI software suite. However, some components of the OSI model are popularly implemented today. For example, OSI network service access point (NSAP) network layer addresses often are used for signaling in Asynchronous Transfer Mode (ATM) networks. In short, OSI was a great idea that never fully made it to market.

So, why have a whole chapter on OSI? As a CCNA, you'll be expected to learn and interpret new technologies and protocols. The OSI seven-layer reference model is an excellent point of reference for describing the concepts and functions behind these new technologies and protocols. References to Layer 2 switching and Layer 3 switching, which are popular topics today, refer to the comparison between Layers 2 and 3 of the OSI model. Cisco courses make generous use of the OSI model as a reference for comparison with other network protocol implementations. So, this chapter will not actually help you understand OSI fully, but it will discuss OSI functions in comparison with popularly implemented protocols.

How to Best Use This Chapter

By taking the following steps, you can make better use of your study time:

- Keep your notes and the answers for all your work with this book in one place, for easy reference.
- Take the "Do I Know This Already?" quiz, and write down your answers. Studies show that retention is significantly increased through writing down facts and concepts, even if you never look at the information again.
- Use the diagram in Figure 3-1 to guide you to the next step.

Figure 3-1 *How to Use This Chapter*

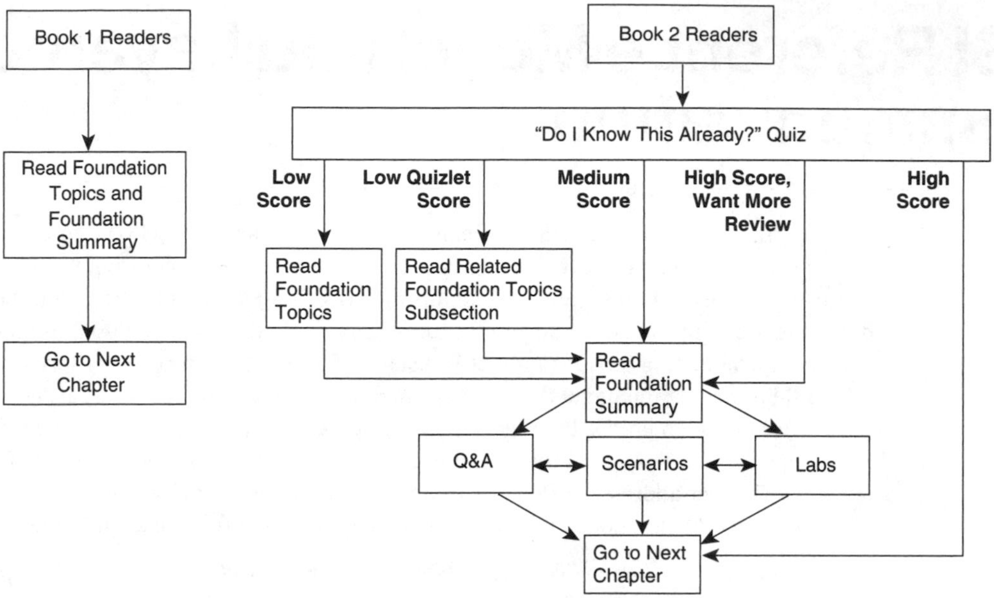

"Do I Know This Already?" Quiz

The purpose of the "Do I Know This Already?" quiz is to help you decide what parts of this chapter to use. If you already intend to read the entire chapter, you do not necessarily need to answer these questions now.

This 16-question quiz helps you determine how to spend your limited study time. The quiz is sectioned into four smaller four-question "quizlets," which correspond to the four major headings in the "Foundation Topics" section of the chapter. Figure 3-1 outlines suggestions on how to spend your time in this chapter. Use Table 3-1 to record your score.

Table 3-1 *Scoresheet for Quiz and Quizlets*

Quizlet Number	Foundation Topics Section Covering These Questions	Questions	Score
1	The OSI, TCP/IP, and NetWare Protocol Architectures	1 to 4	
2	OSI Transport Layer Functions	5 to 8	
3	OSI Data Link Layer Functions	9 to 12	
4	OSI Network Layer Functions	13 to 16	
All questions		1 to 16	

1 Name the seven layers of the OSI model.

2 What is the main purpose(s) of Layer 3?

3 What is the main purpose(s) of Layer 2?

4 What OSI layer typically encapsulates using both a header and a trailer?

5 Describe the features required for a protocol to be considered connectionless.

6 Describe the features required for a protocol to be considered connection-oriented.

7 In a particular error-recovering (reliable) protocol, the sender sends three frames, labeled 2, 3, and 4. On its next sent frame, the receiver of these frames sets an acknowledgment field to 4. What does this typically imply?

8 Name three connection-oriented protocols.

____

____

____

9 Name three terms popularly used as synonyms for *MAC address*.

____

____

____

10 What portion of a MAC address encodes an identifier representing the manufacturer of the card?

____

____

____

11 Are DLCI addresses defined by a Layer 2 or a Layer 3 protocol?

____

____

____

12 How many bits are present in a MAC address?

____

____

____

13 How many bits are present in an IPX address?

____

____

____

14 Name the two main parts of an IP address. Which part identifies the "group" of which this address is a member?

____

____

____

15 Describe the differences between a routed protocol and a routing protocol.

____

____

____

16 Name at least three routed protocols.

____

____

____

The answers to the "Do I Know This Already?" quiz are found in Appendix A, "Answers to the 'Do I Know This Already?' Quizzes and Q&A Sections." The suggested choices for your next step are as follows:

- **8 or less overall score**—Read the entire chapter. This includes the "Foundation Topics" and "Foundation Summary" sections, the Q&A section, and the scenarios at the end of the chapter.
- **2 or less on any quizlet**—Review the subsection(s) of the "Foundation Topics" part of this chapter, based on Table 3-1. Then move into the "Foundation Summary" section, the quiz, and the scenarios at the end of the chapter.
- **9 to 12 overall score**—Begin with the "Foundation Summary" section, and then go to the Q&A section and the scenarios at the end of the chapter.
- **13 or more overall score**—If you want more review on these topics, skip to the "Foundation Summary" section and then go to the Q&A section and the scenarios at the end of the chapter. Otherwise, move to the next chapter.

Foundation Topics

OSI: Concepts, Layers, and Encapsulation

7 List the key internetworking functions of the OSI network layer.

8 Identify at least three reasons why the industry uses a layered model.

10 Define and explain the five conversion steps of data encapsulation.

Four topics of particular importance for the CCNA exam are covered in this chapter:

- **The OSI reference model**—Expect questions on the functions of each layer and examples at each layer in the CCNA exam.
- **Transport layer protocols**—This section on Layer 4 of the OSI reference model is important to properly understand end-to-end transport.
- **Network layer protocols**—This section on Layer 3 of the OSI reference model is important to properly understand routing.
- **Data link protocols**—This section on Layer 2 of the OSI reference model is important to properly understand LAN switching.

The last three sections all use the terminology discussed in the first section.

OSI Reference Model: Origin and Evolution

To pass the CCNA exam, you must be conversant in a protocol specification with which you are very unlikely to ever have any hands-on experience. The difficulty these days when using the OSI protocol specifications as a point of reference is that almost no one uses those specifications. You cannot typically walk down the hall and see a computer whose main, or even optional, networking protocols are defined by OSI.

OSI is the Open System Interconnection reference model for communications. OSI is a rather well-defined set of protocol specifications with many options for accomplishing similar tasks. Some participants in OSI's creation and development wanted it to become *the* networking protocol used by all applications. The U.S. government went so far as to require OSI support on every computer that it would buy (as of a certain date in the early 1990s) with an edict called the

Government OSI Profile (GOSIP), which certainly gave vendors some incentive to write OSI code. In fact, in my old IBM days, the company even had charts showing how the TCP/IP–installed base would start declining by 1994, how OSI installations would take off, and how OSI would be *the* protocol from which the 21st century Internet was built. (In IBM's defense, moving the world to OSI might have been yet another case of "You just can't get there from here.")

What is OSI today? Well, the protocols are still in existence and are used around the world, to some degree. The U.S. government reversed its GOSIP directive officially in May 1994, which was probably the final blow to the possibility of pervasive OSI implementations. Cisco routers will route OSI. OSI NSAP addresses are used in Cisco ATM devices for signaling. Digital Equipment's DECnet Phase V uses several portions of OSI, including the network layer (Layer 3) addressing and routing concepts. More often than not, however, the OSI model now is mainly used as a point of reference for discussing other protocol specifications.

OSI Layers

The OSI reference model consists of seven layers, each of which can (and typically does) have several sublayers. Cisco requires that CCNAs demonstrate an understanding of each layer as well as the protocols that correspond to each OSI layer. The names of the OSI reference model layers and their main functions are simply good things to memorize. And frankly, if you want to pursue your Cisco certifications beyond CCNA, these names and functional areas will come up continually. You also will need to know some example protocols and the OSI layers that they most closely match.

The upper layers of the OSI reference model (application, presentation, session, and transport—Layers 7, 6, 5, and 4) define functions focused on the application. The lower three layers (network, data link, and physical—Layers 3, 2, and 1) define functions focused on end-to-end delivery of the data. CCNAs work mostly with issues in the lower layers, in particular with Layer 2, upon which switching is based, and Layer 3, upon which routing is based. Table 3-2 diagrams the seven OSI layers, with a thorough description and a list of example protocols.

Table 3-2 *OSI Reference Model*

Layer Name	Functional Description	Examples
Application (Layer 7)	An application that communicates with other computers is implementing OSI application layer concepts. The application layer refers to communications services to applications. For example, a word processor that lacks communications capabilities would not implement code for communications, and word processor programmers would not be concerned about OSI Layer 7. However, if an option for transferring a file were added, the word processor would need to implement OSI Layer 7 (or the equivalent layer in another protocol specification).	Telnet, HTTP, FTP, WWW browsers, NFS, SMTP gateways (Eudora, CC:mail), SNMP, X.400 mail, FTAM

continues

Table 3-2 *OSI Reference Model (Continued)*

Layer Name	Functional Description	Examples
Presentation (Layer 6)	This layer's main purpose is defining data formats, such as ASCII text, EBCDIC text, binary, BCD, and JPEG. Encryption also is defined by OSI as a presentation layer service. For example, FTP enables you to choose binary or ASCII transfer. If binary is selected, the sender and receiver do not modify the contents of the file. If ASCII is chosen, the sender translates the text from the sender's character set to a standard ASCII and sends the data. The receiver translates back from the standard ASCII to the character set used on the receiving computer.	JPEG, ASCII, EBCDIC, TIFF, GIF, PICT, encryption, MPEG, MIDI
Session (Layer 5)	The session layer defines how to start, control, and end conversations (called sessions). This includes the control and management of multiple bidirectional messages so that the application can be notified if only some of a series of messages are completed. This allows the presentation layer to have a seamless view of an incoming stream of data. The presentation layer can be presented with data if all flows occur in some cases. For example, an automated teller machine transaction in which you withdraw cash from your checking account should not debit your account and then fail before handing you the cash, recording the transaction even though you did not receive money. The session layer creates ways to imply which flows are part of the same session and which flows must complete before any are considered complete.	RPC, SQL, NFS, NetBios names, AppleTalk ASP, DECnet SCP
Transport (Layer 4)	Layer 4 includes the choice of protocols that either do or do not provide error recovery. Multiplexing of incoming data for different flows to applications on the same host (for example, TCP sockets) is also performed. Reordering of the incoming data stream when packets arrive out of order is included.	TCP, UDP, SPX

Table 3-2 *OSI Reference Model (Continued)*

Layer Name	Functional Description	Examples
Network (Layer 3)	This layer defines end-to-end delivery of packets. To accomplish this, the network layer defines logical addressing so that any endpoint can be identified. It also defines how routing works and how routes are learned so that the packets can be delivered. The network layer also defines how to fragment a packet into smaller packets to accommodate media with smaller maximum transmission unit sizes. (*Note:* Not all Layer 3 protocols use fragmentation.) The network layer of OSI defines most of the details that a Cisco router considers when routing. For example, IP running in a Cisco router is responsible for examining the destination IP address of a packet, comparing that address to the IP routing table, fragmenting the packet if the outgoing interface requires smaller packets, and queuing the packet to be sent out to the interface.	IP, IPX, AppleTalk DDP, ICMP
Data link (Layer 2)	The data link (Layer 2) specifications are concerned with getting data across one particular link or medium. The data link protocols define delivery across an individual link. These protocols are necessarily concerned with the type of media in question; for example, 802.3 and 802.2 are specifications from the IEEE, which are referenced by OSI as valid data link (Layer 2) protocols. These specifications define how Ethernet works. Other protocols, such as High-Level Data Link Control (HDLC) for a point-to-point WAN link, deal with the different details of a WAN link. As with other protocol specifications, OSI often does not create any original specification for the data link layer but instead relies on other standards bodies such as IEEE to create new standards for the data link layer and the physical layer.	IEEE 802.3/802.2, HDLC, Frame Relay, PPP, FDDI, ATM, IEEE 802.5/802.2

continues

Table 3-2 *OSI Reference Model (Continued)*

Layer Name	Functional Description	Examples
Physical (Layer 1)	These physical layer (Layer 1) specifications, which are also typically standards from other organizations that are referred to by OSI, deal with the physical characteristics of the transmission medium. Connectors, pins, use of pins, electrical currents, encoding, and light modulation are all part of different physical layer specifications. Multiple specifications are sometimes used to complete all details of the physical layer. For example, RJ-45 defines the shape of the connector and the number of wires or pins in the cable. Ethernet and 802.3 define the use of wires or pins 1, 2, 3, and 6. So, to use a Category 5 cable with an RJ-45 connector for an Ethernet connection, Ethernet and RJ-45 physical layer specifications are used.	EIA/TIA-232, V.35, EIA/TIA-449, V.24, RJ45, Ethernet, 802.3, 802.5, FDDI, NRZI, NRZ, B8ZS

Some protocols define details of multiple layers. For example, because the TCP/IP application layer correlates to OSI Layers 5 through 7, the Network File System (NFS) implements elements matching all three upper OSI layers. Likewise, the 802.3, 802.5, and Ethernet standards define details for the data link and physical layers.

CCNAs deal with many aspects of Layers 1 through 4 on a daily basis, but the upper layers are not as important to CCNAs. In addition, most networking people know about the OSI model, but there is no need to memorize everything about it. Table 3-2 shows plenty of detail and explanation for a more in-depth idea of the OSI model components. If you are daunted by the task of memorizing all the examples in Table 3-2, you can refer to Table 3-3, which offers a more condensed description of the layer characteristics and examples. This table is taken directly from Cisco's ICND course, so if you are just not willing to try to remember all of Table 3-2, the information in Table 3-3 is a good compromise. (ICND is the instructor-led course in the official CCNA training path.)

Table 3-3 *OSI Reference Model (Condensed Information)*

OSI Layer Name	Functional Description	Examples
Application (Layer 7)	Interface between network and application software	Telnet, HTTP
Presentation (Layer 6)	How data is presented Special processing, such as encryption	JPEG, ASCII, EBCDIC
Session (Layer 5)	Keeping data separate from different applications	Operating systems and application access scheduling

Table 3-3 *OSI Reference Model (Condensed Information) (Continued)*

OSI Layer Name	Functional Description	Examples
Transport (Layer 4)	Reliable or unreliable delivery Multiplexing	TCP, UDP, SPX
Network (Layer 3)	Logical addressing, which routers use for path determination	IP, IPX
Data link (Layer 2)	Combination of bits into bytes, and bytes into frames Access to the media using MAC address Error detection and error recovery	802.3/802.2, HDLC
Physical (Layer 1)	Moving of bits between devices Specification of voltage, wire speed, and cable pinouts	EIA/TIA-232, V.35

Layering Concepts and Benefits

Many benefits can be gained from the process of breaking up the functions or tasks of networking into smaller chunks, called *layers,* and defining standard interfaces between these layers. The layers break a large, complex set of concepts and protocols into smaller pieces, making it easier to talk about, to implement with hardware and software, and to troubleshoot. The following list summarizes the benefits of layered protocol specifications:

- Humans can more easily discuss and learn about the many details of a protocol specification.
- Standardized interfaces among layers facilitate modular engineering. Different products can provide functions of only some layers (such as a router with Layers 1 to 3), or some products could supply parts of the functions of the protocol (such as Microsoft TCP/IP built into Win95, or the Eudora e-mail application providing TCP/IP application layer support).
- A better environment for interoperability is created. One vendor can write software that implements higher layers—for example, a Web browser—and another can write software that implements the lower layers—for example, Microsoft's built-in TCP/IP software in its operating systems.
- Reduced complexity allows easier program changes and faster product evolution.
- One layer uses the services of the layer immediately below it. Therefore, remembering what each layer does is easier. (For example, the network layer needs to deliver data from end to end. To do this, it uses data links to forward data to the next successive device along that end-to-end path.)

An analogy between the U.S. Postal Service and protocol layers might help. If I write a letter to my boss, Mike Z, at Skyline Computer in Campbell, California, I write the letter on a piece of paper. I then put it in an envelope and write the address on the front. After I put it in the mailbox, I assume that the USPS will deliver it. I don't have to know anything about where my letter goes after the postman picks up the letter. It would be irritating if I had to tell the postman to send my letter to some series of post office sorting centers to deliver the letter. Likewise, layering lets one software package or hardware device perform some of the functions, assuming that other software/hardware will perform the others.

Interaction Between OSI Layers

Imagine a Web browser displaying a Web page that it received from a Web server. Before that happened, the browser somehow interacted with the software implementing other layers of TCP/IP on the client computer, causing a request to flow to the server. Likewise, the broswer application somehow communicated with the Web server application, telling the server what Web page the browser wanted to display. A fancy way to describe these two ideas that is "interaction between OSI layers." The process of how layers interact on the same computer, as well as how the same layer processes on different computers communicate with each other, is all interrelated. The software or hardware products implementing the logic of some of the OSI protocol layers provide two general functions:

- Each layer provides a service to the layer above it in the protocol specification.
- Each layer communicates some information with the same layer's software or hardware on other computers. In some cases, the other computer is connected to the same media; in other cases, the other computer is on the other end of the network.

Interactions Between Adjacent Layers on the Same Computer

The post office analogy provides an easy comparison to networking and interactions between adjacent layers. The words in my letter to Mike Z are the application data. While still at my office, I put the letter in an envelope because the USPS will not just deliver the paper; it requires me to provide an envelope. On that envelope, I provide an address that meets USPS specifications for addresses. Having done that, and after putting on the correct postage stamp, I expect the USPS to deliver the letter. That's exactly the same concept of the interactions between layers on the same computer. When sending data, the higher layers expect the lower layers to help deliver the data. However, the lower layers expect the higher layers to give them the data in a certain format, with certain header and address information attached. (The header acts like the envelope in the analogy.)

So, to provide services to the next higher layer, the layer must know about the standard interfaces defined between itself and the next higher layer. These interfaces include definitions of what Layer *N*+1 must provide to Layer *N* to get services, as well as what information Layer *N* must provide back to Layer *N*+1 when data has been received. And these details are all part of the protocol specifications.

Figure 3-2 presents a graphical representation of two computers and provides an excellent backdrop for a discussion of interactions between layers on the same computer.

Figure 3-2 *Example for Discussion of Adjacent-Layer Interactions*

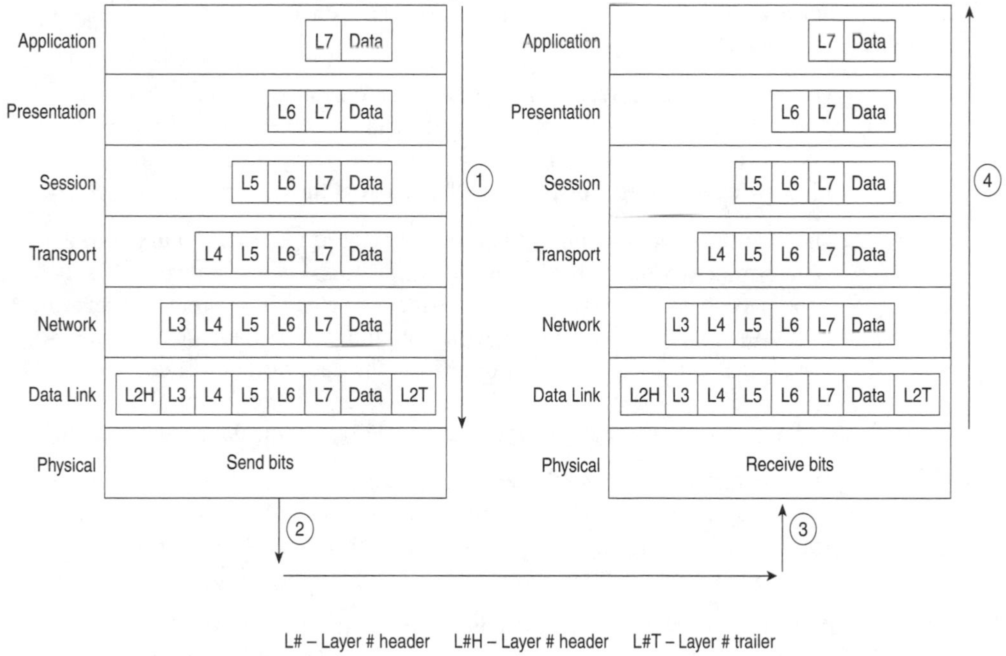

The data is created by some application on Host A. For example, an e-mail message is typed by the user. Each layer creates a header and passes the data down to the next layer. (The arrows in Figure 3-2, Step 1, denote the passing of data between layers.) Just as I had to put an envelope around my letter to Mike, a layer typically has to put some header around its data before giving it to the next lower layer that is providing service. Passing the data down to the next layer implies that the lower layer needs to perform some services for the higher layer; to perform these services, the lower layer adds some information in a header or trailer. For example, the transport layer hands off its data and header; the network layer adds a header with the correct destination network layer address so that the packet can be delivered to the other computer.

From each layer's perspective, the bits after that layer's header are considered to be data. For instance, Layer 4 considers the Layer 5, 6, and 7 headers, along with the original user data, to be one large data field.

After the application creates the data, the software and hardware implementing each layer perform their work, adding the appropriate header and trailer. The physical layer can use the media to send a signal for physical transmission, as shown in Step 2 in Figure 3-2.

Upon receipt (Step 3), Host B begins the adjacent layer interactions on Host B. The right side of Figure 3-2 shows an arrow pointing next to the computer (Step 4), signifying that the received data is being processed as it goes up the protocol stack. In fact, thinking about what each layer does in the OSI model can help you decide what information could be in each header.

The following sequence outlines the basics of processing at each layer and shows how each lower layer provides a service to the next higher layer. Consider the *receipt of data* by the host on the right side of Figure 3-2:

Step 1 The physical layer (Layer 1) ensures bit synchronization and places the received binary pattern into a buffer. It notifies the data link layer that a frame has been received after decoding the incoming signal into a bit stream. Therefore, Layer 1 has provided delivery of a stream of bits across the medium.

Step 2 The data link layer examines the frame check sequence (FCS) in the trailer to determine whether errors occurred in transmission (error detection). If an error has occurred, the frame is discarded. (Some data link protocols perform error *recovery*, and some do not.) The data link address(es) are examined so that Host B can decide whether to process the data further. If the data is addressed to host B, the data between the Layer 2 header and trailer is given to the Layer 3 software. The data link has delivered the data across that link.

Step 3 The network layer (Layer 3) destination address is examined. If the address is Host B's address, processing continues (logical addressing) and the data after the Layer 3 header is given to the transport layer (Layer 4) software. Layer 3 has provided the service of end-to-end delivery.

Step 4 If error recovery was an option chosen for the transport layer (Layer 4), the counters identifying this piece of data are encoded in the Layer 4 header along with acknowledgment information (error recovery). After error recovery and reordering of the incoming data, the data is given to the session layer.

Step 5 The session layer (Layer 5) can be used to ensure that a series of messages is completed. For example, this data could be meaningless if the next four exchanges are not completed. The Layer 5 header could include fields signifying that this is a middle flow in a chain, not an ending flow. After the session layer ensures that all flows are completed, it passes the data after the Layer 5 header to the Layer 6 software.

Step 6 The presentation layer (Layer 6) defines and manipulates data formats. For example, if the data is binary instead of character data, the header denotes that fact. The receiver does not attempt to convert the data using the default ASCII character set of Host B. Typically, this type of header is included only for initialization flows, not with every message being transmitted (data formats). After the data formats have been converted, the data (after the Layer 6 header) is then passed to the application layer (Layer 7) software.

Step 7 The application layer (Layer 7) processes the final header and then can examine the true end-user data. This header signifies agreement to operating parameters by the applications on Host A and Host B. The headers are used to signal the values for all parameters; therefore, the header typically is sent and received at application initialization time only. For example, for file transfer, the size of the file to be transferred and the file formats used would be communicated (application parameters).

Interactions Between the Same Layers on Different Computers

Layer *N* must interact with Layer *N* on another computer to successfully implement its functions. For example, the transport layer (Layer 4) can send data, but if another computer does not acknowledge that the data was received, the sender will not know when to perform error recovery. Likewise, the sending computer encodes a destination network layer address (Layer 3) in the network layer header. If the intervening routers do not cooperate by performing their network layer tasks, the packet will not be delivered to the true destination.

The post office analogy can help in this case as well. If I write the letter to Mike and put the address but not his name on the envelope, the letter gets to the office because I gave the USPS enough information to deliver the letter. No one knows to whom to give the letter, though. In real life, someone would open the letter and see that it's addressed to Mike—but, of course, the office might have more than one Mike! With real networking, the sending application needs to put some header around the data so that the receiving computer knows what application should receive the data.

To interact with the same layer on another computer, each layer defines a header and, in some cases, a trailer. Headers and trailers are additional data bits, created by the sending computer's software or hardware, that are placed before or after the data given to Layer *N* by Layer *N+1*. The information needed for this layer to communicate with the same layer process on the other computer is encoded in the header and trailer. The receiving computer's Layer *N* software or hardware interprets the headers and trailers created by the sending computer's Layer *N*, learning how Layer *N*'s processing is being handled, in this case.

Figure 3-3 provides a conceptual perspective on the same-layer interactions. The application layer on Host A communicates with the application layer on Host B. Likewise, the transport, session, and presentation layers on Host A and Host B also communicate. The bottom three layers of the OSI model have to do with delivery of the data; Router 1 is involved in that process.

Host A's network, physical, and data link layers communicate with Router 1; likewise, Router 1 communicates with Host B's physical, data link, and network layers. Figure 3-3 provides a visual representation of the same-layer interaction concepts.

Figure 3-3 *Same-Layer Interactions on Different Computers*

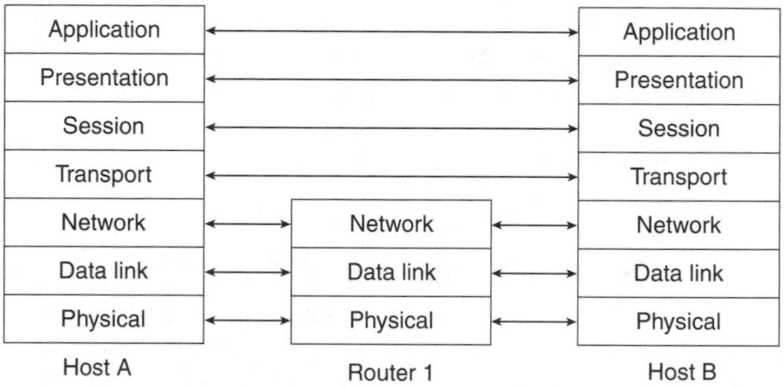

The post office analogy again helps. I, Wendell, the letter writer, is the equivalent of Host A. I write the letter, put it in the envelope, address and stamp the envelope, and drop it off at the local post office. The post office forwards the letter through many other mail-sorting centers because our home office, where Mike is, is 2,000 miles away. The mailing centers look at only the address—in fact, only at the ZIP code—until the letter makes it to Campbell, California. So I, the sender (Host A), put the address on the letter, which is used by many mailing centers (routers) who deliver the letter to our home office (host B), where the letter is given to the correct individual (correct application).

Data Encapsulation

The term *encapsulation* describes the process of putting headers and trailers around some data. Encapsulation puts the data in the correct, expected format so that another adjacent layer can provide a service or so that the same layer on another computer knows what needs to be done. For example, I put an envelope around my letter to Mike because that was required by the USPS, which provided me a service. I put Mike's name on the envelope so that the people in our home office would know to whom to give the letter—the equivalent of the "same" layer on another computer.

As seen previously in Figure 3-2, when each layer creates its header, it places the data given to it by the next-higher layer behind its own header, thereby encapsulating the higher layer's data. In the case of a data link (Layer 2) protocol, the Layer 3 header and data are placed between the Layer 2 header and the Layer 2 trailer. The physical layer does not use encapsulation because it does not use headers or trailers.

Again referring to Figure 3-2, Step 1, the following list describes the encapsulation process for sending data by Host A:

Step 1 The application has already created the data. The application layer creates the application header and places the data behind it. This data structure is passed to the presentation layer.

Step 2 The presentation layer creates the presentation header and places the data behind it. This data structure is passed to the session layer.

Step 3 The session layer creates the session header and places the data behind it. This data structure is passed to the transport layer.

Step 4 The transport layer creates the transport header and places the data behind it. This data structure is passed to the network layer.

Step 5 The network layer creates the network header and places the data behind it. This data structure is passed to the data link layer.

Step 6 The data link layer creates the data link header and places the data behind it. The data link trailer is added to the end of the structure. This data structure is passed to the physical layer.

Step 7 The physical layer encodes a signal onto the medium to transmit the frame.

This seven-step process accurately describes what happens for the seven-layer OSI model. However, encapsulation by each layer does not typically happen for each transmission of data by the application. Normally, Layers 5 through 7 use headers during initialization—and occasionally after initialization—but, in most flows, there is no Layer 5, 6, or 7 header. This is because there is no new information to exchange for every flow of data.

An analogy can help in this case. A friend of mine from church spent several summers teaching English in a communist country. When I wrote to her, she assumed that I would write in English, but I could not write about "church" without the sensors tossing the letter. So, we agreed on encryption before she left. Under our code, God was called "Phil," and I could write things such as, "I saw Fred at Phil's house yesterday, and he said hi." I still had to address the letters before I mailed them, just like the lower OSI layers need to exchange some information for every piece of data sent. I didn't need to repeat what "Phil" really meant in each letter, just like the upper layers do not need to repeat encryption rules.

Previous CCNA exams referred to a five-step process for encapsulation. This included the typical encapsulation by the transport, network, and data link layers as steps 2 through 4 in the seven-step process. The first step in the five-step process was the application's creation of the data, and the fifth step was the physical layer's transmission of the bit stream. In case any questions remain in the CCNA question database referring to a five-step encapsulation process, the following list provides the details and explanation.

NOTE The term *LxPDU*, where *x* represents the number of one of the layers, is used to represent the bits that include the headers and trailers for that layer, as well as the encapsulated data. For instance, an IP packet is an L3PDU, which includes the IP header and any encapsulated data.

Step 1 **Create the data**—This simply means that the application has data to send.

Step 2 **Package the data for transport**—In other words, the transport layer creates the transport header and places the data behind it. The L4PDU is created here.

Step 3 **Add the destination network layer address to the data**—The network layer creates the network header, which includes the network layer address, and places the data (L4PDU) behind it. In other words, the L3PDU is created here.

Step 4 **Add the destination data link address to the data**—The data link layer creates the data link header, places the data (L3PDU) behind it, and places the data link trailer at the end. In other words, the L2PDU is created here.

Step 5 **Transmit the bits**—The physical layer encodes a signal onto the medium to transmit the frame.

This five-step process happens to match the TCP/IP network model very well. Figure 3-4 depicts the concept; the numbers shown represent each of the five steps.

Figure 3-4 *Five Steps of Data Encapsulation—TCP/IP*

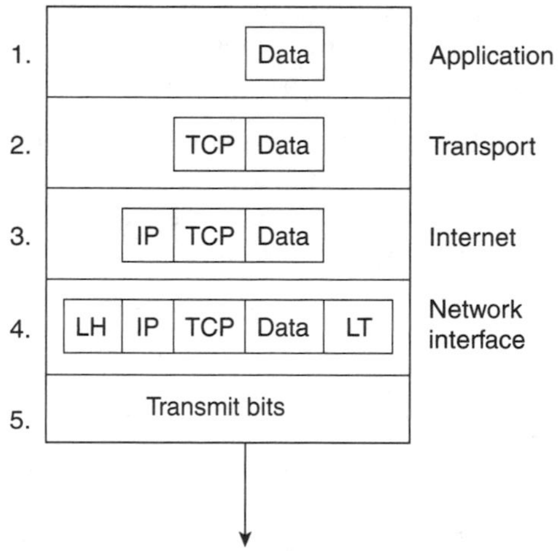

Several very important terms describe details about encapsulation. *Layer N PDU* (protocol data unit) is a term used to describe a set of bytes that includes the Layer *N* header and trailer and the user data. From Layer *N*'s perspective, the higher-layer headers and the user data form one large *data* or *information* field. A few other terms describe some of these PDUs. The Layer 2

PDU (including the data link header and trailer) is called a *frame*. Similarly, the Layer 3 PDU is called a *packet*, or sometimes a *datagram*. Finally, the Layer 4 PDU is called a *segment*. Figure 3-5 illustrates the construction of frames, packets, and segments and the different layers' perspectives on what is considered to be *data*.

Figure 3-5 *Frames, Packets, and Segments*

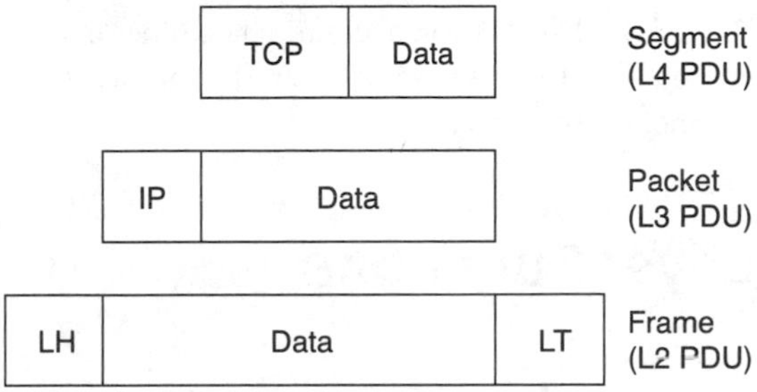

The TCP/IP and NetWare Protocols

Two of the most pervasively deployed protocols are TCP/IP and Novell NetWare; these also are the two key protocol architectures covered on the CCNA exam. TCP/IP and NetWare are covered in much more detail in the upcoming chapters.

This short section compares TCP/IP, Novell, and OSI. The goal is to provide some insight into what some popularly used terminology really means. In particular, routing is defined as a *Layer 3 process*; this section reviews how that term relates to TCP/IP and NetWare.

For perspective, Figure 3-6 shows the layers of these two protocols as compared with OSI.

Figure 3-6 *OSI, TCP/IP, and NetWare Protocols*

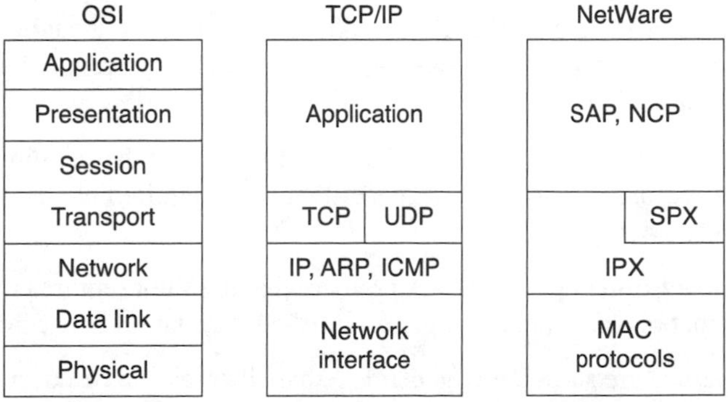

As Figure 3-6 illustrates, the IP and IPX protocols most closely match the OSI network layer—Layer 3. Many times, even on the CCNA exam, IP and IPX will be called *Layer 3 protocols*. Clearly, IP is in TCP/IP's Layer 2, but for consistent use of terminology, it is commonly called a

Layer 3 protocol because its functions most closely match OSI's Layer 3. Both IP and IPX define logical addressing, routing, the learning of routing information, and end-to-end delivery rules.

As with OSI Layers 1 and 2 (physical and data link, respectively), the lower layers of each stack simply refer to other well-known specifications. For example, the lower layers all support the IEEE standards for Ethernet and Token Ring, the ANSI standard for FDDI, the ITU standard for ISDN, and the Frame Relay protocols specified by the Frame Relay Forum, ANSI, and the ITU. The protocol stacks can accommodate other evolving Layer 1 and Layer 2 specifications more easily by referring to emerging international standards rather than trying to evolve these standards themselves.

OSI Transport Layer Functions

1 Describe connection-oriented network service and connectionless network service, and identify their key differences.

The transport layer (Layer 4) defines several functions, the most important of which are error recovery and flow control. Routers discard packets for many reasons, including bit errors, congestion that has caused a lack of buffer space, and instances in which no correct routes are known. The transport layer may provide for retransmission (error recovery) and can help avoid congestion (flow control), or it might not. When you compare similar protocols, you typically want to know whether they perform error recovery or flow control.

Connection-Oriented Versus Connectionless Protocols

The terms *connection-oriented* and *connectionless* have some relatively well-known connotations inside the world of networking protocols. The meaniing of the terms is intertwined with error recovery and flow control, but they are not the same. So, first, some basic definitions are in order:

> **Connection-oriented protocol**—A protocol either that requires an exchange of messages before data transfer begins or that has a required pre-established correlation between two endpoints
>
> **Connectionless protocol**—A protocol that does not require an exchange of messages and that does not require a pre-established correlation between two endpoints

The definitions are sufficiently general so that all cases can be covered. TCP is connection-oriented because a set of three messages must be completed before data is exchanged. Likewise, SPX is connection-oriented. When using PVCs, Frame Relay does not require any messages be sent ahead of time, but it does require predefinition in the Frame Relay switches, establishing a connection between two Frame Relay–attached devices. ATM PVCs are also connection-oriented, for similar reasons.

NOTE Some documentation refers to the terms *connected* or *connection-oriented*. These terms are used synonymously. You will most likely see the use of the term *connection-oriented* in Cisco documentation.

Many people confuse the real meaning of *connection-oriented* with the definition of a reliable, or error-recovering, protocol. A great example that you will learn more about in this book is Frame Relay. Frame Relay requires that some connection be established before any data can flow between two endpoints. However, there is no error receovery. Table 3-4 lists some popular protocols and tells whether they are connected or reliable.

Table 3-4 *Protocol Characteristics: Recovery and Connections*

Connected?	Reliable?	Examples
Connection-oriented	Yes	LLC Type 2 (802.2), TCP (TCP/IP), SPX (NetWare), X.25
Connection-oriented	No	Frame Relay virtual circuits, ATM virtual connections, PPP
Connectionless	Yes	TFTP, NetWare NCP (without Packet Burst)
Connectionless	No	UDP, IP, IPX, AppleTalk DDP, most Layer 3 protocols, 802.3, 802.5

Error Recovery

Cisco expects CCNAs to be able to distinguish between *error detection* and *error recovery*. Any header or trailer with a frame check sequence (FCS) or similar field can be used to detect bit errors in the PDU. The FCS uses some magic math against the contents of the frame, with the result recorded in the FCS field. If the receiving device repeats the same math but gets a different value than what is in the FCS field, there were bit errors in transmission. Error detection uses the FCS to detect the error, which results in discarding the PDU. However, error recovery implies that the protocol reacts to the lost data and somehow causes the data to be retransmitted.

Many protocols offer error recovery, and these protocols accomplish the task in the same general way. Generically, the transmitted data is labeled or numbered. After receipt, the receiver signals back to the sender that the data was received, using the same label or number to identify the data. Figure 3-7 summarizes the operation.

Figure 3-7 *Forward Acknowledgement*

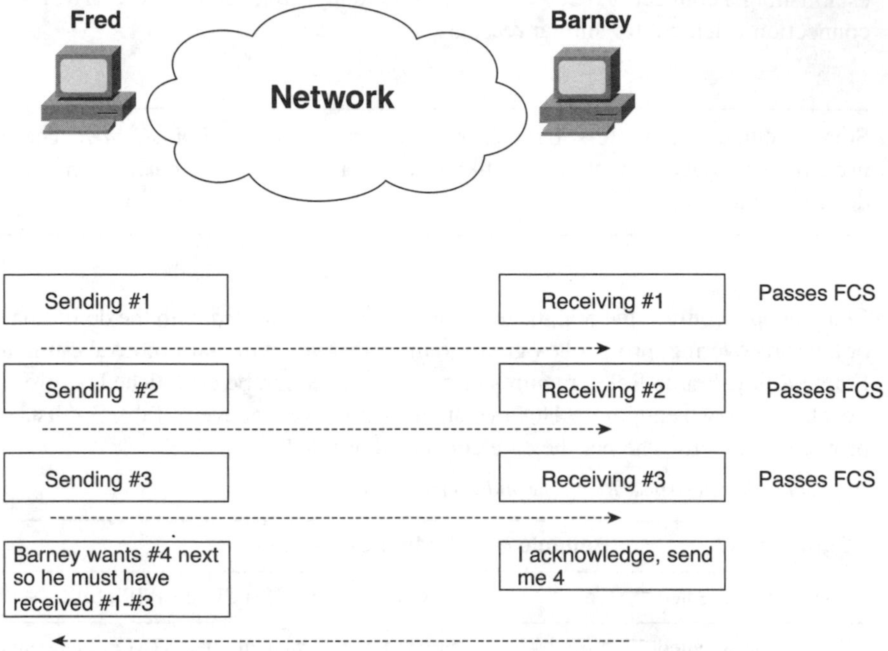

As Figure 3-7 illustrates, the data is numbered, as shown with the numbers 1, 2, and 3. These numbers are placed into the header used by that particular protocol; for example, the TCP header contains similar numbering fields. When Barney sends his next segment to Fred, Barney acknowledges that all three segments were received by setting his acknowledgment field to 4. The number 4 refers to the next data to be received, which is called *forward acknowledgment*. This means that the acknowledgment number in the header identifies the next data that is to be received, not the last one received. (In this case, 4 is next to be received.)

In some protocols, such as LLC2, the numbering always starts with zero. In other protocols, such as TCP, the number is stated during initialization by the sending machine. Also, some protocols count the frame/packet/segment as 1; others count the number of bytes sent. In any case, the basic idea is the same.

Of course, error recovery has not been covered yet. Take the case of Fred and Barney again, but notice Barney's reply in Figure 3-8.

Figure 3-8 *Recovery Example*

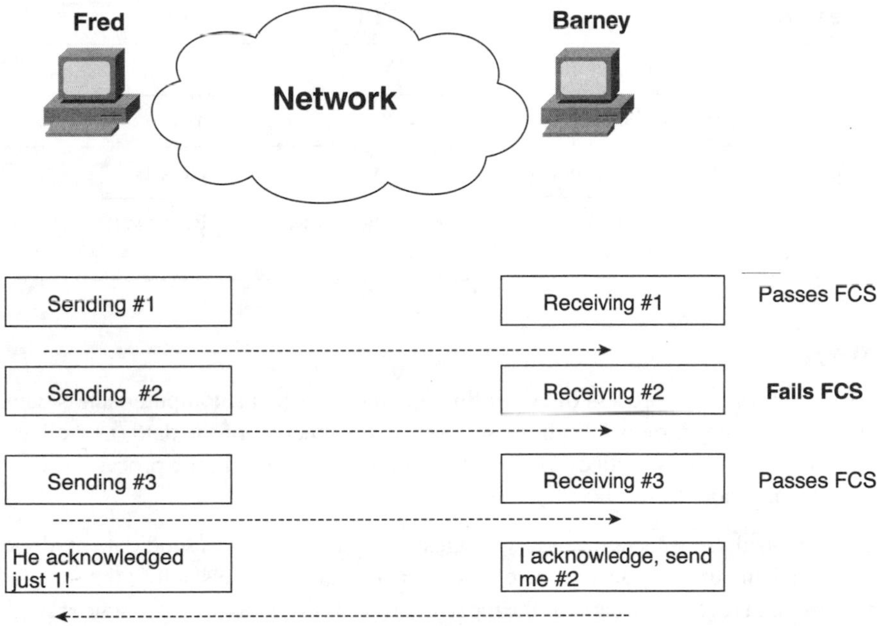

What should Fred do next? Well, Fred certainly should resend number 2. However, should Fred resend number 3? Two choices exist. Fred could send numbers 2 and 3 again, or Fred could send number 2 and wait, hoping that Barney's next acknowledgment will say 4, indicating that Barney just got number 2 and already had number 3 from earlier. What happens in real life is dependant on the praticular protocol.

Finally, error recovery typically uses two sets of counters: one to count data in one direction, and one to count data in the opposite direction. So, the numbers 1, 2, and 3 in the segments sent by Fred would be in the Number Sent field of some header. Barney acknowledges packet number 2 with the Number Acknowledged field in the header. Similarly, segments sent by Barney also have a Number Sent field that identifies the data in Barney's packet, and the Number Acknowledged field in Fred's segments would be used to acknowledge segments sent by Barney.

Table 3-5 summarizes the concepts behind error recovery and lists the behavior of three popular error-recovery protocols.

Table 3-5 *Examples of Error-Recovery Protocols and Their Features*

Feature	TCP	SPX	LLC2
Acknowledges data in both directions?	Yes	Yes	Yes
Uses forward acknowledgment?	Yes	Yes	Yes
Counts bytes or frame/packets?	Bytes	Packets	Frames
Necessitates resending of all data, or just one part and wait when resending?	One and wait	Resend all	Resend all

Flow Control

Flow control is the process of controlling the rate at which a computer sends data. Depending on the particular protocol, both the sender and the receiver of the data (as well as any intermediate routers, bridges, or switches) might participate in the process of controlling the flow from sender to receiver.

Flow control prevents unnecessary congestion by attempting to send data at a rate that the network can currently accomodate. A sender of data might be sending the data faster than the receiver can receive the data, so the receiver discards the data. Also, the sender might be sending the data faster than the intermediate switching devices (switches and routers) can forward the data, also causing discards. Packets can be lost because of transmission errors as well. This happens in every network, sometimes temporarily and sometimes regularly, depending on the network and the traffic patterns. The receiving computer can have insufficient buffer space to receive the next incoming frame, or possibly the CPU is too busy to process the incoming frame. Intermediate routers might need to discard the packets based on temporary lack of buffers or processing as well.

Flow control attempts to reduce unnecessary discarding of data. Comparing flows when flow control is used and when it is not used is helpful for understanding why flow control can be useful. Without flow control, some PDUs are discarded. If some reliable protocol in use happens to implement error recovery, the data is resent. The sender keeps sending as fast as possible. With flow control, the sender can be slowed enough that the original PDU can be forwarded to the receiving computer, and the receiving computer can process the PDU. Flow-control protocols do not prevent the loss of data as a result of congestion; these protocols simply reduce the amount of lost data, which, in turn, reduces the amount of retransmitted traffic, which hopefully reduces overall congestion. However, with flow control, the sender is artificially slowed or throttled so that it sends data less quickly than it could without flow control.

The CCNA exam requires that you be familiar with three features, or methods, of implementing flow control:

- Buffering
- Congestion avoidance
- Windowing

Buffering

Buffering simply means that the computers reserve enough buffer space that bursts of incoming data can be held until processed. No attempt is made to actually slow the transmission rate of the sender of the data. In fact, buffering is such a common method of dealing with changes in the rate of arrival of data that most of us probably would just assume that it is happening. However, some older documentation refers to "three methods of flow control," of which buffering is one of the methods, so be sure to remember it as a separate function.

Congestion Avoidance

Congestion avoidance is the second method of flow control covered here. The computer receiving the data notices that its buffers are filling. This causes either a separate PDU or a field in a header to be sent toward the sender, signaling the sender to stop transmitting. Figure 3-9 shows an example.

Figure 3-9 *Congestion-Avoidance Flow Control*

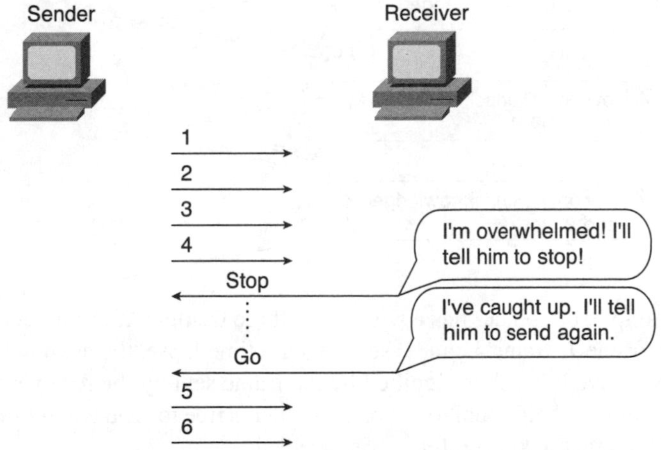

"Hurry up and wait" is a popular expression used to describe the process used in this congestion-avoidance example. This process is used by Synchronous Data Link Control (SDLC) and Link Access Procedure, Balanced (LAPB) serial data-link protocols.

A preferred method might be to get the sender to simply slow down instead of stopping altogether. This method would still be considered congestion avoidance, but instead of signaling the sender to stop, the signal would mean to slow down. One example is the TCP/IP Internet Control Message Protocol (ICMP) source quench message. This message is sent by the receiver or some intermediate router to slow the sender. The sender can slow down gradually until source quench messages are no longer received.

Windowing

The third category of flow-control methods is called *windowing*. A window is the maximum amount of data that the sender can send without getting an acknowledgment. If no acknowledgment is received by the time the window is filled, the sender must wait for acknowledgment. Figure 3-10 shows an example. The slanted lines indicate the time difference between sending a PDU and its receipt.

Figure 3-10 *Windowing Flow Control*

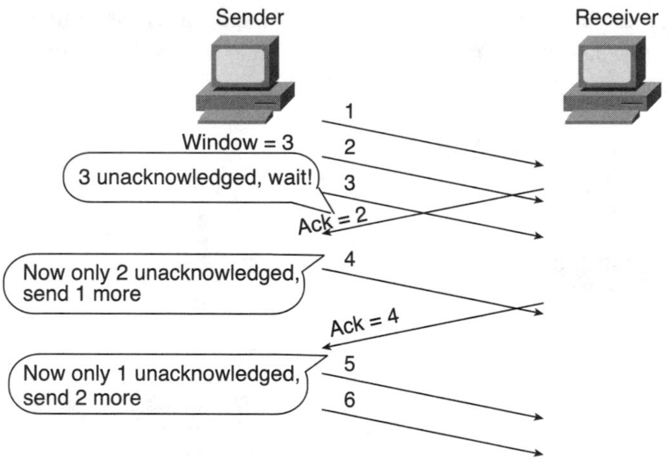

In this example, the sender has a window of three frames. After the receiver acknowledges the receipt of frame 1, frame 4 can be sent. After a time lapse, the acknowledgment for frames 2 and 3 are received, which is signified by the frame sent by the receiver with the Acknowledgment field equal to 4. So, the sender is free to send two more frames—frames 5 and 6—before another acknowledgment is received.

Table 3-6 summarizes the flow-control terms and provides examples of each type. Memorizing these terms should help trigger your memory of flow-control concepts.

Table 3-6 *Flow-Control Methods—Summary*

Name Used in This Book	Other Names	Example Protocols
Buffering	N/A	N/A
Congestion avoidance	Stop/start, RNR, source quench	SDLC, LAPB, LLC2
Windowing	N/A	TCP, SPX, LLC2

OSI Data Link Layer Functions

5 Describe data-link and network addresses, and identify key differences between them.

6 Define and describe the function of a MAC address.

As a CCNA, you'll need to understand both the abstract concepts about the OSI layers and particular instances of such protocols. This section focuses on more of the abstract concepts. Later chapters provide more details about particular LAN and WAN data-link protocols, as well as their configuration in the IOS.

This section examines four different protocols: Ethernet, Token Ring, HDLC, and Frame Relay. A generalized definition of the function of a data-link protocol will be used to guide you through the comparison of these four data-link protocols. This definition could be used to examine any other data-link protocol. The four components of this definition of the functions of data-link (Layer 2) protocols are as follows:

- **Arbitration**—Determines when it is appropriate to use the physical medium.
- **Addressing**—Ensures that the correct recipient(s) receives and processes the data that is sent.
- **Error detection**—Determines whether the data made the trip across the medium successfully.
- **Identifying the encapsulated data**—Determines the type of header that follows the data-link header. This feature is included in a subset of data-link protocols.

Engineers deploy Ethernet as the chosen type of LAN, but, for the sake of comparison, Token Ring concepts are covered here briefly. These protocols are defined by the IEEE in specifications 802.3 and 802.5, respectively. Because 802.3 and 802.5 define how a station accesses the media, the IEEE calls these protocols *Media Access Control (MAC)* protocols.

Also, both 802.3 and 802.5 call for the use of another IEEE specification as a separate part of the data link layer—namely, 802.2 Logical Link Control (LLC). 802.2 purposefully is designed to provide functions common to both Ethernet and Token Ring, whereas 802.3 and 802.5 were designed specifically for data-link functions pertinent to either Ethernet or Token Ring topologies, respectively.

The IEEE created 802.3 and 802.2 after the original creation of Ethernet. The original specification is called *DIX Ethernet*, with the letters DIX representing Digital, Intel, and Xerox, giving credit to the creators. DIX Version 2 (the latest and final DIX specification) defines similar functions to both the 802.3 and 802.2 specifications.

HDLC is the default data-link protocol (encapsulation) on Cisco routers' serial interfaces. Frame Relay headers coincidentally are based on the HDLC specification, but Frame Relay was created for multiaccess networks (with more than two devices). The clear differences between Frame Relay and HDLC provide a good backdrop to examine the functions of the data link layer (Layer 2).

Data Link Function 1: Arbitration

Arbitration is needed only when there are instants in time during which it is not appropriate to send data across the media. It's like trying to get through an intersection in your car when all the traffic signals are out—you all want to use the intersection, but you had better use it one at a time! The arbitration methods vary greatly, depending on how conservative you are, how big the other cars are, how new or old your car is, and how much you value your own life! LANs originally were defined as a shared medium on which each device must wait until the appropriate time to send data. The specifications for these data-link protocols define how to arbitrate the use of the physical medium.

Ethernet uses the *carrier sense multiple access collision detect (CSMA/CD)* algorithm for arbitration. The basic algorithm for using an Ethernet when there is data to be sent consists of the following steps:

1. Listen to find out whether a frame is currently being received.
2. If no other frame is on the Ethernet, send.
3. If another frame is on the Ethernet, wait and then listen again.
4. While sending, if a collision occurs, stop, wait, and listen again.

With Token Ring, a totally different mechanism is used. A free-token frame rotates around the ring while no device has data to send. When sending, a device claims the free token, which really means changing bits in the 802.5 header to signify "token busy." The data then is placed onto the ring after the Token Ring header. The basic algorithm for using a Token Ring when there is data to be sent consists of the following steps:

1. Listen for the passing token.
2. If token is *busy*, listen for the next token.

3. If the token is *free*, mark the token as a *busy* token, append the data, and send the data onto the ring.
4. When the header with the busy token returns to the sender of that frame, after completing a full revolution around the ring, the sender removes the data from the ring.
5. The same device that just sent the frame sends a free token to allow another station to send a frame.

The algorithm for Token Ring does have other rules and variations, but these are beyond the depth of what is needed for the CCNA exam. Network Associates (the "Sniffer" people) have an excellent class covering Token Ring in detail. To find out more about these classes, go to www.nai.com.

With HDLC, arbitration is a nonissue today. HDLC is used on point-to-point links, which are typically full-duplex (four-wire) circuits. In other words, either endpoint can send at any time on a full-duplex link. Full-duplex operation is analogous to driving down a two-lane road—cars pass you going the other direction with no problem because there is a lane for each direction.

From a physical perspective, Frame Relay is comprised of a leased line between a router and the Frame Relay switch. These links are also typically full-duplex links, so no arbitration is needed. The Frame Relay network is shared among many data terminal equipment (DTE) devices, whereas the access link is not shared, so arbitration of the medium is not an issue.

NOTE As used in this book and in the ICND course, the word *frame* refers to particular parts of the data as sent on a link. In particular, *frame* implies that the data-link header and trailer are part of the bits being examined and discussed. Figure 3-11 shows frames for the four data-link protocols.

Figure 3-11 *Popular Frame Formats*

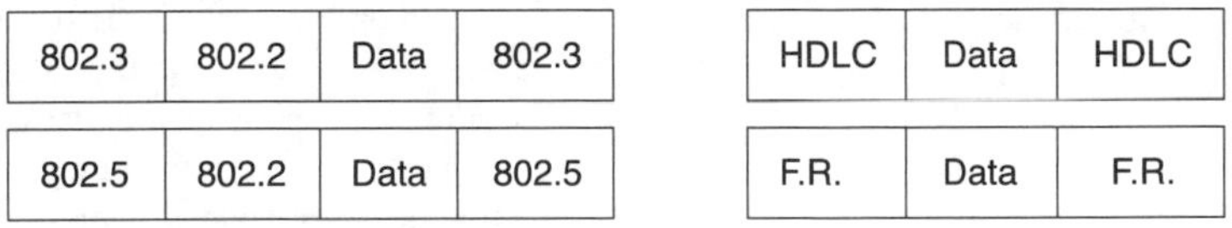

Data Link Function 2: Addressing

Cisco requires that CCNAs master the formats and meanings of data link layer and network layer addresses. LANs need addressing because there can be many possible recipients of data—that is, there could be more than two devices on the link. LANs behave much like people when you have a meeting with three or more people: If you want to say something to someone in particular, you first say that person's name—or at least look at him. Or, if you want to tell everyone in the meeting something, you just say it because they can all hear you. Likewise, LANs are *broadcast media*—a term signifying that all devices on the media receive the same data.

With Ethernet and Token Ring, the addresses are very similar. Each uses Media Access Control (MAC) addresses, which are 6 bytes long and are represented as a 12-digit hexadecimal number. Table 3-7 summarizes most of the details about MAC addresses.

Table 3-7 *LAN MAC Address Terminology and Features*

LAN Addressing Terms and Features	Description
MAC	Media Access Control. 802.3 (Ethernet) and 802.5 (Token Ring) are the MAC sublayers of these two LAN data-link protocols.
Ethernet address, NIC address, LAN address, Token Ring address, card address	Other names often used instead of MAC address. These terms describe the 6-byte address of the LAN interface card.
Burned-in address	The 6-byte address assigned by the vendor making the card. It usually is burned into a ROM or EEPROM on the LAN card and begins with a 3-byte organizationally unique identifier (OUI) assigned by the IEEE.
Locally administered address	Through configuration, an address that is used instead of the burned-in address.
Unicast address	Fancy term for a MAC that represents a single LAN interface.
Broadcast address	An address that means "all devices that reside on this LAN right now."
Multicast address	Not valid on Token Ring. On Ethernet, a multicast address implies some subset of all devices currently on the LAN.
Functional address	Not valid on Ethernet. On Token Ring, these addresses are reserved to represent the device(s) on the ring performing a particular function. For example, all source-route bridges supply the ring number to other devices; to do so, they each listen for the Ring Parameter Server (RPS) functional address.

HDLC includes a meaningless address field because it is used only on point-to-point serial links. The recipient is implied; if one device sent a frame, the other device is the only possible intended recipient. In the earlier analogy of three or more people in a meeting, point-to-point links are more like a meeting with two people—you do not have to say someone's name before you speak because the other person is the only one you can talk to!

Frame Relay acts more like a LAN than a point-to-point link, regarding the need for addressing. With Frame Relay, there is one physical link that has many logical circuits called *virtual circuits*

(VCs). (See Chapter 10, "Frame Relay Concepts and Configuration," for more background on Frame Relay.) The address field in Frame Relay defines a data-link connection identifier (DLCI), which identifies each VC. For example, in Figure 3-12, the Frame Relay switch to which router Timbuktu is connected receives frames; the switch forwards the frame to either Kalamazoo or East Egypt based on the DLCI, which identifies each VC. So, Timbuktu has one physical connection but multiple logical connections.

Figure 3-12 *Frame Relay Network*

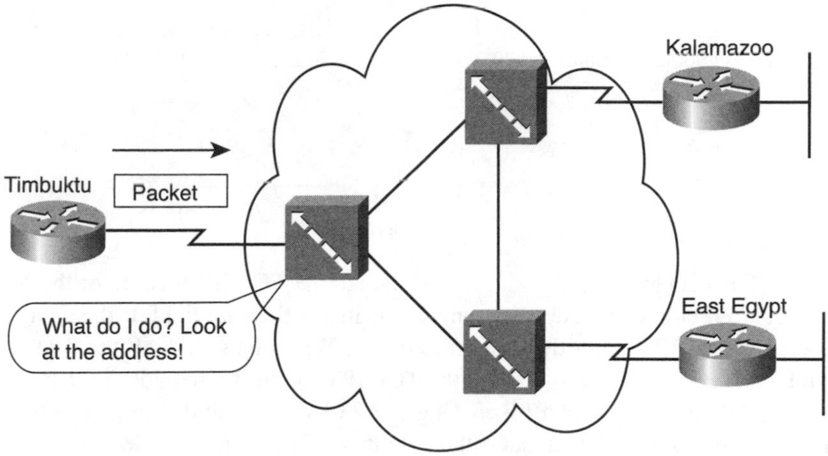

Data Link Function 3: Error Detection

Error detection discovers whether bit errors occurred during the transmission of the frame. To do this, most data links include a *frame check sequence (FCS)* or *cyclical redundancy check (CRC)* field in the data link trailer. This field contains a value that is the result of a mathematical formula applied to the data in the frame. The FCS value calculated and sent by the sender should match the value calculated by the receiver. All four data links discussed in this section contain an FCS field in the frame trailer.

Error detection does not imply recovery; most data links, including 802.5 Token Ring and 802.3 Ethernet, do not provide error recovery. In these two cases, however, an option in the 802.2 protocol, called LLC Type 2, does perform error recovery. (SNA and NetBIOS are the typical higher-layer protocols in use that request the services of LLC2.) Neither HDLC or Frame Relay does error recovery.

Data Link Function 4: Identifying the Encapsulated Data

Finally, the fourth part of a data link identifies the contents of the data field in the frame. Figure 3-13 helps make the usefulness of this feature apparent.

Figure 3-13 *Multiplexing Using Data Link Type and Protocol Fields*

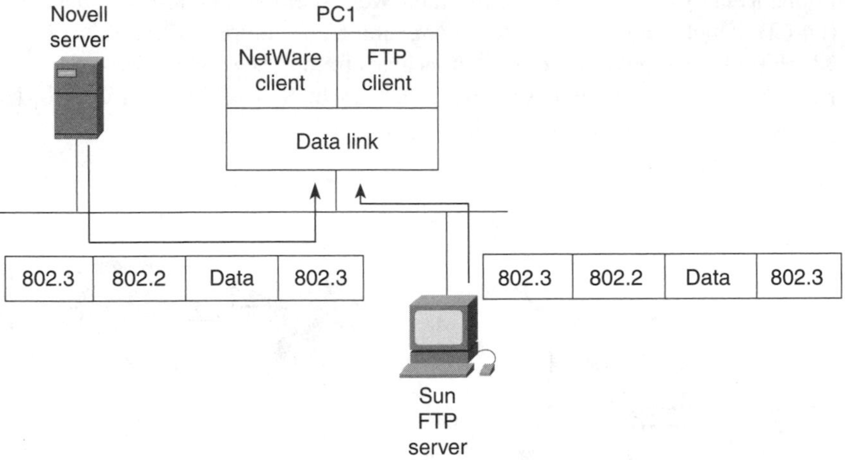

When PC1 receives data, does it give the data to the TCP/IP software or the NetWare client software? Of course, that depends on what is inside the data field. If the data came from the Novell server, PC1 hands the data off to the NetWare client code. If the data comes from the Sun FTP server, PC1 hands it off to the TCP/IP code. But what does PC1 look at to make this decision? Well, Ethernet and Token Ring 802.2 LLC use a field in its header to identify the type of data in the data field, and that is the field that PC1 examines to decide whether the packet is an IP packet or an IPX packet.

Each data-link header has a field with a code that means IP, IPX, or some other designation defining the type of protocol header that follows. For example, in the first frame in Figure 3-14, the destination service access point (DSAP) field has a value of E0, which means that the next header is a Novell IPX header. Why is that? Well, when the IEEE created 802.2, they saw the need for a protocol type field. They called it DSAP, and anyone could register favorite protocols to use a reserved value in the DSAP field; Novell registered IPX and was assigned hex E0 by the IEEE.

However, the IEEE did not plan for a large number of protocols—in fact, the 1-byte-long DSAP field is not big enough to number them all. In the second frame of Figure 3-14, the DSAP field is AA, which implies that a *subnetwork access protocol (SNAP)* header follows. The SNAP header uses a 2-byte protocol type field, which has a value of 0800 in this case, signifying that the next header is an IP header. RFC 1700, the "Assigned Numbers" RFC (http://www.isi.edu/in-notes/rfc1700.txt), lists the SAP and SNAP Type field values and the protocol types that they imply.

Figure 3-14 *802.2 SAP and SNAP Type Fields*

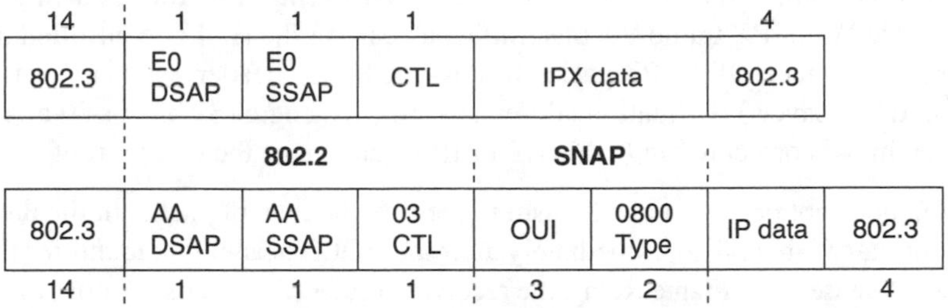

Similarly, HDLC and Frame Relay need to identify the contents of the data field. Of course, it is atypical to have end-user devices attached to either of these types of data links. In this case, routers provide an example more typically found in most WAN environments, as shown in Figure 3-15.

Figure 3-15 *Identifying Protocols over HDLC and Frame Relay*

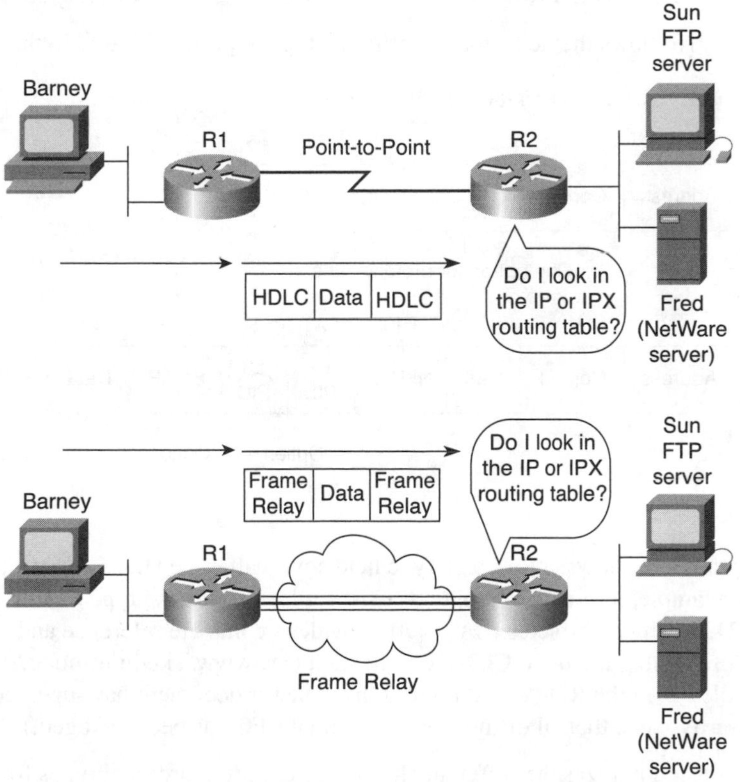

Referring to the top part of Figure 3-15, if Barney is using FTP to transfer files to the Sun system and also is connected to the NetWare server (Fred) using IPX, Barney will generate both TCP/IP and NetWare IPX traffic. As this traffic passes over the HDLC-controlled link, R2 will need to know whether an IP or IPX packet follows the HDLC header. Mainly, this is so that the router can find the Layer 3 destination address, assume its length (32 bits or 80 bits), perform table lookup in the correct routing table (IP or IPX), and make the correct routing decision.

HDLC does not provide a mechanism to identify the type of packet in the data field. IOS adds a proprietary 2-byte field immediately after the HDLC header that identifies the contents of the data. Likewise, with Frame Relay, the receiving router (R2) needs to know whether an IP or IPX packet follows the Frame Relay header. Frame Relay headers originally did not address this issue, either, because the headers were based on HDLC. However, the IETF created a specification called RFC 1490 that defined additional headers that followed the standard Frame Relay header. These headers include several fields that can be used to identify the data so that the receiving device knows what type is hidden inside.

The ITU and ANSI picked up the specifications of RFC 1490 and added it to their official Frame Relay standards: ITU T1.617 Annex F and ANSI Q.933 Annex E, respectively.

Figure 3-16 shows the fields that identify the type of protocol found in the data field.

Figure 3-16 *Identifying Protocols over HDLC and Frame Relay*

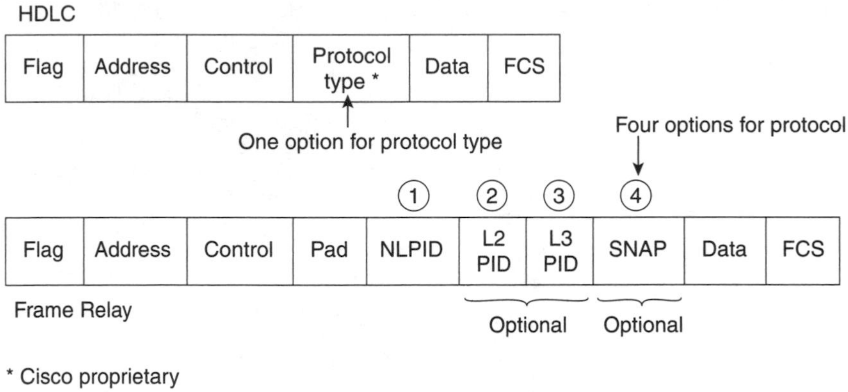

As Figure 3-16 shows, a Protocol Type field comes after the HDLC Control field. In the Frame Relay example, four different options exist for identifying the type of data inside the frame. RFC 2427, which obsoletes RFC 1490, provides a complete reference and is useful reading for those of you moving on to CCNP certification (see www.isi.edu/in-notes/rfc2427.txt). ("Obsoletes" in the RFC world implies that a newer document has superceded it but does not necessarily mean that all or most of the original RFC has been changed.)

Table 3-8 summarizes the different choices for encoding protocol types for each of the four data-link protocols. Notice that the length of some of these fields is only 1 byte, which historically has led to the addition of other headers that have a 2-byte Protocol Type field because 1 byte is just not enough to number all the different protocols. For example, the SNAP header contains a 2-byte type field because a 1-byte DSAP field is not big enough to number all the available options for what type of protocol is inside the data.

Table 3-8 *Different Choices for Encoding Protocol Types for Each of the Four Example Data-Link Protocols*

Data-Link Protocol	Field	Header in Which It Is Found	Size
802.3 Ethernet and 802.5 Token Ring	DSAP	802.2 header	1 byte
802.3 Ethernet and 802.5 Token Ring	SSAP	802.2 header	1 byte
802.3 Ethernet and 802.5 Token Ring	Protocol Type	SNAP header	2 bytes
Ethernet (DIX)	Ethertype	Ethernet header	2 bytes
HDLC	Cisco-proprietary Protocol ID field	Extra Cisco header	2 bytes
Frame Relay RFC 2427	NLPID	RFC 1490	1 byte
Frame Relay RFC 2427	L2 or L3 Protocol ID	Q.933	2 bytes each
Frame Relay RFC 2427	SNAP Protocol Type	SNAP Header	2 bytes

Summary: Data Link Functions

Table 3-9 summarizes the basic functions of data-link protocols.

Table 3-9 *Data-Link Protocol Functions*

Function	Ethernet	Token Ring	HDLC	Frame Relay
Arbitration	CSMA/CD algorithm (part of MAC)	Token passing (part of MAC)	N/A	N/A
Addressing	Source and destination MAC addresses	Source and destination MAC addresses	Single 1-byte address; unimportant on point-to-point links	DLCI used to identify virtual circuits
Error detection	FCS in trailer	FCS in trailer	FCS in trailer	FCS in trailer

continues

Table 3-9 *Data-Link Protocol Functions (Continued)*

Function	Ethernet	Token Ring	HDLC	Frame Relay
Identifying contents of data	802.2 DSAP, SNAP header, or Ethertype, as needed	802.2 DSAP or SNAP header, as needed	Proprietary Type field	RFC 1490/2427 headers, with NLPID, L2 and L3 protocol IDs, or SNAP header

OSI Network Layer Functions

9 Identify the parts in specific protocol address examples.

12 Describe the two parts of network addressing, and then identify the parts in specific protocol address examples.

OSI Layer 3 equivalent protocols use *routing* and *addressing* to accomplish their goals. The choices made by the people who made up addressing greatly affect how routing works, so the two topics are best described together.

Network layer (Layer 3) addressing will be covered in enough depth to describe IP, IPX, and AppleTalk addresses. Also, now that data link layer and network layer addresses have been covered in this chapter, this section undertakes a comparison between the two.

Routing

Routing can be thought of as a three-step process, as seen in Figure 3-17. Thinking about routing in these three separate steps helps make some of the details more obvious. However, most people will not think of routing as a three-step process when going about their normal jobs—this is just a tool to make a few points more clearly.

As illustrated in Figure 3-17, the three steps of routing include the following:

Step 1 Sending the data from the source computer to some nearby router

Step 2 Delivering the data from the router near the source to a router near the destination

Step 3 Delivering the data from the router near the destination to the end destination computer

Figure 3-17 *Three Steps of Routing*

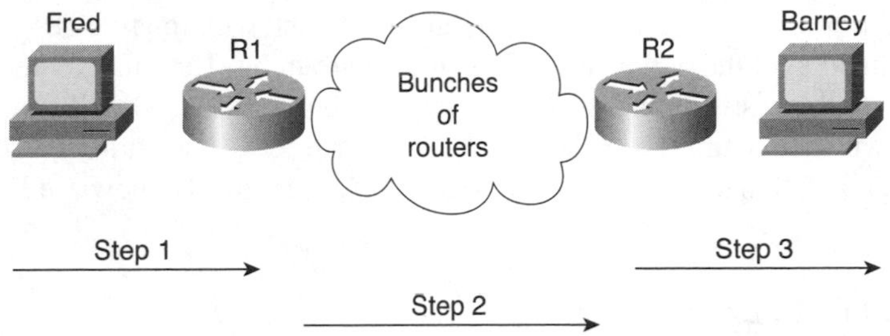

Sending Data to a Nearby Router

The creator of the data, who is also the sender of the data, decides to send data to a device in another group. A mechanism must be in place so that the sender knows of some router on a *common data link with the sender* to ensure that data can be sent to that router. The sender sends a data-link frame across the medium to the nearby router; this frame includes the packet in the data portion of the frame. That frame uses data link layer (Layer 2) addressing in the data-link header to ensure that the nearby router receives the frame. The main point here is that the originator of the data does not know much about the network—just how to get the data to some nearby router. In the post office analogy, I know how to get to the local post office, but that's all I need to know to send that letter to Mike in Califonia.

Routing Data Across the Network

The routing table for that particular network layer protocol contains a list of network layer address *groupings*. Instead of a single entry in the routing table per destination address, there is one entry per group. The router compares the destination network layer address in the packet to the entries in the routing table in memory, and a match is made. This matching entry in the routing table tells this router where to forward the packet next.

The concept of network layer address grouping is identical to the U.S. ZIP code system. Everyone living in the same vicinity is in the same ZIP code, and the postal sorters just look for the ZIP codes, ignoring the rest of the address.

Any intervening routers repeat the same process. The destination network layer (Layer 3) address in the packet identifies the group in which the destination resides. The routing table is searched for a matching entry, which tells this router where to forward the packet next. Eventually, the packet is delivered to the router connected to the network or subnet of the destination host, as previously shown in Figure 3-17.

Delivering Data to the End Destination

The final router in the path also needs a list of all the address groupings, but because the destination is on the same LAN as the router, this final router needs to look at the entire address. When the packet arrives at a router sharing a data link with the true destination, the router and the destination of the packet are in the same L3 grouping. That final router can forward the data directly to the destination. As usual, a new data-link header and trailer are created before a frame (which contains the packet that made the trip across the entire network) can be sent on to the media. This matches the final step (Step 3), as previously shown in Figure 3-17.

A Comment About Data Links

Because the routers build new data-link headers and trailers, and because the new headers contain data-link addresses, the routers must have some way to decide what data-link addresses to use. An example of how the router determines which data-link address to use is the IP Address Resolution Protocol (ARP) protocol. *ARP is used to dynamically learn the data-link address of some IP host.*

An example specific to TCP/IP will be useful to solidify the concepts behind routing. Imagine that PC1 is sending packets to PC2. (If you do not understand the basics of IP addressing already, you might want to bookmark this page and refer to it after you have reviewed Chapter 5, which covers IP addressing.) Figure 3-18 provides an example network so that you can review the routing process.

Figure 3-18 *Routing Logic and Encapsulation—PC1 Sending to PC2*

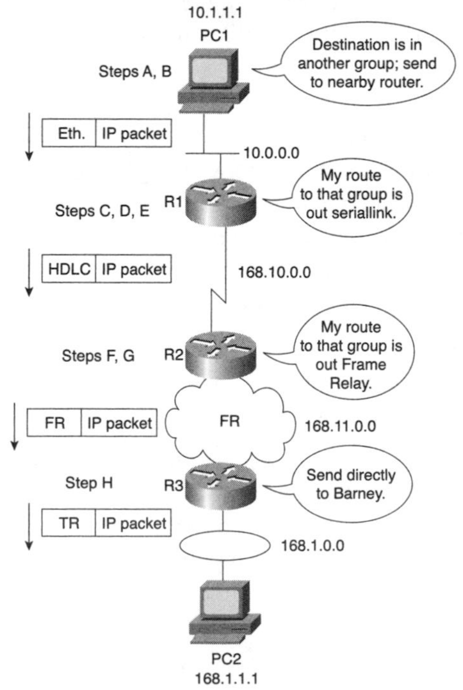

The logic behind the earlier three-step routing process is described in the following more detailed steps:

Step A PC1 needs to know its nearby router. PC1 first knows of R1's IP address by having either a *default router* or a *default gateway* configured. The default router defined on some host is the router to which that host forwards packets that are destined for subnets other than the directly attached subnet. Assume that a default router of 10.1.1.100 is configured on PC1 and that it is R1's Ethernet IP address.

Step B PC1 needs to know R1's Ethernet MAC address before PC1 can finish building the Ethernet header (see Figure 3-18). In the case of TCP/IP, the ARP process is used to dynamically learn R1's MAC address. (See Chapter 5 for a discussion of ARP.) When R1's MAC address is known, PC1 completes the Ethernet header with the destination MAC address being R1's MAC address and sends the packet to R1.

Step C At Step 2 of the routing process, the router has many items to consider. First, the incoming frame (Ethernet interface) is processed only if the Ethernet FCS is passed and the router's MAC address is in the destination address field. Then the appropriate Protocol Type field is examined so that R1 knows what type of packet is in the data portion of the frame. At this point, R1 discards the Ethernet header and trailer.

Step D The next part of Step 2 involves finding an entry in the routing table for network 168.1.0.0, the network of which PC2 is a member. In this case, the route in R1 references 168.1.0.0 and lists R1's serial interface as the interface by which to forward the packet.

Step E To complete Step 2, R1 builds an HDLC header and trailer to place around the IP packet. Because the HDLC data link uses the same address field every time, no process such as ARP is needed to allow R1 to build the HDLC header.

Step F Routing Step 2 is repeated by R2 when it receives the HDLC frame. The HDLC FCS is checked; the type field is examined to learn that the packet inside the frame is an IP packet, and then the HDLC header and trailer are discarded. The IP routing table in R2 is examined for network 168.1.0.0, and a match is made. The entry directs R2 to forward the packet to its Frame Relay serial interface. The routing entry also identifies the next router's IP address—namely, R3's IP address on the other end of the Frame Relay VC.

Step G Before R2 can complete its Step 2 of this end-to-end routing algorithm, R2 must build a Frame Relay header and trailer. Before it can complete the task, the correct DLCI for the VC to R3 must be decided. In most cases today, the dynamic Inverse ARP process will have associated R3's IP address with the DLCI that R2 uses to send frames to R3. (See Chapter 8 for more details on Inverse ARP and Frame Relay mapping.) With that mapping information, R2 can complete the Frame Relay header and send the frame to R3.

Step H Step 3 of the original algorithm is performed by R3. Like R1 and R2 before it, R3 checks the FCS in the data link trailer, looks at the type field to decide whether the packet inside the frame is an IP packet, and then discards the Frame Relay header and trailer. The routing table entry for 168.1.0.0 shows that the outgoing interface is R3's Token Ring interface. However, there is no next-router IP address because there is no need to forward the packet to another router. R3 simply needs to build a Token Ring header and trailer and forward the frame that contains the original packet to PC2. Before R3 can finish building the Token Ring header, an IP ARP must be used to find PC2's MAC address (assuming that R3 doesn't already have that information in its IP ARP cache).

Network Layer (Layer 3) Addressing

Cisco requires that CCNAs master the details of Layer 3 addressing, both the concepts and the particulars of IP and IPX. One key feature of network layer addresses is that they were designed to allow logical grouping of addresses. In other words, something about the numeric value of an address implies a group or set of addresses, all of which are considered to be in the same grouping. In TCP/IP, this group is called a *network* or a *subnet*. In IPX, it is called a *network*. In AppleTalk, the grouping is called a *cable range*. These groupings work just like USPS ZIP codes, allowing the routers (mail sorters) to speedily route (sort) lots of packets (letters).

Just like street addresses, network layer addresses are grouped based on physical location in a network. The rules differ for some network layer protocols, but the grouping concept is identical for IP, IPX, and AppleTalk. In each of these network layer protocols, all devices with addresses in the same group cannot be separated from each other by a router that is configured to route that protocol, respectively. Stated differently, all devices in the same group (IP subnet/IPX network/AppleTalk cable range) must be connected to the same data link; for example, all devices must be connected to the same Ethernet to be in the same group.

Routing relies on the fact that Layer 3 addresses are grouped together. The routing tables for each network layer protocol can have one entry for the group, not one entry for each individual address. Imagine an Ethernet with 100 Novell clients. A router needing to forward packets to any of those clients needs only one entry in its IPX routing table. If those clients in the same IPX network were not required to be attached to the same data link, and if there was no way to encode the IPX network number as part of the IPX address of the client, routing would not be capable of using just one entry in the table. This basic fact is one of the key reasons that routers can scale to allow tens and hundreds of thousands of devices. It's very similar to the USPS ZIP code system—it would be ridiculous to have people in the same ZIP code as me live somewhere far away. Likewise, devices in the same IP subnet, IPX network, or AppleTalk cable range are physically close, relatively speaking.

With that in mind, most network layer (Layer 3) addressing schemes were created with the following goals:

- The address space should be large enough to accommodate the largest network for which the designers imagined the protocol would be used.
- The addresses should allow for unique assignment so that little or no chance of address duplication exists.
- The address structure should have some grouping implied so that many addresses are considered to be in the same group.
- Dynamic address assignment for clients is desired.

A great analogy for this concept of network addressing is the addressing scheme used by the U.S. Postal Service. Instead of getting involved with every small community's plans for what to name new streets, the post office simply has a nearby office with a ZIP code. The rest of the post offices in the country are already prepared to send mail to new businesses and residences on the new streets because they care only about the ZIP code, which they already know. It is the local postmaster's job to assign a mail carrier to deliver and pick up mail on those new streets. There might be hundreds of Main streets in different ZIP codes, but as long as there is just one per ZIP code, the address is unique—and with an amazing percentage of success, the U.S. Postal Service delivers the mail to the correct address.

Example Layer 3 Address Structures

Each Layer 3 address structure contains at least two parts. One (or more) part at the beginning of the address works like the ZIP code and essentially identifies the grouping. All instances of addresses with the same value in these first bits of the address are considered to be in the same group—for example, the same IP subnet or IPX network or AppleTalk cable range. The last part of the address acts as a local address, uniquely identifying that device in that particular group. Table 3-10 outlines several Layer 3 address structures.

Table 3-10 *Layer 3 Address Structures*

Protocol	Size of Address (Bits)	Name and Size of Grouping Field	Name and Size of Local Address Field
IP	32	Network or subnet (variable, between 8 and 30 bits)	Host (variable, between 2 and 24 bits)
IPX	80	Network (32)	Node (48)
AppleTalk	24	Network (16) (Consecutively numbered values in this field can be combined into one group, called a cable range.)	Node (8)
OSI	Variable	Many formats, many sizes	Domain Specific Part (DSP) (typically 56, including NSAP)

Routing Protocols

Conveniently, the routing tables in the example based on Figure 3-18 had the correct routing information already in their routing tables. In most cases, these entries are built dynamically by use of a *routing protocol*. Routing protocols define message formats and procedures, just like any other protocol. With routing protocols, however, the goal is not to help with end-user data delivery—the end goal is to fill the routing table with all known destination groups and with the best route to reach each group.

A technical description of the logic behind two underlying routing protocol algorithms, *distance vector* and *link-state*, is found in Chapter 7, "Routing and Routing Protocols."

Nonroutable Protocols

Start Extra Credit

In the early and mid-1990s, one of the reasons that Cisco sold a lot of routers is that the IOS could route more Layer 3 protocols than most—if not all—competitors. However, some protocols are not routable. To support those, Cisco supported and evolved variations of bridging to support nonroutable protocols.

What makes a protocol nonroutable? Basically, a protocol stack that does not define an OSI Layer 3 equivalent, including a logical Layer 3 address structure, cannot be routed. To be fair, because the answer to the question "Is a protocol routable?" for any particular protocol is more of a geek-party discussion, no hard-and-fast rules govern what has to be true for a protocol to be considered routable. As this chapter shows, however, forwarding packets (L3PDUs) based on a destination Layer 3—equivalent address involves routing; a protocol stack with no Layer 3 is considered nonroutable.

If a protocol is not routable, bridging must be enabled to support those protocols. (Bridging concepts are covered in Chapter 4, "LANs, Bridges, and Switches.") To support nonroutable protocols over WAN links, some other protocol must be used, such as encapsulated transparent bridging and data-link switching (a form of remote bridging for SNA and NetBIOS).

The details of how to support nonroutable protocols is beyond the scope of CCNA. What is reasonably expected to be in the scope of CCNA is to know the most popular nonroutable protocols. Consider Table 3-11, which lists protocols that some people consider to be nonroutable.

Table 3-11 *Purported Nonroutable Protocols*

Protocol	Do Protocol Specifications Allow Routing?	Does IOS Support Routing This Protocol?
DEC Local Area Transport (LAT)	No	No
NetBIOS	No	No
SNA (Traditional Subarea SNA)	Yes; routed by IBM products running VTAM and NCP	No
SNA (APPN)	Yes	Yes

DEC LAT and NetBIOS (sometimes referred to as NetBEUI, for NetBIOS End User Interface) are definitely nonroutable. IBM's SNA has two general categories: Subarea SNA is the traditional Mainframe DataCenter SNA and advanced peer-to-peer networking (APPN) is a newer, more easily routable variation. Both are routable, have Layer 3 addressing, and can be routed by products that you can purchase today. However, be careful—Cisco folklore has it that SNA is not routable because Cisco IOS Software did not route SNA. If CCNA exam questions touch on this topic, focus on the context and be sure to remember that LAT and NetBIOS are truly nonroutable.

End Extra Credit

The section that follows, however, presents an anecdote that might help you remember the difference among the terms *routing*, *routed protocols*, and *routing protocols*.

The Story of Ted and Ting

NOTE This somewhat silly story is the result of the Cisco World Wide Training division's proctors for the instructor certification process, who emphasize that the instructors should be creative in the use of tools to help students remember important details. After I tried this story during certification, it was propagated by other instructors. I am curious—if you have heard this story or a variation, please let me know when you heard it and from whom (wendell@lacidar.com).

Ted and Ting both work for the same company at a facility in Snellville, Georgia. They work in the same department; their job is to make lots of widgets. (Widgets are imaginary products; the term *widget* is used in the United States often to represent a product when the actual product is not the topic of discussion.)

Ted worked quickly and was a hard worker. In fact, because he was a very intense person, Ted tended to make more widgets than anyone else in Snellville, including Ting. Ted also liked to have everything he needed instantly available when and where he wanted it so that he could make the widgets more quickly.

Ting, on the other hand, also worked very hard but was much more of a planner. He tended to think first and then act. Ting planned very well and had all supplies well stocked, including all the instructions needed to make the different kinds of widgets. In fact, all the information about how to build each type of widget was on a table by his door. He had a problem with the table getting "reallocated" (that is, stolen), so he applied a nonremovable label with the words "Ting's Table" to the surface so that he could find the table in case someone stole it.

It turns out that Ted's productivity was partly a result of sitting next to Ting. In fact, Ted often was ready to make the next widget but needed something, such as the instruction sheet for a particular unique widget. By swinging into Ting's office, Ted could be back at it in just a few seconds. In fact, part of the reason Ting kept the instruction sheets on Ting's Table by the door was that he was tired of Ted always interrupting him looking for something.

Well, Ted got lots of bonuses for being the most productive worker, and Ting did not. Being fair, though, Ted realized that he would not be as successful without Ting, so Ted shared his bonuses with Ting. (Hey, it's an imaginary story!)

Then one day the president decided to franchise the company because it was the best widget-making company in the world. The president, Dr. Rou (pronounced like the word "ouch"), decided to create a manual to be used by all the franchisees to build their business. So, Dr. Rou went to the most productive widget maker, Ted, and asked him what he did every day. Along the way, Dr. Rou noticed that Ted went next door a lot. So, being the bright guy that he was, Dr. Rou visited Ting next and asked him what he did.

The next day Dr. Rou emerged with the franchise manual. Being an ex–computer networking professional, he had called the manual "Protocols for Making Widgets." One part of the protocol defined how Ted made widgets very quickly. Another part described how Ting kept everything needed by Ted at arm's length, including all the instructions that Ted needed. It even mentioned Ting's Table as the place to store the instruction sheets. To give credit where credit was due—but not too much credit—the names of these protocols were as follows:

- **The "Rou-Ted Protocol"**—How to make widgets really quickly
- **The "Rou-Ting Protocol"**—How to plan and collect information so that the other guy can make widgets fast
- **The "Rou-Ting Table"**—The place to store your widget-making instruction sheets

Similarly, with networking, the *routed protocol* is the one being routed, such as IP, IPX, OSI, DECnet, and so forth. The *routing protocol* is the one preparing the information needed to perform the routing process quickly, such as RIP, IGRP, OSPF, NLSP, and so forth. The *routing table* is where the information needed to perform routing is held, as built by the routing protocol and used by the routing process to forward the packets of the routed protocol.

That's all just to distinguish among the terms *routed protocol*, *routing protocol*, and *routing table*.

Foundation Summary

The "Foundation Summary" is a collection of tables and figures that provide a convenient review of many key concepts in this chapter. For those of you already comfortable with the topics in this chapter, this summary could help you recall a few details. For those of you who just read this chapter, this review should help solidify some key facts. For any of you doing your final prep before the exam, these tables and figures will be a convenient way to review the day before the exam.

Table 3-12 offers a more condensed description of the layer characteristics and examples. This table is taken directly from Cisco's ICND course.

Table 3-12 *OSI Reference Model (Condensed Information)*

OSI Layer Name	Functional Description	Examples
Application (Layer 7)	Interface between network and application software	Telnet, HTTP
Presentation (Layer 6)	How data is presented Special processing, such as encryption	JPEG, ASCII, EBCDIC
Session (Layer 5)	Keeping data separate from different applications	Operating systems and application access scheduling
Transport (Layer 4)	Reliable or unreliable delivery Multiplexing	TCP, UDP, SPX
Network (Layer 3)	Logical addressing, which routers use for path determination	IP, IPX
Data link (Layer 2)	Combination of bits into bytes, and bytes into frames Access to the media using MAC address Error detection and error recovery	802.3/802.2, HDLC
Physical (Layer 1)	Moving of bits between devices Specification of voltage, wire speed, and cable pinouts	EIA/TIA-232, V.35

The following list summarizes the benefits of layered protocol specifications:

- Humans can more easily discuss and learn about the many details of a protocol specification.
- Standardized interfaces among layers facilitate modular engineering. Different products can provide functions of only some layers (such as a router with Layers 1 to 3), or some products could supply parts of the functions of the protocol (such as Microsoft TCP/IP built into Win95, or the Eudora e-mail application providing TCP/IP application layer support).
- A better environment for interoperability is created. One vendor can write software that implements higher layers—for example, a Web browser—and another can write software that implements the lower layers—for example, Microsoft's built-in TCP/IP software in its operating systems.
- Reduced complexity allows easier program changes and faster product evolution.
- One layer uses the services of the layer immediately below it. Therefore, remembering what each layer does is easier. (For example, the network layer needs to deliver data from end to end. To do this, it uses data links to forward data to the next successive device along that end-to-end path.)

Figure 3-19 provides a visual representation of the same-layer interaction concepts.

Figure 3-19 *Same-Layer Interactions on Different Computers*

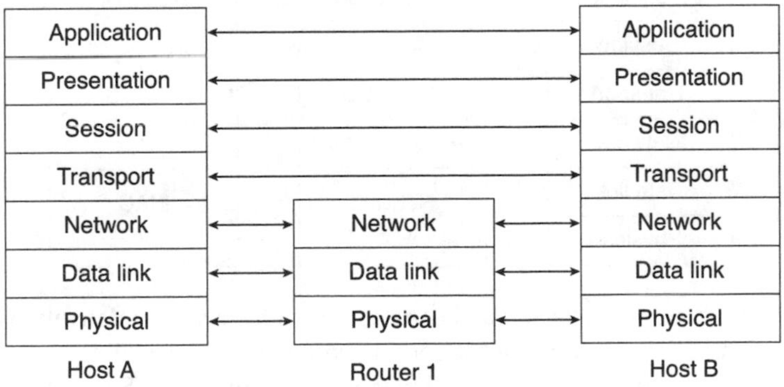

This five-step process happens to match the TCP/IP network model very well. Figure 3-20 depicts the concept; the numbers shown represent each of the five steps.

Figure 3-20 *Five Steps of Data Encapsulation—TCP/IP*

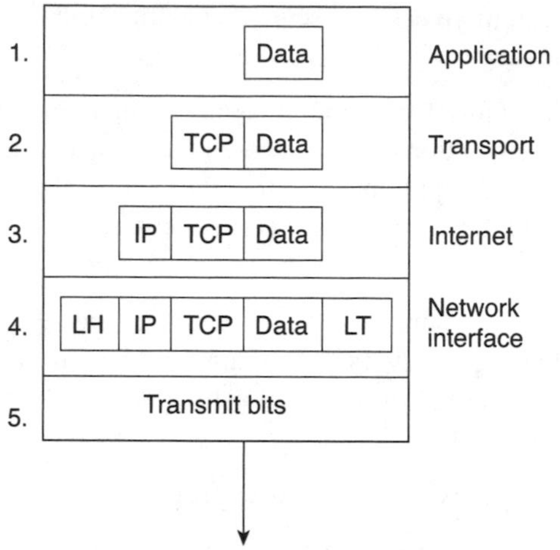

Figure 3-21 shows the layers of TCP/IP and NetWare, as compared with OSI.

Figure 3-21 *OSI, TCP/IP, and NetWare Protocols*

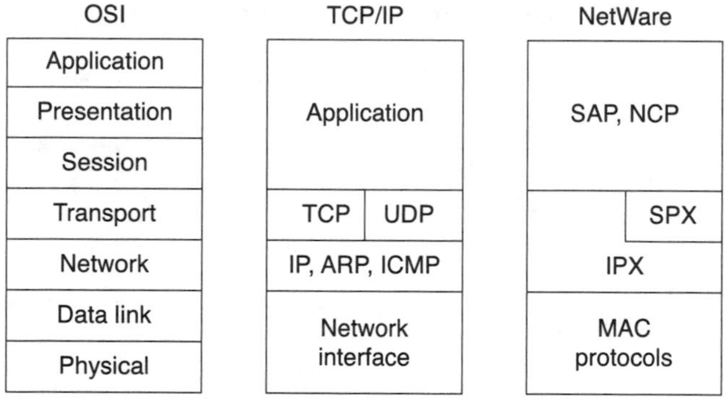

The terms *connection-oriented* and *connectionless* have some relatively well-known connotations inside the world of networking protocols. The meaniing of the terms is intertwined with error recovery and flow control, but they are not the same. So, first, some basic definitions are in order:

> **Connection-oriented protocol**—A protocol either that requires an exchange of messages before data transfer begins or that has a required pre-established correlation between two endpoints

> **Connectionless protocol**—A protocol that does not require an exchange of messages and that does not require a pre-established correlation between two endpoints

Table 3-13 summarizes the concepts behind error recovery and lists the behavior of three popular error-recovery protocols.

Table 3-13 *Examples of Error-Recovery Protocols and Their Features*

Feature	TCP	SPX	LLC2
Acknowledges data in both directions?	Yes	Yes	Yes
Uses forward acknowledgment?	Yes	Yes	Yes
Counts bytes or frame/packets?	Bytes	Packets	Frames
Necessitates resending of all data, or just one part and wait when resending?	One and wait	Resend all	Resend all

Figure 3-22 shows frames for the four data-link protocols.

Figure 3-22 *Popular Frame Formats*

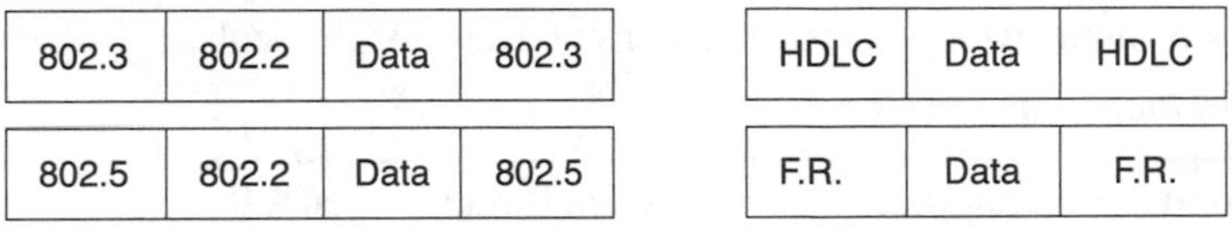

Table 3-14 summarizes most of the details about MAC addresses.

Table 3-14 *LAN MAC Address Terminology and Features*

LAN Addressing Terms and Features	Description
MAC	Media Access Control. 802.3 (Ethernet) and 802.5 (Token Ring) are the MAC sublayers of these two LAN data-link protocols.
Ethernet address, NIC address, LAN address, Token Ring address, card address	Other names often used instead of MAC address. These terms describe the 6-byte address of the LAN interface card.
Burned-in address	The 6-byte address assigned by the vendor making the card. It is usually burned in to a ROM or EEPROM on the LAN card and begins with a 3-byte organizationally unique identifier (OUI) assigned by the IEEE.
Locally administered address	Through configuration, an address that is used instead of the burned-in address.
Unicast address	Fancy term for a MAC that represents a single LAN interface.

continues

Table 3-14 *LAN MAC Address Terminology and Features (Continued)*

LAN Addressing Terms and Features	Description
Broadcast address	An address that means "all devices that reside on this LAN right now."
Multicast address	Not valid on Token Ring. On Ethernet, a multicast address implies some subset of all devices currently on the LAN.
Functional address	Not valid on Ethernet. On Token Ring, these addresses are reserved to represent the device(s) on the ring performing a particular function. For example, all source-route bridges supply the ring number to other devices; to do so, they each listen for the Ring Parameter Server (RPS) functional address.

Table 3-15 summarizes the basic functions of data-link protocols.

Table 3-15 *Data-Link Protocol Functions*

Function	Ethernet	Token Ring	HDLC	Frame Relay
Arbitration	CSMA/CD algorithm (part of MAC)	Token passing (part of MAC)	N/A	N/A
Addressing	Source and destination MAC addresses	Source and destination MAC addresses	Single 1-byte address; unimportant on point-to-point links	DLCI used to identify virtual circuits
Error detection	FCS in trailer	FCS in trailer	FCS in trailer	FCS in trailer
Identifying contents of data	802.2 DSAP, SNAP header, or Ethertype, as needed	802.2 DSAP or SNAP header, as needed	Proprietary Type field	RFC 1490/2427 headers, with NLPID, L2 and L3 protocol IDs, or SNAP header

Table 3-16 outlines several Layer 3 address structures.

Table 3-16 *Layer 3 Address Structures*

Protocol	Size of Address (Bits)	Name and Size of Grouping Field	Name and Size of Local Address Field
IP	32	Network or subnet (variable, between 8 and 30 bits)	Host (variable, between 2 and 24 bits)
IPX	80	Network (32)	Node (48)
AppleTalk	24	Network (16) (Consecutively numbered values in this field can be combined into one group, called a cable range.)	Node (8)
OSI	Variable	Many formats, many sizes	Domain Specific Part (DSP) (typically 56, including NSAP)

Q&A

As mentioned in Chapter 1, "All About the Cisco Certified Network Associate Certification," the questions and scenarios in this book are more difficult than what you should experience on the actual exam. The questions do not attempt to cover more breadth or depth than the exam; however, they are designed to make sure that you know the answer. Rather than allowing you to derive the answer from clues hidden inside the question itself, the questions challenge your understanding and recall of the subject. Questions from the "Do I Know This Already?" quiz from the beginning of the chapter are repeated here to ensure that you have mastered the chapter's topic areas. Hopefully, these questions will help limit the number of exam questions on which you narrow your choices to two options and then guess.

The answers to these questions can be found in Appendix A.

1 Name the seven layers of the OSI model.

____

____

____

2 What is the main purpose(s) of Layer 7?

____

____

____

3 What is the main purpose(s) of Layer 6?

____

____

____

4 What is the main purpose(s) of Layer 5?

____

____

____

5 What is the main purpose(s) of Layer 4?

____

____

____

6 What is the main purpose(s) of Layer 3?

7 What is the main purpose(s) of Layer 2?

8 What is the main purpose(s) of Layer 1?

9 Describe the process of data encapsulation as data is processed from creation until it exits a physical interface to a network. Use the OSI model as an example.

10 Describe the features required for a protocol to be considered connectionless.

11 Name at least three connectionless protocols.

12 Describe the features required for a protocol to be considered connection-oriented.

13 In a particular error-recovering protocol, the sender sends three frames, labeled 2, 3, and 4. On its next sent frame, the receiver of these frames sets an acknowledgment field to 4. What does this typically imply?

14 Name three connection-oriented protocols.

15 What does MAC stand for?

16 Name three terms popularly used as a synonym for *MAC address*.

17 Are IP addresses defined by a Layer 2 or Layer 3 protocol?

18 Are IPX addresses defined by a Layer 2 or Layer 3 protocol?

19 Are OSI NSAP addresses defined by a Layer 2 or Layer 3 protocol?

20 What portion of a MAC address encodes an identifier representing the manufacturer of the card?

21 Are MAC addresses defined by a Layer 2 or a Layer 3 protocol?

22 Are DLCI addresses defined by a Layer 2 or a Layer 3 protocol?

23 Name two differences between Layer 3 addresses and Layer 2 addresses.

24 How many bits are present in an IP address?

25 How many bits are present in an IPX address?

26 How many bits are present in a MAC address?

27 Name the two main parts of an IPX address. Which part identifies which "group" this address is a member of?

____

____

____

28 Name the two main parts of an IP address. Which part identifies which "group" this address is a member of?

____

____

____

29 Name the two main parts of a MAC address. Which part identifies which "group" this address is a member of?

____

____

____

30 Name three benefits to layering networking protocol specifications.

____

____

____

31 What header and/or trailer does a router discard as a side effect of routing?

____

____

____

32 Describe the differences between a routed protocol and a routing protocol.

____

____

____

33 Name at least three routed protocols.

34 Name at least three routing protocols.

35 How does an IP host know what router to send a packet to? In which cases does an IP host choose to send a packet to this router instead of directly to the destination host?

36 How does an IPX host know which router to send a packet to? In which case does an IPX host choose to send a packet to this router instead of directly to the destination host?

37 Name three items in an entry in any routing table.

38 What OSI layer typically encapsulates using both a header and a trailer?

Scenarios

Scenario 3-1

Given the network in Figure 3-23 and the address table in Table 3-17, perform the tasks that follow. This scenario uses an imaginary Layer 3 addressing structure as a method to review concepts. When in doubt, concentrate on the concepts. Also, the imaginary Layer 3 used in this example is here only to allow you to concentrate on the concepts instead of a particular protocol; there is no need to memorize this scheme or expect questions like this on the exam.

Figure 3-23 *Musketeer Network for Scenario*

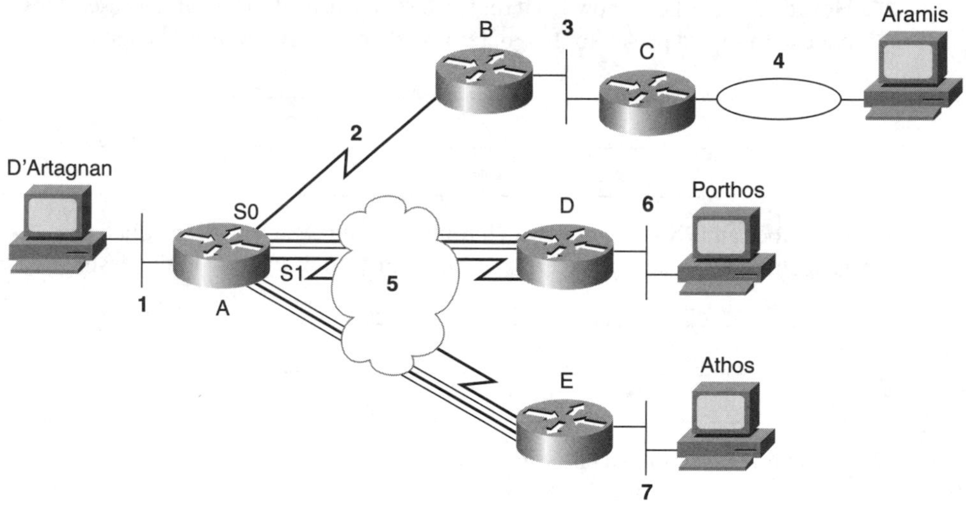

Table 3-17 provides the routing table for the network setup in Figure 3-23.

Table 3-17 *Layer 3 Address Table for Network in Figure 3-23*

Router	Interface	Address
A	E0	group-1.local-A
A	S0	group-2.local-A
A	S1	group-5.local-A
B	S0	group-2.local-B

Table 3-17 *Layer 3 Address Table for Network in Figure 3-23 (Continued)*

Router	Interface	Address
B	E0	group-3.local-B
C	E0	group-3.local-C
C	T0	group-4.local-C
D	S0	group-5.local-D
D	E0	group-6.local-D
E	S0	group-5.local-E
E	E0	group-7.local-E
D'Artagnan		group-1.local-M
Aramis		group-4.local-M
Porthos		group-6.local-M
Athos		group-7.local-M

Task 1 for Scenario 3-1

Create the routing table in Router A; assume that all parts of the network are up and working properly. Table 3-18 provides an empty routing table to record your answers.

Table 3-18 *Scenario 3-1 Task 1 Routing Table Answer Form*

Group	Outgoing Interface	Next Router

Task 2 for Scenario 3-1

D'Artagnan sends a packet to Aramis (source group-1.local-M, destination group-4.local-M). D'Artagnan sends this packet inside an Ethernet frame to Router A. Given this information, determine the following:

1. List the routing table entries in each router that are necessary for the packet to be delivered to Aramis.
2. What type of data-link header or trailer is discarded by each router in that route?
3. What destination data-link addresses are placed into the new data-link headers by each router?
4. What routes must be in which routers to ensure that Aramis can send a return packet to D'Artagnan?

Task 3 for Scenario 3-1

D'Artagnan sends a packet to Porthos (source group-1.local-M, destination group-6.local-M). D'Artagnan sends this packet inside an Ethernet frame to Router A. Given this information, determine the following:

1. List the routing table entries in each router that are necessary for the packet to be delivered to Porthos.
2. What type of data-link header or trailer is discarded by each router in that route?
3. What destination data-link addresses are placed into the new data-link headers by each router?
4. What routes must be in which routers to ensure that Porthos can send a return packet to D'Artagnan?

Scenario Answers

Answers to Task 1 for Scenario 3-1

Based on the network design illustrated in Figure 3-23, Task 1 for Scenario 3-1 asks you to create the routing table in Router A; assume that all parts of the network are up and working properly. The routing table for Router A is as follows:

Group	Outgoing Interface	Next Router
group-1	Ethernet 0	N/A
group-2	serial 0	N/A
group-3	serial 0	group-2.local-B
group-4	serial 0	group-2.local-B
group-5	serial 1	N/A
group-6	serial 1	group-5.local-D
group-7	serial 1	group-5.local-E

Answers to Task 2 for Scenario 3-1

Based on the network design illustrated in Figure 3-23, Task 2 for Scenario 3-1 states that D'Artagnan sends a packet to Aramis (source group-1.local-M, destination group-4.local-M). D'Artagnan sends this packet inside an Ethernet frame to Router A. The following are the solutions to exercises 1 through 4 for Task 2.

1 The routing tables are as follows:

In Router A:

Group	Outgoing Interface	Next Router
group-2	serial 0	N/A
group-4	serial 0	group-2.local-B

In Router B:

Group	Outgoing Interface	Next Router
group-3	Ethernet 0	N/A
group-4	Ethernet 0	group-3.local-C

In Router C:

Group	Outgoing Interface	Next Router
group-4	Token Ring 0	N/A

2 Router A discards the Ethernet header and adds an HDLC header. Router B discards the HDLC header and adds an Ethernet header. Router C discards the Ethernet header and adds a Token Ring header.

3 Router A places the never-changing HDLC address (Hex 03) into the header. Router B places Router C's Ethernet MAC address into the destination address field. Router C places Aramis's Token Ring MAC address into the destination address field.

4 This is all noise if Aramis cannot get a packet back to D'Artagnan. The following routing tables show the routes needed for both directions; the routes with asterisks signify routes required for the routes back to D'Artagnan.

In Router A:

Group	Outgoing Interface	Next Router
group-1*	Ethernet 0	N/A
group-2	serial 0	N/A
group-4	serial 0	group-2.local-B

In Router B:

Group	Outgoing Interface	Next Router
group-1*	serial 0	group-2.local-A
group-2*	serial 0	N/A
group-3	Ethernet 0	N/A
group-4	Ethernet 0	group-3.local-C

In Router C:

Group	Outgoing Interface	Next Router
group-1*	Ethernet 0	group-3.local-B
group-3*	Ethernet 0	N/A
group-4	Token ring 0	N/A

Answers to Task 3 for Scenario 3-1

Based on the network design illustrated in Figure 3-23, Task 3 for Scenario 3-1 states that D'Artagnan sends a packet to Porthos (source group-1.local-M, destination group-6.local-M). D'Artagnan sends this packet inside an Ethernet frame to Router A. The following are the solutions to exercises 1 through 4 for Task 3.

1 The routing tables are as follows:

In Router A:

Group	Outgoing Interface	Next Router
group-5	serial 1	N/A
group-6	serial 1	group-5.local-D

In Router D:

Group	Outgoing Interface	Next Router
group-6	Ethernet 0	N/A

2 Router A discards the Ethernet header and adds a Frame Relay header. Router D discards the Frame Relay header and adds an Ethernet header.

3 Router A places the Frame Relay DLCI for the VC connecting it to Router D into the address field in the header. Router D places Porthos's Ethernet MAC address into the destination address field.

4 This is all noise if Porthos cannot get a packet back to D'Artagnan. The following routing tables show the routes needed for both directions; the routes with asterisks signify routes required for the routes back to D'Artagnan.

In Router A:

Group	Outgoing Interface	Next Router
group-1*	Ethernet 0	N/A
group-5	serial 1	N/A
group-6	serial 1	group-5.local-D

In Router D:

Group	Outgoing Interface	Next Router
group-1*	serial 0	group-5.local-A
group-5*	serial 0	N/A
group-6	Ethernet 0	N/A

Exam Topics in This Chapter

1 Name and describe two switching methods.

2 Distinguish between cut-through and store-and-forward LAN switching.

13 Describe the advantages of LAN segmentation.

14 Describe LAN segmentation using bridges.

15 Describe LAN segmentation using routers.

16 Describe LAN segmentation using switches.

17 Describe the benefits of network segmentation with bridges.

18 Describe the benefits of network segmentation with routers.

19 Describe the benefits of network segmentation with switches.

38 Describe full- and half-duplex Ethernet operation.

39 Describe network congestion problems in Ethernet networks.

40 Describe the features and benefits of Fast Ethernet.

41 Describe the guidelines and distance limitations of Fast Ethernet.

CHAPTER 4

LANs, Bridges, and Switches

Cisco's LAN switch revenue surpassed router revenues about the time that the CCNA exam was first announced, back in 1998. There is little doubt about the importance of LAN switch revenue to Cisco. However, router concepts and configuration consume a much larger share of the CCNA exam's questions—a seemingly odd fact. So, if switches drive more revenue for Cisco, why is most of the popular Cisco certification about routers and routing issues?

Simply put, LAN switches are simpler than routers. LAN switches operate at OSI Layer 2, and Layer 2 issues are generally less complicated than Layer 3 issues. But before you take exception with me, that in no way means that LAN issues are not complicated! There are simply fewer concepts and issues to consider. Furthermore, because Layer 3–aware devices, such as routers, make extensive use of Layer 2 features to forward packets, the routing-centric topics can never totally ignore LAN and WAN Layer 2 concepts. However, when discussing LAN concepts, Layer 3 issues can be ignored, making the discussion of LANs and LAN switches much briefer and to the point. So, this book includes two LAN-specific chapters in addition to the more lengthy coverage of routing.

This chapter describes the core basic concepts of Ethernet LANs, bridging, and LAN switches. Along the way, Cisco LAN switch configuration also will be covered. Some historical perspectives about Ethernet are important in this chapter because Cisco definitely expects you to understand why installing a switch for ten users is better than using a hub, a router, or a bridge, or simply using a single coax cable, as the older Ethernet specifications called for.

How to Best Use This Chapter

By taking the following steps, you can make better use of your study time:

- Keep your notes and the answers for all your work with this book in one place, for easy reference.
- Take the "Do I Know This Already?" quiz, and write down your answers. Studies show that retention is significantly increased through writing down facts and concepts, even if you never look at the information again.
- Use the diagram in Figure 4-1 to guide you to the next step.

Figure 4-1 *How to Use This Chapter*

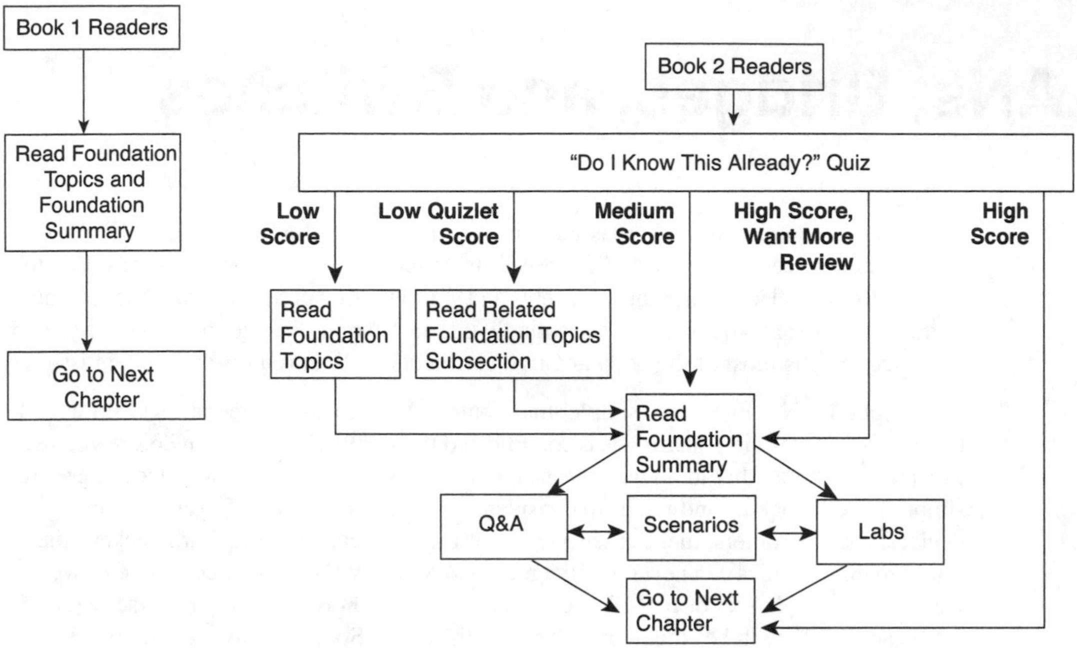

"Do I Know This Already?" Quiz

The purpose of the "Do I Know This Already?" quiz is to help you decide what parts of this chapter to use. If you already intend to read the entire chapter, you do not necessarily need to answer these questions now.

This 12-question quiz helps you determine how to spend your limited study time. The quiz is sectioned into four smaller four-question "quizlets" that correspond to the three major headings in the chapter. Suggestions on how to spend your time in this chapter, based on your quiz scores, are outlined in Figure 4-1. Use Table 4-1 to record your score.

Table 4-1 *Scoresheet for Quiz and Quizlets*

Quizlet Number	Foundation Topics Section Covering These Questions	Questions	Score
1	LAN Overview	1 to 4	
2	Bridging and Switching	5 to 8	
3	LAN Switch Configuration	9 to 12	
All questions		1 to 12	

1 What do the letters *MAC* stand for? What other terms have you heard to describe the same or similar concept?

2 If a Fast Ethernet NIC currently is receiving a frame, can it begin sending a frame?

3 What are the two key differences between a 10-Mbps NIC and a 10/100 NIC?

4 What is the distance limitation of a single cable for 10BaseT? 100BaseTX?

5 What routing protocol does a transparent bridge use to learn about Layer 3 addressing groupings?

6 Name two of the methods of internal switching on typical switches today. Which provides less latency for an individual frame?

7 Describe how a transparent bridge decides whether it should forward a frame, and tell how it chooses the interface out which to forward the frame.

8 Define the term *collision domain*.

9 How many IP addresses must be configured for network management on a Cisco Catalyst 1900 switch if eight ports are to be used with three VLANs?

10 How do exec and configuration commands refer to the two Fast Ethernet ports on a Catalyst 1912 switch?

11 Configuration is added to the running configuration in RAM when commands are typed in Catalyst 1900 configuration mode. What causes these commands to be saved into NVRAM?

12 What command erases the startup config in a Catalyst 1900 switch?

The answers to the quiz are found in Appendix A, 'Answers to the 'Do I Know This Already?' Quizzes and Q&A Sections." The uggested choices for your next step are as follows:

- **8 or less overall score**—Read the entire chapter. This includes the "Foundation Topics" and "Foundation Summary" sections and the Q&A section at the end of the chapter.
- **2 or less on any quizlet**—Review the subsection(s) of the "Foundation Topics" part of this chapter, based on Table 4-1. Then move into the "Foundation Summary" section and the Q&A section at the end of the chapter.
- **9 to 10 overall score**—Begin with the "Foundation Summary" section, and then go to the Q&A section and the scenarios at the end of the chapter.
- **11 or more overall score**—If you want more review on these topics, skip to the "Foundation Summary" section and then go to the Q&A section at the end of the chapter. Otherwise, move to the next chapter.

Foundation Topics

LAN Overview

38 Describe full- and half-duplex Ethernet operation.

39 Describe network-congestion problems in Ethernet networks.

40 Describe the features and benefits of Fast Ethernet.

41 Describe the guidelines and distance limitations of Fast Ethernet.

Network engineers install Ethernet variants more than any other type of LAN today. Not surprisingly, the CCNA exam covers Ethernet. But most everyone would guess that Ethernet is relatively important on the exam—the trick is to make sure that you know what details about Ethernet LANs are on the exam. This chapter and Chapter 5, "Intermediate LANs: Spanning Tree, VLANs, and Trunking" describe those details.

The CCNA exam covers the functions and protocol specifications for the more popular types of Ethernet. 10BaseT, Fast Ethernet, and Gigabit Ethernet are all on the exam. But to appreciate how some of the features of Ethernet work, a historical knowledge of 10Base2 and 10Base5 Ethernet is helpful. Similarly, LAN switching concepts and configuration will definitely be covered on the exam. Developing an understanding of how transparent bridges work gives you a historical perspective that lets you appreciate how LAN switches work and why they work that way. All these topics help your understanding, but expect more questions about Fast Ethernet than 10Base2, and more questions about LAN switching than transparent bridging.

Engineers make important design decisions when implementing LANs, and the CCNA exam attempts to test your knowledge of these decisions by comparing several options. In particular, a comparison of a single LAN segment with multiple segments with a transparent bridge between them and with multiple segments with a hub, or a switch, or a router among them—all these comparisons get at the heart of the reasons behind how you design a LAN today. CCNA does not test your ability to design a LAN site with 30 switches, but it does test your ability to think through all the building-block concepts that you would need to make good choices in building that network.

This chapter details all the basics of Ethernet LANs that are on the CCNA exam. First, a historical view of 10-Mbps Ethernet provides the basis for understanding some of the reasons behind why switches act as they do. LAN addressing and LAN framing define somewhat mundane but important parts of the networking puzzle and are found in the next section. Fast Ethernet and Gigabit Ethernet follow.

The second "Foundation Topics" section details bridging and switching. In this section, comparisons of using a single segment and segmenting into multiple segments using either a hub, a bridge, a switch, or a router are made. Finally, in the third section, configuration details on Cisco IOS-based switches is covered.

By the end of the "Foundation Topics" section of this chapter, you should be able to describe everything that happens in a typical LAN today that uses a single switch. In the next chapter, the details of what happens in a network with multiple switches are described fully.

10-Mbps Ethernet

Ethernet is best understood by first considering the early *10Base5* and *10Base2* specifications. These two Ethernet specifications defined the details of the physical layer of early Ethernet networks. With these two specifications, the engineer installs a series of coaxial cables to each device on the Ethernet network—there is no hub, switch, or wiring panel. The series of cables creates an electrical bus that is shared among all devices on the Ethernet. Because it is a single bus, only one electrical signal can flow at a single time. If two or more signals were sent, the two would overlap, making both signals unintelligible.

Not surprisingly, Ethernet also defined a specification for how to ensure that only one device sends traffic on the Ethernet at one time—otherwise, the Ethernet would have been unusable. The algorithm, known as the carrier sense multiple access collision detect (CSMA/CD) algorithm, defines how the bus is accessed. In human terms, CSMA/CD is similar to what happens in a meeting room with many attendees. Some people talk much of the time. Some do not talk, but they listen. Others talk occasionally. Being humans, it's hard to understand what two people are saying at the same time, so generally, one person is talking and the rest are listening. Imagine that Bob and Larry both want to reply to the current speaker's comments. As soon as the speaker takes a breath, Bob and Larry might both try to speak. If Larry hears Bob's voice before Larry actually makes a noise, Larry might stop and let Bob speak. Or, maybe they both start at almost the same time, so they talk over each other, and many others in the room can't hear what was said. Then there's the proverbial "Excuse me, you talk next . . . " and eventually Larry or Bob talks. Or, in some cases, another person jumps in and talks while Larry and Bob are both backing off. These "rules" are based on your culture; CSMA/CD is based on Ethernet protocol specifications and achieves the same type of goal.

Figure 4-2 shows the basic logic of an old Ethernet 10Base2 network, which literally uses a single electrical bus, created with coaxial cable.

The CSMA/CD algorithm works like this:

1. A device with a frame to send listens until the Ethernet is not busy.
2. When the Ethernet is not busy, the sender begins sending the frame.
3. The sender listens to make sure that no collision occurred.
4. If there was a collision, the sender randomizes a timer and waits that long.
5. When the timer expires, the process starts over with Step 1.

Figure 4-2 *Small Ethernet 10Base2 Network*

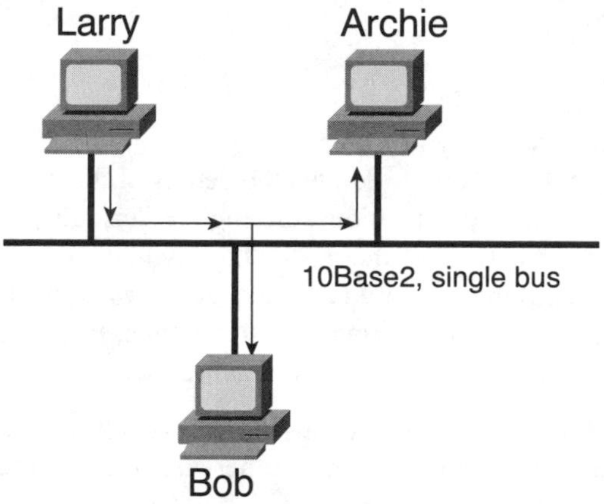

10Base2 and 10Base5 Ethernet would not work without some method to arbitrate use of the bus. However, because of the CSMA/CD algorithm, Ethernet becomes more inefficient under higher loads. In fact, two particular negative features of the CSMA/CD algorithm are as follows:

- All collided frames become corrupted, so each sending station must resend the frames. This wastes time on the bus and increases the latency for delivering the collided frames.
- Latency increases for stations waiting for the Ethernet to be silent before sending their frames. Because there are more frames per second, each sender has a longer wait time before sending. This increases latency while waiting for the incoming frame to complete.

10BaseT solved several problems with the early Ethernet specifications. 10BaseT allowed the use of telephone cabling that was already installed, or simply allowed the use of cheaper, easier-to-install cabling when new cabling was required. The use of 10BaseT *hubs* gave Ethernet much higher availability because a single cable problem does not affect the other users. These hubs are essentially multiport repeaters; they extend the bus concept of 10Base2 and 10Base5 by regenerating the same electrical signal sent by the original sender of a frame out every other port. Therefore, collisions can still occur, so CSMA/CD access rules continue to be used. Figure 4-3 shows the same network as Figure 4-2, after migration to using hubs and twisted-pair cabling instead of co-ax cabling.

Figure 4-3 *Small Ethernet 10BaseT Network*

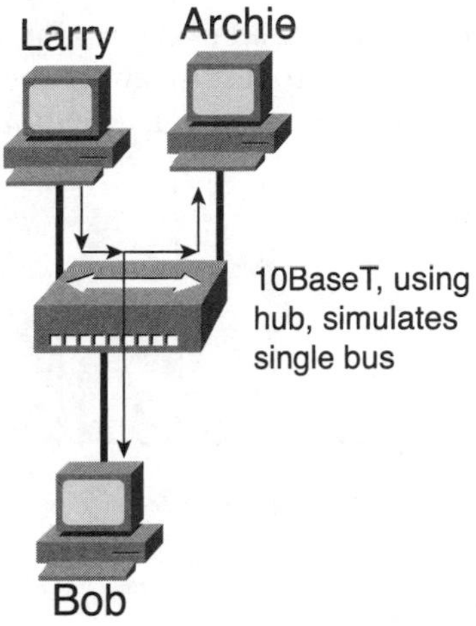

The concept of cabling each device to a central hub, with that hub creating the same electrical bus as in the older types of Ethernet, was a core fact of 10BaseT Ethernet. Because hubs continued the concept and physical reality of a single electrical path that is shared by all devices, today we call this *shared Ethernet*: All devices are sharing a single 10-Mbps bus.

So, hubs solved some cabling and availability problems. However, the degrading performance of CSMA/CD when the Ethernet utilization increased was still not addressed. The next step was to make the hub smart enough to ensure that collisions simply did not happen—which means that CSMA/CD would no longer be needed. First, you need a deeper knowledge of 10BaseT hubs before the solution to the congestion problem becomes obvious. Figure 4-4 outlines the operation of half-duplex 10BaseT with hubs.

Figure 4-4 outlines how a 10BaseT hub behaves to create an electrical bus. The chronological steps illustrated in Figure 4-4 are as follows:

1. The network interface card (NIC) sends a frame.
2. The NIC loops the sent frame onto its receive pair.
3. The hub receives the frame.
4. The hub sends the frame across an internal bus so that all other NICs can receive the electrical signal. It does not forward the electrical signal back out to the device that sent the original signal.
5. The hub repeats the signal to each receive pair to all other devices. In other words, the hub sends so that the attached stations receive on their receive pair. (Similarly, the hub listens on the transmit pair because that is the pair used by each station for transmissions.)

The figure details how the hub works, with one device sending and no collision. If PC1 and PC2 sent a frame at the same time, a collision would occur. At Step 4, the hub would forward both electrical signals, which would cause the overlapping signals to be sent to all the NICs. CSMA/CD logic is still needed to have PC1 and PC2 wait and try again.

The term *collision domain* defines the set of devices for which their frames could collide. All devices on a 10Base2, 10Base5, or 10BaseT network using a hub risk collisions between the frames that they send, so all devices on one of these types of Ethernet networks are in the same collision domain.

Figure 4-4 *10BaseT Half-Duplex Operation*

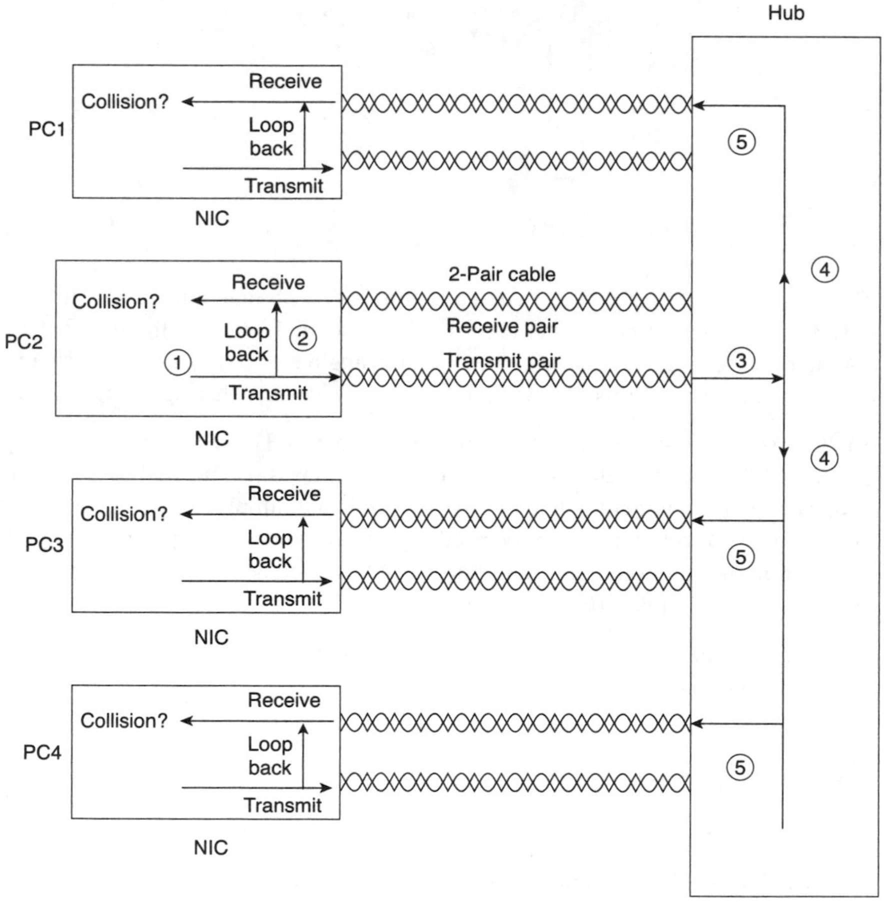

NOTE PC2 would sense a collision because of its loopback circuitry on the NIC. The hub does not forward the signal that PC2 sent back to PC2—if the hub did that, PC2 would think that there was a collision on every frame. So, each NIC loops the frame that it sends back to its own receive pair on the NIC, as shown in Step 2 of the figure. The signal sent by PC1 is sent to PC2 on PC2's receive pair, so the incoming signal from the hub, plus the looped signal on PC2's NIC, let it notice that there is a collision. Who cares? Well, to appreciate full-duplex LAN operation, you need to know about the NIC's loopback feature.

The original Ethernet specifications implied half-duplex behavior. Just like having a single speaker in a meeting room, there is a single sender on an Ethernet (so far). Essentially, if the topology allows collisions, CSMA/CD is used to react to the collisions. With a shared 10BaseT hub—or with 10Base2 or 10Base5, for that matter—if a station is receiving a frame, it would not choose to also start sending another frame because sending a frame would cause a collision.

LAN switches overcome the problems created by collisions and the CSMA/CD algorithm. Switches do not create a single shared bus, but rather they treat each individual physical port as a separate bus. Switches use memory buffers to hold incoming frames as well. So, as seen in Figure 4-5, collisions can be avoided.

Figure 4-5 *Basic Switch Operation*

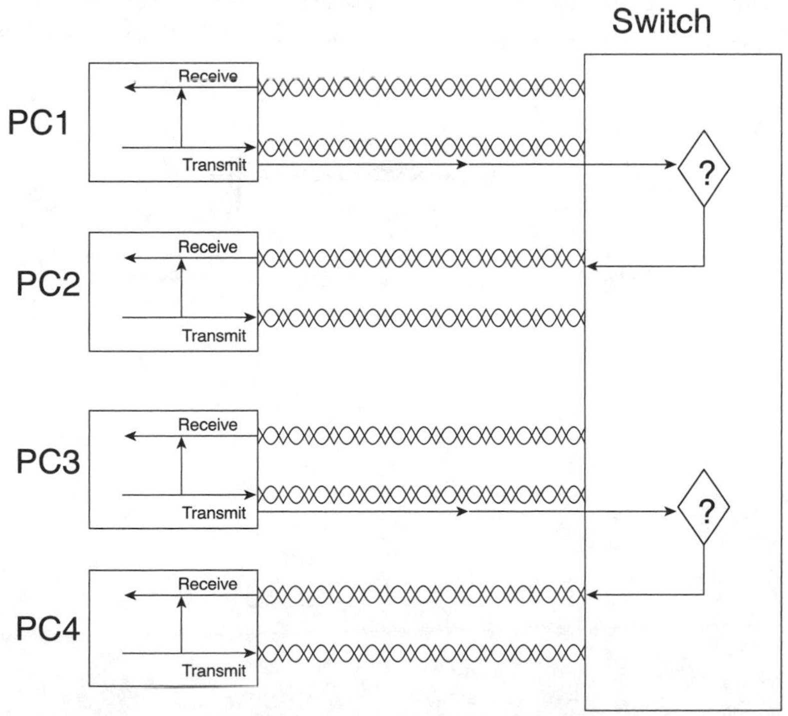

In Figure 4-5, both PC1 and PC3 are sending at the same time. The switch looks at the destination Ethernet address, and sends only the frame from PC1 to PC2 and the frame sent by PC3 to PC4. The big difference between the hub and the switch is that the switch interpreted the electrical signal as an Ethernet frame and processed the frame to make a decision. (The details of Ethernet addressing and framing are coming up in the next two sections.) A hub simply repeats the electrical signal and makes no attempt to interpret the electrical signal (Layer 1) as a LAN frame (Layer 2).

Buffering also helps prevent collisions. Imagine that PC1 had sent a broadcast, which needs to be sent out all ports in Figure 4-3. PC3 is sending another frame to PC4. The switch, knowing that forwarding both frames to PC4 would cause a collision, buffers one frame until the first one has been completely sent to PC4.

So, back to the historical picture. 10BaseT switches added forwarding logic based on the address of the frame, which avoids collisions. Switches also added buffering so that additional collisions were avoided. In short:

> If only one device is cabled to each port of a switch, no collisions occur.

The final concept in this section requires the assumption that no collision can occur. If no collision can occur, CSMA/CD is not needed—at least, not the collision detection and recovery part. If CSMA/CD is not needed, the implied half-duplex operation no longer is needed. In short, LAN switches with only one device cabled to the switch allow the use of *full-duplex* operation.

Full-duplex means that an Ethernet card can send and receive concurrently. Consider Figure 4-6, which shows the full-duplex circuitry used with a single PC cabled to a LAN switch.

Figure 4-6 *10BaseT Full-Duplex Operation*

Because no collisions are possible, the NIC disabled its loopback circuitry. Both ends can send and receive simultaneously. This reduces Ethernet congestion and provides the following advantages, as compared to half-duplex 10BaseT operation:

- Collisions do not occur; therefore, time is not wasted retransmitting frames.
- There is no latency waiting for others to send their frames.
- There are 10 Mbps in each direction, doubling the available capacity (bandwidth).

So far in this chapter, you have seen 12 years of Ethernet evolution. Table 4-2 summarizes some of the key points as they relate to what is covered in this initial section of the chapter. More of the specification details are listed later in this chapter.

Table 4-2 *Summary of Some Basic Ethernet Features*

10Base2, 10Base5	Single bus cabled serially between devices using coaxial cable.
10BaseT with a Hub	One electrical bus shared among all devices creating a single collision domain, cabled in a star topology using twisted-pair cabling.
10BaseT with a Switch	One electrical bus per switch port creating multiple collision domains, cabled in a star topology using twisted-pair cabling.
Half Duplex	Logic that requires a card to only send or receive at a single point in time. Used to avoid collisions.
Full Duplex	Logic that enables concurrent sending and receiving, allowed when one device is attached to a switch port, ensuring that no collisions can occur.

LAN Addressing

LAN addressing identifies either individual devices or groups of devices on a LAN. On the CCNA exam, you are expected to confidently understand and interpret LAN addresses.

Unicast addresses identify a single LAN card. Frames between a pair of LAN stations use a source and destination address field to identify each other. These addresses are called unicast addresses, or *individual addresses*, because they identify an individual LAN interface card. (The term *unicast* was chosen mainly for contrast with the terms *broadcast*, *multicast*, and *group addresses*.) It's a fancy term but a simple concept.

The IEEE defines the format and assignment of LAN addresses. The IEEE requires globally unique unicast Media Access Control (MAC, another term for LAN address) addresses on all LAN interface cards. The manufacturers encode the MAC address onto the LAN card, usually in a ROM chip. The first half of the address identifies the manufacturer of the card. This code, which is assigned to each manufacturer by the IEEE, is called the *organizationally unique identifier (OUI)*. The manufacturer assigns a MAC address with its own OUI as the first half of the address, with the second half of the address being assigned a number that this manufacturer has never used on another card. These addresses are called *burned-in addresses (BIAs)* because they are burned into ROM chips. They also are sometimes called *universally administered addresses (UAA)* because the IEEE universally (well, at least worldwide) administers address assignment.

Group addresses identify more than one LAN interface card. The IEEE defines three general categories of group addresses:

- **Broadcast addresses**—The most often used of IEEE group MAC address, the broadcast address, has a value of FFFF.FFFF.FFFF (hexadecimal notation). The broadcast address implies that all devices on the LAN should process the frame.
- **Multicast addresses**—Used by Ethernet and FDDI, multicast addresses fulfill the requirement to address a subset of all the devices on a LAN. Multicast addresses are not burned into the card, but they are added by the software on the NIC in the direction of the software in the computer. If the software on the computer wants to listen for frames sent to a particular multicast address, the software configures the NIC to listen for that address. An example of multicast addresses is a range of addresses—0100.5exx.xxxx—with different values assigned in the last 3 bytes; these MAC addresses are used in conjunction with the Internet Group Multicast Protocol (IGMP) and IP multicast. IP hosts on an Ethernet that want to receive IP packets to a particular IP multicast address all use the same Ethernet MAC address, which begins with 0100.5E.
- **Functional addresses**—Valid only on Token Ring, functional addresses identify one or more interfaces that provide a particular function. For example, c000.0000.0001 is used by the device on a Token Ring that is currently implementing the Active Monitor function.

The following list summarizes many of the key features of MAC addresses:

- Unicast MAC addresses address an individual LAN interface card.
- Broadcast MAC addresses address all devices on a LAN.
- Multicast MAC addresses address a subset of the devices on an Ethernet or FDDI LAN.
- Functional MAC addresses identify devices performing a specific IEEE-defined function on Token Ring only.

LAN Framing

Framing defines how a string of binary numbers is interpreted. For example, Ethernet defines how the first several bytes of a received electrical signal are interpreted after that signal is received and converted into a binary string. Figure 4-7 shows the details of several type LAN frames.

Figure 4-7 *LAN Header Formats*

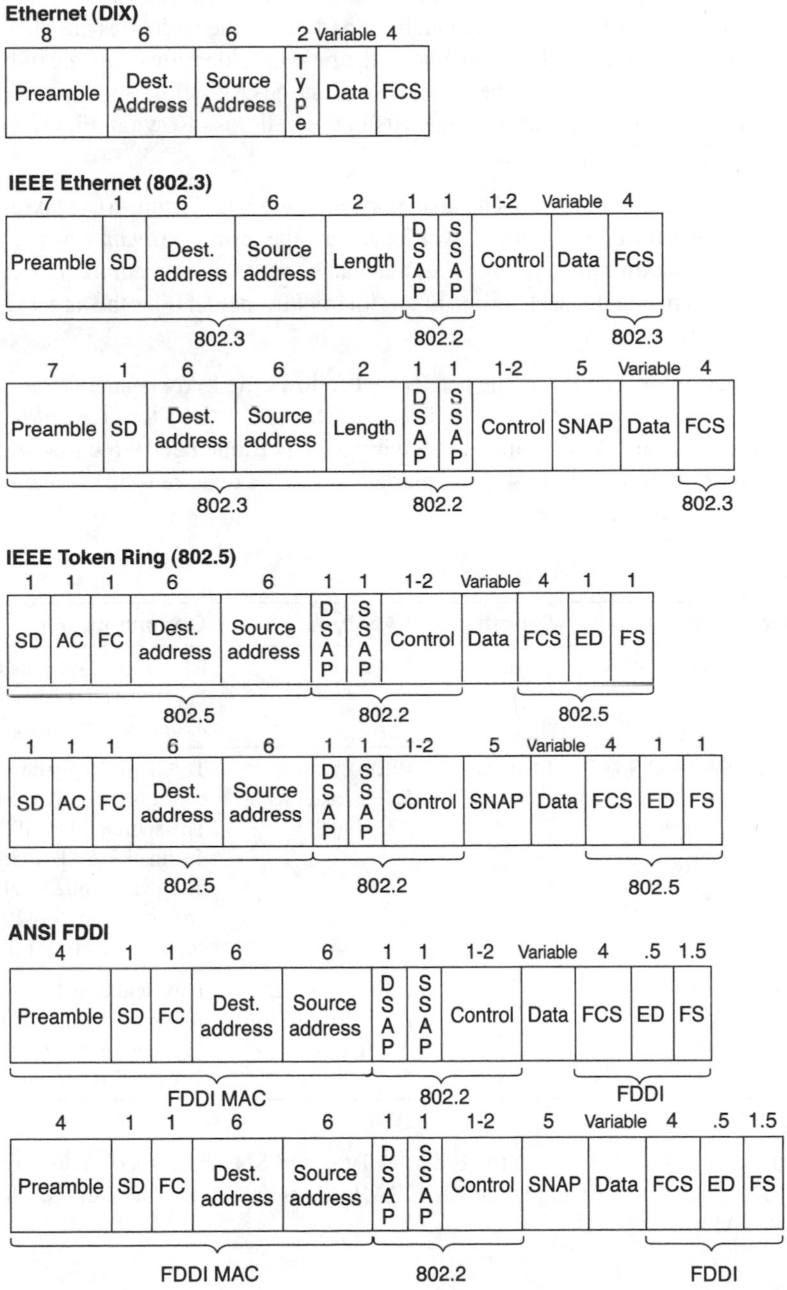

Don't be alarmed—it is unlikely that you would get CCNA exam questions asking about all these LAN framing fields! You should remember some details about the contents of the headers and trailers for each LAN type, though. In particular, the addresses and their location in the headers are important. Also, the name of the field that identifies the type of header that follows the LAN headers—namely, the Type, DSAP, and SNAP fields—is important. Finally, the fact that a frame check sequence (FCS) exists in the trailer is also vital. Figure 4-7 summarizes the various header formats.

The 802.3 specification limits the data portion of the 802.3 frame to a maximum of 1500 bytes. The data was designed to hold Layer 3 packets; the term *maximum transmission unit (MTU)* defines the maximum Layer 3 packet that can be sent over a medium. Because the Layer 3 packet rests inside the data portion of an Ethernet frame, 1,500 is the largest MTU allowed over an Ethernet.

The function of identifying the header that follows the LAN header (what's in the data in Figure 4-7) is covered rather extensively in Chapter 3, "OSI Reference Model and Layered Communication." Any computer receiving a LAN frame needs to know what is in the data portion of the frame. Table 4-3 summarizes the fields that are used for identifying the types of data contained in a frame.

Table 4-3 *Protocol Type Fields in LAN Headers*

Field Name	Length	LAN Type	Comments
Ethernet Type	2 bytes	Ethernet	RFC 1700 ("Assigned Numbers" RFC) lists the values. Xerox owns the assignment process.
802.2 DSAP and SSAP	1 byte each	IEEE Ethernet, IEEE Token Ring, ANSI FDDI	The IEEE Registration Authority controls the assignment of valid values. The source SAP (SSAP) and destination SAP (DSAP) do not have to be equal, so 802.2 calls for the sender's protocol type (SSAP) and the destination's type (DSAP).
SNAP Protocol	2 bytes	IEEE Ethernet, IEEE Token Ring, ANSI FDDI	This field uses Ethernet Type values and is used only when DSAP is hex AA. It is needed because the DSAP and SSAP fields are only 1 byte in length.

Some examples of values in the Ethernet Type and SNAP Protocol fields are 0800 for IP and 8137 for NetWare. Examples of IEEE SAP values are E0 for NetWare, 04 for SNA, and AA for SNAP.

Fast Ethernet and Gigabit Ethernet

Fast Ethernet and Gigabit Ethernet provide faster Ethernet options. Both have gained widespread acceptance in networks today, with Fast Ethernet most likely being used to the desktop and Gigabit Ethernet being used between networking devices or to servers.

Fast Ethernet retains many familiar features of 10-Mbps Ethernet variants. The age-old CSMA/CD logic still exists, but it can be disabled for full-duplex point-to-point topologies in which no collisions can occur. A variety of cabling options is allowed—unshielded and shielded copper cabling as well as multimode and single-mode fiber. Both Fast Ethernet shared hubs and switches can be deployed. However, because Fast Ethernet gained market acceptance around the same time that LAN switching became popular, most Fast Ethernet cards either are connected to a switch or are directly cabled to another device.

The two key additional features of Fast Ethernet, as compared to 10-Mbps Ethernet, are higher bandwidth and autonegotiation.

Fast Ethernet operates at 100 Mbps—enough said. The other key difference, autonegotiation, allows an Ethernet card or switch to operate at 10 or 100 Mbps. Also, support for half-duplex or full-duplex operation is negotiated. If the other device, such as a 10BaseT NIC, does not support autonegotiation, autonegotiation settles for half-duplex operation at 10 Mbps.

The autonegotiation process has been known to fail. Cisco recommends that, for devices that seldom move, you should configure the LAN switch and the device to use the identical desired setting rather than depend on autonegotiation. Generally, for ports that are used for end-user devices, autonegotiation is enabled because these devices are moved frequently relative to servers or other network devices, such as routers.

Gigabit Ethernet also retains many familiar features of slower Ethernet variants. CSMA/CD is still used and can be disabled for full-duplex support. Although gigabit hubs are allowed, it is more likely that Gigabit Ethernet switch ports will be the most popular use for Gigabit Ethernet, along with use as a trunk between high-throughput switches and routers.

Gigabit Ethernet is similar to its slower cousins in several ways. The most important similarity is that the same Ethernet headers and trailers are used, no matter whether it's 10 Mbps, 100 Mbps, or 1000 Mbps. If you understand how Ethernet works for 10 and 100 Mbps, then you know most of what you need to know about Gigabit Ethernet.

Gigabit Ethernet differs from the slow specifications in how it encodes the signals onto the cable. Gigabit Ethernet is obviously faster, at 1000 Mbps, or 1 Gbps. The physical layer differences are truly beyond the scope of the CCNA exam.

Both Fast Ethernet (FE) and Gigabit Ethernet (GE) relieve congestion in some fairly obvious ways. Collisions and wait time are decreased when compared to 10-Mbps Ethernet simply because it takes 90 percent (FE) or 99 percent (GE) less time to transmit the same frame on the faster LANs. Capacity is greatly increased as well: If all frames were 1250 bytes long, a theoretical maximum of 10,000 frames per second could be reached on Fast Ethernet, and a theoretical maximum of 100,000 frames per second could be reached on Gigabit Ethernet. (Of course, this little math problem ignores such details as interframe gaps and the unlikely case of identical length frames; it's just an example to give you perspective.)

LAN Standards

The IEEE defines most of the standards for Ethernet and Token Ring, with ANSI defining standards for FDDI. These specifications match OSI Layer 2 and typically are divided into two parts: the Media Access Control (MAC) and Logical Link Control (LLC) sublayers. The MAC sublayer is very specific to that particular type of LAN, whereas the LLC sublayer performs functions that are relevant to several types of LANs. For instance, all LANs need some form of protocol type field; the LLC specification, rather than the MAC, defines the use of the DSAP field for that purpose. Table 4-4 lists the various protocol specifications.

Table 4-4 *MAC and LLC Details for Three Types of LANs*

Name	MAC Sublayer Spec	LLC Sublayer Spec	Other Comments
Ethernet Version 2 (DIX Ethernet)	Ethernet	N/A	This spec is owned by Digital, Intel, and Xerox.
IEEE Ethernet	IEEE 802.3	IEEE 802.2	This is also popularly called 802.3 Ethernet. It is built upon details of DIX Ethernet.
IEEE Token Ring	IEEE 802.5	IEEE 802.2	IBM helped with development before the IEEE took over.
ANSI FDDI	ANSI X3T9.5	IEEE 802.2	ANSI liked 802.2, so it just refers to the IEEE spec.

Start Extra Credit

With the advent of Fast Ethernet and Gigabit Ethernet, the variety of Ethernet standards has increased to the point that most networking personnel do not memorize all the standards. The CCNA exam probably will not require you to be that familiar with Ethernet standards—or, at least, not the full list. Table 4-5 lists the key Ethernet specifications and several related details about the operation of each.

Table 4-5 *Ethernet Standards*

Standard	MAC Sublayer Specification	Maximum Cable Length	Cable Type	Pairs Required
10Base5	802.3	500 m[1]	50-ohm thick coaxial cable	
10Base2	802.3	185 m[1]	50-ohm thin coaxial cable	
10BaseT	802.3	100 m[1]	Category 3, 4, or 5 UTP	2
10BaseFL	802.3	2000 m[2]	Fiber	1
100BaseTx	802.3u	100 m[2]	Category 5 UTP	2
100BaseT4	802.3u	100 m[2]	Category 3 UTP	4
100BaseT2	802.3u	100 m[2]	Category 3, 4, or 5 UTP	2
100BaseFx	802.3u	400/2,000 m[3]	Multimode fiber	1
100BaseFx	802.3u	10,000 m	Single-mode fiber	1
1000BaseSx	802.3z	220-550 m	Multimode fiber	1
1000BaseLx	802.3z	3000 m	Single-mode or multimode fiber	1
1000BaseCx	802.3z	25 m	Shielded copper	2
1000BaseT	802.3ab	100 m	Category 5 UTP	2

[1]For entire bus, without using a repeater
[2]From device to hub/switch
[3]Numbers shown are for half- or full-duplex operation

For more information on Fast Ethernet and information on Gigabit Ethernet, try the following Web pages:

- www.host.ots.utexas.edu/ethernet/ethernet-home.html
- www.ots.utexas.edu/ethernet/descript-100quickref.html
- www.iol.unh.edu/training
- www.cisco.com/warp/customer/cc/so/neso/lnso/lnmnso/feth_tc.htm
- www.cisco.com/warp/customer/cc/techno/media/lan/gig/tech/index.shtml
- www.10gea.org

NOTE A Cisco.com login is required for the preceding Cisco URLs.

End Extra Credit

Bridging and Switching

1 Name and describe two switching methods.

2 Distinguish between cut-through and store-and-forward LAN switching.

13 Describe the advantages of LAN segmentation.

14 Describe LAN segmentation using bridges.

15 Describe LAN segmentation using routers.

16 Describe LAN segmentation using switches.

17 Describe the benefits of network segmentation with bridges.

18 Describe the benefits of network segmentation with routers.

19 Describe the benefits of network segmentation with switches.

So far in this chapter, you have learned the fundamental components of Ethernet. The varied Ethernet specifications define different characteristics, but more similarities exist among the various types of Ethernet. You have seen that the early Ethernet specifications used a single shared bus, whether it was truly a long Ethernet cable or a bus created inside a shared-media Ethernet hub. You have seen that a switch creates multiple buses, which reduces or eliminates collisions and greatly improves performance. In spite of these differences, the various Ethernet specifications use the same framing and MAC addresses, which makes your job as a network engineer much easier when you migrate to a different physical specification for Ethernet.

Like the first major section of this chapter, a historical perspective gives you a chance to see why Ethernet has evolved to where it is today. You would not likely deploy a device called a transparent bridge today, and there is only a small chance that you might enable transparent bridging features in a Cisco router. So why bother to talk about bridging? Well, to understand bridging is to understand LAN switching. And you might infer that bridging concepts might well be on a test soon as well.

An old adage best describes LAN switching: Switches are bridges on steroids. The underlying logic between the two is similar, so both are described in this section. Also, a comparison of what happens when a single Ethernet is migrated to a pair of Ethernets—separated by a bridge in one case, a switch in another case, and a router in the third case—serves as a good review of the concepts behind all three types of campus forwarding devices. The trade-offs when using bridges, switches, and routers are important for two reasons. First, the concepts are still at the core of your decisions when designing a campus LAN today; second, the comparisons are a great tool for Cisco to test your knowledge about how the various devices work.

Transparent Bridging

Transparent bridges connect two or more LAN segments. The term *segment* defines a LAN in terms of older Ethernet terminology. For example, a 10Base2 network was a series of coaxial cables with taps for each device, so the whole series of cables was one segment. As a LAN segment grew, eventually it became too crowded with collisions or exceeded cabling length restrictions. So, the one segment was separated into two segments, and a bridge was placed between the two segments. As you will soon see, this separated the world into two collision domains, meaning that frames sent by devices on one side of the bridge could not collide with frames sent by devices on the other side of the bridge. Because the bridge does not forward all traffic, traffic to each node was reduced. In short, transparent bridges were created to alleviate congestion problems on a single Ethernet segment and to extend allowed cabling distances because the segments on each side of the bridge conformed to the same distance limitation as a single segment.

Transparent bridging is called "transparent" because the endpoint devices do not need to know that the bridge(s) exist(s). In other words, the computers attached to the LAN do not behave any differently in the presence or absence of transparent bridges.

Transparent bridges forward frames when necessary and do not forward when there is no need to do so, thus reducing overhead. To accomplish this, transparent bridges perform three actions:

- Learning MAC addresses by examining the source MAC address of each frame received by the bridge
- Deciding when to forward a frame or when to filter (not forward) a frame, based on the destination MAC address
- Creating a loop-free environment with other bridges by using the Spanning Tree Protocol

To fully understand transparent bridging logic, consider Figure 4-8. A client first asks for DNS name resolution and then connects to a Web server. All three devices are on the same LAN segment. The LAN segment is drawn as if it is a 10Base2 or 10Base5 network, but it could be 10BaseT using a shared hub. Regardless, focus on the Ethernet addresses and the bridges actions in the figure.

Figure 4-8 *Example Protocol Flows—Single Ethernet Segment*

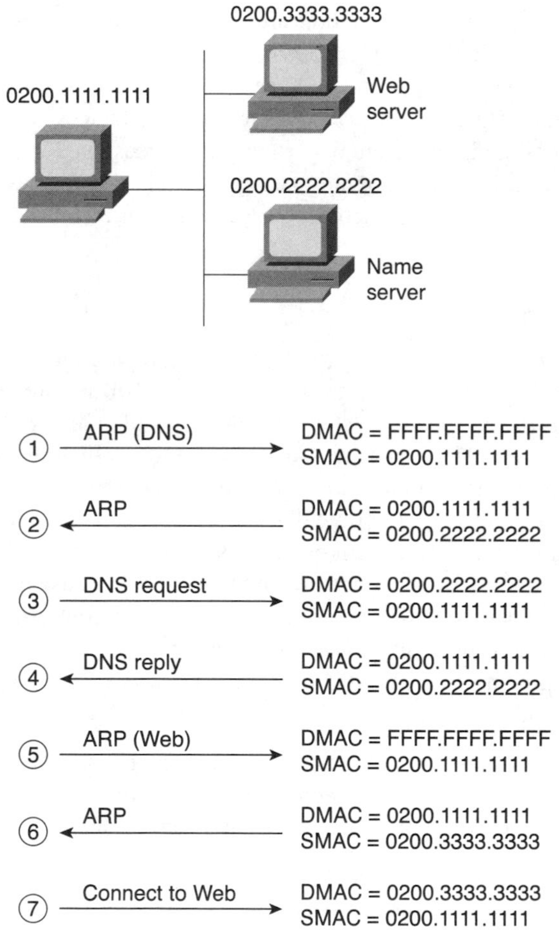

In this example, the devices send messages just like they would if the user, the Web server, and the DNS were on the same segment. The destination and source MAC addresses are listed in the figure. The following list provides some additional text relating the steps shown in Figure 4-8:

1 The PC is preconfigured with the IP address of the DNS; it must use ARP to find the DNS's MAC address.

2 The DNS replies to the ARP request with its MAC address, 0200.2222.2222.

3 The PC requests name resolution by the DNS for the Web server's name.

4 The DNS returns the IP address of the Web server to the PC.

5 The PC does not know the Web server's MAC address, but it does know its IP address, so the PC sends an ARP broadcast to learn the MAC address of the Web server.

6 The Web server replies to the ARP, stating that its MAC address is 0200.3333.3333.

7 The PC now can send frames directly to the Web server.

One somewhat obvious point must be made: All frames are received by all devices. In this case, the single LAN segment is a bus, or a 10BaseT hub, which creates a single bus. Ethernet is considered a *broadcast medium* because when one device sends, all the rest receive the electrical signal. Each device then must decide whether to process the frame.

Why bother to point out that everyone gets each frame? Well, a transparent bridge would not always forward a copy of each frame on each segment. Now consider the same protocol flow, but with the DNS on a separate segment and a transparent bridge separating the segments, as shown in Figure 4-9. The computers act no differently, sending the same frames and packets. (Remember, "transparent" bridges are transparent to the end user devices.) The transparent bridge forwards all broadcasts, all unicast destination frames not in its bridge table, and multicasts.

Figure 4-9 *Example Protocol Flows—Using a Transparent Bridge*

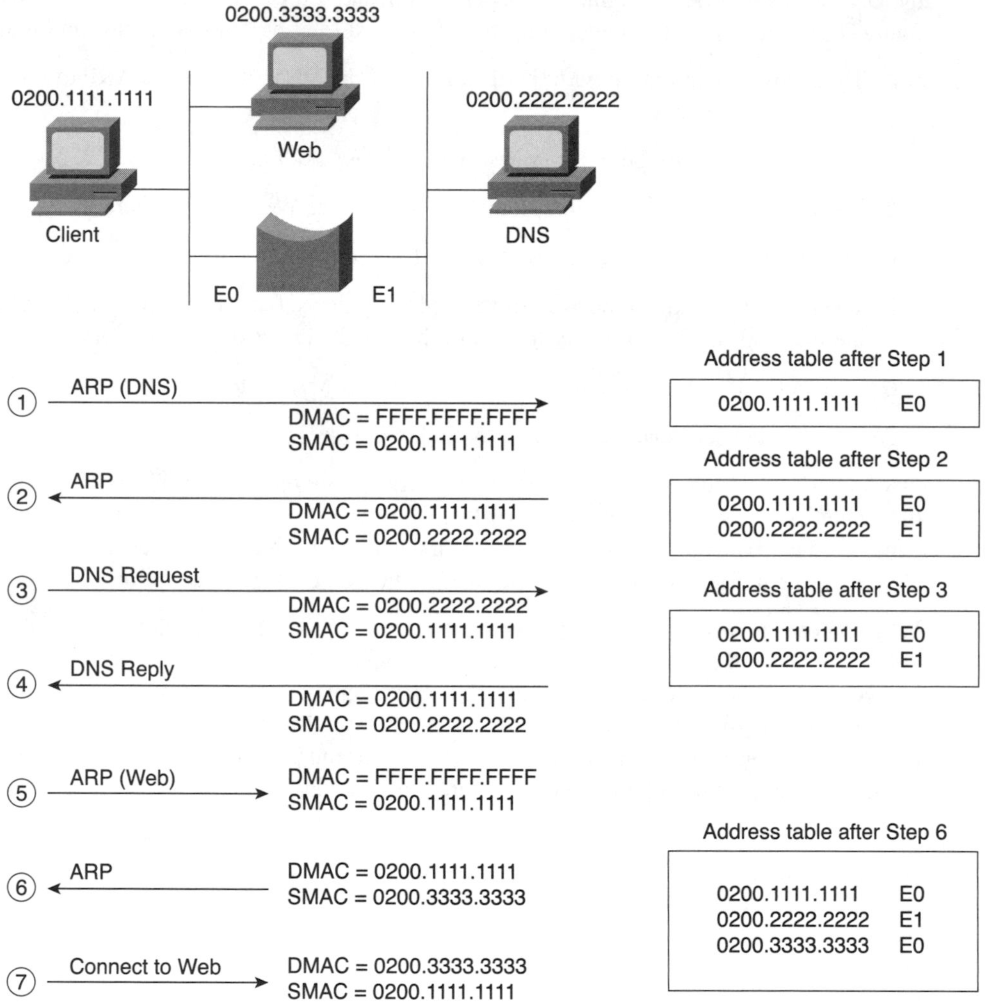

Figure 4-9 illustrates several important ideas related to segmentation. To see the real end goal of the bridge, consider Step 7 and the state of the address table after Step 6. Because the bridge knows the unicast MAC addresses of all three devices, when the client sends the frame to the Web server (Step 7), the bridge simply asks itself, "Should I forward this frame?" Because the frame came in the bridge's E0 port and the Web server (0200.3333.3333) is also out its E0 port, there is no need to forward the frame.

The following list outlines the logic used at each step in the process of Figure 4-9:

1. The first frame is a broadcast, so the bridge forwards the frame. The source MAC address, 0200.1111.1111, is added to the address table.

2. The ARP reply is a unicast destined to 0200.1111.1111, so the bridge knows to forward it out its E0 port, according to the address table. The source MAC of the frame, 0200.2222.2222, is added to the address table.

3. The DNS request is a unicast frame, and the bridge knows where the destination, 0200.2222.222, is. The bridge forwards the frame. The bridge checks the source address (0200.1111.1111) and notices that it is already in the table.

4. The DNS reply is a unicast, with a known destination (0200.1111.1111) and a known source (0200.2222.2222). The bridge forwards the frame.

5. The ARP broadcast is destined to MAC address FFFF.FFFF.FFFF, so it is forwarded by the bridge, in spite of the fact that the ARP broadcast will reach the Web server without the bridge forwarding the frame.

6. The ARP reply from the Web server is a unicast to 0200.1111.1111, and the bridge has that MAC in its address table. The bridge does not forward the frame because it came in its E0 interface and it is destined out that same interface. The source MAC address, 0200.3333.3333, is added to the address table.

7. The last frame is a unicast whose destination MAC (0200.3333.3333) is in the address table, and the bridge should not forward it.

   Networks using bridges have the following general characteristics:

- Broadcasts and multicast frames are forwarded by a bridge.

- Transparent bridges perform switching of frames using Layer 2 headers and Layer 2 logic and are Layer 3 protocol-independent. This means that installation is simple because no Layer 3 address group planning or address changes are necessary. For example, because the bridge retains a single broadcast domain, all devices on all segments attached to the bridge can look like a single subnet.

- Store-and-forward operation is typical in transparent bridging devices. Because an entire frame is received before being forwarded, additional latency is introduced (as compared to a single LAN segment).

- The transparent bridge must perform processing on the frame, which also can increase latency (as compared to a single LAN segment).

LAN Switching

An Ethernet switch uses the same logic as a transparent bridge. However, switches perform more functions, have more features, and have more physical ports. Switches use hardware to learn addresses and to make forwarding and filtering decisions. Bridges use software running on general-purpose processors, so they tend to run much more slowly than switches. The reason behind this difference is simply the time frame in which each technology was developed: Switches came later and took advantage of newer hardware capabilities, such as application-specific integrated circuits (ASICs). But if you look at the basic forward/filter logic, just as with a transparent bridge, the basic logic of a LAN switch is as follows:

1. A frame is received.
2. If the destination is a broadcast or multicast, forward on all ports.
3. If the destination is a unicast and the address is not in the address table, forward on all ports.
4. If the destination is a unicast and the address is in the address table, and if the associated interface is not the interface in which the frame arrived, forward the frame.

Consider Figure 4-10, which separates LANs with a switch.

Figure 4-10 *Example Protocol Flows—Using a Switch*

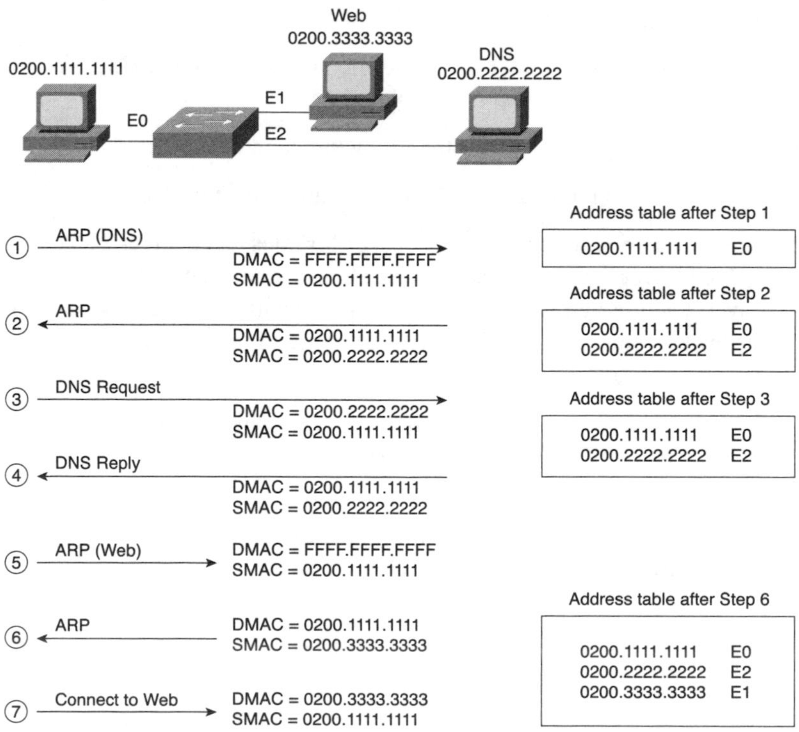

It appears that exactly the same thing happened in Figure 4-10 with a switch as it did in Figure 4-9 using a bridge. The basic logic is similar, but there are some differences. The key physical difference is that each device is attached to a separate port on the switch, whereas, in Figure 4-9, the client and the Web server share the same port on the bridge.

The following list provides some additional insights relating to the steps shown in Figure 4-10, including where this figure describes a slightly different action than in Figure 4-9:

1. The PC is preconfigured with the IP address of the DNS. The PC notices that the DNS IP address is in the same subnet as its own IP address; therefore, the PC sends an ARP broadcast hoping to learn the DNS's MAC address. *This frame is forwarded out all other ports by the switch,* just like the transparent bridge did in Figure 4-9.
2. The DNS replies to the ARP request with its MAC address, 0200.2222.2222. The destination MAC is 0200.1111.1111, which is already in the address table, *so the switch forwards this frame only out port E0.*
3. The PC requests name resolution for the Web server by sending a packet with the destination IP address of the DNS. The destination MAC is 0200.2222.2222, which is already in the address table, *so the switch forwards this frame only out port E2.*
4. The DNS returns the IP address of the Web server to the PC in the DNS reply. The destination MAC is 0200.1111.1111, which is already in the address table, *so the switch forwards this frame only out port E0.*
5. The PC does not know the Web server's MAC address, so it sends an ARP broadcast to learn the MAC address. Because it is a MAC broadcast, *the switch forwards the frame on all ports.*
6. The Web server replies to the ARP, stating that its MAC address is 0200.3333.3333. This frame has a destination MAC of 0200.1111.1111, which is already in the address table, *so the switch forwards this frame only out port E0.*
7. The PC now can connect to the Web server. This frame has a destination MAC of 0200.3333.3333, which is already in the address table, *so the switch forwards this frame only out port E1.*

The switch behaves exactly like a transparent bridge would if the bridge used three ports instead of two. The switch learned the MAC addresses by examining the source MAC addresses and made forwarding decisions based on the contents of the address table.

The switch reduces the possibility of collisions. For example, imagine a fourth device, on port E3. If that new device sent a frame to the DNS's address of 0200.2222.2222 at the same time that the client sent a frame to the Web server (0200.3333.3333), the switch's basic logic would prevent a collision. For different reasons, the switch prevents a broadcast sent by this new device from colliding with the frame that the client sent to the server. The switch buffers one of the frames until the first frame has been sent and then forwards the second frame.

Collisions can occur on segments attached to switches. Consider Figure 4-11, which shows the same switch but with a shared hub connected to E0.

Figure 4-11 *Switch Connected to a Hub*

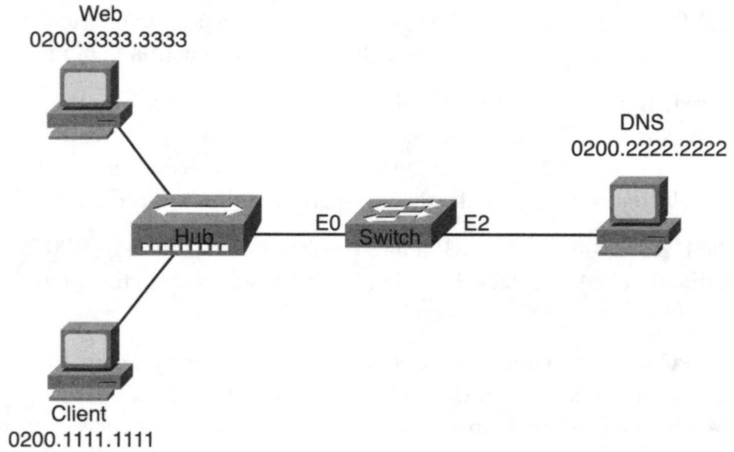

The switch connects to a shared hub, to which the client and the Web server are attached. As you might recall, the shared-media hub does not perform any Layer 2 logic—it just forwards all incoming electrical signals out all other ports. So, if the switch forwarded a frame out E0 to the client, and if the client is sending a frame to the Web server, a collision could occur. However, a frame sent by the client should never collide with frames sent by the DNS because they are on different switch ports. So, a more general statement should be made about switches and collisions:

> Switches prevent collisions for ports with only one device connected to the port. If a hub is attached to the switch port with multiple devices attached to the hub, collisions can occur between frames sent by those devices. These frames would not collide with frames sent from devices on other switch ports.

To better discuss LANs, bridging, and switching, a term is needed to describe the set of devices whose frames could collide. *Collision domain* is the set of LAN interfaces whose frames could collide with each other but not with any other devices in the network. The switch network in Figure 4-10 has created three separate Ethernet segments, and each is a separate collision domain. For example, frames sent by the client in Figure 4-10 would not collide with frames sent by the DNS and the Web server. However, the switch could forward a frame out E0 toward the client at the same instant that the client sends a frame and would create a collision—unless the switch and the client are using full-duplex operation, as covered in the earlier section of this chapter. Regardless, transparent bridges, switches, and routers all create separate collision domains, one per interface.

Figure 4-12 shows a typical example of the definition of collision domains.

Figure 4-12 *Collision Domains*

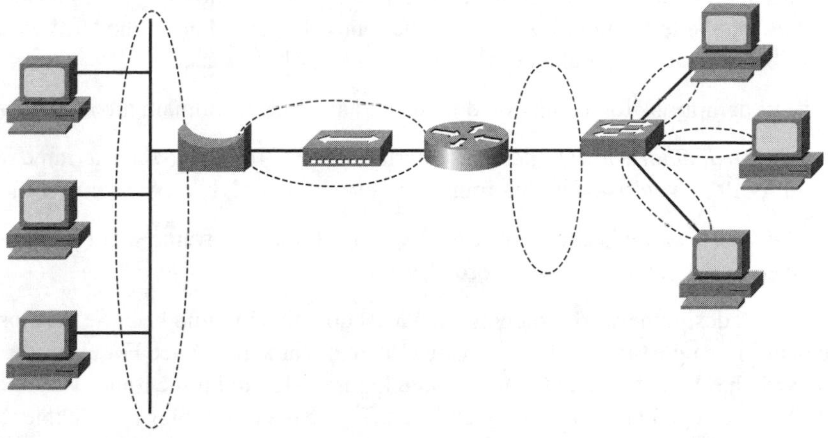

Bridges and switches forward broadcasts and multicasts on all ports. (Actually, the forwarding of multicasts can be optimized using several switch features, such as the Cisco Group Management Protocol (CGMP), but these are beyond the scope of CCNA.) Because broadcast frames are sent out all ports, a bridge or switch creates only a single *broadcast domain*. A broadcast domain is the set of devices for which, when one of the devices sends a broadcast, all the other devices receive a copy of the broadcast.

The broadcast domain concept is similar to the concept of collision domains; however, only routers stop the flow of broadcasts. Figure 4-13 provides the broadcast domains for the same network depicted in Figure 4-12.

Figure 4-13 *Broadcast Domains*

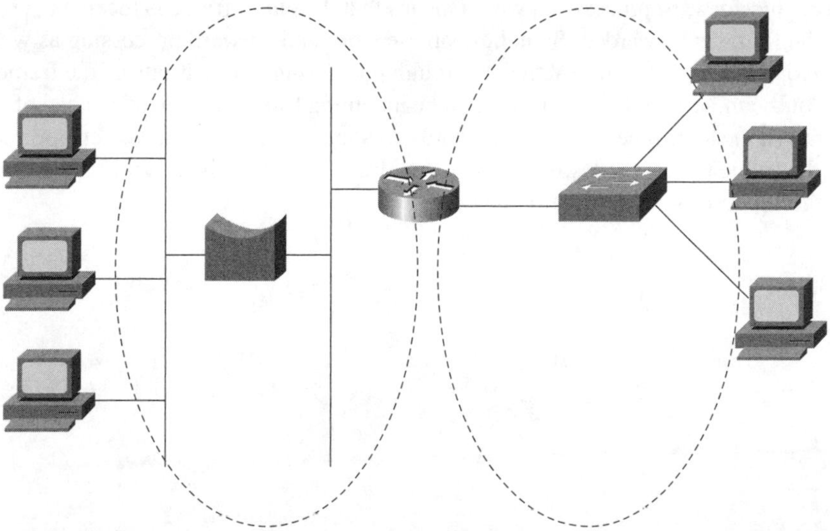

Broadcasts sent by a device in one broadcast domain are not forwarded to devices in another broadcast domain. In this example, there are two broadcast domains. For instance, an ARP sent by a PC on the left is not forwarded by the router. In the old days, the term *broadcast firewall* described the fact that routers did not forward LAN broadcasts.

General definitions for a collision domain and a broadcast domain are as follows:

A *collision domain* is a set of network interface cards (NICs) for which a frame sent by one NIC could result in a collision with a frame sent by any other NIC in the same collision domain.

A *broadcast domain* is a set of NICs for which a broadcast frame sent by one NIC will be received by all other NICs in the broadcast domain.

Engineers design networks keeping broadcast domains in mind because, in most cases, all the devices in a single broadcast domain are also in the same IP subnet. For example, if only bridges and switches had existed in the network in Figure 4-13, and if the router was later added, some IP addresses would have had to be changed. To use the terminology in Chapter 3, two separate address groupings (for example, IP subnets) would be used for IP in Figure 4-13—one for the devices to the left of the router and another for devices to the right of the router. A definition of Layer 3 address groupings on LANs will help you understand VLANs better:

NOTE All devices in the same broadcast domain (Layer 2) typically will be in the same Layer 3 address grouping—in other words, the same IP subnet or same IPX network.

Internal Switching Paths

The internal processing on a switch can decrease latency for frames. Transparent bridges use store-and-forward processing, which means that the entire frame is received before the first bit of the frame is forwarded. Switches can use store-and-forward processing as well as *cut-through* processing logic. With cut-through processing, the first bits of the frame are sent out the outbound port before the last bit of the incoming frame is received instead of waiting for the entire frame to be received. In other words, as soon as the incoming switch port receives enough of the frame to see the destination MAC address, the frame is transmitted out the appropriate outgoing port to the destination device.

Cut-through processing can help, and it can hurt. Because the frame check sequence (FCS) is in the Ethernet trailer, a cut-through forwarded frame might have bit errors that the switch will not notice before sending most of the frame. And, of course, if the outbound port is busy, the switch stores the frame until the output port is available, gaining no advantage of store-and-forward switching.

The internal processing algorithms used by switches vary among models and vendors; regardless, the internal processing can be categorized as one of the methods listed in Table 4-6.

Table 4-6 *Switch Internal Processing*

Switching Method	Description
Store-and-forward	The switch fully receives all bits in the frame (store) before forwarding the frame (forward). This allows the switch to check the FCS before forwarding the frame. (FCS is in the Ethernet trailer.)
Cut-through	The switch performs the address table lookup as soon as the destination address field in the header is received. The first bits in the frame can be sent out the outbound port before the final bits in the incoming frame are received. This does not allow the switch to discard frames that fail the FCS check. (FCS is in the Ethernet trailer.)
FragmentFree	This performs like cut-through switching, but the switch waits for 64 bytes to be received before forwarding the first bytes of the outgoing frame. According to Ethernet specifications, collisions should be detected during the first 64 bytes of the frame; frames in error because of a collision will not be forwarded. The FCS still cannot be checked.

Comparison of LAN Segmentation Using Bridges, Switches, and Routers

The CCNA exam tests your ability to compare networks that use bridges, switches, and routers to separate LAN segments. The basic workings of a bridge and a switch have already been covered in this chapter. To compare these three options, first routing logic is covered. Afterward, comparisons will be made among the three options.

Routing is covered more fully in other chapters. For comparison, a router separates two segments in Figure 4-14. The client initiates the same example flow that was used in the earlier examples. Figure 4-14 illustrates a couple of key features of routing.

Figure 4-14 *Example Protocol Flows—Using a Router*

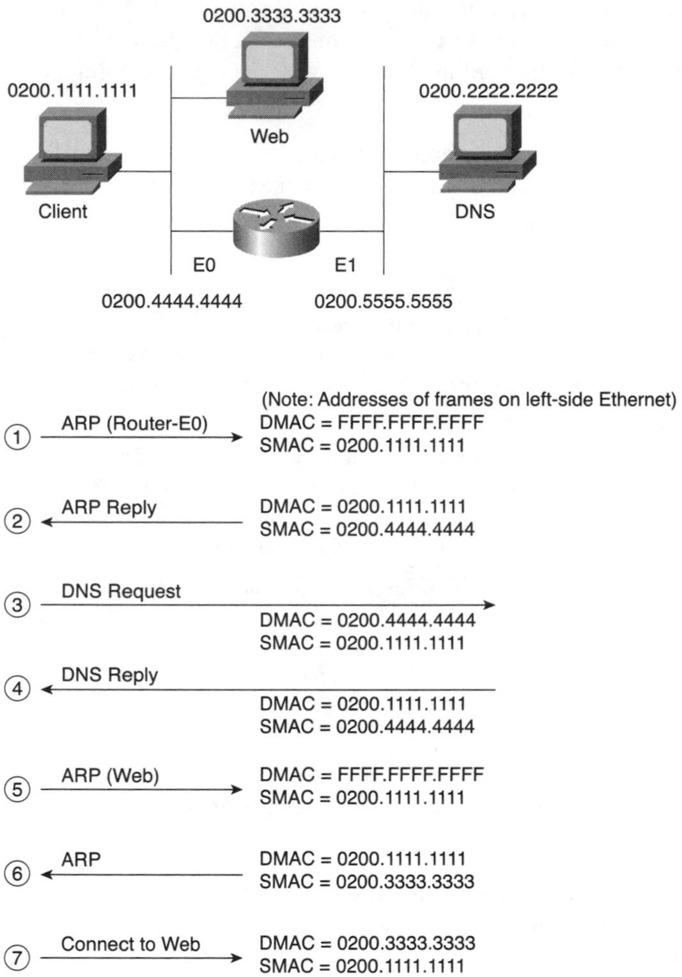

The flows in Figure 4-14 match the numbers in this list, which explains the meaning and implications of the flows in the figure:

1 The PC is preconfigured with the IP address of the DNS. The PC notices that the IP address of the DNS is on a different subnet, so the PC wants to forward the packet to its default router. However, the PC does not know its default router's MAC address yet, so *it must use ARP to find that router's MAC address. The ARP broadcast is not forwarded by the router.*

2 The router replies to the ARP request with its MAC address, 0200.4444.4444.

3. The PC requests name resolution for the Web server by sending a packet with the destination IP address of the DNS. The destination MAC address in the frame sent by the PC is the router's E0 MAC address. The router receives the frame, extracts the packet, and forwards it.
4. The DNS returns the IP address of the Web server to the PC in the DNS reply.
5. The PC does not know the Web server's MAC address, so it sends an ARP broadcast to learn the MAC address. The router has no need to forward the ARP broadcast.
6. The Web server replies to the ARP, stating that its MAC address is 0200.3333.3333.
7. The PC can now connect to the Web server.

The router does not forward ARP broadcasts. In fact, the logic in Step 1 begins with an ARP looking for the MAC address of the client's default router—namely, the router's E0 MAC address. This broadcast was not forwarded by the router, a fact that causes a router to be called a *broadcast firewall*. Comparing this to a transparent bridge or a LAN switch, this difference in broadcast treatment is the biggest advantage of routers.

Table 4-7 lists several features relating to segmenting LANs with bridges, switches, and routers. Essentially, this chart summarizes features that might differ among the three devices. Table 4-8 lists features that describe how each device performs when separating two Ethernet segments, compared to using a single Ethernet segment with no bridge, switch, or router. The two tables together provide the necessary details when comparing the three types of devices.

Table 4-7 *Comparison of Segmentation Options*

Feature	Single Segment	Bridging	Switching	Routing
Number of broadcast domains	1	1	1	1 per router interface
Number of collision domains	1	1 per bridge port	1 per switch port	1 per router interface
Forwards LAN broadcasts?	N/A	Yes	Yes	No
Forwards LAN multicasts?	N/A	Yes	Yes; can be optimized for less forwarding	No[1]
OSI layer used when making forwarding decision	N/A	Layer 2	Layer 2	Layer 3
Internal processing variants	N/A	Store-and-forward	Store-and-forward, cut-through, FragmentFree	Store-and-forward

continues

Table 4-7 *Comparison of Segmentation Options (Continued)*

Feature	Single Segment	Bridging	Switching	Routing
Frame/packet fragmentation allowed?	N/A	No	No	Yes
Multiple concurrent equal-cost paths to same destination allowed?	N/A	No	No	Yes

[1]Routers can forward IP multicast packets, if configured to do so. However, this does not mean that the LAN multicast frame is forwarded.

Table 4-8 lists features that should be interpreted within the following context: If I migrated from a single Ethernet segment to a network with two segments separated by a bridge/switch/router, and if traffic loads and destinations stayed constant, the result would be _______.

Table 4-8 *Benefits when Moving from One Ethernet Segment to Multiple Segments Using Bridges, Switches, and Routers*

Feature	Bridging	Switching	Routing
Greater cabling distances allowed	Yes	Yes	Yes
Decrease in collisions, assuming equal traffic loads	Yes	Yes	Yes
Decreased adverse impact of broadcasts	No	No	Yes
Decreased adverse impact of multicasts	No	No, unless mcast optimizations enabled	Yes
Increase in bandwidth	Yes	Yes	Yes
Filtering on Layer 2 header allowed	Yes	Yes	No
Filtering on Layer 3 header allowed	No	No	Yes

Certainly, the most important distinction among the three segmentation methods is their treatment of broadcasts and multicasts. Remembering the concepts of collision domains, broadcast domains, and how each device separates LANs into different domains is one key to understanding campus LAN design and troubleshooting.

LAN Switch Configuration

Cisco expects CCNAs to master the concepts behind LAN switching and VLANs. This mastery includes the ability to configure IOS-based LAN switches using the IOS CLI. This section outlines the similarities of the switch IOS CLI to the router IOS CLI, and contrasts the commands, syntax, and required configuration elements unique to switches.

Not all Cisco LAN switches provide an IOS CLI interface to the network engineer. Cisco wants its certifications to prove that the candidate knows the technology and can implement it; that proof would be onerous if all switch families' user interfaces were required on the CCNA exam. This book covers some implementation details and examples on the 1900 series switch, which is the same (and only) switch user interface covered by the ICND course.

The similarities between the 1900 series switch CLI and the router IOS CLI far outnumber the differences. In fact, most of the differences relate to the commands needed on a switch, which are simply not needed on a router. The up arrow retrieves the previous command. The ? key requests help. The Tab key completes a parameter after you have typed in a unique set of beginning characters. The **configure terminal** command takes you from privileged exec mode to configuration mode. The **show running-config** command lists the currently used configuration. In fact, when in doubt, assume that the switch and router IOS CLIs are identical. The important differences are mentioned as appropriate in this section.

Basic 1900 Switch Configuration

On the Catalyst 1900 switch, three different configuration methods exist:

- Menu-driven interface from the console port
- Web-based Visual Switch Manager (VSM)
- IOS command-line interface (CLI)

As mentioned earlier, this book focuses on using the CLI to configure the switch. Table 4-9 lists the switch commands referred to in this section.

Table 4-9 *Commands for Catalyst 1900 Switch Configuration*

Command	Description
ip address *address subnet-mask*	Sets the IP address for in-band management of the switch
ip default-gateway	Sets the default gateway so that the management interface can be reached from a remote network
show ip	Displays IP address configuration
show interfaces	Displays interface information
mac-address-table permanent *mac-address type module/port*	Sets a permanent MAC address
mac-address-table restricted static *mac-address type module/port src-if-list*	Sets a restricted static MAC address

continues

Table 4-9 *Commands for Catalyst 1900 Switch Configuration (Continued)*

Command	Description
port secure [**max-mac-count** *count*]	Sets port security
show mac-address-table {**security**}	Displays the MAC address table; the **security** option displays information about the restricted or static settings
address-violation {**suspend** | **disable** | **ignore**}	Sets the action to be taken by the switch if there is a security address violation
show version	Displays version information
copy tftp://*host/src_file* {**opcode** [*type module*] | **nvram**}	Copies a configuration file from the TFTP server into NVRAM
copy nvram tftp://*host/dst_file*	Saves a configuration file to the TFTP server
delete nvram [*type module*]	Removes all configuration parameters and returns the switch to factory default settings

Default 1900 Configuration

The default values vary depending on the features of the switch. The following list provides some of the default settings for the Catalyst 1900 switch. (Not all the defaults are shown in this example.)

- IP address: 0.0.0.0
- CDP: Enabled
- Switching mode: FragmentFree
- 100BaseT port: Autonegotiate duplex mode
- 10BaseT port: Half duplex
- Spanning Tree: Enabled
- Console password: None

Numbering Ports (Interfaces)

The terms *interface* and *port* both are used to describe the physical connectors on the switch hardware. For instance, the **show running-config** command uses the term *interface*; the **show spantree** command uses the term *port*. The numbering of the interfaces is relatively straightforward; the interface numbering convention for the 1912 and 1924 switches is shown in Table 4-10. Example 4-1 shows three exec commands and highlights the use of the terms *interface* and *port*.

Table 4-10 *Catalyst 1912 and 1924 Interface/Port Numbering*

	Catalyst 1912	Catalyst 1924
10BaseT ports	12 total (e0/1 to e0/12)	24 total (e0/1 to e0/24)
AUI port	e0/25	e0/25
100BaseT uplink ports	fa0/26 (port A) fa0/27 (port B)	fa0/26 (port A) fa0/27 (port B)

Example 4-1 **show run** *Output Refers to Port e0/1 as Interface Ethernet 0/1*

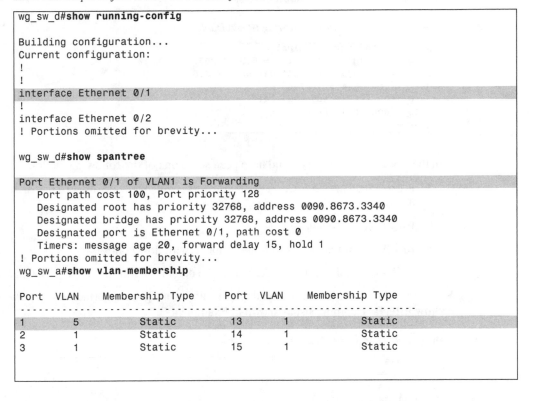

```
wg_sw_d#show running-config

Building configuration...
Current configuration:
!
!
interface Ethernet 0/1
!
interface Ethernet 0/2
! Portions omitted for brevity...

wg_sw_d#show spantree

Port Ethernet 0/1 of VLAN1 is Forwarding
   Port path cost 100, Port priority 128
   Designated root has priority 32768, address 0090.8673.3340
   Designated bridge has priority 32768, address 0090.8673.3340
   Designated port is Ethernet 0/1, path cost 0
   Timers: message age 20, forward delay 15, hold 1
! Portions omitted for brevity...
wg_sw_a#show vlan-membership

Port  VLAN    Membership Type      Port  VLAN    Membership Type
-----------------------------------------------------------------
1        5           Static         13       1           Static
2        1           Static         14       1           Static
3        1           Static         15       1           Static
```

Basic IP and Port Duplex Configuration

Two features commonly configured during switch installation are TCP/IP support and the setting of duplex on key switch ports. Switches support IP, but in a different way than a router. The switch acts more like a normal IP host, with a single address/mask for the switch and a default router. Each port/interface does not need an IP address because the switch is not performing Layer 3 routing. In fact, if there were no need to manage the switch, IP would not be needed on the switch at all.

The second feature typically configured at installation time is to preconfigure some ports to always use half- or full-duplex operation rather than allow negotiation. At times, autonegotiation can produce unpredictable results. For example, if a device attached to the switch does not support autonegotiation, the Catalyst switch sets the corresponding switch port to half-duplex mode by default. If the attached device is configured for full-duplex operation, a duplex mismatch occurs. To avoid this situation, manually set the duplex parameters of the switch to match the attached device.

Similar to the router IOS, the Catalyst 1900 switch has various configuration modes. Example 4-2 shows the initial configuration of IP and duplex, with the actual prompts showing the familiar exec and configuration modes.

Example 4-2 *Configuration Modes for Configuring IP and Duplex*

```
wg_sw_a# configure terminal
wg_sw_a(config)#ip address 10.5.5.11 255.255.255.0
wg_sw_a(config)#ip default-gateway 10.5.5.3
wg_sw_a(config)# interface e0/1
wg_sw_a(config-if)#duplex  half
wg_sw_a(config-if)#end
wg_sw_a
```

In the example, the duplex could have been set to one of the following modes:

- **auto**—Sets autonegotiation of duplex mode. This is the default option for 100-Mbps TX ports.
- **full**—Sets full-duplex mode.
- **full-flow-control**—Sets full-duplex mode with flow control.
- **half**—Sets half-duplex mode. This is the default option for 10-Mbps TX ports.

To verify the IP configuration and duplex settings on a given interface, use the **show ip** and **show interface** commands, as shown in Example 4-3.

Example 4-3 **show ip** *and* **show interfaces** *Output*

```
wg_sw_a#show ip
IP address: 10.5.5.11
Subnet mask: 255.255.255.0
Default gateway: 10.5.5.3
Management VLAN:  1
Domain name:
Name server 1: 0.0.0.0
Name server 2: 0.0.0.0
HTTP server: Enabled
HTTP port:  80
RIP: Enabled

wg_sw_a#show interfaces
```

Example 4-3 **show ip** *and* **show interfaces** *Output (Continued)*

```
Ethernet 0/1 is Enabled
Hardware is Built-in 10Base-T
Address is 0090.8673.3341
MTU 1500 bytes, BW 10000 Kbits
802.1d STP State:  Forwarding     Forward Transitions:  1
Port monitoring: Disabled
Unknown unicast flooding: Enabled
Unregistered multicast flooding:  Enabled
Description:
Duplex setting: Half duplex
Back pressure: Disabled

    Receive Statistics                        Transmit Statistics
-------------------------------------     -------------------------------------
Total good frames                  44841     Total frames                    404502
Total octets                     4944550     Total octets                  29591574
Broadcast/multicast frames         31011     Broadcast/multicast frames      390913
Broadcast/multicast octets       3865029     Broadcast/multicast octets    28478154
Good frames forwarded              44832     Deferrals                            0
Frames filtered                        9     Single collisions                    0
Runt frames                            0     Multiple collisions                  0
No buffer discards                     0     Excessive collisions                 0
                                             Queue full discards                  0
Errors:                                      Errors:
  FCS errors                           0       Late collisions                    0
  Alignment errors                     0       Excessive deferrals                0
  Giant frames                         0       Jabber errors                      0
  Address violations                   0       Other transmit errors              0
```

No IP address is in the **show interface** output because the IP address is associated with the entire switch, not just a single interface. The spanning-tree state of the interface is shown, as is the duplex setting. If duplex was mismatched with the device on the other end, the late collisions counter most likely would increment rapidly.

Viewing and Configuring Entries in the MAC Address Table

The switching/bridging table concept discussed earlier in this chapter is called the *MAC address table* on the 1900 family of switches. The MAC address table contains dynamic entries, which are learned when the switch receives frames and examines the source MAC address. Two other variations of entries in the MAC address table are important to switch configuration and are outlined along with dynamic entries in the following list:

- **Dynamic addresses**—MAC addresses are added to the MAC address table through normal bridge/switch processing. In other words, when a frame is received, the source MAC of the frame is associated with the incoming port/interface. These entries in the table time out with disuse (default 300 seconds on a 1900 series switch) and are cleared whenever the entire table is cleared.

- **Permanent MAC addresses**—Through configuration, a MAC address is associated with a port, just as it would have been associated as a dynamic address. However, permanent entries in the table never time out.
- **Restricted-static entries**—Through configuration, a MAC address is configured to be associated only with a particular port, with an additional restriction: Frames destined to that MAC address must have entered through a particular set of incoming ports.

Figure 4-15 provides a simple example to show the use of permanent and restricted-static addresses. A popular server (Server 1) is on port E0/3, and there is never a case when its MAC address should not be in the table. The payroll server is also on this switch, and only the company comptroller is allowed access. The configuration and resulting MAC address table are shown in Example 4-4, which follows the figure.

Figure 4-15 *MAC Address Table Manipulation—Sample Network*

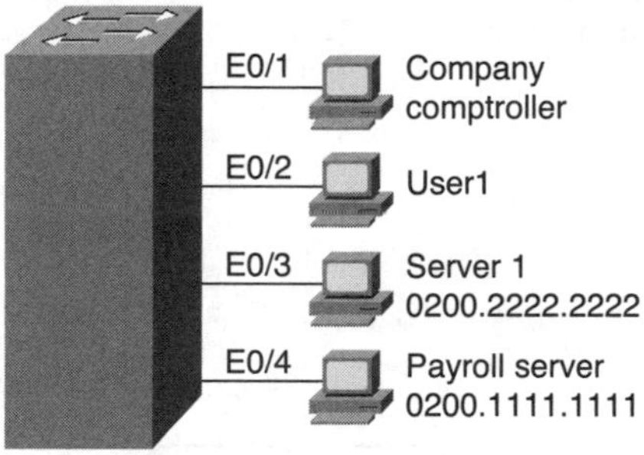

Example 4-4 *The MAC Address Table, with Dynamic, Permanent, and Restricted Static Entries*

```
wg_sw_a(config)#mac-address-table permanent 0200.2222.2222 ethernet 0/3
wg_sw_a(config)#mac-address-table restricted static 0200.1111.1111 e0/4 e0/1
wg_sw_a(config)#End
wg_sw_a#
wg_sw_a#show mac-address-table
Number of permanent addresses : 1
Number of restricted static addresses : 1
Number of dynamic addresses : 5

Address          Dest Interface      Type         Source Interface List
----------------------------------------------------------------------
0200.4444.4444   Ethernet 0/1        Dynamic      All
00E0.1E5D.AE2F   Ethernet 0/2        Dynamic      All
0200.2222.2222   Ethernet 0/3        Permanent    All
0200.1111.1111   Ethernet 0/4        Static       Et0/1
00D0.588F.B604   FastEthernet 0/26   Dynamic      All
00E0.1E5D.AE2B   FastEthernet 0/26   Dynamic      All
00D0.5892.38C4   FastEthernet 0/27   Dynamic      All
```

In the example, Server 1 is always in the address table as the permanent entry. The payroll server is always in the table off port 0/4, and only devices on port 0/1 are allowed to send frames to it.

Another feature affecting the MAC address table is called *port security.* Port security is a feature that, when enabled, limits the number of MAC addresses associated with a port in the MAC address table. In other words, there is a preset limit to the number of sources that can forward frames into that switch port.

An example is particularly useful for understanding this concept; the configuration is straightforward. Consider Figure 4-16, which shows a similar configuration to Figure 4-15, except that the finance department has increased to three employees. These three employees are on the same shared hub, which then is cabled to switch port 0/1.

Figure 4-16 *Sample Network with Port Security*

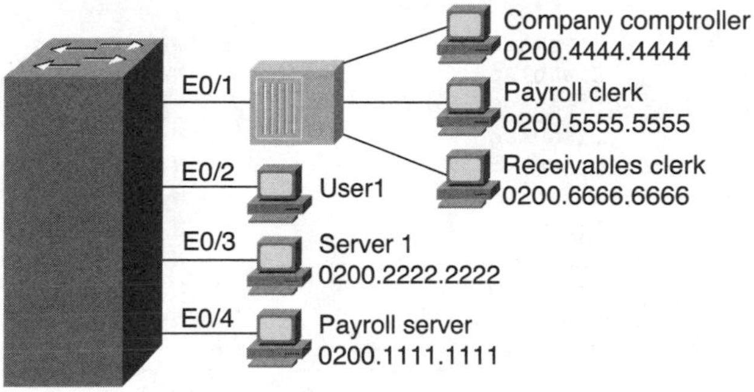

Port security can be used to restrict port 0/1 so that only three MAC addresses can source frames that enter port 0/1; this is because only the finance department is expected to use the shared hub. Any permanent or restricted-static MAC addresses count against this total of three. Example 4-5 shows a sample configuration, with **show** commands.

Example 4-5 *Port Security Example*

```
wg_sw_a(config)#mac-address-table permanent 0200.2222.2222 ethernet 0/3
wg_sw_a(config)#mac-address-table permanent 0200.4444.4444 ethernet 0/1
wg_sw_a(config)#mac-address-table restricted static 0200.1111.1111 e0/4 e0/1
wg_sw_a(config)#interface ethernet 0/1
wg_sw_a(config-if)#port secure max-mac-count 3
wg_sw_a(config-if)#End
wg_sw_a#
wg_sw_a#show mac-address-table
Number of permanent addresses : 2
Number of restricted static addresses : 1
Number of dynamic addresses : 6
```

continues

Example 4-5 *Port Security Example (Continued)*

```
Address          Dest Interface      Type         Source Interface List
-------------------------------------------------------------------------
0200.4444.4444   Ethernet 0/1        Permanent    All
0200.5555.5555   Ethernet 0/1        Dynamic      All
0200.6666.6666   Ethernet 0/1        Dynamic      All
00E0.1E5D.AE2F   Ethernet 0/2        Dynamic      All
0200.2222.2222   Ethernet 0/3        Permanent    All
0200.1111.1111   Ethernet 0/4        Static       Et0/1
00D0.588F.B604   FastEthernet 0/26   Dynamic      All
00E0.1E5D.AE2B   FastEthernet 0/26   Dynamic      All
00D0.5892.38C4   FastEthernet 0/27   Dynamic      All
wg_sw_a#show mac-address-table security
Action upon address violation : Suspend

Interface        Addressing Security      Address Table Size
-------------------------------------------------------------
Ethernet 0/1      Enabled                     3
Ethernet 0/2      Disabled                    N/A
Ethernet 0/3      Disabled                    N/A
Ethernet 0/4      Disabled                    N/A
Ethernet 0/5      Disabled                    N/A
Ethernet 0/6      Disabled                    N/A
Ethernet 0/7      Disabled                    N/A
Ethernet 0/8      Disabled                    N/A
Ethernet 0/9      Disabled                    N/A
Ethernet 0/10     Disabled                    N/A
Ethernet 0/11     Disabled                    N/A
Ethernet 0/12     Disabled                    N/A
```

In this example, the permanently defined MAC address of 0200.4444.444, the comptroller's MAC address, is always associated with port e0/1. Notice that the two new employees' MAC addresses are also in the MAC address table. The **port secure max-mac-count 3** command means that a total of three addresses can be learned on this port.

What should the switch do when a fourth MAC address sources a frame that enters E0/1? An address violation occurs when a secured port receives a frame from a new source address that, if added to the MAC table, would cause the switch to exceed its address table size limit for that port. When a port security address violation occurs, the options for action to be taken on a port include suspending, ignoring, or disabling the port. When a port is suspended, it is re-enabled when a frame containing a valid address is received. When a port is disabled, it must be manually re-enabled. If the action is ignored, the switch ignores the security violation and keeps the port enabled.

Use the **address-violation** global configuration command to specify the action for a port address violation. The syntax for this command is as follows:

```
address-violation {suspend | disable | ignore}
```

Use the **no address-violation** command to set the switch to its default value, which is **suspend**.

Managing Configuration and System Files

Commands that are used to manage and control the configuration and system software files are slightly different on the 1900 switch family than on IOS-based routers. One of the reasons for the difference is that the switch does not actually run IOS—it has many features similar to IOS, including the IOS CLI, but there are and probably always will be some differences. For example, in Example 4-6, the familiar **show version** command is used to display uptime and software levels, but it does not show the IOS level because IOS is not running.

Example 4-6 **show version** *Output Displays Switch Hardware and Cisco IOS Software Information*

```
wg_sw_a#show version
Cisco Catalyst 1900/2820 Enterprise Edition Software
Version V9.00.00(12) written from 171.071.114.222
Copyright  Cisco Systems, Inc.  1993-1999
DS2820-1 uptime is 2day(s) 19hour(s) 34minute(s) 41second(s)
cisco Catalyst 2820 (486sxl) processor with 2048K/1024K bytes of memory
Hardware board revision is 1
Upgrade Status: No upgrade currently in progress.
Config File Status: No configuration upload/download is in progress
25 Fixed Ethernet/IEEE 802.3 interface(s)
SLOT A:
 FDDI (Fiber DAS Model), Version 00
  v1.14 written from 172.031.004.151: valid
SLOT B:
 100Base-TX(1 Port UTP Model), Version 0
Base Ethernet Address: 00-E0-1E-87-21-40
```

Another difference is that when the configuration is changed, the running config is modified but the startup config file in NVRAM is automatically updated. In other words, there is no need for a **copy running-config startup-config** command on the 1900 family of switches, as there would be on a router. Configuration files can be copied to an external TFTP server, but instead of using the keyword **startup-config** (used by routers), **NVRAM** is used.

The syntax of the **copy** command is slightly different than what was covered in Chapter 2, "Cisco IOS Software Fundamentals," relating to the router IOS **copy** command. The syntax of the command used to copy the NVRAM configuration file to host 10.1.1.1 into file mybackup.cfg is **copy nvram tftp://10.1.1.1/mybackup.cfg**. Unlike the router IOS, the switch IOS CLI will not prompt for the server name or IP address or the name of the file. Instead, the address or server host name and the filename are entered at the command line. The fact that the command does not prompt you is certainly different than with the router IOS. However, the same general syntax is available on the router IOS as of Cisco IOS Software release 12.0. For example, a similar, valid router IOS command would be **copy startup-config tftp://10.1.1.1/myrouter.cfg**.

Table 4-11 summarizes some of the key differences between the router IOS CLI and the 1900 IOS CLI.

Table 4-11 *IOS CLI Differences: Router Versus 1900 Switch*

Function	Router Command, Features	Switch Command, Features
Finding software version	**show version** command; shows IOS version.	**show version** command; shows switch software version.
Copying configuration files to TFTP server	**copy startup-config tftp** command; router IOS prompts for TFTP parameters.	**copy nvram tftp://server/file** command; switch IOS CLI does not prompt for TFTP parameters. "Server" can be IP address or host name.
Updating the config file used at reload time	**copy running-config startup-config** command.	Changes made to running configuration using config mode automatically are reflected in NVRAM config file.
Erasing the config file used at reload time	**write erase** or **erase startup-config** command.	**delete nvram** command.

Foundation Summary

The "Foundation Summary" is a collection of tables and figures that provide a convenient review of many key concepts in this chapter. For those of you already comfortable with the topics in this chapter, this summary could help you recall a few details. For those of you who just read this chapter, this review should help solidify some key facts. For any of you doing your final prep before the exam, these tables and figures will be a convenient way to review the day before the exam.

Table 4-12 summarizes the basic features of Ethernet.

Table 4-12 *Summary of Some Basic Ethernet Features*

10Base2, 10Base5	Single bus cabled serially between devices using coaxial cable.
10BaseT with a hub	One electrical bus shared among all devices creating a single collision domain cabled in a star topology, using twisted-pair cabling.
10BaseT with a switch	One electrical bus per switch port, creating multiple collision domains, cabled in a star topology using twisted-pair cabling.
Half duplex	Logic that requires a card to only send or receive at a single point in time. Used to avoid collisions.
Full duplex	Logic that enables concurrent sending and receiving, allowed when one device is attached to a switch port, ensuring that no collisions can occur.

The following list summarizes many of the key features of MAC addresses:

- Unicast MAC addresses address an individual LAN interface card.
- Broadcast MAC addresses address all devices on a LAN.
- Multicast MAC addresses address a subset of the devices on an Ethernet or FDDI LAN.
- Functional MAC addresses identify devices performing a specific IEEE-defined function on Token Ring only.

Figure 4-17 outlines the various LAN framing fields. Focus on the addressing fields, the location of the FCS, and the different "type" fields.

Figure 4-17 *LAN Header Formats*

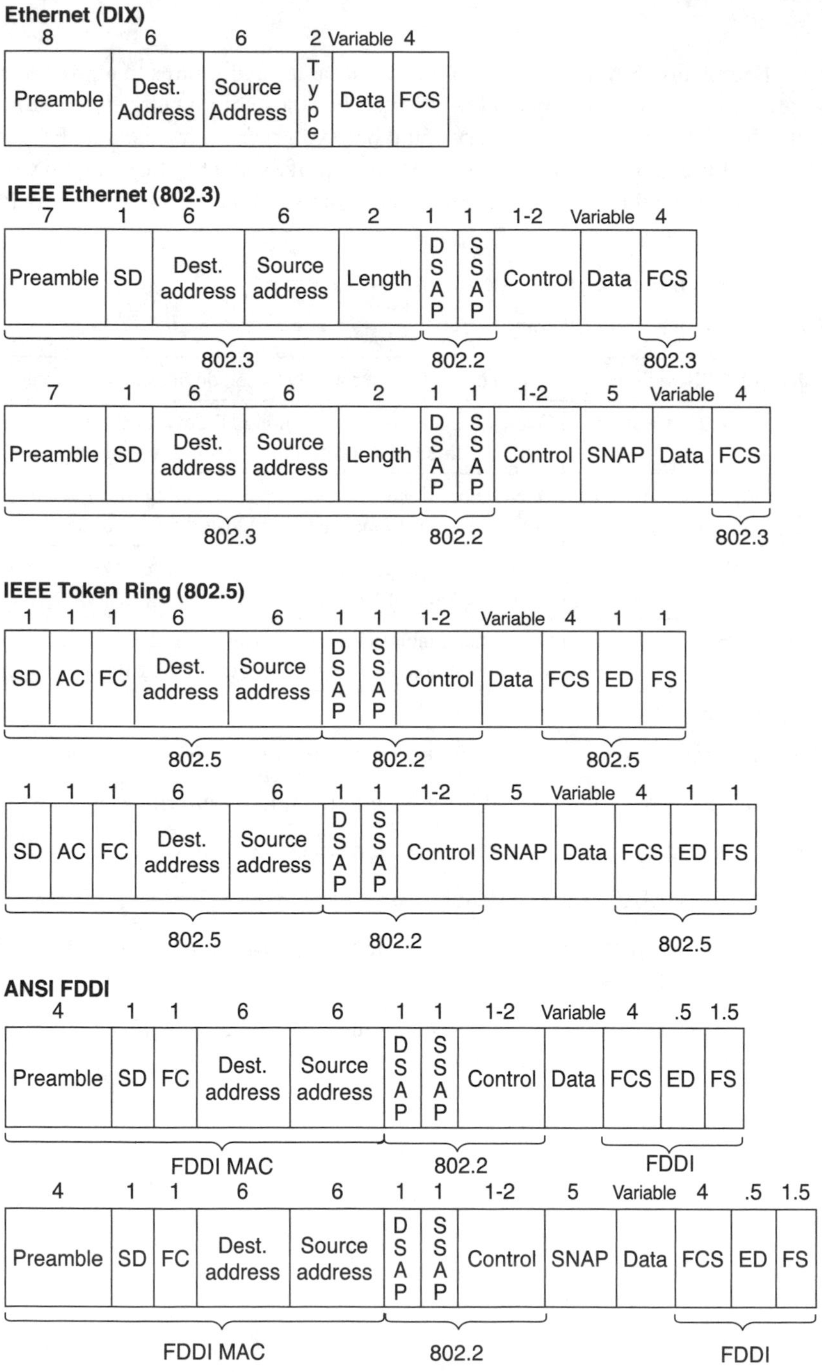

Table 4-13 summarizes the fields used for identifying the types of data contained in a frame.

Table 4-13 *Protocol Type Fields in LAN Headers*

Field Name	Length	LAN Type	Comments
Ethernet Type	2 bytes	Ethernet	RFC 1700 ("Assigned Numbers" RFC) lists the values. Xerox owns the assignment process.
802.2 DSAP and SSAP	1 byte each	IEEE Ethernet, IEEE Token Ring, ANSI FDDI	The IEEE Registration Authority controls the assignment of valid values. The source SAP (SSAP) and destination SAP (DSAP) do not have to be equal, so 802.2 calls for the sender's protocol type (SSAP) and the destination's type (DSAP).
SNAP Protocol	2 bytes	IEEE Ethernet, IEEE Token Ring, ANSI FDDI	Uses Ethernet Type values and is used only when DSAP is hex AA. It is needed because the DSAP and SSAP fields are only 1 byte in length.

Table 4-14 lists the specification that defines the Media Access Control (MAC) and Logical Link Control (LLC) sublayers of the three LAN types, for comparison.

Table 4-14 *MAC and LLC Details for Three Types of LANs*

Name	MAC Sublayer Spec	LLC Sublayer Spec	Other Comments
Ethernet Version 2 (DIX Ethernet)	Ethernet	N/A	This spec is owned by Digital, Intel, and Xerox.
IEEE Ethernet	IEEE 802.3	IEEE 802.2	This is also popularly called 802.3 Ethernet. It is built upon details of DIX Ethernet.
IEEE Token Ring	IEEE 802.5	IEEE 802.2	IBM helped with development before the IEEE took over.
ANSI FDDI	ANSI X3T9.5	IEEE 802.2	ANSI liked 802.2, so it just refers to the IEEE spec.

Transparent bridges forward frames when necessary and do not forward when there is no need to do so, thus reducing overhead. To accomplish this, transparent bridges perform three actions:

- Learning MAC addresses by examining the source MAC address of each frame received by the bridge

- Deciding when to forward a frame or when to filter (not forward) a frame, based on the destination MAC address
- Creating a loop-free environment with other bridges by using the Spanning Tree Protocol

Figures 4-18 and 4-19 detail the concepts of a collision domain and a broadcast domain.

Figure 4-18 *Collision Domains*

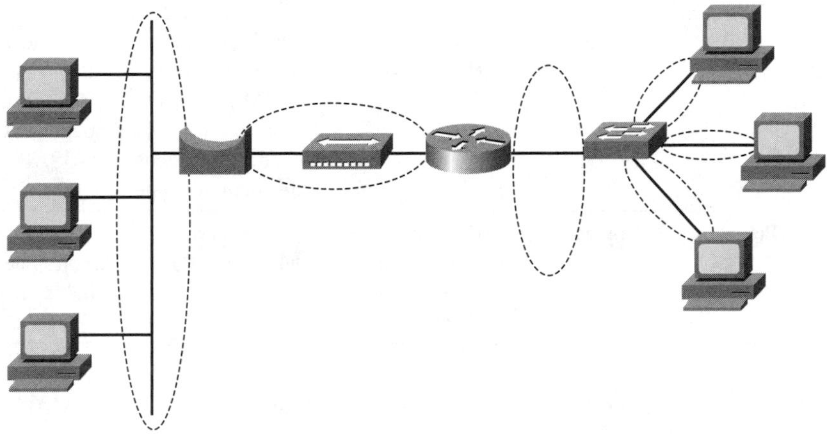

Figure 4-19 *Broadcast Domains*

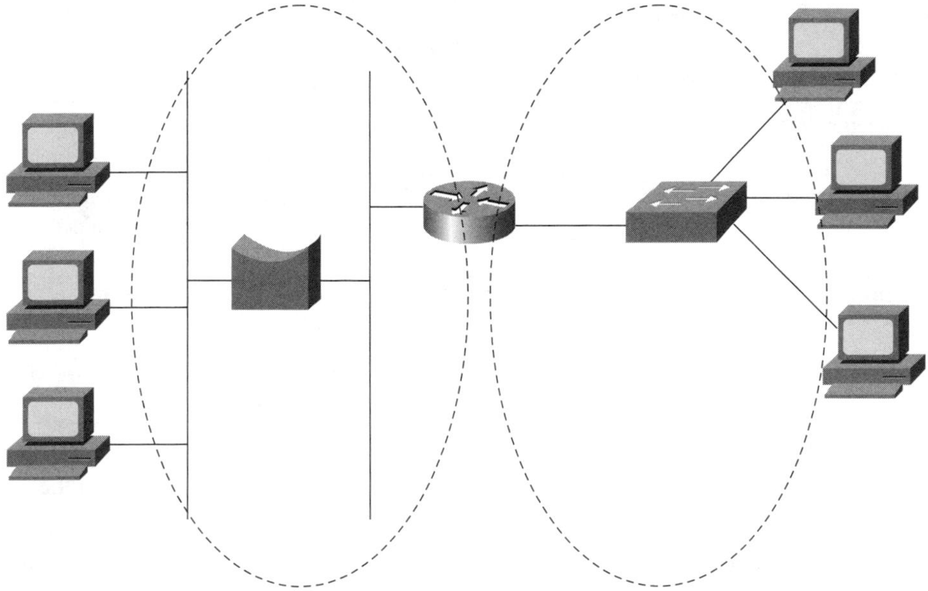

General definitions for *collision domain* and *broadcast domain* are as follows:

A *collision domain* is a set of network interface cards (NICs) for which a frame sent by one NIC could result in a collision with a frame sent by any other NIC in the same collision domain.

A *broadcast domain* is a set of NICs for which a broadcast frame sent by one NIC will be received by all other NICs in the broadcast domain.

Table 4-15 lists the internal processing methods of LAN switches.

Table 4-15 *Switch Internal Processing*

Switching Method	Description
Store-and-forward	The switch fully receives all bits in the frame (store) before forwarding the frame (forward). This allows the switch to check the FCS before forwarding the frame. (FCS is in the Ethernet trailer.)
Cut-through	The switch performs the address table lookup as soon as the destination address field in the header is received. The first bits in the frame can be sent out the outbound port before the final bits in the incoming frame are received. This does not allow the switch to discard frames that fail the FCS check. (FCS is in the Ethernet trailer.)
FragmentFree	This performs like cut-through switching, but the switch waits for 64 bytes to be received before forwarding the first bytes of the outgoing frame. According to Ethernet specifications, collisions should be detected during the first 64 bytes of the frame; frames in error because of a collision will not be forwarded. The FCS still cannot be checked.

Table 4-16 lists several features relating to segmenting LANs with bridges, switches, and routers.

Table 4-16 *Comparison of Segmentation Options*

Feature	Single Segment	Bridging	Switching	Routing
Number of broadcast domains	1	1	1	1 per router interface
Number of collision domains	1	1 per bridge port	1 per switch port	1 per router interface
Forwards LAN broadcasts?	N/A	Yes	Yes	No
Forwards LAN multicasts?	N/A	Yes	Yes; can be optimized for less forwarding	No[1]
OSI layer used when making forwarding decision	N/A	Layer 2	Layer 2	Layer 3

continues

Table 4-16 *Comparison of Segmentation Options (Continued)*

Feature	Single Segment	Bridging	Switching	Routing
Internal processing variants	N/A	Store-and-forward	Store-and-forward, cut-through, FragmentFree	Store-and-forward
Frame/packet fragmentation allowed?	N/A	No	No	Yes
Multiple concurrent equal-cost paths to same destination allowed?	N/A	No	No	Yes

[1]Routers can forward IP multicast packets, if configured to do so. However, this does not mean that the LAN multicast frame is forwarded.

Table 4-17 lists features that must be interpreted within the following context: If I migrated from a single Ethernet segment to a network with two segments separated by a bridge/switch/router, and if traffic loads and destinations stayed constant, the result would be _______.

Table 4-17 *Benefits when Moving from One Ethernet Segment to Multiple Segments Using Bridges, Switches, and Routers*

Feature	Bridging	Switching	Routing
Greater cabling distances allowed	Yes	Yes	Yes
Decrease in collisions, assuming equal traffic loads	Yes	Yes	Yes
Decreased adverse impact of broadcasts	No	No	Yes
Decreased adverse impact of multicasts	No	No, unless mcast optimizations enabled	Yes
Increase in bandwidth	Yes	Yes	Yes
Filtering on Layer 2 header allowed	Yes	Yes	No
Filtering on Layer 3 header allowed	No	No	Yes

Table 4-18 lists the 1900 switch commands used to perform basic switch configuration.

Table 4-18 *Commands for Catalyst 1900 Switch Configuration*

Command	Description
ip address *address subnet-mask*	Sets the IP address for in-band management of the switch
ip default-gateway	Sets the default gateway so that the management interface can be reached from a remote network
show ip	Displays IP address configuration
show interfaces	Displays interface information
mac-address-table permanent *mac-address type module/port*	Sets a permanent MAC address
mac-address-table restricted static *mac-address type module/port src-if-list*	Sets a restricted static MAC address
port secure [**max-mac-count** *count*]	Sets port security
show mac-address-table {**security**}	Displays the MAC address table; the **security** option displays information about the restricted or static settings
address-violation {**suspend** | **disable** | **ignore**}	Sets the action to be taken by the switch if there is a security address violation
show version	Displays version information
copy tftp://*host/src_file* {**opcode** [*type module*] | **nvram**}	Copies a configuration file from the TFTP server into NVRAM
copy nvram tftp://*host/dst_file*	Saves a configuration file to the TFTP server
delete nvram [*type module*]	Removes all configuration parameters and returns the switch to factory default settings

Table 4-19 lists the port-numbering conventions for the 1912 and 1924 series switches.

Table 4-19 *Catalyst 1912 and 1924 Interface/Port Numbering*

	Catalyst 1912	Catalyst 1924
10BaseT ports	12 total (e0/1 to e0/12)	24 total (e0/1 to e0/24)
AUI port	e0/25	e0/25
100BaseT uplink ports	fa0/26 (port A) fa0/27 (port B)	fa0/26 (port A) fa0/27 (port B)

Table 4-20 lists the key differences between the switch CLI and the router CLI.

Table 4-20 *IOS CLI Differences: Router Versus 1900 Switch*

Function	Router Command, Features	Switch Command, Features
Finding software version	**show version** command; shows IOS version	**show version** command; shows switch software version.
Copying configuration files to TFTP server	**copy startup-config tftp** command; router IOS prompts for TFTP parameters	**copy nvram tftp://server/file** command; switch IOS CLI does not prompt for TFTP parameters. "Server" can be IP address or host name.
Updating the config file used at reload time	**copy running-config startup-config** command	Changes made to running configuration using config mode automatically are reflected in NVRAM config file.
Erasing the config file used at reload time	**write erase** or **erase startup-config** command	**delete nvram** command.

Q&A

As mentioned in Chapter 1, "All About the Cisco Certified Network Associate Certification," the questions and scenarios in this book are more difficult than what you should experience on the actual exam. The questions do not attempt to cover more breadth or depth than the exam; however, they are designed to make sure that you know the answer. Rather than allowing you to derive the answer from clues hidden inside the question itself, the questions challenge your understanding and recall of the subject. Questions from the "Do I Know This Already?" quiz from the beginning of the chapter are repeated here to ensure that you have mastered the chapter's topic areas. Hopefully, these questions will help limit the number of exam questions on which you narrow your choices to two options and then guess.

The answers to these questions can be found in Appendix A.

1 What do the letters *MAC* stand for? What other terms have you heard to describe the same or similar concept?

____

____

____

2 Name two benefits of LAN segmentation using transparent bridges.

____

____

____

3 What routing protocol does a transparent bridge use to learn about Layer 3 addressing groupings?

____

____

____

4 If a Fast Ethernet NIC is currently receiving a frame, can it begin sending a frame?

____

____

____

5 Why did Ethernet networks' performance improve with the advent of bridges?

6 Why did Ethernet networks' performance improve with the advent of switches?

7 What are two key differences between a 10-Mbps NIC and a 10/100 NIC?

8 Assume that a building has 100 devices attached to the same Ethernet. These users then are migrated onto two separate shared Ethernet segments, each with 50 devices, with a transparent bridge between them. List two benefits that would be derived for a typical user.

9 What standards body owns the process of ensuring unique MAC addresses worldwide?

10 Assume that a building has 100 devices attached to the same Ethernet. These devices are migrated to two different shared Ethernet segments, each with 50 devices. The two segments are connected to a Cisco LAN switch to allow communication between the two sets of users. List two benefits that would be derived for a typical user.

11 Name two of the methods of internal switching on typical switches today. Which provides less latency for an individual frame?

12 What is the distance limitation of a single cable for 10BaseT? 100BaseTX?

13 Describe how a transparent bridge decides whether it should forward a frame, and tell how it chooses the interface out which to forward the frame.

14 How fast is Fast Ethernet?

15 How does a transparent bridge build its address table?

16 How many bytes long is a MAC address?

17 Assume that a building has 100 devices attached to the same Ethernet. These users then are migrated onto two separate Ethernet segments, each with 50 devices and separated by a router. List two benefits that would be derived for a typical user.

____

____

____

18 Does a bridge/switch examine just the incoming frame's source MAC, the destination MAC, or both? Why does it examine the one(s) that it examines?

____

____

____

19 Define the term *collision domain.*

____

____

____

20 Define the difference between broadcast and multicast MAC addresses.

____

____

____

21 Excluding the preamble and starting delimiter fields, but including all other Ethernet headers and trailers, what is the maximum number of bytes in an Ethernet frame?

____

____

____

22 Define the term *broadcast domain.*

____

____

____

23 Describe the benefits of creating 3 VLANs of 25 ports each, versus a single VLAN of 75 ports, in each case using a single switch. Assume that all ports are switched ports (each port is a different collision domain).

____

____

____

24 Explain the function of the loopback and collision-detection features of an Ethernet NIC in relation to half-duplex and full-duplex operations.

____

____

____

25 How many IP addresses must be configured for network management on a Cisco Catalyst 1900 switch if eight ports are to be used and with three VLANs?

____

____

____

26 What command on a 1900 series switch would cause the switch to block frames destined to 0200.7777.7777 entering interface 0/5 from going out port 0/6?

____

____

____

27 What Catalyst 1900 switch command displays the version of IOS running in the switch?

____

____

____

28 What does the Catalyst 1900 switch command **address violation disable** do?

____

____

____

29 What command erases the startup config in a Catalyst 1900 switch?

____

____

____

30 Configuration is added to the running configuration in RAM when commands are typed in Catalyst 1900 configuration mode. What causes these commands to be saved into NVRAM?

____

____

____

31 How do exec and configuration commands refer to the two Fast Ethernet ports on a Catalyst 1912 switch?

____

____

____

32 What Catalyst 1900 switch command displays the switching table?

____

____

____

Scenarios

Scenario 4-1: LAN Switch Configuration

Your job is to deploy a new LAN switch at a remote site. Figure 4-20 depicts the network. Perform the activities in the list that follows the diagram.

Figure 4-20 *Scenario 4-1: Basic LAN Switch Configuration*

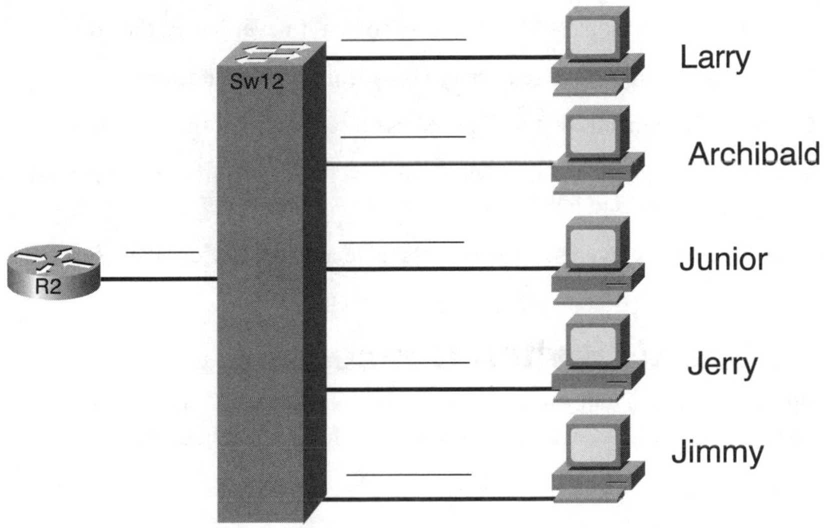

1 Clear the saved configuration before starting.
2 Assign IP address 172.16.2.254, mask 255.255.255.0, to SW12. Assign it an appropriate default gateway, and configure SW12 to use a DNS, which is at 172.16.1.250.
3 Assign a host name of SW12.
4 Choose port numbers to be used for each device, as if you were planning the physical installation. Write down these numbers on the diagram.
5 Configure so that the router uses 100-Mbps full-duplex operation.
6 Configure Archibald's MAC address so that it never leaves the address table.
7 Configure Junior so it gets frames only from Jimmy and Jerry.
8 List the commands that you would use to verify all of these features.
9 Identify the command that you would use to examine the running configuration, saved configuration, and IOS level.
10 Describe the contents of the address table after all devices have sent at least one frame.

Scenario 4-2: LAN Switch Concepts

In this scenario, you will answer some questions about a simple network diagram. Figure 4-21 depicts the network. Answer the questions that follow the diagram.

Figure 4-21 *Scenario 4-2: Basic LAN Switch Concepts*

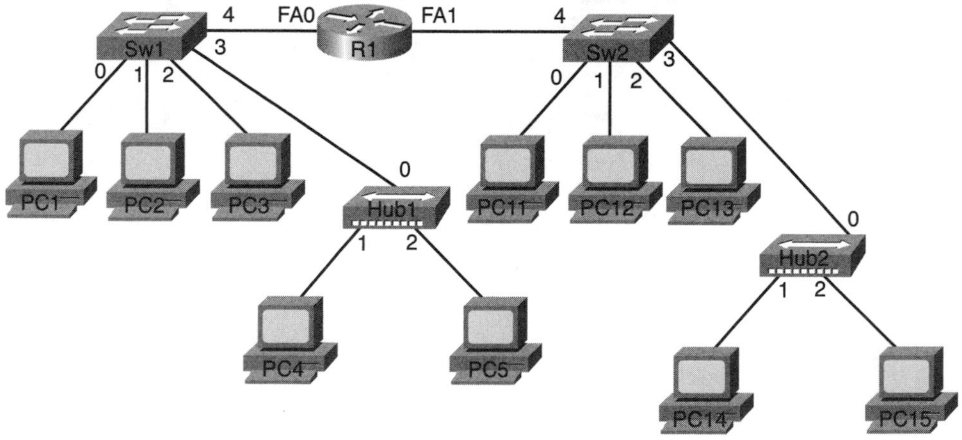

1 How many collision domains exist in this network?

2 How many broadcast domains exist in this network?

3 Assuming that all cards, switches, and router interfaces are 10/100 cards, how many ports total on each switch could run full duplex?

4 Assuming that all cards, switches, and router interfaces are 10/100 cards, how many ports total on each switch could run 100 Mbps?

5 The first frames to flow in this network are the following: PC5 sends an IP ARP, encapsulated in an Ethernet frame, to its default gateway, which is R1's FA0 interface's IP address. The Ethernet frame containing the ARP reply is the second frame. Describe what ports each frame is sent out. Use Table 4-21 to list where the frame flowed, or is draw on the diagram. If you use the table, write "received" if the frame was received in that port, or write "sent" if the frame was sent out that port.

Table 4-21 *List of Hub/Switch/Router Ports for Figure 4-21*

Port	Was Frame 1 Either Received in or Sent out This Port?	Was Frame 2 Either Received in or Sent out This Port?
Hub1—port 0		
Hub1—port 1		
Hub1—port 2		
SW1—port 0		
SW1—port 1		
SW1—port 2		
SW1—port 3		
SW1—port 4		
Hub2—port 0		
Hub2—port 1		
Hub2—port 2		
SW2—port 0		
SW2—port 1		
SW2—port 2		
SW2—port 3		
SW2—port 4		
R1—FA0		
R1—FA1		

Scenario Answers

Answers to Scenario 4-1: LAN Switch Configuration

This scenario should have forced you to perform basic LAN configuration. Figure 4-22 lists the port numbers and MAC addresses used for the solution. Example 4-7 lists the output from actually performing these steps sequentially on a 1900 series switch. An explanation of the steps follows the example.

Figure 4-22 *MAC Address Format*

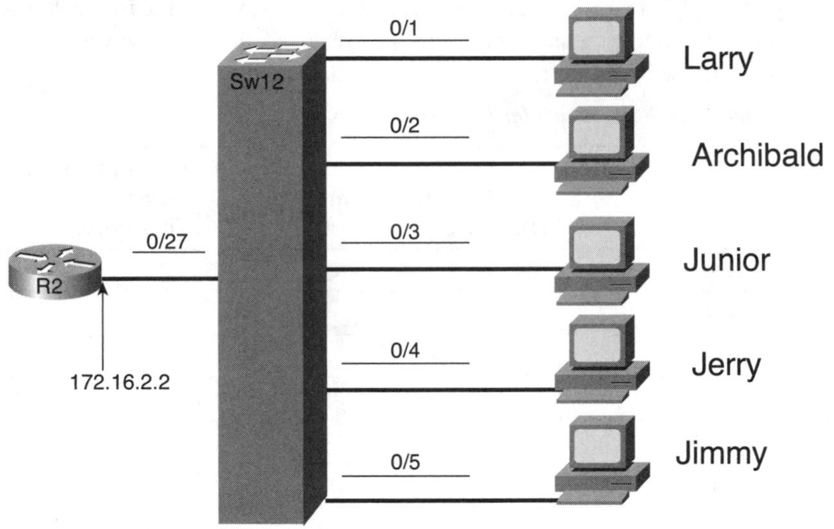

Example 4-7 *Scenario 4-1 Configuration and* **show** *Commands*

```
#delete nvram
This command resets the switch with factory defaults.  All system
parameters will revert to their default factory settings.  All static
and dynamic addresses will be removed.

Reset system with factory defaults, [Y]es or [N]o?  Yes

(some time passes…)
Catalyst 1900 Management Console
Copyright (c) Cisco Systems, Inc.  1993-1999
All rights reserved.
Enterprise Edition Software
Ethernet Address:      00-10-29-DE-7B-C0

PCA Number:            73-2241-04
PCA Serial Number:     SAD02030649
```

Example 4-7 *Scenario 4-1 Configuration and* **show** *Commands (Continued)*

```
Model Number:            WS-C1924C-EN
System Serial Number:  FAA0208T0BH
-----------------------------------------------

1 user(s) now active on Management Console.

        User Interface Menu

     [M] Menus
     [K] Command Line
     [I] IP Configuration
     [P] Console Password

Enter Selection:  K


      CLI session with the switch is open.
      To end the CLI session, enter [Exit].

>enable

#configure terminal
Enter configuration commands, one per line.  End with CNTL/Z
(config)#ip address 172.16.2.254 255.255.255.0
(config)#ip default-gateway 172.16.2.2
(config)#hostname SW12
SW12(config)#interface fastethernet 0/27
SW12(config-if)#duplex ?
  auto                 Enable auto duplex configuration
  full                 Force full duplex operation
  full-flow-control  Force full duplex with flow control
  half                 Force half duplex operation
SW12(config-if)#duplex full
SW12(config-if)#interface e 0/1
SW12(config-if)#duplex auto
Error: Invalid configuration for this interface
SW12(config)#mac-address-table permanent 0000.0c3E.5183 e 0/2
SW12(config)#mac-address-table restricted static 0100.3333.3333 e0/3 e0/4 e0/5
12(config)#exit
SW12#show mac-address-table
Number of permanent addresses : 1
Number of restricted static addresses : 1
Number of dynamic addresses : 2

Address             Dest Interface    Type         Source Interface List
----------------------------------------------------------------------------
0000.0C3E.5183    Ethernet 0/2      Permanent    All
0100.3333.3333    Ethernet 0/3      Static       Et0/4,Et0/5
0000.0C4A.8BCA    Ethernet 0/1      Dynamic      All
0004.5A0A.EBBE    Ethernet 0/6      Dynamic      All
SW12#show version
Cisco Catalyst 1900/2820 Enterprise Edition Software
Version V9.00.04
```

continues

Example 4-7 *Scenario 4-1 Configuration and* **show** *Commands (Continued)*

```
Copyright (c) Cisco Systems, Inc.  1993-1999
SW12 uptime is 0day(s) 00hour(s) 05minute(s) 45second(s)
cisco Catalyst 1900 (486sxl) processor with 2048K/1024K bytes of memory
Hardware board revision is 1
Upgrade Status: No upgrade currently in progress.
Config File Status: No configuration upload/download is in progress
27 Fixed Ethernet/IEEE 802.3 interface(s)
Base Ethernet Address: 00-10-29-DE-7B-C0

SW12#show running-config
Building configuration...
Current configuration:
!
mac-address-table permanent 0000.0C3E.5183 Ethernet 0/2
mac-address-table restricted static 0100.3333.3333 Ethernet 0/3 Ethernet 0/4
Ethernet 0/5
!
hostname "SW12"
!
ip address 172.16.2.254 255.255.255.0
ip default-gateway 172.16.2.2
ip domain-name  "atl.mediaone.net"
ip name-server 24.88.1.66
ip name-server 24.88.1.67
!
interface Ethernet 0/1

!
interface Ethernet 0/2

!
interface Ethernet 0/3
!
interface Ethernet 0/4
!
interface Ethernet 0/5
!
interface Ethernet 0/6
!
interface Ethernet 0/7
!
interface Ethernet 0/8
!
interface Ethernet 0/9
!
interface Ethernet 0/10
!
interface Ethernet 0/11
!
interface Ethernet 0/12
!
```

Example 4-7 *Scenario 4-1 Configuration and* **show** *Commands (Continued)*

```
interface Ethernet 0/13
!
interface Ethernet 0/14
!
interface Ethernet 0/15
!
interface Ethernet 0/16
!
interface Ethernet 0/17
!
interface Ethernet 0/18
!
interface Ethernet 0/19
!
interface Ethernet 0/20
!
interface Ethernet 0/21
!
interface Ethernet 0/22
!
interface Ethernet 0/23
!
interface Ethernet 0/24
!
interface Ethernet 0/25
!
interface FastEthernet 0/26
!
interface FastEthernet 0/27
  duplex full
!
line console
end
SW12#show startup
          ^
% Invalid input detected at '^' marker.
SW12#show config
          ^
% Invalid input detected at '^' marker.
SW12#
```

Example 4-7 begins with the startup config being deleted using the **delete nvram** configuration. Because only one configuration file exists, the command also clears the running config. As shown in the example, some time passes (about 10 seconds) and then the console is presented with the usual option for the menu system or the command line. In this case, the command line is chosen. The **delete nvram** command does clear the MAC table and put everything in VLAN 1 (the default), so it interrupts typical switch operation. The global commands for setting the IP address, default gateway, and host name are straightforward.

You need to know some information about 1900 switch architecture to get the configuration completely correct. For example, the 1900 has only 10-Mbps or 100-Mbps ports, but no autosensing 10/100 ports. Also, full-duplex operation is supported only on 100-Mbps ports. So, the only ports that can do any negotiation are the two uplink ports, namely 0/26 and 0/27. (To prove the point, in Example 4-7, the **duplex auto** command failed on interface E 0/1.) In this case, 0/27 is used to connect to R2, and it is set to full-duplex mode.

The static entry in the MAC table and the restricted port pose the most challenging part of the configuration. Although the entry is indeed static, the term used for Cisco IOS switches for statically configured entries in the MAC table is *permanent*. So, the **mac-address-table permanent 0000.0c3E.5183 e 0/2** command permanently places the MAC address in the MAC table, off port e 0/2. The command that restricts traffic to Junior so that only Jimmy and Jerry can reach him is **mac-address-table restricted static 0100.3333.3333 e0/3 e0/4 e0/5.** The **show mac-address-table** command lists the results of these two commands—one permanent entry and one MAC address with restrictions so that it is accessible only from ports 0/4 and 0/5.

Finally, you view the configuration file with the **show running-config** command. Because there is only one config file, there is no need for a **show startup-config** command or a **show config** command. Notice that both commands are rejected at the end of Example 4-7.

Answers to Scenario 4-2: LAN Switch Concepts

This scenario tests your recollection of a few of the core concepts for LAN switching. The answers are listed in succession:

1. Ten collision domains exist in the network for this scenario. Routers and switches separate LANs into separate collision domains, but shared hubs do not. In this diagram, each switch port and the device(s) connected to it form the individual collision domains.
2. Two broadcast domains exist in this network. Switches and hubs do not separate the LAN segments into different broadcast domains, but routers do. The two broadcast domains consist of the devices to the left of R1 and the devices to the right of R1.
3. Eight total switch ports could run full-duplex operation. Port 3 on each switch could not because there is a shared hub attached to this port, so collisions could happen. When collisions could happen, FDX is not allowed.
4. All ten switch ports could run 100 Mbps Fast Ethernet. Router FastEthernet interfaces support 100 Mbps, and the assumption was made that all the PCs support 100 Mbps. Shared hubs also can support 100 Mbps. So, all switch ports could run at 100 Mbps, but port 3 on each switch could not use full-duplex operation.
5. Figures 4-23 and 4-24 depict the flows of frame 1 and frame 2. Frame 1 has a source of PC5 and a broadcast destination. Frame 2 has a source of R1's FA0 MAC address and a destination of PC5's MAC address. Table 4-22 also describes the ports that the frames came in and out on their journeys, respectively.

Figure 4-23 *Scenario 4-2: Path of First Frame in Question Number 5*

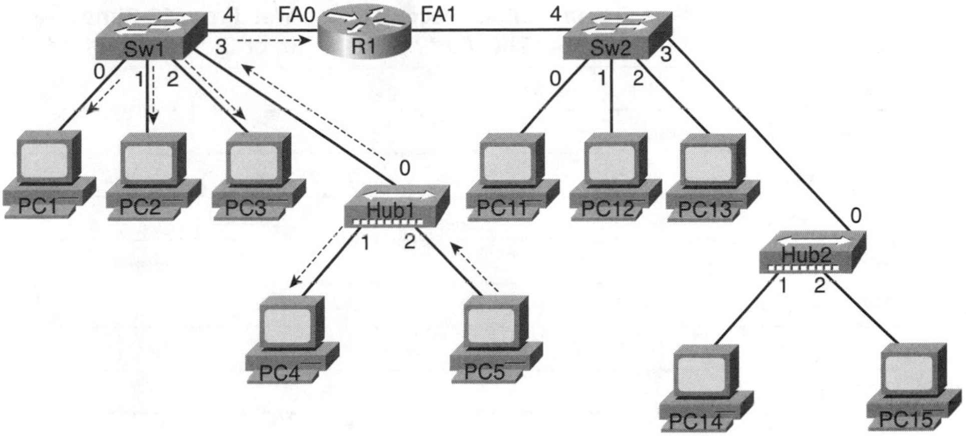

Figure 4-24 *Scenario 4-2: Path of Second Frame in Question Number 5*

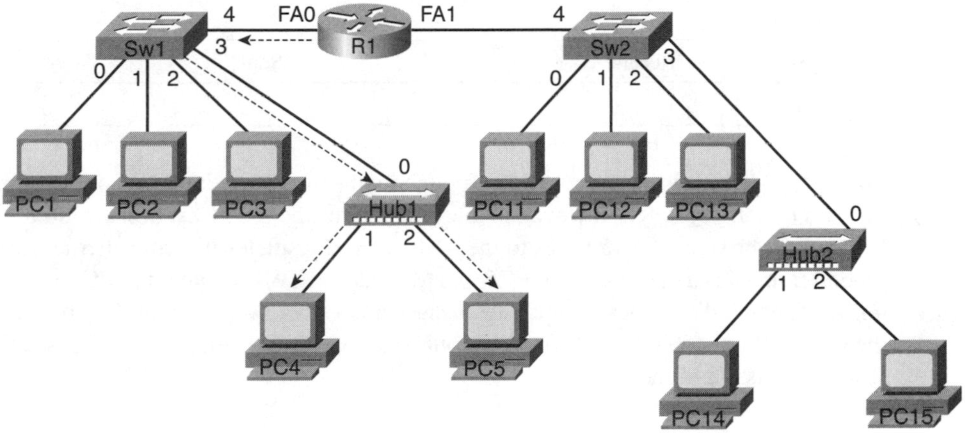

Table 4-22 *Table of Incoming and Outgoing Ports for Frames in Scenario 4-2, Question 5*

Port	Was Frame 1 Either Received in or Sent out This Port?	Was Frame 2 Either Received in or Sent out This Port?
Hub1—port 0	Sent	Received
Hub1—port 1	Sent	Sent
Hub1—port 2	Received	Sent
SW1—port 0	Sent	

continues

Table 4-22 *Table of Incoming and Outgoing Ports for Frames in Scenario 4-2, Question 5 (Continued)*

Port	Was Frame 1 Either Received in or Sent out This Port?	Was Frame 2 Either Received in or Sent out This Port?
SW1—port 1	Sent	
SW1—port 2	Sent	
SW1—port 3	Received	Sent
SW1—port 4	Sent	Received
Hub2—port 0		
Hub2—port 1		
Hub2—port 2		
SW2—port 0		
SW2—port 1		
SW2—port 2		
SW2—port 3		
SW2—port 4		
R1—FA0	Received	Sent
R1—FA1		

Frame 1 is a broadcast, so it must flow throughout the broadcast domain. So, Hub1 and Switch1 forward out all ports. R1, however, is the boundary of the broadcast domain, so R1 does not forward the broadcast. R1 replies to the ARP and encapsulates it in an Ethernet frame. This second frame has a destination of PC5's MAC address. SW1 learned that PC5's MAC is out its port 3. The hub did not learn anything because it does not keep an address table. So, R1 sends the second frame to PC5. SW1 forwards only out port 3, according to its address table. The hub still forwards out all ports.

Exam Topics in This Chapter

3 Describe the operation of the Spanning Tree Protocol and its benefits.

4 Describe the benefits of virtual LANs.

CHAPTER 5

Intermediate LANs: Spanning Tree, VLANs, and Trunking

Engineers need a basic knowledge of LANs and Ethernet to plan, design, build, and troubleshoot a small site with a single LAN. However, when building a larger intermediate-sized LAN, several additional LAN features must be understood. You can install LANs that use VLANs and multiple switches without understanding a lot of what is in this chapter, but if you want the network to work well, you should understand these topics.

Most LANs with multiple interconnected switches have redundant Ethernets between the switches. For such a LAN to be usable, the Spanning Tree Protocol (STP) must be used. The first topic in this chapter describes how STP prevents loops while allowing the redundancy to be used for backup purposes. STP, however, solves a large problem but creates smaller ones—but Cisco provides several features to optimize networks that must use STP. So, STP and one feature that helps optimize STP, called EtherChannel, are covered in the first section.

The second section in this chapter covers virtual LANs (VLANs). VLANs allow the engineer to create multiple broadcast domains in a single switch or spanning multiple interconnected switches. Because typical designs imply that a single IP subnet is the same set of devices that are in the same Layer 2 broadcast domain, VLANs allow multiple subnets to be designed into a single LAN switch infrastructure. Engineers design networks using VLANs in almost every LAN that is bigger than 100 devices at the site, making VLANs a very important topic on the CCNA exam.

Designing networks using VLANs requires consideration of two related topics. First, the switches must "tag" a frame with the VLAN identifier when sending the frame to another switch so that the receiving switch knows what VLAN the frame is in. *Trunking* is the term that Cisco uses to describe a link over which frame tagging is done. The second related topic uses the word trunking in its name, but it's different than trunking. Namely, the VLAN Trunking Protocol (VTP) defines a Cisco-proprietary method of exchanging VLAN configuration information so that VLAN configuration is more consistent and correct. Both trunking and VTP are key concepts in building LANs using Cisco switches.

Cisco does not list many "exam topics" for CCNA that happen to match the topics in this chapter. In fact, no exam topic listed on the Cisco Web site mentions configuration of LAN switches or, specifically, the 1900 series switch; nonetheless, these topics are on the exam. However, there will probably be more coverage on the average test on the LAN topics from the previous chapter than this chapter.

How to Best Use This Chapter

By taking the following steps, you can make better use of your study time:

- Keep your notes and the answers for all your work with this book in one place, for easy reference.
- Take the "Do I Know This Already?" quiz, and write down your answers. Studies show that retention is significantly increased through writing down facts and concepts, even if you never look at the information again.
- Use the diagram in Figure 5-1 to guide you to the next step.

Figure 5-1 *How to Use This Chapter*

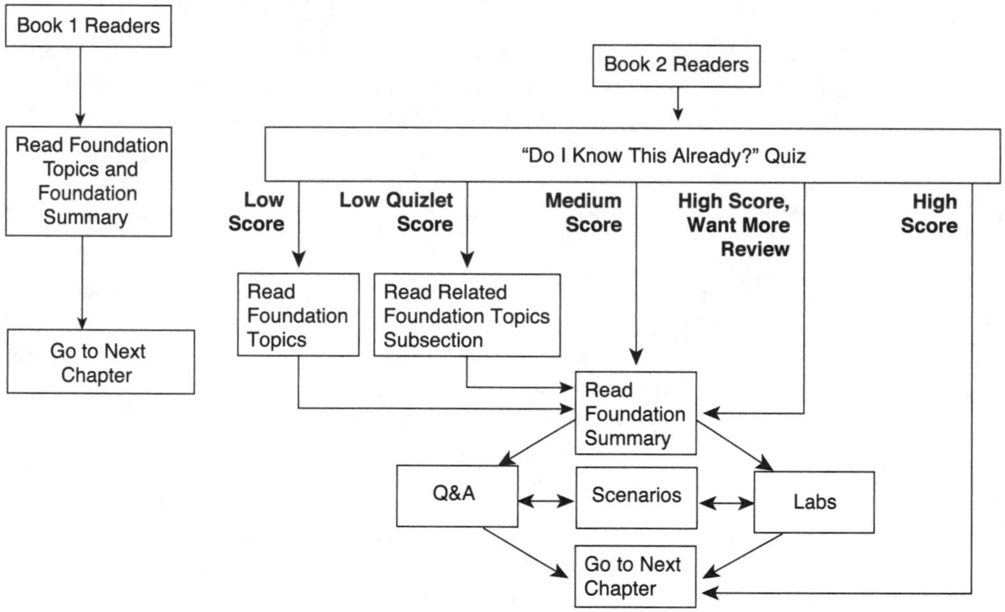

"Do I Know This Already?" Quiz

The purpose of the "Do I Know This Already?" quiz is to help you decide what parts of this chapter to use. If you already intend to read the entire chapter, you do not necessarily need to answer these questions now.

This 12-question quiz helps you determine how to spend your limited study time. The quiz is sectioned into four smaller four-question "quizlets," which correspond to the three major headings in the chapter. Suggestions on how to spend your time in this chapter, based on your quiz scores, are outlined in 5-1. Use Table 5-1 to record your score.

Table 5-1 *Scoresheet for Quiz and Quizlets*

Quizlet Number	Foundation Topics Section Covering These Questions	Questions	Score
1	Spanning Tree Protocol	1 to 4	
2	Virtual LANs and Trunking	5 to 8	
3	LAN Switch Configuration	9 to 12	
All questions		1 to 12	

1 What routing protocol does a transparent bridge use to learn about Layer 3 addressing groupings?

____

____

____

2 What settings are examined by a bridge or switch to determine which should be elected as root of the spanning tree?

____

____

____

3 If a switch hears three different hello BPDUs from three different neighbors on three different interfaces, and if all three specify that Bridge 1 is the root, how does the switch choose which interface is its root port?

____

____

____

4 Can the root bridge/switch ports be placed in blocking state?

____

____

____

5 Define the term *VLAN*.

____

____

____

6 Describe the benefits of creating 3 VLANs of 25 ports each versus creating a single VLAN of 75 ports, in each case using a single switch. Assume that all ports are switched ports (each port is a different collision domain).

____

____

____

7 If two Cisco LAN switches are connected using Fast Ethernet, what VLAN trunking protocols could be used? If only one VLAN spanned both switches, is a VLAN trunking protocol needed?

____

____

____

8 Must all members of the same VLAN be in the same collision domain, the same broadcast domain, or both?

____

____

____

9 What Catalyst 1900 switch command assigns a port to a particular VLAN?

____

____

____

10 What Catalyst 1900 switch command creates VLAN 10 and assigns it a name of bigbadvlan?

11 What Catalyst 1900 switch command lists the details about VLAN 10?

12 What two 1900 series exec commands list information about the spanning tree for VLAN 2?

The answers to the quiz are found in Appendix A, "Answers to the 'Do I Know This Already?' Quizzes and Q&A Sections." The suggested choices for your next step are as follows:

- **8 or less overall score**—Read the entire chapter. This includes the "Foundation Topics" and "Foundation Summary" sections and the Q&A section at the end of the chapter.
- **2 or less on any quizlet**—Review the subsection(s) of the "Foundation Topics" part of this chapter, based on Table 5-1. Then move into the "Foundation Summary" section and the Q&A section at the end of the chapter.
- **9 to 10 overall score**—Begin with the "Foundation Summary" section, and then go to the Q&A section and the scenarios at the end of the chapter.
- **11 or more overall score**—If you want more review on these topics, skip to the "Foundation Summary" section, and then go to the Q&A section at the end of the chapter. Otherwise, move to the next chapter.

Foundation Topics

Spanning-Tree Protocol

1 Describe the operation of the Spanning Tree Protocol and its benefits.

In the absence of STP, frames would loop for an indefinite period of time in networks with physically redundant links. STP blocks some ports so that only one active path exists between any pair of LAN segments (collision domains). The result of STP is both good and bad: Frames do not loop infinitely, which makes the LAN usable, which is good. However, the network does not actively take advantage of some of the redundant links because they are blocked to prevent frames from looping. Some users' traffic travels a seemingly longer path through the network because a shorter physical path is blocked, which is bad. However, the net result (yep, I wrote that on purpose!) is good: If frames looped indefinitely, the LAN would be unusable, anyway. So, STP has some minor unfortunate side effects compared to the major benefit of letting us build redundant LANs.

To avoid loops, all bridging devices, including switches, use STP. STP causes each interface on a bridging device to settle into a *blocking* state or a *forwarding* state. Blocking means that the interface cannot forward or receive data frames, but it can send and receive bridge protocol data units (BPDUs); forwarding means that the interface can both send and receive data frames as well as BPDUs. By having a correct subset of the interfaces blocked, a single currently active logical path will exist between each pair of LANs.

STP behaves identically for a transparent bridge and a switch. So, in this section, the terms *bridge, switch*, and *bridging device* refer to a device that can run STP.

A simple example makes the need for STP more obvious. Remember, frames destined for unknown MAC addresses, or broadcasts, will be forwarded out all interfaces. Figure 5-2 shows a single frame, sent by Larry, looping forever because the network has redundancy but STP is not enabled.

Figure 5-2 *Network with Redundant Links but Without STP—Frame Loops Forever*

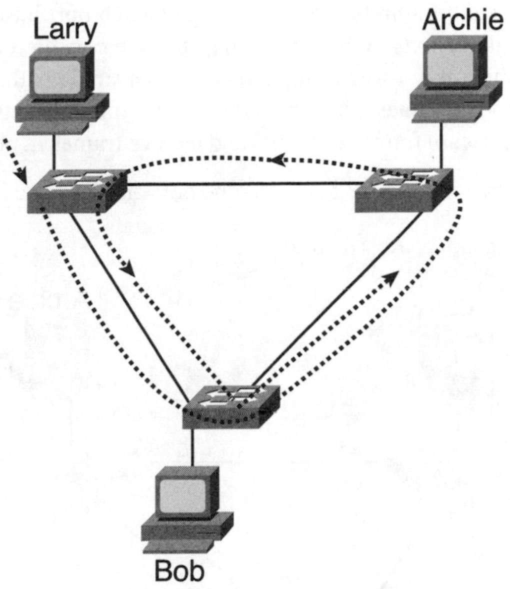

Larry sends a single unicast frame to Bob's MAC address, but Bob is powered off and none of the switches has learned Bob's MAC address yet. Frames addressed to Bob's MAC address will loop forever—or at least until time is no more! Because the switches never learn Bob's MAC address, they keep forwarding the frame out all ports, and copies of the frame go around and around. Ethernet does not define a mechanism to mark a frame so that it can be thrown away by a bridge if it the frame loops. (IP does have that feature, using the Time To Live field.) The frame would loop until one of the links that create the redundancy fails.

Similarly, bridges and switches forward broadcasts on all interfaces, so if any of the PCs sent a broadcast, the broadcast would loop indefinitely as well.

Most engineers will not design a multiswitch LAN without physical redundancy between the switches. Without STP, a LAN design with redundancy will become simply unusable. So, good design practices require physical redundancy, and STP allows physical redundancy to exist and work well. The right solution includes bridged/switched networks with physical redundancy, using spanning tree to dynamically block some interface(s) so that *only one active path exists at any instant in time*.

What Spanning Tree Does

The spanning-tree algorithm places each bridge/switch port into either a *forwarding* state or a *blocking* state. All the ports in the forwarding state are considered to be in the current *spanning tree*. The collective set of forwarding ports creates a single path over which frames are sent. Switches can forward frames out ports and receive frames in ports that are in a forwarding state; switches do not forward frames out ports and receive frames in ports that are in a blocking state.

Figure 5-3 shows a simple STP tree with one port on SW3 in a blocking state.

Figure 5-3 *Network with Redundant Links, with STP*

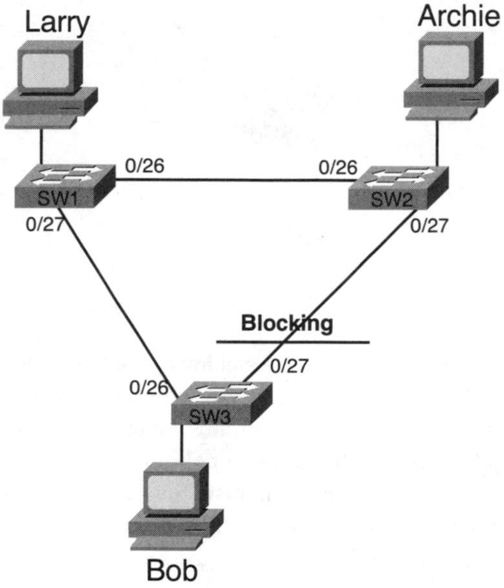

Now when Larry sends a frame to Bob's MAC address, the frame does not loop. SW1 sends a copy to SW3, but SW3 cannot forward it to SW2 out its port 0/27 because it is blocking. However, STP happens to cause some frames to use a longer physical path for the sake of preventing loops. For instance, if Archie wants to send a frame to Bob, it has to go from SW2, to SW1, and then to SW3—a longer path than is physically required. You must prevent the loops, but you then have to live with a less efficient path for some traffic.

If the link between SW1 and SW3 fails, STP would reconverge so that SW3 would no longer block. For instance, in Figure 5-4, that link has failed and STP has changed.

Figure 5-4 *Network with Redundant Links and with STP, After Link Failure*

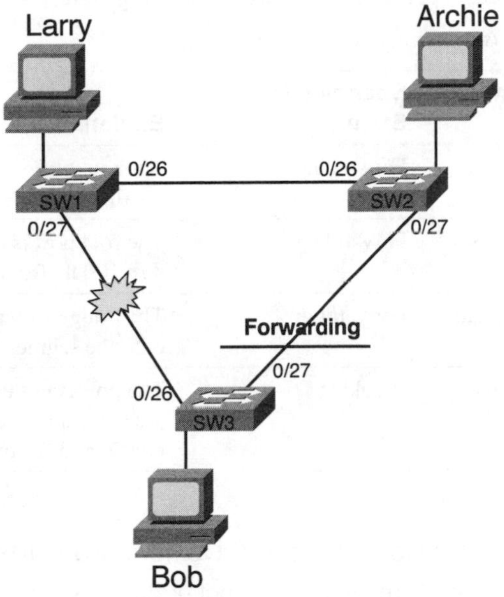

How does STP manage to make switches block or forward on each interface? And how does it reconverge to change state from blocking to forwarding to take advantage of redundant links in response to network outages? The rest of the section on STP answers those questions.

How Spanning Tree Works

The STP algorithm creates a spanning tree of interfaces that either forward or block. STP actually places interfaces into forwarding state; by default, if an interface has no reason to be in forwarding state, it is placed into a blocking state. In other words, STP simply picks which interfaces should forward.

So, how does STP choose whether to put an interface into forwarding state? Well, it uses three criteria:

- STP elects a root bridge. All interfaces on the root bridge are in forwarding state.
- Each nonroot bridge considers one of its ports to have the least administrative cost between itself and the root bridge. STP places this least-root-cost interface, called that bridge's *root port*, into the forwarding state.
- Many bridges can attach to the same segment. These bridges advertise BPDUs declaring their administrative cost to the root bridge. The bridge with the lowest such cost of all bridges on that segment is called the *designated bridge*. The interface on the *designated bridge* that sends this lowest-cost BPDU is the *designated port* on that LAN segment, and that port is placed in a forwarding state.

All other interfaces are placed in a blocking state. Table 5-2 summarizes the reasons why spanning tree places a port in forwarding or blocking state.

Table 5-2 *Spanning Tree: Reasons for Forwarding or Blocking*

Characterization of Port	Spanning Tree State	Explanation
All root bridge's ports	Forwarding	The root bridge is always the designated bridge on all connected segments.
Each nonroot bridge's root port	Forwarding	The root port is the port receiving the lowest-cost BPDU from the root.
Each LAN's designated port	Forwarding	The bridge forwarding the lowest-cost BPDU onto the segment is the designated bridge.
All other ports	Blocking	The port is not used for forwarding frames, nor are any frames received on these interfaces considered for forwarding.

Electing the Root, Discovering Root Ports and Designated Ports

Each bridge begins by claiming to be the root bridge by sending STP messages. STP defines these messages used to exchange information with other bridges, which are called *bridge protocol data units (BPDUs)*. Each bridge begins by sending a BPDU stating the following:

- **The root bridge's bridge ID**—At the beginning of the process, each bridge claims to be root, so this value is the same as the bridge ID of this bridge.
- **An administratively set priority**—This is the priority of the root bridge. At the beginning of the process, each bridge claims to be root, so this value is the priority of this bridge.
- **The cost to reach the root from this bridge**—At the beginning of the process, each bridge claims to be root, so the value is set to 0, which is this bridge's cost to reach itself.
- **The bridge ID of the sender of this BPDU**—This value is always the bridge ID of the sender of the BPDU, regardless of whether this bridge is the root.

The bridges elect a root bridge to begin the process. The root bridge will be the bridge with the lowest priority value. If a tie occurs based on priority, the root bridge with the lowest ID will be the root. The bridge IDs should be unique; bridges and switches use one of their own MAC addresses as their bridge ID, so the bridge IDs are unique because MAC addresses are supposed to be unique.

The message used to identify the root and its priority, ID, and cost is called a hello BPDU.

STP elects a root bridge, in a manner not unlike a political election. The process of choosing the root begins with all bridges claiming to be the root by sending hello BPDUs with their bridge IDs and priorities. If a bridge hears of a better candidate, it stops advertising itself as root and starts forwarding the hello sent by the better political candidate, much like a candidate does when leaving a political race: the lesser candidate throws support behind another candidate. Eventually, someone wins and everyone supports the elected switch, which is where the political race analogy falls apart.

Figure 5-5 outlines a part of the process. Imagine that SW1 has advertised itself as root, as have SW2 and SW3. SW2 now believes that SW1 is a better root.

Figure 5-5 *Root Election Process*

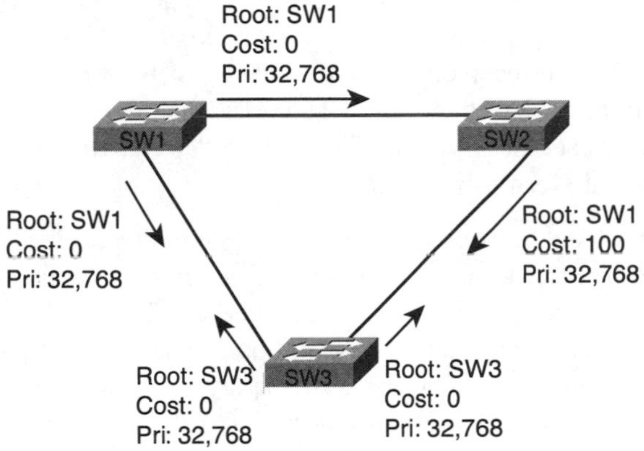

Two candidates still exist in Figure 5-5—namely, SW1 and SW3. So who wins? Well, the lower-priority switch wins; if there is a tie, the lower MAC address wins. For the sake of discussion, imagine that SW1 wins. Figure 5-6 shows the hello messages sent by the switches.

Figure 5-6 *SW1 Wins Election*

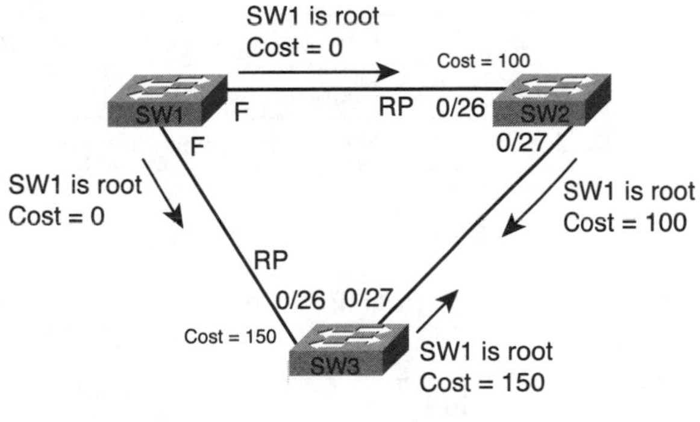

SW1's interfaces are placed into a forwarding state because SW1 won the election. All interfaces on the root switch forward. But what about SW2 and SW3's interfaces? Well, the second reason that an interface forwards is if it is the root port on that switch. Each switch has one root port, which is the port receiving the least-cost BPDU from the root. From Figure 5-6, SW2's best cost is seen in the hello entering its port 0/26. Likewise, SW3's best cost is seen entering its 0/26 port. So, the figure lists the acronym "RP" beside each of those ports. SW2 and SW3 place those ports into a forwarding state, respectively.

NOTE If root hello BPDUs enter both interfaces and the costs are identical, Cisco switches choose the lowest-numbered port—so, the same ports would have been chosen as in this example.

Finally, interfaces forward if they advertise the lowest-cost hello onto a LAN segment. In Figure 5-6, both SW2 and SW3 forward hello messages onto the link between them. The cost is calculated by adding the cost in the received hello (0, in this case), to the cost of the interface in which the hello was received. So, SW2 added cost 100 to 0, and SW3 added 150 to 0. The costs can be configured, or they can default. (The defaults are listed later.) So, because SW2 advertises the lowest cost, SW2's 0/27 port is the *designated port* on that LAN segment. SW2 places that port into forwarding state.

The only interface on the three switches that does not forward is SW3's 0/27 port, which is the same spanning-tree topology listed in Figure 5-3. The process is now complete, with all ports in forwarding state except for SW3's E0/27 interface. Table 5-3 outlines the state of each port and shows why it is in that state. The default port costs defined by IEE are listed in Table 5-4. The cost values were revised once because the original values, set in the early 1980s, did not anticipate the growth of Ethernet to support 10-Gigabit Ethernet.

Table 5-3 *The State of Each Interface*

Bridge Interface	State	Reason Interface Is in Forwarding State
SW1, E 0/26	Forwarding	Interface is on root bridge
SW1, E 0/27	Forwarding	Interface is on root bridge
SW2, E 0/26	Forwarding	Root port
SW2, E 0/27	Forwarding	Designated port on the LAN segment to SW3
SW3, E 0/26	Forwarding	Root port
SW3, E 0/27	Blocking	Not root bridge, not root port, not designated port

Table 5-4 *Default Port Costs According to IEEE*

Speed of Ethernet	Original IEEE Cost	Revised IEEE Cost
10 Mbps	100	100
100 Mbps	10	19
1 Gbps	1	4
10 Gbps	1	2

Reacting to Changes in the Network

After the STP topology has been set, it does not change unless the network topology changes. Although some of the basics about STP convergence might be on the CCNA exam, the details of all the variations on how this occurs are beyond the scope of the exam. If you want more information, a great detailed explanation is contained in *Cisco LAN Switching*, by Clark and Hamilton. But it is worth the time to think about a single example of how STP changes its topology when reacting to network changes because you can learn a couple of important terms that you will see in real life when working with STP.

The root bridge sends a new BPDU, called a hello, every 2 seconds, by default. Each bridge forwards the hello, changing the cost to reflect that bridge's added cost to reach the root. When a bridge ceases to receive the hellos, it reacts and starts the process of changing the spanning tree, under the assumption that the reason that the hello BPDUs quit arriving is that something has failed in the network.

The hello BPDU defines the timers used by all the bridges when choosing when to react:

- **Hello time**—The time that the root waits before sending the periodic hello BPDUs, which then are forwarded by successive switches/bridges. The default is 2 seconds.
- **MaxAge**—The time that any bridge should wait before deciding that the topology has changed. Usually it is a multiple of the hello time; the default is 20 seconds.
- **Forward delay**—Delay that affects the time involved when an interface changes from a blocking state to a forwarding state; this timer is covered in more depth shortly.

When the network is up and no problems are occurring, the process works like this:

1. The root sends a hello BPDU, with a cost of 0, out all its interfaces.
2. The neighboring bridges forward hello BPDUs out their nonroot, designated ports, referring to the root but with their cost added.
3. Step 2 is repeated by each bridge in the network as it receives these hello BPDUs.
4. The root repeats Step 1 every hello time.
5. If a bridge does not get a Hello BPDU in hello time, it continues as normal. If a bridge fails to receive a Hello BPDU in MaxAge time, the bridge reacts.

For example, imagine that the link between SW1 and SW3 fails, as depicted in Figure 5-7.

Figure 5-7 *Reacting to Link Failure Between SW1 and SW3*

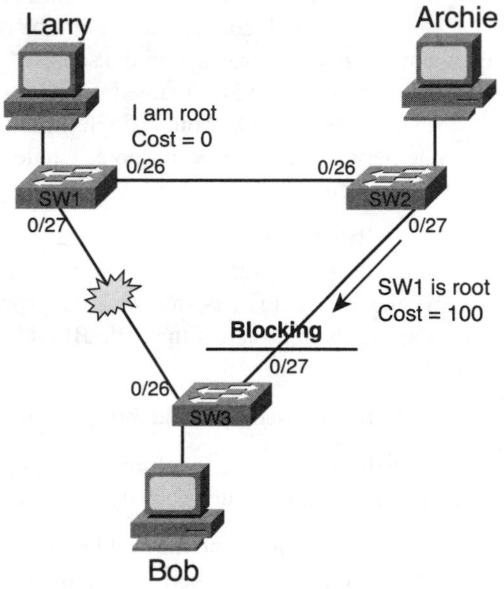

SW3 reacts to the change, but SW2 does not. SW3 ceases to receive the hello message in its 0/26 interface—SW3's "best" hello, with cost=0. Remember, when a switch ceases to hear its best hello message after MaxAge time, it reacts. However, SW2 continues to receive its best hello BPDU, so it does not react.

After MaxAge expires, SW3 either advertises itself as root again or believes the next-best claim to who should be root. Because SW2 is forwarding SW1's claim to be root and SW1 was already root, SW1 must have a better (lower) priority or better (lower) MAC address than SW3. So, SW3 does the following:

- Decides that its 0/27 interface is now its root port because SW3 is receiving a hello with a lower priority. (If SW3 had a lower priority, it would already have been root!) So, SW3 places 0/27 in forwarding state.
- Interface 0/26 probably has physically failed, so that interface is in blocking state.
- SW3 flushes its address table for those two interfaces because the location of MAC addresses, relative to itself, might have changed. For instance, Larry's MAC address formerly was reachable out 0/26 and will now be reachable out 0/27.

However, SW3 cannot immediately transition from blocking for forwarding on its 0/27 port. If SW3 immediately transitioned to forwarding on 0/27 and other bridges/switches also were converging, loops could occur. To prevent this, two intermediate states are used. The first, *listening*, allows each device to wait to make sure that there are no new, better Hellos with a new, better root. The second state, *learning*, is used to learn the new location of MAC addresses, without allowing forwarding. This prevents the switches from flooding frames until all the switches have converged and learned the new MAC addresses. Table 5-5 summarizes the intermediate states of the spanning tree.

Table 5-5 *Spanning Tree Interface States*

State	Forward Data Frames?	Learn MACs Based on Received Frames?	Transitory or Stable State?
Blocking	No	No	Stable
Listening	No	No	Transitory
Learning	No	Yes	Transitory
Forwarding	Yes	Yes	Stable

Spanning-Tree Protocol Summary

Spanning trees accomplish the goals of allowing physical redundancy, but with only one currently active path through a bridged network. Spanning tree uses the following features to accomplish the goal:

- All bridge interfaces eventually stabilize at either a forwarding state or a blocking state. The forwarding interfaces are considered to be a part of the spanning tree.
- One of the bridges is elected as root. The election process includes all bridges claiming to be root, until one is considered best by all. All root bridge interfaces are in forwarding state.
- Each bridge receives hello BPDUs from the root, either directly or forwarded by some other bridge. Each bridge can receive more than one such message on its interfaces, but the port in which the least-cost BPDU is received is called the root port of a bridge, and that port is placed in forwarding state.
- For each LAN segment, one bridge sends the forwarded BPDU with the lowest cost. That bridge is the designated bridge for that segment. That bridge's interface on that segment is placed in forwarding state.
- All other interfaces are placed in blocking state.
- The root sends BPDUs every hello time seconds. The other bridges expect to receive copies of these BPDUs so that they know that nothing has changed. Hello time is defined in the BPDU itself, so all bridges use the same value.

- If a bridge does not receive a BPDU for MaxAge time, it begins the process of causing the spanning tree to change. The reaction can vary from topology to topology. (MaxAge is defined in the BPDU itself, so all bridges use the same value.)
- One or more bridges decide to change interfaces from blocking to forwarding, or vice versa, depending on the change in the network. If moving from blocking to forwarding, the interim listening state is entered first. After forward delay time (another timer defined in the root BPDU), the state is changed to learning. After another forward delay time, the interface is placed in forwarding state.
- The Spanning-Tree Protocol includes these delays to help ensure that no temporary loops occur.

Virtual LANs

4 Describe the benefits of virtual LANs.

This chapter focuses on some of the additional features that are required to implement intermediate-sized LANs. Chapter 4, "LANs, Bridges, and Switches," focused on the basics of LANs. Frankly, though you probably could have bought several Cisco switches, cabled them together, and made them work with absolutely no configuration required, ignoring everything we have covered so far. Why is that? Well, Cisco switches with 10/100 ports autonegotiate by default. Cisco switches place all ports in VLAN 1 by default, which effectively means that the switch behaves as if the concept of VLANs did not exist at all. And STP is enabled by default, so even if you cabled the switches in a redundant configuration, it still would have worked. The only thing not spelled out here was whether to use a straight-through or cross-over Ethernet cable. Sure, you would be missing a few things if you had not configured anything on the switches, such as some basic administrative information, but the switches would work for the attached devices.

When creating a LAN design, there is a good chance that you will use VLANs. Using VLANs make technological sense and economic sense. However, implementing switches that use VLANs requires some configuration on your part. The configuration is not hard; to reduce mistakes, Cisco even provides tools to dynamically exchange VLAN information among switches.

A *virtual LAN (VLAN)* is a broadcast domain created by one or more switches. The VLAN is created by configuration in the switch. So, instead of all ports on a switch forming a single broadcast domain, the switch separates them into many, based on configuration. It's really that simple.

Two example networks provide enough context to see the great benefit of VLANs. Before VLANs existed, if a design specified three separate broadcast domains, three switches would be used—one for each broadcast domain. And because a switch can forward frames only between devices in the same VLAN, each switch also would be connected to a router so that the router could forward packets among the three broadcast domains. So, if there was a need for three different broadcast domains, three switches would be purchased and three router Ethernet ports would be needed as well. Figure 5-8 shows just such a network.

Figure 5-8 *Example Network with Three Broadcast Domains and No VLANs*

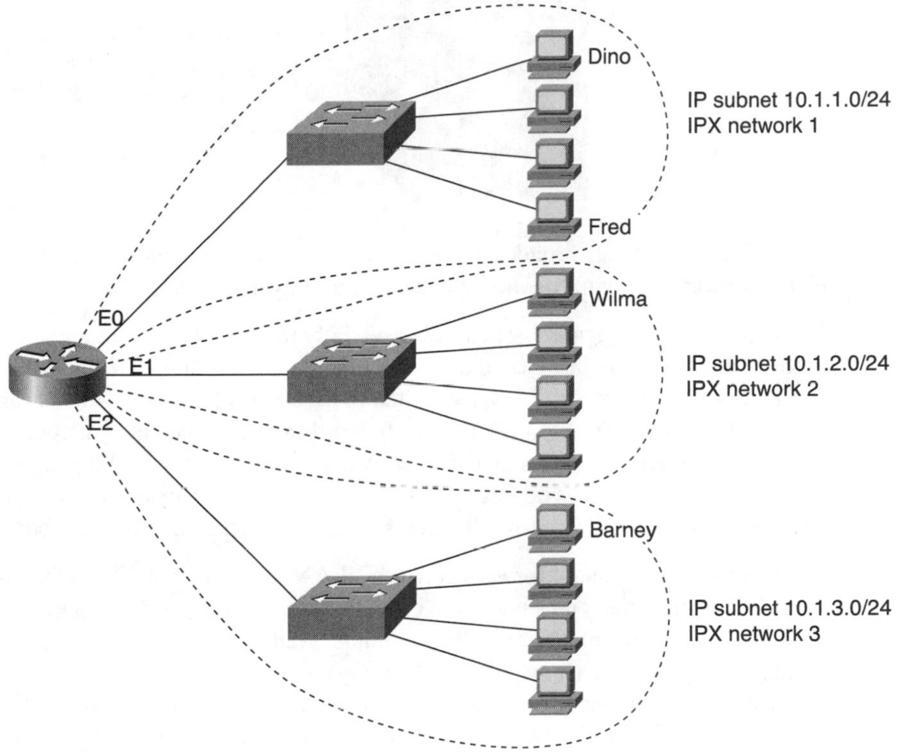

Three separate hardware switches were required in Figure 5-8 because three broadcast domains were needed. If a switch could logically separate ports into different broadcast domains, only one switch would be required. So, a switch supporting VLANs would be configured to place each port into one of three different groups, with each group being a VLAN. For instance, in Figure 5-9, one switch is used; the switch is configured so that each port is considered to be in one of three different broadcast domains or VLANs.

In both cases, separate broadcast domains imply separate Layer 3 groupings; a router is needed for forwarding traffic among the different Layer 3 groups.

Figure 5-9 *Example with Three Broadcast Domains and Three VLANs*

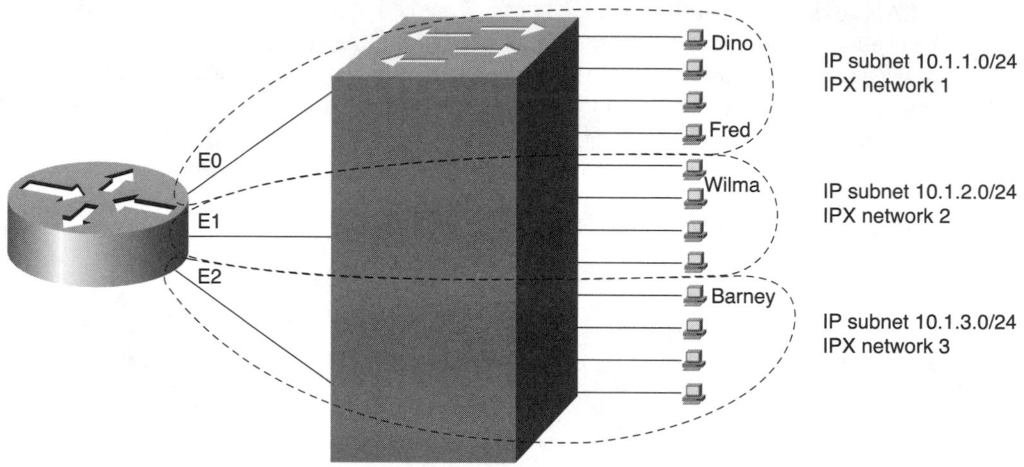

In both figures, separate broadcast domains imply separate Layer 3 groupings; a router is needed for forwarding traffic among the different Layer 3 groups.

The single switch in Figure 5-9 behaves identically to each of the three switches in Figure 5-8, but for each VLAN. For instance, the top switch in Figure 5-8 forwards broadcasts that it receives from Dino out all ports; similarly, the switch in Figure 5-8 forwards Dino's broadcasts out all ports in VLAN 1. The single switch *never* forwards a frame that enters an port that is in one VLAN out another port that is in a different VLAN. (Well, ever heard the saying "Never say never"? With multilayer switching, which is not on the CCNA exam, you could argue that this last statement is wrong. For now, the rule is that the switch cannot forward between VLANs.)

Although the switch cannot forward between VLANs, a router can. The switch in Figure 5-9 forwards frames to the router interfaces only if the frame is a broadcast or is destined for one of the MAC addresses of the router. For example, Fred eventually will want to talk to Barney, probably to find out when they are going bowling later. Fred will send an IP packet to Barney, and Fred will encapsulate the IP packet inside an Ethernet frame. Fred encodes a destination MAC address of the router's E0 MAC address because Fred's default router should be the router's E0 interface. The switch forwards this frame to the router, which routes it out E2 to Barney.

Of course, the switch can forward frames directly between devices in the same VLAN. For instance, when Fred sends frames to Dino, the destination MAC address of the frame is Dino's MAC address, and there is no need for the switch to get the router involved. Broadcasts sent by Fred do not go to the other VLANs because each VLAN is a separate broadcast domain, and you know the rule: Switches forward frames only out other ports in the same VLAN.

VLANs allow easy moves, additions, and changes. For example, if Barney moved to a different office that was cabled to a different port on the switch, he still can be configured to be in VLAN 3. No Layer 3 address changes are necessary, which means that no changes need to be made on Barney.

Switches create a separate address table for each VLAN. For instance, if a frame is received on a port in VLAN 2, the VLAN 2 address table will be searched. When a frame is received, the source address is checked against the address table so that it can be added if the address is currently unknown. Also, the destination address is checked so that a forwarding decision can be made. In other words, the switch learns addresses and makes forwarding decisions the same way as always, except that it uses a separate address table per VLAN.

Implementing VLANs with multiple switches adds more complexity that is not necessarily obvious. Consider Figure 5-10, which uses two switches connected with a Fast Ethernet. Two VLANs are configured.

Figure 5-10 *Two Switches, Two VLANs*

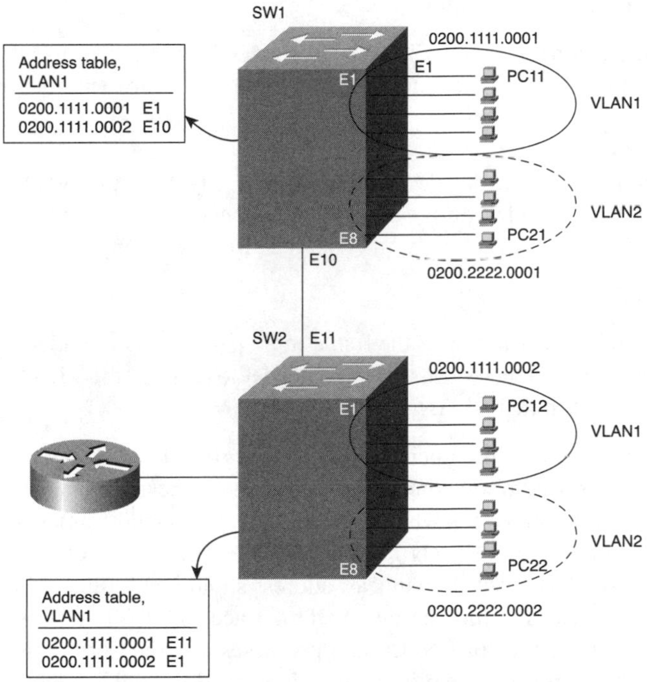

To see the problem and then the solution, consider a frame sent by PC11, addressed to PC12. The address table for VLAN 1 lists the two MAC addresses for the two PCs. The following steps outline the logic and then give you three different alternatives for how Step 6 could work:

1 PC11 generates the frame with destination MAC 0200.1111.0002.

2 Switch 1 receives the frame on port E1.

3 Switch 1 performs address table lookup in VLAN 1's address table because incoming port E1 is in VLAN 1.

4 Switch 1 forwards the frame out its E10 port.

5 Switch 2 receives the frame in its E11 port.

The creators of LAN switching might have considered the next three options for what should happen next. Just to let you consider some of the issues, there are three alternatives to the next step (Step 6) that the people who made this up might have considered. They did only one of these—but some of the choices for how they could have designed Switch 2 to react to the incoming frame are as follows:

6 Switch 2 considers port E11 to be in VLAN 1, so it performs table lookup for 0200.1111.0002 in that address table and correctly forward the frame to PC12.

   Or . . .

   Switch 2 does not consider port E11 to be in any particular VLAN, so it does table lookup in all tables and forwards out all ports matched. Because PC12 is only in VLAN 1, it would possibly match only VLAN 1's address table anyway.

   Or . . .

   Before Switch 1 forwards the frame in Step 4, it adds a header that identifies the VLAN. Then Switch 2 can look at the frame header to identify the VLAN number and can do table lookup just in that VLAN's address table.

LAN switches use the third alternative: frame tagging. The first option would work fine for one VLAN, and it is used when connecting multiple switches without using VLANs. However, the logic in this first option fails when devices in VLAN 2 send frames because their addresses would never be found in VLAN 1's address table. The second option would work well for unicasts, particularly because a unicast address should be found in only a single address table. However, broadcasts would be sent on all interfaces in all VLANs, which would cause horrendous side effects for OSI Layer 3 processes. So, the third option, called *VLAN tagging*, is used. VLAN tagging is the process of adding an additional header to a LAN frame to identify the VLAN to which the frame belongs. Cisco refers to this as *trunking*.

Cisco provides two trunking options on Ethernet. Inter-Switch Link (ISL) tags frames using Cisco-proprietary framing, which is shown in Figure 5-11. The CCNA exam does not require that you know the entire ISL header format. However, a few items are fair game. First, the ISL header encapsulates the LAN frame, which lengthens the frame. IEEE 802.1Q, the alternative trunking protocol on Ethernet, actually modifies the existing Ethernet header to accomplish the same tagging goal. The second important feature is the VLAN ID field, which exists in both ISL and 802.1Q. The VLAN ID simply identifies the VLAN to which the encapsulated frame belongs.

Figure 5-11 *ISL Framing*

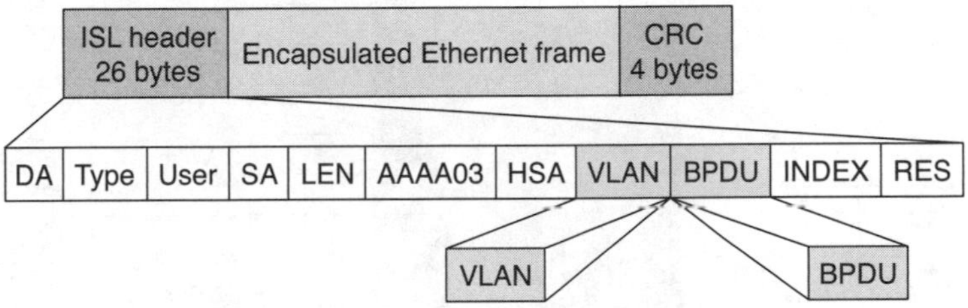

Back to the original point in Figure 5-11: PC11 sends a frame to PC12, and now ISL trunking is configured between the two switches. The following list outlines what happens:

1. PC11 generates the frame with destination MAC 0200.1111.0002.
2. Switch 1 receives the frame on port E1.
3. Switch 1 performs address table lookup in VLAN 1's address table because incoming port E1 is in VLAN 1.
4. Switch 1 forwards the frame out its E10 port after adding an ISL header that includes VLAN 1 as the VLAN ID.
5. Switch 2 receives the frame in its E11 port. Expecting an ISL-encapsulated frame, Switch 2 de-encapsulates the original frame, noting that it is in VLAN 1.
6. Switch 2 performs address table lookup in VLAN 1's address table only and forwards the frame out port E1 based on the table.

Trunking, in this case, simply enables the two switches to identify which VLAN a frame belongs to.

Engineers use trunking between two switches, as well as between a switch and a router. Trunking between a switch and a router reduces the number of router interfaces needed. Figure 5-12 shows a router with a single Fast Ethernet interface and a single connection to Switch 2. The same tagging method used between switches is used for frames sent to the router so that the router knows from which VLAN the frame originated. For frames that the router routes between the two VLANs, the incoming frame is tagged with one VLAN ID, and the outgoing frame is tagged with the other VLAN ID by the router before sending the frame back to the switch.

Figure 5-12 shows an example network, with flows from VLAN 1 to VLAN 2. Example 5-1 shows the router configuration required to support ISL encapsulation and forwarding between these VLANs.

Figure 5-12 *Example of a Router Forwarding Between VLANs*

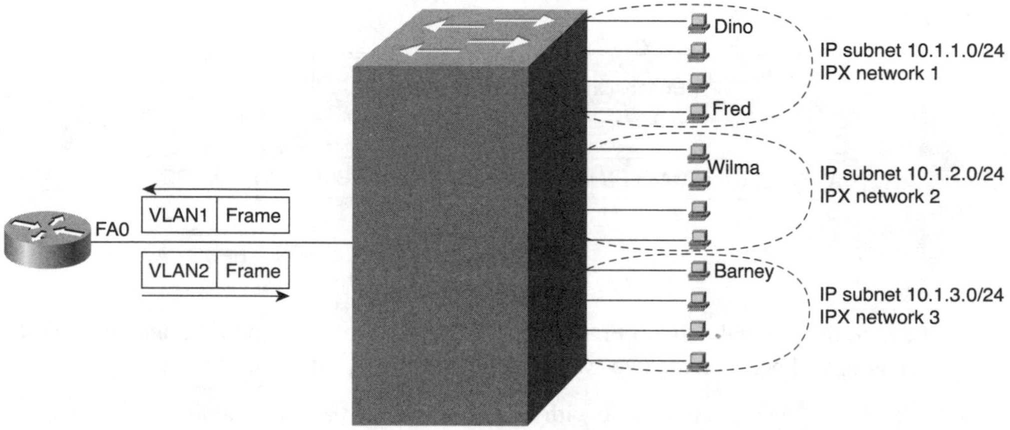

Example 5-1 *Router Configuration for ISL Encapsulation in Figure 5-12*

```
interface fastethernet 0.1
ip address 10.1.1.1 255.255.255.0
encapsulation isl 1
!
interface fastethernet 0.2
ip address 10.1.2.1 255.255.255.0
encapsulation isl 2
!
interface fastethernet 0.3
ip address 10.1.3.1 255.255.255.0
encapsulation isl 3
```

Example 5-1 shows the configuration for three subinterfaces of the Ethernet interface on the router. Each is assigned an IP address because the interface is actually a part of three VLANs, implying three IP subnets. So, instead of three physical interfaces, each attached to a different subnet and broadcast domain, there is one physical router interface, with three logical subinterfaces, each attached to a different subnet and broadcast domain. The **encapsulation** command numbers the VLANs, which must match the configuration for VLAN IDs in the switch.

Table 5-6 lists the various types of tagging used by Cisco and the types of interfaces on which they are used.

Table 5-6 *Frame Trunking/Tagging Protocols*

Tagging Method	Medium
Inter-Switch Link (ISL)	Fast Ethernet
802.1Q	Fast Ethernet
802.10	FDDI
LAN Emulation (LANE)	ATM

VLAN Trunking Protocol (VTP)

VTP is a Layer 2 messaging protocol that maintains VLAN configuration consistency throughout a common administration domain. VTP manages the additions, deletions, and name changes of VLANs across multiple switches, minimizing misconfigurations and configuration inconsistencies that can cause problems, such as duplicate VLAN names or incorrect VLAN-type specifications.

VTP makes VLAN configuration easier. However, you have not yet seen how to configure VLANs. To appreciate VTP, consider this example. If a network has ten switches that are interconnected, and parts of VLAN 3 were on all ten switches, you would have to type the same config command on all ten switches to "create" the VLAN. With VTP, you would do that once and the other nine switches would learn about VLAN 3 dynamically.

VTP distributes and synchronizes identifying information about VLANs configured throughout a switched network. Configurations made to a single switch, which is called the VTP server, are propagated across trunk links to all switches in the same VTP domain. VTP allows switched network solutions to scale to large sizes by reducing the manual configuration needs in the network.

The VTP domain is created by having each switch in the domain configure the same domain name. The network administrator chooses which switches are in the same domain by deciding which switches share common VLANs. One (or more) switch creates VLANs as the VTP server; then the others are configured as clients for full VTP operation. (VTP transparent mode, a third option, is covered shortly.)

How VTP Works

VTP advertisements are flooded throughout the management domain every 5 minutes, or whenever there is a change in VLAN configurations. Included in a VTP advertisement is a configuration revision number, as well as VLAN names and numbers, and information about which switches have ports assigned to each VLAN. By configuring the details on one server and propagating the information through advertisements, all switches know the names and numbers of all VLANs.

One of the most important components of the VTP advertisements is the *configuration revision number*. Each time a VTP server modifies its VLAN information, it increments the configuration revision number by one. The VTP server then sends out a VTP advertisement that includes the new configuration revision number. When a switch receives a VTP advertisement with a larger configuration revision number, it updates its VLAN configuration. Figure 5-13 illustrates how VTP operates in a switched network.

Figure 5-13 *VTP Operation*

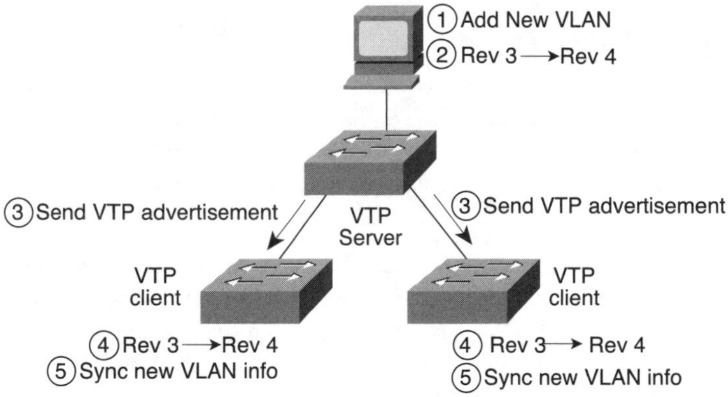

VTP operates in one of three modes:

- Server mode
- Client mode
- Transparent mode

VTP servers can create, modify, and delete VLANs and other configuration parameters for the entire VTP domain; this information, in turn, is propagated to the VTP clients in that same domain. VTP servers save VLAN configurations in the Catalyst NVRAM, whereas, in clients, the VLAN configuration is not stored. VTP messages are transmitted by the server out all trunk connections.

A VTP client cannot create, change, or delete VLANs, nor can it save VLAN configurations in nonvolatile memory. So, why be a VTP client? Well, if one engineer designs and implements the network, it's a lot more convenient to configure the VLANs in one switch (the VTP server) and have the information propagated to VTP clients.

In some cases, a VLAN exists in multiple switches, but administrative control of those switches is among different departments. VTP transparent mode provides an option so that some switches can use VTP but other switches can ignore VTP, while not stopping the other switches from using it. A switch in transparent mode forwards VTP advertisements received from other switches that are part of the same management domain, while ignoring the information in the VTP message. A switch configured in VTP transparent mode can create, delete, and modify VLANs, but the changes are not transmitted to other switches in the domain; they affect only that local switch. Choosing to use transparent mode is typical when there is a need for distributed administrative control of the switches, in spite of the fact that they each control parts of the same VLANs.

Table 5-7 offers a comparative overview of the three VTP modes.

Table 5-7 *VTP Modes*

Function	Server Mode	Client Mode	Transparent Mode
Originates VTP advertisements	Yes	No	No
Processes received advertisements and synchronizes VLAN configuration information with other switches	Yes	Yes	No
Forwards VTP advertisements received in a trunk	Yes	Yes	Yes
Saves VLAN configuration in NVRAM	Yes	No	Yes
Can create, modify, or delete VLANs using configuration commands	Yes	No	Yes

VTP Pruning

Start Extra Credit

Because ISL trunk lines carry VLAN traffic for all VLANs, some traffic might be needlessly broadcast across links that do not need to carry that traffic. VTP pruning uses VTP advertisements to determine when parts of the network do not have any members in a particular VLAN. By knowing what switches do not have members of a VLAN, VTP can prune some trunks, meaning these trunks do not forward broadcast for that VLAN. By default, a trunk connection carries traffic for all VLANs in the VTP management domain. Commonly, some switches in an enterprise network do not have local ports configured in each VLAN, so VTP pruning provides a way to be ready for future expansion but not waste trunk capacity with needless broadcasts. Figure 5-14 provides an example of VTP pruning.

Figure 5-14 *VTP Pruning Example*

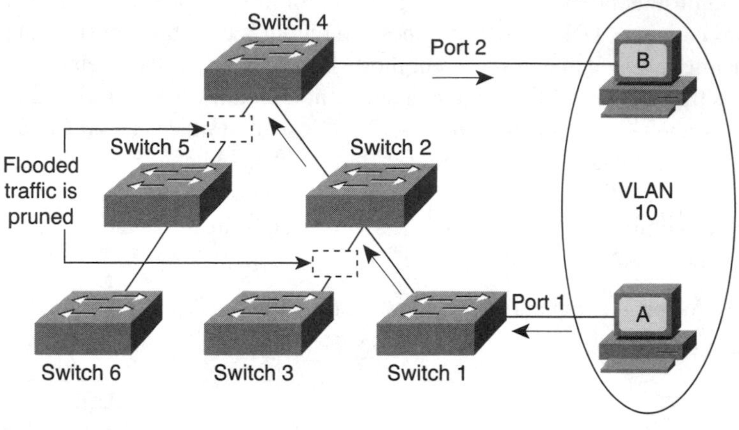

In Figure 5-14, switches 1 and 4 support ports in VLAN 10. As illustrated, with VTP pruning enabled, when Station A sends a broadcast, the broadcast is flooded only toward any switch with ports assigned to VLAN 10. As a result, broadcast traffic from Station A is not forwarded to switches 3, 5, and 6 because traffic for VLAN 10 has been pruned on the links indicated on switches 2 and 4.

VTP pruning increases available bandwidth by restricting flooded traffic, which consists of broadcasts and unknown destination unicasts. VTP pruning is one of the two most compelling reasons to use VTP—the other reason is to make VLAN configuration easier and more consistent.

End Extra Credit

VLAN and Trunking Configuration

You can purchase Cisco switches, install devices with the correct cabling, turn on the switches, and see it all work. You would never need to configure the switch and it would work fine, even if you interconnected switches—until you needed more than one VLAN. With redundant links between switches, STP would be needed, but it is enabled by default. So, on the CCNA exam, VLAN configuration is covered partly because it is one of the items that you must configure on a Cisco switch, assuming that you want to use VLANs.

VTP also can be configured, but it is on by default. However, the details of how you might configure VLANs are affected by the VTP configuration, so this is covered here as well.

LAN switch configuration on the CCNA exam assumes the use of a 1900 series switch.

Basic VLAN Configuration

You should remember several items before you begin VLAN configuration:

- The maximum number of VLANs is switch-dependent. The Catalyst 1900 supports 64 VLANs with a separate spanning tree per VLAN.
- VLAN 1 is one of the factory-default VLANs.
- CDP and VTP advertisements are sent on VLAN 1.
- Catalyst 1900 IP address is in the VLAN 1 broadcast domain.
- The switch must be in VTP server mode or transparent mode to create, add, or delete VLANs.

Table 5-8 represents the commands covered in this section and gives a brief description of each command's function.

Table 5-8 *VLAN Command List*

Command	Description
delete vtp	Resets all VTP parameters to defaults and resets the configuration revision number to 1
vtp [**server** | **transparent** | **client**] [**domain** *domain-name*] [**trap** {**enable** | **disable**}] [**password** *password*] [**pruning** {**enable** | **disable**}]	Defines VTP parameters
vtp trunk pruning-disable *vlan-list*	Disables pruning for specified VLANs on a particular trunk interface (interface subcommand)
show vtp	Displays VTP status
trunk [**on** | **off** | **desirable** | **auto** | **nonegotiate**]	Configures a trunk interface
show trunk {**A** | **B** | **port-channel**} [**allowed-vlans** | **prune-eligible** | **joined-vlans** | **joining-vlans**]	Displays trunk status
vlan *vlan* [**name** *vlan-name*] [**state** {**operational** | **suspended**}]	Defines a VLAN and its name
show vlan [*vlan*]	Displays VLAN information
vlan-membership {static {*vlan***} | dynamic}**	Assigns a port to a VLAN
show vlan-membership	Displays VLAN membership
show spantree [*bridge-group* | *vlan*]	Displays spanning tree information for a VLAN

VLAN Configuration for a Single Switch

If only one switch is in use, there is no real benefit to using VTP. However, VTP is on in server mode by default. Because VTP does not help when using a single switch, the first example shows VTP functions being turned off by enabling VTP transparent mode. The steps taken in this example are listed here:

1. Enabling VTP transparent mode
2. Creating the VLAN numbers and names
3. Configuring each port's assigned VLAN

First, use the **vtp** global configuration command to configure VTP transparent mode. Use the **vlan** global command to define each VLAN number (required) and associated name (optional). Then assign each port to its associated VLAN using the **vlan-membership** interface subcommand. Example 5-2 shows an example based on Figure 5-15.

Figure 5-15 *Sample Network with One Switch and Three VLANs*

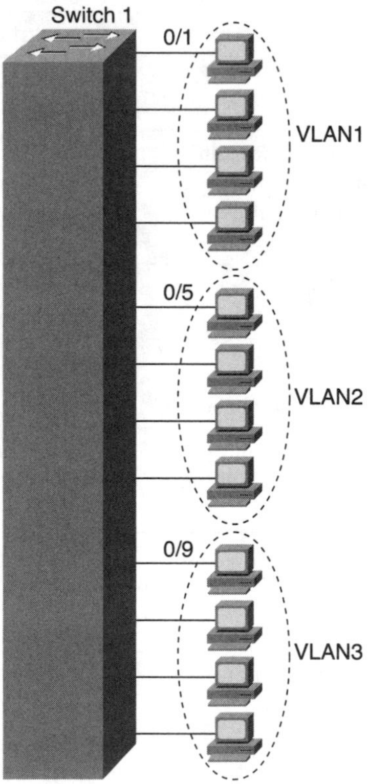

Example 5-2 *Single-Switch VLAN Configuration Matching Figure 5-15*

```
switch(config)# vtp transparent domain dummy
switch(config)# vlan 2 name VLAN2
switch1(config)# vlan 3 name VLAN3
switch1(config)# interface e 0/5
switch1(config-if)# vlan-membership static 2
switch1(config-if)# interface e 0/6
switch1(config-if)# vlan-membership static 2
switch1(config-if)# interface e 0/7
switch1(config-if)# vlan-membership static 2
switch1(config-if)# interface e 0/8
switch1(config-if)# vlan-membership static 2
switch1(config-if)# interface e 0/9
switch1(config-if)# vlan-membership static 3
switch1(config-if)# interface e 0/10
switch1(config-if)# vlan-membership static 3
switch1(config-if)# interface e 0/11
switch1(config-if)# vlan-membership static 3
switch1(config-if)# interface e 0/12
switch1(config-if)# vlan-membership static 3
```

Notice that some configuration seems to be missing. VLAN 1, with name VLAN 1, is not configured because it is configured automatically. In fact, the name cannot be changed. Also, any ports without a specific static VLAN configuration are considered to be in VLAN 1. Also, the IP address of the switch is considered to be in VLAN 1's broadcast domain. Ports 5 through 8 are statically configured for VLAN 2; similarly, VLAN 3 comprises ports 9 through 12. In addition, VTP is set to transparent mode, with a meaningless domain name of dummy.

After the VLANs are configured, the parameters for that VLAN should be confirmed to ensure validity. To verify the parameters of a VLAN, use the **show vlan** *vlan#* privileged exec command to display information about a particular VLAN. Use **show vlan** to show all configured VLANs. Example 5-3 demonstrates the **show** command output, which shows the switch ports assigned to the VLAN.

Example 5-3 **show vlan** *Output*

```
Switch1#show vlan 3

VLAN Name                 Status      Ports
--------------------------------------------------
3    VLAN3                Enabled     9-12
--------------------------------------------------

VLAN Type             SAID   MTU    Parent RingNo BridgeNo Stp  Trans1 Trans2
----------------------------------------------------------------------------
3    Ethernet         100003 1500      0      1      1     Unkn    0      0
----------------------------------------------------------------------------
```

Other VLAN parameters shown in Example 5-3 include the type (default is Ethernet), SAID (used for FDDI trunk), MTU (default is 1500 for Ethernet VLAN), Spanning-Tree Protocol (the 1900 supports only the 802.1D Spanning-Tree Protocol standard), and other parameters used for Token Ring or FDDI VLANs.

Sample Configuration for Multiple Switches

To allow VLANs to span multiple switches, you must configure *trunks* to interconnect the switches. Trunks are simply LAN segments that connect switches and use one of two methods of tagging the frames with the VLAN number. Cisco calls the use of a trunking protocol such as ISL or 802.1Q *trunking*, so the command to enable these protocols is **trunk**.

Use the **trunk** interface configuration command to set a Fast Ethernet port to trunk mode. On the Catalyst 1900, the two Fast Ethernet ports are interfaces fa0/26 and fa0/27. Enabling and defining the type of trunking protocol can be done statically or dynamically for ISL. The syntax for the **trunk** Fast Ethernet interface configuration subcommand is as follows:

```
switch(config-if)# trunk [on | off | desirable | auto | nonnegotiate]
```

The options for the **trunk** command function are as follows:

- **on**—Configures the port into permanent ISL trunk mode and negotiates with the connected device to convert the link to trunk mode.
- **off**—Disables port trunk mode and negotiates with the connected device to convert the link to nontrunk.
- **desirable**—Triggers the port to negotiate the link from nontrunking to trunk mode. The port negotiates to a trunk port if the connected device is either in the **on**, **desirable**, or **auto** states. Otherwise, the port becomes a nontrunk port.
- **auto**—Enables a port to become a trunk only if the connected device has the state set to **on** or **desirable**.
- **nonegotiate**—Configures a port to permanent ISL trunk mode, and no negotiation takes place with the partner.

As seen in the list, many options exist. Choices for these options are mostly personal preference. Because trunks seldom change, my preference is to configure either **on** or **off**.

Figure 5-16 and Examples 5-4 and 5-5 provide an expanded sample network, along with the additional configuration required for trunking and VTP server configuration.

Figure 5-16 *Sample Network with Two Switches and Three VLANs*

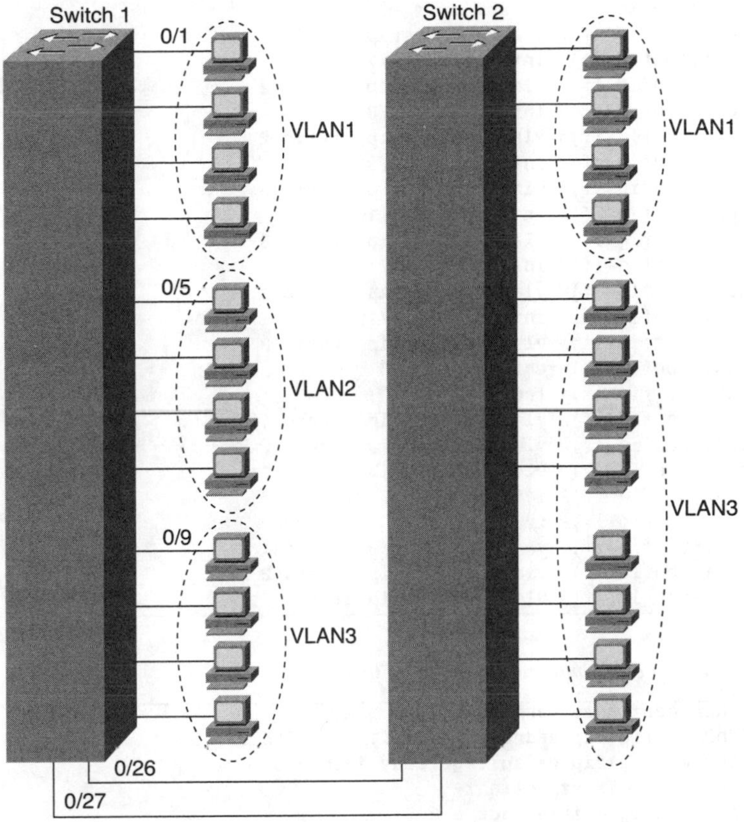

Example 5-4 *Switch 1 Complete Configuration as VTP Server*

```
switch1# configure terminal
switch1(config)#ip address 10.5.5.11 255.255.255.0
switch1(config)#ip default-gateway 10.5.5.3
switch1(config)# vtp server domain Hartsfield pruning enable
switch1(config)# vlan 2 name VLAN2
switch1(config)# vlan 3 name VLAN3
switch1(config)# interface e 0/5
switch1(config-if)# vlan-membership static 2
```

continues

Example 5-4 *Switch 1 Complete Configuration as VTP Server (Continued)*

```
switch1(config-if)# interface e 0/6
switch1(config-if)# vlan-membership static 2
switch1(config-if)# interface e 0/7
switch1(config-if)# vlan-membership static 2
switch1(config-if)# interface e 0/8
switch1(config-if)# vlan-membership static 2
switch1(config-if)# interface e 0/9
switch1(config-if)# vlan-membership static 3
switch1(config-if)# interface e 0/10
switch1(config-if)# vlan-membership static 3
switch1(config-if)# interface e 0/11
switch1(config-if)# vlan-membership static 3
switch1(config-if)# interface e 0/12
switch1(config-if)# vlan-membership static 3
Switch1(config)# interface fa 0/26
switch1(config-if)# trunk on
switch1(config-if)# vlan-membership static 1
switch1(config-if)# vlan-membership static 2
switch1(config-if)# vlan-membership static 3
switch1(config-if)# interface fa 0/27
switch1(config-if)# trunk on
switch1(config-if)# vlan-membership static 1
switch1(config-if)# vlan-membership static 2
switch1(config-if)# vlan-membership static 3
```

Example 5-5 *Switch 2 Complete Configuration as VTP Client*

```
switch2# configure terminal
switch2(config)#ip address 10.5.5.12 255.255.255.0
switch2(config)#ip default-gateway 10.5.5.3
switch2(config)# vtp client
switch2(config)# interface e 0/5
switch2(config-if)# vlan-membership static 2
switch2(config-if)# interface e 0/6
switch2(config-if)# vlan-membership static 2
switch2(config-if)# interface e 0/7
switch2(config-if)# vlan-membership static 2
switch2(config-if)# interface e 0/8
switch2(config-if)# vlan-membership static 2
switch2(config-if)# interface e 0/9
switch2(config-if)# vlan-membership static 2
switch2(config-if)# interface e 0/10
switch2(config-if)# vlan-membership static 2
switch2(config-if)# interface e 0/11
switch2(config-if)# vlan-membership static 2
switch2(config-if)# interface e 0/12
switch2(config-if)# vlan-membership static 2
switch2(config-if)# interface fa 0/27
switch2(config-if)# trunk on
switch2(config-if)# vlan-membership static 1
switch2(config-if)# vlan-membership static 2
```

Several items are particularly important in these configurations. The **vtp** global command in Example 5-4 shows Switch 1 as the server, with domain Hartsfield. No password is used in this case. Switch 2 is not configured with the domain name but will learn it with the first advertisement. Missing from Example 5-5 is the definition of the VLANs, which not only is unnecessary but also is not allowed when in VTP client mode. And because pruning was enabled in the **vtp** command on Switch 1, VTP prunes VLAN 2 from Switch 2 because Switch 2 has no ports in VLAN 3. VLAN 3 broadcasts received by Switch 1 are not forwarded to Switch 2.

Notice that not only was trunking enabled on both Fast Ethernet ports, but each of the three VLANs was statically configured on those ports. By also configuring the VLANs, the switch treats the trunk ports as part of those VLANs.

To verify a recent configuration change, or to just view the VTP configuration information, use the **show vtp** privileged exec command, as demonstrated in Example 5-6. Also displayed is the IP address of the device that last modified the configuration and a time stamp of the time the modification was made. VTP has two versions: VTP Version 1 supports only Ethernet; VTP Version 2 supports Ethernet and Token Ring.

Example 5-6 **show vtp** *Command Output*

```
switch1# show vtp
VTP version: 1
Configuration revision: 4
Maximum VLANs supported locally: 1005
Number of existing VLANs: 3
VTP domain name:Hartsfield
VTP password:
VTP operating mode: Server
VTP pruning mode: Enabled
VTP traps generation: Enabled
Configuration last modified by: 10.5.5.3 at 00-00-0000 00:00:00
```

To verify a trunk configuration, use the **show trunk** privileged exec command to display the trunk parameters, as demonstrated in Example 5-7. The syntax is as follows:

```
switch1# show trunk [a | b]
```

The parameters **a** and **b** represent the Fast Ethernet ports:

- Port a represents Fast Ethernet 0/26.
- Port b represents Fast Ethernet 0/27.

Example 5-7 shows a sample of the **show trunk** command as well as the **show vlan-membership** command.

Example 5-7 **show trunk** *and* **show vlan-membership** *Sample Output*

```
Switch1# show trunk a
DISL state: Off, Trunking: On, Encapsulation type: ISL
```

continues

Example 5-7 **show trunk** *and* **show vlan-membership** *Sample Output (Continued)*

```
Switch1#show vlan-membership

  Port  VLAN    Membership Type        Port    VLAN    Membership Type
  ------------------------------------------------------------------------------
 1       1      Static                  14       1        Static
 2       1      Static                  15       1        Static
 3       1      Static                  16       1        Static
 4       1      Static                  17       1        Static
 5       2      Static                  18       1        Static
 6       2      Static                  19       1        Static
 7       2      Static                  20       1        Static
 8       2      Static                  21       1        Static
 9       3      Static                  22       1        Static
 10      3      Static                  23       1        Static
 11      3      Static                  24       1        Static
 12      3      Static                  AUI      1        Static
 13      1      Static
 A       1-3    Static
 B       1-3    Static
```

Although the CCNA exam coverage does not include configuration to tune the behavior of spanning tree, you can see some basic information about STP using the **show spantree** privileged exec command, as demonstrated in Example 5-8.

Example 5-8 **show spantree** *Output*

```
switch1# show spantree 1
VLAN1 is executing the IEEE compatible Spanning-Tree Protocol
   Bridge Identifier has priority 32768, address 0050.F037.DA00
   Configured hello time 2, max age 20, forward delay 15
   Current root has priority 0, address 00D0.588F.B600
   Root port is FastEthernet 0/27, cost of root path is 10
   Topology change flag not set, detected flag not set
   Topology changes 53, last topology change occurred 0d00h17m14s ago
   Times:  hold 1, topology change 8960
           hello 2, max age 20, forward delay 15
   Timers: hello 2, topology change 35, notification 2
Port Ethernet 0/1 of VLAN1 is Forwarding
   Port path cost 100, Port priority 128
   Designated root has priority 0, address 00D0.588F.B600
   Designated bridge has priority 32768, address 0050.F037.DA00
   Designated port is Ethernet 0/1, path cost 10
   Timers: message age 20, forward delay 15, hold 1
```

Example 5-8 displays various spanning tree information for VLAN 1, including the following:

- Port e0/1 is in the forwarding state for VLAN 1.
- The root bridge for VLAN 1 has a bridge priority of 0, with a MAC address of 00D0.588F.B600.
- The switch is running the IEEE 802.1d Spanning-Tree Protocol.

Foundation Summary

The "Foundation Summary" is a collection of tables and figures that provide a convenient review of many key concepts in this chapter. For those of you already comfortable with the topics in this chapter, this summary could help you recall a few details. For those of you who just read this chapter, this review should help solidify some key facts. For any of you doing your final prep before the exam, these tables and figures will be a convenient way to review the day before the exam.

Table 5-9 summarizes the reasons why spanning tree places a port in forwarding or blocking state.

Table 5-9 *Spanning Tree: Reasons for Forwarding or Blocking*

Characterization of Port	Spanning Tree State	Explanation
All root bridge's ports	Forwarding	The root bridge is always the designated bridge on all connected segments.
Each nonroot bridge's root port	Forwarding	The root port is the port receiving the lowest-cost BPDU from the root.
Each LAN's designated port	Forwarding	The bridge forwarding the lowest-cost BPDU onto the segment is the designated bridge.
All other ports	Blocking	The port is not used for forwarding frames, nor are any frames received on these interfaces considered for forwarding.

Each bridge begins by claiming to be the root bridge by sending STP messages. STP defines these messages used to exchange information with other bridges, which are called *bridge protocol data units (BPDUs)*. Each bridge begins by sending a BPDU stating the following:

- **The root bridge's bridge ID**—At the beginning of the process, each bridge claims to be root, so this value is the same as the bridge ID of this bridge.
- **An administratively set priority**—This is the priority of the root bridge. At the beginning of the process, each bridge claims to be root, so this value is the priority of this bridge.
- **The cost to reach the root from this bridge**—At the beginning of the process, each bridge claims to be root, so the value is set to 0, which is this bridge's cost to reach itself.
- **The bridge ID of the sender of this BPDU**—This value is always the bridge ID of the sender of the BPDU, regardless of whether this bridge is the root.

The default port costs defined by IEE are listed in Table 5-10.

Table 5-10 *Default Port Costs According to IEEE*

Speed of Ethernet	Original IEEE Cost	Revised IEEE Cost
10 Mbps	100	100
100 Mbps	10	19
1 Gbps	1	4
10 Gbps	1	2

The Hello BPDU defines the timers used by all the bridges when choosing when to react:

- **Hello time**—The time that the root waits before sending the periodic hello BPDUs, which then are forwarded by successive switches/bridges. The default is 2 seconds.
- **MaxAge**—The time that any bridge should wait before deciding that the topology has changed. Usually this is a multiple of the hello time; the default is 20 seconds.
- **Forward delay**—Delay that affects the time involved when an interface changes from a blocking state to a forwarding state; this timer is covered in more depth shortly.

Table 5-11 summarizes the intermediate states of the spanning tree.

Table 5-11 *Spanning Tree Interface States*

State	Forward Data Frames?	Learn MACs Based on Received Frames?	Transitory or Stable State?
Blocking	No	No	Stable
Listening	No	No	Transitory
Learning	No	Yes	Transitory
Forwarding	Yes	Yes	Stable

Table 5-12 lists the various types of tagging used by Cisco and the types of interfaces on which they are used.

Table 5-12 *Frame Trunking/Tagging Protocols*

Tagging Method	Media
Inter-Switch Link (ISL)	Fast Ethernet
802.1Q	Fast Ethernet
802.10	FDDI
LAN Emulation (LANE)	ATM

Table 5-13 offers a comparative overview of the three VTP modes.

Table 5-13 *VTP Modes*

Function	Server Mode	Client Mode	Transparent Mode
Originates VTP advertisements	Yes	No	No
Processes received advertisements and synchronizes VLAN configuration information with other switches	Yes	Yes	No
Forwards VTP advertisements received in a trunk	Yes	Yes	Yes
Saves VLAN configuration in NVRAM	Yes	No	Yes
Can create, modify, or delete VLANs using configuration commands	Yes	No	Yes

Table 5-14 represents the commands covered in this chapter and gives a brief description of each command's function.

Table 5-14 *LAN Command List*

Command	Description
delete vtp	Resets all VTP parameters to defaults and resets the configuration revision number to 1
vtp [**server** | **transparent** | **client**] [**domain** *domain-name*] [**trap** {**enable** | **disable**}] [**password** *password*] [**pruning** {**enable** | **disable**}]	Defines VTP parameters
vtp trunk pruning-disable *vlan-list*	Disables pruning for specified VLANs on a particular trunk interface (interface subcommand)
show vtp	Displays VTP status
trunk [**on** | **off** | **desirable** | **auto** | **nonegotiate**]	Configures a trunk interface
show trunk {**A** | **B** | **port-channel**} [**allowed-vlans** | **prune-eligible** | **joined-vlans** | **joining-vlans**]	Displays trunk status
vlan *vlan* [**name** *vlan-name*] [**state** {**operational** | **suspended**}]	Defines a VLAN and its name
show vlan [*vlan*]	Displays VLAN information
vlan-membership {**static** {*vlan*} | **dynamic**}	Assigns a port to a VLAN
show vlan-membership	Displays VLAN membership
show spantree [*bridge-group* | *vlan*]	Displays spanning tree information for a VLAN

Q&A

As mentioned in Chapter 1, "All About the Cisco Certified Network Associate Certification," the questions and scenarios in this book are more difficult than what you should experience on the actual exam. The questions do not attempt to cover more breadth or depth than the exam; however, they are designed to make sure that you know the answer. Rather than allowing you to derive the answer from clues hidden inside the question itself, the questions challenge your understanding and recall of the subject. Questions from the "Do I Know This Already?" quiz from the beginning of the chapter are repeated here to ensure that you have mastered the chapter's topic areas. Hopefully, these questions will help limit the number of exam questions on which you narrow your choices to two options and then guess.

The answers to these questions can be found in Appendix A.

1 What routing protocol does a transparent bridge use to learn about Layer 3 addressing groupings?

2 What settings are examined by a bridge or switch to determine which should be elected as root of the spanning tree?

3 Define the term *VLAN.*

4 Describe the benefit of the Spanning-Tree Protocol as used by transparent bridges and switches.

5 If a switch hears three different hello BPDUs from three different neighbors on three different interfaces, and if all three specify that Bridge 1 is the root, how does the switch choose which interface is its root port?

6 When a bridge or switch using Spanning-Tree Protocol first initializes, who does it assert should be the root of the tree?

7 Name the three reasons why a port is placed in forwarding state as a result of spanning tree.

8 Describe the benefits of creating 3 VLANs of 25 ports each versus creating a single VLAN of 75 ports, in each case using a single switch. Assume that all ports are switched ports (each port is a different collision domain).

9 If two Cisco LAN switches are connected using Fast Ethernet, what VLAN trunking protocols could be used? If only one VLAN spanned both switches, is a VLAN trunking protocol needed?

10 Name the three interface states that the Spanning-Tree Protocol uses, other than forwarding. Which of these states is transitory?

11 What are the two reasons that a nonroot bridge/switch places a port in forwarding state?

12 Can the root bridge/switch ports be placed in blocking state?

13 What does VTP do, and what does the abbreviation stand for?

14 Name the three VTP modes. Which of these does not allow VLANs to be added or modified?

15 What Catalyst 1900 switch command assigns a port to a particular VLAN?

16 What Catalyst 1900 switch command creates VLAN 10 and assigns it a name of bigbadvlan?

17 What Catalyst 1900 switch command lists the details about VLAN 10?

18 What Catalyst 1900 switch command configures ISL trunking on fastethernet port 26 so that as long as the switch port on the other end of the trunk is not disabled (off) or configured to not negotiate to become a trunk, the trunk will definitely be placed in trunking mode?

19 What type of VTP mode allows a switch to create VTP advertisements?

20 Must all members of the same VLAN be in the same collision domain, the same broadcast domain, or both?

21 What is the acronym and complete name of Cisco's proprietary trunking protocol over Ethernet?

22 Switch 1 has VLANs 1, 2, and 3 configured. Switch 2 has VLANs 1 and 3 configured. The two switches are connected by a single 10-Mbps Ethernet link. How many address tables will Switch 1 have? Switch 2? Why?

____

____

____

23 What two 1900 series exec commands list information about the spanning tree for VLAN 2?

____

____

____

24 What if the costs of all the ports in the previous answer are the same?

____

____

____

Scenarios

Scenario 5-1: LAN Switch Configuration

Your job is to deploy a new LAN switch at a remote site. Figure 5-17 depicts the network. Perform the activities in the list that follows the diagram. Assume that all basic administrative configuration, as covered in Chapter 4, is complete.

Figure 5-17 *Scenario 5-1: Intermediate LAN Switch Configuration*

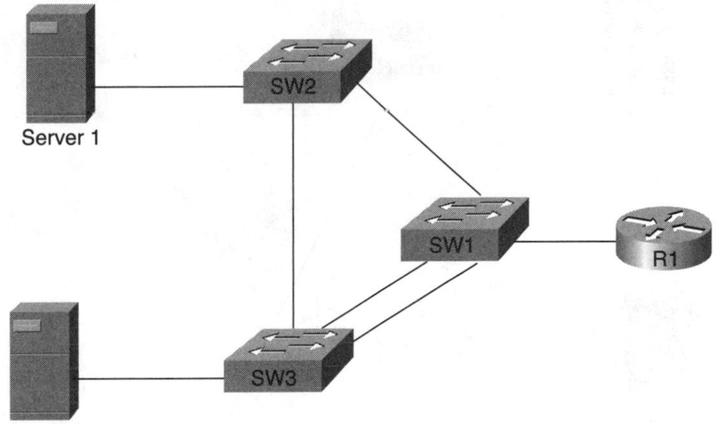

1. Choose port numbers to be used for each device, as if you were planning the physical installation. Write down these numbers on the diagram.
2. Place Server 1 and Server 2 in VLANs 1 and 2, respectively.
3. Use ISL trunking, where appropriate.
4. Use VTP to minimize the possibility of configuration errors.
5. Explain how STP could converge so that SW2 blocks on its trunk connected to SW1.

Answers to Scenario 5-1: LAN Switch Configuration

The first task required you to assign port numbers to the diagram. The task ends up being much more tricky than just picking the ports. 1900 series switches have two 100-Mbps ports, and because ISL and 802.1Q trunking require at least 100-Mbps Ethernet, these two ports are the only ports over which trunking can be used. So, trunking between R1 and SW1 requires one 100-Mbps port, leaving only one additional trunk port on SW1 for connection to the other two switches.

In this scenario, the problem of lack of ports is solved by using two 10-Mbps Ethernet links between SW1 and SW3. Two are required because one is used for VLAN 1 and one is used for VLAN 2. In most networks today, 1900 series switches are not used, and you would have more 10/100 ports available, most likely. Interestingly, the low port density for Fast and Gigabit Ethernet in the 1900 series gives you a good reminder about some of the design details when doing trunking.

Figure 5-18 shows the diagram, with port numbers included.

Figure 5-18 *Scenario 5-1 Solution: Port Numbers Used*

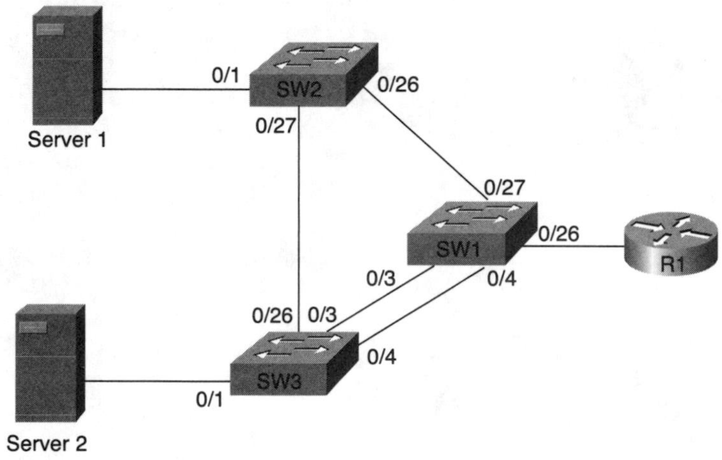

Tasks 2, 3, and 4 are all configuration-oriented. Examples 5-9, 5-10, and 5-11 list the commands used on SW1, SW2, and SW3, respectively.

Example 5-9 *Scenario 5-1 Configuration and* **show** *Commands, SW1*

```
sw1# show running-config

Building configuration...
Current configuration:
!
!
vtp domain "Veggies"
!
vlan 2 name "veggie2" sde 100002 state Operational mtu 1500
!
hostname "sw1"
!
interface Ethernet 0/1
!
interface Ethernet 0/2

!
```

Example 5-9 *Scenario 5-1 Configuration and* **show** *Commands, SW1 (Continued)*

```
interface Ethernet 0/3

!
interface Ethernet 0/4
  vlan-membership static 2
!
interface Ethernet 0/5
!
interface Ethernet 0/6
!
interface Ethernet 0/7
!
interface Ethernet 0/8
!
interface Ethernet 0/9
!
interface Ethernet 0/10
!
interface Ethernet 0/11
!
interface Ethernet 0/12
!
interface Ethernet 0/25
!
interface FastEthernet 0/26
!
  trunk On
!
interface FastEthernet 0/27
!
  trunk On
!
line console
end

sw1# show vtp

     VTP version: 1
     Configuration revision: 1
     Maximum VLANs supported locally: 1005
     Number of existing VLANs: 6
     VTP domain name         : Veggies
     VTP password            :
     VTP operating mode      : Server
     VTP pruning mode        : Disabled
     VTP traps generation    : Enabled
     Configuration last modified by: 0.0.0.0 at 00-00-0000 00:00:00
sw1#show vtp stat
          Receive Statistics                     Transmit Statistics
-----------------------------------    -----------------------------------
Summary Adverts                   1    Summary Adverts                  16
Subset Adverts                    0    Subset Adverts                    8
```

continues

Example 5-9 *Scenario 5-1 Configuration and* **show** *Commands, SW1 (Continued)*

```
Advert Requests                   1     Advert Requests                  0

Configuration Errors:
  Revision Errors                 0
  Digest Errors                   0


VTP Pruning Statistics:

Port    Join Received    Join Transmitted    Summary Adverts received
                                             with no pruning support
----    -------------    ----------------    ------------------------
A       0                0                   0
B       0                0                   0
sw1#show spantree

VLAN1 is executing the IEEE compatible Spanning Tree Protocol
   Bridge Identifier has priority 32768, address 00B0.6426.8C80
   Configured hello time 2, max age 20, forward delay 15
   Current root has priority 32768, address 00B0.6426.8C80
   Root port is N/A, cost of root path is 0
   Topology change flag not set, detected flag not set
   Topology changes 14, last topology change occurred 0d00h05m22s ago
   Times:  hold 1, topology change 8960
           hello 2, max age 20, forward delay 15
   Timers: hello 2, topology change 35, notification 2
Port Ethernet 0/1 of VLAN1 is Forwarding
   Port path cost 100, Port priority 128
   Designated root has priority 32768, address 00B0.6426.8C80
   Designated bridge has priority 32768, address 00B0.6426.8C80
   Designated port is Ethernet 0/1, path cost 0
   Timers: message age 20, forward delay 15, hold 1
Port Ethernet 0/2 of VLAN1 is Forwarding
   Port path cost 100, Port priority 128
   Designated root has priority 32768, address 00B0.6426.8C80
   Designated bridge has priority 32768, address 00B0.6426.8C80
   Designated port is Ethernet 0/2, path cost 0
   Timers: message age 20, forward delay 15, hold 1
--More--
Port Ethernet 0/3 of VLAN1 is Forwarding
   Port path cost 100, Port priority 128
   Designated root has priority 32768, address 00B0.6426.8C80
   Designated bridge has priority 32768, address 00B0.6426.8C80
   Designated port is Ethernet 0/3, path cost 0
   Timers: message age 20, forward delay 15, hold 1
Port Ethernet 0/5 of VLAN1 is Forwarding
   Port path cost 100, Port priority 128
   Designated root has priority 32768, address 00B0.6426.8C80
   Designated bridge has priority 32768, address 00B0.6426.8C80
   Designated port is Ethernet 0/5, path cost 0
   Timers: message age 20, forward delay 15, hold 1
Port Ethernet 0/6 of VLAN1 is Forwarding
```

Example 5-9 *Scenario 5-1 Configuration and* **show** *Commands, SW1 (Continued)*

```
   Port path cost 100, Port priority 128
   Designated root has priority 32768, address 00B0.6426.8C80
   Designated bridge has priority 32768, address 00B0.6426.8C80
   Designated port is Ethernet 0/6, path cost 0
   Timers: message age 20, forward delay 15, hold 1
Port Ethernet 0/7 of VLAN1 is Forwarding
   Port path cost 100, Port priority 128
   Designated root has priority 32768, address 00B0.6426.8C80
   Designated bridge has priority 32768, address 00B0.6426.8C80
   Designated port is Ethernet 0/7, path cost 0
   Timers: message age 20, forward delay 15, hold 1
Port Ethernet 0/8 of VLAN1 is Forwarding
   Port path cost 100, Port priority 128
   Designated root has priority 32768, address 00B0.6426.8C80
   Designated bridge has priority 32768, address 00B0.6426.8C80
   Designated port is Ethernet 0/8, path cost 0
   Timers: message age 20, forward delay 15, hold 1
Port Ethernet 0/9 of VLAN1 is Forwarding
   Port path cost 100, Port priority 128
   Designated root has priority 32768, address 00B0.6426.8C80
   Designated bridge has priority 32768, address 00B0.6426.8C80
   Designated port is Ethernet 0/9, path cost 0
   Timers: message age 20, forward delay 15, hold 1
Port Ethernet 0/10 of VLAN1 is Forwarding
   Port path cost 100, Port priority 128
   Designated root has priority 32768, address 00B0.6426.8C80
   Designated bridge has priority 32768, address 00B0.6426.8C80
   Designated port is Ethernet 0/10, path cost 0
   Timers: message age 20, forward delay 15, hold 1
Port Ethernet 0/11 of VLAN1 is Forwarding
   Port path cost 100, Port priority 128
   Designated root has priority 32768, address 00B0.6426.8C80
   Designated bridge has priority 32768, address 00B0.6426.8C80
   Designated port is Ethernet 0/11, path cost 0
   Timers: message age 20, forward delay 15, hold 1
Port Ethernet 0/12 of VLAN1 is Forwarding
   Port path cost 100, Port priority 128
   Designated root has priority 32768, address 00B0.6426.8C80
   Designated bridge has priority 32768, address 00B0.6426.8C80
   Designated port is Ethernet 0/12, path cost 0
   Timers: message age 20, forward delay 15, hold 1
Port Ethernet 0/25 of VLAN1 is Forwarding
   Port path cost 100, Port priority 128
   Designated root has priority 32768, address 00B0.6426.8C80
   Designated bridge has priority 32768, address 00B0.6426.8C80
   Designated port is Ethernet 0/25, path cost 0
   Timers: message age 20, forward delay 15, hold 1
Port FastEthernet 0/26 of VLAN1 is Forwarding
   Port path cost 10, Port priority 128
   Designated root has priority 32768, address 00B0.6426.8C80
   Designated bridge has priority 32768, address 00B0.6426.8C80
```

continues

Example 5-9 *Scenario 5-1 Configuration and* **show** *Commands, SW1 (Continued)*

```
   Designated port is FastEthernet 0/26, path cost 0
   Timers: message age 20, forward delay 15, hold 1
Port FastEthernet 0/27 of VLAN1 is Forwarding
   Port path cost 10, Port priority 128
   Designated root has priority 32768, address 00B0.6426.8C80
   Designated bridge has priority 32768, address 00B0.6426.8C80
   Designated port is FastEthernet 0/27, path cost 0
   Timers: message age 20, forward delay 15, hold 1
VLAN2 is executing the IEEE compatible Spanning Tree Protocol
   Bridge Identifier has priority 32768, address 00B0.6426.8C81
   Configured hello time 2, max age 20, forward delay 15
   Current root has priority 32768, address 00B0.6426.8C81
   Root port is N/A, cost of root path is 0
   Topology change flag not set, detected flag not set
   Topology changes 10, last topology change occurred 0d00h06m00s ago
   Times:  hold 1, topology change 8960
           hello 2, max age 20, forward delay 15
   Timers: hello 2, topology change 35, notification 2
Port Ethernet 0/4 of VLAN2 is Forwarding
   Port path cost 100, Port priority 128
   Designated root has priority 32768, address 00B0.6426.8C81
   Designated bridge has priority 32768, address 00B0.6426.8C81
   Designated port is Ethernet 0/4, path cost 0
   Timers: message age 20, forward delay 15, hold 1
Port FastEthernet 0/26 of VLAN2 is Forwarding
   Port path cost 10, Port priority 128
   Designated root has priority 32768, address 00B0.6426.8C81
   Designated bridge has priority 32768, address 00B0.6426.8C81
   Designated port is FastEthernet 0/26, path cost 0
   Timers: message age 20, forward delay 15, hold 1
Port FastEthernet 0/27 of VLAN2 is Forwarding
   Port path cost 10, Port priority 128
   Designated root has priority 32768, address 00B0.6426.8C81
   Designated bridge has priority 32768, address 00B0.6426.8C81
   Designated port is FastEthernet 0/27, path cost 0
   Timers: message age 20, forward delay 15, hold 1
```

Example 5-10 *Scenario 5-1 Configuration and* **show** *Commands, SW2*

```
sw2#show running-config

Building configuration...
Current configuration:
!
! Note from author - the domain name was NOT configured - it was learned with VTP!
vtp domain "Veggies"
vtp client
!
! Note from author - VLAN2 was NOT configured - it was learned with VTP!

vlan 2 name "veggie2" sde 100002 state Operational mtu 1500
!
```

Example 5-10 *Scenario 5-1 Configuration and* **show** *Commands, SW2 (Continued)*

```
hostname "SW2"
!
interface Ethernet 0/1
!
interface Ethernet 0/2
!
interface Ethernet 0/3
!
interface Ethernet 0/4
!
interface Ethernet 0/5
!
interface Ethernet 0/6
!
interface Ethernet 0/7
!
interface Ethernet 0/8
!
interface Ethernet 0/9
!
interface Ethernet 0/10
!
interface Ethernet 0/11
!
interface Ethernet 0/12
!
interface Ethernet 0/25
!
interface FastEthernet 0/26
!
  trunk Desirable
!
interface FastEthernet 0/27
!
  trunk Desirable
!
line console
```

Example 5-11 *Scenario 5-1 Configuration and* **show** *Commands, SW3*

```
sw3# show running-config
Building configuration...
Current configuration:
!
! Note from author - the domain name was NOT configured - it was learned with VTP!
vtp domain "Veggies"
vtp client
!
! Note from author - VLAN2 was NOT configured - it was learned with VTP!
vlan 2 name "veggie2" sde 100002 state Operational mtu 1500
!
hostname "sw3"
```

continues

Example 5-11 *Scenario 5-1 Configuration and* **show** *Commands, SW3 (Continued)*

```
!
interface Ethernet 0/1
  vlan-membership static 2
!
interface Ethernet 0/2
!
interface Ethernet 0/3
!
interface Ethernet 0/4
  vlan-membership static 2
!
interface Ethernet 0/5
!
interface Ethernet 0/6
!
interface Ethernet 0/7
!
interface Ethernet 0/8
!
interface Ethernet 0/9
!
interface Ethernet 0/10
!
interface Ethernet 0/11
!
interface Ethernet 0/12
!
interface Ethernet 0/25
!
interface FastEthernet 0/26
!
  trunk On
!
interface FastEthernet 0/27
!
line console
end
```

Task 2 required the creation of VLANs. You needed more configuration on the VTP server switch; in this case, SW1 is the VTP server. VLANs 1 and 2 did not need to be created on SW2 or SW3 because they learned it with VTP, but the ports for Server 1 (SW2) and Server 2 (SW3) needed to be added to the correct VLAN.

For Task 3, trunking needed to be configured. First, you must decide where trunking would be useful. If enough trunk ports were available, all the links between switched should be trunks, along with the link to R1. Because there are only two trunk ports per 1900 series switch, and because SW1 would need three trunk ports (one for the connection to the router and one each for the connections to the other two switches), this scenario uses two nontrunk 10-Mbps Ethernet links between SW1 and SW3. Why two? Well, because trunking is not allowed on 10-Mbps Ethernet and there are two VLANs, one Ethernet link is placed into VLAN 1 and the other is placed into VLAN 2 because only one VLAN is allowed per port unless trunking is used.

Task 4 asks that you use VTP, which indeed is configured on all three switches, with SW1 being the VTP server. Notice the output of the **show vtp** command in each example listing—VLANs 1 and 2 indeed are listed identically in each case. The commands **vlan 2 name "veggie2" sde 100002 state Operational mtu 1500** and **vtp domain "veggies"** were typed in only on SW1, which is the VTP server.

Task 5 asks for a simple explanation of how STP could be affected. You should not see STP configuration details on the CCNA exam, but you should expect to see questions about how it works. Two alternatives could be used to get SW2 to block on port 0/26. One method is to artificially increase the port cost on SW2's 0/26 port using the **spantree cost x** interface subcommand. However, if SW2 is elected root, its port costs do not matter because all ports on the root switch forward. So, to make sure, also ensure that another switch is root by lowering its priority. For instance, if SW3's priority was lowered to 15,000 instead of the default 32,768, SW3 would become root. SW2's root port would be 0/27, and SW1's root port would be 0/3 or 0/4 for VLAN 1 and 2, respectively. Either SW2's 0/26 or SW1's 0/27 would become the designated port on that segment—and if SW2's 0/26 cost was increased beyond the default cost on SW1, SW1's port would win, leaving SW2's 0/26 to block.

Exam Topics in This Chapter

20 Describe the different classes of IP addresses (and subnetting).

21 Identify the functions of the TCP/IP network-layer protocols.

22 Identify the functions performed by ICMP.

23 Configure IP addresses.

24 Verify IP addresses.

26 Define flow control and describe the three basic methods used in networking.

CHAPTER 6

TCP/IP and IP Routing

The TCP/IP suite includes the most important protocols covered on the CCNA exam and the protocols used most often in networks today. This chapter covers the TCP/IP protocols, including IP addressing and subnetting. Cisco expects CCNAs not just to know IP addressing and routing, but also to know the concepts behind many other TCP/IP protocols. In addition, CCNAs should be able to easily recall the commands used to examine the details of IP processing in a router. Of course, Cisco also requires you to continually prove your understanding of IP subnetting on the CCNA exam and on almost all other Cisco exams.

This chapter begins by describing TCP and UDP, the two main options for OSI Layer 4 protocols in TCP/IP. Routers care about TCP and UDP because they can examine TCP and UDP headers when making filtering decisions with access lists. Also, a deep understanding of TCP helps with many other parts of networking, including topics that you will see on the CCNP exam. After TCP and UDP, a couple of other short topics, ARP and ICMP, are covered. The TCP/IP protocols require ARP and ICMP to work.

You need solid skills with IP addressing and subnetting to succeed as a network engineer or to do well on the CCNA exam. For the exam, you need to be able to answer subnetting questions quickly and confidently. In real life, you need to apply these same concepts in a variety of ways. The second section of this chapter details IP addressing and subnetting, including some tricks that make the math required to answer test questions a bit easier.

Finally, you need to be able to configure TCP/IP on a Cisco router. Actually, that part of the chapter is a bit anticlimatic—configuring IP is pretty easy. Included in that section are some additional features about how to troubleshoot and manage an IP network.

How to Best Use This Chapter

By taking the following steps, you can make better use of your study time:

- Keep your notes and the answers for all your work with this book in one place, for easy reference.
- Take the "Do I Know This Already?" quiz, and write down your answers. Studies show that retention is significantly increased through writing down facts and concepts, even if you never look at the information again.
- Use the diagram in Figure 6-1 to guide you to the next step.

Figure 6-1 *How to Use This Chapter*

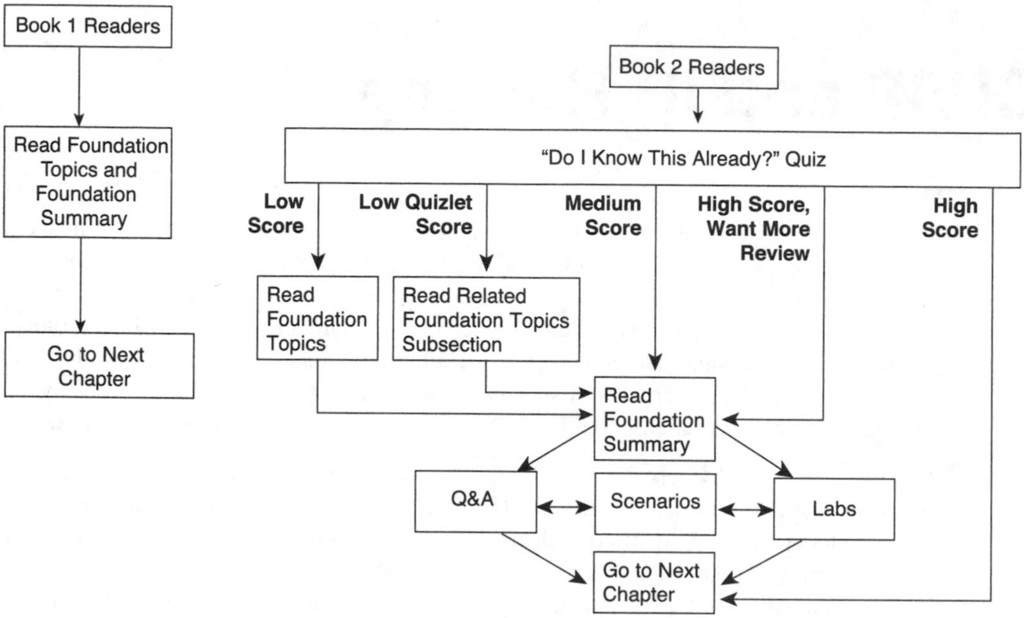

"Do I Know This Already?" Quiz

The purpose of the "Do I Know This Already?" quiz is to help you decide what parts of this chapter to use. If you already intend to read the entire chapter, you do not necessarily need to answer these questions now.

This 12-question quiz helps you determine how to spend your limited study time. The quiz is sectioned into three smaller four-question "quizlets," which correspond to the three major headings in the chapter. Figure 6-1 outlines suggestions on how to spend your time in this chapter. Use Table 6-1 to record your score.

Table 6-1 *Scoresheet for Quiz and Quizlets*

Quizlet Number	Foundation Topics Section Covering These Questions	Questions	Score
1	TCP/IP Protocols	1 to 4	
2	IP Addressing and Subnetting	5 to 8	
3	IP Configuration	9 to 12	
All questions	N/A	1 to 12	

1 What do *TCP, UDP, IP,* and *ICMP* stand for? Which protocol is considered to be Layer 3–equivalent when comparing TCP/IP to the OSI protocols?

2 Describe how to view the IP ARP cache in a Cisco router. Also describe the three key elements of each entry.

3 Does FTP or TFTP perform error recovery? If so, describe the basics of how error recovery is performed.

4 How many TCP segments are exchanged to establish a TCP connection? How many are required to terminate a TCP connection?

5 Given the IP address 134.141.7.11 and the mask 255.255.255.0, what is the subnet number?

6 Given the IP address 134.141.7.11 and the mask 255.255.255.0, what is the subnet broadcast address?

7 Given the IP address 200.1.1.130 and the mask 255.255.255.224, what are the assignable IP addresses in this subnet?

____

____

____

8 Given the IP address 220.8.7.100 and the mask 255.255.255.240, what are all the subnet numbers if the same (static) mask is used for all subnets in this network?

____

____

____

9 Create a minimal configuration enabling IP on each interface on a 2501 router (two serial, one Ethernet). The NIC assigned you network 8.0.0.0. Your boss says that you need, at most, 200 hosts per subnet. You decide against using VLSM. Your boss says to plan your subnets so that you can have as many subnets as possible rather than allowing for larger subnets later. When choosing the actual IP address values and subnet numbers, you decide to start with the lowest numerical values. Assume that point-to-point serial links will be attached to this router and that RIP is the routing protocol.

____

____

____

10 Describe the question and possible responses in setup mode when a router wants to know the mask used on an interface. How can the router derive the correct mask from the information supplied by the user?

____

____

____

11 Define the purpose of the **trace** command. What type of messages does it send, and what type of messages does it receive?

____

____

____

12 What causes the output from an IOS **ping** command to display "UUUUU"?

____

____

____

The answers to the quiz are found in Appendix A, "Answers to the 'Do I Know This Already?' Quizzes and Q&A Sections." The suggested choices for your next step are as follows:

- **8 or less overall score**—Read the entire chapter. This includes the "Foundation Topics" and "Foundation Summary" sections and the Q&A section at the end of the chapter.
- **2 or less on any quizlet**—Review the subsection(s) of the "Foundation Topics" part of this chapter, based on Table 6-1. Then move into the "Foundation Summary" section and the Q&A section at the end of the chapter.
- **9 to 10 overall score**—Begin with the "Foundation Summary" section, and then go to the Q&A section and the scenarios at the end of the chapter.
- **11 or more overall score**—If you want more review on these topics, skip to the "Foundation Summary" section and then go to the Q&A section at the end of the chapter. Otherwise, move to the next chapter.

Foundation Topics

TCP/IP Protocols

21 Identify the functions of the TCP/IP network-layer protocols.

22 Identify the functions performed by ICMP.

26 Define flow control and describe the three basic methods used in networking.

CCNAs work with multiple protocols on a daily basis; none of these is more important than TCP/IP. This section examines the TCP, UDP, ICMP, and ARP protocols in detail. TCP and UDP are the two transport layer (Layer 4) protocols most often used by applications in a TCP/IP network. ICMP and ARP are actually parts of the network layer (Layer 3) of TCP/IP and are used in conjunction with IP. As you'll see on the exam, IP addressing is something that all CCNAs must master to confidently pass the exam. Because of the importance of IP, IP addressing will be covered in great detail in the next section of this chapter.

Overview of a Sample TCP/IP Network

TCP/IP encompasses a lot of smaller protocols—in fact, the name itself is a combination of two of the most popular of these many protocols, the Transmission Control Protocol and the Internet Protocol. The best way to get a sense of how some of these varied TCP/IP protocols work together is to examine a simple TCP/IP network with some simple applications. After that, we will look at each protocol more closely.

The sample network consists of two PCs, labeled Hannah and Jessie. Hannah uses an application that she wrote to send advertisements that display on Jessie's screen. The application sends a new ad to Jessie every 10 seconds. Hannah also uses a wire-transfer application to send Jessie some money. Finally, Hannah uses a web browser to access the web server that runs on Jessie's PC. The ad application and wire-transfer application are imaginary, just for this example. The web application works just like it would in real life.

We begin with the ad and wire-transfer applications behaving normally. Figure 6-2 shows the network, with flows for both applications.

Figure 6-2 *Sample Network, Ad, and Wire Applications Working*

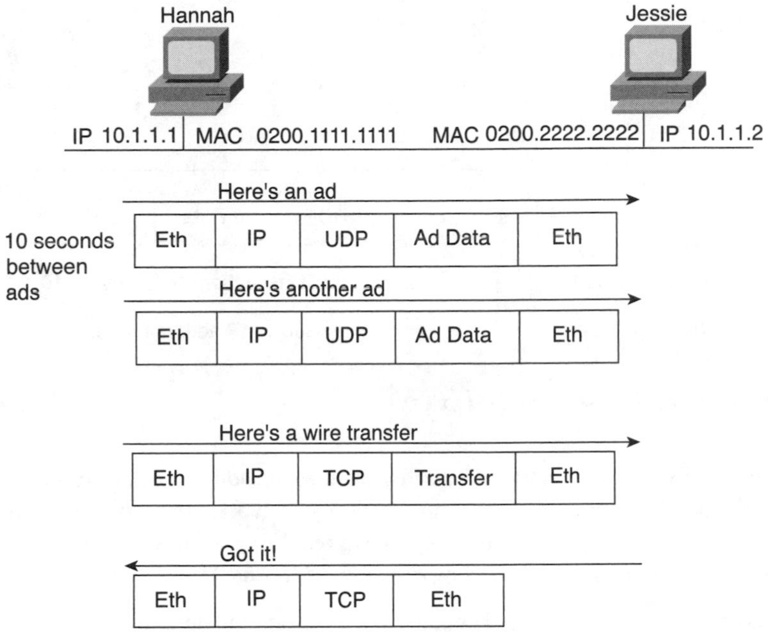

Hannah designed the ad application to not use acknowledgments—because another ad will be sent in 10 seconds anyway, there is little value to knowing whether the last ad got to the other user. For the wire transfer, Hannah included the capability to acknowledge the data. The ad application uses the User Datagram Protocol (UDP), and the wire application uses TCP because UDP does not use acknowledgments and TCP does.

However, these two applications cannot work until some overhead occurs. For example, the Ethernet frames going from Hannah to Jessie have information in them that Hannah did not know in advance—namely the destination IP and Ethernet addresses, as seen in Figure 6-3.

Figure 6-3 *Sample Network, with Addresses Shown in Headers*

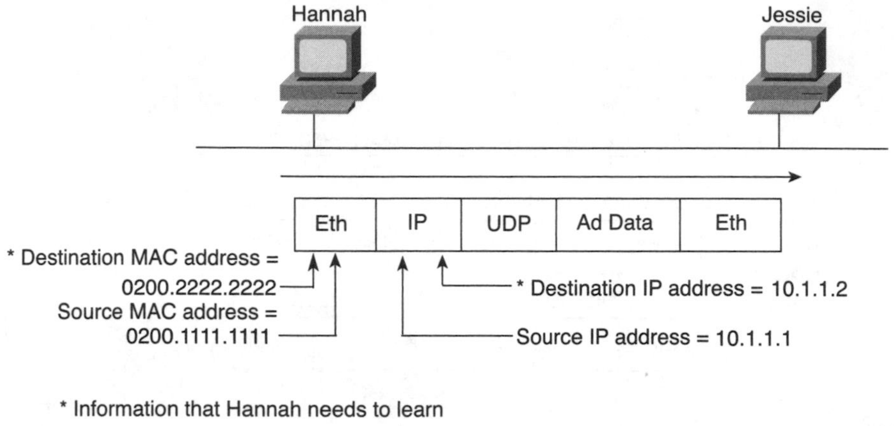

Hannah knows her own name, IP address, and MAC address because those things are configured in advance. Before the applications can work, somehow Hannah needs to know Jessie's host name. (They are first cousins in real life, so knowing the names shouldn't be too hard!) *What Hannah does not know are Jessie's IP and MAC addresses.*

To find the two missing facts, Hannah uses the Domain Name System (DNS) and the Address Resolution Protocol (ARP). Hannah knows the IP address of the DNS because the address was preconfigured on Hannah's machine. Hannah now sends a *DNS request* to the DNS, asking for Jessie's IP address. The DNS replies with the address, 10.1.1.2. Hannah still needs to know the Ethernet MAC address used by 10.1.1.2, so Hannah issues something called an *ARP broadcast*. An ARP broadcast is sent to a broadcast Ethernet address, so everyone on the LAN receives it. Because Jessie is on the LAN, Jessie receives the ARP broadcast. Because Jessie's IP address is 10.1.1.2 and the ARP broadcast is looking for the MAC address associated with 10.1.1.2, Jessie replies with her own MAC address. Figure 6-4 outlines the process.

Figure 6-4 *Sample Network, DNS, and ARP Process*

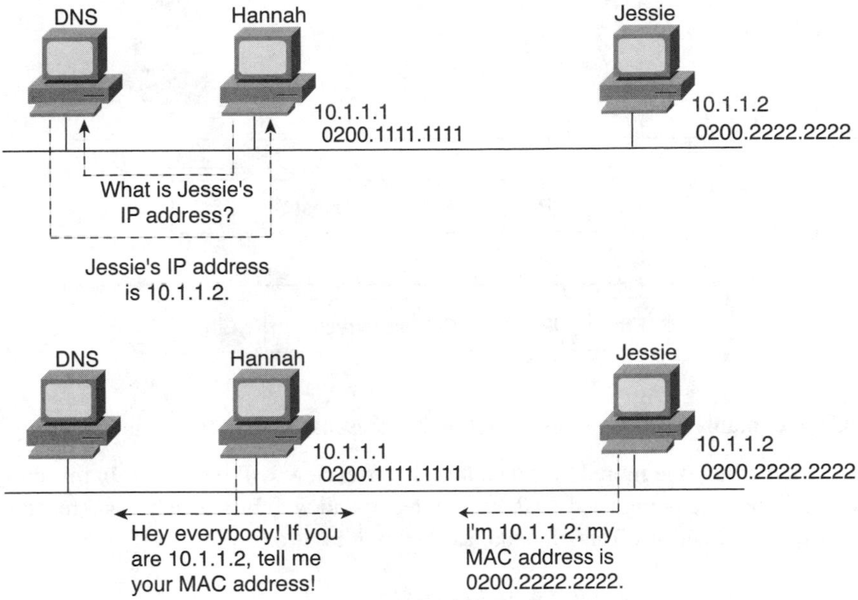

Now Hannah knows the destination IP and Ethernet addresses that she should use when sending frames to Jessie, and the messages in Figure 6-2 can be sent successfully.

But what if all this overhead happens and the applications still do not work? Well, as any network engineer will tell you, it's probably the application! But if you ask the application support personnel, the problem is in the network! Hannah, being a great network troubleshooter (in spite of being my one-year-old daughter), decides to simply test basic network connectivity using the **ping** command. Ping (Packet INternet Groper) uses the *Internet Control Message Protocol (ICMP)* protocol, sending a message called an *ICMP echo request* to another IP address. The computer with that IP address should reply with an *ICMP echo reply.* If that works, you have successfully tested the IP network, and if it works, the problem is more likely related to the application. ICMP does not rely on any application, so it really just tests basic IP connectivity—Layers 1, 2, and 3 of the OSI model. Figure 6-5 outlines the basic process.

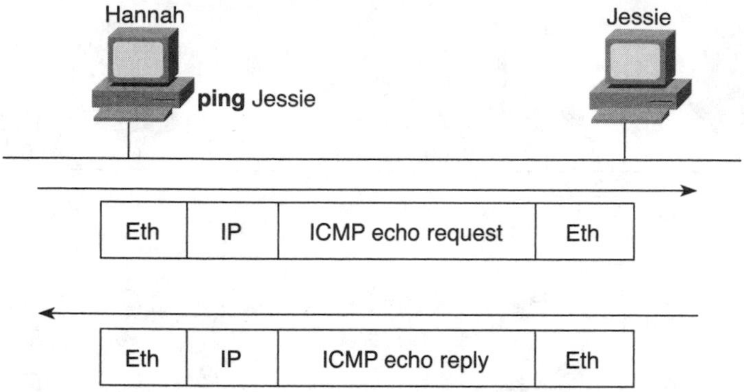

Figure 6-5 *Sample Network,* **ping** *Command*

ICMP contains many features, which will be discussed in detail in an upcoming section.

Understanding one more key concept in this overview will be useful. In this case, all three applications are being used—ad, wire transfer, and web browsing. Jessie receives packets for all three applications from Hannah, as shown in Figure 6-6.

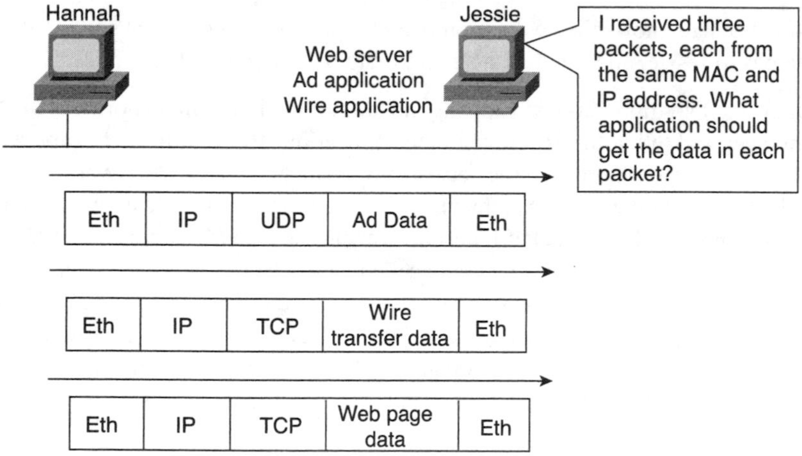

Figure 6-6 *Hannah Sending Packets to Jessie, with Three Applications*

Jessie needs to know which application to give the data to, but all three packets are from the same Ethernet and IP address. You might think that Jessie could look at whether the packet contains a UDP or a TCP header, but, as you see in the figure, two applications (wire transfer and web) both are using TCP. Fortunately, UDP and TCP designers purposefully included a field in the TCP and UDP headers to allow multiplexing, called the port number. *Multiplexing* is the term used to generally describe the capability to determine which application gets the data for each packet. Each of Hannah's applications uses a different port number, so Jessie knows which application to give the data to.

Figure 6-7 *Hannah Sending Packets to Jessie, with Three Applications Using Port Numbers to Multiplex*

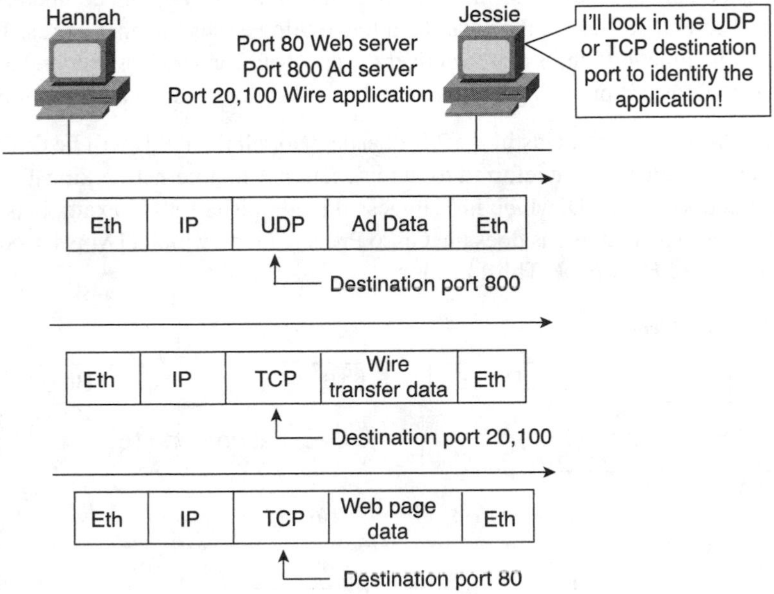

This overview provides a basic understanding of how a TCP/IP network behaves. More details will be covered in the next several sections of the book.

Transmission Control Protocol

Routers and hosts discard packets for a variety of reasons. A router might not have a route telling it where to forward a packet. A router or host might examine the FCS field in the frame trailer and discover that there were bit errors in transmission. Regardless, packets can be lost.

TCP provides a variety of useful features, including error recovery. In fact, TCP is best known for its error-recovery feature—but it does more. In fact, the CCNA exam covers the basics of five different features of TCP. Will every test taker see questions on all of these topics? Probably not. But TCP functions are within the scope of the test, so it pays to be ready.

The Transmission Control Protocol (TCP), defined in RFC 793, performs the following functions:

- Multiplexing
- Error recovery (reliability)

- Flow control using windowing
- Connection establishment and termination
- Data transfer

TCP accomplishes these goals through mechanisms at the endpoint computers. TCP relies on IP for end-to-end delivery of the data, including routing issues. In other words, TCP performs only part of the functions necessary to deliver the data between applications, and the role that it plays is directed toward providing services for the applications that sit at the endpoint computers.

Figure 6-8 shows the fields in the TCP header. Not all the fields will be described in this text, but several fields will be referred to in this section. The Internetworking Technologies Multimedia (ITM) CD, which is a suggested prerequisite for the exam, lists the fields along with brief explanations, as does the Cisco Press book on which ITM is based: *Internetworking Technologies Handbook,* Third Edition.

Figure 6-8 *TCP Header Fields*

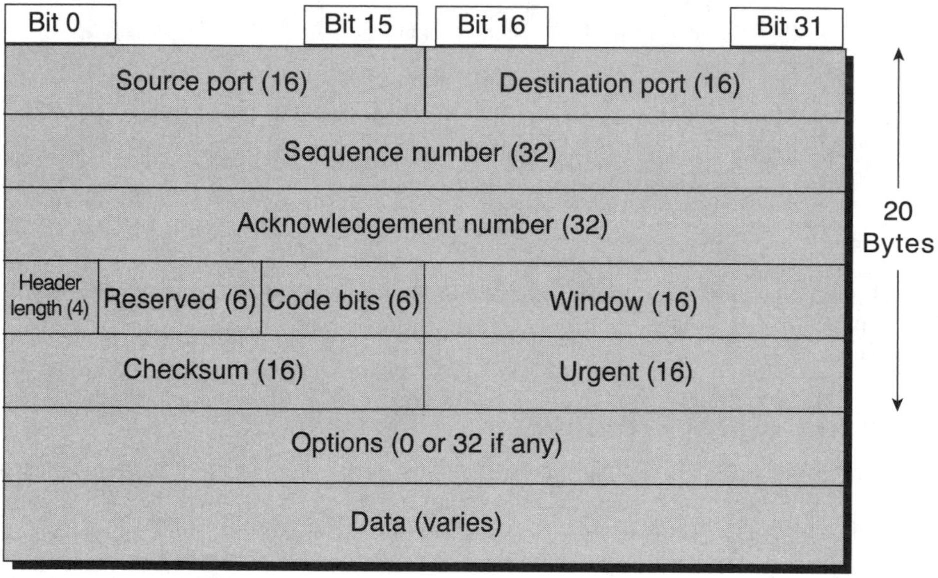

Multiplexing

In this context, multiplexing defines the process by which a host decides, among all its applications, which one should be given the incoming data. In the overview in the previous section, Jessie needed to decide whether to give the incoming data to the ad application, the wire-transfer application, or the web server application—that process is what we call multiplexing.

Multiplexing relies on the use of a concept called a *socket*. A socket consists of three things: an IP address, a transport protocol, and a port number. So for a web server application on Jessie, the socket would be (10.1.1.2, TCP, port 80) because, by default, web servers use the well-known port 80. When Hannah's web browser connected to the web server, Hannah used a socket as well—possibly one like this: (10.1.1.1, TCP, 1030). Why 1030? Well, Hannah just needs a port number that is unique on Hannah, so Hannah saw that port 1030 was available and used it. In fact, hosts typically allocate dynamic port numbers starting at 1024 because the ports below 1024 are reserved for well-known applications, such as web services.

In the overview section, Hannah and Jessie used three applications at the same time—hence, there were three socket connections open. Because a socket on a single computer should be unique, a connection between two sockets should identify a unique connection between two computers. The fact that each connection between two sockets is unique allows you each to use multiple applications at the same time, talking to applications running on the same or different computers; multiplexing, based on sockets, ensures that the data is delivered to the correct applications. Figure 6-9 shows the three socket connections between Hannah and Jessie.

Figure 6-9 *Connections Between Sockets*

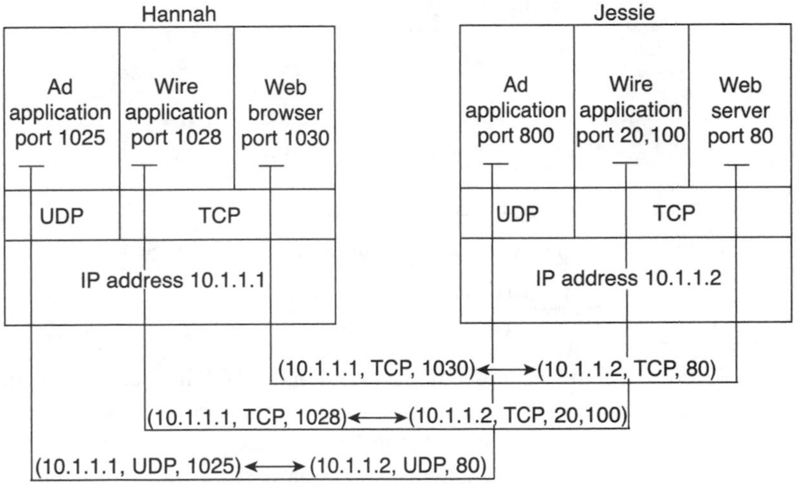

Port numbers are a vital part of the socket concept. Well-known port numbers are used by servers; other port numbers are used by clients. Applications that provide a service, such as FTP, Telnet, and web servers, open a socket using a well-known port and listen for connection requests. Because these connection requests from clients are required to include both the source and the destination port numbers, the port numbers used by the servers must be well known. Therefore, each server has a hard-coded, well-known port number, as defined in the well-known numbers RFC. On client machines, where the requests originate, any unused port number can be allocated. The result is that each client on the same host uses a different port number, but a server uses the same port number for all connections. For example, 100 Telnet clients on the same host would each use a different port number, but the Telnet server with 100 clients connected to it would have only one socket and, therefore, only one port number. The combination of source and destination sockets allows all participating hosts to distinguish the source and destination of the data. (Look to www.rfc-editor.org to find RFCs such as the well-known numbers RFC 1700.)

Error Recovery (Reliability)

TCP provides for reliable data transfer, which is also called reliability or error recovery, depending on what document you read. To accomplish reliability, TCP numbers data bytes using the sequence and acknowledgment fields in the TCP header. TCP achieves reliability in both directions, using the Sequence Number field of one direction combined with the Acknowledgment Field in the opposite direction. If you remember error recovery from Chapter 3, "OSI Reference Model and Layered Communication," TCP performs it the same way. Figure 6-10 shows the basic operation.

Figure 6-10 *TCP Acknowledgment Without Errors*

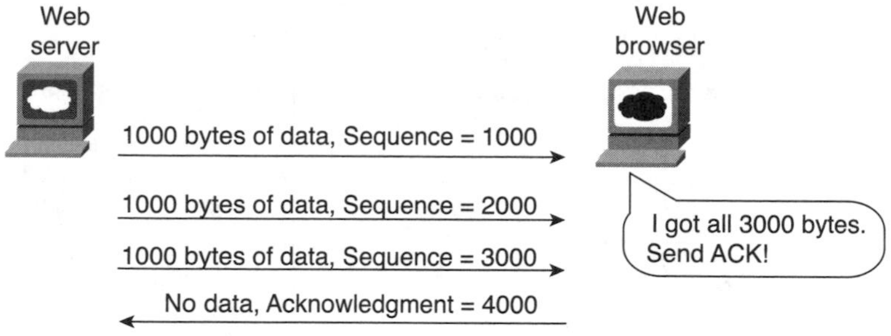

In Figure 6-10, the acknowledgment field in the TCP header sent by the web client (4000) implies the next byte to be received; this is called *forward acknowledgment*. The sequence number reflects the number of the first byte in the segment. In this case, each TCP segment is 1000 bytes in length; the sequence and acknowledgment fields count the number of bytes.

Figure 6-11 depicts the same scenario, but the second TCP segment was lost or was in error. The web client's reply has an ACK field equal to 2000, implying that the web client is expecting byte number 2000 next. The TCP function at the web server then could recover lost data by resending the second TCP segment. The TCP protocol allows for resending just that segment and then waiting, hoping that the web client will reply with an acknowledgment that equals 4000.

Figure 6-11 *TCP Acknowledgment with Errors*

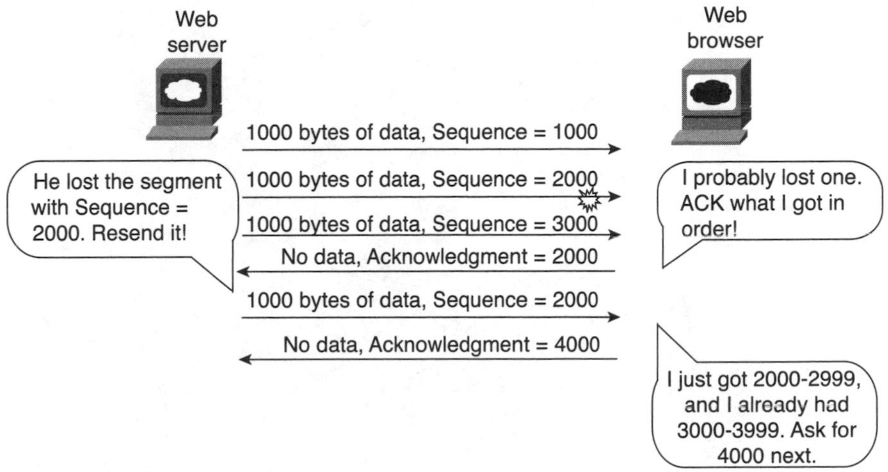

Flow Control Using Windowing

TCP implements flow control by taking advantage of the sequence and acknowledgment fields in the TCP header, along with another field called the *Window* field. This Window field implies the maximum number of unacknowledged bytes allowed outstanding at any instant in time. The window starts small and then grows until errors occur. The window then "slides" up and down based on network performance, so it is sometimes called a *sliding window*. When the window is full, the sender will not send, which controls the flow of data. Figure 6-12 shows windowing with a current window size of 3000. Each TCP segment has 1000 bytes of data.

Notice that the web server must wait after sending the third segment because the window is exhausted. When the acknowledgment has been received, another window can be sent. Because there have been no errors, the web client grants a larger window to the server, so now 4000 bytes can be sent before an acknowledgment is received by the server. In other words, the Window field is used by the receiver to tell the sender how much data it can send before it must stop and wait for the next acknowledgment. As with other TCP features, windowing is symmetrical—both sides send and receive, and, in each case, the receiver grants a window to the sender using the Window field.

Figure 6-12 *TCP Windowing*

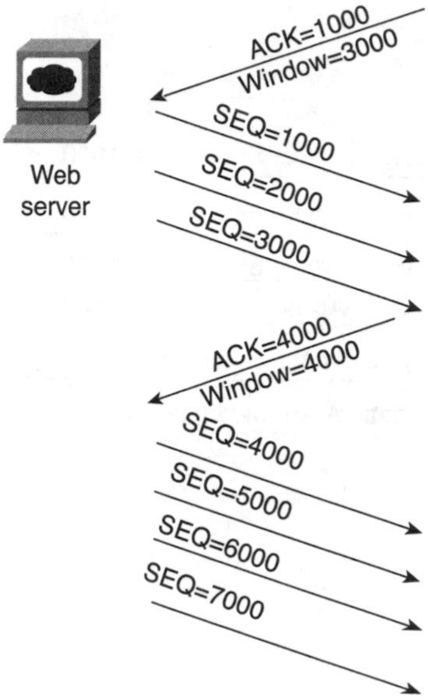

Windowing does not require that the sender stop sending in all cases. If an acknowledgment is received before the window is exhausted, a new window begins and the sender continues to send data until the current window is exhausted.

Connection Establishment and Termination

TCP connection establishment occurs before any of the other TCP features can begin their work. Connection establishment refers to the process of initializing sequence and acknowledgment fields and agreeing to the port numbers used. Figure 6-13 shows an example of connection establishment flow.

Figure 6-13 *TCP Connection Establishment*

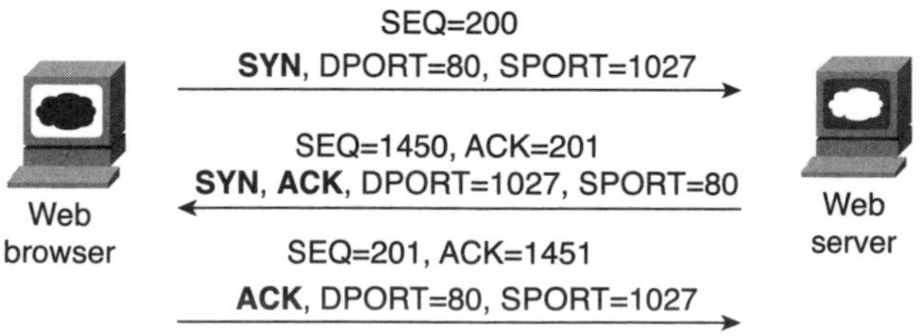

This three-way connection-establishment flow must complete before data transfer can begin. The connection exists between the two sockets, although there is no single socket field in the TCP header. Of the three parts of a socket, the IP addresses are implied based on the source and destination IP addresses in the IP header. TCP is implied because a TCP header is in use, as specified by the protocol field value in the IP header. Therefore, the only parts of the socket that need to be encoded in the TCP header are the port numbers.

TCP signals connection establishment using two bits inside the flag fields of the TCP header. Called the SYN and ACK flags, these bits have a particularly interesting meaning. SYN means "synchronize the sequence numbers," which is one necessary component in initialization for TCP. The ACK field means "the acknowledgment field is valid in this header." Until the sequence numbers are initialized, the acknowledgment field cannot be very useful. Also notice that in the initial TCP segment in Figure 6-13, no acknowledgment number is shown; this is because that number is not valid yet. Because the ACK field must be present in all the ensuing segments, the ACK bit will continue to be set until the connection is terminated.

TCP initializes the Sequence Number and Acknowledgment Number fields to any number that fits into the four-byte fields; the actual values shown in Figure 6-13 are simply example values. The initialization flows are each considered to have a single byte of data, as reflected in the Acknowledgment Number fields in the example.

Figure 6-14 shows TCP connection termination.

Figure 6-14 *TCP Connection Termination*

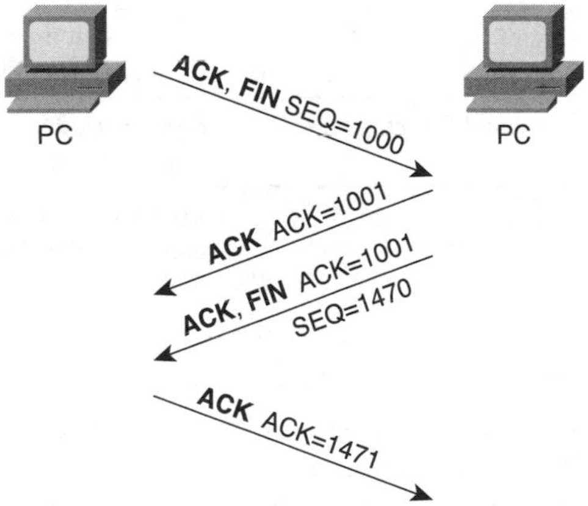

This four-way termination sequence is straightforward and uses an additional flag, called the FIN bit. (FIN is short for "finished," as you might guess.) *One interesting note:* Before the device receiving the first FIN segment sends the third TCP segment in the sequence, TCP notifies the application that the connection is coming down. TCP waits on an acknowledgment from the application before sending the third segment in the figure. That's why the second segment is required: to acknowledge the first segment so that the side taking down the connection doesn't start resending the first TCP segment.

Ordered Data Transfer

TCP not only causes retransmissions when segments are lost, but it also reorders segments that arrive out of sequence. The process is not hard to imagine: If segments arrive with sequence numbers 1000, 3000, and 2000, each with 1000 bytes of data, the receiver can reorder them, and no retransmissions are required.

TCP Function Summary

Table 6-2 summarizes TCP functions.

Table 6-2 *TCP Function Summary*

Function	Description
Multiplexing	Function that allows receiving hosts to decide the correct application for which the data is destined, based on the port number
Error recovery (reliability)	Process of numbering and acknowledging data with sequence and acknowledgment header fields
Flow control using windowing	Process that uses window sizes to protect buffer space and routing devices
Connection establishment and termination	Process used to initialize port numbers and sequence and acknowledgement fields
Ordered data transfer	Continuous stream of bytes from upper-layer process that is "segmented" for transmission

User Datagram Protocol

The CCNA exam requires that you be able to compare and contrast the User Datagram Protocol (UDP) with TCP. UDP provides a service for applications to exchange messages. Unlike TCP, UDP is connectionless and provides no reliability, no windowing, and no function to ensure that the data is received in the order in which it was sent. However, UDP provides some functions of TCP, such as data transfer and multiplexing, and it does so with fewer bytes of overhead in the UDP header.

UDP multiplexes using port numbers in an identical fashion to TCP. The only difference in UDP (compared to TCP) sockets is that, instead of designating TCP as the transport protocol, the transport protocol is UDP. An application could open identical port numbers on the same host but use TCP in one case and UDP in the other—that is not typical, but it certainly is allowed. If a particular service supports both TCP and UDP transport, it uses the same value for the TCP and UDP port number, as shown in the assigned numbers RFC (currently RFC 1700—see www.isi.edu/in-notes/rfc1700.txt).

UDP data transfer differs from TCP data transfer in that no reordering or recovery is accomplished. Applications using UDP are tolerant of the lost data, or they have some application mechanism to recover lost data. For example, DNS requests use UDP because the user will retry an operation if the DNS resolution fails. The Network File System (NFS) performs recovery with application layer code, so UDP features are acceptable to NFS.

Table 6-3 contrasts typical transport layer functions as performed (or not performed) by UDP or TCP.

Table 6-3 *TCP and UDP Functional Comparison*

Function	Description (TCP)	Description (UDP)
Data transfer	This involves a continuous stream of ordered data.	This involves message (datagram) delivery.
Multiplexing	Receiving hosts decide the correct application for which the data is destined, based on the port number.	Receiving hosts decide the correct application for which the data is destined, based on the port number.
Reliable transfer	Acknowledgment of data uses the sequence and acknowledgment fields in the TCP header.	This is not a feature of UDP.
Flow control	This process is used to protect buffer space and routing devices.	This is not a feature of UDP.
Connections	This process is used to initialize port numbers and other TCP header fields.	UDP is connectionless.

Figure 6-15 shows TCP and UDP header formats. Note the existence of both Source Port and Destination Port fields in the TCP and UDP headers but the absence of Sequence Number and Acknowledgment Number fields in the UDP header. UDP does not need these fields because it makes no attempt to number the data for acknowledgments or resequencing.

Figure 6-15 *TCP and UDP Headers*

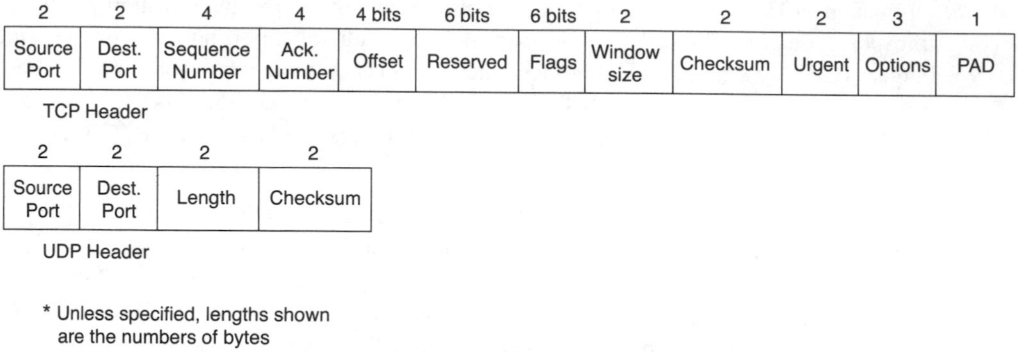

UDP gains some advantages over TCP by not using the sequence and acknowledgment fields. The most obvious advantage of UDP over TCP is that there are fewer bytes of overhead. Not as obvious is the fact that UDP does not require waiting on acknowledgments or holding the data in memory until it is acknowledged. This means that UDP applications are not artificially slowed by the acknowledgment process, and memory is freed more quickly.

Address Resolution Protocol

The Address Resolution Protocol (ARP) answers this question: Given an IP address of another device on the same LAN, what is its MAC address? ARP is needed because, to send an IP packet across some LANs, the data-link header and trailer (which encapsulate the packet) must first be created. The source MAC address in this new header is known because it is the MAC address of the sender. However, the destination MAC is not known in advance; ARP is the method that IP uses to discover the destination MAC address. Figure 6-16 shows an example of the ARP process.

Figure 6-16 *The ARP Process*

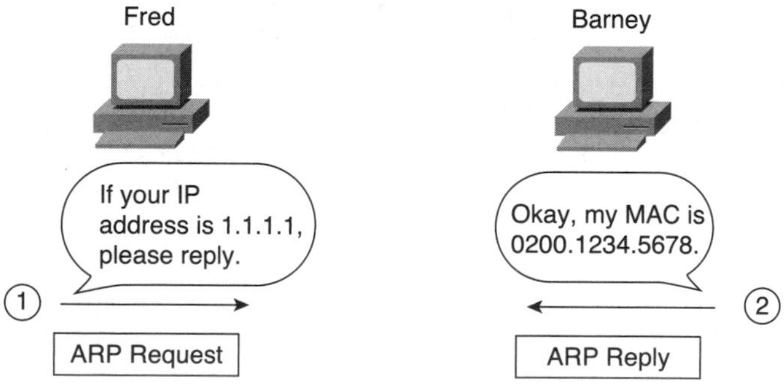

The ARP reply includes Barney's MAC address, in this example. An ARP cache holds the ARP entries (IP address and MAC address in each entry) for each interface. After a period of disuse for an entry, the entry in the table is removed. After the ARP entry times out, another ARP exchange is required.

From an architectural perspective, ARP is a Layer 3 function and is defined in RFC 826. In fact, ARP does not use IP—ARP is carried inside a frame, just like IP. Note the location of ARP in the architectural model in Figure 6-17.

Figure 6-17 *TCP/IP Architectural Model*

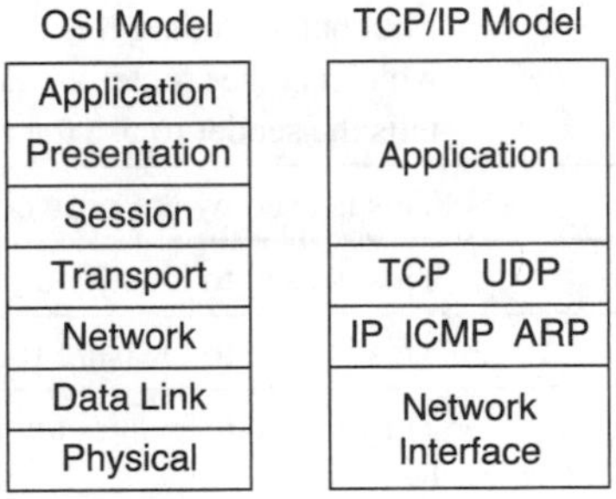

Internet Control Message Protocol

You should know both the general concepts and several specifics about the Internet Control Message Protocol (ICMP) for the CCNA exam. *Control Message* is the most descriptive part of the name— ICMP helps control and manage the work of IP and, therefore, is considered to be part of TCP/IP's network layer. RFC 792 defines ICMP and includes the following excerpt, which describes the protocol well:

> Occasionally a gateway or destination host will communicate with a source host, for example, to report an error in datagram processing. For such purposes, this protocol, the Internet Control Message Protocol (ICMP), is used. ICMP uses the basic support of IP as if it were a higher level protocol; however, ICMP is actually an integral part of IP and must be implemented by every IP module.

ICMP uses messages to accomplish its tasks. Many of these messages are used in even the smallest IP network. Table 6-4 lists several ICMP messages, with the ones most likely to be on the exam noted with an asterisk. Not surprisingly, these are the same messages used most often. The Destination Unreachable, Time Exceeded, and Redirect messages will be described in more detail following Table 6-4.

Table 6-4 *ICMP Message Types*

Message	Purpose
*Destination Unreachable	This tells the source host that there is a problem delivering a packet.
*Time Exceeded	The time that it takes a packet to be delivered has become too long; the packet has been discarded.
Source Quench	The source is sending data faster than it can be forwarded; this message requests that the sender slow down.
*Redirect	The router sending this message has received some packet for which another router would have had a better route; the message tells the sender to use the better route.
*Echo	This is used by the **ping** command to verify connectivity.
Parameter Problem	This is used to identify a parameter that is incorrect.
Timestamp	This is used to measure round-trip time to particular hosts.
Address Mask Request/Reply	This is used to inquire about and learn the correct subnet mask to be used.
Router Advertisement and Selection	This is used to allow hosts to dynamically learn the IP addresses of the routers attached to the subnet.

*Most likely to be on the CCNA exam

Start Extra Credit

Each ICMP message contains a Type field and a Code field, as shown in Figure 6-18. The Type field implies the message types from Table 6-4. The Code field implies a subtype; several subtypes will be shown in the following examples. I do not expect any ICMP header format questions on the exam; it's just good for perspective with the upcoming explanations.

Figure 6-18 *ICMP Header Formats*

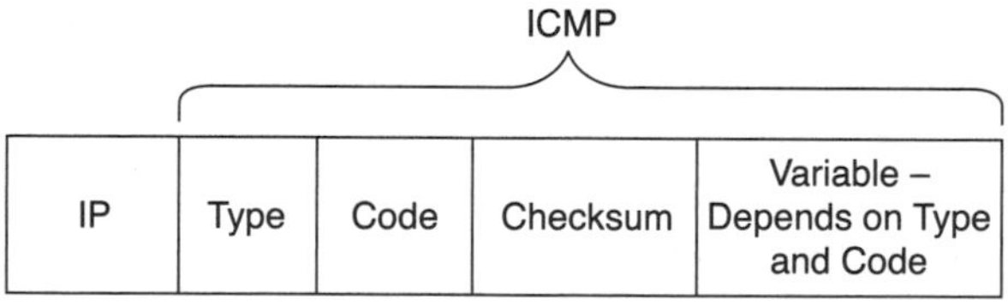

End Extra Credit

ICMP Echo Request and Echo Reply

The ICMP Echo Request and Echo Reply messages are sent and received by the **ping** command. In fact, when people say that they sent a ping packet, they really mean that they sent an ICMP Echo Request. These two messages are very self-explanatory. The Echo Request simply means that the host to which it is addressed should reply to the packet. The Echo Reply is the ICMP message type that should be used in the reply. The Echo Request includes some data that can be specified by the **ping** command; whatever data is sent in the Echo Request is sent back in the Echo Reply.

The **ping** command itself supplies many creative ways to use Echo Requests and Replies. For instance, the **ping** command enables you to specify the length as well as the source and destination addresses, and it also enables you to set other fields in the IP header. Example 6-6, later in this chapter, shows a good example of the capabilities of the **ping** command.

Destination Unreachable ICMP Message

The ICMP unreachable message is sent when a message cannot be delivered completely to the application at the destination host. However, packet delivery could fail for many reasons, so there are five separate unreachable functions (codes) using this single ICMP unreachable message. All five code types pertain directly to some IP, TCP, or UDP feature and are better described by using Figure 6-19 as an example network.

Assume that Fred is trying to connect to the web server, called Web. (Web uses TCP as the transport layer protocol.) Three of the ICMP unreachable codes would possibly be used by Routers A and B. The other two codes would be used by the web server. These ICMP codes would be sent to Fred as a result of the packet originally sent by Fred.

Figure 6-19 *Sample Network for Discussing ICMP Unreachable Codes*

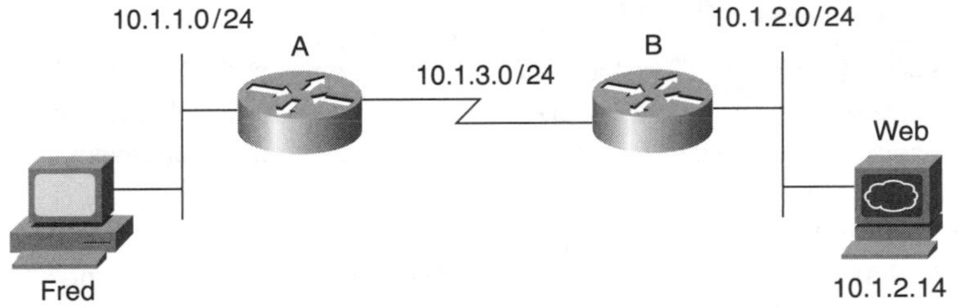

Table 6-5 summarizes the more common ICMP unreachable codes.

Table 6-5 *ICMP Unreachable Codes*

Unreachable Code	When Used	Typically Sent By
Network unreachable	There is no match in a routing table for the destination of the packet.	Router
Host unreachable	The packet can be routed to a router connected to the destination subnet, but the host is not responding.	Router
Can't fragment	The packet has the Don't Fragment bit set, and a router must fragment to forward the packet.	Router
Protocol unreachable	The packet is delivered to the destination host, but the transport layer protocol is not available on that host.	Endpoint host
Port unreachable	The packet is delivered to the destination host, but the destination port has not been opened by an application.	Endpoint host

The list that follows explains each code in Table 6-5 in greater detail:

- **Network unreachable**—A code meaning "network unreachable" will be used by Router A if Router A does not have a route telling it where to forward the packet. In this case, Router A needs a route to subnet 10.1.2.0. The ICMP unreachable message, with the code "network unreachable," is sent by Router A to Fred, in response to Fred's packet destined for 10.1.2.14.

- **Host unreachable**—This code implies that the single destination host is unavailable. If Router A has a route to 10.1.2.0, the packet will be delivered to Router B. However, if the web server is down, Router B will not get an ARP reply from web. The ICMP unreachable message, with code "host unreachable," will be sent by Router B to Fred, in response to Fred's packet destined for 10.1.2.14.

- **Can't fragment**—This code is the last of the three ICMP unreachable codes that might be sent by a router. Fragmentation defines a process in which a router needs to forward a packet, but the outgoing interface allows only packets that are smaller than the forwarded packet. The router can break the packet into pieces. However, if Router A or Router B needs to fragment the packet but the Do Not Fragment bit is set in the IP header, the router will discard the packet. The ICMP unreachable message, with code "can't fragment," will be sent by Router A or B to Fred, in response to Fred's packet destined for 10.1.2.14.

- **Protocol unreachable**—If the packet successfully arrives at the web server, two other unreachable codes are possible. One implies that the protocol above IP, typically TCP or UDP, is not running on that host. This is highly unlikely because most operating systems that use TCP/IP use a single software package that provides IP, TCP and UDP functions. But if the host receives the IP packet and TCP or UDP is not available, the ICMP unreachable message, with code "protocol unreachable," will be sent by the web server host to Fred, in response to Fred's packet destined for 10.1.2.14.

- **Port unreachable**—The final code field value is more likely today. If the server is up but the web server software is not running, the packet can get to the server but cannot be delivered to the web server software. The ICMP unreachable message, with code "port unreachable," will be sent by the web server host to Fred, in response to Fred's packet destined for 10.1.2.14.

Time Exceeded ICMP Message

The ICMP Time Exceeded message notifies a host when a packet that it sent has been discarded because it was "out of time." Packets are not actually timed, but to prevent packets from being forwarded forever when there is a routing loop, each IP header uses a Time to Live (TTL) field. Routers decrement TTL by one every time they forward a packet; if a router decrements TTL to zero, it throws away the packet. This prevents packets from rotating forever. Figure 6-20 shows the basic process.

Figure 6-20 *TTL Decremented to Zero*

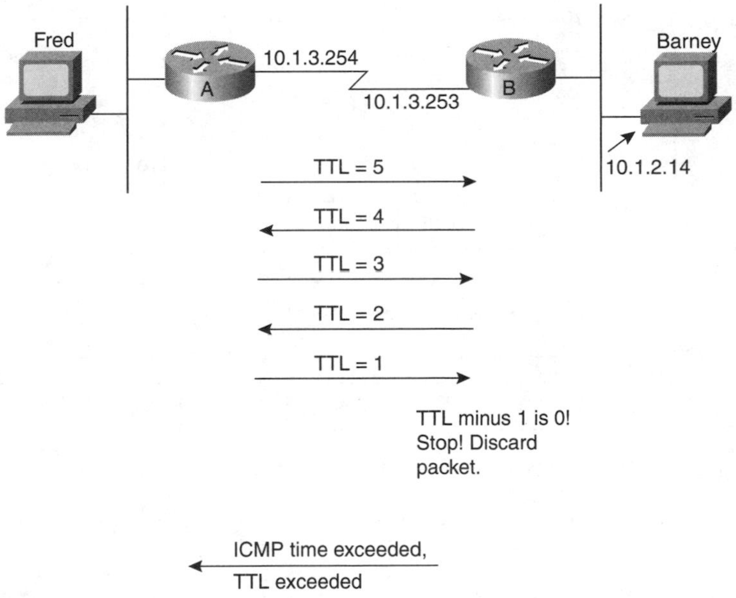

As you see in the figure, the router that discards the packet also sends an ICMP Time Exceeded message, with a code field of "time exceeded." That way, the sender knows that the packet was not delivered. Getting a Time Exceeded message can also help you when troubleshooting a network. Hopefully, you do not get too many of these; otherwise, you have routing problems.

The IOS **trace** command uses the Time Exceeded message and the IP TTL field to its advantage. By purposefully sending IP packets (with a UDP transport layer) with the TTL set to one, an ICMP Time Exceeded message is returned by the first router in the route. That's because that router decrements TTL to zero, causing it to discard the packet, and also sends the Time Exceeded message. The **trace** command learns the IP address of the first router by receiving the Time Exceeded message from that router. (The **trace** command actually sends three successive packets with TTL = 1.) Another set of three IP packets, this time with TTL = 2, is sent by the **trace** command. These messages make it through the first router but are discarded by the second router because the TTL is decremented to zero. The original packets sent by the host **trace** command use a destination port number that is very unlikely to be used so that the destination host will return the Port Unreachable message. The ICMP Port Unreachable message signifies that the packets reached the true destination host without having time exceeded, so the **trace** command knows that the packets are getting to the true endpoint. Figure 6-21 outlines the process, in which Router A is using the **trace** command trying to find the route to Barney. Example 6-1 shows this **trace** command on Router A, with debug messages from Router B, showing the resulting Time Exceeded messages.

Figure 6-21 *Cisco IOS Software* **trace** *Command—Messages Generated*

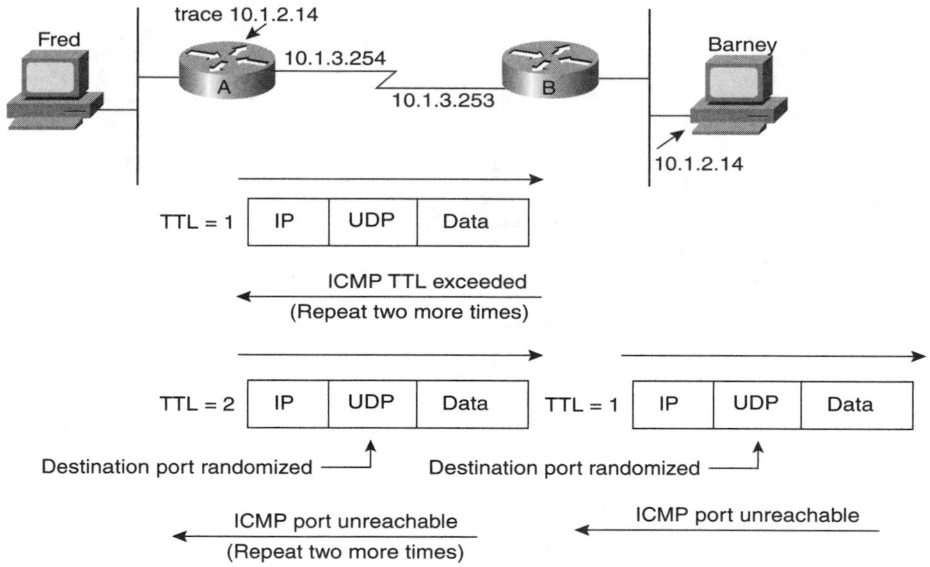

Example 6-1 *ICMP* **debug** *on Router B When Running* **trace** *Command on Router A*

```
RouterA#trace 10.1.2.14

Type escape sequence to abort.
Tracing the route to 10.1.2.14

  1 10.1.3.253 8 msec 4 msec 4 msec
  2 10.1.2.14 12 msec 8 msec 4 msec
```

Example 6-1 *ICMP* **debug** *on Router B When Running* **trace** *Command on Router A (Continued)*

```
RouterA#
```

```
RouterB#
ICMP: time exceeded (time to live) sent to 10.1.3.251 (dest was 10.1.2.14)
ICMP: time exceeded (time to live) sent to 10.1.3.251 (dest was 10.1.2.14)
ICMP: time exceeded (time to live) sent to 10.1.3.251 (dest was 10.1.2.14)
```

Redirect ICMP Message

ICMP redirect messages provide a very important element in routed IP networks. Many hosts are preconfigured with a default router IP address. When sending packets destined to subnets other than the one to which they are directly connected, these hosts send the packets to their default router. If there is a better local router to which the host should send the packets, an ICMP redirect can be used to tell the host to send the packets to this different router.

For example, in Figure 6-22, the PC uses Router B as its default router. However, Router A's route to subnet 10.1.4.0 is a better route. (Assume use of mask 255.255.255.0 in each subnet in Figure 6-22.) The PC sends a packet to Router B (Step 1 in Figure 6-22). Router B then forwards the packet based on its own routing table (Step 2); that route points through A, which has a better route. Finally, Router B sends the ICMP redirect message to the PC (Step 3), telling it to forward future packets destined for 10.1.4.0 to Router A instead. Ironically, the host can ignore the redirect and keep sending the packets to Router B.

Figure 6-22 *Example of an ICMP Redirect*

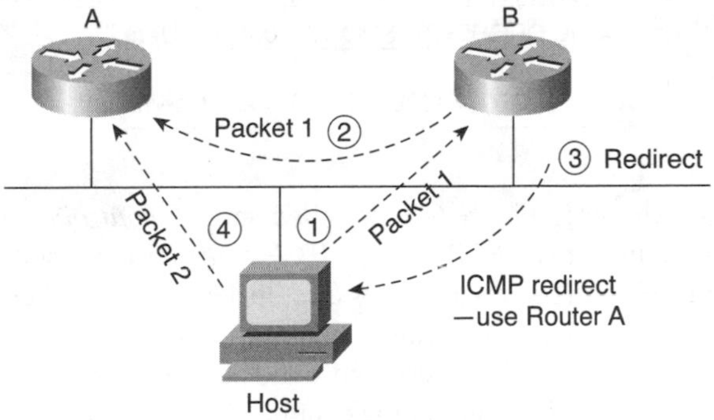

In summary, ICMP defines several message types and several subtypes, called codes. Popular use of terminology treats each different code as a different message; the exam is likely to treat these codes as different messages as well, although it is unlikely that the level of granularity will be important in getting the right answer. Pay particular attention to the messages denoted with asterisks in Table 6-5. Finally, RFC 792 is a short and straightforward RFC to read if you want more information.

Start Extra Credit

FTP and TFTP

The File Transfer Protocol (FTP) and the Trivial File Transfer Protocol (TFTP) are two popularly used file-transfer protocols in a typical IP network. Most users use FTP; whereas, router and switch administrators use TFTP. Which is "better" depends partially on what is being done. A more important question might be, "Which is supported on the devices that need to transfer the file?" Given a choice today, most users will choose FTP because it has more robust features. However, IOS did not support FTP for moving files in and out of the router originally, so many people continue to use TFTP out of habit.

FTP

FTP is a TCP-based application that has many options and features, including the capabilities to change directories, list files using wildcard characters, transfer multiple files with a single command, and use a variety of character sets or file formats. More important in this context is the basic operation of FTP. Figures 6-23 and 6-24 show a typical FTP connection—or, better stated, connections.

Figure 6-23 *FTP Control Connection*

The connection shown in Figure 6-23 is called an *FTP control connection*. When a user (FTP client) asks to connect to an FTP server, a TCP connection is established to the FTP server's well-known port (21). The connection is established like any other TCP connection. The user typically is required to enter a username and password, which the server uses to authenticate the files available to that user for read and write permissions. This security is based on the file security on the server's platform. All the commands used to control the transfer of a file are sent across this connection—hence the name *FTP control connection*.

At this point, the user has a variety of commands available to enable settings for transfer, change directories, list files, and so forth. However, whenever a **get** or a **put** command is entered (or **mget** or **mput**—*m* is for *multiple*) or the equivalent button is clicked, a file is transferred. The data is transferred over a separate *FTP data connection*. Figure 6-24 outlines the FTP data-connection process.

Figure 6-24 *FTP Data Connection*

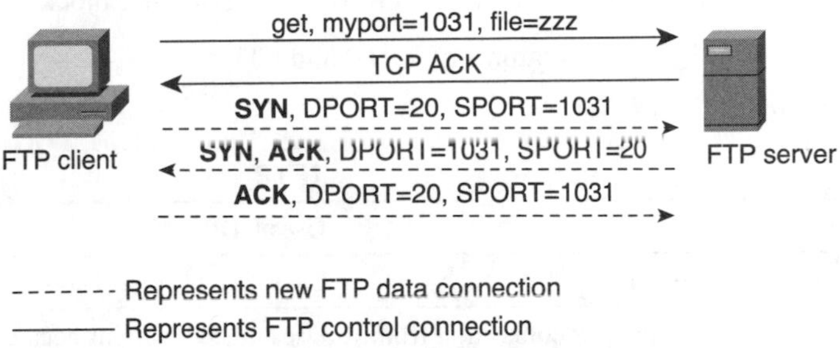

As shown in Figure 6-24, another TCP connection is established for the actual data transfer, this time to well-known port 20. Using this convention, a file can be transferred without getting in the way of the control connection. If many files are to be transferred rather than making a single control/data connection for each file, the control connection is made once. The environment is defined using the control connection, and these settings affect the functioning of the data connection. For example, the default directory to use in future transfers can be defined using commands on the control connection as well as the type of data (binary or ASCII). The control connection stays up until the user breaks it or the connection times out. While the control connection is up, a separate data connection is established for each file transfer.

An additional step helps prevent hackers from breaking in and transferring files, as shown in Figure 6-24. Rather than just creating a new connection, the client tells the server with an application layer message over the control connection which port number will be used for the new data connection. The server will not transfer the file (zzz, in this case) over any other data connection except the one to the correct socket—the one with the client's IP address, TCP, and the port number declared to the server (1031, in this case).

TFTP

The Trivial File Transfer Protocol (TFTP) performs basic file transfer with a small set of features. One of the reasons that such an application is needed, even when the more robust FTP is available, is that TFTP takes little memory to load and little time to program. With the advent of extremely low-cost memory and processing, such advantages seem trivial. Practically speaking, if you intend to transfer files frequently from your PC, you probably will use FTP. However, Cisco has supported TFTP for a much longer time, many people still use it, and basic exams might still use TFTP rather than FTP in examples.

TFTP uses UDP, so there is no connection establishment and no error recovery by the transport layer. However, TFTP uses application layer recovery by embedding a small header between the UDP header and the data. This header includes codes—for example, read, write, and acknowledgment—along with a numbering scheme that numbers 512-byte blocks of data.

These block numbers are used to acknowledge receipt and resend the data. TFTP sends one block and waits on an acknowledgment before sending another block.

Table 6-6 summarizes some features of TFTP and FTP.

Table 6-6 *Comparison of FTP and TFTP*

FTP	TFTP
Uses TCP	Uses UDP
Uses robust control commands	Uses simple control commands
Sends data over a separate TCP connection from control commands	Uses no connections because of UDP
Requires more memory and programming effort	Requires less memory and programming effort

End Extra Credit

IP Addressing and Subnetting

20 Describe the different classes of IP addresses (and subnetting).

No one reading this book should be shocked to hear that IP addressing is one of the most important topics on the CCNA exam. You need a comfortable, confident understanding of IP addressing and subnetting for success on any Cisco certification. For CCNA, the exam questions will ask for an interpretation of an address, its network number, its subnet number, the other IP addresses in the same subnet, the broadcast address, and the other subnets that could be used if the same mask were in use. In other words, you had better know subnetting!

Network engineers need to understand subnetting very well. Engineers who work with multiple networks must decipher IP addresses quickly, without running off to use a subnet calculator tool. For example, someone with a problem might call and tell you his IP address. After finding out the mask that's used, you do a **show ip route** command on a router, but that typically lists subnets—so you need to be able to easily figure out the subnet of which the address is a member. And not all networks will be using nice, easy subnet masks.

You need the same understanding and tricks to get the right answers quickly and easily to pass the CCNA exam with confidence. After reading this section, you will be able to confidently understand subnetting and quickly derive all the information related to an IP address.

IP Addressing and Subnetting

Engineers use IP addressing terminology in many different ways—and sometimes people use the terms to mean slightly different things. Table 6-7 lists the IP terms used in the upcoming sections, giving an exact definition. Feel free to refer to this table as you read.

Table 6-7 *IP Addressing Terminology*

Term	Definition
IP address	A 32-bit number, usually written in dotted-decimal form, that uniquely identifies an interface of some computer.
Host address	Another term for IP address.
Network	A group of hosts, all of which have an identical beginning portion of their IP addresses.
Network number	A 32-bit number, usually written in dotted-decimal form, that represents a network. This number cannot be assigned as an IP address to an interface of some computer. The host portion of the network number has a value of all binary 0s.
Network address	Another term for the network number.
Broadcast address	A 32-bit number, usually written in dotted-decimal form, that is used to address all hosts in the network. This number cannot be assigned as an IP address to an interface of some computer. The host portion of the network number has a value of all binary 1s.
Subnet	A group of hosts, all of which have an identical beginning portion of their IP addresses. A subnet differs from a network in that a subnet is a further subdivision of a network, with a longer portion of the addresses being identical.
Subnet number	A 32-bit number, usually written in dotted-decimal form, that represents a subnet. This number cannot be assigned as an IP address to an interface of some computer. The host portion of the network number has a value of all binary 0s.
Subnet address	Another term for the subnet number.
Subnet broadcast address	A 32-bit number, usually written in dotted-decimal form, that is used to address all hosts in the subnet. This number cannot be assigned as an IP address to an interface of some computer. The host portion of the network number has a value of all binary 1s.

continues

Table 6-7 *IP Addressing Terminology (Continued)*

Term	Definition
Subnetting	The process of subdividing networks into smaller subnets. This is jargon—for example, "Are you subnetting your network?"
Network mask	A 32-bit number, usually written in dotted-decimal form. The mask is used by computers to calculate the network number of a given IP address by performing a Boolean AND of the address and mask. The mask also defines the number of host bits in an address.
Mask	A generic term for a mask, whether it is a default mask or a subnet mask.
Address mask	Another term for a mask.
Default Class A mask	The mask used for Class A networks when no subnetting is used. The value is 255.0.0.0.
Default Class B mask	The mask used for Class B networks when no subnetting is used. The value is 255.255.0.0.
Default Class C mask	The mask used for Class C networks when no subnetting is used. The value is 255.255.255.0.
Subnet mask	A nondefault mask that is used when subnetting.
Network part or network field	Term used to describe the first part of an IP address. The network part is 8, 16, or 24 bits for Class A, B, and C networks, respectively.
Host part or host field	Term used to describe the last part of an IP address. The host part is 24, 16, or 8 bits for Class A, B, and C networks, respectively, when subnetting is not used. When subnetting, the size of the host part depends on the subnet mask chosen for that network.
Subnet part or subnet field	Term used to describe the middle part of an IP address. The subnet part is variable in size, based on how subnetting is implemented.

To fully appreciate IP addressing, you first must understand the concepts behind the grouping of IP addresses. The first visions of what we call the Internet were for connecting research sites. A typical network diagram might have looked like Figure 6-25.

Figure 6-25 *Sample Network Using Class A, B, and C Network Numbers*

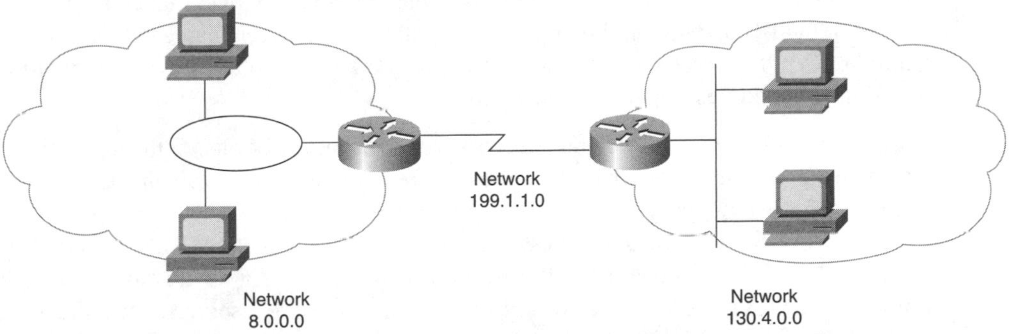

The conventions of IP addressing and IP address grouping make routing easy. For example, all IP addresses that begin with 8 are on the Token Ring on the left. Likewise, all IP addresses that begin with 130.4 are on the right. Along the same lines, 199.1.1 is the prefix on the serial link. By following this convention, the routers build a routing table with three entries, one for each prefix, or network number.

The convention fails if you do not follow these rules:

- IP addresses are assigned to interfaces, not to entire computers. Therefore, routers will have multiple IP addresses, one per interface.
- All IP addresses in the same group must not be separated by a router.
- IP addresses separated by a router must be in different groups.

In Figure 6-25, all IP addresses assigned to interfaces on the Token Ring are in the same group. Likewise, both serial interfaces, one on each router, are in a second group. Finally, all the interfaces on the Ethernet are in the third IP address grouping.

IP addressing behaves similarly to ZIP codes. Everyone living in my ZIP code lives in my town. If some members of my ZIP code were in California, some of my mail might be sent out there (I live in Georgia, by the way). Just as it would be silly for addresses in the same ZIP code to be in different states, having IP addresses in the same network grouping be on different sites in the network topology is silly.

Classes of Networks

RFC 790 defines the IP protocol, including three different sizes of networks. By definition, all addresses in the same network have the same numeric value *network* portion of the addresses. The rest of the address is called the *host* portion of the address. Using the post office example, the network part is the ZIP code, and the host part is the street address. Just as a letter-sorting machine three states away from you cares only about the ZIP code on a letter addressed to you, a router three hops away from you cares only about the subnet number that your address resides in. Individual IP addresses in the same network all have a different value in the host part of the addresses, but they have identical values in the network part, just as everyone in my town has a different street address but the same ZIP code.

Class A networks have a 1-byte-long network part. That leaves 24 bits for the rest of the address, or the host part. That means that 2^{24} addresses are numerically possible in a Class A network. Similarly, Class B networks have a 2-byte-long network part, leaving 16 bits for the host portion of the address. So 2^{16} possible addresses exist in a single Class B network. Finally, Class C networks have a 3-byte-long network part, leaving only 8 bits for the host part, which implies only 2^8 addresses in a Class C network. However, there are two reserved host addresses in each network, as shown in the last column of Table 6-8. The table summarizes the characteristics of Class A, B, and C networks.

Table 6-8 *Sizes of Network and Host Parts of IP Addresses with No Subnetting*

Any Network of This Class	Number of Network Bytes (Bits)	Number of Host Bytes (Bits)	Number of Addresses per Network*
A	1 (8)	3 (24)	2^{24}, minus two special cases
B	2 (16)	2 (16)	2^{16}, minus two special cases
C	3 (24)	1 (8)	2^8, minus two special cases

*There are two reserved host addresses per network.

For example, Figure 6-25 shows a small network with the IP network numbers filled in. Network 8.0.0.0 is a Class A network, network 130.4.0.0 is a Class B network, and network 199.1.1.0 is a Class C network.

Network numbers look like addresses because they are in dotted-decimal format. However, network numbers cannot be assigned to an interface as an IP address. Conceptually, network numbers represent the group of all IP addresses in the network, much like a ZIP code represents the group of all addresses in a community. Numerically, the network number is built with the network number in the network part, but with all binary 0s in the host part. Based on the three examples from Figure 6-25, Table 6-9 provides a closer look at the numerical version of the three network numbers: 8.0.0.0, 130.4.0.0, and 199.1.1.0.

Table 6-9 *Example Network Numbers, Decimal and Binary*

Network Number	Binary Representation, with Host Part Bold
8.0.0.0	0000 1000 **0000 0000 0000 0000 0000 0000**
130.4.0.0	1000 0010 0000 0100 **0000 0000 0000 0000**
199.1.1.0	1100 0111 0000 0001 0000 0001 **0000 0000**

The binary values provide a little more insight into the IP address structure. By convention, Class A networks have a one-octet network part and a three-octet host part. With 24 host bits, you can number 2^{24} hosts—except that two of those are reserved. Of course, who cares if you have to waste two addresses when you have more than 16 million addresses? One of the two reserved values is the network number itself—the value shown in Table 6-9. The other reserved value is the one with all binary 1s in the host part of the address—this number is the network broadcast address. And as you might guess, all the numbers between the network number and the broadcast address are the valid, useful IP addresses that can be used to address interfaces in the network.

Many different Class A, B, and C networks exist. If your firm connects to the Internet without using a form of Address Translating Gateway (such as the Cisco PIX), it must use registered, unique network numbers. To that end, the Network Information Center (NIC) assigns network numbers so that uniqueness is achieved. Table 6-10 summarizes the possible network numbers, the total number of each type, and the number of hosts in each Class A, B, and C network.

Table 6-10 *List of All Possible Valid Network Numbers**

Class	First Octet Range	Valid Network Numbers	Total Number of This Class of Network	Number of Hosts per Network	Number of Bytes in Network Part of Address	Number of Bytes in Host Part of Address
A	1 to 126	1.0.0.0 to 126.0.0.0	2^7, minus two special cases	2^{24}, minus two special cases	1	3
B	128 to 191	128.1.0.0 to 191.254.0.0	2^{14}, minus two special cases	2^{16}, minus two special cases	2	2
C	192 to 223	192.0.1.0 to 223.255.254.0	2^{21}, minus two special cases	2^8, minus two special cases	3	1

*The Valid Network Numbers column shows actual network numbers. There are several reserved cases. For example, network 0.0.0.0 (originally defined for use as a broadcast address) and 127.0.0.0 (still available for use as the loopback address) are reserved. Networks 128.0.0.0, 191.255.0.0, 192.0.0.0, and 223.255.255.0 also are reserved.

Engineers should classify a network as Class A, B, or C with ease. If you have not already done so, you should memorize the first octet ranges in Table 6-11. It's on the exam—reason enough. However, if you plan on having a job for which you work with lots of different installations, as you would if you worked for a vendor, reseller, service provider, or consulting company, classifying a network as Class A, B, or C should become an instantaneous process. Also memorize the number of octets in the network part of Class A, B, and C addresses, as shown in Table 6-8.

For example, Figure 6-26 shows three example IP addresses, one for each of the three networks shown in Figure 6-25. One address is in a Class A network, one is in a Class B network, and one is in a Class C network.

Figure 6-26 *Example Class A, B, and C IP Addresses and Their Formats*

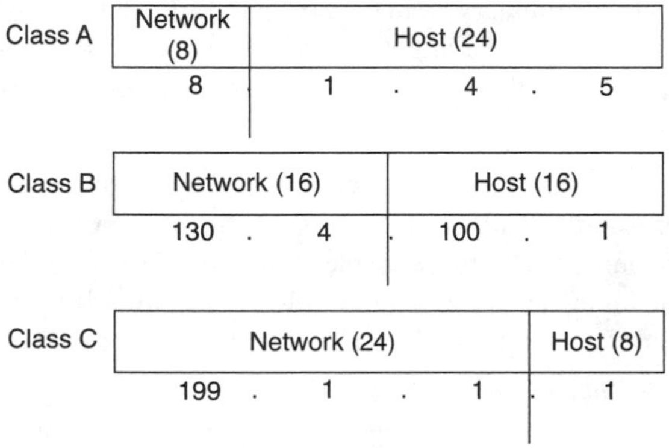

By definition, an address that begins with 8 is in a Class A network, so the network part of the address is the first byte, or first octet. (Refer to Table 6-10 for a reminder of the Class A, B, and C ranges in the first octet.) An address that begins with 130 is in a Class B network, and, by definition, Class B addresses have a two-byte network part, as shown. Finally, any address that begins with 199 is in a Class C network, which has a three-byte network part. Also by definition, a Class A address has a three-byte host part, Class B has a two-byte host part, and Class C has a three-byte host part.

Humans can simply remember the numbers in Table 6-10 and the concepts in Figure 6-26 and then quickly determine the network and host part of an IP address. Computers, however, use a mask to define the size of the network and host parts of an address. The logic behind the mask results in the same conventions of Class A, B, and C networks that you already know, but the computer can deal with it better as a binary math problem. The mask is a 32-bit binary number, usually written in dotted-decimal format, that defines the structure of an IP address. In short, the mask defines the size of the host parts of an IP address, representing the host part of the IP address with binary 0s. Class A mask has its last 24 bits as binary 0, which means that the last three octets of the mask, in decimal, are 0s. Table 6-11 summarizes the default masks and reflects the sizes of the two parts of an IP address.

Table 6-11 *Class A, B, and C Networks—Network and Host Parts and Default Masks*

Class of Address	Size of Network Part of Address, in Bits	Size of Host Part of Address, in Bits	Default Mask for Each Class of Network
A	8	24	255.0.0.0
B	16	16	255.255.0.0
C	24	8	255.255.255.0

IP Grouping Concepts and Subnetting

The creators of the Internet realized the impracticality of the original network-numbering conventions early on. Computing history shows many examples of people being unable to conceive the idea that computing technology would grow as fast as it has. Needless to say, the Internet would have run out of Class A, B, and C networks long ago if additional addressing features had not been created. Subnetting provided the first significant addressing feature that conserved the global IP address space.

IP subnetting creates vastly larger numbers of smaller groups of IP addresses, compared with simply using Class A, B, and C conventions. The Class A, B, and C rules still exist—but now, a single Class A, B, or C network can be subdivided into many smaller groups. Subnetting treats a subdivision of a single Class A, B, or C network as if it were a network itself. By doing so, a single Class A, B, or C network can be subdivided into many nonoverlapping subnets.

The needs for subnetting are both technical and administrative, as documented in the following list:

- All organizations connected to the Internet (and not using IP address translation) are required to use IP networks registered with the NIC.
- IP protocols enforce the following grouping concept: All hosts in the same group must not be separated by an IP router.
- A corollary to the grouping concept is this: Hosts separated by an IP router must be in separate groups.
- Without subnetting, the smallest group is a single, entire Class A, B, or C network number.
- Without subnetting, the NIC would be woefully short of assignable networks.
- With subnetting, the NIC can assign one or a few network numbers to an organization, and then the organization can subdivide those networks into subnets of more usable sizes.

An example drives these points home. Consider all network interfaces in Figure 6-27, and note which ones are not separated by a router.

Figure 6-27 *Backdrop for Discussing Numbers of Different Networks/Subnetworks*

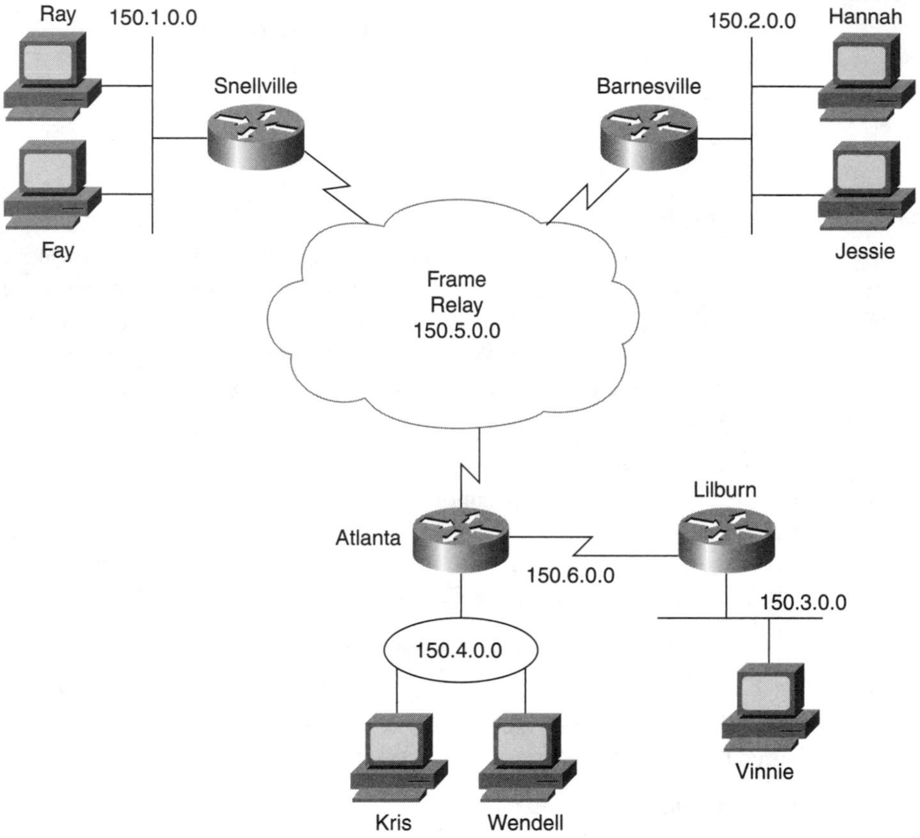

The design in Figure 6-27 requires six groups, each of which is a Class B network. The four LANs each use a single Class B network. In other words, the LANs attached to routers A, B, C, and D are each a separate network. Additionally, the two serial interfaces composing the point-to-point serial link between routers C and D use the same network because these two interfaces are not separated by a router. Finally, the three router interfaces composing the Frame Relay network with routers A, B, and C are not separated by an IP router and would compose the sixth network. (*Note:* Other Frame Relay IP addressing options would require one or two more IP network numbers for this physical network.)

However, this design would not be allowed if it were connected to the Internet. The NIC would not assign six separate registered Class B network numbers—in fact, you probably would not even get one Class B because most of the Class B addresses already are assigned. You are more likely to get a couple of Class C networks, and the NIC would expect you to use subnetting.

Figure 6-28 illustrates a more realistic example that uses basic subnetting.

Figure 6-28 *Using Subnets*

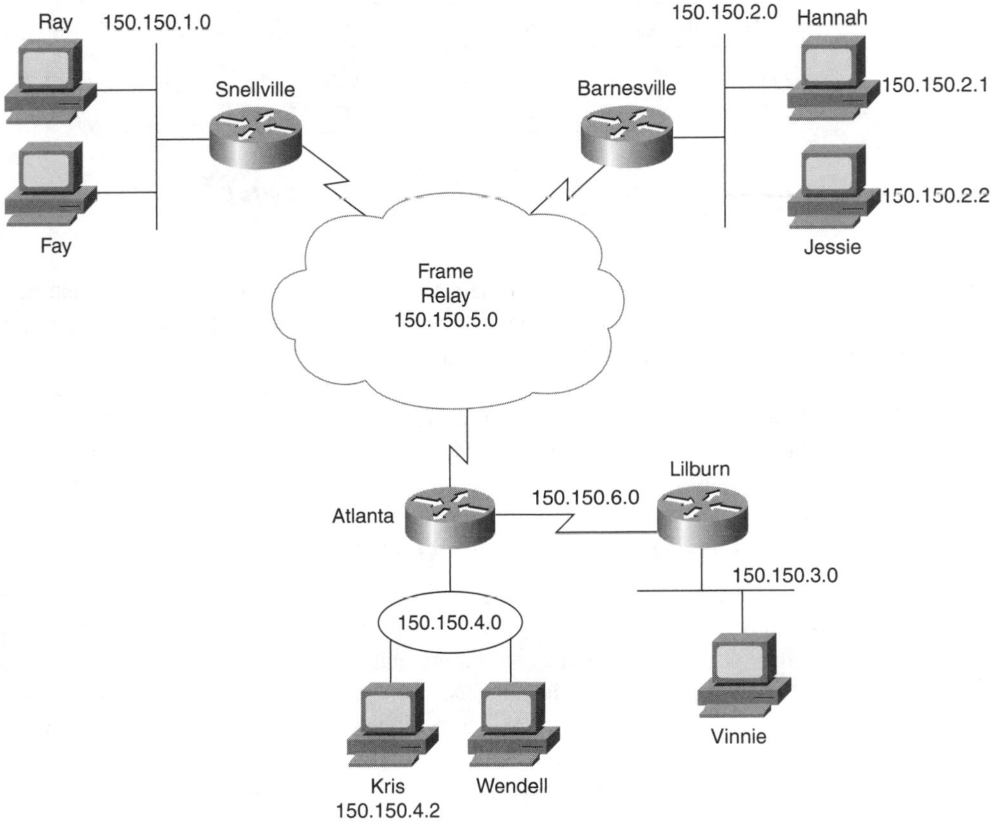

As in Figure 6-27, the design in Figure 6-28 requires six groups. Unlike Figure 6-27, this figure uses six subnets, each of which is a subnet of a single Class B network. This design subnets Class B network 150.150.0.0, which has been assigned by the NIC. The IP network designer has chosen a mask of 255.255.255.0, the last octet of which implies 8 host bits. Because it is a Class B network, there are 16 network bits. Therefore, there are 8 subnet bits, which happen to be bits 17 through 24—in other words, the third octet. Notice that each subnet number in the figure shows a different value in the third octet, representing each different subnet number. In other words, this design numbers or identifies each different subnet using the third octet.

When subnetting, a third part of an IP address appears in the middle of the address—namely, the subnet part of the address. This field is created by "stealing" bits from the host part of the address. The size of the network part of the address never shrinks—in other words, Class A, B, and C rules still apply when defining the size of the network part of an address. Figure 6-29 shows the format of addresses when subnetting.

Figure 6-29 *Address Formats When Subnetting Is Used*

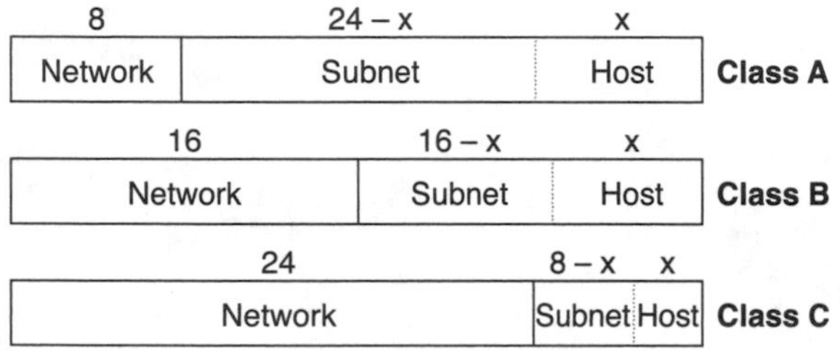

Three portions of the address now exist: network, subnet, and host. Class rules determine the size of the network part. The subnet mask determines the size of the host part—the number of bits of value 0 in the subnet mask defines the number of host bits. The remaining bits define the size of the subnet part of the address. For example, a mask of 255.255.255.224, used with a Class C network, implies five host bits. (The mask can be more easily converted to decimal using the table in Appendix B, "Decimal to Hexadecimal Binary Conversion Table.") The mask has five binary 0s at the end, implying five host bits. As shown in Figure 6-29, a Class C network has 24 network bits. That leaves three subnet bits—not many, but it still provides more groupings than if this Class C network was not subnetted at all!

The number of host bits implies how many valid host addresses exist in the subnet; $2^{hostbits}$ minus 2 special reserved cases is the formula. Similarly, the number of subnet bits implies the number of valid subnets of a network, assuming that the same mask is used on all subnets; $2^{subnetbits}$ is the formula. Two special subnets, the "zero subnet" and the "broadcast subnet," were reserved in years past but are now usable. However, when you get a test question about the number of possible subnets, the "right" answer is $2^{subnetbits} - 2$.

Binary View of Subnetting

Computers, especially routers, do not think about IP addresses in terms of conventions. They think in terms of 32-bit binary numbers, which is fine because, technically, that's what IP addresses really are. Also, computers use a mask to define the structure of these binary IP addresses. A full understanding of what that means is not difficult—in fact, if you understood the last section of the book, you already understand the structure of an IP address. However, getting accustomed to doing the binary math in your head is challenging for most of us, particularly if you don't do it every day.

Understanding Binary-to-Decimal and Decimal-to-Binary Conversion If you already know how binary works, how binary-to-decimal and decimal-to-binary conversion works, and how to convert IP addresses from decimal to binary and back, skip this note.

IP addresses are 32-bit binary numbers, written as a series of decimal numbers, separated by periods. To examine an address in its true form, binary, you need to convert from decimal to binary. To put a 32-bit binary number in the decimal form that is needed when configuring a router, you need to convert the 32-bit number back to decimal, 8 bits at a time.

One key to the conversion process for IP addresses is remembering these facts: When converting from one format to the other, each decimal number represents eight bits. When converting from decimal to binary, each decimal number converts to an eight-bit number. So address 150.150.2.1, 150, when converted to its eight-bit binary equivalent, is 10010010. How do you know that? For now, look in the conversion chart in Appendix B. The next byte, another decimal 150, is converted to 10010010. The third byte, decimal 2, is converted to 00000010; finally, the fourth byte, decimal 1, is converted to 00000001. The combined series of 8-bit numbers is the 32-bit IP address—in this case, 10010010 10010010 00000010 00000001.

If you start with the binary version of the IP address, you first separate it into four sets of eight digits. *Then you convert each set of eight binary digits to its binary equivalent.* For example, 10010010100100100000001000000001 is not a useful way to write an IP address. First, separate it into four sets of eight digits: 10010010 10010010 00000010 00000001. Then look in the conversion chart in Appendix B, and find that the first 8-bit number converts to 150, and so does the second set. The third set of 8 bits converts to 2, and the fourth converts to 1—giving you 150.150.2.1.

Using the chart in Appendix B makes this much easier—but you will not have the chart on the exam, of course! So you can do a couple of things. First, you can learn how to do the conversion. The book does not cover it, but a couple of web sites referenced at the end of this note can help. The other alternative is to use the chart when studying, and study the examples that show you how to manipulate IP addresses and find the right answers to the test questions without doing any binary math. If that works for you, you actually do not need to be speedy and proficient at doing binary-to-decimal and decimal-to-binary, conversions.

One last important fact: When subnetting, the subnet and host parts of the address might span only part of a byte of the IP address. So when converting from binary to decimal and decimal to binary, the rule of doing this using an eight-bit binary number is indeed true. However, when thinking about subnetting, you will need to ignore byte boundaries and think about IP addresses as 32-bit numbers without specific byte boundaries. But that will be explained later.

Some sites that might help you if you want more information are

For basic information on base 10, base 2 (binary), and conversion practice, visit www.ibilce.unesp.br/courseware/datas/numbers.htm#mark2.

For a description of the conversion process, try doit.ort.org/course/inforep/135.htm.

For another description of the conversion process, try www.goshen.edu/compsci/mis200/decbinary.htm.

For some free video classes that cover binary, conversion, and subnetting, go to www.learntosubnet.com.

An example of several IP addresses, in binary, will make subnetting a little clearer. The subnet part of an address identifies the different subdivisions of this network. An address with a different value in the subnet field, as compared with a second address, is considered to be in a different subnet. For example, examine the following three IP addresses that are part of Table 6-12 and are valid addresses in Figure 6-28.

Table 6-12 *Subnet Part of Sample Addresses*

Address in Decimal	Address in Binary
150.150.2.1	1001 0110 1001 0110 **0000 0010** 0000 0001
150.150.2.2	1001 0110 1001 0110 **0000 0010** 0000 0010
150.150.4.2	1001 0110 1001 0110 **0000 0100** 0000 0010

The example shows that the subnet field consists of bits 17 through 24 (the entire third byte). 150.150.2.1 and 150.150.2.2 are in the same subnet because they are in the same Class B network and because *their subnet fields have the same value* (0000 0010). 150.150.4.2 is in a different subnet of the same Class B network because the subnet field has a different value than the first two addresses (0000 0100). 150.150.4.2 must be physically located with at least one IP router between itself and 150.150.2.1 and 150.150.2.2. Similarly, addresses 150.150.2.1 and 150.150.2.2 must not be separated by a router, as is shown in Figure 6-28.

Routers understand the format of addresses using a mask. When subnetting is used, the mask is called a subnet mask. The mask is useful in that it defines the size and location of the host part of the address. In the example of network 150.150.0.0, using the third octet as the subnet part of the address, subnet mask 255.255.255.0 is used. Logically, the mask is interpreted this way:

- The subnet mask, 255.255.255.0, in binary is 11111111 11111111 11111111 00000000.
- The size of the network field is based on Class A, B, and C rules and does not consider the subnet mask. In this case, the network part is 16 bits long because the address is a Class B address.
- The size of the host part of the address is defined by the number of binary 0s in the subnet mask. There are eight binary 0s at the end of the mask.
- The subnet part is the remaining part of the address—bits 17 through 24, or, in other words, the third octet.

Routers and other computers take advantage of the subnet masks to answer a very frequently considered question:

What subnet is this address in?

For a computer, it's simple binary math—a Boolean AND between the IP address and the subnet mask. An example will help. Consider the following binary example. (*Note:* Appendix B has a binary-to-decimal conversion chart.)

Address	150.150.2.1	1001 0110 1001 0110 0000 0010 0000 0001
Mask	255.255.255.0	1111 1111 1111 1111 1111 1111 0000 0000
Result	150.150.2.0	1001 0110 1001 0110 0000 0010 0000 0000

A Boolean AND between the address and the mask results in the subnet number. The term *mask* comes from the idea that, because all the host bits are binary 0s in the mask, all those same bits in the IP address fall out to binary 0 as well. That's because, in a Boolean AND, both bits must be binary 1 for the result to be binary 1. Otherwise, the result is binary 0. So the mask of 255.255.255.0 masks out the last octet, leaving a subnet number that contains the same first three octets as the address, but a decimal 0 in the last octet.

If you understand the basic idea but would like additional examples to make it more clear, read on. In the next section, the four-step method to answer all IP addressing questions will be described. Also, in Appendix C, "Subnetting Practice: 25 Subnetting Questions," 25 IP addressing practice questions are available, each with the binary math worked out for performing the Boolean AND.

Finally, any Cisco-oriented IP addressing coverage would be incomplete without a discussion of *prefix notation*. Prefix notation describes a mask, but with fewer characters. Therefore, output from commands is briefer.

Prefix notation simply denotes the number of binary 1s in a mask, preceded by a "/". In other words, for subnet mask 255.255.255.0, the equivalent prefix notation would be /24 because there are 24 consecutive binary 1s in the mask. When talking about subnets, you can say things like, "That subnet uses a slash 24 prefix" instead of saying something like, "That subnet uses a mask of 255.255.255.0." The first option is simply easier to say, and it is often more convenient to use when you get used to it.

So far, you have read about all the basic information you need to understand IP addressing for a typical networking job. Now, for further preparation for the exam, the next section takes you through a process that will help you answer questions on the exam quickly and accurately.

Four Steps to Answering IP Addressing Questions

You must master IP addressing and subnetting to succeed as a network engineer. To pass the CCNA exam, you must at least be able to answer a few questions about subnetting. For most networking jobs, the ability to think about IP addresses and quickly decipher the structure and meaning of the address is a prerequisite for the job.

The exam will test your abilities with questions that go something like this:

- Given a network number and a mask, how many subnets are there, and how many hosts are there per subnet?
- Given an address and a mask, what is the subnet number?
- Given an address and a mask, what is the subnet broadcast address?
- Given an address and a mask, what are the valid IP addresses in the subnet?

This section teaches a process by which you can ignore the four preceding questions and think about IP addressing and subnetting like you normally would for your job. Coincidentally, if you follow the four-step process in this section, you would answer all of the preceding questions without much binary math. This four-step process is designed to help you learn how to do the math in your head—when you get the idea, you will not need to memorize every little step. In fact, with five examples in this chapter and 25 more in an appendix, you will be able to practice enough to easily memorize the process.

For reference, the steps in the process are as follows:

Step 1 Identify the structure of the IP address.

Step 2 Create the chart that will be used in Steps 3 and 4.

Step 3 Derive the subnet number and the first valid IP address.

Step 4 Derive the broadcast address and the last valid IP address.

In this section, you will see two different examples worked out in great detail and three examples worked out with less detail. With these five examples, plus the extra practice in Appendix C, you will be able to master the process of answering the previous questions about any IP address. If you already can answer those questions about the five examples, you know plenty about IP subnetting for passing the CCNA exam! Here are the examples:

8.1.4.5, mask 255.255.0.0
130.4.102.1, mask 255.255.255.0
199.1.1.100, mask 255.255.255.0
130.4.102.1, mask 255.255.252.0
199.1.1.100, mask 255.255.255.224

If you can confidently answer all four questions for all five example address/mask pairs, you might want to skip the rest of the IP addressing section. If you look at the examples and think that you simply need more practice, turn to Appendix C, which has 25 additional examples completely worked out. If you want to see how I got the answers to these five, along with the process to do it quickly without needing a binary-to-decimal conversion chart, read on! By the way, you can check your work against Table 6-13, which summarizes the results of all the steps for each of the five sample addresses and masks.

Table 6-13 *Five Addresses/Masks, with IP Addressing Information Explained*

	8.1.4.5/16	130.4.102.1/24	199.1.1.100/24	130.4.102.1/22	199.1.1.100/27
Mask	255.255.0.0	255.255.255.0	255.255.255.0	255.255.252.0	255.255.255.224
Number of network bits	8	16	24	16	24
Number of host bits	16	8	8	10	5
Number of subnet bits	8	8	0	6	3
Number of hosts per subnet	$2^{16} - 2$	$2^8 - 2$	$2^8 - 2$	$2^{10} - 2$	$2^5 - 2$
Number of subnets	$2^8 - 2$	$2^8 - 2$	0	$2^6 - 2$	$2^3 - 2$
Subnet number	8.1.0.0	130.4.102.0	199.1.1.0	130.4.100.0	199.1.1.96
First valid IP address	8.1.0.1	130.4.102.1	199.1.1.1	130.4.100.1	199.1.1.97
Broadcast address	8.1.255.255	130.4.102.255	199.1.1.255	130.4.103.255	199.1.1.127
Last valid IP address	8.1.255.254	130.4.102.254	199.1.1.254	130.4.103.254	199.1.1.126
Range of valid IP addresses	8.1.0.1–8.1.255.254	130.4.102.1–130.4.102.254	199.1.1.1–199.1.1.254	130.4.100.1–130.4.103.254	199.1.1.97–199.1.1.126

Step 1: Identify the Structure of the IP Address

Two tasks must be performed in Step 1. First, the rules that define the three parts of an IP address must be remembered and applied. In other words, you must decide how many of the 32 bits in the address comprise the network, subnet, and host portions of the address. The second task is to remember and apply two easy formulas that tell you how many subnets exist and how many hosts there are per subnet.

The first task requires that you remember these three facts:

The network part of the address is always defined by class rules.

The host part of the address is always defined by the mask; binary 0s in the mask mean that the corresponding address bits are part of the host field.

The subnet part of the address is what's left over in the 32-bit address.

Table 6-14 lists these three key facts, beside the first example. If you have forgotten the ranges of values in the first octet for addresses in Class A, B, and C networks, refer to Table 6-10 earlier in the chapter.

Table 6-14 *First Example, with Rules for Learning Network, Subnet, and Host Part Sizes*

Step	Example	Rules to Remember
Address	8.1.4.5	N/A
Mask	255.255.0.0	N/A
Number of network bits	8	Always defined by Class A, B, C
Number of host bits	16	Always defined as number of binary 0s in mask
Number of subnet bits	8	32 – (network size + host size)

In this example, there are eight network bits because the address is in a Class A network, 8.0.0.0. There are 16 host bits because, when you convert 255.255.0.0 to binary, there are 16 binary 0s—the last 16 bits in the mask. (If you do not believe me, look at Appendix B, in the binary-to-decimal conversion chart. 255 decimal is eight binary 1s, and 0 decimal is eight binary 0s.) The size of the subnet part of the address is what's left over, or 8 bits.

The same logic applies to all five examples in Table 6-13. For example, 130.4.102.1 is in a Class B network, so there are 16 network bits. The prefix of /24 has only eight binary 0s, implying eight host bits, which leaves eight subnet bits. The third example, 199.1.1.100, with mask 255.255.255.0, is not using subnetting at all. How do you know? Well, 199.1.1.100 is in a Class C network, which means that there are 24 network bits. The mask has eight binary 0s, yielding eight host bits, with no bits remaining for the subnet part of the address. In fact, if you remembered that the default mask for Class C networks is 255.255.255.0, you might have already realized that no subnetting was being used.

Most of us can calculate the number of host bits easily if the mask uses only decimal 255s and 0s. When the mask uses other values besides 0 and 255, deciphering the number of host bits is more difficult. Examining the subnet masks in binary help overcome the challenge. Consider the masks used in the last two examples of Table 6-13, as shown in Table 6-15.

Table 6-15 *Masks Used in Examples 4 and 5*

Mask in Decimal	Mask in Binary
255.255.252.0	1111 1111 1111 1111 1111 1100 0000 0000
255.255.255.224	1111 1111 1111 1111 1111 1111 1110 0000

The number of host bits implied by a mask becomes more apparent after converting the mask to binary. In the first mask, 255.255.252.0, there are 10 binary 0s, implying a 10-bit host field. Because that mask is used with a Class B address (130.4.102.1), implying 16 network bits, there are six remaining subnet bits. In the last example, the mask has only five binary 0s, for five host bits. Because the mask is used with a Class C address, there are 24 network bits, leaving only three subnet bits.

The process so far is straightforward: The class rules define the network part, the mask binary 0s define the host part, and what's left over defines the size of the subnet part. The only big problem occurs when the mask is tricky, which is true in examples 4 and 5. When the mask is tricky, you have two alternatives for deciding how many host bits are defined:

Convert the mask to binary, using any method for conversion at your disposal, and count the number of zeros.

Convert the mask to binary after memorizing the nine decimal and binary values in Table 6-16—these are the only nine valid decimal values used in a subnet mask. Converting a mask to binary without the use of any tools will be much faster.

Table 6-16 lists the only valid decimal values in a mask and their binary equivalents.

Table 6-16 *Decimal and Binary Values in a Single Octet of a Valid Subnet Mask*

Decimal	Binary
0	0000 0000
128	1000 0000
192	1100 0000
224	1110 0000
240	1111 0000
248	1111 1000
252	1111 1100
254	1111 1110
255	1111 1111

Binary conversion of a subnet mask, without the use of a calculator, PC, or decimal-to-binary conversion chart, becomes easy after memorizing this chart. The binary equivalents of 255 and decimal 0 are obvious. The other seven values are not! But notice the values in succession: Each value has an additional binary 1 and one less binary 0. Each mask value, in succession, shows a mask value that reduces the number of host bits by 1 and adds 1 to the size of the subnet field. If you simply memorize each decimal value and its binary equivalent, converting masks from decimal to binary will be a breeze.

This section on subnetting outlines a four-step process that helps you answer most subnetting questions. Step 1 includes two tasks, as mentioned in the first paragraph of the description of Step 1. The first task is to figure out how many network, host, and subnet bits exist in the address. However, the exam probably will not include simple questions like, "Given this address and mask, how big is the host part of the address?" A question that could be on your exam would be something more like this: "Given an address and mask, how many subnets are there? And how many hosts are there in a single subnet?" Well, two simple formulas provide the answers, and the formulas are based on the information that you just learned how to derive:

Number of subnets = $2^{\text{number-of-subnet-bits}} - 2$
Number of hosts per subnet = $2^{\text{number-of-host-bits}} - 2$

The formulas calculate the number of things that can be numbered using a binary number and subtract 2 for the two special cases. IP addressing conventions define that two subnets per network not be used and that two hosts per subnet not be used. One reserved subnet, the subnet that has all binary 0s in the subnet field, is called the zero subnet. The subnet with all binary 1s in the subnet field is called the broadcast subnet—and it also is reserved. (Well, in fact, you can use both these subnets on a Cisco router, but it is recommended that you avoid using them. On the exam, the "right" answer is that you do not use them—hence the $2^{\text{number-of-subnet-bits}} - 2$ formula.) IP addressing conventions also reserve two IP addresses per subnet: the first (all binary 0s in the host field) and last (all binary 1s in the host field) addresses. No tricks exist to make these two addresses usable—they are indeed always reserved.

Now you have seen how to identify the components of an IP address and to derive how many subnets are allowed and how many hosts exist per subnet. However, the right answer in real life might not be so simple! In some networks, the network design engineer chooses an identical subnet mask to be used for all subnets of the same network. However, the engineer could choose different masks for each and every subnet. Consider, for example, the network in Figure 6-30.

This design requires only two hosts in the subnet for each serial link, but the mask allows for 2^8-2, or 254, hosts per subnet! If the network engineer had wanted to conserve the address space because the network was going to grow a lot, he might have chosen to use a different mask for the serial link's subnet. Likewise, the LAN where Server1 resides might have more than 254 hosts on it—in which case a single subnet with 8 host bits would not be big enough. A mask such as 255.255.252.0 with 10 host bits might have been a better choice.

Figure 6-30 *Sample Network, with Router IP Addresses Shown*

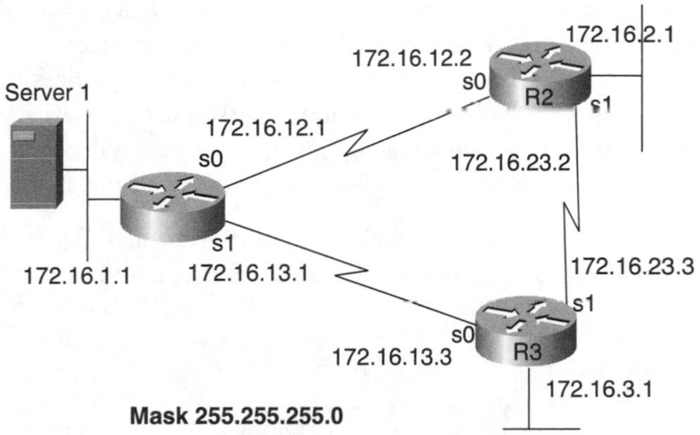

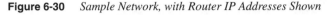

The term *variable-length subnet mask* (VLSM) describes a single Class A, B, or C network in which more than one subnet mask is used. Before you complete your CCNP certification, you will need to fully understand how to implement a VLSM design. If you understood the previous paragraph, you already understand the concepts behind VLSM. Planning, implementing, and operating a network that uses VLSM requires a full, comfortable understanding of subnetting.

On the CCNA exam, if you are asked, "How many subnets of network *x* are there when using mask *y*?", assume that the mask is identical for all subnets of the network and that no VLSM is in use.

Now you can complete a chart similar to Table 6-14 for each of the five examples. Completing charts such as Table 6-14 covers all the parts of Step 1 in the four-step process of answering all IP address questions. Table 6-13 contains answers for all five example for Step 1. The details of Step 1 are as follows:

Step 1 Identify the structure of the IP address.

- **A** Identify the size of the network part of the address, based on Class A, B, and C rules.
- **B** Identify the size of the host part of the address, based on the number of binary 0s in the mask. If the mask is tricky, use the chart of typical mask values to convert the mask to binary more quickly.
- **C** The size of the subnet part is what's "left over"; mathematically, it is 32 – (number of network + host bits).
- **D** Declare the number of subnets, which is $2^{\text{number-of-subnet-bits}} - 2$.
- **E** Declare the number of hosts per subnet, which is $2^{\text{number-of-host-bits}} - 2$.

Step 2: Create the Chart to Be Used in Steps 3 and 4

Step 2 simply introduces you to a tool that you can use to teach yourself how to quickly derive the subnet number and first valid address (Step 3) and the broadcast address and last valid address (Step 4). This tool, which is a chart that you will complete, organizes the given information (address and mask) along with the information that you need to derive. This tool will help you learn to perform subnetting with no binary math, which you will need to do in most networking jobs.When you become accustomed to the logic, you will simply skip this step mentally.

All the examples in this chapter, as well as those in Appendix C, use this chart to explain the process of deriving the subnet number, broadcast address, and valid IP addresses in the subnet.

Table 6-17 is an example subnet chart

Table 6-17 *Subnet Chart—Generic*

	Octet 1	Octet 2	Octet 3	Octet 4
Address				
Mask				
Subnet number				
First valid address				
Broadcast				
Last valid address				

A typical exam question might supply the address and mask and then ask you for one of the other four values—the subnet number, the first valid address, the broadcast address, or the last valid address. The subnet chart begins with the address and mask. The subnet number and the subnet broadcast address are what you are after, along with the first and the last valid IP addresses in the subnet. In real life, you seldom care about the broadcast address, but you do care about the range of valid IP addresses in the subnet. Finding the last valid IP address in the subnet is much easier if you know the broadcast address, so calculating the broadcast is still very useful. And of course, it might be on the exam.

Four tasks must be completed in Step 2:

- **A** Create a generic subnet chart, as in Table 6-17.
- **B** Write in the IP address and subnet mask.
- **C** Draw a vertical line between the columns with 255 and 0 in the mask if the mask is "easy" (those with all mask octets either 0 or 255). Draw a box around the column with the mask octet that is not 0 or 255 if the mask is not easy.
- **D** Copy the values of the address to the left of the line or box into the final four rows. After that, you are ready for the more important concepts of Steps 3 and 4.

Tables 6-18 and 6-19 list two of the examples from Table 6-13, after the first two tasks of Step 1 have been completed.

Table 6-18 *Subnet Chart—130.102.1/24, After Two of Four Tasks in Step 2 Are Complete*

	Octet 1	Octet 2	Octet 3	Octet 4
Address	130	4	102	1
Mask	255	255	255	0
Subnet number				
First valid address				
Broadcast				
Last valid address				

Table 6-19 *Subnet Chart—130.102.1/22, After Two of Four Tasks in Step 2 Are Complete*

	Octet 1	Octet 2	Octet 3	Octet 4
Address	130	4	102	1
Mask	255	255	252	0
Subnet number				
First valid address				
Broadcast				
Last valid address				

The table simply lists the information provided in a typical question, up to this point. The only difficulty might be if the question lists the prefix, as did Table 6-13, and the subnet chart wants the mask. The prefix is the number of binary 1s that start the mask. With a 24-bit prefix (Table 6-18's example), the mask is pretty easy to derive—you need three 255s to start the mask to get 24 prefix bits. The example in Table 6-19, using a 22-bit prefix, is tougher—two 255s to start the mask get you 16 prefix bits. You need 6 more prefix bits, so you remember that 252 decimal has six binary 1s, to create a mask with 22 prefix bits. Refer to Table 6-16 for a reminder of the mask values in decimal and binary.

The third task of Step 2 requires you to draw either a line or a box. You use a line when the mask is "easy," and you use a box when the mask is "hard." Easy masks use only 255s or 0s in the mask; whereas, hard masks have one octet in which the mask is something besides 255 or 0. I call a mask octet that's not a 255 or 0 the *interesting* octet because it is the octet that gives everyone heartburn when first learning subnetting. The line separates the 255s from the 0s when the mask is easy, and the box both separates the host part from the rest of the address and draws attention to the tricky part of the logic used in this four-step process.

You decide where to draw either the line or the box based on some easy rules. When an easy mask is used, you draw a vertical line between the host part of the address and the rest—in other words, a line between the 255s and the 0s in the mask. When a hard mask is used, a decimal math trick can be used to complete the subnet chart—and the math trick applies to the octet with the non-255 or 0 value in the mask. So, with a hard mask, instead of drawing a line, you draw a box around the column of the interesting octet. Table 6-20 gives an example of using a line when the mask is easy, and Table 6-21 gives an example of using a box around the interesting octet when the mask is hard.

Table 6-20 *Subnet Chart—130.102.1/24, After Drawing the Vertical Line*

	Octet 1	Octet 2	Octet 3	Octet 4
Address	130	4	102	1
Mask	255	255	255	0
Subnet number				
First valid address				
Broadcast				
Last valid address				

Table 6-21 *Subnet Chart—130.102.1/22, After Drawing a Box Around the Interesting Octet*

	Octet 1	Octet 2	Octet 3	Octet 4
Address	130	4	102	1
Mask	255	255	252	0
Subnet number				
First valid address				
Broadcast				
Last valid address				

Finally, you should complete the chart for everything to the left of the line or the box. To complete the chart, look at the original IP address octets to the left of the line or box, and copy those into the subnet, first valid address, broadcast, and last valid address fields. Note that only octets to the left of the line or box should be copied—the interesting octet, which is inside the box, should not be copied. Tables 6-22 and 6-23 show the same two examples, at the end of Step 2 of the process.

Table 6-22 *Subnet Chart—130.102.1/24, at the End of Step 2*

	Octet 1	Octet 2	Octet 3	Octet 4
Address	130	4	102	1
Mask	255	255	255	0
Subnet number	130	4	102	
First valid address	130	4	102	
Broadcast	130	4	102	
Last valid address	130	4	102	

Table 6-23 *Subnet Chart—130.102.1/22, at the End of Step 2*

	Octet 1	Octet 2	Octet 3	Octet 4
Address	130	4	102	1
Mask	255	255	252	0
Subnet number	130	4		
First valid address	130	4		
Broadcast	130	4		
Last valid address	130	4		

Keep in mind that Step 2 gives you a tool to derive the right answers without binary math. At the end of Step 2, you do not have the answers yet! Step 3 will give you two more answers—namely, the subnet number and first valid IP address. Step 4 will give you the broadcast address, along with the last valid IP address in the subnet. So be patient—the usefulness of the chart will be apparent in the coming steps.

For completeness, Tables 6-24, 6-25, and 6-26 show the completed subnet charts for the other three examples in Table 6-13.

Table 6-24 *Subnet Chart—8.1.4.5/16, at the End of Step 2*

	Octet 1	Octet 2	Octet 3	Octet 4
Address	8	1	4	5
Mask	255	255	0	0
Subnet number	8	1		
First valid address	8	1		
Broadcast	8	1		
Last valid address	8	1		

Table 6-25 *Subnet Chart—199.1.1.100/24, at the End of Step 2*

	Octet 1	Octet 2	Octet 3	Octet 4
Address	199	1	1	100
Mask	255	255	255	0
Subnet number	199	1	1	
First valid address	199	1	1	
Broadcast	199	1	1	
Last valid address	199	1	1	

Table 6-26 *Subnet Chart—199.1.1.100/27, at the End of Step 2*

	Octet 1	Octet 2	Octet 3	Octet 4
Address	199	1	1	100
Mask	255	255	255	224
Subnet number	199	1	1	
First valid address	199	1	1	
Broadcast	199	1	1	
Last valid address	199	1	1	

Now you are ready to see how to complete the chart in Steps 3 and 4. First, a summary of Steps 1 and 2:

Step 1 Identify the structure of the IP address.

A Identify the size of the network part of the address, based on Class A, B, and C rules.

B Identify the size of the host part of the address, based on the number of binary 0s in the mask. If the mask is tricky, use the chart of typical mask values to convert the mask to binary more quickly.

C The size of the subnet part is what's "left over"; mathematically, it is 32 – (number of network + host bits).

D Declare the number of subnets, which is $2^{\text{number-of-subnet-bits}} - 2$.

E Declare the number of hosts per subnet, which is $2^{\text{number-of-host-bits}} - 2$.

Step 2 Create the chart that will be used in Steps 3 and 4.

A Create a generic subnet chart.

B Write down the IP address and subnet mask in the first two rows of the chart.

C If an easy mask is used, draw a vertical line between the 255s and the 0s in the mask, from top to bottom of the chart. If a hard mask is used, draw a box around the column of the interesting octet.

D Copy the address octets to the left of the line or the box into the final four rows of the chart.

Step 3: Derive the Subnet Number and the First Valid IP Address

NOTE Before beginning the explanations in Steps 3 and 4 of this process, you might want to choose to not read parts of this section. If you are not yet comfortable with subnetting when easy masks are used, you might benefit from focusing on the example that covers the easy masks used and ignoring the hard example. Then, when you are comfortable with the easy ones, reread all of Steps 3 and 4.

To help you focus on the easy example, the parts of the text that cover the difficult example are shaded. If you want to focus on the easier part, get good at that, and then read these steps a second time, you should ignore the parts that are shaded—for now.

Earlier, you learned that computers perform a Boolean AND of the address and mask to find the subnet number. If you want a way to find the subnet number without using any binary math or binary conversions, read on! In Step 3, you will see how to quickly derive the subnet number, even when the mask is a tricky one.

You should understand how to perform the Boolean AND, so the ANDs for each of the five examples from Table 6-13 follow. However, if you already understand Boolean ANDs, feel free to go right past these next five examples and on to the rest of the four-step process.

Address	8.1.4.5	0000 1000 0000 0001 0000 0100 0000 0101
Mask	255.255.0.0	1111 1111 1111 1111 **0000 0000 0000 0000**
AND result (subnet number)	8.1.0.0	0000 1000 0000 0001 0000 0000 0000 0000

Address	130.4.102.1	1000 0010 0000 0100 0110 0110 0000 0001
Mask	255.255.255.0	1111 1111 1111 1111 1111 1111 **0000 0000**
AND result (Subnet number)	130.4.102.0	1000 0010 0000 0100 0110 0110 0000 0000

Address	199.1.1.100	1100 0111 0000 0001 0000 0001 0110 0100
Mask	255.255.255.0	1111 1111 1111 1111 1111 1111 **0000 0000**
AND result (subnet number)	199.1.1.0	1100 0111 0000 0001 0000 0001 0000 0000

Address	130.4.102.1	1000 0010 0000 0100 0110 0110 0000 0001
Mask	255.255.252.0	1111 1111 1111 1111 1111 11**00 0000 0000**
AND result (subnet number)	130.4.100.0	1000 0010 0000 0100 0110 0100 0000 0000

Address	199.1.1.100	1100 0111 0000 0001 0000 0001 0110 0100
Mask	255.255.255.224	1111 1111 1111 1111 1111 1111 111**0 0000**
AND result (subnet number)	199.1.1.96	1100 0111 0000 0001 0000 0001 0110 0000

The four-step process avoids all binary conversions and Boolean AND operations. On the exam, you will not have a binary conversion chart, and in real life, you will not always be sitting at your desk near your tools for deriving the subnet number. Mastering this simple process gives you the subnet number, if you already know the address and mask.

At Step 3 of the four-step process, you must complete one more task to derive the subnet number if the mask is easy, or two more tasks if the mask is hard. When that is finished, a single task derives the first valid IP address in the subnet. The hardest part requires you to do a little arithmetic.

First, in the subnet number row, write down a decimal 0 for all octets to the right of the line or the box. Do not write down a 0 in the octet inside the box. If the mask is easy (all 255s or 0s), you should have a complete subnet number. If the mask is hard (one mask octet with something besides a 255 or a 0), you should have three octets of the subnet number completed, with the interesting octet not yet filled in. Tables 6-27 and 6-28 show two examples, with this first task in Step 3 completed.

The subnet number in example in Table 6-27 is complete. In Step 2, you wrote down all the parts of the subnet number to the left of the line in the chart—the ones that were identical to the IP address. In Step 3, you wrote 0s to the right of the line—that's it! In fact, because the mask is easy, many of you probably would have been able to answer the question, "Given 130.4.102.1/24, what is the subnet number?" well before this point in the process. If you are new to subnetting, feel free to use the subnet chart even for examples with an easy mask—it still gives you the right answer.

Table 6-27 *Subnet Chart—130.4.102.1/24, at Step 3's First Task, Placing 0s After the Line*

	Octet 1	Octet 2	Octet 3	Octet 4
Address	130	4	102	1
Mask	255	255	255	0
Subnet number	130	4	102	**0**
First valid address	130	4	102	
Broadcast	130	4	102	
Last valid address	130	4	102	

Table 6-28 *Subnet Chart—130.4.102.1/22, after Step 3's Task of Placing 0s After the Box*

	Octet 1	Octet 2	Octet 3	Octet 4
Address	130	4	102	1
Mask	255	255	252	0
Subnet number	130	4		**0**
First valid address	130	4		
Broadcast	130	4		
Last valid address	130	4		

You must complete the second task of Step 3 for the example in Table 6-18 because this is a difficult example. The box in the chart should remind you that additional work needs to be done. Now, if you could already look at the mask and derive the subnet number of 130.4.100.0, you probably would not need to use this process!

For the rest of you who do not do this often enough to be able to do the math in your head, the next task gives you the right value for the subnet number's interesting octet. First, you find what I will call the *magic number*—which is 256 minus the mask's interesting octet. In this case, you have 256 – 252, or a magic number of 4. Then you find the multiple of the magic number that is the closest to the address's interesting octet but less than or equal to it. In this example, 100 is a multiple of the magic number (4 × 25), and this multiple is ≤ 102. The next multiple of the magic number, which is 104, is, of course, more than 102, so that's not the right number. The multiple of the magic number closest to but not more than the address's interesting octet is the subnet's interesting octet value.

In other words, plug in 100 for the third octet of the subnet number in Table 6-28.

Finally, the third task in Step 3 requires you to derive the first valid IP address in the subnet. You might recall that two values are reserved in each subnet. The first of these reserved values is the subnet number itself. The number that is one bigger than the subnet number is the first valid IP address in the subnet. As you might guess, finding the first valid IP address is easy when you know the subnet number:

> To find the first valid IP address in the subnet, copy the subnet number, but add 1 to the fourth octet.

That's all! Table 6-29 shows the same examples as Table 6-27 at the completion of Step 3.

Table 6-29 *Subnet Chart—130.4.102.1/24, After Step 3*

	Octet 1	Octet 2	Octet 3	Octet 4
Address	130	4	102	1
Mask	255	255	255	0
Subnet number	130	4	102	**0**
First valid address	130	4	102	**1**
Broadcast	130	4	102	
Last valid address	130	4	102	

In Table 6-29, the first three octets of the subnet number and first valid address were already filled in. Because this example uses an easy mask, you just write down a 0 in all the octets to the right of the line—the last octet—to get the subnet number. To get the first valid address, just add 1 to the last octet of the subnet number.

Tables 6-30 shows the same examples as Table 6-28 at the completion of Step 3.

Table 6-30 *Subnet Chart—130.4.102.1/22, After Step 3*

	Octet 1	Octet 2	Octet 3	Octet 4	Comments
Address	130	4	102	1	
Mask	255	255	252	0	
Subnet number	130	4	**100**	**0**	Magic = 256 – 252 = 4; 4 × 25 = 100, closest multiple ≤ 102.
First valid address	130	4	**100**	**1**	Add 1 to subnet's last octet
Broadcast	130	4			
Last valid address	130	4			

In Table 6-30, the first two octets of the subnet number and first valid address were already filled in because they are to the left of the box around the third octet—the interesting octet, in this case. In the subnet number, the last octet is 0 because it is to the right of the box. To find the interesting octet value, just find the closest multiple of the magic number that's not bigger than that octet of the address—100 in this case. The subnet number is 130.4.100.0. To get the first valid address, just add 1 to the last octet of the subnet number, giving you 130.4.100.1.

For completeness, Tables 6-31, 6-32, and 6-33 list the other three examples from Table 6-13, with the subnet number and first IP address rows completed.

Table 6-31 *Subnet Chart—8.1.4.5/16, at the End of Step 3*

	Octet 1	Octet 2	Octet 3	Octet 4
Address	8	1	4	5
Mask	255	255	0	0
Subnet number	8	1	**0**	**0**
First valid address	8	1	**0**	**1**
Broadcast	8	1		
Last valid address	8	1		

Table 6-32 *Subnet Chart—199.1.1.100/24, at the End of Step 3*

	Octet 1	Octet 2	Octet 3	Octet 4
Address	199	1	1	100
Mask	255	255	255	0
Subnet number	199	1	1	**0**
First valid address	199	1	1	**1**
Broadcast	199	1	1	
Last valid address	199	1	1	

Table 6-33 *Subnet Chart—199.1.1.100/27, At the End of Step 3*

	Octet 1	Octet 2	Octet 3	Octet 4	Comments
Address	199	1	1	100	
Mask	255	255	255	224	
Subnet number	199	1	1	**96**	Magic = 256 – 224 = 32; 3 ×32 = 96, closest multiple ≤ 100
First valid address	199	1	1	**97**	Add 1 to fourth octet of subnet
Broadcast	199	1	1		
Last valid address	199	1	1		

For Step 3, you have two main alternatives to find the subnet number: Use a Boolean AND or use the process with the subnet chart. The following summary encapsulates the logic for using first three steps of the four-step process that avoids any binary math.

Step 1 Identify the structure of the IP address.

- **A** Identify the size of the network part of the address, based on Class A, B, and C rules.
- **B** Identify the size of the host part of the address, based on the number of binary 0s in the mask. If the mask is tricky, use the chart of typical mask values to convert the mask to binary more quickly.
- **C** The size of the subnet part is what's "left over"; mathematically, it is 32 – (number of network + host bits).
- **D** Declare the number of subnets, which is $2^{\text{number-of-subnet-bits}} - 2$.
- **E** Declare the number of hosts per subnet, which is $2^{\text{number-of-host-bits}} - 2$.

Step 2 Create the chart that will be used in Steps 3 and 4.

- **A** Create a generic subnet chart.
- **B** Write down the IP address and subnet mask in the first two rows of the chart.
- **C** If an easy mask is used, draw a vertical line between the 255s and the 0s in the mask, from top to bottom of the chart. If a hard mask is used, draw a box around the column of the interesting octet.
- **D** Copy the address octets to the left of the line or the box into the final four rows of the chart.

Step 3 Derive the subnet number and the first valid IP address.

A Write down 0s in the subnet octets to the right of the line or the box.

B If the mask is hard and there is a box in the chart, use the magic number trick to find the value of the subnet's interesting octet.

C To derive the first valid IP address, copy the first three octets of the subnet number, and add 1 to the fourth octet of the subnet number.

Step 4: Derive the Subnet Broadcast Address and the Last Valid IP Address

NOTE *Reminder:* If you want to focus on the easy example and then come back and reread this section when you are comfortable with the easy one, continue to avoid reading the shaded areas of this section.

Step 4 completes the process using the subnet chart to answer the most typical subnetting questions. You need to know how to calculate the subnet broadcast address as well as the last IP address in the subnet, which is one less than the broadcast address. After you calculate the broadcast address, finding the last valid IP address is easy.

You should know how to derive the subnet broadcast address using binary math, and you also should know how to do it with this four-step decimal math process. The binary math is easy when you have the subnet number in binary: Simply change all the host bit values in the subnet number to binary 1s. You can examine the math behind the five examples from Table 6-13 from the information that follows. The host parts of the addresses, masks, subnet numbers, and broadcast addresses are in bold.

Address	8.1.4.5	0000 1000 0000 0001 **0000 0100 0000 0101**
Mask	255.255.0.0	1111 1111 1111 1111 **0000 0000 0000 0000**
AND result (subnet number)	8.1.0.0	0000 1000 0000 0001 **0000 0000 0000 0000**
Broadcast address	8.1.255.255	0000 1000 0000 0001 **1111 1111 1111 1111**

Address	130.4.102.1	1000 0010 0000 0100 0110 0110 **0000 0001**
Mask	255.255.255.0	1111 1111 1111 1111 1111 1111 **0000 0000**
AND result (subnet number)	130.4.102.0	1000 0010 0000 0100 0110 0110 **0000 0000**
Broadcast address	130.4.102.255	1000 0010 0000 0100 0110 0110 **1111 1111**

Address	199.1.1.100	1100 0111 0000 0001 0000 0001 0110 0100
Mask	255.255.255.0	1111 1111 1111 1111 1111 1111 **0000 0000**
AND result (subnet number)	199.1.1.0	1100 0111 0000 0001 0000 0001 0000 0000
Broadcast address	199.1.1.255	1100 0111 0000 0001 0000 0001 **1111 1111**

Address	130.4.102.1	1000 0010 0000 0100 0110 01**10 0000 0001**
Mask	255.255.252.0	1111 1111 1111 1111 1111 11**00 0000 0000**
AND result (subnet number)	130.4.100.0	1000 0010 0000 0100 0110 01**00 0000 0000**
Broadcast address	130.4.103.255	1000 0010 0000 0100 0110 01**11 1111 1111**

Address	199.1.1.100	1100 0111 0000 0001 0000 0001 011**0 0100**
Mask	255.255.255.224	1111 1111 1111 1111 1111 1111 111**0 0000**
AND result (subnet number)	199.1.1.96	1100 0111 0000 0001 0000 0001 011**0 0000**
Broadcast address	199.1.1.127	1100 0111 0000 0001 0000 0001 011**1 1111**

The four-step process avoids all binary conversions and Boolean AND operations. On the exam, you will not have a binary conversion chart, and in real life, you will not always be sitting at your desk near your tools for deriving the subnet number and broadcast address. So mastering this four-step process gives you the broadcast address and highest valid IP address.

For Step 4 in the four-step process, you must complete one more task to derive the broadcast address if the mask is easy, or two more tasks if the mask is hard. When that is finished, a single step is used to derive the last valid IP address in the subnet. The hardest part requires you to do a little arithmetic.

First, in the broadcast address, write down a decimal 255 for all octets to the right of the line or the box. Do not write down a 255 in the octet inside the box. If the mask is easy (all 255s or 0s), you should have a complete broadcast address. If the mask is hard (one mask octet with something besides a 255 or a 0), you should have three octets of the broadcast address, with the interesting octet not yet filled in. Tables 6-34 and 6-35 show the same two familiar examples, with this first task in Step 4 completed.

Table 6-34 *Subnet Chart—130.4.102.1/24, After Step 4's First Task, Placing 255s After the Line*

	Octet 1	Octet 2	Octet 3	Octet 4
Address	130	4	102	1
Mask	255	255	255	0
Subnet number	130	4	102	0
First valid address	130	4	102	1
Broadcast	130	4	102	**255**
Last valid address	130	4	102	

Table 6-35 *Subnet Chart—130.4.102.1/22, After Step 4's First Task, Placing 255s After the Box*

	Octet 1	Octet 2	Octet 3	Octet 4
Address	130	4	102	1
Mask	255	255	252	0
Subnet number	130	4	100	0
First valid address	130	4	100	1
Broadcast	130	4		**255**
Last valid address	130	4		

The broadcast address in example in Table 6-34 is complete. In Step 2, you wrote down all the parts of the broadcast address to the left of the line in the chart—the ones that were identical to the IP address. In Step 4, you wrote 255s to the right of the line—that's it! In fact, because the mask is easy, many of you probably would have been able to answer the question, “Given 130.4.102.1/24, what is the broadcast address?” well before this point in the process. If you are new to subnetting, feel free to use the subnet chart even for examples with an easy mask—it still gives you the right answer.

For the more difficult example, you must complete the second task of Step 4 for the example in Table 6-36. The box in the chart, as well as the mask value of 252, should remind you that additional work needs to be done, and it is obvious that one octet of the broadcast address simply is not filled in yet.

The next task in Step 4 gives you the right value for the broadcast address’s interesting octet in the difficult example. First, remind yourself about the magic number. The magic number is 256 minus the mask’s interesting octet. In this case, you have 256 – 252, or a magic number of 4. Then you add the magic number to the interesting octet value of the subnet number and subtract 1. The result is the broadcast address’s value in the interesting octet. In this case, the value is 100 + 4 (magic number) – 1 = 103.

Finally, the third task in Step 4 requires you to derive the last valid IP address in the subnet. You might recall that two values are reserved in each subnet. The first of these values is the subnet number itself, and the other reserved value is the broadcast address. Numerically, the subnet number has the lowest numeric value, and the broadcast address has the largest. The last valid IP address in the subnet can be calculated easily: *Copy the broadcast address, except subtract 1 from the fourth octet.* That’s all! Tables 6-36 and 6-37 show the same examples as Tables 6-34 and 6-35, at the completion of Step 4.

Table 6-36 *Subnet Chart—130.4.102.1/24, After Step 4*

	Octet 1	Octet 2	Octet 3	Octet 4
Address	130	4	102	1
Mask	255	255	255	0
Subnet number	130	4	102	0
First valid address	130	4	102	1
Broadcast	130	4	102	**255**
Last valid address	130	4	102	**254**

Table 6-37 *Subnet Chart—130.4.102.1/22, After Step 4*

	Octet 1	Octet 2	Octet 3	Octet 4
Address	130	4	102	1
Mask	255	255	252	0
Subnet number	130	4	100	0
First valid address	130	4	100	1
Broadcast	130	4	**103**	**255**
Last valid address	130	4	**103**	**254**

On the exam, you are more likely to see questions that ask you about the range of valid IP addresses in a subnet than those that simply ask you for the broadcast address for the subnet. By finding the subnet number and broadcast addresses, however, you can easily derive the lowest valid IP address and the highest, and easily answer the questions.

Tables 6-38, 6-39, and 6-40 shows the remaining three examples from Table 6-13.

Table 6-38 *Subnet Chart—8.1.4.5/16, at the End of Step 4*

	Octet 1	Octet 2	Octet 3	Octet 4
Address	8	1	4	5
Mask	255	255	0	0
Subnet number	8	1	0	0
First valid address	8	1	0	1
Broadcast	8	1	**255**	**255**
Last valid address	8	1	**255**	**254**

Table 6-39 *Subnet Chart—199.1.1.100/24, at the End of Step 4*

	Octet 1	Octet 2	Octet 3	Octet 4
Address	199	1	1	100
Mask	255	255	255	0
Subnet number	199	1	1	0
First valid address	199	1	1	1
Broadcast	199	1	1	**255**
Last valid address	199	1	1	**254**

Table 6-40 *Subnet Chart—199.1.1.100/27, at the End of Step 4*

	Octet 1	Octet 2	Octet 3	Octet 4	Comments
Address	199	1	1	100	N/A
Mask	255	255	255	224	N/A
Subnet number	199	1	1	96	Magic = 256 – 224 = 32; 3 × 32 = 96, closest multiple ≤ 100
First valid address	199	1	1	97	Add 1 to fourth octet of subnet
Broadcast	199	1	1	**127**	96 + magic (32) – 1 = 127
Last valid address	199	1	1	**126**	Subtract 1 from fourth octet of broadcast address

The four-step process for dissecting IP addresses is now complete. The following list summarizes the tasks in each step:

Step 1 Identify the structure of the IP address.

A Identify the size of the network part of the address, based on Class A, B, and C rules.

B Identify the size of the host part of the address, based on the number of binary 0s in the mask. If the mask is tricky, use the chart of typical mask values to convert the mask to binary more quickly.

C The size of the subnet part is what's "left over"; mathematically, it is 32 – (number of network + host bits).

D Declare the number of subnets, which is $2^{\text{number-of-subnet-bits}} - 2$.

E Declare the number of hosts per subnet, which is $2^{\text{number-of-host-bits}} - 2$.

Step 2 Create the chart that will be used in Steps 3 and 4.

A Create a generic subnet chart.

B Write down the IP address and subnet mask in the first two rows of the chart.

C If an easy mask is used, draw a vertical line between the 255s and the 0s in the mask, from top to bottom of the chart. If a hard mask is used, draw a box around the column of the interesting octet.

D Copy the address octets to the left of the line or the box into the final four rows of the chart.

Step 3 Derive the subnet number and the first valid IP address.

A Write down 0s in the subnet octets to the right of the line or the box.

B If the mask is hard and there is a box in the chart, use the magic number trick to find the value of the subnet's interesting octet.

C To derive the first valid IP address, copy the first three octets of the subnet number, and add 1 to the fourth octet of the subnet number.

Step 4 Derive the broadcast address and the last valid IP address.

A Write down 255s in the broadcast address octets to the right of the line or the box.

B If the mask is hard and there is a box in the chart, use the magic number trick to find the value of the broadcast address's interesting octet.

C To derive the last valid IP address, copy the first three octets of the broadcast address, and subtract 1 from the fourth octet of the broadcast address.

So now what? Well, if you are confident that you can answer subnetting questions easily, move on to the next major section. If not, you might want to work on Appendix C, which has many practice examples.

Deciding What the Other Subnets Are

When I wrote the four-step process section for IP subnetting, I had two goals in mind. As I mentioned earlier, you need to answer subnetting questions quickly and confidently on the exam. Network engineers also think about subnetting every day, so it's great to be able to do the math in your head.

So far, you have dealt with questions regarding a single subnet. You might also need to address the question: "What are the other valid subnets of this network?" The details of answering this question follow next.

First, the question needs a better definition—or at least a more complete one. The question you might get on the CCNA exam might be better stated like this: "If the same subnet mask is used for all subnets of this Class A, B, or C network, what are the valid subnets?" IP design conventions do not require the engineer to use the same mask for every subnet. If you recall, the topic of VLSMs was explained briefly back in Step 1 of the four-step process to analyze a single address. On the CCNA exam, the question "What are all the subnets" assumes that

VLSMs are not in use. The question is, simply put, if the same mask is used for all subnets, what are the subnet numbers?

Another easy decimal process (three steps, this time!) lists all the valid subnets, given the network number and the only mask used on that network. This three-step process assumes that the size of the subnet part of the address is, at most, eight bits in length. The same general process can be expanded to work when the size of the subnet part of the address is more than eight bits, but that expanded process is not described here.

The three-step process uses a chart that I call the subnet list chart. I made up the name just for this book, simply as another tool to use. Table 6-41 presents a generic version of the subnet list chart.

Table 6-41 *Three-Step Process Generic Subnet List Chart*

	Octet 1	Octet 2	Octet 3	Octet 4
Network number				
Mask				
Subnet zero				
First valid subnet				
Next valid subnet				
Last valid subnet				
Broadcast subnet				

You list the known network number and subnet mask as the first step in the process. If the question gives you an IP address and mask instead of the network number and mask, just write down the network number of which that IP address is a member. (Remember, this three-step process assumes that the subnet part of the addresses is eight bits or less.) The second of the three steps is to copy the network number into the row labeled Subnet zero. *Subnet zero*, or the *zero subnet*, is numerically the first subnet, but it is one of the two reserved subnet numbers in a network. You can use the zero subnet on a Cisco router if you configure the global configuration command **ip zero-subnet**. For the purposes of answering questions on the exam about the number of valid subnets in a network, consider the zero subnet unusable. In real life, do not use the zero subnet if you do not have to.

Tables 6-42 and 6-43 list two familiar examples, with the first two steps completed.

Table 6-42 *Subnet List Chart—130.4.0.0/24*

	Octet 1	Octet 2	Octet 3	Octet 4
Network number	130	4	0	0
Mask	255	255	255	0
Subnet zero	130	4	0	0

Table 6-43 *Subnet List Chart—130.4.0.0/22*

	Octet 1	Octet 2	Octet 3	Octet 4
Network number	130	4	0	0
Mask	255	255	252	0
Subnet zero	130	4	0	0

Step 3 is the last step, but it is repeated many times. This last step uses the magic number—remember, the magic number is 256 minus the mask octet value in the interesting octet. With this process of finding all the subnet numbers, the interesting octet is the octet that contains *all* of the subnet part of the addresses. (Remember, the process assumes eight or less subnet bits!) In both Tables 6-42 and 6-43, the interesting octet is the third octet.

The third and final step in the process to find all the subnet numbers goes like this: Starting with the last row that's completed in the table, do the following:

1. Copy all three noninteresting octets from the previous line.
2. Add the magic number to the previous interesting octet, and write that down as the value of the interesting octet.
3. Repeat the last two tasks until the next number that you would write down in the interesting column is 256. (Don't write that one down—it's not valid.)

The idea behind the process of finding all the subnets becomes apparent by reviewing the same two examples used earlier. First, Table 6-44 lists the example with the easy mask.

Table 6-44 *Subnet List Chart—130.4.0.0/24 Completed*

	Octet 1	Octet 2	Octet 3	Octet 4
Network number	130	4	0	0
Mask	255	255	255	0
Subnet zero	130	4	0	0
First valid subnet	130	4	1	0
Next valid subnet	130	4	2	0
Next valid subnet	130	4	3	0
Next valid subnet	130	4	4	0
(Skipping a bunch)	130	4	X	0
Last valid subnet	130	4	254	0
Broadcast subnet	130	4	255	0

The logic behind how the process works might be better understood by looking at the first few entries and then the last few entries. The zero subnet is easily found because it's the same number as the network number. The magic number is 256 – 255 = 1 in this case. Essentially, you increment the third octet (in this case) by the magic number for each successive subnet number.

In the middle of the table, one row is labeled Skipping a bunch. Rather than make the book even bigger, I left out several entries but included enough that you could see that the subnet number's third octet just gets bigger by 1, in this case, for each successive subnet number.

Looking at the end of the table, the last entry lists 255 in the third octet. 256 decimal is never a valid value in any IP address, and the directions said to not write down a subnet with 256 in it, so the last number in the table is 130.4.255.0. *The last subnet is the broadcast subnet, which is the other reserved subnet number. The subnet before the broadcast subnet is the highest, or last, valid subnet number.*

Many people might even refer to these subnets using just the third octet. If all subnets of a particular organization were in network 130.4.0.0, with mask 255.255.255.0, you might simply say "subnet five" when referring to subnet 130.4.5.0.

You might see an exam question such as, "How many valid subnets are there for network 130.4.0.0, mask 255.255.255.0?" Table 6-44 lists them—well, at least some of them. Intuitively, there are 254 valid subnets with this numbering scheme—subnets 1 through 254, using common terminology.

The process works the same with difficult subnet masks, even though the answers are not as intuitive. Table 6-45 lists the answers for the second example, using a 22-bit prefix.

Table 6-45 *Subnet List Chart—130.4.0.0/22*

	Octet 1	Octet 2	Octet 3	Octet 4
Network number	130	4	0	0
Mask	255	255	252	0
Subnet zero	130	4	0	0
First valid subnet	130	4	4	0
Next valid subnet	130	4	8	0
Skip a lot	130	4	X	0
Last valid subnet	130	4	248	0
Broadcast subnet	130	4	252	0

Most of us would not guess that 130.4.252.0 was the broadcast subnet for this latest example. However, adding the magic number 4 to 252 would give you 256 as the next subnet number, which is not valid—so, 130.4.252.0 is indeed the broadcast subnet.

The three-step process to find all the subnet numbers of a network is:

1. Write down the network number and subnet mask in the first two rows of the subnet list chart.
2. Write down the network number in the third row. This is the zero subnet, which is one of the two reserved subnets.
3. Do the following two tasks, stopping when the next number that you would write down in the interesting column is 256. (Don't write that one down—it's not valid.)
   - Copy all three noninteresting octets from the previous line.
   - Add the magic number to the previous interesting octet, and write that down as the value of the interesting octet.

Start Extra Credit

CIDR, Private Addressing, and NAT

Connecting to the Internet using only a registered network number or several registered network numbers uses a very straightforward and obvious convention. With registered network numbers, no other organization connected to the Internet will have conflicting IP addresses. In fact, this convention is part of the reason the global Internet functions well.

In the early and mid-1990s, concern arose that the available networks would be completely assigned so that some organizations would not be capable of connecting to the Internet. This one fact was the most compelling reason for the advent of IP Version 6 (IPv6). (The version discussed in this book is Version 4. Version 5 was defined for experimental reasons and was never deployed.) Version 6 calls for a much larger address structure so that the convention of all organizations using unique groupings (networks) of IP addresses would still be reasonable—the numbers of IPv6-style networks would reach into the trillions and beyond. That solution is still technically viable and possibly one day will be used because IPv6 is still evolving in the marketplace.

Three other functions of IP have been used to reduce the need for IP Version 4 (IPv4) registered network numbers. Network Address Translation (NAT), often used in conjunction with private addressing, allows organizations to use unregistered IP network numbers internally and still communicate well with the Internet. Classless interdomain routing (CIDR) is a feature used by Internet service providers (ISPs) to reduce the wasting of IP addresses and to delay the day when we run out of IP addresses.

CIDR

CIDR is a convention, defined in RFC 1817 (www.ietf.org/rfc/rfc1817.txt), that calls for aggregating multiple network numbers into a single routing entity. CIDR was actually created to help the scalability of Internet routers—imagine a router in the Internet with a route to every Class A, B, and C network on the planet! By aggregating the routes, fewer routes would need to exist in the routing table. Consider Figure 6-31.

Figure 6-31 *Typical Use of CIDR*

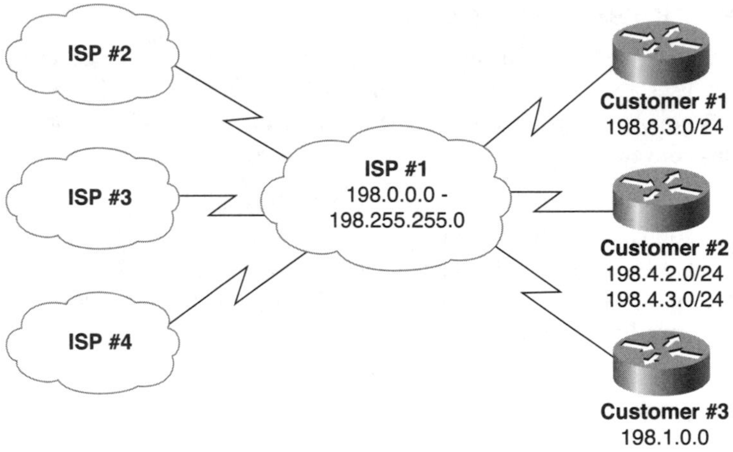

Class C networks 198.0.0.0 through 198.255.255.0 (they might look funny, but they are valid Class C network numbers) are registered networks for an ISP. All other ISPs' routing tables would have a separate route to each of the 2^{16} networks without CIDR. However, as the illustration shows, now the other ISPs' routers will have a single route to 198.0.0.0/8—in other words, a route to all hosts whose IP address begins with 198. More than two million Class C networks alone exist, but CIDR has helped Internet routers reduce their routing tables to a more manageable size, in the range of 70,000 routes at the end of 1999.

By using a routing protocol that exchanges the mask as well as the subnet/network number, a "classless" view of the number can be attained. In other words, treat the grouping as a math problem, ignoring the Class A, B, and C rules. For instance, 198.0.0.0/8 (198.0.0.0, mask 255.0.0.0) defines a set of addresses whose first 8 bits are equal. This route is advertised by ISP 1 to the other ISPs, who need a route only to 198.0.0.0/8. In its routers, ISP 1 knows which Class C networks are at which customer sites. This is how CIDR gives Internet routers a much more scalable routing table, by reducing the number of entries in the tables.

Historically, ISPs found ways to use CIDR to allow better use of the IP Version 4 address space. Imagine that Customer 1 and Customer 3 will need a maximum of 10 and 20 IP addresses, respectively—ever. Each customer has only a router and a single Ethernet. Each customer could register its own Class C network, but if both did so, it would not be in the range already registered to the ISP.

To help CIDR work in the Internet, ISP 1 wants its customers to use IP addresses in the 198.*x*.*x*.*x* range. As a service, the ISP suggests to Customer 1 something like this: Use IP subnet 198.8.3.16/28, with assignable addresses 198.8.17 to 198.8.30. To Customer 3, who needs 20 addresses, ISP 1 suggests 198.8.3.32/27, with 30 assignable addresses (198.8.3.33 to 198.8.3.62). (Feel free to check the math with the IP addressing algorithms listed earlier.)

NOTE The notation with the " / " followed by the number is a common designation on Cisco routers meaning that the mask has that number of 1 bits. This number of 1 bits is called the *prefix*. In this case, the mask implied with prefix /27 would be 255.255.255.224.

The need for registered IP network numbers is reduced through CIDR. Instead of the two customers consuming two whole Class C networks, each consumes a small portion of a single Class C network. The ISP has customers use its IP addresses in a convenient range of values, so CIDR works well and enables the Internet to grow.

Private Addressing

A legitimate need exists for IP addresses that will never be used in the interconnected IP networks called the Internet. So when designing the IP addressing convention for such a network, an organization could pick and use any network number(s) it wanted, and all would be well. Of course, that's true until the organization decides to connect to the Internet—but that will be covered in the section "Network Address Translation."

When building a private network that will have no Internet connectivity, you can use IP network numbers called private Internets, as defined in RFC 1918, "Address Allocation for Private Internets" (www.ietf.org/rfc/rfc1918.txt). This RFC defines a set of networks that will never be assigned to any organization as a registered network number. Instead of using someone else's registered network numbers, you can use numbers in a range that are not used by anyone else. Table 6-46 shows the private address space defined by RFC 1918.

Table 6-46 *RFC 1918 Private Address Space*

Range of IP Addresses	Class of Networks	Number of Networks
10.0.0.0 to 10.255.255.255	A	1
172.16.0.0 to 172.31.255.255	B	16
192.168.0.0 to 192.168.255.255	C	256

In other words, any organization can use these network numbers. However, no organization is allowed to advertise these networks using a routing protocol on the Internet.

The IP Version 4 address space is conserved if all organizations use private addresses in cases for which there will never be a need for Internet connectivity. So the dreaded day of exhausting the registered IP Version 4 network numbers has been delayed again, in part by CIDR and in part by private addressing.

Private addressing's requirement that the privately addressed hosts cannot communicate with others through the Internet can be a particularly onerous restriction. The solution: private addressing with the use of Network Address Translation (NAT).

Network Address Translation

NAT is an RFC-defined function implemented in IOS that allows a host that does not have a valid registered IP address to communicate with other hosts through the Internet. The hosts might be using private addresses or addresses assigned to another organization; in either case, NAT allows these addresses that are not Internet-ready to continue to be used but still allow communication with hosts across the Internet.

NAT achieves its goal by using a valid registered IP address to represent the invalid address to the rest of the Internet. The NAT function changes the IP addresses as necessary inside each IP packet, as shown in Figure 6-32.

Notice that the packet's source IP address is changed when leaving the private organization, and the destination address is changed each time a packet is forwarded back into the private network. Network 200.1.1.0 has been registered as a network owned by Cisco in Figure 6-32, with address 200.1.1.1 configured as part of the NAT configuration. The NAT feature, configured in the router labeled NAT, performs the translation. As you might expect, NAT certainly requires more processing than simply routing the packet. Cisco does not recommend using NAT for a large volume of different hosts.

Figure 6-32 *NAT IP Address Swapping—Private Addressing*

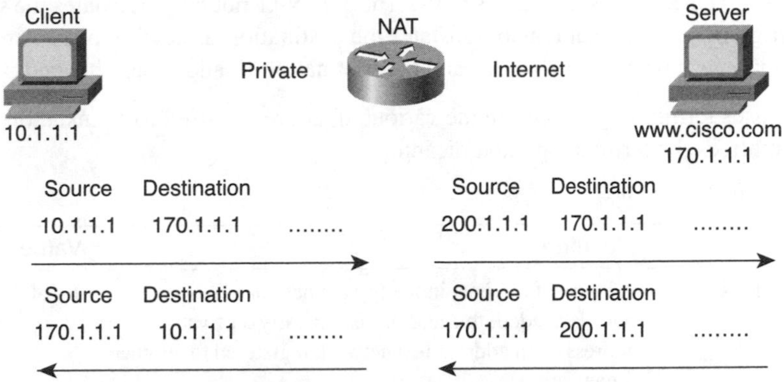

NAT also can be used when the private organization is not using private addressing but is instead using a network number registered to another company. (A client company of mine originally had done just that—ironically, the company was using a network number registered to Cabletron, which my client saw used in a presentation by an ex-Cabletron employee who then worked at 3COM. The 3COM SE explained IP addressing using the Cabletron registered network number; my client liked the design and took him at his word—literally.) If one company inappropriately uses the same network number that is registered appropriately to a different company, NAT can be used, but both the source and the destination IP addresses will need to be translated. For instance, consider Figure 6-33, with Company A using a network that is registered to Cisco (170.1.0.0).

Figure 6-33 *NAT IP Address Swapping—Unregistered Networks*

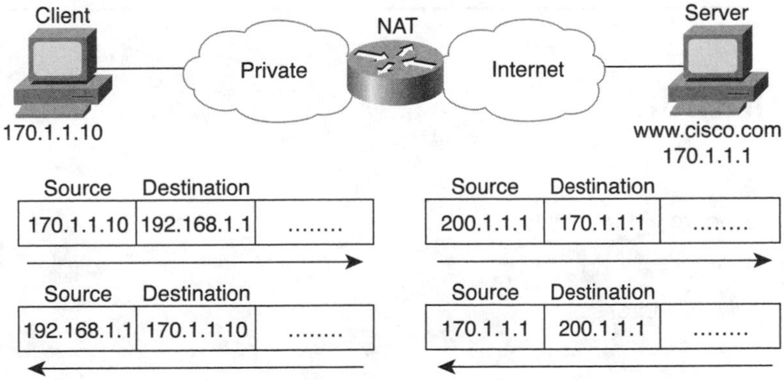

In this case, the client in Company A cannot send a packet to 170.1.1.1—or, at least, if it did, the packet would never get to the real 170.1.1.1 in Cisco's network. That is because there is a very reasonable possibility that the private network has a route matching 170.1.1.1 in its routing table that points to some subnet inside the private company. When the DNS reply comes back past the NAT router, the DNS reply is changed by NAT so that the client in Company A thinks that www.cisco.com's IP address is 192.168.1.1. NAT not only translates the source IP address in outgoing packets, but it also translates the destination. Likewise, packets returning to Company A have both the source and the destination IP addresses changed.

NAT uses terminology to define the various IP addresses used for translation. Table 6-47 summarizes the terminology and meaning.

Table 6-47 *NAT Addressing Terms*

Term	Meaning	Value in Figure 6-32
Inside local	Address of the host in the private network. When NAT is needed, this address is typically a private address or an address in a network registered to another organization.	170.1.1.10
Inside global	The Internet (global network) view of the inside local address. This address is in a network registered to the company responsible for the NAT router.	200.1.1.1
Outside global	This is the Internet (global network) view of the address of the host correctly attached to the Internet.	170.1.1.1
Outside local	When the private company reuses a network number registered to someone else, the outside local address represents the outside global address in the local (private) network. Because this address is used only in the private organization, it can be any IP address.	192.168.1.1

End Extra Credit

IP Configuration

23 Configure IP addresses.

24 Verify IP addresses.

You can easily configure a Cisco router to forward IP traffic when you know the details covered in this chapter so far. Tables 6-48 and 6-49 summarize many of the most common commands used for IP configuration and verification. Two sample network configurations, with both configuration and exec command output, follow. The Cisco IOS documentation is an excellent reference for additional IP commands; the Cisco Press book *Interconnecting Cisco Network Devices* is an excellent reference, particularly if you are not able to attend the instructor-led version of the class.

Table 6-48 *IP Configuration Commands*

Command	Configuration Mode
ip address *ip-address mask* [**secondary**]	Interface mode
ip host *name* [*tcp-port-number*] *address1* [*address2...address8*]	Global
ip route *network-number network-mask* {*ip-address* | *interface*} [*distance*] [**name** *name*]	Global
ip name-server *server-address1* [[*server- address2*]…*server-address6*]	Global
ip domain-lookup	Global
ip routing	Global
ip netmask-format {**bitcount** | **decimal** | **hexadecimal**}	Interface mode
ip default-network *network*	Global
ip classless	Global
ip host ***name*** [*tcp-port-number*] *address1* [*address2…address8*]	Global

Table 6-49 *IP Exec Commands*

Command	Function
show hosts	Lists all host names and corresponding IP addresses
show interfaces [*type number*]	Lists interface statistics, including IP address
show ip interface [*type number*]	Provides a detailed view of IP parameter settings, per interface
show ip interface brief	Provides a summary of all interfaces and their IP addresses
show ip route [*ip-address* [*mask*] [**longer-prefixes**]] | [*protocol* [*process-id*]]	Shows entire routing table or a subset if other parameters are entered
show ip arp [*ip-address*] [*host-name*] [*mac-address*] [*type number*]	Displays IP ARP cache
debug ip packet	Issues log messages for each IP packet

continues

Table 6-49 *IP Exec Commands (Continued)*

Command	Function
terminal ip netmask-format {**bitcount** | **decimal** | **hexadecimal**}	Sets type of display for subnet masks in **show** commands
ping [*protocol* | **tag**] {*host-name* | *system-address*}	Sends and receives ICMP echo messages to verify connectivity
trace [*protocol*] [*destination*]	Sends a series of UDP packets with increasing TTL values to verify the current route to a host

Collectively, Figure 6-34 and Examples 6-2 through 6-4 show three sites, each with two serial links and one Ethernet. The following site guidelines were used when choosing configuration details:

- Use name servers at 10.1.1.100 and 10.1.2.100.
- Use host names from Figure 6-34.
- The router's IP addresses are to be assigned from the last few valid IP addresses in their attached subnets; use a mask of 255.255.255.0.

Figure 6-34 *Sample Network with Three Routers, with Point-to-Point Serial Links*

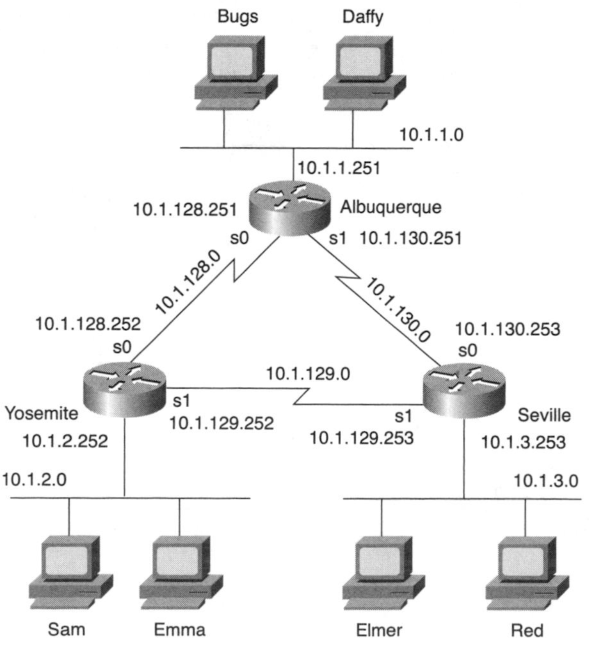

Example 6-2 *Albuquerque Router Configuration and Exec Commands*

```
Albuquerque#configure terminal
Enter configuration commands, one per line.  End with CNTL/Z.
Albuquerque(config)#interface serial 0
Albuquerque(config-if)#ip address 10.1.128.251 255.255.255.0
Albuquerque(config)#interface serial 1
Albuquerque(config-if)#ip address 10.1.130.251 255.255.255.0
Albuquerque(config)#interface ethernet 0
Albuquerque(config-if)#ip address 10.1.1.251 255.255.255.0

Albuquerque#show running-config
Building configuration...

Current configuration : 872 bytes
!
version 12.2
service timestamps debug uptime
service timestamps log uptime
no service password-encryption
!
hostname Albuquerque
!
enable secret 5 $1$J3Fz$QaEYNIiI2aMu.3Ar.q0Xm.
!
!
ip name-server 10.1.1.100
ip name-server 10.1.2.100
!
interface Serial0
 ip address 10.1.128.251 255.255.255.0
!
interface Serial1
 ip address 10.1.130.251 255.255.255.0
!
interface Ethernet0
 ip address 10.1.1.251 255.255.255.0
!
no ip http server

banner motd ^C
  Should've taken a left turn here! This is Albuquerque...  ^C
!
line con 0
 password cisco
 login
line aux 0
line vty 0 4
 password cisco
 login
!
end
```

continues

Example 6-2 *Albuquerque Router Configuration and Exec Commands (Continued)*

```
Albuquerque#show ip route
Codes: C - connected, S - static, I - IGRP, R - RIP, M - mobile, B - BGP
       D - EIGRP, EX - EIGRP external, O - OSPF, IA - OSPF inter area
       N1 - OSPF NSSA external type 1, N2 - OSPF NSSA external type 2
       E1 - OSPF external type 1, E2 - OSPF external type 2, E - EGP
       i - IS-IS, L1 - IS-IS level-1, L2 - IS-IS level-2, ia - IS-IS inter area
       * - candidate default, U - per-user static route, o - ODR
       P - periodic downloaded static route

Gateway of last resort is not set

     10.0.0.0/24 is subnetted, 3 subnets
C       10.1.1.0 is directly connected, Ethernet0
C       10.1.130.0 is directly connected, Serial1
C       10.1.128.0 is directly connected, Serial0

Albuquerque#terminal ip netmask-format decimal
Albuquerque#show ip route
Codes: C - connected, S - static, I - IGRP, R - RIP, M - mobile, B - BGP
       D - EIGRP, EX - EIGRP external, O - OSPF, IA - OSPF inter area
       N1 - OSPF NSSA external type 1, N2 - OSPF NSSA external type 2
       E1 - OSPF external type 1, E2 - OSPF external type 2, E - EGP
       i - IS-IS, L1 - IS-IS level-1, L2 - IS-IS level-2, ia - IS-IS inter area
       * - candidate default, U - per-user static route, o - ODR
       P - periodic downloaded static route

Gateway of last resort is not set

     10.0.0.0 255.255.255.0 is subnetted, 3 subnets
C       10.1.1.0 is directly connected, Ethernet0
C       10.1.130.0 is directly connected, Serial1

C       10.1.128.0 is directly connected, Serial0
Albuquerque#
```

Example 6-3 *Yosemite Router Configuration and Exec Commands*

```
Yosemite#show running-config
Building configuration...

Current configuration : 867 bytes
!
version 12.2
service timestamps debug uptime
service timestamps log uptime
no service password-encryption
!
hostname Yosemite
!
enable secret 5 $1$J3Fz$QaEYNIiI2aMu.3Ar.q0Xm.
!
!
ip name-server 10.1.1.100
```

Example 6-3 *Yosemite Router Configuration and Exec Commands (Continued)*

```
ip name-server 10.1.2.100
!
interface Serial0
 ip address 10.1.128.252 255.255.255.0
 no fair-queue
!
interface Serial1
 ip address 10.1.129.252 255.255.255.0
!
interface Ethernet0
 ip address 10.1.2.252 255.255.255.0
!
no ip http server

banner motd ^C
   This is the Rootin-est Tootin-est Router in these here parts!  ^C
!
line con 0
 password cisco
 login
line aux 0
line vty 0 4
 password cisco
 login
!
end

Yosemite#show ip interface brief
Interface              IP-Address      OK? Method Status                Protocol
Serial0                10.1.128.252    YES manual up                    up
Serial1                10.1.129.252    YES manual up                    up
Ethernet0              10.1.2.252      YES manual up                    up
Yosemite#
```

Example 6-4 *Seville Router Configuration and Exec Commands*

```
Seville#show running-config
Building configuration...

Current configuration : 869 bytes
!
version 12.2
service timestamps debug uptime
service timestamps log uptime
no service password-encryption
!
hostname Seville
!
!
enable secret 5 $1$J3Fz$QaEYNIiI2aMu.3Ar.q0Xm.
!
ip name-server 10.1.1.100
```

continues

Example 6-4 *Seville Router Configuration and Exec Commands (Continued)*

```
ip name-server 10.1.2.100
!
interface Serial0
 ip address 10.1.130.253 255.255.255.0
 no fair-queue
!
interface Serial1
 ip address 10.1.129.253 255.255.255.0
!
Ethernet0
 ip address 10.1.3.253 255.255.255.0
!
no ip http server
banner motd ^C
  Take a little off the top, Wabbit!  (Elmer)   ^C
!
line con 0
 password cisco
 login
line aux 0
line vty 0 4
 password cisco
 login
!
end

Seville#show ip route
Codes: C - connected, S - static, I - IGRP, R - RIP, M - mobile, B - BGP
       D - EIGRP, EX - EIGRP external, O - OSPF, IA - OSPF inter area
       N1 - OSPF NSSA external type 1, N2 - OSPF NSSA external type 2
       E1 - OSPF external type 1, E2 - OSPF external type 2, E - EGP
       i - IS-IS, L1 - IS-IS level-1, L2 - IS-IS level-2, ia - IS-IS inter area
       * - candidate default, U - per-user static route, o - ODR
       P - periodic downloaded static route


Gateway of last resort is not set


10.0.0.0/24 is subnetted, 3 subnets
C       10.1.3.0 is directly connected, Ethernet0
C       10.1.130.0 is directly connected, Serial0
C       10.1.129.0 is directly connected, Serial1


Seville#show ip interface serial 1
Serial1 is up, line protocol is up
  Internet address is 10.1.129.253/24
  Broadcast address is 255.255.255.255
  Address determined by non-volatile memory
  MTU is 1500 bytes
  Helper address is not set
  Directed broadcast forwarding is disabled
```

Example 6-4 *Seville Router Configuration and Exec Commands (Continued)*

```
  Outgoing access list is not set
  Inbound  access list is not set
  Proxy ARP is enabled
  Security level is default
  Split horizon is disabled
  ICMP redirects are always sent
  ICMP unreachables are always sent
  ICMP mask replies are never sent
  IP fast switching is enabled
  IP fast switching on the same interface is enabled
  IP Flow switching is disabled
  IP Feature Fast switching turbo vector
  IP multicast fast switching is disabled
  IP multicast distributed fast switching is disabled
  IP route-cache flags are Fast
  Router Discovery is disabled
  IP output packet accounting is disabled
  IP access violation accounting is disabled
  TCP/IP header compression is disabled
  RTP/IP header compression is disabled
  Probe proxy name replies are disabled
  Policy routing is disabled
  Network address translation is disabled
  WCCP Redirect outbound is disabled
  WCCP Redirect inbound is disabled
  WCCP Redirect exclude is disabled
  BGP Policy Mapping is disabled

Seville#show interface serial 0
Serial0 is up, line protocol is up
  Hardware is HD64570
  Internet address is 10.1.130.253/24
  MTU 1500 bytes, BW 1544 Kbit, DLY 20000 usec,
     reliability 255/255, txload 1/255, rxload 1/255
  Encapsulation HDLC, loopback not set
  Keepalive set (10 sec)
  Last input never, output never, output hang never
  Last clearing of "show interface" counters never
  Input queue: 0/75/0/0 (size/max/drops/flushes); Total output drops: 0
  Queueing strategy: weighted fair
  Output queue: 0/1000/64/0 (size/max total/threshold/drops)
     Conversations  0/0/256 (active/max active/max total)
     Reserved Conversations 0/0 (allocated/max allocated)
     Available Bandwidth 1158 kilobits/sec
  5 minute input rate 0 bits/sec, 0 packets/sec
  5 minute output rate 0 bits/sec, 0 packets/sec
     0 packets input, 0 bytes, 0 no buffer
     Received 0 broadcasts, 0 runts, 0 giants, 0 throttles
     0 input errors, 0 CRC, 0 frame, 0 overrun, 0 ignored, 0 abort
     0 packets output, 0 bytes, 0 underruns
     0 output errors, 0 collisions, 1 interface resets
     0 output buffer failures, 0 output buffers swapped out
     0 carrier transitions
```

continues

Example 6-4 *Seville Router Configuration and Exec Commands (Continued)*

```
     DCD=up  DSR=up  DTR=up  RTS=up  CTS=up

Seville#show ip arp
Protocol  Address          Age (min)  Hardware Addr   Type   Interface
Internet  10.1.3.102              0   0060.978b.1301  ARPA   Ethernet0
Internet  10.1.3.253              -   0000.0c3e.5183  ARPA   Ethernet0

Seville#debug ip packet
IP packet debugging is on
Seville#ping 10.1.130.251
Type escape sequence to abort.
Sending 5, 100-byte ICMP Echos to 10.1.130.251, timeout is 2 seconds:
!!!!!
Success rate is 100 percent (5/5), round-trip min/avg/max = 80/81/84 ms
Seville#
00:09:38: IP: s=10.1.130.251 (local), d=10.1.130.251 (Serial1), len 100, sending
00:09:38: IP: s=10.1.130.251 (Serial1), d=10.1.130.253 (Serial1), len 100, rcvd 3
00:09:38: IP: s=10.1.130.253 (local), d=10.1.130.251 (Serial1), len 100, sending
00:09:38: IP: s=10.1.130.251 (Serial1), d=10.1.130.253 (Serial1), len 100, rcvd 3
00:09:38: IP: s=10.1.130.253 (local), d=10.1.130.251 (Serial1), len 100, sending
00:09:38: IP: s=10.1.130.251 (Serial1), d=10.1.130.253 (Serial1), len 100, rcvd 3
00:09:38: IP: s=10.1.130.253 (local), d=10.1.130.251 (Serial1), len 100, sending
00:09:38: IP: s=10.1.130.251 (Serial1), d=10.1.130.253 (Serial1), len 100, rcvd 3
00:09:38: IP: s=10.1.130.253 (local), d=10.1.130.251 (Serial1), len 100, sending
00:09:38: IP: s=10.1.130.251 (Serial1), d=10.1.130.253 (Serial1), len 100, rcvd 3
Seville#
```

As you see in Figure 6-34, the IP addresses chosen for the interfaces are shown. At the beginning of Example 6-2, the engineer uses configuration mode to configure the IP addresses. The **show running-config** command displays the results of the configuration, along with some other details that were already configured.

Notice that the configuration matches the output of the **show interface**, **show ip interface**, and **show ip interface brief** commands. In Example 6-3, the IP addresses in the configuration match the output of **show ip interface brief**. If these details did not match, one common oversight would be that you are looking at the configuration in NVRAM, not in RAM. Be sure to use the **show running-config** or **write terminal** commands to see the active configuration.

The subnet mask in the output of **show** commands uses prefix notation. For example, 10.1.4.0/24 means 24 network and subnet bits, leaving 8 host bits with this subnetting scheme. The **terminal ip netmask** command can be used to change this formatting for screen output during this session, as seen in Example 6-2.

Example 6-4 shows the ARP cache generated by the **show ip arp** output. The first entry shows the IP address (10.1.3.102) and MAC address of another host on the Ethernet. The timer value of 0 implies that the entry is very fresh—the value grows with disuse and eventually times out. One entry is shown for the router's Ethernet interface itself, which never times out of the ARP table.

The **debug ip packet** output in Example 6-4 lists one entry per IP packet sent and received. This command is a very dangerous one—it could crash almost any production router because of the added overhead of processing the debug messages. Imagine a router that forwards 50,000 packets per second, needing to send 50,000 messages per second to a console that's running at 9600 bps! The router would buffer the messages and exhaust all its memory doing so, and the router would crash. Also notice that the output shows both the source and destination IP addresses.

As compared with a working, real configuration in a production network, these examples omit the needed routing protocol configuration. The routing table in Example 6-4 does not list all subnets because the routing protocol configuration has not been added—notice that all the routers have a value of C beside them, which, according to the legend shown at the beginning of the command, means that the route describes a connected subnet. However, because you also need to know how to configure static routes rather than show the configuration of a routing protocol next, the **ip route** commands in Example 6-5 have been added to Albuquerque, which adds static routes. Examples 6-6 and 6-7 contain **show** commands executed after the new configuration was added.

Example 6-5 *Static Routes Added to Albuquerque*

```
ip route 10.1.2.0 255.255.255.0 10.1.128.252
ip route 10.1.3.0 255.255.255.0 10.1.130.253
```

Example 6-6 *Albuquerque Router Exec Commands, After Adding Static Routes for 10.1.2.0 and 10.1.3.0*

```
Albuquerque#show ip route
Codes: C - connected, S - static, I - IGRP, R - RIP, M - mobile, B - BGP
       D - EIGRP, EX - EIGRP external, O - OSPF, IA - OSPF inter area
       N1 - OSPF NSSA external type 1, N2 - OSPF NSSA external type 2
       E1 - OSPF external type 1, E2 - OSPF external type 2, E - EGP
       i - IS-IS, L1 - IS-IS level-1, L2 - IS-IS level-2, ia - IS-IS inter area
       * - candidate default, U - per-user static route, o - ODR
       P - periodic downloaded static route


Gateway of last resort is not set

     10.0.0.0/24 is subnetted, 5 subnets
S       10.1.3.0 [1/0] via 10.1.130.253
S       10.1.2.0 [1/0] via 10.1.128.252
C       10.1.1.0 is directly connected, Ethernet0
C       10.1.130.0 is directly connected, Serial1
C       10.1.128.0 is directly connected, Serial0
Albuquerque#ping 10.1.128.252

Type escape sequence to abort.
Sending 5, 100-byte ICMP Echos to 10.1.128.252, timeout is 2 seconds:
!!!!!
Success rate is 100 percent (5/5), round-trip min/avg/max = 4/4/8 ms
```

continues

Example 6-6 *Albuquerque Router Exec Commands, After Adding Static Routes for 10.1.2.0 and 10.1.3.0 (Continued)*

```
! Note: the following extended ping command will result in some debug messages
! on Yosemite in Example 6-7.

Albuquerque#ping
Protocol [ip]:
Target IP address: 10.1.2.252
Repeat count [5]:
Datagram size [100]:
Timeout in seconds [2]:
Extended commands [n]: y
Source address or interface: 10.1.1.251
Type of service [0]:
Set DF bit in IP header? [no]:
Validate reply data? [no]:
Data pattern [0xABCD]:
Loose, Strict, Record, Timestamp, Verbose[none]:
Sweep range of sizes [n]:
Type escape sequence to abort.
Sending 5, 100-byte ICMP Echos to 10.1.2.252, timeout is 2 seconds:
.....
Success rate is 0 percent (0/5)
Albuquerque#
```

Example 6-7 **show ip route** *on Yosemite, After Adding Static Routes to Albuquerque*

```
Yosemite#show ip route
Codes: C - connected, S - static, I - IGRP, R - RIP, M - mobile, B - BGP
       D - EIGRP, EX - EIGRP external, O - OSPF, IA - OSPF inter area
       N1 - OSPF NSSA external type 1, N2 - OSPF NSSA external type 2
       E1 - OSPF external type 1, E2 - OSPF external type 2, E - EGP
       i - IS-IS, L1 - IS-IS level-1, L2 - IS-IS level-2, ia - IS-IS inter area
       * - candidate default, U - per-user static route, o - ODR
       P - periodic downloaded static route

Gateway of last resort is not set

     10.0.0.0/24 is subnetted, 3 subnets
C       10.1.2.0 is directly connected, Ethernet0
C       10.1.129.0 is directly connected, Serial1
C       10.1.128.0 is directly connected, Serial0
Yosemite#ping 10.1.128.251

Type escape sequence to abort.
Sending 5, 100-byte ICMP Echos to 10.1.128.251, timeout is 2 seconds:
!!!!!
Success rate is 100 percent (5/5), round-trip min/avg/max = 4/4/8 ms
Yosemite#ping 10.1.1.251

Type escape sequence to abort.
```

Example 6-7 **show ip route** *on Yosemite, After Adding Static Routes to Albuquerque (Continued)*

```
Sending 5, 100-byte ICMP Echos to 10.1.1.251, timeout is 2 seconds:
.....
Success rate is 0 percent (0/5)
Yosemite#debug ip icmp
ICMP packet debugging is on
Yosemite#
Yosemite#show debug
Generic IP:
  ICMP packet debugging is on
Yosemite#

!NOTE: the following debug messages are a result of the extended ping
!command issued on Albuquerque in Example 6-6;
!these messages are generated by Yosemite!

ICMP: echo reply sent, src 10.1.2.252, dst 10.1.1.251
ICMP: echo reply sent, src 10.1.2.252, dst 10.1.1.251
ICMP: echo reply sent, src 10.1.2.252, dst 10.1.1.251
ICMP: echo reply sent, src 10.1.2.252, dst 10.1.1.251
ICMP: echo reply sent, src 10.1.2.252, dst 10.1.1.251
```

First, you should examine the static routes in Example 6-5. On Albuquerque, one route defines a route to 10.1.2.0, off Yosemite, so the next-hop IP address is configured as 10.1.128.252, which is Yosemite's Serial 0 IP address. Similarly, a route to 10.1.3.0, the subnet off Seville, points to Seville's Serial 0 IP address, 10.1.130.253. Presumably, Albuquerque can forward packets to these subnets now; as seen in Example 6-6's first **ping** command, the ping works.

However, if you look at just the syntax but not the rest of these two examples, you will miss an important concept about routing and some necessary details about the **ping** command. First, two subtleties of the **ping** command are used in these two example console dialogs of Examples 6-6 and 6-7:

- Cisco **ping** commands use the output interface's IP address as the source address of the packet, unless otherwise specified in an extended ping. The first ping in Example 6-6 uses a source of 10.1.128.251; the extended ping uses the source address that the user typed in (10.1.1.251).
- ICMP Echo Reply messages (ping responses) reverse the IP addresses used in the ICMP Echo Request to which they are responding.

To make the ping options appear more obvious, this configuration does not contain routes on Yosemite or Seville, pointing back to the subnet off Albuquerque—namely, 10.1.1.0. In a real network, routing protocols would be used instead. If static routes were used, you would need routes pointing in both directions. But because the needed static route on Yosemite, pointing back to 10.1.1.0, is missing, packets from subnet 10.1.1.0 can get to 10.1.2.0 but cannot get back.

When you troubleshoot this network, you can use the extended **ping** command to act like you issued a ping from a computer on that subnet, without having to call a user and ask him to type a **ping** command for you on his PC. The extended version of the **ping** command can be used to more fully refine the underlying cause of the problem. In fact, when a ping from a router works but a ping from a host does not, the extended ping could help in re-creating the problem without needing to work with the end user on the phone. For example, the extended **ping** command on Albuquerque sent an Echo Request from 10.1.1.251 (Albuquerque's Ethernet) to 10.1.2.252 (Yosemite's Ethernet); no response was received by Albuquerque. Normally, the echoes are sourced from the IP address of the outgoing interface; with the use of the extended **ping** source address option, the source IP address of the echo packet can be changed. Because the ICMP echo generated by the extended ping is sourced from an address in 10.1.1.0, it looks more like a packet from an end user in that subnet. It appears that the ICMP Echo Requests generated by the extended ping were received by Yosemite because the debug messages on Yosemite imply that it sent ICMP Echo Replies back to 10.1.1.251. Somewhere between Yosemite creating the ICMP echo replies and Albuquerque receiving them, a problem occurred.

The problem, as mentioned earlier, is that Yosemite has no routes that tell it how to forward packets back to 10.1.1.0. An examination of the steps after the Echo Replies were created by Yosemite is needed to understand the problem in this example. ICMP asks the IP software in Yosemite to deliver the packets. The IP code performs IP routing table lookup to find the correct route for these packets, whose destination is 10.1.1.251. However, the **show ip route** command output in Example 6-7 shows that Yosemite has no route to subnet 10.1.1.0. It seems that Yosemite created the Echo Reply messages but failed to send them because it has no route to 10.1.1.0/24. This is just one example in which the route in one direction is working fine, but the route in the reverse direction is not.

Other options for extended ping are also quite useful. The Don't Fragment (DF) bit can be set, along with the amount of data to send in the echo so that the MTU for the entire route can be discovered through experimentation. Echo packets that are too large to pass over a link because MTU restrictions will be discarded because the DF bit is set. The timeout value can be set so that the **ping** command will wait longer than the default two seconds for an Echo Reply. Furthermore, not only can a single size for the ICMP Echo be set, but a range of sizes can be used to give a more realistic set of packets.

One key to troubleshooting with the **ping** command is understanding the various codes the command uses to signify the various responses that it can receive. Table 6-50 lists the various codes that the Cisco IOS Software **ping** command can supply.

Table 6-50 *Explanation of the Codes That the* **ping** *Command Receives in Response to Its ICMP Echo Request*

ping Command Code	Explanation
!	ICMP Echo Reply received
.	Nothing received

Table 6-50 *Explanation of the Codes That the* **ping** *Command Receives in Response to Its ICMP Echo Request (Continued)*

ping Command Code	Explanation
U	ICMP unreachable (destination) received
N	ICMP unreachable (network) received
P	ICMP unreachable (port) received
Q	ICMP source quench received
M	ICMP Can't Fragment message received
?	Unknown packet received

Using Secondary Addresses

As a CCNA, Cisco expects you to be comfortable and familiar with IP address planning issues. One such issue involves what to do when there are no more unassigned IP addresses in a subnet. One alternative solution is to change the mask used on that subnet, making the existing subnet larger. However, changing the mask could cause an overlap. For example, if 10.1.4.0/24 is running out of addresses and you make a change to mask 255.255.254.0 (9 host bits, 23 network/subnet bits), an overlap can occur. 10.1.4.0/23 includes addresses 10.1.4.0 to 10.1.5.255; this is indeed an overlap with a different existing subnet, 10.1.5.0/24. If subnet 10.1.5.0/24 already exists, using 10.1.4.0/23 would not work.

Another alternative for continued growth is to place all the existing addresses in the mostly full subnet into another larger subnet. There must be a valid subnet number that is unassigned, that does not create an overlap, and that is larger than the old subnet. However, this solution causes administrative effort to change the IP addresses. In either case, both solutions that do not use secondary addressing imply a strategy of using different masks in different parts of the network. Use of these different masks is called variable-length subnet masking (VLSM), which brings up another set of complex routing protocol issues.

The issue of running out of addresses in this subnet can be solved by the use of IP secondary addressing. Secondary addressing uses multiple subnets on the same data link. Secondary IP addressing is simple in concept. Because more than one subnet is used on the same medium, the router needs to have more than one IP address on the interface attached to that medium. For example, Figure 6-35 has subnet 10.1.2.0/24; assume that the subnet has all IP addresses assigned. Assuming secondary addressing to be the chosen solution, subnet 10.1.7.0/24 also could be used on the same Ethernet. Example 6-8 shows the configuration for secondary IP addressing on Yosemite.

Figure 6-35 *TCP/IP Network with Secondary Addresses*

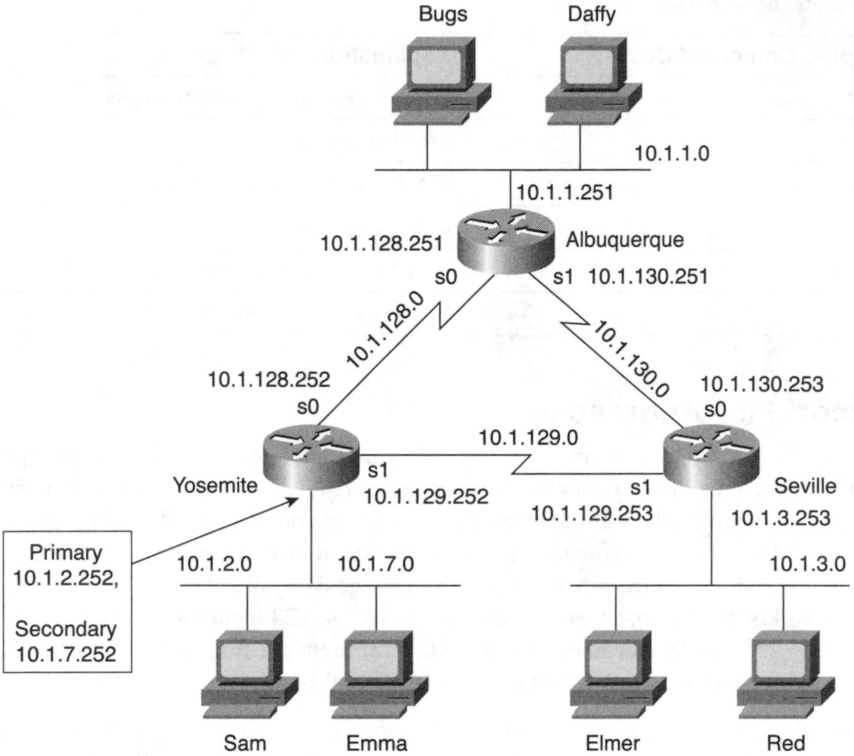

Example 6-8 *Secondary IP Addressing Configuration and* **show ip route** *Command on Yosemite*

```
! Excerpt from show running-config follows...
Hostname Yosemite
ip domain-lookup
ip name-server 10.1.1.100 10.1.2.100
interface ethernet 0
ip address 10.1.7.252  255.255.255.0 secondary
ip address 10.1.2.252  255.255.255.0
interface serial 0
ip address 10.1.128.252  255.255.255.0
interface serial 1
ip address 10.1.129.252  255.255.255.0

Yosemite#show ip route
Codes: C - connected, S - static, I - IGRP, R - RIP, M - mobile, B - BGP
       D - EIGRP, EX - EIGRP external, O - OSPF, IA - OSPF inter area
```

Example 6-8 *Secondary IP Addressing Configuration and* **show ip route** *Command on Yosemite (Continued)*

```
       N1 - OSPF NSSA external type 1, N2 - OSPF NSSA external type 2
       E1 - OSPF external type 1, E2 - OSPF external type 2, E - EGP
       i - IS-IS, L1 - IS-IS level-1, L2 - IS-IS level-2, ia - IS-IS inter area
       * - candidate default, U - per-user static route, o - ODR
       P - periodic downloaded static route

Gateway of last resort is not set

     10.0.0.0/24 is subnetted, 4 subnets
C       10.1.2.0 is directly connected, Ethernet0
C       10.1.7.0 is directly connected, Ethernet0
C       10.1.129.0 is directly connected, Serial1
C       10.1.128.0 is directly connected, Serial0
Yosemite#
```

The router has routes to subnets 10.1.2.0/24 and 10.1.7.0/24, so it can forward packets to each subnet. The router also can receive packets from hosts in one subnet and can forward the packets to the other subnet using the same interface.

IP Addressing with Frame Relay Subinterfaces

Frame Relay behaves like a WAN in some ways and more like a LAN in other ways. To overcome some routing protocol issues that will be discussed in Chapter 7, "Routing and Routing Protocols," and Chapter 10, "Frame Relay Concepts and Configuration," Cisco provides three different ways to configure IP addresses on Frame Relay serial interfaces:

1. Configure the IP addresses on the normal physical interface, just like for other interfaces. By doing so, all routers on the Frame Relay network are in the same subnet.
2. Configure IP addresses on a point-to-point subinterface of the physical interface. A subinterface is a logical subdivision of the physical interface, which, in this case, allows you to correlate a single VC to the point-to-point subinterface. The IP address is configured under the subinterface. Every VC results in a separate subnet.
3. Configure IP addresses on a multipoint subinterface of the physical interface. A subinterface is a logical subdivision of the physical interface, which, in this case, allows you to correlate multiple VCs to the multipoint subinterface. (The addressing subtleties in this case are better left until Chapter 10.)

Figures 6-36 and 6-37 give a graphical representation of the first two options for the same network. Examples 6-9, 6-10, 6-11, and 6-12 show the configurations on routers A, B, C, and D when point-to-point subinterfaces are used, respectively.

Figure 6-36 *Frame Relay Subnets with No Subinterfaces*

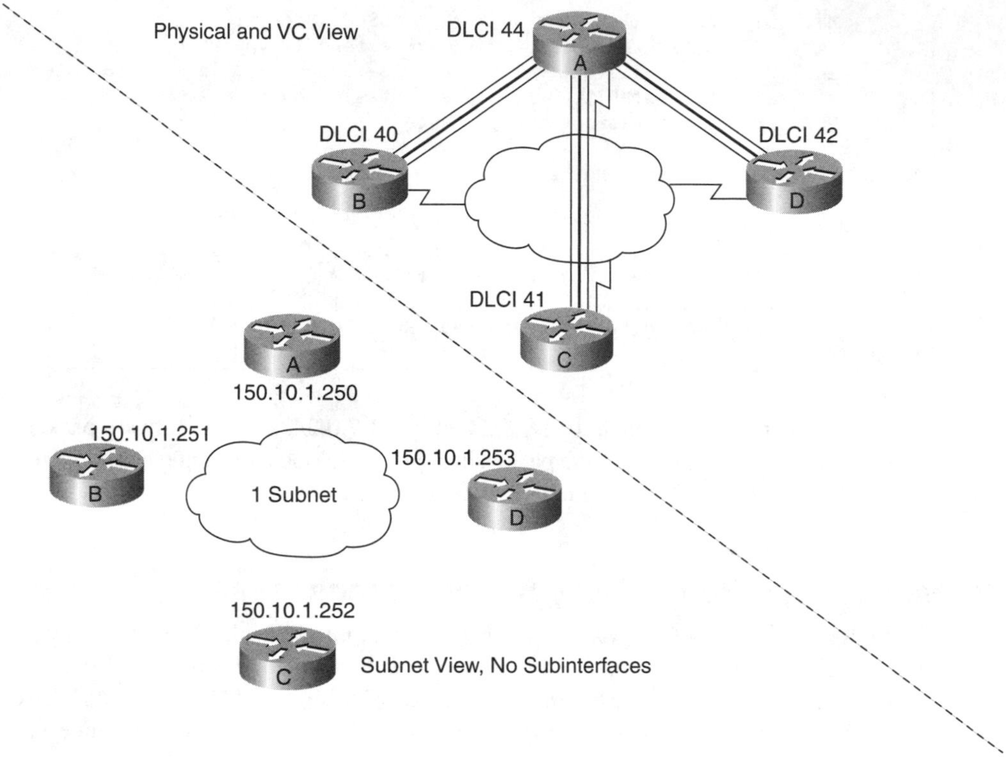

Example 6-9 *Router A Configuration*

```
hostname routerA
interface serial 0
encapsulation frame-relay
!
interface serial 0.1 point-to-point
ip address 150.10.1.250   255.255.255.0
frame-relay interface-dlci 40
description this is for the VC to site B
!
interface serial 0.2 point-to-point
ip address 150.10.2.250   255.255.255.0
frame-relay interface-dlci 41
description this is for the VC to site C
!
interface serial 0.3 point-to-point
ip address 150.10.3.250   255.255.255.0
frame-relay interface-dlci 42
description this is for the VC's to sites D
```

Figure 6-37 *Frame Relay Subnets with Point-to-Point Subinterfaces*

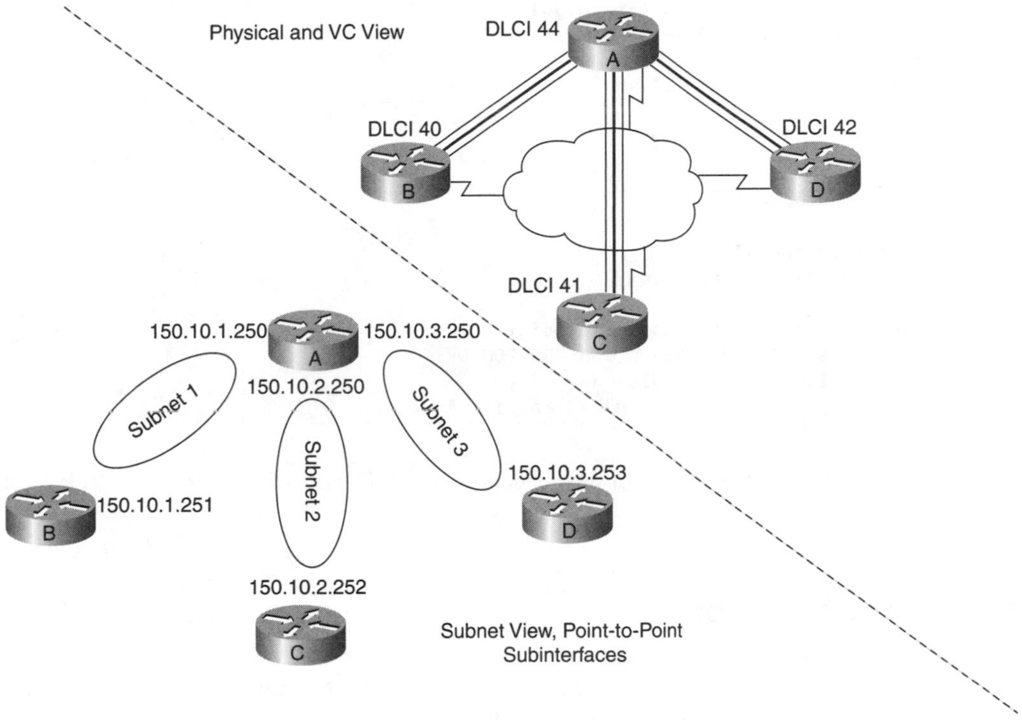

Example 6-10 *Router B Configuration*

```
hostname routerB
!
interface serial 0
encapsulation frame-relay
!
interface serial 0.1 point-to-point
ip address 150.10.1.251   255.255.255.0
frame-relay interface-dlci 44
description this is for the VC to site A
```

Example 6-11 *Router C Configuration*

```
hostname routerC
!
interface serial 0
encapsulation frame-relay
!
```

continues

Example 6-11 *Router C Configuration (Continued)*

```
interface serial 0.2 point-to-point
ip address 150.10.2.252   255.255.255.0
frame-relay interface-dlci 44
description this is for the VC to site A
```

Example 6-12 *Router D Configuration*

```
hostname routerD
!
interface serial 0
encapsulation frame-relay
!
interface serial 0.3 point-to-point
ip address 150.10.3.253   255.255.255.0
frame-relay interface-dlci 44
description this is for the VC to site A
```

For a more complete review of the concepts behind IP addressing over Frame Relay, refer to Chapter 10.

MTU and Fragmentation

The maximum transmission unit (MTU) is a concept that implies the largest Layer 3 packet that can be forwarded out an interface. The maximum MTU value allowed is based on the data-link protocol; essentially, the maximum size of the data portion of the data-link frame (where the packet is placed) is the maximum setting for the MTU on an interface. The default MTU value on Ethernet and serial interfaces is 1,500.

If an interface's MTU is smaller than a packet that must be forwarded, fragmentation is performed by the router. *Fragmentation* is the process of simply breaking the packet into smaller packets, each of which is less than or equal to the MTU value. For example, consider Figure 6-38, with a point-to-point serial link whose MTU has been lowered to 1000.

As Figure 6-38 illustrates, Koufax threw a 1500-byte packet toward Router LA. LA removed the Ethernet header but could not forward the packet because it was 1500 bytes and the HDLC link supported only an MTU of 1000. LA fragmented the original packet into two packets. After forwarding the two packets, Boston receives the packets and forwards them, without reassembling them—reassembly is done by the endpoint host, which, in this case, is Clemens.

The IP header contains fields useful for reassembly of the fragments into the original packet. The IP header includes an ID value that is the same in each fragmented packet, as well as an offset value that defines which part of the original packet is held in each fragment. Fragmented packets arriving out of order can be identified as part of the same original packet and can be reassembled into the correct order using the offset field in each fragment.

Figure 6-38 *IP Fragmentation*

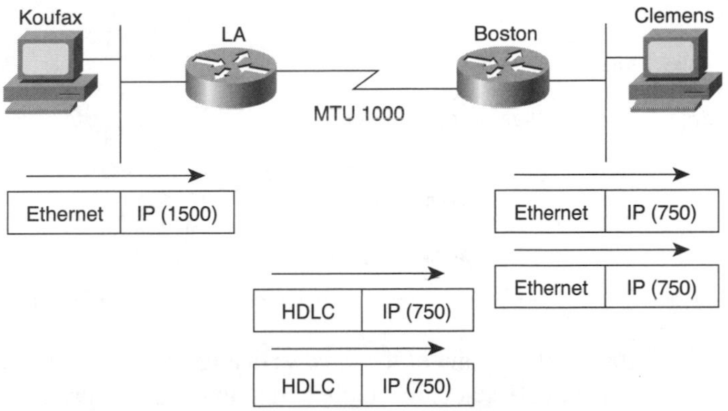

Two configuration commands can be used to change the IP MTU size on an interface: the **mtu** interface subcommand and the **ip mtu** interface subcommand. The **mtu** command sets the MTU for all Layer 3 protocols; unless there is a need to vary the setting per Layer 3 protocol, this command is preferred. If a different setting is desired for IP, the **ip mtu** command sets the value used for IP.

A few nuances relate to the two MTU-setting commands. If both are configured on an interface, the IP MTU setting takes precedence on the interface. However, if the **mtu** command is configured after the **ip mtu** is configured, the **ip mtu** value is reset to the same value as that of the **mtu** command. Care must be taken when changing these values.

IP Naming Commands and Telnet

When using the IOS CLI, you will want to refer to names instead of IP addresses. Particularly for the **trace**, **ping**, and **telnet** commands, the IP address or host name must be supplied. This section describes the use of host names on an IOS-based device. Along the way, some nuances of the use of Telnet are covered.

The IOS can use statically configured names as well as refer to one or more DNSs. Example 6-13 shows some names statically configured, with configuration pointing to two different DNSs.

Example 6-13 *IP Naming Configuration and* **show ip host** *Command*

```
hostname Cooperstown
!
ip host Mays 10.1.1.1
ip host Aaron 10.2.2.2
ip host Mantle 10.3.3.3
!
ip domain-name lacidar.com
ip name-server 10.1.1.200  10.2.2.200
```

continues

Example 6-13 *IP Naming Configuration and* **show ip host** *Command (Continued)*

```
ip domain-lookup

Seville#show hosts
Default domain is lacidar.com
Name/address lookup uses static mappings

Host                     Flags      Age Type   Address(es)
Mays                     (perm, OK)  0   IP    10.1.1.1
Aaron                    (perm, OK)  0   IP    10.2.2.2
Mantle                   (perm, OK)  0   IP    10.3.3.3
Seville#
```

Router Cooperstown will use any of the three statically configured host name–to–IP address mappings. Three names are statically configured in this case—Mays, Aaron, and Mantle. Any command referring to Mays, Aaron, or Mantle will resolve into the IP addresses shown in the **ip host** command.

Router Cooperstown also will ask a DNS for name resolution if it does not know the name and IP address already. The DNS configuration is shown toward the end of the configuration. The IP addresses of the name servers are shown in the **ip name-server** command. Up to six DNSs can be listed; they are searched for each request sequentially based on the order in the command. Finally, the **ip domain-lookup** command enables IOS to ask a name server. IP domain lookup is the default; **no ip domain-lookup** disables the DNS client function. For names that do not include the full domain name, the **ip domain-name** command defines the domain name that should be assumed by the router.

The **show ip host** command lists the static entries, in addition to any entries learned from a DNS request. Only the three static entries were in the table, in this case. The term *perm* in the output implies that the entry is static.

Telnet and Suspend

The **telnet** IOS exec command allows you to Telnet from one Cisco device to another; in practical use, it is typically to another Cisco device. One of the most important features of the **telnet** command is the *suspend* feature. To understand the suspend function, you will need to refer to the network diagram in Figure 6-39.

Figure 6-39 *Telnet Suspension*

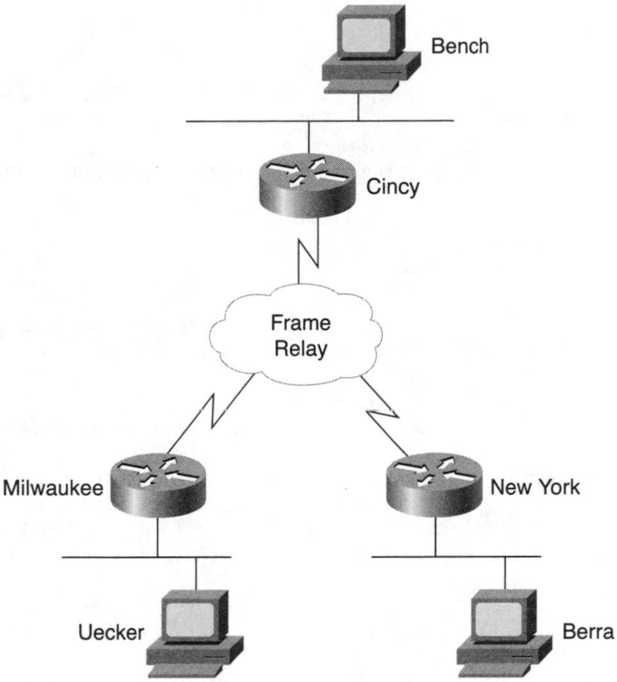

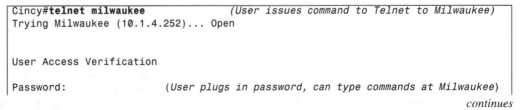

In the figure, the router administrator is using Bench to Telnet into the Cincy router. When in Cincy, the user Telnets to Milwaukee. When in Milwaukee, the user suspends the Telnet by pressing Ctrl-Shift-6, followed by pressing the letter *x*. The user then Telnets to New York and again suspends the connection. The example begins with Bench already logged into Cincy. Example 6-14 shows example output, with annotations to the side.

Example 6-14 *Telnet Suspensions*

```
Cincy#telnet milwaukee                (User issues command to Telnet to Milwaukee)
Trying Milwaukee (10.1.4.252)... Open


User Access Verification

Password:                    (User plugs in password, can type commands at Milwaukee)
```

continues

Example 6-14 *Telnet Suspensions (Continued)*

```
Milwaukee>
Milwaukee>
Milwaukee>
                         (Note: User pressed Ctrl-Shift-6 and then x)
Cincy#telnet NewYork          (User back at Cincy because Telnet was suspended)
Trying NewYork (10.1.6.253)... Open
               (User is getting into New York now, based on telnet NewYork command)


User Access Verification

Password:
NewYork>                                (User can now type commands on New York)
NewYork>
NewYork>
NewYork>
                                    (Note: User pressed Ctrl-Shift-6 and then x)

Cincy#show sessions                (This command lists suspended Telnet sessions)
Conn Host                Address             Byte  Idle Conn Name
   1 milwaukee           10.1.4.252             0     0 milwaukee
*  2 NewYork             10.1.6.253             0     0 NewYork

Cincy#where                       (where does the same thing)
Conn Host                Address             Byte  Idle Conn Name
   1 milwaukee           10.1.4.252             0     0 milwaukee
*  2 NewYork             10.1.6.253             0     0 NewYork

Cincy#resume 1       (Resume connection 1 (see show session) to Milwaukee)
[Resuming connection 1 to milwaukee ... ]

Milwaukee>                              (User can type commands on Milwaukee)
Milwaukee>
Milwaukee>
(Note: User pressed Ctrl-Shift-6 and then x)    (User wants to go back to Cincy)
Cincy#         (WOW! User just pressed Enter and resumes the last Telnet)
 [Resuming connection 1 to milwaukee ... ]

Milwaukee>
Milwaukee>
Milwaukee>
                                  (Note: User pressed Ctrl-Shift-6 and then x)
                                (Tired of Milwaukee again - can't imagine why!)
Cincy#disconnect 1           (No more need to use Milwaukee - Telnet terminated!)
Closing connection to milwaukee [confirm]         (User presses Enter to confirm)
Cincy#
[Resuming connection 2 to NewYork ... ]
                  (Pressing Enter resumes most recently suspended active Telnet)
```

Example 6-14 *Telnet Suspensions (Continued)*

```
NewYork>
NewYork>
NewYork>
                                    (Note: User pressed Ctrl-Shift-6 and then x)
Cincy#disconnect 2                     (Done with New York, terminate Telnet)
Closing connection to NewYork [confirm]          (Just press Enter to confirm)
Cincy#
```

The play-by-play notes in the example explain most of the details. Example 6-14 begins with the Cincy command prompt that would be seen in Bench's Telnet window because the user at Bench Telnetted into Cincy first. After Telnetting to Milwaukee, the Telnet connection was suspended. Then, after Telnetting to New York, that connection was suspended. The two connections can be suspended or resumed easily. The **resume** command can be used to resume either connection; however, the **resume** command requires a connection ID, which is shown in the **show sessions** command. (The **where** command provides the same output.)

The interesting and potentially dangerous nuance here is that if a Telnet session is suspended and you simply press Enter, *Cisco IOS Software resumes the connection to the most recently suspended Telnet connection.* That is fine, until you realize how much you tend to press the Enter key occasionally to clear some of the clutter from the screen. With a suspended Telnet connection, you also just happened to reconnect to another router. This is particularly dangerous when you are changing the configuration or using potentially damaging exec commands—be careful about what router you are actually using when you have suspended Telnet connections!

Default Routes and the ip classless Command

When a router needs to route a packet and there is no route matching that packet's destination in the routing table, the router discards the packet. Default routing lets the router forward the packet to some default next-hop router. Default routing is that simple! However, two configuration options for default routing make it a little tricky. Also one other option changes the algorithm of how the router decides whether there is a routing table match, which affects when the default route is used.

First, default routes work best when there is one path to a part of the network. In Figure 6-40, R1, R2, and R3 are connected to the rest of this network only through R1's Token Ring interface. All three routers can forward packets to the rest of the network, as long as the packets get to R1, which forwards them to Dist1.

Figure 6-40 *Example Network Using a Default Route*

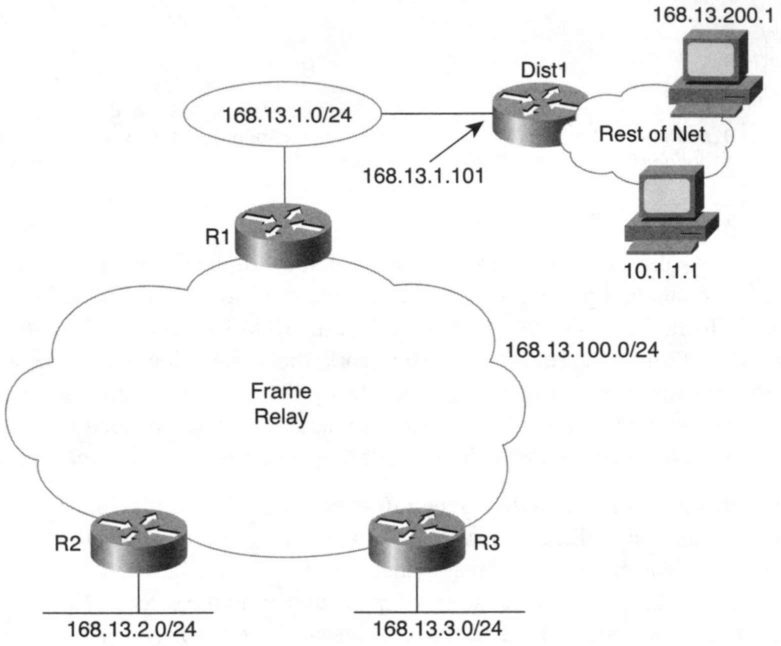

By coding a default route on R1 that points to router Dist1 in Figure 6-40 and having R1 advertise the default to R2 and R3, default routing can be accomplished. Examples 6-15 and 6-16, along with Figure 6-40, show an example of a default route on R1.

Example 6-15 *R1 Static Default Route Configuration and Routing Table*

```
R1(config)#ip route 0.0.0.0 0.0.0.0 168.13.1.101

R1#show ip route
Codes: C - connected, S - static, I - IGRP, R - RIP, M - mobile, B - BGP
       D - EIGRP, EX - EIGRP external, O - OSPF, IA - OSPF inter area
       N1 - OSPF NSSA external type 1, N2 - OSPF NSSA external type 2
       E1 - OSPF external type 1, E2 - OSPF external type 2, E - EGP
       i - IS-IS, L1 - IS-IS level-1, L2 - IS-IS level-2, ia - IS-IS inter area
       * - candidate default, U - per-user static route, o - ODR
       P - periodic downloaded static route

Gateway of last resort is 168.13.1.101 to network 0.0.0.0

     168.13.0.0/24 is subnetted, 4 subnets
C       168.13.1.0 is directly connected, TokenRing0
R       168.13.3.0 [120/1] via 168.13.100.3, 00:00:05, Serial0.1
R       168.13.2.0 [120/1] via 168.13.100.2, 00:00:21, Serial0.1
C       168.13.100.0 is directly connected, Serial0.1
S*   0.0.0.0/0 [1/0] via 168.13.1.101
R1#
```

Example 6-16 *R3—Nuances with Successful Use of Static Route on R1*

```
R3#show ip route
Codes: C - connected, S - static, I - IGRP, R - RIP, M - mobile, B - BGP
       D - EIGRP, EX - EIGRP external, O - OSPF, IA - OSPF inter area
       N1 - OSPF NSSA external type 1, N2 - OSPF NSSA external type 2
       E1 - OSPF external type 1, E2 - OSPF external type 2, E - EGP
       i - IS-IS, L1 - IS-IS level-1, L2 - IS-IS level-2, ia - IS-IS inter area
       * - candidate default, U - per-user static route, o - ODR
       P - periodic downloaded static route

Gateway of last resort is 168.13.100.1 to network 0.0.0.0

     168.13.0.0/24 is subnetted, 4 subnets
R       168.13.1.0 [120/1] via 168.13.100.1, 00:00:13, Serial0.1
C       168.13.3.0 is directly connected, Ethernet0
R       168.13.2.0 [120/1] via 168.13.100.2, 00:00:06, Serial0.1
C       168.13.100.0 is directly connected, Serial0.1
R3#ping 10.1.1.1

Type escape sequence to abort.
Sending 5, 100-byte ICMP Echos to 10.1.1.1, timeout is 2 seconds:
!!!!!
Success rate is 100 percent (5/5), round-trip min/avg/max = 84/89/114 ms
R3#
R3#ping 168.13.200.1

Type escape sequence to abort.
Sending 5, 100-byte ICMP Echos to 168.13.200.1, timeout is 2 seconds:
.....
Success rate is 0 percent (0/5)
R3#
R3#conf t
Enter configuration commands, one per line.  End with CNTL/Z.
R3(config)#ip classless
R3(config)#^Z
R3#ping 168.13.200.1

Type escape sequence to abort.
Sending 5, 100-byte ICMP Echos to 168.13.200.1, timeout is 2 seconds:
!!!!!
Success rate is 100 percent (5/5), round-trip min/avg/max = 80/88/112 ms
R3#
```

The default route is defined with a static **ip route** command on R1, with destination 0.0.0.0, mask 0.0.0.0. This route matches all destinations, by convention. R1 advertises to R2 and R3, as seen in the output of the **show ip route** command on R3 in Example 6-16. So the **ping 10.1.1.1** command on R3 works, just like it should. However, the **ping 168.13.200.1** command does not work—why?

The key to knowing why one ping worked and one did not is based on what Cisco IOS Software thinks is a "match" of the routing table. If the router first matches the Class A, B, or C network number that a destination resides in and then looks for the specific subnet, the router is considered to be *classful*. If the router simply looks for the best subnet match, ignoring Class A, B, and C rules, the router is *classless*. What you need in this case is a router with no class! Seriously, here's R3's logic when the ping failed:

1. I need to send a packet to 168.13.200.1.
2. I match Class B network 168.13.0.0, so there is a match.
3. I do not match a specific subnet that contains 168.13.200.1.
4. I use the default route only if there is no match, and there was a match, so I discard the packet.

If you make R3 act in a classless manner, the ping will work, as in the second **ping 168.13.200.1** command in Example 6-16. The logic works something like this:

1. I need to send a packet to 168.13.200.1.
2. I do not match a specific subnet that contains 168.13.200.1.
3. I use the default route only if there is no match, and there was no match, so I use the default route.

The **no ip classless** command makes the router behave as a classful router. The **ip classless** command makes it act as a classless router, which would be preferred in this case. It seems like classless would always be better, but it is not. What if the networks on the other side of Dist1 were on the Internet and 168.13.0.0 was your registered Class B network? Well, there should not be any part of 168.13.0.0 to the right of Dist1, so it would be pointless to send packets for unknown subnets of 168.13.0.0 to Dist1 because they will be discarded at some point anyway. There are uses for both modes—just be aware of how each works.

The gateway of last resort, highlighted in the **show ip route** command output, sounds like a pretty desperate feature. There are worse things than having to discard a packet in a router, and "gateway of last resort" simply references the current default route. It is possible that several default routes have been configured and then distributed with a routing protocol; the gateway of last resort is the currently used default on a particular router. Be careful—multiple defaults can cause a routing loop.

Another style of configuration for the default route uses the **ip default-network** command. This command is used most typically when you want to reach other Class A, B, or C networks by default, but all the subnets of your own network are expected to be in your own routing tables. For example, imagine that the cloud next to Dist1 in Figure 6-40 has subnets of network 10.0.0.0 in it as well as other networks. (Dist1 could be an ISP router.) The network in Figure 6-40 is still in use, but instead of using the **ip route 0.0.0.0 0.0.0.0 168.13.1.101** command, the **ip default-network 10.0.0.0** command is used on R1. R1 uses its route to network 10.0.0.0 as its default and advertises this route as a default route to other routers. Examples 6-17 and 6-18 show several details on R1 and R3.

Example 6-17 *R1's Use of the* **ip default-network** *Command*

```
R1#configure terminal
R1(config)#ip default-network 10.0.0.0
R1(config)#exit
R1#show ip route
Codes: C - connected, S - static, I - IGRP, R - RIP, M - mobile, B - BGP
       D - EIGRP, EX - EIGRP external, O - OSPF, IA - OSPF inter area
       N1 - OSPF NSSA external type 1, N2 - OSPF NSSA external type 2
       E1 - OSPF external type 1, E2 - OSPF external type 2, E - EGP
       i - IS-IS, L1 - IS-IS level-1, L2 - IS-IS level-2, ia - IS-IS inter area
       * - candidate default, U - per-user static route, o - ODR
       P - periodic downloaded static route

Gateway of last resort is 168.13.1.101 to network 10.0.0.0

     168.13.0.0/24 is subnetted, 5 subnets
R       168.13.200.0 [120/1] via 168.13.1.101, 00:00:12, TokenRing0
C       168.13.1.0 is directly connected, TokenRing0
R       168.13.3.0 [120/1] via 168.13.100.3, 00:00:00, Serial0.1
R       168.13.2.0 [120/1] via 168.13.100.2, 00:00:00, Serial0.1
C       168.13.100.0 is directly connected, Serial0.1
R*   10.0.0.0/8 [120/1] via 168.13.1.101, 00:00:12, TokenRing0
R1#
```

Example 6-18 *R3 Routing Table and* **trace** *Command Samples*

```
R3#show ip route
Codes: C - connected, S - static, I - IGRP, R - RIP, M - mobile, B - BGP
       D - EIGRP, EX - EIGRP external, O - OSPF, IA - OSPF inter area
       N1 - OSPF NSSA external type 1, N2 - OSPF NSSA external type 2
       E1 - OSPF external type 1, E2 - OSPF external type 2, E - EGP
       i - IS-IS, L1 - IS-IS level-1, L2 - IS-IS level-2, ia - IS-IS inter area
       * - candidate default, U - per-user static route, o - ODR
       P - periodic downloaded static route

Gateway of last resort is 168.13.100.1 to network 0.0.0.0

     168.13.0.0/24 is subnetted, 5 subnets
R       168.13.200.0 [120/2] via 168.13.100.1, 00:00:26, Serial0.1
R       168.13.1.0 [120/1] via 168.13.100.1, 00:00:26, Serial0.1
C       168.13.3.0 is directly connected, Ethernet0
R       168.13.2.0 [120/1] via 168.13.100.2, 00:00:18, Serial0.1
C       168.13.100.0 is directly connected, Serial0.1
R    10.0.0.0/8 [120/2] via 168.13.100.1, 00:00:26, Serial0.1
R*   0.0.0.0/0 [120/2] via 168.13.100.1, 00:00:26, Serial0.1
R3#trace 168.13.222.2

Type escape sequence to abort.
Tracing the route to 168.13.222.2

  1 168.13.100.1 68 msec 56 msec 52 msec
  2 168.13.1.101 52 msec 56 msec 52 msec
R3#trace 10.1.1.1
```

continues

Example 6-18 *R3 Routing Table and* **trace** *Command Samples (Continued)*

```
Type escape sequence to abort.
Tracing the route to 10.1.1.1

  1 168.13.100.1 68 msec 56 msec 52 msec
  2 168.13.1.101 48 msec 56 msec 52 msec
R3#
```

Both R1 and R3 have default routes, but they are shown differently in their respective routing tables. R1 shows a route to network 10.0.0.0 with an *, meaning that it is a candidate to be the default route. In R3, 0.0.0.0 shows up in the routing table as the candidate default route. The reason that R3 shows this information differently is that RIP advertises default routes using network number 0.0.0.0. If IGRP or EIGRP were in use, there would be no route to 0.0.0.0 on R3, and network 10.0.0.0 would be the candidate default route. That's because IGRP and EIGRP would flag 10.0.0.0 as a candidate default route in their routing updates rather than advertise the special case of 0.0.0.0.

The default route on R3 is used for destinations in network 168.13.0.0, 10.0.0.0, or any other network because **ip classless** is still configured. The **trace** commands in Example 6-18, which show destinations in two different networks, both succeed. The **trace** commands each show that the first router in the route was R1, then comes Dist1, and then the command finished. If *n* other routers had been present in the network of Figure 6-40, these routers could have shown up in the **trace** output as well. (In each case, the destination address was the address of some loopback interface in Dist1, so there were no routers beyond Dist1.) **ip classless** still was configured; it is recommended that you configure **ip classless** if using any form of default routes.

Cisco Discovery Protocol

The Cisco Discovery Protocol (CDP) discovers basic information about neighboring routers and switches, without needing to know the passwords for the neighboring devices. CDP supports any LAN, HDLC, Frame Relay, and ATM interface. CDP supports any interface that supports the use of SNAP headers. The router or switch can discover Layer 2 and Layer 3 addressing details of neighboring routers without even configuring that Layer 3 protocol—this is because CDP is not dependent on any particular Layer 3 protocol.

CDP discovers several useful details from the neighboring device:

- **Device identifier**—Typically the host name
- **Address list**—Network and data-link addresses
- **Port identifier**—Text that identifies the port, which is another name for an interface

- **Capabilities list**—Information on what type of device it is—for instance, a router or a switch
- **Platform**—The model and OS level running in the device

CDP is enabled in the configuration by default. The **no cdp run** global command disables CDP for the entire device, and the **cdp run** global command re-enables CDP. Likewise, the **no cdp enable** interface subcommand disables CDP just on that interface, and the **cdp enable** command switches back to the default state of CDP being enabled.

A variety of **show cdp** command options are available. Example 6-19 lists the output of the commands, with some commentary following.

Example 6-19 **show cdp** *Command Options*

```
Seville#show cdp neighbor
Capability Codes: R - Router, T - Trans Bridge, B - Source Route Bridge
                  S - Switch, H - Host, I - IGMP, r - Repeater

Device ID        Local Intrfce     Holdtme    Capability  Platform  Port ID
fred                Ser 1           172          R        2500      Ser 1
Yosemite            Ser 0.2         161          R        2500      Ser 0.2

Seville#show cdp entry fred
-------------------------
Device ID: fred
Entry address(es):
  IP address: 163.5.8.3
Platform: cisco 2500,  Capabilities: Router
Interface: Serial1,  Port ID (outgoing port): Serial1
Holdtime : 168 sec

Version :
Cisco Internetwork Operating System Software
IOS (tm) 2500 Software (C2500-DS-L), Version 12.2(3), RELEASE SOFTWARE (fc1)
Copyright (c) 1986-2001 by cisco Systems, Inc.
Compiled Wed 18-Jul-01 21:10 by pwade

advertisement version: 2

Seville#show cdp neighbor detail
-------------------------
Device ID: fred
Entry address(es):
  IP address: 163.5.8.3
Platform: cisco 2500,  Capabilities: Router
Interface: Serial1,  Port ID (outgoing port): Serial1
Holdtime : 164 sec

Version :
```

continues

Example 6-19 show cdp *Command Options (Continued)*

```
Cisco Internetwork Operating System Software
IOS (tm) 2500 Software (C2500-DS-L), Version 12.2(3), RELEASE SOFTWARE (fc1)
Copyright (c) 1986-2001 by cisco Systems, Inc.
Compiled Wed 18-Jul-01 21:10 by pwade

advertisement version: 2

-------------------------
Device ID: Yosemite
Entry address(es):
  IP address: 10.1.5.252
  Novell address: 5.0200.bbbb.bbbb
Platform: cisco 2500,  Capabilities: Router
Interface: Serial0.2,  Port ID (outgoing port): Serial0.2
Holdtime : 146 sec

Version :
Cisco Internetwork Operating System Software
IOS (tm) 2500 Software (C2500-DS-L), Version 12.2(3), RELEASE SOFTWARE (fc1)
Copyright (c) 1986-2001 by cisco Systems, Inc.
Compiled Wed 18-Jul-01 21:10 by pwade

advertisement version: 2

Seville#show cdp interface
Ethernet0 is up, line protocol is down
  Encapsulation ARPA
  Sending CDP packets every 60 seconds
  Holdtime is 180 seconds
Serial0.2 is up, line protocol is up
  Encapsulation FRAME-RELAY
  Sending CDP packets every 60 seconds
  Holdtime is 180 seconds
Serial1 is up, line protocol is up
  Encapsulation HDLC
  Sending CDP packets every 60 seconds
  Holdtime is 180 seconds

Seville#show cdp traffic
CDP counters :
        Total packets output: 31, Input: 41
        Hdr syntax: 0, Chksum error: 0, Encaps failed: 9
        No memory: 0, Invalid packet: 0, Fragmented: 0
        CDP version 1 advertisements output: 0, Input: 0
        CDP version 2 advertisements output: 31, Input: 41
```

The commands provide information about both the neighbors and the behavior of the CDP protocol itself. In the **show cdp entry fred** command in Example 6-19, all the details learned by CDP are shown and highlighted. To know that fred is the device identifier of a neighbor, the **show cdp neighbor** command can be used to summarize the information about each neighbor. **show cdp neighbor detail** lists the detail of all neighbors, in the same format as **show cdp entry**. In addition, **show cdp traffic** lists the overhead that CDP introduces to perform its functions.

Foundation Summary

The "Foundation Summary" is a collection of tables and figures that provides a convenient review of many key concepts in this chapter. For those of you already comfortable with the topics in this chapter, this summary could help you recall a few details. For those of you who just read this chapter, this review should help solidify some key facts. For any of you doing your final prep before the exam, these tables and figures will hopefully be a convenient way to review the day before the exam.

Figure 6-41 outlines the basic process with DNS name resolution and IP ARP.

Figure 6-41 *Sample Network, DNS and ARP Processes*

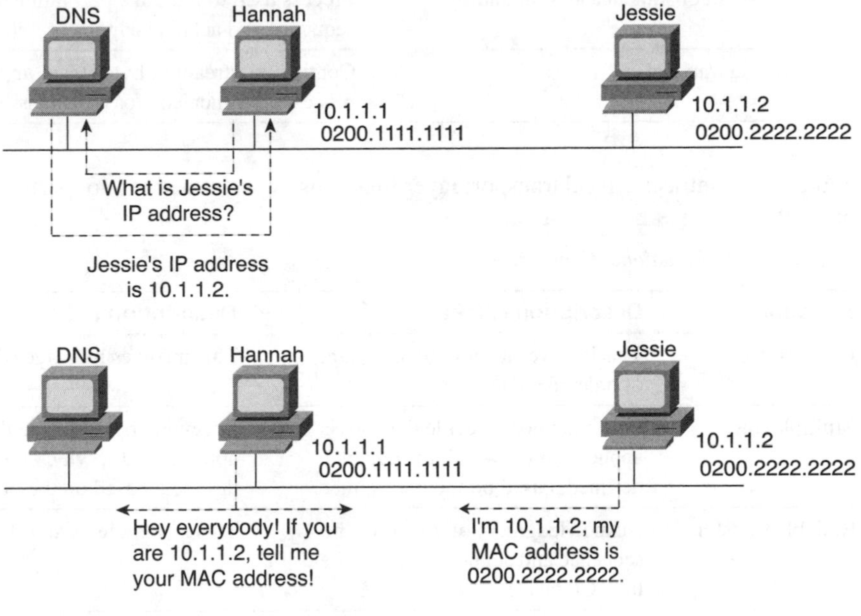

Figure 6-42 shows an example of TCP connection establishment flow.

Figure 6-42 *TCP Connection Establishment*

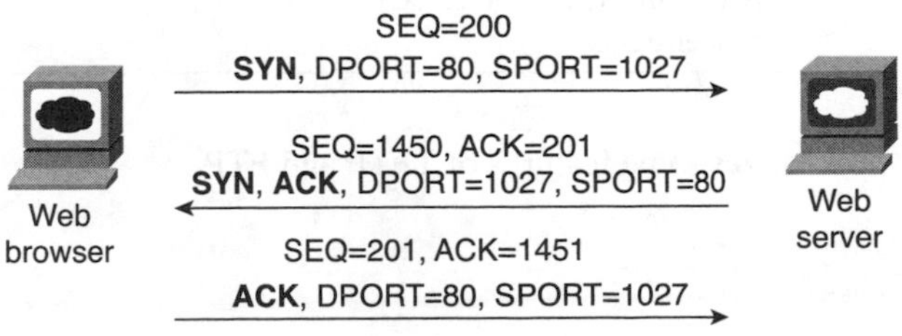

Table 6-51 summarizes TCP functions.

Table 6-51 *TCP Function Summary*

Function	Description
Multiplexing	Function that allows receiving hosts to decide the correct application for which the data is destined, based on the port number
Error recovery (reliability)	Process of numbering and acknowledging data with sequence and acknowledgment header fields
Flow control using windowing	Process that uses window sizes to protect buffer space and routing devices
Connection establishment and termination	Process used to initialize port numbers and sequence and acknowledgement fields
Ordered data transfer	Continuous stream of bytes from upper-layer process, "segmented" for transmission

Table 6-52 contrasts typical transport layer functions as performed (or not performed) by UDP or TCP.

Table 6-52 *TCP and UDP Functional Comparison*

Function	Description (TCP)	Description (UDP)
Data transfer	This involves a continuous stream of ordered data.	This involves message (datagram) delivery.
Multiplexing	Receiving hosts decide the correct application for which the data is destined, based on the port number.	Receiving hosts decide the correct application for which the data is destined, based on the port number.
Reliable transfer	Acknowledgment of data uses the sequence and acknowledgment fields in the TCP header.	This is not a feature of UDP.
Flow control	This process is used to protect buffer space and routing devices.	This is not a feature of UDP.
Connections	This process is used to initialize port numbers and other TCP header fields.	UDP is connectionless.

Table 6-53 summarizes some features of TFTP and FTP.

Table 6-53 *Comparison of FTP and TFTP*

FTP	TFTP
Uses TCP	Uses UDP
Uses robust control commands	Uses simple control commands
Sends data over a separate TCP connection from control commands	Uses no connections because of UDP
Requires more memory and programming effort	Requires less memory and programming effort

Table 6-54 lists the IP terms used in the upcoming sections, giving an exact definition.

Table 6-54 *IP Addressing Terminology*

Term	Definition
IP address	A 32-bit number, usually written in dotted-decimal form, that uniquely identifies an interface of some computer.
Host address	Another term for IP address.
Network	A group of hosts, all of which have an identical beginning portion of their IP addresses.
Network number	A 32-bit number, usually written in dotted-decimal form, that represents a network. This number cannot be assigned as an IP address to an interface of some computer. The host portion of the network number has a value of all binary 0s.
Network address	Another term for network number.
Broadcast address	A 32-bit number, usually written in dotted-decimal form, that is used to address all hosts in the network. This number cannot be assigned as an IP address to an interface of some computer. The host portion of the network number has a value of all binary 1s.
Subnet	A group of hosts, all of which have an identical beginning portion of their IP addresses. A subnet differs from a network in that a subnet is a further subdivision of a network, with a longer portion of the addresses being identical.
Subnet number	A 32-bit number, usually written in dotted-decimal form, that represents a subnet. This number cannot be assigned as an IP address to an interface of some computer. The host portion of the network number has a value of all binary 0s.
Subnet address	Another term for subnet number.

continues

Table 6-54 *IP Addressing Terminology (Continued)*

Term	Definition
Subnet broadcast address	A 32-bit number, usually written in dotted-decimal form, that is used to address all hosts in the subnet. This number cannot be assigned as an IP address to an interface of some computer. The host portion of the network number has a value of all binary 1s.
Subnetting	The process of subdividing networks into smaller subnets. This is jargon—for example, "Are you subnetting your network?"
Network mask	A 32-bit number, usually written in dotted-decimal form. The mask is used by computers to calculate the network number of a given IP address by performing a Boolean AND of the address and mask. The mask also defines the number of host bits in an address.
Mask	A generic term for a mask, whether it is a default mask or a subnet mask.
Address mask	Another term for a mask.
Default Class A mask	The mask used for Class A networks when no subnetting is used. The value is 255.0.0.0.
Default Class B mask	The mask used for Class B networks when no subnetting is used. The value is 255.255.0.0.
Default Class C mask	The mask used for Class C networks when no subnetting is used. The value is 255.255.255.0.
Subnet mask	A nondefault mask that is used when subnetting.
Network part or network field	Term used to describe the first part of an IP address. The network part is 8, 16, or 24 bits for Class A, B, and C networks, respectively.
Host part or host field	Term used to describe the last part of an IP address. The host part is 24, 16, or 8 bits for Class A, B, and C networks, respectively, when subnetting is not used. When subnetting, the size of the host part depends on the subnet mask chosen for that network.
Subnet part of subnet field	Term used to describe the middle part of an IP address. The subnet part is variable in size, based on how subnetting is implemented.

Table 6-55 summarizes the possible network numbers, the total number of each type, and the number of hosts in each Class A, B, and C network.

Table 6-55 *List of All Possible Valid Network Numbers*

Class	First Octet Range	Valid Network Numbers	Total Number of This Class of Network	Number of Hosts per Network
A	1 to 126	1.0.0.0 to 126.0.0.0	2^7, minus two special cases	2^{24}, minus two special cases

Table 6-55 *List of All Possible Valid Network Numbers (Continued)*

Class	First Octet Range	Valid Network Numbers	Total Number of This Class of Network	Number of Hosts per Network
B	128 to 191	128.1.0.0 to 191.254.0.0	2^{14}, minus two special cases	2^{16}, minus two special cases
C	192 to 223	192.0.1.0 to 223.255.254.0	2^{21}, minus two special cases	2^{8}, minus two special cases

Figure 6-43 shows the format of addresses when subnetting.

Figure 6-43 *Address Formats When Subnetting Is Used*

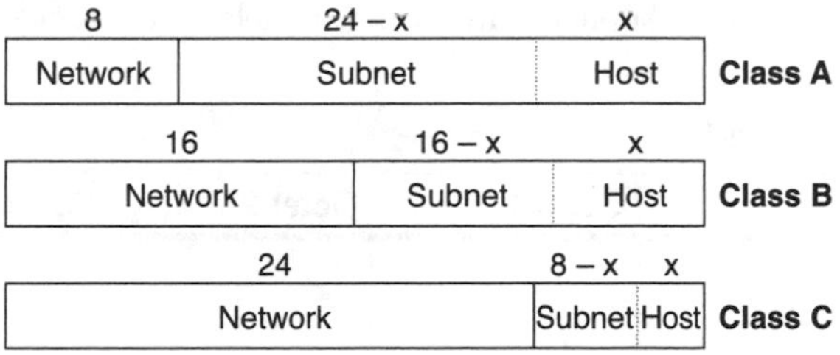

Table 6-56 lists the key rules to deconstructing an IP address, alongside an example.

Table 6-56 *First Example, with Rules for Learning Network, Subnet, and Host Part Sizes*

Step	Example	Rules to Remember
Address	8.1.4.5	
Mask	255.255.0.0	
Number of network bits	8	Always defined by Class A, B, C
Number of host bits	16	Always defined as number of binary 0s in mask
Number of subnet bits	8	32 – (network size + host size)

Table 6-57 lists the only valid decimal values in a mask and their binary equivalents.

Table 6-57 *Decimal and Binary Values in a Single Octet of a Valid Subnet Mask*

Decimal	Binary
0	0000 0000
128	1000 0000

continues

Table 6-57 *Decimal and Binary Values in a Single Octet of a Valid Subnet Mask (Continued)*

Decimal	Binary
192	1100 0000
224	1110 0000
240	1111 0000
248	1111 1000
252	1111 1100
254	1111 1110
255	1111 1111

Table 6-58 is an example subnet chart, used to help learn the easy subnetting process using no binary math.

Table 6-58 *Subnet Chart—Generic*

	Octet 1	Octet 2	Octet 3	Octet 4
Address				
Mask				
Subnet number				
First valid address				
Broadcast				
Last valid address				

The four-step process for dissecting IP addresses is summarized in the following list:

Step 1 Identify the structure of the IP address.

A Identify the size of the network part of the address, based on Class A, B, and C rules.

B Identify the size of the host part of the address, based on the number of binary 0s in the mask. If the mask is tricky, use the chart of typical mask values to convert the mask to binary more quickly.

C The size of the subnet part is what's "left over"; mathematically, it is 32 – (number of network + host bits).

D Declare the number of subnets, which is $2^{\text{number-of-subnet-bits}} - 2$.

E Declare the number of hosts per subnet, which is $2^{\text{number-of-host-bits}} - 2$.

Step 2 Create the chart that will be used in Steps 3 and 4.

A Create a generic subnet chart.

B Write down the IP address and subnet mask in the first two rows of the chart.

C If an easy mask is used, draw a vertical line between the 255s and the 0s in the mask, from top to bottom of the chart. If a hard mask is used, draw a box around the column of the interesting octet.

D Copy the address octets to the left of the line or the box into the final four rows of the chart.

Step 3 Derive the subnet number and the first valid IP address.

A Write down 0s in the subnet octets to the right of the line or the box.

B If the mask is hard and there is a box in the chart, use the magic number trick to find the value of the subnet's interesting octet.

C To derive the first valid IP address, copy the first three octets of the subnet number, and add 1 to the fourth octet of the subnet number.

Step 4 Derive the broadcast address and the last valid IP address.

A Write down 255s in the broadcast address octets to the right of the line or the box.

B If the mask is hard and there is a box in the chart, use the magic number trick to find the value of the broadcast address's interesting octet.

C To derive the last valid IP address, copy the first three octets of the broadcast address, and subtract 1 from the fourth octet of the broadcast address.

The three-step process to find all the subnet numbers of a network is listed next:

Step 1 Write down the network number and subnet mask in the first two rows of the subnet list chart.

Step 2 Write down the network number in the third row. This is the zero subnet, which is one of the two reserved subnets.

Step 3 Do the following two tasks, stopping when the next number that you would write down in the interesting column is 256. (Don't write that one down—it's not valid.)

A Copy all three noninteresting octets from the previous line.

B Add the magic number to the previous interesting octet, and write that down as the value of the interesting octet.

Tables 6-59 and 6-60 summarize many of the most common commands used for IP configuration and verification.

Table 6-59 *IP Configuration Commands*

Command	Configuration Mode
ip address *ip-address mask* [**secondary**]	Interface mode
ip host *name* [*tcp-port-number*] *address1* [*address2...address8*]	Global
ip route *network-number network-mask* {*ip-address* | *interface*} [*distance*] [**name** *name*]	Global
ip name-server *server-address1* [[*server- address2*] …*server-address6*]	Global
ip domain-lookup	Global
ip routing	Global
ip netmask-format {**bitcount** | **decimal** | **hexadecimal**}	Interface mode
ip default-network *network*	Global
ip classless	Global
ip host ***name*** [*tcp-port-number*] *address1* [*address2…address8*]	Global

Table 6-60 *IP Exec Commands*

Command	Function
show hosts	Lists all host names and corresponding IP addresses
show interfaces [*type number*]	Lists interface statistics, including IP address
show ip interface [*type number*]	Provides a detailed view of IP parameter settings, per interface
show ip interface brief	Provides a summary of all interfaces and their IP addresses

Table 6-60 *IP Exec Commands (Continued)*

Command	Function
show ip route [*ip-address* [*mask*] [**longer-prefixes**]] | [*protocol* [*process-id*]]	Shows entire routing table or a subset if other parameters are entered
show ip arp [*ip-address*] [*host-name*] [*mac-address*] [*type number*]	Displays IP ARP cache
debug ip packet	Issues log messages for each IP packet
terminal ip netmask-format {**bitcount** | **decimal** | **hexadecimal**}	Sets type of display for subnet masks in **show** commands
ping [*protocol* | **tag**] {*host-name* | *system-address*}	Sends and receives ICMP echo messages to verify connectivity
trace [*protocol*] [*destination*]	Sends series of UDP packets with increasing TTL values to verify the current route to a host

Q&A

As mentioned in Chapter 1, "All About the Cisco Certified Network Associate Certification," the questions and scenarios in this book are more difficult than what you should experience on the actual exam. The questions do not attempt to cover more breadth or depth than the exam; however, they are designed to make sure that you know the answer. Rather than allowing you to derive the answer from clues hidden inside the question itself, the questions challenge your understanding and recall of the subject. Questions from the "Do I Know This Already?" quiz from the beginning of the chapter are repeated here to ensure that you have mastered the chapter's topic areas. Hopefully, these questions will help limit the number of exam questions on which you narrow your choices to two options and then guess.

The answers to these questions can be found in Appendix A.

1. What do *TCP, UDP, IP,* and *ICMP* stand for? Which protocol is considered to be Layer 3–equivalent when comparing TCP/IP to the OSI protocols?

2. Name the parts of an IP address.

3. Define the term *subnet mask*. What do the bits in the mask whose values are binary 0 tell you about the corresponding IP address(es)?

4. Given the IP address 134.141.7.11 and the mask 255.255.255.0, what is the subnet number?

5 Given the IP address 193.193.7.7 and the mask 255.255.255.0, what is the subnet number?

6 Given the IP address 10.5.118.3 and the mask 255.255.0.0, what is the subnet number?

7 Given the IP address 190.1.42.3 and the mask 255.255.255.0, what is the subnet number?

8 Given the IP address 200.1.1.130 and the mask 255.255.255.224, what is the subnet number?

9 Given the IP address 220.8.7.100 and the mask 255.255.255.240, what is the subnet number?

10 Given the IP address 140.1.1.1 and the mask 255.255.255.248, what is the subnet number?

11 Given the IP address 167.88.99.66 and the mask 255.255.255.192, what is the subnet number?

12 Given the IP address 134.141.7.11 and the mask 255.255.255.0, what is the subnet broadcast address?

13 Given the IP address 193.193.7.7 and the mask 255.255.255.0, what is the broadcast address?

14 Given the IP address 10.5.118.3 and the mask 255.255.0.0, what is the broadcast address?

15 Given the IP address 190.1.42.3 and the mask 255.255.255.0, what is the broadcast address?

16 Given the IP address 200.1.1.130 and the mask 255.255.255.224, what is the broadcast address?

17 Given the IP address 220.8.7.100 and the mask 255.255.255.240, what is the broadcast address?

____

____

____

18 Given the IP address 140.1.1.1 and the mask 255.255.255.248, what is the broadcast address?

____

____

____

____

____

19 Given the IP address 167.88.99.66 and the mask 255.255.255.192, what is the broadcast address?

____

____

____

20 Given the IP address 134.141.7.11 and the mask 255.255.255.0, what are the assignable IP addresses in this subnet?

____

____

____

21 Given the IP address 193.193.7.7 and the mask 255.255.255.0, what are the assignable IP addresses in this subnet?

____

____

____

22 Given the IP address 10.5.118.3 and the mask 255.255.0.0, what are the assignable IP addresses in this subnet?

23 Given the IP address 190.1.42.3 and the mask 255.255.255.0, what are the assignable IP addresses in this subnet?

24 Given the IP address 200.1.1.130 and the mask 255.255.255.224, what are the assignable IP addresses in this subnet?

25 Given the IP address 220.8.7.100 and the mask 255.255.255.240, what are the assignable IP addresses in this subnet?

26 Given the IP address 140.1.1.1 and the mask 255.255.255.248, what are the assignable IP addresses in this subnet?

27 Given the IP address 167.88.99.66 and the mask 255.255.255.192, what are the assignable IP addresses in this subnet?

28 Given the IP address 134.141.7.7 and the mask 255.255.255.0, what are all the subnet numbers if the same (static) mask is used for all subnets in this network?

29 Given the IP address 10.5.118.3 and the mask 255.255.255.0, what are all the subnet numbers if the same (static) mask is used for all subnets in this network?

30 Given thc IP address 220.8.7.100 and the mask 255.255.255.240, what are all the subnet numbers if the same (static) mask is used for all subnets in this network?

31 Given the IP address 220.8.7.1 and the mask 255.255.255.240, what are all the subnet numbers if the same (static) mask is used for all subnets in this network?

32 How many IP addresses could be assigned in each subnet of 134.141.0.0, assuming that a mask of 255.255.255.0 is used? If the same (static) mask is used for all subnets, how many subnets are there?

33 How many IP addresses could be assigned in each subnet of 10.0.0.0, assuming that a mask of 255.255.255.0 is used? If the same (static) mask is used for all subnets, how many subnets are there?

34 How many IP addresses could be assigned in each subnet of 220.8.7.0, assuming that a mask of 255.255.255.240 is used? If the same (static) mask is used for all subnets, how many subnets are there?

____

____

____

35 How many IP addresses could be assigned in each subnet of 140.1.0.0, assuming that a mask of 255.255.255.248 is used? If the same (static) mask is used for all subnets, how many subnets are there?

____

____

____

36 You design a network for a customer, and the customer insists that you use the same subnet mask on every subnet. The customer will use network 10.0.0.0 and needs 200 subnets, each with 200 hosts maximum. What subnet mask would you use to allow the largest amount of growth in subnets? Which mask would work and would allow for the most growth in the number of hoses per subnet?

____

____

____

37 Create a minimal configuration enabling IP on each interface on a 2501 router (two serial, one Ethernet). The NIC assigned you network 8.0.0.0. Your boss says that you need, at most, 200 hosts per subnet. You decide against using VLSM. Your boss also says to plan your subnets so that you can have as many subnets as possible rather than allow for larger subnets later. When choosing the actual IP address values and subnet numbers, you decide to start with the lowest numerical values. Assume that point-to-point serial links will be attached to this router and that RIP is the routing protocol.

____

____

____

38 In the previous question, what would be the IP subnet of the link attached to serial 0? If another user wanted to answer the same question but did not have the enable password, what command(s) might provide this router's addresses and subnets?

39 Describe the question and possible responses in setup mode when a router wants to know the mask used on an interface. How can the router derive the correct mask from the information supplied by the user?

40 Name the three classes of unicast IP addresses and list their default masks, respectively. How many of each type could be assigned to companies and organizations by the NIC?

41 Describe how TCP performs error recovery. What role do the routers play?

42 Define the purpose of an ICMP redirect message.

43 Define the purpose of the **trace** command. What type of messages does it send, and what type of ICMP messages does it receive?

44 What does *IP* stand for? What does *ICMP* stand for? Which protocol is considered to be a Layer 3 protocol when comparing TCP/IP to the OSI protocols?

45 What causes the output from an IOS **ping** command to display "UUUUU?"

46 Describe how to view the IP ARP cache in a Cisco router. Also describe the three key elements of each entry.

47 How many hosts are allowed per subnet if the subnet mask used is 255.255.255.192? How many hosts are allowed for 255.255.255.252?

48 How many subnets could be created if using static-length masks in a Class B network when the mask is 255.255.255.224? What about when the mask is 255.255.252.0?

49 Name the two commands typically used to create a default gateway for a router.

____

____

____

50 Assume that subnets of network 10.0.0.0 are in the IP routing table in a router but that no other network and subnets are known, except that there is also a default route (0.0.0.0) in the routing table. A packet destined for 192.1.1.1 arrives at the router. What configuration command determines whether the default route will be used in this case?

____

____

____

51 Assume that subnets of network 10.0.0.0 are in the IP routing table in a router but that no other network and their subnets are known, except that there is also a default route (0.0.0.0) in the routing table. A packet destined for 10.1.1.1 arrives at the router, but there is no known subnet of network 10 that matches this destination address. What configuration command determines whether the default route will be used in this case?

____

____

____

52 What does the acronym *CIDR* stand for? What is the original purpose of CIDR?

____

____

____

53 Define the term *private addressing* as defined in RFC 1918.

____

____

____

54 Define the acronym *NAT* and the basics of its operation.

____

____

____

55 Which requires more lines of source code, FTP or TFTP? Justify your answer.

____

____

____

56 Does FTP or TFTP perform error recovery? If so, describe the basics of how they perform error recovery.

____

____

____

57 Describe the process used by IP routers to perform fragmentation and reassembly of packets.

____

____

____

58 How many TCP segments are exchanged to establish a TCP connection? How many are required to terminate a TCP connection?

____

____

____

59 How many Class B–style networks are reserved by RFC 1918 private addressing?

____

____

____

Scenarios

Scenario 6-1: IP Addressing and Subnet Calculation

Assume that you just took a new job. No one trusts you yet, so they will not give you any passwords to the router. Your mentor at your new company has left you at his desk while he goes to a meeting. He has left up a Telnet window, logged in to one router in user mode. In other words, you can issue only user-mode commands.

Assuming that you had issued the following commands (see Example 6-20), draw the most specific network diagram that you can. Write the subnet numbers used on each link onto the diagram.

Example 6-20 *Command Output on Router Fred*

```
fred>show interface
Serial0 is up, line protocol is up
  Hardware is HD64570
  Internet address is 199.1.1.65/27
MTU 1500 bytes, BW 1544 Kbit, DLY 20000 usec,
     reliability 255/255, txload 1/255, rxload 1/255
  Encapsulation HDLC, loopback not set
  Keepalive set (10 sec)
  Last input never, output never, output hang never
  Last clearing of "show interface" counters never
  Input queue: 0/75/0/0 (size/max/drops/flushes); Total output drops: 0
  Queueing strategy: weighted fair
  Output queue: 0/1000/64/0 (size/max total/threshold/drops)
     Conversations  0/0/256 (active/max active/max total)
     Reserved Conversations 0/0 (allocated/max allocated)
     Available Bandwidth 1158 kilobits/sec

  5 minute input rate 0 bits/sec, 0 packets/sec
  5 minute output rate 0 bits/sec, 0 packets/sec
     27 packets input, 2452 bytes, 0 no buffer
     Received 27 broadcasts, 0 runts, 0 giants, 0 throttles
     0 input errors, 0 CRC, 0 frame, 0 overrun, 0 ignored, 0 abort
     29 packets output, 2044 bytes, 0 underruns
     0 output errors, 0 collisions, 28 interface resets
     0 output buffer failures, 0 output buffers swapped out
     7 carrier transitions
     DCD=up  DSR=up  DTR=up  RTS=up  CTS=up
Serial1 is up, line protocol is up
  Hardware is HD64570
  Internet address is 199.1.1.97/27
MTU 1500 bytes, BW 1544 Kbit, DLY 20000 usec,
     reliability 255/255, txload 1/255, rxload 1/255
  Encapsulation HDLC, loopback not set
  Keepalive set (10 sec)
  Last input never, output never, output hang never
  Last clearing of "show interface" counters never
  Input queue: 0/75/0/0 (size/max/drops/flushes); Total output drops: 0
```

continues

Example 6-20 *Command Output on Router Fred (Continued)*

```
  Queueing strategy: weighted fair
  Output queue: 0/1000/64/0 (size/max total/threshold/drops)
     Conversations  0/0/256 (active/max active/max total)
     Reserved Conversations 0/0 (allocated/max allocated)
     Available Bandwidth 1158 kilobits/sec
  5 minute input rate 0 bits/sec, 0 packets/sec
  5 minute output rate 0 bits/sec, 0 packets/sec
     125 packets input, 7634 bytes, 0 no buffer
     Received 124 broadcasts, 0 runts, 0 giants, 0 throttles
     0 input errors, 0 CRC, 0 frame, 0 overrun, 0 ignored, 0 abort
     161 packets output, 9575 bytes, 0 underruns
     0 output errors, 0 collisions, 1 interface resets
     0 output buffer failures, 0 output buffers swapped out
     4 carrier transitions
     DCD=up  DSR=up  DTR=up  RTS=up  CTS=up
Ethernet0 is up, line protocol is up
Hardware is MCI Ethernet, address is 0000.0c55.AB44 (bia 0000.0c55.AB44)
  Internet address is 199.1.1.33/27
  MTU 1500 bytes, BW 10000 Kbit, DLY 1000 usec,
     reliability 255/255, txload 1/255, rxload 1/255
  Encapsulation ARPA, loopback not set
  Keepalive set (10 sec)
  ARP type: ARPA, ARP Timeout 04:00:00
  Last input 00:00:00, output 00:00:00, output hang never
     Output queue 0/40, 0 drops; input queue 0/75, 0 drops
     Five minute input rate 4000 bits/sec, 4 packets/sec
     Five minute output rate 6000 bits/sec, 6 packets/sec
           22197 packets input, 309992 bytes, 0 no buffer
           Received 2343 broadcasts, 0 runts, 0 giants
           0 input errors, 0 CRC, 0 frame, 0 overrun, 0 ignored, 0 abort
           4456 packets output, 145765 bytes, 0 underruns
           3 output errors, 10 collisions, 2 interface resets, 0 restarts


fred>show ip route
Codes: C - connected, S - static, I - IGRP, R - RIP, M - mobile, B - BGP
       D - EIGRP, EX - EIGRP external, O - OSPF, IA - OSPF inter area
       N1 - OSPF NSSA external type 1, N2 - OSPF NSSA external type 2
       E1 - OSPF external type 1, E2 - OSPF external type 2, E - EGP
       i - IS-IS, L1 - IS-IS level-1, L2 - IS-IS level-2, ia - IS-IS inter area
       * - candidate default, U - per-user static route, o - ODR
       P - periodic downloaded static route

Gateway of last resort is not set

     199.1.1.0/27 is subnetted, 6 subnets
R       199.1.1.192 [120/1] via 199.1.1.98, 00:00:01, Serial1
R       199.1.1.128 [120/1] via 199.1.1.98, 00:00:01, Serial1
                    [120/1] via 199.1.1.66, 00:00:20, Serial0
R       199.1.1.160 [120/1] via 199.1.1.66, 00:00:20, Serial0
C       199.1.1.64 is directly connected, Serial0
C       199.1.1.96 is directly connected, Serial1
C       199.1.1.32 is directly connected, Ethernet0

fred>show ip protocol
```

Example 6-20 *Command Output on Router Fred (Continued)*

```
Routing Protocol is "rip"
  Sending updates every 30 seconds, next due in 23 seconds
  Invalid after 180 seconds, hold down 180, flushed after 240
 Outgoing update filter list for all interfaces is not set
  Incoming update filter list for all interfaces is not set
  Redistributing: rip
  Default version control: send version 1, receive any version
    Interface        Send  Recv   Key-chain
    Serial0          1     1 2
    Serial1          1     1 2
    Ethernet0        1     1 2
  Automatic network summarization is in effect
  Maximum path: 4
 Routing for Networks:

    199.1.1.0
  Routing Information Sources:
    Gateway         Distance      Last Update
    199.1.1.66           120      00:00:04
    199.1.1.98           120      00:00:14
  Distance: (default is 120)

fred>show cdp neighbor detail
-------------------------
Device ID: dino
Entry address(es):
  IP address: 199.1.1.66
Platform: Cisco 2500,  Capabilities: Router
Interface: Serial0,  Port ID (outgoing port): Serial0
Holdtime : 148 sec

Version :
Cisco Internetwork Operating System Software
IOS (tm) 2500 Software (C2500-DS-L), Version 12.2(1), RELEASE SOFTWARE (fc2)
Copyright (c) 1986-2001 by cisco Systems, Inc.
Compiled Fri 27-Apr-01 14:43 by cmong

advertisement version: 2
-------------------------
Device ID: Barney
Entry address(es):
  IP address: 199.1.1.98
Platform: Cisco 2500,  Capabilities: Router
Interface: Serial1,  Port ID (outgoing port): Serial0
Holdtime : 155 sec

Version :
Cisco Internetwork Operating System Software
IOS (tm) 2500 Software (C2500-DS-L), Version 12.2(1), RELEASE SOFTWARE (fc2)
Copyright (c) 1986-2001 by cisco Systems, Inc.
Compiled Fri 27-Apr-01 14:43 by cmong

advertisement version: 2
```

Scenario 6-2: IP Subnet Design with a Class B Network

Your job is to plan a new network. The topology required includes three sites, one Ethernet at each site, and point-to-point serial links for connectivity, as shown in Figure 6-44. The network might grow to need at most 100 subnets, with 200 hosts per subnet maximum. Use network 172.16.0.0, and use the same subnet mask for all subnets. Use Table 6-61 to record your choices, or use a separate piece of paper.

Figure 6-44 *Scenario 6-2 Network Diagram*

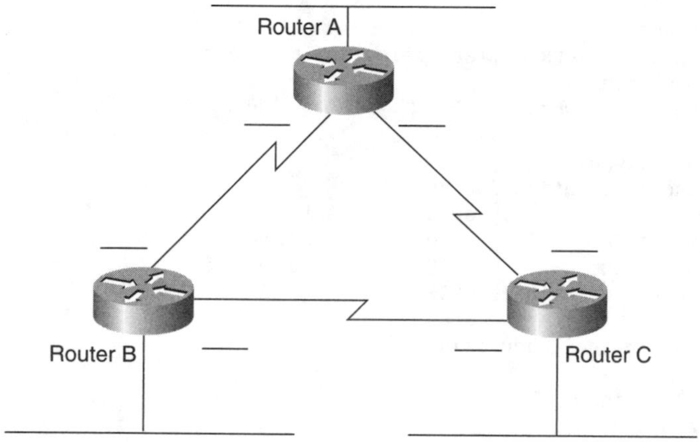

Table 6-61 *Scenario 6-2 Planning Chart*

Location of Subnet Geographically	Subnet Mask	Subnet Number	Router's IP Address
Ethernet off Router A			
Ethernet off Router B			
Ethernet off Router C			
Serial between A and B			
Serial between A and C			
Serial between B and C			

Given the information in Figure 6-44 and Table 6-61, perform the following activities:

1. Determine all subnet masks that meet the criteria in the introduction to this scenario.
2. Choose a mask and pick enough subnets to use for the original topology (refer to Figure 6-44).
3. Create IP-related configuration commands for each router.

Scenario 6-3: IP Subnet Design with a Class C Network

Your job is to plan yet another network. The topology required includes four sites, one Ethernet at each site, and partially meshed Frame Relay for connectivity, as shown in Figure 6-45. The number of subnets will never grow. Choose a mask that will maximize the number of hosts per subnet. Use network 200.1.1.0. Use Table 6-62 to record your choices, or use a separate piece of paper.

Figure 6-45 *Scenario 6-3 Network Diagram*

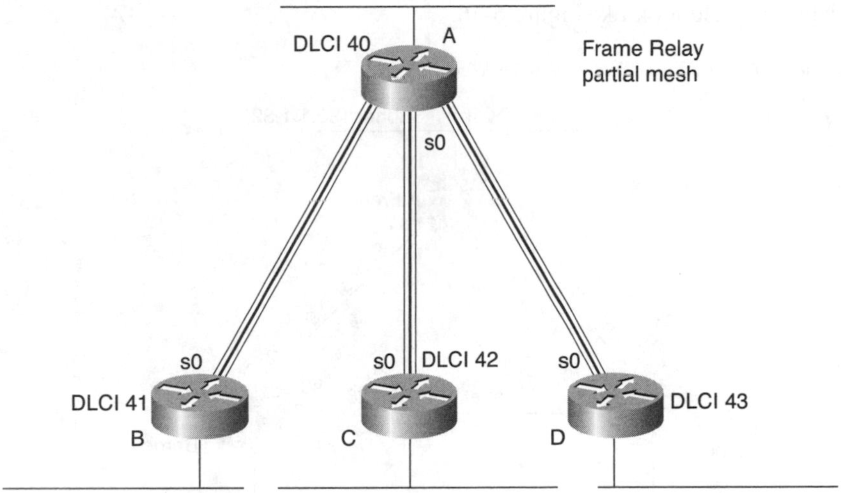

Table 6-62 *Scenario 6-3 Planning Chart*

Location of Subnet	Subnet Mask	Subnet Number	Router's IP Address
Ethernet off Router A			
Ethernet off Router B			
Ethernet off Router C			
Ethernet off Router D			
VC between A and B			
VC between A and C			
VC between A and D			

Given the network setup in Figure 6-45, perform the following tasks:

1 Choose the best subnet mask that meets the criteria.

2 Use Table 6-62 to plan which subnet numbers will be used.

3 Create IP-related configuration commands for each router. Use the DLCIs from Figure 6-45.

Scenario Answers

Answers to Scenario 6-1: IP Addressing and Subnet Calculation

Assuming that you had issued the commands in Example 6-20, the most specific network diagram would look like Figure 6-46.

Figure 6-46 *Scenario 6-1 Answer—Network with Router Fred*

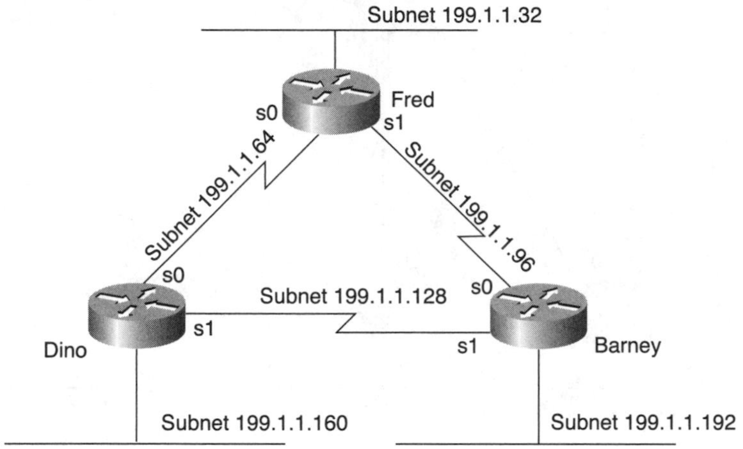

The clues that you should have found in the **show** commands are as follows:

- The types and IP addresses of the interfaces on Fred were in the **show interface** and **show ip interface brief** command output.
- The subnets could be learned from the **show ip route** command or derived from the IP addresses and masks shown in the **show interface** command output.
- The neighboring routers' IP addresses could be learned from the **show ip protocol** command.
- The neighboring routers' IP addresses and host names could be learned from the **show cdp neighbor detail** command.
- The metric for subnet 199.1.1.128/27 in RIP updates implies that both neighbors have an equal-cost route to the same subnet. Because two separate but duplicate networks would be a bad design, you can assume that the neighboring routers are attached to the same medium.

- If you are completely bored, the **telnet 199.1.1.x** command could have been issued for all IP addresses in subnets not directly connected to Fred, hoping to get a router login prompt. That would identify the IP addresses of other router interfaces.

There is no way to know what physical media are beyond the neighboring routers. However, because CDP claims that both routers are 2500 series routers, the possible interfaces on these neighboring routers are limited. Figure 6-46 shows the other subnets as Ethernet segments. Similarly, the figure shows the two neighboring routers attached to the same medium, which is shown as a serial link in Figure 6-46.

Answers to Scenario 6-2: IP Subnet Design with a Class B Network

Figure 6-47 shows one correct answer for the network skeleton presented in Figure 6-44.

Figure 6-47 *Scenario 6-2 Diagram Scratch Pad*

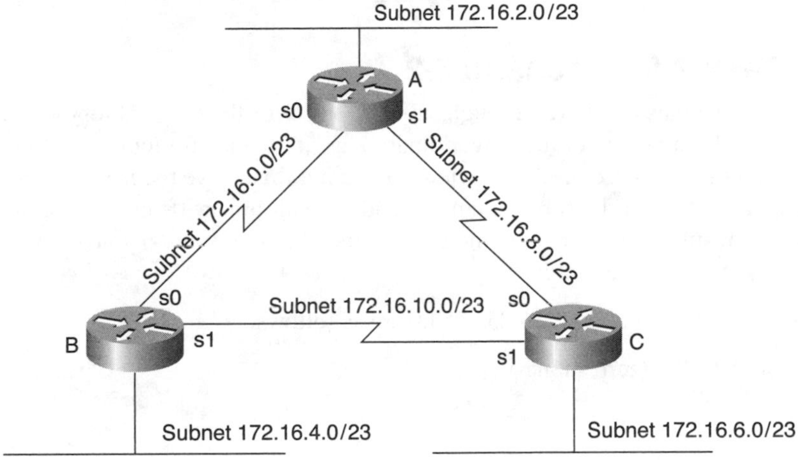

Answers to Task 1 for Scenario 6-2

Given the details in Figure 6-44 and Table 6-61 for Scenario 6-2, the subnet mask criteria are as follows:

- 200 hosts in a subnet, maximum
- 100 subnets, maximum
- Static size masks used all over this network

The mask must have at least eight host bits because $2^7 \times 128$ is not enough and $2^8 \times 256$ is more than enough for numbering 200 hosts in a subnet. The mask must have at least seven subnet bits, likewise, because 2^7 is the smallest power of 2 that is larger than 100, which is the required number of subnets. The first 16 bits in the mask must be binary 1 because a Class B network (172.16.0.0) is used. Figure 6-48 diagrams the possibilities.

Figure 6-48 *Subnet Mask Options for Scenario 6-2*

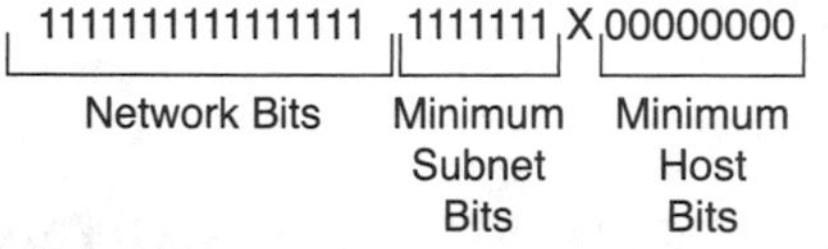

The only bit position in which a decision can be made is the 24th bit, shown with an X in Figure 6-48. That leaves two mask possibilities: 255.255.254.0 and 255.255.255.0. This sample shows the 255.255.254.0 mask just so you can have a little more practice with harder masks. Given the choice in a real network, choose the easy mask!

Answers to Task 2 for Scenario 6-2

To choose a mask and pick enough subnets to use for the original topology illustrated in Figure 6-44, a review of the longer binary algorithm and shortcut algorithm for deriving subnet numbers is required. To review, subnet numbers have the network number value in the network portion of the subnet numbers and have all binary 0s in the host bits. The bits that vary from subnet to subnet are the subnet bits—in other words, you are numbering different subnets in the subnet field.

Valid subnets with mask 255.255.254.0 are as follows:

172.16.0.0 (zero subnet)
172.16.2.0
172.16.4.0
172.16.6.0
.
.
.
172.16.252.0
172.16.254.0 (broadcast subnet)

The first six subnets, including the zero subnet, were chosen for this example, as listed in Table 6-63.

Table 6-63 *Scenario 6-2 Subnets and Addresses*

Location of Subnet Geographically	Subnet Mask	Subnet Number	Router's IP Address
Ethernet off Router A	255.255.254.0	172.16.2.0	172.16.2.1
Ethernet off Router B	255.255.254.0	172.16.4.0	172.16.4.2
Ethernet off Router C	255.255.254.0	172.16.6.0	172.16.6.3
Serial between A and B	255.255.254.0	172.16.0.0	172.16.0.1 (A) and .2 (B)
Serial between A and C	255.255.254.0	172.16.8.0	172.16.8.1 (A) and .3 (C)
Serial between B and C	255.255.254.0	172.16.10.0	172.16.10.2 (B) and .3 (C)

Answers to Task 3 for Scenario 6-2

Given the details in Figure 6-44 and Table 6-61 for Scenario 6-2, the configurations in Examples 6-21 through 6-23 satisfy the exercise of creating IP-related configuration commands for each router. These examples include only the IP-related commands.

Example 6-21 *Router A Configuration, Scenario 6-2*

```
ip subnet-zero
no ip domain-lookup
!
interface serial0
ip address 172.16.0.1 255.255.254.0
interface serial 1
ip address 172.16.8.1 255.255.254.0
interface ethernet 0
ip address 172.16.2.1 255.255.254.0
!
router igrp 6
network 172.16.0.0
```

Example 6-22 *Router B Configuration, Scenario 6-2*

```
ip subnet-zero
no ip domain-lookup
!
interface serial0
ip address 172.16.0.2 255.255.254.0
interface serial 1
ip address 172.16.10.2 255.255.254.0
interface ethernet 0
ip address 172.16.4.2 255.255.254.0
!
router igrp 6
network 172.16.0.0
```

Example 6-23 *Router C Configuration, Scenario 6-2*

```
ip subnet-zero
no ip domain-lookup
!
interface serial0
ip address 172.16.8.3 255.255.254.0
interface serial 1
ip address 172.16.10.3  255.255.254.0
interface ethernet 0
ip address 172.16.6.3 255.255.254.0
!
router igrp 6
network 172.16.0.0
```

Answers to Scenario 6-3: IP Subnet Design with a Class C Network

Planning the network in this scenario requires a topology that includes four sites, one Ethernet at each site, and partially meshed Frame Relay for connectivity, as shown previously in Figure 6-45. The number of subnets will never grow. You must choose a mask that will maximize the number of hosts per subnet, and you must use network 200.1.1.0.

Answers to Task 1 for Scenario 6-3

Given the design criteria and the network setup illustrated in Figure 6-45, this scenario requires tricky subnet masks because a Class C network is used and because subnetting is needed. Using Frame Relay subinterfaces, there will be a need for seven different subnets—one for each Ethernet and one for each Frame Relay VC.

If three subnet bits are used, eight mathematical possibilities exist for subnet numbers. However, one is the zero subnet and the other is the broadcast subnet. In this case, use of one of these is desired because the design called for maximizing the number of hosts per subnet. Deciding against use of the zero and broadcast subnets then would require four subnet bits, leaving only four host bits, implying 14 hosts per subnet. So, three subnet bits and five host bits will be used in this solution (mask of 255.255.255.224). Figure 6-49 summarizes the subnets on the network diagram.

Figure 6-49 *Scenario 6-3 Network, with Subnets Written on Diagram*

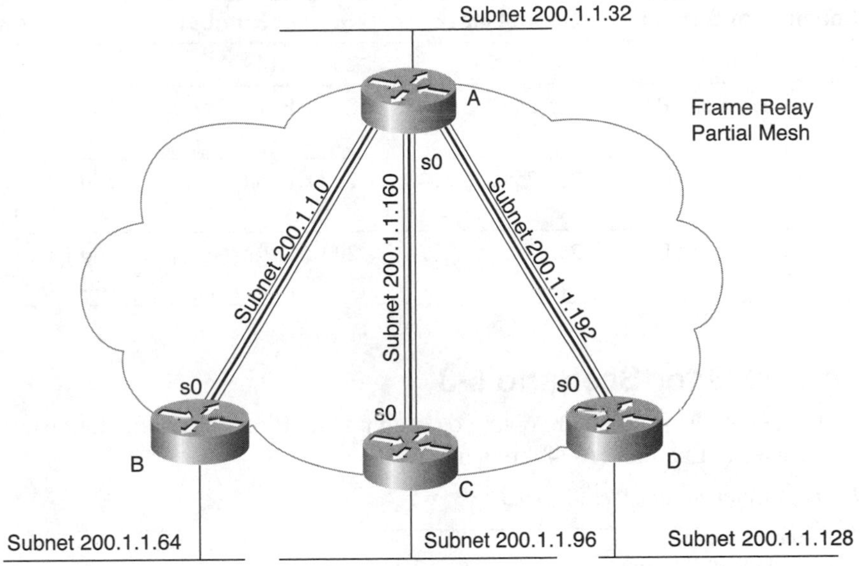

Answers to Task 2 for Scenario 6-3

Given the design criteria and the network setup illustrated in Figure 6-45 for Scenario 6-3, Table 6-64 shows the choices of subnets and addresses in this example. Only one subnet, 200.1.1.224, which is the broadcast subnet, is not used. Of course, you could have chosen a different set of subnets and used them on different links, but the mask you used should have been 255.255.255.224, based on the criteria to maximize the number of hosts per subnet.

Table 6-64 *Scenario 6-3 Subnets and Addresses*

Location of Subnet	Subnet Mask	Subnet Number	Router's IP Address
Ethernet off Router A	255.255.255.224	200.1.1.32	200.1.1.33
Ethernet off Router B	255.255.255.224	200.1.1.64	200.1.1.65
Ethernet off Router C	255.255.255.224	200.1.1.96	200.1.1.97

continues

Table 6-64 *Scenario 6-3 Subnets and Addresses (Continued)*

Location of Subnet	Subnet Mask	Subnet Number	Router's IP Address
Ethernet off Router D	255.255.255.224	200.1.1.128	200.1.1.129
VC between A and B	255.255.255.224	200.1.1.0	200.1.1.1 (A) and .2 (B)
VC between A and C	255.255.255.224	200.1.1.160	200.1.1.161 (A) and .162 (B)
VC between A and D	255.255.255.224	200.1.1.192	200.1.1.193 (A) and .194 (B)

Answers to Task 3 for Scenario 6-3

Using the DLCIs from Figure 6-45, you can find the IP-related configuration commands for each router in Examples 6-24 through 6-27.

Example 6-24 *Router A Configuration, Scenario 6-3*

```
ip subnet-zero
no ip domain-lookup
!
interface serial0
encapsulation frame-relay
interface serial 0.1
ip address 200.1.1.1 255.255.255.224
frame-relay interface-dlci 41
!
interface serial 0.2
ip address 200.1.1.161 255.255.255.224
frame-relay interface-dlci 42
!
interface serial 0.3
ip address 200.1.1.193 255.255.255.224
frame-relay interface-dlci 43
!
interface ethernet 0
ip address 200.1.1.33 255.255.255.224
!
router igrp 6
network 200.1.1.0
```

Example 6-25 *Router B Configuration, Scenario 6-3*

```
ip subnet-zero
no ip domain-lookup
!
interface serial0
```

Example 6-25 *Router B Configuration, Scenario 6-3 (Continued)*

```
encapsulation frame-relay
interface serial 0.1
ip address 200.1.1.2 255.255.255.224
frame-relay interface-dlci 40
!
interface ethernet 0
ip address 200.1.1.65 255.255.255.224
!
router igrp 6
network 200.1.1.0
```

Example 6-26 *Router C Configuration, Scenario 6-3*

```
ip subnet-zero
no ip domain-lookup
!
interface serial0
encapsulation frame-relay
interface serial 0.1
ip address 200.1.1.162 255.255.255.224
frame-relay interface-dlci 40
!
interface ethernet 0
ip address 200.1.1.97 255.255.255.224
!
router igrp 6
network 200.1.1.0
```

Example 6-27 *Router D Configuration, Scenario 6-3*

```
ip subnet-zero
no ip domain-lookup
!
interface serial0
encapsulation frame-relay
interface serial 0.1
ip address 200.1.1.194 255.255.255.224
frame-relay interface-dlci 40
!
interface ethernet 0
ip address 200.1.1.129 255.255.255.224
!
router igrp 6
network 200.1.1.0
```

Exam Topics in This Chapter

27 Add the RIP routing protocol to your configuration.

52 Add the IGRP routing protocol to your configuration.

52 List problems that each routing type encounters when dealing with topology changes, and describe techniques to reduce the number of these problems.

CHAPTER 7

Routing and Routing Protocols

The United States Postal Service routes a huge number of letters and packages each day. Most of us have seen pictures of huge sorting machines—even more so after the recent, horrible Anthrax attacks through the mail in the U.S. The sorting machine can run fast, sorting lots of letters—and then the letters are placed in the correct container, and onto the correct truck or plane, to reach the final destination. However, if no one programs the letter sorter to know where letters to each zip code should be sent, the sorter can't do its job. Similarly, Cisco routers can route many packets, but if the router doesn't know any routes, it can't do its job.

This chapter deals with the concepts and configuration required to fill a router's routing table. Cisco expects CCNAs to demonstrate a comfortable understanding of the logic behind the routing of packets, and the different but related logic behind routing protocols—the protocols used to discover routes. To fully appreciate the nuances of routing protocols, you need a thorough understanding of routing—the process of forwarding packets. You might want to review the section on Layer 3 in Chapter 3, "OSI Reference Model and Layered Communication," before proceeding with this chapter.

The CCNA exam covers the details of distance vector logic, which is covered in the first section of this chapter. This is the logic used by the Routing Information Protocol (RIP) and Interior Gateway Routing Protocol (IGRP), as well as IPX RIP. Along the way, alternative routing protocol algorithms (link-state and Diffusing Update Algorithm [DUAL]) are mentioned briefly.

Implementation details of RIP (Version 1 and Version 2) and IGRP are covered after that. Because EIGRP configuration is similar to IGRP, it is also covered briefly. As you'll find on the CCNA exam, knowledge and skills for routing protocol configuration and troubleshooting are topics required of CCNAs.

How to Best Use This Chapter

By following these steps, you can make better use of your study time:

- Keep your notes and the answers for all your work with this book in one place, for easy reference.

- Take the "Do I Know This Already?" quiz, and write down your answers. Studies show that retention is significantly increased through writing down facts and concepts, even if you never look at the information again.
- Use Figure 7-1 to guide you to the next step.

Figure 7-1 *How to Use This Chapter*

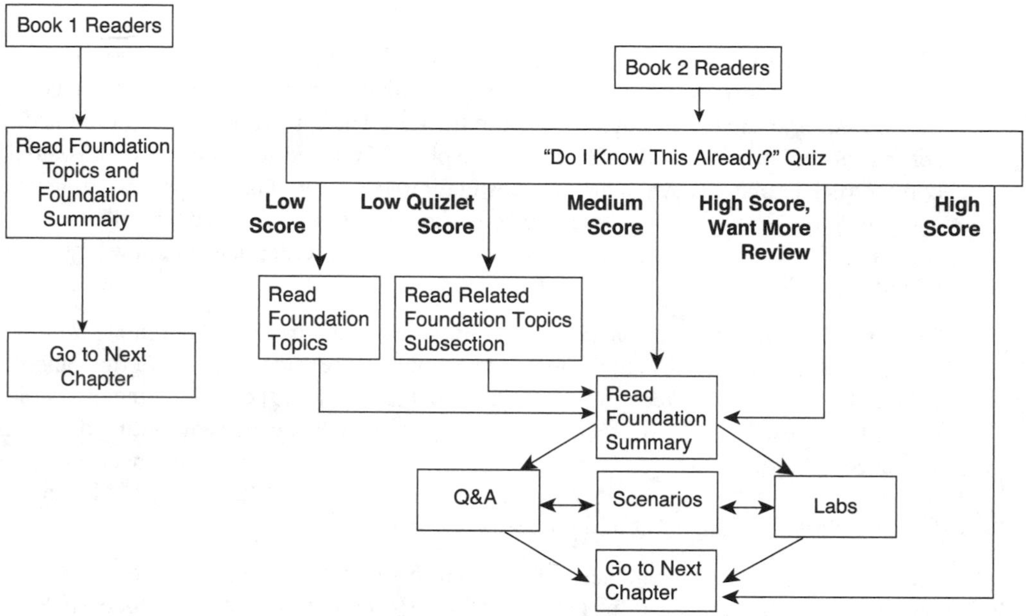

"Do I Know This Already?" Quiz

The "Do I Know This Already?" quiz helps you decide what parts of this chapter to use. If you already intend to read the entire chapter, you do not necessarily need to answer these questions now.

This 12-question quiz helps you determine how to spend your limited study time. The quiz is sectioned into two smaller six-question "quizlets" that help you select the sections of the chapter on which to focus. Figure 7-1 outlines suggestions on how to spend your time in this chapter based on your quiz score. Use Table 7-1 to record your scores.

Table 7-1 *Scoresheet for Quiz and Quizlets*

Quizlet Number	Foundation Topics Section Covering These Questions	Questions	Score
1	Distance Vector Routing Protocols	1 to 6	
2	Configuring RIP and IGRP	7 to 12	
All questions		1 to 12	

1 Define what split horizon means to the contents of a routing update. Does this apply to both the distance vector algorithm and the link-state algorithm?

____

____

____

2 Describe the purpose and meaning of route poisoning.

____

____

____

3 What term describes the underlying logic behind the OSPF routing protocol?

____

____

____

4 Describe the meaning and purpose of triggered updates.

____

____

____

5 List the interior IP routing protocols that have autosummarization enabled by default. Which of these protocols allow autosummarization to be disabled using a configuration command?

____

____

____

6 True or false: Distance vector routing protocols learn routes by transmitting routing updates.

____

____

____

7 Write down the steps you would take to migrate from RIP to IGRP in a router whose current RIP configuration includes only **router rip** followed by a **network 10.0.0.0** command.

____

____

____

8 How does the Cisco IOS Software designate a subnet in the routing table as a directly connected network? What about a route learned with IGRP or RIP?

____

____

____

9 From a router's user mode, without using debugs or privileged mode, how can you determine what routers are sending you routing updates?

____

____

____

10 If the command **router rip** followed by **network 10.0.0.0**, with no other **network** commands, is configured in a router that has an Ethernet0 interface with IP address 168.10.1.1, does RIP send updates out Ethernet0?

____

____

____

11 If the commands **router igrp 1** and **network 10.0.0.0** are configured in a router that has an Ethernet0 interface with IP address 168.10.1.1, does IGRP advertise 168.10.0.0?

____

____

____

12 Create a configuration for IGRP on a router with these interfaces and addresses: e0 using 10.1.1.1, e1 using 224.1.2.3, s0 using 10.1.2.1, and s1 using 199.1.1.1. Use process ID 5.

____

____

____

The answers to the "Do I Know This Already?" quiz are found in Appendix A, "Answers to the 'Do I Know This Already?' Quizzes and Q&A Sections." The suggested choices for your next step are as follows:

- **6 or less overall score**—Read the entire chapter. This includes the "Foundation Topics" and "Foundation Summary" sections, the "Q&A" section, and the scenarios at the end of the chapter.
- **3 or less on any quizlet**—Review the subsections of the "Foundation Topics" section, based on Table 7-1. Then move to the "Foundation Summary" section, the "Q&A" section, and the scenarios at the end of the chapter.
- **9 to 10 overall score**—Begin with the "Foundation Summary" section, and then go to the "Q&A" section and the scenarios at the end of the chapter.
- **11 or 12 overall score**—If you want more review of these topics, skip to the "Foundation Summary" section and then go to the "Q&A" section and the scenarios at the end of the chapter. Otherwise, move to the next chapter.

Foundation Topics

Distance Vector Routing Protocols

52 List problems that each routing type encounters when dealing with topology changes, and describe techniques to reduce the number of these problems.

To succeed on the CCNA exam, you need to be able to describe the logic behind distance vector routing protocols, as well as describe the operation of two IP distance vector routing protocols, RIP and IGRP. You also need to be able to configure and examine the operation of RIP and IGRP. If you understood most of the preceding chapter, you can learn enough to configure and use RIP and IGRP in about two pages of this book. However, you will not learn enough about how routing protocols do their job—and that underlying theory is covered on the exam. The first section of this chapter covers the basics of distance vector routing protocols, including terminology and operation. Then details are given. If you are looking to save a little time, consider skipping the more detailed section on how distance vector logic works.

Terminology can get in the way when you're learning about routing protocols. This book's terminology relating to routing and routing protocols is consistent with the courses in the Cisco CCNA training path, as well as with most Cisco documentation. The first term that needs to be defined is *routing protocol*. This term can be contrasted with *routed protocol*. Chapter 3 provides a silly, but I hope memorable, story (the "Ted and Ting" story) that can help distinguish between these two terms. Three definitions follow:

- A *routing protocol* fills the routing table with routing information. Examples include RIP and IGRP.
- A *routed protocol* is a protocol that has an OSI Layer 3 equivalent specification that defines logical addressing and routing. The packets defined by the network layer (Layer 3) portion of these protocols can be routed. Examples of protocols include IP and IPX.
- The term *routing type* might appear on questions remaining from the older CCNA exam, #640-407. This term refers to the type of routing protocol, such as link-state.

IP routing protocols fill the IP routing table with valid, (hopefully) loop-free routes. As you will see later, distance vector routing protocols have many features that prevent loops. Each route includes a subnet number, the interface out which to forward packets so that they are delivered to that subnet, and the IP address of the next router that should receive packets destined for that subnet (if needed). An analogy to routing is the process a stubborn man might use when taking a trip to somewhere he has never been. He might look for a road sign referring to the destination town and pointing him to the next turn. By repeating the process at each intersection, he should eventually make it to the correct town. Of course, if a routing loop occurs (in other words, he's lost!) and he stubbornly never asks for directions, he could loop forever—or at least until he runs out of gas.

Before I discuss the underlying logic, you need to consider the goals of a routing protocol. The goals described in the following list are common for any IP routing protocol, regardless of its underlying logic type:

- To dynamically learn and fill the routing table with a route to all subnets in the network.
- If more than one route to a subnet is available, to place the best route in the routing table.
- To notice when routes in the table are no longer valid, and to remove those routes from the routing table.
- If a route is removed from the routing table and another route through another neighboring router is available, to add the route to the routing table. (Many people view this goal and the preceding one as a single goal.)
- To add new routes, or to replace lost routes with the best currently available route, as quickly as possible. The time between losing the route and finding a working replacement route is called *convergence* time.
- To prevent routing loops.

Overview of Routing Protocols

Several routing protocols for TCP/IP exist. IP's long history and continued popularity have called for the specification and creation of several different competing options. So, classifying IP routing protocols based on their differences is useful—and also is a fair topic for exam questions.

For the CCNA exam, you must know the terminology and routing protocols discussed here. You must also have a deeper understanding of distance vector protocols, which are described in upcoming sections.

Routing protocols fill each router's routing table with valid, useful routes. With good routes in the routing table, a router can forward packets—which is what a router is supposed to do. One story that helps describe the process is to equate routing and routing protocols to your taking a trip, and the government workers who create road signs. You can take a trip without a map, relying on road signs to tell you which road to take at each intersection, until you get to your destination. However, if you eliminate the overhead function of the government employees who create road signs that tell you where to turn, you will not know where to go, and you will never get there. Likewise, routing protocols are overhead functions, but really useful ones.

Routing protocols can be categorized in several ways, and each requires a definition. One distinction is whether the protocol is more useful between two companies or inside a single company. Another distinction depends on how the routing protocol's internal logic behaves.

Table 7-2 lists some of the terms you need to know for the CCNA exam. After that, you will read about the basics, followed by a summary table that pretty much completes the level of understanding you need for the exam for most routing protocols. More details will follow about RIP and IGRP.

Table 7-2 *Routing Protocol Terminology*

Term	Definition
Routing protocol	A protocol whose purpose is to learn the available routes, place the best routes into the routing table, and remove routes when they are no longer valid.
Exterior routing protocol	A routing protocol designed for use between two different networks that are under the control of two different organizations. These are typically used between ISPs or between a company and an ISP. For example, a company would run BGP, an exterior routing protocol, between one of its routers and a router inside an ISP.
Interior routing protocol	A routing protocol designed for use in a network whose parts are under the control of a single organization. For example, an entire company might choose the IGRP routing protocol, which is an interior routing protocol.
Distance vector	The logic behind the behavior of some interior routing protocols, such as RIP and IGRP.
Link state	The logic behind the behavior of some interior routing protocols, such as OSPF.
Balanced hybrid	The logic behind the behavior of EIGRP, which is more like distance vector than link state but is different from these other two types of routing protocols.
Dijkstra Shortest Path First (SPF) algorithm	Magic math used by link-state protocols, such as OSPF, when the routing table is calculated.
Diffusing Update Algorithm (DUAL)	The process by which EIGRP routers collectively calculate routing tables.
Convergence	The time required for routers to react to changes in the network, removing bad routes and adding new, better routes so that the currently best routes are in all the routers' routing tables.

The CCNA exam focuses on interior routing protocols. If you are interested in pursuing CCIE or CCNP certification, understanding exterior routing protocols is important. An excellent learning tool and reference for IP routing and routing protocols is the Cisco Press book *Routing TCP/IP*, Volume I by Jeff Doyle.

OSPF and Link-State Protocols

One type of interior routing protocol is the *link-state protocol*. Link-state protocols use a topological database that is created on each router. Entries describing every router, every router's attached links, and every router's neighboring routers are included in the database so that each router can build a complete map of the network. The topology database is processed by an algorithm called the Dijkstra Shortest Path First (SPF) algorithm for choosing the best routes to add to the routing table. This detailed topology information, along with the Dijkstra algorithm, helps link-state protocols avoid loops and converge quickly.

Open Shortest Path First (OSPF) is a link-state routing protocol used for IP. Link-state protocols avoid routing loops by transmitting and keeping more detailed topology information, which allows the protocol to use calculations that prevent loops. With OSPF, the subnet mask information is also transmitted, allowing features such as VLSM and route summarization.

EIGRP and Balanced Hybrid Protocols

A second type of routing protocol is the *balanced hybrid protocol*. Balanced hybrid is a term created by Cisco to describe the inner workings of EIGRP, which uses the Diffusing Update Algorithm (DUAL) to calculate routes. A balanced hybrid protocol exchanges more topology information than a distance vector routing protocol, but it does not require full topology or the computation-intensive Dijkstra algorithm to compute loop-free routes.

Enhanced IGRP (EIGRP) is a balanced hybrid routing protocol. DUAL is the underlying algorithm. DUAL defines a method for each router to not only calculate the best current route to each subnet, but also to calculate alternative routes that could be used if the current route fails. An alternative route, using what DUAL defines as a neighboring *feasible successor route,* is guaranteed to be loop-free, so convergence can happen quickly. EIGRP also transmits the subnet mask for each routing entry. Therefore, features such as VLSM and route summarization are easily supported.

RIP, IGRP, and Distance Vector Protocols

RIP Version 1 (RIP-1) and IGRP are two distance vector routing protocols that are covered in depth on the CCNA exam. RIP and IGRP are similar in most details, with the big exception being that IGRP uses a much more robust metric. Both RIP-1 and IGRP are covered in more detail later in this chapter.

Some routing protocols are less likely to be covered on the CCNA exam, including RIP Version 2 (RIP-2). RIP-2 includes many improvements over RIP-1. Most notably, the subnet mask associated with each advertised route is included in the routing update. The mask allows routers to use features such as variable-length subnet masks (VLSMs) and route summarization—features sure to be covered on the CCNP exam.

Table 7-3 lists interior IP routing protocols and their types. A column specifying whether the routing protocol includes subnet mask information in the routing updates is listed for future reference.

Table 7-3 *Interior IP Routing Protocols and Types*

Routing Protocol	Type	Loop-Prevention Mechanisms	Mask Sent in Updates, Which Allows VLSM?
RIP-1	Distance vector	Hold-down timer, split horizon	No
RIP-2	Distance vector	Hold-down timer, split horizon	Yes
IGRP	Distance vector	Hold-down timer, split horizon	No
EIGRP	Balanced hybrid	DUAL and feasible successors	Yes
OSPF	Link-state	Dijkstra SPF algorithm and full topology knowledge	Yes

Distance Vector Routing Protocol Behavior

CCNAs deal with routing problems on a daily basis. Some of these problems are the result of the logic behind distance vector routing protocols. Understanding what distance vector routing means is to understand how a routing protocol accomplishes the following goals:

- Learning routing information
- Noticing failed routes
- Adding the current best route after one has failed
- Preventing loops

The following list summarizes the behavior of a router that uses the RIP-1 or IGRP distance vector routing protocols:

- Routers add *directly connected* subnets to their routing tables. Routers do not need to run a routing protocol to learn connected routes, but connected subnet routes are advertised to neighboring routers by the routing protocol.
- Routers broadcast or multicast *routing updates* to their neighboring routers. This is so that all neighboring routers can learn routes via the single broadcast or multicast update.
- Routers listen for *routing updates* from their neighbors so that they can learn new routes.
- Routers measure how good one route is versus another using a *metric*. The metric describes how good the route is in case a router hears of more than one route to a particular subnet. If multiple routes to the same subnet are learned, the lower-metric route is used.
- Routers include basic *topology* information in routing updates, including, at a minimum, the subnet and metric information.

- Routers send *periodic updates* and expect to receive periodic updates from neighboring routers. Failure to receive updates from a neighbor in a timely manner results in the removal of the routes previously learned from that neighbor.
- A router assumes that, for a route advertised by Router X, the *next-hop router* in that route is Router X.

Figure 7-2 demonstrates how Router A's directly connected subnets are advertised to Router B. In this case, Router A advertises two directly connected routes.

Figure 7-2 *Router A Advertising Directly Connected Routes*

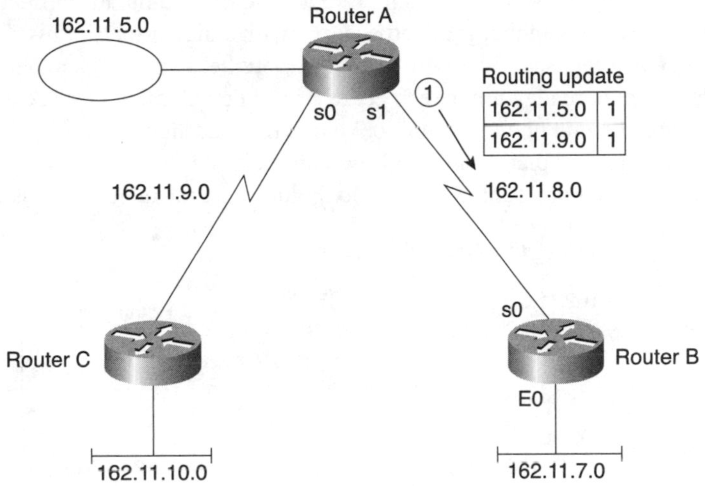

Table 7-4 shows the resulting routing table on Router B.

Table 7-4 *Routing B Routing Table After Receiving the Update Shown in Figure 7-2*

Group (Mask Is 255.255.255.0)	Outgoing Interface	Next-Hop Router	Comments
162.11.5.0	S0	162.11.8.1	This is one of two routes learned via the update in the figure.
162.11.7.0	E0	N/A	This is a directly connected route.
162.11.8.0	S0	N/A	This is a directly connected route.
162.11.9.0	S0	162.11.8.1	This is one of two routes learned via the update in the figure.

Two interesting facts about what a Cisco IOS Software-based Cisco router puts in the routing table become obvious in this example. First, just like for any other directly connected route, the two directly connected routes on Router B do not have an entry in the Next-Hop Router field, because packets to those subnets can be sent directly to hosts in those subnets. In other words, there is no need for Router B to forward packets to another router, because Router B is attached. The second interesting fact is that the Next-Hop Router entries for the routes learned from Router A show Router A's IP address as the next router. In other words, a route learned from a neighboring router goes through that router. Router B typically learns Router A's IP address for these routes simply by looking at the routing update's source IP address.

The next example gives some insight into the metric's cumulative effect. A subnet learned via an update from a neighbor is advertised, but with a higher metric. Just like a road sign in Decatur, Ga. might say "Turn here to get to Snellville, 14 miles," another road sign farther away in Atlanta might read "Turn here to get to Snellville, 22 miles." By taking the turn in Atlanta, 8 miles later, you end up in Decatur, looking at the road sign that tells you the next turn to get to Snellville, which is then 14 miles away. This example shows you exactly what happens with RIP, which uses hop count as the metric. Figure 7-3 and Table 7-5 illustrate this concept.

Figure 7-3 *Router A Advertising Routes Learned from Router C*

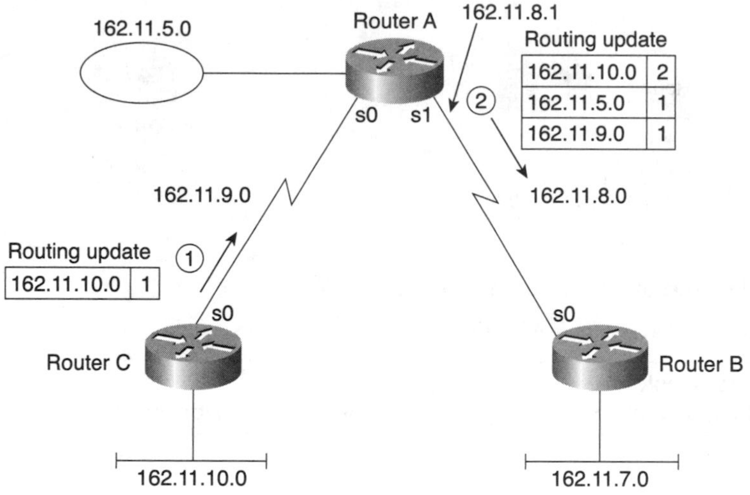

Table 7-5 *Router B Routing Table After Receiving the Update Shown in Figure 7-3*

Group	Outgoing Interface	Next-Hop Router	Metric	Comments
162.11.5.0	S0	162.11.8.1	1	This is the same route that was learned earlier.
162.11.7.0	E0	N/A	0	This is a directly connected route.

Table 7-5 *Router B Routing Table After Receiving the Update Shown in Figure 7-3 (Continued)*

Group	Outgoing Interface	Next-Hop Router	Metric	Comments
162.11.8.0	S0	N/A	0	This is a directly connected route.
162.11.9.0	S0	162.11.8.1	1	This one was also learned earlier.
162.11.10.0	S0	162.11.8.1	2	This one was learned from Router A, which learned it from Router C.

Router B believes some subnets are nearer than others, based on the metric. Router B's metric for connected routes is 0 because there is no router between B and those subnets. B's metric for routes directly connected to the router is 1 because Router A is between B and those subnets. Finally, the metric for subnet 162.11.10.0 is 2, because, from B's perspective, two routers separate it from that subnet—namely, Router A and Router C.

The origin of the term *distance vector* becomes more apparent with this example. The route to 162.11.10.0 that Router B adds to its routing table refers to Router A as the next router because Router B learned the route from Router A; Router B knows nothing about the network topology on the "other side" of Router A. So, B has a vector (send packets to Router A) and a distance (2) for the route to subnet 10, but no other details!

The next core concept of distance vector routing protocols relates to when to doubt the validity of routing information. Each router sends periodic routing updates. A routing update timer, which is equal on all routers, determines how often the updates are sent. The absence of routing updates for a preset number of routing timer intervals results in the removal of the routes previously learned from the router that has become silent.

You have read about the basic, core concepts for distance vector protocols. The next section provides a little deeper look into issues when redundancy exists in the network.

Distance Vector: Advanced Concepts

Two general categories of topics are explained in the rest of this section. First, when multiple physical paths exist in a network, multiple routes to the same network can exist. If that occurs, the metrics could tie, so which one do you use? Well, it depends, so we will take a closer look.

The second category of topics relates to loop avoidance. Just like Spanning-Tree Protocol avoids loops in a switched or bridged LAN, IP routing protocols avoid loops in the routed IP network. Distance vector protocols have several features that are needed in order to prevent loops—and these features are covered here.

Issues When Multiple Routes to the Same Subnet Exist

A router might learn one route and then learn a better route. Of course, the better route should replace the higher-metric route when this happens. Figure 7-4 outlines just such a case. Table 7-6 shows Router B's routing table when only one route to 162.11.10.0 is known, before the serial link between B and C comes up. Table 7-7 shows Router B's routing table after the link between B and C comes up, learning about another route to that same subnet.

Figure 7-4 *Routers A and C Advertising to Router B*

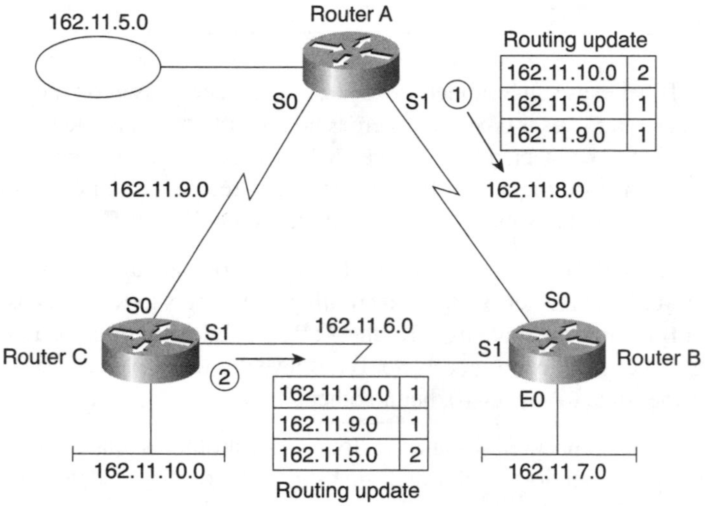

NOTE The routing updates in Figure 7-4 show only the information needed for the point being made in this example. Other routes that would normally be in the routing update have been omitted.

Table 7-6 *Router B Routing Table While Router B Serial 1 Is Down*

Group	Outgoing Interface	Next-Hop Router	Metric	Comments
162.11.5.0	S0	162.11.8.1	1	N/A
162.11.7.0	E0	N/A	0	N/A
162.11.8.0	S0	N/A	0	N/A
162.11.9.0	S0	162.11.8.1	1	The metric 1 route is learned from Router A.
162.11.10.0	S0	162.11.8.1	2	Currently, the best route is through Router A because the link to C is down.

Table 7-7 *Router B Routing Table After Learning a Second Valid Route to Subnet 162.11.10.0*

Group	Outgoing Interface	Next-Hop Router	Metric	Comments
162.11.5.0	S0	162.11.8.1	1	N/A
162.11.6.0	S1	N/A	0	This route was added because it is directly connected to S1, which is now up and operational.
162.11.7.0	E0	N/A	0	N/A
162.11.8.0	S0	N/A	0	N/A
162.11.9.0	S0	162.11.8.1	1	The metric 1 route was learned from Router A, but Router C also advertises a metric 1 route! Only one route is chosen—the first one that was learned.
162.11.10.0	S1	162.11.6.2	1	A better route replaces the old route. The new route has a smaller metric and points directly out S1 toward Router C.

Router B changed only one route in this case in reaction to the new routing updates from Router C. B changed its route to 162.11.10.0 because the metric for the route through Router C (metric 1) is smaller than the one from Router A (metric 2).

Router B added only one route in this example—the directly connected subnet 162.11.6.0. The route was added not because of this distance vector routing protocol; it was added by Router B because it is a directly connected subnet and because that interface is now up.

Router B did not change its route to subnet 162.11.9.0, pointing through Router A, even though another metric 1 route through Router C was learned. *In this case, the route that was already in the table is left in the table, which is a reasonable choice.* Other options in the Cisco IOS Software include adding up to six equal-cost routes in the routing table and balancing across those routes instead of using just a single route.

Avoiding Loops with Distance Vector Protocols

Start Extra Credit

Routing protocols carry out their most important functions when redundancy exists in the network. Most importantly, routing protocols ensure that the currently best routes are in the routing tables by reacting to network topology changes. Routing protocols also prevent loops.

Distance vector protocols need several mechanisms to prevent loops. Table 7-8 summarizes these issues and lists the solutions, which are explained in the upcoming text.

Table 7-8 *Issues Relating to Distance Vector Routing Protocols in Networks with Multiple Paths*

Issue	Solution
Multiple routes to the same subnet have equal metrics	Implementation options involve either using the first route learned or putting multiple routes to the same subnet in the routing table.
Routing loops occur due to updates passing each other over a single link	**Split horizon**—The routing protocol advertises routes out an interface only if they were not learned from updates entering that interface. **Split horizon with poison reverse**—The routing protocol uses split-horizon rules unless a route fails. In that case, the route is advertised out all interfaces, but with infinite-distance metrics.
Routing loops occur due to updates passing each other over alternative paths	**Route poisoning**—When a route to a subnet fails, the subnet is advertised with an infinite-distance metric.
Counting to infinity	**Hold-down timer**—After finding out that a route to a subnet has failed, a router waits a certain period of time before believing any other routing information about that subnet. **Triggered updates**—When a route fails, an update is sent immediately rather than waiting on the update timer to expire. Used in conjunction with route poisoning, this ensures that all routers know of failed routes before any hold-down timers can expire.

Split Horizon Routing loops can occur with distance vector routing protocols due to how quickly a router learns about a failed route. In other words, if a route fails, but Router B does not yet know it is bad, Router B advertises a route to that subnet as still being a good route. Split horizon overcomes timing issues over a single full-duplex link. Figure 7-5 shows an example of this problem.

NOTE The routing updates in Figure 7-5 show only the information needed for the point being made in this example. Other routes that would normally be in the routing update have been omitted.

Figure 7-5 *Advertisements Passing on the Serial Link for Subnet 162.11.7.0*

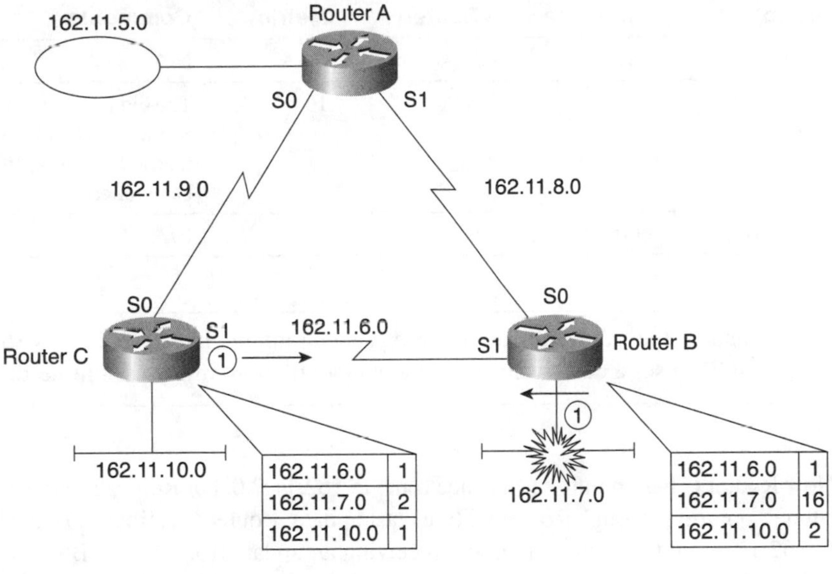

In Figure 7-5, the routing updates are sent periodically, and every router's timer is independent of the others! There is no requirement to make the updates flow from Routers C and B at the same time; however, in this case, Routers B and C are sending updates at the exact same time. How often does this happen? Well, statistically, more often than you might think. And if everything is working, there is no problem. It becomes a problem when Router B advertises an infinite-distance (metric) route to 162.11.7.0, because the subnet just failed. However, Router C advertises a metric 2 route to subnet 162.11.7.0, across the serial link to Router B, that passes the update from Router B. Tables 7-9 and 7-10 show the resulting routing table entries, with a reference to the metric values.

Table 7-9 *Router B Routing Table After Subnet 162.11.7.0 Fails and an Update from Router C Is Received*

Group	Outgoing Interface	Next-Hop Router	Metric	Comments
162.11.6.0	S1	N/A	0	N/A
162.11.7.0	S1	N/A	2	The old route failed, but this one is heard from Router C.
162.11.10.0	S1	162.11.6.2	1	N/A

Table 7-10 *Router C Routing Table After Subnet 162.11.7.0 Fails and an Update from Router B Is Received*

Group	Outgoing Interface	Next-Hop Router	Metric	Comments
162.11.6.0	S1	N/A	0	N/A
162.11.7.0	S1	N/A	16	The old route was metric 1 through Router B. Now B claims that the metric is infinite, so the route must have failed!
162.11.10.0	E0	N/A	1	N/A

NOTE In this chapter, the value 16 is used to represent an infinite metric. RIP uses 16 to represent infinite. IGRP uses a delay value of more than 4 billion to imply an infinite-distance route.

Now Router C has an infinite-distance route to 162.11.7.0, but Router B has a route to the same subnet, pointing through Router C. In its last update, Router C claimed to have a metric 2 route to 162.11.7.0 at the same time it was receiving an update from Router B that the route to 162.11.7.0 was no longer valid. (Infinity is shown as the value 16 in Table 7-10, which is RIP's value for infinity.) So Router B now thinks that 162.11.7.0 can be reached through Router C, and Router C thinks that 162.11.7.0 is unreachable.

This process repeats itself with the next routing update, because it is sent the next time the routing protocol timer expires. This time, Router B advertises metric 3 and Router C advertises an infinite (bad) metric for subnet 162.11.7.0. This continues until both numbers reach infinity. Thankfully, each distance vector routing protocol implementation sets a metric value for which the number is considered infinite. For example, 16 is infinite for RIP, and 4,294,967,295 is infinite for IGRP.

In this case, *split horizon* is the solution to the problem of counting to infinity. Split horizon can be briefly summarized as follows:

> All routes with outgoing interface *x* are not included in updates sent out that same interface *x*.

For example, in Figure 7-6, C's route to subnet 162.11.7.0 points out Serial 1, so its update sent out Serial 1 does not advertise subnet 162.11.7.0. So, when Routers B and C's updates pass each other, one update shows the route with an infinite metric, and the other says nothing about the route, so the counting-to-infinity problem goes away.

Figure 7-6 *Split Horizon Preventing Subnet 162.11.7.0 from Being Advertised by Router C*

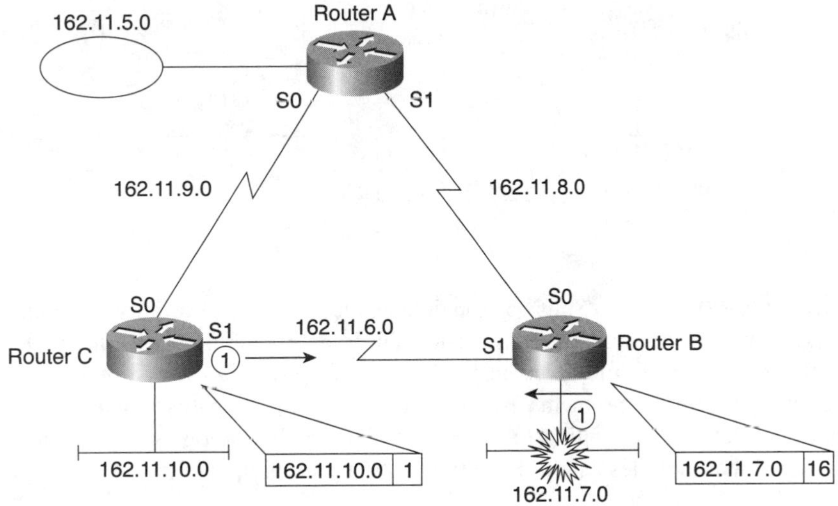

So far, you have read about how split horizon works. However, Cisco distance vector routing protocols actually use a variant of split horizon called *split horizon with poison reverse* (or simply *poison reverse*). When the network is stable, it works just like plain old split horizon. When a route is advertised with an infinite metric, the recipient of the update advertises an infinite-metric route to that subnet out *all* interfaces—including interfaces typically prevented by split horizon. Figure 7-7 lists the pertinent contents of the routing update from Router C, using split horizon with poison reverse.

Figure 7-7 *Split Horizon Enabled with Poison Reverse*

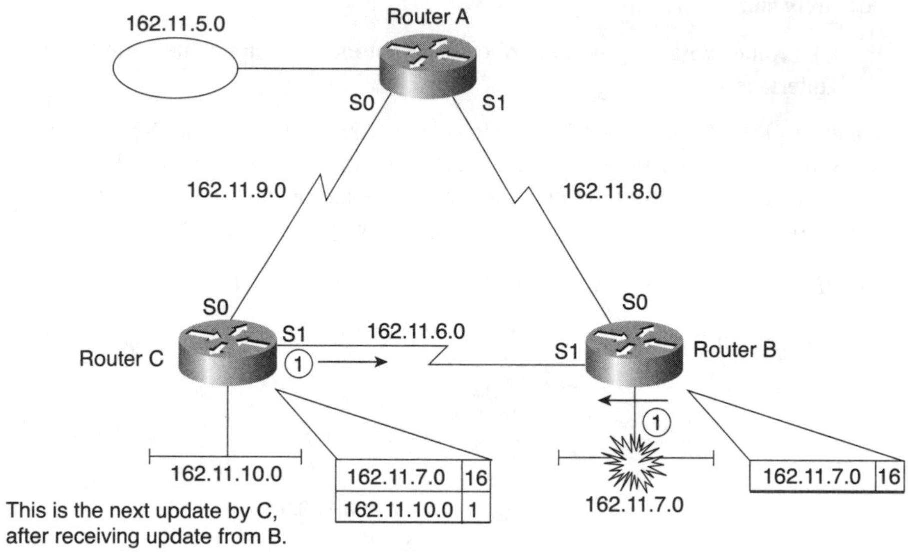

Hold-Down Timer Split horizon defeats the counting-to-infinity problem over a single link. However, counting to infinity can occur in redundant networks (networks with multiple paths) even with split horizon enabled. The *hold-down timer* is part of a solution to the counting-to-infinity problem when networks have multiple paths to many subnets. Split horizon does not defeat the counting-to-infinity problem in all topologies. An additional solution is required that includes a hold-down timer and a routing update feature called route poisoning.

Figure 7-8 shows the version of the counting-to-infinity problem that split horizon does not solve but that holddown does. Subnet 162.11.7.0 fails again (someone should check the cabling!), and Router B advertises an infinite-metric route to 162.11.7.0. However, Router A's update timer expires at the same time (shown as number 1 in the figure), so the updates sent by Routers A and B occur at the same time. Router C hears of an infinite-distance metric to that subnet from Router B and a metric 2 route from Router A, so Router C uses the metric 2 route. Table 7-11 lists the pertinent information about Router C's routing table entry for subnet 162.11.7.0, after the updates shown in Figure 7-8.

Figure 7-8 *Counting to Infinity with a Need for Holddown*

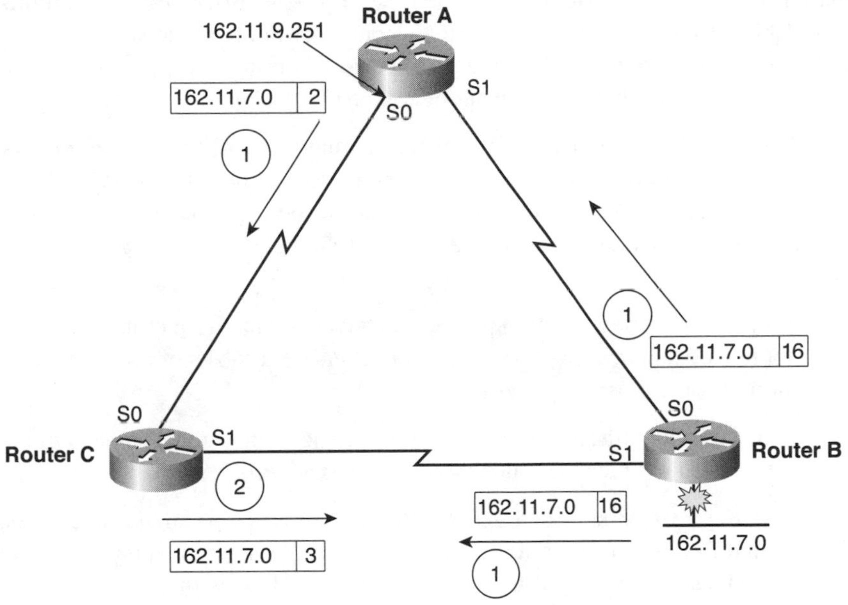

Table 7-11 *Router C's Routing Table After the Updates Shown in Figure 7-8 Are Received*

Group	Outgoing Interface	Next-Hop Router	Metric	Comments
162.11.7.0	S0	162.11.9.251	2	Used to point directly to Router B. Now the route points through Router A, metric 2.

Router C now thinks it has a valid route to 162.11.7.0, pointing back to Router A. On Router B's next update, shown in Step 2 of Figure 7-8, Router C does not advertise subnet 162.11.7.0 out S0 due to split-horizon rules. However, Router C advertises 162.11.7.0 to Router B out Serial1 with metric 3. Router C incorrectly believes that the route to 162.11.7.0 exists through Router B. Router C, in its next update, also tells Router A that it has a route to 162.11.7.0. So, counting to infinity occurs.

The solution is to enable a hold-down timer. The concept is simple—once you see the problem. Holddown is defined as follows:

> When learning that a route has failed, ignore any information about an alternative route to that subnet for a time equal to the hold-down timer.

With holddown enabled, Router C would not believe the metric 2 route learned from Router A in Step 1 of Figure 7-8. During the same time, Router B would advertise infinite-metric routes to 162.11.7.0 to Routers A and C, and then Router A would start advertising an infinite-distance route to Router C. In effect, all routers ignore good routing information about that subnet until enough time passes that everyone has heard the old, bad information.

Route Poisoning When a route fails, a routing protocol could choose to simply stop advertising that route. In fact, distance-vector protocols did just that when they were first created. However, there was no way for a router receiving updates to know the difference between the silence after a route fails and a lost routing update due to noise on the link. So route poisoning was added.

Route poisoning causes a routing protocol to advertise infinite-metric routes for a failed route. It's a lot like poison reverse—in fact, poison reverse is a subset of route poisoning. The formal definition of route poisoning is as follows:

> When a route fails, advertise an infinite-metric route for that subnet out the same interfaces on which the route previously was advertised.

In fact, in Figure 7-8, the update sent by Router B in Step 1 is an example of route poisoning. There is a difference between route poisoning and split horizon with poison reverse. Route poisoning does not break split-horizon rules. Split horizon with poison reverse is essentially route poisoning, but specifically out links on which split horizon would normally not allow routing information to flow. In either case, the result is that failed routes are advertised with infinite metrics!

Triggered (Flash) Updates When a router notices that a directly connected subnet has changed state, it waits until its update timer expires before sending another routing update. The update includes an infinite-metric route based on route poisoning and poison reverse. However, why not go ahead and send updates because routing information has changed! That is exactly what flash or triggered updates are. The router immediately sends another routing update on its other interfaces rather than waiting on the routing update timer to expire. This causes the information about the route whose status has changed to be forwarded more quickly and also starts the hold-down timers more quickly on the neighboring routers.

End Extra Credit

RIP and IGRP

To pass the CCNA exam, you need to know the particulars of how RIP and IGRP implement distance vector logic. RIP and IGRP both use distance vector logic, so they are similar in many respects. A couple of major differences exist, however; they are explained in the upcoming section. Table 7-12 outlines the features of RIP and IGRP.

Table 7-12 *RIP and IGRP Feature Comparison*

Feature	RIP (Default)	IGRP (Default)
Update timer	30 seconds	90 seconds
Metric	Hop count	Function of bandwidth and delay (the default). Can include reliability, load, and MTU.
Hold-down timer	180	280
Flash (triggered) updates	Yes	Yes
Mask sent in update	No for RIP-1; yes for RIP-2	No
Infinite-metric value	16	4,294,967,295

The IGRP metric provides a better measurement of how good a route is, as compared with RIP's metric. IGRP's metric is calculated using the bandwidth and delay settings on the interface on which the update was received. When bandwidth and delay are used, the metric is more meaningful than hop count; longer hop routes that go over faster links are considered better routes by IGRP.

RIP uses hop count as its metric. When an update is received, the metric for each subnet in the update signifies the number of routers between the router receiving the update and each subnet. Before sending an update, a router increments its metric for routes to each subnet by 1.

Finally, the issue of whether the mask is sent is particularly important if VLSMs in the same network are desired. This topic is discussed in the next section.

Configuring RIP and IGRP

27 Add the RIP routing protocol to your configuration.

28 Add the IGRP routing protocol to your configuration.

The CCNA exam covers configuration for two routing protocols—RIP and IGRP. You can configure each of them if you master the use of the **network** command. Other than that, configuration is relatively easy. You should also know the more-popular **show** and **debug** commands, which help you examine and troubleshoot routing protocols.

Of course, you can configure many optional parameters. Some optional features simply are not within the scope of the CCNA exam—and those features are not discussed in this book. I have included some coverage of the additional features that are fair game on the exam. However, you might not see many, if any, more-detailed routing protocol configuration questions on the exam. Therefore, how much you study the additional features is up to you.

Tables 7-13 and 7-14 summarize the more popular commands used for RIP and IGRP configuration and verification. Two configuration examples follow.

Table 7-13 *IP RIP and IGRP Configuration Commands*

Command	Configuration Mode
router rip	Global
router igrp *as-number*	Global
network *net-number*	Router subcommand
passive-interface [**default**] {*interface-type interface-number*}	Router subcommand
maximum-paths *number-paths*	Router subcommand
variance *multiplier*	Router subcommand
traffic-share {*balanced* | *min*}	Router subcommand

Table 7-14 *IP RIP and IGRP EXEC Commands*

Command	Description
show ip route [*ip-address* [*mask*] [**longer-prefixes**]] | [*protocol* [*process-id*]]	Shows the entire routing table, or a subset if parameters are entered.
show ip protocols	Shows routing protocol parameters and current timer values.
debug ip rip	Issues log messages for each RIP update.
debug ip igrp transactions [*ip-address*]	Issues log messages with details of the IGRP updates.
debug ip igrp events [*ip-address*]	Issues log messages for each IGRP packet.
ping [*protocol* | **tag**] {*host-name* | *system-address*}	Sends and receives ICMP echo messages to verify connectivity.
trace [*protocol*] [*destination*]	Sends a series of ICMP echoes with increasing TTL values to verify the current route to a host.

Basic RIP and IGRP Configuration

Each **network** command enables RIP or IGRP on a set of interfaces. You must understand the subtleties of the **network** command, as explained in this section. However, what "enables" really means in this case is not obvious from the Cisco IOS Software documentation. Also, the parameters for the **network** command are not intuitive to many people who are new to Cisco IOS configuration commands. Therefore, routing protocol configuration, including the **network** command, is a likely topic for tricky questions on the exam.

The **network** command "matches" one or more interfaces on a router. For each interface, the **network** command causes the router to do three things:

- The router broadcasts or multicasts routing updates out an interface.
- The router listens for incoming updates on that same interface.
- The router, when sending an update, includes the subnet off that interface in the routing update.

All you need to know is how to match interfaces using the **network** command. The router matches interfaces with the **network** command by asking this simple question:

> Which of my interfaces have IP addresses with the same network number referenced in this **network** subcommand?

For all interfaces that match the **network** command, the router does the three things just listed.

Examples give you a much better understanding of the **network** command, so examine Figure 7-9 and Example 7-1.

Figure 7-9 *Sample Router with Five Interfaces*

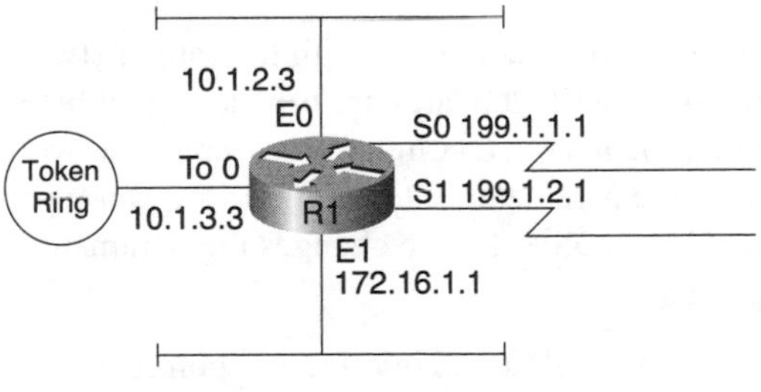

Example 7-1 *Sample Router Configuration with RIP Partially Enabled*

```
interface ethernet 0
ip address 10.1.2.3 255.255.255.0
interface ethernet 1
ip address 172.16.1.1 255.255.255.0
interface tokenring 0
ip address 10.1.3.3 255.255.255.0
interface serial 0
ip address 199.1.1.1 255.255.255.0
interface serial 1
ip address 199.1.2.1 255.255.255.0
!
router rip
network 10.0.0.0
network 199.1.1.0
```

The RIP configuration includes three commands in this case. The **router rip** global command moves the user from global configuration mode to RIP configuration mode. Then, two network commands appear, each with a different Class A, B, or C network number. So what interfaces were matched, and what did this accomplish? Well, if the goal is to enable RIP on *all* interfaces, the configuration is incomplete. Table 7-15 summarizes what this configuration accomplishes and what it does not.

Table 7-15 *What Happens with the RIP Configuration Shown in Example 7-1*

network Command	Interfaces Matched	Actions Taken
network 10.0.0.0	Token0, Ethernet0	Updates are sent out Token0 and Ethernet0. Listen for updates entering Token0 and Ethernet0. Advertise subnets 10.1.3.0 (Token0's subnet) and 10.1.2.0 (Ethernet0's subnet).
network 199.1.1.0	Serial0	Updates are sent out Serial0. Listen for updates entering Serial0. Advertise subnet 199.1.1.0 (Serial0's subnet).

For any interfaces that have IP addresses with the same network number referenced in this **network** subcommand, routing updates are broadcast and listened for, and the connected subnet is advertised. The **network** command requires a network number, not a subnet number, for the parameter. Interestingly, you can type a subnet number in the command, and the Cisco IOS Software changes the parameter to the network number in which that subnet resides.

If the goal was to configure RIP for all interfaces, a common mistake was made in this example. No **network** command matches interfaces Serial1 and Ethernet1. Example 7-2 shows the configuration process to add the additional network commands.

Example 7-2 *Completing the RIP Configuration from Example 7-1*

```
Router1#configure terminal
Router1(config)#router rip
Router1(config-router)#network 199.1.2.0
Router1(config-router)#network 172.16.0.0
Router1(config-router)#CTL-Z
Router1#
```

IGRP Configuration

You configure IGRP just like RIP, except that the **router igrp** command has an additional parameter—the AS number. All that is needed is for all routers to use the same process-id in order for IGRP to work. In Example 7-3, a complete sample IGRP configuration causes the router to advertise all connected subnets, to listen on all interfaces for IGRP updates, and to advertise on all interfaces.

Example 7-3 *Sample IGRP Configuration and* **show ip route** *Command Output*

```
interface ethernet 0
ip address 10.1.2.3 255.255.255.0
interface ethernet 1
ip address 172.16.1.1 255.255.255.0
interface tokenring 0
ip address 10.1.3.3 255.255.255.0
interface serial 0
ip address 199.1.1.1 255.255.255.0
interface serial 1
ip address 199.1.2.1 255.255.255.0
!
router igrp 1
 network 10.0.0.0
 network 199.1.1.0
 network 199.1.2.0
 network 172.16.0.0

Router1#show ip route
Codes: C - connected, S - static, I - IGRP, R - RIP, M - mobile, B - BGP
       D - EIGRP, EX - EIGRP external, O - OSPF, IA - OSPF inter area
       N1 - OSPF NSSA external type 1, N2 - OSPF NSSA external type 2
       E1 - OSPF external type 1, E2 - OSPF external type 2, E - EGP
       i - IS-IS, L1 - IS-IS level-1, L2 - IS-IS level-2, ia - IS-IS inter area
       * - candidate default, U - per-user static route, o - ODR
       P - periodic downloaded static route

Gateway of last resort is not set

     10.0.0.0/24 is subnetted, 3 subnets
C       10.1.3.0 is directly connected, TokenRing0
C       10.1.2.0 is directly connected, Ethernet0
  I       10.1.4.0 [100/8539] via 10.1.2.14, 00:00:50, Ethernet0
     172.16.0.0/24 is subnetted, 2 subnets
C       172.16.1.0 is directly connected, Ethernet1
I       172.16.2.0 [100/6244] via 172.16.1.44, 00:00:20, Ethernet1
C    199.1.1.0/24 is directly connected, Serial0
C    199.1.2.0/24 is directly connected, Serial1
```

IGRP configuration begins with the **router igrp 1** global configuration command. Then, four consecutive network commands match all the interfaces on the router, so that IGRP is fully enabled. In fact, the **network** commands are identical to the **network** commands in the complete RIP configuration.

IGRP Metrics

IGRP uses a composite metric. This metric is calculated as a function of bandwidth, delay, load, and reliability. By default, only bandwidth and delay are considered; the other parameters are considered only if they are enabled via configuration. Delay and bandwidth are not measured values but are set via the **delay** and **bandwidth** interface subcommands. (The same formula is used to calculate the metric for EIGRP, but with a scaling factor so that the actual metric values are larger, allowing more granularity in the metric.)

The **show ip route** command in Example 7-3 shows the IGRP metric values in brackets. For example, the route to 10.1.4.0 shows the value [100/8539] beside the subnet number. The metric 8539 is a single value, as calculated based on bandwidth and delay. The metric is calculated (by default) as the sum of the inverse of the minimum bandwidth, plus the cumulative delay on all links in the route. *In other words, the higher the bandwidth, the lower the metric; the lower the cumulative delay, the lower the metric.*

Examination of RIP and IGRP **debug** and **show** Commands

This section on basic RIP and IGRP configuration closes with one more sample network that is first configured with RIP and then is configured with IGRP. Advanced distance vector protocol concepts, such as split horizon and route poisoning, become more obvious when you look at these examples. RIP and IGRP implement split horizon and route poisoning. You can better understand them by examining the upcoming **debug** messages.

First, Figure 7-10 and Example 7-4 show a stable RIP network with split-horizon rules that affect the RIP updates. Then Ethernet 0 on Yosemite is shut down, and Yosemite advertises an infinite-distance route to 10.1.2.0 because route poisoning is in effect, as shown in Example 7-5. The numbered arrows in the figure represent routing updates. The numbers are referred to with comments inside Example 7-4.

Figure 7-10 *Sample Three-Router Network with Subnet 10.1.2.0 Failing*

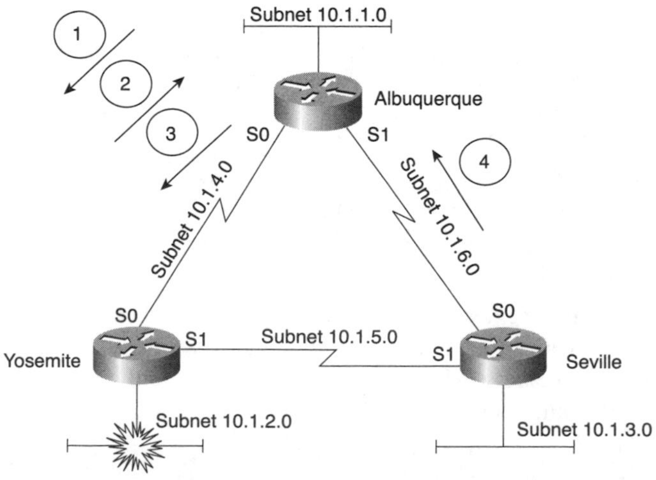

Example 7-4 *RIP Configuration and* **debug***s on Albuquerque*

```
interface ethernet 0
ip addr 10.1.1.251 255.255.255.0
interface serial 0
ip addr 10.1.4.251 255.255.255.0
interface serial 1
ip addr 10.1.6.251 255.255.255.0
!
router rip
network 10.0.0.0

Albuquerque#debug ip rip
RIP: received v1 update from 10.1.6.253 on Serial1
     10.1.3.0 in 1 hops
     10.1.2.0 in 2 hops
     10.1.5.0 in 1 hops
RIP: sending v1 update to 255.255.255.255 via Serial0 (10.1.4.251)
!            (POINT NUMBER 1)
     subnet  10.1.3.0, metric 2
     subnet  10.1.1.0, metric 1
     subnet  10.1.6.0, metric 1
RIP: sending v1 update to 255.255.255.255 via Serial1 (10.1.6.251)
     subnet  10.1.2.0, metric 2
     subnet  10.1.1.0, metric 1
     subnet  10.1.4.0, metric 1
RIP: sending v1 update to 255.255.255.255 via Ethernet0 (10.1.1.251)
     subnet  10.1.3.0, metric 2
     subnet  10.1.2.0, metric 2
     subnet  10.1.6.0, metric 1
     subnet  10.1.5.0, metric 2
     subnet  10.1.4.0, metric 1
RIP: received v1 update from 10.1.4.252 on Serial0
     10.1.3.0 in 2 hops
     10.1.2.0 in 1 hops
     10.1.5.0 in 1 hops
Albuquerque#
(Yosemite E0 shutdown at this time...)

RIP: received v1 update from 10.1.4.252 on Serial0
!            (POINT NUMBER 2)
     10.1.3.0 in 2 hops
     10.1.2.0 in 16 hops (inaccessible)
     10.1.5.0 in 1 hops
RIP: sending v1 update to 255.255.255.255 via Serial0 (10.1.4.251)
!            (POINT NUMBER 3)
     subnet  10.1.3.0, metric 2
     subnet  10.1.2.0, metric 16
     subnet  10.1.1.0, metric 1
     subnet  10.1.6.0, metric 1
RIP: sending v1 update to 255.255.255.255 via Serial1 (10.1.6.251)
     subnet  10.1.2.0, metric 16
     subnet  10.1.1.0, metric 1
```

continues

Example 7-4 *RIP Configuration and* **debug***s on Albuquerque (Continued)*

```
     subnet  10.1.4.0, metric 1
RIP: sending v1 update to 255.255.255.255 via Ethernet0 (10.1.1.251)
     subnet  10.1.3.0, metric 2
     subnet  10.1.2.0, metric 16
     subnet  10.1.6.0, metric 1
     subnet  10.1.5.0, metric 2
     subnet  10.1.4.0, metric 1
RIP: received v1 update from 10.1.6.253 on Serial1
!            (POINT NUMBER 4)
     10.1.3.0 in 1 hops
     10.1.2.0 in 16 hops (inaccessible)
     10.1.5.0 in 1 hops
```

Example 7-5 *RIP Configuration on Yosemite*

```
interface ethernet 0
ip addr 10.1.2.252 255.255.255.0
interface serial 0
ip addr 10.1.4.252 255.255.255.0
interface serial 1
ip addr 10.1.5.252 255.255.255.0

router rip
network 10.0.0.0
```

First, examine the configuration on Albuquerque (Example 7-4) and Yosemite (Example 7-5). Because all interfaces on each router are part of network 10.0.0.0, RIP needs only a single **network** command on each router, so the configuration is relatively easy.

For the rest of the explanation, refer to the phrase "Point Number *X*" in Example 7-4. The following list describes what happens at each point in the process:

- **Point Number 1**—Albuquerque sends an update out Serial0, obeying split-horizon rules. Notice that 10.1.2.0, Yosemite's Ethernet subnet, is not in the update sent out Albuquerque's S0 interface.

- **Point Number 2**—This point begins right after Yosemite's E0 has been shut down, simulating a failure. Albuquerque receives an update from Yosemite, entering Albuquerque's S0 interface. The route to 10.1.2.0 has an infinite metric, which, in this case, is 16.

- **Point Number 3**—Albuquerque formerly did not mention subnet 10.1.2.0 due to split-horizon rules (point 1). The update at point 3 includes a poisoned route for 10.1.2.0 with metric 16. This is an example of split horizon with poison reverse.

- **Point Number 4**—Albuquerque receives an update in S1 from Seville. The update includes a metric 16 (infinite) route to 10.1.2.0. Seville does not suspend any split-horizon rules in order to send this route because it saw the advertisement of that route earlier, so this is a simple case of route poisoning.

Example 7-6 shows the steps needed to migrate to IGRP. It also lists some **debug** and **show** commands. Example 7-6 lists the configuration added to each of the three routers shown in Figure 7-10 to migrate to IGRP. The logic of the **network** commands works just like with RIP. The output of the **show** and **debug** commands provides some insight into the differences between RIP and IGRP.

NOTE The following configuration commands would be used on all three routers.

Example 7-6 *Migration to IGRP with Sample* **show** *and* **debug** *Commands*

```
no router rip
router igrp 5
 network 10.0.0.0

Albuquerque#show ip route
Codes: C - connected, S - static, I - IGRP, R - RIP, M - mobile, B - BGP
       D - EIGRP, EX - EIGRP external, O - OSPF, IA - OSPF inter area
       N1 - OSPF NSSA external type 1, N2 - OSPF NSSA external type 2
       E1 - OSPF external type 1, E2 - OSPF external type 2, E - EGP
       i - IS-IS, L1 - IS-IS level-1, L2 - IS-IS level-2, ia - IS-IS inter area
       * - candidate default, U - per-user static route, o - ODR
       P - periodic downloaded static route

Gateway of last resort is not set

     10.0.0.0/24 is subnetted, 6 subnets
I       10.1.3.0 [100/8539] via 10.1.6.253, 00:00:28, Serial1
I       10.1.2.0 [100/8539] via 10.1.4.252, 00:00:18, Serial0
C       10.1.1.0 is directly connected, Ethernet0
C       10.1.6.0 is directly connected, Serial1
I       10.1.5.0 [100/10476] via 10.1.4.252, 00:00:18, Serial0
                 [100/10476] via 10.1.6.253, 00:00:29, Serial1
C       10.1.4.0 is directly connected, Serial0
Albuquerque#debug ip igrp transactions
IGRP protocol debugging is on
Albuquerque#
07:43:40: IGRP: sending update to 255.255.255.255 via Serial0 (10.1.4.251)
07:43:40:       subnet 10.1.3.0, metric=8539
07:43:40:       subnet 10.1.1.0, metric=688
07:43:40:       subnet 10.1.6.0, metric=8476
07:43:40: IGRP: sending update to 255.255.255.255 via Serial1 (10.1.6.251)
07:43:40:       subnet 10.1.2.0, metric=8539
07:43:40:       subnet 10.1.1.0, metric=688
07:43:40:       subnet 10.1.4.0, metric=8476
07:43:40: IGRP: sending update to 255.255.255.255 via Ethernet0 (10.1.1.251)
07:43:40:       subnet 10.1.3.0, metric=8539
07:43:40:       subnet 10.1.2.0, metric=8539
07:43:40:       subnet 10.1.6.0, metric=8476
07:43:40:       subnet 10.1.5.0, metric=10476
07:43:40:       subnet 10.1.4.0, metric=8476
```

continues

Example 7-6 *Migration to IGRP with Sample* **show** *and* **debug** *Commands (Continued)*

```
07:43:59: IGRP: received update from 10.1.6.253 on Serial1
07:43:59:       subnet 10.1.3.0, metric 8539 (neighbor 688)
07:43:59:       subnet 10.1.5.0, metric 10476 (neighbor 8476)
07:44:18: IGRP: received update from 10.1.4.252 on Serial0
07:44:18:       subnet 10.1.2.0, metric 8539 (neighbor 688)
07:44:18:       subnet 10.1.5.0, metric 10476 (neighbor 8476)
Albuquerque#no debug all
All possible debugging has been turned off
Albuquerque#
Albuquerque#debug ip igrp events
IGRP event debugging is on
Albuquerque#
07:45:00: IGRP: sending update to 255.255.255.255 via Serial0 (10.1.4.251)
07:45:00: IGRP: Update contains 3 interior, 0 system, and 0 exterior routes.
07:45:00: IGRP: Total routes in update: 3
07:45:00: IGRP: sending update to 255.255.255.255 via Serial1 (10.1.6.251)
07:45:00: IGRP: Update contains 3 interior, 0 system, and 0 exterior routes.
07:45:00: IGRP: Total routes in update: 3
07:45:00: IGRP: sending update to 255.255.255.255 via Ethernet0 (10.1.1.251)
07:45:01: IGRP: Update contains 5 interior, 0 system, and 0 exterior routes.
07:45:01: IGRP: Total routes in update: 5
07:45:21: IGRP: received update from 10.1.6.253 on Serial1
07:45:21: IGRP: Update contains 2 interior, 0 system, and 0 exterior routes.
07:45:21: IGRP: Total routes in update: 2
07:45:35: IGRP: received update from 10.1.4.252 on Serial0
07:45:35: IGRP: Update contains 2 interior, 0 system, and 0 exterior routes.
07:45:35: IGRP: Total routes in update: 2
Albuquerque#no debug all
All possible debugging has been turned off
Albuquerque#show ip protocol
Routing Protocol is "igrp 5"
  Sending updates every 90 seconds, next due in 34 seconds
  Invalid after 270 seconds, hold down 280, flushed after 630
  Outgoing update filter list for all interfaces is
  Incoming update filter list for all interfaces is
  Default networks flagged in outgoing updates
  Default networks accepted from incoming updates
  IGRP metric weight K1=1, K2=0, K3=1, K4=0, K5=0
  IGRP maximum hopcount 100
  IGRP maximum metric variance 1
  Redistributing: igrp 5
  Maximum path: 4
  Routing for Networks:
    10.0.0.0
  Routing Information Sources:
    Gateway         Distance      Last Update
    10.1.6.253           100      00:00:23
    10.1.4.252           100      00:00:08
  Distance: (default is 100)
```

You can migrate from RIP to IGRP in this case with only three configuration commands per router. As highlighted in Example 7-6, the **no router rip** command removes all RIP configuration on the router, including any **network** subcommands. The three routers each must use the same IGRP process-id (5, in this case), and because all interfaces on each of the routers are in network 10.0.0.0, only a single **network 10.0.0.0** subcommand is needed.

The **show ip route** command provides the most direct view into what a routing protocol does. First, the legend at the beginning of the **show ip route** command in Example 7-6 defines the letter codes that identify the source of the routing information—for example, **C** for connected routes, **R** for RIP, and **I** for IGRP. Each of the Class A, B, and C networks is listed, along with each of the subnets of that network. If a static mask is used within that network, the mask is shown only in the line referring to the network. Each routing entry lists the subnet number and the outgoing interface. In most cases, the next-hop router's IP address is also listed.

IGRP learns the same routes that RIP learned, but using different metrics. The output of the **show ip route** command lists six subnets, just as it did when RIP was used. Also, notice the two routes to 10.1.5.0/24—one through Yosemite and one through Seville. Both routes are included in the routing table, because the default setting for **ip maximum-paths** is 4, and because the routes have an equal metric. Looking further into the output of the **debug ip igrp transactions** command, you can see the equal-cost routes being advertised. One route is seen in the update received on Serial1; the other route in the update is received on Serial0.

The output of the **debug ip igrp transactions** command shows the details of the routing updates, whereas the **debug ip igrp events** command simply mentions that routing updates have been received.

Finally, the **show ip protocol** command lists several important details about the routing protocol. The update timer is listed, shown with the time remaining until the next routing update is to be sent. Also, the elapsed time since an update was received from each neighboring router is listed at the end of the output. This command also lists each of the neighbors from which routing information has been received. If you are in doubt as to whether updates have been received during the recent past and from what routers, the **show ip protocol** command is the place to find out.

Advanced RIP and IGRP Configuration

Start Extra Credit

The next several sections describe some of the more advanced features of these two protocols. These topics might be on the exam. However, if you are trying to focus on the most important details, taking a small risk by not covering some of the less-important details, you might want to skip these sections and move to the section, "Troubleshooting Routing and Routing Protocols."

RIP-1 and IGRP: No Subnet Masks

RIP-1 and IGRP do not transmit the subnet mask in the routing updates, as seen in the **debug** output in earlier examples. Cisco expects you to be able to explain why routing protocols that do not transmit a mask can have problems in some networks. This section explains these problems, which all originate from the same root cause.

NOTE Routers must assume the subnet mask that should be used with a subnet number listed in a routing update.

Routing protocols that do not transmit masks, such as RIP and IGRP, behave predictably:

- Updates sent out an interface in network X, when containing routes about subnets of network X, contain the subnet numbers of the subnets of network X but not the corresponding masks.
- Updates sent out an interface in network X, when containing routes about subnets of network Y, contain one route about the entire network Y, but not any routes about subnets of network Y.
- When receiving a routing update containing routes referencing subnets of network X, the receiving router assumes that the mask in use is the same mask it uses on an interface with an address in network X.
- When receiving an update about network X, if the receiving router has no interfaces in network X, it treats the route as a route to the entire Class A, B, or C network X.

Examples 7-7, 7-8, and 7-9 contain **show** and **debug** command output on Albuquerque, Yosemite, and Seville with the effects described in the preceding list. The network of Figure 7-10 is still in use, but the subnet on Seville's Ethernet has been changed from 10.1.3.0/24 to 10.1.3.192/26. Because RIP-1 does not send the mask in the update, Seville chooses *not* to address 10.1.3.192/26 onto its serial links (which use mask 255.255.255.0), because the update would be ambiguous.

Example 7-7 *Configuration and* **debug ip rip** *Output on Albuquerque*

```
interface ethernet 0
ip addr 10.1.1.251 255.255.255.0
interface serial 0
ip addr 10.1.4.251 255.255.255.0
interface serial 1
ip addr 10.1.6.251 255.255.255.0
!
router rip
network 10.0.0.0

Albuquerque#debug ip rip
RIP protocol debugging is on
```

Example 7-7 *Configuration and* **debug ip rip** *Output on Albuquerque (Continued)*

```
Albuquerque#
00:38:23: RIP: received v1 update from 10.1.4.252 on Serial0
00:38:23:      10.1.2.0 in 1 hops
00:38:23:      10.1.5.0 in 1 hops
00:38:33: RIP: sending v1 update to 255.255.255.255 via Serial0 (10.1.4.251)
00:38:33:      subnet  10.1.1.0, metric 1
00:38:33:      subnet  10.1.6.0, metric 1
00:38:33: RIP: sending v1 update to 255.255.255.255 via Serial1 (10.1.6.251)
00:38:33:      subnet  10.1.2.0, metric 2
00:38:33:      subnet  10.1.1.0, metric 1
00:38:33:      subnet  10.1.4.0, metric 1
00:38:33: RIP: sending v1 update to 255.255.255.255 via Ethernet0 (10.1.1.251)
00:38:33:      subnet  10.1.2.0, metric 2
00:38:33:      subnet  10.1.6.0, metric 1
00:38:33:      subnet  10.1.5.0, metric 2
00:38:33:      subnet  10.1.4.0, metric 1
00:38:40: RIP: received v1 update from 10.1.6.253 on Serial1
00:38:40:      10.1.2.0 in 2 hops
00:38:40:      10.1.5.0 in 1 hops
undebug all
All possible debugging has been turned off
Albuquerque#show ip route
Codes: C - connected, S - static, I - IGRP, R - RIP, M - mobile, B - BGP
       D - EIGRP, EX - EIGRP external, O - OSPF, IA - OSPF inter area
       N1 - OSPF NSSA external type 1, N2 - OSPF NSSA external type 2
       E1 - OSPF external type 1, E2 - OSPF external type 2, E - EGP
       i - IS-IS, L1 - IS-IS level-1, L2 - IS-IS level-2, ia - IS-IS inter area
       * - candidate default, U - per-user static route, o - ODR
       P - periodic downloaded static route

Gateway of last resort is not set

     10.0.0.0/24 is subnetted, 5 subnets
R       10.1.2.0 [120/1] via 10.1.4.252, 00:00:26, Serial0
C       10.1.1.0 is directly connected, Ethernet0
C       10.1.6.0 is directly connected, Serial1
R       10.1.5.0 [120/1] via 10.1.4.252, 00:00:27, Serial0
                 [120/1] via 10.1.6.253, 00:00:10, Serial1
C       10.1.4.0 is directly connected, Serial0
Albuquerque#
(Suspended telnet resumed to Seville....)

Seville#show ip route
Codes: C - connected, S - static, I - IGRP, R - RIP, M - mobile, B - BGP
       D - EIGRP, EX - EIGRP external, O - OSPF, IA - OSPF inter area
       N1 - OSPF NSSA external type 1, N2 - OSPF NSSA external type 2
       E1 - OSPF external type 1, E2 - OSPF external type 2, E - EGP
       i - IS-IS, L1 - IS-IS level-1, L2 - IS-IS level-2, ia - IS-IS inter area
       * - candidate default, U - per-user static route, o - ODR
       P - periodic downloaded static route

Gateway of last resort is not set
```

continues

Example 7-7 *Configuration and* **debug ip rip** *Output on Albuquerque (Continued)*

```
      10.0.0.0/8 is variably subnetted, 6 subnets, 2 masks
R        10.1.2.0/24 [120/1] via 10.1.5.252, 00:00:19, Serial1
R        10.1.1.0/24 [120/1] via 10.1.6.251, 00:00:22, Serial0
C        10.1.6.0/24 is directly connected, Serial0
C        10.1.5.0/24 is directly connected, Serial1
R        10.1.4.0/24 [120/1] via 10.1.6.251, 00:00:22, Serial0
                     [120/1] via 10.1.5.252, 00:00:19, Serial1
C        10.1.3.192/26 is directly connected, Ethernet0
Seville#
```

Example 7-8 *Configuration on Yosemite*

```
interface ethernet 0
ip addr 10.1.2.252 255.255.255.0
interface serial 0
ip addr 10.1.4.252 255.255.255.0
interface serial 1
ip address 10.1.2.252 255.255.255.0

router rip
network 10.0.0.0
```

Example 7-9 *Configuration on Seville*

```
interface ethernet 0
ip addr 10.1.3.253  255.255.255.192
interface serial 0
ip addr 10.1.6.253  255.255.255.0
interface serial 1
ip address 10.1.5.253  255.255.255.0
!
router rip
network 10.0.0.0
```

As shown in the highlighted portions of Example 7-7, subnet 10.1.3.192/26 is not advertised by Seville, as seen in its update received into Albuquerque's Serial1 interface. Essentially, *RIP does not advertise the route with a mask of 255.255.255.192 out an interface that is in the same network but that has a different mask.* If RIP on Seville had advertised the route to 10.1.3.192, Albuquerque and Yosemite would have believed there was a problem, because the subnet number is 10.1.3.192, which is not a subnet number with the mask that Albuquerque and Yosemite think is in use (255.255.255.0). So, RIP and IGRP simply do not advertise the route into the same network on an interface that uses a different mask. The use of different masks in parts of the same network is called *variable-length subnet masking* (VLSM). As shown in this example, VLSM is not supported by RIP-1 or IGRP.

RIP Version 2

RIP-2, defined by RFC 1723, adds advanced features to RIP-1. Many features are the same: Hop count is still used for the metric, it is still a distance vector protocol, and it still uses hold-down timers and route poisoning. Several features have been added. They are listed in Table 7-16.

Table 7-16 *RIP-2 Features*

Feature	Description
Transmits a subnet mask with the route	This feature allows VLSM by passing the mask along with each route so that the subnet is exactly defined.
Provides authentication	Both clear text (RFC-defined) and MD5 encryption (a Cisco-added feature) can be used to authenticate the source of a routing update.
Includes a next-hop router IP address in its routing update	A router can advertise a route but direct any listeners to a different router on that same subnet. This is done only when the other router has a better route.
Uses external route tags	RIP can pass information about routes learned from an external source and redistributed into RIP.
Provides multicast routing updates	Instead of sending updates to 255.255.255.255, the destination IP address is 224.0.0.9, an IP multicast address. This reduces the amount of processing required on non-RIP-speaking hosts on a common subnet.

RIP-2 supports the new features listed in the table, but most importantly, it supports the use of VLSM through transmitting mask information. For instance, the preceding example showed a problem using VLSM on Seville (subnet 10.1.3.192/26). RIP-2 works fine in the same network, as shown in Example 7-10. This example lists the RIP-2 configuration on each of the three routers, and Example 7-11 shows a sample RIP **debug** on Albuquerque.

Example 7-10 *RIP-2 Sample Configuration for the Routers Shown in Figure 7-10*

```
router rip
network 10.0.0.0
version 2
```

Example 7-11 *RIP-2 Routing Updates, Without Autosummarization, on Albuquerque*

```
Albuquerque#debug ip rip
RIP protocol debugging is on
Albuquerque#
```

continues

Example 7-11 *RIP-2 Routing Updates, Without Autosummarization, on Albuquerque (Continued)*

```
00:36:04: RIP: received v2 update from 10.1.4.252 on Serial0
00:36:04:      10.1.2.0/24 -> 0.0.0.0 in 1 hops
00:36:04:      10.1.5.0/24 -> 0.0.0.0 in 1 hops
00:36:04:      10.1.3.192/26 -> 0.0.0.0 in 2 hops
00:36:08: RIP: sending v2 update to 224.0.0.9 via Serial0 (10.1.4.251)
00:36:08:      10.1.1.0/24 -> 0.0.0.0, metric 1, tag 0
00:36:08:      10.1.6.0/24 -> 0.0.0.0, metric 1, tag 0
00:36:08:      10.1.3.192/26 -> 0.0.0.0, metric 2, tag 0
00:36:08: RIP: sending v2 update to 224.0.0.9 via Serial1 (10.1.6.251)
00:36:08:      10.1.2.0/24 -> 0.0.0.0, metric 2, tag 0
00:36:08:      10.1.1.0/24 -> 0.0.0.0, metric 1, tag 0
00:36:08:      10.1.4.0/24 -> 0.0.0.0, metric 1, tag 0
00:36:08: RIP: sending v2 update to 224.0.0.9 via Ethernet0 (10.1.1.251)
00:36:08:      10.1.2.0/24 -> 0.0.0.0, metric 2, tag 0
00:36:08:      10.1.6.0/24 -> 0.0.0.0, metric 1, tag 0
00:36:08:      10.1.5.0/24 -> 0.0.0.0, metric 2, tag 0
00:36:08:      10.1.4.0/24 -> 0.0.0.0, metric 1, tag 0
00:36:08:      10.1.3.192/26 -> 0.0.0.0, metric 2, tag 0
00:36:20: RIP: received v2 update from 10.1.6.253 on Serial1
00:36:20:      10.1.2.0/24 -> 0.0.0.0 in 2 hops
00:36:20:      10.1.5.0/24 -> 0.0.0.0 in 1 hops
00:36:20:      10.1.3.192/26 -> 0.0.0.0 in 1 hops
00:36:30: RIP: received v2 update from 10.1.4.252 on Serial0
00:36:30:      10.1.2.0/24 -> 0.0.0.0 in 1 hops
00:36:30:      10.1.5.0/24 -> 0.0.0.0 in 1 hops
00:36:30:      10.1.3.192/26 -> 0.0.0.0 in 2 hops

Albuquerque#no debug all
All possible debugging has been turned off

Albuquerque#show ip route
Codes: C - connected, S - static, I - IGRP, R - RIP, M - mobile, B - BGP
       D - EIGRP, EX - EIGRP external, O - OSPF, IA - OSPF inter area
       N1 - OSPF NSSA external type 1, N2 - OSPF NSSA external type 2
       E1 - OSPF external type 1, E2 - OSPF external type 2, E - EGP
       i - IS-IS, L1 - IS-IS level-1, L2 - IS-IS level-2, ia - IS-IS inter area
       * - candidate default, U - per-user static route, o - ODR
       P - periodic downloaded static route

Gateway of last resort is not set

     10.0.0.0/8 is variably subnetted, 6 subnets, 2 masks
R       10.1.2.0/24 [120/1] via 10.1.4.252, 00:00:09, Serial0
C       10.1.1.0/24 is directly connected, Ethernet0
C       10.1.6.0/24 is directly connected, Serial1
R       10.1.5.0/24 [120/1] via 10.1.4.252, 00:00:09, Serial0
                    [120/1] via 10.1.6.253, 00:00:19, Serial1
C       10.1.4.0/24 is directly connected, Serial0
R       10.1.3.192/26 [120/1] via 10.1.6.253, 00:00:19, Serial1
Albuquerque#
```

A couple of important items should be noted in the **debug** output of Example 7-11. (As always, the specific portions that are referred to are highlighted.) The updates sent by Albuquerque are sent to multicast IP address 224.0.0.9 as opposed to a broadcast address; this allows the devices that are not using RIP-2 to ignore the updates and not waste processing cycles. The **show ip route** output on Albuquerque lists the previously missing subnet, 10.1.3.192/26; this is expected, as highlighted in the **debug ip rip** messages received by Albuquerque from Seville (10.1.6.253). The subnet masks are shown in the prefix style, with /26 representing mask 255.255.255.192. Also, note the **debug** output designating **tag 0**. This means that all the external route tags have value 0, which is the default.

Migrating from RIP-1 to RIP-2 requires some planning. RIP-1 sends updates to the broadcast address, whereas RIP-2 uses a multicast. A RIP-1-only router and a RIP-2-only router will not succeed in exchanging routing information. To migrate to RIP-2, one option is to migrate all routers at the same time. This might not be a reasonable political or administrative option, however. If not, some coexistence between RIP-1 and RIP-2 is required.

The **ip rip send version** command can be used to overcome this problem. Essentially, the configuration tells the router whether to send RIP-1-style updates, RIP-2-style updates, or both for each interface. Consider the familiar Figure 7-10 network, with RIP-1 still configured on all three routers. If two of the routers are migrated—for instance, Albuquerque and Seville—they can communicate with RIP-2 easily. However, by default these two routers now send only RIP-2 updates, which Yosemite cannot understand, because it is still running RIP-1. The configurations shown in Examples 7-12, 7-13, and 7-14 overcome this problem by having Albuquerque and Seville send only RIP-1 updates to Yosemite.

Example 7-12 *Configuration on Albuquerque*

```
interface ethernet 0
ip addr 10.1.1.251 255.255.255.0
interface serial 0
ip addr 10.1.4.251 255.255.255.0
ip rip send version 1
ip rip receive version 1
interface serial 1
ip address 10.1.6.251 255.255.255.0
!
router rip
network 10.0.0.0
version 2
```

Example 7-13 *Configuration on Yosemite*

```
interface ethernet 0
ip addr 10.1.2.252 255.255.255.0
interface serial 0
ip addr 10.1.4.252 255.255.255.0
```

continues

Example 7-13 *Configuration on Yosemite (Continued)*

```
interface serial 1
ip address 10.1.5.252 255.255.255.0
!
router rip
network 10.0.0.0
```

Example 7-14 *Configuration on Seville*

```
interface ethernet 0
ip addr 10.1.2.252 255.255.255.0
interface serial 0
ip addr 10.1.4.252 255.255.255.0
interface serial 1
ip address 10.1.5.252 255.255.255.0
ip rip send version 1
ip rip receive version 1
!
router rip
network 10.0.0.0
version 2
```

The RIP-2 configuration logic works just like RIP-1. Updates are sent and received on each interface that is matched by a **network** command. But because Yosemite sends and receives only RIP-1 updates, the other two routers need the appropriate interface subcommands to tell the router to send and receive RIP-1 updates to and from Yosemite. Both Albuquerque and Seville continue to send and receive RIP-2 updates on all interfaces, so when Yosemite upgrades to RIP-2, no immediate configuration changes are required in Albuquerque and Seville.

Autosummarization and Route Aggregation

Cisco IOS Software is optimized to perform routing as fast as possible. Most of the Layer 3 routing performance improvement in the brief history of routers has been through improved algorithms. Many times those improved algorithms later have been implemented in hardware to provide even lower latency. Although these improvements have been a great benefit, it is typically true that any algorithm that searches a list runs more quickly if the list is short, as compared to searching a similar list that is long.

Autosummarization and route aggregation (also known as route summarization) are two Cisco IOS Software features that reduce the size of the IP routing table, thereby reducing latency per packet. Autosummarization is a routing protocol feature that operates using this rule:

> When advertised on an interface whose IP address is not in network X, routes about subnets in network X are summarized and advertised as one route. That route is for the entire Class A, B, or C network X.

RIP and IGRP perform autosummarization, and it cannot be disabled. Essentially, it must be a side effect of routing protocols that transmit the mask. For RIP-2 and EIGRP, autosummarization can be enabled or disabled.

As usual, an example makes the concept much clearer. Consider Figure 7-11, which shows two networks in use: 10.0.0.0 and 172.16.0.0. Seville has four (connected) routes to subnets of network 10.0.0.0. Example 7-15 shows the output of a **show ip route** command on Albuquerque, as well as RIP-2 **debug ip rip** output.

Figure 7-11 *Autosummarization*

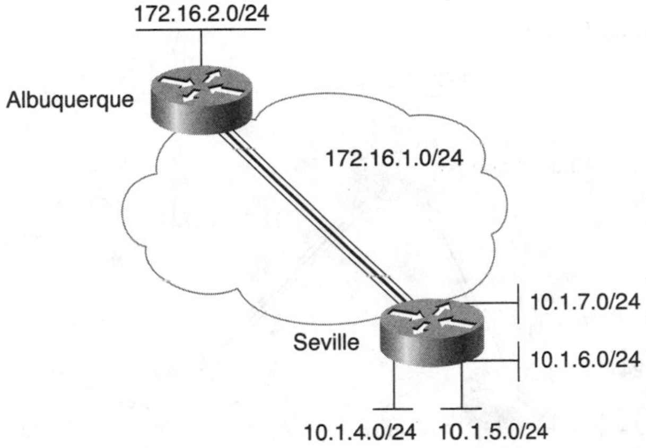

Example 7-15 *Configuration on Seville*

```
Albuquerque#debug ip rip
02:20:42: RIP: sending v2 update to 224.0.0.9 via Serial0.2 (172.16.1.251)
02:20:42:       172.16.2.0/24 -> 0.0.0.0, metric 1, tag 0
02:20:42: RIP: sending v2 update to 224.0.0.9 via Ethernet0 (172.16.2.251)
02:20:42:       172.16.1.0/24 -> 0.0.0.0, metric 1, tag 0
02:20:42:       10.0.0.0/8 -> 0.0.0.0, metric 2, tag 0
02:20:46: RIP: received v2 update from 172.16.1.253 on Serial0.2
02:20:46:       10.0.0.0/8 -> 0.0.0.0 in 1 hops
Albuquerque#undebug all
All possible debugging has been turned off
Albuquerque#show ip route
Codes: C - connected, S - static, I - IGRP, R - RIP, M - mobile, B - BGP
       D - EIGRP, EX - EIGRP external, O - OSPF, IA - OSPF inter area
       N1 - OSPF NSSA external type 1, N2 - OSPF NSSA external type 2
       E1 - OSPF external type 1, E2 - OSPF external type 2, E - EGP
       i - IS-IS, L1 - IS-IS level-1, L2 - IS-IS level-2, ia - IS-IS inter area
       * - candidate default, U - per-user static route, o - ODR
       P - periodic downloaded static route

Gateway of last resort is not set

     172.16.0.0/24 is subnetted, 2 subnets
C       172.16.1.0 is directly connected, Serial0.2
C       172.16.2.0 is directly connected, Ethernet0
R    10.0.0.0/8 [120/1] via 172.16.1.253, 00:00:09, Serial0.2
```

Notice, as highlighted in Example 7-15, that Albuquerque's received update on Serial0.2 from Seville advertises only the entire Class A network 10.0.0.0/8 because autosummarization is enabled on Seville (by default). The IP routing table lists just one route to network 10.0.0.0. This works fine, as long as network 10.0.0.0 is contiguous. Consider Figure 7-12, in which Yosemite also has subnets of network 10.0.0.0 but has no connectivity to Seville other than through Albuquerque.

Figure 7-12 *Autosummarization Pitfalls*

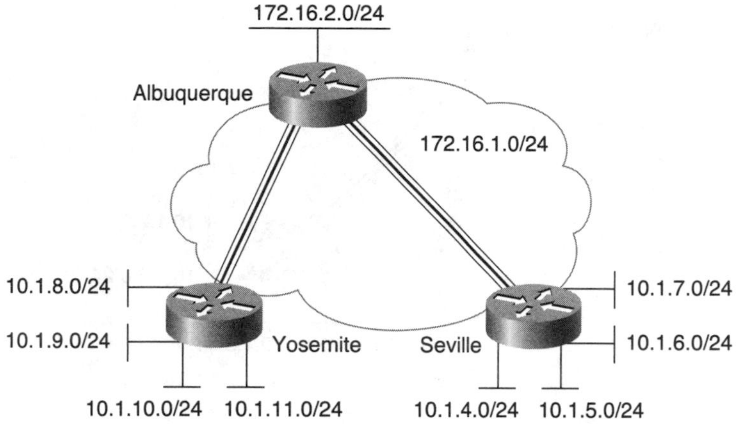

IP subnet design traditionally has not allowed *discontiguous networks*. A *contiguous network* is a single Class A, B, or C network for which all routes to subnets of that network pass through only other subnets of that same single network. *Discontiguous networks* refers to the concept that, in a single Class A, B, or C network, there is at least one case in which the only routes to one subnet pass through subnets of a different network. An easy analogy for residents of the United States is the term *contiguous 48,* referring to the 48 states besides Alaska and Hawaii. To drive to Alaska from the contiguous 48, for example, you must drive through another country (Canada, for the geographically impaired!), so Alaska is not contiguous with the 48 states—in other words, it is discontiguous.

Figure 7-12 breaks that rule. In this figure, there could be a PVC between Yosemite and Seville that uses a subnet of network 10.0.0.0, but that PVC might be down, causing the discontiguous network. The temporarily discontiguous network can be overcome with the use of a routing protocol that transmits masks, because the rule of discontiguous subnets can be ignored if no autosummarization, or configured summarization, is performed. Consider the routing updates and routing table on Albuquerque in Example 7-16, where RIP-2 is used so that autosummarization is disabled on all routers.

Example 7-16 *Albuquerque's Routing Table When Seville Is Not Summarizing*

```
Albuquerque#debug ip rip
RIP protocol debugging is on
Albuquerque#
02:48:58: RIP: received v2 update from 172.16.1.253 on Serial0.2
02:48:58:      10.1.7.0/24 -> 0.0.0.0 in 1 hops
02:48:58:      10.1.6.0/24 -> 0.0.0.0 in 1 hops
02:48:58:      10.1.5.0/24 -> 0.0.0.0 in 1 hops
02:48:58:      10.1.4.0/24 -> 0.0.0.0 in 1 hops
02:49:14: RIP: received v2 update from 172.16.3.252 on Serial0.1
02:49:14:      10.1.11.0/24 -> 0.0.0.0 in 1 hops
02:49:14:      10.1.10.0/24 -> 0.0.0.0 in 1 hops
02:49:14:      10.1.9.0/24 -> 0.0.0.0 in 1 hops
02:49:14:      10.1.8.0/24 -> 0.0.0.0 in 1 hops
02:49:16: RIP: sending v2 update to 224.0.0.9 via Serial0.1 (172.16.3.251)
02:49:16:      172.16.1.0/24 -> 0.0.0.0, metric 1, tag 0
02:49:16:      172.16.2.0/24 -> 0.0.0.0, metric 1, tag 0
02:49:16:      10.0.0.0/8 -> 0.0.0.0, metric 2, tag 0
02:49:16: RIP: sending v2 update to 224.0.0.9 via Serial0.2 (172.16.1.251)
02:49:16:      172.16.2.0/24 -> 0.0.0.0, metric 1, tag 0
02:49:16:      172.16.3.0/24 -> 0.0.0.0, metric 1, tag 0
02:49:16:      10.0.0.0/8 -> 0.0.0.0, metric 2, tag 0
02:49:16: RIP: sending v2 update to 224.0.0.9 via Ethernet 0 (172.16.2.251)
02:49:16:      172.16.1.0/24 -> 0.0.0.0, metric 1, tag 0
02:49:16:      172.16.3.0/24 -> 0.0.0.0, metric 1, tag 0
02:49:16:      10.0.0.0/8 -> 0.0.0.0, metric 2, tag 0
Albuquerque#no debug all
All possible debugging has been turned off
Albuquerque#show ip route
Codes: C - connected, S - static, I - IGRP, R - RIP, M - mobile, B - BGP
       D - EIGRP, EX - EIGRP external, O - OSPF, IA - OSPF inter area
       N1 - OSPF NSSA external type 1, N2 - OSPF NSSA external type 2
       E1 - OSPF external type 1, E2 - OSPF external type 2, E - EGP
       i - IS-IS, L1 - IS-IS level-1, L2 - IS-IS level-2, ia - IS-IS inter area
       * - candidate default, U - per-user static route, o - ODR
       P - periodic downloaded static route

Gateway of last resort is not set

     172.16.0.0/24 is subnetted, 3 subnets
C       172.16.1.0 is directly connected, Serial0.2
C       172.16.2.0 is directly connected, Ethernet0
C       172.16.3.0 is directly connected, Serial0.1
     10.0.0.0/24 is subnetted, 8 subnets
R       10.1.11.0 [120/1] via 172.16.3.252, 00:00:15, Serial0.1
R       10.1.10.0 [120/1] via 172.16.3.252, 00:00:15, Serial0.1
R       10.1.9.0 [120/1] via 172.16.3.252, 00:00:15, Serial0.1
R       10.1.8.0 [120/1] via 172.16.3.252, 00:00:15, Serial0.1
R       10.1.7.0 [120/1] via 172.16.1.253, 00:00:03, Serial0.2
R       10.1.6.0 [120/1] via 172.16.1.253, 00:00:03, Serial0.2
R       10.1.5.0 [120/1] via 172.16.1.253, 00:00:03, Serial0.2
R       10.1.4.0 [120/1] via 172.16.1.253, 00:00:03, Serial0.2
Albuquerque#
```

As highlighted in Example 7-16, the routing updates include the individual subnets. Therefore, Albuquerque can see routes to all subnets of network 10 and can route packets to the correct destinations in Seville and Yosemite. With autosummarization enabled, Albuquerque would think that both Seville and Yosemite had an equal-metric route to network 10.0.0.0, and some packets would be routed incorrectly.

Route summarization (also called route aggregation) works like autosummarization, except that there is no requirement to summarize into a Class A, B, or C network. Consider the network shown in Figure 7-12. Albuquerque has eight routes to subnets of network 10.0.0.0; four of those routes are learned from Seville. Consider the subnet, broadcast, and assignable addresses in each of the subnets, as shown in Table 7-17.

Table 7-17 *Route Aggregation Comparison of Subnet Numbers*

Subnet	Mask	Broadcast	Assignable Addresses
10.1.4.0	255.255.255.0	10.1.4.255	10.1.4.1 to 10.1.4.254
10.1.5.0	255.255.255.0	10.1.5.255	10.1.5.1 to 10.1.5.254
10.1.6.0	255.255.255.0	10.1.6.255	10.1.6.1 to 10.1.6.254
10.1.7.0	255.255.255.0	10.1.7.255	10.1.7.1 to 10.1.7.254

Now consider the concept of a subnet 10.1.4.0 with mask 255.255.252.0. In this case, 10.1.4.0/22 (the same subnet written differently) has a subnet broadcast address of 10.1.7.255 and assignable addresses of 10.1.4.1 to 10.1.7.254. Because 10.1.4.0/22 includes all the assignable addresses of the original four subnets, a single route to 10.1.4.0/22 is just as good as the four separate routes, assuming that the next-hop information is the same for each of the original four routes.

Route aggregation is simply a tool used to tell a routing protocol to advertise a single, larger subnet rather than individual, smaller subnets. In this case, the routing protocol advertises 10.1.4.0/22 rather than the four individual subnets. Albuquerque's routing table is then smaller. EIGRP and OSPF are the only interior IP routing protocols that support route aggregation.

Example 7-17 shows route summarization of the subnets off Seville. Still using the network shown in Figure 7-12, the routers are all migrated to EIGRP. Example 7-17 shows the EIGRP configuration on Albuquerque, the EIGRP configuration on Seville, and the resulting IP routing table on Albuquerque. (Yosemite is migrated to EIGRP as well; the configuration is not shown because the example shows only aggregation by Seville.)

Example 7-17 *Route Aggregation Example Using EIGRP*

```
On Seville:
router eigrp 9
 Network 10.0.0.0
```

Example 7-17 *Route Aggregation Example Using EIGRP (Continued)*

```
 Network 172.16.0.0
 No auto-summary
!
interface serial 0.1 point-to-point
 ip address 172.16.1.253 255.255.255.0
 frame-relay interface-dlci 901
 ip summary-address eigrp 9 10.1.4.0 255.255.252.0
```

```
On Albuquerque:
router eigrp 9
  network 172.16.0.0
  no auto-summary
Albuquerque#show ip route
Codes: C - connected, S - static, I - IGRP, R - RIP, M - mobile, B - BGP
       D - EIGRP, EX - EIGRP external, O - OSPF, IA - OSPF inter area
       N1 - OSPF NSSA external type 1, N2 - OSPF NSSA external type 2
       E1 - OSPF external type 1, E2 - OSPF external type 2, E - EGP
       i - IS-IS, L1 - IS-IS level-1, L2 - IS-IS level-2, ia - IS-IS inter area
       * - candidate default, U - per-user static route, o - ODR
       P - periodic downloaded static route

Gateway of last resort is not set

     172.16.0.0/24 is subnetted, 3 subnets
C       172.16.1.0 is directly connected, Serial0.2
C       172.16.2.0 is directly connected, Ethenet0
C       172.16.3.0 is directly connected, Serial0.1
     10.0.0.0/8 is variably subnetted, 5 subnets, 2 masks
D       10.1.11.0/24 [120/1] via 172.16.3.252, 00:00:15, Serial0.1
D       10.1.10.0/24 [120/1] via 172.16.3.252, 00:00:15, Serial0.1
D       10.1.9.0/24 [120/1] via 172.16.3.252, 00:00:15, Serial0.1
D       10.1.8.0/24 [120/1] via 172.16.3.252, 00:00:15, Serial0.1
D       10.1.4.0/22 [90/2185984] via 172.16.1.253, 00:00:58, Serial0.2
```

The **ip summary-address** interface subcommand on Seville's Serial0.1 interface is used to define the superset of the subnets that should be advertised. Notice the route in Albuquerque's routing table, which indeed shows 10.1.4.0/22 rather than the four individual subnets.

When summarizing, the superset of the original subnets can actually be smaller than the Class A, B, or C network; larger than the network; or exactly matched to a network. For instance, 192.168.4.0, 192.168.5.0, 192.168.6.0, and 192.168.7.0 can be summarized into 192.168.4.0/22, which represents four consecutive Class C networks. Summarizing when the summarized group is a set of networks is sometimes called *supernetting*.

Table 7-18 lists the features for summarizing the interior IP routing protocols.

Table 7-18 *Interior IP Routing Protocol Summarization Features*

Routing Protocol	Autosummarization Enabled?	Can Autosummarization Be Disabled?	Route Aggregation/ Summarization Allowed?
RIP-1	Yes, by default	No	No
IGRP	Yes, by default	No	No
RIP-2	Yes, by default	Yes	No
Enhanced IGRP	Yes, by default	Yes	Yes
OSPF	No, but the equivalent can be done with aggregation	N/A	Yes

Multiple Routes to the Same Subnet

What if a router learns two routes whose metrics are equal? By default, the Cisco IOS Software supports four equal-cost routes to the same IP subnet in the routing table at the same time. The traffic is balanced across the equal-metric routes on a per-destination address basis by default. You can change the number of equal-cost routes to between 1 and 6 using the **ip maximum-paths** *x* router configuration subcommand, where *x* is the maximum number of routes to any subnet.

The metric formula used for IGRP (and EIGRP) poses an interesting problem when considering equal-metric routes. IGRP can learn more than one route to the same subnet with different metrics; however, the metrics are very likely to never be exactly equal. The **variance** router subcommand is used to define how variable the metrics can be in order for routes to be considered to have equal metrics. For example, if the metric for the better of two routes is 100, and the variance is set to 2, a second route with a metric less than 200 would be considered equal-cost and would be added to the routing table.

For many years, equal-cost routes were treated equally—which seems to make sense. But what if the routes are not really equal and you use variance to add them? Well, with one more router subcommand, you can make the router either always use the truly best route or balance across the routes based on the metrics' ratios. In other words, the **traffic-share min** router IGRP subcommand tells the router to ignore all equal-metric routes in the routing table, except the route that truly has the smallest metric. So why not just add only the truly lowest metric route to the routing table? Well, if the other pretty good routes are in the table, and the best one fails, convergence time is practically instantaneous!

An alternative to using the single, truly best route, even when multiple routes are in the routing table, is to use the **traffic-share balanced** router subcommand. It tells the router to use all the routes proportionally based on the metrics for each route.

End Extra Credit

Troubleshooting Routing and Routing Protocols

Cisco would like all its certification exams—CCNA included—to prove that the test taker can build and troubleshoot live networks. Some people work with Cisco routers daily. Others' job function does not allow frequent access to routers. If the latter description applies to you, you might be trying to pass this certification so that you can move into jobs that involve routers and switches. Regardless, this section gives you some final insights into some tricky problems with routing protocols.

The **show ip route** command has a myriad of options that are helpful when you're troubleshooting a large network. The **show ip protocol** command also can provide some useful information when you're troubleshooting a routing problem. With a small network, most of the options with the **show ip route** command are unnecessary. However, knowing the options and what each can do is useful for your work with larger networks.

Example 6-21 lists the options of the **show ip route** command and gives examples of several of them. Figure 7-13 shows the network; it should look familiar from previous examples. In this case, EIGRP is used between Albuquerque and Seville, and RIP-2 is used between Albuquerque and Yosemite. There is no PVC between Yosemite and Seville. The configurations of the three routers are listed in Examples 7-18, 7-19, and 7-20. Example 7-21 lists the **show ip route** options.

Figure 7-13 *Network Environment for Use with the* **show ip route** *Options*

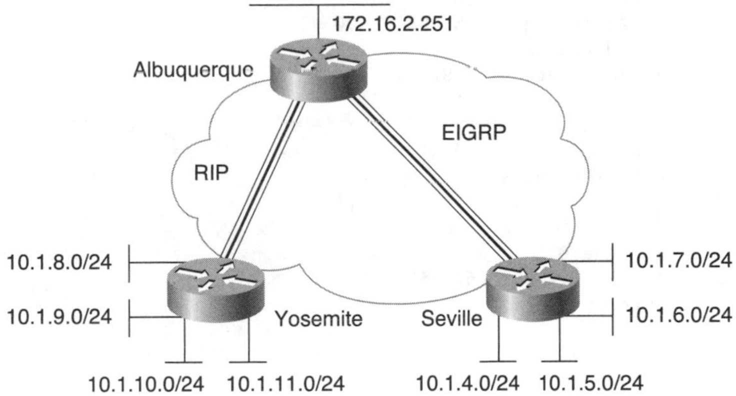

Example 7-18 *Albuquerque Configuration for the* **show ip route** *Options in Example 7-21*

```
Albuquerque#show running-config
Current configuration : 964 bytes
!
version 12.2
```

continues

Example 7-18 *Albuquerque Configuration for the* **show ip route** *Options in Example 7-21 (Continued)*

```
service timestamps debug uptime
service timestamps log uptime
no service password-encryption
!
hostname Albuquerque
!
enable secret 5 $1$J3Fz$QaEYNIiI2aMu.3Ar.q0Xm.
enable password fred
!
ip subnet-zero
no ip domain-lookup
!
interface Serial0
 no ip address
 no ip directed-broadcast
 encapsulation frame-relay IETF
 clockrate 56000
 frame-relay lmi-type cisco
!
interface Serial0.1 point-to-point
 ip address 172.16.3.251 255.255.255.0
 no ip directed-broadcast
 frame-relay interface-dlci 902
!
interface Serial0.2 point-to-point
 ip address 172.16.1.251 255.255.255.0
 no ip directed-broadcast
 frame-relay interface-dlci 903
!
interface Serial1
 no ip address
 no ip directed-broadcast
 shutdown
!
interface Ethernet0
 ip address 172.16.2.251 255.255.255.0
 no ip directed-broadcast
!
router eigrp 9
 passive-interface Serial0.1
 network 172.16.0.0
 no auto-summary
!
router rip
 version 2
 passive-interface Serial0.2
 network 172.16.0.0
 no auto-summary
!
ip classless
no ip http server
!
access-list 1 permit 10.0.0.0 0.255.255.255
```

Example 7-19 *Yosemite Configuration for the* **show ip route** *Options in Example 7-21*

```
Yosemite#show running-config
Current configuration : 968 bytes
!
version 12.2
service timestamps debug uptime
service timestamps log uptime
no service password-encryption
!
hostname Yosemite
!
enable secret 5 $1$J3Fz$QaEYNIiI2aMu.3Ar.q0Xm.
!
ip subnet-zero
no ip domain-lookup
!
interface Serial0
 no ip address
 no ip directed-broadcast
 encapsulation frame-relay IETF
 no fair-queue
 frame-relay lmi-type cisco
!
interface Serial0.1 point-to-point
 ip address 172.16.3.252 255.255.255.0
 no ip directed-broadcast
 frame-relay interface-dlci 901
!
interface Serial1
 no ip address
 no ip directed-broadcast
 shutdown
!
!
interface Ethernet0
 ip address 10.1.8.253 255.255.255.0
!
interface Ethernet1
 ip address 10.1.9.253 255.255.255.0
!
interface Ethernet2
 ip address 10.1.10.253 255.255.255.0
!
interface Ethernet3
 ip address 10.1.11.253 255.255.255.0
!
router rip
 version 2
 network 10.0.0.0
 network 172.16.0.0
 no auto-summary
!
ip classless
no ip http server
```

Example 7-20 *Seville Configuration for the* **show ip route** *Options in Example 7-21*

```
Seville#show running-config
Current configuration : 960 bytes
!
version 12.2
service timestamps debug uptime
service timestamps log uptime
no service password-encryption
!
hostname Seville
!
enable secret 5 $1$J3Fz$QaEYNIiI2aMu.3Ar.q0Xm.
!
ip subnet-zero
no ip domain-lookup
!
interface Serial0
 no ip address
 no ip directed-broadcast
 encapsulation frame-relay IETF
 no fair-queue
 frame-relay lmi-type cisco
!
interface Serial0.1 multipoint
 ip address 172.16.1.253 255.255.255.0
 no ip directed-broadcast
 ip summary-address eigrp 9 10.1.4.0 255.255.252.0
 frame-relay interface-dlci 901
!
interface Serial1
 no ip address
 no ip directed-broadcast
 shutdown
!
interface Ethernet0
 ip address 10.1.4.253 255.255.255.0
!
interface Ethernet1
 ip address 10.1.5.253 255.255.255.0
!
interface Ethernet2
 ip address 10.1.6.253 255.255.255.0
!
interface Ethernet3
 ip address 10.1.7.253 255.255.255.0
!
router eigrp 9
 network 10.0.0.0
 network 172.16.0.0
 no auto-summary
!
ip classless
no ip http server
```

Example 7-21 **show ip route**: *Albuquerque*

```
Albuquerque#show ip route
Codes: C - connected, S - static, I - IGRP, R - RIP, M - mobile, B - BGP
       D - EIGRP, EX - EIGRP external, O - OSPF, IA - OSPF inter area
       N1 - OSPF NSSA external type 1, N2 - OSPF NSSA external type 2
       E1 - OSPF external type 1, E2 - OSPF external type 2, E - EGP
       i - IS-IS, L1 - IS-IS level-1, L2 - IS-IS level-2, ia - IS-IS inter area
       * - candidate default, U - per-user static route, o - ODR
       P - periodic downloaded static route

Gateway of last resort is not set

     172.16.0.0/24 is subnetted, 3 subnets
C       172.16.1.0 is directly connected, Serial0.2
C       172.16.2.0 is directly connected, Ethernet0
C       172.16.3.0 is directly connected, Serial0.1
     10.0.0.0/8 is variably subnetted, 5 subnets, 2 masks
R       10.1.11.0/24 [120/1] via 172.16.3.252, 00:00:17, Serial0.1
R       10.1.10.0/24 [120/1] via 172.16.3.252, 00:00:17, Serial0.1
R       10.1.9.0/24 [120/1] via 172.16.3.252, 00:00:17, Serial0.1
R       10.1.8.0/24 [120/1] via 172.16.3.252, 00:00:17, Serial0.1
D       10.1.4.0/22 [90/2185984] via 172.16.1.253, 00:28:01, Serial0.2

Albuquerque#show ip route ?
   Hostname or A.B.C.D  Network to display information about or hostname
  bgp                   Border Gateway Protocol (BGP)
  connected             Connected
  egp                   Exterior Gateway Protocol (EGP)
  eigrp                 Enhanced Interior Gateway Routing Protocol (EIGRP)
  igrp                  Interior Gateway Routing Protocol (IGRP)
  isis                  ISO IS-IS
  list                  IP Access list
  mobile                Mobile routes
  odr                   On Demand stub Routes
  ospf                  Open Shortest Path First (OSPF)
  profile               IP routing table profile
  rip                   Routing Information Protocol (RIP)
  static                Static routes
  summary               Summary of all routes
  supernets-only        Show supernet entries only
  vrf                   Display routes from a VPN Routing/Forwarding instance
  |                     Output modifiers


Albuquerque#show ip route 10.1.5.8
Routing entry for 10.1.4.0/22
  Known via "eigrp 9", distance 90, metric 2185984, type internal
  Redistributing via eigrp 9
  Last update from 172.16.1.253 on Serial0.2, 00:28:36 ago
  Routing Descriptor Blocks:
  * 172.16.1.253, from 172.16.1.253, 00:28:36 ago, via Serial0.2
      Route metric is 2185984, traffic share count is 1
      Total delay is 20630 microseconds, minimum bandwidth is 1544 Kbit
```

continues

Example 7-21 show ip route: *Albuquerque (Continued)*

```
            Reliability 255/255, minimum MTU 1500 bytes
            Loading 1/255, Hops 1

Albuquerque#show ip route rip
     10.0.0.0/8 is variably subnetted, 5 subnets, 2 masks
R       10.1.11.0/24 [120/1] via 172.16.3.252, 00:00:22, Serial0.1
R       10.1.10.0/24 [120/1] via 172.16.3.252, 00:00:22, Serial0.1
R       10.1.9.0/24 [120/1] via 172.16.3.252, 00:00:22, Serial0.1
R       10.1.8.0/24 [120/1] via 172.16.3.252, 00:00:22, Serial0.1
Albuquerque#show ip route igrp

Albuquerque#show ip route eigrp
     10.0.0.0/8 is variably subnetted, 5 subnets, 2 masks
D       10.1.4.0/22 [90/2185984] via 172.16.1.253, 00:29:42, Serial0.2

Albuquerque#show ip route connected
     172.16.0.0/24 is subnetted, 3 subnets
C       172.16.1.0 is directly connected, Serial0.2
C       172.16.2.0 is directly connected, Ethernet0
C       172.16.3.0 is directly connected, Serial0.1

Albuquerque#show ip route list 1
     10.0.0.0/8 is variably subnetted, 5 subnets, 2 masks
R       10.1.11.0/24 [120/1] via 172.16.3.252, 00:00:22, Serial0.1
R       10.1.10.0/24 [120/1] via 172.16.3.252, 00:00:22, Serial0.1
R       10.1.9.0/24 [120/1] via 172.16.3.252, 00:00:22, Serial0.1
R       10.1.8.0/24 [120/1] via 172.16.3.252, 00:00:22, Serial0.1
D       10.1.4.0/22 [90/2185984] via 172.16.1.253, 00:29:58, Serial0.2

Albuquerque#show ip route summary
Route Source    Networks    Subnets     Overhead    Memory (bytes)
connected       0           3           156         420
static          0           0           0           0
rip             0           4           208         560
eigrp 9         0           1           52          140
internal        2                                   2320
Total           2           8           416         3440

Albuquerque#show ip route supernet
Codes: C - connected, S - static, I - IGRP, R - RIP, M - mobile, B - BGP
       D - EIGRP, EX - EIGRP external, O - OSPF, IA - OSPF inter area
       N1 - OSPF NSSA external type 1, N2 - OSPF NSSA external type 2
       E1 - OSPF external type 1, E2 - OSPF external type 2, E - EGP
       i - IS-IS, L1 - IS-IS level-1, L2 - IS-IS level-2, * - candidate default
       U - per-user static route, o - ODR

Gateway of last resort is not set
```

The **show ip route** command with no options has been seen many times in this book. A review of some of the more important bits of the output is in order; most comments refer to a highlighted portion. First, the legend at the beginning of Example 7-21 defines the letter codes that identify the source of the routing information—for example, **C** for connected routes, **R** for RIP, and **I** for IGRP. Each of the Class A, B, and C networks is listed, along with each of the subnets of that network. If a static mask is used within that network, the mask is shown only in the line referring to the network (as is the case in Example 7-21, network 172.16.0.0). If the network uses VLSM, as network 10.0.0.0 appears to do because of the route summarization done by Seville, the mask information is listed on the lines referring to each of the individual subnets.

Each routing entry lists the subnet number and the outgoing interface. In most cases, the next-hop router's IP address is also listed. The outgoing interface is needed so that the router can choose the type of data link header to use to encapsulate the packet before transmission on that interface. The next-hop router's IP address is needed on interfaces for which the router needs the IP address so that it can find the associated data-link address to put in the newly built data link header. For instance, knowing the next-hop IP address of 172.16.3.252, Yosemite's IP address on the Frame Relay VC allows Albuquerque to find the corresponding DLCI in the Frame Relay map.

The numbers in brackets in the **show ip route** output for each route are interesting. The second number in brackets represents the metric value for this route. The first number defines the administrative distance.

Administrative distance is important only if multiple IP routing protocols are in use in a single router. When this is true, both routing protocols can learn routes to the same subnets. Because their metric values are different (for example, hop count or a function of bandwidth and delay), there is no way to know which routing protocol's routes are better. Therefore, Cisco supplies a method of defining which routing protocol's routes are better. The Cisco IOS Software implements this concept using something called *administrative distance*.

Administrative distance is an integer value; a value is assigned to each source of routing information. The lower the administrative distance, the better the source of routing information. IGRP's default is 100, OSPF's is 110, RIP's is 120, and EIGRP's is 90. The value 100 in brackets in the **show ip route** output signifies that the administrative distance used for IGRP routes is 100. In other words, the default value is in use. So, if RIP and IGRP are both used, and if both learn routes to the same subnets, only IGRP's routing information for those subnets is added to the routing table. If RIP learns about a subnet that IGRP does not know about, that route is added to the routing table.

Moving down Example 7-21, the **show ip route ?** command lists several options, many of which are shown in the ensuing commands in the example. You can limit the **show ip route** output to the routes learned by a particular routing protocol by referring to that routing protocol. Likewise, the output can be limited to show just connected routes.

One of the more important options for the **show ip route** command is to simply pass an IP address as the last parameter. This tells the router to perform routing table lookup, just as it would for a packet destined for that address. In Example 7-21, **show ip route 10.1.5.8** returns a set of messages, the first of which identifies the route to 10.1.4.0/22 as the route matched in the routing table. The route that is matched is listed so that you can always know the route that would be used by this router to reach a particular IP address.

Finally, another feature of **show ip route** that is useful in large networks is filtering the command's output based on an access list. Notice the command **show ip route list 1** in Example 7-21. Access list 1 is configured so that any route with information about network 10.0.0.0 is matched (permitted by the access list) and all others are denied. By referring to the access list, the **show ip route** output is filtered, showing only a portion of the routes. This is particularly useful when there are many routes in the routing table.

The many options of the **show ip route** command can be particularly useful for troubleshooting larger networks.

Foundation Summary

The Foundation Summary is a collection of tables that provides a convenient review of many key concepts in this chapter. If you are already comfortable with the topics in this chapter, this summary can help you recall a few details. If you just read this chapter, this review should help solidify some key facts. If you are doing your final preparation before the exam, these tables are a convenient way to review the day before the exam.

Table 7-19 lists some of the routing protocol terms you need to know for the CCNA exam.

Table 7-19 *Routing Protocol Terminology*

Term	Definition
Routing protocol	A protocol whose purpose is to learn the available routes, place the best routes into the routing table, and remove routes when they are no longer valid.
Exterior routing protocol	A routing protocol designed for use between two different networks that are under the control of two different organizations. These are typically used between ISPs or between a company and an ISP. For instance, a company would run BGP, an exterior routing protocol, between one of its routers and a router inside an ISP.
Interior routing protocol	A routing protocol designed for use in a network whose parts are under the control of a single organization. For example, an entire company might choose the IGRP routing protocol, which is an interior routing protocol.
Distance vector	The logic behind the behavior of some Interior routing protocols, such as RIP and IGRP.
Link state	The logic behind the behavior of some interior routing protocols, such as OSPF.
Balanced hybrid	The logic behind the behavior of EIGRP, which is more like distance vector than link state but is different from these other two types of routing protocols.
Dijkstra Shortest-Path First (SPF) algorithm	Magic math used by link-state protocols, such as OSPF, when the routing table is calculated.

continues

Table 7-19 *Routing Protocol Terminology (Continued)*

Term	Definition
DUAL	The process by which EIGRP routers collectively calculate routing tables.
Convergence	The time required for routers to react to changes in the network, removing bad routes and adding new, better routes so that the currently best routes are in all the routers' routing tables.

Table 7-20 lists interior IP routing protocols and their types. A column referring to whether the routing protocol includes subnet mask information in the routing updates is listed for future reference.

Table 7-20 *Interior IP Routing Protocols and Types*

Routing Protocol	Type	Loop-Prevention Mechanisms	Mask Sent in Updates, Which Allows VLSM?
RIP-1	Distance vector	Hold-down timer, split horizon	No
RIP-2	Distance vector	Hold-down timer, split horizon	Yes
IGRP	Distance vector	Hold-down timer, split horizon	No
EIGRP	Balanced hybrid	DUAL and feasible successors	Yes
OSPF	Link-state	Dijkstra SPF algorithm and full topology knowledge	Yes

Table 7-21 summarizes distance vector routing issues and describes solutions.

Table 7-21 *Issues Relating to Distance Vector Routing Protocols in a Network with Multiple Paths*

Issue	Solution
Multiple routes to the same subnet have equal metrics	Implementation options involve either using the first route learned or putting multiple routes to the same subnet in the routing table.

Table 7-21 *Issues Relating to Distance Vector Routing Protocols in a Network with Multiple Paths (Continued)*

Issue	Solution
Routing loops occur due to updates passing each other over a single link	**Split horizon**—The routing protocol advertises routes out an interface only if they were not learned from updates entering that interface. **Split horizon with poison reverse**—The routing protocol uses split-horizon rules unless a route fails. In that case, the route is advertised out all interfaces, but with infinite-distance metrics.
Routing loops occur due to updates passing each other over alternative paths	**Route poisoning**—When a route to a subnet fails, the subnet is advertised with an infinite-distance metric.
Counting to infinity	**Hold-down timer**—After finding out that a route to a subnet has failed, a router waits a certain period of time before believing any other routing information about that subnet. **Triggered updates**—When a route fails, an update is sent immediately rather than waiting on the update timer to expire. Used in conjunction with route poisoning, this ensures that all routers know of failed routes before any hold-down timers can expire.

Table 7-22 outlines the features of RIP and IGRP.

Table 7-22 *RIP and IGRP Feature Comparison*

Feature	RIP (Default)	IGRP (Default)
Update timer	30 seconds	90 seconds
Metric	Hop count	Function of bandwidth and delay (the default). Can include reliability, load, and MTU.
Hold-down timer	180	280
Flash (triggered) updates	Yes	Yes
Mask sent in update	No for RIP-1; yes for RIP-2	No
Infinite-metric value	16	4,294,967,295

Tables 7-23 and 7-24 summarize the more-popular commands used for RIP and IGRP configuration and verification.

Table 7-23 *IP RIP and IGRP Configuration Commands*

Command	Configuration Mode
router rip	Global
router igrp *as-number*	Global
network *net-number*	Router subcommand
passive-interface [**default**] {*interface-type interface-number*}	Router subcommand
maximum-paths *number-paths*	Router subcommand
variance *multiplier*	Router subcommand
traffic-share {*balanced* | *min*}	Router subcommand

Table 7-24 *IP RIP and IGRP EXEC Commands*

Command	Function
show ip route [*ip-address* [*mask*] [**longer-prefixes**]] | [*protocol* [*process-id*]]	Shows the entire routing table, or a subset if parameters are entered.
show ip protocols	Shows routing protocol parameters and current timer values.
debug ip rip	Issues log messages for each RIP update.
debug ip igrp transactions [*ip-address*]	Issues log messages with details of the IGRP updates.
debug ip igrp events [*ip-address*]	Issues log messages for each IGRP packet.
ping [*protocol* | **tag**] {*host-name* | *system-address*}	Sends and receives ICMP echo messages to verify connectivity.
trace [*protocol*] [*destination*]	Sends a series of ICMP echoes with increasing TTL values to verify the current route to a host.

Table 7-25 summarizes RIP-2 features.

Table 7-25 *RIP-2 Features*

Feature	Description
Transmits a subnet mask with the route	This feature allows VLSM by passing the mask along with each route so that the subnet is exactly defined.
Provides authentication	Both clear text (RFC-defined) and MD5 encryption (a Cisco-added feature) can be used to authenticate the source of a routing update.
Includes a next-hop router IP address in its routing update	A router can advertise a route but direct any listeners to a different router on that same subnet. This is done only when the other router has a better route.
Uses external route tags	RIP can pass information about routes learned from an external source and redistributed into RIP.
Provides multicast routing updates	Instead of sending updates to 255.255.255.255, the destination IP address is 224.0.0.9, an IP multicast address. This reduces the amount of processing required on non-RIP-speaking hosts on a common subnet.

Table 7-26 lists the features for summarization of the interior IP routing protocols.

Table 7-26 *Interior IP Routing Protocol Summarization Features*

Routing Protocol	Autosummarization Enabled?	Can Autosummarization Be Disabled?	Route Aggregation/ Summarization Allowed?
RIP-1	Yes, by default	No	No
IGRP	Yes, by default	No	No
RIP-2	Yes, by default	Yes	No
Enhanced IGRP	Yes, by default	Yes	Yes
OSPF	No, but the equivalent can be done with aggregation	N/A	Yes

Q&A

As mentioned in Chapter 1, "All About the Cisco Certified Network Associate Certification," the questions and scenarios in this book are more difficult than what you should experience on the exam. The questions do not attempt to cover more breadth or depth than the exam, but they are designed to make sure that you know the answer. Rather than allowing you to derive the answer from clues hidden in the question, the questions challenge your understanding and recall of the subject. Questions from the "Do I Know This Already?" quiz at the beginning of this chapter are repeated here to ensure that you have mastered this chapter's topics. Hopefully these questions will help limit the number of exam questions on which you narrow your choices to two options and then guess.

The answers to these questions can be found in Appendix A.

1 What type of routing protocol algorithm uses a hold-down timer? What is its purpose?

2 Define what split horizon means to the contents of a routing update. Does this apply to both the distance vector algorithm and the link-state algorithm?

3 Write down the steps you would take to migrate from RIP to IGRP in a router whose current RIP configuration includes only **router rip** followed by a **network 10.0.0.0** command.

4 How does the Cisco IOS Software designate a subnet in the routing table as a directly connected network? What about a route learned with IGRP or RIP?

5 Create a configuration for IGRP on a router with these interfaces and addresses: e0 using 10.1.1.1, e1 using 224.1.2.3, s0 using 10.1.2.1, and s1 using 199.1.1.1. Use process ID 5

____

____

____

6 Create a configuration for IGRP on a router with these interfaces and addresses: to0 using 200.1.1.1, e0 using 128.1.3.2, s0 using 192.0.1.1, and s1 using 223.254.254.1.

____

____

____

7 From a router's user mode, without using debugs or privileged mode, how can you determine what routers are sending you routing updates?

____

____

____

8 If the command **router rip** followed by **network 10.0.0.0**, with no other **network** commands, is configured in a router that has an Ethernet0 interface with IP address 168.10.1.1, does RIP send updates out Ethernet0?

____

____

____

9 If the commands **router igrp 1** and **network 10.0.0.0** are configured in a router that has an Ethernet0 interface with IP address 168.10.1.1, does IGRP advertise 168.10.0.0?

____

____

____

10 If the commands **router igrp 1** and **network 10.0.0.0** are configured in a router that has an Ethernet0 interface with IP address 168.10.1.1, mask 255.255.255.0, does this router have a route to 168.10.1.0?

____

____

____

11 Must IGRP metrics for multiple routes to the same subnet be exactly equal for the multiple routes to be added to the routing table? If not, how close in value do the metrics have to be?

12 When you're using RIP, what configuration command controls the number of equal-cost routes that can be added to the routing table at the same time? What is the maximum number of equal-cost routes to the same destination that can be included in the IP routing table at once?

13 When you're using IGRP, what configuration command controls the number of equal-cost routes that can be added to the routing table at the same time? What is the maximum number of equal-cost routes to the same destination that can be included in the IP routing table at once?

14 What feature supported by RIP-2 allows it to support variable-length subnet masks (VLSM)?

15 Name three features of RIP-2 that are not features of RIP-1.

16 What configuration commands are different between a router configured for RIP-1 and a router configured for only the support of RIP-2?

17 List the interior IP routing protocols that have autosummarization enabled by default. Which of these protocols allow autosummarization to be disabled using a configuration command?

18 Which interior IP routing protocols support route aggregation?

19 Which command lists all IP routes learned via RIP?

20 Which command or commands list all IP routes in network 172.16.0.0?

21 Assume that several subnets of network 172.16.0.0 exist in a router's routing table. What must be true about those routes so that the output of the **show ip route** command lists mask information only on the line that lists network 172.16.0.0 but doesn't show mask information on each route for each subnet?

22 True or false: Distance vector routing protocols learn routes by transmitting routing updates.

23 Assume that a router is configured to allow only one route in the routing table to each destination network. If more than one route to a particular subnet is learned, and if each route has the same metric value, which route is placed in the routing table if the routing protocol uses distance vector logic?

____

____

____

24 Describe the purpose and meaning of route poisoning.

____

____

____

25 Describe the meaning and purpose of triggered updates.

____

____

____

26 What term describes the underlying logic behind the OSPF routing protocol?

____

____

____

Scenarios

Scenario 7-1: IP Configuration 1

Your job is to deploy a new network. The network engineering group has provided a list of addresses and a network diagram, as shown in Figure 7-14 and Table 7-27.

Figure 7-14 *Scenario 7-1 Network Diagram*

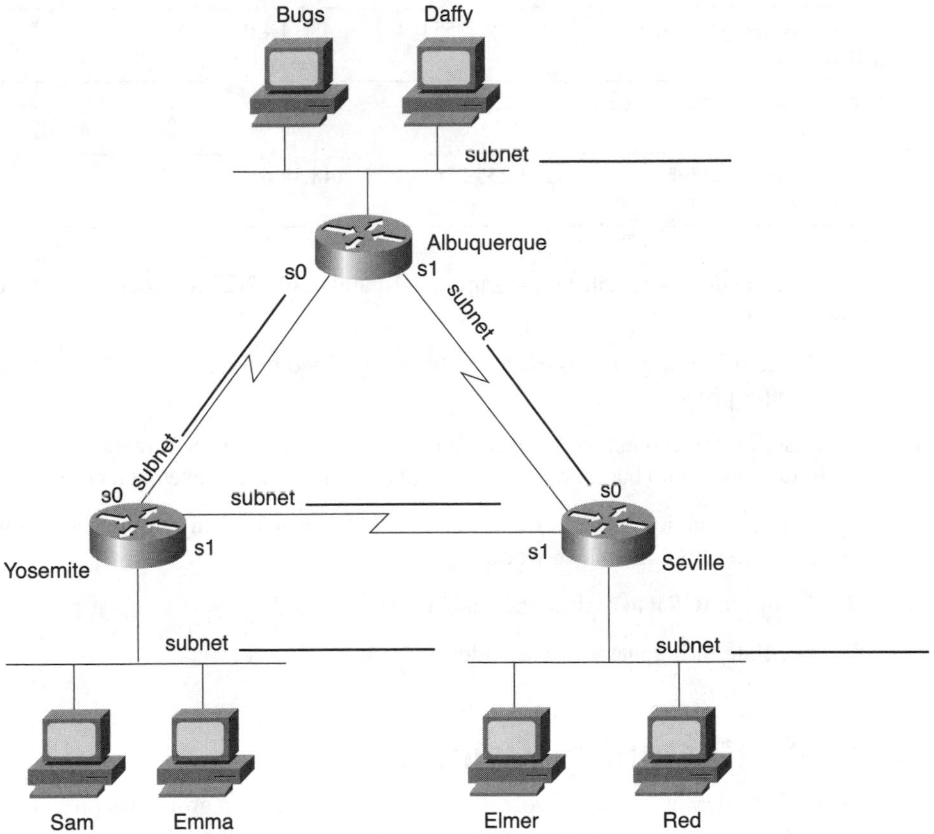

Table 7-27 *Scenario 7-1 IP Addresses*

Location of Subnet Geographically	Subnet Mask	Subnet Number	Subnet Broadcast
Ethernet off router in Albuquerque	255.255.255.0	148.14.1.0	
Ethernet off router in Yosemite	255.255.255.0	148.14.2.0	
Ethernet off router in Seville	255.255.255.0	148.14.3.0	
Serial between Albuquerque and Yosemite	255.255.255.0	148.14.4.0	
Serial between Albuquerque and Seville	255.255.255.0	148.14.5.0	
Serial between Seville and Yosemite	255.255.255.0	148.14.6.0	

Assuming the details established in Figure 7-14 and Table 7-27 for Scenario 7-1, complete or answer the following:

1. Create the configurations to enable IP as described in Table 7-27. Choose IP addresses as appropriate.
2. Describe the contents of the routing table on Seville after the routers are installed and all interfaces are up but no routing protocols or static routes have been configured.
3. Configure static routes for each router so that any host in any subnet can communicate with other hosts in this network.
4. Configure IGRP to replace the static routes in task 3.
5. Calculate the subnet broadcast address for each subnet.

Scenario 7-2: IP Configuration 2

Your job is to deploy a new network. The network engineering group has provided a list of addresses and a network diagram, with Frame Relay global DLCIs, as shown in Figure 7-15 and Table 7-28.

Figure 7-15 *Scenario 7-2 Network Diagram*

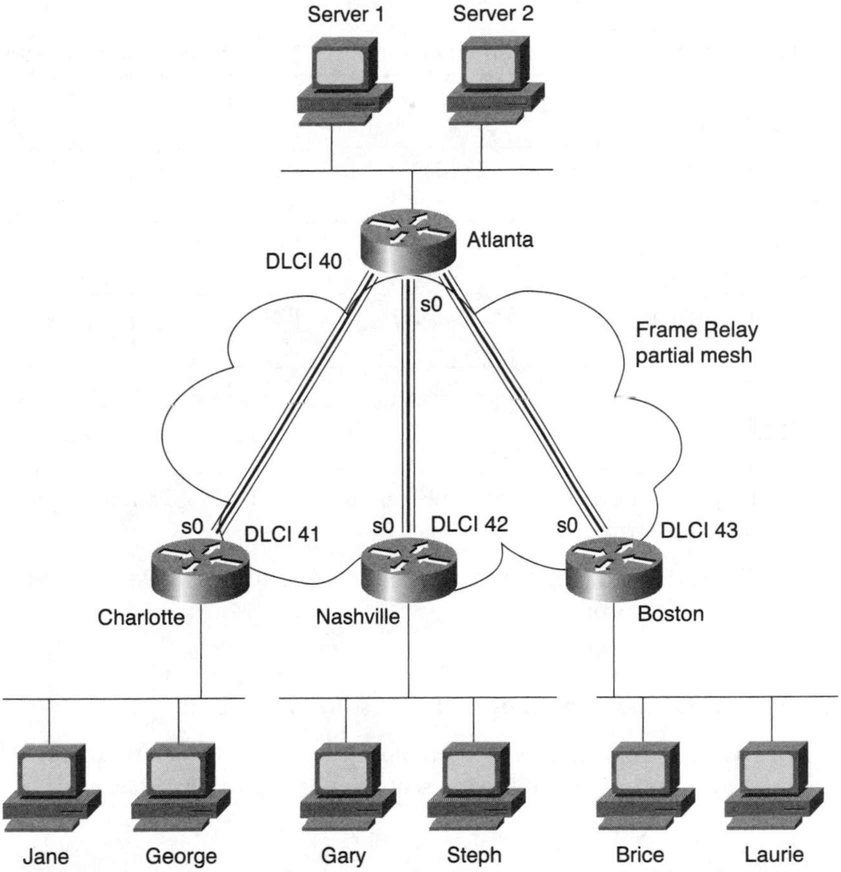

Table 7-28 *Scenario 7-2 IP Addresses*

Location of Subnet Geographically	Subnet Mask	Subnet Number	Subnet Broadcast
Ethernet off router in Atlanta	255.255.255.0	10.1.1.0	
Ethernet off router in Charlotte	255.255.255.0	10.1.2.0	

continues

Table 7-28 *Scenario 7-2 IP Addresses (Continued)*

Location of Subnet Geographically	Subnet Mask	Subnet Number	Subnet Broadcast
Ethernet off router in Nashville	255.255.255.0	10.1.3.0	
Ethernet off router in Boston	255.255.255.0	10.1.4.0	
VC between Atlanta and Charlotte	255.255.255.0	10.2.1.0	
VC between Atlanta and Nashville	255.255.255.0	10.2.2.0	
VC between Atlanta and Boston	255.255.255.0	10.2.3.0	

Assuming the details established in Figure 7-15 and Table 7-28 for Scenario 7-2, complete or answer the following:

1. Create the configurations to enable IP as described in Table 7-28. Do not enable a routing protocol.
2. Configure RIP.
3. Calculate the subnet broadcast address for each subnet.
4. Describe the contents of the RIP update sent from Boston to Atlanta. Also describe the contents of the RIP update sent from Atlanta to Charlotte.

Scenario 7-3: IP Addressing and Subnet Derivation

Complete the tasks and answer the questions following the upcoming figures and examples. Figure 7-16 shows the network diagram for Scenario 7-3, and Examples 7-22, 7-23, and 7-24 contain **show** command output from the three routers. Use Table 7-29 to record the subnet numbers and broadcast addresses as directed in the upcoming tasks.

Figure 7-16 *Scenario 7-3 Network Diagram*

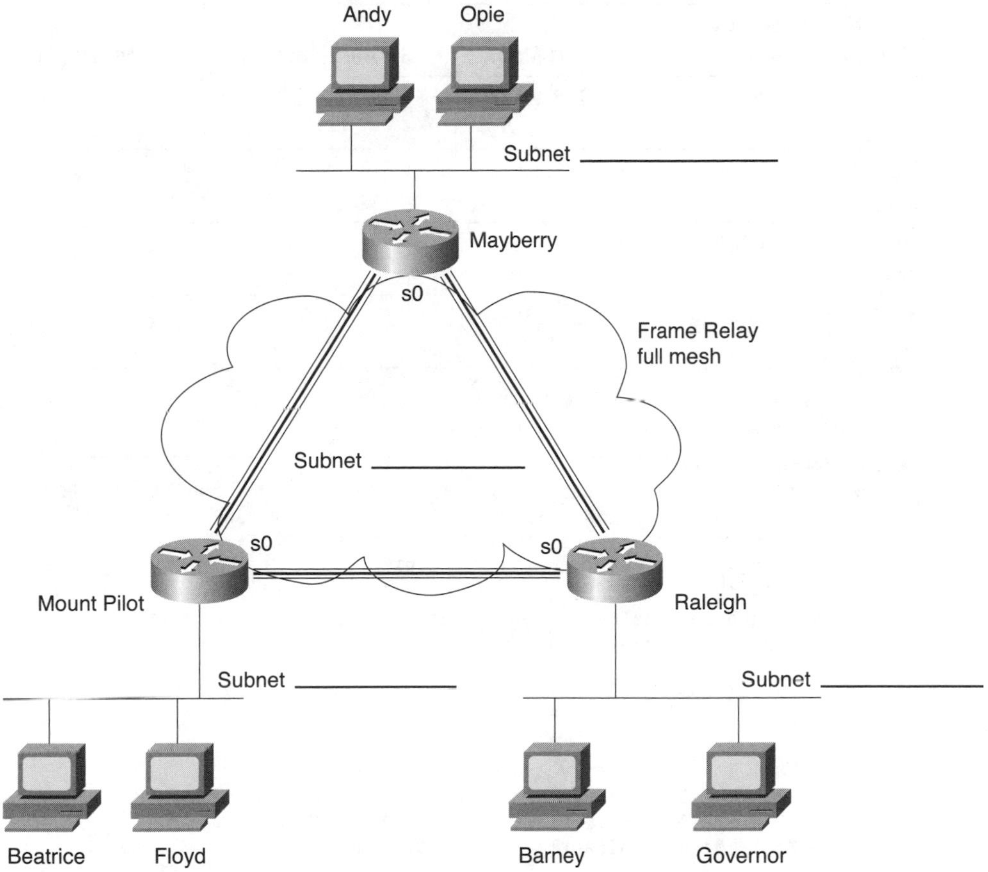

Table 7-29 *Subnets and Broadcast Addresses*

Location of Subnet Geographically	Subnet Mask	Subnet Number	Subnet Broadcast
Ethernet off router in Mayberry	255.255.255.0		
Ethernet off router in Mount Pilot	255.255.255.0		

continues

Table 7-29 *Subnets and Broadcast Addresses (Continued)*

Location of Subnet Geographically	Subnet Mask	Subnet Number	Subnet Broadcast
Ethernet off router in Raleigh	255.255.255.0		
VC between Mayberry and Mount Pilot	255.255.255.0		
VC between Mayberry and Raleigh	255.255.255.0		
VC between Mount Pilot and Raleigh	255.255.255.0		

Example 7-22 *Scenario 7-3:* **show** *Commands on Router Mayberry*

```
Mayberry#show ip route
Codes: C - connected, S - static, I - IGRP, R - RIP, M - mobile, B - BGP
       D - EIGRP, EX - EIGRP external, O - OSPF, IA - OSPF inter area
       N1 - OSPF NSSA external type 1, N2 - OSPF NSSA external type 2
       E1 - OSPF external type 1, E2 - OSPF external type 2, E - EGP
       i - IS-IS, L1 - IS-IS level-1, L2 - IS-IS level-2, ia - IS-IS inter area
       * - candidate default, U - per-user static route, o - ODR
       P - periodic downloaded static route

Gateway of last resort is not set

     170.1.0.0/24 is subnetted, 4 subnets
C       170.1.1.0 is directly connected, Serial0
I       170.1.103.0 [100/8539] via 170.1.1.3, 00:00:50, Serial0
I       170.1.102.0 [100/8539] via 170.1.1.2, 00:00:32, Serial0
C       170.1.101.0 is directly connected, Ethernet0

Mayberry#show ip interface brief
Interface              IP-Address      OK? Method Status                Protocol
Serial0                170.1.1.1       YES NVRAM  up                    up
Serial1                10.1.6.251      YES NVRAM  administratively down down
Ethernet0             170.1.101.1     YES NVRAM  up                    up

Mayberry#debug ip igrp transactions
IGRP protocol debugging is on
Mayberry#debug ip igrp events
IGRP event debugging is on
Mayberry#
IGRP: received update from 170.1.1.3 on Serial0
      subnet 170.1.1.0, metric 10476 (neighbor 8476)
      subnet 170.1.103.0, metric 8539 (neighbor 688)
      subnet 170.1.102.0, metric 10539 (neighbor 8539)
      subnet 170.1.101.0, metric 10539 (neighbor 8539)
IGRP: Update contains 4 interior, 0 system, and 0 exterior routes.
IGRP: Total routes in update: 4
```

Example 7-22 *Scenario 7-3:* **show** *Commands on Router Mayberry (Continued)*

```
IGRP: received update from 170.1.1.2 on Serial0
      subnet 170.1.1.0, metric 10476 (neighbor 8476)
      subnet 170.1.103.0, metric 10539 (neighbor 8539)
      subnet 170.1.102.0, metric 8539 (neighbor 688)
      subnet 170.1.101.0, metric 10539 (neighbor 8539)
IGRP: Update contains 4 interior, 0 system, and 0 exterior routes.
IGRP: Total routes in update: 4
IGRP: sending update to 255.255.255.255 via Serial0 (170.1.1.1)
      subnet 170.1.1.0, metric=8476
      subnet 170.1.103.0, metric=8539
      subnet 170.1.102.0, metric=8539
      subnet 170.1.101.0, metric=688
IGRP: Update contains 4 interior, 0 system, and 0 exterior routes.
IGRP: Total routes in update: 4
IGRP: sending update to 255.255.255.255 via Ethernet0 (170.1.101.1)
      subnet 170.1.1.0, metric=8476
      subnet 170.1.103.0, metric=8539
      subnet 170.1.102.0, metric=8539
IGRP: Update contains 3 interior, 0 system, and 0 exterior routes.
IGRP: Total routes in update:
```

Example 7-23 *Scenario 7-3:* **show** *Commands on Router Mount Pilot*

```
MountPilot#show frame-relay pvc

PVC Statistics for interface Serial0 (Frame Relay DTE)

DLCI = 47, DLCI USAGE = LOCAL, PVC STATUS = ACTIVE, INTERFACE = Serial0

  input pkts 38           output pkts 37           in bytes 3758
  out bytes 3514          dropped pkts 0           in FECN pkts 0
  in BECN pkts 0          out FECN pkts 0          out BECN pkts 0
  in DE pkts 0            out DE pkts 0
  out bcast pkts 36        out bcast bytes 3436
  pvc create time 00:17:39, last time pvc status changed 00:17:39

DLCI = 49, DLCI USAGE = LOCAL, PVC STATUS = ACTIVE, INTERFACE = Serial0

  input pkts 31           output pkts 31           in bytes 3054
  out bytes 3076          dropped pkts 0           in FECN pkts 0
  in BECN pkts 0          out FECN pkts 0          out BECN pkts 0
  in DE pkts 0            out DE pkts 0
  out bcast pkts 31        out bcast bytes 3076
  pvc create time 00:17:40, last time pvc status changed 00:16:40

MountPilot#show frame-relay map

Serial0 (up): ip 170.1.1.1 dlci 47(0x2F,0x8F0), dynamic,
              broadcast,, status defined, active
Serial0 (up): ip 170.1.1.3 dlci 49(0x31,0xC10), dynamic,
              broadcast,, status defined, active
```

continues

Example 7-23 *Scenario 7-3:* **show** *Commands on Router Mount Pilot*

```
MontPilot#debug ip igrp packet
IGRP: sending update to 255.255.255.255 via Serial0 (170.1.1.2)
      subnet 170.1.1.0, metric=8476
      subnet 170.1.103.0, metric=8539
      subnet 170.1.102.0, metric=688
      subnet 170.1.101.0, metric=8539
IGRP: Update contains 4 interior, 0 system, and 0 exterior routes.
IGRP: Total routes in update: 4
IGRP: sending update to 255.255.255.255 via Ethernet0 (170.1.102.2)
      subnet 170.1.1.0, metric=8476
      subnet 170.1.103.0, metric=8539
      subnet 170.1.101.0, metric=8539
IGRP: Update contains 3 interior, 0 system, and 0 exterior routes.
IGRP: Total routes in update: 3
IGRP: received update from 170.1.1.1 on Serial0
      subnet 170.1.1.0, metric 10476 (neighbor 8476)
      subnet 170.1.103.0, metric 10539 (neighbor 8539)
      subnet 170.1.102.0, metric 10539 (neighbor 8539)
      subnet 170.1.101.0, metric 8539 (neighbor 688)
IGRP: Update contains 4 interior, 0 system, and 0 exterior routes.
IGRP: Total routes in update: 4
IGRP: received update from 170.1.1.3 on Serial0
      subnet 170.1.1.0, metric 10476 (neighbor 8476)
      subnet 170.1.103.0, metric 8539 (neighbor 688)
      subnet 170.1.102.0, metric 10539 (neighbor 8539)
      subnet 170.1.101.0, metric 10539 (neighbor 8539)
IGRP: Update contains 4 interior, 0 system, and 0 exterior routes.
IGRP: Total routes in update: 4

%FR-5-DLCICHANGE: Interface Serial0 - DLCI 47 state changed to DELETED
MountPilot#

IGRP: received update from 170.1.1.3 on Serial0
      subnet 170.1.1.0, metric 10476 (neighbor 8476)
      subnet 170.1.103.0, metric 8539 (neighbor 688)
      subnet 170.1.102.0, metric 10539 (neighbor 8539)
      subnet 170.1.101.0, metric 10539 (neighbor 8539)
IGRP: Update contains 4 interior, 0 system, and 0 exterior routes.
IGRP: Total routes in update: 4
```

Example 7-24 *Scenario 7-3:* **show** *Commands on Router Raleigh*

```
Raleigh#show ip route
Codes: C - connected, S - static, I - IGRP, R - RIP, M - mobile, B - BGP
       D - EIGRP, EX - EIGRP external, O - OSPF, IA - OSPF inter area
       N1 - OSPF NSSA external type 1, N2 - OSPF NSSA external type 2
       E1 - OSPF external type 1, E2 - OSPF external type 2, E - EGP
       i - IS-IS, L1 - IS-IS level-1, L2 - IS-IS level-2, ia - IS-IS inter area
       * - candidate default, U - per-user static route, o - ODR
       P - periodic downloaded static route

Gateway of last resort is not set
```

Example 7-24 *Scenario 7-3:* **show** *Commands on Router Raleigh (Continued)*

```
     170.1.0.0/24 is subnetted, 4 subnets
C       170.1.1.0 is directly connected, Serial0
C       170.1.103.0 is directly connected, Ethernet0
I       170.1.102.0 [100/8539] via 170.1.1.2, 00:00:09, Serial0
I       170.1.101.0 [100/8539] via 170.1.1.1, 00:00:42, Serial0

Raleigh#show ip interface brief
Interface              IP-Address      OK? Method Status                Protocol
Serial0                170.1.1.3       YES NVRAM  up                    up
Serial1                180.1.1.253     YES NVRAM  administratively down down
Ethernet0              170.1.103.3     YES NVRAM  up                    up

Raleigh#show ip protocol
Routing Protocol is "igrp 4"
  Sending updates every 90 seconds, next due in 56 seconds
  Invalid after 270 seconds, hold down 280, flushed after 630
  Outgoing update filter list for all interfaces is not set
  Incoming update filter list for all interfaces is not set
  Default networks flagged in outgoing updates
  Default networks accepted from incoming updates
  IGRP metric weight K1=1, K2=0, K3=1, K4=0, K5=0
  IGRP maximum hopcount 100
  IGRP maximum metric variance 1
  Redistributing: igrp 4
  Maximum path: 4
  Routing for Networks:
    170.1.0.0
  Routing Information Sources:
    Gateway         Distance      Last Update
    170.1.1.2            100      00:00:20
    170.1.1.1            100      00:00:53
  Distance: (default is 100)

Raleigh#show frame-relay pvc

PVC Statistics for interface Serial0 (Frame Relay DTE)

DLCI = 47, DLCI USAGE = LOCAL, PVC STATUS = ACTIVE, INTERFACE = Serial0

  input pkts 36            output pkts 35           in bytes 3674
  out bytes 3436           dropped pkts 0           in FECN pkts 0
  in BECN pkts 0           out FECN pkts 0          out BECN pkts 0
  in DE pkts 0             out DE pkts 0
  out bcast pkts 34         out bcast bytes 3358
  pvc create time 00:22:07, last time pvc status changed 00:21:58

DLCI = 48, DLCI USAGE = LOCAL, PVC STATUS = ACTIVE, INTERFACE = Serial0

  input pkts 35            output pkts 35           in bytes 3444
  out bytes 3422           dropped pkts 0           in FECN pkts 0
  in BECN pkts 0           out FECN pkts 0          out BECN pkts 0
  in DE pkts 0             out DE pkts 0
  out bcast pkts 34         out bcast bytes 3358
  pvc create time 00:22:08, last time pvc status changed 00:21:58
```

Assuming the details established in Figure 7-16, Table 7-29, and Examples 7-22, 7-23, and 7-24 for Scenario 7-3, complete or answer the following:

1 Examining the **show** commands on the various routers, complete Table 7-29 with the subnet numbers and broadcast addresses used in this network.

2 Describe the contents of the IGRP update from Raleigh, sent out its virtual circuit to Mount Pilot. How many routes in Raleigh's IGRP update are sent to Mount Pilot? How many routes are in Raleigh's routing table? Is the number different? Why? (Hint: Look at the IGRP debug output in Example 7-23 and the IP routing table in Example 7-24.)

3 If the VC between Mount Pilot and Mayberry fails and routing protocol convergence completes, will Mayberry have a route to 170.1.1.0/24? Why or why not?Answers to Scenarios

Answers to Scenario 7-1: IP Configuration 1

Refer to the network illustrated in Figure 7-14 and Table 7-27 to establish the Scenario 7-1 design details and the context of the answers to the five tasks for this scenario.

Answers to Task 1 for Scenario 7-1

Task 1 for Scenario 7-1 asks for completed configurations. They are shown in Examples 7-25, 7-26, and 7-27. You could have chosen different IP addresses, but your choices must have the same first three octets as those shown in Example 7-25.

Example 7-25 *Albuquerque Configuration for Scenario 7-1*

```
hostname Albuquerque
!
enable secret 5 $1$ZvR/$Gpk5a5K5vTVpotd3KUygA1
!
interface Serial0
 ip address 148.14.4.1 255.255.255.0
!
interface Serial1
 ip address 148.14.5.1 255.255.255.0
!
interface ethernet0
 ip address 148.14.1.1 255.255.255.0
```

Example 7-26 *Yosemite Configuration for Scenario 7-1*

```
hostname Yosemite
enable secret 5 $1$ZvR/$Gpk5a5K5vTVpotd3KUygA1
!
interface Serial0
 ip address 148.14.4.2 255.255.255.0
```

Example 7-26 *Yosemite Configuration for Scenario 7-1 (Continued)*

```
!
interface Serial1
 ip address 148.14.6.2 255.255.255.0
!
interface ethernet0
 ip address 148.14.2.2 255.255.255.0
```

Example 7-27 *Seville Configuration for Scenario 7-1*

```
hostname Seville
enable secret 5 $1$ZvR/$Gpk5a5K5vTVpotd3KUygA1
!
interface Serial0
 ip address 148.14.5.3 255.255.255.0
!
interface Serial1
 ip address 148.14.6.3 255.255.255.0
!
interface ethernet0
 ip address 148.14.3.3 255.255.255.0
```

Answers to Task 2 for Scenario 7-1

Task 2 for Scenario 7-1 asks for a description of the IP routing table on Seville. This is shown in Table 7-30. This table exists before static and dynamic routes are added.

Table 7-30 *Routing Table in Seville*

Group	Outgoing Interface	Next-Hop Router
148.14.3.0	e0	
148.14.5.0	s0	
148.14.6.0	s1	

The Next-Hop Router field is always the IP address of another router, or it is null if the route describes a directly connected network.

Answers to Task 3 for Scenario 7-1

Task 3 for Scenario 7-1 asks for static route configuration. The routes to allow users on LANs to reach each other are shown in upcoming examples. However, routes to the subnets on serial links are not shown in these examples for the sake of brevity. The users should not need to send packets to IP addresses on the serial links' subnets, but rather to other hosts on the LANs. Examples 7-28, 7-29, and 7-30 show the configurations on the three routers.

Example 7-28 *Albuquerque Configuration for Scenario 7-1*

```
ip route 148.14.2.0 255.255.255.0 148.14.4.2
ip route 148.14.3.0 255.255.255.0 serial1
```

Example 7-29 *Yosemite Configuration for Scenario 7-1*

```
ip route 148.14.1.0 255.255.255.0 148.14.4.1
ip route 148.14.3.0 255.255.255.0 serial1
```

Example 7-30 *Seville Configuration for Scenario 7-1*

```
ip route 148.14.1.0 255.255.255.0 148.14.5.1
ip route 148.14.2.0 255.255.255.0 serial1
```

Both valid styles of static route configuration are shown. In any topological case, the style of static route command using the next router's IP address is valid. If the route points to a subnet that is on the other side of a point-to-point serial link, the static route command can simply refer to the outgoing serial interface.

Answers to Task 4 for Scenario 7-1

Task 4 for Scenario 7-1 asks for IGRP configuration. The same configuration is used on each router. It is shown in Example 7-31. The IGRP process-id must be the same on each router. If an IGRP update is received but lists a different process-id, the update is ignored.

Example 7-31 *IGRP Configuration for Scenario 7-1*

```
router igrp 1
network 148.14.0.0
```

Answers to Task 5 for Scenario 7-1

Task 5 for Scenario 7-1 asks for the broadcast addresses for each subnet. Table 7-31 shows these.

Table 7-31 *Completed Scenario 7-1 IP Addresses*

Location of Subnet Geographically	Subnet Mask	Subnet Number	Subnet Broadcast
Ethernet off router in Albuquerque	255.255.255.0	148.14.1.0	148.14.1.255
Ethernet off router in Yosemite	255.255.255.0	148.14.2.0	148.14.2.255
Ethernet off router in Seville	255.255.255.0	148.14.3.0	148.14.3.255
Serial between Albuquerque and Yosemite	255.255.255.0	148.14.4.0	148.14.4.255
Serial between Albuquerque and Seville	255.255.255.0	148.14.5.0	148.14.5.255
Serial between Seville and Yosemite	255.255.255.0	148.14.6.0	148.14.6.255

Answers to Scenario 7-2: IP Configuration 2

Refer to the network illustrated in Figure 7-15 and Table 7-28 to establish the Scenario 7-2 design details and the context of the answers to the four tasks for this scenario.

Answers to Task 1 for Scenario 7-2

Task 1 for Scenario 7-2 asks for completed configurations. They are shown in Examples 7-32 through 7-35.

Example 7-32 *Atlanta Configuration for Scenario 7-2*

```
hostname Atlanta
no ip domain-lookup
!
interface serial0
encapsulation frame-relay
interface serial 0.1
ip address 10.2.1.1 255.255.255.0
frame-relay interface-dlci 41
!
interface serial 0.2
ip address 10.2.2.1 255.255.255.0
frame-relay interface-dlci 42
!
interface serial 0.3
ip address 10.2.3.1 255.255.255.0
frame-relay interface-dlci 43
!
interface ethernet 0
ip address 10.1.1.1 255.255.255.0
```

Example 7-33 *Charlotte Configuration for Scenario 7-2*

```
hostname Charlotte
no ip domain-lookup
!
interface serial0
encapsulation frame-relay
interface serial 0.1
ip address 10.2.1.2 255.255.255.0
frame-relay interface-dlci 40
!
interface ethernet 0
ip address 10.1.2.2 255.255.255.0
```

Example 7-34 *Nashville Configuration for Scenario 7-2*

```
hostname nashville
no ip domain-lookup
!
interface serial0
encapsulation frame-relay
```

continues

Example 7-34 *Nashville Configuration for Scenario 7-2 (Continued)*

```
interface serial 0.1
ip address 10.2.2.3 255.255.255.0
frame-relay interface-dlci 40
!
interface ethernet 0
ip address 10.1.3.3 255.255.255.0
```

Example 7-35 *Boston Configuration for Scenario 7-2*

```
hostname boston
no ip domain-lookup
!
interface serial0
encapsulation frame-relay
interface serial 0.1
ip address 10.2.3.4 255.255.255.0
frame-relay interface-dlci 40
!
interface ethernet 0
ip address 10.1.4.4 255.255.255.0
```

Answers to Task 2 for Scenario 7-2

Task 2 for Scenario 7-2 asks for RIP configuration. The same configuration is used on each router. It is shown in Example 7-36.

Example 7-36 *RIP Configuration for Scenario 7-2*

```
router rip
network 10.0.0.0
```

Answers to Task 3 for Scenario 7-2

Task 3 for Scenario 7-2 asks for the broadcast addresses for each subnet. Table 7-32 shows these.

Table 7-32 *Completed Scenario 7-2 IP Addresses*

Location of Subnet Geographically	Subnet Mask	Subnet Number	Subnet Broadcast
Ethernet off router in Atlanta	255.255.255.0	10.1.1.0	10.1.1.255
Ethernet off router in Charlotte	255.255.255.0	10.1.2.0	10.1.2.255
Ethernet off router in Nashville	255.255.255.0	10.1.3.0	10.1.3.255
Ethernet off router in Boston	255.255.255.0	10.1.4.0	10.1.4.255
VC between Atlanta and Charlotte	255.255.255.0	10.2.1.0	10.2.1.255
VC between Atlanta and Nashville	255.255.255.0	10.2.2.0	10.2.2.255
VC between Atlanta and Boston	255.255.255.0	10.2.3.0	10.2.3.255

Answers to Task 4 for Scenario 7-2

Task 4 for Scenario 7-2 requires that you consider the effects of split horizon. Split-horizon logic considers subinterfaces to be separate interfaces, in spite of the fact that several subinterfaces share the same physical interface. Boston advertises 10.1.4.0 in its RIP update only out its subinterface 1. All other routes in Boston's routing table are learned through RIP updates from Atlanta via updates entering that same subinterface. Therefore, Boston does not advertise those routes in updates it sends on that same subinterface.

The RIP updates from Atlanta to Charlotte out Atlanta's subinterface 1 advertise all subnets not learned from RIP updates entering that same subinterface. All subnets except 10.1.2.0 (learned from Charlotte) and 10.2.1.0 (subinterface 1's subnet) are listed in Atlanta's RIP update to Charlotte. Subnet 10.1.4.0, learned from Boston, is indeed included in updates to Charlotte. Split horizon considers subinterfaces to be separate interfaces.

Answers to Scenario 7-3: IP Addressing and Subnet Derivation

Refer to the network illustrated in Figure 7-16 and Examples 7-22, 7-23, and 7-24 to establish the Scenario 7-3 design details and the context of the answers to the three tasks for this scenario.

Answers to Task 1 for Scenario 7-3

Task 1 for Scenario 7-3 asks you to complete a table with the subnet numbers and broadcast addresses used in this scenario's network after examining the **show** commands on the various routers in Examples 7-22, 7-23, and 7-24. Table 7-33 lists the subnet numbers and broadcast addresses requested in this task.

Table 7-33 *Completed Subnets and Broadcast Addresses*

Location of Subnet Geographically	Subnet Mask	Subnet Number	Subnet Broadcast
Ethernet off router in Mayberry	255.255.255.0	170.1.101.0	170.1.101.255
Ethernet off router in Mount Pilot	255.255.255.0	170.1.102.0	170.1.102.255
Ethernet off router in Raleigh	255.255.255.0	170.1.103.0	170.1.103.255
VC between Mayberry and Mount Pilot	255.255.255.0	170.1.1.0	170.1.1.255
VC between Mayberry and Raleigh	255.255.255.0	170.1.1.0	170.1.1.255
VC between Mount Pilot and Raleigh	255.255.255.0	170.1.1.0	170.1.1.255

Notice that the same subnet is used for all three virtual circuits. A full mesh of virtual circuits is used, and a single subnet was chosen rather than one subnet per virtual circuit.

Answers to Task 2 for Scenario 7-3

Task 2 for Scenario 7-3 asks you to describe the contents of the IGRP update from Raleigh, sent out its virtual circuit to Mount Pilot. Notice that there are four routes in the routing table and four routes in the routing update. Split horizon is disabled on serial interfaces using Frame Relay as configured without subinterfaces. Split horizon is disabled by the Cisco IOS Software if Frame Relay multipoint subinterfaces are used as well. Therefore, all four routes in the IP routing table are advertised in routing updates sent out Serial0.

Answers to Task 3 for Scenario 7-3

Mayberry still has a route to 170.1.1.0/24, which is the subnet covering all the Frame Relay interfaces in this scenario. Because only one VC went down and the other VC is still up, it is reasonable to expect that the physical interface is still up. No subinterfaces are configured in this scenario, so Mayberry still has a connected route for each interface that's currently up, including 170.1.1.0/24 on Serial0.

Exam Topics in This Chapter

35 Configure standard access lists to filter IP traffic.

36 Configure extended access lists to filter IP traffic.

37 Monitor and verify selected access list operations on the router.

CHAPTER 8

Understanding Access List Security

When deciding on the name of this chapter, the first title I chose was "Understanding Network Security." Then I thought to myself (that's what you do when you spend weeks on end in your home office writing), "You could easily write a whole book just on this topic!" So I changed the title to better reflect the scope of the security topics in this book, which of course reflects Cisco's expectations of CCNA candidates. Cisco expects CCNAs to understand security from the perspective of filtering traffic using access lists. Cisco also expects CCNAs to master the ideas and configuration behind the Telnet, auxiliary, console, and enable passwords. These topics are covered in Chapter 2, "Cisco IOS Software Fundamentals."

The reason that access lists are so important to CCNA candidates is that practically every network uses them. If you do more than basic filtering, access lists can become very tricky. In fact, when I was getting certified to teach Cisco classes in 1993, the Cisco Worldwide Training folks said that the TAC's most frequent question topic area was how to configure access lists. Access lists are likely to remain a core competency issue for router support personnel for a long time. Also, several other Cisco IOS software features call on access list logic to perform packet-matching features.

When studying access lists in this book or others, keep in mind that there are usually many ways to configure an access list to achieve the same result. Focus on the syntax of the commands and the nuances of the logic. If a particular example (given a set of criteria) is configured differently than you would have configured it, do not be concerned. In this book, I attempt to point out when a particular list could have been written differently.

How to Best Use This Chapter

Two main approaches to using this book are described in Chapter 1, "All About the Cisco Certified Network Associate Certification." They are called "Book 1" and "Book 2." Book 1 is for readers who need a thorough foundation before their final study time, and Book 2 is intended for readers who are reviewing and filling in the missing parts of their CCNA knowledge. Using Figure 8-1 as a guide, you should either read the Foundation sections of this chapter or begin with the "Do I Know This Already?" quiz.

Figure 8-1 *How to Use This Chapter*

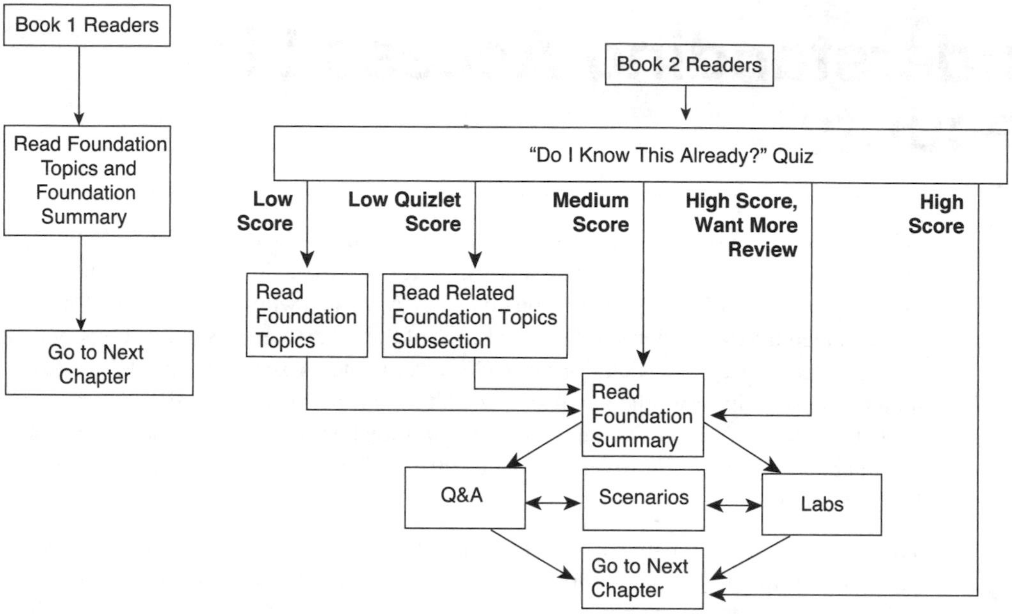

"Do I Know This Already?" Quiz

The purpose of the "Do I Know This Already?" quiz is to help you decide what parts of this chapter to use. If you already intend to read the entire chapter, you do not necessarily need to answer these questions now.

This 12-question quiz helps you determine how to spend your limited study time. The quiz is sectioned into three smaller four-question "quizlets" that correspond to the three major topic headings in this chapter. Figure 8-1 outlines suggestions on how to spend your time in this chapter based on your quiz score. Use Table 8-1 to record your scores.

Table 8-1 *Scoresheet for Quiz and Quizlets*

Quizlet Number	Foundation Topics Section Covering These Questions	Questions	Score
1	Standard IP Access Lists	1 to 4	
2	Extended IP Access Lists	5 to 8	
3	Named IP Access Lists	9 to 12	
All questions		1 to 12	

1 Configure a numbered IP access list that stops packets from subnet 134.141.7.0 255.255.255.0 from exiting serial 0 on a router. Allow all other packets.

____

____

____

2 How would a user who does not have the enable password find out what access lists have been configured and where they are enabled?

____

____

____

3 Name all the items that a standard IP access list can examine to make a match.

____

____

____

4 How many IP access lists of either type can be active on an interface at the same time?

____

____

____

5 Configure and enable an IP access list that allows packets from subnet 10.3.4.0/24, to any Web server, to get out serial interface S0. Also allow packets from 134.141.5.4 going to all TCP-based servers using a well-known port to enter serial 0. Deny all other traffic.

____

____

____

6 Name all the items that an extended IP access list can examine to make a match.

____

____

____

7 How many IP extended **access-list** commands are required to check a particular port number on all IP packets?

8 What command lists the IP extended access lists enabled on serial 1 without showing other interfaces?

9 Configure a named IP access list that allows only packets from subnet 193.7.6.0 255.255.255.0, going to hosts in network 128.1.0.0 and using a Web server in 128.1.0.0, to enter serial 0 on a router.

10 Name all the items that a named standard IP access list can examine to make a match.

11 List the types of IP access lists (numbered standard, numbered extended, named standard, named extended) that can be enabled to prevent Telnet access into a router. What commands would be used to enable this function, assuming that **access-list 2** was already configured to match the right packets?

12 Name all the items that a named extended IP access list can examine to make a match.

____

____

____

The answers to the "Do I Know This Already?" quiz are found in Appendix A, "Answers to the 'Do I Know This Already?' Quizzes and Q&A Sections." The suggested choices for your next step are as follows:

- **6 or less overall score**—Read the entire chapter. This includes the "Foundation Topics" and "Foundation Summary" sections, the "Q&A" section, and the scenarios at the end of the chapter.
- **2 or less on any quizlet**—Review the subsections of the "Foundation Topics" section, based on Table 8-1. Then move to the "Foundation Summary" section, the "Q&A" section, and the scenarios at the end of the chapter.
- **7, 8, or 9 overall score**—Begin with the "Foundation Summary" section, and then go to the "Q&A" section and the scenarios at the end of the chapter.
- **10 or more overall score**—If you want more review of these topics, skip to the "Foundation Summary" section and then go to the "Q&A" section and the scenarios at the end of the chapter. Otherwise, move to the next chapter.

Foundation Topics

Standard IP Access Lists

35 Configure standard access lists to filter IP traffic.

37 Monitor and verify selected access list operations on the router.

IP access lists cause a router to discard some packets based on criteria defined by the network engineer. The goal of these filters is to prevent unwanted traffic in the network—whether to prevent hackers from penetrating the network, or just to prevent employees from using systems that they should not be using. Access lists should simply be part of an organization's security policy, but for CCNA study purposes, we do not need to consider the business goals that drive the security policy. As long as you can configure access lists to filter packets, you know what you need to know about filtering for the CCNA exam.

By the way, IP access lists can also be used to filter routing updates, to match packets for prioritization, and to match packets for implementing quality of service features, but these additional features are not covered on the CCNA exam.

As soon as you know what needs to be filtered, the next goal is to decide where to filter the traffic. Figure 8-2 serves as an example. In this case, imagine that Bob is not allowed to access Server1, but Larry is.

Figure 8-2 *Locations Where Access List Logic Can Be Applied in the Network*

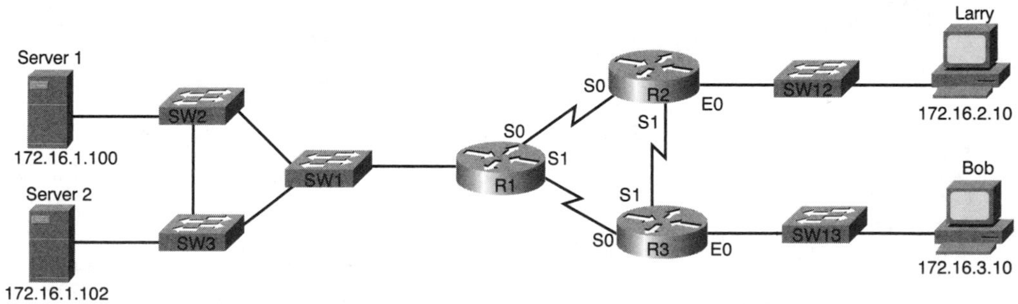

Filtering logic could be configured on any of the three routers and on any of their interfaces. However, some choices simply would not work (but others would). Because Bob's traffic is the only traffic that needs to be filtered, and the goal is to stop access to Server1, the access list could be applied at either R1 or R3. And because Bob's attempted traffic to Server1 would not need to go through R2, R2 would not be a good place to put the access list logic. For the sake of discussion, I'll pick R1.

As soon as you have chosen where you want to place the access list, you must choose the interface on which to apply the access logic. You must also decide whether to apply the logic for inbound or outbound packets. For instance, imagine that you wanted to filter Bob's packets sent to Server1. Figure 8-3 shows the options for filtering the packet.

Figure 8-3 *Locations Where Access List Logic Can Be Applied on Router R1*

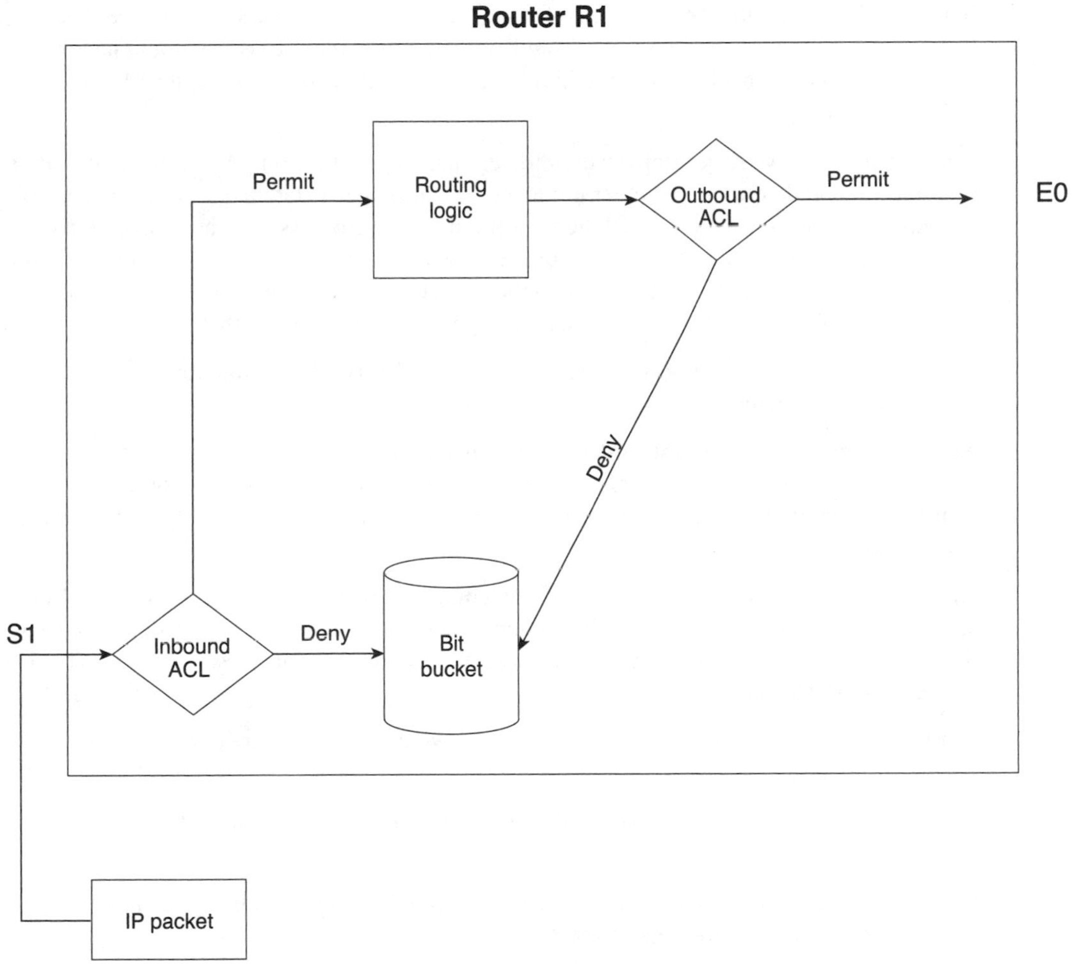

Filtering logic can be applied to packets entering S1 or to packets exiting E0 on R1 in order to match the packet sent by Bob to Server1. In general, you can filter packets by creating and enabling access lists for both incoming and outgoing packets on each interface. Here are some key features of Cisco access lists:

- Packets can be filtered as they enter an interface, before the routing decision.
- Packets can be filtered before they exit an interface, after the routing decision.

- *Deny* is the term used in Cisco IOS software to imply that the packet will be filtered.
- *Permit* is the term used in Cisco IOS software to imply that the packet will not be filtered.
- The filtering logic is configured in the access list.
- At the end of every access list is an implied "deny all traffic" statement. Therefore, if a packet does not match any of your access list statements, it is blocked.

For example, you might create an access list in R1 and enable it on R1's S1 interface. The access list would look for packets that came from Bob. Therefore, the access list would need to be enabled for inbound packets, because in this network, packets from Bob enter S1, and packets to Bob exit S1.

Access lists have two major steps in their logic: matching and action. Matching logic examines each packet and determines whether it matches the **access-list** statement. For instance, Bob's IP address would be used for matching packets sent from Bob. As soon as an **access-list** statement is matched, there are two actions to choose from: deny and permit. Deny means to discard the packet, and permit implies that the packet should continue on its way. So the access list for preventing Bob's traffic to the server might go something like this:

> Look for packets with Bob's source IP address and Server1's destination IP address. When you see them, discard them.

Not surprisingly, it can get a lot harder than that in real life. Even a short list of matching criteria can create complicated access lists on a variety of interfaces in a variety of routers. I've even heard of a couple of large networks with a couple of full-time people who do nothing but plan and implement access lists!

Access lists are a series of statements with matching criteria and the resulting actions. When an access list has multiple entries, the first statement matched determines the action. The two diamond-shaped symbols in Figure 8-3 represent the application of access list logic. That logic can be summarized as follows:

Step 1 The matching parameters of the first **access-list** statement are compared to the packet.

Step 2 If a match is made, the action defined in this **access-list** statement (permit or deny) is performed.

Step 3 If a match is not made in Step 2, Steps 1 and 2 are repeated using the next sequential **access-list** statement.

Step 4 If no match is made with an entry in the access list, the deny action is performed.

Access list logic is applicable whether you're using standard or extended access lists; the only difference between the two is in what constitutes a match.

The matching criteria available to access lists is based on fields inside the IP, TCP, and UDP headers. Extended access lists can check source and destination IP addresses, as well as source and destination port numbers, along with several other fields. However, standard IP access lists can examine only the source IP address.

You can configure the portion of the IP address that is checked by the **access-list** command. For instance, if you wanted to stop Bob from sending packets to Server1, you would look at the entire IP address of Bob and Server1 in the access list. But what if the criteria were to stop all hosts in Bob's subnet from getting to Server1? Because all hosts in Bob's subnet have the same numbers in their first three octets, the access list could just check the first three octets of the address in order to match all packets with a single **access-list** statement.

Cisco *wildcard masks* are access list parameters that define the portion of the IP address that should be examined. For example, suppose that one mask implies that the whole packet should be checked and another implies that only the first three octets need to be examined. To perform this matching, Cisco access lists use wildcard masks. Table 8-2 lists some of the more popular wildcard masks, as well as a few that are not quite as common.

Table 8-2 *Sample Access List Wildcard Masks*

Wildcard Mask	Binary Version of the Mask	Description
0.0.0.0	00000000.00000000.00000000.00000000	The entire IP address must match.
0.0.0.255	00000000.00000000.00000000.11111111	Just the first 24 bits must match.
0.0.255.255	00000000.00000000.11111111.11111111	Just the first 16 bits must match.
0.255.255.255	00000000.11111111.11111111.11111111	Just the first 8 bits must match.
255.255.255.255	11111111.11111111.11111111.11111111	Don't even bother to compare; it's automatically considered to match (0 bits need to match).
0.0.15.255	00000000.00000000.00001111.11111111	Just the first 20 bits must match.
0.0.3.255	00000000.00000000.00000011.11111111	Just the first 22 bits must match.
32.48.0.255	00100000.00110000.00000000.11111111	All bits except the 3rd, 11th, 12th, and last 8 must match.

The first several examples show the typical use of the wildcard mask. As you can see, it is not a subnet mask. A wildcard of 0.0.0.0 means that the entire IP address must be examined, and be equal, in order to be considered a match. 0.0.0.255 means that the last octet automatically matches, but the first three must be examined, and so on. More generally, the wildcard mask means the following:

> Bit positions of binary 0 mean that the access list compares the corresponding bit position in the IP address and makes sure it is equal to the same bit position in the address configured in the **access-list** statement. Bit positions of binary 1 are wildcards—those bit positions are immediately considered to be a match.

The next two rows of Table 8-2 show two reasonable but not obvious wildcard masks. 0.0.5.255, as seen in binary, is 20 0s followed by 12 1s. This means that the first 20 bits must match. Similarly, 0.0.3.255 means that the first 22 bits must be examined to find out if they match. Why are these useful? If the subnet mask is 255.255.240.0, and you want to match all hosts in the same subnet, the 0.0.15.255 wildcard means that all network and subnet bits must be matched, and all host bits are automatically considered to match. Likewise, if you want to filter all hosts in a subnet that uses subnet mask 255.255.252.0, the wildcard mask 0.0.3.255 matches the network and subnet bits. In general, if you want a wildcard mask that helps you match all hosts in a subnet, invert the subnet mask, and you have the correct wildcard mask.

The last entry in Table 8-2 is unreasonable for real networks, but it is included to make a point. The wildcard mask just defines which bits must be compared and which are automatically assumed to match. You should not expect such strange masks on the exam! The point is that although subnet masks must use a sequential set of binary 1s followed by only binary 0s, wildcard masks do not have to follow any such rule.

Standard IP Access List Configuration

Standard IP access list configuration works much like a simple programming language. The logic is something like this:

> If statement 1 is matched, carry out the action defined in that statement. If it isn't, examine the next statement. If it matches, carry out the action it defines. Continue looping through the list until a statement is matched or until the last statement in the list is not matched.

A standard access list is used to match a packet and then take the directed action. Each standard access list can match all or only part of the packet's source IP address. The only two actions taken when an **access-list** statement is matched are to either deny (discard) or permit (forward) the packet.

Table 8-3 lists the configuration commands related to standard IP access lists. Table 8-4 lists the related EXEC commands. Several examples follow the lists of commands.

Table 8-3 *Standard IP Access List Configuration Commands*

Command	Configuration Mode and Description
access-list *access-list-number* {**deny** | **permit**} *source* [*source-wildcard*] [**log**]	Global command for standard numbered access lists
ip access-group {*number* | *name* [**in** | **out**]}	Interface subcommand to enable access lists
access-class *number* | *name* [**in** | **out**]	Line subcommand for standard or extended access lists

Table 8-4 *Standard IP Access List EXEC Commands*

Command	Description
show ip interface [*type number*]	Includes a reference to the access lists enabled on the interface
show access-lists [*access-list-number* | *access-list-name*]	Shows details of configured access lists for all protocols
show ip access-list [*access-list-number* | *access-list-name*]	Shows IP access lists

The first example is basic in order to cover the statements' syntax. As shown in Figure 8-2, Bob is not allowed to access Server1, but Larry is allowed. In Example 8-1, the access list is enabled for all packets going out R1's Ethernet0 interface. Example 8-1 shows the configuration on R1.

Example 8-1 *Standard Access List Stopping Bob from Reaching Server*

```
interface Ethernet0
ip address 172.16.1.1 255.255.255.0
ip access-group 1 out


access-list 1 deny 172.16.3.10 0.0.0.0
access-list 1 permit 0.0.0.0 255.255.255.255
```

There are several small details in this example. Standard IP access lists use a number between 1 and 99, inclusive. Number 1 is used here for no particular reason, other than it's in the right range. The **access-list** command is a global configuration command, *not* a subcommand under the Ethernet0 interface. (The **access-list** commands do appear toward the end of the configuration file, after the interfaces.) The **ip access-group** command enables the logic on Ethernet0 for packets going out.

Access list 1 stops packets sent by Bob from exiting R1's Ethernet interface based on the matching logic of the first **access-list** statement. It forwards any other packets based on the matching logic of the second statement.

The configuration in Example 8-1 is not what shows up in the output of the **show running-config** command. Example 8-2 shows what would actually be placed in the configuration file.

Example 8-2 *Standard Access List Stopping Bob from Reaching Server1: Revised*

```
interface Ethernet0
ip address 172.16.1.1 255.255.255.0
ip access-group 1


access-list 1 deny host 172.16.3.10
access-list 1 permit any
```

The commands in Example 8-1 are changed based on three factors. First, "out" is the default direction for access lists, so the router would omit the **out** keyword of the **ip access-group** command. Second, the use of a wildcard mask of 0.0.0.0 is the old way to configure an access list to match a specific host's IP address. The new style is to code the **host** keyword in front of the IP address. When you type a wildcard of 0.0.0.0, the router replaces the configuration with the newer **host** keyword. Finally, when you use an IP address and a wildcard mask of 255.255.255.255, the keyword **any** is used to replace both parameters. **any** simply means that any IP address is matched.

The second example is more involved. Figure 8-4, Example 8-3, and Example 8-4 show a basic use of standard IP access lists, with two typical oversights in the first attempt at a complete answer. The criteria for the access lists are as follows:

- Sam is not allowed access to Bugs or Daffy.
- Hosts on the Seville Ethernet are not allowed access to hosts on the Yosemite Ethernet.
- All other combinations are allowed.

Figure 8-4 *Network Diagram for Standard Access List Example*

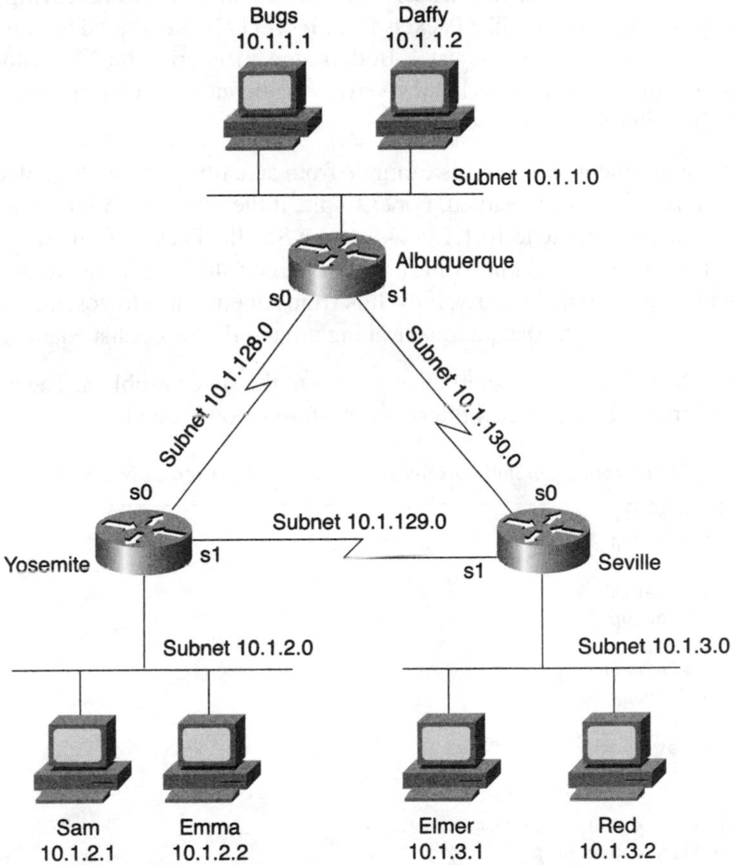

Example 8-3 *Yosemite Configuration for Standard Access List Example*

```
interface serial 0
ip access-group 3
!
access-list 3 deny host 10.1.2.1
access-list 3 permit any
```

Example 8-4 *Seville Configuration for Standard Access List Example*

```
interface serial 1
ip access-group 4
!
access-list 4 deny 10.1.3.0   0.0.0.255
access-list 4 permit any
```

At first glance, these two access lists seem to perform the desired function. Criterion 1 is met in Yosemite. In Yosemite, the packets from Sam are filtered before leaving S0 using access list 3. Criterion 2 is met in Seville: Packets from 10.1.3.0/24 are filtered before leaving Seville's S1 toward Yosemite, using access list 4. Both routers meet criterion 3: A wildcard **permit any** is used at the end of each access list to override the default, which is to discard all other packets. So, all the criteria appear to be met.

One subtle problem prevents this example from actually meeting the stated goals. If certain links fail, new routes are learned. For example, if the link from Albuquerque to Yosemite fails, Yosemite learns a route to 10.1.1.0/24 through Seville. Packets from Sam, forwarded by Yosemite and destined for hosts in Albuquerque, would leave Yosemite's serial1 interface without being filtered. Similarly, if the link from Albuquerque to Yosemite failed, Seville would route packets through Albuquerque, routing around the access list enabled on Seville.

Example 8-5 illustrates an alternative answer to the stated problem. The access list has been removed from Seville, and all filtering is performed on Yosemite.

Example 8-5 *Yosemite Configuration for Standard Access List Example: Alternative Solution to Example 8-3*

```
interface serial 0
ip access-group 3
!
interface serial 1
ip access-group 3
!
interface ethernet 0
ip access-group 4
!
access-list 3 deny host 10.1.2.1
access-list 3 permit any
!
access-list 4 deny 10.1.3.0   0.0.0.255
access-list 4 permit any
```

The configuration in Example 8-5 solves the problem of the earlier example, but it creates another problem. Example 8-5 denies all traffic that should be denied, but it also denies more traffic than the first of the three criteria says it should! In many cases, the meaning of the criteria for the access lists greatly affects your configuration choices. In this example, the problem of Sam's traffic going through Seville to reach Albuquerque when the link directly to Albuquerque is down is solved. The access list denies traffic from Sam (10.1.2.1) in an outbound access list on both of Yosemite's serial interfaces. However, that also prevents Sam from communicating with anyone outside Yosemite. This does not meet the spirit of the filtering goals, because it filters more than it should. An alternative would be to use the same **access-list 3** logic but use it as an inbound access list on Albuquerque's serial interfaces. However, that achieves the real goal only if there are no other servers in Albuquerque that Sam should be allowed to access. And if that were the case, criterion 1 should be rewritten to say something like "Sam is not allowed to access devices on the Albuquerque Ethernet."

The main point is this: With three simple criteria and three routers, the configuration was simple. However, it is easy to introduce problems that are not obvious.

As shown in Example 8-5, **access-list 4** does an effective job of meeting the second of the three criteria. Because the goal was to stop Seville hosts from communicating with Yosemite's hosts, and because the only LAN hosts off Yosemite are the ones on the local Ethernet, the access list is effective in stopping packets from exiting Ethernet 0.

Extended IP Access Lists

35 Configure extended access lists to filter IP traffic.

37 Monitor and verify selected access list operations on the router

Extended IP access lists are almost identical to standard IP access lists in their use. The key difference between the two is the variety of fields in the packet that can be compared for matching by extended access lists. To pass the CCNA exam, you must remember all the items that an extended IP access list can check to make a match. As with standard lists, extended access lists are enabled for packets entering or exiting an interface. The list is searched sequentially; the first statement matched stops the search through the list and defines the action to be taken. All these features are true of standard access lists as well. The matching logic, however, is different than that used with standard access lists and makes extended access lists much more complex.

Table 8-5 lists the configuration commands associated with creating extended IP access lists. Table 8-6 lists the associated EXEC commands. Several examples follow the lists of commands.

Table 8-5 *Extended IP Access List Configuration Commands*

Command	Configuration Mode and Description
access-list *access-list-number* [**dynamic** *dynamic-name* [**timeout** *minutes*]] {**deny** | **permit**} *protocol source source-wildcard destination destination-wildcard* [**precedence** *precedence*] [**tos** *tos*] [**log** | **log-input**] [**time-range** *time-range-name*]	Global command for extended numbered access lists
ip access-group {*number* | *name* [**in** | **out**]}	Interface subcommand to enable access lists
access-class *number* | *name* [**in** | **out**]	Line subcommand for standard or extended access lists

Table 8-6 *Extended IP Access List EXEC Commands*

Command	Description
show ip interface [*type number*]	Includes a reference to the access lists enabled on the interface
show access-lists [*access-list-number* | *access-list-name*]	Shows details of configured access lists for all protocols
show ip access-list [*access-list-number* | *access-list-name*]	Shows IP access lists

Extended access lists create powerful matching logic by examining many parts of a packet. Figure 8-5 shows several of the fields in the packet headers that can be matched. The top set of headers shows the IP protocol type, which identifies what header follows the IP header. The source and destination IP addresses are also shown. In the second set of headers, an example with a TCP header following the IP header is shown. The TCP source and destination port numbers are listed in the abbreviated TCP header. Table 8-7 provides the complete list of items that can be matched with an IP extended access list.

Figure 8-5 *Extended Access List Matching Options*

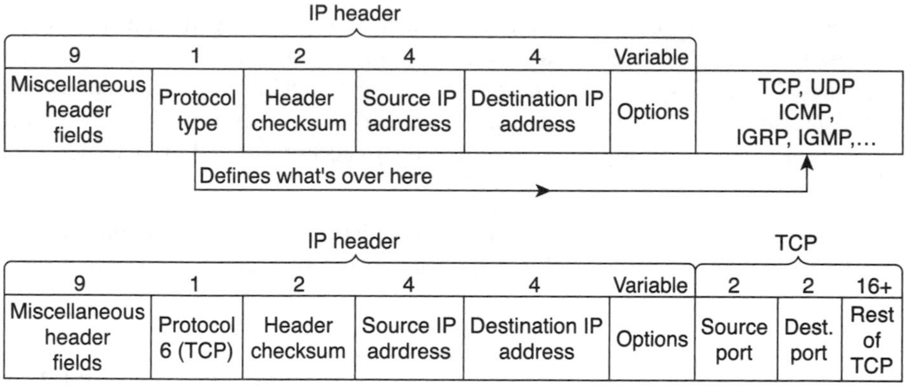

Table 8-7 *Standard and Extended IP Access Lists: Matching*

Type of Access List	What Can Be Matched
IP standard	Source IP address
	Portions of the source IP address using a wildcard mask

Table 8-7 *Standard and Extended IP Access Lists: Matching (Continued)*

Type of Access List	What Can Be Matched
IP extended	Source IP address
	Portions of the source IP address using a wildcard mask
	Destination IP address
	Portions of the destination IP address using a wildcard mask
	Protocol type (TCP, UDP, ICMP, IGRP, IGMP, and others)
	Source port
	Destination port
	Established—matches all TCP flows except the first
	IP TOS
	IP precedence

A statement is considered to match if all options in the statement match. If one option does not match, the statement is skipped, and the next entry in the list is examined. Table 8-8 provides several sample **access-list** statements.

Table 8-8 *Standard* **access-list** *Commands and Logic Explanations*

access-list Statement	What It Matches
access-list 101 deny tcp any host 10.1.1.1 eq 23	A packet with any source address. The destination must be 10.1.1.1, with a TCP header and a destination of port 23.
access-list 101 deny tcp any host 10.1.1.1 eq telnet	The same as the preceding function. The **telnet** keyword is used instead of port 23.
access-list 101 deny udp 1.0.0.0 0.255.255.255 lt 1023 any	A packet with a source in network 1.0.0.0 to any destination, using UDP with a source port less than 1023.
access-list 101 deny udp 1.0.0.0 0.255.255.255 lt 1023 44.1.2.3 0.0.255.255	A packet with a source in network 1.0.0.0 to destinations beginning with 44.1 using UDP with a source port less than 1023.
access-list 101 deny ip 33.1.2.0 0.0.0.255 44.1.2.3 0.0.255.255	A packet with a source in 33.1.2.0/24 to destinations beginning with 44.1.
access-list 101 deny icmp 33.1.2.0 0.0.0.255 44.1.2.3 0.0.255.255 echo	A packet with a source in 33.1.2.0/24 to destinations beginning with 44.1 that are ICMP echo requests and replies.

The sequence of the parameters is very important—and very tricky, in some cases. When checking port numbers, the parameter on the **access-list** command checking the port checks the source port number when placed immediately after the check of the source IP address. Likewise, if the port parameter follows the check of the destination address, the logic matches the destination port. For example, the command **access-list 101 deny tcp any eq telnet any** matches all packets that use TCP and whose source TCP port is 23 (Telnet). Likewise, the command **access-list 101 deny tcp any any eq telnet** matches all packets that use TCP and whose destination TCP port is 23 (Telnet).

Extended IP Access Lists: Example 1

The first example is basic in order to cover the statements'' syntax. In this case, Bob is denied access to all FTP servers on R1's Ethernet, and Larry is denied access to Server1's Web server. Figure 8-6 is a reminder of the network topology. In Example 8-6, an access list is created on R1. Example 8-6 shows the configuration on R1.

Figure 8-6 *Network Diagram for Extended Access List Example 1*

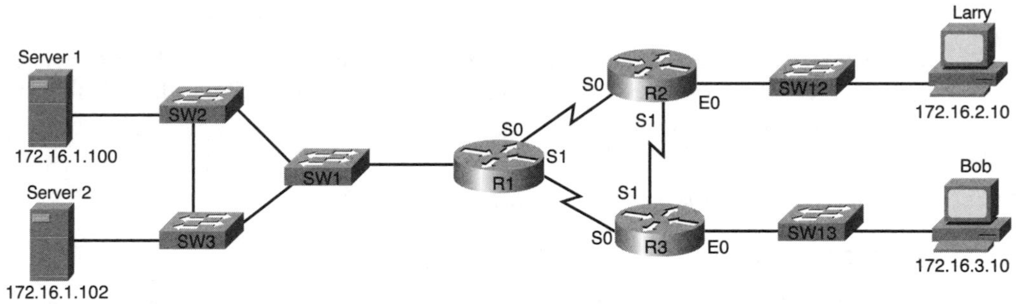

Example 8-6 *R1's Extended Access List: Example 1*

```
interface Serial0
ip address 172.16.12.1 255.255.255.0
ip access-group 101 in

interface Serial1
ip address 172.16.13.1 255.255.255.0
ip access-group 101 in

access-list 101 deny tcp host 172.16.3.10 172.16.1.0 0.0.0.255 eq ftp
access-list 101 deny tcp host 172.16.2.10 host 172.16.1.100 eq http
access-list 101 permit ip any any
```

Focusing on the syntax for a moment, there are several new items to review. First, the access list number for extended access lists is from 100 to 199, inclusive. A protocol parameter is the first option after the permit or deny action. When checking for TCP or UDP port numbers, the TCP or UDP protocol must be specified. The **eq** parameter means "equals." It implies that you are checking the port numbers—in this case, the destination port numbers. You can use the numeric values—or, for the more popular options, a more obvious text version is valid. (If you were to type **eq 80**, the config would show **eq http**.)

The single access list, checking inbound traffic on both serial interfaces of R1, overcomes the rerouting issue that was covered with standard access lists. Because extended access lists can check the packets more exactly, they can perform the exact function much more easily.

An important question can be raised with this first example—and it's probably covered on the exam: Where should you put access lists? For instance, Example 8-6 is implemented on R1. And, unless a link is down, the access list is checking for packets that will never be matched. The three strategies that Cisco has advanced for quite some time are as follows:

- Place access lists as close as possible to the packet's source.
- Place more frequently matched statements at the top of the access list to improve performance.
- Achieve both goals without changing what actually gets denied.

So, in this example, the access lists should have been placed on R2 and R3, respectively. And because the goal is to put the most frequently matched statements first, the **permit any** should be first in the list, right? Of course not! The first entry in the list that is matched determines the action. So, changing the **permit any** action at the beginning changes what is actually denied, which goes against the strategy and also goes against what Example 1 is trying to achieve. Example 8-7 defines an access list on R3 that prevents Bob from reaching all FTP servers off R1's Ethernet. The requirement to prevent Larry from reaching Server1's Web server is left as an exercise.

Example 8-7 *R3's Extended Access List Stopping Bob from Reaching FTP Servers Near R1*

```
interface Serial0
ip address 172.16.13.3 255.255.255.0
ip access-group 101 out

interface Serial1
ip address 172.16.12.3 255.255.255.0
ip access-group 101 out

access-list 101 deny tcp host 172.16.3.10 172.16.1.0 0.0.0.255 eq ftp
access-list 101 permit ip any any
```

The access list in Example 8-7 conforms to Cisco's design goals. It is close to the source, being in R3. It does not try to prevent Larry from getting to Server1, because that will presumably be done close to the source, at R2. Omitting checks for Larry should reduce the number of comparisons made by the access list. The **permit any any** at the end of the list needs to be at the end, even if it is matched more than the other statement in the list, because moving it would change the access list's behavior.

Extended IP Access Lists: Example 2

Example 8-8, based on the network shown in Figure 8-4, shows the use of extended IP access lists. Extended access list Example 2 uses the same criteria as standard access list Example 2:

- Sam is not allowed access to Bugs or Daffy.
- Hosts on the Seville Ethernet are not allowed access to hosts on the Yosemite Ethernet.
- All other combinations are allowed.

Example 8-8 *Yosemite Configuration for Extended Access List Example 2*

```
interface serial 0
ip access-group 110
!
interface serial 1
ip access-group 110
!
access-list 110 deny ip host 10.1.2.1 10.1.1.0 0.0.0.255
access-list 110 deny ip 10.1.2.0 0.0.0.255 10.1.3.0 0.0.0.255
access-list 110 permit ip any any
```

Two important side effects occur with the configuration shown in Example 8-8, compared to the standard access list configuration shown in Examples 8-3 and 8-4. The issue of having packets routed around the access list is taken care of, because the access lists are enabled for output packets on both serial interfaces. Also, most of the packets are filtered at the router nearest the source of the packets, which reduces network overhead. Access lists could have been added at Seville as well, to deny the packets originating from Seville's Ethernet.

Extended IP Access Lists: Example 3

Figure 8-7 shows the network for another example of extended IP access lists.

The filtering criteria for this extended access list example are more complicated:

- The Web server (Daffy) is available to all users.

- UDP-based clients and servers on Bugs are unavailable to hosts whose IP addresses are in the upper half of the valid IP addresses in each subnet. (The subnet mask used is 255.255.255.0.)
- Packets between hosts on the Yosemite Ethernet and the Seville Ethernet are allowed only if packets are routed across the direct serial link.
- Clients Porky and Petunia can connect to all hosts except Red.
- Any other connections are permitted.

Figure 8-7 *Network Diagram for Extended Access List Example 3*

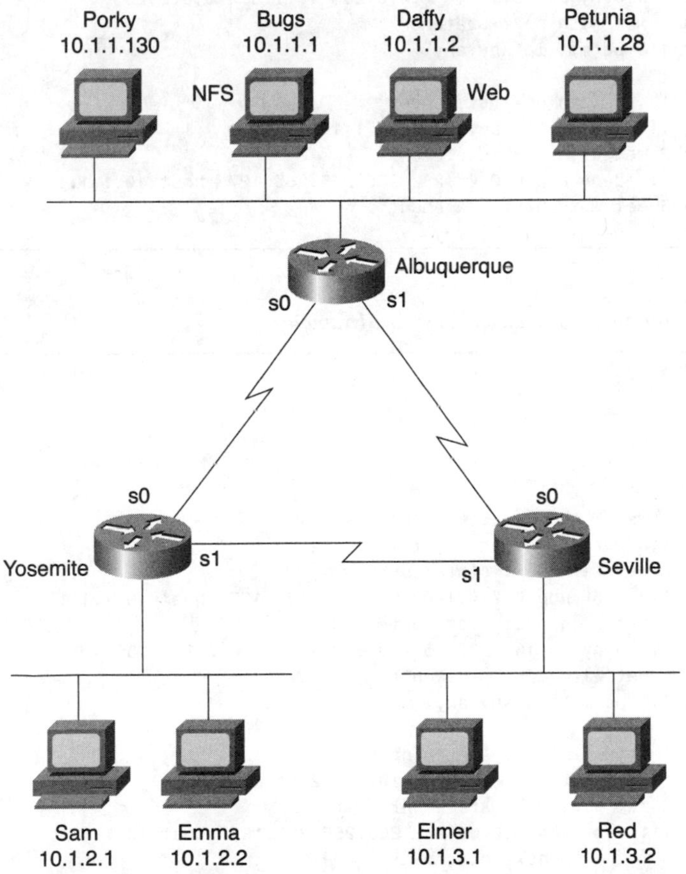

Examples 8-9, 8-10, and 8-11 show one solution for this third extended access list example.

Example 8-9 *Yosemite Configuration for Extended Access List Example 3*

```
interface serial 0
ip access-group 110
!
interface serial 1
ip access-group 111
!
! Criterion 1 met with next statement
access-list 110 permit tcp any host 10.1.1.2 eq www
! Criterion 2 met with next statement
access-list 110 deny udp 0.0.0.128  255.255.255.127  host 10.1.1.1
! Criterion 3 met with next statement
access-list 110 deny ip 10.1.2.0 0.0.0.255 10.1.3.0 0.0.0.255
! Criterion 5 met with next statement
access-list 110 permit ip any any
!
! Criterion 1 met with next statement
access-list 111 permit tcp any host 10.1.1.2 eq www
! Criterion 2 met with next statement
access-list 111 deny udp 0.0.0.128  255.255.255.127  host 10.1.1.1
! Criterion 5 met with next statement
access-list 111 permit ip any any
```

Example 8-10 *Seville Configuration for Extended Access List Example 3*

```
interface serial 0
ip access-group 110
!
interface serial 1
ip access-group 111
!
! Criterion 1 met with next statement
access-list 110 permit tcp any host 10.1.1.2 eq www
! Criterion 2 met with next statement
access-list 110 deny udp 0.0.0.128  255.255.255.127  host 10.1.1.1
! Criterion 3 met with next statement
access-list 110 deny ip 10.1.3.0 0.0.0.255 10.1.2.0 0.0.0.255
! Criterion 5 met with next statement
access-list 110 permit ip any any
!
! Criterion 1 met with next statement
access-list 111 permit tcp any host 10.1.1.2 eq www
! Criterion 2 met with next statement
access-list 111 deny udp 0.0.0.128  255.255.255.127  host 10.1.1.1
! Criterion 5 met with next statement
access-list 111 permit ip any any
```

Example 8-11 *Albuquerque Configuration for Extended Access List Example 3*

```
interface serial 0
ip access-group 112
!
interface serial 1
ip access-group 112
!
! Criterion 4 met with next four statements
access-list 112 deny ip host 10.1.1.130  host 10.1.3.2
access-list 112 deny ip host 10.1.1.28  host 10.1.3.2
access-list 112 permit ip host 10.1.1.130 any
access-list 112 permit ip host 10.1.1.28 any
! Criterion 5 met with next statement
access-list 112 permit ip any any
```

The access lists on Yosemite and Seville are almost identical; each is focused on the first three criteria. List 110 is used as outbound access lists on the Yosemite and Seville links connected to Albuquerque. The first three statements in list 110 in each router complete the first three criteria for this example; the only difference is in the source and destination addresses used in the third statement, which checks for the respective subnet numbers at each site.

Both Yosemite and Seville have a list 111 that is used on the link between the two. Each list 111 on Yosemite and Seville is identical to list 110, except that list 111 is missing one statement. This missing statement (relative to list 110) is the one that meets criterion 3, which says to not filter this traffic from going across the direct serial link. Because list 111 is used on that link, there is no need for the extra statement. The final statement in lists 110 and 111 in Seville and Yosemite provides coverage for the fifth criterion for this example—allowing all other packets to flow.

The second **access-list** statement in lists 110 and 111 on Seville and Yosemite is trickier than you will see on the CCNA exam. This example is representative of the types of nuances you might see on the CCNP and CCIE exams. The mask has only one binary 0 in it, in bit 25 (the first bit in the last byte). The corresponding bit in the address has value 1; in decimal, the address and mask imply addresses whose fourth byte is between 128 and 255, inclusive. Regardless of subnet number, hosts in the upper half of the assignable addresses in each subnet are matched with this combination. (Because the subnet mask is 255.255.255.0, all host addresses in the upper half of the address range are between 128 and 254 in the last octet.)

Two major problems exist when you use extensive detailed criteria for access lists. First, the criteria are open to interpretation. Many people tend to create the lists to match the order in which each point of the criteria are written; no attempt at optimization is made. Finally, it is easy to create the lists in such a way that the criteria are not actually met, as in extended IP access list Example 2.

Example 8-12 shows an alternative solution to the extended access list Example 3 solution that was shown in Examples 8-9, 8-10, and 8-11. All access lists have been removed from Seville and Yosemite, as compared to that earlier solution.

Example 8-12 *Albuquerque Configuration for Extended Access List Example 3: Second Solution*

```
interface serial 0
ip access-group 112
!
interface serial 1
ip access-group 112
!
! Next statement meets criterion 1
access-list 112 permit tcp host 10.1.1.2 eq www any
! Next statement meets criterion 2
access-list 112 deny udp  host 10.1.1.1   0.0.0.128  255.255.255.127
! Next statements meet criterion 3
access-list 112 deny ip 10.1.3.0 0.0.0.255 10.1.2.0 0.0.0.255
access-list 112 deny ip 10.1.2.0 0.0.0.255 10.1.3.0 0.0.0.255
! Next statement meets criterion 4
access-list 112 deny ip host 10.1.1.130  host 10.1.3.2
access-list 112 deny ip host 10.1.1.28  host 10.1.3.2

! Next statement meets criterion 5
access-list 112 permit ip any any
```

Several differences exist between the first solution in Examples 8-9, 8-10, and 8-11, and the second solution in Example 8-12. First, all the filtering is performed in Albuquerque. Criterion point 4 is completed more concisely, allowing the **permit all** final statement to let Porky and Petunia talk to other hosts besides Red. Packets are sent by Yosemite and Seville to Albuquerque hosts, as well as packets sent back from servers in Albuquerque to the Albuquerque router, before being filtered. However, the number of these packets will be small, because the filter prevents the client from sending more than the first packet used to connect to the service.

Named IP Access Lists

35 Configure standard access lists to filter IP traffic.

36 Configure extended access lists to filter IP traffic.

37 Monitor and verify selected access list operations on the router.

Named IP access lists allow the same logic to be configured as with numbered standard and extended access lists. As a CCNA, you will need to remember the configuration commands' syntax differences and also be able to create both numbered and named lists with the same logic. The key differences between numbered and named IP access lists are as follows:

- A name is a more intuitive reminder of a list's function.
- Names allow for more access lists than 99 standard and 100 extended, which is the restriction with numbered access lists.
- Named access lists allow individual statements to be deleted. Numbered lists allow only for the deletion of the entire list. Insertion of the new statement into a named list requires the deletion and re-addition of all statements that should be later in the list than the newly added statement.
- The actual names used must be unique across all named access lists of all protocols and types on an individual router. Names can be duplicated on different routers.

The configuration syntax is very similar between named and numbered IP access lists. The items that can be matched with a numbered standard IP access list are identical to the items that can be matched with a named standard IP access list. Likewise, the items are identical with both numbered and named extended IP access lists.

Two important differences exist between numbered and named access lists. One key difference is that named access lists use a global command, which moves the user into a named IP access list submode under which the matching and permit/deny logic is configured. The other key difference is that when a named matching statement is deleted, only that one statement is deleted. With numbered lists, the deletion of any statement in the list deletes all the statements in the list. (This feature is demonstrated in more detail in an upcoming example.)

Table 8-9 lists the key configuration commands and shows their differences and similarities.

Table 8-9 *Comparison of Named and Numbered IP Access List Configuration Commands*

	Numbered	Named
Commands for matching packets: standard IP ACLs	**access-list 1-99 permit | deny ...**	**ip access-list standard** *name* **permit | deny ...***
Commands for matching packets: extended IP ACLs	**access-list 100-199 permit | deny ...**	**ip access-list extended** *name* **permit | deny ...***
Commands for enabling ACLs	**ip access-group 1-99 in | out**	**ip access-group** *name* **in | out**
Commands for enabling ACLs	**ip access-group 100-199 in | out**	**ip access-group** *name* **in | out**

*This command is a subcommand of the preceding command.

The word *name* represents a name created by the administrator. This name must be unique among all named access lists of all types in this router. Also, note that because the named list does not imply standard or extended by the value of the list's number, the command explicitly states the type of access list. Also, the ... represents all the matching parameters, which are identical in meaning and syntax when comparing the respective numbered and named IP access lists. Also note that the same command is used to enable the list on an interface for both numbered and named lists.

One difference between the two types of lists is that individual matching statements can be removed from named lists. Example 8-13 shows the configuration mode output when entering the access list used on Albuquerque in access list 112 of Example 8-12, but this time as a named access list instead of a numbered access list. One typo is shown in the original creation of the access list in Example 8-13, with changes made to delete and add the statement shown later in this same example. (The statement that is a typo is **deny ip 10.1.2.0 0.0.0.255 10.2.3.0 0.0.0.255**. It is a typo because there is no subnet 10.2.3.0; the intent was to configure 10.1.3.0 instead.)

Example 8-13 *Named Access List Configuration*

```
conf t
Enter configuration commands, one per line.  End with Ctrl-Z.
Router(config)#ip access-list extended barney
Router(config-ext-nacl)#permit tcp host 10.1.1.2 eq www any
Router(config-ext-nacl)#deny udp host 10.1.1.1 0.0.0.128 255.255.255.127
Router(config-ext-nacl)#deny ip 10.1.3.0 0.0.0.255 10.1.2.0 0.0.0.255
! The next statement is purposefully wrong so that the process of changing
! the list can be seen.
Router(config-ext-nacl)#deny ip 10.1.2.0 0.0.0.255 10.2.3.0 0.0.0.255

Router(config-ext-nacl)#deny ip host 10.1.1.130 host 10.1.3.2
Router(config-ext-nacl)#deny ip host 10.1.1.28 host 10.1.3.2
Router(config-ext-nacl)#permit ip any any
Router(config-ext-nacl)#^Z
Router#show running-config
Building configuration...

Current configuration:

.
. (unimportant statements omitted)
.
!
ip access-list extended barney
 permit tcp host 10.1.1.2 eq www any
 deny   udp host 10.1.1.1 0.0.0.128 255.255.255.127
 deny   ip 10.1.3.0 0.0.0.255 10.1.2.0 0.0.0.255
 deny   ip 10.1.2.0 0.0.0.255 10.2.3.0 0.0.0.255
 deny   ip host 10.1.1.130 host 10.1.3.2
 deny   ip host 10.1.1.28 host 10.1.3.2
 permit ip any any

Router#conf t
```

Example 8-13 *Named Access List Configuration (Continued)*

```
Enter configuration commands, one per line.  End with Ctrl-Z.
Router(config)#ip access-list extended barney
Router(config-ext-nacl)#no deny ip 10.1.2.0 0.0.0.255 10.2.3.0 0.0.0.255
Router(config-ext-nacl)#^Z
Router#show access-list

Extended IP access list barney
    permit tcp host 10.1.1.2 eq www any
    deny   udp host 10.1.1.1 0.0.0.128 255.255.255.127
    deny   ip 10.1.3.0 0.0.0.255 10.1.2.0 0.0.0.255
    deny   ip host 10.1.1.130 host 10.1.3.2
    deny   ip host 10.1.1.28 host 10.1.3.2
    permit ip any any
Router#conf t
Enter configuration commands, one per line.  End with Ctrl-Z.
Router(config)#ip access-list extended barney
Router(config-ext-nacl)#no permit ip any any
Router(config-ext-nacl)#no deny ip host 10.1.1.130 host 10.1.3.2
Router(config-ext-nacl)#no deny ip host 10.1.1.28 host 10.1.3.2
Router(config-ext-nacl)#deny ip 10.1.2.0 0.0.0.255 10.1.3.0 0.0.0.255
Router(config-ext-nacl)#deny ip host 10.1.1.130 host 10.1.3.2
Router(config-ext-nacl)#deny ip host 10.1.1.28 host 10.1.3.2
Router(config-ext-nacl)#permit ip any any
Router(config-ext-nacl)#^Z
Router#show ip access-list

Extended IP access list barney
    permit tcp host 10.1.1.2 eq www any
    deny   udp host 10.1.1.1 0.0.0.128 255.255.255.127
    deny   ip 10.1.3.0 0.0.0.255 10.1.2.0 0.0.0.255
    deny   ip 10.1.2.0 0.0.0.255 10.1.3.0 0.0.0.255
    deny   ip host 10.1.1.130 host 10.1.3.2
    deny   ip host 10.1.1.28 host 10.1.3.2
    permit ip any any
```

If an access list is not configured but is enabled on an interface with the **ip access-group** command, no packets are filtered because of this command. After the access list's first command is configured, Cisco IOS software implements the access list's logic. This is true of IP standard access lists as well as extended and named access lists. Access lists that filter other types of packets follow this same logic.

Controlling vty Access with IP Access Lists

Access into and out of the virtual terminal line (vty) ports of the Cisco IOS software can be controlled by IP access lists. (vty is used for Telnet access to and from the Cisco IOS software.) The inbound case is the more obvious case. For instance, imagine that only hosts in subnet 10.1.1.0/24 are supposed to be capable of Telnetting into any of the Cisco routers in a network.

In such a case, the configuration in Example 8-14 could be used on each router to deny access from IP addresses not in that one subnet.

Example 8-14 *vty Access Control Using the* **access-class** *Command*

```
line vty 0 4
 login
 password cisco
 access-class 3 in
!
! Next command is a global command
 access-list 3 permit 10.1.1.0 0.0.0.255
```

The **access-class** command refers to the matching logic in **access-list 3**. The keyword **in** refers to packets that are entering the router when you are trying to Telnet to that router's vtys. The **out** keyword is used both with outbound Telnet from a router and when using the reverse Telnet feature of the Cisco IOS software (which is unlikely to be on the exam). The **out** keyword implies that the packets originated by the Telnet client in the router are checked using the packets' destination address.

IP Access List Summary

To pass the CCNA exam, you must be proficient in using IP access lists. Here are the most important details to recall:

- The order of the list is important.
- All matching parameters must be true before a statement is "matched."
- An implied **deny all** is at the end of the list.

The strategy of choosing the location for access lists is covered in more depth on the CCNP exam than on the CCNA exam. However, it's generally better to filter packets closer to their source, because soon-to-be discarded packets waste less bandwidth than if they are allowed to flow over additional links before being denied.

Be particularly careful of questions relating to existing lists. For example, suppose a question suggests that one more **access-list** command should be added. Simply adding that command places the statement at the end of the list. However, the statement might need to be earlier in the list to accomplish the goal described in the question. Also focus on the differences between named and numbered IP access lists.

Foundation Summary

The Foundation Summary is a collection of tables and figures that provide a convenient review of many key concepts in this chapter. If you are already comfortable with the topics in this chapter, this summary can help you recall a few details. If you just read this chapter, this review should help solidify some key facts. If you are doing your final preparation before the exam, these tables and figures are a convenient way to review the day before the exam.

The logic for any access list can be summarized as follows:

Step 1 The matching parameters of the first **access-list** statement are compared to the packet.

Step 2 If a match is made, the action defined in this **access-list** statement (permit or deny) is performed.

Step 3 If a match is not made in Step 2, Steps 1 and 2 are repeated using the next sequential **access-list** statement.

Step 4 If no match is made with an entry in the access list, the deny action is performed.

Here are some key features of Cisco access lists:

- Packets can be filtered as they enter an interface, before the routing decision.
- Packets can be filtered before they exit an interface, after the routing decision.
- *Deny* is the term used in the Cisco IOS software to imply that the packet will be filtered.
- *Permit* is the term used in the Cisco IOS software to imply that the packet will not be filtered.
- The filtering logic is configured in the access list.
- At the end of every access list is an implied "deny all traffic" statement. Therefore, if a packet does not match any of your **access-list** statements, it is blocked.

Table 8-10 shows several examples of masks, packet source addresses, and addresses in **access-list** commands.

Table 8-10 *Sample Access List Wildcard Masks*

Wildcard Mask	Binary Version of Mask	Description
0.0.0.0	00000000.00000000.00000000.00000000	The entire IP address must match.
0.0.0.255	00000000.00000000.00000000.11111111	Just the first 24 bits must match.
0.0.255.255	00000000.00000000.11111111.11111111	Just the first 16 bits must match.
0.255.255.255	00000000.11111111.11111111.11111111	Just the first 8 bits must match.
255.255.255.255	11111111.11111111.11111111.11111111	Don't even bother to compare; it's automatically considered to match (0 bits need to match).
0.0.15.255	00000000.00000000.00001111.11111111	Just the first 20 bits must match.
0.0.3.255	00000000.00000000.00000011.11111111	Just the first 22 bits must match.
32.48.0.255	00100000.00110000.00000000.11111111	All bits except the 3rd, 11th, 12th, and last 8 must match.

Table 8-11 lists the configuration commands related to standard IP access lists. Table 8-12 lists the related exec commands.

Table 8-11 *Standard IP Access List Configuration Commands*

Command	Configuration Mode and Purpose
access-list *access-list-number* {**deny** | **permit**} *source* [*source-wildcard*] [**log**]	Global command for standard numbered access lists
ip access-group {*number* | *name* [**in** | **out**]}	Interface subcommand to enable access lists
access-class *number* | *name* [**in** | **out**]	Line subcommand for standard or extended access lists

Table 8-12 *Standard IP Access List exec Commands*

Command	Function
show ip interface [*type number*]	Includes a reference to the access lists enabled on the interface
show access-lists [*access-list-number* | *access-list-name*]	Shows details of configured access lists for all protocols
show ip access-list [*access-list-number* | *access-list-name*]	Shows IP access lists

Table 8-13 lists the configuration commands associated with creating extended IP access lists. Table 8-14 lists the associated EXEC commands.

Table 8-13 *Extended IP Access List Configuration Commands*

Command	Configuration Mode and Purpose
access-list *access-list-number* [**dynamic** *dynamic-name* [**timeout** *minutes*]] {**deny** | **permit**} *protocol source source-wildcard destination destination-wildcard* [**precedence** *precedence*] [**tos** *tos*] [**log** | **log-input**] [**time-range** *time-range-name*]	Global command for extended numbered access lists
ip access-group {*number* | *name* [**in** | **out**]}	Interface subcommand to enable access lists
access-class *number* | *name* [**in** | **out**]	Line subcommand for standard or extended access lists

Table 8-14 *Extended IP Access List Configuration Commands*

Command	Function
show ip interface [*type number*]	Includes a reference to the access lists enabled on the interface
show access-lists [*access-list-number* | *access-list-name*]	Shows details of configured access lists for all protocols
show ip access-list [*access-list-number* | *access-list-name*]	Shows IP access lists

The three strategies that Cisco has advanced for quite some time are as follows:

- Place access lists as close as possible to the packet's source.
- Place more frequently matched statements at the top of the access list to improve performance.
- Achieve both goals without changing what actually gets denied.

The key differences between numbered and named IP access lists are as follows:

- A name is a more intuitive reminder of a list's function.
- Names allow for more access lists than 99 standard and 100 extended, which is the restriction using numbered access lists.
- Named access lists allow individual statements to be deleted. Numbered lists only allow for the deletion of the entire list. Insertion of the new statement into a named list requires the deletion and re-addition of all statements that should be later in the list than the newly added statement.
- The actual names used must be unique across all named access lists of all protocols and types on an individual router. Names can be duplicated on different routers.

Table 8-15 lists the key configuration commands and shows their differences and similarities.

Table 8-15 *Comparison of Named and Numbered IP Access List Configuration Commands*

	Numbered	Named
Commands for matching packets: standard IP ACLs	**access-list 1-99 permit | deny ...**	**ip access-list standard** *name* **permit | deny ...***
Commands for matching packets: extended IP ACLs	**access-list 100-199 permit | deny ...**	**ip access-list extended** *name* **permit | deny ...***
Commands for enabling ACLs	**ip access-group 1-99 in | out**	**ip access-group** *name* **in | out**
Commands for enabling ACLs	**ip access-group 100-199 in | out**	**ip access-group** *name* **in | out**

*This command is a subcommand of the preceding command.

Q&A

As mentioned in Chapter 1, the questions and scenarios in this book are more difficult than what you should experience on the exam. The questions do not attempt to cover more breadth or depth than the exam, but they are designed to make sure that you know the answer. Rather than allowing you to derive the answer from clues hidden in the question, the questions challenge your understanding and recall of the subject. Questions from the "Do I Know This Already?" quiz at the beginning of this chapter are repeated here to ensure that you have mastered this chapter's topics. Hopefully these questions will help limit the number of exam questions on which you narrow your choices to two options and then guess. Also be sure to use the CD and take the simulated exams.

The answers to these questions can be found in Appendix A.

1 Configure a numbered IP access list that stops packets from subnet 134.141.7.0 255.255.255.0 from exiting serial 0 on a router. Allow all other packets.

____

____

____

2 Configure an IP access list that allows only packets from subnet 193.7.6.0 255.255.255.0, going to hosts in network 128.1.0.0 and using a Web server in 128.1.0.0, to enter serial 0 on a router.

____

____

____

3 How would a user who does not have the enable password find out what access lists have been configured and where they are enabled?

____

____

____

4 Configure and enable an IP access list that stops packets from subnet 10.3.4.0/24 from getting out serial interface S0 and that stops packets from 134.141.5.4 from entering S0. Permit all other traffic.

5 Configure and enable an IP access list that allows packets from subnet 10.3.4.0/24, to any Web server, to get out serial interface S0. Also allow packets from 134.141.5.4 going to all TCP-based servers using a well-known port to enter serial 0. Deny all other traffic.

6 Can standard IP access lists be used to check the source IP address when enabled with the **ip access-group 1 in** command, and can they check the destination IP addresses when using the **ip access-group 1 out** command?

7 How many IP extended **access-list** commands are required to check a particular port number on all IP packets?

8 True or false: If all IP or IPX **access-list** statements in a particular list define the deny action, the default action is to permit all other packets.

9 How many IP access lists of either type can be active on an interface at the same time?

For questions 10 through 12, assume that all parts of the network shown in Figure 8-8 are up and working. IGRP is the IP routing protocol in use. Answer the questions following Example 8-15, which contains an additional configuration in the Mayberry router.

Figure 8-8 *Network Diagram for Questions 10 Through 12*

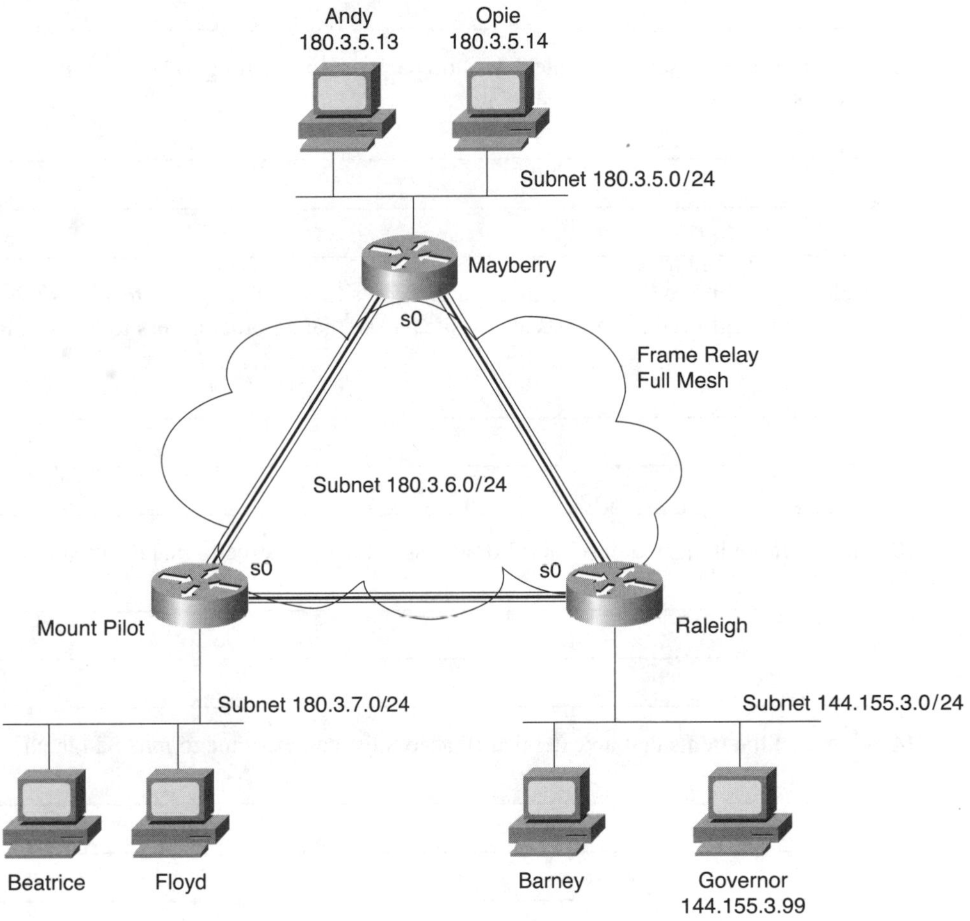

Example 8-15 *Access List at Mayberry*

```
access-list 44 permit 180.3.5.13 0.0.0.0
!
interface serial 0
ip access-group 44
```

10 Describe the types of packets that this filter would discard, and specify at what point they would be discarded.

____

____

____

11 Does the access list in Example 8-15 stop packets from getting to Web server Governor? Why or why not?

____

____

____

12 Referring to Figure 8-8, create and enable access lists so that access to Web server Governor is allowed from hosts at any site and so that no other access to hosts in Raleigh is allowed.

____

____

____

13 Name all the items that a standard IP access list can examine to make a match.

____

____

____

14 Name all the items that an extended IP access list can examine to make a match.

____

____

____

15 True or false: When you use extended IP access lists to restrict vty access, the matching logic is a best match of the list rather than a first match in the list.

____

____

____

16 In a standard numbered IP access list with three statements, a **no** version of the first statement is issued in configuration mode. Immediately following, another access list configuration command is added for the same access list. How many statements are in the list now, and in what position is the newly added statement?

____

____

____

17 In a standard named IP access list with three statements, a **no** version of the first statement is issued in configuration mode. Immediately following, another access list configuration command is added for the same access list. How many statements are in the list now, and in what position is the newly added statement?

____

____

____

18 Name all the items that a named standard IP access list can examine to make a match.

____

____

____

19 Configure a named IP access list that stops packets from subnet 134.141.7.0 255.255.255.0 from exiting serial 0 on a router. Allow all other packets.

____

____

____

20 Configure a named IP access list that allows only packets from subnet 193.7.6.0 255.255.255.0, going to hosts in network 128.1.0.0 and using a Web server in 128.1.0.0, to enter serial 0 on a router.

____

____

____

21 List the types of IP access lists (numbered standard, numbered extended, named standard, named extended) that can be enabled to prevent Telnet access into a router. What commands would be used to enable this function, assuming that **access-list 2** was already configured to match the right packets?

____

____

____

22 What command lists the IP extended access lists enabled on serial 1 without showing other interfaces?

____

____

____

23 Name all the items that a named extended IP access list can examine to make a match.

____

____

____

Scenarios

Scenario 8-1: IP Filtering Sample 1

Scenarios 8-1 through 8-3 use Figure 8-9, each with a different set of requirements for filtering. In each case, configure a correct access list for the routers and enable the access list. Place the access list in the router that filters the unneeded packets as quickly as possible—that is, before the packets are sent far from the originator.

Figure 8-9 *Network Diagram for IP Filtering Scenarios 8-1, 8-2, and 8-3*

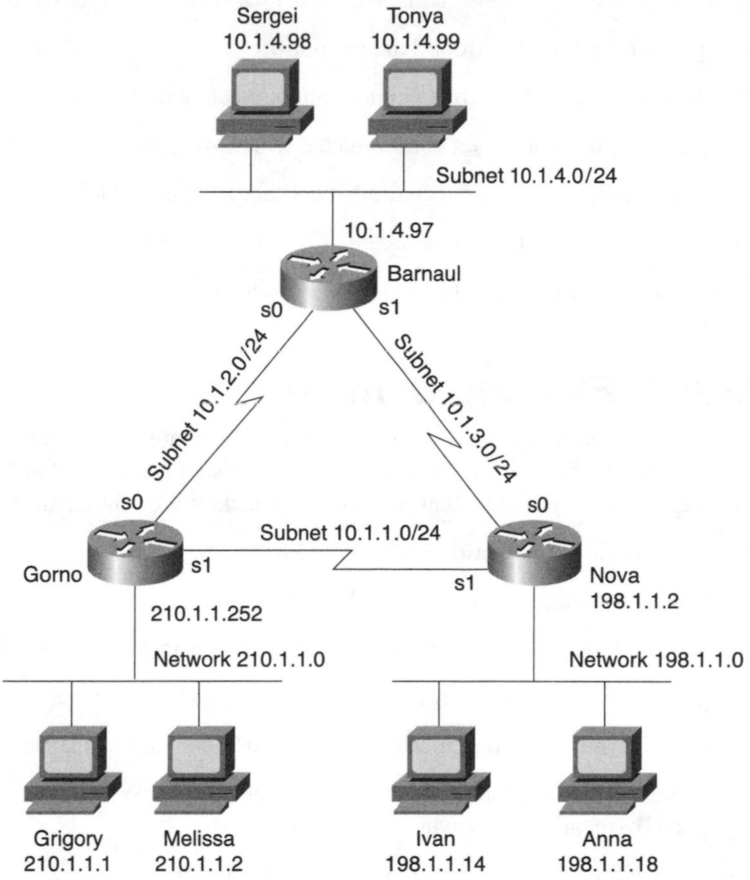

The filtering criteria for Scenario 8-1 are as follows:

1. Grigory can use the hosts on Nova's Ethernet.
2. All other hosts on Gorno (besides Grigory) cannot use the hosts on Nova's Ethernet.
3. All other communications are allowed.

Scenario 8-2: IP Filtering Sample 2

Again using the network diagram shown in Figure 8-9, create and enable access lists for a totally different set of requirements. Place the access list in the routers to filter the unneeded packets as quickly as possible—that is, before the packets are sent far from the originator.

The filtering criteria for Scenario 8-2 are as follows:

1. Hosts on the Barnaul Ethernet cannot communicate with hosts on the Gorno Ethernet.
2. Grigory and Melissa cannot communicate with hosts on the Nova Ethernet.
3. Other communications between the Nova Ethernet and the Gorno Ethernet are allowed.
4. Sergei (in Barnaul) can communicate only with other hosts in Barnaul.
5. Any communication paths not specified are allowed.

Scenario 8-3: IP Filtering Sample 3

Again using the network diagram shown in Figure 8-9, create and enable access lists for a totally different set of requirements. Place the access list in the router that filters the unneeded packets as quickly as possible—that is, before the packets are sent far from the originator.

The filtering criteria for Scenario 8-3 are as follows:

1. Grigory and Melissa can access any Web server in Nova.
2. Grigory and Melissa cannot access any other servers in Nova using TCP.
3. Sergei (Barnaul) can use only the Web services—and no other services—in Nova.
4. Hosts in Gorno can communicate with hosts in Nova unless otherwise stated.
5. Web clients in Barnaul are not allowed to connect to the Web server in Nova unless specifically mentioned elsewhere in these criteria.
6. Any unspecified communication should be disallowed.

Answers to Scenarios

Answers to Scenario 8-1: IP Filtering Sample 1

The solution to fulfilling the criteria stipulated for this access list is straightforward. Simply matching Grigory to permit his traffic and denying packets from 210.1.1.0 is all that is needed for the first two criteria. A **permit all** needs to be explicitly configured at the end of the list.

Example 8-16 provides the solution for this scenario. The access list is enabled on Nova. The problem with list 43 is that if the link from Barnaul to Gorno goes down, and if Gorno learns a route to Barnaul's subnets via Nova, Nova filters all inbound packets from (non-Grigory) Gorno hosts. A better list would be to use an extended access list that matches both the source and the destination addresses. **access-list 143** also is shown in Example 8-16, which avoids the problem seen with **access-list 43**. (**access-list 43** is enabled in the example.)

Example 8-16 *Solution to Scenario 8-1: Nova*

```
access-list 43 permit host 210.1.1.1
access-list 43 deny 210.1.1.0 0.0.0.255
access-list 43 permit any
!
access-list 143 permit ip host 210.1.1.1 198.1.1.0 0.0.0.255
access-list 143 deny ip 210.1.1.0 0.0.0.255 198.1.1.0 0.0.0.255
access-list 143 permit ip any any
!
interface serial 0
ip access-group 43 in
!
interface serial 1
ip access-group 43 in
```

Answers to Scenario 8-2: IP Filtering Sample 2

Many solutions could fulfill the criteria stipulated for this scenario. The solutions provided in Examples 8-17 and 8-18 attempt to filter packets as close to the source of the packet as possible. It is impossible to determine whether your correct solution is better than the one given here without more information about traffic loads and business needs in the network. The comments included in Examples 8-17 and 8-18 provide most of the detailed commentary.

Example 8-17 *Solution to Scenario 8-2: Barnaul Access List*

```
! Next statement meets Criterion 1
access-list 101 deny ip 10.1.4.0 0.0.0.255 210.1.1.0 0.0.0.255
! Next statement meets Criterion 4
access-list 101 deny ip host 10.1.4.98 any
! Criterion 5 met in the next statement
```

continues

Example 8-17 *Solution to Scenario 8-2: Barnaul Access List (Continued)*

```
access-list 101 permit ip any any
interface serial 0
ip access-group 101
!
interface serial 1
ip access-group 101
```

Example 8-18 *Solution to Scenario 8-2: Gorno Access List*

```
! Next statements meet Criterion 2
access-list 101 deny ip host 210.1.1.1 198.1.1.0 0.0.0.255
access-list 101 deny ip host 210.1.1.2 198.1.1.0 0.0.0.255
! Next statement meets Criterion 3, but it's not required, due to the final statement
access-list 101 permit ip 210.1.1.0 0.0.0.255 198.1.1.0 0.0.0.255
access-list 101 permit ip any any
!
interface serial 0
ip access-group 101
!
interface serial 1
ip access-group 101
```

Answers to Scenario 8-3: IP Filtering Sample 3

Many solutions could fulfill the criteria stipulated for this scenario. The solutions provided in Examples 8-19 and 8-20 attempt to filter packets as close to the source of the packet as possible. It is impossible to determine whether your correct solution is better than the one given here without more information about traffic loads and business needs in the network. The comments included in Examples 8-19 and 8-20 provide most of the detailed commentary.

Example 8-19 *Solution to Scenario 8-3: Barnaul Access List*

```
! Next statements meet Criterion 3
access-list 101 permit tcp host 10.1.4.98 198.1.1.0 0.0.0.255 eq www
access-list 101 deny tcp host 10.1.4.98 198.1.1.0.0.0.0.25 lt 1023
! Next statement meets Criterion 5, but it's not really needed
access-list 101 deny ip 10.1.4.0 0.0.0.255 198.1.1.0 0.0.0.255 eq www
! Criterion 6 is met in the default
!
interface serial 0
ip access-group 101
!
interface serial 1
ip access-group 101
```

Example 8-20 *Solution to Scenario 8-3: Gorno Access List*

```
! Next statements meet Criterion 1
access-list 101 permit tcp host 210.1.1.1 198.1.1.0 0.0.0.255 eq www
access-list 101 permit tcp host 210.1.1.2 198.1.1.0 0.0.0.255 eq www
! Next statements meet Criterion 2
access-list 101 deny tcp host 210.1.1.1 198.1.1.0 0.0.0.255 lt 1023
access-list 101 deny tcp host 210.1.1.2 198.1.1.0 0.0.0.255 lt 1023
! Next statement meets Criterion 4
access-list 101 permit ip 210.1.1.0 0.0.0.255 198.1.1.0 0.0.0.255
!Default meets Criterion 6
!
interface serial 0
ip access-group 101
!
interface serial 1
ip access-group 101
```

The default action can be used to shorten the list. For example, in Example 8-19, the commands **access-list 101 deny tcp host 10.1.4.98 198.1.1.0 0.0.0.255 lt 1023** and **access-list 101 deny ip 10.1.4.0 0.0.0.255 198.1.1.0 0.0.0.255 eq www** in access list 101 are not really needed, because the default is to deny these anyway. So, list 101 would perform the same function if it had only one statement in it (**access-list 101 permit tcp host 10.1.4.98 198.1.1.0 0.0.0.255 eq www**).

Exam Topics in This Chapter

32 State a relevant use and context for ISDN networking.

33 Identify ISDN protocols, function groups, reference points, and channels.

34 Identify PPP operations to encapsulate WAN data on Cisco routers.

CHAPTER 9

WAN Protocols and Design

Most people new to working with networking have never actually installed, or even seen the cabling for, a WAN connection. Cisco sells more LAN switches than routers these days. The cabling from your desk to the wiring closet is probably Category 5 twisted pair connected to a LAN switch. And for all connectivity from a typical building, there might be only one or two WAN connections. So, from a statistical perspective, the time spent actually planning and installing a single WAN connection is small compared to installing devices on the LAN.

WAN connectivity is still important, of course. You just don't get as many chances to work with WAN connections until you have a job as a network operator or engineer. In this chapter and Chapter 10, "Frame relay Concepts and Configuration," you learn about the details of WAN connectivity (at least, the details that might be on the CCNA exam). This chapter covers the two popular data-link protocols used on point-to-point links—HDLC and PPP. HDLC is relatively simple, and PPP has a few more interesting features. ISDN concepts and configuration are also covered, with a fair number of examples covering dial-on-demand routing (DDR), which is one way of causing a dialed ISDN connection to be established between routers.

How to Best Use This Chapter

By following these steps, you can make better use of your study time:

- Keep your notes and the answers for all your work with this book in one place, for easy reference.
- Take the "Do I Know This Already?" quiz, and write down your answers. Studies show that retention is significantly increased through writing down facts and concepts, even if you never look at the information again.
- Use Figure 9-1 to guide you to the next step.

Figure 9-1 *How to Use This Chapter*

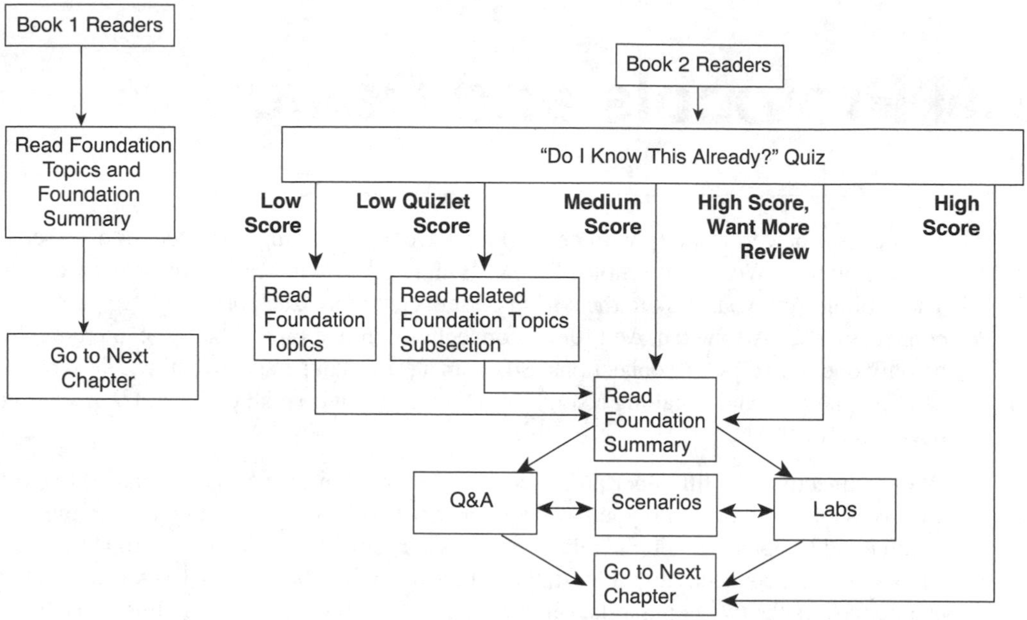

"Do I Know This Already?" Quiz

The purpose of the "Do I Know This Already?" quiz is to help you decide what parts of this chapter to use. If you already intend to read the entire chapter, you do not necessarily need to answer these questions now.

This 12-question quiz helps you determine how to spend your limited study time. The quiz is sectioned into three smaller four-question "quizlets" that correspond to the three major headings in this chapter. Figure 9-1 outlines suggestions on how to spend your time in this chapter based on your quiz score. Use Table 9-1 to record your scores.

Table 9-1 *Scoresheet for Quiz and Quizlets*

Quizlet Number	Foundation Topics Sections Covering These Questions	Questions	Score
1	Point-to-Point Leased Lines	1 to 4	
2	ISDN Protocols and Design	5 to 8	
3	Typical ISDN Configurations	9 to 12	
All questions		1 to 12	

1 Can PPP dynamically assign IP addresses? If so, is this feature always enabled?

2 Create a configuration to enable PPP on serial 0 for IP and IPX. Make up IP and IPX Layer 3 addresses as needed.

3 What data link (OSI Layer 2) protocols are valid on an ISDN B channel?

4 What field has Cisco added to the HDLC header, making it proprietary?

5 What does LAPD stand for? Is it used as the Layer 2 protocol on dialed ISDN bearer channels? If not, what is?

6 Define the term *reference point*. List two examples of reference points.

7 What do ISDN, BRI, and PRI stand for?

8 How many bearer channels are in a BRI? What about a PRI in North America? What about a PRI in Europe?

____

____

____

9 Describe the decision process performed by the Cisco IOS Software to attempt to dial a connection using legacy DDR.

____

____

____

10 CHAP configuration uses names and passwords. Given Routers A and B, describe what names and passwords must match in the respective CHAP configurations.

____

____

____

11 Define the terms PAP and CHAP. Which one sends passwords in clear-text format?

____

____

____

12 Define MLPPP. Describe the typical home or small office use of MLPPP.

____

____

____

The answers to the "Do I Know This Already?" quiz are found in Appendix A, "Answers to the 'Do I Know This Already?' Quizzes and Q&A Sections." The suggested choices for your next step are as follows:

- **6 or less overall score**—Read the entire chapter. This includes the "Foundation Topics" and "Foundation Summary" sections, the "Q&A" section, and the scenarios at the end of the chapter.
- **2 or less on any quizlet**—Review the subsections of the "Foundation Topics" section, based on Table 9-1. Then move to the "Foundation Summary" section, the "Q&A" section, and the scenarios at the end of the chapter.
- **7, 8, or 9 overall score**—Begin with the "Foundation Summary" section and then go to the "Q&A" section and the scenarios at the end of the chapter.
- **10 or more overall score**—If you want more review of these topics, skip to the "Foundation Summary" section and then go to the "Q&A" section and the scenarios at the end of the chapter. Otherwise, move to the next chapter.

Foundation Topics

Point-to-Point Leased Lines

34 Identify PPP operations to encapsulate WAN data on Cisco routers.

WAN protocols used on point-to-point serial links provide the basic function of data delivery across that one link. As a CCNA, you will be required to understand and configure a variety of protocols used on point-to-point links, including Link Access Procedure Balanced (LAPB), High-Level Data Link Control (HDLC), and Point-to-Point Protocol (PPP). Each of these WAN protocols has the following functions in common:

- LAPB, HDLC, and PPP provide for the delivery of data across a single point-to-point serial link.
- LAPB, HDLC, and PPP deliver data on synchronous serial links. (PPP also supports asynchronous functions.)

Each synchronous serial data-link protocol uses the concept of *framing*. Each of these protocols defines the beginning and end of the frame, the information and format of a header and trailer, and the location of the packet between the header and trailer. In other words, synchronous WAN data-link protocols are frame-oriented, not bit- or byte-oriented.

PPP, LAPB, and HDLC are so frame-oriented that even when there is no data to send, they send idle frames, which are frames that have no data in them. Why bother? Well, these WAN protocols are used on synchronous links. *Synchronous* simply means that there is an imposed time ordering at the link's sending and receiving ends. Essentially, the sides agree to a certain speed, but because it is expensive to build devices that can truly operate at exactly the same speed, the devices operate at close to the same speed and listen to the speed of the other device on the other side of the link. One side makes small adjustments in its rate to match the other side, called a clock source. The process works almost like the scenes in spy novels in which the spies synchronize their watches; in this case, the watches or clocks are synchronized automatically several times per minute. Unlike asynchronous links, in which no bits are sent during idle times, synchronous data links define idle frames. These frames do nothing more than provide plenty of signal transitions so that clocks can be adjusted on the receiving end, consequently maintaining synchronization.

Before I describe the features of these data-link protocols, a brief reference to some popularly used WAN terminology is useful. Table 9-2 lists the terms.

Table 9-2 *WAN Terminology*

Term	Definition
Synchronous	The imposition of time ordering on a bit stream. Practically speaking, a device will try to use the same speed as another device on the other end of a serial link. However, by examining transitions between voltage states on the link, the device can notice slight variations in the speed on each end and can adjust its speed accordingly.
Asynchronous	The lack of an imposed time ordering on a bit stream. Practically speaking, both sides agree to the same speed, but there is no check or adjustment of the rates if they are slightly different. However, because only 1 byte per transfer is sent, slight differences in clock speed are not an issue. A start bit is used to signal the beginning of a byte.
Clock source	The device to which the other devices on the link adjust their speed when using synchronous links.
DSU/CSU	Data Service Unit/Channel Service Unit. Used on digital links as an interface to the telephone company in the United States. Routers typically use a short cable from a serial interface to a DSU/CSU, which is attached to the line from the telco with a similar configuration at the other router on the other end of the link. The routers use their attached DSU/CSU as the clock source.
Telco	Telephone company.
Four-wire circuit	A line from the telco with four wires, comprised of two twisted-pair wires. Each pair is used to send in one direction, so a four-wire circuit allows full-duplex communication.
Two-wire circuit	A line from the telco with two wires, comprised of one twisted-pair wire. The pair is used to send in only one direction at a time, so a two-wire circuit allows only half-duplex communication.
T1	A line from the telco that allows transmission of data at 1.544 Mbps. It can be used with a T1 multiplexor.
T1 mux	A multiplexor that separates the T1 into 24 different 64 kbps channels. In the United States, the telco can use 1 of every 8 bits in each channel, so the channels are effectively 56 kbps channels.
E1	Similar to a T1, but used in Europe. It uses a rate of 2.048 Mbps and 32 64 kbps channels.

Three key attributes help differentiate among these synchronous serial data-link protocols (LAPB, HDLC, and PPP):

- Whether the protocol supports synchronous communications, asynchronous communications, or both.
- Whether the protocol provides error recovery. (The LAPB, HDLC, and PPP protocols all provide error detection.)
- Whether an architected Protocol Type field exists. In other words, the protocol specifications define a field in the header that identifies the type of packet contained in the data portion of the frame.

First, a few words about the criteria used to compare these WAN protocols might prove helpful. Synchronous protocols allow more throughput over a serial link than asynchronous protocols. However, asynchronous protocols require less-expensive hardware because there is no need to watch transitions and adjust the clock rate. For links between routers, synchronous links are typically desired and used. All the protocols covered in this section support synchronous links.

Another comparison criteria is error recovery. Error recovery is covered in detail in Chapter 3, "OSI Reference Model and Layered Communication," but a brief review is in order here. All the data-link protocols described here use a field in the trailer, usually called the frame check sequence (FCS), that is used to verify whether bit errors occurred during transmission of the frame. If so, the frame is discarded. Error recovery is the process that causes retransmission of the lost frame(s). Error recovery can be performed by the data-link protocol or a higher-layer protocol, or it might not be performed at all. Regardless, all WAN data-link protocols perform error detection, which involves noticing the error and discarding the frame.

Finally, the people who made up these protocols might or might not have defined a Protocol Type field. As described in more detail in Chapter 3, each data-link protocol that supports multiple network layer protocols needs a method of defining the type of packet encapsulated inside the WAN data-link frame. If such a field is part of the protocol specification, it is considered *architected*—in other words, specified in the protocol. If the protocol specification does not include a Protocol Type field, Cisco might add some other header information to create a Protocol Type field.

Table 9-3 lists these point-to-point data-link protocols and their attributes. (For a review of the Protocol Type field, see Chapter 3.)

Table 9-3 *Point-to-Point Data-Link Protocol Attributes*

Protocol	Error Correction?	Architected Type Field?	Other Attributes
Synchronous Data Link Control (SDLC)	Yes	None	SDLC supports multipoint links. It assumes that the SNA header occurs after the SDLC header.

Table 9-3 *Point-to-Point Data-Link Protocol Attributes (Continued)*

Protocol	Error Correction?	Architected Type Field?	Other Attributes
Link Access Procedure Balanced (LAPB)	Yes	None	Assumes a single configurable protocol after LAPB. LAPB is used mainly with X.25. Cisco uses a proprietary type field to support multiprotocol traffic.
Link Access Procedure on the D channel (LAPD)	No	No	LAPD is not used between routers, but is used on the D channel from the router to the ISDN switch for signaling.
High-Level Data Link Control (HDLC)	No	No	HDLC serves as Cisco's default on serial links. Cisco uses a proprietary type field to support multiprotocol traffic.
Point-to-Point Protocol (PPP)	Supported but not enabled by default.	Yes	PPP was meant for multiprotocol interoperability from its inception, unlike all the others. PPP also supports asynchronous communication.

Be careful not to confuse LAPB and LAPD. The D can help remind you that LAPD is for an ISDN D channel, but don't let that make you think that the B is for an ISDN B channel.

HDLC and PPP Configuration

One common task for CCNAs is to enable an appropriate point-to-point data-link protocol. The configuration is straightforward, with LAPB being the exception. Be sure to configure the same WAN data-link protocol on each end of the serial link. Otherwise, the routers will misinterpret the incoming frames, and the link will not work. Tables 9-4 and 9-5 summarize the configuration commands and the **show** and **debug** commands used for HDLC and PPP configuration.

Table 9-4 *PPP and HDLC Configuration Commands*

Command	Configuration Mode
encapsulation {**hdlc** | **ppp** | **lapb**}	Interface subcommand
compress [**predictor** | **stac** | **mppc** [**ignore-pfc**]]	Interface subcommand

Table 9-5 *Point-to-Point-Related* **show** *and* **debug** *Commands*

Command	Description
show interfaces [*type number*]	Lists statistics and details of interface configuration, including the encapsulation type.
show compress	Lists compression ratios.
show processes [**cpu**]	Lists processor and task utilization. Is useful for watching for increased utilization due to compression.

Example 9-1 shows the configuration for PPP, followed by the changed configuration for a migration to HDLC. Assume that Router A and Router B have a serial link attached to their serial 0 ports, respectively.

Example 9-1 *Configuration for PPP and HDLC*

```
Router A                                 Router B

interface serial 0                       interface serial 0
encapsulation ppp                        encapsulation ppp
.                                        .
. later, changed to...                   . later, changed to...
.                                        .
interface serial 0                       interface serial 0
encapsulation hdlc                       encapsulation hdlc
```

Changing serial encapsulations in configuration mode is tricky compared to some other configuration commands in a Cisco router. In Example 9-1, converting back to HDLC (the default) is done with the **encapsulation hdlc** command, not by using a command such as **no encapsulation ppp**. Additionally, any other interface subcommands that are pertinent only to PPP are also removed when the **encapsulation hdlc** command is used.

PPP provides several other features in addition to synchronization and framing. These features fall into two categories: those needed regardless of the Layer 3 protocol sent across the link, and those specific to each Layer 3 protocol.

The PPP Link Control Protocol (LCP) provides the core features needed regardless of the Layer 3 protocol sent across the link. A series of PPP control protocols, such as IP Control Protocol (IPCP), provide features for a particular Layer 3 protocol to function well across the link. For example, IPCP provides for IP address assignment; this feature is used extensively with Internet dialup connections today.

Only one LCP is needed per link, but multiple control protocols are needed. If a router is configured for IPX, AppleTalk, and IP on a PPP serial link, the router configured for PPP encapsulation automatically tries to bring up the appropriate control protocols for each Layer 3 protocol. Table 9-6 summarizes the features of LCP, which performs functions not specific to a particular Layer 3 protocol.

Table 9-6 *PPP LCP Features*

Function	LCP Feature	Description
Error detection	Link Quality Monitoring (LQM)	PPP can take down a link based on the percentage of errors on the link. LQM exchanges statistics about lost packets versus sent packets in each direction. When compared to packets and bytes sent, this yields a percentage of errored traffic. The percentage of loss that causes a link to be taken down is enabled and defined by a configuration setting.
Looped link detection	Magic number	Using different magic numbers, routers send messages to each other. If you ever receive your own magic number, the link is looped. A configuration setting determines whether the link should be taken down when looped.
Authentication	PAP and CHAP	Mostly used on dial links, PAP and CHAP can be used to authenticate the device on the other end of the link.
Compression	STAC and Predictor	This is software compression.
Multilink support	Multilink PPP	Fragments of packets are load-balanced across multiple links. This feature is more often used with dial. The later section, "Multilink PPP" covers this concept in greater detail.

Error Detection and Looped Link Detection

Error detection and looped link detection are two key features of PPP. Looped link detection allows for faster convergence when a link fails because it is looped. (Links are typically looped for testing purposes.) When this occurs, a router continues to receive the looped Cisco proprietary keepalive messages, so the router might not think that the link has failed. For example, the absence of routing updates from a neighbor for a certain length of time is used to drive convergence. Waiting on such an event when the link is looped increases convergence time.

Looped link detection defeats this problem using a PPP feature called *magic numbers*. The router sends PPP messages instead of keepalives; these messages include a magic number, which is different on each router. If a line is looped, the router receives a message with its own magic number instead of getting a message with the magic number identifying the router on the other end of the link. A router receiving its own magic number knows that the frame it sent has been looped back. If configured to do so, the router can take down the interface, which speeds convergence.

Error detection (not error recovery) is accomplished through a PPP feature called *Link Quality Monitoring (LQM)*. PPP at each end of the link sends messages describing the number of correctly received packets and bytes. This is compared to the number of packets and bytes sent to calculate a percentage loss. The router can be configured to take down the link after a configured error rate has been exceeded so that future packets are sent over a longer—but hopefully better—path.

Compression

Compression can be performed on LAPB, HDLC, and PPP point-to-point serial links. The goal of compression is to reduce the number of bytes sent across the link. However, there is a price to pay for compression—CPU cycles and possibly increased latency for the packets. The following list summarizes the trade-offs when you're considering whether to use compression:

- More processing is required on the router to compress each frame, as compared with no compression.
- Latency per frame increases because of the processing required.
- Latency per frame decreases in cases in which the uncompressed packets have waited in the output queue due to link congestion. With compressed frames, however, the queue is shorter.
- Link utilization decreases.

So, in cases in which the leased lines are expensive or a faster line cannot be justified, compression can be desirable. However, care must be taken to avoid excessive CPU utilization. Cisco recommends avoiding sustained CPU utilization exceeding between 40 and 65 percent, depending on the platform.

Compression can be performed in software or hardware. Any IOS router can perform LAPB, HDLC, and PPP link compression in software. When software compression is used, CPU utilization is affected. For hardware compression, either a VIP2 card or a Compression Service Adapter (CSA) on a 72*xx* or 75*xx* series router is required. When hardware compression is performed, the CPU is not affected.

Several compression algorithms are available in the Cisco IOS Software to perform PPP compression: the *STAC, Predictor,* and *Microsoft Point-to-Point Compression* algorithm (MPPC). The details of these algorithms are beyond the scope of the CCNA exam. However, the MPPC algorithm and protocols can be used between a router and a PC on a dial connection when compression is desired.

HDLC supports compression only with the STAC algorithm. LAPB supports the STAC and Predictor algorithms. Only PPP supports the MPPC algorithm. Table 9-7 summarizes the support for each type.

Table 9-7 *Compression Types for Serial Encapsulations*

Encapsulation Type	Type of Compression Supported in the Cisco IOS Software
PPP	STAC, Predictor, MPPC
LAPB	STAC, Predictor
HDLC	STAC

Configuration for PPP and HDLC compression is straightforward. Consider Figure 9-2 and Example 9-2. A pair of routers is using a serial link and is configured for PPP STAC compression.

Figure 9-2 *Serial Link Configured for Compression*

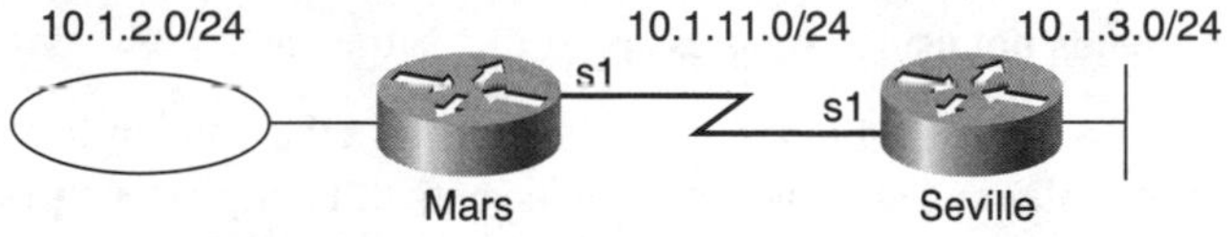

Example 9-2 *PPP Compression Configuration and Verification*

```
! Seville's Pertinent configuration:
!
interface Serial1
 ip address 10.1.11.253 255.255.255.0
 encapsulation ppp
 compress stac
```

```
! Mars's Pertinent configuration:
!
interface Serial1
 ip address 10.1.11.1 255.255.255.0
 encapsulation ppp
 compress stac
!

Seville#show compress
 Serial1
        Software compression enabled
        uncompressed bytes xmt/rcv 260596/222296
        compressed   bytes xmt/rcv 0/0
        1  min avg ratio xmt/rcv 7.752/14.439
        5  min avg ratio xmt/rcv 7.731/14.439
        10 min avg ratio xmt/rcv 7.731/14.439
        no bufs xmt 0 no bufs rcv 0
        resyncs 0
      Additional Stacker Stats:
      Transmit bytes:  Uncompressed =      288 Compressed =      31188
      Received bytes:  Compressed =      15241 Uncompressed =        0
```

continues

Example 9-2 *PPP Compression Configuration and Verification (Continued)*

```
Seville#show process
CPU utilization for five seconds: 15%/15%; one minute: 27%; five minutes: 26%
 PID QTy       PC Runtime (ms)    Invoked   uSecs    Stacks TTY Process
   1 Csp  31C084C         4024      13359     301  720/1000   0 Load Meter
```

The configuration in Example 9-2, compared to a scenario that doesn't use compression, simply requires that the interfaces on each end of the link have the same compression algorithm enabled with the **compress** command. The **show compress** command in the example does not have any particularly interesting numbers, mainly because of the lack of traffic in the network. The 1-, 5-, and 10-minute averages are the transmit and receive compression ratios. They are particularly useful for discovering whether the compression is effective. In fact, if most of the traffic being sent has been compressed already, the compression ratios probably will be low. Cisco recommends not using compression if this is the case.

The **show process** output, which is abbreviated, shows the CPU utilization. The numbers seem to be in a reasonable range. However, for perspective, I simply let a **ping** command run on the Seville router for a few minutes to create the output. No true user traffic was generated for Example 9-2. It's important to watch for compression that drives the CPU utilization too high.

WAN Cabling Standards

Cisco expects CCNAs to understand the cabling options for LAN and WAN interfaces. For any of the point-to-point serial links or Frame Relay links in this chapter, all that is needed on the router is a synchronous serial interface. Traditionally, this interface is a 60-pin D-shell connector. This interface must then be cabled to a CSU/DSU, which in turn is connected to the cable supplied by the service provider. Figure 9-3 shows a typical connection, with the serial cabling options listed.

Figure 9-3 *Serial Cabling Options*

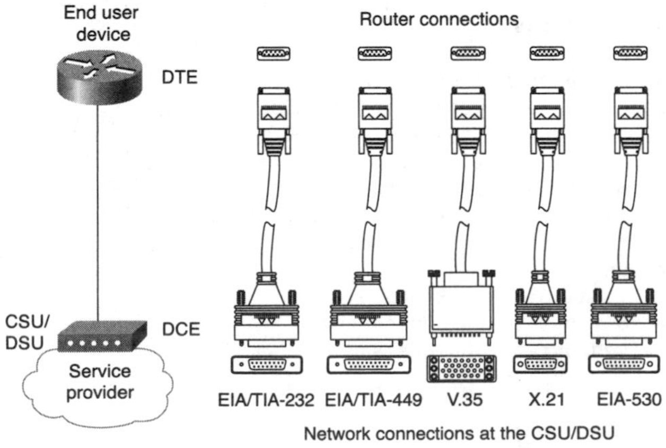

Table 9-8 summarizes the variety of standards that define the types of connectors and physical signaling protocols used on WAN interfaces.

Table 9-8 *WAN Interface Standards*

Standard	Standards Body	Number of Pins on the Interface
EIA/TIA-232	Telecommunications Industry Association	25
EIA/TIA-449	Telecommunications Industry Association	37
EIA/TIA-530	Telecommunications Industry Association	25
V.35	International Telecommunications Union	34
X.21	International Telecommunications Union	15

These cables provide connectivity to the external DSU/CSU, as shown in Figure 9-3. The interface to the service provider depends on the type of connection; the connector could be RJ-11, RJ-48, RJ-45, or possibly coaxial.

Some serial interfaces have an integrated DSU/CSU and do not require a cable of the types shown in the figure. Depending on the expected type of line, a variety of physical interfaces are used. These interfaces are the same as those used for external CSU/DSU devices.

The TIA is accredited by ANSI for the development of telecommunications standards. The TIA also works with the International Telecommunications Union (ITU) on international standards. For more information on these standards bodies, and for the opportunity to spend money to get copies of the standards, refer to the Web sites www.tiaonline.org and www.itu.int.

When building a lab to study for the exam, you do not need to buy DSU/CSUs. You can buy two routers, a DTE serial cable for one router, and a DCE serial cable for the other. The two cables can then be connected, and with one additional configuration command on one of the routers, you have a point-to-point serial link! The secret is simple: The serial cables have a bunch of conductors—just look at the pins on the end of a serial cable. One of these is the transmit pin, and one is the receive pin. The DCE cable swaps the transmit and receive pins. So, when the router with the DCE cable sends on its transmit pin, the electricity for that pin enters the other router's receive pin, and vice versa. A few more pins are also crossed, such as the transmit and receive clock pins. Figure 9-4 gives you the general idea.

So, you buy two routers and the correct two cables and plug them in together. (The DCE cable has a female connector, and the DTE has a male connector.) All you need to do then is use the **clock rate** command, which tells the router to supply clocking (synchronization) on the link. In real life, the CSU/DSU provides the clocking, because it's connected to the phone company, and that's the best place to get clocking for synchronization. Because there is no phone company or CSU/DSU in this case, the router provides the clocking. For example, the **clock rate 56000** interface subcommand, on the router in which the DCE cable is installed, starts clocking the link at 56 kbps.

Figure 9-4 *Serial Cabling Uses a DTE and DCE Cable*

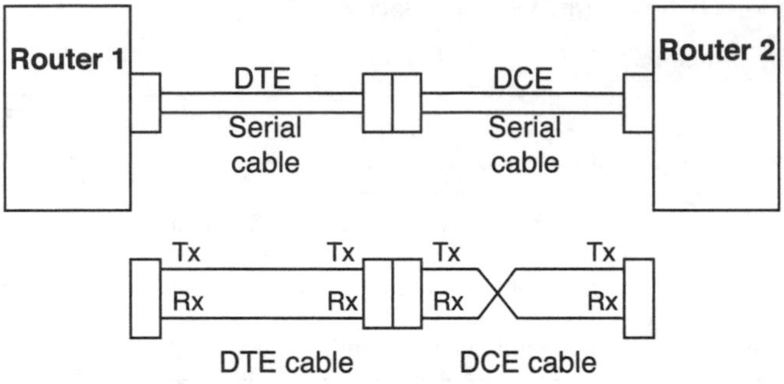

ISDN Protocols and Design

33 Identify ISDN protocols, function groups, reference points, and channels.

Integrated Services Digital Network (ISDN) provides switched (dialed) digital WAN services in increments of 64 kbps. The phone companies of the world created ISDN as a key building block for digital services of the future—things such as faster computing devices that can take advantage of speeds greater than 9600 bps. Another possibility is digital phones. And because ISDN uses 64 kbps bearer channels, and the phone companies use networks whose smallest component is a 64 kbps DS0 channel, ISDN made a lot of sense.

ISDN was created more than 20 years ago, and it began being widely deployed in the U.S. by the early 1990s. Competing technologies might overtake the need for ISDN. For example, the many flavors of DSL technologies, cable modems, Long-Reach Ethernet to the home, and fiber gigabit Ethernet to businesses might become the more popular access technologies of the future. But for the time being, ISDN is on the CCNA exam, and DSL is not, so take a closer look!

This section covers the concepts behind ISDN. The third section of this chapter covers some of the typical configurations you need to use to make ISDN work in a router.

ISDN Channels

The IOS documentation focuses on two types of ISDN interfaces: Basic Rate Interface (BRI) and Primary Rate Interface (PRI). Both BRI and PRI provide multiple digital bearer channels over which temporary connections can be made and data can be sent. The result is concurrent digital dial access to multiple sites. Table 9-9 summarizes the features of BRI and PRI.

Table 9-9 *BRI and PRI Features*

Type of Interface	Number of Bearer Channels (B Channels)	Number of Signaling Channels (D Channels)
BRI	2	1 (16 kbps)
PRI (T1)	23	1 (64 kbps)
PRI (E1)	30	1 (64 kbps)

Bearer channels (B channels) are used to transport data. B channels are called bearer channels because they bear the burden of transporting the data. B channels operate at speeds of up to 64 kbps, although the speed might be lower depending on the service provider. The section, "Typical ISDN Configurations" discusses how to configure the correct speed for bearer channels. D channels are used for signaling.

ISDN Protocols

Coverage of ISDN protocols and their specifications on the CCNA exam poses a particularly difficult problem for the CCNA candidate. The ITU defines the most well-known specifications for ISDN, but there are far more specifications than anyone could memorize. The problem is choosing what to memorize and what to ignore. My personal philosophy is that standards information is best kept in a book rather than in my own memory. With Cisco's emphasis on proving your hands-on skills using the CCNA and CCNP exams, hopefully a de-emphasis on memorizing standards will be a convenient side effect. However, these standards are fair game for the exam.

The characterizations of several key protocols made by the Cisco ICND course are important for the exam. Table 9-10 is directly quoted from the ICND course. Be sure to learn the information in the Issue column. Knowing what each series of specifications is about will be useful.

Table 9-10 *ISDN Protocols*

Issue	Protocol	Key Examples
Telephone network and ISDN	E-series	**E.163**—International telephone numbering plan **E.164**—International ISDN addressing
ISDN concepts, aspects, and interfaces	I-series	**I.100 series**—Concepts, structures, terminology **I.400 series**—User-Network Interface (UNI)
Switching and signaling	Q-series	**Q.921**—LAPD **Q.931**—ISDN network layer

The OSI layers correlating to the different ISDN specifications are also mentioned in both the ITM and ICND CCNA prerequisite courses. It's also useful to memorize the specifications listed in Table 9-11, as well as which OSI layer each specification matches.

Table 9-11 *ISDN I-Series and Q-Series Mentioned in ICND and ITM: OSI Layer Comparison*

Layer as Compared to OSI	I-Series	Equivalent Q-Series Specification	General Purpose
1	ITU-T I.430 ITU-T I.431	N/A	Defines connectors, encoding, framing, and reference points.
2	ITU-T I.440 ITU-T I.4411	ITU-T Q.920 ITU-T Q.921	Defines the LAPD protocol used on the D channel to encapsulate signaling requests.
3	ITU-T I.450 ITU-T I.451	ITU-T Q.930 ITU-T Q.931	Defines signaling messages, such as call setup and takedown messages.

NOTE A tool to help you remember the specifications and layers is that the second digit in the Q-series numbers matches the OSI layer. For example, in ITU-T Q.920, the second digit, 2, corresponds to OSI Layer 2. In the I-series, the second digit of the specification numbers is 2 more than the corresponding OSI layer. For example, I.430, with its second digit of 3, defines OSI Layer 1 equivalent functions.

LAPD is used to deliver signaling messages to the ISDN switch, such as a call setup message. Figure 9-5 shows the use of LAPD versus PPP on B channels.

The call is established through the service provider network. PPP is used as the data-link protocol on the B channel from end to end. LAPD is used between the router and the ISDN switch at each local central office (CO) and remains up so that new signaling messages can be sent and received. Because the signals are sent outside the channel used for data, this is called *out-of-band signaling*.

The BRI encodes bits at 192 kbps, with most of the bandwidth (144 kbps) being used for the two B channels and the D channel. The additional bits are used for framing.

NOTE For further reading, refer to Cisco Press's *Internetworking Technologies Handbook,* Third Edition, ISBN 1-58705-001-3.

Figure 9-5 *LAPD and PPP on D and B Channels*

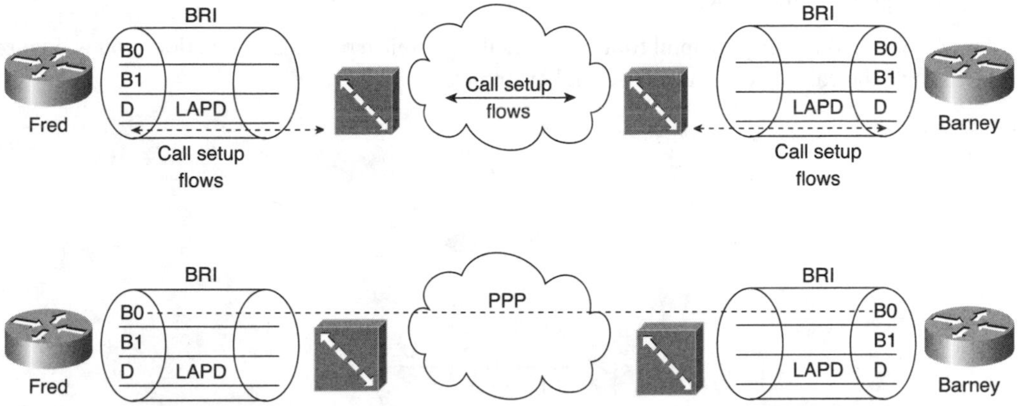

The service profile identifier (SPID) used in signaling is important to the configuration of ISDN and is likely to be mentioned on the exam. The SPID works like an ISDN phone number. In fact, if you buy ISDN for home use, the service provider personnel probably will call it the *ISDN phone number* instead of the SPID. Call setup messages refer to both the called and the calling SPIDs. If a router wants to call another router, a SPID is used for call setup.

ISDN Function Groups and Reference Points

Many people are confused about the ISDN terms *reference point* and *function group*. One key reason for the confusion is that only some function groups—and therefore some reference points—are used in a single topology. Cisco expects CCNAs to be familiar with all function groups and reference points. In an effort to clear up these two topics, consider the following inexact but more-familiar definitions of the two:

- **Function group**—A set of functions implemented by a device and software
- **Reference point**—The interface between two function groups, including cabling details

Most people understand concepts better if they can visualize or actually implement a network. However, for a good understanding of function groups and reference points, keep the following facts in mind:

- Not all reference points are used in any one topology; in fact, one or two might never be used in a particular part of the world.
- After the equipment is ordered and working, there is no need to think about function groups and reference points.

- The router configuration does not refer to reference points and function groups, so many people ignore these details.

A cabling diagram is helpful for examining the reference points and function groups. Figure 9-6 shows the cabling diagram for several examples.

Figure 9-6 *ISDN Function Groups and Reference Points*

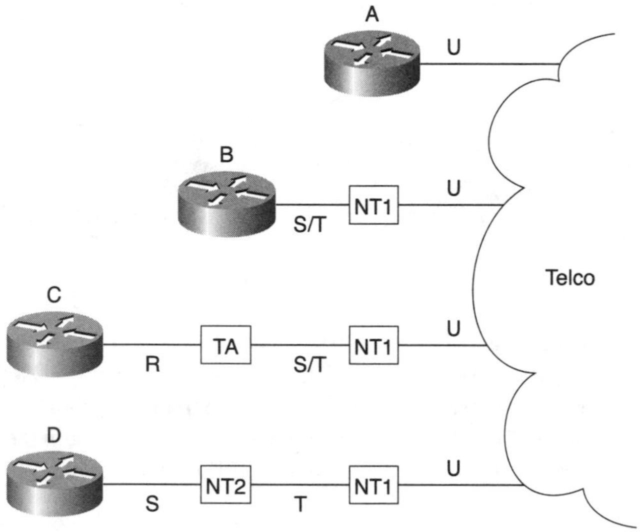

Router A is ordered with an ISDN BRI U reference point, referring to the I.430 reference point defining the interface between the customer premises and the telco in North America. Router B is bought with an ISDN BRI S/T interface, implying that it must be cabled to a function group NT1 device in North America. An NT1 function group device must be connected to the telco line through a U reference point in North America; the S/T interface defines the connection to Router B. Router B is called a TE1 (Terminal Equipment 1) function group device. Non-ISDN equipment is called a TE2 (Terminal Equipment 2) device and is attached using the R reference point to a terminal adapter (TA) function group device. Alternatively, a TE1 can connect using an S reference point to an NT2 function group, as shown in case D of Figure 9-6.

Table 9-12 summarizes the types shown in Figure 9-6. Tables 9-13 and 9-14 summarize the formal definitions.

Table 9-12 *Function Groups and Reference Point Summary*

Router	Function Group(s)	Connected to Which Reference Point(s)	Type of Interface Used in Router
A	TE1, NT1	U	ISDN card, U interface
B	TE1	S/T (combined S and T)	ISDN card, S/T interface
C	TE2	R	Serial interface—no ISDN hardware/software in router
D	TE1	S	Serial interface—no ISDN hardware/software in router

Table 9-13 *Definitions for the Function Groups Shown in Figure 9-6*

Function Group	What the Acronym Stands For	Description
TE1	Terminal Equipment 1	ISDN-capable four-wire cable. Understands signaling and 2B+D. Uses an S reference point.
TE2	Terminal Equipment 2	Equipment that does not understand ISDN protocols and specifications (no ISDN awareness). Uses an R reference point, typically an RS-232 or V.35 cable, to connect to a TA.
TA	Terminal adapter	Equipment that uses R and S reference points. Can be thought of as the TE1 function group on behalf of a TE2.
NT1	Network Termination Type 1	CPE equipment in North America. Connects with a U reference point (two-wire) to the telco. Connects with T or S reference points to other customer premises equipment.
NT2	Network Termination Type 2	Equipment that uses a T reference point to the telco outside North America, or to an NT1 inside North America. Uses an S reference point to connect to other customer premises equipment.
NT1/NT2	N/A	A combined NT1 and NT2 in the same device. This is relatively common in North America.

Table 9-14 *Definitions for the Reference Points Shown in Figure 9-6*

Reference Point	Connection Between
R	TE2 and TA.
S	TE1 or TA and NT2.
T	NT2 and NT1.
U	NT1 and telco.
S/T	TE1 or TA, connected to an NT1, when no NT2 is used. Alternatively, the connection from a TE1 or TA to a combined NT1/NT2.

Jargon definitely confuses the issue with home ISDN services. Figure 9-7 outlines the problem.

Figure 9-7 *Home ISDN User and Reference Points*

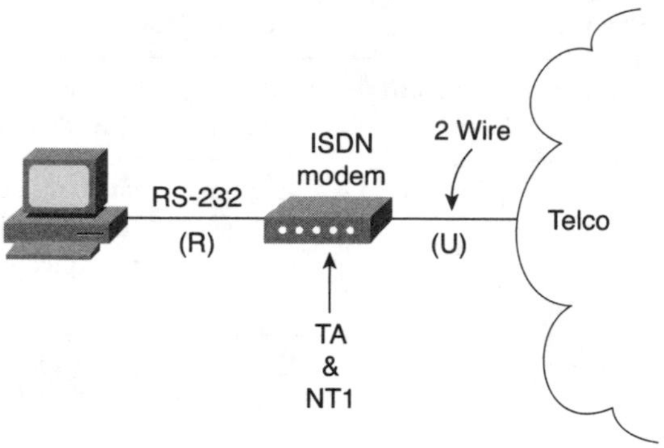

Popularly used, ISDN terminology for home-based consumers sometimes muddles the terminology from the ISDN specifications. The home user orders the service, and the telco offers to sell the user one of several "ISDN modems." What is actually received is a TA and NT1 in one device. A PC uses a serial port to connect to the TA, which uses reference point R. However, the terms reference point, TA, and NT1 are almost never used by providers—hence the confusion.

One other detail of the ISDN protocols that might be on the exam is the ISDN SBus. The ISDN SBus allows multiple devices to share the same BRI by sharing the S reference point. SBus is a great idea, but it has not been deployed extensively. SBus takes the S reference point and allows multiple TE1s to connect to the same NT1. This allows multiple TE1s to use the same BRI. If all the TE1s were data devices, instead of using an SBus, a better solution would be to place all TE1s on a LAN and use an ISDN-capable router. However, the SBus can be used to support ISDN phones, fax, video, and data TE1 devices. Figure 9-8 shows a basic SBus topology.

Figure 9-8 *ISDN SBus*

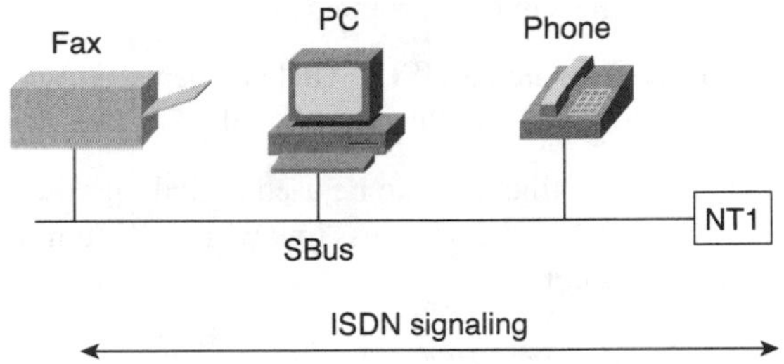

ISDN signaling can be created by TE1s and responded to by TE1s. However, because the BRI is shared among the TE1s, the SPID received in a call setup request no longer uniquely identifies the TE1. Therefore, a suffix called a *subaddress* is added to the SPID. Each TE1 on the SBus uses a different subaddress. The service provider connected to this NT1 and to any other NT1 from which calls are set up must support subaddressing before the user can use the SBus.

Typical ISDN Configurations

32 State a relevant use and context for ISDN networking.

ISDN can be used in many different ways on a Cisco router, but all the possibilities revolve around some basic concepts. The ISDN B channels need to be set up, or dialed. Traffic needs to be directed over those B channels. At some point, the B channels should be taken down.

Temporary connections between routers are another typical use of ISDN, both for backup and for occasional connections. "Occasional" connections might be used by a site for which instant access to data is not needed, but for which access is needed a few times per day. For example, a store might send in sales and resupply information overnight. Most of the configuration needed for these occasional connections is related to dial-on-demand routing (DDR), which is covered in the section, "Dial-on-Demand Routing." In most cases, because the connection is dialed, some form of authentication is also needed.

Figure 9-9 shows some typical network topologies when you're using ISDN. The scenarios in Figure 9-9 can be described as follows:

- Case 1 shows dial-on-demand routing. Logic is configured in the routers to trigger the dial when the user sends traffic that needs to get to another site.
- Case 2 shows a typical telecommuting environment.

- Case 3 shows a typical dial-backup topology. The leased line fails, so an ISDN call is established between the same two routers.
- Case 4 shows a case in which an ISDN BRI can be used to dial directly to another router to replace a Frame Relay access link or a failed VC.
- Case 5 depicts an ISDN line that can be used to dial into the Frame Relay provider's network, replacing a failed VC or access link with a VC running over an ISDN connection to the Frame Relay switch.

Figure 9-9 *Typical Occasional Connections Between Routers*

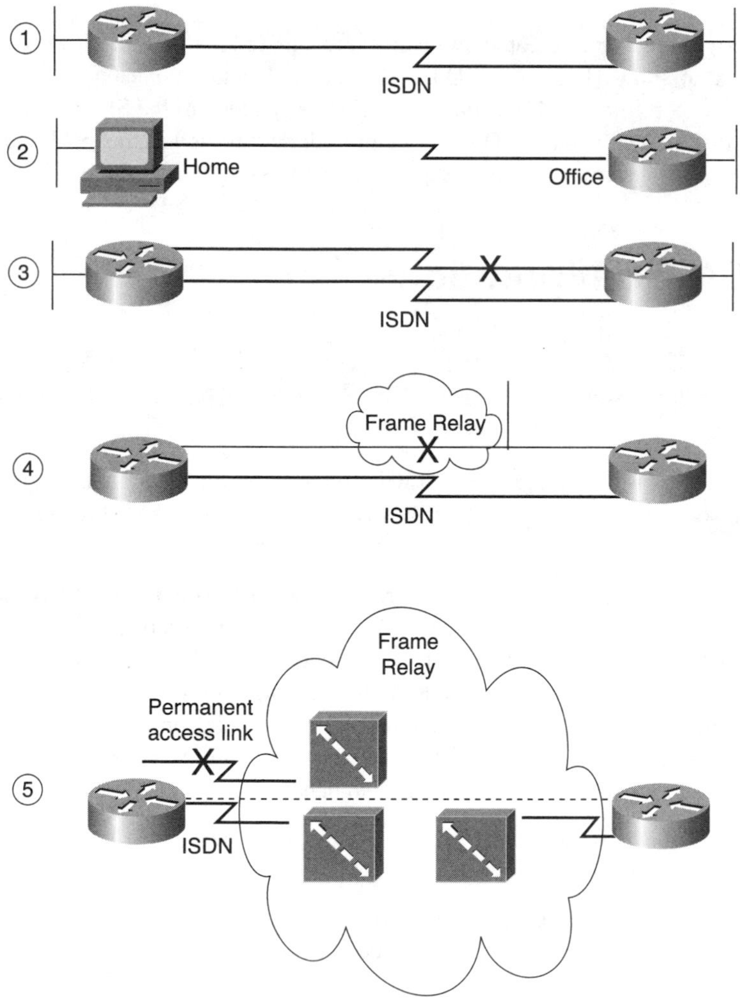

PAP and CHAP

PPP and HDLC can be used on B channels, but PPP provides several features that make it the preferred choice in a dial environment. HDLC and PPP overhead per data frame is identical; however, PPP provides LQM, as well as CHAP and PAP authentication, and Layer 3 address assignment through several of the control protocols. Each of these features is particularly important in a dial environment.

Password Authentication Protocol (PAP) and Challenge Handshake Authentication Protocol (CHAP) are used to authenticate (verify) that the endpoints on a dial connection are allowed to connect. CHAP is the preferred method today because the identifying codes flowing over the link are created using a Message Digest 5 (MD5) one-way hash, which is more secure than the clear-text passwords sent by PAP.

Both PAP and CHAP require the exchange of messages between devices. The dialed-to router expects to receive a username and password from the dialing router with both PAP and CHAP. With PAP, the username and password are sent by the dialing router. With CHAP, the dialed-to router sends a message (called a challenge) that asks the dialing router to send its username and password. The challenge includes a random number, which is part of the input into the MD5 hash algorithm. The dialing router replies with the MD5 hash value, which is a function of its ID (host name), its password, and the random number supplied in the challenge. The dialed-to router repeats the same hash algorithm; if the received value matches the computed value, the CHAP authentication is passed. Figure 9-10 illustrates the message flow in PAP and CHAP environments. Example 9-3 shows the CHAP configuration for Figure 9-10.

Figure 9-10 *PAP and CHAP Messages*

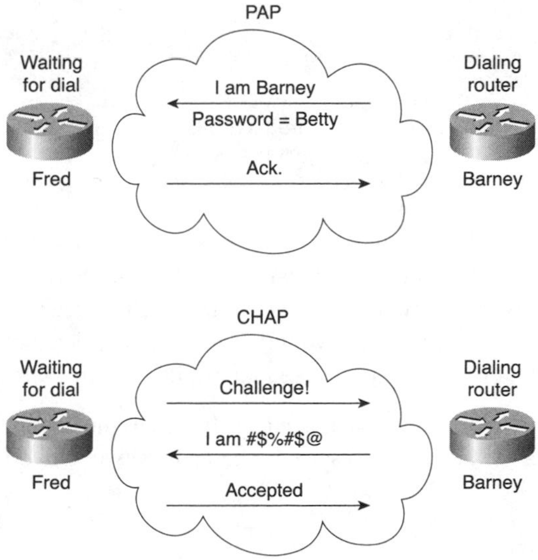

Example 9-3 *CHAP Configuration Example*

Router Fred	Router Barney
username Barney password Bedrock	**username Fred password Bedrock**
!	**!**
interface serial 0	**interface serial 0**
encapsulation ppp	**encapsulation ppp**
ppp authentication chap	**ppp authentication chap**
.	.

Notice that each router refers to the other router's host name; each router uses its own host name in CHAP flows unless overridden by configuration. Each codes the same password. When Router Barney receives a challenge from Router Fred, Router Barney sends an encrypted value, which is the value Fred should compute given the name Barney, the password Bedrock, and the original random number. CHAP authentication is completed if the two values match.

Multilink PPP

Multilink PPP is a function that allows multiple links between a router and some other device over which traffic is balanced. The need for this function is straightforward; some other considerations about when to use it are subtle. Figure 9-11 illustrates the most obvious need for multilink PPP.

Figure 9-11 *Multilink PPP for a Dial-In Device*

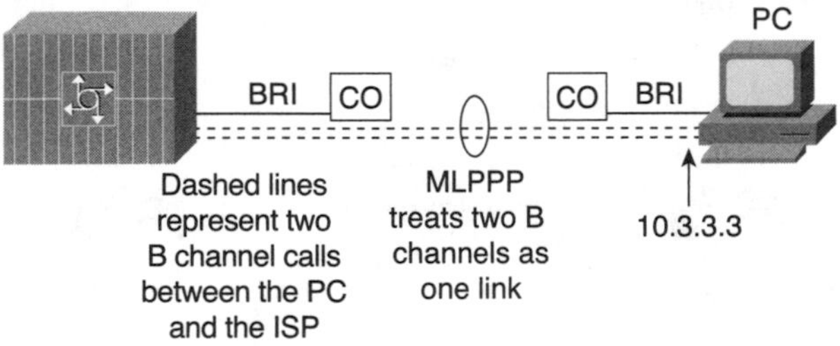

For faster service, the PC that has dialed in would want to use both B channels efficiently. Figure 9-11 shows two dotted lines between the PC and the access server, signifying that two B channels are in use between the devices. Multilink PPP breaks a packet into fragments, sends some fragments across each of the two links, and reassembles them at the other end of the link. The net result is that the links are utilized approximately the same amount.

Multilink PPP is also useful between routers. For example, in Figure 9-12, videoconferencing between Atlanta and Nashville uses six B channels between two routers.

Figure 9-12 *Multilink B Channels Between Routers*

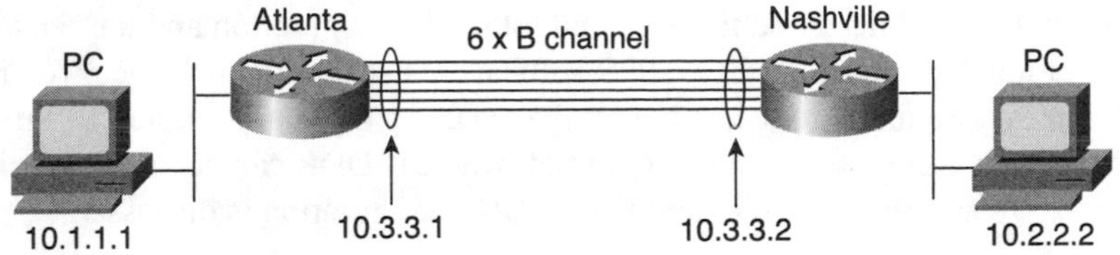

In this example, if multilink PPP is used, the links have almost identical utilization. The downside is that the routers must fragment and reassemble every packet. However, the 384 KB needed for the videoconference is available.

Now consider the alternative—without multilink PPP, but with PPP on each of the six links. Six routes to subnet 10.2.2.0/24 would exist in Router A's routing table. With any of the faster internal switching methods in a Cisco router (fast switching, optimum switching, NetFlow switching), the balancing effect is that *all packets to the same IP address use the same link*. The result is that router Atlanta sends some packets over one link and some over the other, but the balancing is unpredictable. More importantly, all packets to the videoconference system's single IP address in Nashville will use the same link, effectively limiting the videoconference to 64 kbps. An alternative is to disable the faster switching methods in the router so that multiple routes to the same subnet are used in a round-robin fashion. However, this is not recommended because it significantly slows the router's internal processing. For that reason, multilink PPP is a better choice in this case.

Example 9-4 shows a sample multilink PPP configuration. The Atlanta and Nashville routers use two B channels of the same BRI.

Example 9-4 *Multilink PPP Configuration for Atlanta*

```
username Nashville password Robert
interface bri 0
ip addr 10.3.3.1 255.255.255.0
encapsulation ppp
dialer idle-timeout 300
dialer load-threshold 25 either
dialer map 10.3.3.2 name Nashville 16155551234
dialer-group 1
ppp authentication chap
ppp multilink
```

The two key commands are **ppp multilink** and **dialer load-threshold**. **ppp multilink** enables multilink PPP. **dialer load-threshold** tells the router to dial another B channel if the utilization average on the currently used links is more than 25 percent for either inbound or outbound utilization.

Dial-on-Demand Routing

As a CCNA, you'll need to understand both ISDN configuration and the related DDR configuration that causes the Cisco IOS Software to use the BRI interface. You must understand DDR configuration and concepts before the ISDN configuration topics will make complete sense. ISDN configuration can be very brief, whereas DDR can become quite involved. In this section, DDR is explained first, and then ISDN configuration is discussed.

DDR defines the logic behind when a router chooses to dial another site, whether ISDN, synchronous serial, or asynchronous serial interfaces are used. The examples in this chapter reflect ISDN, but the DDR logic is the same for any of the three types of dial interfaces. DDR includes several variations; the variation called DDR legacy is covered in this chapter. If you want to pursue CCNP and CCIE certification, you should expand your knowledge of DDR—especially DDR dialer profiles.

Little additional ISDN configuration is required in addition to the core DDR configuration. In fact, one detail that was covered in detail in an earlier section was the use of certain reference points by Cisco's products. There is no need to configure the Cisco IOS Software to know which interface is used. Cisco's BRI implementation includes a choice of an S/T interface or a U interface. In either case, BRI configuration in the router is identical.

Hands-on experience is the best way to fully learn the details of configuration. In lieu of that, this section lists commands, provides examples, and points out tricky features. Tables 9-15 and 9-16 summarize the more-popular commands used for ISDN configuration and verification. The Cisco IOS Software documentation is an excellent reference for additional IP commands. The Cisco Press book *Interconnecting Cisco Network Devices* is another good reference, particularly if you can't attend the instructor-led version of the class.

Table 9-15 *ISDN Configuration Commands*

Command	Configuration Mode	Description
isdn switch-type *switch-type*	Global or interface	Defines to the router the type of ISDN switch to which the ISDN line is connected at the central office.
isdn spid1 *spid*	Interface	Defines the first SPID.
isdn spid2 *spid*	Interface	Defines the second SPID.
isdn caller *phone-number* [**callback**]	Interface	Defines a valid number for incoming calls when using call screening.
isdn answer1 [*called-party-number*][*:subaddress*]	Interface	Specifies the ISDN number or subaddress that must be used on incoming calls for this router to answer.

Table 9-15 *ISDN Configuration Commands (Continued)*

Command	Configuration Mode	Description
isdn answer2 [*called-party-number*][*:subaddress*]	Interface	Specifies a second ISDN number or subaddress that must be used on incoming calls for this router to answer.
dialer-list *dialer-group* **protocol** *protocol-name* {**permit** | **deny** | **list** *access-list-number* | *access-group*}	Global	Defines the types of traffic that are considered interesting.
dialer-group *n*	Interface	Enables a dialer list on this interface.
dialer in-band [**no-parity** | **odd-parity**]	Interface	Enables dial-out and dial-in on this interface. This command is used only for serial lines that connect to a TA, not for native ISDN interfaces that use the out-of-band D channel.
dialer string *string*	Interface	The dial string used when dialing only one site.
dialer map *protocol next-hop-address* [**name** *host-name*] [**spc**] [**speed 56** | **speed 64**] [**broadcast**] [*dial-string*[*:isdn-subaddress*]]	Interface	The dial string to reach the next hop. However, the **map** command is used when dialing more than one site. This also is the name used for authentication. **broadcast** ensures that copies of broadcasts go to this next-hop address.

Table 9-16 *ISDN-Related Exec Commands*

Command	Description
show interfaces bri *number* [*:b-channel*]	Includes a reference to the access lists enabled on the interface.
show controllers bri *number*	Shows Layer 1 statistics and status for B and D channels.
show isdn {**active** | **history** | **memory** | **status** | **timers**}	Shows various ISDN status information.
show interfaces bri *number*[[**:***bchannel*] | [*first*] [*last*]] [**accounting**]	Displays interface information about the D channel or the B channel(s).

continues

Table 9-16 *ISDN-Related Exec Commands (Continued)*

Command	Description
show dialer interface bri *number*	Lists DDR parameters on the BRI interface. Shows whether a number is currently dialed by indicating the current status. Also shows previous attempts to dial and whether they were successful.
debug isdn q921	Lists ISDN Layer 2 messages.
debug isdn q931	Lists ISDN Layer 3 messages (call setup/teardown).
debug dialer {**events** | **packets** | **map**}	Lists information when a packet is directed out a dial interface, specifying whether the packet is interesting.

DDR Legacy Concepts and Configuration

You can configure DDR in two ways—*DDR legacy* and *DDR dialer profiles*. The main difference between the two is that DDR legacy associates dial details with a physical interface, whereas DDR dialer profiles disassociate the dial configuration from a physical interface, allowing a great deal of flexibility. The concepts behind DDR legacy apply to DDR dialer profiles as well, but DDR legacy is a little less detailed. Although it's not overly stated in the course, the DDR coverage in the ICND class is for DDR legacy.

DDR can be used to cause the router to dial or to receive a dial on asynchronous serial interfaces, synchronous serial interfaces, and ISDN BRI and PRI interfaces. All examples in this chapter use ISDN BRI.

The following list identifies the four key concepts behind DDR configuration. The first two concepts are not actually related to the dial process, but they relate to the process of choosing when to dial and when not to dial. The other two concepts relate to dialing, or signaling. The term *signaling* is used in ISDN to describe the processes of call setup and takedown. It is used synonymously with the term *dialing* here. The four key concepts are as follows:

1. Routing packets out the interface to be dialed
2. Determining the subset of the packets that trigger the dialing process
3. Dialing (signaling)
4. Determining when the connection is terminated

Each of these is addressed in succession, followed by a discussion of DDR legacy configuration. After learning about the basic DDR concepts and configuration procedures, you learn about ISDN-specific configuration. Finally, this section concludes with a complete DDR and ISDN example.

DDR Step 1: Routing Packets Out the Interface to Be Dialed

Figure 9-13 provides the backdrop for these discussions. In these discussions, the SanFrancisco router dials into the main site in LosAngeles.

Figure 9-13 *Sample DDR Network*

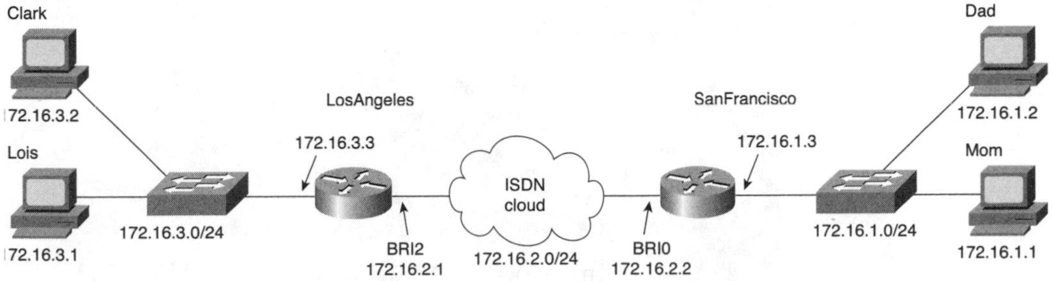

The router must choose when to dial. The first step in this process relates to the following fact:

> DDR does not dial until some traffic is directed (routed) out the dial interface.

The router needs to route packets so that they are queued to go out the dial interface. Cisco's design for DDR defines that the router receives some user-generated traffic and, through normal routing processes, decides to route the traffic out the interface to be dialed. The router (SanFrancisco) can receive a packet that must be routed out BRI0; routing the packet out BRI0 triggers the Cisco IOS Software, causing the dial to occur.

Of course, routes are not learned over a dial link while the dial link is down. In Figure 9-13, for example, SanFrancisco has no routes to 172.16.3.0/24 learned via a routing protocol. Therefore, static routes are configured on SanFrancisco. This can be done for any protocol that is supported by DDR for the purpose of triggering the dial. All routable protocols can be configured to trigger the dial; IP is used in the upcoming examples. Any traffic that could be routed or bridged across a leased link is supported after the link is up.

To begin the process of building a DDR configuration, IP routes are added to the configuration so that packets can be directed out BRI0 on SanFrancisco:

```
! SanFrancisco Static routes.
ip route 172.16.3.0 255.255.255.0 172.16.2.1
```

DDR Step 2: Determining the Subset of the Packets That Trigger the Dialing Process

Together, Steps 1 and 2 of legacy DDR logic determine when the dial is attempted. These combined steps are typically called *triggering the dial*. In Step 1, a packet is routed out an interface to be dialed, but that packet alone does not necessarily cause the dial to occur. The Cisco IOS Software allows the second step to define a subset of the packets routed in Step 1 to actually cause the route to dial. The logic flow is as shown in Figure 9-14.

Figure 9-14 *DDR Logic for Triggering the Data*

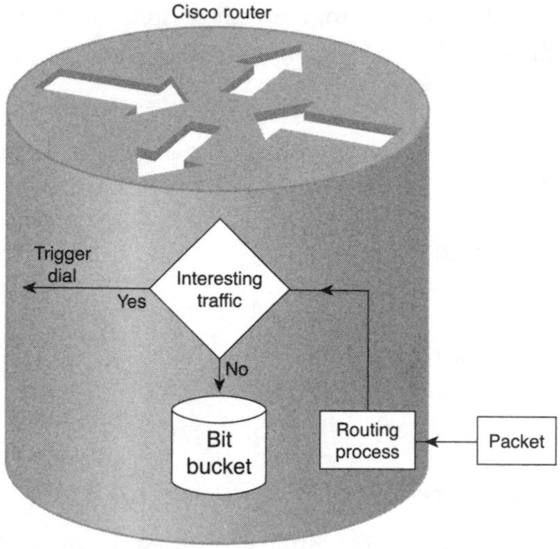

The choice in Step 2 is simply put like this: "Is this packet, which is being routed out this dial interface, worthy of causing the dial to occur?" Cisco calls packets that are worthy of causing the device to dial *interesting packets*. Cisco does not categorize packets that are not worthy of causing the dial; in effect, they are "boring." The capability to exactly determine interesting packets grants the router administrator control over when the dial is made. This is particularly important if the dialed connection is incrementally charged by the minute.

Two different methods can be used to define interesting packets. *Interesting* can be defined as all packets of one or more Layer 3 protocols (for example, all IP packets). In that case, any user in SanFrancisco can send a packet to any host in 172.16.3.0/24 and trigger the dial connection. That might be exactly what is desired, or it might not be. The second method is that *interesting* can be defined as packets permitted by an access list. In this case, if the access list permits the packet, it is considered interesting.

Example 9-5 shows additional configuration on SanFrancisco, in two cases. One shows all IP packets being considered interesting, and the other shows all packets to the Web server Lois (refer to Figure 9-13) considered interesting.

Example 9-5 *Defining Interesting Packets to Activate the Circuit from SanFrancisco to LosAngeles*

```
ip route 172.16.3.0 255.255.255.0 172.16.2.1
access-list 101 permit tcp any host 172.16.3.1 eq 80
dialer-list 1 protocol ip permit
dialer-list 2 protocol ip list 101
interface bri 0
encapsulation ppp
ip address 172.16.2.2 255.255.255.0
!Use this one if all IP is considered interesting ...
```

Example 9-5 *Defining Interesting Packets to Activate the Circuit from SanFrancisco to LosAngeles (Continued)*

```
dialer-group 1
! OR Use next statement to trigger for Web to Server Lois
dialer-group 2
```

The **dialer-group** interface subcommand enables the logic that determines what is interesting. It refers to a dialer list, which can refer to either an entire protocol suite or an access list, as shown. (After the link is up, packets are not filtered using list 101. The logic is used just to determine what is interesting and what is boring.)

DDR Step 3: Dialing (Signaling)

The dialing router needs additional information before the dial can occur. First, for non-ISDN interfaces, it is necessary to communicate the dial string to the external dialing device. In-band signaling (dialing) must be enabled on these interfaces using the command **dialer in-band**. This is not necessary on a BRI interface, because it uses the out-of-band D channel for signaling. Table 9-17 summarizes what this command implies on different interfaces.

Table 9-17 *Effect of the* **dialer in-band** *Command*

Type of Interface	Type of Signaling Used
Async	AT command set (in-band)
Sync	V.25 bis (in-band)
ISDN	ISDN D channel with Q.921/Q.931 (out-of-band)

The second piece of information needed before dialing is the phone number. With the network shown in Figure 9-13, the configuration is straightforward. The command is **dialer string** *string,* where *string* is the phone number. Example 9-6 completes the DDR configuration associated with Figure 9-13 that allows the dial to occur.

Example 9-6 *SanFrancisco Configuration: Dial Now Can Occur*

```
ip route 172.16.3.0 255.255.255.0 172.16.2.1
!
access-list 101 permit tcp any host 172.16.3.1 eq 80
!
dialer-list 2 protocol ip list 101
!
interface bri 0
 ip address 172.16.2.2 255.255.255.0
 encapsulation ppp
 dialer string 14045551234
 dialer-group 2
```

The **dialer in-band** command is omitted because an ISDN BRI is used in this case. The only new command added here is **dialer string**, which shows the phone number that is to be used to signal a connection. The signaling occurs on the BRI's D channel.

When more than one site is dialed from the same interface, several dial strings are needed. For example, Figure 9-15 adds a third site, GothamCity, to the network. The client's FTP connections to the FTP server running on Commissioner are considered interesting traffic for causing dial connections to GothamCity.

The dilemma for SanFrancisco now is how to determine which ISDN telephone number to signal. The key is in the **ip route** commands and the new **dialer map** command. Of course, there are unique ISDN telephone numbers for both LosAngeles and GothamCity. Because the static routes direct the router to send the packet to either 172.16.2.1 or 172.16.2.3, all that is needed is a mapping between these next-hop addresses and their respective ISDN telephone numbers. The **dialer map** command does exactly that. Example 9-7 shows the mostly complete configuration.

Figure 9-15 *Mapping Between the Next Hop and the Dial String*

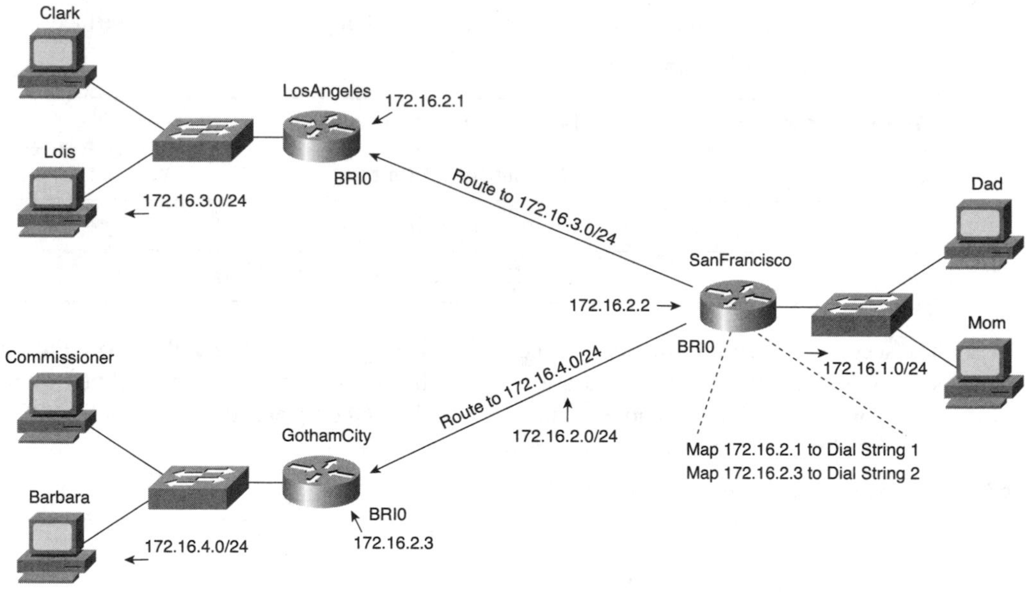

Example 9-7 *SanFrancisco Configuration: Two Dial-To Sites with a Dialer Map in Use*

```
ip route 172.16.3.0 255.255.255.0 172.16.2.1
ip route 172.16.4.0 255.255.255.0 172.16.2.3
! Added usernames for CHAP support!
username LosAngeles password Clark
username GothamCity password Bruce
access-list 101 permit tcp any host 172.16.3.1 eq 80
! Added next statement to make The Client's FTP connection interesting!
```

Example 9-7 *SanFrancisco Configuration: Two Dial-To Sites with a Dialer Map in Use (Continued)*

```
access-list 101 permit tcp any host 172.16.4.1 eq 21
!
dialer-list 2 protocol ip list 101
!
interface bri 0
 ip address 172.16.2.2 255.255.255.0
 encapsulation ppp
 ppp authentication chap
 dialer map ip 172.16.2.1 broadcast name LosAngeles 14045551234
 dialer map ip 172.16.2.3 broadcast name GothamCity 1999999999901
 dialer-group 2
!
router igrp 6
network 172.16.0.0
```

The **dialer map** commands imply that if the interesting packet were routed to 172.16.2.1, the dial to LosAngeles would occur. Conversely, if the interesting packet were routed to 172.16.2.3, the dial to GothamCity would occur. The definition of *interesting* is expanded to include packets to the FTP server in GothamCity.

Two other important configuration elements are included in Example 9-7. First, CHAP authentication is configured. PAP or CHAP is required if you're dialing to more than one site with ISDN—and PAP and CHAP require PPP. The username expected from the other router is coded in the corresponding **dialer map** command.

Broadcast handling is the final configuration element that must be addressed. Just as with any other point-to-point serial link, there is no true data-link broadcast. If a broadcast must be sent on the interface, however, it is necessary to issue the **broadcast** command to tell the interface to forward the packet across the link.

DDR Step 4: Determining When the Connection Is Terminated

The dialed link acts just like a leased line while it is up. If a particular Layer 3 protocol is enabled on the link, it can be routed across the link. Transparent (encapsulated) bridging can be used just like any other point-to-point link. Routing updates, IPX SAPs, AppleTalk ZIP, and other broadcasts are sent across the link if the **broadcast** keyword is coded. Most importantly, any access list used to define which packets are interesting does not filter the traffic on the interface. If packet filters are desired, an access list must be enabled on the interface.

Additional parallel links can be dialed if more capacity is desired. To do so, dialer profiles must be configured. Additionally, the **dialer load-threshold** *load* command defines the link utilization that must be exceeded for another link to be dialed.

The decision to take down the link is the most intriguing part about what happens while the link is up. Although any type of packets can be routed across the link, only interesting packets are considered worthy of keeping the link up. An idle timer counts the time since the last interesting packet went across the link. If that time expires, the link is brought down.

Two idle timers can be set. With the **dialer idle-timeout** *seconds* command, the idle time as previously described is set. However, if interesting traffic that needs to flow to another dial site is occurring, another, shorter idle timer can be used. The **dialer fast-idle** *seconds* command lets you configure a typically lower number than the idle timer so that when other sites need to be dialed, the link that is currently up can be brought down earlier in the process of idling out as per the **dialer idle-timeout** command.

ISDN Configuration

Examples 9-8 and 9-9 show the DDR configuration for the network shown in Figure 9-15. ISDN configuration details have been added. The text following these two examples describes the ISDN commands shown.

Example 9-8 *Completed SanFrancisco Configuration*

```
ip route 172.16.3.0 255.255.255.0 172.16.2.1
ip route 172.16.4.0 255.255.255.0 172.16.2.3
! Added usernames for CHAP support!
username LosAngeles password Clark
username GothamCity password Bruce
!
access-list 101 permit tcp any host 172.16.3.1 eq 80
access-list 101 permit tcp any host 172.16.4.1 eq 21
!
dialer-list 2 protocol ip list 101
!
interface bri 0
 encapsulation ppp
 ppp authentication chap
 isdn spid1 555555111101
 isdn spid2 555555222202
 dialer idle-timeout 300
 dialer fast-idle 120
 dialer map ip 172.16.2.1 broadcast name LosAngeles 14045551234
 dialer map ip 172.16.2.3 broadcast speed 56 name GothamCity 1999999999901
 dialer-group 2
!
router igrp 6
network 172.16.0.0
```

Example 9-9 *LosAngeles Configuration: Receive Only*

```
username SanFrancisco password Clark
!
interface bri 0
 encapsulation ppp
 ppp authentication chap
 isdn switch-type basic-ni1
!
router igrp 6
network 172.16.0.0
```

The ISDN configuration commands are highlighted in the examples and are described in the upcoming text. The switch types are a required parameter for connection to DMS-100 or National ISDN switches; ask your service provider for the type of switch at each site. The LosAngeles BRI is attached to a National ISDN switch in this case. The switch type can be configured with the **isdn switch-type** command, which can be used as a global command or with an interface subcommand if the router is connected to many different types of ISDN switches. The SPIDs might not be required; the switch uses them as a form of authentication. The SPIDs are configured with BRI interface subcommands on SanFrancisco. Also, hidden in part of the DDR configuration, the speed of the B channel from SanFrancisco to GothamCity is 56 kbps, according to the speed parameter in the **dialer map** command on SanFrancisco.

PAP or CHAP authentication is required for ISDN BRI dial connections. PAP and CHAP configuration were covered earlier in the section, "PAP and CHAP."

As shown in Example 9-10, a DDR dial connection over BRI0 occurs from SanFrancisco to LosAngeles.

Example 9-10 *SanFrancisco DDR Commands*

```
SanFrancisco# show interfaces bri 0:1

BRI0:1 is down, line protocol is down
  Hardware is BRI
  MTU 1500 bytes, BW 64 Kbit, DLY 20000 usec, rely 255/255, load 1/255
  Encapsulation PPP, loopback not set, keepalive set (10 sec)
  LCP Open
  Open: IPCP, CDPCP
  Last input 00:00:05, output 00:00:05, output hang never
  Last clearing of "show interface" counters never
  Input queue: 0/75/0 (size/max/drops); Total output drops: 0
  Queuing strategy: weighted fair
  Output queue: 0/1000/64/0 (size/max total/threshold/drops)
     Conversations  0/1/256 (active/max active/max total)
     Reserved Conversations 0/0 (allocated/max allocated)
  5 minute input rate 0 bits/sec, 0 packets/sec
  5 minute output rate 0 bits/sec, 0 packets/sec
     44 packets input, 1986 bytes, 0 no buffer
     Received 0 broadcasts, 0 runts, 0 giants, 0 throttles
     0 input errors, 0 CRC, 0 frame, 0 overrun, 0 ignored, 0 abort
     49 packets output, 2359 bytes, 0 underruns
     0 output errors, 0 collisions, 7 interface resets
     0 output buffer failures, 0 output buffers swapped out
     11 carrier transitions
     DCD=up  DSR=up  DTR=up  RTS=up  CTS=up



SanFrancisco# show dialer interface bri 0

BRI0 - dialer type = ISDN

Dial String      Successes   Failures    Last called   Last status
```

continues

Example 9-10 *SanFrancisco DDR Commands (Continued)*

```
0 incoming call(s) have been screened.

BRI0: B-Channel 1
Idle timer (300 secs), Fast idle timer (120 secs)
Wait for carrier (30 secs), Re-enable (15 secs)

Dialer state is data link layer up

Dial reason: ip (s=172.16.1.1, d=172.16.3.1)


Time until disconnect 18 secs
Current call connected 00:14:00
Connected to 14045551234 (LosAngeles)

BRI0: B-Channel 2
Idle timer (300 secs), Fast idle timer (120 secs)
Wait for carrier (30 secs), Re-enable (15 secs)
Dialer state is idle

 SanFrancisco# show isdn active
 --------------------------------------------------------------------------------
                              ISDN ACTIVE CALLS
--------------------------------------------------------------------------------
History Table MaxLength = 320 entries
History Retain Timer = 15 Minutes
--------------------------------------------------------------------------------
Call Calling      Called         Duration  Remote     Time until   Recorded Charges
Type Number       Number         Seconds   Name       Disconnect   Units/Currency
--------------------------------------------------------------------------------
Out              14045551234     Active(847) LosAngeles     11       u
--------------------------------------------------------------------------------



SanFrancisco# show isdn status
The current ISDN Switchtype = ntt
ISDN BRI0 interface
    Layer 1 Status:
        ACTIVE
    Layer 2 Status:
        TEI = 64, State = MULTIPLE_FRAME_ESTABLISHED
    Layer 3 Status:
        1 Active Layer 3 Call(s)
    Activated dsl 0 CCBs = 1
        CCB:callid=8003, callref=0, sapi=0, ces=1, B-chan=1
    Number of active calls = 1
    Number of available B-channels = 1
    Total Allocated ISDN CCBs = 1
```

Example 9-10 *SanFrancisco DDR Commands (Continued)*

```
SanFrancisco# debug isdn q931
ISDN q931 protocol debugging is on
TX -> SETUP pd = 8 callref = 0x04
 Bearer Capability i = 0x8890
 Channel ID i = 0x83
 Called Party Number i = 0x80, '14045551234'
SanFrancisco#no debug all
All possible debugging has been turned off

SanFrancisco# debug dialer events
Dialer event debugging is on
Dialing cause: BRI0: ip (s=172.16.1.1, d=172.16.3.1)
SanFrancisco#no debug all
All possible debugging has been turned off

SanFrancisco# debug dialer packets
Dialer packet debugging is on
BRI0: ip (s=172.16.1.1, d=172.16.3.1) 444 bytes, interesting (ip PERMIT)
```

The second command in Example 9-10, **show dialer interface bri 0**, lists the current timer values and call setup reason. The call has been up for 14 minutes, and 18 seconds are left before the 300-second inactivity timer will expire and take the connection down. The **show isdn active** command indicates that a single active call exists to LosAngeles, with only 11 seconds left until disconnect. The **show isdn status** command lists the switch type (ntt) and indicates that one call is active, which leaves one inactive B channel.

Remembering the general idea behind the **debug** command output is also useful for CCNAs so that the right options can be enabled quickly. The **debug isdn q921** command (not shown) lists details of the LAPD protocol between the router and the ISDN switch. The **debug isdn q931** command lists output for call setup and disconnect. The output in Example 9-10 shows output typical of what happens on SanFrancisco when a call to LosAngeles is made. The **debug dialer events** and **debug dialer packets** commands provide similar information when a packet is a candidate for causing the dial to occur—in other words, when a packet is routed out the dial interface.

Comparison of WAN Options

Networking professionals need to know about many WAN options when designing networks. Certainly, Cisco requires CCNAs to have a solid foundation of the WAN technologies described in this chapter. Cisco also expects CCNAs to be able to compare and contrast these different WAN technologies. This section summarizes many of the concepts found earlier in this chapter, with a focus on comparison.

The permanent WAN connectivity options can be categorized into two main groups: synchronous serial leased lines and packet-switching services. PPP, HDLC, and LAPB are the three data-link protocols most typical on leased lines, and Frame Relay is the most pervasive packet-switched service. In fact, Frame Relay is more accurately called a *frame-switching* service to imply that the protocol is a Layer 2 protocol. But when discussing similar services as a group, *packet switching* is the typical term used. X.25 and ATM services also fall into the packet-switching category.

X.25 and ATM are not discussed in this book in any depth. (For more information, refer to the documents mentioned in Appendix B, "Decimal to Hexadecimal and Binary Conversion Table.") X.25 is similar to Frame Relay because it uses VCs and has error recovery built in to each link and each end-to-end VC. ATM is similar in its use of virtual connections, which are conceptually equivalent to VCs. However, ATM includes the concept of segmentation and reassembly (SAR), in which the device at the edge of the ATM network breaks the frames to be sent into smaller cells (53 bytes) that are reassembled at the other end of the VC. The details of how each of these three packet-switching protocols are implemented vary; however, each creates a multiaccess network, with direct packet forwarding allowed only between pairs of devices that have a VC between them.

Table 9-18 summarizes these types of permanent connections and lists some of their strengths and weaknesses.

Table 9-18 *Comparison of Leased Lines and Packet Switching*

Type of WAN Service	Data-Link Protocol	Strengths and Weaknesses
Leased line		Delivers pervasive availability. Can be expensive for long circuits. Is more expensive for providers to engineer than are packet services.
	PPP	Can improve the speed of routing protocol convergence. Allows multivendor interoperability. Has an error-recovery option.
	HDLC	The Cisco IOS Software default. Requires a Cisco router on each end.
	LAPB	Provides error recovery, but this can result in throttling (slowing) the data rate.

Table 9-18 *Comparison of Leased Lines and Packet Switching (Continued)*

Type of WAN Service	Data-Link Protocol	Strengths and Weaknesses
Packet-switched		Allows new sites to be added quickly. Typically involves a lower cost.
	Frame Relay	Allows bursting past CIR, giving the perception of "free" capacity. Is pervasive in the United States.
	ATM	As a WAN technology, is not as pervasively available as Frame Relay. Has an attractive built-in Quality of Service feature.
	X.25	Is available pervasively in some parts of the world. Offers beneficial error-recovery features when links have higher error rates. Typically is the third choice of these three if all are available to all connected sites.

The product selection phase of any design project can and should necessarily include key individuals from the organization that will be purchasing or leasing the hardware, Cisco (or the reseller), and any contracted service companies participating in the future deployment of the new equipment. (You might fall into one or more of these categories.) When choosing products, having the vendor or reseller involved can help avoid the problem of trying to be aware of all possible products and options, particularly for new or impending products.

To combat some of the challenges of choosing products from a widely varied product line, Cisco developed the use of three key words to describe the type of product deployed in a typical enterprise network: core, distribution, and access. Figure 9-16 provides a basic network, and Table 9-19 summarizes the meaning of these three categorizations.

Figure 9-16 *Core, Distribution, and Access Layers*

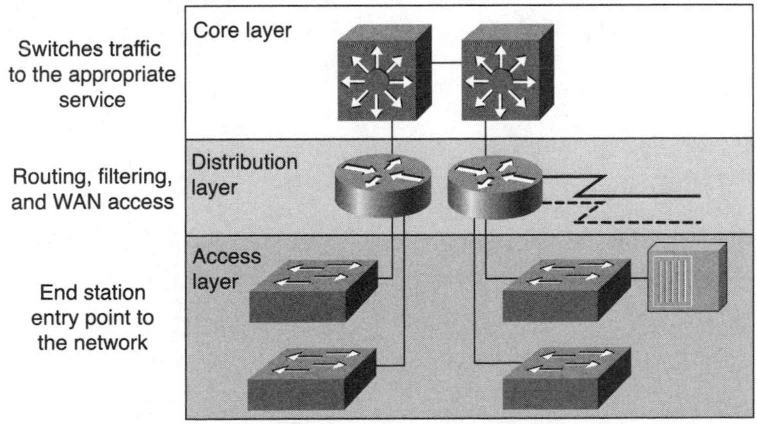

Table 9-19 *Comparison of the Core, Distribution, and Access Layers*

Layer	Features	Desired Device Characteristics
Core	Fast transport, often at the network's topological center. Packet manipulation is not performed here.	Fastest forwarding speed.
Distribution	Aggregation of access points. Any media translation or security (such as access lists) is performed here.	High interface density. Large processing capacity per interface for packet manipulation.
Access	Entry point for end-user devices, both LAN and dial.	Large variety of interface types. Less processing capacity is required (versus distribution).

Foundation Summary

The Foundation Summary is a collection of tables and figures that provide a convenient review of many key concepts in this chapter. If you are already comfortable with the topics in this chapter, this summary can help you recall a few details. If you just read this chapter, this review should help solidify some key facts. If you are doing your final preparation before the exam, these tables and figures are a convenient way to review the day before the exam.

Table 9-20 is a brief reference of some popularly used WAN terminology.

Table 9-20 *WAN Terminology*

Term	Definition
Synchronous	The imposition of time ordering on a bit stream. More practically speaking, a device will try to use the same speed as another device on the other end of a serial link. However, by examining transitions between voltage states on the link, the device can notice slight variations in the speed on each end and can adjust its speed accordingly.
Asynchronous	The lack of an imposed time ordering on a bit stream. More practically speaking, both sides agree to the same speed, but there is no check or adjustment of the rates if they are slightly different. However, because only 1 byte per transfer is sent, slight differences in clock speed are not an issue. A start bit is used to signal the beginning of a byte.
Clock source	The device to which the other devices on the link adjust their speed when using synchronous links.
DSU/CSU	Data Service Unit/Channel Service Unit. This is used on digital links as an interface to the telephone company in the United States. Routers typically use a short cable from a serial interface to a DSU/CSU, which is attached to the line from the telco with a similar configuration at the other router on the other end of the link. The routers use their attached DSU/CSU as the clock source.
Telco	Telephone company.
Four-wire circuit	A line from the telco with four wires, comprised of two twisted-pair wires. Each pair is used to send in one direction, so a four-wire circuit allows full-duplex communication.
Two-wire circuit	A line from the telco with two wires, comprised of one twisted-pair wire. The pair is used to send in only one direction at a time, so a two-wire circuit allows only half-duplex communication.
T1	A line from the telco that allows transmission of data at 1.544 Mbps. It can be used with a T1 multiplexor.

continues

Table 9-20 *WAN Terminology (Continued)*

Term	Definition
T1 mux	A multiplexor that separates the T1 into 24 different 64 kbps channels. In the United States, the telco can use 1 of every 8 bits in each channel, so the channels are effectively 56 kbps channels.
E1	Like a T1, but used in Europe. It uses a rate of 2.048 Mbps and 32 64 kbps channels.

Table 9-21 lists point-to-point data-link protocols and their attributes. (For a review of the Protocol Type field, see Chapter 3.)

Table 9-21 *Point-to-Point Data-Link Protocol Attributes*

Protocol	Error Correction?	Architected Type Field?	Other Attributes
Synchronous Data Link Control (SDLC)	Yes	None	SDLC supports multipoint links. It assumes that the SNA header occurs after the SDLC header.
Link Access Procedure Balanced (LAPB)	Yes	None	Assumes a single configurable protocol after LAPB. LAPB is used mainly with X.25. Cisco uses a proprietary type field to support multiprotocol traffic.
Link Access Procedure on the D channel (LAPD)	No	No	LAPD is not used between routers, but is used on the D channel from the router to the ISDN switch for signaling.
High-Level Data Link Control (HDLC)	No	No	HDLC serves as Cisco's default on serial links. Cisco uses a proprietary type field to support multiprotocol traffic.
Point-to-Point Protocol (PPP)	Lets the user choose whether error correction is performed. Correction uses LAPB.	Yes	PPP was meant for multiprotocol interoperability from its inception, unlike all the others. PPP also supports asynchronous communication.

NOTE Be careful not to confuse LAPB and LAPD. The D can help remind you that LAPD is for an ISDN D channel, but don't let that make you think that the B is for an ISDN B channel.

Tables 9-22 and 9-23 summarize the configuration commands and the **show** and **debug** commands used for HDLC and PPP configuration.

Table 9-22 *PPP and HDLC Configuration Commands*

Command	Configuration Mode
encapsulation {**hdlc** | **ppp** | **lapb**}	Interface subcommand
compress [**predictor** | **stac** | **mppc** [**ignore-pfc**]]	Interface subcommand

Table 9-23 *Point-to-Point-Related* **show** *and* **debug** *Commands*

Command	Description
show interfaces [*type number*]	Lists statistics and details of interface configuration, including the encapsulation type.
show compress	Lists compression ratios.
show processes [**cpu**]	Lists processor and task utilization. Is useful for watching for increased utilization due to compression.

Table 9-24 summarizes the features of LCP, which performs functions not specific to a particular Layer 3 protocol.

Table 9-24 *PPP LCP Features*

Function	LCP Feature	Description
Error detection	Link Quality Monitoring (LQM)	PPP can take down a link based on the percentage of errors on the link. LQM exchanges statistics about lost packets versus sent packets in each direction. When compared to packets and bytes sent, this yields a percentage of errored traffic. The percentage of loss that causes a link to be taken down is enabled and defined by a configuration setting.

continues

Table 9-24 *PPP LCP Features (Continued)*

Function	LCP Feature	Description
Looped link detection	Magic number	Using different magic numbers, routers send messages to each other. If you ever receive your own magic number, the link is looped. A configuration setting determines whether the link should be taken down when looped.
Authentication	PAP and CHAP	Mostly used on dial links, PAP and CHAP can be used to authenticate the device on the other end of the link.
Compression	STAC and Predictor	This is software compression.
Multilink support	Multilink PPP	Fragments of packets are load-balanced across multiple links. This feature is more often used with dial. The section, "Multilink PPP" covers this concept in greater detail.

Table 9-25 summarizes the features of BRI and PRI.

Table 9-25 *BRI and PRI Features*

Type of Interface	Number of Bearer Channels (B Channels)	Number of Signaling Channels (D Channels)
BRI	2	1 (16 kbps)
PRI (T1)	23	1 (64 kbps)
PRI (E1)	30	1 (64 kbps)

Table 9-26 is directly quoted from the ICND course. Be sure to learn the information in the Issue column. Knowing what each series of specifications is about will be useful.

Table 9-26 *ISDN Protocols*

Issue	Protocol	Key Examples
Telephone network and ISDN	E-series	**E.163**—International telephone numbering plan **E.164**—International ISDN addressing
ISDN concepts, aspects, and interfaces	I-series	**I.100 series**—Concepts, structures, terminology **I.400 series**—User-Network Interface (UNI)
Switching and signaling	Q-series	**Q.921**—LAPD **Q.931**—ISDN network layer

Figure 9-17 shows the cabling diagram for several examples.

Figure 9-17 *ISDN Function Groups and Reference Points*

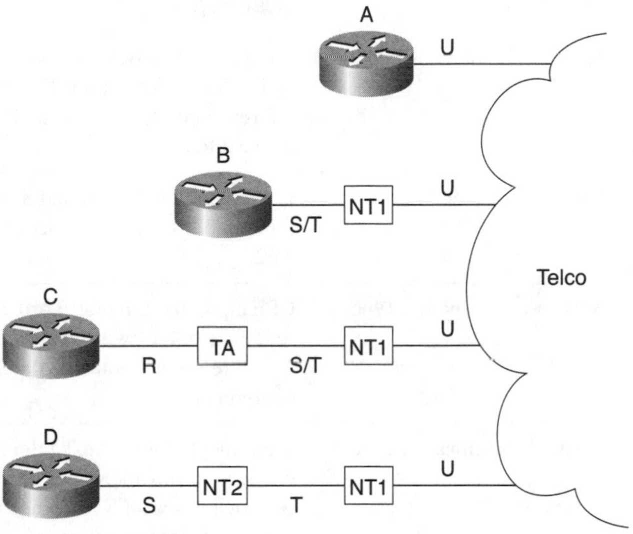

Table 9-27 summarizes the types shown in Figure 9-17. Tables 9-28 and 9-29 summarize the formal definitions.

Table 9-27 *Figure 9-17 Function Groups and Reference Point Summary*

Router	Function Group(s)	Connected to Which Reference Point(s)
A	TE1, NT1	U
B	TE1	S/T (combined S and T)
C	TE2	R
D	TE1	S

Table 9-28 *Definitions for the Function Groups Shown in Figure 9-17*

Function Group	What the Acronym Stands for	Description
TE1	Terminal Equipment 1	ISDN-capable four-wire cable. Understands signaling and 2B+D. Uses an S reference point.

continues

Table 9-28 *Definitions for the Function Groups Shown in Figure 9-17 (Continued)*

Function Group	What the Acronym Stands for	Description
TE2	Terminal Equipment 2	Equipment that does not understand ISDN protocols and specifications (no ISDN awareness). Uses an R reference point, typically an RS-232 or V.35 cable, to connect to a TA.
TA	Terminal adapter	Equipment that uses R and S reference points. Can be thought of as the TE1 function group on behalf of a TE2.
NT1	Network Termination Type 1	CPE equipment in North America. Connects with a U reference point (two-wire) to the telco. Connects with T or S reference points to other customer premises equipment.
NT2	Network Termination Type 2	Equipment that uses a T reference point to the telco outside North America, or to an NT1 inside North America. Uses an S reference point to connect to other customer premises equipment.
NT1/NT2	—	A combined NT1 and NT2 in the same device. This is relatively common in North America.

Table 9-29 *Definitions for the Reference Points Shown in Figure 9-17*

Reference Point	Connection Between
R	TE2 and TA.
S	TE1 or TA and NT2.
T	NT2 and NT1.
U	NT1 and telco.
S/T	TE1 or TA, connected to an NT1, when no NT2 is used. Alternatively, the connection from a TE1 or TA to a combined NT1/NT2.

Figure 9-18 shows some typical network topologies when you're using ISDN. The scenarios in Figure 9-18 can be described as follows:

- Case 1 shows dial-on-demand routing. Logic is configured in the routers to trigger the dial when the user sends traffic that needs to get to another site.
- Case 2 shows a typical telecommuting environment.

- Case 3 shows a typical dial-backup topology. The leased line fails, so an ISDN call is established between the same two routers.
- Case 4 shows a case in which an ISDN BRI can be used to dial directly to another router to replace a Frame Relay access link or a failed VC.
- Case 5 depicts an ISDN line that can be used to dial into the Frame Relay provider's network, replacing a failed VC or access link with a VC running over an ISDN connection to the Frame Relay switch.

Figure 9-18 *Typical Occasional Connections Between Routers*

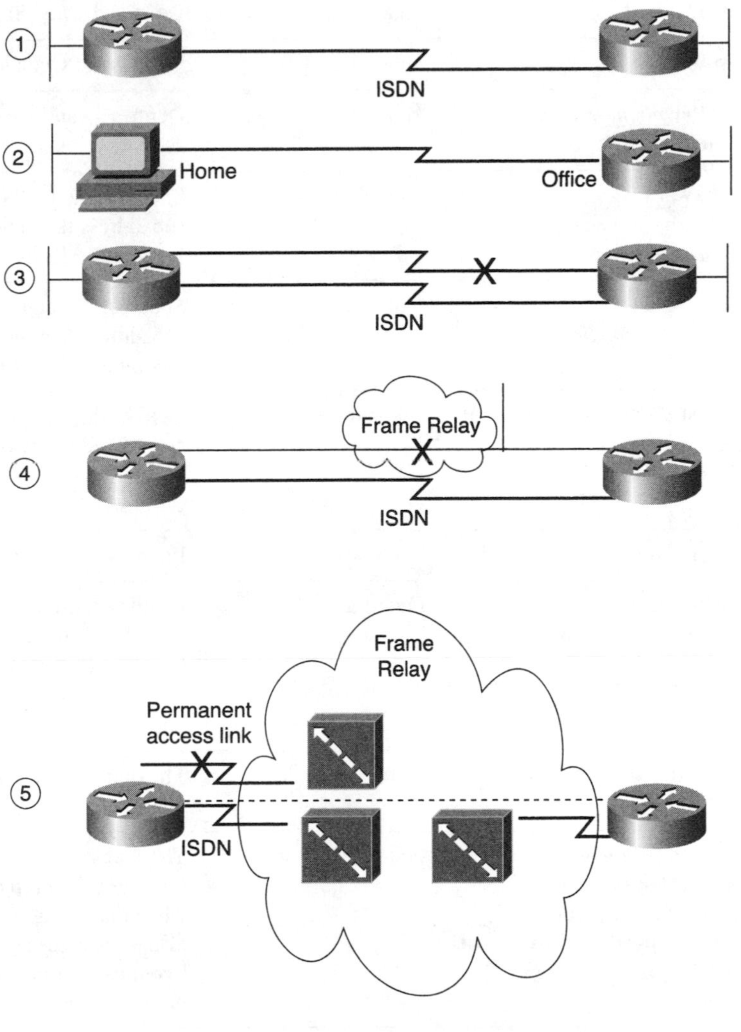

Tables 9-30 and 9-31 summarize the more popular commands used for ISDN configuration and verification.

Table 9-30 *ISDN Configuration Commands*

Command	Configuration Mode	Description
isdn switch-type *switch-type*	Global or interface	Defines to the router the type of ISDN switch to which the ISDN line is connected at the central office.
isdn spid1 *spid*	Interface	Defines the first SPID.
isdn spid2 *spid*	Interface	Defines the second SPID.
isdn caller *phone-number* [**callback**]	Interface	Defines a valid number for incoming calls when using call screening.
isdn answer1 [*called-party- number*] [*:subaddress*]	Interface	Specifies the ISDN number or subaddress that must be used on incoming calls for this router to answer.
isdn answer2 [*called-party- number*] [*:subaddress*]	Interface	Specifies a second ISDN number or subaddress that must be used on incoming calls for this router to answer.
dialer-list *dialer-group* **protocol** *protocol-name* {**permit** | **deny** | **list** *access-list-number* | *access-group*}	Global	Defines the types of traffic that are considered interesting.
dialer-group *n*	Interface	Enables a dialer list on this interface.
dialer in-band [**no-parity** | **odd-parity**]	Interface	Enables dial-out and dial-in on this interface. This command is used only for serial lines that connect to a TA, not for native ISDN interfaces that use the out-of-band D channel.
dialer string *string*	Interface	The dial string used when dialing only one site.
dialer map *protocol next-hop-address* [**name** *host-name*] [**spc**] [**speed 56** | **speed 64**] [**broadcast**] [*dial-string*[*:isdn-subaddress*]]	Interface	The dial string to reach the next hop. However, the **map** command is used when dialing more than one site. This also is the name used for authentication. **broadcast** ensures that copies of broadcasts go to this next-hop address.

Table 9-31 *ISDN-Related Exec Commands*

Command	Description
show interfaces bri *number*[*:b-channel*]	Includes a reference to the access lists enabled on the interface.
show controllers bri *number*	Shows Layer 1 statistics and status for B and D channels.
show isdn {**active** | **history** | **memory** | **status** | **timers**}	Shows various ISDN status information.
show interfaces bri *number*[[**:***bchannel*] | [*first*] [*last*]] [**accounting**]	Displays interface information about the D channel or the B channel(s).
show dialer interface bri *number*	Lists DDR parameters on the BRI interface. Shows whether a number is currently dialed by indicating the current status. Also shows previous attempts to dial and whether they were successful.
debug isdn q921	Lists ISDN Layer 2 messages.
debug isdn q931	Lists ISDN Layer 3 messages (call setup/teardown).
debug dialer {**events** | **packets** | **map**}	Lists information when a packet is directed out a dial interface, specifying whether the packet is interesting.

Table 9-32 summarizes types of permanent connections and lists some of their strengths and weaknesses.

Table 9-32 *Comparison of Leased Lines and Packet Switching*

Type of WAN Service	Data-Link Protocol	Strengths and Weaknesses
Leased line		Delivers pervasive availability. Can be expensive for long circuits. Is more expensive for providers to engineer than are packet services.
	PPP	Can improve the speed of routing protocol convergence. Allows multivendor interoperability. Has an error-recovery option.
	HDLC	The Cisco IOS Software default. Requires a Cisco router on each end.
	LAPB	Provides error recovery, but this can result in throttling (slowing) the data rate.

continues

Table 9-32 *Comparison of Leased Lines and Packet Switching (Continued)*

Type of WAN Service	Data-Link Protocol	Strengths and Weaknesses
Packet-switched		Allows new sites to be added quickly. Typically involves a lower cost.
	Frame Relay	Allows bursting past CIR, giving the perception of "free" capacity. Is pervasive in the United States.
	ATM	As a WAN technology, is not as pervasively available as Frame Relay. Has an attractive built-in Quality of Service feature.
	X.25	Is available pervasively in some parts of the world. Offers beneficial error-recovery features when links have higher error rates. Typically is the third choice of these three if all are available to all connected sites.

Q&A

As mentioned in Chapter 1, “All About the Cisco Certified Network Associate Certification,” the questions and scenarios in this book are more difficult than what you should experience on the exam. The questions do not attempt to cover more breadth or depth than the exam, but they are designed to make sure that you know the answer. Rather than allowing you to derive the answer from clues hidden in the question, the questions challenge your understanding and recall of the subject. Questions from the “Do I Know This Already?” quiz at the beginning of this chapter are repeated here to ensure that you have mastered this chapter’s topics. Hopefully, these questions will help limit the number of exam questions on which you narrow your choices to two options and then guess.

The answers to these questions can be found in Appendix A.

1. Name two WAN data-link protocols for which the standards define a protocol type field that is used to define the type of header that follows the WAN data-link header.

2. Name two WAN data-link protocols that define a method of announcing the interface’s Layer 3 addresses to other devices attached to the WAN.

3. What does LAPD stand for? Is it used as the Layer 2 protocol on dialed ISDN bearer channels? If not, what is?

4. What does NBMA stand for? Does it apply to PPP links? What about X.25 networks or Frame Relay networks?

5 Can PPP dynamically assign IP addresses? If so, is this feature always enabled?

6 Create a configuration to enable PPP on serial 0 for IP and IPX. Make up IP and IPX Layer 3 addresses as needed.

7 Create a configuration for Router1 that has Frame Relay VCs to Router2 and Router3 (DLCIs 202 and 203, respectively) for Frame Relay on Router1's serial 1 interface. Use any IP and IPX addresses you like. Assume that the network is not fully meshed.

8 What do ISDN, BRI, and PRI stand for?

9 Define the term *function group*. List two examples of function groups.

10 Define the term *reference point*. List two examples of reference points.

11 How many bearer channels are in a BRI? What about a PRI in North America? What about a PRI in Europe?

____

____

____

12 True or false: ISDN defines protocols that can be functionally equivalent to OSI Layers 1, 2, and 3. Explain your answer.

____

____

____

13 What reference points are used by ISDN BRI interfaces on Cisco routers?

____

____

____

14 Is LAPD used on ISDN channels? If so, which ones?

____

____

____

15 Name the standards body that defines ISDN protocols.

____

____

____

16 What ISDN functions do standards ITU-T Q.920 and Q.930 define? Does either standard correlate to an OSI layer?

____

____

____

17 What ISDN functions does standard ITU-T I.430 define? Does it correlate to an OSI layer?

18 What does SPID stand for? What does it mean?

19 Define the terms TE1, TE2, and TA. Which implies that one of the other two must be in use?

20 What reference point is used between the customer premises and the phone company in North America? What about in Europe?

21 Define the term SBus, and give an example of when it is useful.

22 What data link (OSI Layer 2) protocols are valid on an ISDN B channel?

23 Define the terms PAP and CHAP. Which one sends passwords in clear-text format?

24 Define MLPPP. Describe the typical home or small office use of MLPPP.

25 CHAP configuration uses names and passwords. Given Routers A and B, describe what names and passwords must match in the respective CHAP configurations.

26 Configure ISDN interface BRI1, assuming that it is attached to a DMS-100 ISDN switch, that it uses only one SPID of 404555121201, and that you want to screen calls so that only calls from 404555999901 are accepted.

27 List the types of compression that are available on PPP links.

28 Describe the decision process performed by the Cisco IOS Software to attempt to dial a connection using legacy DDR.

29 If packets from 10.1.1.0/24 are "interesting" in relation to DDR configuration, such that packets from 10.1.1.0/24 caused a DDR connection out interface BRI0, list the configuration commands that would make the Cisco IOS Software think that those packets were interesting on BRI0.

30 List the typical EIA/TIA standard interfaces used for serial cables with a Cisco router.

____

____

____

31 What field has Cisco added to the HDLC header, making it proprietary?

____

____

____

Scenarios

Scenario 9-1: Point-to-Point Verification

Use Examples 9-11, 9-12, and 9-13 when completing the exercises and answering the questions that follow.

Example 9-11 *Albuquerque Command Output for Scenario 9-1*

```
Albuquerque#show ip interface brief
Interface              IP-Address      OK? Method Status                Protocol
Serial0                199.1.1.129     YES NVRAM  up                    up
Serial1                199.1.1.193     YES NVRAM  up                    up
Ethernet0              199.1.1.33      YES NVRAM  up                    up

Albuquerque#show ip route
Codes: C - connected, S - static, I - IGRP, R - RIP, M - mobile, B - BGP
       D - EIGRP, EX - EIGRP external, O - OSPF, IA - OSPF inter area
N1 - OSPF NSSA external type 1, N2 - OSPF NSSA external type 2
       E1 - OSPF external type 1, E2 - OSPF external type 2, E - EGP
       i - IS-IS, L1 - IS-IS level-1, L2 - IS-IS level-2, * - candidate default
       U - per-user static route, o - ODR

Gateway of last resort is not set

     199.1.1.0/24 is variably subnetted, 7 subnets, 2 masks
C       199.1.1.192/27 is directly connected, Serial1
C       199.1.1.130/32 is directly connected, Serial0
C       199.1.1.128/27 is directly connected, Serial0
I       199.1.1.160/27 [100/10476] via 199.1.1.130, 00:00:01, Serial0
                       [100/10476] via 199.1.1.194, 00:00:54, Serial1
I       199.1.1.64/27 [100/8539] via 199.1.1.130, 00:00:01, Serial0
I       199.1.1.96/27 [100/8539] via 199.1.1.194, 00:00:54, Serial1
C       199.1.1.32/27 is directly connected, Ethernet0

Albuquerque#show ipx route
Codes: C - Connected primary network,    c - Connected secondary network
       S - Static, F - Floating static, L - Local (internal), W - IPXWAN
       R - RIP, E - EIGRP, N - NLSP, X - External, A - Aggregate
       s - seconds, u - uses

6 Total IPX routes. Up to 1 parallel paths and 16 hops allowed.

No default route known.

C       1001 (SAP),          E0
C       2001 (PPP),          Se0
C       2003 (HDLC),         Se1
R       1002 [07/01] via    2001.0200.bbbb.bbbb,    50s, Se0
R       1003 [07/01] via    2003.0200.cccc.cccc,    57s, Se1
R       2002 [07/01] via    2001.0200.bbbb.bbbb,    51s, Se0
```

continues

Example 9-11 *Albuquerque Command Output for Scenario 9-1 (Continued)*

```
Albuquerque#debug ppp negotiation
PPP protocol negotiation debugging is on

%LINK-3-UPDOWN: Interface Serial0, changed state to up

Se0 PPP: Treating connection as a dedicated line
Se0 PPP: Phase is ESTABLISHING, Active Open
Se0 LCP: O CONFREQ [Closed] id 15 len 10
Se0 LCP:    MagicNumber 0x003C2A1F (0x0506003C2A1F)
Se0 LCP: I CONFREQ [REQsent] id 34 len 10
Se0 LCP:    MagicNumber 0x0648CFD3 (0x05060648CFD3)
Se0 LCP: O CONFACK [REQsent] id 34 len 10
Se0 LCP:    MagicNumber 0x0648CFD3 (0x05060648CFD3)
Se0 LCP: TIMEout: Time = 0xBA0E0 State = ACKsent
Se0 LCP: O CONFREQ [ACKsent] id 16 len 10
Se0 LCP:    MagicNumber 0x003C2A1F (0x0506003C2A1F)
Se0 LCP: I CONFACK [ACKsent] id 16 len 10
Se0 LCP:    MagicNumber 0x003C2A1F (0x0506003C2A1F)
Se0 LCP: State is Open
Se0 PPP: Phase is UP
Se0 IPCP: O CONFREQ [Closed] id 3 len 10
Se0 IPCP:    Address 199.1.1.129 (0x0306C7010181)
Se0 CDPCP: O CONFREQ [Closed] id 3 len 4
Se0 LLC2CP: O CONFREQ [Closed] id 3 len 4
Se0 IPXCP: O CONFREQ [Closed] id 3 len 18
Se0 IPXCP:    Network 0x00002001 (0x010600002001)
Se0 IPXCP:    Node 0200.aaaa.aaaa (0x02080200AAAAAAAA)
Se0 IPCP: I CONFREQ [REQsent] id 4 len 10
Se0 IPCP:    Address 199.1.1.130 (0x0306C7010182)
Se0 IPCP: O CONFACK [REQsent] id 4 len 10
Se0 IPCP:    Address 199.1.1.130 (0x0306C7010182)
Se0 CDPCP: I CONFREQ [REQsent] id 6 len 4
Se0 CDPCP: O CONFACK [REQsent] id 6 len 4
Se0 LLC2CP: I CONFREQ [REQsent] id 6 len 4
Se0 LLC2CP: O CONFACK [REQsent] id 6 len 4
Se0 IPXCP: I CONFREQ [REQsent] id 4 len 18
Se0 IPXCP:    Network 0x00002001 (0x010600002001)
Se0 IPXCP:    Node 0200.bbbb.bbbb (0x02080200BBBBBBBB)
Se0 IPXCP: O CONFACK [REQsent] id 4 len 18
Se0 IPXCP:    Network 0x00002001 (0x010600002001)
Se0 IPXCP:    Node 0200.bbbb.bbbb (0x02080200BBBBBBBB)
```

Example 9-12 *Yosemite Command Output for Scenario 9-1*

```
Yosemite#show ipx interface brief
Interface            IPX Network Encapsulation Status                IPX State
Serial0              2001        PPP           up                    [up]
Serial1              2002        LAPB          up                    [up]
Ethernet0            1002        SAP           up                    [up]

Yosemite#show ipx route
Codes: C - Connected primary network,    c - Connected secondary network
```

Example 9-12 *Yosemite Command Output for Scenario 9-1 (Continued)*

```
       S - Static, F - Floating static, L - Local (internal), W - IPXWAN
       R - RIP, E - EIGRP, N - NLSP, X - External, A - Aggregate
       s - seconds, u - uses

6 Total IPX routes. Up to 1 parallel paths and 16 hops allowed.

No default route known.

C       1002 (SAP),            E0
C       2001 (PPP),            Se0
C       2002 (LAPB),           Se1
R       1001 [07/01] via     2001.0200.aaaa.aaaa,   46s, Se0
R       1003 [13/02] via     2001.0200.aaaa.aaaa,   47s, Se0
R       2003 [07/01] via     2001.0200.aaaa.aaaa,   47s, Se0

Yosemite#show interface serial 1 accounting
Serial1
                Protocol    Pkts In   Chars In   Pkts Out  Chars Out
                      IP         37       2798         41       3106

Yosemite#ping ipx 2002.0200.cccc.cccc

Type escape sequence to abort.
Sending 5, 100-byte IPX Cisco Echoes to 2002.0200.cccc.cccc, timeout is 2 seconds:
.....
Success rate is 0 percent (0/5)

Yosemite#ping 199.1.1.162

Type escape sequence to abort.
Sending 5, 100-byte ICMP Echos to 199.1.1.162, timeout is 2 seconds:
!!!!!
Success rate is 100 percent (5/5), round-trip min/avg/max = 8/8/8 ms

Yosemite#ping ipx 1003.0000.30ac.70ef

Type escape sequence to abort.
Sending 5, 100-byte IPX Cisco Echoes to 1003.0000.30ac.70ef, timeout is 2 seconds:
!!!!!
Success rate is 100 percent (5/5), round-trip min/avg/max = 8/8/12 ms

Seville#show ip route
Codes: C - connected, S - static, I - IGRP, R - RIP, M - mobile, B - BGP
       D - EIGRP, EX - EIGRP external, O - OSPF, IA - OSPF inter area
       N1 - OSPF NSSA external type 1, N2 - OSPF NSSA external type 2
       E1 - OSPF external type 1, E2 - OSPF external type 2, E - EGP
       i - IS-IS, L1 - IS-IS level-1, L2 - IS-IS level-2, * - candidate default
       U - per-user static route, o - ODR

Gateway of last resort is not set
```

continues

Example 9-12 *Yosemite Command Output for Scenario 9-1 (Continued)*

```
      199.1.1.0/27 is subnetted, 6 subnets
C        199.1.1.192 is directly connected, Serial0
I        199.1.1.128 [100/10476] via 199.1.1.161, 00:00:36, Serial1
                     [100/10476] via 199.1.1.193, 00:01:09, Serial0
C        199.1.1.160 is directly connected, Serial1
I        199.1.1.64 [100/8539] via 199.1.1.161, 00:00:36, Serial1
C        199.1.1.96 is directly connected, Ethernet0
I        199.1.1.32 [100/8539] via 199.1.1.193, 00:01:09, Serial0

Seville#show ipx route
Codes: C - Connected primary network,    c - Connected secondary network
       S - Static, F - Floating static, L - Local (internal), W - IPXWAN
       R - RIP, E - EIGRP, N - NLSP, X - External, A - Aggregate
       s - seconds, u - uses

6 Total IPX routes. Up to 1 parallel paths and 16 hops allowed.

No default route known.

C        1003 (SAP),          E0
C        2002 (LAPB),         Se1
C        2003 (HDLC),         Se0
R        1001 [07/01] via     2003.0200.aaaa.aaaa,    2s, Se0
R        1002 [13/02] via     2003.0200.aaaa.aaaa,    2s, Se0
R        2001 [07/01] via     2003.0200.aaaa.aaaa,    2s, Se0

Seville#show interface serial 0 accounting
Serial0
                Protocol    Pkts In   Chars In   Pkts Out  Chars Out
                      IP         44       3482         40       3512
                     IPX         46       3478         44       2710
                     CDP         21       6531         26       7694

Seville#debug lapb
LAPB link debugging is on

%LINK-3-UPDOWN: Interface Serial1, changed state to up

Serial1: LAPB O SABMSENT (2) SABM P
Serial1: LAPB I SABMSENT (2) UA F
Serial1: LAPB I CONNECT (104) IFRAME 0 0
Serial1: LAPB O CONNECT (76) IFRAME 0 1Serial1: LAPB I CONNECT (76) IFRAME 1 1
Serial1: LAPB O CONNECT (2) RR (R) 2
Seville#
Seville#ping 199.1.1.161


Type escape sequence to abort.
Sending 5, 100-byte ICMP Echos to 199.1.1.161, timeout is 2 seconds:
```

Example 9-12 *Yosemite Command Output for Scenario 9-1 (Continued)*

```
!!!!!
Success rate is 100 percent (5/5), round-trip min/avg/max = 8/8/12 ms
Seville#
Serial1: LAPB O CONNECT (102) IFRAME 1 3
Serial1: LAPB I CONNECT (102) IFRAME 3 2
Serial1: LAPB O CONNECT (2) RR (R) 4
Serial1: LAPB O CONNECT (102) IFRAME 2 4
Serial1: LAPB I CONNECT (102) IFRAME 4 3
Serial1: LAPB O CONNECT (2) RR (R) 5
Serial1: LAPB O CONNECT (102) IFRAME 3 5
Serial1: LAPB I CONNECT (2) RR (R) 4
Serial1: LAPB I CONNECT (102) IFRAME 5 4
Serial1: LAPB O CONNECT (2) RR (R) 6
Serial1: LAPB O CONNECT (102) IFRAME 4 6
Serial1: LAPB I CONNECT (102) IFRAME 6 5
Serial1: LAPB O CONNECT (2) RR (R) 7
Serial1: LAPB O CONNECT (102) IFRAME 5 7
Serial1: LAPB I CONNECT (102) IFRAME 7 6
Serial1: LAPB O CONNECT (2) RR (R) 0
```

Example 9-13 *Seville Command Output for Scenario 9-1*

```
Seville#show ip route
Codes: C - connected, S - static, I - IGRP, R - RIP, M - mobile, B - BGP
       D - EIGRP, EX - EIGRP external, O - OSPF, IA - OSPF inter area
       N1 - OSPF NSSA external type 1, N2 - OSPF NSSA external type 2
       E1 - OSPF external type 1, E2 - OSPF external type 2, E - EGP
       i - IS-IS, L1 - IS-IS level-1, L2 - IS-IS level-2, * - candidate default
       U - per-user static route, o - ODR

Gateway of last resort is not set

     199.1.1.0/27 is subnetted, 6 subnets
C       199.1.1.192 is directly connected, Serial0
I       199.1.1.128 [100/10476] via 199.1.1.161, 00:00:36, Serial1
                    [100/10476] via 199.1.1.193, 00:01:09, Serial0
C       199.1.1.160 is directly connected, Serial1
I       199.1.1.64 [100/8539] via 199.1.1.161, 00:00:36, Serial1
C       199.1.1.96 is directly connected, Ethernet0
I       199.1.1.32 [100/8539] via 199.1.1.193, 00:01:09, Serial0

Seville#show ipx route
Codes: C - Connected primary network,    c - Connected secondary network
       S - Static, F - Floating static, L - Local (internal), W - IPXWAN
       R - RIP, E - EIGRP, N - NLSP, X - External, A - Aggregate
       s - seconds, u - uses

6 Total IPX routes. Up to 1 parallel paths and 16 hops allowed.
```

continues

Example 9-13 *Seville Command Output for Scenario 9-1 (Continued)*

```
No default route known.

C       1003 (SAP),          E0
C       2002 (LAPB),         Se1
C       2003 (HDLC),         Se0
R       1001 [07/01] via     2003.0200.aaaa.aaaa,    2s, Se0
R       1002 [13/02] via     2003.0200.aaaa.aaaa,    2s, Se0
R       2001 [07/01] via     2003.0200.aaaa.aaaa,    2s, Se0

Seville#show interface serial 0 accounting
Serial0
                Protocol    Pkts In   Chars In   Pkts Out  Chars Out
                      IP         44       3482         40       3512
                     IPX         46       3478         44       2710
                     CDP         21       6531         26       7694

Seville#debug lapb
LAPB link debugging is on

%LINK-3-UPDOWN: Interface Serial1, changed state to up

Serial1: LAPB O SABMSENT (2) SABM P
Serial1: LAPB I SABMSENT (2) UA F
Serial1: LAPB I CONNECT (104) IFRAME 0 0
Serial1: LAPB O CONNECT (76) IFRAME 0 1Serial1: LAPB I CONNECT (76) IFRAME 1 1
Serial1: LAPB O CONNECT (2) RR (R) 2
Seville#
Seville#ping 199.1.1.161


Type escape sequence to abort.
Sending 5, 100-byte ICMP Echos to 199.1.1.161, timeout is 2 seconds:
!!!!!
Success rate is 100 percent (5/5), round-trip min/avg/max = 8/8/12 ms
Seville#
Serial1: LAPB O CONNECT (102) IFRAME 1 3
Serial1: LAPB I CONNECT (102) IFRAME 3 2
Serial1: LAPB O CONNECT (2) RR (R) 4
Serial1: LAPB O CONNECT (102) IFRAME 2 4
Serial1: LAPB I CONNECT (102) IFRAME 4 3
Serial1: LAPB O CONNECT (2) RR (R) 5
Serial1: LAPB O CONNECT (102) IFRAME 3 5
Serial1: LAPB I CONNECT (2) RR (R) 4
Serial1: LAPB I CONNECT (102) IFRAME 5 4
Serial1: LAPB O CONNECT (2) RR (R) 6
```

Example 9-13 *Seville Command Output for Scenario 9-1 (Continued)*

```
Serial1: LAPB O CONNECT (102) IFRAME 4 6
Serial1: LAPB I CONNECT (102) IFRAME 6 5
Serial1: LAPB O CONNECT (2) RR (R) 7
Serial1: LAPB O CONNECT (102) IFRAME 5 7
Serial1: LAPB I CONNECT (102) IFRAME 7 6
Serial1: LAPB O CONNECT (2) RR (R) 0
```

Assuming the details established in Examples 9-11, 9-12, and 9-13 for Scenario 9-1, complete or answer the following:

1 Create a diagram for the network.

2 Complete Table 9-33.

Table 9-33 *Layer 3 Addresses on the PPP Serial Links*

Router	Serial Port	Encapsulation	IP Address	IPX Address
Albuquerque	s0			
Albuquerque	s1			
Yosemite	s0			
Yosemite	s1			
Seville	s0			
Seville	s1			

3 Why are there seven IP routes in Albuquerque and Yosemite and only six in Seville?

Scenario 9-2: Point-to-Point Configuration

Your job is to deploy a new network for an environmental research firm. Two main research sites are in Boston and Atlanta; a T1 line has been ordered between them. The field site in Alaska will need occasional access; ISDN BRI will be used. Another field site in the rain forest of Podunk has a digital 56 kbps link, but it has bursts of errors because parts of the line are microwave.

Figure 9-19 shows the routers and links.

Figure 9-19 *Scenario 9-2 Environmental Research Network*

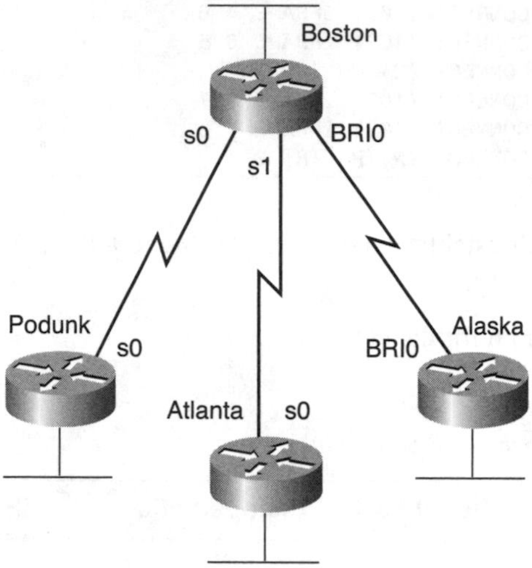

The design criteria are as follows:

- Use two different WAN data-link protocols. (This criterion is designed to force you to configure different features.)
- ISDN BRI will be used between Boston and Alaska. Boston's phone number is 1115551111; Alaska's is 2225552222.
- Both ISDN BRIs are attached to DMS-100 switches.
- Use the IP subnets and IPX networks listed in Table 9-34. Allocate addresses as needed.
- All IP user traffic is considered interesting for DDR.
- IPX RIP and IP IGRP are the routing protocols of choice.

Table 9-34 *Scenario 9-2 Chart of Layer 3 Groups for the Network Shown in Figure 9-19*

Data Link	IP Subnet	IPX Network
Boston Ethernet	200.1.1.0/24	101
Podunk Ethernet	200.1.2.0/24	102
Atlanta Ethernet	200.1.3.0/24	103
Alaska Ethernet	200.1.4.0/24	104
Boston-Podunk	200.1.5.4/30	202
Boston-Atlanta	200.1.5.8/30	203
Boston-Alaska	200.1.5.12/30	204

Assuming the specified design criteria and the information listed in Table 9-34 for Scenario 9-2, complete or answer the following:

1 Create configurations for all four routers.

2 Defend your choices for the different data-link protocols.

3 Name all methods that Boston uses in your configuration to learn the Layer 3 addresses on the other end of each link.

Answers to Scenarios

Answers to Scenario 9-1: Point-to-Point Verification

Figure 9-20 is a diagram that matches the configuration.

Figure 9-20 *Sample Cartoon Network*

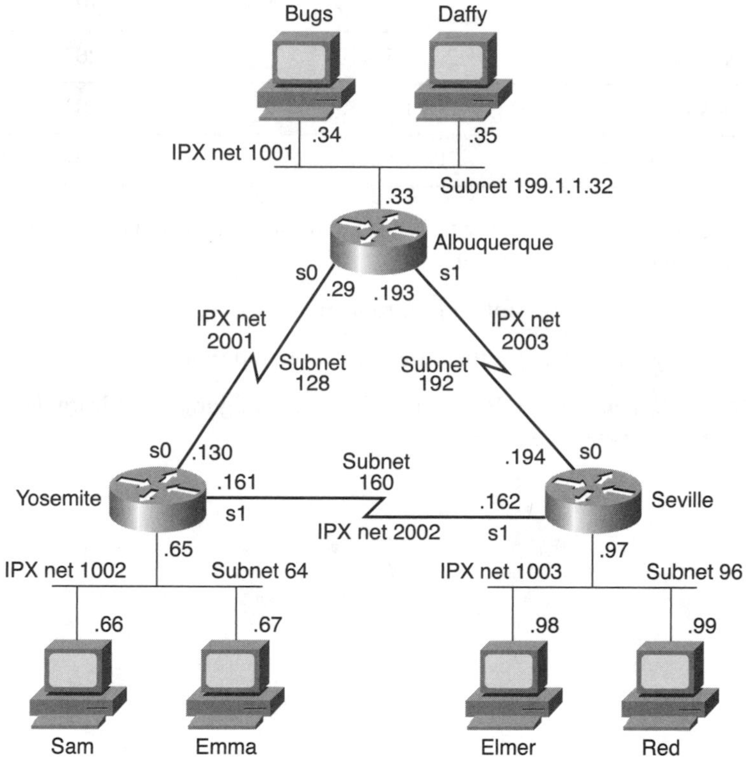

The IP and IPX addresses used on the various router interfaces were one of the tasks for this scenario. Table 9-35 is a completed version of Table 9-33, which was the blank table in which you recorded your answers for this task. Finding all the IP and IPX addresses in Examples 9-11, 9-12, and 9-13 requires some persistence. The best plan of attack is to find all the IP addresses and masks that you can, then find all the IPX network numbers, and finally decide which addresses are in the same IP subnet and IPX network.

The full IPX addresses are a little more difficult to find. The best method with the commands shown is via the **show ipx interface brief** and **show ipx route** commands. In particular, the routing table lists the full IPX addresses, not just the network numbers.

The encapsulations are not easy to notice from the commands listed. The **show interface** command would list the answer. However, in this case, a few subtle clues were included. The **debug** output on Albuquerque and Seville shows PPP output on Albuquerque's S0 interface and LAPB output for Seville's S1 interface. The **show ipx route** commands also list the encapsulation for connected networks. Table 9-35 summarizes the details.

Table 9-35 *Completed Scenario 9-1 Layer 3 Addresses on the Point-to-Point Serial Links*

Router	Serial Port	Encapsulation	IP Address	IPX Address
Albuquerque	s0	PPP	199.1.1.129	2001.0200.aaaa.aaaa
Albuquerque	s1	HDLC	199.1.1.193	2003.0200.aaaa.aaaa
Yosemite	s0	PPP	199.1.1.130	2001.0200.bbbb.bbbb
Yosemite	s1	LAPB	199.1.1.161	2002.0200.bbbb.bbbb
Seville	s0	HDLC	199.1.1.194	2003.0200.cccc.cccc
Seville	s1	LAPB	199.1.1.162	2002.0200.cccc.cccc

An extra IP route is included in the routing tables on the PPP-connected routers. When the IPCP announces the IP addresses on each end of the link, the Cisco IOS Software decides to add a host route specifically to that IP address. For example, Albuquerque has a route to 199.1.1.128/27 (a subnet on a serial link to Yosemite) and to 199.1.1.130/32 (Yosemite's address on that same link). The /32 signifies that the route is a host route.

Answers to Scenario 9-2: Point-to-Point Configuration

Examples 9-14 through 9-17 show the configurations.

Example 9-14 *Boston Configuration for Scenario 9-2*

```
hostname Boston
ipx routing 0200.aaaa.aaaa
no ip domain-lookup
username Alaska password Larry
isdn switch-type basic-dms100
!
interface serial0
encapsulation hdlc
ip address 200.1.5.5 255.255.255.252
ipx network 202
!
interface serial1
encapsulation hdlc
ip address 200.1.5.9 255.255.255.252
ipx network 203
!
```

continues

Example 9-14 *Boston Configuration for Scenario 9-2 (Continued)*

```
interface bri0
encapsulation ppp
isdn spid1 1115551111
ip address 200.1.5.13 255.255.255.252
ipx network 204
ppp authentication chap
!
interface ethernet 0
ip address 200.1.1.1 255.255.255.0
ipx network 101
!
router igrp 1
network 200.1.1.0
network 200.1.5.0
```

Example 9-15 *Podunk Configuration for Scenario 9-2*

```
hostname Podunk
ipx routing 0200.bbbb.bbbb
no ip domain-lookup
!
interface serial0
encapsulation hdlc
ip address 200.1.5.6 255.255.255.252
ipx network 202
!
interface ethernet 0
ip address 200.1.2.1 255.255.255.0
ipx network 102
!
router igrp 1
network 200.1.2.0
network 200.1.5.0
```

Example 9-16 *Atlanta Configuration for Scenario 9-2*

```
hostname Atlanta
ipx routing 0200.cccc.cccc
no ip domain-lookup
!
interface serial0
encapsulation hdlc
ip address 200.1.5.10 255.255.255.252
ipx network 203
!
interface ethernet 0
ip address 200.1.3.1 255.255.255.0
ipx network 103
!
router igrp 1
network 200.1.3.0
network 200.1.5.0
```

Example 9-17 *Alaska Configuration for Scenario 9-2*

```
hostname Alaska
no ip domain-lookup
ipx routing 0200.dddd.dddd
!
isdn switch-type basic-dms100
username Boston password Larry
!
interface BRI 0
encapsulation ppp
ip address 200.1.5.14 255.255.255.252
ipx network 204
isdn spid1 22255522220
ppp authentication chap
!
dialer-group 1
dialer idle-timeout 120
dialer map ip 200.1.5.13  name Boston 11115551111
!
interface ethernet 0
ip address 200.1.4.1 255.255.255.0
ipx network 104
!
router igrp 1
network 200.1.4.0
network 200.1.5.0
!
dialer-list 1 protocol ip permit
```

The choices for serial encapsulation in this solution are HDLC and PPP. PPP was chosen on the ISDN B channel because it provides CHAP authentication. Because the problem statement also requests two different encapsulations, HDLC was chosen. In fact, the encapsulation commands are not actually needed to enable HDLC, because it is the default on Cisco serial interfaces.

As you progress through your certifications, Cisco will sometimes ask questions that force you to deduce a fact from a limited amount of information. The final question in this scenario requires that you think beyond the topic of serial encapsulations. Boston uses PPP control protocols on the PPP link to discern the Layer 3 addresses on the other end of the link. However, LAPB and HDLC do not perform this function. CDP is enabled on each of these links by default and sends messages to discover information about Boston's neighbors. Also, Boston examines the source address of routing updates to learn its neighbors' Layer 3 addresses.

Exam Topics in This Chapter

29 Recognize key Frame Relay terms and features.

30 List commands to configure Frame Relay LMIs, maps, and subinterfaces.

31 List commands to monitor Frame Relay operation in the router.

CHAPTER 10

Frame Relay Concepts and Configuration

Frame Relay networks deliver variable-sized data frames between devices connected to the network. Engineers deploy Frame Relay more than any other WAN protocol today, so it's no surprise that Frame Relay is an important topic on the CCNA exam. This chapter reviews the details of how Frame Relay accomplishes its goal of delivering frames to multiple WAN-connected sites.

Frame Relay is considered a data link layer protocol (Layer 2). If you remember that the word *frame* describes the data link layer protocol data unit, it will be easy to remember that Frame Relay relates to OSI Layer 2. Because Frame Relay is a Layer 2 protocol, it can be used to deliver packets (Layer 3 protocol data units) between routers. Frame Relay protocol headers and trailers are simply used to let a packet traverse the Frame Relay network, just like Ethernet headers and trailers are used to help a packet traverse an Ethernet segment. (Refer to Chapter 3, "OSI Reference Model and Layered Communication," for a review of OSI layers.)

This chapter summarizes the Frame Relay protocol details that are expected to be on the exam.

How to Best Use This Chapter

By following these steps, you can make better use of your study time:

- Keep your notes and the answers for all your work with this book in one place for easy reference.
- Take the "Do I Know This Already?" quiz, and write down your answers. Studies show that retention is significantly increased through writing down facts and concepts, even if you never look at the information again.
- Use Figure 10-1 to guide you to the next step.

Figure 10-1 *How to Use This Chapter*

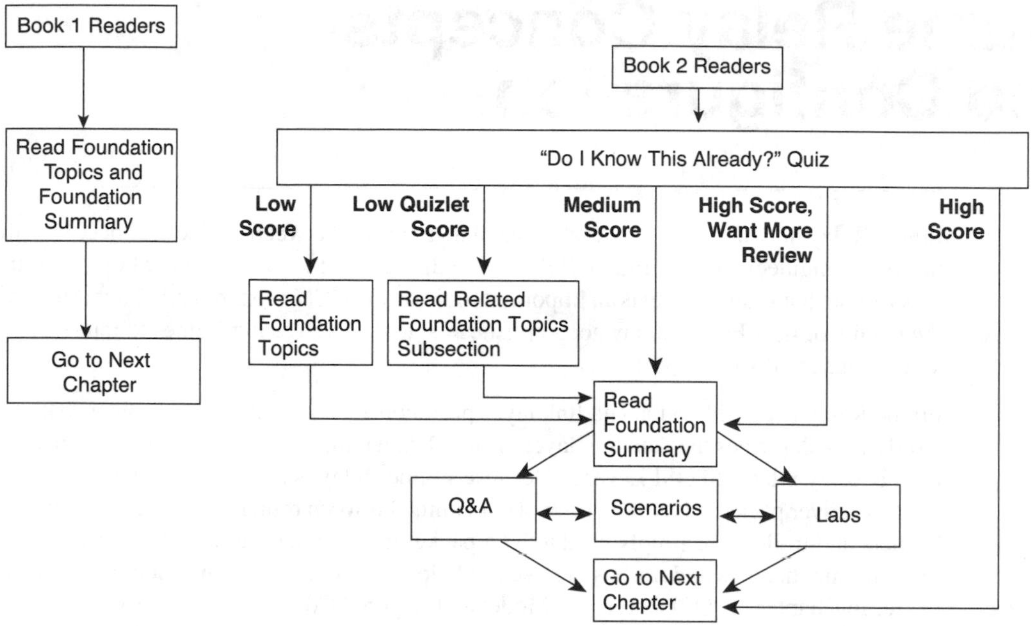

"Do I Know This Already?" Quiz

The purpose of the "Do I Know This Already?" quiz is to help you decide what parts of this chapter to use. If you already intend to read the entire chapter, you do not necessarily need to answer these questions now.

This eight-question quiz helps you determine how to spend your limited study time. The quiz is sectioned into two smaller four-question "quizlets" that correspond to the two major headings in this chapter. Figure 10-1 outlines suggestions on how to spend your time in this chapter based on your quiz score. Use Table 10-1 to record your scores.

Table 10-1 *Scoresheet for Quiz and Quizlets*

Quizlet Number	Foundation Topics Section Covering These Questions	Questions	Score
1	Frame Relay Protocols	1 to 4	
2	Frame Relay Configuration	5 to 8	
All questions		1 to 8	

1 Explain the purpose of Inverse ARP. Explain how Inverse ARP uses Frame Relay broadcasts.

____

____

____

2 What does NBMA stand for? Does it apply to X.25 networks or Frame Relay networks?

____

____

____

3 What is the name of the field that identifies, or addresses, a Frame Relay virtual circuit?

____

____

____

4 Which layer or layers of OSI are most closely related to the functions of Frame Relay? Why?

____

____

____

5 Would a Frame Relay switch connected to a router behave differently if the IETF option were deleted from the **encapsulation frame-relay ietf** command on that attached router? Would a router on the other end of the VC behave any differently if the same change were made?

____

____

____

6 What **show** command tells you when a PVC became active? How does the router know what time the PVC became active?

____

____

____

7 What **debug** option shows Inverse ARP messages?

____

____

____

8 What **show** command lists Frame Relay information about mapping? In what instances does the information displayed include the Layer 3 addresses of other routers?

____

____

____

The answers to the "Do I Know This Already?" quiz are found in Appendix A, "Answers to the 'Do I Know This Already?' Quizzes and Q&A Sections." The suggested choices for your next step are as follows:

- **4 or less overall score**—Read the entire chapter. This includes the "Foundation Topics" and "Foundation Summary" sections, the "Q&A" section, and the scenarios at the end of the chapter.
- **2 or less on any quizlet**—Review the subsections of the "Foundation Topics" section, based on Table 10-1. Then move to the "Foundation Summary" section, the "Q&A" section, and the scenarios at the end of the chapter.
- **5 or 6 overall score**—Begin with the "Foundation Summary" section, and then go to the "Q&A" section and the scenarios at the end of the chapter.
- **7 or 8 overall score**—If you want more review of these topics, skip to the "Foundation Summary" section and then go to the "Q&A" section and the scenarios at the end of the chapter. Otherwise, move to the next chapter.

Foundation Topics

Frame Relay Protocols

29 Recognize key Frame Relay terms and features.

Frame Relay networks provide more features and benefits than simple point-to-point WAN links, but in order to do that, Frame Relay protocols are more detailed. For example, Frame Relay networks are *multiaccess* networks, which means that more than two devices can attach to the network, similar to LANs. Because Frame Relay is multiaccess, Frame Relay addressing is important. First, consider Figure 10-2, which shows some connectivity concepts for Frame Relay.

Figure 10-2 *Frame Relay Components*

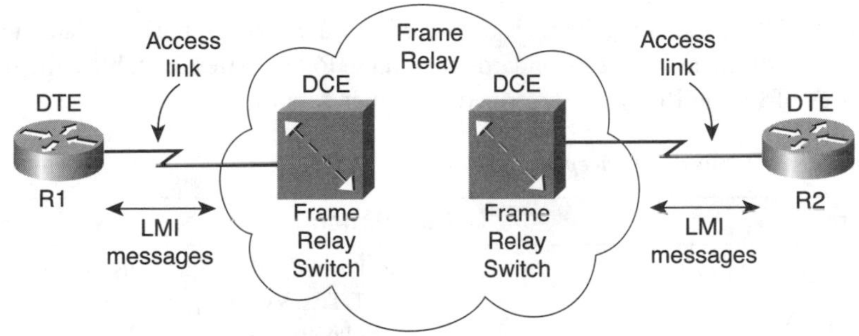

Figure 10-2 shows the most basic components of a Frame Relay network. A leased line is installed between the router and a nearby Frame Relay switch; this link is called the *access link*. To ensure that the link is working, the *Local Management Interface* (LMI) protocol is used between the router and the switch to notify each other of status and problems on the link. The routers are considered *data terminal equipment* (DTE), and the switches are *data communications equipment* (DCE).

Whereas, Figure 10-2 shows the physical and logical connectivity at each connection to the Frame Relay network, Figure 10-3 shows the end-to-end connectivity associated with a virtual circuit.

Figure 10-3 *Frame Relay PVC Concepts*

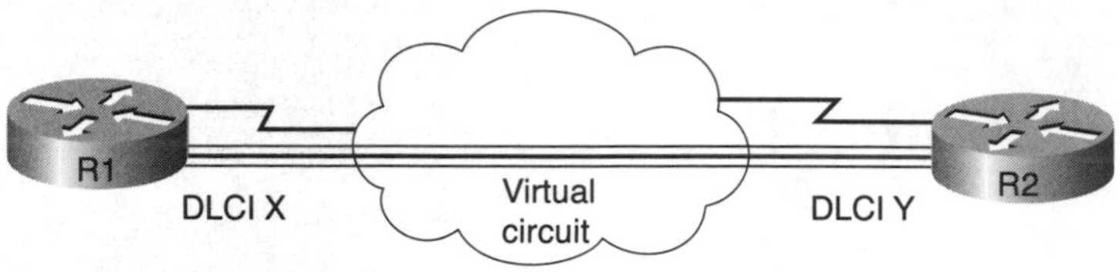

The logical path between each pair of DTEs is called a *virtual circuit* (VC). It is represented by the trio of parallel lines in the figure. Typically, the service provider preconfigures all the required details of a VC; these VCs are called permanent virtual circuits (PVCs). When R1 needs to forward a packet to R2, it encapsulates the Layer 3 packet into a Frame Relay header and trailer, and then sends the frame. R1 uses a Frame Relay address called a *data-link connection identifier* (DLCI) in the Frame Relay header. This allows the switches to deliver the frame to R2, ignoring the details of the Layer 3 packet, only caring to look at the Frame Relay header and trailer. Just like on a point-to-point serial link, when the service provider forwards the frame over a physical circuit between R1 and R2, with Frame Relay the provider forwards the frame over a logical virtual circuit from R1 to R2.

Table 10-2 lists the components shown in Figure 10-2 and some associated terms. Table 10-3 lists some of the associated standards for Frame Relay. After the tables, the most important features of Frame Relay are described in further detail.

Table 10-2 *Frame Relay Terms and Concepts*

Term	Description
Virtual circuit (VC)	A logical concept that represents the path that frames travel between DTEs. VCs are particularly useful when comparing Frame Relay to leased physical circuits.
Permanent virtual circuit (PVC)	A predefined VC. A PVC can be equated to a leased line in concept.
Switched virtual circuit (SVC)	A VC that is set up dynamically when needed. An SVC can be equated to a dial connection in concept.
Data terminal equipment (DTE)	DTEs are connected to a Frame Relay service from a telecommunications company and typically reside at sites used by the company buying the Frame Relay service.
Data communications equipment (DCE)	Frame Relay switches are DCE devices. DCEs are also known as data circuit-terminating equipment. DCEs are typically in the service provider's network.
Access link	The leased line between DTE and DCE.
Access rate (AR)	The speed at which the access link is clocked. This choice affects the price of the connection.

Table 10-2 *Frame Relay Terms and Concepts (Continued)*

Term	Description
Committed information rate (CIR)	The rate at which the DTE can send data for an individual VC, for which the provider commits to deliver that amount of data. The provider sends any data in excess of this rate for this VC if its network has capacity at the time. This choice typically affects the price of each VC.
Burst rate	The rate and length of time which, for a particular VC, the DTE can send faster than the CIR, and the provider agrees to forward the data. Often it is expressed as a *burst size*. A Frame Relay DTE can send burst size bits, wait a moment, send burst size bits, wait, and so on, with the average being the CIR. This choice typically affects the price of each VC.
Data-link connection identifier (DLCI)	A Frame Relay address used in Frame Relay headers to identify the VC.
Forward explicit congestion notification (FECN)	The bit in the Frame Relay header that signals to anyone receiving the frame (switches and DTEs) that congestion is occurring in the same direction as the frame. Switches and DTEs can react by slowing the rate at which data is sent in that direction.
Backward explicit congestion notification (BECN)	The bit in the Frame Relay header that signals to anyone receiving the frame (switches and DTEs) that congestion is occurring in the opposite (backward) direction as the frame. Switches and DTEs can react by slowing the rate at which data is sent in that direction.
Discard eligibility (DE)	The bit in the Frame Relay header that, if frames must be discarded, signals a switch to choose this frame to discard instead of another frame without the DE bit set.
Nonbroadcast multiaccess (NBMA)	A network in which broadcasts are not supported, but more than two devices can be connected.
Local Management Interface (LMI)	The protocol used between a DCE and DTE to manage the connection. Signaling messages for SVCs, PVC status messages, and keepalives are all LMI messages.
Link Access Procedure Frame Mode Bearer Services (LAPF)	Defines the basic Frame Relay header and trailer. The header includes DLCI, FECN, BECN, and DE bits.

The definitions for Frame Relay are contained in documents from the International Telecommunications Union (ITU) and the American National Standards Institute (ANSI). The Frame Relay Forum, a vendor consortium, also defines several Frame Relay specifications, many of which have been added to the standards bodies' documents. Table 10-3 lists the most important of these specifications.

Table 10-3 *Frame Relay Protocol Specifications*

What the Specification Defines	ITU Document	ANSI Document
Data-link specifications, including LAPF header/trailer	Q.922 Annex A	T1.618
PVC management, LMI	Q.933 Annex A	T1.617 Annex D
SVC signaling	Q.933	T1.617
Multiprotocol encapsulation (originated in RFC 1490/2427)	Q.933 Annex E	T1.617 Annex F

Virtual Circuits

Frame Relay provides significant advantages over simply using point-to-point leased lines. The primary advantage has to do with virtual circuits. Consider Figure 10-4, which is a typical Frame Relay network with three sites.

Figure 10-4 *Typical Frame Relay Network with Three Sites*

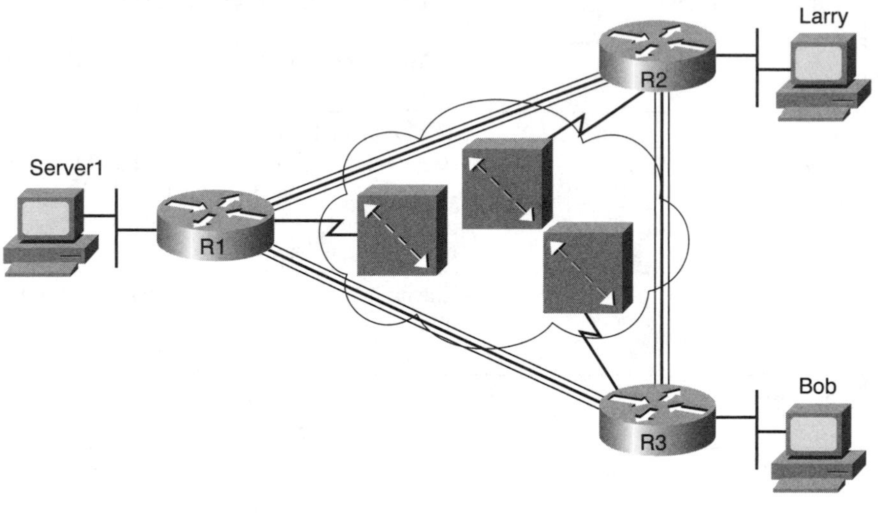

A virtual circuit is a concept that describes a logical path between two Frame Relay DTEs. The term *virtual circuit* describes the concept well. It acts like a point-to-point circuit, but physically it is not, so it's virtual. For example, R1 terminates two VCs—one whose other endpoint is R2, and one whose other endpoint is R3. R1 can send traffic directly to either of the other two routers by sending it over the appropriate VC. R1 has only one physical access link to the Frame Relay network.

VCs share the access link and the Frame Relay network. For example, both VCs terminating at R1 use the same access link. In fact, many customers share the same Frame Relay network.

Originally, people with leased-line networks were reluctant to migrate to Frame Relay, because they would be competing with other customers for the provider's capacity inside the cloud. To address these fears, Frame Relay is designed with the concept of a committed information rate (CIR). Each VC has a CIR, which is a guarantee by the provider that a particular VC gets at least that much bandwidth.

It's interesting that, even in this three-site network, it's probably less expensive to use Frame Relay than to use point-to-point links. Now imagine an organization with 100 sites that needs any-to-any connectivity. How many leased lines are required? 4950! And besides that, you would need 99 serial interfaces per router. Or you could have 100 access links to local Frame Relay switches, one per router, and have 4950 VCs running over them. Also, you would need only one serial interface on each router! The Frame Relay topology is easier for the service provider to implement, costs the provider less, and makes better use of the core of the provider's network. As you would expect, that makes it less expensive to the Frame Relay customer as well. For connecting many WAN sites, Frame Relay is simply more cost-effective than leased lines.

Two types of VCs are allowed—permanent (PVC) and switched (SVC). PVCs are predefined by the provider; whereas, SVCs are created dynamically. PVCs are by far the more popular of the two. PVCs are covered on the CCNA exam, but SVCs are not.

When the Frame Relay network is engineered, the design might not include a PVC between each pair of sites. Figure 10-4 includes PVCs between each pair of sites, which is called a full-mesh Frame Relay network. When not all pairs have a direct PVC, it is called a partial-mesh network. Figure 10-5 shows the same network, but this time with only two PVCs. This is typical when R1 is at the main site and R2 and R3 are at remote offices that rarely need to communicate directly.

Figure 10-5 *Typical Partial-Mesh Frame Relay Network*

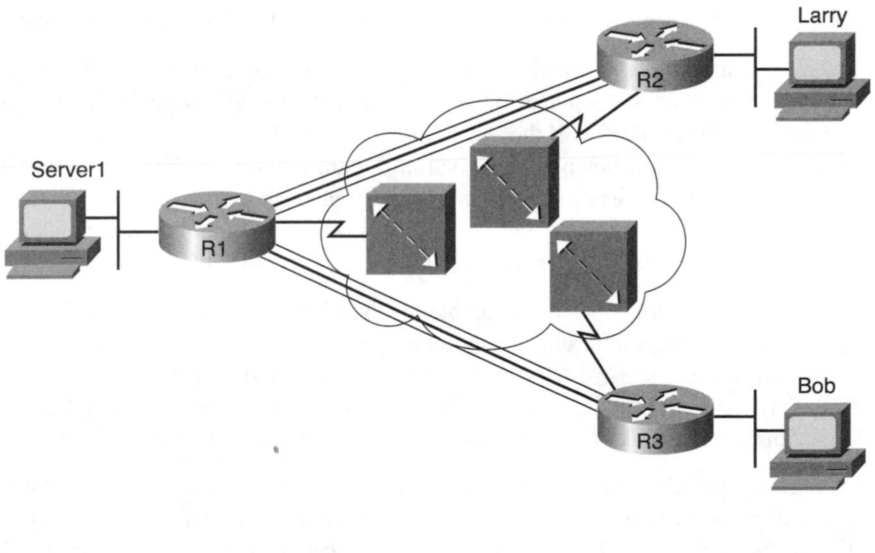

The partial mesh has some advantages and disadvantages when compared to a full mesh. The primary advantage is that partial mesh is cheaper, because the provider charges per VC and because there are fewer VCs. The downside is that traffic from R2's site to R3's site must go to R1 first and then be forwarded. If that's a small amount of traffic, it's a small price to pay. If it's a lot of traffic, a full mesh is probably worth the extra money.

One conceptual hurdle with PVCs is that there is typically a single access link, but multiple PVCs flow across the one link. For example, consider Figure 10-5 from R1's perspective. Server1 sends a packet to Larry. It comes across the Ethernet, R1 gets it and matches his routing table, which tells him to send the packet out Serial0, which is R1's access link. He encapsulates the packet in a Frame Relay header and trailer and then sends it. Which PVC does it use? The Frame Relay switch should forward it to R2, but why does it? Well, Frame Relay uses an address to differentiate one PVC from another. This address is called a data-link connection identifier (DLCI). The name is descriptive: The address is for an OSI Layer 2 (data link) protocol, and it identifies a VC, which is sometimes called a virtual connection. So, in this example, R1 uses the DLCI that identifies the PVC to R2, so the provider forwards the frame correctly over the PVC to R2.

LMI and Encapsulation Types

When you're first learning about Frame Relay, it's often easy to confuse the LMI and the encapsulation used with Frame Relay, but Cisco expects CCNAs to master the differences. The LMI is a definition of the messages used between the DTE (for example, a router) and the DCE (for example, the Frame Relay switch owned by the service provider). The encapsulation defines the headers used by a DTE in order to communicate some information to the DTE on the other end of a VC. The switch and its connected router care about using the same LMI; the switch does not care about the encapsulation. The endpoint routers (DTEs) do care about the encapsulation.

The most important LMI message relating to topics on the exam is the LMI *status inquiry* message. Status messages perform two key functions. First, they perform a keepalive function between the DTE and DCE. If the access link has a problem, the absence of keepalive messages implies that the link is down. The second important function of the status message is to signal whether a PVC is active or inactive. Even though each PVC is predefined, its status can change. So an access link might be up, but it could be down. The router could then remove all routes using that PVC but leave other routes that use other working PVCs alone.

Three LMI protocol options are available in Cisco IOS Software: Cisco, ITU, and ANSI. Each LMI option is slightly different and, therefore, incompatible with the other two. For example, the Cisco and ANSI Q.933-A LMIs call for the use of DLCI 1023 for LMI messages; whereas, T1.617-D specifies DLCI 0. Some of the messages have different fields in their headers. The DTE simply needs to know which of the three LMIs to use, and the local switch must agree.

Configuring the LMI type is easy. Today's most popular option is to use the default LMI setting, which uses the LMI autosense feature. Because the default LMI setting is supported by Cisco IOS Software Release 11.2 and later, you do not need to code the LMI type. The LMI type can be configured, but this disables the autosense feature.

Table 10-4 outlines the three LMI types, their origin, and the keyword used in the Cisco **frame-relay lmi-type** interface subcommand.

Table 10-4 *Frame Relay LMI Types*

Name	Document	IOS LMI-Type Parameter
Cisco	Proprietary	**cisco**
ANSI	T1.617 Annex D	**ansi**
ITU	Q.933 Annex A	**q933a**

A Frame Relay header and trailer are used to encapsulate a packet before it is sent out an access link. Frame Relay uses the standard Link Access Procedure Frame Bearer Services (LAPF) header, defined by ITU Q.922-A. The sparse LAPF framing provides error detection with an FCS in the trailer, as well as the DLCI, DE, FECN, and BECN fields in the header (which are discussed later). Figure 10-6 diagrams the frame.

Figure 10-6 *LAPF Header*

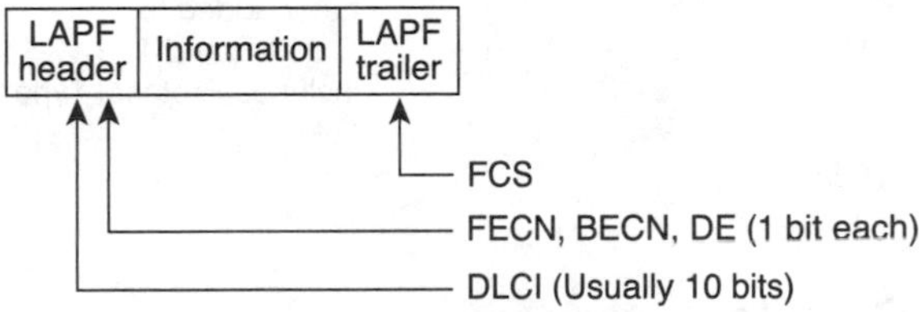

The LAPF header and trailer do not provide all the fields typically needed by routers. In particular, Figure 10-6 does not show the presence of a Protocol Type field. As discussed in Chapter 3, a field in the header must define the type of header, typically a Layer 3 packet, that follows the data-link header. If Frame Relay is using only the LAPF header, DTEs (including routers) cannot support multiprotocol traffic, because there is no way to identify the type of protocol in the Information field. (See Chapter 3 for more information on the concept of a Protocol Type field in data-link headers.)

Two solutions were created to compensate for the lack of a Protocol Type field. Cisco and three other companies created an additional header, which comes first in the Information field shown in Figure 10-6. It includes a two-byte Protocol Type field, with values matching the same field used for HDLC by Cisco. The second solution was defined in RFC 1490, "Multiprotocol Interconnect over Frame Relay," which was written to ensure multivendor interoperability between Frame Relay DTEs. This solution includes use of a Protocol Type field and adds many other options, including support for bridged frames. ITU and ANSI later incorporated RFC 1490 headers into specs Q.933 Annex E and T1.617 Annex F, respectively. The encapsulation option defined by Cisco and others, and the option as originally defined in RFC 1490, are the two encapsulation options in the Cisco IOS Software today. They are called cisco and ietf.

NOTE RFC 1490 has been superceded by RFC 2427. You will want to remember both numbers, particularly the older 1490, because it is referred to often in documentation from Cisco and other vendors.

DTEs use and react to the fields specified by these two types of encapsulation; Frame Relay switches ignore these fields. Figure 10-7 provides a conceptual diagram of the two forms of encapsulation. *Because the frames flow from DTE to DTE, both DTEs must agree to the encapsulation used.* The switches do not care. However, each VC can use a different encapsulation.

Figure 10-7 *Cisco and RFC 1490/2427 Encapsulation*

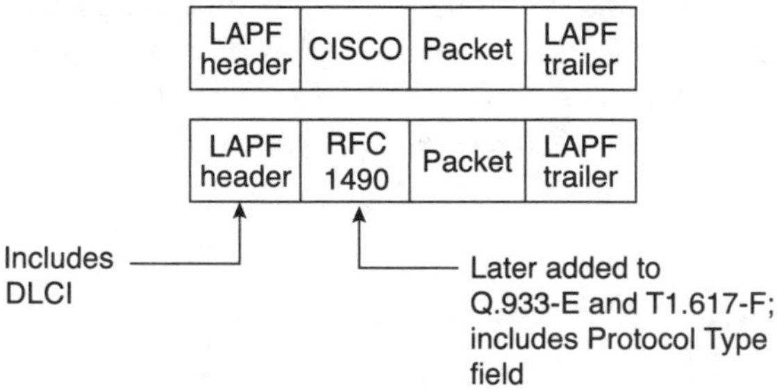

DLCI Addressing Details

So far, you know some basic information about Frame Relay. First, the routers (DTEs) connect to the Frame Relay switches (DCEs) over an access link, which is a leased line between the router and the switch. The logical path between a pair of DTEs is called a virtual circuit (VC). Permanent virtual circuits (PVCs) are typically used, and the data-link connection identifier (DLCI) is used to address or identify each individual PVC. The LMI protocol is used to manage the access link, and the LMI type must match between the router and the local switch. Finally, the routers agree to the style of encapsulation used. Both encapsulation types include a protocol type field, which identifies the next header that follows the Frame Relay header.

DLCIs can be both simple and confusing. The earlier explanation simply states that the DLCI is used to identify a VC, so when multiple VCs use the same access link, the Frame Relay switches know how to forward the frames correctly. You could know just that, look at the configuration examples later in this chapter, and probably learn to create new configurations. You would probably even get all the exam questions right with that depth of knowledge. However, a closer look at DLCIs shows how they really work. This is important for actually understanding the configurations you create. If you want to get a deeper understanding, read on. If you prefer to get the basics right now and fill in more details later, you might want to jump ahead to the "Frame Relay Configuration" section.

Start Extra Credit

Frame Relay addressing and switching define how to deliver frames across a Frame Relay network. Because a router uses a single access link but can send to many other routers, there must be something to identify the other device—in other words, an address. The DLCI is the Frame Relay address. However, DLCIs are used to address VCs. The logic and use of DLCIs are different from the addresses seen for other protocols covered in this book. This difference is mainly due to the use of the DLCI and the fact that *there is a single DLCI field in the header—there are not both source and destination DLCI fields.*

A few characteristics of DLCIs are important to understand before getting into their actual use. Frame Relay DLCIs are locally significant; this means that the addresses need to be unique only on the local access link. A popular analogy that explains local addressing is that there can be only a single street address of 2000 Pennsylvania Avenue, Washington, DC, but there can be a 2000 Pennsylvania Avenue in every town in the United States. Likewise, DLCIs must be unique on each access link. In Figure 10-8, notice that DLCI 40 is used on two access links to describe two different PVCs. Because DLCI 40 is used on two different access links, there is no conflict.

Figure 10-8 *Frame Relay Addressing with A Sending to B and C*

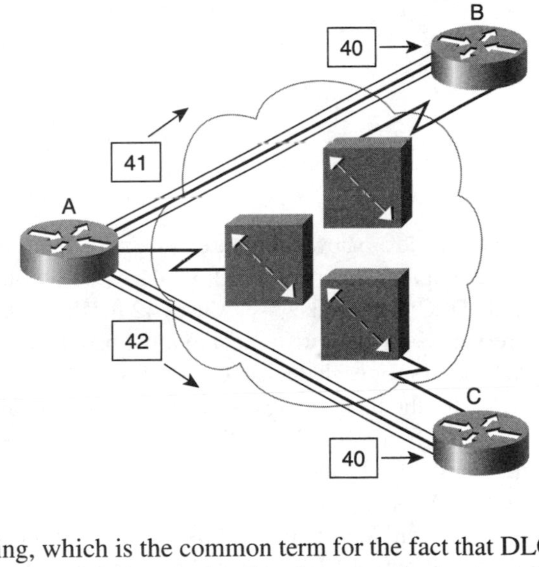

Local addressing, which is the common term for the fact that DLCIs are locally significant, is a fact. It is how Frame Relay works. Simply put, a single access link cannot use one DLCI to represent more than one VC on the same link. Otherwise, the Frame Relay switch would not know how to forward frames correctly.

Most people get confused about DLCIs the first time they think about the local significance of DLCIs and the existence of only a single DLCI field in the Frame Relay header. Global addressing solves this problem by making DLCI addressing look like LAN addressing in concept. Global addressing is simply a way of choosing DLCI numbers when planning a Frame Relay network. Because local addressing is a fact, global addressing does not change the rules. Global addressing just makes DLCI assignment more obvious—once you get used to it. Here's how it works: The service provider hands out a planning spreadsheet and a diagram. Figure 10-9 is an example of such a diagram, with the "global" DLCIs shown.

Figure 10-9 *Frame Relay Global DLCIs*

Global addressing is planned as shown in Figure 10-9, with the resulting use of DLCIs as shown in Figure 10-8. For example, Router A uses DLCI 41 when sending a frame to Router B, because B's "global" DLCI is 41. Likewise, A uses 42 for the PVC to Router C. The nice thing is that global addressing is much more logical to most people, because it works like a LAN, with a single MAC address for each device. On a LAN, if the MAC addresses are MAC-A, MAC-B, and MAC-C for the three routers, Router A uses destination address MAC-B when sending frames to Router B and MAC-C as the destination to reach Router C. Likewise, with DLCIs 40, 41, and 42 used for Routers A, B, and C, respectively, the same concept applies. Because DLCIs address VCs, the logic is something like this when Router A sends a frame to Router B: "Hey, local switch! When you get this frame, send it over the VC that we agreed to number with DLCI 41." Figure 10-10 outlines this example.

Figure 10-10 *Frame Relay Global Addressing from the Sender's Perspective*

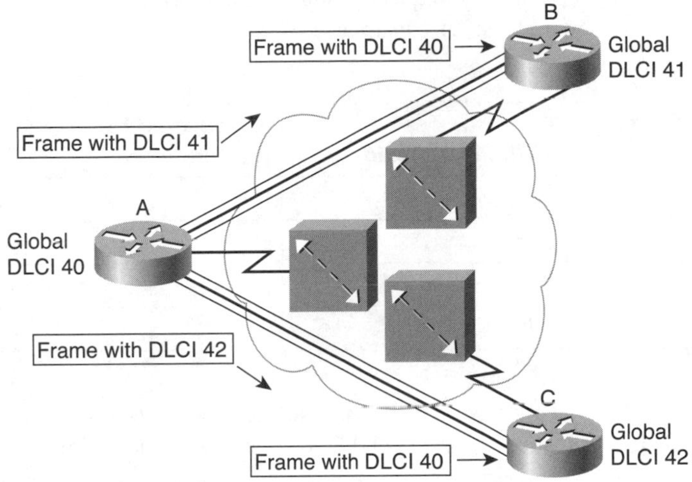

Router A sends frames with DLCI 41, and they reach the local switch. The local switch sees the DLCI field and forwards the frame through the Frame Relay network until it reaches the switch connected to Router B. Then Router B's local switch forwards the frame out the access link to Router B. The same process happens between Router A and Router C when Router A uses DLCI 42. The beauty of global addressing is that you think of each router as having an address, like LAN addressing. If I want to send a frame to someone, I put his or her DLCI in the header, and the network delivers the frame to the correct DTE.

The final key to global addressing is that the Frame Relay switches actually change the DLCI value before delivering the frame. Did you notice that Figure 10-10 shows a different DLCI value as the frames are received by Routers B and C? For example, Router A is sending a frame to Router B, and Router A puts DLCI 41 in the frame. The last switch changes the field to DLCI 40 before forwarding it to Router B. The result is that when B and C receive their frames, the DLCI value is actually the DLCI of the sender. Why? Well, when B receives the frame, because the DLCI is 40, it knows that the frame came in on the PVC between itself and Router A. In general:

- The sender treats the DLCI field as a destination address, using the destination's global DLCI in the header.
- The receiver thinks of the DLCI field as the source address, because it contains the global DLCI of the frame's sender.

Figure 10-10 describes what really happens in a typical Frame Relay network. Service providers supply a planning spreadsheet and diagrams with global DLCIs listed. Table 10-5 gives a tabular view of what DLCIs are used.

Table 10-5 *DLCI Swapping in the Frame Relay Cloud*

Frame Sent by Router	With DLCI Field	Is Delivered to Router	With DLCI Field
A	41	B	40
A	42	C	40
B	40	A	41
C	40	A	42

One benefit of global addressing is that new sites can be added more conveniently. Examine Figure 10-11, which adds Routers D and E. The service provider simply states that global DLCI 43 and 44 are used for these two routers. If these two routers also have only one PVC to Router A, all the DLCI planning is complete. You know that Router D and Router E use DLCI 40 to reach Router A and that Router A uses DLCI 43 to reach Router D and DLCI 44 to reach Router E.

Figure 10-11 *Adding Frame Relay Sites: Global Addressing*

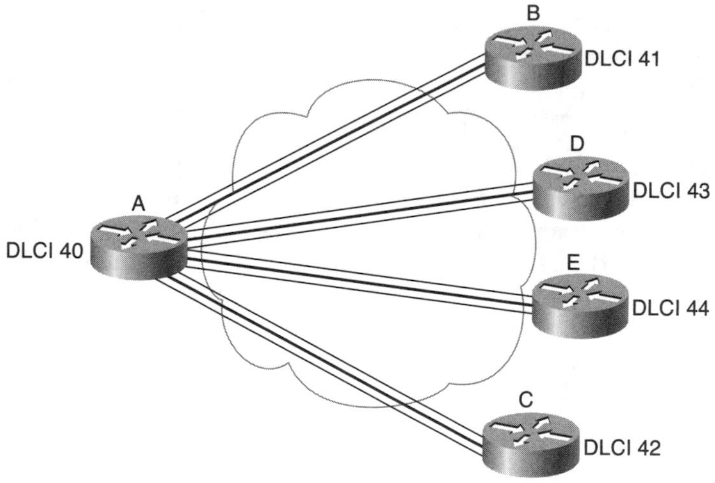

The remaining examples in this chapter use global addressing in any planning diagrams unless otherwise stated. One practical way to determine whether the diagram lists the local DLCIs or the global DLCI convention is this: If two VCs terminate at the same DTE and a single DLCI is shown, it probably represents the global DLCI convention. If one DLCI is shown per VC, local DLCI addressing is depicted.

NOTE If you're taking the ICND course or reading the ICND book, you might notice that it does not cover the concepts behind global addressing. Can you build router configurations if you just understand local DLCI addressing? Yes. But if you expect to work with Frame Relay, understanding both local and global addressing concepts is very important, because some people will want to use one convention, and some will want to use the other.

End Extra Credit

Network Layer Concerns with Frame Relay

Most of the important Frame Relay concepts have been covered. First, the routers (DTEs) connect to the Frame Relay switches (DCEs) over an access link, which is a leased line between the router and the switch. The LMI protocol is used to manage the access link, and the LMI type must match between the router and the local switch. The routers agree to the style of encapsulation used. The single DLCI field in the Frame Relay header identifies the VC used to deliver the frame. The DLCI is used like a destination address when the frame is being sent and like a source address as the frame is received. The switches actually swap the DLCI in transit.

Frame Relay is both similar to and a little different from LAN and point-to-point WAN links. These differences introduce some additional considerations for passing Layer 3 packets across a Frame Relay network. As a CCNA, you need to concern yourself with three key issues relating to Layer 3 flows over Frame Relay:

- Choices for Layer 3 addresses on Frame Relay interfaces
- Broadcast handling
- Split horizon

The following sections cover these three issues in depth.

Layer 3 Addressing with Frame Relay

Cisco's Frame Relay implementation defines three different options for assigning subnets and IP addresses on Frame Relay interfaces:

- One subnet containing all Frame Relay DTEs
- One subnet per VC
- A hybrid of the first two options

Figure 10-12 shows the first alternative, which is to use a single subnet. The illustration shows a fully meshed Frame Relay network because the single-subnet option is typically used when a full mesh of VCs exists. In a full mesh, each router has a VC to every other router, which makes the

Frame Relay network behave like a LAN, at least in how IP addressing works. (These concepts also apply to IPX networks. In this case, a single IPX network is needed.) Figure10-12 also shows IPX and IP addresses. The IPX and IP addresses are configured as subcommands on the serial interface. (Configuration details are shown in a later section.) Table 10-6 summarizes the addresses used in Figure 10-12.

Figure 10-12 *Full Mesh with IP and IPX Addresses*

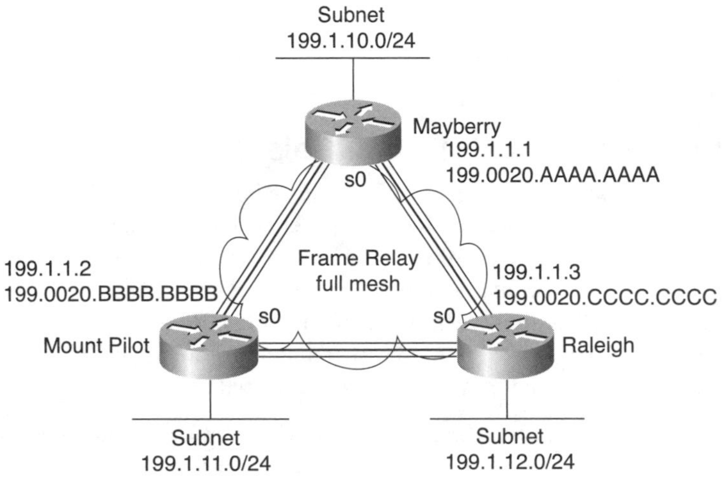

Table 10-6 *IP and IPX Addresses with No Subinterfaces*

Router	IP Address of Frame Relay Interface	IPX Network of Frame Relay Interface	IPX Address
Mayberry	199.1.1.1	199	199.0200.aaaa.aaaa
Mount Pilot	199.1.1.2	199	199.0200.bbbb.bbbb
Raleigh	199.1.1.3	199	199.0200.cccc.cccc

The single-subnet alternative is straightforward, and it conserves your IP address space. It also looks like what you are used to with LANs, which makes it easier to conceptualize. The problems are that most Frame Relay networks are not full mesh, and the single-subnet option has some deficiencies when the network is a partial mesh.

The second IP addressing alternative, the single-subnet-per-VC alternative, is most useful with a partially meshed Frame Relay network (see Figure 10-13). Boston cannot forward frames directly to Charlotte, because no VC is defined between the two. This is a more typical Frame Relay network, because most organizations with many sites tend to group applications onto servers at a few locations, and most of the traffic is between a remote site and those servers.

Figure 10-13 *Partial Mesh with IP and IPX Addresses*

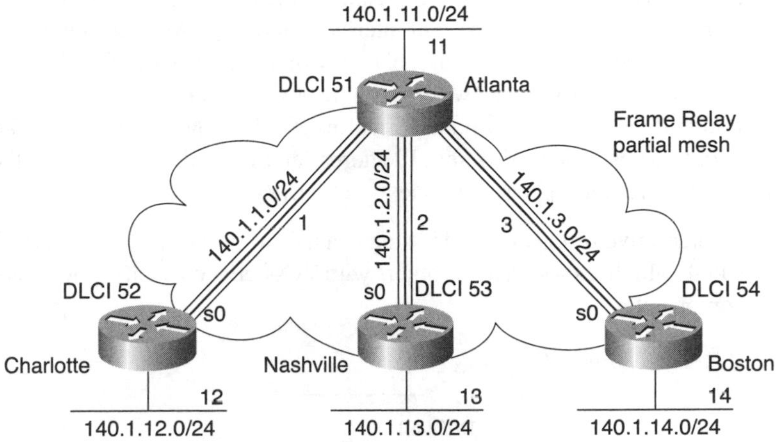

The single-subnet-per-VC alternative matches the logic behind a set of point-to-point links. Because there is a separate subnet for each point-to-point link, using a single subnet per VC has some advantages in this case. Table 10-7 shows the IP and IPX addresses for the partially meshed Frame Relay network illustrated in Figure 10-13. The addresses would be configured as subcommands on serial subinterfaces.

NOTE The notation /24 signifies a subnet mask with 24 binary 1s—in other words, 255.255.255.0.

Table 10-7 *IP and IPX Addresses with Point-to-Point Subinterfaces*

Router	Subnet	IP Address	IPX Network	IPX Address
Atlanta	140.1.1.0/24	140.1.1.1	1	1.0200.aaaa.aaaa
Charlotte	140.1.1.0/24	140.1.1.2	1	1.0200.bbbb.bbbb
Atlanta	140.1.2.0/24	140.1.2.1	2	2.0200.aaaa.aaaa
Nashville	140.1.2.0/24	140.1.2.3	2	2.0200.cccc.cccc
Atlanta	140.1.3.0/24	140.1.3.1	3	3.0200.aaaa.aaaa
Boston	140.1.3.0/24	140.1.3.4	3	3.0200.dddd.dddd

Frame Relay VCs essentially create a subdivision of the traffic on a serial interface per VC. Cisco IOS Software has a configuration feature called *subinterfaces* that creates a logical subdivision of a physical interface. Subinterfaces allow the Atlanta router to have three IP addresses and three IPX addresses associated with its Serial0 interface by configuring three separate subinterfaces associated with the single physical interface. Subinterfaces can treat each VC as though it were a point-to-point serial link. Each of the three subinterfaces of Serial0 on Atlanta would be assigned a different IP address and IPX address from the list in Table 10-7. (Sample configurations appear in the next section.)

The third alternative of Layer 3 addressing is a hybrid of the first two alternatives. Consider Figure 10-14, which shows a trio of routers with VCs between each of them, as well as two other VCs to remote sites.

Figure 10-14 *Hybrid of Full and Partial Mesh*

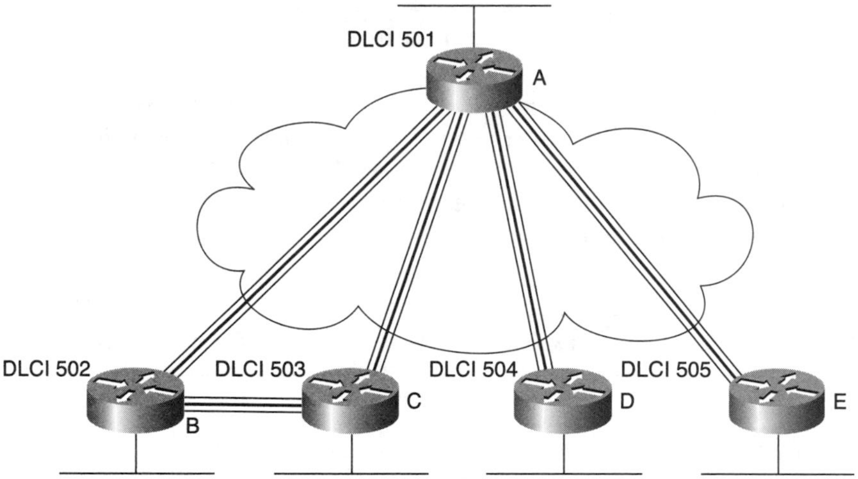

Two options exist for Layer 3 addressing in this case. The first is to treat each VC as a separate Layer 3 group; five subnets and five IPX networks are needed for the Frame Relay network. However, Routers A, B, and C create a full mesh between each other. This allows Routers A, B, and C to use one subnet and IPX network. The other two VCs—one between A and D and one between A and E—are treated as two separate Layer 3 groups. The result is a total of three subnets and three IPX network numbers.

To accomplish either style of Layer 3 addressing in this third and final case, subinterfaces are used. Point-to-point subinterfaces are used when a single VC is considered to be all that is in the group. Multipoint subinterfaces are used among Routers A, B, and C in Figure 10-14. (A multipoint subinterface is a subinterface that is used when multiple VCs terminate at a router.) Table 10-8 summarizes the addresses and subinterfaces that are used.

Table 10-8 *IP and IPX Addresses with Point-to-Point and Multipoint Subinterfaces*

Router	Subnet	IP Address	IPX Network	IPX Address	Subinterface Type
A	140.1.1.0/24	140.1.1.1	1	1.0200.aaaa.aaaa	Multipoint
B	140.1.1.0/24	140.1.1.2	1	1.0200.bbbb.bbbb	Multipoint
C	140.1.1.0/24	140.1.1.3	1	1.0200.cccc.cccc	Multipoint
A	140.1.2.0/24	140.1.2.1	2	2.0200.aaaa.aaaa	Point-to-point
D	140.1.2.0/24	140.1.2.4	2	2.0200.dddd.dddd	Point-to-point
A	140.1.3.0/24	140.1.3.1	3	3.0200.aaaa.aaaa	Point-to-point
E	140.1.3.0/24	140.1.3.5	3	3.0200.eeee.eeee	Point-to-point

What will you see in a real network? Most of the time, point-to-point subinterfaces are used, with a single subnet and IPX network per PVC. All three alternatives are fair game on the exam, however!

The later section "Frame Relay Configuration" provides full configurations for all three cases illustrated in Figures 10-12, 10-13, and 10-14.

Broadcast Handling

The second consideration for Layer 3 over Frame Relay is how to deal with Layer 3 broadcasts. Frame Relay can send copies of a broadcast over all VCs, but there is no equivalent to LAN broadcasts. In other words, no capability exists for a Frame Relay DTE to send a single frame into the Frame Relay network and have that frame replicated and delivered across multiple VCs to multiple destinations. However, routers need to send broadcasts in order for several features to work. In particular, routing protocol updates and SAP updates are broadcasts.

The solution to the broadcast dilemma for Frame Relay has two parts. First, Cisco IOS Software sends copies of the broadcasts across each VC that you tell it to. If there are only a few VCs, this is not a big problem. However, if hundreds of VCs terminate in one router, for each broadcast, hundreds of copies could be sent.

As the second part of the solution, the router tries to minimize the impact of the first part of the solution. The router places these broadcasts into a different output queue than the one for user traffic so that the user does not experience a large spike in delay each time a broadcast is replicated and sent over every VC. Cisco IOS Software can also be configured to limit the amount of bandwidth that is used for these replicated broadcasts.

NOTE Although the CCNP exam, not the CCNA exam, covers such issues as dealing with overhead, a short example shows the significance of this overhead. If a router knows 1000 routes, uses RIP, and has 50 VCs, 1.072 MB of RIP updates are sent every 30 seconds. That averages out to 285 Kbps. (The math is as follows: 536-byte RIP packets, with 25 routes in each packet, for 40 packets per update, with copies sent over 50 VCs. 536 * 40 * 50 = 1.072 MB per update interval. 1.072 * 8 / 30 seconds = 285 Kbps.)

Knowing how to tell the router to forward these broadcasts to each VC is important on the CCNA exam and, therefore, is covered later in the section "Frame Relay Configuration." The issues that relate to dealing with the volume of these updates are more likely a topic for the CCNP and CCIE exams.

Start Extra Credit

Split Horizon

The third network layer consideration when you're using Frame Relay is understanding how split horizon works over Frame Relay. Split horizon is useful for preventing routing loops by preventing a router from advertising a route onto the same interface on which the route was learned. (Refer to Chapter 7, "Routing and Routing Protocols," for a full explanation.) However, split horizon can cause some problems with Frame Relay. Thankfully, several configuration options help you deal with this issue.

Understanding the problem is difficult without an example. Refer back to Figure 10-13. Atlanta uses a single serial interface—say, Serial0. With split horizon enabled on Atlanta's Serial0, Atlanta learns about 140.1.12.0/24 from Charlotte, but Atlanta does not advertise Charlotte's 140.1.12.0/24 subnet in its updates to Nashville or Boston. So no traffic could flow from Boston or Nashville to Charlotte.

Two solutions to this problem are supported in the Cisco IOS Software. First, split-horizon logic applies to subinterfaces, as if they were separate interfaces. In other words, Atlanta uses a different subinterface for each VC to the three remote sites. Split horizon is enabled on each subinterface. However, because the routing updates from Charlotte are considered to enter Atlanta via one subinterface, and because routing updates to Nashville and Boston exit two other subinterfaces, advertising 140.1.12.0/24 to Nashville and Boston is allowed. No special action is required.

The other solution is to disable split horizon. Normally that would be a bad idea, but with Frame Relay, it is generally more acceptable. Consider Figure 10-12. When all three VCs are up, no problem exists. However, if the VC from Mount Pilot to Raleigh went down, split horizon on Mayberry would be harmful. Mount Pilot advertises its route to 199.1.11.0 on its local subnet to Mayberry. Mayberry receives that route. However, because subinterfaces are not used, Mayberry does not advertise Mount Pilot's 199.1.11.0 subnet to Raleigh when split horizon is enabled.

The multipoint subinterfaces used between Routers A, B, and C in Figure 10-14 would experience the same problems for the same reasons described for Figure 10-12.

The second solution to the split horizon problem is to disable split horizon when not using subinterfaces or when using multipoint subinterfaces. Conveniently, the Cisco IOS Software defaults to disabling split horizon on Frame Relay interfaces in all cases except for point-to-point subinterfaces. Table 10-9 summarizes these settings and shows that the current default settings work around the split horizon issues just described.

Table 10-9 *Split Horizon and Frame Relay Interfaces*

Type of Configuration	Split Horizon Is
No subinterfaces	Disabled
Point-to-point subinterfaces	Enabled
Multipoint subinterfaces	Disabled

If the default value for split horizon is not what you want, the **ip split horizon** interface configuration command can be used to enable split horizon. Similarly, the **no ip split horizon** interface configuration command disables split horizon on that interface.

End Extra Credit

Frame Relay Configuration

30 List commands to configure Frame Relay LMIs, maps, and subinterfaces.

31 List commands to monitor Frame Relay operation in the router.

This chapter describes Frame Relay concepts. For example, three LMI types and two encapsulation types are available. Depending on the placement of your VCs, you might want to use one subnet for the whole Frame Relay network, one subnet per VC, or a mixture of the two. You might need to configure static mapping of IP addresses and their corresponding DLCIs. And you will definitely need to tell the router that its serial interface is using Frame Relay instead of the default of HDLC.

Basic configuration of Frame Relay in a Cisco router is relatively straightforward. The Cisco IOS Software uses good default values. Of course, Cisco expects CCNAs to know the optional parameters that are described in this section and the methods of changing the default values.

There is no substitute for hands-on experience! However, in lieu of hands-on experience, this section lists commands, provides examples, and points out tricky features. Tables 10-10 and 10-11 summarize the more popular commands used for Frame Relay configuration and verification. Two configuration examples follow. If you are interested in other references as well, the Cisco IOS Software documentation is an excellent reference for additional IP commands. The Cisco Press book *Interconnecting Cisco Network Devices* is also a good reference, particularly if you can't attend the instructor-led version of the ICND class.

Table 10-10 *Frame Relay Configuration Commands*

Command	Configuration Mode	Description
encapsulation frame-relay [**ietf** | **cisco**]	Interface	Defines the Frame Relay encapsulation that is used rather than HDLC, PPP, and so on.
frame-relay lmi-type {**ansi** | **q933a** | **cisco**}	Interface	Defines the type of LMI messages sent to the switch.
bandwidth *num*	Interface	Sets the router's perceived interface speed. Bandwidth is used by some routing protocols to influence the metric and is used in link utilization calculations seen with the **show interfaces** command.
frame-relay map {*protocol protocol-address dlci*} **payload-compression frf9 stac caim** [*element-number*] [**broadcast**] [**ietf** | **cisco**]	Interface	Statically defines a mapping between a network layer address and a DLCI.
keepalive *sec*	Interface	Defines whether and how often LMI status inquiry messages are sent and expected.
interface serial *number.sub* [**point- to-point** | **multipoint**]	Global	Creates a subinterface or references a previously created subinterface.
frame-relay interface-dlci *dlci* [**ietf** | **cisco**] [**voice-cir** *cir*] [**ppp** *virtual-template-name*]	Subinterface	Links or correlates a DLCI to the subinterface.

Table 10-11 *Frame Relay-Related Exec Commands*

Command	Function
show interfaces [*type number*]	Shows the physical interface status.
show frame-relay pvc [**interface** *interface*][*dlci*]	Lists information about the PVC status.
show frame-relay lmi [*type number*]	Lists LMI status information.

The network engineer plans the Frame Relay configuration based on several factors. When the service is ordered, the service provider specifies the LMI type that will be used. The engineer chooses the endpoints of the VCs, including whether to use a full mesh or partial mesh. Based on the location of the VCs, the engineer then decides which IP addressing option to use: single subnet, single subnet per VC, or a combination of the two. Finally, the encapsulation type is chosen. Because Frame Relay switches do not care about the encapsulation type, nor do they care about IP addressing, the only details that have to be discussed with the carrier are the VCs and the LMI type, along with the CIR and burst rates.

Three examples of Layer 3 addressing were given earlier in this chapter, with the networks diagrammed in Figures 10-12, 10-13, and 10-14. The configurations matching those networks and addresses are shown next.

Fully-Meshed Network with One IP Subnet/IPX Network

The network engineer designed a fully-meshed network for the first example. This first sample network, based on the environment depicted in Figure 10-12, does not use subinterfaces, but rather includes all Frame Relay configuration under the physical interface. Multipoint subinterfaces could have been used instead. Examples 10-1, 10-2, and 10-3 show the configuration for the network shown in Figure 10-15.

Figure 10-15 *Full Mesh with IP and IPX Addresses*

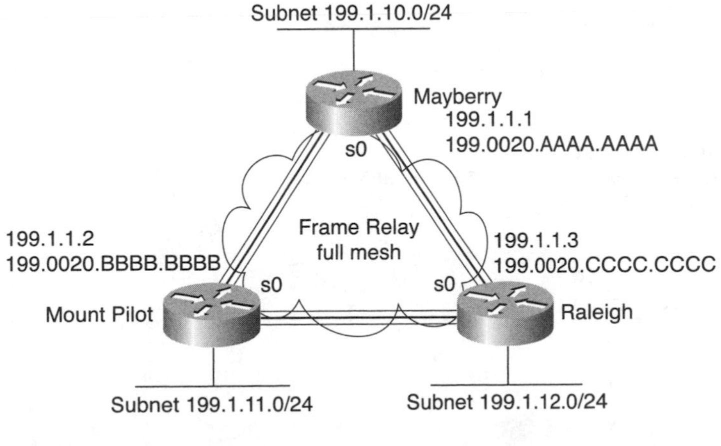

Example 10-1 *Mayberry Configuration*

```
ipx routing 0200.aaaa.aaaa
!
interface serial0
encapsulation frame-relay
ip address  199.1.1.1  255.255.255.0
ipx network  199
!
interface ethernet 0
ip address  199.1.10.1  255.255.255.0
ipx network  1
!
router igrp 1
network  199.1.1.0
network 199.1.10.0
```

Example 10-2 *Mount Pilot Configuration*

```
ipx routing 0200.bbbb.bbbb
!
interface serial0
encapsulation frame-relay
ip address  199.1.1.2  255.255.255.0
ipx network  199
!
interface ethernet 0
ip address  199.1.11.2   255.255.255.0
ipx network  2
!
router igrp 1
network  199.1.1.0
network 199.1.11.0
```

Example 10-3 *Raleigh Configuration*

```
ipx routing 0200.cccc.cccc
!
interface serial0
encapsulation frame-relay
ip address  199.1.1.3  255.255.255.0
ipx network  199
!
interface ethernet 0
ip address  199.1.12.3   255.255.255.0
ipx network  3
!
router igrp 1
network  199.1.1.0
network 199.1.12.0
```

The configuration is simple in comparison with the protocol concepts. All default settings (Cisco IOS Software Release 12.2) are used. They are as follows:

- The LMI type is automatically sensed.
- The encapsulation is Cisco instead of IETF.
- PVC DLCIs are learned via LMI status messages.
- Inverse ARP is enabled (by default) and is triggered when the status message declaring that the VCs are up has been received.
- Because either RIP or IGRP is being used, and all the configuration is on the real interface, split horizon is disabled.

In some cases, the default values are inappropriate. For example, if one router is not a Cisco router and does not support Cisco encapsulation, IETF encapsulation is required. For the purpose of showing an alternative configuration, suppose that the following requirements were added:

- The Raleigh router requires IETF encapsulation on both VCs.
- Mayberry's LMI type should be ANSI, and LMI autosense should not be used.

Examples 10-4 and 10-5 show the changes that would be made to Mayberry and Raleigh.

Example 10-4 *Mayberry Configuration with New Requirements*

```
ipx routing 0200.aaaa.aaaa
!
interface serial0
encapsulation frame-relay
frame-relay lmi-type ansi
frame-relay interface-dlci 42 ietfip address  199.1.1.1  255.255.255.0
ipx network  199
! rest of configuration unchanged from Example 10-1.
```

Example 10-5 *Raleigh Configuration with New Requirements*

```
ipx routing 0200.cccc.cccc
!
interface serial0
encapsulation frame-relay ietf
ip address  199.1.1.3  255.255.255.0
ipx network  199
!
! rest of configuration unchanged from Example 10-3.
```

The encapsulation was changed in two ways. Raleigh changed its encapsulation for both its PVCs with the **ietf** keyword on the **encapsulation** command. This keyword applies to all VCs on the interface. However, Mayberry could not change its encapsulation in the same way, because only one of the two VCs to Mayberry was directed to use IETF encapsulation. So Mayberry was forced to code the **frame-relay interface-dlci** command, coding the DLCI for the VC to Raleigh, with the **ietf** keyword being used to change the encapsulation just for this VC.

The LMI configuration in Mayberry would have been fine without any changes, because autosense would have recognized ANSI. However, by coding the **frame-relay lmi-type ansi**, Mayberry is forced to use ANSI, because this command disables autonegotiation of the LMI type.

Mount Pilot needs to configure a **frame-relay interface-dlci** command with the **ietf** keyword, just like Mayberry. This change is not shown in the examples.

Frame Relay Address Mapping

The DLCIs are missing from Figure 10-16 and the original configurations (Examples 10-1, 10-2, and 10-3). The configurations work as stated, and frankly, if you never knew the DLCIs, this network would work! However, knowing why you can make it work with no knowledge of the DLCIs means that you need to understand an important concept related to Frame Relay—namely, Frame Relay address mapping.

Figure 10-16 *Full Mesh with IP and IPX Addresses*

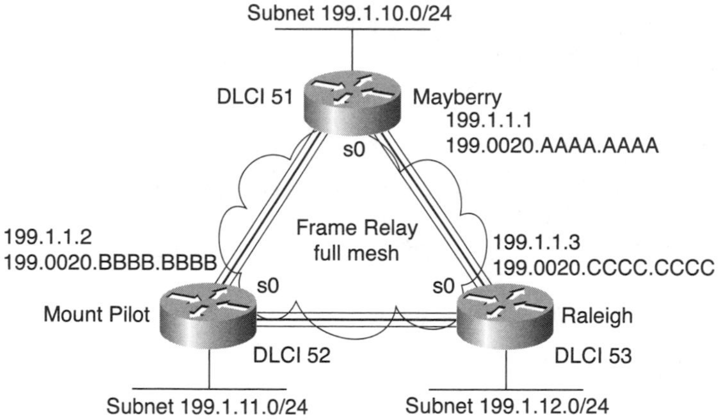

Mapping, as used here, means a correlation between a Layer 3 address and its corresponding Layer 2 address. For example, the IP ARP cache is an example of mapping. With IP ARP, you know the IP address of another device on the same LAN. When the ARP completes, you know another device's LAN (Layer 2) address. (For a review of IP ARP, see Chapter 6, "TCP/IP and IP Routing.") Likewise, we need a mapping between a router's Layer 3 address and the DLCI we use to reach that other router.

This section discusses the basics of why mapping is needed for LAN connections and Frame Relay, with a focus on Frame Relay. A more general definition of mapping follows:

> The information that correlates to the next-hop router's Layer 3 address, and the Layer 2 address used to reach it, is called mapping. Mapping is needed on multiaccess networks.

The need for mapping is more apparent when you think about the routing process. A host in Mayberry sends an IP packet to a host in Mount Pilot. The packet arrives at the Mayberry router, which discards the Ethernet header and trailer. Mayberry looks at the routing table, which lists a route to 199.1.11.0, outgoing interface Serial0, and next-hop router 199.1.1.2, which is Mount Pilot's Frame Relay IP address. 199.1.11.0 is Mount Pilot's subnet on its Ethernet interface.

The issue is simply this: What DLCI does Mayberry put into the Frame Relay header? We configured no DLCIs. However, the LMI uses status messages to tell Mayberry about the DLCIs. If the network works, obviously Mayberry knows the right DLCI value to use. To see the answer, consider Example 10-6, which shows some important commands that can be used to see how Mayberry makes the right choice for the DLCI.

Example 10-6 show *Commands on Mayberry, Showing the Need for Mapping*

```
Mayberry#show ip route
Codes: C - connected, S - static, I - IGRP, R - RIP, M - mobile, B - BGP
       D - EIGRP, EX - EIGRP external, O - OSPF, IA - OSPF inter area
       N1 - OSPF NSSA external type 1, N2 - OSPF NSSA external type 2
       E1 - OSPF external type 1, E2 - OSPF external type 2, E - EGP
       i - IS-IS, L1 - IS-IS level-1, L2 - IS-IS level-2, ia - IS-IS inter area
       * - candidate default, U - per-user static route, o - ODR
       P - periodic downloaded static route

Gateway of last resort is not set

I     199.1.11.0/24 [100/8576] via 199.1.1.2, 00:00:26, Serial0
C     199.1.10.0/24 is directly connected, Ethernet0
I     199.1.12.0/24 [100/8539] via 199.1.1.3, 00:01:04, Serial0
C     199.1.1.0/24 is directly connected, Serial0
C     192.68.1.0/24 is directly connected, Ethernet0
C     192.168.1.0/24 is directly connected, Ethernet0

Mayberry#show frame-relay pvc

PVC Statistics for interface Serial0 (Frame Relay DTE)

              Active     Inactive      Deleted       Static
  Local          2           0            0             0
  Switched       0           0            0             0
  Unused         0           0            0             0

DLCI = 52, DLCI USAGE = LOCAL, PVC STATUS = ACTIVE, INTERFACE = Serial0

  input pkts 46              output pkts 22              in bytes 2946
  out bytes 1794             dropped pkts 0              in FECN pkts 0
  in BECN pkts 0             out FECN pkts 0             out BECN pkts 0
  in DE pkts 0               out DE pkts 0
  out bcast pkts 21          out bcast bytes 1730
  pvc create time 00:23:07, last time pvc status changed 00:21:38

DLCI = 53, DLCI USAGE = LOCAL, PVC STATUS = ACTIVE, INTERFACE = Serial0
```

continues

Example 10-6 show *Commands on Mayberry, Showing the Need for Mapping (Continued)*

```
  input pkts 39            output pkts 18           in bytes 2564
  out bytes 1584           dropped pkts 0           in FECN pkts 0
  in BECN pkts 0           out FECN pkts 0          out BECN pkts 0
  in DE pkts 0             out DE pkts 0
  out bcast pkts 18        out bcast bytes 1584
  pvc create time 00:23:08, last time pvc status changed 00:21:20

Mayberry#show frame-relay map
Serial0 (up): ip 199.1.1.2 dlci 52(0x34,0xC40), dynamic,
              broadcast,, status defined, active
Serial0 (up): ip 199.1.1.3 dlci 53(0x35,0xC50), dynamic,
              broadcast,, status defined, active
Serial0 (up): ipx 1.0200.bbbb.bbbb dlci 52(0x34,0xC40), dynamic,
              broadcast,, status defined, active
Serial0 (up): ipx 199.0000.3089.b170 dlci 53(0x35,0xC50), dynamic,
              broadcast,, status defined, active
```

All the information needed for Mayberry to pick DLCI 52 is in the command output. The route to 199.1.11.0 points out Serial0 to 199.1.1.2 as the next-hop address. The **show frame-relay pvc** command lists two DLCIs, 52 and 53, and both are active. Which one should be used? The **show frame-relay map** command output holds the answer. Notice the phrase **ip 199.1.1.2 dlci 52** in the output. Somehow, Mayberry has mapped 199.1.1.2, which is the next-hop address in the route, to the correct DLCI, which is 52.

Mayberry can use two methods to build the mapping shown in the example. One uses a statically configured mapping, and the other uses a dynamic process called *Inverse ARP*. Before these two options are described, you need more background information. Table 10-12 lists the IP and IPX addresses of the three routers shown in Figure 10-16.

Table 10-12 *Layer 3 Addresses and DLCIs Used with Figure 10-16*

Router	Global DLCI	IP Address	IPX Address
Mayberry	51	199.1.1.1	199.0200.aaaa.aaaa
Mount Pilot	52	199.1.1.2	199.0200.bbbb.bbbb
Raleigh	53	199.1.1.3	199.0200.cccc.cccc

Example 10-7 lists the static Frame Relay map for the three routers shown in Figure 10-12. The DLCIs in Table 10-12 are the same as those used in Figure 10-16.

Example 10-7 frame-relay map *Commands*

```
Mayberry
interface serial 0
frame-relay map ip 199.1.1.2 52 broadcast
frame-relay map ipx 199.0200.bbbb.bbbb 52 broadcast
frame-relay map ip 199.1.1.3 53 broadcast
frame-relay map ipx 199.0200.cccc.cccc 53 broadcast
```

Example 10-7 frame-relay map *Commands (Continued)*

```
Mount Pilot
interface serial 0
frame-relay map ip 199.1.1.1 51 broadcast
frame-relay map ipx 199.0200.aaaa.aaaa 51 broadcast
frame-relay map ip 199.1.1.3 53 broadcast
frame-relay map ipx 199.0200.cccc.cccc 53 broadcast
```

```
Raleigh
interface serial 0
frame-relay map ip 199.1.1.1 51 broadcast
frame-relay map ipx 199.0200.aaaa.aaaa 51 broadcast
frame-relay map ip 199.1.1.2 52 broadcast
frame-relay map ipx 199.0200.bbbb.bbbb 52 broadcast
```

The **frame-relay map** command entry for Mayberry, referencing 199.1.1.2, is used for packets in Mayberry going to Mount Pilot. When Mayberry creates a Frame Relay header, expecting it to be delivered to Mount Pilot, Mayberry must use DLCI 52. Mayberry's **map** statement correlates Mount Pilot's IP address, 199.1.1.2, to the DLCI used to reach Mount Pilot—namely, DLCI 52. Likewise, a packet sent back from Mount Pilot to Mayberry causes Mount Pilot to use its **map** statement to refer to Mayberry's IP address of 199.1.1.1. Mapping is needed for each next-hop Layer 3 address for each Layer 3 protocol being routed. Even with a network this small, the configuration process can be laborious.

The alternative mapping solution is a dynamic protocol called Inverse ARP. Inverse ARP still creates a mapping between the Layer 3 address (for example, the IP address) and Layer 2 address (the DLCI). The process it uses is different from ARP on a LAN. After the VC is up, each DTE announces its network layer address to the DTE on the other end of the VC. It works as shown in Figure 10-17.

Figure 10-17 *Inverse ARP Process*

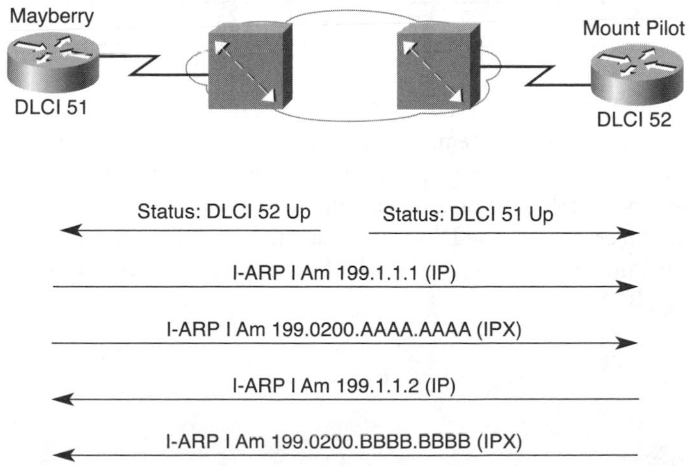

As shown in Figure 10-17, Inverse ARP announces its Layer 3 addresses as soon as the LMI signals that the PVCs are up. IP ARP reacts to an incoming packet and begins knowing the IP address but not the data link layer LAN address. Inverse ARP starts by learning the DLCI data link layer address and announces its own Layer 3 addresses right away. Inverse ARP is enabled by default in Cisco IOS Software Release 11.2 and later. Table 10-13 summarizes what occurs in the network shown in Figure 10-16.

Table 10-13 *Inverse ARP Messages for Figure 10-16*

Sending Router	DLCI in Header of Inverse ARP Frame When Sent	Receiving Router	DLCI in Header of Inverse ARP Frame When Received	Information in Inverse ARP
Mayberry	52	Mount Pilot	51	I am 199.1.1.1.
Mayberry	52	Mount Pilot	51	I am 199.0200.aaaa.aaaa.
Mayberry	53	Raleigh	51	I am 199.1.1.1.
Mayberry	53	Raleigh	51	I am 199.0200.aaaa.aaaa.
Mount Pilot	51	Mayberry	52	I am 199.1.1.2.
Mount Pilot	51	Mayberry	52	I am 199.0200.bbbb.bbbb.
Mount Pilot	53	Raleigh	52	I am 199.1.1.2.
Mount Pilot	53	Raleigh	52	I am 199.0200.bbbb.bbbb.
Raleigh	51	Mayberry	53	I am 199.1.1.3.
Raleigh	51	Mayberry	53	I am 199.0200.cccc.cccc.
Raleigh	52	Mount Pilot	53	I am 199.1.1.3.
Raleigh	52	Mount Pilot	53	I am 199.0200.cccc.cccc.

To understand Inverse ARP, focus on the last two columns of Table 10-13. Each router receives some Inverse ARP "announcements." The Inverse ARP contains the Layer 3 address of the sender, and the Frame Relay header, of course, has a DLCI in it. These two values are placed into the Inverse ARP cache on the receiving router. For example, in the fifth row, Mayberry receives an Inverse ARP. The DLCI is 52, and the IP address is 199.1.1.2. This is added to the Frame Relay map table in Mayberry, which is seen with the **show frame-relay map** command in Example 10-6.

Partially-Meshed Network with One IP Subnet/IPX Network Per VC

The second sample network, based on the environment shown in Figure 10-18, uses point-to-point subinterfaces. Examples 10-8 through 10-11 show the configuration for this network. The command prompts are included in the first example because they change when you're configuring subinterfaces.

Figure 10-18 *Partial Mesh with IP and IPX Addresses*

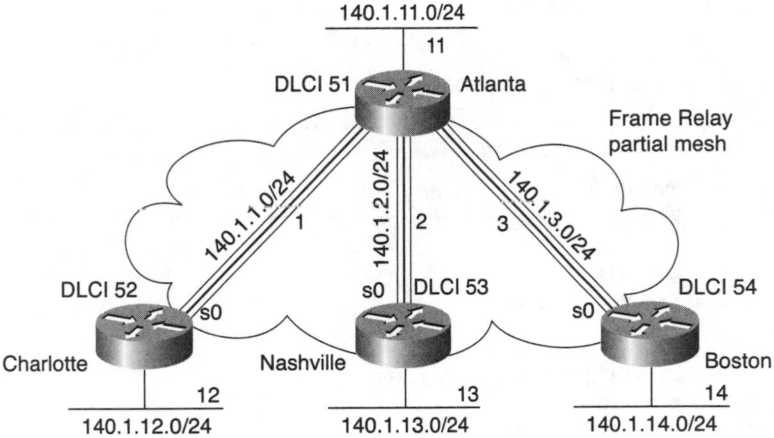

Example 10-8 *Atlanta Configuration*

```
Atlanta(config)#ipx routing 0200.aaaa.aaaa
Atlanta(config)#interface serial0
Atlanta(config-if)#encapsulation frame-relay

Atlanta(config-if)#interface serial 0.1 point-to-point
Atlanta(config-subif)#ip address 140.1.1.1  255.255.255.0
Atlanta(config-subif)#ipx network 1
Atlanta(config-subif)#frame-relay interface-dlci 52
 Atlanta(config-fr-dlci)#interface serial 0.2 point-to-point
Atlanta(config-subif)#ip address 140.1.2.1 255.255.255.0
Atlanta(config-subif)#ipx network 2
Atlanta(config-subif)#frame-relay interface-dlci 53

Atlanta(config-fr-dlci)#interface serial 0.3 point-to-point
Atlanta(config-subif)#ip address 140.1.3.1 255.255.255.0
Atlanta(config-subif)#ipx network 3
Atlanta(config-subif)#frame-relay interface-dlci 54

Atlanta(config-fr-dlci)#interface ethernet 0
Atlanta(config-if)#ip address 140.1.11.1 255.255.255.0
Atlanta(config-if)#ipx network 11
```

Example 10-9 *Charlotte Configuration*

```
ipx routing 0200.bbbb.bbbb
!
interface serial0
encapsulation frame-relay
!
interface serial 0.1 point-to-point
ip address 140.1.1.2  255.255.255.0
ipx network 1
frame-relay interface-dlci 51
!
interface ethernet 0
ip address 140.1.12.2 255.255.255.0
ipx network 12
```

Example 10-10 *Nashville Configuration*

```
ipx routing 0200.cccc.cccc
!
interface serial0
encapsulation frame-relay
!
interface serial 0.2 point-to-point
ip address 140.1.2.3 255.255.255.0
ipx network 2
frame-relay interface-dlci 51
!
interface ethernet 0
ip address 140.1.13.3 255.255.255.0
ipx network 13
```

Example 10-11 *Boston Configuration*

```
ipx routing 0200.dddd.dddd
!
interface serial0
encapsulation frame-relay
!
interface serial 0.3 point-to-point
ip address 140.1.3.4 255.255.255.0
ipx network 3
frame-relay interface-dlci 51
!
interface ethernet 0
ip address 140.1.14.4  255.255.255.0
ipx network 14
```

Again, defaults abound in this configuration, but some defaults are different than when you're configuring on the main interface, as in the preceding example. The LMI type is autosensed, and Cisco encapsulation is used, which is just like the fully-meshed example. However, Inverse ARP is disabled and split horizon is enabled, because these are the defaults when you're using a point-point subinterface. As you will see, Inverse ARP is not needed, and because there is only one VC per subinterface, the split horizon problem described earlier is not an issue.

Point-to-point subinterfaces are used in this configuration because the network is not fully meshed. If only the main interface were used, or if multipoint subinterfaces were used, the routing problems described in the preceding section would prevent remote sites from communicating with each other.

Two new commands create the configuration required with point-to-point subinterfaces. First, the **interface serial 0.1 point-to-point** command creates logical subinterface number 1 under physical interface Serial0. The **frame-relay interface-dlci** subinterface subcommand is needed when you're using subinterfaces. Consider router Atlanta in Figure 10-18. Atlanta receives LMI messages on Serial0 stating that three PVCs, with DLCIs 52, 53, and 54, are up. Which PVC goes with which subinterface? Cisco IOS Software needs to associate the correct PVC with the correct subinterface. This is accomplished with the **frame-relay interface-dlci** command.

The subinterface numbers do not have to match on the router on the other end of the PVC. I just numbered them to be easier to remember! In real life, it is useful to encode some information about your network numbering scheme into the subinterface number. One client I worked with encoded part of the carrier's circuit ID in the subinterface number so that the operations staff could find the correct information to call during a failed access link. Many sites use the DLCI as the subinterface number. In any case, there are no requirements for matching subinterface numbers. Here, all I did was match the subinterface number to the third octet of the IP address.

Example 10-12 shows the output from the most popular Cisco IOS Software Frame Relay EXEC commands for monitoring Frame Relay, as issued on router Atlanta.

Example 10-12 *Output from EXEC Commands on Atlanta*

```
Atlanta#show frame-relay pvc

PVC Statistics for interface Serial0 (Frame Relay DTE)

              Active     Inactive      Deleted       Static
  Local          3           0            0             0
  Switched       0           0            0             0
  Unused         0           0            0             0
DLCI = 52, DLCI USAGE = LOCAL, PVC STATUS = ACTIVE, INTERFACE = Serial0.1

  input pkts 843            output pkts 876          in bytes 122723
  out bytes 134431          dropped pkts 0           in FECN pkts 0
  in BECN pkts 0            out FECN pkts 0          out BECN pkts 0
  in DE pkts 0              out DE pkts 0
  out bcast pkts 876         out bcast bytes 134431
  pvc create time 05:20:10, last time pvc status changed 05:19:31
 --More--
DLCI = 53, DLCI USAGE = LOCAL, PVC STATUS = ACTIVE, INTERFACE = Serial0.2

  input pkts 0              output pkts 875          in bytes 0
```

continues

Example 10-12 *Output from EXEC Commands on Atlanta (Continued)*

```
  out bytes 142417         dropped pkts 0            in FECN pkts 0
  in BECN pkts 0           out FECN pkts 0           out BECN pkts 0
  in DE pkts 0             out DE pkts 0
  out bcast pkts 875        out bcast bytes 142417
  pvc create time 05:19:51, last time pvc status changed 04:55:41
 --More--
DLCI = 54, DLCI USAGE = LOCAL, PVC STATUS = ACTIVE, INTERFACE = Serial0.3

  input pkts 10            output pkts 877           in bytes 1274
  out bytes 142069         dropped pkts 0            in FECN pkts 0
  in BECN pkts 0           out FECN pkts 0           out BECN pkts 0
  in DE pkts 0             out DE pkts 0
  out bcast pkts 877        out bcast bytes 142069
  pvc create time 05:19:52, last time pvc status changed 05:17:42

Atlanta#show frame-relay map
Serial0.3 (up): point-to-point dlci, dlci 54(0x36,0xC60), broadcast
          status defined, active
Serial0.2 (up): point-to-point dlci, dlci 53(0x35,0xC50), broadcast
          status defined, active
Serial0.1 (up): point-to-point dlci, dlci 52(0x34,0xC40), broadcast
          status defined, active

Atlanta#debug frame-relay lmi
Frame Relay LMI debugging is on
Displaying all Frame Relay LMI data

Serial0(out): StEnq, myseq 163, yourseen 161, DTE up
datagramstart = 0x45AED8, datagramsize = 13
FR encap = 0xFCF10309
00 75 01 01 01 03 02 A3 A1

Serial0(in): Status, myseq 163
RT IE 1, length 1, type 1
KA IE 3, length 2, yourseq 162, myseq 163
```

The **show frame-relay pvc** command lists useful management information. For instance, the packet counters for each VC, plus the counters for FECN and BECN, can be particularly useful. Likewise, comparing the packets/bytes sent on one router versus the counters of what is received on the router on the other end of the VC is also quite useful, because it reflects the number of packets/bytes lost inside the Frame Relay cloud. Also, the PVC status is a great place to start when troubleshooting. In addition, all this information can be better gathered by an SNMP manager with this command.

The **show frame-relay map** command lists mapping information. With the earlier example of a fully-meshed network, in which the configuration did not use any subinterfaces, a Layer 3 address was listed with each DLCI. In this example, a DLCI is listed in each entry, but no mention of corresponding Layer 3 addresses is made. The whole point of mapping was to correlate a Layer 3 address to a Layer 2 address, but there is no Layer 3 address in the **show frame-relay map** command output! The reason is that the information is stored somewhere else. Subinterfaces require the use of the **frame-relay interface-dlci** configuration command. Because these subinterfaces are point-to-point, when a route points out a single subinterface, the DLCI is implied by the configuration. Mapping is needed only when more than two devices are attached to the link, and with a point-to-point subinterface, logically speaking, there are only two DTEs.

The **debug frame-relay lmi** output lists information for the sending and receiving LMI inquiries. The status message is sent by the switch; whereas, the status inquiry is sent by the DTE (router). The default setting with Cisco IOS Software is to send, and expect to receive, these status messages. The Cisco IOS Software **no keepalive** command is used to disable the use of LMI status messages. Unlike other interfaces, Cisco keepalive messages do not flow from router to router over Frame Relay. Instead, they are simply used to detect whether the router has connectivity to its local Frame Relay switch.

Partially-Meshed Network with Some Fully-Meshed Parts

Frame Relay networks built by CCNAs usually include both point-to-point and multipoint subinterfaces. This last sample network (based on the environment shown in Figure 10-19) uses both types of subinterfaces. Examples 10-13 through 10-17 show the configuration for this network. Table 10-14 summarizes the addresses and subinterfaces used.

Figure 10-19 *Hybrid of Full and Partial Mesh*

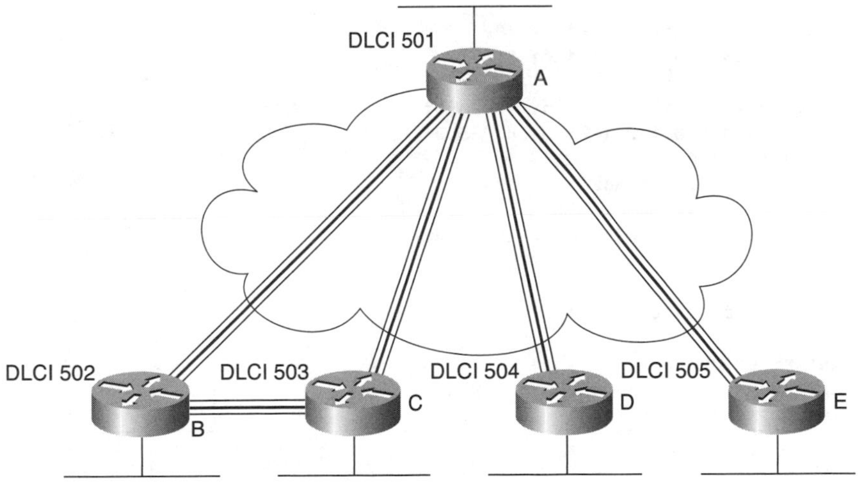

Table 10-14 *IP and IPX Addresses with Point-to-Point and Multipoint Subinterfaces*

Router	Subnet	IP Address	IPX Network	IPX Address	Subinterface Type
A	140.1.1.0/24	140.1.1.1	1	1.0200.aaaa.aaaa	Multipoint
B	140.1.1.0/24	140.1.1.2	1	1.0200.bbbb.bbbb	Multipoint
C	140.1.1.0/24	140.1.1.3	1	1.0200.cccc.cccc	Multipoint
A	140.1.2.0/24	140.1.2.1	2	2.0200.aaaa.aaaa	Point-to-point
D	140.1.2.0/24	140.1.2.4	2	2.0200.dddd.dddd	Point-to-point
A	140.1.3.0/24	140.1.3.1	3	3.0200.aaaa.aaaa	Point-to-point
E	140.1.3.0/24	140.1.3.5	3	3.0200.eeee.eeee	Point-to-point

Example 10-13 *Router A Configuration*

```
hostname RouterA
!
ipx routing 0200.aaaa.aaaa
!
interface serial0
encapsulation frame-relay
!
interface serial 0.1 multipoint
ip address 140.1.1.1  255.255.255.0
ipx network 1
frame-relay interface-dlci 502
frame-relay interface-dlci 503
!
interface serial 0.2 point-to-point
ip address 140.1.2.1 255.255.255.0
ipx network 2
frame-relay interface-dlci 504
!
interface serial 0.3 point-to-point
ip address 140.1.3.1 255.255.255.0
ipx network 3
frame-relay interface-dlci 505
!
interface ethernet 0
ip address 140.1.11.1 255.255.255.0
ipx network 11
```

Example 10-14 *Router B Configuration*

```
hostname RouterB
!
ipx routing 0200.bbbb.bbbb
!
```

Example 10-14 *Router B Configuration (Continued)*

```
interface serial0
encapsulation frame-relay
!
interface serial 0.1 multipoint
ip address 140.1.1.2  255.255.255.0
ipx network 1
frame-relay interface-dlci 501
frame-relay interface-dlci 503
!
interface ethernet 0
ip address 140.1.12.2 255.255.255.0
ipx network 12
```

Example 10-15 *Router C Configuration*

```
hostname RouterC
!
ipx routing 0200.cccc.cccc
!
interface serial0
encapsulation frame-relay
!
interface serial 0.1 multipoint
ip address 140.1.1.3  255.255.255.0
ipx network 1
frame-relay interface-dlci 501
frame-relay interface-dlci 502
!
interface ethernet 0
ip address 140.1.13.3 255.255.255.0
ipx network 13
```

Example 10-16 *Router D Configuration*

```
hostname RouterD
!
ipx routing 0200.dddd.dddd
!
interface serial0
encapsulation frame-relay
!
interface serial 0.1 point-to-point
ip address 140.1.2.4  255.255.255.0
ipx network 2
frame-relay interface-dlci 501
!
interface ethernet 0
ip address 140.1.14.4 255.255.255.0
ipx network 14
```

Example 10-17 *Router E Configuration*

```
hostname RouterE
!
ipx routing 0200.eeee.eeee
!
interface serial0
encapsulation frame-relay
!
interface serial 0.1 point-to-point
ip address 140.1.3.5 255.255.255.0
ipx network 3
frame-relay interface-dlci 501
!
interface ethernet 0
ip address 140.1.15.5 255.255.255.0
ipx network 15
```

On Routers A, B, and C, a multipoint subinterface is used. These three routers each have a PVC to the other two, making the use of multipoint reasonable. The term *multipoint* simply means that there is more than one DTE. Like point-to-point subinterfaces, multipoint subinterfaces use the **frame-relay interface-dlci** command. Notice that there are two for each multipoint subinterface in this case. The reason is that each PVC associated with this subinterface must be identified.

No mapping statements are required for the configurations shown in Examples 10-13 through 10-17 because Inverse ARP is enabled on the multipoint subinterfaces by default. The **show frame-relay map** command lists the mapping information learned by Inverse ARP. Notice that the output now includes the Layer 3 addresses! The reason is that the routes might point out a multipoint interface, but because more than one DLCI is associated with the interface, the router needs mapping information to identify the correct DLCI.

Router A is the only router using both multipoint and point-to-point subinterfaces. On Router A's Serial0.1 interface, multipoint is in use, with DLCIs for Router B and Router C listed. On Router A's other two subinterfaces, which are point-to-point, only a single DLCI needs to be listed. In fact, only one **frame-relay interface-dlci** command is allowed on a point-to-point subinterface, because only one VC is allowed. Otherwise, the configurations between the two types are similar.

Example 10-18 shows the contents of the Frame Relay map table, which are a result of Inverse ARP. This example also shows a copy of the **debug frame-relay events**, showing the contents of the Inverse ARP messages. The **debug** in Example 10-18 provides some insight into Inverse ARP operation.

Example 10-18 *Frame Relay Maps and Inverse ARP on Router C*

```
RouterC#show frame-relay map
Serial0.10 (up): ip 140.1.1.1 dlci 501(0x1F5,0x7C50), dynamic,
              broadcast,, status defined, active
Serial0.10 (up): ip 140.1.1.2 dlci 502(0x1F6,0x7C60), dynamic,
              broadcast,, status defined, active
Serial0.10 (up): ipx 1.0200.aaaa.aaaa dlci 501(0x1F5,0x7C50), dynamic,
              broadcast,, status defined, active
Serial0.10 (up): ipx 1.0200.bbbb.bbbb dlci 502(0x1F6,0x7C60), dynamic,
              broadcast,, status defined, active

RouterC#debug frame-relay events
Frame Relay events debugging is on

RouterC#configure terminal
Enter configuration commands, one per line.  End with Ctrl-Z.
RouterC(config)#interface serial 0.1
RouterC(config-subif)#no shutdown
RouterC(config-subif)#^Z
RouterC#

Serial0.1: FR ARP input
Serial0.1: FR ARP input
Serial0.1: FR ARP input
datagramstart = 0xE42E58, datagramsize = 30
FR encap = 0x7C510300
80 00 00 00 08 06 00 0F 08 00 02 04 00 09 00 00
8C 01 01 01 7C 51 8C 01 01 03

datagramstart = 0xE427A0, datagramsize = 46
FR encap = 0x7C510300
80 00 00 00 08 06 00 0F 81 37 02 0A 00 09 00 00
00 00 00 01 02 00 AA AA AA AA 7C 51 00 00 00 01
02 00 CC CC CC CC 1B 99 D0 CC

datagramstart = 0xE420E8, datagramsize = 30
FR encap = 0x7C610300
80 00 00 00 08 06 00 0F 08 00 02 04 00 09 00 00
8C 01 01 02 7C 61 8C 01 01 03

Serial0.1: FR ARP input
datagramstart = 0xE47188, datagramsize = 46
FR encap = 0x7C610300
80 00 00 00 08 06 00 0F 81 37 02 0A 00 09 00 00
00 00 00 01 02 00 BB BB BB BB 7C 61 00 00 00 01
02 00 CC CC CC CC 1B 99 D0 CC
```

The messages about Inverse ARP in the **debug frame-relay events** output are not so obvious. One easy exercise is to search for the hex version of the IP and IPX addresses in the output. These addresses are highlighted in Example 10-18. For example, the first three bytes of 140.1.1.0 are 8C 01 01 in hexadecimal. This field starts on the left side of the output, so it is easy to recognize. The IPX address should be even easier to recognize, because it is already in hexadecimal format in the configuration.

NOTE Enabling **debug** options increases the router's CPU utilization. Depending on how much processing is required and how many messages are generated, it is possible to significantly degrade performance and possibly crash the router. This is a result of the memory and processing used to look for the requested information and to process the messages. You might want to first type the command **no debug all** and then type your **debug** command. If your **debug** creates too much output, you can easily go back to the **no debug all** command by pressing Ctrl-P twice.

Foundation Summary

The Foundation Summary is a collection of tables and figures that provide a convenient review of many key concepts in this chapter. If you are already comfortable with the topics in this chapter, this summary will help you recall a few details. If you just read this chapter, this review will help solidify some key facts. If you are doing your final preparation before the exam, these tables and figures are a convenient way to review the day before the exam.

Figure 10-20 shows some connectivity used for Frame Relay.

Figure 10-20 *Frame Relay Components*

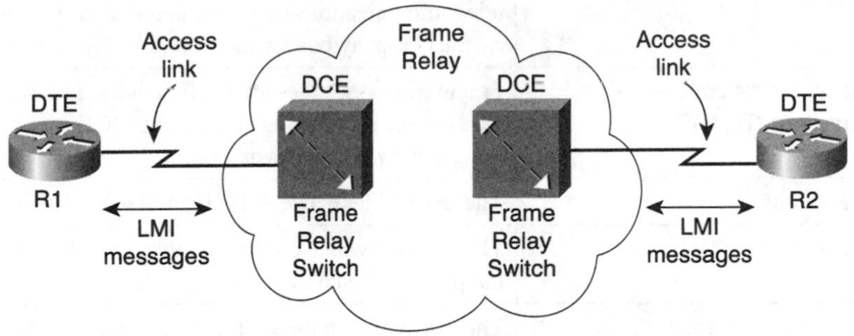

Figure 10-21 shows the physical and logical connectivity at each connection to the Frame Relay network.

Figure 10-21 *Frame Relay Concepts*

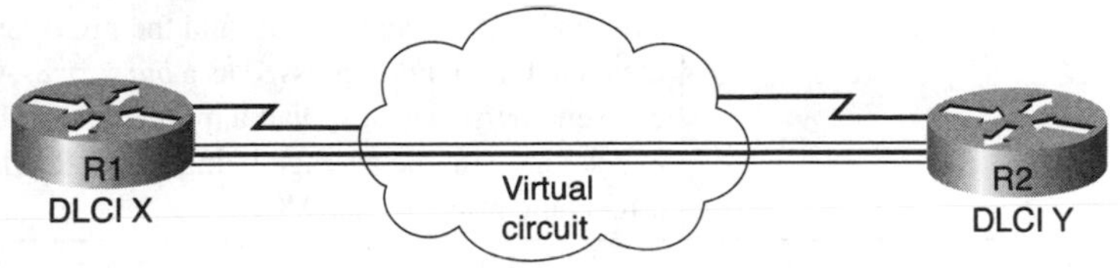

For reference, Table 10-15 lists the components shown in Figure 10-20 and some associated terms.

Table 10-15 *Frame Relay Terms and Concepts*

Term	Description
Virtual circuit (VC)	A logical concept that represents the path that frames travel between DTEs. VCs are particularly useful when comparing Frame Relay to leased physical circuits.
Permanent virtual circuit (PVC)	A predefined VC. A PVC can be equated to a leased line in concept.
Switched virtual circuit (SVC)	A VC that is set up dynamically when needed. An SVC can be equated to a dial connection in concept.
Data terminal equipment (DTE)	DTEs are connected to a Frame Relay service from a telecommunications company and typically reside at sites used by the company buying the Frame Relay service.
Data communications equipment (DCE)	Frame Relay switches are DCE devices. DCEs are also known as data circuit-terminating equipment. DCEs are typically in the service provider's network.
Access link	The leased line between DTE and DCE.
Access rate (AR)	The speed at which the access link is clocked. This choice affects the price of the connection.
Committed information rate (CIR)	The rate at which the DTE can send data for an individual VC, for which the provider commits to deliver that amount of data. The provider sends any data in excess of this rate for this VC if its network has capacity at the time. This choice typically affects the price of each VC.
Burst rate	The rate and length of time which, for a particular VC, the DTE can send faster than the CIR, and the provider agrees to forward the data. Often it is expressed as a *burst size*. A Frame Relay DTE can send burst size bits, wait a moment, send burst size bits, wait, and so on, with the average being the CIR. This choice typically affects the price of each VC.
Data-link connection identifier (DLCI)	A Frame Relay address used in Frame Relay headers to identify the VC.
Forward explicit congestion notification (FECN)	The bit in the Frame Relay header that signals to anyone receiving the frame (switches and DTEs) that congestion is occurring in the same direction as the frame. Switches and DTEs can react by slowing the rate at which data is sent in that direction.
Backward explicit congestion notification (BECN)	The bit in the Frame Relay header that signals to anyone receiving the frame (switches and DTEs) that congestion is occurring in the opposite (backward) direction as the frame. Switches and DTEs can react by slowing the rate at which data is sent in that direction.

Table 10-15 *Frame Relay Terms and Concepts (Continued)*

Term	Description
Discard eligibility (DE)	The bit in the Frame Relay header that, if frames must be discarded, signals a switch to choose this frame to discard instead of another frame without the DE bit set.
Nonbroadcast multiaccess (NBMA)	A network in which broadcasts are not supported, but more than two devices can be connected.
Local Management Interface (LMI)	The protocol used between a DCE and DTE to manage the connection. Signaling messages for SVCs, PVC status messages, and keepalives are all LMI messages.
Link Access Procedure Frame Mode Bearer Services (LAPF)	Defines the basic Frame Relay header and trailer. The header includes DLCI, FECN, BECN, and DE bits.

Table 10-16 lists the most important of the Frame Relay specifications.

Table 10-16 *Frame Relay Protocol Specifications*

What the Specification Defines	ITU Document	ANSI Document
Data-link specifications, including LAPF header/trailer	Q.922 Annex A	T1.618
PVC management, LMI	Q.933 Annex A	T1.617 Annex D
SVC signaling	Q.933	T1.617
Multiprotocol encapsulation (originated in RFC 1490/2427)	Q.933 Annex E	T1.617 Annex F

Table 10-17 outlines the three LMI types, their origin, and the keyword used in the Cisco **frame-relay lmi-type** interface subcommand.

Table 10-17 *Frame Relay LMI Types*

Name	Document	IOS LMI-Type Parameter
Cisco	Proprietary	**cisco**
ANSI	T1.617 Annex D	**ansi**
ITU	Q.933 Annex A	**q933a**

Table 10-18 summarizes the default split horizon settings used for each type of Frame Relay interface.

Table 10-18 *Split Horizon and Frame Relay Interfaces*

Type of Configuration	Split Horizon Is
No subinterfaces	Disabled
Point-to-point subinterfaces	Enabled
Multipoint subinterfaces	Disabled

Tables 10-19 and 10-20 summarize the more popular commands used for Frame Relay configuration and verification.

Table 10-19 *Frame Relay Configuration Commands*

Command	Configuration Mode	Description
encapsulation frame-relay [**ietf** | **cisco**]	Interface	Defines the Frame Relay encapsulation that is used rather than HDLC, PPP, and so on.
frame-relay lmi-type {**ansi** | **q933a** | **cisco**}	Interface	Defines the type of LMI messages sent to the switch.
bandwidth *num*	Interface	Sets the router's perceived interface speed. Bandwidth is used by some routing protocols to influence the metric and is used in link utilization calculations seen with the **show interfaces** command.
frame-relay map {*protocol protocol-address dlci*} **payload-compression frf9 stac caim** [*element-number*] [**broadcast**] [**ietf** | **cisco**]	Interface	Statically defines a mapping between a network layer address and a DLCI.
keepalive *sec*	Interface	Defines whether and how often LMI status inquiry messages are sent and expected.
interface serial *number.sub* [**point-to-point** | **multipoint**]	Global	Creates a subinterface or references a previously created subinterface.
frame-relay interface-dlci *dlci* [**ietf** | **cisco**] [**voice-cir** *cir*] [**ppp** *virtual-template-name*]	Subinterface	Links or correlates a DLCI to the subinterface.

Table 10-20 *Frame Relay-Related EXEC Commands*

Command	Function
show interfaces [*type number*]	Shows the physical interface status.
show frame-relay pvc [**interface** *interface*][*dlci*]	Lists information about the PVC status.
show frame-relay lmi [*type number*]	Lists LMI status information.

Q&A

As mentioned in Chapter 1, "All About the Cisco Certified Network Associate Certification," the questions and scenarios in this book are more difficult than what you should experience on the exam. The questions do not attempt to cover more breadth or depth than the exam, but they are designed to make sure that you know the answer. Rather than allowing you to derive the answer from clues hidden in the question, the questions challenge your understanding and recall of the subject. Questions from the "Do I Know This Already?" quiz at the beginning of this chapter are repeated here to ensure that you have mastered this chapter's topics. Hopefully these questions will help limit the number of exam questions on which you narrow your choices to two options and then guess.

The answers to these questions can be found in Appendix A.

1. Name two WAN data-link protocols that define a method of announcing the interface's Layer 3 addresses to other devices attached to the WAN.

   ____

   ____

   ____

2. Explain the purpose of Inverse ARP. Explain how Inverse ARP uses Frame Relay broadcasts.

   ____

   ____

   ____

3. Would a Frame Relay switch connected to a router behave differently if the IETF option were deleted from the **encapsulation frame-relay ietf** command on that attached router? Would a router on the other end of the VC behave any differently if the same change were made?

   ____

   ____

   ____

4. What does NBMA stand for? Does it apply to X.25 networks or Frame Relay networks?

   ____

   ____

   ____

5 Define the terms DCE and DTE in the context of the physical layer and a point-to-point serial link.

____

____

____

6 Which layer or layers of OSI are most closely related to the functions of Frame Relay? Why?

____

____

____

7 When Inverse ARP is used by default, what additional configuration is needed to get IGRP routing updates to flow over each VC?

____

____

____

8 Define the attributes of a partial-mesh and full-mesh Frame Relay network.

____

____

____

9 What key pieces of information are required in the **frame-relay map** statement?

____

____

____

10 When creating a partial-mesh Frame Relay network, are you required to use subinterfaces?

____

____

____

11 What benefit related to routing protocols can be gained by using subinterfaces with a partial mesh?

____

____

____

12 Create a configuration for Router1 that has Frame Relay VCs to Router2 and Router3 (DLCIs 202 and 203, respectively) on Router1's Serial1 interface. Use any IP and IPX addresses you like. Assume that the network is not fully meshed.

____

____

____

13 What **show** command tells you when a PVC became active? How does the router know what time the PVC became active?

____

____

____

14 What **show** command lists Frame Relay information about mapping? In what instances does the information displayed include the Layer 3 addresses of other routers?

____

____

____

15 True or false: The **no keepalive** command on a Frame Relay serial interface causes no further Cisco proprietary keepalive messages to be sent to the Frame Relay switch.

____

____

____

16 What **debug** option shows Inverse ARP messages?

17 True or false: The Frame Relay **map** configuration command allows more than one Layer 3 protocol address mapping on the same configuration command.

18 What is the name of the field that identifies, or addresses, a Frame Relay virtual circuit?

Scenarios

Scenario 10-1: Frame Relay Verification

Use Examples 10-19 through 10-22 when completing the exercises and answering the questions that follow.

Example 10-19 *Atlanta Command Output, Scenario 10-1*

```
Atlanta#show interface s 0
Serial0 is up, line protocol is up
  Hardware is HD64570
  MTU 1500 bytes, BW 1544 Kbit, DLY 20000 usec, rely 255/255, load 1/255
  Encapsulation FRAME-RELAY, loopback not set, keepalive set (10 sec)
  LMI enq sent  32, LMI stat recvd 32, LMI upd recvd 0, DTE LMI up
  LMI enq recvd 0, LMI stat sent  0, LMI upd sent  0
  LMI DLCI 1023  LMI type is CISCO  frame relay DTE
  Broadcast queue 0/64, broadcasts sent/dropped 75/0, interface broadcasts 59
  Last input 00:00:00, output 00:00:07, output hang never
  Last clearing of "show interface" counters never
  Queuing strategy: fifo
  Output queue 0/40, 0 drops; input queue 0/75, 0 drops
  5 minute input rate 0 bits/sec, 0 packets/sec
  5 minute output rate 0 bits/sec, 0 packets/sec
     74 packets input, 5697 bytes, 0 no buffer
     Received 32 broadcasts, 0 runts, 0 giants, 0 throttles
     0 input errors, 0 CRC, 0 frame, 0 overrun, 0 ignored, 0 abort
     110 packets output, 9438 bytes, 0 underruns
     0 output errors, 0 collisions, 2 interface resets
     0 output buffer failures, 0 output buffers swapped out
     0 carrier transitions
     DCD=up  DSR=up  DTR=up  RTS=up  CTS=up

Atlanta#show interface s 0.1
Serial0.1 is up, line protocol is up
  Hardware is HD64570
  Internet address is 168.10.202.1/24
  MTU 1500 bytes, BW 1544 Kbit, DLY 20000 usec, rely 255/255, load 1/255
  Encapsulation FRAME-RELAY

Atlanta#show interface s 0.2
Serial0.2 is up, line protocol is up
  Hardware is HD64570
  Internet address is 168.10.203.1/24
  MTU 1500 bytes, BW 1544 Kbit, DLY 20000 usec, rely 255/255, load 1/255
  Encapsulation FRAME-RELAY

Atlanta#show interface s 0.3
Serial0.3 is up, line protocol is up
  Hardware is HD64570
  Internet address is 168.10.204.1/24
```

Example 10-19 *Atlanta Command Output, Scenario 10-1 (Continued)*

```
  MTU 1500 bytes, BW 1544 Kbit, DLY 20000 usec, rely 255/255, load 1/255
Encapsulation FRAME-RELAY

Atlanta#show frame-relay map
Serial0.3 (up): point-to-point dlci, dlci 54(0x36,0xC60), broadcast, IETF
          Status defined, active
Serial0.2 (up): point-to-point dlci, dlci 53(0x35,0xC50), broadcast
          Status defined, active
Serial0.1 (up): point-to-point dlci, dlci 52(0x34,0xC40), broadcast
          Status defined, active

Atlanta#show frame-relay lmi

LMI Statistics for interface Serial0 (Frame Relay DTE) LMI TYPE = CISCO
  Invalid Unnumbered info 0          Invalid Prot Disc 0
  Invalid dummy Call Ref 0           Invalid Msg Type 0
  Invalid Status Message 0           Invalid Lock Shift 0
  Invalid Information ID 0           Invalid Report IE Len 0
  Invalid Report Request 0           Invalid Keep IE Len 0
  Num Status Enq. Sent 43            Num Status msgs Rcvd 43
  Num Update Status Rcvd 0           Num Status Timeouts 0

Atlanta#debug frame-relay events
Frame Relay events debugging is on

Atlanta#configure terminal
Enter configuration commands, one per line.  End with Ctrl-Z.
Atlanta(config)#interface serial 0
Atlanta(config-if)#shutdown

%LINEPROTO-5-UPDOWN: Line protocol on Interface Serial0.1, changed state to down
%LINEPROTO-5-UPDOWN: Line protocol on Interface Serial0.2, changed state to down
%LINEPROTO-5-UPDOWN: Line protocol on Interface Serial0.3, changed state to down
%LINEPROTO-5-UPDOWN: Line protocol on Interface Serial0, changed state to down
%LINK-5-CHANGED: Interface Serial0, changed state to administratively down
%FR-5-DLCICHANGE: Interface Serial0 - DLCI 54 state changed to DELETED
%FR-5-DLCICHANGE: Interface Serial0 - DLCI 53 state changed to DELETED
%FR-5-DLCICHANGE: Interface Serial0 - DLCI 52 state changed to DELETED

Atlanta(config-if)#no shutdown
Atlanta(config-if)#^Z

%LINEPROTO-5-UPDOWN: Line protocol on Interface Serial0.1, changed state to up
%FR-5-DLCICHANGE: Interface Serial0 - DLCI 52 state changed to ACTIVE
%LINEPROTO-5-UPDOWN: Line protocol on Interface Serial0.2, changed state to up
%FR-5-DLCICHANGE: Interface Serial0 - DLCI 53 state changed to ACTIVE
%LINEPROTO-5-UPDOWN: Line protocol on Interface Serial0.3, changed state to up
%FR-5-DLCICHANGE: Interface Serial0 - DLCI 54 state changed to ACTIVE
%SYS-5-CONFIG_I: Configured from console by console
%LINEPROTO-5-UPDOWN: Line protocol on Interface Serial0, changed state to up
%LINK-3-UPDOWN: Interface Serial0, changed state to up
```

continues

Example 10-19 *Atlanta Command Output, Scenario 10-1 (Continued)*

```
Atlanta#show frame map
Serial0.3 (up): point-to-point dlci, dlci 54(0x36,0xC60), broadcast, IETF
          Status defined, active
Serial0.2 (up): point-to-point dlci, dlci 53(0x35,0xC50), broadcast
          Status defined, active
Serial0.1 (up): point-to-point dlci, dlci 52(0x34,0xC40), broadcast
          Status defined, active

Atlanta#debug frame-relay lmi
Frame Relay LMI debugging is on
Displaying all Frame Relay LMI data
Atlanta#

Serial0(out): StEnq, myseq 6, yourseen 5, DTE up
datagramstart = 0x45B25C, datagramsize = 13
FR encap = 0xFCF10309
00 75 01 01 01 03 02 06 05

Serial0(in): Status, myseq 6
RT IE 1, length 1, type 1
KA IE 3, length 2, yourseq 6 , myseq 6
```

Example 10-20 *Charlotte Command Output, Scenario 10-1*

```
Charlotte#show interface s 0.1
Serial0.1 is up, line protocol is up
  Hardware is HD64570
  Internet address is 168.10.202.2/24
  MTU 1500 bytes, BW 1544 Kbit, DLY 20000 usec, rely 255/255, load 1/255
  Encapsulation FRAME-RELAY

Charlotte#show cdp neighbor detail
-------------------------
Device ID: Atlanta
Entry address(es):
  IP address: 168.10.202.1
  Novell address: 202.0200.aaaa.aaaa
Platform: Cisco 2500,  Capabilities: Router
Interface: Serial0.1,  Port ID (outgoing port): Serial0.1
Holdtime : 164 sec

Version :
Cisco Internetwork Operating System Software
IOS (tm) 2500 Software (C2500-AINR-L), Version 11.2(11), RELEASE SOFTWARE (fc1)
Copyright  1986-1997 by Cisco Systems, Inc.
Compiled Mon 29-Dec-97 18:47 by ckralik

Charlotte#show frame-relay map
Serial0.1 (up): point-to-point dlci, dlci 51(0x33,0xC30), broadcast
          status defined, active
Charlotte#show frame-relay pvc
```

Example 10-20 *Charlotte Command Output, Scenario 10-1 (Continued)*

```
PVC Statistics for interface Serial0 (Frame Relay DTE)

DLCI = 51, DLCI USAGE = LOCAL, PVC STATUS = ACTIVE, INTERFACE = Serial0.1

  input pkts 36            output pkts 28           in bytes 4506
  out bytes 2862           dropped pkts 1           in FECN pkts 0
  in BECN pkts 0           out FECN pkts 0          out BECN pkts 0
  in DE pkts 0             out DE pkts 0
  out bcast pkts 26         out bcast bytes 2774
  pvc create time 00:08:54, last time pvc status changed 00:01:26

Charlotte#show frame-relay lmi

LMI Statistics for interface Serial0 (Frame Relay DTE) LMI TYPE = CCITT
  Invalid Unnumbered info 0      Invalid Prot Disc 0
  Invalid dummy Call Ref 0       Invalid Msg Type 0
  Invalid Status Message 0       Invalid Lock Shift 0
  Invalid Information ID 0       Invalid Report IE Len 0
  Invalid Report Request 0       Invalid Keep IE Len 0
  Num Status Enq. Sent 54        Num Status msgs Rcvd 37
  Num Update Status Rcvd 0       Num Status Timeouts 17
```

Example 10-21 *Nashville Command Output, Scenario 10-1*

```
Nashville#show cdp neighbor detail
-------------------------
Device ID: Atlanta
Entry address(es):
  IP address: 168.10.203.1
  Novell address: 203.0200.aaaa.aaaa
Platform: Cisco 2500,  Capabilities: Router
Interface: Serial0.1,  Port ID (outgoing port): Serial0.2
Holdtime : 139 sec

Version :
Cisco Internetwork Operating System Software
IOS (tm) 2500 Software (C2500-AINR-L), Version 11.2(11), RELEASE SOFTWARE (fc1)
Copyright  1986-1997 by Cisco Systems, Inc.
Compiled Mon 29-Dec-97 18:47 by ckralik

Nashville#show frame-relay pvc

PVC Statistics for interface Serial0 (Frame Relay DTE)

DLCI = 51, DLCI USAGE = LOCAL, PVC STATUS = ACTIVE, INTERFACE = Serial0.1

  input pkts 52            output pkts 47           in bytes 6784
  out bytes 6143           dropped pkts 0           in FECN pkts 0
  in BECN pkts 0           out FECN pkts 0          out BECN pkts 0
  in DE pkts 0             out DE pkts 0
  out bcast pkts 46         out bcast bytes 6099
  pvc create time 00:13:50, last time pvc status changed 00:06:51
```

continues

Example 10-21 *Nashville Command Output, Scenario 10-1 (Continued)*

```
Nashville#show frame-relay traffic
Frame Relay statistics:
    ARP requests sent 0, ARP replies sent 0
    ARP requests recvd 0, ARP replies recvd 0

Nashville#show frame-relay lmi

LMI Statistics for interface Serial0 (Frame Relay DTE) LMI TYPE = CISCO
  Invalid Unnumbered info 0       Invalid Prot Disc 0
  Invalid dummy Call Ref 0        Invalid Msg Type 0
  Invalid Status Message 0        Invalid Lock Shift 0
  Invalid Information ID 0        Invalid Report IE Len 0
  Invalid Report Request 0        Invalid Keep IE Len 0
  Num Status Enq. Sent 84         Num Status msgs Rcvd 84
  Num Update Status Rcvd 0        Num Status Timeouts 0
```

Example 10-22 *Boston Command Output, Scenario 10-1*

```
Boston#show interface s 0.1
Serial0.1 is up, line protocol is up
  Hardware is HD64570
  Internet address is 168.10.204.4/24
  MTU 1500 bytes, BW 1544 Kbit, DLY 20000 usec, rely 255/255, load 1/255
  Encapsulation FRAME-RELAY

Boston#show cdp neighbor detail
-------------------------
Device ID: Atlanta
Entry address(es):
  IP address: 168.10.204.1
  Novell address: 204.0200.aaaa.aaaa
Platform: Cisco 2500,  Capabilities: Router
Interface: Serial0.1,  Port ID (outgoing port): Serial0.3
Holdtime : 125 sec

Version :
Cisco Internetwork Operating System Software
IOS (tm) 2500 Software (C2500-AINR-L), Version 11.2(11), RELEASE SOFTWARE (fc1)
Copyright  1986-1997 by Cisco Systems, Inc.
Compiled Mon 29-Dec-97 18:47 by ckralik

Boston#show frame-relay map
Serial0.1 (up): point-to-point dlci, dlci 51(0x33,0xC30), broadcast, IETF
          status defined, active

Boston#show frame-relay pvc

PVC Statistics for interface Serial0 (Frame Relay DTE)

DLCI = 51, DLCI USAGE = LOCAL, PVC STATUS = ACTIVE, INTERFACE = Serial0.1
```

Example 10-22 *Boston Command Output, Scenario 10-1 (Continued)*

```
  input pkts 65            output pkts 54           in bytes 8475
  out bytes 6906           dropped pkts 1           in FECN pkts 0
  in BECN pkts 0           out FECN pkts 0          out BECN pkts 0
  in DE pkts 0             out DE pkts 0
  out bcast pkts 52        out bcast bytes 6792
  pvc create time 00:15:43, last time pvc status changed 00:07:54
Num Update Status Rcvd 0   Num Status Timeouts 0
```

Assuming the details established in Examples 10-19 through 10-22 for Scenario 10-1, do the following:

1 Create a diagram for the network based on the command output shown in Examples 10-19 through 10-22.

2 Complete Table 10-21 with the Layer 3 addresses on the serial links.

Table 10-21 *Layer 3 Addresses for Scenario 10-1*

Router	Port	Subinterface	IP Address	IPX Address
Atlanta	S0			
Atlanta	S0			
Atlanta	S0			
Atlanta	S0			
Charlotte	S0			
Charlotte	S0			
Nashville	S0			
Nashville	S0			
Boston	S0			
Boston	S0			

3 Complete Table 10-22 with the LMI types and encapsulations used.

Table 10-22 *LMIs and Encapsulations Used in Scenario 10-1*

Router	Port	Subinterface	LMI Type	Encapsulation
Atlanta	s0			
Atlanta	s0			
Atlanta	s0			
Atlanta	s0			

continues

Table 10-22 *LMIs and Encapsulations Used in Scenario 10-1 (Continued)*

Router	Port	Subinterface	LMI Type	Encapsulation
Charlotte	s0			
Charlotte	s0			
Nashville	s0			
Nashville	s0			
Boston	s0			
Boston	s0			

Scenario 10-2: Frame Relay Configuration

Your job is to deploy a new network. Site A is the main site, with PVC connections to the other four sites. Sites D and E also have a PVC between them. Examine Figure 10-22 and perform the following activities.

Figure 10-22 *Scenario 10-2 Frame Relay Network*

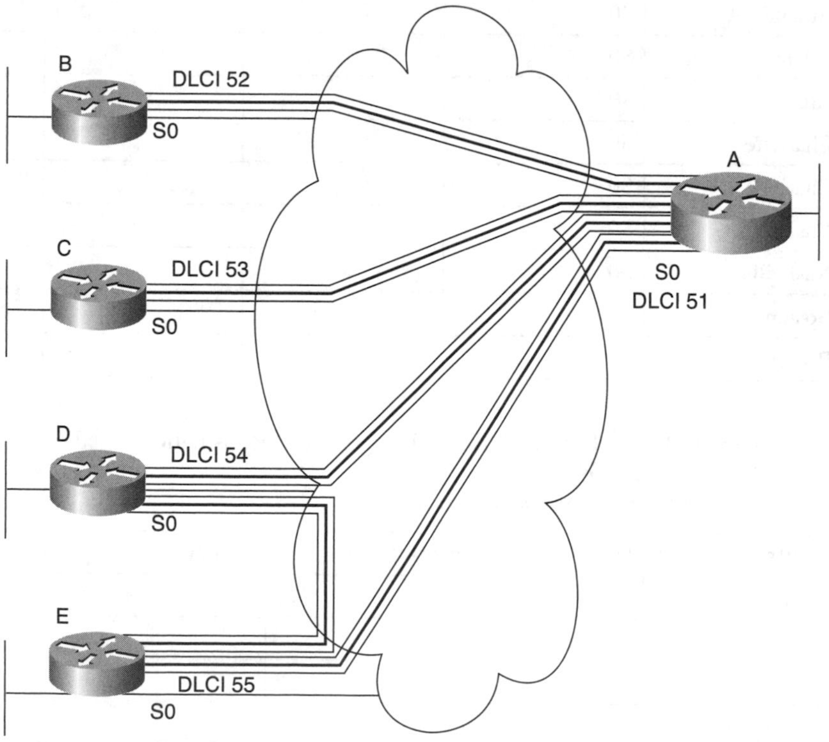

1 Plan the IP and IPX addresses to be used. Use Table 10-23 if helpful. Use IP network 168.15.0.0.

2 Using the DLCIs shown in Figure 10-22, create configurations for Routers A, B, and E. Use multipoint subinterfaces for the VCs between Routers A, D, and E.

3 Create alternative configurations for Routers A and E using point-to-point subinterfaces instead of multipoint.

4 Describe the contents of the IP and IPX routing tables on Router A, assuming that the network you just created is working properly. Describe the routing table, assuming that you are using point-to-point subinterfaces only, as in Step 3. Use Table 10-24 if useful.

Table 10-23 *Layer 3 Address Planning Chart*

Interface	Subinterface	IP Address	IPX Address
A's Ethernet			
B's Ethernet			
C's Ethernet			
D's Ethernet			
E's Ethernet			
A's S0			
A's S0			
A's S0			
A's S0			
A's S0			
B's S0			
C's S0			
D's S0			
D's S0			
E's S0			
E's S0			

Table 10-24 *Frame Relay Configuration Commands*

Layer 3 Group	Outgoing Interface	Next-Hop IP Address, or Connected	Next-Hop IPX Address, or Connected

Scenario 10-3: Frame Relay Configuration Dissection

A four-router Frame Relay network has been configured. Consider the configurations in Examples 10-23 through 10-26, and answer the questions that follow.

Example 10-23 *Scenario 10-3, Atlanta Configuration*

```
hostname Atlanta
!
ipx routing 0200.1111.1111
!
interface serial0
encapsulation frame-relay
!
interface serial 0.1
ip address 180.1.1.1 255.255.255.0
ipx network AAA1801
frame-relay interface-dlci 501
!
interface serial 0.2
ip address 180.1.2.1 255.255.255.0
ipx network AAA1802
frame-relay interface-dlci 502
!
interface serial 0.3
ip address 180.1.3.1 255.255.255.0
ipx network AAA1803
frame-relay interface-dlci 503
!
interface ethernet 0
ip address 180.1.10.1 255.255.255.0
ipx network AAA18010
!
router igrp 1
network 180.1.0.0
```

Example 10-24 *Scenario 10-3, Charlotte Configuration*

```
hostname Charlotte
!
ipx routing 0200.2222.2222
!
interface serial0
encapsulation frame-relay
!
interface serial 0.1
ip address 180.1.1.2 255.255.255.0
ipx network AAA1801
frame-relay interface-dlci 500
!
interface ethernet 0
ip address 180.1.11.2 255.255.255.0
ipx network AAA18011
!
router igrp 1
network 180.1.0.0
```

Example 10-25 *Scenario 10-3, Nashville Configuration*

```
hostname Nashville
!
ipx routing 0200.3333.3333
!
interface serial0
encapsulation frame-relay
!
interface serial 0.1
ip address 180.1.2.3 255.255.255.0
ipx network AAA1802
frame-relay interface-dlci 500
!
interface ethernet 0
ip address 180.1.12.3 255.255.255.0
ipx network AAA18012
!
router igrp 1
network 180.1.0.0
```

Example 10-26 *Scenario 10-3, Boston Configuration*

```
hostname Boston
!
ipx routing 0200.4444.4444
!
interface serial0
encapsulation frame-relay
!
```

continues

Example 10-26 *Scenario 10-3, Boston Configuration (Continued)*

```
interface serial 0.1
ip address 180.1.3.4 255.255.255.0
ipx network AAA1803
frame-relay interface-dlci 500
!
interface ethernet 0
ip address 180.1.13.4 255.255.255.0
ipx network AAA18013
!
router igrp 1
network 180.1.0.0
```

Assuming the details established in Examples 10-23 through 10-26 for Scenario 10-3, complete or answer the following:

1 Draw a diagram of the network.

2 Is IGRP split horizon on or off? How can you tell?

3 What type of Frame Relay encapsulation is used?

4 Create the commands on Router 1 and Router 2 to disable Inverse ARP and instead use static mapping.

Answers to Scenarios

Answers to Scenario 10-1: Frame Relay Verification

Figure 10-23 is a diagram that matches the configuration.

Figure 10-23 *Scenario 10-1 Network Derived from* **show** *and* **debug** *Commands*

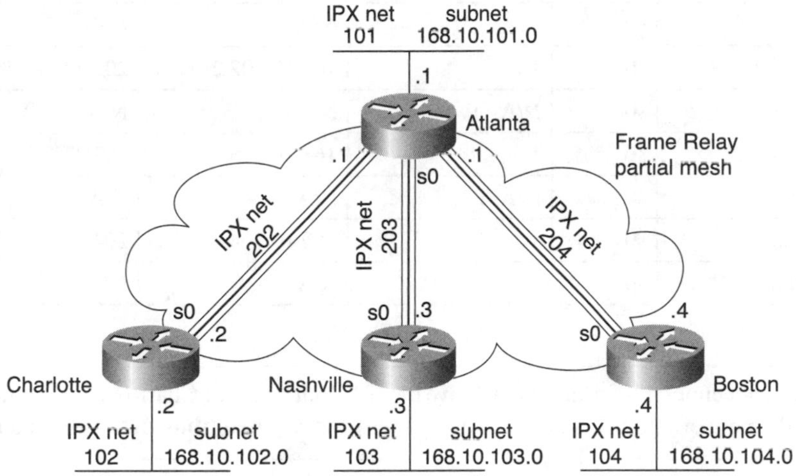

Discovering the IP addresses and subinterfaces is relatively straightforward. The **show** commands for most subinterfaces are provided. They list the IP address and mask used. The **show cdp neighbor detail** commands also mention the IP address of the connected routers.

The full IPX addresses are more challenging to deduce. The only command that lists the IPX addresses is the **show cdp neighbor detail** command, which is used in Examples 10-20, 10-21, and 10-22. The **show frame-relay map** command should seemingly provide that information, but because all the subinterfaces are point-to-point, no direct mapping is needed. The subinterface acts like a point-to-point link, so the neighboring router's IPX address is not shown in the **show frame-relay map** command output. A **debug frame-relay events** command, which shows output for Inverse ARP flows, could have identified the IPX addresses, but Inverse ARP is not enabled on point-to-point subinterfaces because it is not needed.

In short, there is no way to deduce all IPX addresses from the scenario.

Table 10-25 completes Table 10-21 by listing the Layer 3 addresses and subinterface numbers.

Table 10-25 *Completed Layer 3 Addresses for Scenario 10-1*

Router	Port	Subinterface	IP Address	IPX Address
Atlanta	S0	1	168.10.202.1	202.0200.AAAA.AAAA
Atlanta	S0	2	168.10.203.1	203.0200.AAAA.AAAA
Atlanta	S0	3	168.10.204.1	204.0200.AAAA.AAAA
Atlanta	s0	N/A	N/A	N/A
Charlotte	s0	1	168.10.202.2	202.????.????.????
Charlotte	s0	N/A	N/A	N/A
Nashville	s0	1	168.10.203.3	203.????.????.????
Nashville	s0	N/A	N/A	N/A
Boston	s0	1	168.10.204.4	204.????.????.????
Boston	s0	N/A	N/A	N/A

NOTE There is not enough information to derive the IPX addresses for Charlotte, Nashville, and Boston. The IPX network numbers are implied by the **show cdp neighbor detail** command output.

The LMI type is discovered only by examining the output of the **show frame-relay lmi** command. However, this command does not list whether the LMI type was learned via autosensing or whether it was configured.

The encapsulation type is more obscure. The **show frame-relay map** command output holds the answer. Table 10-26 completes Table 10-22 by summarizing the answers.

Table 10-26 *Completed LMIs and Encapsulations for Scenario 10-1*

Router	Port	Subinterface	LMI Type	Encapsulation
Atlanta	S0	N/A	Cisco	N/A
Atlanta	S0	1	N/A	cisco
Atlanta	S0	2	N/A	cisco
Atlanta	S0	3	N/A	ietf
Charlotte	S0	N/A	Q933A	N/A
Charlotte	s0	1	N/A	cisco
Nashville	s0	N/A	Cisco	N/A

Table 10-26 *Completed LMIs and Encapsulations for Scenario 10-1 (Continued)*

Router	Port	Subinterface	LMI Type	Encapsulation
Nashville	s0	1	N/A	cisco
Boston	s0	N/A	Cisco	N/A
Boston	s0	1	N/A	ietf

Answers to Scenario 10-2: Frame Relay Configuration

Check your IP and IPX address design against the ones chosen in Table 10-27. Of course, your choices most likely are different. However, you should have one subnet per VC when using only point-to-point subinterfaces. With the original criteria of Routers A, D, and E each using multipoint subinterfaces, these three subinterfaces should have been in the same IP subnet and IPX network. Table 10-27 lists the planned Layer 3 addresses for the configurations using multipoint among these three routers.

Table 10-27 *Layer 3 Planning Chart, Multipoint A-D-E*

Interface	Subinterface	IP Address	IPX Address
A's Ethernet	N/A	168.15.101.1	101.0200.AAAA.AAAA
B's Ethernet	N/A	168.15.102.1	102.0200.BBBB.BBBB
C's Ethernet	N/A	168.15.103.1	103.0200.CCCC.CCCC
D's Ethernet	N/A	168.15.104.1	104.0200.DDDD.DDDD
E's Ethernet	N/A	168.15.105.1	105.0200.EEEE.EEEE
A's S0	2	168.15.202.1	202.0200.AAAA.AAAA
A's S0	3	168.15.203.1	203.0200.AAAA.AAAA
A's S0	1	168.15.200.1	200.0200.AAAA.AAAA
B's S0	2	168.15.202.2	202.0200.BBBB.BBBB
C's S0	3	168.15.203.3	203.0200.CCCC.CCCC
D's S0	1	168.15.200.4	200.0200.DDDD.DDDD
E's S0	1	168.15.200.5	200.0200.EEEE.EEEE

Assuming the DLCIs shown in Figure 10-22, Examples 10-27, 10-28, and 10-29 show the configurations for Routers A, B, and E, respectively, using multipoint subinterfaces for the VCs between A, D, and E.

Example 10-27 *Router A Configuration, Scenario 10-2*

```
ipx routing 0200.aaaa.aaaa
!
interface serial0
encapsulation frame-relay
!
interface serial 0.1 multipoint
ip address 168.15.200.1  255.255.255.0
ipx network 200
frame-relay interface-dlci 54
frame-relay interface-dlci 55
!
interface serial 0.2 point-to-point
ip address 168.15.202.1  255.255.255.0
ipx network 202
interface-dlci 52
!
interface serial 0.3 point-to-point
ip address 168.15.203.1  255.255.255.0
ipx network 203
interface-dlci 53
!

interface ethernet 0
ip address 168.15.101.1 255.255.255.0
ipx network 101
!
router igrp 1
network 168.15.0.0
```

Example 10-28 *Router B Configuration, Scenario 10-2*

```
ipx routing 0200.bbbb.bbbb
!
interface serial0
encapsulation frame-relay
!
interface serial 0.2 point-to-point
ip address 168.15.202.2  255.255.255.0
ipx network 202
frame-relay interface-dlci 51
!
interface ethernet 0
ip address 168.15.102.1 255.255.255.0
ipx network 102
!
router igrp 1
network 168.15.0.0
```

Example 10-29 *Router E Configuration, Scenario 10-2*

```
ipx routing 0200.eeee.eeee
!
interface serial0
encapsulation frame-relay
!
interface serial 0.1 multipoint
ip address 168.15.200.5  255.255.255.0
ipx network 200
frame-relay interface-dlci 51
frame-relay interface-dlci 54
!
interface ethernet 0
ip address 168.15.105.1 255.255.255.0
ipx network 105
!
router igrp 1
network 168.15.0.0
```

Multipoint subinterfaces work perfectly well in this topology. Using multipoint also conserves IP subnets, as you will see in the next task of this scenario. When you change strategy to use only point-to-point subinterfaces, each of the three VCs in the triangle of Routers A, D, and E requires a different subnet and IPX network number. Table 10-28 shows the choices made here. Examples 10-30 and 10-31 show alternative configurations for Routers A and E using point-to-point instead of multipoint subinterfaces.

Table 10-28 *Scenario 10-2 Layer 3 Address Planning Chart, All Point-to-Point Subinterfaces*

Interface	Subinterface	IP Address	IPX Address
A's Ethernet	N/A	168.15.101.1	101.0200.AAAA.AAAA
B's Ethernet	N/A	168.15.102.1	102.0200.BBBB.BBBB
C's Ethernet	N/A	168.15.103.1	103.0200.CCCC.CCCC
D's Ethernet	N/A	168.15.104.1	104.0200.DDDD.DDDD
E's Ethernet	N/A	168.15.105.1	105.0200.EEEE.EEEE
A's S0	2	168.15.202.1	202.0200.AAAA.AAAA
A's S0	3	168.15.203.1	203.0200.AAAA.AAAA
A's S0	4	168.15.204.1	204.0200.AAAA.AAAA
A's S0	5	168.15.205.1	205.0200.AAAA.AAAA

continues

Table 10-28 *Scenario 10-2 Layer 3 Address Planning Chart, All Point-to-Point Subinterfaces (Continued)*

Interface	Subinterface	IP Address	IPX Address
B's S0	2	168.15.202.2	202.0200.BBBB.BBBB
C's S0	3	168.15.203.3	203.0200.CCCC.CCCC
D's S0	4	168.15.204.4	204.0200.DDDD.DDDD
D's S0	1	168.15.190.4	190.0200.DDDD.DDDD
E's S0	5	168.15.205.5	205.0200.EEEE.EEEE
E's S0	1	168.15.190.5	190.0200.EEEE.EEEE

Example 10-30 *Router A Configuration, Scenario 10-2, All Point-to-Point Subinterfaces*

```
ipx routing 0200.aaaa.aaaa
!
interface serial0
encapsulation frame-relay
!
interface serial 0.2 point-to-point
ip address 168.15.202.1  255.255.255.0
ipx network 202
frame-relay interface-dlci 52
!
interface serial 0.3 point-to-point
ip address 168.15.203.1  255.255.255.0
ipx network 203
frame-relay interface-dlci 53
!
interface serial 0.4 point-to-point
ip address 168.15.204.1  255.255.255.0
ipx network 204
frame-relay interface-dlci 54
!
interface serial 0.5 point-to-point
ip address 168.15.205.1  255.255.255.0
ipx network 205
frame-relay interface-dlci 55
!
interface ethernet 0
ip address 168.15.101.1 255.255.255.0
ipx network 101
!
router igrp 1
network 168.15.0.0
```

Example 10-31 *Router E Configuration, Scenario 10-2, Subinterfaces*

```
ipx routing 0200.eeee.eeee
!
interface serial0
encapsulation frame-relay
!
interface serial 0.1 point-to-point
ip address 168.15.190.5  255.255.255.0
ipx network 190
interface-dlci 54
!
interface serial 0.5 point-to-point
ip address 168.15.200.5  255.255.255.0
ipx network 200
interface-dlci 51
!
interface ethernet 0
ip address 168.15.105.1 255.255.255.0
ipx network 105
!
router igrp 1
network 168.15.0.0
```

The contents of the IP and IPX routing tables asked for in task 4 of this scenario are listed in shorthand in Table 10-29. The third byte of the IP address is shown in the Layer 3 Group column because the third byte (octet) fully comprises the subnet field. Not coincidentally, the IPX network number was chosen as the same number, mainly to make network operation easier.

Table 10-29 *Scenario 10-2 IP and IPX Routing Table Contents, Router A*

Layer 3 Group	Outgoing Interface	Next-Hop IP Address, or Connected	Next-Hop IPX Address, or Connected
101	E0	Connected	Connected
102	S0.2	168.15.202.2	202.0200.bbbb.bbbb
103	S0.3	168.15.203.3	203.0200.cccc.cccc
104	S0.4	168.15.204.4	204.0200.dddd.dddd
105	S0.5	168.15.205.5	205.0200.eeee.eeee

Answers to Scenario 10-3: Frame Relay Configuration Dissection

Figure 10-24 supplies the network diagram described in Scenario 10-3. The subinterfaces are all point-to-point, which is a clue that each VC has a subnet and IPX network associated with it. An examination of the IP addresses or IPX network numbers should have been enough for you to deduce which routers are attached to each end of each VC.

Figure 10-24 *Diagram of Scenario 10-3 Frame Relay Network*

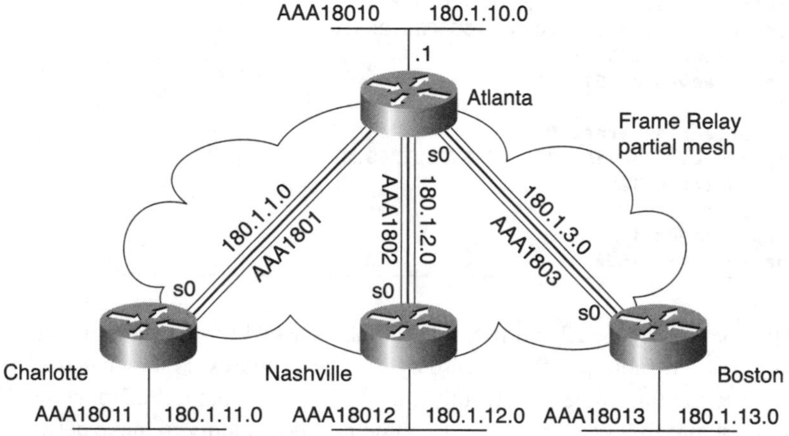

Split horizon is turned off on all interfaces because that is the default with point-to-point subinterfaces and because no command has been configured to turn it on.

Cisco encapsulation is used in each case. The **encapsulation frame-relay** command defaults to the use of Cisco encapsulation.

Disabling Inverse ARP is unlikely in real networks. However, this exercise was included so that you are ready for the exam. Examples 10-32 and 10-33 show the commands used to migrate to not using Inverse ARP. The maps are necessary for both IP and IPX because both need to be routed across the Frame Relay network.

Example 10-32 *Scenario 10-3, Atlanta Router: Changes for Static Mapping*

```
Atlanta(config)# interface serial 0.1
Atlanta(config-subif)#no frame-relay inverse-arp
Atlanta(config-subif)#frame-relay map ip 180.1.1.2 501 broadcast
Atlanta(config-subif)#frame-relay map ipx aaa1801.0200.2222.2222 501 broadcast
Atlanta(config-subif)# interface serial 0.2
Atlanta(config-subif)#no frame-relay inverse-arp
Atlanta(config-subif)#frame-relay map ip 180.1.2.3 502 broadcast
Atlanta(config-subif)#frame-relay map ipx aaa1802.0200.3333.3333 502 broadcast
Atlanta(config-subif)# interface serial 0.3
Atlanta(config-subif)#no frame-relay inverse-arp
Atlanta(config-subif)#frame-relay map ip 180.1.3.4 503 broadcast
Atlanta(config-subif)#frame-relay map ipx aaa1803.0200.4444.4444 503 broadcast
```

Example 10-33 *Scenario 10-3, Charlotte Router: Changes for Static Mapping*

```
Charlotte(config)# interface serial 0.1
Charlotte(config-subif)#no frame-relay inverse-arp
Charlotte(config-subif)#frame-relay map ip 180.1.1.1 500 broadcast
Charlotte(config-subif)#frame-relay map ipx aaa1801.0200.1111.1111 500 broadcast
```

Exam Topic in This Chapter

25 List the required IPX address and encapsulation type.

CHAPTER 11

Novell IPX

Novell's NetWare protocols have been well established and widely implemented for more than a decade. Novell also has chosen to move toward using TCP/IP as the underlying protocol used by NetWare clients and servers. So, very few changes that affect the router's role in forwarding NetWare traffic have been made in recent years. If you already understand Novell protocols from previous classes or work experience, picking up the rest of the details needed for the CCNA exam should be relatively easy.

Novell protocols, including the Layer 3 Internet Packet Exchange (IPX) protocol, were created with the Novell client/server model in mind. So, some features of Novell protocols are useful when you can assume that the client always wants to—or, indeed, must—connect to a server for communications to happen. Routing for IP and IPX is similar, so, if you understand IP routing, you likely will find IPX routing easy to grasp. Routing protocols for IP and IPX are also similar. However, unlike TCP/IP, Novell relies on a capability for clients to find their servers, so Novell uses protocols such as the Service Advertisement Protocol (SAP) to advertise information about servers. This chapter briefly reviews the concepts that are similar to TCP/IP, details the concepts specific to Novell, and helps you refine your retention and recall of the configuration with questions and scenarios.

For those of you looking to save some time studying, of all chapters in this book, this chapter is the best one to consider simply reviewing the highlights. Fewer and fewer networks will be configured to support Novell IPX protocols over time. One key reason is that Novell is using TCP/IP as the underlying protocol, not IPX, at their latest releases. Also, NetWare servers have lost significant market share to Microsoft, Linux, and Unix server platforms. Likewise, the emphasis on Novell protocols on the CCNA exam has lessened with the successive exams. Should you understand and master this chapter if you want to make sure you pass the exam? Yes! But if you have time to spend mastering only TCP/IP or Novell but not both, devote the extra time to TCP/IP, being sure to memorize IPX addressing, encapsulation, and basic configuration.

How to Best Use This Chapter

By taking the following steps, you can make better use of your study time:

- Keep your notes and the answers for all your work with this book in one place, for easy reference.

- Take the "Do I Know This Already?" quiz, and write down your answers. Studies show that retention is significantly increased through writing down facts and concepts, even if you never look at the information again.
- Use the diagram in Figure 11-1 to guide you to the next step.

Figure 11-1 *How to Use This Chapter*

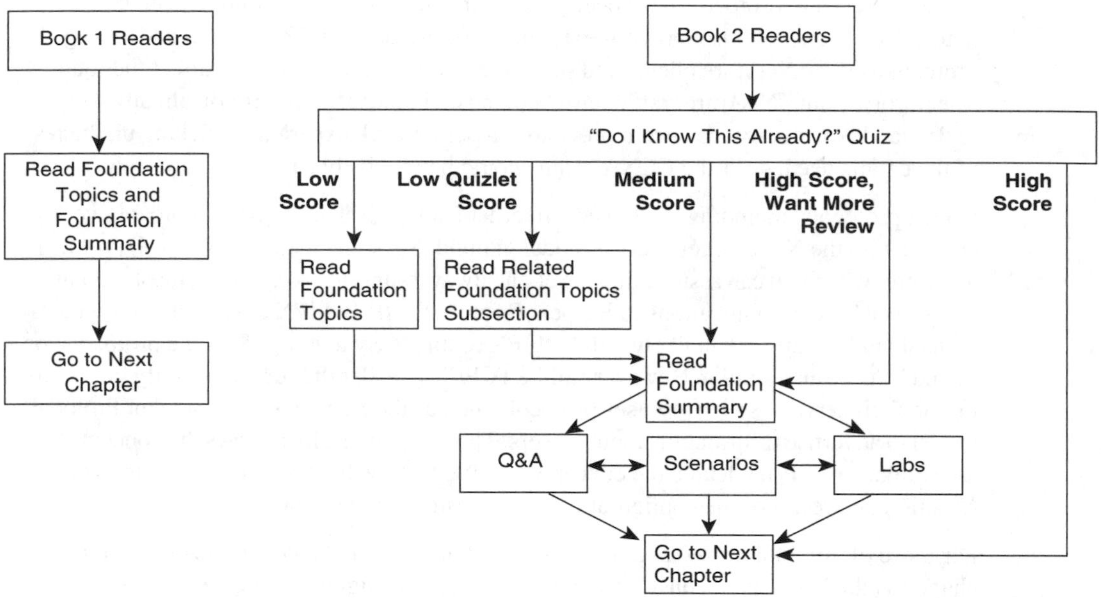

"Do I Know This Already?" Quiz

The purpose of the "Do I Know This Already?" quiz is to help you decide what parts of this chapter to use. If you already intend to read the entire chapter, you do not necessarily need to answer these questions now.

This 12-question quiz helps you determine how to spend your limited study time. The quiz is sectioned into four smaller four-question "quizlets," which correspond to the four major headings in the chapter. Figure 11-1 outlines suggestions on how to spend your time in this chapter. Use Table 11-1 to record your score.

Table 11-1 *Scoresheet for Quiz and Quizlets*

Quizlet Number	Foundation Topics Section Covering These Questions	Questions	Score
1	Novell IPX Concept	1 to 4	
2	Novell IPX Configuration	5 to 8	
3	IPX Access Lists	9 to 12	
All questions		1 to 12	

1 How often does IPX RIP send routing updates, by default?

____

____

____

2 What does *GNS* stand for? What creates GNS requests, and what creates GNS replies?

____

____

____

3 How many bytes comprise an IPX address?

____

____

____

4 Give an example of an IPX network mask used when subnetting.

____

____

____

5 Name the command that lists all the SAP entries in a Cisco router.

____

____

____

6 What **show** command lists the IPX address(es) of interfaces in a Cisco router?

7 A router is attached to an Ethernet LAN. Some clients on the LAN use Novell's Ethernet_II encapsulation, and some use Ethernet_802.3. If the only subcommand on Ethernet0 reads **ipx network 1**, which of the clients are working? (All, Ethernet_II, or Ethernet_802.3?)

8 What IOS IPX encapsulation keyword implies use of an 802.2 header but no SNAP header? On what types of interfaces is this type of encapsulation valid?

9 Name all the items that a SAP access list can examine to make a match.

10 True or false: If all IP or IPX access list statements in a particular list define the deny action, the default action is to permit all other packets.

11 In an IPX access list with five statements, a **no** version of the third statement is issued in configuration mode. Immediately following, another access list configuration command is added for the same access list. How many statements are in the list now, and in what position is the newly added statement?

12 Name all the items that a standard IPX access list can examine to make a match.

____

____

____

The answers to the quiz are found in Appendix A, "Answers to the 'Do I Know This Already?' Quizzes and Q&A Sections." The suggested choices for your next step are as follows:

- **8 or less overall score**—Read the entire chapter. This includes the "Foundation Topics" and "Foundation Summary" sections and the Q&A section at the end of the chapter.
- **2 or less on any quizlet**—Review the subsection(s) of the "Foundation Topics" part of this chapter, based on Table 11-1. Then move into the "Foundation Summary" section and the Q&A section at the end of the chapter.
- **9 to 10 overall score**—Begin with the "Foundation Summary" section, and then go to the Q&A section and the scenarios at the end of the chapter.
- **11 or more overall score**—If you want more review on these topics, skip to the "Foundation Summary" section and then go to the Q&A section at the end of the chapter. Otherwise, move to the next chapter.

Foundation Topics

Novell IPX Concepts

25 List the required IPX address and encapsulation type.

Cisco requires a thorough knowledge of two protocol stacks for the CCNA exam—TCP/IP and Novell NetWare. Novell's NetWare protocol stack defines Internetwork Packet Exchange (IPX) as a network layer–equivalent protocol. Novell also specifies several routing protocols, with Novell RIP being the one covered on the CCNA exam. NetWare also defines the Service Advertisement Protocol (SAP), which is used by servers and routers to exchange information about servers, their locations, and the services they offer.

To understand Novell, after understanding TCP/IP, you simply keep the same general concepts in mind, while remembering that Novell requires a client to talk to a server before anything useful can happen. IPX defines addressing, which, in concept, is similar to TCP/IP. It defines routing and routing protocols—and the concepts are the same as TCP/IP. Most of the new concepts in this chapter relate to the additional features found in Novell, as compared with TCP/IP—the features that help a client learn about servers and their services. For instance, consider Figure 11-2, which shows a sample Novell network. Two servers are located at the main site, with one client at the main site in San Francisco and a remote client in Los Angeles.

For this network to function, each device will need an IPX address per interface, just like TCP/IP. And just like IP RIP, the IPX RIP protocol could be used to exchange routing information about the networks. But Client 1, in LA, needs to be capable of logging in to a server—something for which there is no direct equivalent using TCP/IP. In fact, Client 1 can be configured to connect to a "preferred" server—in which case it needs to find a specific server. In this section, the concepts behind the simple process of Client 1 connecting to its preferred server will be covered.

Figure 11-2 *Sample Novell Network*

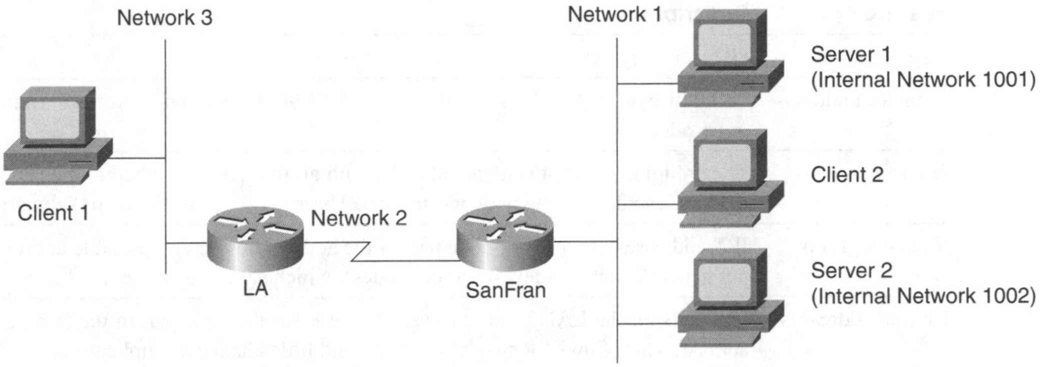

IPX Addressing

Novell uses Internet Packet Exchange (IPX) as its network layer protocol, as seen in Figure 11-3. IPX defines the 80-bit address structure, which uses a 32-bit network part and a 48-bit node part. As with IP and AppleTalk, all interfaces attached to the same data link use addresses in the same network. Table 11-2 lists four features of IPX addressing. The features listed in Table 11-2 are the same features used to generically describe a well-designed Layer 3 addressing scheme in Chapter 3, "OSI Reference Model and Layered Communication."

Figure 11-3 *Novell NetWare Protocols*

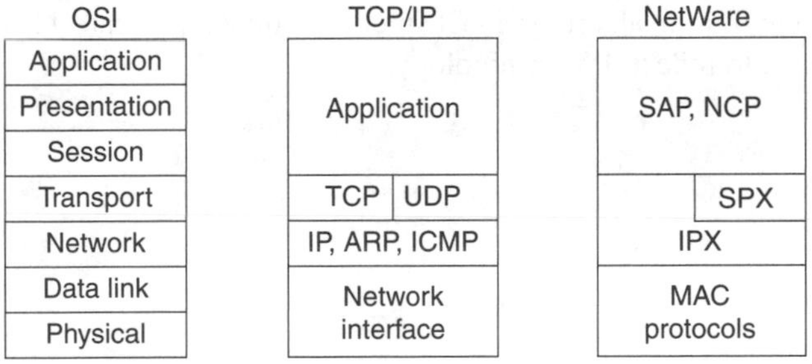

Table 11-2 *IPX Addressing Details*

Feature	Description
Size of address	80 bits (10 bytes).
Format of address	32-bit (4-byte) network part, followed by a 48-bit (6-byte) node number. Written in hexadecimal.
Grouping	The grouping concept is identical to IP, with all interfaces attached to the same medium using the same network number. There is no equivalent of IP subnetting.
Size of a group	IPX addresses use a 48-bit node part of the address, giving 2^{48} possible addresses per network (minus a few reserved values), which should be big enough.
Unique addresses	IPX calls for the LAN MAC address to be used as the node part of the IPX address. This allows for easy assignment and little chance of duplication. Ensuring that no duplicates of the network numbers are made is the biggest concern because the network numbers are configured.
Dynamic address assignment	Client IPX addresses are dynamically assigned as part of the protocol specifications. Servers and routers are configured with the network number(s) on their physical interfaces. Servers can choose to automatically generate an internal network number at installation time.
Internal networks	Servers create their own internal IPX network, in addition to the IPX networks covering the interfaces the server is attached to. When connecting to the server, a client connects to the server's internal IPX address, which is comprised of its internal network number and a node address of 0000.0000.0001.

IPX routing works just like routing, as described in the section "Routing" in Chapter 3. The logic from the routing algorithm in Chapter 3 is shown in Figure 11-4 for reference, with changes made to reflect IPX terminology.

Figure 11-4 *IPX Routing Algorithm*

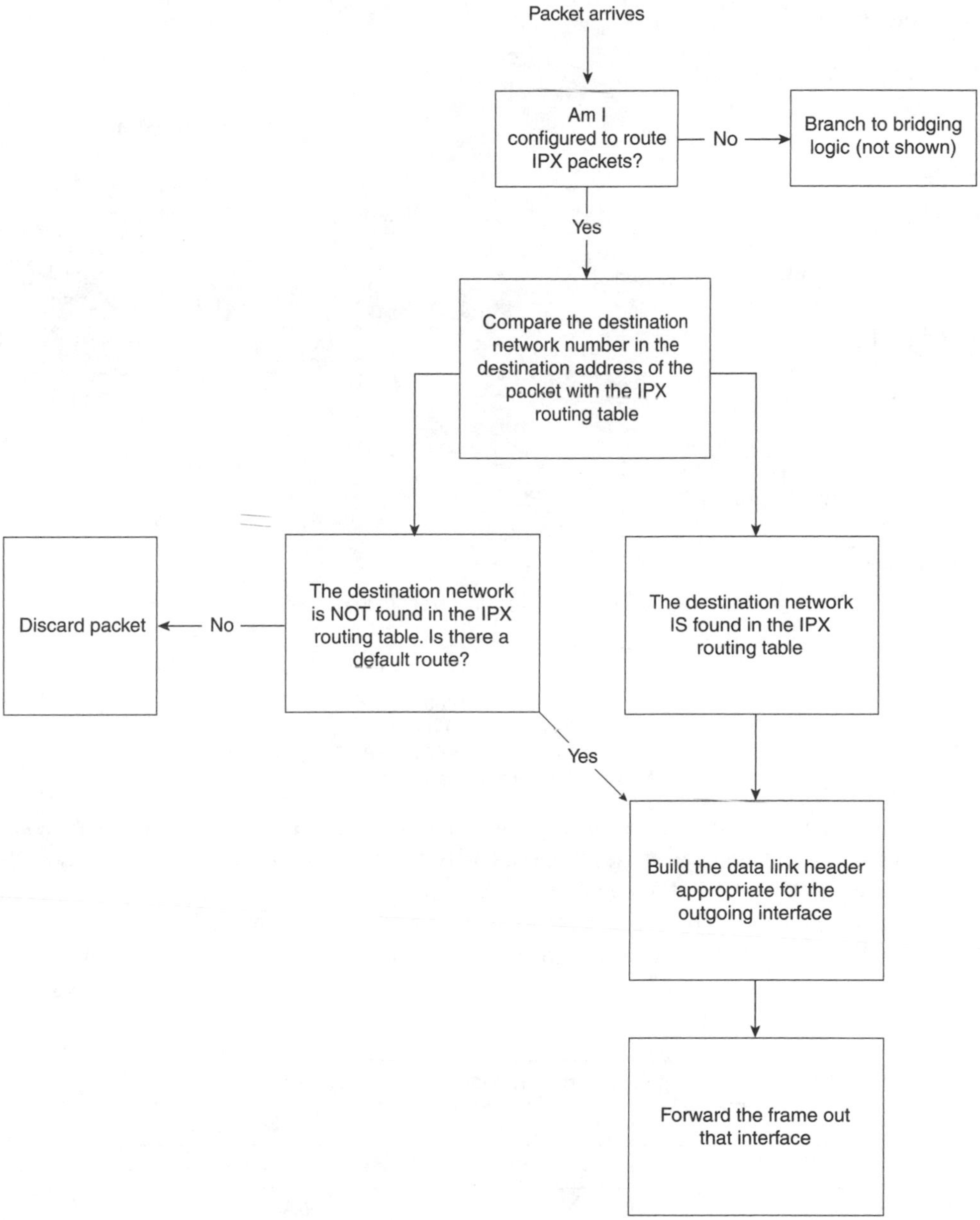

IPX addressing becomes more obvious with a simple example. Consider the example seen in Figure 11-5.

Figure 11-5 *Sample IPX Network*

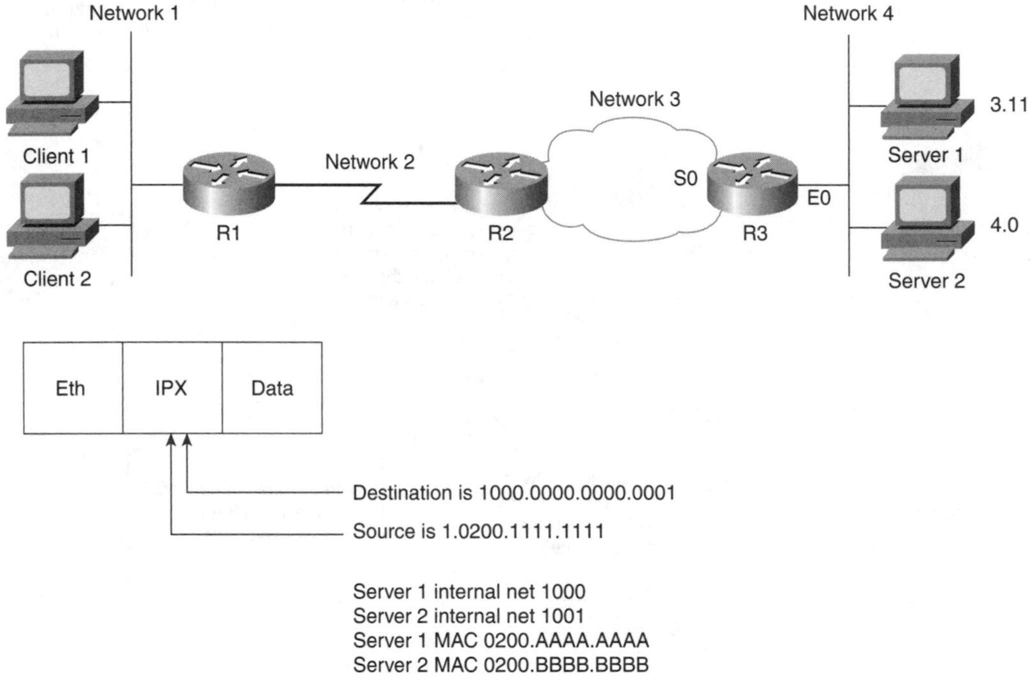

In the example, Client 1 has already logged in to Server 1 and is busily sending packets. Because NetWare servers use an internal network number, the destination of packets from Client 1 to Server 1 is 1000.0000.0000.0001 (Server 1's internal network number is configured as network 1000). The source address of these packets is Client 1's IPX address (1.0200.1111.1111, in this case). Of course, the routers need network 1000 in their IPX routing tables. For example, Table 11-3 shows the contents of the IPX routing table of R3:

Table 11-3 *IPX Routing Table, R3*

Network	Outgoing Interface	Next Router
1	s0	3.0200.0000.2222
2	s0	3.0200.0000.2222
3	s0	N/A
4	E0	N/A
1000	E0	4.0200.AAAA.AAAA
1001	E0	4.0200.BBBB.BBBB

R3 learned the routes to Network 3 and Network 4 because they are directly attached. The other four routes were learned through a routing protocol, which can be RIP, EIGRP, or NLSP. (NLSP is not covered on the CCNA exam.) Server 1 and Server 2 send RIP updates advertising networks 1000 and 1001, respectively. That is one reason why NetWare servers send RIP updates even if they have only one interface, as is the case with Server 1.

So, servers' internal network numbers must be in the routing tables of the routers because their internal addresses are used as the destination address of packets.

Encapsulation

Routers encapsulate Layer 3 packets inside Layer 2 frames before sending out the frames onto a network. Both Chapter 3 and Chapter 6, "TCP/IP and IP Routing," covered the process of encapsulation. So why cover it again? Well, on Ethernet LANs, Novell supports four different styles of Ethernet header. Why so many? Simply put, Novell has been around a while; as new releases of software emerged, new options were added to support a larger variety of devices on NICs, which required supporting different types of Ethernet headers. And because the clients and servers may support only one of the four types, a router needs to know which type to build when forwarding an IPX packet.

The types of encapsulating Ethernet headers are shown in Figure 11-6 and are listed in Table 11-4. Novell uses one set of names for the four Ethernet encapsulation types, and Cisco uses another set of names. So, when talking to a Novell server administrator, you need to be ready to translate between the terminology. First, here's a brief summary of encapsulation:

> Data-link encapsulation defines the details of data-link headers and trailers created by a router and placed around a packet before completing the routing process by forwarding the frame out an interface.

Figure 11-6 *IPX Ethernet Encapsulations*

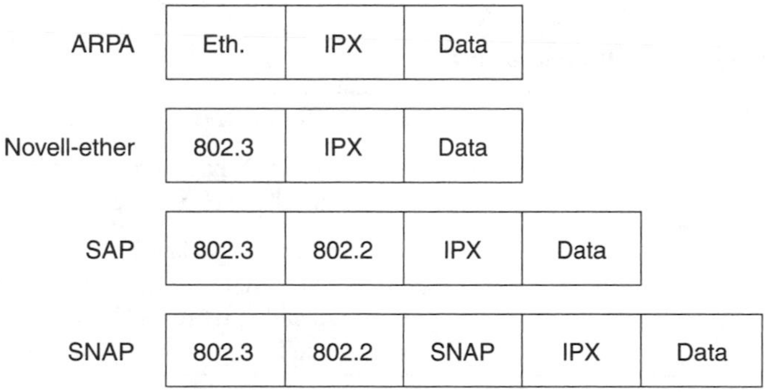

Table 11-4 *IPX Ethernet Encapsulations*

Novell's Name	Cisco IOS Software's Name	Hints for Remembering the Names and Meanings
Ethernet_II	ARPA	One way to help correlate the two names is to remember that ARPA was the original agency that created TCP/IP and that Ethernet_II is the older version of Ethernet; remember that the "old" names go together.
Ethernet_802.3	Novell-ether	Novell's name refers to the final header before the IPX header, in this case. There are no suggestions on easier ways to recall the IOS name Novell-ether. This setting is Novell's default on NetWare 3.11 and earlier releases.
Ethernet_802.2	SAP	Novell's name refers to the final header before the IPX header, in this case. Novell's name refers to the committee and complete header that defines the SAP field; Cisco's name refers to the SAP part of the 802.2 header. (The SAP field denotes that an IPX packet follows the 802.2 header.) This setting is Novell's default on NetWare 3.12 and later releases.
Ethernet_SNAP	SNAP	Novell's name refers to the final header before the IPX header, in this case. Cisco's name refers to this same header.

The key for remembering the Novell encapsulation names is that each name refers to the header that directly precedes the IPX packet. This can help you recall header formats as well. Remembering the names in the order in this book also can help because the size of the headers increases with the third and fourth options, as compared with the first two options (see Figure 11-6).

The same encapsulation issue exists on Token Ring and FDDI interfaces. Table 11-5 outlines the options.

Table 11-5 *IPX Token Ring and FDDI Encapsulations*

Novell's Name	Cisco IOS's Name	Description and Hints for Remembering
FDDI_Raw	Novell-fddi	The IPX packet follows directly after the FDDI header. No Type field of any kind is used.
FDDI_802.2	SAP	The IPX packet follows the 802.2 header. Novell's name refers to the committee and complete header that defines the SAP field; Cisco's name refers to the SAP part of the 802.2 header.

Table 11-5 *IPX Token Ring and FDDI Encapsulations (Continued)*

Novell's Name	Cisco IOS's Name	Description and Hints for Remembering
FDDI_SNAP	SNAP	Novell's name refers to the final header before the IPX header, in this case. Cisco's name refers to this same header.
Token-Ring	SAP	The IPX packet follows the 802.2 header. Novell's name refers to the committee and complete header that defines the SAP field; Cisco's name refers to the SAP part of the 802.2 header.
Token-Ring_SNAP	SNAP	Novell's name refers to the final header before the IPX header. Cisco's name refers to this same header.

Sometimes more than one encapsulation is needed per Ethernet interface. If all NetWare clients/servers on the Ethernet use the same encapsulation, just that single encapsulation is needed. However, if more than one encapsulation is used by the clients and servers, multiple encapsulations are needed on the router.

To configure multiple encapsulations in IOS, multiple IPX network numbers must be used on the same Ethernet, one per encapsulation. In other words, only one encapsulation type is allowed per network.

Two methods of configuration can be used to create multiple IPX networks on the same link, allowing multiple encapsulations. The first method uses IPX secondary addresses, and the other uses subinterfaces. Both require one IPX network number per encapsulation type per physical interface. Both methods cause the same protocol flows to occur. The subinterface style of configuration allows the use of NLSP, whereas secondary interface configuration does not. Figure 11-7 illustrates the concept of IPX secondary addressing. Server 1 uses Novell-ether, and Server 2 uses SAP encapsulation. Network 4 devices use Novell-ether, and Network 5 devices use SAP.

Figure 11-7 *Multiple IPX Encapsulations on One Ethernet*

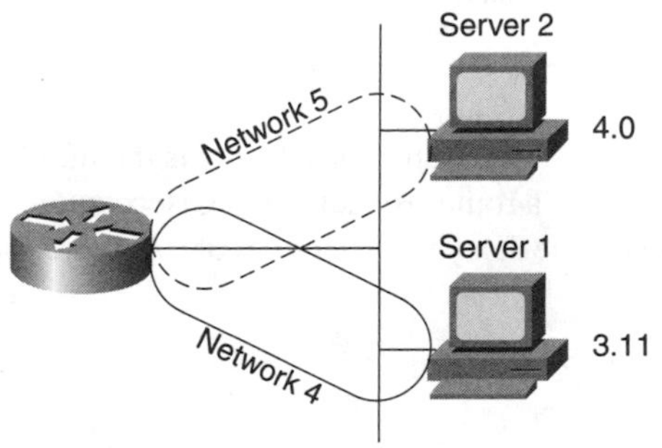

The router's choice of encapsulation for forwarding packets is relatively straightforward. If the route refers to a next router in Network 4, the router uses Novell-ether encapsulation. If the route refers to a next router in Network 5, the router uses SAP encapsulation. For RIP and SAP updates, the router sends updates to both IPX networks using the two different encapsulations, respectively. This is also true if the subinterface style of supporting multiple encapsulations is used instead of secondary addressing.

Troubleshooting can be more challenging because clients or servers using only a single encapsulation cannot communicate directly if they are using different encapsulations. Also, clients and servers on the same LAN that happen to use different encapsulations will require that their packets be routed by the router so that the encapsulation is changed. Therefore, there are many advantages to not using multiple encapsulations on the same LAN segment. In most cases, supporting multiple Novell encapsulations is useful when migrating between releases of server software or client code.

RIP and SAP

The CCNA exam requires you not only to know the differences between IPX RIP and IP RIP, but also to know another NetWare protocol used by the router: the Service Advertisement Protocol (SAP). Because IPX RIP and IP RIP originally were based on the same protocol (XNS RIP), the two are very similar. SAP has no equivalent feature in TCP/IP. RIP for IPX works in a similar manner to IP RIP. The most obvious difference is that IPX RIP advertises IPX network numbers, not IP subnet numbers. Table 11-6 lists the similarities and differences.

Table 11-6 *RIP for IPX and IP Compared*

Novell RIP	IP RIP
Uses distance vector	Uses distance vector
Is based on XNS RIP	Is based on XNS RIP
Uses 60-second update timer (default)	Uses 30-second update timer (default)
Uses timer ticks (delay) as primary metric and hop count as secondary metric	Uses hop count as only metric

IPX RIP uses two metrics: delay and hops. Delay is the number of time ticks (ticks are 1/18 of 1 second) associated with a route. By default, a Cisco router treats a link as having a certain number of ticks delay—the delay is not measured. LAN interfaces default to one tick, and WAN interfaces default to six ticks. The number of hops is considered only when the number of ticks is a tie. By using ticks as the primary metric, better routes can be chosen instead of just using hop count. For example, a three-hop, three-tick route that uses three Ethernets will be chosen over a two-hop, eight-tick route that uses two Ethernets and a serial link.

Service Advertisement Protocol

The Service Advertisement Protocol (SAP) is one of the most important parts of the NetWare protocol specification, but it is also one of the biggest challenges when trying to scale an IPX network. SAP is used by servers to propagate information that describes their services. CCNAs are expected to be very familiar with SAP and the routers' roles in forwarding SAP information.

The SAP process works very much like the process used by a distance vector routing protocol. Each server sends SAP updates, by default every 60 seconds, that include the IPX address, server name, and service type. Every other server and router listens for these updates but does not forward the SAP packet(s). Instead, the SAP information is added to a SAP table in the server or router; then the packets are discarded. When that router or server's SAP timer expires, new SAP broadcasts are sent. As with IPX RIP for routing information, IPX SAP propagates service information until all servers and routers have learned about all servers.

Get Nearest Server and Automatic IPX Address Assignment

Client initialization flows provide some insight into why routers need to learn SAP information. Consider Figure 11-8, which includes the use of the Get Nearest Server (GNS) request and shows a typical startup with a client configured with a preferred server of Server 2.

The overall goal of Client 1 is to log in to its preferred server, Server 2. The first step is to connect to some server that has a full SAP table so that the client can learn the IPX address of its preferred server. (The preferred server *name*, not the preferred server's *address*, is configured on the client.) The router might have the preferred server's name and IPX address in its SAP table, but no IPX message defined allows the client to query the router for name resolution. However, an IPX broadcast message asking for any nearby server is defined by IPX: the GNS request. The router can supply the IPX address of some nearby server (see Step 2 in Figure 11-8) because the router has a SAP table.

Figure 11-8 *Client Initialization Flows, Including GNS*

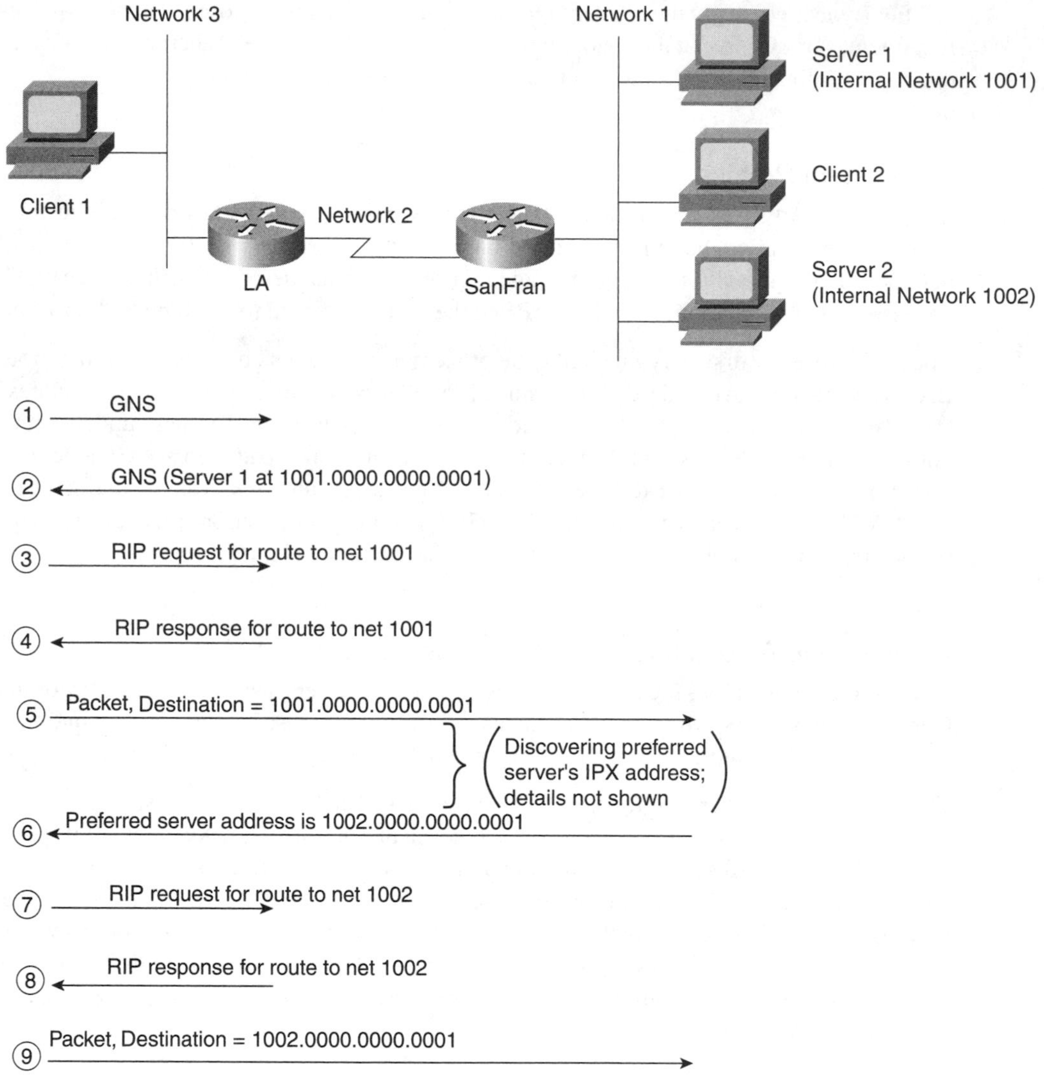

Next, the client needs to learn which router to use to forward packets to the server discovered by its GNS request. RIP requests and replies are used by the client to learn the route from any router (or server) on the same LAN, as seen in steps 3 and 4 in Figure 11-8. As a result, Client 1 knows to use the LA router to deliver packets to network 1001.

After connecting to Server 1, the client learns the IPX address of Server 2, its preferred server (see steps 5 and 6 in Figure 11-8). The client needs to know the best route to the preferred server's network; therefore, a RIP request and reply to learn the best next-hop router to network 1002 are shown in steps 7 and 8, in Figure 11-8. Finally, packets are sent between the client and Server 2 so that the client can log in; the intervening routers are simply routing the packets.

IPX clients create their own IPX address using the network number in the source address field of the GNS reply. The GNS reply always is sent by a router or server on the same network as the client. The client examines the source IPX address of the GNS reply to learn its own IPX network number. The complete client IPX address is formed by putting that network number with the MAC address of the client's LAN interface.

IPX Configuration

Configuration of IPX and IPX RIP on a Cisco router is relatively straightforward. Hands-on experience is the best way to fully learn the details of configuration. In lieu of that, this section lists commands, provides examples, and points out any tricky features. Tables 11-7 and 11-8 summarize the more popular commands used for IPX configuration and verification. Two configuration samples follow. The Cisco IOS Software documentation serves as an excellent reference for additional IPX commands; the Cisco Press book *Installing Cisco Network Devices* also is an excellent reference, particularly if you are not able to attend the instructor-led version of the class.

Table 11-7 *IPX and IPX RIP Configuration Commands*

Command	Configuration Mode
ipx routing [*node*]	Global
ipx maximum-paths *paths*	Global
ipx network *network* [**encapsulation** *type*] [**secondary**]	Interface mode

Table 11-8 *IPX Exec Commands*

Command	Function
show ipx interface	Gives detailed view of IPX parameter settings, per interface
show ipx route [*network*]	Shows the entire routing table, or one entry if **network** is entered

continues

Table 11-8 *IPX Exec Commands (Continued)*

Command	Function
show ipx servers	Shows the SAP table
show ipx traffic	Shows IPX traffic statistics
debug ipx routing [*events* | *activity*]	Gives messages describing each routing update
debug ipx sap [*events* | *activity*]	Gives messages describing each SAP update
ping *ipx-address*	Sends IPX packets to verify connectivity

The first sample is a basic configuration for the network in Figure 11-9. Examples 11-1, 11-2, and 11-3 provide the configuration.

NOTE The IPX samples also contain IP configuration. This is not required for correct operation of IPX. However, to Telnet to the routers to issue commands, IP must be configured. In fact, in almost every network with Cisco routers, IP is indeed configured. Therefore, the IPX examples generally include IP configuration.

Figure 11-9 *IPX Network with Point-to-Point Serial Links*

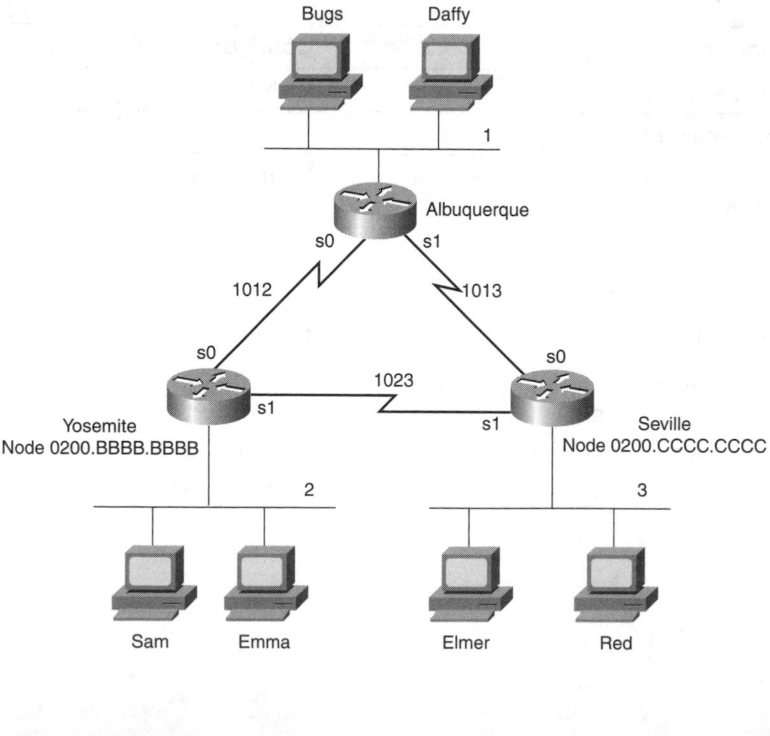

Example 11-1 *Albuquerque Configuration for IPX, Sample 1*

```
ipx routing
!
interface serial0
ip address 10.1.12.1 255.255.255.0
ipx network 1012
bandwidth 56
!
interface serial1
ip address 10.1.13.1 255.255.255.0
ipx network 1013
!
interface ethernet 0
ip address 10.1.1.1 255.255.255.0
ipx network 1
```

Example 11-2 *Yosemite Configuration for IPX, Sample 1*

```
ipx routing 0200.bbbb.bbbb
!
interface serial0
ip address 10.1.12.2 255.255.255.0
ipx network 1012
bandwidth 56
!
interface serial1
ip address 10.1.23.2 255.255.255.0
ipx network 1023
!
interface ethernet 0
ip address 10.1.2.2 255.255.255.0
ipx network 2
```

Example 11-3 *Seville Configuration for IPX, Sample 1*

```
ipx routing 0200.cccc.cccc
!
interface serial0
ip address 10.1.13.3 255.255.255.0
ipx network 1013
!
interface serial1
ip address 10.1.23.3 255.255.255.0
ipx network 1023
!
interface ethernet 0
ip address 10.1.3.3 255.255.255.0
ipx network 3
```

Enabling IPX routing globally as well as on each interface is all that is required to route IPX in a Cisco router. The **ipx routing** command enables IPX in this router and initializes the RIP and SAP processes. The individual **ipx network** commands on each interface enable IPX routing into and out of each interface and enable RIP and SAP on each interface, respectively.

The IPX addresses are not completely defined, however. Only the network number is configured. The full IPX network number is created by adding the MAC address of each interface to the configured IPX network number. For non-LAN interfaces, the MAC address of a LAN interface is used by default. However, for easier troubleshooting, a MAC address to be used as the node part of the IPX address on non-LAN interfaces can be configured. Notice the difference in the two commands in Example 11-4. The first is on Albuquerque, and the second is on Seville.

Example 11-4 show ipx interface serial 0 *on Albuquerque and Seville*

```
Albuquerque#show ipx interface serial 0
Serial0 is up, line protocol is up
  IPX address is 1012.0000.0ccf.21cd [up]
  Delay of this IPX network, in ticks is 6 throughput 0 link delay 0
  IPXWAN processing not enabled on this interface.
  IPX SAP update interval is 1 minute(s)
  IPX type 20 propagation packet forwarding is disabled
  Incoming access list is not set
  Outgoing access list is not set
  IPX helper access list is not set
  SAP GNS processing enabled, delay 0 ms, output filter list is not set
  SAP Input filter list is not set
  SAP Output filter list is not set
  SAP Router filter list is not set
  Input filter list is not set
  Output filter list is not set
  Router filter list is not set
  Netbios Input host access list is not set
  Netbios Input bytes access list is not set
  Netbios Output host access list is not set
  Netbios Output bytes access list is not set
  Updates each 60 seconds, aging multiples RIP: 3 SAP: 3
  SAP interpacket delay is 55 ms, maximum size is 480 bytes
  RIP interpacket delay is 55 ms, maximum size is 432 bytes
  Watchdog processing is disabled, SPX spoofing is disabled, idle time 60
  IPX accounting is disabled
  IPX fast switching is configured (enabled)
  RIP packets received 39, RIP packets sent 44
  SAP packets received 27, SAP packets sent 29
Albuquerque#
```

```
Seville#show ipx interface serial 0
Serial0 is up, line protocol is up
  IPX address is 1013.0200.cccc.cccc [up]
  Delay of this IPX network, in ticks is 6 throughput 0 link delay 0
  IPXWAN processing not enabled on this interface.
  IPX SAP update interval is 1 minute(s)
  IPX type 20 propagation packet forwarding is disabled
```

Example 11-4 **show ipx interface serial 0** *on Albuquerque and Seville (Continued)*

```
  Incoming access list is not set
  Outgoing access list is not set
  IPX helper access list is not set
  SAP GNS processing enabled, delay 0 ms, output filter list is not set
  SAP Input filter list is not set
  SAP Output filter list is not set
  SAP Router filter list is not set
  Input filter list is not set
  Output filter list is not set
  Router filter list is not set
  Netbios Input host access list is not set
  Netbios Input bytes access list is not set
  Netbios Output host access list is not set
  Netbios Output bytes access list is not set
  Updates each 60 seconds, aging multiples RIP: 3 SAP: 3
  SAP interpacket delay is 55 ms, maximum size is 480 bytes
  RIP interpacket delay is 55 ms, maximum size is 432 bytes
  Watchdog processing is disabled, SPX spoofing is disabled, idle time 60
  IPX accounting is disabled
  IPX fast switching is configured (enabled)
  RIP packets received 51, RIP packets sent 51
  SAP packets received 2, SAP packets sent 28
Seville#
```

The **show ipx interface** command provides a lot of information about IPX, including the complete IPX address. In this case, you can see that the node part of Seville's IPX address is easily recognizable, whereas Albuquerque's is not. Seville's node address is 0200.cccc.cccc based on its **ipx routing 0200.cccc.cccc** configuration command (refer to Example 11-3). However, because the node parameter was omitted from the **ipx routing** command on Albuquerque (refer to Example 11-1), the router chooses a MAC on one of the LAN interfaces to use as the node portion of the IPX addresses on non-LAN interfaces.

NOTE After the **ipx routing** command is entered, the router saves the command with the node value. In other words, even if Albuquerque's configuration were typed as in Example 11-1, the node number chosen from a LAN interface would be shown at the end of the **ipx routing** command when viewing the configuration in the future.

Several nuances are involved in how the node parts of the addresses are assigned. The first is that if the node part of the IPX address on WAN interfaces is derived from the MAC of a LAN interface, and if there is more than one LAN interface, the IOS must choose one MAC address to use. The algorithm uses the MAC address of the "first" Ethernet interface—or the first Token Ring interface, if no Ethernet exists, or the first FDDI interface, if no Ethernet or Token Ring exists. The lowest-numbered interface number is considered to be "first." The next nuance is that if no LAN interfaces exist, the node parameter on the **ipx routing** command *must* be configured, or IPX routing will not work on a WAN interface. The final nuance is that the node part of IPX addresses on router LAN interfaces ignores the node parameter of the **ipx routing** command and uses its specific MAC address as the node part of the address.

Some RIP and SAP **show** and **debug** commands provide a lot of insight into how IPX works, with very little output from the commands. Example 11-5 lists the output of the **show ipx route** and **show ipx servers** commands, as well as some **debug** output.

Example 11-5 *Routing and SAP Information on Yosemite*

```
Yosemite#show ipx route
Codes: C - Connected primary network,    c - Connected secondary network
       S - Static, F - Floating static, L - Local (internal), W - IPXWAN
       R - RIP, E - EIGRP, N - NLSP, X - External, A - Aggregate
       s - seconds, u - uses

7 Total IPX routes. Up to 1 parallel paths and 16 hops allowed.

No default route known.

C          2 (SAP),          E0_
C       1012 (HDLC),         Se0
C       1023 (HDLC),         Se1
R          1 [07/01] via    1012.0200.aaaa.aaaa,   14s, Se0
R          3 [07/01] via    1023.0200.cccc.cccc,    1s, Se1
R       1001 [08/03] via    1023.0200.cccc.cccc,    1s, Se1
R       1013 [12/01] via    1023.0200.cccc.cccc,    1s, Se1
Yosemite#show ipx servers
Codes: S - Static, P - Periodic, E - EIGRP, N - NLSP, H - Holddown, + = detail
1 Total IPX Servers

Table ordering is based on routing and server info

   Type Name                        Net     Address    Port     Route Hops Itf
P     4 Server1                    1001.0000.0000.0001:0451      8/03   3  Se1

Yosemite#debug ipx routing activity
IPX routing debugging is on

Yosemite#
IPXRIP: positing full update to 2.ffff.ffff.ffff via Ethernet0 (broadcast)
IPXRIP: src=2.0200.bbbb.bbbb, dst=2.ffff.ffff.ffff, packet sent
    network 1, hops 2,  delay 8
    network 1001, hops 4,  delay 9
    network 1012, hops 1,  delay 2
    network 3, hops 2,  delay 8
    network 1013, hops 2,  delay 8
    network 1023, hops 1,  delay 2
```

Example 11-5 *Routing and SAP Information on Yosemite (Continued)*

```
IPXRIP: positing full update to 1012.ffff.ffff.ffff via Serial0 (broadcast)
IPXRIP: src=1012.0200.bbbb.bbbb, dst=1012.ffff.ffff.ffff, packet sent
    network 1001, hops 4,  delay 14
    network 3, hops 2,  delay 13
    network 1013, hops 2,  delay 13
    network 1023, hops 1,  delay 7
    network 2, hops 1,  delay 7

IPXRIP: update from 1012.0200.aaaa.aaaa
    1013 in 1 hops, delay 7
    1 in 1 hops, delay 7
    1001 in 4 hops, delay 14
    3 in 2 hops, delay 13
IPXRIP: 1023 FFFFFFFF not added, entry in table is static/connected/internal
    1023 in 2 hops, delay 13

IPXRIP: update from 1023.0200.cccc.cccc
    1 in 2 hops, delay 13
    1001 in 3 hops, delay 8
    3 in 1 hops, delay 7
    1013 in 1 hops, delay 7
IPXRIP: positing full update to 1023.ffff.ffff.ffff via Serial1 (broadcast)
IPXRIP: src=1023.0200.bbbb.bbbb, dst=1023.ffff.ffff.ffff, packet sent
    network 1, hops 2,  delay 13
    network 1012, hops 1,  delay 7
    network 2, hops 1,  delay 7

Yosemite#debug ipx sap activity
IPX service debugging is on

IPXSAP: positing update to 1012.ffff.ffff.ffff via Serial0 (broadcast) (full)
IPXSAP: Update type 0x2 len 96 src:1012.0200.bbbb.bbbb
dest:1012.ffff.ffff.ffff(452)
 type 0x4, "Server1", 1001.0000.0000.0001(451), 4 hops

IPXSAP: Response (in) type 0x2 len 96 src:1012.0200.aaaa.aaaa
dest:1012.ffff.ffff.ffff(452)
 type 0x4, "Server1", 1001.0000.0000.0001(451), 4 hops

IPXSAP: positing update to 1023.ffff.ffff.ffff via Serial1 (broadcast) (full)
IPXSAP: suppressing null update to 1023.ffff.ffff.ffff
IPXSAP: Response (in) type 0x2 len 96 src:1023.0200.cccc.cccc
dest:1023.ffff.ffff.ffff(452)
 type 0x4, "Server1", 1001.0000.0000.0001(451), 3 hops

IPXSAP: positing update to 2.ffff.ffff.ffff via Ethernet0 (broadcast) (full)
IPXSAP: Update type 0x2 len 96 src:2.0000.3089.b170 dest:2.ffff.ffff.ffff(452)
 type 0x4, "Server1", 1001.0000.0000.00011(451), 4 hops
```

Some of the most important portions of the output are highlighted in the example. These features are described in the upcoming paragraphs. The **show ipx route** command lists the metric values in brackets; the number of ticks is listed before the hop count. The number of seconds listed at the end of each line for RIP-derived routes is the time since the routing information was heard; the ticks metric shows only as a number of ticks, never as a number of seconds. For example, in Example 11-5, Yosemite lists a route to network 3, with the numbers [7,1] shown beside the IPX network number. Seven is the number of ticks, which, in this case, is the sum of six ticks for the serial link to Seville and one tick for the Ethernet in Seville. The one in brackets represents the hop count.

The **show ipx servers** command purposely was kept small for this example; in many networks, there are thousands of SAP entries. The name of the server and the SAP type are listed; SAP type is important for SAP filters. The IPX address and socket used by the server for this service also are listed; the socket might be important when filtering IPX packets. The metric values for the route to network 1001 are shown under the word *route*. By having metric information handy, good choices for GNS replies can be made easily. In Example 11-5, Server 1 is listed with SAP type 4, which is file servers; its IPX address is 1001.0000.0000.0001, and it uses IPX port 0451. The route to network 1001 has a metric of eight ticks and three hops; when packets are sent to Server 1, they are sent out Yosemite's interface Serial1.

The **debug ipx routing activity** command enables output describing every RIP update sent and received. The number of ticks on LAN interfaces defaults to 1 and on WAN interfaces defaults to 6. Although Albuquerque and Yosemite have coded a bandwidth parameter of 56 on the serial link between them, and although the other links default to 1,544, the ticks are not affected. The **ipx delay** *ticks* interface subcommand can be used to change the metric for a particular interface.

Finally, the **debug ipx sap activity** command (highlighted near the end of Example 11-5) enables output describing every SAP update sent and received. Notice the update Yosemite wants to send out network 1023; it is time to send a SAP broadcast, but the SAP update is null. This is because the only SAP in the table (Server 1, SAP type 4) was learned from Seville over network 1023, so Yosemite is using split-horizon rules to not send information about this SAP back to Seville.

Only one route to each network is allowed in the routing table, by default. Looking back to the beginning of Example 11-5, notice that the route to network 1013, metric [7/1], points to the next hop 1023.0200.cccc.cccc (Seville), out Yosemite's Serial 1 interface. However, 1012.0200.aaaa.aaaa (Albuquerque) is sending RIP updates describing a route to network 1013, with seven ticks and one hop, into Yosemite's S0 interface (see RIP debug output). Yosemite heard from Seville first; therefore, only that route is included. If the **ipx maximum-paths 2** global command had been configured on Yosemite, both routes would have been included. Unlike with IP, when two routes are in the IPX routing table, per-packet load balancing across these paths occurs even if fast switching is enabled.

NOTE The default per-packet load balancing used for IPX when multiple routes to the same network are in the routing table might not be desired because packets can arrive out of order. By having the router send all packets to an individual IPX address over the same route every time, those packets should be received in order. The **ipx per-host-load-share** configuration command disables per-packet balancing and enables balancing based on the destination address. Of course, the penalty is that the traffic will not be completely balanced, based on the numbers of packets to each destination.

The second sample network (illustrated in Figure 11-10) uses Frame Relay with point-to-point subinterfaces. Examples 11-6, 11-7, 11-8, and 11-9 show the configuration for this network.

Figure 11-10 *IPX Network with Frame Relay and Point-to-Point Subinterfaces*

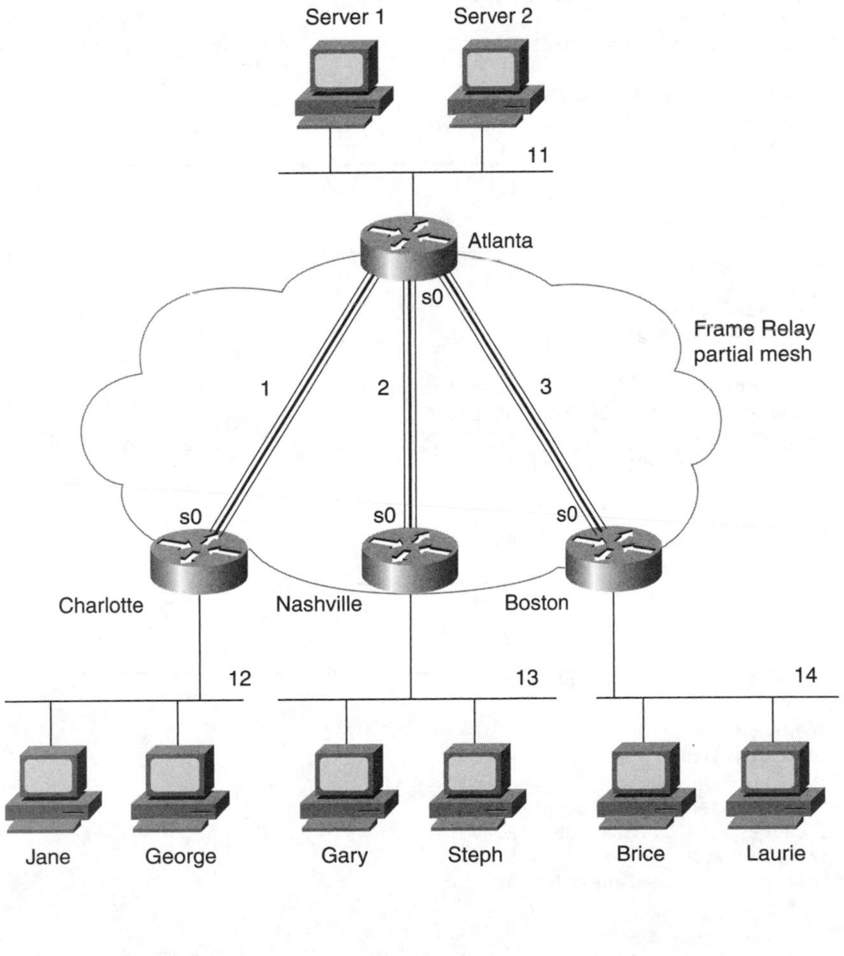

Example 11-6 *Atlanta Configuration*

```
ipx routing 0200.aaaa.aaaa
!
interface serial0
encapsulation frame-relay
!
interface serial 0.1 point-to-point
ip address 140.1.1.1  255.255.255.0
ipx network 1
frame-relay interface-dlci 52
!
interface serial 0.2 point-to-point
ip address 140.1.2.1 255.255.255.0
ipx network 2
frame-relay interface-dlci 53
!
interface serial 0.3 point-to-point
ip address 140.1.3.1 255.255.255.0
ipx network 3
frame-relay interface-dlci 54
!
interface ethernet 0
ip address 140.1.11.1 255.255.255.0
ipx network 11
```

Example 11-7 *Charlotte Configuration*

```
ipx routing 0200.bbbb.bbbb
!
interface serial0
encapsulation frame-relay
!
interface serial 0.1 point-to-point
ip address 140.1.1.2  255.255.255.0
ipx network 1
frame-relay interface-dlci 51
!
interface ethernet 0
ip address 140.1.12.2 255.255.255.0
ipx network 12
```

Example 11-8 *Nashville Configuration*

```
ipx routing 0200.cccc.cccc
!
interface serial0
encapsulation frame-relay
!
interface serial 0.2 point-to-point
ip address 140.1.2.3 255.255.255.0
ipx network 2
frame-relay interface-dlci 51
!
```

Example 11-8 *Nashville Configuration (Continued)*

```
interface ethernet 0
ip address 140.1.13.3 255.255.255.0
ipx network 13
```

Example 11-9 *Boston Configuration*

```
ipx routing 0200.dddd.dddd
!
interface serial0
encapsulation frame-relay
!
interface serial 0.3 point-to-point
ip address 140.1.3.4 255.255.255.0
ipx network 3
frame-relay interface-dlci 51
!
interface ethernet 0
ip address 140.1.14.4  255.255.255.0
ipx network 14
```

The configuration is very similar to the point-to-point network of Figure 11-9. The biggest difference is that each point-to-point subinterface is a different IPX network, as seen in Figure 11-10. Otherwise, SAP and RIP are enabled globally with the **ipx routing** command; each is allowed to be broadcast on interfaces (or subinterfaces) with the **ipx network** interface subcommand. SAP and RIP updates are sent out each subinterface—this means that Atlanta will replicate and send three copies of the RIP update and three copies of the SAP update on its serial0 interface, one per subinterface, every 60 seconds.

Configuration when using multiple Ethernet encapsulations is the final configuration option to be reviewed. In Figure 11-10, assume that Gary is an old NetWare client running NetWare version 3.11 client software and using the Ethernet_802.3 Novell encapsulation. Stephanie is newer and uses the Ethernet_802.2 encapsulation. Two IPX networks are used on Nashville's Ethernet 0 interface in this case.

Gary will be in Network 13, and Stephanie will be in Network 23. Example 11-10 shows just the Ethernet configuration for the Nashville network, with a secondary IPX network on Ethernet 0. Example 11-10 also shows an alternative configuration using subinterfaces.

Example 11-10 *Nashville Configuration with Secondary IPX Network on Ethernet 0*

```
ipx routing 0200.cccc.cccc

!
interface ethernet 0

ipx network 13 encapsulation novell-ether
ipx network 23 encapsulation sap secondary
! Or instead of the previous 3 lines, use the following 4 lines:
interface ethernet 0.1
```

continues

Example 11-10 *Nashville Configuration with Secondary IPX Network on Ethernet 0 (Continued)*

```
ipx network 13 encapsulation novell-ether
interface ethernet 0.2
ipx network 23 encapsulation sap
```

Example 11-11 shows the output of the **debug ipx sap events** and **debug ipx routing events** commands. The network in Figure 11-11 was used to gather the sample output.

Figure 11-11 *Sample Network Used for IPX* **debug** *Commands*

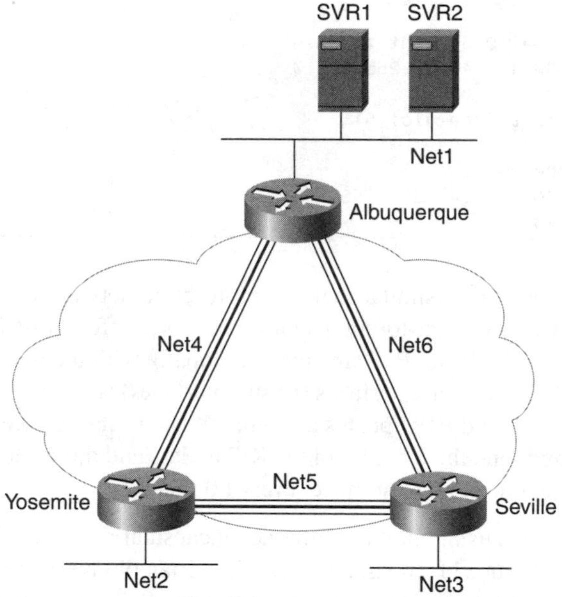

Example 11-11 *IPX* **debug** *Commands*

```
Seville#show ipx route
Codes: C - Connected primary network,    c - Connected secondary network
       S - Static, F - Floating static, L - Local (internal), W - IPXWAN
       R - RIP, E - EIGRP, N - NLSP, X - External, A - Aggregate
       s - seconds, u - uses, U - Per-user static

9 Total IPX routes. Up to 1 parallel paths and 16 hops allowed.

No default route known.

C          3 (NOVELL-ETHER),  Et0
C          5 (FRAME-RELAY),   Se0.2
C          6 (FRAME-RELAY),   Se0.1
```

Example 11-11 *IPX* **debug** *Commands (Continued)*

```
R          1 [07/01] via       6.0200.aaaa.aaaa,   51s, Se0.1
R          2 [07/01] via       5.0200.bbbb.bbbb,   40s, Se0.2
R          4 [07/01] via       5.0200.bbbb.bbbb,   40s, Se0.2
R         11 [08/03] via       6.0200.aaaa.aaaa,   51s, Se0.1
R         22 [08/03] via       6.0200.aaaa.aaaa,   51s, Se0.1
R        200 [08/02] via       6.0200.aaaa.aaaa,   51s, Se0.1
Seville#
Seville#debug ipx routing events
IPX routing events debugging is on

01:04:03: IPXRIP: 5 FFFFFFFF not added, entry in table is static/connected/internal
01:04:12: IPXRIP: positing full update to 6.ffff.ffff.ffff via Serial0.1
  (broadcast)
01:04:14: IPXRIP: 6 FFFFFFFF not added, entry in table is static/connected/internal
01:04:14: IPXRIP: positing full update to 5.ffff.ffff.ffff via Serial0.2
  (broadcast)
01:04:20: IPXRIP: positing full update to 3.ffff.ffff.ffff via Ethernet0
  (broadcast)
01:05:03: IPXRIP: 5 FFFFFFFF not added, entry in table is static/connected/internal
01:05:11: IPXRIP: positing full update to 6.ffff.ffff.ffff via Serial0.1
  (broadcast)
01:05:14: IPXRIP: 6 FFFFFFFF not added, entry in table is static/connected/internal
01:05:14: IPXRIP: positing full update to 5.ffff.ffff.ffff via Serial0.2
  (broadcast)
01:05:20: IPXRIP: positing full update to 3.ffff.ffff.ffff via Ethernet0
  (broadcast)
Seville#debug ipx routing activity
IPX routing debugging is on
Seville#
01:07:02: IPXRIP: update from 6.0200.aaaa.aaaa
01:07:02: IPXRIP: 5 FFFFFFFF not added, entry in table is static/connected/internal
01:07:02:     5 in 2 hops, delay 13
01:07:02:     200 in 2 hops, delay 8
01:07:02:     11 in 3 hops, delay 8
01:07:02:     22 in 3 hops, delay 8
01:07:02:     1 in 1 hops, delay 7
01:07:02:     2 in 2 hops, delay 13
01:07:02:     4 in 1 hops, delay 7
01:07:10: IPXRIP: positing full update to 6.ffff.ffff.ffff via Serial0.1
  (broadcast)
01:07:10: IPXRIP: Update len 64 src=6.0200.cccc.cccc, dst=6.ffff.ffff.ffff(453)
01:07:10:     network 3, hops 1,  delay 7
01:07:10:     network 4, hops 2,  delay 13
01:07:10:     network 2, hops 2,  delay 13
01:07:10:     network 5, hops 1,  delay 7
01:07:13: IPXRIP: positing full update to 5.ffff.ffff.ffff via Serial0.2
  (broadcast)
01:07:13: IPXRIP: Update len 80 src=5.0200.cccc.cccc, dst=5.ffff.ffff.ffff(453)
```

continues

Example 11-11 *IPX* **debug** *Commands (Continued)*

```
01:07:13:     network 1, hops 2,  delay 13
01:07:13:     network 22, hops 4,  delay 14
01:07:13:     network 11, hops 4,  delay 14
01:07:13:     network 200, hops 3,  delay 14
01:07:13:     network 3, hops 1,  delay 7
01:07:13:     network 6, hops 1,  delay 7
01:07:13: IPXRIP: update from 5.0200.bbbb.bbbb
01:07:13: IPXRIP: 6 FFFFFFFF not added, entry in table is static/connected/internal
01:07:13:     6 in 2 hops, delay 13
01:07:13:     22 in 4 hops, delay 14
01:07:13:     11 in 4 hops, delay 14
01:07:13:     200 in 3 hops, delay 14
01:07:13:     1 in 2 hops, delay 13
01:07:13:     2 in 1 hops, delay 7
01:07:13:     4 in 1 hops, delay 7


Seville#undebug all
All possible debugging has been turned off

Seville#show ipx servers
Codes: S - Static, P - Periodic, E - EIGRP, N - NLSP, H - Holddown, + = detail
U - Per-user static
4 Total IPX Servers

Table ordering is based on routing and server info

   Type Name                       Net     Address    Port     Route Hops Itf
P     4 SVR1                       200.0000.0000.0001:0452      8/02   3  Se0.1
P     4 SVR2                       200.0000.0000.0001:0452      8/02   3  Se0.1
P     7 SVR1                       200.0000.0000.0001:0452      8/02   3  Se0.1
P     7 SVR2                       200.0000.0000.0001:0452      8/02   3  Se0.1
Seville#debug ipx sap activity
IPX service debugging is on
Seville#
00:13:21: IPXSAP: Response (in) type 0x2 len 288 src:6.0200.aaaa.aaaa
  dest:6.ffff.ffff.ffff(452)
00:13:21:  type 0x4, "SVR2", 200.0000.0000.0001(452), 3 hops
00:13:21:  type 0x4, "SVR1", 200.0000.0000.0001(452), 3 hops
00:13:21:  type 0x7, "SVR2", 200.0000.0000.0001(452), 3 hops
00:13:21:  type 0x7, "SVR1", 200.0000.0000.0001(452), 3 hops
00:13:27: IPXSAP: positing update to 6.ffff.ffff.ffff via Serial0.1
  (broadcast) (full)
00:13:27: IPXSAP: suppressing null update to 6.ffff.ffff.ffff
Seville#
Seville#
00:13:30: IPXSAP: Response (in) type 0x2 len 288 src:5.0200.bbbb.bbbb
  dest:5.ffff.ffff.ffff(452)
00:13:30:  type 0x7, "SVR1", 200.0000.0000.0001(452), 4 hops
00:13:30:  type 0x7, "SVR2", 200.0000.0000.0001(452), 4 hops
```

Example 11-11 *IPX* **debug** *Commands (Continued)*

```
00:13:30:  type 0x4, "SVR1", 200.0000.0000.0001(452), 4 hops
00:13:30:  type 0x4, "SVR2", 200.0000.0000.0001(452), 4 hops
undebug all
All possible debugging has been turned off
Seville#
```

The **debug ipx SAP events** command lists the details of each sent and received SAP update. Notice that the number of hops to the server is shown, as is the type of service and the server name. The source and destination of the update packets also are listed. The **debug ipx routing events** command lists just summary information about routing updates, whereas the **debug ipx routing activity** command gives the details.

Filtering IPX Traffic and SAPs

IPX access lists can be used to filter IPX packets sent by clients and servers, just as IP access lists are used to filter IP packets. However, similar functions can be performed by using Service Advertising Protocol (SAP) filters, which filter SAP updates sent by servers and routers. SAP filters are more common because they can be used to prevent clients and servers from trying to send packets, as well as to reduce the overhead of SAP updates.

CCNAs deal with SAPs and SAP filtering on a regular basis and with IPX packet filtering a little less often. Both numbered and named IPX access lists are available. Table 11-9 lists the configuration commands used for these filters; Table 11-10 lists the exec commands related to IPX filtering.

Table 11-9 *IPX Access List Configuration Commands*

Command	Configuration Mode and Purpose
access-list {*800-899*} {**permit** | **deny**} *source-network* [.*source-node* [*source-node-mask*]] [*destination-network* [.*destination-node* [*destination-node-mask*]]]	Global command to create numbered standard IPX access lists
access-list {*900-999*} {**permit** | **deny**} *protocol* [*source-network*] [[[.*source-node* [*source-node-mask*]] | [.*source-node source-network-mask.source-node-mask*]] [*source-socket*] [*destination-network*] [[[.*destination-node* [*destination-node-mask*] | [.*destination-node destination-network-mask. destination-node-mask*]] [*destination-socket*] **log**	Global command to create numbered extended IPX access lists

continues

Table 11-9 *IPX Access List Configuration Commands (Continued)*

Command	Configuration Mode and Purpose
access-list {*1000-1099*} {**permit** | **deny**} *network* [*.node*] [*network-mask.node-mask*] [*service-type* [*server-name*]]	Global command to create numbered SAP access lists
ipx access-list {**standard** | **extended** | **sap** } *name*	Global command to begin creation of a named standard, extended, or SAP access list
{**permit** | **deny**} *source-network* [*.source-node* [*source-node-mask*]] [*destination-network* [*.destination-node* [*destination-node-mask*]]]	Named access list subcommand for standard access lists
{**permit** | **deny**} *protocol* [*source-network*] [[[*.source-node* [*source-node-mask*]] | [*.source-node source-network-mask.source-node-mask*]] [*source-socket*] [*destination-network*] [[[*.destination-node* [*destination-node-mask*] | [*.destination-node destination-network-mask. destination-node-mask*]] [*destination-socket*] **log**	Named access list subcommand for extended access lists
{**permit** | **deny**} *network* [*.node*] [*network-mask.node-mask*] [*service-type* [*server-name*]]	Named access list subcommand for SAP access lists
ipx access-group {*number* | *name* [**in** | **out**] }	Interface subcommand to enable a named or numbered, standard or extended IPX access list
ipx output-sap-filter *list-number*	Interface subcommand to enable SAP access lists used for outbound SAP packets
ipx input-sap-filter *list-number*	Interface subcommand to enable SAP access lists used for inbound SAP packets

Table 11-10 *IPX Access List EXEC Commands*

Command	Function
show ipx interface	Includes a reference to the access lists enabled on the interface
show access-list *number*	Shows details of all configured access lists for all protocols
show ipx access-list	Shows details of all IPX access lists

Access lists for filtering packets are covered next; SAP filters are covered in the section "SAP Access Lists."

IPX Packet Filters (Access Lists)

Packet filters in the Cisco IOS use the same general logic for any Layer 3 protocol. Figure 11-12 outlines the path that an IPX packet can take through a router. The comments following the figure describe the basic logic behind IPX access lists.

Features of the process described in Figure 11-12 are as follows:

- Packets can be filtered as they enter an interface, before the routing decision.
- Packets can be filtered before they exit an interface, after the routing decision.
- "Deny" is the term used in IOS to imply that the packet will be filtered.
- "Permit" is the term used in IOS to imply that the packet will not be filtered.
- The filtering logic is configured in the access list.

The logic created by an access list, as shown in the diamond-shaped symbols in Figure 11-12, is best summarized by the following sequence of events:

Step 1 The matching parameters of the first access list statement are compared to the packet.

Step 2 If a match is made, the action defined in this access list statement (permit or deny) is performed, as shown in Figure 11-12.

Step 3 If a match is not made in Step 2, repeat steps 1 and 2 using the next sequential access list statement.

Step 4 If no match is made with an entry in the access list, the deny action is performed.

Figure 11-12 *Locations Where Access List Logic Can Be Applied*

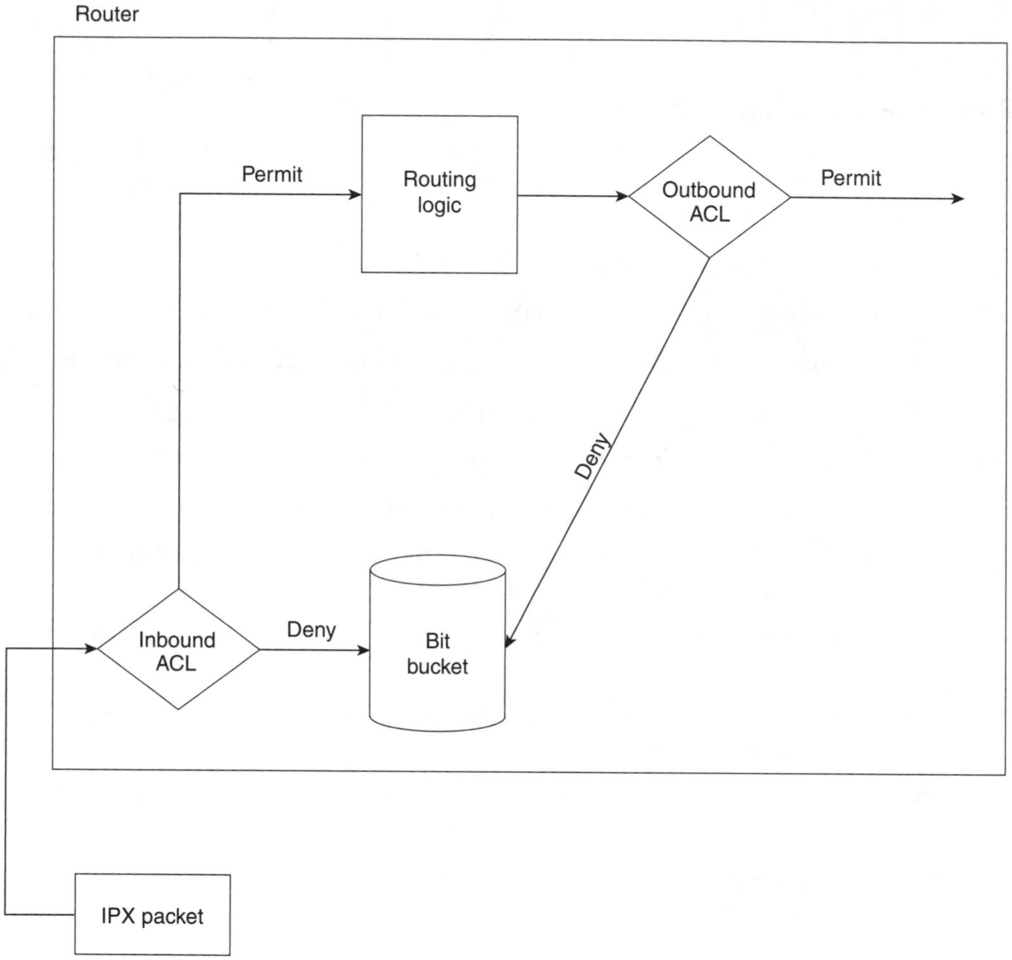

The logic for access lists is true whether using standard or extended access lists. The only difference is that extended access lists include more comparisons to determine a match. These differences are outlined in the next few sections on standard IPX access lists, extended IPX access lists, and SAP access lists.

Standard IPX Access Lists

When deciding what this book should really try to accomplish, I decided that the text of the book should cover the topics in two ways. First, the voluminous details should be summarized in tables and lists whenever possible, to allow easy review for a reader who already knows the topic pretty well. The explanations then should focus on topics that are less obvious from reading the manual; these are the types of tidbits that you get from the instructor in a well-taught class. When discussing IPX packet filters, I will be focusing on these tidbits. If you are new to IPX access lists, you probably will want to read the IOS documentation or the Cisco Press book *Interconnecting Cisco Network Devices*.

Standard IPX access lists can check the source and destination network number. They also can check the node part of the source and destination addresses, and they use a wildcard mask to examine the node part of the IPX addresses.

Figure 11-13 and Example 11-12 provide an example network and configuration.

Figure 11-13 *IPX Standard Access List Example*

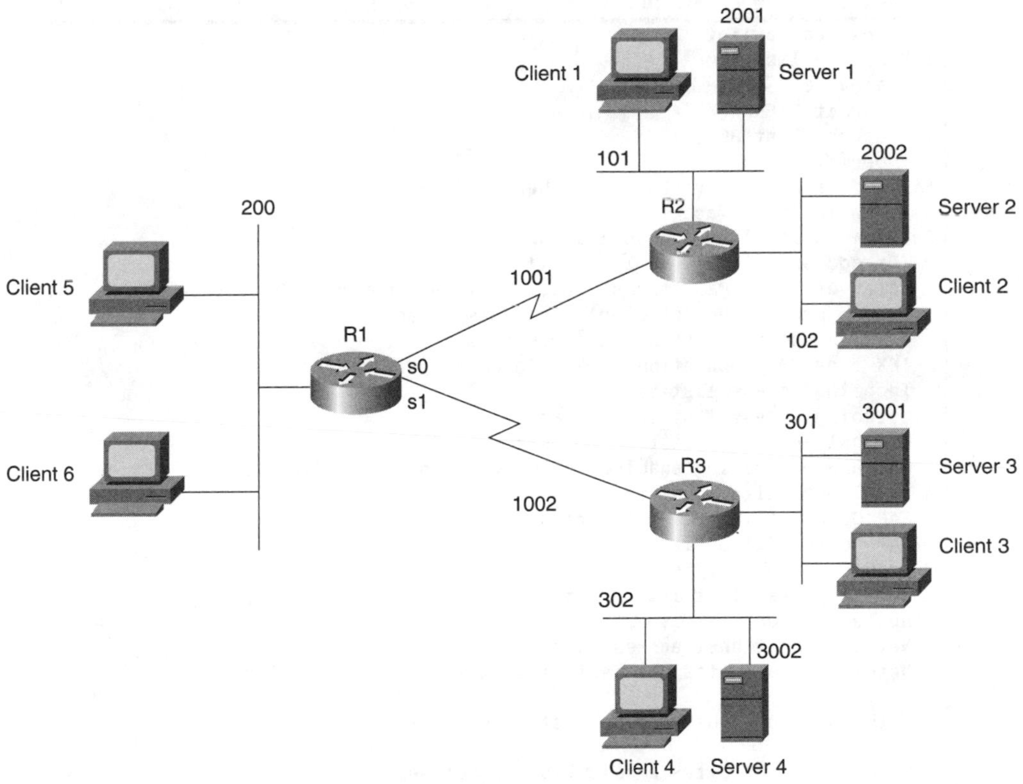

Example 11-12 *R1 Configuration for Standard IPX Access Lists*

```
ipx routing 0200.1111.1111
!
interface serial0
ip address 10.1.1.1 255.255.255.0
ipx network 1001
!
interface serial1
ip address 10.1.2.1 255.255.255.0
ipx network 1002
ipx access-group 820 in
!
interface ethernet 0
ip address 10.1.200.1 255.255.255.0
ipx network 200
ipx access-group 810
!
access-list 810 deny 101
access-list 810 permit -1
!
access-list 820 permit 302
```

```
R2#show access-list
IPX access list 810
    deny 101
    permit FFFFFFFF
IPX access list 820
    permit 302
***Production, insert 2 pt rule here
R1#show ipx interface s 1
Serial1 is up, line protocol is up
  IPX address is 1002.0200.1111.1111 [up]
  Delay of this IPX network, in ticks is 6 throughput 0 link delay 0
  IPXWAN processing not enabled on this interface.
  IPX SAP update interval is 1 minute(s)
  IPX type 20 propagation packet forwarding is disabled
  Incoming access list is 820
  Outgoing access list is not set
  IPX helper access list is not set
  SAP GNS processing enabled, delay 0 ms, output filter list is not set
  SAP Input filter list is not set
  SAP Output filter list is not set
  SAP Router filter list is not set
  Input filter list is not set
  Output filter list is not set
  Router filter list is not set
  Netbios Input host access list is not set
  Netbios Input bytes access list is not set

  Netbios Output host access list is not set

  Netbios Output bytes access list is not set
```

The following criteria will be used in this IPX standard access list example established in Figure 11-13 and Example 11-12:

1. Packets from network 101 are not allowed onto network 200.
2. Packets from network 102 are allowed onto network 200.
3. Packets from network 301 are not allowed onto network 200, 101, or 102.
4. Packets from network 302 are allowed to go anywhere.

The example shows one way to accomplish the goals, but other alternatives exist. Access list 810 implements the first two criteria for the example by filtering packets exiting Ethernet 0 on R1. Access list 820 implements the last two criteria for the example by filtering packets entering serial1 on R1.

First, consider the logic in **access-list 810**, which is used to meet the first two criteria. The list denies access from source network 101 and permits all other source network numbers through the explicitly defined "permit all else" as the second statement in the list. If the list had been used as an inbound access list on serial0 of R1, packets from network 101 would not be capable of entering R1 for forwarding on to R3. By placing the filter on Ethernet0 as an outbound filter, R1 could forward packets from 101 and 102 on to R3, but only packets from network 102 would make it to network 200.

Next consider the logic in **access-list 820**. This permits only source network 302 and denies all other source networks because of the implied "deny all else" at the end of the list. By applying the list as an inbound list on R1's serial 1, criterion 3 will be met by the default "deny all," and criterion 4 will be met by the explicit "permit" of source network 302.

Several nuances of access-list operation are seen (or implied, by omission) in the syntax shown in Example 11-12. **access-list 810** uses the keyword **–1**, which means any and all network numbers. No destination networks are checked with either access list, which is allowed with IPX standard access lists. Also, the optional node mask is not used and is not useful very often. For example, imagine that a requirement was added so that packets from clients 5 and 6 were not allowed to be sent to network 302. If the IPX addresses for clients 5 and 6 were 200.0200.1234.0000 and 200.0200.1234.0001, and if no other client's IPX addresses began with 200.0200.1234, the following **access-list** command could match packets from these two clients:

```
access-list 830 deny 200.0200.1234.0000 0000.0000.ffff
```

The wildcard mask works like the wildcard mask used in IP access lists; the only difference is that it is configured as a hexadecimal number. The final four **f** digits mean that the final four hex digits in the node part of the address automatically are considered to match, but the first eight digits do need to be checked. However, because almost everyone who uses IPX uses the burned-in MAC address for the node part of the IPX address, the IPX addresses on these clients almost never have a convenient number to allow packets from both to be matched in the same access list statement. Even if the numbers were convenient for using a wildcard mask, the IPX address would change if the LAN adapter ever was replaced, giving undesired results from the access list. So, unless you are using locally administered MAC addresses on your IPX nodes, the node mask almost never will be useful.

Cisco expects CCNAs to be familiar enough with TCP/IP and IPX protocols to recognize oversights in an access list design before the access lists are deployed. Such an oversight is true of Example 11-12—or, more accurately, the criteria used for Example 11-12. Note that the criteria all mentioned network numbers but not servers. The oversight is that when clients connect to servers whose code level is NetWare 3.11 and beyond, the address used by the server to communicate with the client uses the server's internal network number. So, in Example 11-12, the effect is an interesting mental exercise. **access-list 810**, with the explicit "permit all," would permit the client/server traffic exiting R1's Ethernet0, while **access-list 820**, with the implied "deny all" would prevent all client/server traffic from entering R1's serial1 interface.

Now thinking in terms of client/server flows with NetWare, consider the following changes in the criteria for these access lists:

1. Packets from Server 1 are not allowed onto network 200.
2. Packets from Server 2 are allowed onto network 200.
3. Packets from Server 3 are not allowed onto networks 200, 101, or 102.
4. Packets from Server 4 are allowed to go anywhere.
5. All combinations not mentioned should be permitted.

The new configuration in Example 11-13 successfully focuses on the servers' network numbers, not the network numbers on the LAN segments.

Example 11-13 *Configuration for Standard IPX Access Lists, Modified*

```
ipx routing 0200.1111.1111
!
interface serial0
ip address 10.1.1.1 255.255.255.0
ipx network 1001
!
interface serial1
ip address 10.1.2.1 255.255.255.0
ipx network 1002
ipx access-group 820 in
!
interface ethernet 0
ip address 10.1.200.1 255.255.255.0
ipx network 200
ipx access-group 810
!
```

Example 11-13 *Configuration for Standard IPX Access Lists, Modified (Continued)*

```
access-list 810 deny 2001
access-list 810 permit -1
!
access-list 820 deny 3001
access-list 820 permit -1
```

Extended IPX Access Lists

Extended access lists for IPX can check several additional fields in the IPX packet header, as compared to standard IPX access lists. Cisco expects CCNAs to remember all the items that can be matched using a standard or extended IPX **access-list** command. Table 11-11 summarizes those items, and Figure 11-14 shows the relative location of the fields in the headers.

Figure 11-14 *Header Fields Matchable Using IPX Access Lists*

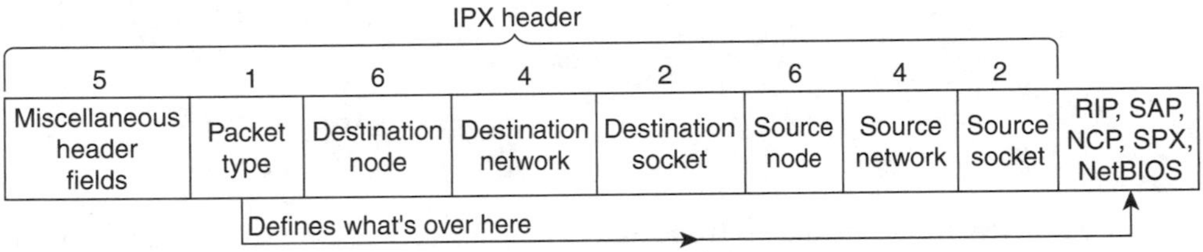

Table 11-11 *IPX Standard and Extended Access Lists—Matching*

Type of Access List	What Can Be Matched
IPX Standard	Source network
	Source IPX address (network and node)
	Source network and portions of the node address, using a node mask
	Destination network
	Destination IPX address (network and node)
	Destination network and portions of the node address, using a node mask
IPX Extended	Same points as with an IPX standard access list, in addition to items in the rows that follow
	Portions of entire source IPX address, using a wildcard mask
	Portions of entire destination IPX address, using a wildcard mask
	Protocol type
	Source socket
	Destination socket

The protocol type is a field that is not shown in many examples in other references, such as the Cisco IOS documentation CD. Figure 11-15 shows example packets that would be matched by the various protocol types.

Figure 11-15 *Extended Access List Protocol Types*

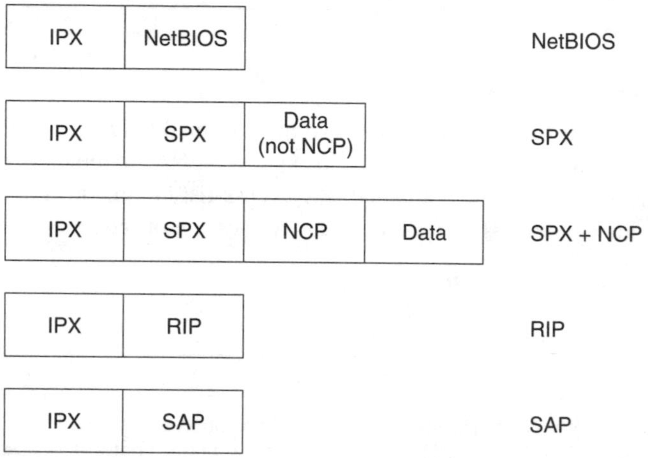

The protocol names, particularly the SAP protocol type, can be misleading. Extended access lists can be used to filter entire SAP packets; the protocol type SAP would be useful to match those packets. For filtering the content of the SAP updates, which is a hugely popular function, access lists for filtering SAP information would be used. The SAP filters, which use list numbers between 1000 and 1099, are covered in the section "SAP Filters," later in this chapter. SAP filtering does not use extended IPX access lists with a SAP protocol type.

Similarly, extended IPX access lists with protocol type RIP can allow matching of RIP packets, but not the routing information in the RIP update. The most practical use of the *protocol type* parameter is for NetBIOS. If NetBIOS is not an issue, most sites use the **any** keyword for the protocol type.

The *socket* parameter is similar to a TCP or UDP port number. Novell assigns socket values to applications to create the equivalent of a TCP or UDP well-known port. Clients dynamically assign sockets in the range of 4000 to 7FFF, and Novell assigns sockets to applications in the range of 8000 to FFFF. As with IP, there is both a source and a destination socket, used for multiplexing.

NOTE Do not confuse SAP type with socket. A file server advertises SAP Type 4 but does not use socket number 4 for file services.

The most useful extended access list feature that is not supported by standard access lists is the network wildcard mask. Figure 11-16 and Example 11-14 provide a sample to show when this mask is useful. The access list is configured in R2. The criteria for this packet filter is as follows:

1 Clients in networks 100 and 101 are allowed access to Server 3 and Server 4.

2 Clients in network 300 are not allowed to access Server 1 and Server 2.

Figure 11-16 *IP Extended Access List Example*

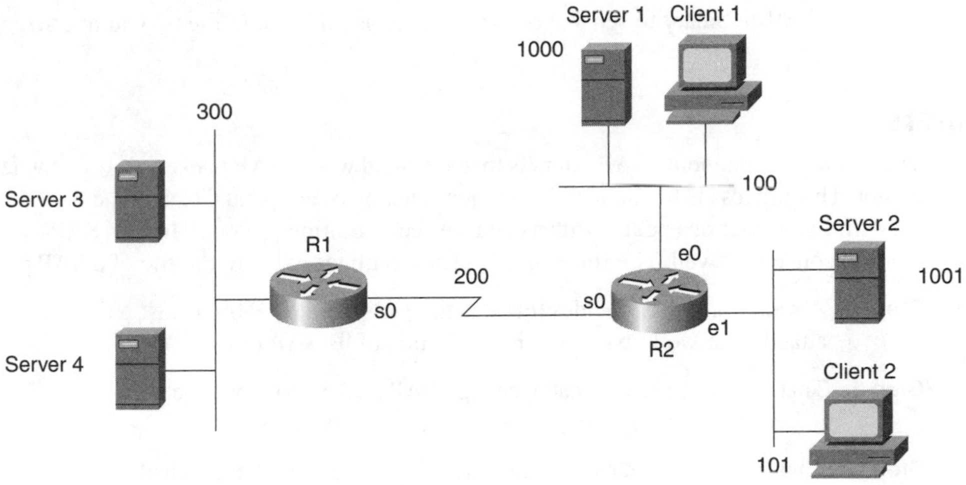

Example 11-14 *Configuration for Extended IPX Access Lists*

```
hostname R2
!
ipx routing 0200.2222.2222
!
interface serial0
ip address 10.1.1.2 255.255.255.0
ipx network 200
ipx access-group 910
!
interface ethernet 0
ip address 10.1.100.2 255.255.255.0
ipx network 100
!
interface ethernet 1
ip address 10.1.101.2 255.255.255.0
ipx network 101
!
access-list 910 deny any 1000 0000000F
access-list 910 permit any -1
```

access-list 910 actually checks for packets sourced from networks 1000 to 100F. The network number is eight hex digits long; the leading 0s are not shown. For the network wildcard mask, all digits are shown in the book, but the leading zeroes are omitted in an actual router configuration. The mask 0000000F means that the first seven hex digits must match 0000100, which are the first seven hex digits of the network number in this case, with leading 0s shown. The last hex digit can be any value. Therefore, networks 1000, 1001, and 14 others are matched.

To exactly match the two networks 1000 and 1001, the mask 00000001 could be used. This mask implies that all bits are checked except the one low-order bit. (Feel free to convert hex 1000 and 1001 to binary to see that only the last bit is different in the two numbers.)

SAP Filters

The key to understanding SAP filters is to understand where SAP packets flow and where they do not. This process is fundamental to the job function of a typical CCNA. The SAP process is very similar to routing updates with a distance vector routing protocol. In fact, SAP uses a split-horizon concept as well. The following sequence outlines a day in the life of a SAP packet:

Step 1 A router or server decides that it is time to send a SAP broadcast on its attached network, based on the expiration of its SAP timer.

Step 2 That router or server creates enough SAP packets to advertise all its SAP information (up to seven services per packet, by default).

Step 3 That router or server sends the SAP packets out into the attached network.

Step 4 Other routers and servers are attached to the same medium; these routers and servers receive all the SAP packets.

Step 5 The receiving routers and servers examine the information inside the SAP packets and update their SAP tables as necessary.

Step 6 The receiving routers and servers discard the SAP packets.

Step 7 Every server and router uses a SAP timer, which is not synchronized with the other servers and routers. When the timer expires, each server and router performs steps 1 through 3, and their neighboring servers and routers react and perform steps 4 through 6.

In other words, the SAP packets are never forwarded by a router or server. This process is effectively the same process used by distance vector routing protocols. So, packet filters filter packets going through a router. Therefore, the IOS uses *distribute lists* (instead of packet filters) to filter routing information. Likewise, IOS uses SAP filters to filter SAP information.

SAP filtering provides two functions: filtering the services listed in outgoing SAP updates and filtering services listed in received SAP updates. The first function reduces the information sent to the router's neighboring IPX servers and routers. The second function limits what a router adds to its SAP table when an update is received. Unlike packet filters, SAP filters examine the data inside the packet as well. Figure 11-17 outlines the process.

Figure 11-17 *SAP Filter Flow Diagram*

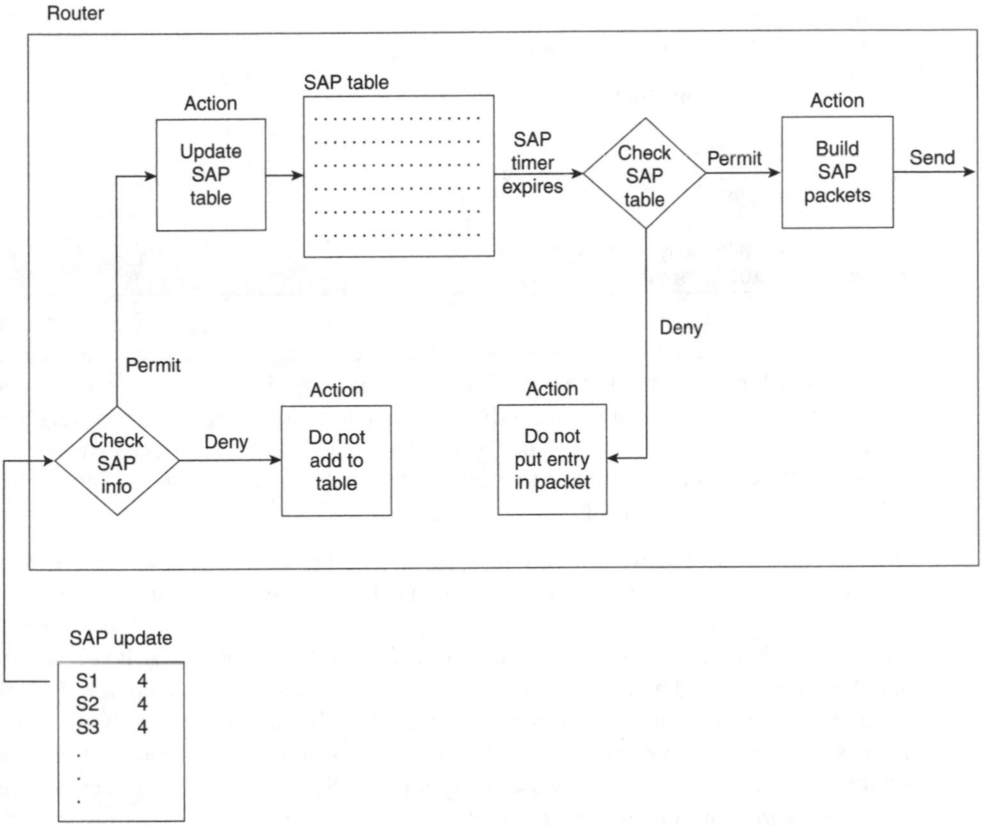

Two main reasons exist for using SAP filters. First, SAP updates can consume a large amount of bandwidth, particularly in nonbroadcast multiaccess (NBMA) networks. If clients in one division never need services from servers in another division, there is no need to waste bandwidth advertising the services. The second reason for SAP filters is that they can accomplish the same task as most IPX packet filters, but with less overhead. (This second reason will be outlined in the SAP filtering sample in Example 11-15.) SAP filters will be used to accomplish the same set of criteria that was mentioned with Example 11-14 and Figure 11-16. As a reminder, the criteria for that filter is as follows:

1. Clients in networks 100 and 101 are allowed to access Server 3 and Server 4.
2. Clients in network 300 are not allowed to access Server 1 and Server 2.

Example 11-15 *R1 Configuration for SAP Filters*

```
hostname  R1
!
ipx routing 0200.1111.111
!
interface serial0
ip address 10.1.1.1 255.255.255.0
ipx network 200
ipx input-sap-filter 1005
!
interface ethernet 0
ip address 10.1.30.1 255.255.255.0
ipx network 300
!
access-list 1005 deny 1000 0000000F
access-list 1005 permit -1
```

The effect of the SAP filter on R1 is somewhat obvious. How the filter stops clients in network 300 from reaching Server 1 and Server 2 is not as obvious. The filter examines inbound SAP updates from R2. Services in networks 1000 to 100F are filtered. All other services are not filtered; the **–1** keyword signifies all networks. (Extended IPX access lists can use the keyword **any**. SAP filters do not currently use that keyword.) So, there will never be an entry in R1's SAP table for networks 1000 to 100F.

The key to understanding what stops clients from reaching Server 1 and Server 2 is to recall the GNS process and its purpose. (Figure 11-8 outlined the process earlier in the chapter.) Either Server 3 or Server 4 will be used as the GNS server for clients in network 300. (The router will not reply to GNS requests if a real server exists on the LAN at some later IOS release; before that, the router delayed replying so that any local servers would send the first reply.) Neither Server 3 nor Server 4 will know of Server 1 or Server 2 because both are relying on R1 to advertise SAP information and R1 has filtered SAPs about networks 1000 to 100F. Therefore, network 300 clients will not be capable of logging in to Server 1 or Server 2 because *clients can connect only to servers in the SAP table of their GNS server.*

SAP filtering to disallow certain clients from using certain servers is more efficient than IPX packet filters. SAPs are sent once every 60 seconds, whereas packet filters cause the IOS to examine every IPX packet, a much more frequent task. So, you are more likely to use SAP filers in real networks, and you also are more likely to see SAP filters on the exam than IPX packet filters.

The following list shows the fields that can be matched for each service advertised, or to be advertised, in a SAP update:

- Source network
- Source IPX address (network and node)

- Portions of the source address, using a wildcard mask
- Destination network
- Destination IPX address (network and node)
- Portions of the destination address, using a wildcard mask
- Service type
- Server name

Named IPX Access Lists

Start Extra Credit

Named IPX access lists allow the same logic to be configured as with numbered standard, extended, and SAP access lists. As a CCNA, you will need to remember the differences in syntax of the configuration commands and be able to create both numbered and named lists with the same logic. The key differences between numbered and named IP access lists are listed here:

- Names are more intuitive reminders of the function of the list.
- Names allow more access lists than 100 standard, extended, and SAP access lists, which is the restriction using numbered access lists.
- Named access lists allow individual statements to be deleted. Numbered lists allow for deletion only of the entire list. Insertion of the new statement into a named list requires deletion and readdition of all statements that should follow the newly added statement.
- The actual names used must be unique across all named access lists of all protocols and types on an individual router. Names can be duplicated on different routers.

The configuration syntax is very similar between named and numbered IPX access lists. The items that can be matched with a numbered standard IPX access list are identical to the items that can be matched with a named standard IPX access list. Likewise, the items are identical with both numbered and named extended IPX access lists, as well as with numbered and named SAP access lists.

One key difference is that named access lists use a global command, which moves the user into a named IPX access list submode, under which the matching and permit/deny logic is configured. The other key difference is that when a named matching statement is deleted, only that specific statement is deleted. With numbered lists, the deletion of any statement in the list deletes all the statements in the list. (This feature will be demonstrated in more detail in an upcoming example.)

Table 11-12 lists the key IPX access list configuration commands and shows their differences and similarities.

Table 11-12 *Comparison of Named and Numbered IPX Access List Configuration Commands*

	Numbered	Named
Standard matching command	**access-list 800-899 permit | deny . . .**	**ipx access-list standard** *name* ***permit | deny . . .**
Extended matching command	**access-list 900-999 permit | deny . . .**	**ipx access-list extended** *name* ***permit | deny . . .**
SAP matching command	**access-list 1000-1099 permit | deny . . .**	**ipx access-list sap** *name* ***permit | deny . . .**
Standard access list–enabling command	**ipx access-group 800–899 in | out**	**ipx access-group** *name* **in | out**
Extended access list–enabling command	**ipx access-group 900–999 in | out**	**ipx access-group** *name* **in | out**
SAP filter–enabling command	**ipx output-sap-filter 1000–1099** **ipx input-sap-filter 1000–1099**	**ipx output-sap-filter** *name* **ipx input-sap-filter** *name*

*The **permit** and **deny** commands are subcommands to the **ipx access-list** command.

The word *name* represents a name created by the administrator. This name must be unique among all named access lists of all types in this router. Also, note that because the named list does not imply standard, extended, or SAP by the value of the number of the list, the command explicitly states the type of access list. Also, the ellipsis (. . .) represents all the matching parameters that are identical in meaning and syntax when comparing the respective numbered and named IPX access lists. Also note that the same command is used to enable the list on an interface for both numbered and named lists.

One difference between the two types of lists is that individual matching statements can be removed from the named lists. Example 11-16 shows the configuration mode output when entering a named SAP access list on R1. The key to this example is to notice the changes. One statement is deleted and then readded to the list, but this changes the order of the list. Example 11-16 shows the details.

Example 11-16 *Named IPX SAP Access List Configuration*

```
configure terminal
Enter configuration commands, one per line.  End with CNTL/Z.
R1(config)#ipx access-list sap fred
R1(config-ipx-sap-nacl)#deny 2 7
R1(config-ipx-sap-nacl)#deny 3
R1(config-ipx-sap-nacl)#deny 4 7
```

Example 11-16 *Named IPX SAP Access List Configuration (Continued)*

```
R1(config-ipx-sap-nacl)#permit -1
R1(config-ipx-sap-nacl)#^Z

R1#show ipx access-lists
IPX sap access list fred
    deny 2 7
    deny 3
    deny 4 7
    permit FFFFFFFF
R1#config t
Enter configuration commands, one per line.  End with CNTL/Z.
R1(config)#ipx access-list sap fred
R1(config-ipx-sap-nacl)#no deny 4 7
R1(config-ipx-sap-nacl)#^Z

R1#show ipx access-lists
IPX sap access list fred
    deny 2 7
    deny 3
    permit FFFFFFFF

R1#config t
Enter configuration commands, one per line.  End with CNTL/Z.
R1(config)#ipx access-list sap fred
R1(config-ipx-sap-nacl)#deny 4 7
R1(config-ipx-sap-nacl)#^Z

R1#show ipx access-lists
IPX sap access list fred
    deny 2 7
    deny 3
    permit FFFFFFFF
    deny 4 7

R1#config t
Enter configuration commands, one per line.  End with CNTL/Z.
R1(config)#ipx access-list sap fred
R1(config-ipx-sap-nacl)#no permit -1
R1(config-ipx-sap-nacl)#permit -1
R1(config-ipx-sap-nacl)#^Z

R1#show ipx access-lists
IPX sap access list fred
    deny 2 7
    deny 3
    deny 4 7
    permit FFFFFFFF

R1#configure t
Enter configuration commands, one per line.  End with CNTL/Z.
R1(config)#interface s 0.1
```

continues

Example 11-16 *Named IPX SAP Access List Configuration (Continued)*

```
R1(config-subif)#ipx output-sap-filter fred
R1(config-subif)#^Z

R1#show running
Building configuration...

Current configuration:
!
version 12.0
service timestamps debug uptime
service timestamps log uptime
no service password-encryption
!
hostname R1
!
enable secret 5 $1$chuM$zon5bAnWNCu38hzCmAr.k.
!
ip subnet-zero
no ip domain-lookup
ipx routing 0000.3089.b170
!
!
!
interface Serial0
 no ip address
 no ip directed-broadcast
 encapsulation frame-relay IETF
 clockrate 56000
 frame-relay lmi-type cisco
!
interface Serial0.1 multipoint
 ip address 168.13.100.1 255.255.255.0
 no ip directed-broadcast
 ipx network 100
 ipx output-sap-filter fred
 frame-relay interface-dlci 902
 frame-relay interface-dlci 903
!
! Additional configuration not shown...
```

End Extra Credit

Foundation Summary

The "Foundation Summary" is a collection of tables and figures that provides a convenient review of many key concepts in this chapter. For those of you already comfortable with the topics in this chapter, this summary could help you recall a few details. For those of you who just read this chapter, this review should help solidify some key facts. For any of you doing your final prep before the exam, these tables and figures will hopefully be a convenient way to review the day before the exam.

Novell uses Internet Packet Exchange (IPX) as its network layer protocol, as seen in Figure 11-18. The features listed in Table 11-13 are the same features used to generically describe a well-designed Layer 3 addressing scheme in Chapter 3.

Figure 11-18 *Novell NetWare Protocols*

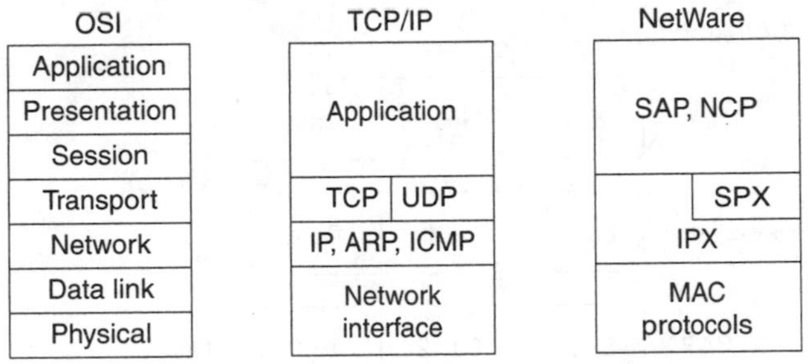

Table 11-13 *IPX Addressing Details*

Feature	Description
Size of address80 bits (10 bytes).	Format of address32-bit (4-byte) network part, followed by a 48-bit (6-byte) node number. Written in hexadecimal.
Grouping	The grouping concept is identical to IP, with all interfaces attached to the same medium using the same network number. There is no equivalent of IP subnetting.
Size of a group	IPX addresses use a 48-bit node part of the address, giving 2^{48} possible addresses per network (minus a few reserved values), which should be big enough.
Unique addresses	IPX calls for the LAN MAC address to be used as the node part of the IPX address. This allows for easy assignment and little chance of duplication. Ensuring that no duplicates of the network numbers are made is the biggest concern because the network numbers are configured.

continues

Table 11-13 *IPX Addressing Details (Continued)*

Feature	Description
Dynamic address assignment	Client IPX addresses are dynamically assigned as part of the protocol specifications. Servers and routers are configured with the network number(s) on their physical interfaces. Servers can choose to automatically generate an internal network number at installation time.
Internal networks	Servers create their own internal IPX network, in addition to the IPX networks covering the interfaces the server is attached to. When connecting to the server, a client connects to the server's internal IPX address, which is comprised of its internal network number and a node address of 0000.0000.0001.

Figure 11-19 shows the types of encapsulating Ethernet headers as also listed in Table 11-14.

Figure 11-19 *IPX Ethernet Encapsulations*

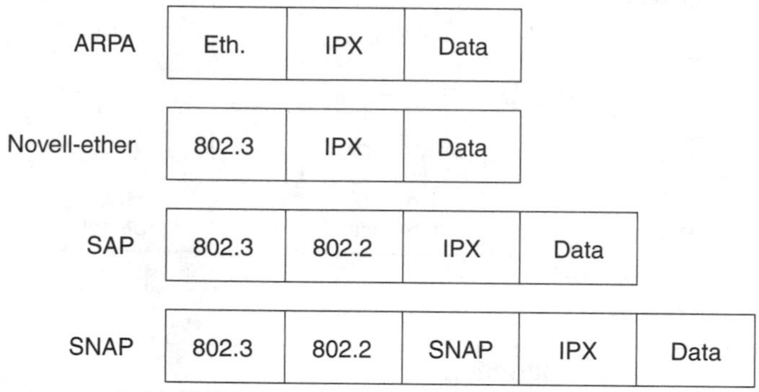

Table 11-14 *IPX Ethernet Encapsulations*

Novell's Name	Cisco IOS Software's Name	Hints for Remembering the Names and Meanings
Ethernet_II	ARPA	One way to help correlate the two names is to remember that ARPA was the original agency that created TCP/IP and that Ethernet_II is the older version of Ethernet; remember that the "old" names go together.
Ethernet_802.3	Novell-ether	Novell's name refers to the final header before the IPX header, in this case. There are no suggestions on easier ways to recall the IOS name Novell-ether. This setting is Novell's default on NetWare 3.11 and earlier releases.

Table 11-14 *IPX Ethernet Encapsulations (Continued)*

Novell's Name	Cisco IOS Software's Name	Hints for Remembering the Names and Meanings
Ethernet_802.2	SAP	Novell's name refers to the final header before the IPX header, in this case. Novell's name refers to the committee and complete header that defines the SAP field; Cisco's name refers to the SAP part of the 802.2 header. (The SAP field denotes that an IPX packet follows the 802.2 header.) This setting is Novell's default on NetWare 3.12 and later releases.
Ethernet_SNAP	SNAP	Novell's name refers to the final header before the IPX header, in this case. Cisco's name refers to this same header.

The same encapsulation issue exists on Token Ring and FDDI interfaces. Table 11-15 outlines the options.

Table 11-15 *IPX Token Ring and FDDI Encapsulations*

Novell's Name	Cisco IOS Software's Name	Description and Hints for Remembering
FDDI_Raw	Novell-fddi	The IPX packet follows directly after the FDDI header. No Type field of any kind is used.
FDDI_802.2	SAP	The IPX packet follows the 802.2 header. Novell's name refers to the committee and complete header that defines the SAP field; Cisco's name refers to the SAP part of the 802.2 header.
FDDI_SNAP	SNAP	Novell's name refers to the final header before the IPX header, in this case. Cisco's name refers to this same header.
Token-Ring	SAP	The IPX packet follows the 802.2 header. Novell's name refers to the committee and complete header that defines the SAP field; Cisco's name refers to the SAP part of the 802.2 header.
Token-Ring_SNAP	SNAP	Novell's name refers to the final header before the IPX header. Cisco's name refers to this same header.

Table 11-16 lists the similarities and differences.

Table 11-16 *RIP for IPX and IP Compared*

Novell RIP	IP RIP
Uses distance vector	Uses distance vector
Is based on XNS RIP	Is based on XNS RIP
Uses 60-second update timer (default)	Uses 30-second update timer (default)
Uses timer ticks as primary metric and hop count as secondary metric	Uses hop count as only metric

Figure 11-20 includes the use of the Get Nearest Server (GNS) request and shows a typical startup with a client configured with a preferred server of Server 2.

Figure 11-20 *Client Initialization Flows, Including GNS*

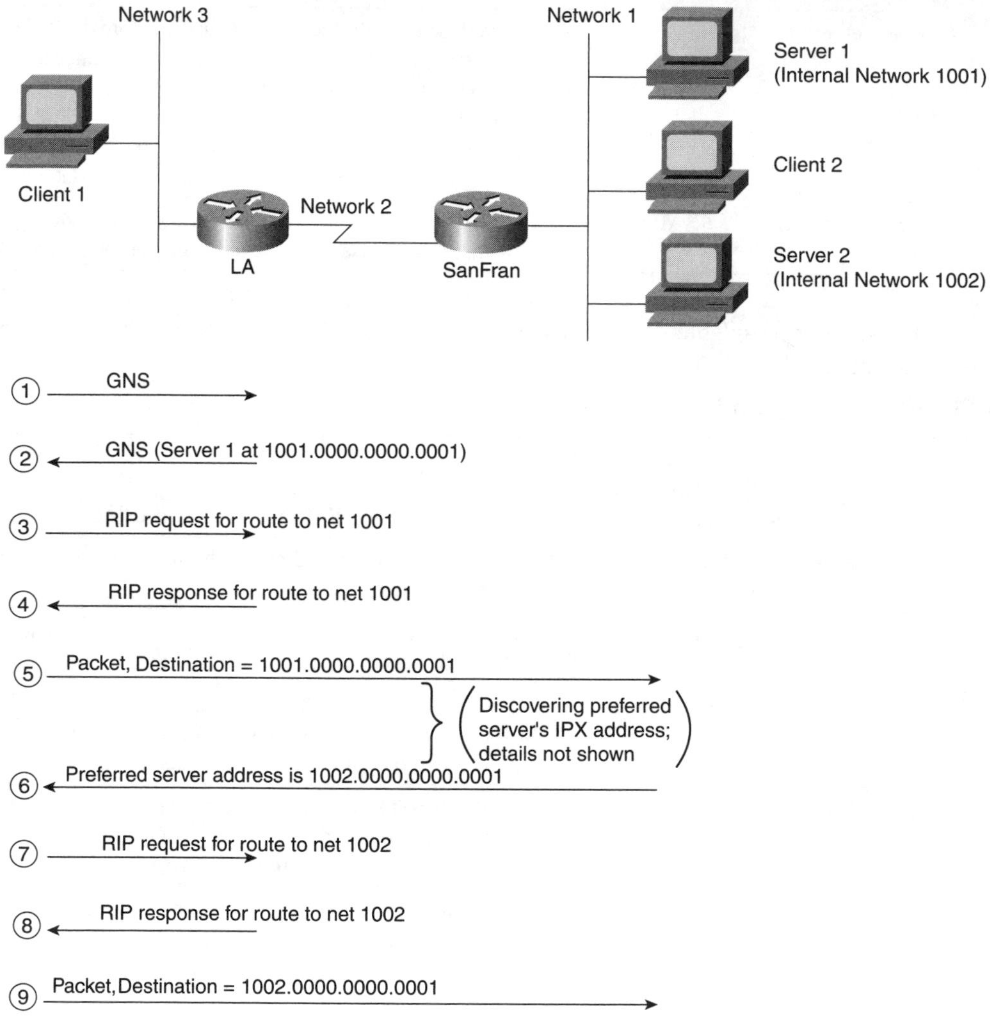

Tables 11-17 and 11-18 summarize the most popular commands used for IPX configuration and verification.

Table 11-17 *IPX and IPX RIP Configuration Commands*

Command	Configuration Mode
ipx routing [*node*]	Global
ipx maximum-paths *paths*	Global
ipx network *network* [**encapsulation** *type*] [**secondary**]	Interface mode

Table 11-18 *IPX Exec Commands*

Command	Function
show ipx interface	Gives detailed view of IPX parameter settings, per interface
show ipx route [*network*]	Shows entire routing table, or one entry if **network** is entered
show ipx servers	Shows SAP table
show ipx traffic	Shows IPX traffic statistics
debug ipx routing [*events* | *activity*]	Gives messages describing each routing update
debug ipx sap [*events* | *activity*]	Gives messages describing each SAP update
ping *ipx-address*	Sends IPX packets to verify connectivity

Table 11-19 lists the configuration commands used for IPX access lists, while Table 11-20 lists the Exec commands related to IPX filtering.

Table 11-19 *IPX Access Lists Configuration Commands*

Command	Configuration Mode and Purpose
access-list {*800-899*} {**permit** | **deny**} *source-network* [*.source-node* [*source-node-mask*]] [*destination-network* [*.destination-node* [*destination-node-mask*]]]	Global command to create numbered standard IPX access lists
access-list {*900-999*} {**permit** | **deny**} *protocol* [*source-network*] [[[*.source-node* [*source-node-mask*]] | [*.source-node source-network-mask.source-node-mask*]] [*source-socket*] [*destination-network*] [[[*.destination-node* [*destination-node-mask*] | [*.destination-node destination-network-mask. Destination-node-mask*]] [*destination-socket*] **log**	Global command to create numbered extended IPX access lists

Table 11-19 *IPX Access Lists Configuration Commands (Continued)*

Command	Configuration Mode and Purpose
access-list {*1000-1099*} {**permit** | **deny**} *network* [*.node*] [*network-mask.node-mask*] [*service-type* [*server-name*]]	Global command to create numbered SAP access lists
ipx access-list {**standard** | **extended** | **sap** } *name*	Global command to begin creation of a named standard, extended, or SAP access list
{**permit** | **deny**} *source-network* [*.source-node* [*source-node-mask*]] [*destination-network* [*.destination-node* [*destination-node-mask*]]]	Named access list subcommand for standard access lists
{**permit** | **deny**} *protocol* [*source-network*] [[[*.source-node* [*source-node-mask*]] | [*.source-node source-network-mask.source-node-mask*]] [*source-socket*] [*destination-network*] [[[*.destination-node* [*destination-node-mask*] | [*.destination-node destination-network-mask. Destination-node-mask*]] [*destination-socket*] **log**	Named access list subcommand for extended access lists
{**permit** | **deny**} *network* [*.node*] [*network-mask.node-mask*] [*service-type* [*server-name*]]	Named access list subcommand for SAP access lists
ipx access-group {*number* | *name* [**in** | **out**] }	Interface subcommand to enable a named or numbered, standard or extended IPX access list
ipx output-sap-filter *list-number*	Interface subcommand to enable SAP access lists used for outbound SAP packets
ipx input-sap-filter *list-number*	Interface subcommand to enable SAP access lists used for inbound SAP packets

Table 11-20 *IPX Access List Exec Commands*

Command	Function
show ipx interface	Includes reference to the access lists enabled on the interface
show access-list *number*	Shows details of all configured access lists for all protocols
show ipx access-list	Shows details of all IPX access lists

Table 11-21 summarizes the items that can be matched by IPX packet access lists, and Figure 11-21 shows the relative location of the fields in the headers.

Figure 11-21 *Header Fields Matchable Using IPX Access Lists*

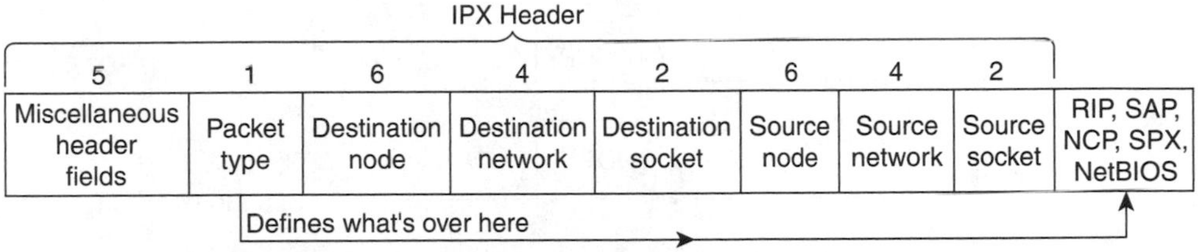

Table 11-21 *Standard and Extended IPX Access Lists—Matching*

Type of Access List	What Can Be Matched
Standard IPX	Source network
	Source IPX address (network and node)
	Source network and portions of the node address, using a node mask
	Destination network
	Destination IPX address (network and node)
	Destination network and portions of the node address, using a node mask
Extended IPX	Same points as with an IPX standard access list, in addition to items in the rows that follow
	Portions of entire source IPX address, using a wildcard mask
	Portions of entire destination IPX address, using a wildcard mask
	Protocol type
	Source socket
	Destination socket

Figure 11-22 shows example IPX packets that would be matched by the various protocol types.

Figure 11-22 *Extended Access List Protocol Types*

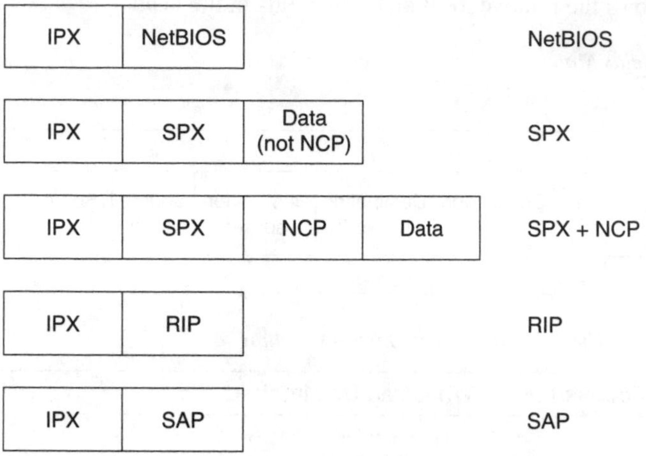

Figure 11-23 outlines the process of where SAP filters may be applied.

Figure 11-23 *SAP Filter Flow Diagram*

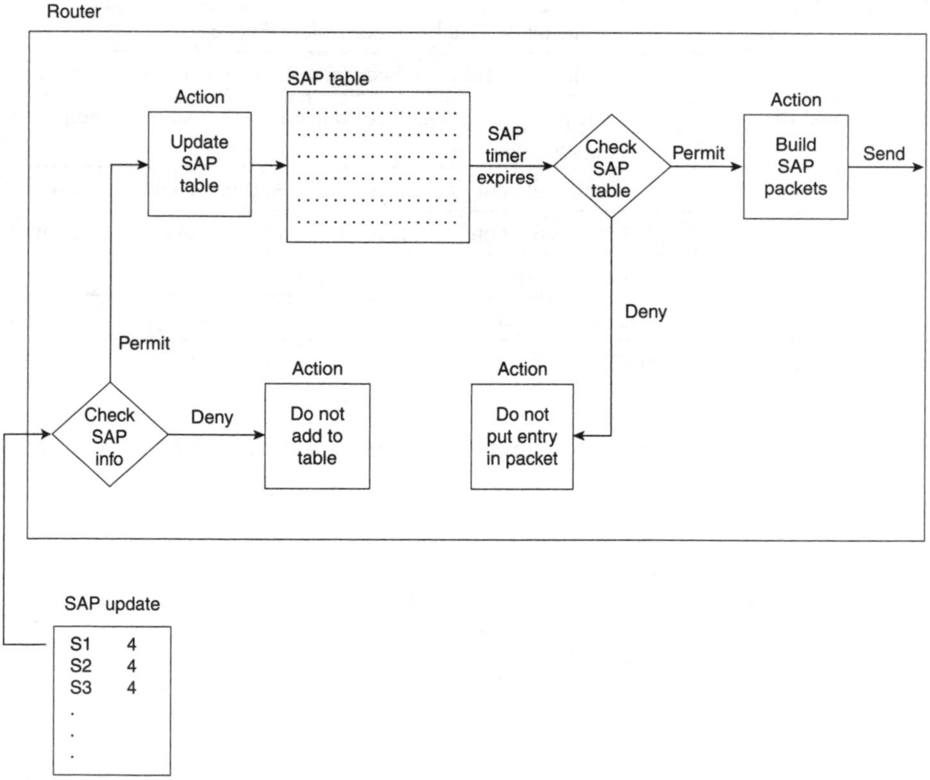

The following list shows the fields that can be matched for each service advertised, or to be advertised, in a SAP update.

- Source network
- Source IPX address (network and node)
- Portions of the source address, using a wildcard mask
- Destination network
- Destination IPX address (network and node)
- Portions of the destination address, using a wildcard mask
- Service type
- Server name

Table 11-22 lists the key IPX access list configuration commands and shows their differences and similarities.

Table 11-22 *Comparison of Named and Numbered IPX Access List Configuration Commands*

	Numbered	**Named**
Standard matching command	**access-list** *800–899* **permit | deny . . .**	**ipx access-list standard** *name* ***permit | deny . . .**
Extended matching command	**access-list** *900–999* **permit | deny . . .**	**ipx access-list extended** *name* ***permit | deny . . .**
SAP matching command	**access-list** *1000–1099* **permit | deny . . .**	**ipx access-list sap** *name* ***permit | deny . . .**
Standard access list–enabling command	**ipx access-group** *800–899* **in | out**	**ipx access-group** *name* **in | out**
Extended access list–enabling command	**ipx access-group** *900–999* **in | out**	**ipx access-group** *name* **in | out**
SAP filter–enabling command	**ipx output-sap-filter** *1000–1099* **ipx input-sap-filter** *1000–1099*	**ipx output-sap-filter** *name* **ipx input-sap-filter** *name*

*The **permit** and **deny** commands are subcommands to the **ipx access-list** command.

Q&A

As mentioned in Chapter 1, "All About the Cisco Certified Network Associate Certification," the questions and scenarios in this book are more difficult than what you should experience on the actual exam. The questions do not attempt to cover more breadth or depth than the exam; however, they are designed to make sure that you know the answer. Rather than allowing you to derive the answer from clues hidden inside the question itself, the questions challenge your understanding and recall of the subject. Questions from the "Do I Know This Already?" quiz from the beginning of the chapter are repeated here to ensure that you have mastered the chapter's topic areas. Hopefully, these questions will help limit the number of exam questions on which you narrow your choices to two options and then guess.

The answers to these questions can be found in Appendix A.

1 How often does IPX RIP send routing updates, by default?

2 Describe the metric(s) used by IPX RIP in a Cisco router.

3 Does IPX RIP use split horizon?

4 True or false: RIP and SAP information is sent in the same packets. If true, can only one of the two be enabled in a router? If false, what commands enable each protocol globally in a router?

5 What does *GNS* stand for? Who creates GNS requests, and who creates GNS replies?

6 How often does a router send SAP updates, by default?

7 If Serial0 has a **bandwidth 1544** interface subcommand and Serial1 has a **bandwidth 56** interface subcommand, what metric will IPX RIP associate with each interface?

8 What **show** commands list IPX RIP metric values in a Cisco router?

9 How many bytes comprise an IPX address?

10 What do *IPX* and *SPX* stand for?

11 Define *encapsulation* in the context of Cisco routers and Novell IPX.

____

____

____

12 Give an example of an IPX network mask used when subnetting.

____

____

____

13 Describe the headers used for two types of Ethernet encapsulation when using IPX.

____

____

____

14 Name the part of the NetWare protocol specifications that, like TCP, provides end-to-end guaranteed delivery of data.

____

____

____

15 Name the command that lists all the SAP entries in a Cisco router.

____

____

____

16 How many different values are possible for IPX network numbers?

____

____

____

17 Create a configuration enabling IPX on each interface, with RIP and SAP enabled on each as well, for a 2501 (two serial, one Ethernet) router. Use networks 100, 200, and 300 for interfaces S0, S1, and E0, respectively. Choose any node values.

____

____

____

18 In the previous question, what would be the IPX address of the serial 0 interface? If another user wanted to know but did not have the enable password, what command(s) might provide this IPX address?

____

____

____

19 What **show** command lists the IPX address(es) of interfaces in a Cisco router?

____

____

____

20 How many Novell encapsulation types are valid in the IOS for Ethernet interfaces? What about for FDDI and Token Ring?

____

____

____

21 A router is attached to an Ethernet LAN. Some clients on the LAN use Novell's Ethernet_II encapsulation, and some use Ethernet_802.3. If the only subcommand on Ethernet0 reads **ipx network 1**, which of the clients are working? (All, Ethernet_II, or Ethernet_802.3?)

____

____

____

22 A router is attached to an Ethernet LAN. Some clients on the LAN use Novell's Ethernet_802.2 encapsulation, and some use Ethernet_SNAP. Create a configuration that allows both types of clients to send and receive packets through this router.

____

____

____

23 True or false: Up to 64 IPX networks can be used on the same Ethernet by using the IPX secondary address feature. If true, describe the largest number that is practically needed. If false, what is the maximum number that is legal on an Ethernet?

____

____

____

24 In the **ipx network 11** interface subcommand, does the IOS assume that 11 is binary, octal, decimal, or hexadecimal? What is the largest valid value that could be configured instead of 11?

____

____

____

25 What IOS IPX encapsulation keyword implies use of an 802.2 header but no SNAP header? On what types of interfaces is this type of encapsulation valid?

____

____

____

26 How would a user who does not have the enable password find out what access lists have been configured and where they are enabled?

____

____

____

27 Create a configuration to add a SAP access list to filter all print services (SAP 7) from being advertised out a router's serial 0 and serial1 interfaces.

28 Name all the items that a SAP access list can examine to make a match.

29 True or false: If all IP or IPX access list statements in a particular list define the deny action, the default action is to permit all other packets.

30 In an IPX access list with five statements, a **no** version of the third statement is issued in configuration mode. Immediately following, another access list configuration command is added for the same access list. How many statements are in the list now, and in what position is the newly added statement?

31 Name all the items that a standard IPX access list can examine to make a match.

32 Name all the items that an extended IPX access list can examine to make a match.

33 In an extended named IPX access list with five statements, a **no** version of the second statement is issued in configuration mode. Immediately following, another access list configuration command is added for the same access list. How many statements are in the list now, and in what position is the newly added statement?

34 Name all the items that a named extended IPX access list can examine to make a match.

35 Configure a SAP numbered access list so that SAPs 4 through 7 are matched in network BEEF with a single command.

36 What command could someone who has only the Telnet password, not the enable password, use to find out what IPX access lists were enabled on which interfaces?

37 What command would display the contents of only IPX **access-list 904**?

Scenarios

Scenario 11-1: IPX Examination

Given the network in Figure 11-24 and the command output in Examples 11-17, 11-18, and 11-19, answer the questions and perform the tasks listed after Example 11-19.

Figure 11-24 *Scenario 11-1 Network Diagram*

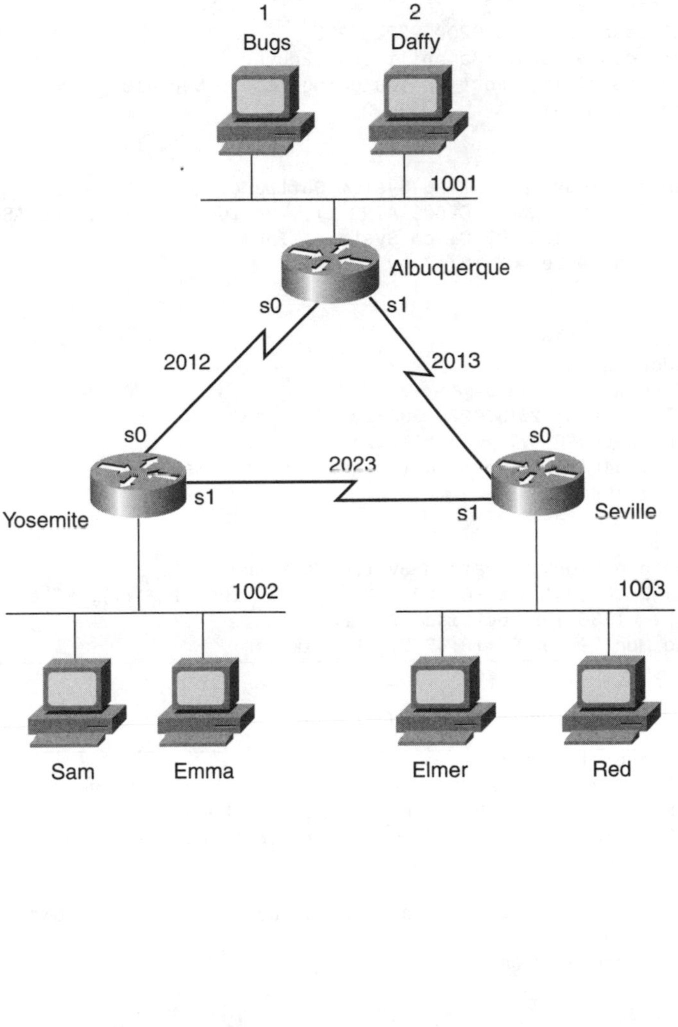

Example 11-17 *Albuquerque Command Output, Scenario 11-1*

```
Albuquerque#show ipx interface brief
Interface          IPX Network Encapsulation Status                IPX State
Serial0            2012        HDLC          up                    [up]
Serial1            2013        HDLC          up                    [up]
Ethernet0          1001        SAP           up                    [up]

Albuquerque#show cdp neighbor detail
-------------------------
Device ID: Yosemite
Entry address(es):
  IP address: 10.1.12.2
  Novell address: 2012.0200.2222.2222
Platform: cisco 2500,  Capabilities: Router
Interface: Serial0,  Port ID (outgoing port): Serial0
Holdtime : 167 sec

Version :
Cisco Internetwork Operating System Software
IOS (tm) 2500 Software (C2500-AINR-L), Version 11.2(11), RELEASE SOFTWARE (fc1)
Copyright  1986-1997 by Cisco Systems, Inc.
Compiled Mon 29-Dec-97 18:47 by ckralik

-------------------------
Device ID: Seville
Entry address(es):
  IP address: 10.1.13.3
  Novell address: 2013.0200.3333.3333
Platform: cisco 2500,  Capabilities: Router
Interface: Serial1,  Port ID (outgoing port): Serial0
Holdtime : 164 sec

Version :
Cisco Internetwork Operating System Software
IOS (tm) 2500 Software (C2500-AINR-L), Version 11.2(11), RELEASE SOFTWARE (fc1)
Copyright  1986-1997 by Cisco Systems, Inc.
Compiled Mon 29-Dec-97 18:47 by ckralik
```

Example 11-18 *Yosemite Command Output, Scenario 11-1*

```
Yosemite#show ipx route
Codes: C - Connected primary network,    c - Connected secondary network
       S - Static, F - Floating static, L - Local (internal), W - IPXWAN
       R - RIP, E - EIGRP, N - NLSP, X - External, A - Aggregate
       s - seconds, u - uses

8 Total IPX routes. Up to 1 parallel paths and 16 hops allowed.

No default route known.

C       1002 (SAP),           E0
```

Example 11-18 *Yosemite Command Output, Scenario 11-1 (Continued)*

```
C       2012 (HDLC),         Se0
C       2023 (HDLC),         Se1
R          1 [08/03] via     2012.0200.1111.1111,   32s, Se0
R          2 [08/03] via     2012.0200.1111.1111,   33s, Se0
R       1001 [07/01] via     2012.0200.1111.1111,   33s, Se0
R       1003 [07/01] via     2023.0200.3333.3333,   32s, Se1
R       2013 [07/01] via     2012.0200.1111.1111,   33s, Se0

Yosemite#show ipx traffic
System Traffic for 0.0000.0000.0001 System-Name: Yosemite
Rcvd:   169 total, 0 format errors, 0 checksum errors, 0 bad hop count,
        8 packets pitched, 161 local destination, 0 multicast
Bcast:  160 received, 242 sent
Sent:   243 generated, 0 forwarded
        0 encapsulation failed, 0 no route
SAP:    2 SAP requests, 0 SAP replies, 2 servers
        0 SAP Nearest Name requests, 0 replies
        0 SAP General Name requests, 0 replies
        60 SAP advertisements received, 57 sent
        6 SAP flash updates sent, 0 SAP format errors
RIP:    1 RIP requests, 0 RIP replies, 9 routes
        98 RIP advertisements received, 120 sent
        45 RIP flash updates sent, 0 RIP format errors
Echo:   Rcvd 0 requests, 0 replies
        Sent 0 requests, 0 replies
        0 unknown: 0 no socket, 0 filtered, 0 no helper
        0 SAPs throttled, freed NDB len 0
Watchdog:
        0 packets received, 0 replies spoofed
Queue lengths:
        IPX input: 0, SAP 0, RIP 0, GNS 0
        SAP throttling length: 0/(no limit), 0 nets pending lost route reply
        Delayed process creation: 0
EIGRP:  Total received 0, sent 0
        Updates received 0, sent 0
        Queries received 0, sent 0
        Replies received 0, sent 0
        SAPs received 0, sent 0
NLSP:   Level-1 Hellos received 0, sent 0
        PTP Hello received 0, sent 0
        Level-1 LSPs received 0, sent 0
        LSP Retransmissions: 0
        LSP checksum errors received: 0
        LSP HT=0 checksum errors received: 0
        Level-1 CSNPs received 0, sent 0
        Level-1 PSNPs received 0, sent 0
        Level-1 DR Elections: 0
        Level-1 SPF Calculations: 0
        Level-1 Partial Route Calculations: 0
```

Example 11-19 *Seville Command Output, Scenario 11-1*

```
Seville#show ipx interface
Serial0 is up, line protocol is up
  IPX address is 2013.0200.3333.3333 [up]
  Delay of this IPX network, in ticks is 6 throughput 0 link delay 0
  IPXWAN processing not enabled on this interface.
  IPX SAP update interval is 1 minute(s)
  IPX type 20 propagation packet forwarding is disabled
  Incoming access list is not set
  Outgoing access list is not set
  IPX helper access list is not set
  SAP GNS processing enabled, delay 0 ms, output filter list is not set
  SAP Input filter list is not set
  SAP Output filter list is not set
  SAP Router filter list is not set
  Input filter list is not set
  Output filter list is not set
  Router filter list is not set
  Netbios Input host access list is not set
  Netbios Input bytes access list is not set
  Netbios Output host access list is not set
  Netbios Output bytes access list is not set
  Updates each 60 seconds, aging multiples RIP: 3 SAP: 3
  SAP interpacket delay is 55 ms, maximum size is 480 bytes
  RIP interpacket delay is 55 ms, maximum size is 432 bytes
  Watchdog processing is disabled, SPX spoofing is disabled, idle time 60
  IPX accounting is disabled
  IPX fast switching is configured (enabled)
  RIP packets received 53, RIP packets sent 55
  SAP packets received 14, SAP packets sent 25
Serial1 is up, line protocol is up
  IPX address is 2023.0200.3333.3333 [up]
  Delay of this IPX network, in ticks is 6 throughput 0 link delay 0
  IPXWAN processing not enabled on this interface.
  IPX SAP update interval is 1 minute(s)
  IPX type 20 propagation packet forwarding is disabled
  Incoming access list is not set
  Outgoing access list is not set
  IPX helper access list is not set
  SAP GNS processing enabled, delay 0 ms, output filter list is not set
  SAP Input filter list is not set
  SAP Output filter list is not set
  SAP Router filter list is not set
  Input filter list is not set
  Output filter list is not set
  Router filter list is not set
  Netbios Input host access list is not set
  Netbios Input bytes access list is not set
  Netbios Output host access list is not set
  Netbios Output bytes access list is not set
  Updates each 60 seconds, aging multiples RIP: 3 SAP: 3
 SAP interpacket delay is 55 ms, maximum size is 480 bytes
  RIP interpacket delay is 55 ms, maximum size is 432 bytes
```

Example 11-19 *Seville Command Output, Scenario 11-1 (Continued)*

```
 Watchdog processing is disabled, SPX spoofing is disabled, idle time 60
  IPX accounting is disabled
  IPX fast switching is configured (enabled)
  RIP packets received 53, RIP packets sent 62
  SAP packets received 13, SAP packets sent 37
Ethernet0 is up, line protocol is up
  IPX address is 1003. 0000.0cac.ab41, SAP [up]
  Delay of this IPX network, in ticks is 1 throughput 0 link delay 0
  IPXWAN processing not enabled on this interface.
  IPX SAP update interval is 1 minute(s)
  IPX type 20 propagation packet forwarding is disabled
  Incoming access list is not set
  Outgoing access list is not set
  IPX helper access list is not set
  SAP GNS processing enabled, delay 0 ms, output filter list is not set
  SAP Input filter list is not set
  SAP Output filter list is not set
  SAP Router filter list is not set
  Input filter list is not set
  Output filter list is not set
  Router filter list is not set
  Netbios Input host access list is not set
  Netbios Input bytes access list is not set
  Netbios Output host access list is not set
  Netbios Output bytes access list is not set
  Updates each 60 seconds, aging multiples RIP: 3 SAP: 3
  SAP interpacket delay is 55 ms, maximum size is 480 bytes
  RIP interpacket delay is 55 ms, maximum size is 432 bytes
  IPX accounting is disabled
  IPX fast switching is configured (enabled)
  RIP packets received 20, RIP packets sent 62
  SAP packets received 18, SAP packets sent 15

Seville#show ipx servers
Codes: S - Static, P - Periodic, E - EIGRP, N - NLSP, H - Holddown, + = detail
2 Total IPX Servers

Table ordering is based on routing and server info

   Type Name                       Net     Address    Port     Route Hops Itf
P     4 Bugs                         1.0000.0000.0001:0451      8/03    3  Se0
P     4 Daffy                        2.0000.0000.0001:0451      8/03    3  Se0
```

Assuming the details established in Figure 11-24 and the command output in Examples 11-17, 11-18, and 11-19 for Scenario 11-1, complete or answer the following:

1. Complete Table 11-23 with all IPX network numbers. List the command(s) that you use to find these network numbers.
2. Complete as much of Table 11-24 as possible.

Table 11-23 *IPX Networks in Scenario 11-1*

IPX Network	Location (Such as "Between Albuquerque and Seville")	Command Used to Find This Information

Table 11-24 *IPX Addresses on Routers in Scenario 11-1*

Router	Interface	IPX Network	IPX Node
Albuquerque	E0		
	S0		
	S1		

Table 11-24 *IPX Addresses on Routers in Scenario 11-1 (Continued)*

Router	Interface	IPX Network	IPX Node
Yosemite	E0		
	S0		
	S1		
Seville	E0		
	S0		
	S1		

Scenario 11-2: IPX Configuration

Assume the network setup in Figure 11-25.

Figure 11-25 *Scenario 11-2 Network Diagram*

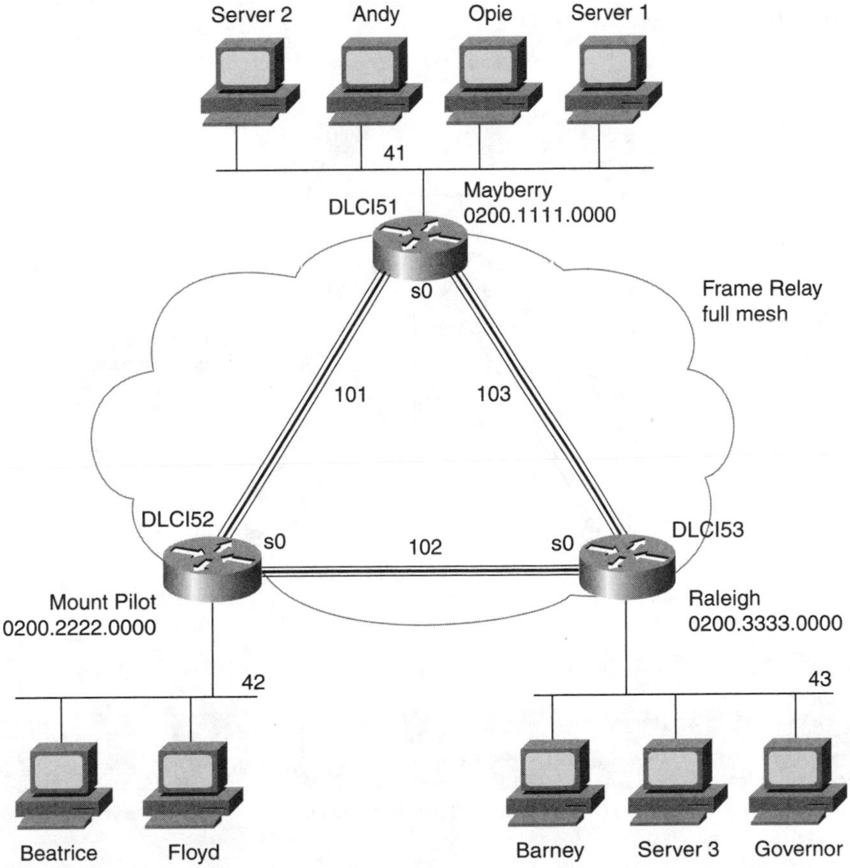

Assuming the details established in Figure 11-25 for Scenario 11-2, complete or answer the following:

1 Configure IPX on all three routers. Use the network numbers listed in the figure. (Do not bother with IP.) Use point-to-point subinterfaces, and use the IPX node addresses shown in the diagram on the serial interfaces.

2 You later find out that Beatrice is using NetWare's Ethernet_II encapsulation, Floyd is using Ethernet_802.3, Barney is using Ethernet_802.2, and Governor is using Ethernet_SNAP. Configure the changes necessary to support each client.

Scenario 11-3: IPX Filtering

IPX packet and SAP filtering concepts and configuration are reviewed in this scenario. Sample configurations are supplied first. Your job is to interpret the current access lists and then create new packet access lists and SAP access lists to meet some additional criteria. The details are listed after Figure 11-26 and Examples 11-20 through 11-23.

Figure 11-26 *Network Diagram for Scenario 11-4*

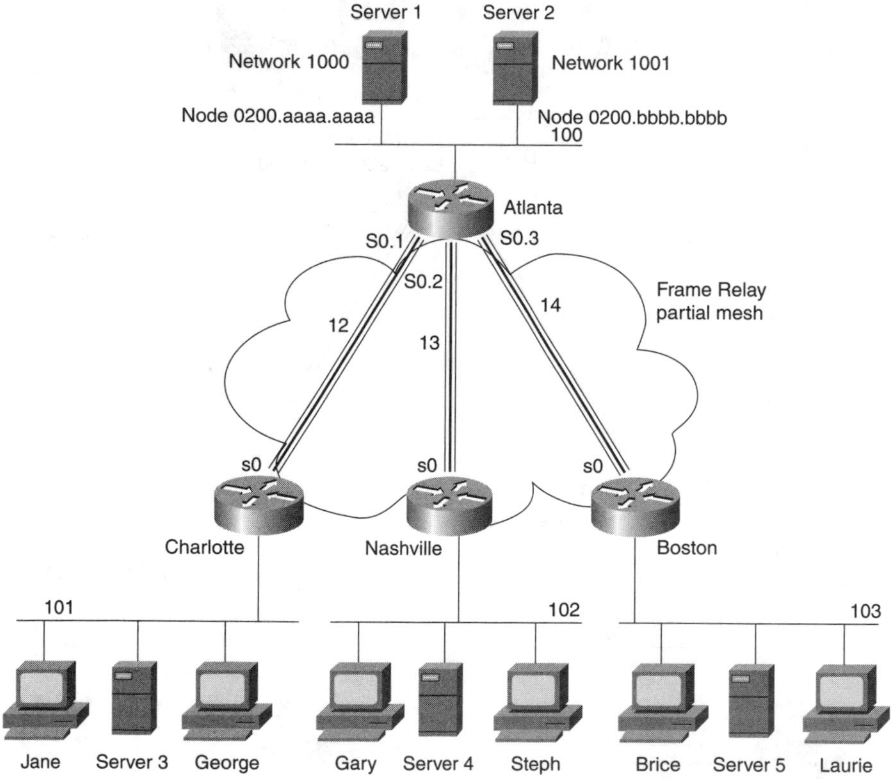

Example 11-20 *Atlanta Configuration*

```
ipx routing 0200.1111.1111
!
interface serial0
encapsulation frame-relay
!
interface serial 0.1 point-to-point
ip address 168.10.12.1  255.255.255.0
ipx network 12
ipx access-group 801 in
frame-relay interface-dlci 52
!
interface serial 0.2 point-to-point
ip address 168.10.13.1 255.255.255.0
ipx network 13
ipx access-group 903 in
frame-relay interface-dlci 53
!
interface serial 0.3 point-to-point
ip address 168.10.14.1 255.255.255.0
ipx network 14
ipx access-group 903 in
frame-relay interface-dlci 54
!
interface ethernet 0
ip address 168.10.100.1 255.255.255.0
ipx network 100
!
access-list 903 deny any 102.0000.0000.0000 1.ffff.ffff.ffff all 100
access-list 903 permit any any
access-list 801 deny 101 100.0200.bbbb.bbbb
access-list 801 permit -1
```

Example 11-21 *Charlotte Configuration*

```
ipx routing 0200.2222.2222
!
interface serial0
encapsulation frame-relay
!
interface serial 0.1 point-to-point
ip address 168.10.12.2 255.255.255.0
ipx network 12
frame-relay interface-dlci 51
!
interface ethernet 0
ip address 168.10.101.2 255.255.255.0
ipx network 101
```

Example 11-22 *Nashville Configuration*

```
ipx routing 0200.3333.3333
!
interface serial0
encapsulation frame-relay
!
interface serial 0.2 point-to-point
ip address 168.10.13.3 255.255.255.0
ipx network 13
frame-relay interface-dlci 51
!
interface ethernet 0
ip address 168.10.102.3 255.255.255.0
ipx network 102
```

Example 11-23 *Boston Configuration*

```
ipx routing 0200.4444.4444
!
interface serial0
encapsulation frame-relay
!
interface serial 0.3 point-to-point
ip address 168.10.14.4 255.255.255.0
ipx network 14
frame-relay interface-dlci 51
!
interface ethernet 0
ip address 168.10.103.4 255.255.255.0
ipx network 103
```

Given the network in Figure 11-26 and the configurations in Example 11-20 through 11-23, answer the questions and perform the tasks that follow.

1 Characterize the traffic that is discarded because of the access lists used on Atlanta. Can clients in the remote sites access the servers in Atlanta?

2 Create IPX packet filters to meet the following criteria:

- Clients in Nashville and Boston are not allowed access to Server 1.
- Clients in Charlotte are not allowed access to Server 2.
- Use standard access lists, if possible.
- Place the access lists close to the source of the packets.
- Assume that all access lists from Task 1 have been disabled and deleted.

3 Create SAP filters that perform the same function as described in Task 2.

Scenario Answers

Answers to Scenario 11-1: IPX Examination

Assuming the details established in Figure 11-24 and the command output in Examples 11-17, 11-18, and 11-19 for Scenario 11-1, the **show ipx interface brief** command and **show ipx route** command are the best methods for learning the network numbers in Table 11-25 (Task 1, for this scenario).

Table 11-25 *IPX Networks in Scenario 11-1—Completed Chart*

IPX Network	Location (Such as "Between Albuquerque and Seville")	Command Used to Find This Information
1001	Albuquerque Ethernet0	**show ipx interface brief** on Albuquerque
		show ipx route on Yosemite
1002	Yosemite Ethernet0	**show ipx route** on Yosemite
1003	Seville Ethernet0	**show cdp neighbor detail** on Albuquerque
		show ipx interface on Seville
2012	Albuquerque–Yosemite	**show cdp neighbor detail** on Albuquerque
		show ipx route on Yosemite
		show ipx interface brief on Albuquerque
2013	Albuquerque–Seville	**show cdp neighbor detail** on Albuquerque
		show ipx route on Yosemite
		show ipx interface brief on Albuquerque
		show ipx interface on Seville
2023	Yosemite–Seville	**show ipx route** on Yosemite
		show ipx interface on Seville
1	Bugs' internal network	**show ipx servers** on Seville
		show ipx route on Yosemite
2	Daffy's internal network	**show ipx servers** on Seville
		show ipx route on Yosemite

Assuming the details established in Figure 11-24 and the command output in Examples 11-17, 11-18, and 11-19 for Scenario 11-1, the network numbers are obtained from several sources, as seen in Table 11-27. The additional requirement for Task 2 is to find the node part of the IPX addresses on each interface. The easy way to learn this information is through the **show ipx interface** command. Of course, only one such command was provided in Examples 11-17, 11-18, and 11-19. The answers that could be found in the examples are listed in Table 11-26.

Table 11-26 *IPX Addresses on Routers in Scenario 11-1—Completed Chart*

Router	Interface	IPX Network	IPX Node
Albuquerque	E0	1001	
	S0	2012	0200.1111.1111
	S1	2013	
Yosemite	E0	1002	
	S0	2012	0200.2222.2222
	S1	2023	
Seville	E0	1003	0000.0cac.ab41
	S0	2013	0200.3333.3333
	S1	2023	0200.3333.3333

Answers to Scenario 11-2: IPX Configuration

Answers to Task 1 for Scenario 11-2

Assuming the details established in Figure 11-25 for Scenario 11-2, you can find in Examples 11-24, 11-25, and 11-26 the IPX configurations on all three routers: Mayberry, Mount Pilot, and Raleigh, respectively.

Example 11-24 *Mayberry Configuration, Scenario 11-2, Task 1*

```
ipx routing 0200.1111.0000
!
interface serial0
encapsulation frame-relay
!
interface serial 0.2 point-to-point
ipx network 101
frame-relay interface-dlci 52
!
interface serial 0.3 point-to-point
ipx network 103
frame-relay interface-dlci 53

!
interface ethernet 0
ipx network 41
```

Example 11-25 *Mount Pilot Configuration, Scenario 11-2, Task 1*

```
ipx routing 0200.2222.0000
!
interface serial0
encapsulation frame-relay
!
interface serial 0.1 point-to-point
ipx network 101
frame-relay interface-dlci 51
!
interface serial 0.3 point-to-point
ipx network 102
frame-relay interface-dlci 53
!
interface ethernet 0
ipx network 42
```

Example 11-26 *Raleigh Configuration, Scenario 11-2, Task 1*

```
ipx routing 0200.3333.0000
!
interface serial0
encapsulation frame-relay
!
interface serial 0.1 point-to-point
ipx network 103
frame-relay interface-dlci 51
!
interface serial 0.2 point-to-point
ipx network 102
frame-relay interface-dlci 52
!
interface ethernet 0
ipx network 43
```

Your answer should match Examples 11-24 through 11-26, with a few minor exceptions. The book does not specify the serial interface, nor does it restrict the subinterface numbers chosen. Likewise, the Ethernet interface number was not specified. Otherwise, the configuration should identically match these examples.

Answers to Task 2 for Scenario 11-2

Assuming the details established in Figure 11-25 for Scenario 11-2, the second task for Scenario 11-2 calls for additional encapsulations. Beatrice is using NetWare's Ethernet_II encapsulation, Floyd is using Ethernet_802.3, Barney is using Ethernet_802.2, and Governor is using Ethernet_SNAP. Hopefully you remembered the encapsulation names used in the IOS; the names supplied in the problem statement use the NetWare names. (In real life, a simple question mark when typing the **ipx network** interface subcommand would remind you of the names, but the objective is to memorize things so that you can pass the test. Refer to Table 11-4 for reminders on how to remember the encapsulation names.) Examples 11-27 and 11-28 show just the configuration commands used to change the configuration on Mount Pilot and Raleigh to support each client.

Example 11-27 *Mount Pilot Configuration, Scenario 11-2, Task 2—Changes Only*

```
interface ethernet 0
ipx network 42 encapsulation arpa
ipx network 142 secondary
```

Example 11-28 *Raleigh Configuration, Scenario 11-2, Task 2—Changes Only*

```
interface ethernet 0.1
ipx network 43 encapsulation sap
interface ethernet 0.2
ipx network 143 encapsulation snap
```

Two new network numbers are needed: 142 and 143 are used, in this case. Any numbers that you use are fine unless they are duplicates of some other network. The **ipx network 142 secondary** command on Mount Pilot has no encapsulation type configured because the default encapsulation type is Novell-ether. The second IPX network command must be configured with the **secondary** keyword, or it will replace the **ipx network** command that was configured first.

Answers to Scenario 11-4: IPX Filtering

Refer to the network illustrated in Figure 11-26 and Examples 11-20 through 11-23 to establish the Scenario 11-4 design details and the context of the answers to the three tasks for this scenario.

Answers to Task 1 for Scenario 11-4

Task 1 for Scenario 11-4 asks you to characterize the traffic that is discarded because of the access lists used on Atlanta. Furthermore, you need to determine whether clients in the remote sites can access the servers in Atlanta. The answer is not obvious in this case. The extended access list is particularly confusing, given all the options. The parameters coded in the first entry in list 903 in Example 11-20 are as follows:

- **Deny**—Direction to throw away packets that match.
- **Any**—Any protocol type.
- **102.0000.0000.0000**—Source IPX address. The node part of the address will be masked, so all 0s are coded in the node part of the address. The node part of the address must be configured; otherwise, the syntax does not allow the right to use the network wildcard mask.

- **1.ffff.ffff.ffff**—Source network and node wildcard mask. With leading zeroes written in, the mask would be 00000001.ffff.ffff.ffff. This mask matches networks 102 and 103, which are identical except for the final bit in the network part of the address. The mask means, "All bits in the network must match network 102, except for the last bit in the network number." (All F's for the node mean that any node number will match.)
- **All**—All sockets.
- **100**—Destination network.

So, the first entry in list 903 matches packets from network 102 and 103, destined for network 100, any protocol, any socket. These packets are denied. The second entry in 903 permits all protocols, all source networks, and, by implication, all destination networks; in other words, this statement changes the default to be "permit all else."

By enabling list 903 for inbound packets on Atlanta's serial 0.2 and serial 0.3 interfaces, clients in Nashville and Boston cannot reach network 100.

Access list 801 stops all packets from network 101 from reaching Server 2's Ethernet IPX address. It also has a "permit everything else" statement at the end of the list, but because standard IPX access lists do not use the **any** keyword, **–1** is used to signify **any**.

Neither list stops access to Server 1 or Server 2 because the destination of packets to these servers will be the internal IPX addresses (1000.0000.0000.0001 and 1001.0000.0000.0001). Packets sent to networks 1000 and 1001 will not be matched until the "permit all" at the end of the lists.

Answers to Task 2 for Scenario 11-4

Task 2 for Scenario 11-4 asks you to create IPX packet filters to meet the following criteria:

- Clients in Nashville and Boston are not allowed access to Server 1.
- Clients in Charlotte are not allowed access to Server 2.
- Use standard access lists, if possible.
- Place the access lists close to the source of the packets.
- Assume that all access lists from Task 1 have been disabled and deleted.

This can be accomplished by configuring standard IPX access lists. Because the goal is to filter packets close to the source, and because the client initiates the process of connecting to a server, the filters all were placed at the remote routers and not in Atlanta. Each filter matches packets sourced in their local IPX networks and destined for network 1000 (if filtering packets destined for Server 1), or destined for network 1001 (if filtering packets destined for Server 2). Examples 11-29 through 11-31 show the configurations necessary to create IPX packet filters to satisfy the criteria.

Example 11-29 *Charlotte with Access List Configured, Scenario 11-4, Task 2*

```
access-list 800 deny 101 1001
access-list 800 permit -1
!
interface serial 0.1 point-to-point
ipx access-group 800
```

Example 11-30 *Nashville with Access List Configured, Scenario 11-4, Task 2*

```
access-list 800 deny 102 1000
access-list 800 permit -1
!
interface serial 0.2 point-to-point
ipx access-group 800
```

Example 11-31 *Boston with Access List Configured, Scenario 11-4, Task 2*

```
access-list 800 deny 103 1000
access-list 800 permit -1
!
interface serial 0.3 point-to-point
ipx access-group 800
```

Answers to Task 3 for Scenario 11-4

Task 3 for Scenario 11-4 asks you to create SAP filters that perform the same function as described in Task 2. Task 3 suggests a very simple solution, but the simple solution works only because there are local servers in Charlotte, Nashville, and Boston. First take a look at the solution; then read over some comments.

Because the local server in each case will be the GNS server for the local clients, respectively, all that is needed is to stop Server 1 and Server 2 SAP information from being advertised into the remote sites. In an effort to reduce overhead, the SAP filters will be placed in Atlanta because SAP information originates in the servers. Example 11-32 provides the solution.

Example 11-32 *Atlanta with SAP Filter Configured, Scenario 11-4, Task 3*

```
access-list 1050 deny 1000
access-list 1050 permit -1
!
access-list 1051 deny 1001
access-list 1051 permit -1
!
interface serial 0.1 point-to-point
ipx output-sap-filter 1051
```

Example 11-32 *Atlanta with SAP Filter Configured, Scenario 11-4, Task 3 (Continued)*

```
!
interface serial 0.2 point-to-point
ipx output-sap-filter 1050
!
interface serial 0.3 point-to-point
ipx output-sap-filter 1050
```

SAPs about Server 1 (network 1000) are filtered from being sent out serial 0.2 and serial 0.3 to Nashville and Boston, respectively. Likewise, SAPs about Server 2 (network 1001) are filtered from being sent out serial 0.1 to Charlotte. Server 3 will not know about Server 2, so it cannot tell Charlotte clients about Server 2. Likewise, Server 4 and Server 5 will not know about Server 1, so they cannot tell Nashville clients and Boston clients about Server 1.

SAP filters are also great for reducing traffic, of course. However, when using them for stopping particular clients and servers from communicating, there are some caveats. If no servers were in place in Charlotte, Nashville, or Boston, the remote clients would have used Server 1 or Server 2 as their GNS server. Server 1 and Server 2 have full knowledge of each other's SAP information because they are on the same Ethernet. Therefore, clients would be capable of connecting to the servers, in spite of efforts to prevent the connections from using SAP filtering.

CHAPTER 12

Scenarios for Final Preparation

This chapter assists you with your final preparation for the CCNA exam by providing additional practice with the core focus of the exam. These exercises and tasks require a broad perspective, which means that you need to draw on the knowledge you acquired in Chapters 2 through 11. This chapter also focuses on configuration and verification commands in ways that help you learn and review better than another set of questions could. These scenarios are designed with the following assumptions in mind:

- You might have forgotten many details by the time you completed the other chapters. These scenarios cover the entire breadth of topics to remind you of many of these details.
- Your understanding of the concepts at this point in your study is complete. Practice and repetition are useful so that you can answer the exam questions quickly and confidently.

This chapter is not the only one you should use when doing your final preparation for the CCNA exam. The concepts in Chapter 3, "OSI Reference Model and Layered Communication," are not covered in this chapter, mainly because Chapter 3 deals with concepts and theory. However, Chapter 3 concepts are an important part of the CCNA exam. Review the questions at the end of that chapter and look at the tables that detail the functions of each OSI layer and the sample protocols at each layer as a final review of OSI.

The "Foundation Summary" section in each chapter is another great way to review the topics as your exam date approaches. Figure 12-1 describes your final preparation options with this book.

Figure 12-1 *Final CCNA Exam Preparation Study Strategy*

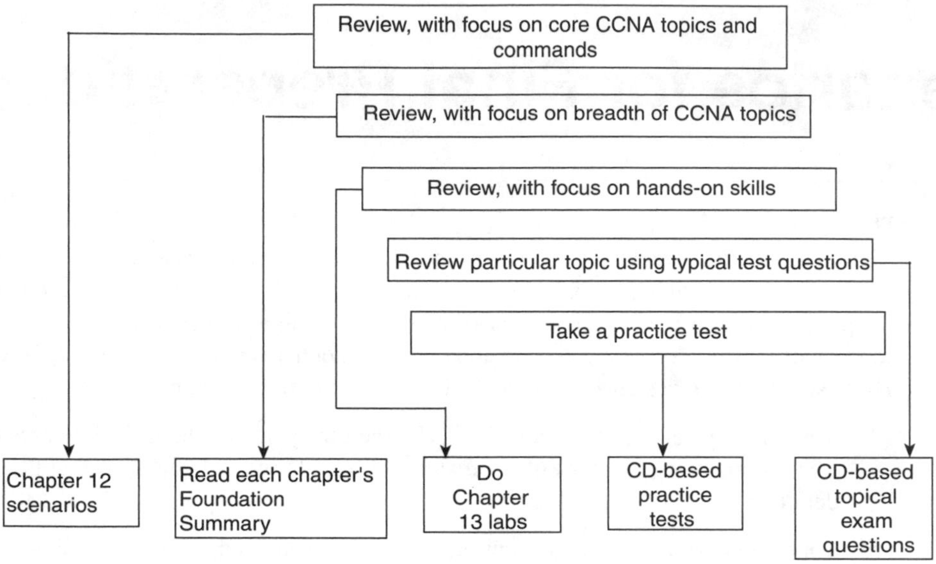

If you want more final preparation, many practice questions are located in each chapter and on the CD. All prechapter quizzes and chapter-ending questions, with answers, are listed in Appendix A, "Answers to the 'Do I Know This Already?' Quizzes and Q&A Sections." You can quickly read and review these conveniently located questions and go over the answers and explanations. In addition, the accompanying CD-ROM includes testing software and many other questions in the format of the CCNA exam (multiple-choice questions). These questions are a valuable resource when you are performing final preparations.

How to Best Use This Chapter

The current CCNA exam includes simulated labs, with the possible future addition of live labs on real gear during the exam. The best way to use this chapter is to get some gear, set it up, and do these lab scenarios. Alternatively, you could rent lab time from one of several sources, such as www.skylinecomputer.com. Regardless, the best way to build hands-on skills with routers is to actually configure and troubleshoot a network!

The scenarios in this chapter focus on easily forgotten items. The first such items are the **show** and **debug** commands. Their options are often ignored, mainly because you can easily get online help for them when using the Cisco CLI. However, questions about the exact command options used to see a particular piece of information are scattered throughout the exam. Be sure to review the output of the commands in these scenarios.

NOTE Do not count on the CCNA exam to have only multiple-choice questions. It also can have fill-in-the blank questions, with particular emphasis on commands and command options.

Another focus of this chapter is a review of command-line tricks and acronym trivia. Like it or not, part of the preparation involves memorization. Hopefully, these reminders will help you answer a question or two on the exam.

Additional examples for IP and IPX addressing are included with each scenario. You can be sure that IP addressing, subnetting, and broadcast addresses will be on the exam. Also be sure to recall the Novell encapsulation options, which are also reviewed in these scenarios.

Finally, this chapter contains more configurations for almost all options covered in this book. If you can configure these options without online help, feel confident that you will be able to choose the correct command from a list of five options in a multiple-choice question.

If you have enough time, review all the parts of each scenario. However, if you have limited time, you might want to review only part of a scenario. For example, the solutions to Part A of each scenario are the background information for Part B, and the solutions to Part B of each scenario are the background information for Part C. So, if you read Part A or B, decide you already know those details, and don't want to take the time to figure out your own answer, just look at the answer in the book. It will lead you into the next part of the scenario.

If you are reading this chapter as your final review before taking the exam, let me take this opportunity to wish you success. Hopefully, you will be relaxed and confident for your exam—and hopefully, this book will have helped you build your knowledge and confidence.

Scenario 12-1

Part A of Scenario 12-1 begins with some planning guidelines that include planning IP addresses, IPX network numbers, the location of SAP filters, and the location of standard IP access lists. After you complete Part A, Part B of the scenario asks you to configure the three routers to implement the planned design and a few other features. Finally, Part C asks you to examine router command output to discover details about the current operation. Part C also lists some questions related to the user interface and protocol specifications.

Scenario 12-1, Part A: Planning

Your job is to deploy a new network with three sites, as shown in Figure 12-2. The decision to use point-to-point serial links has already been made, and the products have been chosen. For Part A of this scenario, perform the following tasks:

1 Plan the IP addressing and subnets used in this network. Class B network 163.1.0.0 has been assigned by the NIC. The maximum number of hosts per subnet is 100. Assign IP addresses to the PCs as well.

2 Plan the IPX network numbers to be used. You can choose the servers' internal network numbers as well.

3 Plan the location and logic of IP access lists to filter for the following criteria: Hosts on the Ethernet attached to R1 are not allowed to send or receive IP traffic to or from hosts on the Ethernet attached to R3. (Do not code the access lists; just code their location and logic. Part B asks for configuration, and because the answer to Part B is based on where the access lists are placed, you probably will want to see the answer in Part A before configuring.)

4 Plan the location and logic of SAP filters to prevent clients on the Ethernet off R2 from logging in to Server 2. Again, do not create the configuration, but simply make notes about the logic and location of the access lists.

Assume that a single VLAN is used on the switches near Router 1 (R1).

Tables 12-1 and 12-2 are provided as a convenient place to record your IP subnets, IPX networks, and IP addresses when performing the planning tasks for this scenario.

Figure 12-2 *Scenario 12-1 Network Diagram*

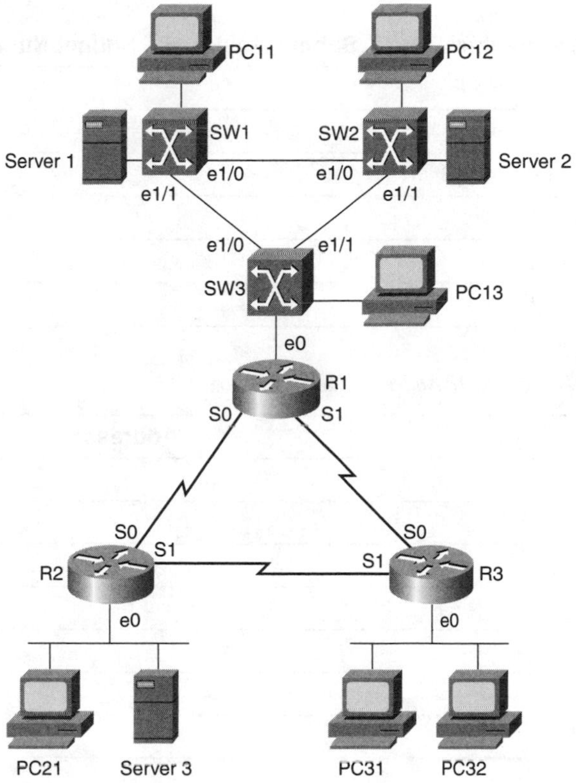

Table 12-1 *Scenario 12-1, Part A: IP Subnet and IPX Network Planning Chart*

Location of Subnet/ Network Geographically	Subnet Mask	Subnet Number	IPX Network
R1 Ethernet			
R2 Ethernet			
R3 Ethernet			

continues

Table 12-1 *Scenario 12-1, Part A: IP Subnet and IPX Network Planning Chart (Continued)*

Location of Subnet/ Network Geographically	Subnet Mask	Subnet Number	IPX Network
Serial between R1 and R2			
Serial between R1 and R3			
Serial between R2 and R3			
Server 1 internal			
Server 2 internal			
Server 3 internal			

Table 12-2 *Scenario 12-1, Part A: IP Address Planning Chart*

Host	Address
PC11	
PC12	
PC13	
PC21	
PC31	
PC32	
R1-E0	
R1-S0	
R1-S1	
R2-E0	
R2-S0	
R2-S1	
R3-E0	
R3-S0	
R3-S1	

Solutions to Scenario 12-1, Part A: Planning

It's a good idea to keep the design as simple as possible, without making it so simple that it will not be useful as the network evolves. The numbering scheme in these suggested answers was chosen because it's easier to remember.

1 The IP subnet design includes the use of mask 255.255.255.128. The design criteria leave enough ambiguity that you could argue that any mask with at least 7 host bits is valid; therefore, the much easier mask of 255.255.255.0 would be valid. However, I chose a more challenging mask to give you more difficult practice.

2 The IPX network number assignment is simply a matter of choosing numbers. These are recorded, along with the IP addresses, in Table 12-3. The IP addresses are assigned in Table 12-4.

Table 12-3 *Scenario 12-1, Part A: The Completed IP Subnet and IPX Network Planning Chart*

Location of Subnet/ Network Geographically	Subnet Mask	Subnet Number	IPX Network
R1 Ethernet	255.255.255.128	163.1.1.128	1
R2 Ethernet	255.255.255.128	163.1.2.128	2
R3 Ethernet	255.255.255.128	163.1.3.128	3
Serial between R1 and R2	255.255.255.128	163.1.12.128	12
Serial between R1 and R3	255.255.255.128	163.1.13.128	13
Serial between R2 and R3	255.255.255.128	163.1.23.128	23
Server 1 internal	N/A	N/A	101
Server 2 internal	N/A	N/A	102
Server 3 internal	N/A	N/A	103

Table 12-4 *Scenario 12-1, Part A: The Completed IP Address Planning Chart*

Host	Address
PC11	163.1.1.211
PC12	163.1.1.212
PC13	163.1.1.213
PC21	163.1.2.221
PC31	163.1.3.231
PC32	163.1.3.232
R1-E0	163.1.1.201

continues

Table 12-4 *Scenario 12-1, Part A: The Completed IP Address Planning Chart (Continued)*

Host	Address
R1-S0	163.1.12.201
R1-S1	163.1.13.201
R2-E0	163.1.2.202
R2-S0	163.1.12.202
R2-S1	163.1.23.202
R3-E0	163.1.3.203
R3-S0	163.1.13.203
R3-S1	163.1.23.203

3 As usual, the access lists can be placed in several areas to achieve the desired function. Also as usual, the criteria for the access list are subject to interpretation. One solution is to filter packets sent from hosts on the Ethernet off R3, filtering them as they enter R1, on either of R1's serial interfaces. If you filter packets in only one direction, applications that require a two-way flow will not successfully communicate. If you filter on both of R1's serial interfaces for inbound traffic, any valid route for the incoming packets will be checked.

4 For the SAP filter, several options also exist; one is shown here. If you stop R2 from adding the SAP for Server 2 to its SAP table, R2 will never advertise that server in a GNS request, nor will Server 3 learn about Server 2's SAPs from R2's SAP updates. So, the plan is to place incoming SAP filters on both serial interfaces on R2, to filter Server 2 from being added to R2's SAP table.

Scenario 12-1, Part B: Configuration

The next step in your job is to deploy the network designed in Scenario 12-1, Part A. Use the solutions for Part A of Scenario 12-1 to help you identify IP and IPX addresses and determine the logic behind the access lists. For Scenario 12-1, Part B, perform the following tasks:

1 Configure IP, IPX, and IP access lists and IPX SAP filters based on the design of Scenario 12-1, Part A.

2 Use RIP as the IP routing protocol.

3 Use PPP as the data link protocol on the link between R2 and R3. Use the default serial encapsulation elsewhere.

Solutions to Scenario 12-1, Part B: Configuration

Examples 12-1, 12-2, and 12-3 show the configurations for Scenario 12-1, Part B, given the criteria in tasks 1, 2, and 3.

Example 12-1 *R1 Configuration*

```
hostname R1
!
ipx routing 0200.1111.1111
!
interface Serial0
 ip address 163.1.12.201 255.255.255.128
 ipx network 12
 ip access-group 83 in
!
interface Serial1
 ip address 163.1.13.201 255.255.255.128
 ipx network 13
 ip access-group 83 in
!
Ethernet0
 ip address 163.1.1.201 255.255.255.128
ipx network 1
!
router rip
network 163.1.0.0
!
access-list 83 deny 163.1.3.128 0.0.0.127
access-list 83 permit any
```

Example 12-2 *R2 Configuration*

```
hostname R2
!
ipx routing 0200.2222.2222
!
interface Serial0
 ip address 163.1.12.202 255.255.255.128
 ipx network 12
 ipx input-sap-filter 1010
!
interface Serial1
 encapsulation ppp
 ip address 163.1.23.202 255.255.255.128
 ipx network 23
 ipx input-sap-filter 1010
!
Ethernet0
 ip address 163.1.2.202 255.255.255.128
 ipx network 2
```

continues

Example 12-2 *R2 Configuration (Continued)*

```
!
router rip
network 163.1.0.0
!
access-list 1010 deny 102
access-list 1010 permit -1
```

Example 12-3 *R3 Configuration*

```
hostname R3
!
ipx routing 0200.3333.3333
!
interface Serial0
 ip address 163.1.13.203 255.255.255.128
 ipx network 13
!
interface Serial1
 encapsulation ppp
 ip address 163.1.23.203 255.255.255.128
 ipx network 23
!
Ethernet0
 ip address 163.1.3.203 255.255.255.128
ipx network 3
!
router rip
network 163.1.0.0
```

Scenario 12-1, Part C: Verification and Questions

The CCNA exam tests you on your memory of the kinds of information you can find in the output of various **show** commands. Using Examples 12-4, 12-5, and 12-6 as references, answer the questions following the examples.

NOTE In the network from which these commands were captured, several administrative settings not mentioned in the scenario were configured. For example, the enable password was configured. Any **show running-config** commands in the examples in this chapter might have other unrelated configurations.

Example 12-4 *Scenario 12-1, Part C: R1* **show** *and* **debug** *Output*

```
R1#show ip interface brief
Interface                IP-Address      OK? Method Status                Protocol
Serial0                  163.1.12.201    YES NVRAM  up                    up
```

Example 12-4 *Scenario 12-1, Part C: R1* **show** *and* **debug** *Output (Continued)*

```
Serial1                 163.1.13.201    YES NVRAM  up                    up
Ethernet0               163.1.1.201     YES NVRAM  up                    up
R1#show access-lists
Standard IP access list 83
    deny   163.1.3.0, wildcard bits 0.0.0.127
    permit any
R1#
R1#debug ipx sap event
IPX service events debugging is on
R1#
IPXSAP: positing update to 1.ffff.ffff.ffff via Ethernet0 (broadcast) (full)
IPXSAP: positing update to 13.ffff.ffff.ffff via Serial1 (broadcast) (full)
IPXSAP: positing update to 12.ffff.ffff.ffff via Serial0 (broadcast) (full)
IPXSAP: positing update to 1.ffff.ffff.ffff via Ethernet0 (broadcast) (full)
R1#undebug all
All possible debugging has been turned off
R1#
R1#debug ipx sap activity
IPX service debugging is on
R1#
IPXSAP: positing update to 13.ffff.ffff.ffff via Serial1 (broadcast) (full)
IPXSAP: Update type 0x2 len 224 src:13.0200.1111.1111 dest:13.ffff.ffff.ffff(452)
 type 0x4, "Server3", 103.0000.0000.0001(451), 4 hops
 type 0x4, "Server1", 101.0000.0000.0001(451), 3 hops
 type 0x4, "Server2", 102.0000.0000.0001(451), 3 hops
IPXSAP: positing update to 12.ffff.ffff.ffff via Serial0 (broadcast) (full)
IPXSAP: Update type 0x2 len 160 src:12.0200.1111.1111 dest:12.ffff.ffff.ffff(452)
 type 0x4, "Server1", 101.0000.0000.0001(451), 3 hops
 type 0x4, "Server2", 102.0000.0000.0001(451), 3 hops
R1#undebug all
All possible debugging has been turned off
R1#
R1#
R1#debug ipx routing event
IPX routing events debugging is on
R1#
IPXRIP: positing full update to 1.ffff.ffff.ffff via Ethernet0 (broadcast)
IPXRIP: positing full update to 13.ffff.ffff.ffff via Serial1 (broadcast)
IPXRIP: positing full update to 12.ffff.ffff.ffff via Serial0 (broadcast)
IPXRIP: 13 FFFFFFFF not added, entry in table is static/connected/internal
IPXRIP: 12 FFFFFFFF not added, entry in table is static/connected/internal
IPXRIP: positing full update to 1.ffff.ffff.ffff via Ethernet0 (broadcast)
R1#undebug all
All possible debugging has been turned off
R1#
R1#debug ipx routing activity
IPX routing debugging is on
R1#
IPXRIP: update from 1.0000.0c89.b130
    102 in 2 hops, delay 2
    101 in 2 hops, delay 2
IPXRIP: positing full update to 13.ffff.ffff.ffff via Serial1 (broadcast)
```

continues

Example 12-4 *Scenario 12-1, Part C: R1* **show** *and* **debug** *Output (Continued)*

```
IPXRIP: src=13.0200.1111.1111, dst=13.ffff.ffff.ffff, packet sent
    network 103, hops 4,  delay 14
    network 23, hops 2,  delay 13
    network 2, hops 3,  delay 8
    network 101, hops 3,  delay 8
    network 102, hops 3,  delay 8
    network 1, hops 1,  delay 7
    network 12, hops 1,  delay 7
IPXRIP: positing full update to 12.ffff.ffff.ffff via Serial0 (broadcast)
IPXRIP: src=12.0200.1111.1111, dst=12.ffff.ffff.ffff, packet sent
    network 3, hops 2,  delay 13
    network 2, hops 3,  delay 8
  network 101, hops 3,  delay 8
network 102, hops 3,  delay 8
    network 1, hops 1,  delay 7
    network 13, hops 1,  delay 7
IPXRIP: update from 12.0200.2222.2222
    103 in 3 hops, delay 8
IPXRIP: 13 FFFFFFFF not added, entry in table is static/connected/internal
    13 in 2 hops, delay 13
    3 in 2 hops, delay 13
    23 in 1 hops, delay 7
    2 in 1 hops, delay 7
IPXRIP: update from 13.0200.3333.3333
    103 in 4 hops, delay 14
IPXRIP: 12 FFFFFFFF not added, entry in table is static/connected/internal
    12 in 2 hops, delay 13
    3 in 1 hops, delay 7
    2 in 2 hops, delay 13
    23 in 1 hops, delay 7
IPXRIP: positing full update to 1.ffff.ffff.ffff via Ethernet0 (broadcast)
IPXRIP: src=1.0000.0ccf.21cd, dst=1.ffff.ffff.ffff, packet sent
    network 103, hops 4,  delay 9
    network 3, hops 2,  delay 8
    network 23, hops 2,  delay 8
    network 13, hops 1,  delay 2
    network 12, hops 1,  delay 2
IPXRIP: update from 1.0000.0c89.b130
    102 in 2 hops, delay 2
    101 in 2 hops, delay 2
    2 in 2 hops, delay 2

R1#undebug all
All possible debugging has been turned off
R1#
R1#debug ip rip events
RIP event debugging is on
R1#
RIP: received v1 update from 163.1.13.203 on Serial1
RIP: Update contains 4 routes
RIP: sending v1 update to 255.255.255.255 via Serial0 (163.1.12.201)
RIP: Update contains 4 routes
```

Example 12-4 *Scenario 12-1, Part C: R1* **show** *and* **debug** *Output (Continued)*

```
RIP: Update queued
RIP: Update sent via Serial0
RIP: sending v1 update to 255.255.255.255 via Serial1 (163.1.13.201)
RIP: Update contains 4 routes
RIP: Update queued
RIP: Update sent via Serial1
RIP: sending v1 update to 255.255.255.255 via Ethernet0 (163.1.1.201)
RIP: Update contains 7 routes
RIP: Update queued
RIP: Update sent via Ethernet0

RIP: received v1 update from 163.1.12.202 on Serial0
RIP: Update contains 4 routes
R1#undebug all
All possible debugging has been turned off
R1#
R1#debug ip rip
RIP protocol debugging is on
R1#
RIP: received v1 update from 163.1.12.202 on Serial0
     163.1.2.128 in 1 hops
     163.1.3.128 in 2 hops
     163.1.23.128 in 1 hops
     163.1.23.203 in 1 hops
RIP: received v1 update from 163.1.13.203 on Serial1
     163.1.2.128 in 2 hops
     163.1.3.128 in 1 hops
     163.1.23.128 in 1 hops
     163.1.23.202 in 1 hops
RIP: sending v1 update to 255.255.255.255 via Serial0 (163.1.12.201)
     subnet  163.1.3.128, metric 2
     subnet  163.1.1.128, metric 1
     subnet  163.1.13.128, metric 1
     host    163.1.23.202, metric 2
RIP: sending v1 update to 255.255.255.255 via Serial1 (163.1.13.201)
     subnet  163.1.2.128, metric 2
     subnet  163.1.1.128, metric 1
     subnet  163.1.12.128, metric 1
     host    163.1.23.203, metric 2
RIP: sending v1 update to 255.255.255.255 via Ethernet0 (163.1.1.201)
     subnet  163.1.2.128, metric 2
     subnet  163.1.3.128, metric 2
     subnet  163.1.12.128, metric 1
     subnet  163.1.13.128, metric 1
     subnet  163.1.23.128, metric 2
     host    163.1.23.203, metric 2
     host    163.1.23.202, metric 2

R1#undebug all
All possible debugging has been turned off
R1#
```

Example 12-5 *Scenario 12-1, Part C: R2* **show** *and* **debug** *Output*

```
R2#show interface
Serial0 is up, line protocol is up
  Hardware is HD64570
  Internet address is 163.1.12.202/25
  MTU 1500 bytes, BW 1544 Kbit, DLY 20000 usec,
     reliability 255/255, txload 1/255, rxload 1/255
  Encapsulation HDLC, loopback not set
  Keepalive set (10 sec)
  Last input never, output never, output hang never
  Last clearing of "show interface" counters never
  Input queue: 0/75/0/0 (size/max/drops/flushes); Total output drops: 0
  Queueing strategy: weighted fair
  Output queue: 0/1000/64/0 (size/max total/threshold/drops)
     Conversations  0/0/256 (active/max active/max total)
     Reserved Conversations 0/0 (allocated/max allocated)
     Available Bandwidth 1158 kilobits/sec
  5 minute input rate 0 bits/sec, 0 packets/sec
  5 minute output rate 0 bits/sec, 0 packets/sec
     1242 packets input, 98477 bytes, 0 no buffer
     Received 898 broadcasts, 0 runts, 0 giants, 0 throttles
     0 input errors, 0 CRC, 0 frame, 0 overrun, 0 ignored, 0 abort
     1249 packets output, 91395 bytes, 0 underruns
     0 output errors, 0 collisions, 2 interface resets
     0 output buffer failures, 0 output buffers swapped out
     12 carrier transitions
     DCD=up  DSR=up  DTR=up  RTS=up  CTS=up
Serial1 is up, line protocol is up
  Hardware is HD64570
  Internet address is 163.1.23.202/25
    MTU 1500 bytes, BW 1544 Kbit, DLY 20000 usec,
       reliability 255/255, txload 1/255, rxload 1/255
    Encapsulation PPP, loopback not set
    Keepalive set (10 sec)
    LCP Open
    Open: IPCP, CDPCP
    Last input 00:00:03, output 00:00:03, output hang never
    Last clearing of "show interface" counters 00:00:15
    Input queue: 0/75/0/0 (size/max/drops/flushes); Total output drops: 0
    Queueing strategy: weighted fair
    Output queue: 0/1000/64/0 (size/max total/threshold/drops)
       Conversations  0/1/256 (active/max active/max total)
       Reserved Conversations 0/0 (allocated/max allocated)
       Available Bandwidth 1158 kilobits/sec
  5 minute input rate 0 bits/sec, 0 packets/sec
  5 minute output rate 0 bits/sec, 0 packets/sec
     1654 packets input, 90385 bytes, 0 no buffer
     Received 1644 broadcasts, 0 runts, 0 giants, 0 throttles
     0 input errors, 0 CRC, 0 frame, 0 overrun, 0 ignored, 0 abort
     1674 packets output, 96130 bytes, 0 underruns
     0 output errors, 0 collisions, 8 interface resets
     0 output buffer failures, 0 output buffers swapped out
     13 carrier transitions
```

Example 12-5 *Scenario 12-1, Part C: R2* **show** *and* **debug** *Output (Continued)*

```
     DCD=up  DSR=up  DTR=up  RTS=up  CTS=up
Ethernet0 is up, line protocol is up
  Hardware is MCI Ethernet, address is 0000.0c89.b170 (bia 0000.0c89.b170)
  Internet address is 163.1.2.202, subnet mask is 255.255.255.128
    MTU 1500 bytes, BW 10000 Kbit, DLY 1000 usec,
     reliability 255/255, txload 1/255, rxload 1/255
  Encapsulation ARPA, loopback not set, keepalive set (10 sec)
  ARP type: ARPA, ARP Timeout 4:00:00
Last input 00:00:00, output 00:00:04, output hang never
  Last clearing of "show interface" counters never
  Queuing strategy: fifo
  Output queue 0/40, 0 drops; input queue 0/75, 0 drops
  5 minute input rate 0 bits/sec, 0 packets/sec
  5 minute output rate 0 bits/sec, 0 packets/sec
     2274 packets input, 112381 bytes, 0 no buffer
     Received 1913 broadcasts, 0 runts, 0 giants, 0 throttles
     0 input errors, 0 CRC, 0 frame, 0 overrun, 0 ignored, 0 abort
     863 packets output, 110146 bytes, 0 underruns
     0 output errors, 0 collisions, 2 interface resets
     0 output buffer failures, 0 output buffers swapped out
     6 transitions

R2#show ipx interface brief
Interface          IPX Network Encapsulation Status                 IPX State
Serial0            12          HDLC          up                     [up]
Serial1            23          PPP           up                     [up]
Ethernet0          2           SAP           up                     [up]

R2#show ipx route
Codes: C - Connected primary network,    c - Connected secondary network
       S - Static, F - Floating static, L - Local (internal), W - IPXWAN
       R - RIP, E - EIGRP, N - NLSP, X - External, A - Aggregate
       s - seconds, u - uses

9 Total IPX routes. Up to 1 parallel paths and 16 hops allowed.

No default route known.

C          2 (SAP),           E0
C         12 (HDLC),          Se0
C         23 (PPP),           Se1
R          1 [07/01] via       12.0200.1111.1111,   59s, Se0
R          3 [07/01] via       23.0200.3333.3333,    5s, Se1
R         13 [07/01] via       23.0200.3333.3333,    5s, Se1
R        101 [08/03] via       12.0200.1111.1111,    0s, Se0
R        102 [08/03] via       12.0200.1111.1111,    0s, Se0
R        103 [02/02] via        2.0000.0cac.70ef,   21s, E0

R2#show ip protocol
Routing Protocol is "rip"
  Sending updates every 30 seconds, next due in 6 seconds
  Invalid after 180 seconds, hold down 180, flushed after 240
```

continues

Example 12-5 *Scenario 12-1, Part C: R2* **show** *and* **debug** *Output (Continued)*

```
  Outgoing update filter list for all interfaces is not set
  Incoming update filter list for all interfaces is not set
  Redistributing: rip
   Default version control: send version 1, receive any version
    Interface        Send  Recv   Key-chain
    Serial0           1     1 2
    Serial1           1     1 2
    Ethernet0         1     1 2
  Automatic network summarization is in effect
  Maximum path: 4
Routing for Networks:
    163.1.0.0
  Routing Information Sources:
    Gateway         Distance      Last Update
    163.1.13.201         120      00:00:02
    163.1.23.202         120      00:00:09
  Distance: (default is 120)

R2#show ipx servers
Codes: S - Static, P - Periodic, E - EIGRP, N - NLSP, H - Holddown, + = detail
3 Total IPX Servers

Table ordering is based on routing and server info

   Type Name                       Net     Address    Port     Route Hops Itf
P     4 Server3                    103.0000.0000.0001:0451      2/02   2  E0
P     4 Server1                    101.0000.0000.0001:0451      8/03   3  Se0
P     4 Server2                    102.0000.0000.0001:0451      8/03   3  Se0
```

Example 12-6 *Scenario 12-1, Part C: R3* **show** *and* **debug** *Output*

```
R3#show running-config
Building configuration...

Current configuration : 888 bytes
!
version 12.2
service timestamps debug uptime
service timestamps log uptime
no service password-encryption
!
hostname R3
!
enable secret 5 $1$J3Fz$QaEYNIiI2aMu.3Ar.q0Xm.
!
ip subnet-zero
no ip domain-lookup
!
ipx routing 0200.3333.3333
!
interface Serial0
```

Example 12-6 *Scenario 12-1, Part C: R3* **show** *and* **debug** *Output (Continued)*

```
 ip address 163.1.13.203 255.255.255.128
 ipx network 13
 no fair-queue
!
interface Serial1
 ip address 163.1.23.203 255.255.255.128
 encapsulation ppp
 ipx network 23
!
interface Ethernet0
 ip address 163.1.3.203 255.255.255.128
 ipx network 3

!
router rip
 network 163.1.0.0
!
ip classless
no ip http server
!
!
!
!
line con 0
 password cisco
 login
line aux 0
line vty 0 4
 password cisco
 login
!
end

R3#show ip arp
Protocol  Address          Age (min)  Hardware Addr   Type   Interface
Internet  163.1.3.203             -   0000.0c89.b1b0  SNAP   Ethernet0

R3#show ip route
Codes: C - connected, S - static, I - IGRP, R - RIP, M - mobile, B - BGP
       D - EIGRP, EX - EIGRP external, O - OSPF, IA - OSPF inter area
       N1 - OSPF NSSA external type 1, N2 - OSPF NSSA external type 2
       E1 - OSPF external type 1, E2 - OSPF external type 2, E - EGP
       i - IS-IS, L1 - IS-IS level-1, L2 - IS-IS level-2, ia - IS-IS inter area
       * - candidate default, U - per-user static route, o - ODR
       P - periodic downloaded static route

Gateway of last resort is not set

     163.1.0.0/16 is variably subnetted, 7 subnets, 2 masks
R       163.1.2.128/25 [120/1] via 163.1.23.202, 00:00:22, Serial1
C       163.1.3.128/25 is directly connected, Ethernet0
R       163.1.1.128/25 [120/1] via 163.1.13.201, 00:00:28, Serial0
```

continues

Example 12-6 *Scenario 12-1, Part C: R3* **show** *and* **debug** *Output (Continued)*

```
R       163.1.12.128/25 [120/1] via 163.1.13.201, 00:00:28, Serial0
                        [120/1] via 163.1.23.202, 00:00:22, Serial1
C       163.1.13.128/25 is directly connected, Serial0
C       163.1.23.128/25 is directly connected, Serial1
C       163.1.23.202/32 is directly connected, Serial1

R3#trace 163.1.13.203


Type escape sequence to abort.
Tracing the route to 163.1.13.203

  1 163.1.13.201 16 msec 16 msec 16 msec
  2 163.1.13.203 44 msec *  32 msec

R3#ping 163.1.13.203

Type escape sequence to abort.
Sending 5, 100-byte ICMP Echos to 163.1.13.203, timeout is 2 seconds:
!!!!!
Success rate is 100 percent (5/5), round-trip min/avg/max = 64/66/68 ms

R3#ping 13.0200.3333.3333

Type escape sequence
 to abort.
Sending 5, 100-byte IPX Cisco Echoes to 13.0200.3333.3333, timeout is 2 seconds:
!!!!!
Success rate is 100 percent (5/5), round-trip min/avg/max = 68/69/72 ms
```

Answer the following questions. Use Examples 12-4, 12-5, and 12-6 as references when the question refers directly to this scenario:

1. Describe how the switches choose the root of the spanning tree.
2. If Switch1 becomes the root, and if all interface costs are equal on all interfaces on all switches, which ports are considered root ports?
3. If Switch3 blocks on port E1 and then later Switch2's E0 port fails, what notifies Switch3 so that it can forward on its E1 port? What interim spanning tree states is E1 in before it forwards?
4. Describe the contents of an IP RIP update from R1 to R3. What **debug** command options provide the details of what is in the RIP update?
5. Describe the contents of an IPX RIP update from R1 to R2. What **debug** command options provide the details of what is in the IPX RIP update?
6. What command tells you the contents of the ARP cache? Does it contain IP as well as IPX addresses?

7 What commands list the routing metrics used for IP subnets? What about for IPX networks?

8 What command is used to find the path a packet would take from R3 to 163.1.1.1?

9 What **show** command identifies which routes were learned with IP RIP? What about with IPX RIP? What in the command identifies these routing protocols?

10 What **show** command lists SAP information in the router?

11 What **debug** command options create debug messages with the details of the SAP updates? Which options just provide messages referring to the fact that an update is sent, without listing the details?

12 What **debug** command options provide IP RIP update details?

13 Imagine that R3's E0 interface needs to use a new IP address and mask (10.1.1.1, 255.255.255.0). If the user is in user mode, what steps are necessary to change the IP address?

14 When in privileged mode, the user remembers that the IP RIP configuration should be updated, based on the change in the previous question. List the steps necessary to make this change.

15 If an EXEC command you cannot recall begins with the letter C, how can you get help to list all commands that start with C? List the steps, assuming that you are in privileged mode.

16 Name the two commands to list the currently used configuration in a router.

17 Name the two commands to list the configuration that will be used the next time the router is reloaded.

18 What does CDP stand for?

19 Define the metric used by IPX RIP.

20 What does GNS stand for? What role does R2 play in the GNS process? What about R3?

Solutions to Scenario 12-1, Part C: Verification and Questions

The answers to the questions for Scenario 12-1, Part C are as follows:

1 Each bridge and switch sends a BPDU claiming to be the root. The bridge or switch with the lowest bridge priority—or, if a tie occurs, the bridge or switch with the lowest value for root bridge ID—is considered the root.

2 Because all port costs are equal, Switch2 gets BPDUs with a lower cost in E1/0. Likewise, Switch3 receives BPDUs with a lower cost on its E1/0 port. Therefore, each switch considers its E1/0 port to be its root port. This port is placed in a forwarding state.

3 Switch3 reacts after Switch2's MaxAge time expires and Switch2 stops sending BPDU messages to its E1 (the Ethernet segment that Switch2 and Switch3 have in common). Switch3 then transitions its E1 port to listening state, then to learning state, and finally to forwarding state.

4 The **debug ip rip** command provides detailed RIP debug output. The **debug ip rip event** command shows summary information about the same updates. An example of each is shown in Example 12-4. This example shows four routes being described in the update to R3. One of the routes (appropriately) missing in the update is 163.1.13.128, which is the subnet on the serial link between R1 and R3. The other (appropriately) missing route is the route to 163.1.3.128. Thus, R1's best route to that subnet is through R3. Split-horizon rules prevent either route from being advertised.

5 The command **debug ipx routing activity** provides the detailed IPX RIP debug output. This output is shown in Example 12-4. Two routes from R1's routing table are not included in the update—namely, networks 12 and 2. Network 12 is on the common serial link, and R1's route to network 2 points through R2. Both networks are not included due to split-horizon rules.

6 The **show ip arp** command (refer to Example 12-6) contains only MAC and IP addresses, not IPX addresses, because IPX does not use a concept like ARP on LANs.

7 The **show ip route** and **show ipx route** commands list the metric values (refer to Examples 12-5 and 12-6). The metric value for each IP subnet is the second of the two numbers inside brackets. Two IPX metrics are located between brackets for IPX routes: the number of timer ticks and the number of hops.

8 The **trace 163.1.1.1** command would be used (refer to Example 12-6).

9 The **show ip route** and **show ipx route** commands identify the source of the routing information (refer to Examples 12-5 and 12-6). The source of the routing information is coded in a field on the left side of the output line and is based on the legend of such codes that appear at the beginning of the command output before the actual routing table entries are listed.

10 The **show ipx servers** command lists the SAP table (refer to Example 12-5).

11 The **debug ipx sap events** command just displays a message when an update is sent, with no details about the update's contents. The **debug ipx sap activity** command displays the details of what is sent in the update (refer to Example 12-4).

12 The **debug ip rip** command displays the details of what is sent in the update (refer to Example 12-4).

13 Use the following steps:

```
R3> enable
password: password
R3#configure terminal
R3(config)#interface ethernet 0
R3(config-if)#ip address 10.1.1.1 255.255.255.0
R3(config)#Ctrl-Z
R3#
```

14 Use the following steps:

```
R3#configure terminal
R3(config)#router rip
R3(config-router)#network 10.0.0.0
R3(config)#Ctrl-Z
R3#
```

15 Use the following steps:

```
R3#c?
clear  clock  configure  connect  copy

R3#c
```

16 **show running-config** and **write terminal** would be used.

17 **show startup-config** and **show config** would be used.

18 CDP stands for Cisco Discovery Protocol.

19 The primary metric is a counter of timer ticks. If two routes to the same network tie with the ticks metric, the hop count is considered.

20 GNS stands for Get Nearest Server. Any router can respond to GNS requests, which are issued by clients. Both R2 and R3 reply by default. R2's response is unlikely to be used because its GNS delay ensures that its reply is slower than the server on the same Ethernet.

Scenario 12-2

Scenario 12-2 uses the familiar Frame Relay network with three routers and a full mesh of virtual circuits. Some planning exercises begin the scenario (Scenario 12-2, Part A), followed by configuration (Scenario 12-2, Part B). Finally, a series of questions, some based on **show** and **debug** command output, finish the scenario (Scenario 12-2, Part C).

Scenario 12-2, Part A: Planning

Your job is to deploy a new network with three sites, as shown in Figure 12-3. The decision to use Frame Relay has already been made, and the products have been chosen. For Part A of this scenario, perform the following tasks:

1. Subnet planning has been completed. Before implementation, you are responsible for providing a list for the local LAN administrators defining the IP addresses that they can assign to hosts. Using Table 12-5, derive the subnet numbers and broadcast addresses, and define the range of valid IP addresses. A static mask of 255.255.255.192 is used on all subnets.

2. PC11 and PC12 use different IPX encapsulations, as do PC21 and PC22. Figure 12-4 shows the types of headers used by each PC. Plan the encapsulation types to be used, including the correct keywords used in the Cisco IOS software.

3. Plan the IPX network numbers to be used. Use Table 12-6 to record the information.

Figure 12-3 *Scenario 12-2 Network Diagram*

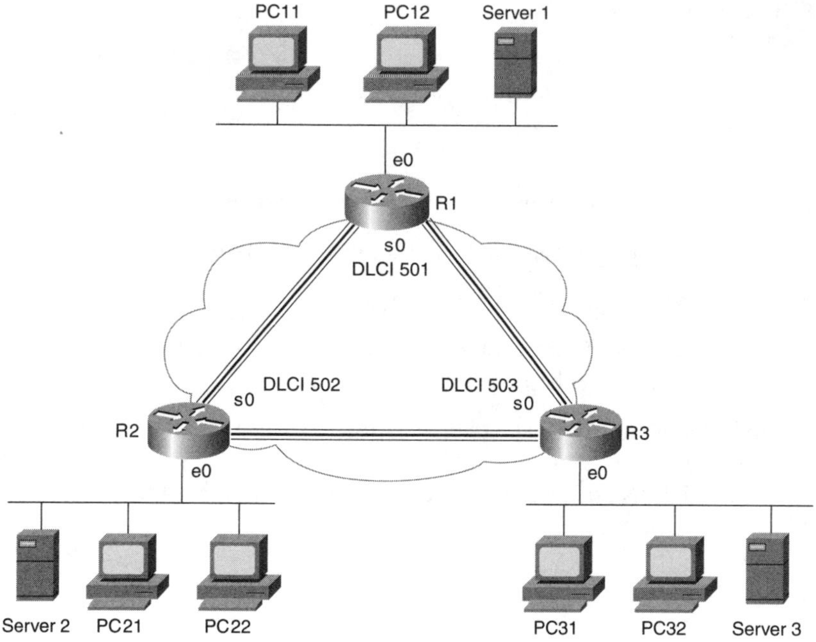

Figure 12-4 *Scenario 12-2, Part A: IPX Encapsulations*

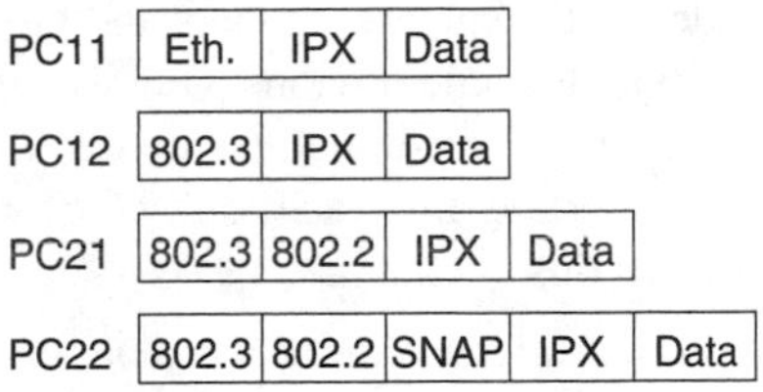

Table 12-5 *Scenario 12-2, Part A: IP Subnet Planning Chart, Mask 255.255.255.192*

Router Interface	IP Address	Subnet Number	Subnet Broadcast Address	Range of Valid Addresses
R1 E0	168.11.11.101			
R2 E0	168.11.12.102			
R3 E0	168.11.13.103			
R1 S0	168.11.123.201			
R2 S0	168.11.123.202			
R3 S0	168.11.123.203			

Table 12-6 *Scenario 12-2, Part A: IPX Network Number Planning Chart*

Location of Network	IPX Network
Attached to R1 E0	
Attached to R2 E0	
Attached to R3 E0	
Frame Relay	
Server 1 Internal	
Server 2 Internal	
Server 3 Internal	

Solutions to Scenario 12-2, Part A: Planning

1 The first task is to derive the subnet numbers and broadcast addresses, so the assignable addresses in each subnet become obvious. One important item is that the three Frame Relay interfaces are in the same subnet, which is a clue that subinterfaces will not be used and that the Frame Relay interfaces will be treated as a single network. Table 12-7 provides the answers to this question.

Table 12-7 *Scenario 12-2, Part A: IP Subnet and IPX Network Planning Chart*

Router Interface	IP Address	Subnet Number	Subnet Broadcast Address	Range of Valid Addresses
R1 E0	168.11.11.101	168.11.11.64	168.11.11.127	65 to 126 in last octet
R2 E0	168.11.12.102	168.11.12.64	168.11.12.127	65 to 126 in last octet
R3 E0	168.11.13.103	168.11.13.64	168.11.13.127	65 to 126 in last octet
R1 S0	168.11.123.201	168.11.123.192	168.11.123.255	193 to 254 in last octet
R2 S0	168.11.123.202	168.11.123.192	168.11.123.255	193 to 254 in last octet
R3 S0	168.11.123.203	168.11.123.192	168.11.123.255	193 to 254 in last octet

2 The second planning item requires remembering the four encapsulations for IPX on Ethernet. The important task here is to correlate the headers used by the devices to the correct name used by Cisco in the encapsulation command. Table 12-8 summarizes the encapsulations for the four PCs.

Table 12-8 *Scenario 12-2, Part A: IPX Encapsulations*

PC	Cisco IOS Software Encapsulation
PC11	ARPA
PC12	Novell-ether
PC21	SAP
PC22	SNAP

3 Choosing IPX network numbers is not a particularly challenging task. However, realizing that two network numbers are needed on R1's E0 and on R2's E0 is the hidden part of the objective. As long as your network numbers are not duplicated, and as long as you planned for two IPX networks for the two aforementioned Ethernet interfaces, any network numbers are fine. Table 12-9 lists the network numbers that are used as the basis of the configuration in Scenario 12-2, Part B.

Table 12-9 *Scenario 12-2, Part A: IPX Network Number Planning Chart—Completed*

Host	Address
R1 E0	110 (ARPA)
R1 E0	111 (Novell-ether)
R2 E0	120 (SAP)
R2 E0	121 (SNAP)
R3 E0	130
Frame Relay	123
Server 1 internal	101
Server 2 internal	102
Server 3 internal	103

Scenario 12-2, Part B: Configuration

The next step in your job is to deploy the network designed in Scenario 12-2, Part A. Use the solutions to Scenario 12-2, Part A to help you identify IP and IPX addresses and the encapsulations to be used. For Scenario 12-2, Part B, perform the following tasks:

1. Configure IP and IPX to be routed. Use IP IGRP and IPX RIP as routing protocols. Use IGRP process-id 1.
2. Use secondary IPX addresses to accommodate the multiple IPX encapsulation types described in Scenario 12-2, Part A.
3. Configure Frame Relay without the use of subinterfaces. R1's attached switch uses LMI type ANSI. Cisco encapsulation should be used for all routers.
4. Assume that, after you installed the network, you were forced to disable IP IGRP on R2. Define the required IP static routes to allow hosts on all three Ethernets to communicate. (This is unlikely to happen in real life; it's just an excuse to review IP static routes!)
5. Assume that, after you installed the network, you were forced to disable Inverse ARP on R2. Define static mappings as necessary for all hosts to communicate.

Solutions to Scenario 12-2, Part B: Configuration

Examples 12-7, 12-8, and 12-9 show the configurations for tasks 1, 2, and 3.

Example 12-7 *R1 Configuration*

```
ipx routing 0200.aaaa.aaaa
!
interface serial0
encapsulation frame-relay
ip address  168.11.123.201  255.255.255.192
ipx network  123
frame-relay interface-dlci 502
frame-relay interface-dlci 503
!
interface ethernet 0
ip address  168.11.11.101  255.255.255.192
!
ipx network  110 encapsulation arpa
ipx network  111 encapsulation novell-ether secondary
!
router igrp 1
network 168.11.0.0
```

Example 12-8 *R2 Configuration*

```
ipx routing 0200.bbbb.bbbb
!
interface serial0
encapsulation frame-relay
ip address  168.11.123.202  255.255.255.192
ipx network  123
frame-relay interface-dlci 501
frame-relay interface-dlci 503
!
interface ethernet 0
ip address  168.11.12.102  255.255.255.192
ipx network  120 encapsulation sap
ipx network  121 encapsulation snap secondary
!
router igrp 1
network 168.11.0.0
```

Example 12-9 *R3 Configuration*

```
ipx routing 0200.cccc.cccc
!
interface serial0
encapsulation frame-relay
ip address  168.11.123.203  255.255.255.192
ipx network  123
frame-relay interface-dlci 501
frame-relay interface-dlci 502
!
interface ethernet 0
```

Example 12-9 *R3 Configuration (Continued)*

```
ip address  168.11.13.103  255.255.255.192
ipx network  130
!
router igrp 1
network 168.11.0.0
```

For task 4 in Scenario 12-2, Part B, static routes need to be defined in all three routers. R2 needs routes to the two LAN-based subnets at the other sites. Likewise, R1 and R3 need routes to 168.11.12.64 (Ethernet off R2). Example 12-10 lists the routes in all three routers.

Example 12-10 *Static Routes*

```
R1(config)#ip route 168.11.12.64 255.255.255.192 168.11.123.202

R2(config)#ip route 168.11.11.64 255.255.255.192 168.11.123.201
R2(config)#ip route 168.11.13.64 255.255.255.192 168.11.123.203

R3(config)#ip route 168.11.12.64 255.255.255.192 168.11.123.202
```

Finally, task 5 requests that static **frame-relay map** commands be configured. The **map** commands are necessary for each routed protocol. Also, the **broadcast** keyword is needed so that packets that would normally be broadcast, such as routing updates, will be sent as unicasts across each VC for each protocol. Example 12-11 lists the additional commands.

Example 12-11 frame-relay map *Commands*

```
R1(config)#frame-relay map ip 168.11.123.202 502 broadcast
R1(config)#frame-relay map ipx 123.0200.bbbb.bbbb 502 broadcast

R2(config)#frame-relay map ip 168.11.123.201 501 broadcast
R2(config)#frame-relay map ip 168.11.123.203 503 broadcast
R2(config)#frame-relay map ipx 123.0200.aaaa.aaaa 501 broadcast
R2(config)#frame-relay map ipx 123.0200.cccc.cccc 503 broadcast

R3(config)#frame-relay map ip 168.11.123.202 502 broadcast
R3(config)#frame-relay map ipx 123.0200.bbbb.bbbb 502 broadcast
```

Scenario 12-2, Part C: Verification and Questions

The CCNA exam tests your memory of the kinds of information you can find in the output of various **show** commands. Using Examples 12-12, 12-13, and 12-14 as references, answer the questions following the examples.

NOTE In the network from which these commands were captured, several administrative settings not mentioned in the scenario were configured. For example, the enable password was configured. Any **show running-config** commands in the examples might have other unrelated configurations.

Example 12-12 *Scenario 12-2, Part C: R1* **show** *and* **debug** *Output*

```
R1#show ipx interface brief
Interface            IPX Network Encapsulation Status                 IPX State
Serial0              123         FRAME-RELAY   up                     [up]
Serial1              unassigned  not config'd  administratively down  n/a
Ethernet0            110         ARPA          up                     [up]
Ethernet0            111         Novell-ether  up                     [up]

R1#show ip interface brief
Interface              IP-Address      OK? Method Status                Protocol
Serial0                168.11.123.201  YES NVRAM  up                    up
Serial1                unassigned      YES unset  administratively down down
Ethernet0              168.11.11.101   YES NVRAM  up                    up

R1#debug ipx sap activity
IPX service debugging is on
R1#
IPXSAP: positing update to 110.ffff.ffff.ffff via Ethernet0 (broadcast) (full)
IPXSAP: Update type 0x2 len 96 src:110.0000.0ccf.21cd dest:110.ffff.ffff.ffff(452)
 type 0x4, "Server3", 103.0000.0000.0001(451), 4 hops
IPXSAP: positing update to 111.ffff.ffff.ffff via Ethernet0 (broadcast) (full)
IPXSAP: Update type 0x2 len 224 src:111.0000.0ccf.21cd dest:111.ffff.ffff.ffff(452)
 type 0x4, "Server3", 103.0000.0000.0001(451), 4 hops
 type 0x4, "Server1", 101.0000.0000.0001(451), 3 hops
 type 0x4, "Server2", 102.0000.0000.0001(451), 3 hops
IPXSAP: Response (in) type 0x2 len 160 src:110.0000.0c89.b130
dest:110.ffff.ffff.ffff(452)
 type 0x4, "Server2", 102.0000.0000.0001(451), 2 hops
 type 0x4, "Server1", 101.0000.0000.0001(451), 2 hops
IPXSAP: positing update to 123.ffff.ffff.ffff via Serial0 (broadcast) (full)
IPXSAP: Update type 0x2 len 160 src:123.0200.aaaa.aaaa dest:123.ffff.ffff.ffff(452)
 type 0x4, "Server1", 101.0000.0000.0001(451), 3 hops
 type 0x4, "Server2", 102.0000.0000.0001(451), 3 hops
IPXSAP: Response (in) type 0x2 len 96 src:123.0200.bbbb.bbbb
dest:123.ffff.ffff.ffff(452)
 type 0x4, "Server3", 103.0000.0000.0001(451), 3 hops
R1#undebug all
All possible debugging has been turned off
R1#
R1#debug ipx routing activity
IPX routing debugging is on
R1#
IPXRIP: positing full update to 123.ffff.ffff.ffff via Serial0 (broadcast)
IPXRIP: src=123.0200.aaaa.aaaa, dst=123.ffff.ffff.ffff, packet sent
```

Example 12-12 *Scenario 12-2, Part C: R1* **show** *and* **debug** *Output (Continued)*

```
    network 555, hops 2,  delay 8
    network 101, hops 3,  delay 8
    network 102, hops 3,  delay 8
    network 111, hops 1,  delay 7
    network 110, hops 1,  delay 7
IPXRIP: update from 123.0200.3333.3333
    130 in 1 hops, delay 7
IPXRIP: update from 123.0200.bbbb.bbbb
    444 in 2 hops, delay 8
    103 in 3 hops, delay 8
    121 in 1 hops, delay 7
    120 in 1 hops, delay 7
IPXRIP: positing full update to 110.ffff.ffff.ffff via Ethernet0 (broadcast)
IPXRIP: src=110.0000.0ccf.21cd, dst=110.ffff.ffff.ffff, packet sent
    network 120, hops 2,  delay 8
    network 121, hops 2,  delay 8
    network 103, hops 4,  delay 9
    network 444, hops 3,  delay 9
    network 130, hops 2,  delay 8
    network 111, hops 1,  delay 2
    network 123, hops 1,  delay 2
IPXRIP: positing full update to 111.ffff.ffff.ffff via Ethernet0 (broadcast)
IPXRIP: src=111.0000.0ccf.21cd, dst=111.ffff.ffff.ffff, packet sent
    network 120, hops 2,  delay 8
    network 121, hops 2,  delay 8
    network 103, hops 4,  delay 9
    network 444, hops 3,  delay 9
    network 130, hops 2,  delay 8
    network 555, hops 2,  delay 3
    network 101, hops 3,  delay 3
    network 102, hops 3,  delay 3
    network 110, hops 1,  delay 2
    network 123, hops 1,  delay 2
IPXRIP: update from 110.0000.0c89.b130
    102 in 2 hops, delay 2
    101 in 2 hops, delay 2
    555 in 1 hops, delay 2
R1#
R1#undebug all
All possible debugging has been turned off
R1#
R1#debug ip igrp transactions
IGRP protocol debugging is on
R1#
IGRP: sending update to 255.255.255.255 via Serial0 (168.11.123.201)
      subnet 168.11.123.192, metric=180571
      subnet 168.11.11.64, metric=688
      subnet 168.11.13.64, metric=180634
      subnet 168.11.12.64, metric=180634
IGRP: sending update to 255.255.255.255 via Ethernet0 (168.11.11.101)
      subnet 168.11.123.192, metric=180571
      subnet 168.11.13.64, metric=180634
```

continues

Example 12-12 *Scenario 12-2, Part C: R1* **show** *and* **debug** *Output (Continued)*

```
      subnet 168.11.12.64, metric=180634
IGRP: received update from 168.11.123.202 on Serial0
      subnet 168.11.123.192, metric 182571 (neighbor 180571)
      subnet 168.11.11.64, metric 182634 (neighbor 180634)
      subnet 168.11.13. 64, metric 182634 (neighbor 180634)
      subnet 168.11.12. 64, metric 180634 (neighbor 688)
IGRP: received update from 168.11.123.203 on Serial0
      subnet 168.11.123.192, metric 182571 (neighbor 8476)
      subnet 168.11.11. 64, metric 182634 (neighbor 8539)
      subnet 168.11.13. 64, metric 180634 (neighbor 688)
      subnet 168.11.12. 64, metric 182634 (neighbor 8539)
IGRP: sending update to 255.255.255.255 via Serial0 (168.11.123.201)
      subnet 168.11.123.192, metric=180571
      subnet 168.11.11. 64, metric=688
      subnet 168.11.13. 64, metric=180634
      subnet 168.11.12. 64, metric=180634
IGRP: sending update to 255.255.255.255 via Ethernet0 (168.11.11.101)
      subnet 168.11.123.192, metric=180571
      subnet 168.11.13. 64, metric=180634
      subnet 168.11.12. 64, metric=180634
R1#undebug all
All possible debugging has been turned off
```

Example 12-13 *Scenario 12-2, Part C: R2* **show** *and* **debug** *Output*

```
R2#show interface
Serial0 is up, line protocol is up
  Hardware is HD64570
  Internet address is 168.11.123.202/26
    MTU 1500 bytes, BW 56 Kbit, DLY 20000 usec,
     reliability 255/255, txload 1/255, rxload 1/255
  Encapsulation FRAME-RELAY, loopback not set, keepalive set (10 sec)
  LMI enq sent  1657, LMI stat recvd 1651, LMI upd recvd 0, DTE LMI up
  LMI enq recvd 0, LMI stat sent  0, LMI upd sent  0
  LMI DLCI 0  LMI type is ANSI Annex D  frame relay DTE
  Broadcast queue 0/64, broadcasts sent/dropped 979/0, interface broadcasts 490
  Last input 00:00:01, output 00:00:01, output hang never
  Last clearing of "show interface" counters never
  Queuing strategy: fifo
  Output queue 0/40, 0 drops; input queue 0/75, 0 drops
  5 minute input rate 0 bits/sec, 0 packets/sec
  5 minute output rate 0 bits/sec, 0 packets/sec
     4479 packets input, 165584 bytes, 0 no buffer
     Received 1 broadcasts, 0 runts, 0 giants, 0 throttles
     0 input errors, 0 CRC, 0 frame, 0 overrun, 0 ignored, 0 abort
     4304 packets output, 154785 bytes, 0 underruns
     0 output errors, 0 collisions, 4 interface resets
     0 output buffer failures, 0 output buffers swapped out
     12 carrier transitions
     DCD=up  DSR=up  DTR=up  RTS=up  CTS=up
Serial1 is administratively down, line protocol is down
```

Example 12-13 *Scenario 12-2, Part C: R2* **show** *and* **debug** *Output (Continued)*

```
  Hardware is HD64570
  MTU 1500 bytes, BW 1544 Kbit, DLY 20000 usec, rely 255/255, load 1/255
  Encapsulation PPP, loopback not set, keepalive set (10 sec)
  LCP Closed
  Closed: CDPCP, LLC2
  Last input never, output never, output hang never
  Last clearing of "show interface" counters never
    Input queue: 0/75/0/0 (size/max/drops/flushes); Total output drops: 0
  Queueing strategy: weighted fair
  Output queue: 0/1000/64/0 (size/max total/threshold/drops)
     Conversations  0/1/256 (active/max active/max total)
     Reserved Conversations 0/0 (allocated/max allocated)
     Available Bandwidth 1158 kilobits/sec
  5 minute input rate 0 bits/sec, 0 packets/sec
  5 minute output rate 0 bits/sec, 0 packets/sec
     0 packets input, 0 bytes, 0 no buffer
     Received 0 broadcasts, 0 runts, 0 giants, 0 throttles
     0 input errors, 0 CRC, 0 frame, 0 overrun, 0 ignored, 0 abort
     0 packets output, 0 bytes, 0 underruns
     0 output errors, 0 collisions, 5 interface resets
     0 output buffer failures, 0 output buffers swapped out
     0 carrier transitions
     DCD=down  DSR=down  DTR=down  RTS=down  CTS=down
Ethernet0 is up, line protocol is up
  Hardware is MCI Ethernet, address is 0000.0c89.b170 (bia 0000.0c89.b170)
  Internet address is 168.11.12.102/26, subnet mask is 255.255.255.192
    MTU 1500 bytes, BW 10000 Kbit, DLY 1000 usec,
      reliability 255/255, txload 1/255, rxload 1/255
  Encapsulation ARPA, loopback not set, keepalive set (10 sec)
  ARP type: ARPA, ARP Timeout 4:00:00
  Last input 00:00:04, output 00:00:04, output hang never
  Last clearing of "show interface" counters never
  Queuing strategy: fifo
  Output queue 0/40, 0 drops; input queue 0/75, 0 drops
  5 minute input rate 0 bits/sec, 0 packets/sec
  5 minute output rate 0 bits/sec, 0 packets/sec
     6519 packets input, 319041 bytes, 0 no buffer
     Received 5544 broadcasts, 0 runts, 0 giants, 0 throttles
     0 input errors, 0 CRC, 0 frame, 0 overrun, 0 ignored, 0 abort
     2055 packets output, 192707 bytes, 0 underruns
     0 output errors, 0 collisions, 2 interface resets
     0 output buffer failures, 0 output buffers swapped out
     6 transitions

R2#show ipx interface brief
Interface            IPX Network Encapsulation Status                 IPX State
Serial0              123         FRAME-RELAY   up                     [up]
Serial1              unassigned  not config'd  administratively down  n/a
Ethernet0            120         SAP           up                     [up]
Ethernet0            121         SNAP          up                     [up]

R2#show ip protocol
```

continues

Example 12-13 *Scenario 12-2, Part C: R2* **show** *and* **debug** *Output (Continued)*

```
Routing Protocol is "igrp 1"
  Sending updates every 90 seconds, next due in 6 seconds
  Invalid after 270 seconds, hold down 280, flushed after 630
  Outgoing update filter list for all interfaces is not set
  Incoming update filter list for all interfaces is not set
  Default networks flagged in outgoing updates
  Default networks accepted from incoming updates
  IGRP metric weight K1=1, K2=0, K3=1, K4=0, K5=0
  IGRP maximum hopcount 100
  IGRP maximum metric variance 1
  Redistributing: igrp 1
  Automatic network summarization is in effect
    maximum path: 4
  Routing for Networks:
    168.11.0.0
  Routing Information Sources:
    Gateway         Distance      Last Update
    168.11.123.201       100        00:00:02
    168.11.123.203       100        00:00:09
  Distance: (default is 100)

R2#show ipx route
Codes: C - Connected primary network,    c - Connected secondary network
       S - Static, F - Floating static, L - Local (internal), W - IPXWAN
       R - RIP, E - EIGRP, N - NLSP, X - External, A - Aggregate
       s - seconds, u - uses

9 Total IPX routes. Up to 1 parallel paths and 16 hops allowed.

No default route known.

C        120 (SAP),            E0
c        121 (SNAP),           E0
C        123 (FRAME-RELAY),    Se0
R        101 [08/03] via       123.0200.aaaa.aaaa,    21s, Se0
R        102 [02/02] via       123.0200.0cac.70ef,    22s, E0
R        103 [08/03] via       120.0000.aaaa.aaaa,    29s, Se0
R        110 [07/01] via       123.0200.aaaa.aaaa,    22s, Se0
R        111 [07/01] via       123.0200.aaaa.aaaa,    22s, Se0
R        130 [07/01] via       123.0200.cccc.cccc,    19s, Se0

R2#show ipx servers
Codes: S - Static, P - Periodic, E - EIGRP, N - NLSP, H - Holddown, + = detail
2 Total IPX Servers

Table ordering is based on routing and server info

   Type Name                     Net      Address      Port        Route Hops Itf
P     4 Server3                  103.0000.0000.0001:0451            8/03    3  Se0
P     4 Server1                  101.0000.0000.0001:0451            8/03    3  Se0
P     4 Server2                  102.0000.0000.0001:0451            2/02    2  E0
```

Example 12-13 *Scenario 12-2, Part C: R2* **show** *and* **debug** *Output (Continued)*

```
R2#show frame-relay pvc

PVC Statistics for interface Serial0 (Frame Relay DTE)

DLCI = 501, DLCI USAGE = LOCAL, PVC STATUS = ACTIVE, INTERFACE = Serial0

  input pkts 780            output pkts 529           in bytes 39602
  out bytes 29260           dropped pkts 0            in FECN pkts 0
  in BECN pkts 0            out FECN pkts 0           out BECN pkts 0
  in DE pkts 0              out DE pkts 0
  out bcast pkts 525         out bcast bytes 28924
  pvc create time 04:36:40, last time pvc status changed 04:34:54
DLCI = 503, DLCI USAGE = LOCAL, PVC STATUS = ACTIVE, INTERFACE = Serial0

  input pkts 481            output pkts 493           in bytes 30896
  out bytes 34392           dropped pkts 0            in FECN pkts 0
  in BECN pkts 0            out FECN pkts 0           out BECN pkts 0
  in DE pkts 0              out DE pkts 0
  out bcast pkts 493         out bcast bytes 34392
  pvc create time 04:36:41, last time pvc status changed 04:34:55

R2#show frame-relay map
Serial0 (up): ipx 123.0200.aaaa.aaaa dlci 501(0x1F5,0x7C50), dynamic,
              broadcast,, status defined, active
Serial0 (up): ipx 123.0200.cccc.cccc dlci 503(0x1F7,0x7C70), dynamic,
              broadcast,, status defined, active
Serial0 (up): ip 168.11.123.201 dlci 501(0x1F5,0x7C50), dynamic,
              broadcast,, status defined, active
Serial0 (up): ip 168.11.123.203 dlci 503(0x1F7,0x7C70), dynamic,
              broadcast,, status defined, active
```

Example 12-14 *Scenario 12-2, Part C: R3* **show** *and* **debug** *Output*

```
R3#show running-config
Building configuration...

Current configuration : 912 bytes
!
version 12.2
service timestamps debug uptime
service timestamps log uptime
no service password-encryption
!
hostname R3
!
enable secret 5 $1$J3Fz$QaEYNIiI2aMu.3Ar.q0Xm.
!
ip subnet-zero
no ip domain-lookup
!
```

continues

Example 12-14 *Scenario 12-2, Part C: R3* **show** *and* **debug** *Output (Continued)*

```
ipx routing 0200.cccc.cccc
!
interface Serial0
 ip address 168.11.123.203 255.255.255.192
 encapsulation frame-relay
 ipx network 123
 no fair-queue
 frame-relay interface-dlci 501
 frame-relay interface-dlci 502
!
interface Serial1
 no ip address
 encapsulation ppp
 shutdown
 clockrate 56000
!
interface Ethernet0
 ip address 168.11.13.103 255.255.255.192
 ipx network 130
 ring-speed 16
!
router igrp 1
 network 168.11.0.0
!
ip classless
no ip http server
!
!
!
!
line con 0
 password cisco
 login
line aux 0
line vty 0 4
 password cisco
 login
!
end

R3#show ip arp
Protocol  Address          Age (min)  Hardware Addr   Type   Interface
Internet  168.11.13.103           -   0000.0c89.b1b0  SNAP   Ethernet0

R3#show ip route
Codes: C - connected, S - static, I - IGRP, R - RIP, M - mobile, B - BGP
       D - EIGRP, EX - EIGRP external, O - OSPF, IA - OSPF inter area
       N1 - OSPF NSSA external type 1, N2 - OSPF NSSA external type 2
       E1 - OSPF external type 1, E2 - OSPF external type 2, E - EGP
       i - IS-IS, L1 - IS-IS level-1, L2 - IS-IS level-2, ia - IS-IS inter area
       * - candidate default, U - per-user static route, o - ODR
       P - periodic downloaded static route
```

Example 12-14 *Scenario 12-2, Part C: R3* **show** *and* **debug** *Output (Continued)*

```
Gateway of last resort is not set

     168.11.0.0/26 is subnetted, 4 subnets
C       168.11.123.192 is directly connected, Serial0
I       168.11.11.64 [100/8539] via 168.11.123.201, 00:00:06, Serial0
C       168.11.13. 64 is directly connected, Ethernet0
I       168.11.12. 64 [100/8539] via 168.11.123.202, 00:00:46, Serial0

R3#ping 168.11.11.80

Type escape sequence to abort.
Sending 5, 100-byte ICMP Echos to 168.11.11.80, timeout is 2 seconds:
!!!!!
Success rate is 100 percent (5/5), round-trip min/avg/max = 76/76/76 ms
R3#trace 168.11.11.80

Type escape sequence to abort.
Tracing the route to 168.11.11.80

  1 168.11.123.201 44 msec 44 msec 44 msec
  2 168.11.11.250 44 msec *  40 msec
R3#show ipx servers
Codes: S - Static, P - Periodic, E - EIGRP, N - NLSP, H - Holddown, + = detail
3 Total IPX Servers

Table ordering is based on routing and server info

   Type Name                        Net     Address    Port     Route Hops Itf
P     4 Server1                     101.0000.0000.0001:0451      8/03   3  Se0
P     4 Server2                     102.0000.0000.0001:0451      8/03   3  Se0
P     4 Server3                     103.0000.0000.0001:0451      2/02   2  E0

R3#show frame-relay map
Serial0 (up): ipx 123.0200.aaaa.aaaa dlci 501(0x1F5,0x7C50), dynamic,
              broadcast,, status defined, active
Serial0 (up): ipx 123.0200.bbbb.bbbb dlci 502(0x1F6,0x7C60), dynamic,
              broadcast,, status defined, active
Serial0 (up): ip 168.11.123.201 dlci 501(0x1F5,0x7C50), dynamic,
              broadcast,, status defined, active
Serial0 (up): ip 168.11.123.202 dlci 502(0x1F6,0x7C60), dynamic,
              broadcast,, status defined, active

R3#show frame-relay lmi

LMI Statistics for interface Serial0 (Frame Relay DTE) LMI TYPE = CISCO
  Invalid Unnumbered info 0         Invalid Prot Disc 0
  Invalid dummy Call Ref 0          Invalid Msg Type 0
  Invalid Status Message 0          Invalid Lock Shift 0
```

continues

Example 12-14 *Scenario 12-2, Part C: R3* **show** *and* **debug** *Output (Continued)*

```
Invalid Information ID 0           Invalid Report IE Len 0
Invalid Report Request 0           Invalid Keep IE Len 0
Num Status Enq. Sent 1677          Num Status msgs Rcvd 1677
Num Update Status Rcvd 0           Num Status Timeouts 0
```

Using Examples 12-12, 12-13, and 12-14 as references, answer the following questions:

1 What command tells you how much time must elapse before the next IP IGRP update is sent by a router?

2 What command shows you a summary of the IP addresses on that router?

3 What **show** command identifies which routes were learned with IP IGRP? What about with IPX RIP? What in the command output identifies these routing protocols?

4 What **show** command lists SAP information in the router?

5 Describe the contents of an IP IGRP update from R1 to R3. What **debug** command options provide the details of what is in the IGRP update?

6 What password is required to move from user mode to privileged mode? What configuration command(s) can be used to set the password that is required?

7 If a serial interface configuration subcommand you cannot recall starts with the letter D, how can you get help to list all commands that start with D? List the steps, assuming that you are in privileged mode.

8 After changing the configuration and moving back to privileged mode, you want to save your configuration. Name the two commands that can be used.

9 List all characters displayed on-screen during the process of getting into configuration mode from privileged mode, changing the host name from R1 to R2, and then getting back into privileged mode.

10 In this network, if setup mode were used to configure the IP addresses on the interface, how would the subnet mask information be entered?

11 If a routing loop occurs so that IP packets destined for 168.11.12.66 are routed between routers continually, what stops the packets from rotating forever? Are any notification messages sent when the routers notice what is happening? If so, what is the message?

12 Describe the role of R1 relating to TCP error recovery for an FTP connection between PC11 and PC21.

13 Define integrated multiprotocol routing.

14 Describe how R2 learns that R1's IP address is 168.11.123.201.

15 What does NBMA stand for?

16 When does IGRP use split-horizon rules on interfaces with Frame Relay encapsulation?

17 What effect does the **no keepalive** interface subcommand have on Frame Relay interfaces?

18 If just the VC between R1 and R3 needed to use encapsulation of **ietf**, what configuration changes would be needed?

19 What command lists the total number of Status Enquiry messages received on a Frame Relay interface?

20 List examples of two ISDN function groups.

21 What type of ISDN channel is used for signaling?

Solutions to Scenario 12-2, Part C: Verification and Questions

The answers to the questions for Scenario 12-2, Part C are as follows:

1 The **show ip protocol** command gives this information (refer to Example 12-13).

2 The **show ip interface brief** command gives this information (refer to Example 12-12).

3 The **show ip route** and **show ipx route** commands list the metric values (refer to Examples 12-5 and 12-6). The metric value for each IP subnet is the second of the two numbers inside brackets. Two IPX metrics are located between brackets for IPX routes: the number of timer ticks and the number of hops.

4 The **show ipx servers** command lists this information (refer to Example 12-14).

5 The **debug ip igrp transaction** command provides debug output with details of the IGRP updates. The output immediately follows the **IGRP: sending update to 255.255.255.255 via Serial0 (168.11.123.201)** message in Example 12-12. Notice that all four routes are advertised, because split horizon is disabled on the serial interface when no subinterfaces are used.

6 The enable password is the required password; the user is prompted after typing the **enable** EXEC command. The **enable** and **enable secret** commands define the password; if both are configured, the **enable secret** password is used.

7 The steps are as follows:

```
R3#configure terminal
R3(config)#interface serial 0
R3(config-if)#D?

dce-terminal-timing-enable  default          delay  description  dialer
dialer-group                down-when-looped dspu   dxi
R3(config-if)#d#Ctrl-Z
R3#
```

8 **write memory** and **copy running-config startup-config** are the two commands that could be used.

9 The on-screen code is as follows:

```
R1#configure terminal
R1(config)#hostname R2
R2(config)#Ctrl-Z
R2#
```

The most important part of this question is to realize that configuration changes are immediate. Notice that the prompt changes immediately after the **hostname** command.

10 Enter the mask information as the number of subnet bits rather than simply typing the mask. In this network, mask 255.255.255.192 implies 6 host bits. A Class B network is used, which implies 16 network bits, leaving 10 subnet bits.

11 The Time To Live (TTL) field in the IP header is decremented by each router. After the number is decremented to 0, the router discards the packet. That router also sends an ICMP TTL-exceeded message to the host that originally sent the packet.

12 The router plays no role in TCP error recovery in this case. The endpoint hosts are responsible for the TCP processing.

13 Integrated multiprotocol routing means that routed protocols IP, IPX, and AppleTalk use a common routing protocol, which consolidates routing updates.

14 R1 uses Inverse ARP to announce its IP and IPX addresses on the serial interface used for Frame Relay. The Inverse ARP message is sent over the VC between the two routers. R2 learns based on receiving the message.

15 NBMA stands for nonbroadcast multiaccess.

16 IGRP uses split horizon on point-to-point subinterfaces only. If multipoint subinterfaces are used, or if no subinterfaces are used, split horizon is off by default.

17 LMI keepalive messages, which flow between the router and the switch, are no longer sent. No keepalive messages pass from router to router.

18 The **frame-relay interface-dlci** command could be changed on Router1 and Router3 to include the keyword **ietf** at the end of the command—for example, **frame-relay interface-dlci 501 ietf** on R3.

19 The **show frame-relay lmi** command lists this information (refer to Example 12-14).

20 NT1, NT2, TE1, TE2, and TA are all function groups.

21 D channels are used for signaling.

Scenario 12-3

Part A of the final review scenario begins with some planning guidelines that include planning IP addresses, IPX network numbers, the location of SAP filters, and the location of IP standard access lists. After you complete Part A, Part B of Scenario 12-3 asks you to configure the three routers to implement the planned design and a few other features. Finally, in Part C of Scenario 12-3, some errors have been introduced into the network, and you are asked to examine router command output to find them. Part C of Scenario 12-3 also lists some questions relating to the user interface and protocol specifications.

Scenario 12-3, Part A: Planning

Your job is to deploy a new network with three sites, as shown in Figure 12-5. The decision to use Frame Relay has already been made, and the products have been chosen. To complete Scenario 12-3, Part A, perform the following tasks:

1. Plan the IP addressing and subnets used in this network. Class B network 170.1.0.0 has been assigned by the NIC. The maximum number of hosts per subnet is 300. Assign IP addresses to the PCs as well. Use Tables 12-10 and 12-11 to record your answers.
2. Plan the IPX network numbers to be used. You can choose the servers' internal network numbers as well. Each LAN should support both SAP and SNAP encapsulations.
3. Plan the location and logic of IP access lists to filter for the following criteria:
   - Access to servers in PC11 and PC12 is allowed for Web and FTP clients from anywhere else.
   - All other traffic to or from PC11 and PC12 is not allowed.
   - No IP traffic between the Ethernets off R2 and R3 is allowed.
   - All other IP traffic between any sites is allowed.
4. Plan the location and logic of SAP filters. Ensure that Server 3 is accessed only by clients on the Ethernet off R2.
5. After choosing your subnet numbers, calculate the broadcast addresses and the range of valid IP addresses in each subnet. Use Table 12-12, if convenient.

Figure 12-5 *Scenario 12-3 Network Diagram*

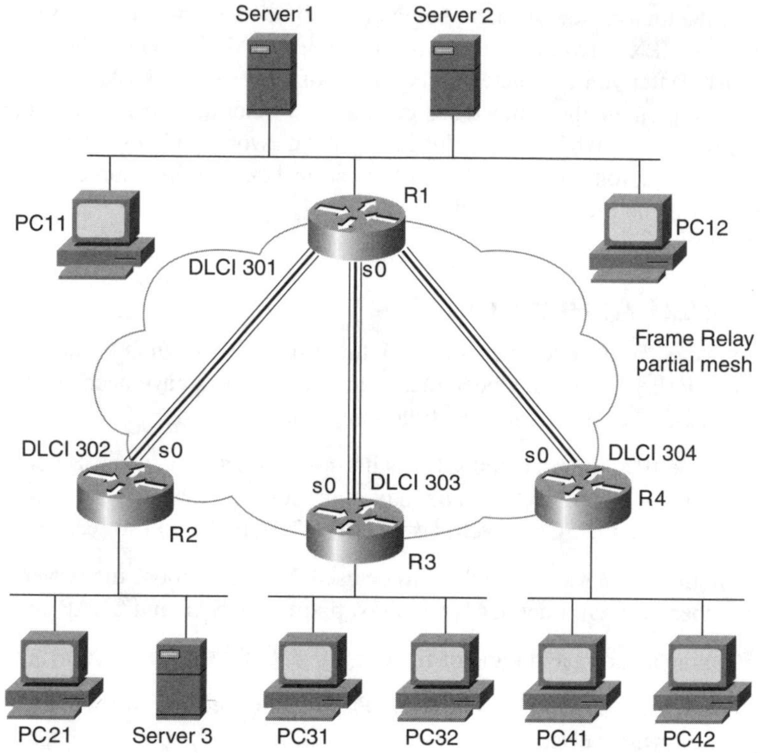

Table 12-10 *Scenario 12-3, Part A: IP Subnet and IPX Network Planning Chart*

Location of Subnet/Network Geographically	Subnet Mask	Subnet Number	IPX Network
Ethernet off R1			
Ethernet off R2			
Ethernet off R3			
Ethernet off R4			
Virtual circuit between R1 and R2			
Virtual circuit between R1 and R3			
Virtual circuit between R1 and R4			
Server 1 internal			
Server 2 internal			
Server 3 internal			

Table 12-11 *Scenario 12-3, Part A: IP Address Planning Chart*

Host	Address
PC11	
PC12	
PC21	
PC31	
PC32	
PC41	
PC42	
R1-E0	
R1-S0-sub ____	
R1-S0-sub ____	
R1-S0-sub ____	
R2-E0	
R2-S0-sub ____	
R3-E0	
R3-S0-sub ____	
R4-E0	
R4-S0-sub ____	
Server 1	
Server 2	
Server 3	

Table 12-12 *Scenario 12-3, Part A: IP Subnet Planning Chart*

Subnet Number	Subnet Broadcast Address	Range of Valid Addresses

continues

Table 12-12 *Scenario 12-3, Part A: IP Subnet Planning Chart (Continued)*

Subnet Number	Subnet Broadcast Address	Range of Valid Addresses

Solutions to Scenario 12-3, Part A: Planning

The IP subnet design includes the use of mask 255.255.254.0. The same mask is used throughout the network. Therefore, at least 9 host bits are needed, because at least one subnet contains 300 hosts.

The IPX network number assignment process is straightforward when you're using multiple encapsulations on the same Ethernet. You simply have to choose two different network numbers—one per encapsulation type. Each encapsulation type on the router requires the use of a separate IPX network. The subnets, networks, and IP addresses are recorded in Tables 12-13 and 12-14.

Table 12-13 *Scenario 12-3, Part A: The Completed IP Subnet and IPX Network Planning Chart*

Location of Subnet/Network Geographically	Subnet Mask	Subnet Number	IPX Network
Ethernet off R1	255.255.254.0	170.1.2.0	2, 3
Ethernet off R2	255.255.254.0	170.1.4.0	4, 5
Ethernet off R3	255.255.254.0	170.1.6.0	6, 7
Ethernet off R4	255.255.254.0	170.1.8.0	8, 9
Virtual circuit between R1 and R2	255.255.254.0	170.1.10.0	10
Virtual circuit between R1 and R3	255.255.254.0	170.1.12.0	12
Virtual circuit between R1 and R4	255.255.254.0	170.1.14.0	14
Server 1 internal	N/A	N/A	101
Server 2 internal	N/A	N/A	102
Server 3 internal	N/A	N/A	103

The choice of IP addresses can conform to any standard you like, as long as the addresses are in the correct subnets. Refer to Table 12-15 for the list of valid addresses for the subnets chosen. Table 12-14 uses a convention in which the numbers reflect the number of the PC. For the routers, the convention uses addresses in the second half of the range of addresses in each subnet. This convention is simply a reminder of the addresses that are valid in this subnetting scheme.

Table 12-14 *Scenario 12-3, Part A: The Completed IP Address Planning Chart*

Host	Address
PC11	170.1.2.11
PC12	170.1.2.12
PC21	170.1.4.21
PC31	170.1.6.31
PC32	170.1.6.32
PC41	170.1.8.41
PC42	170.1.8.42
R1-E0	170.1.3.1
R1-S0-sub 2	170.1.10.1
R1-S0-sub 3	170.1.12.1
R1-S0-sub 4	170.1.14.1
R2-E0	170.1.5.2
R2-S0-sub 2	170.1.10.2
R3-E0	170.1.7.3
R3-S0-sub 3	170.1.12.3
R4-E0	170.1.9.4
R4-S0-sub 4	170.1.14.4
Server 1	170.1.2.101
Server 2	170.1.2.102
Server 3	170.1.4.103

The IP access lists can effectively be placed in several places. Stopping packets in one of the two directions will succeed in stopping users from actually connecting to the servers. For the first set of criteria, an access list stopping packets from entering the serial interface of R1, thus stopping packets destined for PC11 and PC12, will suffice. For the second criteria to disallow traffic between Site 2 and Site 3, the access lists are also placed in R1. The access lists will stop the packets earlier in their life if they are placed in R2 and R3, but the traffic will be minimal because no true application traffic will ever successfully be generated between IP hosts at Sites 2 and 3.

The design shown here calls for all filtered packets to be filtered via access lists enabled on subinterfaces on R1's S0 interface. Other options are valid as well.

The SAP filter can be placed in several places, but there is one obvious location. A SAP filter is added on R2 to filter Server 3 from the SAP table. The filter could filter incoming SAPs on R2's E0 or filter outgoing SAP updates out R2's S0 port. In this case, anticipating the day that a second Ethernet port is used on R2, and anticipating the fact that the objective probably meant that local clients should have access to Server 3, the plan in this case is to filter outbound SAPs on R2's S0 interface.

Finally, the broadcast addresses for each subnet are shown in Table 12-15. As a reminder, to calculate the broadcast address, you need to write down the subnet number in binary. Then copy down the network and subnet portions of the subnet number directly below it, leaving the host bit positions empty. Then write all binary 1s in the host bit positions. Finally, convert the number back to decimal, 8 bits at a time. The result is the subnet broadcast address and is the high end of the range of assignable addresses in that subnet.

Table 12-15 shows the answers, which include the subnet numbers, their corresponding broadcast addresses, and the range of valid assignable IP addresses.

Table 12-15 *Scenario 12-3, Part A: The Completed IP Subnet Planning Chart*

Subnet Number	Subnet Broadcast Address	Range of Valid Addresses (Last 2 Bytes)
170.1.2.0	170.1.3.255	2.1 through 3.254
170.1.4.0	170.1.5.255	4.1 through 5.254
170.1.6.0	170.1.7.255	6.1 through 7.254
170.1.8.0	170.1.9.255	8.1 through 9.254
170.1.10.0	170.1.11.255	10.1 through 11.254
170.1.12.0	170.1.13.255	12.1 through 13.254
170.1.14.0	170.1.15.255	14.1 through 15.254

Scenario 12-3, Part B: Configuration

The next step in your job is to deploy the network designed in Scenario 12-3, Part A. Use the solutions to Scenario 12-3, Part A to help you identify IP and IPX addresses, access lists, and the encapsulations to be used. For Scenario 12-3, Part B, perform the following tasks:

1. Configure IP and IPX to be routed. Use IP IGRP and IPX RIP as routing protocols. Use IGRP process-id 1.
2. Use secondary IPX addresses to accommodate the multiple IPX encapsulation types described in Scenario 12-3, Part A.
3. Configure Frame Relay using point-to-point subinterfaces. R1's attached Frame Relay switch uses LMI type ANSI. Cisco encapsulation should be used for all routers, except for the VC between R1 and R4.

Solutions to Scenario 12-3, Part B: Configuration

Examples 12-15 through 12-18 show the configurations for tasks 1, 2, and 3 for Part B of Scenario 3.

Example 12-15 *R1 Configuration*

```
ipx routing 0200.aaaa.aaaa
!
interface serial0
encapsulation frame-relay
interface serial 0.2 point-to-point
 ip address  170.1.10.1  255.255.254.0
 ipx network  10
 frame-relay interface-dlci 302
 ip access-group 102 in
!
interface serial 0.3 point-to-point
 ip address  170.1.12.1  255.255.254.0
 ipx network  12
 frame-relay interface-dlci 303
 ip access-group 103 in
!
interface serial 0.4 point-to-point
 ip address  170.1.14.1  255.255.254.0
 ipx network  14
 frame-relay interface-dlci 304 ietf
 ip access-group 104 in
!
interface ethernet 0
ip address  170.1.3.1  255.255.254.0
ipx network  2 encapsulation sap
ipx network  3 encapsulation snap secondary
!
router igrp 1
network 170.1.0.0

!
access-list 102 permit tcp any host 170.1.2.11 eq ftp
access-list 102 permit tcp any host 170.1.2.11 eq www
access-list 102 permit tcp any host 170.1.2.12 eq ftp
access-list 102 permit tcp any host 170.1.2.12 eq www
access-list 102 deny ip any host 170.1.2.11
access-list 102 deny ip any host 170.1.2.12
access-list 102 deny ip 170.1.4.0 0.0.1.255 170.1.6.0 0.0.1.255
access-list 102 permit ip any any

access-list 103 permit tcp any host 170.1.2.11 eq ftp
access-list 103 permit tcp any host 170.1.2.11 eq www
access-list 103 permit tcp any host 170.1.2.12 eq ftp
access-list 103 permit tcp any host 170.1.2.12 eq www
access-list 103 deny ip any host 170.1.2.11
```

continues

Example 12-15 *R1 Configuration (Continued)*

```
access-list 103 deny ip any host 170.1.2.12
access-list 103 deny ip 170.1.6.0 0.0.1.255 170.1.4.0 0.0.1.255
access-list 103 permit ip any any

access-list 104 permit tcp any host 170.1.2.11 eq ftp
access-list 104 permit tcp any host 170.1.2.11 eq www
access-list 104 permit tcp any host 170.1.2.12 eq ftp
access-list 104 permit tcp any host 170.1.2.12 eq www
access-list 104 deny ip any host 170.1.2.11
access-list 104 deny ip any host 170.1.2.12
access-list 104 permit ip any any
```

Example 12-16 *R2 Configuration*

```
ipx routing 0200.bbbb.bbbb
!
interface serial0
encapsulation frame-relay
interface serial 0.1 point-to-point
 ip address  170.1.10.2  255.255.254.0
 ipx network  10
 frame-relay interface-dlci 301
 ipx output-sap-filter 1001
!
interface ethernet 0
ip address  170.1.5.2  255.255.254.0
ipx network  4 encapsulation sap
ipx network  5 encapsulation snap secondary
!
router igrp 1
network 170.1.0.0
!
access-list 1001 deny 103
access-list 1001 permit -1
```

Example 12-17 *R3 Configuration*

```
ipx routing 0200.cccc.cccc
!
interface serial0
encapsulation frame-relay
interface serial 0.1 point-to-point
 ip address  170.1.12.3  255.255.254.0
 ipx network  12
 frame-relay interface-dlci 301
```

Example 12-17 *R3 Configuration (Continued)*

```
!
interface ethernet 0
ip address  170.1.7.3  255.255.254.0
ipx network  6 encapsulation sap
ipx network  7 encapsulation snap secondary
!
router igrp 1
network 170.1.0.0
```

Example 12-18 *R4 Configuration*

```
ipx routing 0200.dddd.dddd
!
interface serial0
encapsulation frame-relay ietf
interface serial 0.1 point-to-point
 ip address  170.1.14.4  255.255.254.0
 ipx network  14
 frame-relay interface-dlci 301
!
interface ethernet 0
ip address  170.1.9.4  255.255.254.0
ipx network  8 encapsulation sap
ipx network  9 encapsulation snap secondary
!
router igrp 1
network 170.1.0.0
```

Three different access lists are shown on R1. List 102 is used for packets entering subinterface 2. List 103 is used for packets entering subinterface 3, and list 104 is used for packets entering subinterface 4. Lists 102 and 103 check for packets between sites 2 and 3, and they also check for packets to PC11 and PC12. The mask used to check all hosts in subnets 170.1.4.0 and 170.1.6.0 is rather tricky. The mask represents 23 binary 0s and 9 binary 1s, meaning that the first 23 bits of the number in the access list must match the first 23 bits in the source or destination address in the packet. This matches all hosts in each subnet because there are 23 combined network and subnet bits.

Two IPX networks are used on each Ethernet because two encapsulations are used.

The Frame Relay configuration is relatively straightforward. The LMI type is autosensed. The encapsulation of **ietf** between R1 and R4 is configured in two ways. First, R1 uses the **ietf** keyword on the **frame-relay interface-dlci** command. On R4, the **encapsulation** command lists the **ietf** option, implying **ietf** encapsulation for all VCs on this serial interface.

Scenario 12-3, Part C: Verification and Questions

The CCNA exam tests your memory of the kinds of information you can find in the output of various **show** commands. Using Examples 12-19 through 12-22 as references, answer the questions following the examples.

Example 12-19 *Scenario 12-3, Part C: R1* **show** *and* **debug** *Output*

```
R1#show ip interface brief
Interface              IP-Address       OK? Method Status                Protocol
Serial0                unassigned       YES unset  up                    up
Serial0.2              170.1.10.1       YES NVRAM  up                    up
Serial0.3              170.1.12.1       YES NVRAM  up                    up
Serial0.4              170.1.14.1       YES NVRAM  up                    up
Serial1                unassigned       YES unset  administratively down down
Ethernet0              170.1.3.1        YES NVRAM  up                    up

R1#show cdp neighbor detail
-------------------------
Device ID: R2
Entry address(es):
  IP address: 170.1.10.2
  Novell address: 10.0200.bbbb.bbbb
Platform: cisco 2500,  Capabilities: Router
Interface: Serial0.2,  Port ID (outgoing port): Serial0.1
Holdtime : 132 sec
Version :
Cisco Internetwork Operating System Software
 IOS (tm) 2500 Software (C2500-DS-L), Version 12.2(1), RELEASE SOFTWARE (fc2)
 Copyright (c) 1986-2001 by cisco Systems, Inc.
 Compiled Fri 27-Apr-01 14:43 by cmong

 advertisement version: 2

-------------------------
Device ID: R3
Entry address(es):
  IP address: 170.1.12.3
  Novell address: 12.0200.cccc.cccc
Platform: Cisco 2500,  Capabilities: Router
Interface: Serial0.3,  Port ID (outgoing port): Serial0.1
Holdtime : 148 sec

Version :
Cisco Internetwork Operating System Software
 IOS (tm) 2500 Software (C2500-DS-L), Version 12.2(1), RELEASE SOFTWARE (fc2)
 Copyright (c) 1986-2001 by cisco Systems, Inc.
 Compiled Fri 27-Apr-01 14:43 by cmong

 advertisement version: 2

-------------------------
Device ID: R4
Entry address(es):
```

Example 12-19 *Scenario 12-3, Part C: R1* **show** *and* **debug** *Output (Continued)*

```
  IP address: 170.1.14.4
  Novell address: 14.0200.dddd.dddd
Platform: Cisco 2500,  Capabilities: Router
Interface: Serial0.4,  Port ID (outgoing port): Serial0.1
Holdtime : 149 sec

Version :
Cisco Internetwork Operating System Software
 IOS (tm) 2500 Software (C2500-DS-L), Version 12.2(1), RELEASE SOFTWARE (fc2)
 Copyright (c) 1986-2001 by cisco Systems, Inc.
 Compiled Fri 27-Apr-01 14:43 by cmong

 advertisement version: 2

R1#show ipx servers
Codes: S - Static, P - Periodic, E - EIGRP, N - NLSP, H - Holddown, + = detail
2 Total IPX Servers

Table ordering is based on routing and server info

   Type Name                       Net     Address    Port     Route Hops Itf
P     4 Server1                    101.0000.0000.0001:0451      2/02   2  E0
P     4 Server2                    102.0000.0000.0001:0451      2/02   2  E0
R1#
R1#debug ipx sap activity
IPX service debugging is on

R1#
IPXSAP: positing update to 2.ffff.ffff.ffff via Ethernet0 (broadcast) (full)
IPXSAP: suppressing null update to 2.ffff.ffff.ffff
IPXSAP: positing update to 3.ffff.ffff.ffff via Ethernet0 (broadcast) (full)
IPXSAP: Update type 0x2 len 160 src:3.0000.0ccf.21cd dest:3.ffff.ffff.ffff(452)
 type 0x4, "Server2", 102.0000.0000.0001(451), 3 hops
 type 0x4, "Server1", 101.0000.0000.0001(451), 3 hops
IPXSAP: Response (in) type 0x2 len 160 src:2.0000.0c89.b130 dest:2.ffff.ffff.ffff(452)
 type 0x4, "Server1", 101.0000.0000.0001(451), 2 hops
 type 0x4, "Server2", 102.0000.0000.0001(451), 2 hops
IPXSAP: positing update to 10.ffff.ffff.ffff via Serial0.2 (broadcast) (full)
IPXSAP: Update type 0x2 len 160 src:10.0200.aaaa.aaaa dest:10.ffff.ffff.ffff(452)
 type 0x4, "Server2", 102.0000.0000.0001(451), 3 hops
 type 0x4, "Server1", 101.0000.0000.0001(451), 3 hops
IPXSAP: positing update to 14.ffff.ffff.ffff via Serial0.4 (broadcast) (full)
IPXSAP: Update type 0x2 len 160 src:14.0200.aaaa.aaaa dest:14.ffff.ffff.ffff(452)
 type 0x4, "Server2", 102.0000.0000.0001(451), 3 hops
 type 0x4, "Server1", 101.0000.0000.0001(451), 3 hops
IPXSAP: positing update to 12.ffff.ffff.ffff via Serial0.3 (broadcast) (full)
IPXSAP: Update type 0x2 len 160 src:12.0200.aaaa.aaaa dest:12.ffff.ffff.ffff(452)
 type 0x4, "Server2", 102.0000.0000.0001(451), 3 hops
 type 0x4, "Server1", 101.0000.0000.0001(451), 3 hops

R1#undebug all
All possible debugging has been turned off
```

continues

Example 12-19 *Scenario 12-3, Part C: R1* **show** *and* **debug** *Output (Continued)*

```
R1#
R1#debug ipx routing activity

IPX routing debugging is on
R1#
IPXRIP: update from 12.0200.cccc.cccc
    7 in 1 hops, delay 7
    6 in 1 hops, delay 7
IPXRIP: positing full update to 14.ffff.ffff.ffff via Serial0.4 (broadcast)
IPXRIP: src=14.0200.aaaa.aaaa, dst=14.ffff.ffff.ffff, packet sent
    network 4, hops 2,  delay 13
    network 5, hops 2,  delay 13
    network 103, hops 4,  delay 14
    network 10, hops 1,  delay 7
    network 6, hops 2,  delay 13
    network 7, hops 2,  delay 13
    network 3, hops 1,  delay 7
    network 2, hops 1,  delay 7
    network 101, hops 3,  delay 8
    network 102, hops 3,  delay 8
    network 12, hops 1,  delay 7
IPXRIP: positing full update to 12.ffff.ffff.ffff via Serial0.3 (broadcast)
IPXRIP: src=12.0200.aaaa.aaaa, dst=12.ffff.ffff.ffff, packet sent
    network 8, hops 2,  delay 13
    network 9, hops 2,  delay 13
    network 14, hops 1,  delay 7
    network 4, hops 2,  delay 13
    network 5, hops 2,  delay 13
    network 103, hops 4,  delay 14
    network 10, hops 1,  delay 7
    network 3, hops 1,  delay 7
    network 2, hops 1,  delay 7
    network 101, hops 3,  delay 8
    network 102, hops 3,  delay 8
IPXRIP: update from 14.0200.dddd.dddd
    9 in 1 hops, delay 7
    8 in 1 hops, delay 7
IPXRIP: update from 10.0200.bbbb.bbbb
    444 in 2 hops, delay 8
    103 in 3 hops, delay 8
    5 in 1 hops, delay 7
    4 in 1 hops, delay 7
IPXRIP: positing full update to 3.ffff.ffff.ffff via Ethernet0 (broadcast)
IPXRIP: src=3.0000.0ccf.21cd, dst=3.ffff.ffff.ffff, packet sent
    network 8, hops 2,  delay 8
    network 9, hops 2,  delay 8
    network 14, hops 1,  delay 2
    network 4, hops 2,  delay 8
    network 5, hops 2,  delay 8
    network 103, hops 4,  delay 9
    network 10, hops 1,  delay 2
    network 6, hops 2,  delay 8
```

Example 12-19 *Scenario 12-3, Part C: R1* **show** *and* **debug** *Output (Continued)*

```
    network 7, hops 2,  delay 8
    network 2, hops 1,  delay 2
    network 101, hops 3,  delay 3
    network 102, hops 3,  delay 3
    network 12, hops 1,  delay 2
IPXRIP: update from 2.0000.0c89.b130
    102 in 2 hops, delay 2
    101 in 2 hops, delay 2
IPXRIP: positing full update to 2.ffff.ffff.ffff via Ethernet0 (broadcast)
IPXRIP: src=2.0000.0ccf.21cd, dst=2.ffff.ffff.ffff, packet sent
    network 8, hops 2,  delay 8
    network 9, hops 2,  delay 8
    network 14, hops 1,  delay 2
    network 4, hops 2,  delay 8
    network 5, hops 2,  delay 8
    network 103, hops 4,  delay 9
    network 10, hops 1,  delay 2
    network 6, hops 2,  delay 8
    network 7, hops 2,  delay 8
    network 3, hops 1,  delay 2
    network 12, hops 1,  delay 2
IPXRIP: positing full update to 10.ffff.ffff.ffff via Serial0.2 (broadcast)
IPXRIP: src=10.0200.aaaa.aaaa, dst=10.ffff.ffff.ffff, packet sent
    network 8, hops 2,  delay 13
    network 9, hops 2,  delay 13
    network 14, hops 1,  delay 7
    network 6, hops 2,  delay 13
    network 7, hops 2,  delay 13
    network 3, hops 1,  delay 7
    network 2, hops 1,  delay 7
    network 101, hops 3,  delay 8
    network 102, hops 3,  delay 8
    network 12, hops 1,  delay 7
R1#
R1#undebug all
All possible debugging has been turned off
R1#
R1#debug ip igrp transactions
IGRP protocol debugging is on
R1#
IGRP: received update from 170.1.14.4 on Serial0.4
      subnet 170.1.8.0, metric 8539 (neighbor 688)
IGRP: sending update to 255.255.255.255 via Serial0.2 (170.1.10.1)
      subnet 170.1.8.0, metric=8539
      subnet 170.1.14.0, metric=8476
      subnet 170.1.12.0, metric=8476
      subnet 170.1.2.0, metric=688
      subnet 170.1.6.0, metric=8539
IGRP: sending update to 255.255.255.255 via Serial0.3 (170.1.12.1)
      subnet 170.1.10.0, metric=8476
      subnet 170.1.8.0, metric=8539
      subnet 170.1.14.0, metric=8476
```

continues

Example 12-19 *Scenario 12-3, Part C: R1* **show** *and* **debug** *Output (Continued)*

```
      subnet 170.1.2.0, metric=688
      subnet 170.1.4.0, metric=8539
IGRP: sending update to 255.255.255.255 via Serial0.4 (170.1.14.1)
      subnet 170.1.10.0, metric=8476
      subnet 170.1.12.0, metric=8476
      subnet 170.1.2.0, metric=688
      subnet 170.1.6.0, metric=8539
      subnet 170.1.4.0, metric=8539
IGRP: sending update to 255.255.255.255 via Ethernet0 (170.1.3.1)
      subnet 170.1.10.0, metric=8476
      subnet 170.1.8.0, metric=8539
      subnet 170.1.14.0, metric=8476
      subnet 170.1.12.0, metric=8476
      subnet 170.1.6.0, metric=8539
      subnet 170.1.4.0, metric=8539
IGRP: received update from 170.1.10.2 on Serial0.2
      subnet 170.1.4.0, metric 8539 (neighbor 688)
IGRP: received update from 170.1.12.3 on Serial0.3
      subnet 170.1.6.0, metric 8539 (neighbor 688)
R1#
R1#undebug all
All possible debugging has been turned off
```

Example 12-20 *Scenario 12-3, Part C: R2* **show** *and* **debug** *Output*

```
R2#show interfaces
Serial0 is up, line protocol is up
  Hardware is HD64570
  MTU 1500 bytes, BW 56 Kbit, DLY 20000 usec,
     reliability 255/255, txload 1/255, rxload 1/255
  Encapsulation FRAME-RELAY, loopback not set, keepalive set (10 sec)
  LMI enq sent  144, LMI stat recvd 138, LMI upd recvd 0, DTE LMI up
  LMI enq recvd 0, LMI stat sent  0, LMI upd sent  0
  LMI DLCI 0  LMI type is ANSI Annex D  frame relay DTE
  Broadcast queue 0/64, broadcasts sent/dropped 73/0, interface broadcasts 48
  Last input 00:00:04, output 00:00:04, output hang never
  Last clearing of "show interface" counters never
    Input queue: 0/75/0/0 (size/max/drops/flushes); Total output drops: 0
    Queueing strategy: weighted fair
    Output queue: 0/1000/64/0 (size/max total/threshold/drops)
       Conversations  0/0/256 (active/max active/max total)
       Reserved Conversations 0/0 (allocated/max allocated)
       Available Bandwidth 42 kilobits/sec
  5 minute input rate 0 bits/sec, 0 packets/sec
  5 minute output rate 0 bits/sec, 0 packets/sec
     232 packets input, 17750 bytes, 0 no buffer
     Received 1 broadcasts, 0 runts, 0 giants, 0 throttles
     0 input errors, 0 CRC, 0 frame, 0 overrun, 0 ignored, 0 abort
     225 packets output, 12563 bytes, 0 underruns
     0 output errors, 0 collisions, 4 interface resets
     0 output buffer failures, 0 output buffers swapped out
```

Example 12-20 *Scenario 12-3, Part C: R2* **show** *and* **debug** *Output (Continued)*

```
     12 carrier transitions
     DCD=up  DSR=up  DTR=up  RTS=up  CTS=up
 --More--
Serial0.1 is up, line protocol is up
  Hardware is HD64570
  Internet address is 170.1.10.2/23
  MTU 1500 bytes, BW 1544 Kbit, DLY 20000 usec,
     reliability 255/255, txload 1/255, rxload 1/255
  Encapsulation FRAME-RELAY
 --More--
Serial1 is administratively down, line protocol is down
  Hardware is HD64570
    MTU 1500 bytes, BW 1544 Kbit, DLY 20000 usec,
     reliability 255/255, txload 1/255, rxload 1/255
  Encapsulation PPP, loopback not set, keepalive set (10 sec)
  LCP Closed
  Closed: CDPCP, LLC2
  Last input never, output never, output hang never
  Last clearing of "show interface" counters never
    Input queue: 0/75/0/0 (size/max/drops/flushes); Total output drops: 0
      Queueing strategy: weighted fair
    Output queue: 0/1000/64/0 (size/max total/threshold/drops)
     Conversations  0/1/256 (active/max active/max total)
     Reserved Conversations 0/0 (allocated/max allocated)
     Available Bandwidth 1158 kilobits/sec
  5 minute input rate 0 bits/sec, 0 packets/sec
  5 minute output rate 0 bits/sec, 0 packets/sec
     0 packets input, 0 bytes, 0 no buffer
     Received 0 broadcasts, 0 runts, 0 giants, 0 throttles
     0 input errors, 0 CRC, 0 frame, 0 overrun, 0 ignored, 0 abort
     0 packets output, 0 bytes, 0 underruns
     0 output errors, 0 collisions, 5 interface resets
     0 output buffer failures, 0 output buffers swapped out
     0 carrier transitions
     DCD=down  DSR=down  DTR=down  RTS=down  CTS=down
 --More--
Ethernet0 is up, line protocol is up
  Hardware is TMS380, address is 0000.0c89.b170 (bia 0000.0c89.b170)
  Internet address is 170.1.5.2/23
    MTU 1500 bytes, BW 10000 Kbit, DLY 1000 usec,
       reliability 255/255, txload 1/255, rxload 1/255
  Encapsulation ARPA, loopback not set, keepalive set (10 sec)
  ARP type: ARPA, ARP Timeout 4:00:00
  Last input 00:00:00, output 00:00:01, output hang never
  Last clearing of "show interface" counters never
  Queuing strategy: fifo
Output queue 0/40, 0 drops; input queue 0/75, 0 drops
  5 minute input rate 0 bits/sec, 0 packets/sec
  5 minute output rate 0 bits/sec, 0 packets/sec
     583 packets input, 28577 bytes, 0 no buffer
     Received 486 broadcasts, 0 runts, 0 giants, 0 throttles
     0 input errors, 0 CRC, 0 frame, 0 overrun, 0 ignored, 0 abort
```

continues

Example 12-20 *Scenario 12-3, Part C: R2* **show** *and* **debug** *Output (Continued)*

```
     260 packets output, 31560 bytes, 0 underruns
     0 output errors, 0 collisions, 2 interface resets
     0 output buffer failures, 0 output buffers swapped out
     6 transitions

R2#show ipx interface brief
Interface            IPX Network Encapsulation Status                 IPX State
Serial0              unassigned  not config'd  up                     n/a
Serial0.1            10          FRAME-RELAY   up                     [up]
Serial1              unassigned  not config'd  administratively down  n/a
Ethernet0            4           SAP           up                     [up]
Ethernet0            5           SNAP          up                     [up]
R2#
R2#show ipx route
Codes: C - Connected primary network,    c - Connected secondary network
       S - Static, F - Floating static, L - Local (internal), W - IPXWAN
       R - RIP, E - EIGRP, N - NLSP, X - External, A - Aggregate
       s - seconds, u - uses

14 Total IPX routes. Up to 1 parallel paths and 16 hops allowed.

No default route known.

C          4 (SAP),           E0
c          5 (SNAP),          E0
C         10 (FRAME-RELAY),   Se0.1
R          2 [07/01] via       10.0200.aaaa.aaaa,   47s, Se0.1
R          3 [07/01] via       10.0200.aaaa.aaaa,   48s, Se0.1
R          6 [13/02] via       10.0200.aaaa.aaaa,   48s, Se0.1
R          7 [13/02] via       10.0200.aaaa.aaaa,   48s, Se0.1
R          8 [13/02] via       10.0200.aaaa.aaaa,   48s, Se0.1
R          9 [13/02] via       10.0200.aaaa.aaaa,   48s, Se0.1
R         12 [07/01] via       10.0200.aaaa.aaaa,   48s, Se0.1
R         14 [07/01] via       10.0200.aaaa.aaaa,   48s, Se0.1
R        101 [08/03] via       10.0200.aaaa.aaaa,   48s, Se0.1
R        102 [08/03] via       10.0200.aaaa.aaaa,   48s, Se0.1
R        103 [02/02] via        4.0000.0cac.70ef,   42s, E0

R2#ping 14.0200.dddd.dddd
Translating "14.0200.dddd.dddd"

Type escape sequence to abort.
Sending 5, 100-byte IPX Cisco Echoes to 14.0200.dddd.dddd, timeout is 2 seconds:
!!!!!
Success rate is 100 percent (5/5), round-trip min/avg/max = 140/144/148 ms

R2#show ipx servers
Codes: S - Static, P - Periodic, E - EIGRP, N - NLSP, H - Holddown, + = detail
3 Total IPX Servers

Table ordering is based on routing and server info
```

Example 12-20 *Scenario 12-3, Part C: R2* **show** *and* **debug** *Output (Continued)*

```
   Type Name                       Net     Address    Port     Route Hops Itf
P     4 Server3                    103.0000.0000.0001:0451      2/02   2  E0
P     4 Server1                    101.0000.0000.0001:0451      8/03   3  Se0.1
P     4 Server2                    102.0000.0000.0001:0451      8/03   3  Se0.1

R2#show frame-relay pvc

PVC Statistics for interface Serial0 (Frame Relay DTE)

DLCI = 301, DLCI USAGE = LOCAL, PVC STATUS = ACTIVE, INTERFACE = Serial0.1

  input pkts 102           output pkts 82           in bytes 16624
  out bytes 11394          dropped pkts 0           in FECN pkts 0
  in BECN pkts 0           out FECN pkts 0          out BECN pkts 0
  in DE pkts 0             out DE pkts 0
  out bcast pkts 76         out bcast bytes 10806
  pvc create time 00:25:09, last time pvc status changed 00:23:15

R2#show frame-relay lmi

LMI Statistics for interface Serial0 (Frame Relay DTE) LMI TYPE = ANSI
  Invalid Unnumbered info 0        Invalid Prot Disc 0
  Invalid dummy Call Ref 0        Invalid Msg Type 0
  Invalid Status Message 0        Invalid Lock Shift 0
  Invalid Information ID 0        Invalid Report IE Len 0
  Invalid Report Request 0        Invalid Keep IE Len 0
  Num Status Enq. Sent 151        Num Status msgs Rcvd 145
  Num Update Status Rcvd 0        Num Status Timeouts 7
R2#
```

Example 12-21 *Scenario 12-3, Part C: R3* **show** *and* **debug** *Output*

```
R3#show ipx servers
Codes: S - Static, P - Periodic, E - EIGRP, N - NLSP, H - Holddown, + = detail
2 Total IPX Servers

Table ordering is based on routing and server info

   Type Name                       Net     Address    Port     Route Hops Itf
P     4 Server1                    101.0000.0000.0001:0451      8/03   3  Se0.1
P     4 Server2                    102.0000.0000.0001:0451      8/03   3  Se0.1

R3#show ip arp
Protocol  Address          Age (min)  Hardware Addr   Type   Interface
Internet  170.1.7.3               -   0000.0c89.b1b0  SNAP   Ethernet0

R3#show ip route
Codes: C - connected, S - static, I - IGRP, R - RIP, M - mobile, B - BGP
       D - EIGRP, EX - EIGRP external, O - OSPF, IA - OSPF inter area
       N1 - OSPF NSSA external type 1, N2 - OSPF NSSA external type 2
       E1 - OSPF external type 1, E2 - OSPF external type 2, E - EGP
```

continues

Example 12-21 *Scenario 12-3, Part C: R3* **show** *and* **debug** *Output (Continued)*

```
       i - IS-IS, L1 - IS-IS level-1, L2 - IS-IS level-2, ia - IS-IS inter area
       * - candidate default, U - per-user static route, o - ODR
       P - periodic downloaded static route

Gateway of last resort is not set

     170.1.0.0/23 is subnetted, 7 subnets
I       170.1.10.0 [100/10476] via 170.1.12.1, 00:00:57, Serial0.1
I       170.1.8.0 [100/10539] via 170.1.12.1, 00:00:57, Serial0.1
I       170.1.14.0 [100/10476] via 170.1.12.1, 00:00:57, Serial0.1
C       170.1.12.0 is directly connected, Serial0.1
I       170.1.2.0 [100/8539] via 170.1.12.1, 00:00:57, Serial0.1
C       170.1.6.0 is directly connected, Ethernet0
I       170.1.4.0 [100/10539] via 170.1.12.1, 00:00:57, Serial0.1

R3#trace 170.1.9.4

Type escape sequence to abort.
Tracing the route to 170.1.9.4

  1 170.1.12.1 40 msec 40 msec 44 msec
  2 170.1.14.4 80 msec *  80 msec

R3#trace 170.1.5.2

Type escape sequence to abort.
Tracing the route to 170.1.5.2

  1 170.1.12.1 40 msec 40 msec 40 msec
  2 170.1.10.2 72 msec *  72 msec

R3#ping 170.1.5.2

Type escape sequence to abort.
Sending 5, 100-byte ICMP Echos to 170.1.5.2, timeout is 2 seconds:
!!!!!
Success rate is 100 percent (5/5), round-trip min/avg/max = 136/136/140 ms

R3#ping
Protocol [ip]:
Target IP address: 170.1.5.2
Repeat count [5]:
Datagram size [100]:
Timeout in seconds [2]:
Extended commands [n]: y
Source address or interface: 170.1.7.3
Type of service [0]:
Set DF bit in IP header? [no]:
Validate reply data? [no]:
Data pattern [0xABCD]:
Loose, Strict, Record, Timestamp, Verbose[none]:
Sweep range of sizes [n]:
```

Example 12-21 *Scenario 12-3, Part C: R3* **show** *and* **debug** *Output (Continued)*

```
Type escape sequence to abort.
Sending 5, 100-byte ICMP Echos to 170.1.5.2, timeout is 2 seconds:
UUUUU
Success rate is 0 percent (0/5)

R3#show frame-relay lmi

LMI Statistics for interface Serial0 (Frame Relay DTE) LMI TYPE = CISCO
  Invalid Unnumbered info 0        Invalid Prot Disc 0
  Invalid dummy Call Ref 0        Invalid Msg Type 0
  Invalid Status Message 0        Invalid Lock Shift 0
  Invalid Information ID 0        Invalid Report IE Len 0
  Invalid Report Request 0        Invalid Keep IE Len 0
  Num Status Enq. Sent 172        Num Status msgs Rcvd 172
  Num Update Status Rcvd 0        Num Status Timeouts 0

R3#show frame-relay map
Serial0.1 (up): point-to-point dlci, dlci 301(0x12D,0x48D0), broadcast
          status defined, active
```

Example 12-22 *Scenario 12-3, Part C: R4* **show** *and* **debug** *Output*

```
R4#show ip interface brief
Interface              IP-Address      OK? Method Status                Protocol
Serial0                unassigned      YES unset  up                    up
Serial0.1              170.1.14.4      YES NVRAM  up                    up
Serial1                unassigned      YES unset  administratively down down
Ethernet0              170.1.9.4       YES NVRAM  up                    up

R4#show ipx interface brief
Interface            IPX Network Encapsulation Status                 IPX State
Serial0              unassigned  not config'd  up                     n/a
Serial0.1            14          FRAME-RELAY   up                     [up]
Serial1              unassigned  not config'd  administratively down  n/a
Ethernet0            8           SAP           up                     [up]
Ethernet0            9           SNAP          up                     [up]

R4#show ipx servers
Codes: S - Static, P - Periodic, E - EIGRP, N - NLSP, H - Holddown, + = detail
2 Total IPX Servers

Table ordering is based on routing and server info

   Type Name                    Net     Address    Port     Route Hops Itf
P     4 Server1                 101.0000.0000.0001:0451      8/03   3  Se0.1
P     4 Server2                 102.0000.0000.0001:0451      8/03   3  Se0.1

R4#show ipx route
Codes: C - Connected primary network,    c - Connected secondary network
       S - Static, F - Floating static, L - Local (internal), W - IPXWAN
       R - RIP, E - EIGRP, N - NLSP, X - External, A - Aggregate
```

continues

Example 12-22 *Scenario 12-3, Part C: R4* **show** *and* **debug** *Output (Continued)*

```
       s - seconds, u - uses

14 Total IPX routes. Up to 1 parallel paths and 16 hops allowed.

No default route known.

C          8 (SAP),           E0
c          9 (SNAP),          E0
C         14 (FRAME-RELAY),   Se0.1
R          2 [07/01] via      14.0200.aaaa.aaaa,   33s, Se0.1
R          3 [07/01] via      14.0200.aaaa.aaaa,   34s, Se0.1
R          4 [13/02] via      14.0200.aaaa.aaaa,   34s, Se0.1
R          5 [13/02] via      14.0200.aaaa.aaaa,   34s, Se0.1
R          6 [13/02] via      14.0200.aaaa.aaaa,   34s, Se0.1
R          7 [13/02] via      14.0200.aaaa.aaaa,   34s, Se0.1
R         10 [07/01] via      14.0200.aaaa.aaaa,   34s, Se0.1
R         12 [07/01] via      14.0200.aaaa.aaaa,   34s, Se0.1
R        101 [08/03] via      14.0200.aaaa.aaaa,   34s, Se0.1
R        102 [08/03] via      14.0200.aaaa.aaaa,   34s, Se0.1
R        103 [14/04] via      14.0200.aaaa.aaaa,   34s, Se0.1

R4#show cdp neighbor detail
-------------------------
Device ID: R1
Entry address(es):
  IP address: 170.1.14.1
  Novell address: 14.0200.aaaa.aaaa
Platform: Cisco 2500,  Capabilities: Router
Interface: Serial0.1,  Port ID (outgoing port): Serial0.4
Holdtime : 178 sec

Version :
Cisco Internetwork Operating System Software
IOS (tm) 2500 Software (C2500-DS-L), Version 12.2(1), RELEASE SOFTWARE (fc2)
Copyright (c) 1986-2001 by cisco Systems, Inc.
Compiled Fri 27-Apr-01 14:43 by cmong

advertisement version: 2

R4#show frame-relay pvc

PVC Statistics for interface Serial0 (Frame Relay DTE)

DLCI = 301, DLCI USAGE = LOCAL, PVC STATUS = ACTIVE, INTERFACE = Serial0.1

  input pkts 85            output pkts 63           in bytes 14086
  out bytes 8464           dropped pkts 0           in FECN pkts 0
  in BECN pkts 0           out FECN pkts 0          out BECN pkts 0
  in DE pkts 0             out DE pkts 0
  out bcast pkts 53         out bcast bytes 7614
  pvc create time 00:18:40, last time pvc status changed 00:18:40
```

Using Examples 12-19 through 12-22 as references, answer the following questions:

1 The ping of 170.1.5.2 (R2's E0 interface) from R3 was successful (refer to Example 12-21). Why was it successful if the access lists in R1 are enabled as shown in its configuration?

2 Describe the SAP update entering R1 over its S0.2 subinterface. How many services are described?

3 What **show** commands can be executed on R4 to display R1's IP and IPX addresses?

4 What command lists the IP subnet numbers to which R2 is connected?

5 What commands list the routing metrics used for IP subnets? What about for IPX networks?

6 What command is used to verify that IPX packets can be delivered and returned to another router?

7 If you do not know the enable password, how can you see what access lists are used?

8 You are not physically close to R2 or R3. What two methods can be used to gain access to the user mode command prompt?

9 After typing **show ip route**, you want to type **show ip route 168.11.12.64**. Describe the steps to do so, using the fewest keystrokes.

10 After typing **show ip route**, you want to type **show ip arp**. Describe the steps to do so, using the fewest keystrokes.

11 Name the editing commands (keyboard key sequences) that do the following:

— Move to the beginning of the command line

— Move to the end of the command line

— Move to the beginning of the previous word

— Move to the beginning of the next word

— Move backward one character

— Move forward one character

12 Describe the process of upgrading to a new version of the Cisco IOS software. What memory in the router is affected?

13 What do TCP and UDP stand for? Which one provides error recovery?

14 What does ICMP stand for?

15 Describe how R2 learns that R1's IP address is 170.1.10.1.

16 What does DLCI stand for? How big can a DLCI be?

17 What additional configuration is needed on R3 to get routing updates to flow over the VC to R1?

18 What **show** command lists Frame Relay PVCs and the IP and IPX addresses on the other end of the PVC in this network?

19 What **show** command lists the status of the VC between R1 and R2?

20 What do ISDN, BRI, and PRI stand for?

21 List examples of two ISDN reference points.

22 What layers of the OSI model do the ISDN specifications Q.920 and Q.930 most closely match?

23 What ISDN reference points are supported by Cisco routers?

24 What command(s) can be used to discover details about a neighboring router without logging in to that router?

Solutions to Scenario 12-3, Part C: Verification and Questions

The answers to the questions for Scenario 12-3, Part C are as follows:

1 The **ping** command uses the outgoing interface's IP address as the source address in the packet, which in this case is 170.1.12.3. Access lists 102 and 103 check the source and destination IP addresses, looking for the subnets on the Ethernet segments. Therefore, the packet is not matched. Look further in Example 12-21 to see an extended **ping** with source IP address 170.1.7.3 (R3's E0 IP address), and see that it fails. That's because the extended **ping** calls for the use of 170.1.7.3 as the source IP address.

2 Two services are in the update instead of the three services listed in R2's SAP table. These messages are displayed after the **debug ipx sap activity** command in Example 12-19. This simply shows that the SAP filter on R2 is working properly.

3 The **show ip route** (refer to Example 12-21) and **show ipx route** (refer to Example 12-20) commands list the IP and IPX addresses of the neighboring routers. Because only point-to-point subinterfaces are in use, the **show frame-relay map** command (refer to Example 12-21) does not show details of the neighboring routers' Layer 3 addresses. The **show cdp neighbor detail** command (refer to Example 12-22) also shows information about IP and IPX addresses.

4 The **show ip route** command lists these numbers (refer to Example 12-21). Routes with a C in the left column signify connected subnets.

5 The **show ip route** and **show ipx route** commands list the metric values (refer to Examples 12-21 and 12-20, respectively). The metric value for each IP subnet is the second of the two numbers inside brackets. Two IPX metrics are located between brackets for IPX routes: the number of timer ticks and the number of hops.

6 The **ping** command can be used to verify IPX and IP connectivity, as well as several other network layer (Layer 3) protocols (refer to Example 12-21).

7 Use the **show access-lists** command.

8 You can dial in to a modem attached to the auxiliary port, or you can Telnet.

9 Press the up-arrow key or press Ctrl-P to retrieve the last command. Then type the subnet number, which leaves **show ip route 168.11.12.64** on the command line. Press Enter.

10 Press the up-arrow key or press Ctrl-P to retrieve the last command. Then press the Backspace key until the word **route** is erased. Then type **arp**, which leaves **show ip arp** on the command line. Press Enter.

11 The answers are as follows:

— Beginning of command line—Ctrl-A

— End of command line—Ctrl-E

— Beginning of previous word—Esc-B

— Beginning of next word—Esc-F

— Backward one character—Ctrl-B

— Forward one character—Ctrl-F

12 A file is obtained from Cisco via disk or FTP download over the Internet; this file is the Cisco IOS Software. The file is placed in the default directory on a TFTP server that is accessible to the router. The **copy tftp flash** command is issued on the router, and the user answers questions to tell the router the name and location of the new Cisco IOS Software. Flash memory is updated as a result of this process. The new Cisco IOS Software is not used until the router is reloaded.

13 TCP stands for Transmission Control Protocol; UDP stands for User Datagram Protocol. TCP provides error recovery.

14 ICMP stands for Internet Control Message Protocol.

15 The Inverse ARP process is not used when the subinterface is a point-to-point subinterface. Therefore, R2 can learn of R1's IP and IPX addresses only with CDP, or by looking at the source addresses of the IPX RIP and IP IGRP routing updates.

16 DLCI stands for data-link connection identifier. Lengths between 10 and 14 bits are defined, with a 10-bit number being the most typically implemented size.

17 No other configuration is necessary; this is a trick question. This is the kind of misdirection you might see on the exam. Read the questions slowly, and read them twice.

18 The **show frame-relay pvc** command lists the PVCs. When multipoint subinterfaces are used, or when no subinterfaces are used for Frame Relay configuration, the **show frame-relay map** command lists the IP and IPX addresses. The **show ip route** and **show ipx route** commands, or the **show cdp neighbor detail** command, can be used to see the addresses in either case.

19 The **show frame-relay pvc** command displays the status.

20 ISDN stands for Integrated Services Digital Network. BRI stands for Basic Rate Interface. PRI stands for Primary Rate Interface.

21 A reference point is an interface between function groups. R, S, T, and U are the reference points. S and T are combined in many cases and together are called the S/T reference point.

22 Q.920 performs functions similar to OSI Layer 2, and Q.930 performs functions similar to OSI Layer 3.

23 Cisco routers' ISDN interfaces are either S/T or U interfaces.

24 The **show cdp neighbor detail** command gives these details.

CHAPTER 13

Hands-on Lab Exercises

Some jobs require that you be able to configure routers and switches, but others do not. For instance, many people who sell Cisco products for Cisco or Cisco Channel Partners have never configured a router or switch. However, those same people might know a lot more about other things, like the Cisco product line and what the latest products are. Simply put, some jobs require different skills and knowledge.

Cisco created CCNA as part of an overall plan to assess and verify the skill sets of the various Cisco Channel Partners. The CCNA certification's role was to prove the basic proficiency of a Channel Partner employee in network installation and support. Because CCNA focuses on network installation and support, Cisco wants CCNAs to be able to configure routers and switches.

In order to better test people on whether they have hands-on skills, Cisco will begin including a practical component on the CCNA exam. The exam engine will simulate routers and switches, with the eventual possibility of using remote lab access to configure live routers and switches during the exam! Therefore, this chapter is designed to help you practice your hands-on skills.

Is it a good thing that Cisco is adding simulated labs to CCNA? Absolutely! If you have made it this far in the book, you definitely want to learn this stuff, not just pass a test. And the more Cisco can make the exam like a real implementation, asking you to apply the knowledge you have gained rather than just spew forth memorized answers, the more valuable the CCNA certification becomes. Wouldn't you rather configure a small IP network than memorize that pressing Esc-B backs up a single word in the command line? With more hands-on skills on the exam, there will be less time for trivial questions.

So how should you prepare? In a word, practice! Get some routers and switches and do the lab exercises in this chapter—even if you think you understand it all. Build some "muscle memory" for implementing simple networks. Do you think Michael Jordan figured out how to shoot a jump shot when he was 12 and then quit shooting them? No, he practiced them a lot, so now his muscles remember what to do, and he doesn't think about how to shoot a jump shot every time he does it. So, the more you practice configuring routers and switches, the easier it will be to breeze through the exam instead of being hesitant about taking the exam with the new practical component.

Options for Gaining Hands-on Skills

When I sat down to write this chapter, I thought about the different options available when you want to develop hands-on skills. Each option has advantages and disadvantages:

- **Borrowing gear from your company's test lab**—If you already work in a networking job, chances are you can scrounge around and find some gear to use. Of course, getting a combination of gear that matches the examples in the books you're using might be a little more challenging, and collecting the gear each time you have a few hours to study might be a hassle. However, it's still one of the best ways to get hands-on skills. One key is to have some direction as to what to do with the gear after you get it—and that problem is solved for CCNA with this chapter of lab exercises.
- **Buying some gear on the Internet**—You can always buy your own equipment if you do not have access to it at your job. It takes money, but you can always sell the gear when you're done, as long as it isn't broken or obsolete. Collecting a variety of gear to match a book's different examples and scenarios might be difficult, because most books' examples (this one included) are not written to minimize the amount of equipment needed to build the lab. The lab exercises in this chapter use the minimum amount of equipment needed to let you learn the necessary information, hopefully keeping the price down for you.
- **Leasing the gear**—Some companies will lease you a CCNA lab, but you still have the problem of collecting a variety of gear to match the different examples and scenarios in a book.
- **Simulators**—Simulators vary greatly in quality, but if you have little or no access to actual equipment, it's the next best thing. Cisco offers two different simulators—the Cisco Interactive Mentor and the CCNA Router and Switch eSIM, upon which the CCNA exam simulation tool is based. Although simulators cannot teach everything, they are generally adequate for what you need to learn for CCNA. The labs in this chapter will not help you with simulators, because simulators tend to force you to configure what they want you to configure, not to just configure anything you want to.
- **Lab rentals (e-labs)**—Finally, several companies (including Skyline Computer) will rent lab time on lab pods accessible from the Internet. These typically can be rented by the hour or by the lab exercise, either for specific lab exercises or to do any labs you would like to perform. The labs in this book should work with some of the lab rental offerings.

About the Labs in This Chapter

There are two general categories of labs in this chapter:

- **Familiarization**—The first two labs familiarize you with the CLI of routers and switches. They are designed for people who have not used routers and switches before, so they are very straightforward. They are also designed to be repeatable, until all the features and commands become second nature.

- **Practice**—The rest of the labs are simply practice for the configuration and EXEC commands covered in a particular chapter. These labs assume that you know how to get around the user interface of the router and switch. These practice labs do not tell you exactly what commands and options to type at every step. Instead, they are designed to make you think. Appendix D (included in PDF format on the CD for this book), "Hands-on Lab Exercises: Solutions," has figures for all the labs, worked out on a live lab pod, in case you need help.

Equipment List

You will of course need some equipment in order to do the labs. Because different people might buy different equipment, this list describes the gear generically:

- **Routers (you need two)**—Each router needs IP/IPX enabled in Cisco IOS Software, as well as one Ethernet and one Serial interface. The serial interface can be a synchronous interface or an async/sync interface. These are priced around $500 to $600 on eBay.
- **1900 series switch (you need one or two)**—One lab exercise requires one switch, and the other requires two. The other lab exercises can be done with very inexpensive Ethernet hubs. The second switch lab, Lab 3, requires two 1900 series switches, each with Enterprise-level software. Either a 1912 or 1924 model works fine. These are around $400 to $500 on eBay.
- **Router as Frame Relay switch (you need one)**—In all the examples in this book, the Frame Relay network was created using one or more Cisco routers configured to act as a Frame Relay switch. A sample configuration is included with the Frame Relay lab in this chapter. Any Cisco router with two serial interfaces, along with IP IOS, will work. You need this additional router only for Lab 7.
- **Ethernet hub (you need one)**—One router (R2) in the labs is not attached to the switch, so it needs to be plugged into any available LAN hub. You can alternatively connect R2 to the same 1900 as R1, making sure that R2's port is in a different VLAN.
- **LAN cables (you need two)**—Two Category 5 straight-through cables attach the routers to either the 1900 switch (R1) or the hub (R2). If your two routers use an AUI interface, you need AUI transceivers as well.
- **Serial cables**—You need one DCE cable and one DTE cable, which will be connected to create the serial link between R1 and R2. The connectors are dependent on the connectors on the routers you buy.
- **Serial cables (for Frame Relay)**—You need one DCE cable and one DTE cable, which will be connected, between each router and the router acting as a Frame Relay switch. Depending on the type of interfaces on the Frame Relay router, you might not be able to use the ones you used to create the point-to-point link between R1 and R2.

- **Console kit (you need one)**—You need to access the console of the routers and switches. A console kit contains the correct cable and connector.

For example, you could obtain the following equipment. This list contains currently-popularly-available items on eBay:

- Three 2501 routers
- Two 1912EN switches
- Two Ethernet AUI transceivers
- Two DB60-V.35 DTE cables (part number CAB-v35MT=)
- Two DB60-V.35 DCE cables (part number CAB-v35FC=)
- Two 6-foot Category 5 cables (straight-through)
- Two 6-foot Category 5 cables (cross-over for trunk links)
- One console cable/connector
- One 10BaseT hub

List of Labs

Table 13-1 describes the labs in this chapter.

Table 13-1 *Lab Descriptions*

Lab	Title	Description
1	Router Command-Line Interface Familiarization	The main goal of this lab is to make you familiar with getting around the router CLI. This lab offers you hints, ensuring that you understand the basics.
2	1900 Series Switch Command-Line Interface Familiarization	The main goal of this lab is to make you familiar with getting around the switch CLI. This lab offers you hints, ensuring that you understand the basics.
3	1900 Series Switch VLANs, Trunks, and Spanning Tree	In this lab, the only one that requires two switches, you configure VLANs and trunking. You must exercise your memory of the commands. In this and the rest of the labs, you are told what to do, but not the command you need in order to do it.
4	Basic Router IP Configuration and Management Navigation	This lab exercises your memory of basic IP configuration, as well as how to use the more popular IP troubleshooting commands.
5	IP Routing Configuration	This lab has you configure static IP routes, as well as the RIP and IGRP routing protocols.

Table 13-1 *Lab Descriptions (Continued)*

Lab	Title	Description
6	IP Access List Configuration	This lab has you configure two different extended IP access lists and one named extended IP access list.
7	WAN Configuration	This lab takes you through PPP configuration, as well as several Frame Relay configuration options.

Lab 1: Router Command-Line Interface Familiarization

All the labs in this chapter assume that the routers and switches have no existing configuration in them when the lab starts. Figure 13-1 shows the network diagram used in most of the labs. In this lab, you only need to use R1.

Figure 13-1 *Lab 1 Network*

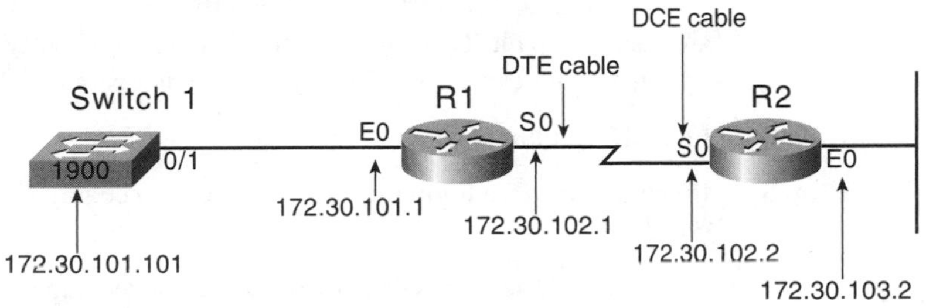

Lab 1: Objectives

When finished with this lab, you will be able to do the following:

- Log in to a Cisco router via the console port
- Configure the passwords needed to log in via the console port and to enter privileged mode
- Get help via the router user interface
- Get help in EXEC and configuration modes
- Configure IP parameters
- Use several basic switch EXEC and configuration mode commands easily
- Navigate the different modes of the Cisco 1900 series switch CLI

This lab is intended to force you to try out several features of the CLI. You can, and should, branch out to try other commands. You should also repeat this lab until you've memorized all its commands and their syntax and you no longer need to ask for help to be able to remember the commands and their options. After the step-by-step instructions for this lab, you will get some hints, ensuring that you understand the basics.

Lab 1: Step-by-Step Instructions

Step 1 Connect the console cable between your PC's COM1 port and a router's console port.

Step 2 Bring up your favorite terminal emulator program. If you do not have a favorite, use HyperTerminal, which comes with Microsoft operating systems. Select Start, Programs, Accessories, Communications, HyperTerminal.

Step 3 Ignore attempts to make you configure a phone number, but configure terminal characteristics of 9600 bps, 8 bits/byte, no parity, and 1 start/stop bit. This combination is often called 9600 8N1. It is what the router expects the console terminal to operate with.

Step 4 From the terminal emulator, press Enter.

Step 5 If you do not see a login prompt, repeat the preceding steps until you do.

Step 6 Using the help facilities described, look at the available commands.

Step 7 Try to enter privileged mode. Are you prompted for a password?

____

Step 8 When you are in privileged mode, use **help** to see the current list of commands.

Step 9 Guessing at some commands that look like they might be destructive or powerful, go back to user mode and use command help again to verify whether those commands are available in user mode.

Step 10 Repeat the last few steps until you have found three commands available in privileged mode but not user mode. List these commands:

____

____

____

Step 11 For the three commands recorded in step 10, use help to find the parameters for each command.

____

____

____

Step 12 How many serial interfaces are on this router? What are their names?

____

Step 13 How many packets and bytes have exited the lowest-numbered serial interface since the counters were last cleared? How long ago were the counters last cleared?

____

Step 14 What version of the Cisco IOS software is running?

____

Step 15 What is the name of the file in Flash memory?

____

Step 16 What was the time of and reason for the last reload?

____

Step 17 Enter configuration mode.

Step 18 Using help, find the command that changes the router's host name.

Step 19 Change your host name to a name you like.

Step 20 Exit configuration mode.

Step 21 Using both old-style and new-style commands, verify that the RAM configuration and NVRAM configuration are different—namely, that the host name in NVRAM is the old name and the one in the RAM configuration is the new name you just specified.

Step 22 Enter configuration mode, and change the host name back to what it was previously.

Step 23 Save your configuration.

Step 24 Using help, find three global configuration commands that are interesting to you, and list them here.

____

____

____

Step 25 Enter interface configuration mode for the Ethernet interface.

Step 26 Using help, find two commands that are interesting to you, and list them here.

____

____

Step 27 In privileged EXEC mode, use the **clock set** command. Using help key sequences, type a syntactically correct **clock set** command. Then retrieve the command and move to the front of the command on the command line, back to the end, back one word, forward one word, back one letter, and forward one letter, each time using a single two-key combination.

Lab 1: Hints

Table 13-2 *Hints for Lab 1*

Step	Hint
1	I searched for "console connection" on www.cisco.com, and I found this pointer that might be helpful: http://www.cisco.com/univercd/cc/td/doc/product/access/acs_fix/cis2500/2520/2520_23/c2520ins.htm#xtocid894612
4	If you do everything right but forget to press Enter, the router or switch will not write anything to the screen. You will not hurt anything by pressing Enter too many times!
5	Always try a different console cable and connector, make sure the cables are connected well, and make sure the cable is plugged into the console port, not the auxiliary port.
6	Use the **?** command.
7	Use the **enable** command.
8	Use the **?** command.
9	Use the **disable** and **enable** commands to move back and forth.
11	For example, if you choose **configure** as one of your commands, use the **configure ?** command to find information about the next option.

Table 13-2 *Hints for Lab 1 (Continued)*

Step	Hint
12	Use the **show interfaces** command.
13	Use the **show interfaces serial** *x* command.
14	Use the **show version** command.
15	Use the **show flash** command.
16	Use the **show version** command, and look closely!
17	Use the **configure terminal** command.
18	Use the **?** command to find the **hostname** command.
19	The right command would be something like **hostname Hannah**.
20	Press Ctrl-Z to exit, or repeatedly enter the **exit** command.
21	Use the **show startup-config** and **show running-config** commands (new) or the **show config** and **write terminal** commands (old).
23	Use the **copy running-config startup-config** command (new) or the **write memory** command (old).
24	Enter configuration mode first! Then, simply use the **?** command.
25	From global configuration mode, use the **interface ethernet** *x* command.
26	Some examples might be the **ip address** command and the **description** command.

Lab 2: 1900 Series Switch Command-Line Interface Familiarization

This lab assumes that the routers and switches have no existing configuration in them when the lab starts.

Lab 2: Objectives

When finished with this lab, you will be able to do the following:

- Log in to a Cisco 1900 series switch via the console port
- Configure the passwords needed to log in via the console port and to enter privileged mode
- Get help in EXEC and configuration modes

- Configure IP parameters on the switch
- Use several basic switch EXEC and configuration mode commands easily
- Navigate the different modes of the Cisco 1900 series switch CLI

This lab, like Lab 1, is intended to force you to try out several features of the CLI. You can, and should, branch out to try other commands. You should also repeat this lab until you've memorized all its commands and their syntax and you no longer need to ask for help to be able to remember the commands and their options. After the step-by-step instructions for this lab, you will get some hints, ensuring that you understand the basics.

Lab 2: Step-by-Step Instructions

Step 1 Connect the console cable between your PC's COM1 port and a switch's console port.

Step 2 Bring up your favorite terminal emulator program. If you do not have a favorite, use HyperTerminal, which comes with Microsoft operating systems. Select Start, Programs, Accessories, Communications, HyperTerminal.

Step 3 Ignore attempts to make you configure a phone number, but configure terminal characteristics of 9600 bps, 8 bits/byte, no parity, and 1 start/stop bit. This combination is often called 9600 8N1. It is what the router expects the console terminal to operate with.

Step 4 Turn on the switch. The 1900 series has no on/off switch—you just plug it in.

Step 5 The switch should display some text, with options. Select option K to use the CLI.

Step 6 If you do not see a login prompt, repeat the preceding steps until you do.

Step 7 Using help facilities, look at the available commands. Do there seem to be more commands, or fewer commands, compared to the router CLI?

Step 8 Try to enter privileged mode. Are you prompted for a password?

____

Step 9 When you are in privileged mode, use **help** to see the current list of commands. Are there more commands than were shown in user mode? Are there more commands in switch CLI enable mode or router CLI enable mode?

____

Step 10 Guessing at some commands that look like they might be destructive or powerful, go back to user mode and look at command help again to verify whether those commands are unavailable in user mode.

Step 11 Repeat the last few steps until you have found three commands available in privileged mode but not user mode. List these commands:

____

____

____

Step 12 For the three commands you recorded in Step 11, use help to find the parameters for each command.

____

____

____

Step 13 How many LAN interfaces are on this switch? What are their names and/or numbers?

____

Step 14 How many packets and bytes have exited the lowest-numbered Ethernet interface since the counters were last cleared?

____

Step 15 What version of the switch IOS is running? Also note the "base MAC address" used by the switch (seen with the same command).

____

Step 16 What is the name of the file in Flash memory?

____

Step 17 What was the time of the last reload?

____

Step 18 Enter configuration mode.

Step 19 Using help, find the command that changes the switch's host name.

Step 20 Change your host name to a name that you like.

Step 21 Exit configuration mode.

Are the RAM configuration and NVRAM configuration different? List the commands you use to verify.

___

___

Step 22 Enter configuration mode, and change the host name back to what it was previously. If the host name was not set, set it to "switch1."

Step 23 Save your configuration. Record the command you use.

___

Step 24 Delete the saved configuration so that next time you boot the switch, the switch will use only default configuration parameters, including not using the host name you just defined. What command did you use?

___

Step 25 Using help, find three global configuration commands that are interesting to you. List them here.

___

___

___

Step 26 Enter interface configuration mode for the Ethernet interface.

Step 27 Using help, find two commands that are interesting to you, and list them here.

___

___

Step 28 Set an enable password so that **cisco** must be typed when a user tries to enter privileged mode. What command did you use?

___

Step 29 Set the switch's IP address and default router based on Figure 13-1. Record the commands you use.

___

Step 30 Verify that STP is on by default. What is the bridge-id of the spanning tree root? What switch is that?

___

Step 31 List all the MAC addresses in the address table. Record the command you use.

____

Step 32 List the switch's IP address and default router without looking at the configuration file. Record your command(s).

____

Lab 2: Hints

Table 13-3 *Hints for Lab 2*

Step	Hint
1	I searched for "console connection" on www.cisco.com, and found this pointer that may be helpful: http://www.cisco.com/univercd/cc/td/doc/product/access/acs_fix/cis2500/2520/2520_23/c2520ins.htm#xtocid894612
6	Always try a different console cable and connector, make sure the cables are connected well, and make sure the cables are plugged into the console port, not the aux port.
7	Use the **?** command.
8	Use the **enable** command.
9	Use the **?** command.
10	Use the **disable** and **enable** commands to move back and forth.
13	Use the **show interfaces** command.
14	Use the **show interfaces ethernet 0/1** command.
15, 17	Use the **show version** command.
18	Use the **configure terminal** command.
19	Use the **?** command to find the **hostname** command.
20	The right command would be something like **hostname Hannah**
21	**Ctrl-z** exits, or repeated use of the **exit** command.
22	Use the **show running-config** command.
23	It's automatic on 1900 series switches—no command required.
24	Use the **delete nvram** EXEC command.
26	Use the **interface ethernet 0/1** command.

continues

Table 13-3 *Hints for Lab 2 (Continued)*

Step	Hint
28	Use the **enable password** or **enable secret** global config commands.
30	Use the **show spantree** command.
31	Use the **show mac-address-table** command.
32	Use the **show ip** command.

Lab 3: 1900 Series Switch VLANs, Trunks, and Spanning Tree

This lab assumes that the routers and switches have no existing configuration in them when the lab starts. This lab also assumes that you know how to get around the user interface on the switches. This lab focuses on reviewing the most important commands from Chapter 5, "Intermediate LANs: Spanning Tree, VLANs, and Trunking." The lab topology for this lab is shown in Figure 13-2.

Figure 13-2 *Cabling Diagram for Lab 3*

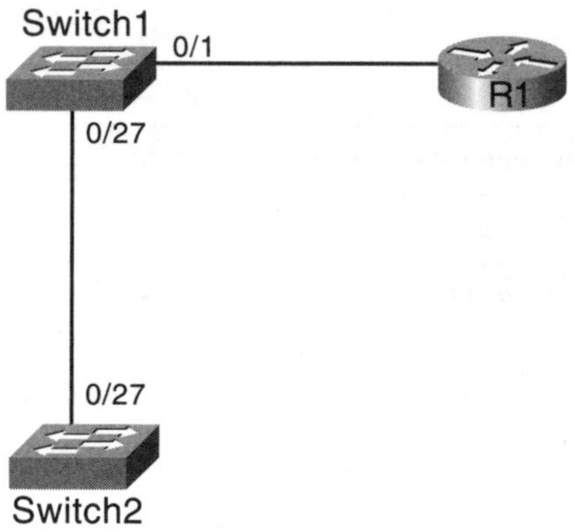

Lab 3: Objectives

When finished with this lab, you will be able to do the following:

- Configure VLANs and VTP on a Cisco 1900 series switch
- Examine STP parameters in a switch network with redundancy
- Configure ISL trunking to allow VLAN traffic to pass between switches

Lab 3: Step-by-Step Instructions

Step 1 Cable the network based on Figure 13-2.

Step 2 Log in to Switch1. Configure a host name for the switch.

Step 3 Configure the VTP server of Switch1, with VTP domain Bees.

Step 4 Configure ports 0/1 through 0/10 in VLAN1 and ports 0/11 through 0/20 in VLAN2.

Step 5 Name VLAN2 something really clever, like VLAN2 or something similar.

Step 6 Turn on ISL trunking on interface 0/27. Allow traffic for both VLANs to pass.

Step 7 Log in to Switch2. Configure an appropriate host name. Also give it an IP address of 172.30.101.102 and a default gateway of R1 (172.30.101.1).

Step 8 Does ISL need to be enabled on 0/27? Is it already on? If it isn't, turn on ISL trunking on interface 0/27. Record the command(s) you use to find out.

____

Step 9 Does your switch already know about VLAN2? Record the command(s) you use to find out.

____

Step 10 If needed, configure VLAN2 on Switch2, with the same clever name you chose in Step 5.

Step 11 On Switch2, put interfaces 0/1 through 0/10 in VLAN 1 and interfaces 0/11 through 0/20 in VLAN2. Ensure that VLAN1 and VLAN2 traffic can pass between switches.

Step 12 Using **show** commands only, verify the VLANs in which all ports on Switch2 reside. Record your command(s).

____

Step 13 Do you think that STP needs to block on any ports? Is STP blocking on any ports? Record the commands you use to verify whether STP is blocking.

____

____

Step 14 Which switch is the root of the spanning tree? Record the commands you use to determine which switch is the root.

____

____

Step 15 What is the VTP revision number?

____

Step 16 On Switch1, configure VLANs 5, 6, and 7. What is the VTP revision number now?

____

Lab 4: Basic Router IP Configuration and Management Navigation

This lab assumes that the routers and switches have no existing configuration in them when the lab starts. This lab also assumes that you know how to get around the user interface on the routers. This lab focuses on reviewing the most important commands from Chapter 6, "TCP/IP and IP Routing." This lab assumes you are using a lab network that matches the Figure 13-1.

Lab 4: Objectives

When finished with this lab, you will be able to do the following:

- Perform initial configuration using setup mode
- Perform initial configuration using configuration mode
- Verify IP connectivity using ping and trace
- Verify basic configuration using CDP
- Suspend and reconnect Telnet sessions

Lab 4: Step-by-Step Instructions

Step 1 Log in to R1, and use the **write erase** command to clear NVRAM.

Step 2 Issue the **reload** command to reload your router. What configuration will the router use when reloading?

____

Step 3 After the router has reloaded, you are asked if you want to enter the "initial configuration dialogue." Type **yes**.

Step 4 You are prompted with a series of commands. These commands expect a response from you. If there is a default answer, it is shown in brackets at the end of the command. You can just press Enter if that is the answer you want. Otherwise, type the appropriate answer, and the router creates the correct configuration for you.

Step 5 Configure a host name, configure all passwords as **cisco**, and configure IP parameters based on Figure 13-1. All subnet masks are 255.255.255.0.

Step 6 When finished, you are asked if you want to use this configuration. If you are happy with what you configured, type **yes** and press Enter. If not, type **no**, press Enter, and start again at Step 1.

Step 7 Log in to R2, and use the **write erase** command to clear NVRAM.

Step 8 Issue the **reload** command to reload your router. What configuration will the router use when reloading?

____

Step 9 When the router has reloaded, you are asked if you want to enter the "initial configuration dialogue." Type **no**.

Step 10 Enter configuration mode, and configure R2. Give it a host name, configure all passwords as **cisco**, and configure IP addresses based on Figure 13-1. All subnet masks are 255.255.255.0.

Step 11 On serial interface 0 (or your equivalent), configure the command **clock rate 56000**. This makes the router provide clocking, because there is no CSU/DSU in the sample network.

Step 12 Exit configuration mode, and save your configuration.

Step 13 Reconnect to R1's console. Using the **ping** command on R1, discover whether you can ping R2's IP addresses. List the IP addresses you can ping and those you cannot.

____

Step 14 Ping these same IP addresses using 1000-byte-long packets.

Step 15 Using the **trace** command on R1, discover the path taken to reach R2's IP addresses. (Hint: If **trace** never seems to want to finish, press Ctrl-Shift-6 to stop the command.)

____

Step 16 Telnet to R2.

Step 17 Using the **ping** command on R2, discover whether you can ping R1's IP addresses. List the IP addresses you can ping and those you cannot.

Step 18 Ping these same IP addresses using 1000-byte-long packets.

Step 19 Using the **trace** command on R2, discover the path taken to reach R1's IP addresses. (Hint: If **trace** never seems to want to finish, press Ctrl-Shift-6 to stop the command.)

Step 20 Suspend your Telnet connection. You should now be at the R1 command prompt.

Step 21 Look at the suspended Telnet connections on R1. What command did you use?

Step 22 Reconnect to R2 without having to type passwords again.

Step 23 On R2, exit (do not suspend) the Telnet connection.

Step 24 Back on R1, configure a host name for R2, referencing both IP addresses on R2.

Step 25 Telnet to R2 using the host name. Exit back to R1 when finished.

Step 26 On R1, use CDP to learn as much as you can about the neighboring switch and router without logging in to either device. What version of software is R2 using? Switch1? What are their IP addresses? What are their capabilities relative to each other?

Step 27 Save your configurations on both routers.

Lab 5: IP Routing Configuration

This lab assumes that you have completed Lab 4, in which you configured IP addresses. This lab assumes that you know how to get around the user interface on the routers. This lab focuses on reviewing the most important commands from Chapter 7, "Routing and Routing Protocols." This lab assumes you are using a lab network that matches the Figure 13-1.

Lab 5: Objectives

When finished with this lab, you will be able to do the following:

- Configure static IP routes
- Configure RIP
- Configure IGRP
- Verify the contents of the IP routing table

Lab 5: Step-by-Step Instructions

Step 1 Log in to R1.

Step 2 You should be able to ping 172.30.102.2, R2's serial IP address, but not 172.30.103.2, R2's Ethernet IP address. The ping to 172.30.103.2 does not work, because R1 does not have a route to 172.30.103.0/24, the subnet in which 172.30.103.2 resides.

Step 3 Verify the contents of the routing table on R1. What command did you use? How many routes are in the routing table?

Step 4 On R1, configure a static route pointing to subnet 172.30.103.0.

Step 5 On R1, ping 172.30.103.2. Does it work now? (It should!) If it doesn't, work on your static route configuration until it does.

Step 6 From R2, try to ping R1's Ethernet IP address, 172.30.101.1. Does it work? (It should not.)

Step 7 Add a static route on R2 that will make the ping to 172.30.101.1 work.

Step 8 How many routes are in R2's routing table?

Step 9 Remove the static route commands from both R1 and R2. How many routes are in each router's routing table now?

Step 10 Configure RIP on both R1 and R2.

Step 11 From R1, try pinging R2's Ethernet IP address. Similarly, ping R1's Ethernet IP address from R2. Does it work?

Step 12 What is the administrative distance associated with the routes learned by RIP? Record the command you use to discover this information.

Step 13 Configure IGRP on R1 and R2. How many routes are in each routing table now?

Step 14 What are the sources of the routing information? Static? Connected? RIP? IGRP? EIGRP?

Step 15 Turn on a debug that shows IGRP routing updates. How often do they occur?

Step 16 Turn on a debug that shows RIP routing updates. How often do they occur?

Step 17 Does it appear that RIP is still sending and receiving routing updates?

Step 18 Turn off RIP on both routers. Are all the routes still in the routing table?

Step 19 Turn off your debugs, and save your configurations on both routers.

Lab 6: IP Access List Configuration

This lab assumes that you have completed Labs 4 and 5, in which you configured IP addresses and routing protocols. This lab assumes that you know how to get around the user interface on the routers. This lab focuses on reviewing the most important commands from Chapter 8, "Understanding Access List Security." This lab assumes you are using a lab network that matches the Figure 13-1.

Lab 6: Objectives

When finished with this lab, you will be able to do the following:

- Configure extended IP access lists
- Configure named extended IP access lists

Lab 6: Step-by-Step Instructions

Step 1 Log in to R1.

Step 2 Verify that you can ping 172.30.103.2, R2's Ethernet0 IP address. Likewise, verify that you can Telnet to that same address.

Step 3 After you have Telnetted to R2, configure the Web server feature on R2 using the **ip http server** configuration command. Save your configuration on R2.

Step 4 Suspend/quit back to R1.

Step 5 From R1, you can use the **telnet** command to test whether the Web server on R2 is responding, using a trick. From R1, use the command **telnet 172.30.103.2 80**. This command uses Telnet, but it tries to Telnet to destination port 80—the port used by the Web server. You should get no error messages if this works correctly. Then, type **?**. You see some messages from the Web server on R2 about HTTP 400 bad request, as shown in Example 13-1.

Example 13-1 *Trick to Test Web Traffic Using Just Routers*

```
R1#telnet 172.30.103.2 80
Trying 172.30.103.2, 80 ... Open
?
HTTP/1.0 400 Bad Request
Date: Mon, 01 Mar 1993 03:08:27 UTC
Content-type: text/html
Expires: Thu, 16 Feb 1989 00:00:00 GMT

<H1>400 Bad Request</H1>



[Connection to 172.30.103.2 closed by foreign host]
```

Step 6 So far, you should have confirmed that ping, Telnet, and Web traffic to 172.30.103.2 work.

Step 7 Create an access list on R2, and enable it for traffic entering R2's S0 interface. In this access list, permit ICMP echoes to the Ethernet subnet off R2, permit Telnet to all IP addresses in that subnet except R2's Ethernet IP address, and allow Web traffic to any Web servers in that same subnet. Also, permit Telnet into 172.30.102.2 so that you can still Telnet into R2 to do your testing.

Step 8 After configuring the access list, from R1, test. A **ping** from R1 to 172.30.103.2 should work, a **telnet** to the same address should not, and the **telnet 172.30.103.2 80** trick should still work.

Step 9 Disable the access list on R2 so that all traffic is now allowed.

Step 10 On R2, create a named access list that achieves the same goal.

Step 11 Test again from R1. A **ping** from R1 to 172.30.103.2 should work, a **telnet** to the same address should not, and the **telnet 172.30.103.2 80** trick should still work.

Step 12 Disable the named access list on R2 so that all traffic is now allowed.

Step 13 Create an access list on R1, enabled for input traffic in R1's S0 interface, that achieves the same function as the first ACL.

Step 14 Test again from R1. A **ping** from R1 to 172.30.103.2 should work, a **telnet** to the same address should not, and the **telnet 172.30.103.2 80** trick should still work.

Step 15 When finished, disable the access list on R1.

Lab 7: WAN Configuration

This lab assumes that you have completed Labs 4 and 5, in which you configured IP addresses and routing protocols. This lab assumes that you know how to get around the user interface on the routers. This lab focuses on reviewing the most important commands from Chapter 9, "WAN Protocols and Design," and Chapter 10, "Frame Relay Concepts and Configuration." This lab requires that you use three routers, with one configured as a Frame Relay switch. Figure 13-3 outlines the physical and logical diagrams for the network.

Lab 7: Objectives

When finished with this lab, you will be able to do the following:

- Configure PPP
- Configure Frame Relay

Figure 13-3 *Frame Relay Network Used in Lab 7*

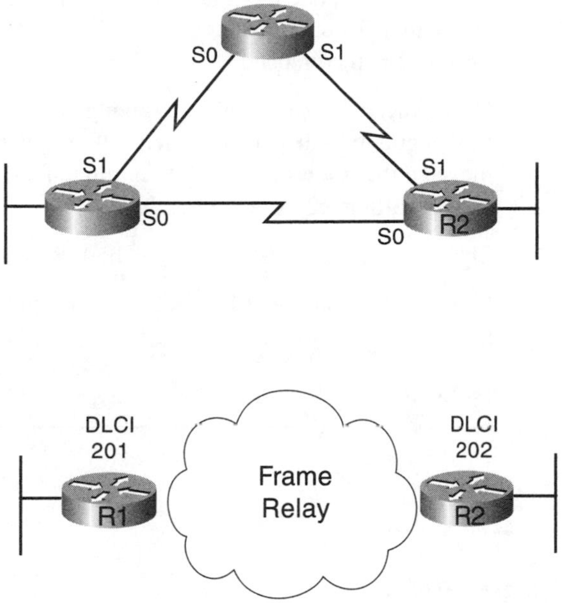

Lab 7: Step-by-Step Instructions

Step 1 The first several steps of this lab use the direct serial link between R1 and R2 that you were using in earlier labs. So, log in to R1 and R2 and ensure that all ACLs from the previous lab have been disabled.

Step 2 On R1, change the encapsulation type on Serial0 to PPP encapsulation. From R1, ping R2's serial IP address. Does it still work?

Step 3 On R2, change the encapsulation type on Serial0 to PPP. Go back to R1. Can R1 ping R2's serial IP address now?

Step 4 Examine the IP routing table. On R1, is there a route to 172.30.102.2? Is there a similar route on R2?

Step 5 On R1, enable PPP debugs using the **debug PPP negotiation** command.

Step 6 On R1, shut down the serial link using the **shutdown** command, wait 5 seconds, and bring it back up with the **no shutdown** command. Get out of configuration mode as soon as you issue the **no shutdown** command.

Step 7 Debug messages should appear, giving you some insight into the PPP negotiation that occurs when PPP initializes. Notice the message that shows PPP on R1 learning about R2's IP address, and R1 telling R2 its own IP address.

Step 8 Shut down the Serial0 interface on both R1 and R2.

Step 9 Log in to the console of R3, and copy the configuration shown in Example 13-2 into R3.

Example 13-2 *Frame Relay Switch Configuration*

```
hostname FRswitch
!
frame-relay switching
!
interface Serial0
 no ip address
 encapsulation frame-relay
 clockrate 56000
 no shutdown
 frame-relay intf-type dce
 frame-relay route 202 interface Serial1 201
!
interface Serial1
 no ip address
 encapsulation frame-relay
 clockrate 56000
 no shutdown
 frame-relay intf-type dce
 frame-relay route 201 interface Serial0 202
```

Step 10 Cable the serial cables between R1 and R3 and between R2 and R3 based on Figure 13-3. Make sure that the DCE cable ends are plugged into the R3. Shutdown the serial link directly between R1 and R2.

Step 11 Configure Frame Relay between R1 and R2 with the following settings: use LMI autosense (the default), use Cisco encapsulation (the default), allow Inverse ARP to work (the default), and do not use subinterfaces. Use a new set of IP addresses instead of the point-to-point link used in the other labs. Use 172.30.104.0/24, using 172.30.104.1 on R1 and 172.30.104.2 on R2.

Step 12 From R1, test the network by pinging R2's IP addresses. Likewise, ping R1 from R2. Do not proceed past this step until it is working. Feel free to refer to Appendix D (included in PDF format on the CD for this book) for an example of a working configuration.

Step 13 From R1, examine the mapping between R2's IP address and the associated DLCI. What is the PVC's DLCI? How long has the associated DLCI been up? Record the commands you use.

____

____

Step 14 Disable Inverse ARP on both routers, and then try to ping the routers on the other side of the network. Record the results.

____

____

Step 15 On both routers, configure static **frame-relay map** statements to map the next-hop IP address to the correct DLCI value. Record the commands that you use. Verify that it works correctly by pinging R2 from R1 and vice versa.

____

____

Step 16 Convert the configuration to use point-to-point subinterfaces on both R1 and R2. Delete the old **frame-relay static map** statements. Can you ping the other routers?

____

Step 17 Look at the current PVC status and the Frame Relay map information. Is there more or less information than with the earlier configuration?

____

Step 18 Confirm that R1 can ping R2. Then change R1's Frame Relay encapsulation type to ietf, and try the ping again. Does it work? Why?

____

Step 19 Change the Frame Relay encapsulation type on R2 to ietf, and try the ping again. Does it work? Why?

Step 20 What LMI type is used by R1? By R2? Record the command you use to discover the LMI type.

Lab 8: Novell IPX Configuration

This lab assumes that you have completed Labs 4 and 5, in which you configured IP addresses and routing protocols. This lab assumes that you know how to get around the user interface on the routers. This lab focuses on reviewing the most important commands from Chapter 11, "Novell IPX." Figure 13-4 outlines the IPX network numbering.

Figure 13-4 *Novell IPX Network Numbers for Lab 8*

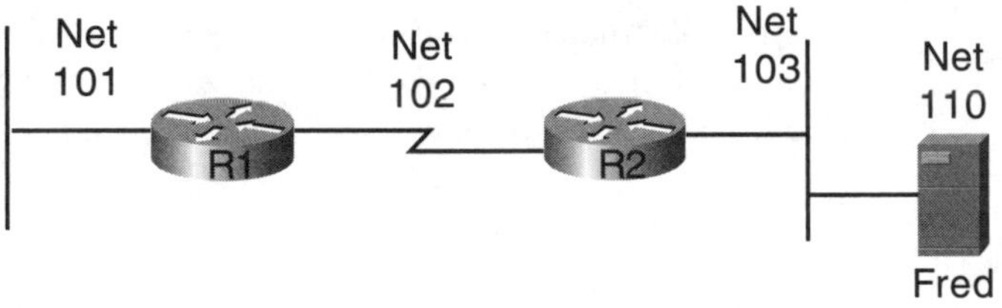

Lab 8: Objectives

When finished with this lab, you will be able to do the following:

- Configure Novell routing and RIP
- Configure SAP filters

Lab 8: Step-by-Step Instructions

Step 1 Revert to the physical and logical topology using a single point-to-point serial link instead of Frame Relay. (You do not have to do this, but this lab assumes that you are using the point-to-point link, not Frame Relay.)

Step 2 On R1 and R2, configure IPX, including IPX RIP.

Step 3 On R1, display the IPX routing table. How many IPX networks are in the table?

Step 4 On R1 and R2, display the IPX addresses for each interface, and record the values.

Step 5 On R1, use the **ping** command to ping R2's S0 and E0 IPX addresses. Likewise, from R2, ping R1's S0 and E0 IPX addresses. If you cannot ping all IPX addresses, troubleshoot your configuration before moving on.

Step 6 On R1, display the list of services available. Are there any?

Step 7 On R2, use the following two configuration commands to create a static SAP entry so that you can see something in the SAP table:

```
ipx sap 4 Fred 110.0000.0000.0001 451 3
ipx route 110 103.0000.0000.0001
```

Step 8 On R2, display the list of services available. Are there any?

Step 9 On R1, display the list of services available. Are there any? If not, wait about 1 minute and try again. You should see on R1 the same SAP you saw on R2.

Step 10 On R1, use the **debug IPX sap activity** command to enable SAP debugging. Wait up to 1 minute. You should see the SAP update entering S0, with information about server Fred.

Step 11 Configure a SAP filter on R1 to filter the Type 4 SAP from server Fred. Enable the SAP access list for incoming traffic on R1's S0 interface.

Step 12 After you apply the SAP filter, the SAP information should time out. Does Fred show up in the SAP table any more?

APPENDIX **A**

Answers to the "Do I Know This Already?" Quizzes and Q&A Sections

Answers to the Chapter 2 "Do I Know This Already?" Quiz

1 What are the two different names for the router's mode of operation that, when accessed, enables you to issue commands that could be disruptive to router operations?

Enable and privileged mode. Both are commonly used and found in Cisco documentation.

2 What command would you use to receive command help if you knew that a show command option begins with a *c* but you could not recall the option?

You would use **show c?**. Help would appear immediately after you typed the **?** symbol. You would not need to press Enter afterward; if you did so, the router would try to execute the command with only the parameters that you had typed after the **?**.

3 After typing **show ip route**, which is the only command that you issued since logging in to the router, you now want to issue the **show ip arp** command. What steps would you take to execute this command by using command-recall keystrokes?

Press the up arrow key, press Backspace five times, and then type **arp**. The up arrow key retrieves the **show ip route** command. The Backspace key moves the cursor backward and erases the character. Typing inserts the characters into the line.

4 What is the name of the user interface mode of operation used when you cannot issue disruptive commands?

User mode.

5 What configuration command causes the router to require a password from a user at the console? What configuration mode context must you be in? (That is, what command(s) must be typed before this command after entering configuration mode?) List the commands in the order in which they must be typed while in config mode.

```
line console 0
 login
```

The **line console 0** command is a context-setting command; it adds no information to the configuration by itself. The command can be typed from any part of configuration mode. The **login** command, which follows the **line console 0** command, tells the IOS that a password prompt is desired at the console.

6 What does the "NV" stand for in NVRAM?

Nonvolatile. NVRAM is used for storing the startup configuration file used when the router is brought up. NVRAM is battery-powered if it is really RAM. In some routers, Cisco has (sneakily) used a small portion of Flash memory for the purpose of NVRAM, but Cisco would not ask such trivia on the test.

7 Name two commands used to view the configuration that is currently used in a router. Which one is a more recent addition to the IOS?

write terminal and **show running-config**. The newer command is **show running-config** and, hopefully, is easier to remember.

8 Name two commands used to view the configuration to be used at the next reload of the router. Which one is a more recent addition to the IOS?

show config and **show startup-config**. **show startup-config** is the newer one and, hopefully, is easier to remember.

9 What two methods could a router administrator use to cause a router to load the IOS stored in ROM?

Setting the configuration register boot field to binary 0001, or adding **boot system rom** to the configuration file and copying it to the startup configuration file. To set the configuration register to hex 2101, which would yield binary 0001 in the boot field, the **config-register 0x2101** global configuration command would be used.

10 What is the process used to update the contents of Flash memory so that a new IOS in a file called c4500-d-mz.120-5.bin, on TFTP server 128.1.1.1, is copied into Flash memory?

copy tftp flash. The other details, namely the IP address of the TFTP server and the filename, are requested through prompts to the user.

11 Two different IOS files are in a router's Flash memory: one called c2500-j-l.111-3.bin and one called c2500-j-l.112-14.bin. Which one does the router use when it boots up? How could you force the other IOS file to be used? Without looking at the router configuration, what command could be used to discover which file was used for the latest boot of the router?

The first IOS file listed in the **show flash** command is the one used at reload time, unless a boot system command is configured. The configuration command **boot system flash xyz123.bin** would override the order of the files in Flash memory. The **show version** command displays the filename of the IOS for the latest reload of a router. The **show version** output tells you the version as well as the name of the file that was used at the last reload. This information is particularly difficult to find in the output of the command; watch for three lines separated by empty lines above and below. The IOS file loaded is in one of those messages.

12 What are the primary purposes of Flash memory in a Cisco router?

To store IOS and microcode files, and to allow remote loading of new versions of these files. In most routers, only an IOS is found. If microcode is upgraded, these files also reside in Flash memory.

Answers to the Chapter 2 Q&A Section

1 What are the two names for the router's mode of operation that, when accessed, enables you to issue commands that could be disruptive to router operations?

Enable mode and privileged mode. Both modes are commonly used and found in Cisco documentation.

2 What are three methods of logging on to a router?

Console, auxiliary port, and Telnet. All three cause the user to enter user EXEC mode.

3 What is the name of the user interface mode of operation used when you cannot issue disruptive commands?

User EXEC mode.

4 Can the auxiliary port be used for anything besides remote modem user access to a router? If so, what other purpose can it serve?

Yes. For direct attachment of a terminal, and dial for the purpose of routing packets. Although it originally was created to support remote administration access, many customers use an auxiliary port for dial backup, particularly when analog lines are desired or when that is all that is available.

5 How many console ports can be installed on a Cisco 7500 router?

One. This is a purposefully strange question. You do not order the console port; every router comes with only one. So, technically, you do not even order one because it is implied by ordering the router.

6 What command would you use to receive command help if you knew that a **show** command option begins with a *c* but you cannot recall the option?

show c?. Help would appear immediately after you typed the **?** symbol. You would not need to press Enter after the **?**. If you did so, the router would try to execute the command with only the parameters that you had typed after the **?**.

7 While you are logged in to a router, you issue the command **copy ?** and get a response of "Unknown command, computer name, or host." Offer an explanation for why this error message appears.

You were in user mode. You must be in enable/privileged mode to use the **copy** command. When in user mode, the router does not provide help for privileged commands, and it treats the request for help as if there is no such command.

8 Is the number of retrievable commands based on the number of characters in each command, or is it simply a number of commands, regardless of their size?

The number of commands. The length (that is, the number of characters) of each command does not affect the command history buffer.

9 How can you retrieve a previously used command? (Name two ways.)

Ctrl-p and up arrow. Up arrow refers literally to the up arrow key on the keyboard. Not all terminal emulators support Ctrl-p or the up arrow, so recalling both methods is useful.

10 After typing **show ip route**, which is the only command that you typed since logging in to the router, you now want to issue the **show ip arp** command. What steps would you take to execute this command by using command-recall keystrokes?

Press the up arrow, press Backspace five times, and type **arp**. The up arrow key retrieves the **show ip route** command. Backspace moves the cursor backward and erases the character. Typing inserts the characters into the line.

11 After typing **show ip route 128.1.1.0**, you now want to issue the command **show ip route 128.1.4.0**. What steps would you take to do so, using command-recall and command-editing keystrokes?

Press the up arrow, Ctrl-b (or left arrow) twice, and Backspace once, and then type **4**. The Ctrl-b and left arrow keys back up one character in the line, without deleting the character. The Backspace key deletes the 1, in this case. Typing inserts into the line.

12 What configuration command causes the router to require a password from a user at the console? What configuration mode context must you be in? (That is, what command(s) must be typed before this command after entering configuration mode?) List the commands in the order in which they must be typed while in config mode.

```
line console 0
login
```

The **line console 0** command is a context-setting command; it adds no information to the configuration. The command can be typed from any part of configuration mode. The **login** command, which follows the **line console 0** command, tells IOS that a password prompt is desired at the console.

13 What configuration command is used to tell the router the password that is required at the console? What configuration mode context must you be in? (That is, what command(s) must you type before this command after entering configuration mode?) List the commands in the order in which they must be typed while in config mode.

```
line console 0
password xxxxxxx
```

The **password** command tells IOS the value that should be typed when a user wants access from the console. This value is requested by IOS because of the login command. The password xxxxxxx must be typed while in console configuration mode, which is reached by typing line console 0.

14 What are the primary purposes of Flash memory in a Cisco router?

To store IOS and microcode files, and to allow remote loading of new versions of these files. In most routers, only IOS is found. If microcode is upgraded, the files also reside in Flash memory.

15 What is the intended purpose of NVRAM memory in a Cisco router?

To store a single configuration file, used at router load time. NVRAM does not support multiple files.

16 What does the "NV" stand for in NVRAM?

Nonvolatile. NVRAM is battery-powered if it is really RAM. In some routers, Cisco has (sneakily) used a small portion of Flash memory for the purpose of NVRAM, but Cisco would not ask such trivia on the test.

17 What is the intended purpose of RAM in a Cisco router?

RAM is used as IOS working memory (storing such things as routing tables or packets) and for IOS code storage. (In some router models, not all IOS is copied into RAM. Some of IOS is left in Flash memory so that more RAM is available for working memory.)

18 What is the main purpose of ROM in a Cisco router?

To store a small, limited-function version of IOS and to store bootstrap code. Typically, this type of IOS is used only during maintenance or emergencies.

19 What configuration command would be needed to cause a router to use an IOS image named c2500-j-l.112-14.bin on TFTP server 128.1.1.1 when the router is reloaded? If you forgot the first parameter of this command, what steps must you take to learn the correct parameters and add the command to the configuration? (Assume that you are not logged in to the router when you start.)

```
boot system tftp 128.1.1.1 c2500-j-l.112-14.bin
```

As for the second part of the question: Log in from con/aux/telnet, type the **enable** command, type the enable password, type the **configure terminal** command, and type **boot ?**. Help appears for the first parameter of the **boot** command.

20 What command sets the password that would be required after typing the **enable** command? Is that password encrypted by default?

enable password or **enable secret**. The password in the **enable** command is not encrypted, by default. The enable secret password is encrypted using MD5.

21 To have the correct syntax, what must you add to the following configuration command?

```
banner This is Ivan Denisovich's Gorno Router--Do Not Use
```

A delimiter character that is not part of the banner is the first parameter, which is followed by the banner text, which is followed by the delimiter character. For example, the "#" is the delimiter in the following command:

```
banner # This is Ivan.... Do Not Use #
```

22 Name two commands that affect the text used as the command prompt.

hostname and **prompt**.

23 When using setup mode, you are prompted at the end of the process for whether you want to use the configuration parameters that you just typed in. Which type of memory is this configuration stored in if you type **yes**?

Both NVRAM and RAM. Setup is the only IOS feature that modifies both the active and the startup configuration files as the result of one action by the user.

24 What two methods could a router administrator use to cause a router to load IOS stored in ROM?

Setting the configuration register boot field to binary 0001, or adding **boot system rom** to the configuration file and copying it to the startup configuration file. To set the configuration register to hex 2101, which would yield binary 0001 in the boot field, the **config-register 0x2101** global configuration command would be used.

25 What could a router administrator do to cause a router to load file xyz123.bin from TFTP server 128.1.1.1 upon the next reload? Is there more than one way to accomplish this?

```
boot system tftp xyz123.bin 128.1.1.1
```

This is the only way to make the router load this file from the TFTP server.

26 What is the process used to update the contents of Flash memory so that a new IOS in a file called c4500-d-mz.120-5.bin on TFTP server 128.1.1.1 is copied into Flash memory?

copy tftp flash. The other details—namely, the IP address of the TFTP server and the filename—are requested through prompts to the user.

27 Name three possible problems that could prevent the command **boot system tftp c2500-j-l.112- 14.bin 128.1.1.1** from succeeding.

The possible reasons include: 128.1.1.1 is not accessible through the network; there is no TFTP server on 128.1.1.1; the file is not in the TFTP default directory; the file is corrupted; a **boot** command could precede this **boot** command in the configuration file; and the IOS referenced in the first **boot** command would be used instead.

28 Two different IOS files are in a router's Flash memory: one called c2500-j-l.111-3.bin and one called c2500-j-l.112-14.bin. Which one does the router use when it boots up? How could you force the other IOS file to be used? Without looking at the router configuration, what command could be used to discover which file was used for the latest boot of the router?

The first IOS file listed in the **show flash** command is the one used at reload time, unless a **boot system** command is configured. The configuration command **boot system flash xyz123.bin** would override the order in Flash memory. **show version** is the command used to display the filename of IOS for the latest reload of a router. The **show version** output tells you the version as well as the name of the file that was used at last reload time. It is particularly difficult to find in the output of the command.

29 Is the password required at the console the same one that is required when Telnet is used to access a router?

No. The Telnet ("virtual terminal") password is not the same password, although many installations use the same value.

30 Which IP routing protocols could be enabled using setup?

RIP and IGRP.

31 Name two commands used to view the configuration to be used at the next reload of the router. Which one is a more recent addition to IOS?

show config and **show startup-config**. **show startup-config** is the newer one and, hopefully, is easier to remember.

32 Name two commands used to view the configuration that is currently used in a router. Which one is a more recent addition to IOS?

write terminal and **show running-config**. **show running-config** is the newer command and, hopefully, is easier to remember.

33 True or false: The **copy startup-config running-config** command always changes the currently used configuration for this router to exactly match what is in the startup configuration file. Explain.

False. Some configuration commands do not replace an existing command but are simply added to a list of related commands. If such a list exists, the **copy startup-config running-config** command simply adds those to the end of the list. Many of these lists in a router configuration are order-dependent.

Answers to the Chapter 3 "Do I Know This Already?" Quiz

1 Name the seven layers of the OSI model.

Application (Layer 7), presentation (Layer 6), session (Layer 5), transport (Layer 4), network (Layer 3), data link (Layer 2), and physical (Layer 1).

2 What is the main purpose(s) of Layer 3?

The network layer defines logical addressing and routing as a means of delivering data across an entire network. IP and IPX are two examples of Layer 3–equivalent protocols.

3 What is the main purpose(s) of Layer 2?

The data link layer defines addressing specific to a particular medium as part of the means of providing delivery of data across that medium. It also includes the protocols used to determine what device(s) access the media at any point in time.

4 What OSI layer typically encapsulates using both a header and a trailer?

The data link layer. The trailer typically includes a frame check sequence (FCS), which is used to perform error detection.

5 Describe the features required for a protocol to be considered connectionless.

Unordered low-overhead delivery of data from one host to another is the service provided in most connectionless protocol services.

6 Describe the features required for a protocol to be considered connection-oriented.

Either the protocol must exchange messages with another device before data is allowed to be sent, or some pre-established correlation between the two endpoints must be defined. TCP is an example of a connection-oriented protocol that exchanges messages before data may be sent; Frame Relay is a connection-oriented protocol for which pre-established correlation between endpoints is defined.

7 In a particular error-recovering (reliable) protocol, the sender sends three frames, labeled 2, 3, and 4. On its next sent frame, the receiver of these frames sets an acknowledgment field to 4. What does this typically imply?

Setting the acknowledgment field to 4 implies that frames through number 3 were received successfully. Most windowing, error-recovery (reliable) protocols use forward acknowledgment.

8 Name three connection-oriented protocols.

TCP, SPX, LLC Type 2, and X.25 are some examples of connection-oriented protocols that happen to provide error recovery. ATM and Frame Relay are also connection-oriented, but without error recovery.

9 Name three terms popularly used as synonyms for *MAC address*.

NIC address, *card address*, *LAN address*, *hardware address*, *Ethernet address*, *Token Ring address*, *FDDI address*, and *burned-in* address are used synonymously with MAC address. All of these names are used casually and in formal documents, and they refer to the same 6-byte MAC address concept as defined by IEEE.

10 What portion of a MAC address encodes an identifier representing the manufacturer of the card?

The first 3 bytes. For instance, Cisco is assigned 0000.0C as one of its organizationally unique identifiers (OUIs). Many Cisco router Ethernet interfaces have MAC addresses beginning with that value. The output of the **show interface** command for a LAN interface lists the burned-in address after the acronym BIA.

11 Are DLCI addresses defined by a Layer 2 or a Layer 3 protocol?

Layer 2. Although they are not specifically covered in this chapter, Frame Relay protocols do not define a logical addressing structure that can usefully exist outside a Frame Relay network; by definition, the addresses would be OSI Layer 2–equivalent.

12 How many bits are present in a MAC address?

MAC addresses comprise 48 bits. The first 24 bits for burned-in addresses represent a code that identifies the manufacturer.

13 How many bits are present in an IPX address?

IPX addresses comprise 80 bits—32 bits in the network portion and 48 bits in the node portion.

14 Name the two main parts of an IP address. Which part identifies the “group” of which this address is a member?

Network and host are the two main parts of an IP address. As described in Chapter 6, “ TCP/IP and IP Routing,” technically there are three portions of the IP address: network, subnet, and host. However, because most people think of the network and subnet portions as one portion, another correct answer to this question, using popular terminology, would be subnet and host.

15 Describe the differences between a routed protocol and a routing protocol.

The routed protocol defines the addressing and Layer 3 header in the packet that is actually forwarded by a router. The routing protocol defines the process of routers exchanging topology data so that the routers know how to forward the data. A router uses the routing table created by the routing protocol to choose how to forward a routed protocol packet.

16 Name at least three routed protocols.

TCP/IP (IP), Novell (IPX), OSI (CLNP), DECnet (CLNP), AppleTalk (DDP), and VINES are some examples of routed protocols.

Answers to the Chapter 3 Q&A Section

1 Name the seven layers of the OSI model.

Application (Layer 7), presentation (Layer 6), session (Layer 5), transport (Layer 4), network (Layer 3), data link (Layer 2), and physical (Layer 1). Some mnemonics to help you recall the names of the layers are: All People Seem To Need Data Processing (Layer 7 to 1), Please Do Not Take Sausage Pizzas Away (Layer 1 to 7), and the ever-popular Pew! Dead Ninja Turtles Smell Particularly Awful (Layer 1 to 7).

2 What is the main purpose(s) of Layer 7?

Layer 7 (application layer) provides standardized services to applications. The definition for this layer is typically ambiguous because it varies. The key is that it does not define a user interface, but instead it is a sort of toolbox used by application developers. For example, a Web browser is an application that uses HTML to format text, as defined by the TCP/IP application layer, to describe the graphics to be displayed onscreen.

3 What is the main purpose(s) of Layer 6?

Layer 6 (presentation layer) defines data formats, compression, and possibly encryption.

4 What is the main purpose(s) of Layer 5?

Layer 5 (session layer) controls the conversation between two endpoints. Although the term used is *session*, the term *conversation* more accurately describes what is accomplished. The session layer ensures that not only communication but also useful sets of communication between endpoints is accomplished.

5 What is the main purpose(s) of Layer 4?

Layer 4 (transport layer) provides end-to-end error recovery, if requested.

6 What is the main purpose(s) of Layer 3?

Layer 3 (network layer) defines logical addressing and routing as a means of delivering data across an entire network. IP and IPX are two examples of Layer 3–equivalent protocols.

7 What is the main purpose(s) of Layer 2?

The data link layer defines addressing specific to a particular medium as part of the means of providing delivery of data across that medium. It also includes the protocols used to determine what device(s) accesses the media at any point in time.

8 What is the main purpose(s) of Layer 1?

Layer 1 (physical layer) is responsible for encoding energy signals onto the medium and interpreting a received energy signal. Layer 1 also defines the connector and cabling details.

9 Describe the process of data encapsulation as data is processed from creation until it exits a physical interface to a network. Use the OSI model as an example.

Data encapsulation represents the process of a layer adding a header (and possibly a trailer) to the data as it is processed by progressively lower layers in the protocol specification. In the context of OSI, each layer could add a header so that—other than the true application data—there would be six other headers (Layers 2 to 7) and a trailer for Layer 2, with this L2PDU being encoded by the physical layer onto the network media.

10 Describe the features required for a protocol to be considered connectionless.

Unordered low-overhead delivery of data from one host to another is the service provided in most connectionless protocol services.

11 Name at least three connectionless protocols.

LLC Type 1, UDP, IPX, IP, and PPP are some examples of connectionless protocols. Remember, Frame Relay, X.25, and ATM are connection-oriented, regardless of whether they define error recovery.

12 Describe the features required for a protocol to be considered connection-oriented.

Either the protocol must exchange messages with another device before data is allowed to be sent, or some pre-established correlation between the two endpoints must be defined. TCP is an example of a connection-oriented protocol that exchanges messages before data may be sent; Frame Relay is a connection-oriented protocol for which pre-established correlation between endpoints is defined.

13 In a particular error-recovering protocol, the sender sends three frames, labeled 2, 3, and 4. On its next sent frame, the receiver of these frames sets an acknowledgment field to 4. What does this typically imply?

Frames up through number 3 were received successfully. Most windowing, error-recovery protocols use forward acknowledgment.

14 Name three connection-oriented protocols.

TCP, SPX, LLC Type 2, and X.25 are some examples of connection-oriented protocols that provide error recovery. ATM and Frame Relay are also connection-oriented, but without error recovery.

15 What does MAC stand for?

MAC stands for Media Access Control.

16 Name three terms popularly used as a synonym for *MAC address*.

NIC address, *card address*, *LAN address*, *hardware address*, *Ethernet address*, *Token Ring address*, *FDDI address*, and *burned-in address* are all synonymous with MAC address. All of these names are used casually and in formal documents, and they refer to the same 6-byte MAC address concept as defined by IEEE.

17 Are IP addresses defined by a Layer 2 or Layer 3 protocol?

IP addresses are defined by the IP part of TCP/IP, which is the second layer of TCP/IP. However, compared to OSI, IP most closely matches OSI Layer 3 in function, so the popular (and CCNA exam) answer is Layer 3.

18 Are IPX addresses defined by a Layer 2 or Layer 3 protocol?

IP addresses are defined by a Layer 3 protocol.

19 Are OSI NSAP addresses defined by a Layer 2 or Layer 3 protocol?

OSI NSAP addresses are defined by a Layer 3 protocol. Of course, they are truly Layer 3 because they are defined by OSI. The number of bits in the address is variable. However, it is highly unlikely that questions about NSAPs would be on the exam because they are not mentioned in any objective and are not covered in any class.

20 What portion of a MAC address encodes an identifier representing the manufacturer of the card?

The first 3 bytes comprise the portion of a MAC address that encodes an identifier representing the manufacturer of the card.

21 Are MAC addresses defined by a Layer 2 or Layer 3 protocol?

MAC addresses are defined by a Layer 2 protocol. Ethernet and Token Ring MAC addresses are defined in the 802.3 and 802.5 specifications.

22 Are DLCI addresses defined by a Layer 2 or Layer 3 protocol?

DLCI addresses are defined by a Layer 2 protocol. Although they are not specifically covered in this chapter, Frame Relay protocols do not define a logical addressing structure that can usefully exist outside a Frame Relay network; by definition, the addresses would be OSI Layer 2–equivalent.

23 Name two differences between Layer 3 addresses and Layer 2 addresses.

Layer 3 addresses can be used regardless of media type, whereas Layer 2 addresses are useful only on a particular medium. Layer 3 addresses are designed with a minimum of two parts, the first of which creates a grouping concept. Layer 2 addresses do not have a grouping concept that allows the setup interfaces on the same medium to share the same value in a portion of the data-link address, which is how Layer 3 addresses are structured.

24 How many bits are present in an IP address?

IP addresses have 32 bits: a variable number in the network portion, and the rest of the 32 in the host portion. IP Version 6 uses a much larger address. Stay tuned!

25 How many bits are present in an IPX address?

IPX addresses have 80 bits: 32 bits in the network portion and 48 bits in the node portion.

26 How many bits are present in a MAC address?

MAC addresses have 48 bits. The first 24 bits for burned-in addresses represent a code that identifies the manufacturer.

27 Name the two main parts of an IPX address. Which part identifies which "group" this address is a member of?

Network number and node number are the two main parts of an IPX address. Addresses with the same network number are in the same group. On LAN interfaces, the node number is made to have the same value as the LAN MAC address.

28 Name the two main parts of an IP address. Which part identifies which "group" this address is a member of?

Network and host are the two main parts of an IP address. As described in Chapter 5, technically there are three portions of the IP address: network, subnet, and host. However, because most people think of the network and subnet portions as one portion, another correct answer to this question, using popular terminology, would be subnet and host.

29 Name the two main parts of a MAC address. Which part identifies which "group" this address is a member of?

There are no parts, and nothing defines a grouping concept in a MAC address. This is a trick question. Although you might have guessed that the MAC address has two parts—the first part dictated to the manufacturer, and the second part made up by the manufacturer—there is no grouping concept.

30 Name three benefits to layering networking protocol specifications.

Some examples of benefits to layering networking protocol specifications include reduced complexity, standardized interfaces, modular engineering, interoperable technology, accelerated evolution, and simplified teaching and learning. Questions such as this on the exam will require some subjective interpretation of the wording on your part.

31 What header and/or trailer does a router discard as a side effect of routing?

A router discards the data-link header and trailer as a side effect of routing. This is because the network layer, where routing is defined, is interested in delivering the network layer (Layer 3) PDU from end to end. Routing uses intermediate data links (Layer 2) to transport the data to the next routers and eventually to the true destination. The data-link header and trailer are useful only to deliver the data to the next router or host, so the header and trailer are discarded by each router.

32 Describe the differences between a routed protocol and a routing protocol.

The routed protocol defines the addressing and Layer 3 header in the packet that is actually forwarded by a router. The routing protocol defines the process of routers exchanging topology data so that the routers know how to forward the data. A router uses the routing table created by the routing protocol to choose how to forward a routed protocol packet.

33 Name at least three routed protocols.

TCP/IP (IP), Novell (IPX), OSI (CLNP), DECnet (CLNP), AppleTalk (DDP), and VINES are some examples of routed protocols.

34 Name at least three routing protocols.

IP RIP, IP IGRP, IP/IPX/AppleTalk EIGRP, IP OSPF, OSI NLSP, AppleTalk RTMP, VINES VTP, and OSI IS-IS are some examples of routing protocols.

35 How does an IP host know what router to send a packet to? In which cases does an IP host choose to send a packet to this router instead of directly to the destination host?

Typically an IP host knows to what router to send a packet based on its configured default router. If the destination of the packet is in another subnet, the host sends the packet to the default router. Otherwise, the host sends the packet directly to the destination host because it is in the same subnet and, by definition, must be on the same data link.

36 How does an IPX host know which router to send a packet to? In which case does an IPX host choose to send a packet to this router instead of directly to the destination host?

An IPX host knows which router to send a packet to by broadcasting a RIP request to locate any servers or routers on the attached IPX network that have a route to the destination network. If the destination is an IPX address on the attached network, a router is not needed and the node forwards the packet directly instead of sending a RIP request.

37 Name three items in an entry in any routing table.

The group identifier, the interface by which to forward the packet, and the Layer 3 address of the next router to send this packet to are three items that you will always find in a routing table entry.

38 What OSI layer typically encapsulates using both a header and a trailer?

The data link layer typically encapsulates using both a header and a trailer. The trailer typically includes a frame check sequence (FCS), which is used to perform error detection.

Answers to the Chapter 4 "Do I Know This Already?" Quiz

1 What do the letters *MAC* stand for? What other terms have you heard to describe the same or similar concept?

Media Access Control (MAC). Many terms are used to describe a MAC address: *NIC*, *LAN*, *hardware*, *BIA*, *universally administered address* (UAA), *locally administered address* (LAA), *Ethernet*, *Token Ring*, *FDDI*, *card*, *wire*, and *real* are all terms used to describe this same address in different instances.

2 If a Fast Ethernet NIC currently is receiving a frame, can it begin sending a frame?

Yes, if the NIC is operating in full-duplex mode.

3 What are the two key differences between a 10-Mbps NIC and a 10/100 NIC?

The obvious benefit is that the 10/100 NIC can run at 100 Mbps. The other benefit is that 10/100 NICs can autonegotiate both speed and duplex between itself and the device that it is cabled to, typically a LAN switch.

4 What is the distance limitation of a single cable for 10BaseT? 100BaseTX?

10BaseT allows 100 meters between the device and the hub or switch, as does 100BaseTX. Table 4-5 summarizes the lengths for all Ethernet LAN types.

5 What routing protocol does a transparent bridge use to learn about Layer 3 addressing groupings?

None. Bridges do not use routing protocols. Transparent bridges do not care about Layer 3 address groupings. Devices on either side of a transparent bridge are in the same Layer 3 group—in other words, the same IP subnet or IPX network.

6 Name two of the methods of internal switching on typical switches today. Which provides less latency for an individual frame?

Store-and-forward, cut-through, and FragmentFree switching. Cut-through switching has less latency per frame but does not check for bit errors in the frame, including errors caused by collisions. Store-and-forward switching stores the entire received frame, verifies that the FCS is correct, and then sends the frame. Cut-through switching sends out the first bytes of the frame before the last bytes of the incoming frame have been received. FragmentFree switching is similar to cut-through switching in that the frame can be sent before the incoming frame is totally received; however, FragmentFree processing waits to receive the first 64 bytes, to ensure no collisions, before beginning to forward the frame.

7 Describe how a transparent bridge decides whether it should forward a frame, and tell how it chooses the interface out which to forward the frame.

The bridge examines the destination MAC address of a frame and looks for the address in its bridge (or address) table. If found, the matching entry tells the bridge which output interface to use to forward the frame. If not found, the bridge forwards the frame out all other interfaces (except for interfaces blocked by spanning tree and the interface in which the frame was received). The bridge table is built by examining incoming frames' source MAC addresses.

8 Define the term *collision domain*.

A collision domain is a set of Ethernet devices for which concurrent transmission of a frame by any two of them will result in a collision. Bridges, switches, and routers separate LAN segments into different collision domains. Repeaters and shared hubs do not separate segments into different collision domains.

9 How many IP addresses must be configured for network management on a Cisco Catalyst 1900 switch if eight ports are to be used with three VLANs?

A single IP address is needed. No need exists for an IP address per port because the switch is not a router. The management IP address is considered to be in VLAN 1.

10 How do EXEC and configuration commands refer to the two Fast Ethernet ports on a Catalyst 1912 switch?

These two ports are known as fastethernet 0/26 and 0/27. 0/25 is always reserved for the AUI port, and 0/1 through 0/24 are always reserved for the (up to) first 24 Ethernet ports.

11 Configuration is added to the running configuration in RAM when commands are typed in Catalyst 1900 configuration mode. What causes these commands to be saved into NVRAM?

Unlike the router IOS, commands are saved in both running config and NVRAM as the user enters the configuration commands. No separate command, such as **copy running-config startup-config** in the router IOS, is needed.

12 What command erases the startup config in a Catalyst 1900 switch?

The **delete nvram** EXEC command erases the configuration file in NVRAM. In fact, although it is easy to call it the startup config, commands instead refer to this configuration file as NVRAM.

Answers to the Chapter 4 Q&A Section

1 What do the letters *MAC* stand for? What other terms have you heard to describe the same or similar concept?

Media Access Control (MAC). Many terms are used to describe a MAC address: *NIC*, *LAN*, *hardware*, *BIA*, *universally administered address* (UAA), *locally administered address* (LAA), *Ethernet*, *Token Ring*, *FDDI*, *card*, *wire*, and *real* are all terms used to describe this same address in different instances.

2 Name two benefits of LAN segmentation using transparent bridges.

The main benefits are reduced collisions and more bandwidth. Multiple 10- or 100-Mbps Ethernet segments are created, and unicasts between devices on the same segment are not forwarded by the bridge, which reduces overhead.

3 What routing protocol does a transparent bridge use to learn about Layer 3 addressing groupings?

None. Bridges do not use routing protocols. Transparent bridges do not care about Layer 3 address groupings. Devices on either side of a transparent bridge are in the same Layer 3 group—in other words, the same IP subnet or IPX network.

4 If a Fast Ethernet NIC is currently receiving a frame, can it begin sending a frame?

Yes, if the NIC is operating in full-duplex mode.

5 Why did Ethernet networks' performance improve with the advent of bridges?

Before bridges and switches existed, all devices were cabled to the same shared Ethernet. The CSMA/CD algorithm was used to determine who got to send across the Ethernet. As the amount of traffic increased, collisions and waiting (because CSMA/CD) increased, so frames took longer to send. Bridges separated the network into multiple collision domains, reducing collisions and allowing devices on opposite sides of the bridge to send concurrently.

6 Why did Ethernet networks' performance improve with the advent of switches?

Before bridges and switches existed, all devices were cabled to the same shared Ethernet. The CSMA/CD algorithm was used to determine who got to send across the Ethernet. As the amount of traffic increased, collisions and waiting (because of CSMA/CD) increased, so frames took longer to send. Switches separated the network into multiple collision domains, typically one per port, reducing collisions and allowing devices on opposite sides of the bridge to send concurrently.

7 What are two key differences between a 10-Mbps NIC and a 10/100 NIC?

The obvious benefit is that the 10/100 NIC can run at 100 Mbps. The other benefit is that 10/100 NICs can autonegotiate both speed and duplex between themselves and the device that they are cabled to—typically a LAN switch.

8 Assume that a building has 100 devices attached to the same Ethernet. These users then are migrated onto two separate shared Ethernet segments, each with 50 devices, with a transparent bridge between them. List two benefits that would be derived for a typical user.

Fewer collisions and less waiting should occur because twice as much capacity exists. Also, if the placement of devices causes a small percentage of traffic to be forwarded by the bridge, fewer collisions and less waiting should occur.

9 What standards body owns the process of ensuring unique MAC addresses worldwide?

The IEEE. The first half of the burned-in MAC address is a value assigned to the manufacturer by the IEEE. As long as the manufacturer uses that prefix and doesn't duplicate values that it assigns in the last 3 bytes, global uniqueness is attained.

10 Assume that a building has 100 devices attached to the same Ethernet. These devices are migrated to two different shared Ethernet segments, each with 50 devices. The two segments are connected to a Cisco LAN switch to allow communication between the two sets of users. List two benefits that would be derived for a typical user.

Two switch ports are used, which reduces the possibility of collisions. Also, each segment has its own 10- or 100-Mbps capacity, allowing more throughput and reducing the likelihood of collisions. Furthermore, although this is unlikely to be on the CCNA exam, some Cisco switches can reduce the flow of multicasts using the Cisco Group Message Protocol (CGMP).

11 Name two of the methods of internal switching on typical switches today. Which provides less latency for an individual frame?

Store-and-forward, cut-through, and FragmentFree switching. Cut-through switching has less latency per frame but does not check for bit errors in the frame, including errors caused by collisions. Store-and-forward switching stores the entire received frame, verifies that the FCS is correct, and then sends the frame. Cut-through switching sends out the first bytes of the frame before the last bytes of the incoming frame have been received. FragmentFree switching is similar to cut-through switching in that the frame can be sent before the incoming frame is totally received; however, FragmentFree processing waits to receive the first 64 bytes, to ensure no collisions, before beginning to forward the frame.

12 What is the distance limitation of a single cable for 10BaseT? 100BaseTX?

10BaseT allows 100 meters between the device and the hub or switch, as does 100BaseTX. Table 4-5 summarizes the lengths for all Ethernet LAN types.

13 Describe how a transparent bridge decides whether it should forward a frame, and tell how it chooses the interface out which to forward the frame.

The bridge examines the destination MAC address of a frame and looks for the address in its bridge (or address) table. If found, the matching entry tells the bridge which output interface to use to forward the frame. If not found, the bridge forwards the frame out all other interfaces (except for interfaces blocked by Spanning Tree and the interface in which the frame was received). The bridge table is built by examining incoming frames' source MAC addresses.

14 How fast is Fast Ethernet?

100 million bits per second (100 Mbps).

15 How does a transparent bridge build its address table?

The bridge listens for incoming frames and examines the source MAC address. If not in the table, the source address is added, along with the port (interface) by which the frame entered the bridge. The bridge also marks an entry for freshness so that entries can be removed after a period of disuse. This reduces table size and allows for easier table changes in case a Spanning Tree change forces more significant changes in the bridge (address) table.

16 How many bytes long is a MAC address?

6 bytes long, or 48 bits.

17 Assume that a building has 100 devices attached to the same Ethernet. These users then are migrated onto two separate Ethernet segments, each with 50 devices and separated by a router. List two benefits that would be derived for a typical user.

Collisions are reduced by creating two collision domains. Broadcasts also are reduced because the router does not forward broadcasts. Routers provide greater control and administration as well.

18 Does a bridge/switch examine just the incoming frame's source MAC, the destination MAC, or both? Why does it examine the one(s) that it examines?

The bridge/switch examines both MAC addresses. The source is examined so that entries can be added to the bridge/address table. The destination address is examined to determine the interface out which to forward the frame. Table lookup is required for both addresses for any frame that enters an interface. That is one of the reasons that LAN switches, which have a much larger number of interfaces than traditional bridges, need to have optimized hardware and logic to perform table lookup quickly.

19 Define the term *collision domain.*

A collision domain is a set of Ethernet devices for which concurrent transmission of a frame by any two of them will result in a collision. Bridges, switches, and routers separate LAN segments into different collision domains. Repeaters and shared hubs do not separate segments into different collision domains.

20 Define the difference between broadcast and multicast MAC addresses.

Both identify more than one device on the LAN. *Broadcast* always implies all devices on the LAN, whereas *multicast* implies some subset of all devices. Multicast is not allowed on Token Ring; broadcast is allowed on all LAN types. Devices that intend to receive frames addressed to a particular multicast address must be aware of the particular multicast address(es) that they should process. These addresses are dependent on the applications used. Read RFC 1112, "The Internet Group Message Protocol (IGMP)," for related information about the use of Ethernet multicast in conjunction with IP multicast. For example, the broadcast address is FFFF.FFFF.FFFF, and one sample multicast address is 0100.5e00.0001.

21 Excluding the preamble and starting delimiter fields, but including all other Ethernet headers and trailers, what is the maximum number of bytes in an Ethernet frame?

1518 bytes. See Figure 4-7 for more detail.

22 Define the term *broadcast domain.*

A broadcast domain is a set of Ethernet devices for which a broadcast sent by any one of them should be received by all others in the group. Unlike routers, bridges and switches do not stop the flow of broadcasts. Two segments separated by a router would each be in a different broadcast domain. A switch can create multiple broadcast domains by creating multiple VLANs, but a router must be used to route packets between the VLANs.

23 Describe the benefits of creating 3 VLANs of 25 ports each, versus a single VLAN of 75 ports, in each case using a single switch. Assume that all ports are switched ports (each port is a different collision domain).

Three different broadcast domains are created with three VLANs, so the devices' CPU utilization should decrease because of decreased broadcast traffic. Traffic between devices in different VLANs will pass through some routing function, which can add some latency for those packets. Better management and control are gained by including a router in the path for those packets.

24 Explain the function of the loopback and collision-detection features of an Ethernet NIC in relation to half-duplex and full-duplex operations.

The loopback feature copies the transmitted frame back onto the receive pin on the NIC interface. The collision-detection logic compares the received frame to the transmitted frame during transmission; if the signals do not match, a collision is occurring. This logic implies that half-duplex operation is being used because if collisions can occur, only one transmitter at a time is allowed. With full-duplex operation, collisions cannot occur, so the loopback and collision-detection features are not needed, and concurrent transmission and reception is allowed.

25 How many IP addresses must be configured for network management on a Cisco Catalyst 1900 switch if eight ports are to be used and with three VLANs?

A single IP address is needed. No need exists for an IP address per port because the switch is not a router. The management IP address is considered to be in VLAN 1.

26 What command on a 1900 series switch would cause the switch to block frames destined to 0200.7777.7777 entering interface 0/5 from going out port 0/6?

The **mac-address-table restricted static 0200.7777.7777 0/6 0/5** global configuration command would block the frames. This also makes address 0200.7777.7777 permanently held in the MAC address table for port 0/6.

27 What Catalyst 1900 switch command displays the version of IOS running in the switch?

This is a trick question. The **show version** command shows the level of switch software, but because the switch does not run IOS, no command will display the level of IOS in the switch.

28 What does the Catalyst 1900 switch command **address violation disable** do?

This global configuration command tells the switch what action to take when the maximum number of addresses on a port has been exceeded. If a new dynamically learned MAC address on some port had caused the maximum (as defined by the **port secure** command) to be exceeded, the port would have been disabled.

29 What command erases the startup config in a Catalyst 1900 switch?

The **delete nvram** EXEC command erases the configuration file in NVRAM. In fact, although it is easy to call it the startup config, commands instead refer to this configuration file as NVRAM.

30 Configuration is added to the running configuration in RAM when commands are typed in Catalyst 1900 configuration mode. What causes these commands to be saved into NVRAM?

Unlike the router IOS, commands are saved in both running config and in NVRAM as the user enters the configuration commands. No separate command, such as **copy running-config startup-config** in the router IOS, is needed.

31 How do EXEC and configuration commands refer to the two Fast Ethernet ports on a Catalyst 1912 switch?

These two ports are known as fastethernet 0/26 and 0/27. 0/25 is always reserved for the AUI port, and 0/1 through 0/24 are always reserved for the (up to) first 24 Ethernet ports.

32 What Catalyst 1900 switch command displays the switching table?

The **show mac-address-table** command displays the table that the switch uses to make switching decisions.

Answers to the Chapter 5 "Do I Know This Already?" Quiz

1 What routing protocol does a transparent bridge use to learn about Layer 3 addressing groupings?

None. Bridges do not use routing protocols. Transparent bridges do not care about Layer 3 address groupings. Devices on either side of a transparent bridge are in the same Layer 3 group—in other words, the same IP subnet or IPX network.

2 What settings are examined by a bridge or switch to determine which should be elected as root of the spanning tree?

The bridge priority is examined first (the lowest wins). In case of a tie, the lowest bridge ID wins. The priority is prepended to the bridge ID in the actual CBPDU message so that the combined fields can be easily compared.

3 If a switch hears three different hello BPDUs from three different neighbors on three different interfaces, and if all three specify that Bridge 1 is the root, how does the switch choose which interface is its root port?

The root port is the port in which the BPDU with the lowest-cost value is received. The root port is placed in forwarding state on each bridge and switch.

4 Can the root bridge/switch ports be placed in blocking state?

The root bridge's ports are always in a forwarding state because they always have cost 0 to the root, which ensures that they are always the designated bridges on their respective LAN segments.

5 Define the term *VLAN*.

Virtual LAN (VLAN) refers to the process of treating one subset of a switch's interfaces as one broadcast domain. Broadcasts from one VLAN are not forwarded to other VLANs; unicasts between VLANs must use a router. Advanced methods, such as Layer 3 switching in a NetFlow feature card in a Catalyst 5000 switch, can be used to allow the LAN switch to forward traffic between VLANs without each individual frame being routed by a router. However, for the depth of CCNA, such detail is not needed.

6 Describe the benefits of creating 3 VLANs of 25 ports each versus creating a single VLAN of 75 ports, in each case using a single switch. Assume that all ports are switched ports (each port is a different collision domain).

Three different broadcast domains are created with three VLANs, so the devices' CPU utilization should decrease because of decreased broadcast traffic. Traffic between devices in different VLANs will pass through some routing function, which can add some latency for those packets. Better management and control are gained by including a router in the path for those packets.

7 If two Cisco LAN switches are connected using Fast Ethernet, what VLAN trunking protocols could be used? If only one VLAN spanned both switches, is a VLAN trunking protocol needed?

ISL and 802.1Q are the trunking protocols used by Cisco over Fast Ethernet. If only one VLAN spans the two switches, a trunking protocol is not needed. Trunking or tagging protocols are used to tag a frame as being in a particular VLAN; if only one VLAN is used, tagging is unnecessary.

8 Must all members of the same VLAN be in the same collision domain, the same broadcast domain, or both?

By definition, members of the same VLAN are all part of the same broadcast domain. They may all be in the same collision domain, but it is unlikely.

9 What Catalyst 1900 switch command assigns a port to a particular VLAN?

The **vlan-membership static** *x* interface subcommand assigns the port to VLAN number *x*.

10 What Catalyst 1900 switch command creates VLAN 10 and assigns it a name of bigbadvlan?

The **vlan 10 name bigbadvlan** global configuration command creates the VLAN.

11 What Catalyst 1900 switch command lists the details about VLAN 10?

The **show vlan 10** command displays VLAN information about VLAN 10.

12 What two 1900 series EXEC commands list information about the spanning tree for VLAN 2?

The **show spantree** command lists details of the current Spanning Tree for all VLANs. **show spantree 2** lists the details just for VLAN 2.

Answers to the Chapter 5 Q&A Section

1 What routing protocol does a transparent bridge use to learn about Layer 3 addressing groupings?

None. Bridges do not use routing protocols. Transparent bridges do not care about Layer 3 address groupings. Devices on either side of a transparent bridge are in the same Layer 3 group—in other words, the same IP subnet or IPX network.

2 What settings are examined by a bridge or switch to determine which should be elected as root of the spanning tree?

The bridge priority is examined first (the lowest wins). In case of a tie, the lowest bridge ID wins. The priority is prepended to the bridge ID in the actual CBPDU message so that the combined fields can be easily compared.

3 Define the term *VLAN*.

Virtual LAN (VLAN) refers to the process of treating one subset of a switch's interfaces as one broadcast domain. Broadcasts from one VLAN are not forwarded to other VLANs; unicasts between VLANs must use a router. Advanced methods, such as Layer 3 switching in a NetFlow feature card in a Catalyst 5000 switch, can be used to allow the LAN switch to forward traffic between VLANs without each individual frame being routed by a router. However, for the depth of CCNA, such detail is not needed.

4 Describe the benefit of the Spanning-Tree Protocol as used by transparent bridges and switches.

Physically redundant paths in the network are allowed to exist and be used when other paths fail. Also, loops in the bridged network are avoided. Loops are particularly bad because bridging uses LAN headers, which do not provide a mechanism to mark a frame so that its lifetime can be limited; in other words, the frame can loop forever.

5 If a switch hears three different hello BPDUs from three different neighbors on three different interfaces, and if all three specify that Bridge 1 is the root, how does the switch choose which interface is its root port?

The root port is the port in which the BPDU with the lowest-cost value is received. The root port is placed in forwarding state on each bridge and switch.

6 When a bridge or switch using Spanning-Tree Protocol first initializes, who does it assert should be the root of the tree?

Each bridge/switch begins by sending BPDUs claiming itself as the root bridge.

7 Name the three reasons why a port is placed in forwarding state as a result of Spanning Tree.

First, all ports on the root bridge are placed in forwarding state. Second, one port on each bridge is considered its root port, which is placed in forwarding state. Finally, on each LAN segment, one bridge is considered to be the designated bridge on that LAN; that designated bridge's interface on the LAN is placed in a forwarding state.

8 Describe the benefits of creating 3 VLANs of 25 ports each versus creating a single VLAN of 75 ports, in each case using a single switch. Assume that all ports are switched ports (each port is a different collision domain).

Three different broadcast domains are created with three VLANs, so the devices' CPU utilization should decrease because of decreased broadcast traffic. Traffic between devices in different VLANs will pass through some routing function, which can add some latency for those packets. Better management and control are gained by including a router in the path for those packets.

9 If two Cisco LAN switches are connected using Fast Ethernet, what VLAN trunking protocols could be used? If only one VLAN spanned both switches, is a VLAN trunking protocol needed?

ISL and 802.1Q are the trunking protocols used by Cisco over Fast Ethernet. If only one VLAN spans the two switches, a trunking protocol is not needed. Trunking or tagging protocols are used to tag a frame as being in a particular VLAN; if only one VLAN is used, tagging is unnecessary.

10 Name the three interface states that the Spanning-Tree Protocol uses, other than forwarding. Which of these states is transitory?

Blocking, listening, and learning. Blocking is the only stable state; the other two are transitory between blocking and forwarding. Table 4-13 summarizes the states and their features.

11 What are the two reasons that a nonroot bridge/switch places a port in forwarding state?

If the port is the designated bridge on its LAN segment, the port is placed in forwarding state. Also, if the port is the root port, it is placed in forwarding state. Otherwise, the port is placed in blocking state.

12 Can the root bridge/switch ports be placed in blocking state?

The root bridge's ports are always in a forwarding state because they always have cost 0 to the root, which ensures that they are always the designated bridges on their respective LAN segments.

13 What does VTP do, and what does the abbreviation stand for?

The VLAN Trunking Protocol is a protocol used to transmit configuration information about VLANs between interconnected switches. VTP helps prevent misconfiguration, eases administration of the switches, and also reduces broadcast overhead by the use of VTP pruning.

14 Name the three VTP modes. Which of these does not allow VLANs to be added or modified?

Server and client modes are used to actively participate in VTP; transparent mode is used to simply stay out of the way of servers and clients while not participating in VTP. Switches in client mode cannot change or add VLANs.

15 What Catalyst 1900 switch command assigns a port to a particular VLAN?

The **vlan-membership static** *x* interface subcommand assigns the port to VLAN number *x*.

16 What Catalyst 1900 switch command creates VLAN 10 and assigns it a name of bigbadvlan?

The **vlan 10 name bigbadvlan** global configuration command creates the VLAN.

17 What Catalyst 1900 switch command lists the details about VLAN 10?

The **show vlan 10** command displays VLAN information about VLAN 10.

18 What Catalyst 1900 switch command configures ISL trunking on fastethernet port 26 so that as long as the switch port on the other end of the trunk is not disabled (off) or configured to not negotiate to become a trunk, the trunk will definitely be placed in trunking mode?

The **trunk desirable** interface subcommand tells this switch to be in trunking mode (in other words, to use ISL) as long as the switch on the other end of the trunk is configured for on, autonegotiate, or desirable. If the other switch has configured the trunk as off or nonegotiate, trunking will not be enabled.

19 What type of VTP mode allows a switch to create VTP advertisements?

Only VTP servers generate VTP advertisements.

20 Must all members of the same VLAN be in the same collision domain, the same broadcast domain, or both?

By definition, members of the same VLAN are all part of the same broadcast domain. They might all be in the same collision domain, but it is unlikely.

21 What is the acronym and complete name of Cisco's proprietary trunking protocol over Ethernet?

Inter-Switch Link (ISL).

22 Switch 1 has VLANs 1, 2, and 3 configured. Switch 2 has VLANs 1 and 3 configured. The two switches are connected by a single 10-Mbps Ethernet. How many address tables will Switch 1 have? Switch 2? Why?

Switch 1 will have three and Switch 2 will have two because Cisco switches have a single address table per VLAN.

23 What two 1900 series EXEC commands list information about the spanning tree for VLAN 2?

The **show spantree** command lists details of the current spanning tree for all VLANs. **show spantree 2** lists the details just for VLAN 2.

24 What if the costs of all the ports in the previous answer are the same?

The switch would use the lowest logically numbered interface.

Answers to the Chapter 6 "Do I Know This Already?" Quiz

1 What do *TCP, UDP, IP,* and *ICMP* stand for? Which protocol is considered to be Layer 3-equivalent when comparing TCP/IP to the OSI protocols?

Transmission Control Protocol, User Datagram Protocol, Internet Protocol, and Internet Control Message Protocol. Both TCP and UDP are Layer 4 protocols. ICMP is considered a Layer 3 protocol because it is used for control and management of IP. IP is the core part of the network layer (Layer 3) of TCP/IP.

2 Describe how to view the IP ARP cache in a Cisco router. Also describe the three key elements of each entry.

show ip arp displays the IP ARP cache in a Cisco router. Each entry contains the IP address, the MAC address, and the interface from which the information was learned. The encapsulation type is also in the table entry.

3 Does FTP or TFTP perform error recovery? If so, describe the basics of how error recovery is performed.

Both FTP and TFTP perform error recovery. FTP relies on TCP, whereas TFTP performs application layer recovery one block of data at a time.

4 How many TCP segments are exchanged to establish a TCP connection? How many are required to terminate a TCP connection?

A three-way connection-establishment sequence is performed, and a four-way connection-termination sequence is used.

5 Given the IP address 134.141.7.11 and the mask 255.255.255.0, what is the subnet number?

The subnet is 134.141.7.0. The binary algorithm is shown in the following table.

Address	134.141.7.11	1000 0110 1000 1101 **0000 0111** 0000 1011
Mask	255.255.255.0	1111 1111 1111 1111 **1111 1111** 0000 0000
Result	134.141.7.0	1000 0110 1000 1101 **0000 0111** 0000 0000

6 Given the IP address 134.141.7.11 and the mask 255.255.255.0, what is the subnet broadcast address?

The broadcast address is 134.141.7.255. The binary algorithm is shown in the following table.

Address	134.141.7.11	1000 0110 1000 1101 **0000 0111** 0000 1011
Mask	255.255.255.0	1111 1111 1111 1111 **1111 1111** 0000 0000
Result	134.141.7.0	1000 0110 1000 1101 **0000 0111** 0000 0000
Broadcast address	134.141.7.255	1000 0110 1000 1101 0000 0111 **1111 1111**

7 Given the IP address 200.1.1.130 and the mask 255.255.255.224, what are the assignable IP addresses in this subnet?

The answer is 200.1.1.128. The table that follows shows the subnet chart used in this chapter to help you learn the way to calculate the subnet number without binary math. The magic number is 256 – 224 = 32.

	Octet 1	Octet 2	Octet 3	Octet 4	Comments
Address	200	1	1	130	N/A
Mask	255	255	255	224	The interesting octet is the fourth octet.
Subnet number	200	1	1	128	128 is the closest multiple of magic not greater than 130.
First valid address	200	1	1	129	Add 1 to the ast octet.
Broadcast	200	1	1	159	Subnet + magic – 1.
Last valid address	200	1	1	158	Subtract 1 from broadcast.

8 Given the IP address 220.8.7.100 and the mask 255.255.255.240, what are all the subnet numbers if the same (static) mask is used for all subnets in this network?

The answer is not as obvious in this question. The Class C network number is 220.8.7.0. The mask implies that bits 25 through 28, which are the first 4 bits in the fourth octet, comprise the subnet field. The answer is 220.8.7.16, 220.8.7.32, 220.8.7.48, and so on, through 220.8.7.224. 220.8.7.0 is the zero subnet, and 220.8.7.240 is the broadcast subnet. The following table outlines the easy decimal algorithm to figure out the subnet numbers

	Octet 1	Octet 2	Octet 3	Octet 4	Comments
Network number	220	8	7	0	N/A
Mask	255	255	255	240	The last octet is interesting; magic number is 256 – 240 = 16.
Subnet zero	220	8	7	0	Copy down network the number; it’s the zero subnet.
First valid subnet	220	8	7	16	Add magic to last subnet number’s interesting octet.
Next valid subnet	220	8	7	32	Add magic to the previous one . . .
Last valid subnet	220	8	7	224	You eventually get to here . . .
Broadcast subnet	220	8	7	240	. . . and to here, the broadcast subnet, because the next one is 256, which is invalid.

9 Create a minimal configuration enabling IP on each interface on a 2501 router (two serial, one Ethernet). The NIC assigned you network 8.0.0.0. Your boss says that you need, at most, 200 hosts per subnet. You decide against using VLSM. Your boss says to plan your subnets so that you can have as many subnets as possible rather than allowing for larger subnets later. When choosing the actual IP address values and subnet numbers, you decide to start with the lowest numerical values. Assume that point-to-point serial links will be attached to this router and that RIP is the routing protocol.

```
router rip
network 8.0.0.0
interface ethernet 0
ip address 8.0.1.1 255.255.255.0
interface serial 0
ip address 8.0.2.1 255.255.255.0
interface serial 1
ip address 8.0.3.1 255.255.255.0
```

The zero subnet was not used in this solution. If desired, the **ip subnet-zero** global command could have been used, enabling subnet 8.0.0.0 as well as the subnets 8.0.1.0, 8.0.2.0, and 8.0.3.0 to be used in the configuration.

10 Describe the question and possible responses in setup mode when a router wants to know the mask used on an interface. How can the router derive the correct mask from the information supplied by the user?

When using versions of the IOS before version 12.0, the question asks for the number of subnet bits. The router creates a subnet mask with *x* more binary 1s than the default mask for the class of network of which the interface's IP address is a member. (*x* is the number in the response.) "Number of subnet bits" from the setup question uses the definition that there are three parts to an address—network, subnet, and host. The size of the network field is based on the class of address; the interface's address was typed in response to an earlier setup question. The mask simply has binary 1s in the network and subnet fields, and binary 0s in the host field.

With IOS version 12.0 and beyond, setup prompts for the subnet mask in canonical decimal format—for example, 255.255.255.0.

11 Define the purpose of the trace command. What type of messages does it send, and what type of messages does it receive?

The **trace** command learns the current route to a destination address. It uses IP packets with UDP as the transport layer protocol, with TTL values beginning at 1 and then incrementing by 1 in successive messages. The result is that intervening routers find that the TTL is exceeded and send ICMP time exceeded messages back to the originator of the packet, which is the router where the **trace** command is being executed. The source addresses of the Time Exceeded packets identify each router on the path. By sending successive packets with TTL = 2, then 3, and so on, eventually the packet is received by the destination host. The host returns a Port Unreachable ICMP message, which lets the **trace** command know that the endpoint host has been reached.

12 What causes the output from an IOS ping command to display "UUUUU"?

A *U* is an indication that an unreachable message was received. The type of unreachable message is not implied by the *U*.

Answers to the Chapter 6 Q&A Section

1 What do *TCP*, *UDP*, *IP*, and *ICMP* stand for? Which protocol is considered to be Layer 3-equivalent when comparing TCP/IP to the OSI protocols?

Transmission Control Protocol, User Datagram Protocol, Internet Protocol, and Internet Control Message Protocol. Both TCP and UDP are Layer 4 protocols. ICMP is considered a Layer 3 protocol because it is used for control and management of IP. IP is the core part of the network layer of TCP/IP.

2 Name the parts of an IP address.

Network, subnet, and host are the three parts of an IP address. However, many people commonly treat the network and subnet parts of an address as a single part, leaving only two parts, the subnet and host parts. On the exam, the multiple-choice format should provide extra clues as to which terminology is used.

3 Define the term *subnet mask*. What do the bits in the mask whose values are binary 0 tell you about the corresponding IP address(es)?

A subnet mask defines the number of host bits in an address. The bits of value 0 define which bits in the address are host bits. The mask is an important ingredient in the formula to dissect an IP address; along with knowledge of the number of network bits implied for Class A, B, and C networks, the mask provides a clear definition of the size of the network, subnet, and host parts of an address.

4 Given the IP address 134.141.7.11 and the mask 255.255.255.0, what is the subnet number?

The subnet is 134.141.7.0. The binary algorithm is shown in the table that follows.

Address	134.141.7.11	1000 0110 1000 1101 **0000 0111** 0000 1011
Mask	255.255.255.0	1111 1111 1111 1111 **1111 1111** 0000 0000
Result	134.141.7.0	1000 0110 1000 1101 **0000 0111** 0000 0000

5 Given the IP address 193.193.7.7 and the mask 255.255.255.0, what is the subnet number?

The network number is 193.193.7.0. Because this is a Class C address and the mask used is 255.255.255.0 (the default), there is no subnetting in use. The binary algorithm is shown in the table that follows.

Address	193.193.7.7	1100 0001 1100 0001 0000 0111 0000 0111
Mask	255.255.255.0	1111 1111 1111 1111 1111 1111 0000 0000
Result	193.193.7.0	1100 0001 1100 0001 0000 0111 0000 0000

6 Given the IP address 10.5.118.3 and the mask 255.255.0.0, what is the subnet number?

The subnet is 10.5.0.0. The binary algorithm math is shown in the table that follows.

Address	10.5.118.3	0000 1010 **0000 0101** 0111 0110 0000 0011
Mask	255.255.0.0	1111 1111 **1111 1111** 0000 0000 0000 0000
Result	10.5.0.0	0000 1010 **0000 0101** 0000 0000 0000 0000

7 Given the IP address 190.1.42.3 and the mask 255.255.255.0, what is the subnet number?

The subnet is 190.1.42.0. The binary algorithm math is shown in the table that follows.

Address	190.1.42.3	1011 1110 0000 0001 **0010 1010** 0000 0011
Mask	255.255.255.0	1111 1111 1111 1111 **1111 1111** 0000 0000
Result	190.1.42.0	1011 1110 0000 0001 **0010 1010** 0000 0000

8 Given the IP address 200.1.1.130 and the mask 255.255.255.224, what is the subnet number?

The answer is 200.1.1.128. The table that follows shows the subnet chart used in this chapter to help you learn the way to calculate the subnet number without binary math. The magic number is 256 – 224 = 32.

	Octet 1	Octet 2	Octet 3	Octet 4	Comments
Address	200	1	1	130	N/A
Mask	255	255	255	224	Interesting octet is the fourth octet (magic = 256 – 224 = 32)
Subnet number	200	1	1	128	128 is the closest multiple of magic not greater than 130.
First valid address	200	1	1	129	Add 1 to the last octet of the subnet number.
Broadcast	200	1	1	159	Subnet + magic – 1.
Last valid address	200	1	1	158	Subtract 1 from broadcast.

9 Given the IP address 220.8.7.100 and the mask 255.255.255.240, what is the subnet number?

The answer is 220.8.7.96. The table that follows shows the subnet chart used in this chapter to help you learn the way to calculate the subnet number without binary math. The magic number is 256–240=16.

	Octet 1	Octet 2	Octet 3	Octet 4	Comments
Address	220	8	7	100	N/A
Mask	255	255	255	240	Interesting octet is the fourth octet.
Subnet number	220	8	7	96	96 is the closest multiple of magic not greater than 100.
First valid address	220	8	7	97	Add 1 to the last octet.
Broadcast	220	8	7	111	Subnet + magic – 1.
Last valid address	220	8	7	110	Subtract 1 from broadcast.

10 Given the IP address 140.1.1.1 and the mask 255.255.255.248, what is the subnet number?

The answer is 140.1.1.0. The table that follows shows the subnet chart used in this chapter to help you learn the way to calculate the subnet number without binary math. The magic number is 256 – 248 = 8.

	Octet 1	Octet 2	Octet 3	Octet 4	Comments
Address	140	1	1	1	N/A
Mask	255	255	255	248	Interesting octet is the fourth octet.
Subnet number	140	1	1	0	0 is the closest multiple of magic not greater than 1.
First valid address	140	1	1	1	Add 1 to the last octet.
Broadcast	140	1	1	7	Subnet + magic – 1.
Last valid address	140	1	1	6	Subtract 1 from broadcast.

11 Given the IP address 167.88.99.66 and the mask 255.255.255.192, what is the subnet number?

The answer is 167.88.99.64. The table that follows shows the subnet chart used in this chapter to help you learn the way to calculate the subnet number without binary math. The magic number is 256–192=64

	Octet 1	Octet 2	Octet 3	Octet 4	Comments
Address	167	88	99	66	N/A
Mask	255	255	255	192	Interesting octet is the fourth octet.
Subnet number	167	88	99	64	64 is the closest multiple of magic not greater than 66.
First valid address	167	88	99	65	Add 1 to the last octet.
Broadcast	167	88	99	127	Subnet + magic – 1.
Last valid address	167	88	99	126	Subtract 1 from broadcast.

12 Given the IP address 134.141.7.11 and the mask 255.255.255.0, what is the subnet broadcast address?

The broadcast address is 134.141.7.255. The binary algorithm is shown in the table that follows.

Address	134.141.7.11	1000 0110 1000 1101 0000 0111 0000 1011
Mask	255.255.255.0	1111 1111 1111 1111 1111 1111 0000 0000
Result	134.141.7.0	1000 0110 1000 1101 0000 0111 0000 0000
Broadcast address	134.141.7.255	1000 0110 1000 1101 0000 0111 **1111 1111**

13 Given the IP address 193.193.7.7 and the mask 255.255.255.0, what is the broadcast address?

The broadcast address is 193.193.7.255. Because this is a Class C address and the mask used is 255.255.255.0 (the default), there is no subnetting in use. The binary algorithm is shown in the table that follows.

Address	193.193.7.7	1100 0001 1100 0001 0000 0111 0000 0111
Mask	255.255.255.0	1111 1111 1111 1111 1111 1111 0000 0000
Result	193.193.7.0	1100 0001 1100 0001 0000 0111 0000 0000
Broadcast address	193.193.7.255	1100 0001 1100 0001 0000 0111 **1111 1111**

14 Given the IP address 10.5.118.3 and the mask 255.255.0.0, what is the broadcast address?

The broadcast address is 10.5.255.255. The binary algorithm math is shown in the table that follows.

Address	10.5.118.3	0000 1010 0000 0101 0111 0110 0000 0011
Mask	255.255.0.0	1111 1111 1111 1111 0000 0000 0000 0000
Result	10.5.0.0	0000 1010 0000 0101 0000 0000 0000 0000
Broadcast address	10.5.255.255	0000 1010 0000 0101 **1111 1111 1111 1111**

15 Given the IP address 190.1.42.3 and the mask 255.255.255.0, what is the broadcast address?

The broadcast address is 190.1.42.255. The binary algorithm math is shown in the table that follows.

Address	190.1.42.3	1011 1110 0000 0001 0010 1010 0000 0011
Mask	255.255.255.0	1111 1111 1111 1111 1111 1111 0000 0000
Result	190.1.42.0	1011 1110 0000 0001 0010 1010 0000 0000
Broadcast address	190.1.42.255	1011 1110 0000 0001 0010 1010 **1111 1111**

16 Given the IP address 200.1.1.130 and the mask 255.255.255.224, what is the broadcast address?

The broadcast address is 200.1.1.159. The binary algorithm math is shown in the table that follows. The easy decimal algorithm is shown in the answer to an earlier question.

Address	200.1.1.130	1100 1000 0000 0001 0000 0001 1000 0010
Mask	255.255.255.224	1111 1111 1111 1111 1111 1111 1110 0000
Result	200.1.1.128	1100 1000 0000 0001 0000 0001 1000 0000
Broadcast address	200.1.1.159	1100 1000 0000 0001 0000 0001 100**1 1111**

17 Given the IP address 220.8.7.100 and the mask 255.255.255.240, what is the broadcast address?

The broadcast address is 220.8.7.111. The binary algorithm is shown in the table that follows.

Address	220.8.7.100	1101 1100 0000 1000 0000 0111 0110 0100
Mask	255.255.255.240	1111 1111 1111 1111 1111 1111 1111 0000
Result	220.8.7.96	1101 1100 0000 1000 0000 0111 0110 0000
Broadcast address	220.8.7.111	1101 1100 0000 1000 0000 0111 0110 **1111**

18 Given the IP address 140.1.1.1 and the mask 255.255.255.248, what is the broadcast address?

The broadcast address is 140.1.1.7. The binary algorithm math is shown in the table that follows.

Address	140.1.1.1	1000 1100 0000 0001 0000 0001 0000 0001
Mask	255.255.255.248	1111 1111 1111 1111 1111 1111 1111 1000
Result	140.1.1.0	1000 1100 0000 0001 0000 0001 0000 0000
Broadcast address	140.1.1.7	1000 1100 0000 0001 0000 0001 0000 0**111**

19 Given the IP address 167.88.99.66 and the mask 255.255.255.192, what is the broadcast address?

The broadcast address is 167.88.99.127. The binary algorithm math is shown in the table that follows.

Address	167.88.99.66	1010 0111 0101 1000 0110 0011 0100 0010
Mask	255.255.255.192	1111 1111 1111 1111 1111 1111 1100 0000
Result	167.88.99.64	1010 0111 0101 1000 0110 0011 0100 0000
Broadcast address	167.88.99.127	1010 0111 0101 1000 0110 0011 01**11 1111**

20 Given the IP address 134.141.7.11 and the mask 255.255.255.0, what are the assignable IP addresses in this subnet?

The subnet number is 134.141.7.0, and the subnet broadcast address is 134.141.7.255. The assignable addresses are all the addresses between the subnet and broadcast addresses, namely 134.141.7.1 to 134.141.7.254.

21 Given the IP address 193.193.7.7 and the mask 255.255.255.0, what are the assignable IP addresses in this subnet?

The subnet number is 193.193.7.0, and the subnet broadcast address is 193.193.7.255. The assignable addresses are all the addresses between the subnet and broadcast addresses, namely 193.193.7.1 to 193.193.7.254.

22 Given the IP address 10.5.118.3 and the mask 255.255.0.0, what are the assignable IP addresses in this subnet?

The subnet number is 10.5.0.0, and the subnet broadcast address is 10.5.255.255. The assignable addresses are all the addresses between the subnet and broadcast addresses, namely 10.5.0.1 to 10.5.255.254.

23 Given the IP address 190.1.42.3 and the mask 255.255.255.0, what are the assignable IP addresses in this subnet?

The subnet number is 190.1.42.0, and the subnet broadcast address is 190.1.42.255. The assignable addresses are all the addresses between the subnet and broadcast addresses, namely 190.1.42.1 to 190.1.42.254.

24 Given the IP address 200.1.1.130 and the mask 255.255.255.224, what are the assignable IP addresses in this subnet?

The subnet number is 200.1.1.128, and the subnet broadcast address is 200.1.1.159. The assignable addresses are all the addresses between the subnet and broadcast addresses, namely 200.1.1.129 to 200.1.1.158.

25 Given the IP address 220.8.7.100 and the mask 255.255.255.240, what are the assignable IP addresses in this subnet?

The subnet number is 220.8.7.96, and the subnet broadcast address is 220.8.7.111. The assignable addresses are all the addresses between the subnet and broadcast addresses, namely 220.8.7.97 to 220.8.7.110.

26 Given the IP address 140.1.1.1 and the mask 255.255.255.248, what are the assignable IP addresses in this subnet?

The subnet number is 140.1.1.0, and the subnet broadcast address is 140.1.1.7. The assignable addresses are all the addresses between the subnet and broadcast addresses, namely 140.1.1.1 to 140.1.1.6.

27 Given the IP address 167.88.99.66 and the mask 255.255.255.192, what are the assignable IP addresses in this subnet?

The subnet number is 167.88.99.64, and the subnet broadcast address is 167.88.99.127. The assignable addresses are all the addresses between the subnet and broadcast addresses, namely 167.88.99.65 to 167.88.99.126.

28 Given the IP address 134.141.7.7 and the mask 255.255.255.0, what are all the subnet numbers if the same (static) mask is used for all subnets in this network?

The answer is 134.141.1.0, 134.141.2.0, 134.141.3.0, and so on, up to 134.141.254.0. 134.141.0.0 is the zero subnet, and 134.141.255.0 is the broadcast subnet.

29 Given the IP address 10.5.118.3 and the mask 255.255.255.0, what are all the subnet numbers if the same (static) mask is used for all subnets in this network?

The answer is 10.0.1.0, 10.0.2.0, 10.0.3.0, and so on, up to 10.255.254.0. The Class A network number is 10.0.0.0. The mask implies that the entire second and third octets, and only those octets, comprise the subnet field. The first subnet number, called the zero subnet (10.0.0.0), and the last subnet number, called the broadcast subnet (10.255.255.0), are reserved.

30 Given the IP address 220.8.7.100 and the mask 255.255.255.240, what are all the subnet numbers if the same (static) mask is used for all subnets in this network?

The answer is not as obvious in this question. The Class C network number is 220.8.7.0. The mask implies that the bits 25 through 28, which are the first 4 bits in the fourth octet, comprise the subnet field. The answer is 220.8.7.16, 220.8.7.32, 220.8.7.48, and so on, through 220.8.7.224. 220.8.7.0 is the zero subnet, and 220.8.7.240 is the broadcast subnet. The following table outlines the easy decimal algorithm to figure out the subnet numbers.

	Octet 1	Octet 2	Octet 3	Octet 4	Comments
Network number	220	8	7	0	N/A
Mask	255	255	255	240	The last octet is interesting; the magic number is 256 – 240 = 16.
Subnet zero	220	8	7	0	Copy the network number; it's the zero subnet.
First valid subnet	220	8	7	16	Add magic to the last subnet number's interesting octet.
Next valid subnet	220	8	7	32	Add magic to the previous one.
Last valid subnet	220	8	7	224	You eventually get here . . .
Broadcast subnet	220	8	7	240	. . . and then here, the broadcast subnet, because the next one is 256, which is invalid.

31 Given the IP address 220.8.7.1 and the mask 255.255.255.240, what are all the subnet numbers *if the same (static) mask is used for all subnets in this network*?

The Class C network number is 220.8.7.0. The mask implies that the bits 25 to 28, which are the first 4 bits in the fourth octet, comprise the subnet field. Essentially, the subnet numbers have the same numbers in the network portion and the same (all binary 0) value in the host portion of the number. Each individual subnet number has a unique value in the subnet portion of the number.

	Octet 1	Octet 2	Octet 3	Octet 4	Comments
Network number	220	8	7	0	N/A
Mask	255	255	255	240	The last octet is interesting.
Subnet zero	220	8	7	0	Copy the network number; it's the zero subnet.
First valid subnet	220	8	7	16	Add magic to the last subnet number's interesting octet.
Next valid subnet	220	8	7	32	Add magic to the previous one.
Last valid subnet	220	8	7	224	You eventually get here . . .
Broadcast subnet	220	8	7	240	. . . and then here, the broadcast subnet, because the next one is 256, which is invalid.

32 How many IP addresses could be assigned in each subnet of 134.141.0.0, assuming that a mask of 255.255.255.0 is used? If the same (static) mask is used for all subnets, how many subnets are there?

There will be $2^{hostbits}$, or 2^8 hosts per subnet, minus two special cases. The number of subnets will be $2^{subnetbits}$, or 2^8, minus 2 special cases.

Network and Mask	Number of Network Bits	Number of Host Bits	Number of Subnet Bits	Number of Hosts per Subnet	Number of Subnets
134.141.0.0, 255.255.255.0	16	8	8	254	254

33 How many IP addresses could be assigned in each subnet of 10.0.0.0, assuming that a mask of 255.255.255.0 is used? If the same (static) mask is used for all subnets, how many subnets are there?

There will be $2^{hostbits}$, or 2^8 hosts per subnet, minus two special cases. The number of subnets will be $2^{subnetbits}$, or 2^{16}, minus 2 special cases.

Network and Mask	Number of Network Bits	Number of Host Bits	Number of Subnet Bits	Number of Hosts per Subnet	Number of Subnets
10.0.0.0, 255.255.255.0	8	8	16	254	65,534

34 How many IP addresses could be assigned in each subnet of 220.8.7.0, assuming that a mask of 255.255.255.240 is used? If the same (static) mask is used for all subnets, how many subnets are there?

There will be $2^{hostbits}$, or 2^4 hosts per subnet, minus two special cases. The number of subnets will be $2^{subnetbits}$, or 2^4, minus 2 special cases.

Network and Mask	Number of Network Bits	Number of Host Bits	Number of Subnet Bits	Number of Hosts per Subnet	Number of Subnets
220.8.7.0, 255.255.255. 240	24	4	4	14	14

35 How many IP addresses could be assigned in each subnet of 140.1.0.0, assuming that a mask of 255.255.255.248 is used? If the same (static) mask is used for all subnets, how many subnets are there?

There will be $2^{hostbits}$, or 2^3 hosts per subnet, minus two special cases. The number of subnets will be $2^{subnetbits}$, or 2^{13}, minus 2 special cases.

Network and Mask	Number of Network Bits	Number of Host Bits	Number of Subnet Bits	Number of Hosts per Subnet	Number of Subnets
140.1.0.0	16	3	13	6	8190

36 You design a network for a customer, and the customer insists that you use the same subnet mask on every subnet. The customer will use network 10.0.0.0 and needs 200 subnets, each with 200 hosts maximum. What subnet mask would you use to allow the largest amount of growth in subnets? Which mask would work and would allow for the most growth in the number of hoses per subnet?

Network 10.0.0.0 is a Class A network, so you have 24 host bits with no subnetting. To number 200 subnets, you will need at least 8 subnet bits because 2^8 is 256. Likewise, to number 200 hosts per subnet, you will need 8 host bits. So, you need to pick a mask with at least 8 subnet bits and 8 host bits. 255.255.0.0 is a mask with 8 subnet bits and 16 host bits. That would allow for the 200 subnets and 200 hosts, while allowing the number of hosts per subnet to grow to $2^{16}-2$—quite a large number. Similarly, a mask of 255.255.255.0 gives you 16 subnet bits, allowing $2^{16}-2$ subnets, each with 2^8-2 hosts per subnet.

37 Create a minimal configuration enabling IP on each interface on a 2501 router (two serial, one Ethernet). The NIC assigned you network 8.0.0.0. Your boss says that you need, at most, 200 hosts per subnet. You decide against using VLSM. Your boss also says to plan your subnets so that you can have as many subnets as possible rather than allow for larger subnets later. When choosing the actual IP address values and subnet numbers, you decide to start with the lowest numerical values. Assume that point-to-point serial links will be attached to this router and that RIP is the routing protocol.

```
router rip
network 8.0.0.0
interface ethernet 0
ip address 8.0.1.1 255.255.255.0
interface serial 0
ip address 8.0.2.1 255.255.255.0
interface serial 1
ip address 8.0.3.1 255.255.255.0
```

The zero subnet was not used in this solution. If desired, the **ip subnet-zero** global command could have been used, enabling subnet 8.0.0.0 as well as the subnets 8.0.1.0, 8.0.2.0, and 8.0.3.0 to be used in the configuration.

38 In the previous question, what would be the IP subnet of the link attached to serial 0? If another user wanted to answer the same question but did not have the enable password, what command(s) might provide this router's addresses and subnets?

The attached subnet is 8.0.2.0, 255.255.255.0. The **show interface**, **show ip interface**, and **show ip interface brief** commands would supply this information, as would **show ip route**. The **show ip route** command would show the actual subnet number instead of the address of the interface.

39 Describe the question and possible responses in setup mode when a router wants to know the mask used on an interface. How can the router derive the correct mask from the information supplied by the user?

When using versions of Cisco IOS Software earlier than Release 12.0, the question asks for the number of subnet bits. The router creates a subnet mask with *x* more binary 1s than the default mask for the class of network of which the interface's IP address is a member. (*x* is the number in the response.) "Number of subnet bits" from the setup question uses the definition that there are three parts to an address—network, subnet, and host. The size of the network field is based on the class of address; the interface's address was typed in response to an earlier setup question. The mask simply has binary 1s in the network and subnet fields, and binary 0s in the host field.

With Cisco IOS Software Release 12.0 and later, setup prompts for the subnet mask in canonical decimal format—for example, 255.255.255.0.

40 Name the three classes of unicast IP addresses and list their default masks, respectively. How many of each type could be assigned to companies and organizations by the NIC?

Class A, B, and C, have default masks 255.0.0.0, 255.255.0.0, and 255.255.255.0, respectively. 2^7 Class A networks are mathematically possible, 2^{14} Class B networks are possible, and 2^{21} Class C networks are possible. There are two reserved network numbers in each range.

41 Describe how TCP performs error recovery. What role do the routers play?

TCP numbers the first byte in each segment with a sequence number. The receiving host uses the acknowledgment field in segments that it sends back to acknowledge receipt of the data. If the receiver sends an acknowledgment number that is a smaller number than the sender expected, the sender believes that the intervening bytes were lost, so the sender resends them. The router plays no role unless the TCP connection ends in the router—for example, a Telnet into a router. A full explanation is provided in the section "Error Recovery (Reliability)."

42 Define the purpose of an ICMP redirect message.

The ICMP redirect message enables a router to tell a host to use a different router than itself because that other router has a better route to the subnet to which the host sent a packet. The redirect also implies that the router sending the redirect, the host sending the original packet, and the better router all have interfaces attached to this same subnet.

43 Define the purpose of the **trace** command. What type of messages does it send, and what type of ICMP messages does it receive?

The **trace** command learns the current route to a destination address. It uses IP packets with UDP as the transport layer protocol, with TTL values beginning at 1 and then incrementing by 1 in successive messages. The result is that intervening routers will find that the TTL is exceeded and will send ICMP Time Exceeded messages back to the originator of the packet, which is the router where the **trace** command is being executed. The source addresses of the Time Exceeded packets identify each router on the path. By sending successive packets with TTL = 2, then 3, and so on, eventually the packet is received by the destination host. The host returns a Port Unreachable ICMP message, which lets the **trace** command know that the endpoint host has been reached.

44 What does *IP* stand for? What does *ICMP* stand for? Which protocol is considered to be a Layer 3 protocol when comparing TCP/IP to the OSI protocols?

Internet Protocol and Internet Control Message Protocol. Both protocols are considered to be part of TCP/IP's protocols equivalent to OSI Layer 3. ICMP also is considered a Layer 3 protocol because it is used for control and management of IP. However, an IP header precedes an ICMP header, so it is common to treat ICMP as another Layer 4 protocol, like TCP and UDP. ICMP does not provide services to a higher layer, however, so it is really an adjunct part of Layer 3.

45 What causes the output from an IOS **ping** command to display "UUUUU?"

U is an indication that an unreachable message was received. The type of unreachable message is not implied by the *U*.

46 Describe how to view the IP ARP cache in a Cisco router. Also describe the three key elements of each entry.

show ip arp displays the IP ARP cache in a Cisco router. Each entry contains the IP address, the MAC address, and the interface from which the information was learned. The encapsulation type is also in the table entry.

47 How many hosts are allowed per subnet if the subnet mask used is 255.255.255.192? How many hosts are allowed for 255.255.255.252?

255.255.255.192 has 6 bits of value 0, giving 2^6 hosts, minus the two reserved numbers, for 62. The 255.255.255.252 mask leaves 2^2 hosts, minus the two reserved numbers, for two hosts. 255.255.255.252 often is used on serial links when using VLSM; point-to-point links need only two IP addresses.

48 How many subnets could be created if using static-length masks in a Class B network when the mask is 255.255.255.224? What about when the mask is 255.255.252.0?

With a Class B network, the first 16 bits are network bits. With mask 255.255.255.224, there are 5 host bits, leaving 11 subnet bits. 2^{11} is 2,048, minus 2 special cases, which leaves 2,046. For the mask 255.255.252.0, there are 10 host bits, leaving 6 subnet bits. 2^6 is 64, minus 2 special cases, which leaves 62.

49 Name the two commands typically used to create a default gateway for a router.

The **ip default-network** command and the **ip route 0.0.0.0 0.0.0.0** command. Both accomplish the goal of having the router use a known route as the default for packets that are not matched in the routing table. The **ip route 0.0.0.0 0.0.0.0** uses the fact that network 0.0.0.0 is used by Cisco IOS Software to represent the default network.

50 Assume that subnets of network 10.0.0.0 are in the IP routing table in a router but that no other network and subnets are known, except that there is also a default route (0.0.0.0) in the routing table. A packet destined for 192.1.1.1 arrives at the router. What configuration command determines whether the default route will be used in this case?

The packet will be routed using the default route, regardless of other configuration commands. In this particular scenario, in which the Class A, B, or C network is known, there is no match for the destination in the known subnets, and a default exists, the default must be used.

51 Assume that subnets of network 10.0.0.0 are in the IP routing table in a router but that no other network and their subnets are known, except that there is also a default route (0.0.0.0) in the routing table. A packet destined for 10.1.1.1 arrives at the router, but there is no known subnet of network 10 that matches this destination address. What configuration command determines whether the default route will be used in this case?

If the command **ip classless** is configured, the packet will be routed using the default route. If **no ip classless** is configured, the packet will be discarded.

52 What does the acronym *CIDR* stand for? What is the original purpose of CIDR?

Classless Interdomain Routing is the concept of grouping multiple sequential network numbers into a single routing table entry, for the purpose of improving scalability of Internet routers by reducing the size of the IP routing table.

53 Define the term *private addressing* as defined in RFC 1918.

Some hosts will never need to communicate with other hosts across the Internet. For such hosts, assignment of IP addresses from registered networks wastes IP addresses. To conserve IP addresses, a set of network numbers, called *private addresses*, has been reserved and can be used in these cases to help conserve IP addresses for use over the Internet.

54 Define the acronym *NAT* and the basics of its operation.

Network Address Translation is a mechanism for allowing hosts with private addresses or addresses that conflict with IP addresses from a registered network to communicate with hosts over the Internet. The basic operation involves the NAT router changing the IP addresses in packets to and from these hosts so that only legitimately registered IP addresses are used in flows through the Internet.

55 Which requires more lines of source code, FTP or TFTP? Justify your answer.

TFTP requires less code. It was designed to be simple (that is, trivial), with the small amount of memory needed to load the code ranking as an advantage to using TFTP. FTP is much more robust, with many more features and more code.

56 Does FTP or TFTP perform error recovery? If so, describe the basics of how they perform error recovery.

Both FTP and TFTP perform error recovery. FTP relies on TCP, whereas TFTP performs application layer recovery one block of data at a time.

57 Describe the process used by IP routers to perform fragmentation and reassembly of packets.

When a packet must be forwarded but the packet is larger than the maximum transmission unit (MTU) size for the outgoing interface, the router fragments the packet, as long as the Don't Fragment bit is not set. No IP router reassembles the fragments; fragments are reassembled at the final destination host.

58 How many TCP segments are exchanged to establish a TCP connection? How many are required to terminate a TCP connection?

A three-way connection-establishment sequence is used, and a four-way connection-termination sequence is used.

59 How many Class B–style networks are reserved by RFC 1918 private addressing?

Sixteen Class B networks are reserved for use as private networks in RFC 1918, networks 172.16.0.0 to 172.31.0.0.

Answers to the Chapter 7 "Do I Know This Already?" Quiz

1 Define what split horizon means to the contents of a routing update. Does this apply to both the distance vector algorithm and the link-state algorithm?

Routing updates sent out an interface do not contain routing information about subnets learned from updates entering the same interface. Split horizon is used only by distance vector routing protocols.

2 Describe the purpose and meaning of route poisoning.

Route poisoning is the distance vector routing protocol feature in which a newly bad route is advertised with an infinite metric. Routers receiving this routing information then can mark the route as a bad route immediately. The purpose is to prevent routing loops.

3 What term describes the underlying logic behind the OSPF routing protocol?

Link state.

4 Describe the meaning and purpose of triggered updates.

A triggered update is the routing protocol feature in which an update is sent immediately when new routing information is learned rather than waiting on a timer to complete before sending another routing update.

5 List the interior IP routing protocols that have autosummarization enabled by default. Which of these protocols allow autosummarization to be disabled using a configuration command?

RIP-1, IGRP, EIGRP, and RIP-2 all have autosummarization enabled by default. EIGRP and RIP-2 can disable this feature.

6 True or false: Distance vector routing protocols learn routes by transmitting routing updates.

False. Routes are learned by receiving routing updates from neighboring routers.

7 Write down the steps you would take to migrate from RIP to IGRP in a router whose current RIP configuration includes only **router rip** followed by a **network 10.0.0.0** command.

Issue the following commands in configuration mode:

```
router igrp 5
network 10.0.0.0
no router rip
```

If RIP still were configured, IGRP's routes would be chosen over RIP. The Cisco IOS Software considers IGRP a better source of routing information by default, as defined in the administrative distance setting (the defaults are 120 for RIP and 100 for IGRP).

8 How does the Cisco IOS Software designate a subnet in the routing table as a directly connected network? What about a route learned with IGRP or RIP?

The **show ip route** command lists routes with a designator on the left side of the command output. **C** represents connected routes, **I** is used for IGRP, and **R** represents routes derived from RIP.

9 From a router's user mode, without using debugs or privileged mode, how can you determine what routers are sending you routing updates?

The **show ip protocol** command output lists the routing sources—the IP addresses of routers sending updates to this router. Knowing how to determine a fact without looking at the configuration will better prepare you for the exam. Also, the **show ip route** command lists next-hop router IP addresses. The next-hop routers listed identify the routers that are sending routing updates.

10 If the command **router rip** followed by **network 10.0.0.0**, with no other **network** commands, is configured in a router that has an Ethernet0 interface with IP address 168.10.1.1, does RIP send updates out Ethernet0?

No. There must be a **network** statement for network 168.10.0.0 before RIP advertises out that interface. The **network** command simply selects the connected interfaces on which to send and receive updates.

11 If the commands **router igrp 1** and **network 10.0.0.0** are configured in a router that has an Ethernet0 interface with IP address 168.10.1.1, does IGRP advertise 168.10.0.0?

No. There must be a **network** statement for network 168.10.0.0 before IGRP advertises that directly connected subnet.

12 Create a configuration for IGRP on a router with these interfaces and addresses: e0 using 10.1.1.1, e1 using 224.1.2.3, s0 using 10.1.2.1, and s1 using 199.1.1.1. Use process ID 5.

```
router igrp 5
network 10.0.0.0
network 199.1.1.0
```

If you noticed that 224.1.2.3 is not a valid Class A, B, or C address, you get full credit. A new address is needed for Ethernet1, with a matching **network** command.

Answers to the Chapter 7 Q&A Section

1 What type of routing protocol algorithm uses a hold-down timer? What is its purpose?

Distance vector. Holddown helps prevent counting-to-infinity problems. Holddown is explained in detail in the section "Distance Vector Routing Protocols" in Chapter 6, "TCP/IP and IP Routing." After learning that a route has failed, a router waits for a hold-down timer before believing any new information about the route.

2 Define what split horizon means to the contents of a routing update. Does this apply to both the distance vector algorithm and the link-state algorithm?

Routing updates sent out an interface do not contain routing information about subnets learned from updates entering the same interface. Split horizon is used only by distance vector routing protocols.

3 Write down the steps you would take to migrate from RIP to IGRP in a router whose current RIP configuration includes only **router rip** followed by a **network 10.0.0.0** command.

Issue the following commands in configuration mode:

```
router igrp 5
network 10.0.0.0
no router rip
```

If RIP still were configured, IGRP's routes would be chosen over RIP. The Cisco IOS Software considers IGRP a better source of routing information by default, as defined in the administrative distance setting (the defaults are 120 for RIP and 100 for IGRP).

4 How does the Cisco IOS Software designate a subnet in the routing table as a directly connected network? What about a route learned with IGRP or RIP?

The **show ip route** command lists routes with a designator on the left side of the command output. **C** represents connected routes, **I** is used for IGRP, and **R** represents routes derived from RIP.

5 Create a configuration for IGRP on a router with these interfaces and addresses: e0 using 10.1.1.1, e1 using 224.1.2.3, s0 using 10.1.2.1, and s1 using 199.1.1.1. Use process ID 5.

```
router igrp 5
network 10.0.0.0
network 199.1.1.0
```

If you noticed that 224.1.2.3 is not a valid Class A, B, or C address, you get full credit. A new address is needed for Ethernet1, with a matching **network** command.

6 Create a configuration for IGRP on a router with these interfaces and addresses: to0 using 200.1.1.1, e0 using 128.1.3.2, s0 using 192.0.1.1, and s1 using 223.254.254.1.

```
router igrp 1
network 200.1.1.0
network 128.1.0.0
network 192.0.1.0
network 223.254.254.0
```

Because four different networks are used, four network commands are required. If you noticed that this question does not specify the process ID (1 in this example) but configured one, you get full credit. A few of these network numbers are used in examples; memorize the range of valid A, B, and C network numbers.

7 From a router's user mode, without using debugs or privileged mode, how can you determine what routers are sending you routing updates?

The **show ip protocol** command output lists the routing sources—the IP addresses of routers sending updates to this router. Knowing how to determine a fact without looking at the configuration will better prepare you for the exam. Also, the **show ip route** command lists next-hop router IP addresses. The next-hop routers listed identify the routers that are sending routing updates.

8 If the command **router rip** followed by **network 10.0.0.0**, with no other **network** commands, is configured in a router that has an Ethernet0 interface with IP address 168.10.1.1, does RIP send updates out Ethernet0?

No. There must be a **network** statement for network 168.10.0.0 before RIP advertises out that interface. The **network** command simply selects the connected interfaces on which to send and receive updates.

9 If the commands **router igrp 1** and **network 10.0.0.0** are configured in a router that has an Ethernet0 interface with IP address 168.10.1.1, does IGRP advertise 168.10.0.0?

No. There must be a **network** statement for network 168.10.0.0 before IGRP advertises that directly connected subnet.

10 If the commands **router igrp 1** and **network 10.0.0.0** are configured in a router that has an Ethernet0 interface with IP address 168.10.1.1, mask 255.255.255.0, does this router have a route to 168.10.1.0?

Yes. The route is in the routing table because it is a directly connected subnet, not because of any action by IGRP.

11 Must IGRP metrics for multiple routes to the same subnet be exactly equal for the multiple routes to be added to the routing table? If not, how close in value do the metrics have to be?

IGRP (and EIGRP) use a concept called variance, which represents how close the metrics to the same subnet must be before they are considered equal. The **variance** router subcommand is used to set the value.

12 When you're using RIP, what configuration command controls the number of equal-cost routes that can be added to the routing table at the same time? What is the maximum number of equal-cost routes to the same destination that can be included in the IP routing table at once?

The **ip maximum-paths** *x* router subcommand is used in RIP configuration mode to set the number. The maximum is 6, and the default is 4.

13 When you're using IGRP, what configuration command controls the number of equal-cost routes that can be added to the routing table at the same time? What is the maximum number of equal-cost routes to the same destination that can be included in the IP routing table at once?

The **ip maximum-paths** *x* router subcommand is used in IGRP configuration mode to set the number. The maximum is 6, and the default is 4.

14 What feature supported by RIP-2 allows it to support variable-length subnet masks (VLSM)?

The association and transmission of mask information with each route allows VLSM support with any routing protocol, RIP-2 included.

15 Name three features of RIP-2 that are not features of RIP-1.

Features included in RIP-2 but not in RIP-1 include transmission of subnet masks with routes, authentication, next-hop router IP addresses in routing update, external route tags, and multicast routing updates.

16 What configuration commands are different between a router configured for RIP-1 and a router configured for only the support of RIP-2?

The **router rip** and **network** commands are identical. The RIP-2 router requires a RIP-2 router subcommand to enable RIP-2.

17 List the interior IP routing protocols that have autosummarization enabled by default. Which of these protocols allow autosummarization to be disabled using a configuration command?

RIP-1, IGRP, EIGRP, and RIP-2 all have autosummarization enabled by default. EIGRP and RIP-2 can disable this feature.

18 Which interior IP routing protocols support route aggregation?

EIGRP and OSPF support route aggregation.

19 Which command lists all IP routes learned via RIP?

The **show ip route rip** command lists only RIP-learned routes.

20 Which command or commands list all IP routes in network 172.16.0.0?

show ip route 172.16.0.0 lists all the routes in 172.16.0.0. Also, the **show ip route list 1** command lists routes in network 172.16.0.0, assuming that the following configuration command also exists: **access-list 1 permit 172.16.0.0 0.0.255.255**.

21 Assume that several subnets of network 172.16.0.0 exist in a router's routing table. What must be true about those routes so that the output of the **show ip route** command lists mask information only on the line that lists network 172.16.0.0 but doesn't show mask information on each route for each subnet?

If all the subnets of 172.16.0.0 use the same mask, the output of the **show ip route** command lists only the mask in the heading line for the network. If VLSM were in use, each route for each subnet would reflect the mask used in that case.

22 True or false: Distance vector routing protocols learn routes by transmitting routing updates.

False. Routes are learned by receiving routing updates from neighboring routers.

23 Assume that a router is configured to allow only one route in the routing table to each destination network. If more than one route to a particular subnet is learned, and if each route has the same metric value, which route is placed in the routing table if the routing protocol uses distance vector logic?

In this scenario, the first route learned is placed in the table. If that route is removed later, the next routing update received after the original route has been removed is added to the routing table.

24 Describe the purpose and meaning of route poisoning.

Route poisoning is the distance vector routing protocol feature in which a newly bad route is advertised with an infinite metric. Routers receiving this routing information then can mark the route as a bad route immediately. The purpose is to prevent routing loops.

25 Describe the meaning and purpose of triggered updates.

A triggered update is the routing protocol feature in which an update is sent immediately when new routing information is learned rather than waiting on a timer to complete before sending another routing update.

26 What term describes the underlying logic behind the OSPF routing protocol?

Link state.

Answers to the Chapter 8 "Do I Know This Already?" Quiz

1 Configure a numbered IP access list that stops packets from subnet 134.141.7.0 255.255.255.0 from exiting serial 0 on a router. Allow all other packets.

```
access-list 4 deny 134.141.7.0 0.0.0.255
access-list 4 permit any
interface serial 0
ip access-group 4
```

The first **access-list** statement denies packets from that subnet. The other statement is needed because the default action to deny packets is not explicitly matched in an **access-list** statement.

2 How would a user who does not have the enable password find out what access lists have been configured and where they are enabled?

The **show access-list** command lists all access lists. The **show ip interfaces** and **show ipx interfaces** commands identify interfaces on which the access lists are enabled.

3 Name all the items that a standard IP access list can examine to make a match.

Source IP address

Subset of the entire source address (using a mask)

4 How many IP access lists of either type can be active on an interface at the same time?

Only one IP access list per interface, per direction. In other words, one inbound and one outbound are allowed, but no more.

5 Configure and enable an IP access list that allows packets from subnet 10.3.4.0/24, to any Web server, to get out serial interface S0. Also allow packets from 134.141.5.4 going to all TCP-based servers using a well-known port to enter serial 0. Deny all other traffic.

```
access-list 101 permit tcp 10.3.4.0 0.0.0.255 any eq www
access-list 102 permit tcp host 134.141.5.4 any lt 1023
interface serial 0
ip access-group 101 out
ip access-group 102 in
```

Two extended access lists are required. List 101 permits packets in the first of the two criteria, in which packets exiting S0 are examined. List 102 permits packets for the second criterion, in which packets entering S0 are examined.

6 Name all the items that an extended IP access list can examine to make a match.

Protocol type

Source port

Source IP address

Subset of the entire source address (using a mask)

Destination port

Destination IP address

Subset of the entire destination address (using a mask)

7 How many IP extended access-list commands are required to check a particular port number on all IP packets?

Two statements are required. If the protocol type IP is configured, the port number is not allowed to be checked. Therefore, the TCP or UDP protocol type must be used to check the port numbers. Thus, if port 25 needs to be checked for both TCP and UDP, two statements are needed: one for TCP and one for UDP.

8 What command lists the IP extended access lists enabled on serial 1 without showing other interfaces?

The **show ip interface serial 1** command lists the names and numbers of the IP access lists enabled on serial 1.

9 Configure a named IP access list that allows only packets from subnet 193.7.6.0 255.255.255.0, going to hosts in network 128.1.0.0 and using a Web server in 128.1.0.0, to enter serial 0 on a router.

```
ip access-list extended barney
 permit tcp 193.7.6.0 0.0.0.255 128.1.0.0 0.0.255.255 eq www
!
interface serial 0
ip access-group barney in
```

A **deny all** is implied at the end of the list.

10 Name all the items that a named standard IP access list can examine to make a match.

Source IP address

Subset of the entire source address (using a mask)

Named standard IP access lists match the same items that numbered IP access lists match.

11 List the types of IP access lists (numbered standard, numbered extended, named standard, named extended) that can be enabled to prevent Telnet access into a router. What commands would be used to enable this function, assuming that access-list 2 was already configured to match the right packets?

Any type of IP access list can be enabled to prevent vty access. The command **line vty 0 4**, followed by **ip access-class 2 in**, enables the feature using access list 2.

12 Name all the items that a named extended IP access list can examine to make a match.

Protocol type

Source port

Source IP address

Subset of the entire source address (using a mask)

Destination port

Destination IP address

Subset of the entire destination address (using a mask)

These are the same things that can be matched with a numbered extended IP access list.

Answers to the Chapter 8 Q&A Section

1 Configure a numbered IP access list that stops packets from subnet 134.141.7.0 255.255.255.0 from exiting serial 0 on a router. Allow all other packets.

```
access-list 4 deny 134.141.7.0 0.0.0.255
access-list 4 permit any
interface serial 0
ip access-group 4
```

The first **access-list** statement denies packets from that subnet. The other statement is needed because the default action to deny packets is not explicitly matched in an **access-list** statement.

2 Configure an IP access list that allows only packets from subnet 193.7.6.0 255.255.255.0, going to hosts in network 128.1.0.0 and using a Web server in 128.1.0.0, to enter serial 0 on a router.

```
access-list 105 permit tcp 193.7.6.0 0.0.0.255
128.1.0.0 0.0.255.255 eq www
!
interface serial 0
ip access-group 105 in
```

A **deny all** is implied at the end of the list.

3 How would a user who does not have the enable password find out what access lists have been configured and where they are enabled?

The **show access-list** command lists all access lists. The **show ip interfaces** and **show ipx interfaces** commands identify interfaces on which the access lists are enabled.

4 Configure and enable an IP access list that stops packets from subnet 10.3.4.0/24 from getting out serial interface S0 and that stops packets from 134.141.5.4 from entering S0. Permit all other traffic.

```
access-list 1 deny 10.3.4.0 0.0.0.255
access-list 1 permit any
access-list 2 deny host 134.141.5.4
access-list 2 permit any
interface serial 0
ip access-group 1
ip access-group 2 in
```

5 Configure and enable an IP access list that allows packets from subnet 10.3.4.0/24, to any Web server, to get out serial interface S0. Also allow packets from 134.141.5.4 going to all TCP-based servers using a well-known port to enter serial 0. Deny all other traffic.

```
access-list 101 permit tcp 10.3.4.0 0.0.0.255 any eq www
access-list 102 permit tcp host 134.141.5.4 any lt 1023
interface serial 0
ip access-group 101 out
ip access-group 102 in
```

Two extended access lists are required. List 101 permits packets in the first of the two criteria, in which packets exiting S0 are examined. List 102 permits packets for the second criterion, in which packets entering S0 are examined.

6 Can standard IP access lists be used to check the source IP address when enabled with the **ip access-group 1 in** command, and can they check the destination IP addresses when using the **ip access-group 1 out** command?

No. Standard IP access lists check only the source IP address, regardless of whether the packets are checked when inbound or outbound.

7 How many IP extended **access-list** commands are required to check a particular port number on all IP packets?

Two statements are required. If the protocol type IP is configured, the port number is not allowed to be checked. Therefore, the TCP or UDP protocol type must be used to check the port numbers. Thus, if port 25 needs to be checked for both TCP and UDP, two statements are needed: one for TCP and one for UDP.

8 True or false: If all IP or IPX **access-list** statements in a particular list define the deny action, the default action is to permit all other packets.

False. The default action at the end of any IP or IPX access list is to deny all other packets.

9 How many IP access lists of either type can be active on an interface at the same time?

Only one IP access list per interface, per direction. In other words, one inbound and one outbound are allowed, but no more.

For questions 10 through 12, assume that all parts of the network shown in Figure 8-8 are up and working. IGRP is the IP routing protocol in use. Answer the questions following Example 8-15, which contains an additional configuration in the Mayberry router.

Figure 8-8 *Network Diagram for Questions 10 Through 12*

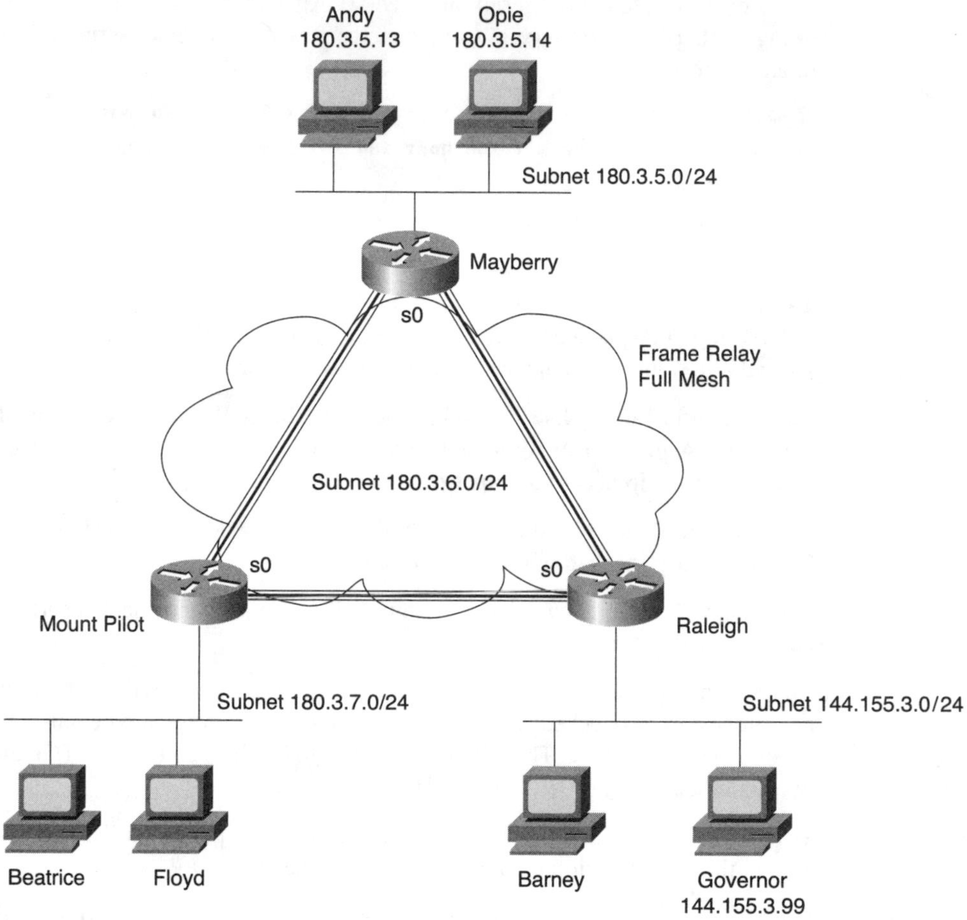

Example 8-15 *Access List at Mayberry*

```
access-list 44 permit 180.3.5.13 0.0.0.0
!
interface serial 0
ip access-group 44
```

10 Describe the types of packets that this filter would discard, and specify at what point they would be discarded.

Only packets coming from Andy exit Mayberry's Serial 0 interface. Packets originating inside the Mayberry router—such as a **ping** command issued from Mayberry—work because the Cisco IOS Software does not filter packets originating in that router. Opie is still out of luck—he'll never get (a packet) out of Mayberry!

11 Does the access list in Example 8-15 stop packets from getting to Web server Governor? Why or why not?

Packets from Andy can get to Web server Governor. Packets from Mount Pilot can be delivered to Governor if the route points directly from Mount Pilot to Raleigh so that the packets do not pass through Mayberry. Therefore, the access list, as coded, stops only hosts other than Andy on the Mayberry Ethernet from reaching Web server Governor.

12 Referring to Figure 8-8, create and enable access lists so that access to Web server Governor is allowed from hosts at any site and so that no other access to hosts in Raleigh is allowed.

```
! this access list is enabled on the Raleigh router
access-list 130 permit tcp 180.3.5.0  0.0.0.255 host 144.155.3.99 eq www
access-list 130 permit tcp 180.3.7.0  0.0.0.255 host 144.155.3.99 eq www
!
interface serial 0
ip access-group 130 in
```

This access list performs the function and also filters IGRP updates. That is part of the danger of inbound access lists. With outbound lists, the router does not filter packets originating in that router. With inbound access lists, all packets entering the interface are examined and can be filtered. An IGRP protocol type is allowed in the extended **access-list** command; therefore, IGRP updates easily can be matched. The command **access-list 130 permit igrp any** performs the needed matching of IGRP updates, permitting those packets. (This command needs to appear before any statements in list 130 that might match IGRP updates.)

13 Name all the items that a standard IP access list can examine to make a match.

Source IP address

Subset of the entire source address (using a mask)

14 Name all the items that an extended IP access list can examine to make a match.

Protocol type

Source port

Source IP address

Subset of the entire source address (using a mask)

Destination port

Destination IP address

Subset of the entire destination address (using a mask)

15 True or false: When you use extended IP access lists to restrict vty access, the matching logic is a best match of the list rather than a first match in the list.

False. Access list logic is always a first match for any application of the list.

16 In a standard numbered IP access list with three statements, a **no** version of the first statement is issued in configuration mode. Immediately following, another access list configuration command is added for the same access list. How many statements are in the list now, and in what position is the newly added statement?

Only one statement remains in the list: the newly added statement. The **no access-list** *x* command deletes the entire access list, even if you type all the parameters in an individual command when issuing the **no** version of the command.

17 In a standard named IP access list with three statements, a **no** version of the first statement is issued in configuration mode. Immediately following, another access list configuration command is added for the same access list. How many statements are in the list now, and in what position is the newly added statement?

Three statements remain in the list, with the newly added statement at the end of the list. The **no deny | permit ...** command deletes only that single named access list subcommand in named lists. However, when the command is added again, it cannot be placed anywhere except at the end of the list.

18 Name all the items that a named standard IP access list can examine to make a match.

Source IP address

Subset of the entire source address (using a mask)

Named standard IP access lists match the same items that numbered IP access lists match.

19 Configure a named IP access list that stops packets from subnet 134.141.7.0 255.255.255.0 from exiting serial 0 on a router. Allow all other packets.

```
ip access-list standard fred
 deny 134.141.7.0 0.0.0.255
 permit any
!
interface serial 0
ip access-group fred
```

The first **access-list** statement denies packets from that subnet. The other statement is needed because the default action to deny packets is not explicitly matched in an **access-list** statement.

20 Configure a named IP access list that allows only packets from subnet 193.7.6.0 255.255.255.0, going to hosts in network 128.1.0.0 and using a Web server in 128.1.0.0, to enter serial 0 on a router.

```
ip access-list extended barney
 permit tcp 193.7.6.0 0.0.0.255 128.1.0.0 0.0.255.255 eq www
!
interface serial 0
ip access-group barney in
```

A **deny all** is implied at the end of the list.

21 List the types of IP access lists (numbered standard, numbered extended, named standard, named extended) that can be enabled to prevent Telnet access into a router. What commands would be used to enable this function, assuming that **access-list 2** was already configured to match the right packets?

Any type of IP access list can be enabled to prevent vty access. The command **line vty 0 4**, followed by **ip access-class 2 in**, enables the feature using access list 2.

22 What command lists the IP extended access lists enabled on serial 1 without showing other interfaces?

The **show ip interface serial 1** command lists the names and numbers of the IP access lists enabled on serial 1.

23 Name all the items that a named extended IP access list can examine to make a match.

Protocol type

Source port

Source IP address

Subset of the entire source address (using a mask)

Destination port

Destination IP address

Subset of the entire destination address (using a mask)

These are the same things that can be matched with a numbered extended IP access list.

Answers to the Chapter 9 "Do I Know This Already?" Quiz

1 Can PPP dynamically assign IP addresses? If so, is this feature always enabled?

PPP's IPCP protocol can assign an IP address to the device on the other end of the link. This process is not required and is not performed by default. PPP usually does address assignment for dial access, such as when a user dials an Internet service provider.

2 Create a configuration to enable PPP on serial 0 for IP and IPX. Make up IP and IPX Layer 3 addresses as needed.

```
interface serial 0
ip addr 1.1.1.1 255.255.255.0
ipx network 1
encapsulation ppp
```

encapsulation ppp is all that is needed for PPP. Having IP and IPX enabled causes PPP to enable the control protocols for each.

3 What data link (OSI Layer 2) protocols are valid on an ISDN B channel?

HDLC, PPP, and LAPB are all valid options. PPP is the preferred choice, however. If you're using DDR to more than one site, PAP or CHAP authentication is required. If used, PPP must be used. PPP also provides automatic IP address assignment, which is convenient for PC dial-in.

4 What field has Cisco added to the HDLC header, making it proprietary?

A Protocol Type field has been added to allow support for multiprotocol traffic. HDLC was not originally designed to allow for multiprotocol support.

5 What does LAPD stand for? Is it used as the Layer 2 protocol on dialed ISDN bearer channels? If not, what is?

LAPD stands for Link Access Procedure on the D channel. LAPD is used not on bearer channels but on the signaling channel. PPP is typically used on bearer channels.

6 Define the term *reference point*. List two examples of reference points.

A reference point is an interface between function groups. R, S, T, and U are reference points. S and T are combined in many cases and are then called the S/T reference point. Reference points refer to cabling, which implies the number of wires used. In particular, the S and T points use a four-wire interface; the U interface uses a two-wire cable.

7 What do ISDN, BRI, and PRI stand for?

ISDN stands for Integrated Services Digital Network. BRI stands for Basic Rate Interface. PRI stands for Primary Rate Interface. BRI is the most likely to be on the exam.

8 How many bearer channels are in a BRI? What about a PRI in North America? What about a PRI in Europe?

BRI uses two bearer channels and one signaling channel (2B+D). PRI uses 23B+D in North America and 30B+D in Europe. The signaling channel on BRI is a 16 kbps channel; on PRI, it is a 64 kbps channel.

9 Describe the decision process performed by the Cisco IOS Software to attempt to dial a connection using legacy DDR.

First, some traffic must be routed out the interface to be dialed; this is typically accomplished by adding static routes pointing out the interface. Then, "interesting" must be defined; any packets routed out the interface that are considered interesting cause the interface to be dialed.

10 CHAP configuration uses names and passwords. Given Routers A and B, describe what names and passwords must match in the respective CHAP configurations.

Router A has name B and a corresponding password configured. Router B has name A and the same password configured. The names used are the host names of the routers unless the CHAP name is configured.

11 Define the terms PAP and CHAP. Which one sends passwords in clear-text format?

PAP stands for Password Authentication Protocol. CHAP stands for Challenge Handshake Authentication Protocol. PAP sends passwords as simple text, whereas CHAP uses MD5 hashing to protect the password contents.

12 Define MLPPP. Describe the typical home or small office use of MLPPP.

MLPPP stands for Multilink Point-to-Point Protocol. MLPPP is used to treat multiple B channels as a single link because MLPPP fragments packets and sends different fragments across the multiple links to balance the traffic. MLPPP is very useful for sharing two B channels in a home or small office. It is not restricted to home use.

Answers to the Chapter 9 Q&A Section

1 Name two WAN data-link protocols for which the standards define a protocol type field that is used to define the type of header that follows the WAN data-link header.

PPP and Frame Relay. The Frame Relay protocol field was added to the standard based on the efforts of the IETF.

2 Name two WAN data-link protocols that define a method of announcing the interface's Layer 3 addresses to other devices attached to the WAN.

PPP and Frame Relay. PPP uses control protocols specific to each Layer 3 protocol supported. Frame Relay uses Inverse ARP.

3 What does LAPD stand for? Is it used as the Layer 2 protocol on dialed ISDN bearer channels? If not, what is?

LAPD stands for Link Access Procedure on the D channel. LAPD is used not on bearer channels but on the signaling channel. PPP is typically used on bearer channels.

4 What does NBMA stand for? Does it apply to PPP links? What about X.25 networks or Frame Relay networks?

NBMA stands for nonbroadcast multiaccess. PPP is nonbroadcast, but not multiaccess. X.25 and Frame Relay are NBMA networks. Multiaccess really means that more than two devices are connected to the data link; therefore, when one device sends data, the intended receiver is not obvious.

5 Can PPP dynamically assign IP addresses? If so, is this feature always enabled?

PPP's IPCP protocol can assign an IP address to the device on the other end of the link. This process is not required and is not performed by default. PPP usually does address assignment for dial access, such as when a user dials an Internet service provider.

6 Create a configuration to enable PPP on serial 0 for IP and IPX. Make up IP and IPX Layer 3 addresses as needed.

```
interface serial 0
ip addr 1.1.1.1 255.255.255.0
ipx network 1
encapsulation ppp
```

encapsulation ppp is all that is needed for PPP. Having IP and IPX enabled causes PPP to enable the control protocols for each.

7 Create a configuration for Router1 that has Frame Relay VCs to Router2 and Router3 (DLCIs 202 and 203, respectively) for Frame Relay on Router1's serial 1 interface. Use any IP and IPX addresses you like. Assume that the network is not fully meshed.

```
interface serial 1
encapsulation frame-relay
interface serial 1.1 point-to-point
ip address 168.10.1.1 255.255.255.0
ipx network 1
frame-relay interface-dlci 202
interface serial 1.2 point-to-point
ip address 168.10.2.1 255.255.255.0
ipx network 2
frame-relay interface-dlci 203
```

This is not the only valid configuration to accomplish the task. However, because there is no full mesh, point-to-point subinterfaces are the best choice. Cisco encapsulation is used by default. The LMI type is autosensed.

8 What do ISDN, BRI, and PRI stand for?

ISDN stands for Integrated Services Digital Network. BRI stands for Basic Rate Interface. PRI stands for Primary Rate Interface. BRI is the most likely to be on the exam.

9 Define the term *function group*. List two examples of function groups.

A function group is a set of ISDN functions that need to be implemented by a device. NT1, NT2, TE1, TE2, and TA are all function groups.

10 Define the term *reference point*. List two examples of reference points.

A reference point is an interface between function groups. R, S, T, and U are reference points. S and T are combined in many cases and are then called the S/T reference point. Reference points refer to cabling, which implies the number of wires used. In particular, the S and T points use a four-wire interface; the U interface uses a two-wire cable.

11 How many bearer channels are in a BRI? What about a PRI in North America? What about a PRI in Europe?

BRI uses two bearer channels and one signaling channel (2B+D). PRI uses 23B+D in North America and 30B+D in Europe. The signaling channel on BRI is a 16 kbps channel; on PRI, it is a 64 kbps channel.

12 True or false: ISDN defines protocols that can be functionally equivalent to OSI Layers 1, 2, and 3. Explain your answer.

True. Reference points in part define the physical interfaces. Used on the signaling channel, LAPD is a data-link protocol. SPIDs define a logical addressing structure and are roughly equivalent to OSI Layer 3. Table 9-11 summarizes ISDN protocols as compared to the OSI model.

13 What reference points are used by ISDN BRI interfaces on Cisco routers?

A BRI interface with an S/T reference point, or a BRI with a U reference point, can be bought from Cisco. With an S/T interface, an external NT1, NT2, or NT1/NT2 device is required. With the U interface, no external device is required.

14 Is LAPD used on ISDN channels? If so, which ones?

LAPD is used only on ISDN D channels to deliver signaling messages to the local ISDN switch. Many people don't understand the function of LAPD, thinking it is used on the B channels after the dial is complete. The encapsulation chosen in the router configuration determines the data-link protocol on the bearer channels. Cisco routers do not have an option to turn off LAPD on the signaling channel.

15 Name the standards body that defines ISDN protocols.

International Telecommunications Union (ITU). This group was formerly called CCITT. The ITU is governed by the United Nations.

16 What ISDN functions do standards ITU-T Q.920 and Q.930 define? Does either standard correlate to an OSI layer?

Q.920 defines ISDN data-link specifications, such as LAPD; Q.930 defines Layer 3 functions, such as call setup messages. I.440 and I.450 are equivalent to Q.920 and Q.930, respectively.

17 What ISDN functions does standard ITU-T I.430 define? Does it correlate to an OSI layer?

I.430 defines ISDN BRI physical layer specifications. It is similar to OSI Layer 1. I.430 has no Q-series equivalent specification.

18 What does SPID stand for? What does it mean?

SPID stands for service profile identifier. It is the ISDN phone number used in signaling.

19 Define the terms TE1, TE2, and TA. Which implies that one of the other two must be in use?

TE1 stands for Terminal Equipment 1. TE2 stands for Terminal Equipment 2. TA stands for terminal adapter. A TE2 device requires a TA. A TE2 uses the R reference point. An S reference point is needed to perform ISDN signaling. It is provided in that case by the TA.

20 What reference point is used between the customer premises and the phone company in North America? What about in Europe?

The U interface is used in North America. Elsewhere, the T interface is used. The NT1 function, the dividing point between the T and U reference points, is implemented in telco equipment outside North America.

21 Define the term SBus, and give an example of when it is useful.

SBus is a bus with many devices sharing the S reference point. ISDN-capable phones, faxes, and computers that want to share the same BRI connect to the same NT1 using an SBus. SPIDs include subaddresses to distinguish among the multiple devices when using an SBus.

22 What data link (OSI Layer 2) protocols are valid on an ISDN B channel?

HDLC, PPP, and LAPB are all valid options. PPP is the preferred choice, however. If you're using DDR to more than one site, PAP or CHAP authentication is required. If used, PPP must be used. PPP also provides automatic IP address assignment, which is convenient for PC dial-in.

23 Define the terms PAP and CHAP. Which one sends passwords in clear-text format?

PAP stands for Password Authentication Protocol. CHAP stands for Challenge Handshake Authentication Protocol. PAP sends passwords as simple text, whereas CHAP uses MD5 hashing to protect the password contents.

24 Define MLPPP. Describe the typical home or small office use of MLPPP.

MLPPP stands for Multilink Point-to-Point Protocol. MLPPP is used to treat multiple B channels as a single link because MLPPP fragments packets and sends different fragments across the multiple links to balance the traffic. MLPPP is very useful for sharing two B channels in a home or small office. It is not restricted to home use.

25 CHAP configuration uses names and passwords. Given Routers A and B, describe what names and passwords must match in the respective CHAP configurations.

Router A has name B and a corresponding password configured. Router B has name A and the same password configured. The names used are the host names of the routers unless the CHAP name is configured.

26 Configure ISDN interface BRI1, assuming that it is attached to a DMS-100 ISDN switch, that it uses only one SPID of 404555121201, and that you want to screen calls so that only calls from 404555999901 are accepted.

```
isdn switch-type basic-dms100
interface bri1
  isdn spid1 404555121201
  isdn caller 404555999901
```

The **switch-type** command is required. SPIDs are required only with some switches. The **isdn caller** command is needed only for call screening.

27 List the types of compression that are available on PPP links.

The STAC, Predictor, and MPPC compression types are available on PPP interfaces in the Cisco IOS Software.

28 Describe the decision process performed by the Cisco IOS Software to attempt to dial a connection using legacy DDR.

First, some traffic must be routed out the interface to be dialed; this is typically accomplished by adding static routes pointing out the interface. Then, "interesting" must be defined; any packets routed out the interface that are considered interesting cause the interface to be dialed.

29 If packets from 10.1.1.0/24 are "interesting" in relation to DDR configuration, such that packets from 10.1.1.0/24 caused a DDR connection out interface BRI0, list the configuration commands that would make the Cisco IOS Software think that those packets were interesting on BRI0.

The following access list defines the packets from 10.1.1.0/24. The **dialer-list** defines the use of **access-list 1** for deciding what is interesting. The **dialer-group** command enables that logic on interface BRI0.

```
access-list 1 permit 10.1.1.0 0.0.0.255
!
dialer-list 2 protocol ip list 1
!
interface bri 0
 dialer-group 2
```

30 List the typical EIA/TIA standard interfaces used for serial cables with a Cisco router.

EIA/TIA-232, EIA/TIA-449, and EIA/TIA-530 are typical. V.35 and X.21, which are ITU standards, are also typical. Be careful on the exam—this question asked for EIA/TIA standards, so V.35 and X.21 would be incorrect.

31 What field has Cisco added to the HDLC header, making it proprietary?

A Protocol Type field has been added to allow support for multiprotocol traffic. HDLC was not originally designed to allow for multiprotocol support.

Answers to the Chapter 10 "Do I Know This Already?" Quiz

1 Explain the purpose of Inverse ARP. Explain how Inverse ARP uses Frame Relay broadcasts.

A router discovers the Layer 3 address(es) of a router on the other end of a VC when that other router sends an Inverse ARP message. The message is not a broadcast.

2 What does NBMA stand for? Does it apply to X.25 networks or Frame Relay networks?

NBMA stands for nonbroadcast multiaccess. X.25 and Frame Relay are NBMA networks. Multiaccess really means that more than two devices are connected to the data link, because many other devices may be reached by a single device. For instance, Router1 might have a PVC to Router2 and Router3, making it multiaccess.

3 What is the name of the field that identifies, or addresses, a Frame Relay virtual circuit?

The data-link connection identifier (DLCI) is used to identify a VC. The number may be different on either side of the VC.

4 Which layer or layers of OSI are most closely related to the functions of Frame Relay? Why?

OSI Layers 1 and 2. Frame Relay refers to well-known physical layer specifications. Frame Relay does define headers for delivery across the Frame Relay cloud, but it provides no addressing structure to allow VCs among many different Frame Relay networks. Thus, it is not considered to match OSI Layer 3 functions. With the advent of Frame Relay SVCs, it could be argued that Frame Relay performs some Layer 3-like functions.

5 Would a Frame Relay switch connected to a router behave differently if the IETF option were deleted from the **encapsulation frame-relay ietf** command on that attached router? Would a router on the other end of the VC behave any differently if the same change were made?

The switch does not behave differently. The other router, however, must also use IETF encapsulation. Otherwise, the routers will not look at the correct fields to learn the packet type.

6 What **show** command tells you when a PVC became active? How does the router know what time the PVC became active?

The **show frame-relay pvc** command lists the time since the PVC came up. You can subtract this time from the current time to derive the time at which the VC came up. The router learns about when PVCs come up and go down from LMI messages.

7 What **debug** option shows Inverse ARP messages?

debug frame-relay events, as shown in Example 10-18.

8 What **show** command lists Frame Relay information about mapping? In what instances does the information displayed include the Layer 3 addresses of other routers?

show frame-relay map lists Frame Relay information about mapping. The mapping information includes Layer 3 addresses when multipoint subinterfaces are used or when no subinterfaces are used. The two cases in which the neighboring routers' Layer 3 addresses are shown are the two cases in which Frame Relay acts like a multiaccess network. With point-to-point subinterfaces, the logic works like a point-to-point link, in which the next router's Layer 3 address is unimportant to the routing process.

Answers to the Chapter 10 Q&A Section

1 Name two WAN data-link protocols that define a method of announcing the interface's Layer 3 addresses to other devices attached to the WAN.

PPP and Frame Relay. PPP uses control protocols specific to each Layer 3 protocol supported. Frame Relay uses Inverse ARP.

2 Explain the purpose of Inverse ARP. Explain how Inverse ARP uses Frame Relay broadcasts.

A router discovers the Layer 3 address(es) of a router on the other end of a VC when that other router sends an Inverse ARP message. The message is not a broadcast.

3 Would a Frame Relay switch connected to a router behave differently if the IETF option were deleted from the **encapsulation frame-relay ietf** command on that attached router? Would a router on the other end of the VC behave any differently if the same change were made?

The switch does not behave differently. The other router, however, must also use IETF encapsulation. Otherwise, the routers will not look at the correct fields to learn the packet type.

4 What does NBMA stand for? Does it apply to X.25 networks or Frame Relay networks?

NBMA stands for nonbroadcast multiaccess. X.25 and Frame Relay are NBMA networks. Multiaccess really means that more than two devices are connected to the data link, because many other devices may be reached by a single device. For instance, Router1 might have a PVC to Router2 and Router3, making it multiaccess.

5 Define the terms DCE and DTE in the context of the physical layer and a point-to-point serial link.

At the physical layer, DTE refers to the device that looks for clocking from the device on the other end of the cable on a link. The DCE supplies that clocking. For example, the computer is typically the DTE, and the modem or CSU/DSU is the DCE. At the data link layer, both X.25 and Frame Relay define a logical DTE and DCE. In this case, the customer premises equipment (CPE), such as a router and CSU/DSU, is the logical DTE, and the service provider equipment (the Frame Relay switch and CSU/DSU) is the DCE.

6 Which layer or layers of OSI are most closely related to the functions of Frame Relay? Why?

OSI Layers 1 and 2. Frame Relay refers to well-known physical layer specifications. Frame Relay does define headers for delivery across the Frame Relay cloud, but it provides no addressing structure to allow VCs among many different Frame Relay networks. Thus, it is not considered to match OSI Layer 3 functions. With the advent of Frame Relay SVCs, it could be argued that Frame Relay performs some Layer 3-like functions.

7 When Inverse ARP is used by default, what additional configuration is needed to get IGRP routing updates to flow over each VC?

No additional configuration is required. The forwarding of broadcasts as unicasts can be enabled on each VC and protocol for which Inverse ARP is received.

8 Define the attributes of a partial-mesh and full-mesh Frame Relay network.

In a partial-mesh network, not all DTEs are directly connected with a VC. In a full-mesh network, all DTEs are directly connected with a VC.

9 What key pieces of information are required in the **frame-relay map** statement?

The Layer 3 protocol, the next-hop router's Layer 3 address, the DLCI to reach that router, and whether to forward broadcasts. Frame Relay maps are not required if Inverse ARP is in use.

10 When creating a partial-mesh Frame Relay network, are you required to use subinterfaces?

No. Subinterfaces can be used and are preferred with a partial mesh because this removes split-horizon issues by treating each VC as its own interface. Likewise, subinterfaces are optional when the network is a full mesh. Most people tend to use subinterfaces today.

11 What benefit related to routing protocols can be gained by using subinterfaces with a partial mesh?

Split-horizon issues can be avoided by treating each VC as a separate interface. Split horizon is still enabled. Routing loops are not a risk, but all routes are learned.

12 Create a configuration for Router1 that has Frame Relay VCs to Router2 and Router3 (DLCIs 202 and 203, respectively) on Router1's Serial1 interface. Use any IP and IPX addresses you like. Assume that the network is not fully meshed.

```
interface serial 1
encapsulation frame-relay
interface serial 1.1 point-to-point
ip address 168.10.1.1 255.255.255.0
ipx network 1
frame-relay interface-dlci 202
interface serial 1.2 point-to-point
ip address 168.10.2.1 255.255.255.0
ipx network 2
frame-relay interface-dlci 203
```

This is not the only valid configuration given the problem statement. However, because there is not a full mesh, point-to-point subinterfaces are the best choice. Cisco encapsulation is used by default. The LMI type is autosensed.

13 What **show** command tells you when a PVC became active? How does the router know what time the PVC became active?

The **show frame-relay pvc** command lists the time since the PVC came up. You can subtract this time from the current time to derive the time at which the VC came up. The router learns about when PVCs come up and go down from LMI messages.

14 What **show** command lists Frame Relay information about mapping? In what instances does the information displayed include the Layer 3 addresses of other routers?

show frame-relay map lists Frame Relay information about mapping. The mapping information includes Layer 3 addresses when multipoint subinterfaces are used or when no subinterfaces are used. The two cases in which the neighboring routers' Layer 3 addresses are shown are the two cases in which Frame Relay acts like a multiaccess network. With point-to-point subinterfaces, the logic works like a point-to-point link, in which the next router's Layer 3 address is unimportant to the routing process.

15 True or false: The **no keepalive** command on a Frame Relay serial interface causes no further Cisco proprietary keepalive messages to be sent to the Frame Relay switch.

False. This command stops LMI status inquiry messages from being sent. They are defined in Frame Relay Forum standards. Cisco sends proprietary keepalive messages on point-to-point serial and LAN interfaces.

16 What **debug** option shows Inverse ARP messages?

debug frame-relay events, as shown in Example 10-18.

17 True or false: The Frame Relay **map** configuration command allows more than one Layer 3 protocol address mapping on the same configuration command.

False. The syntax allows only a single network layer protocol and address to be configured.

18 What is the name of the field that identifies, or addresses, a Frame Relay virtual circuit?

The data-link connection identifier (DLCI) is used to identify a VC. The number may be different on either side of the VC.

Answers to the Chapter 11 "Do I Know This Already?" Quiz

1 How often does IPX RIP send routing updates, by default?

Every 60 seconds.

2 What does *GNS* stand for? What creates GNS requests, and what creates GNS replies?

GNS stands for Get Nearest Server. Clients create the request, which is a broadcast looking for a nearby server. Servers and routers reply, based on their SAP table, with the IPX address of a server whose RIP metric is low.

3 How many bytes comprise an IPX address?

10 bytes. The network portion is 32 bits, and the node portion is 48 bits. The node part conveniently is the same size as a LAN MAC address.

4 Give an example of an IPX network mask used when subnetting.

There is no such thing as subnetting with IPX. This is an example of a question meant to shake your confidence on the exam. Thoughts such as, "I've never read about subnetting IPX!" can destroy your concentration. Be prepared for unusual questions or answers like this on the exam.

5 Name the command that lists all the SAP entries in a Cisco router.

show ipx servers. Many people remember that the command uses either the **servers**, or **server**, or **service**, or **sap** keyword. The exam is likely to list those four keywords as the four answers; spend a little time memorizing the commands summarized at the beginning of each configuration section in most chapters of this book.

6 What **show** command lists the IPX address(es) of interfaces in a Cisco router?

show ipx interface. The other **show** commands list only the IPX network numbers, not the entire IPX addresses.

7 A router is attached to an Ethernet LAN. Some clients on the LAN use Novell's Ethernet_II encapsulation, and some use Ethernet_802.3. If the only subcommand on Ethernet0 reads **ipx network 1**, which of the clients are working? (All, Ethernet_II, or Ethernet_802.3?)

Just those with Ethernet_802.3 are working. The associated IOS keyword is **novell-ether**, and this is the default IPX encapsulation. This question is just trying to test your recall of the default encapsulation for Ethernet.

8 What IOS IPX encapsulation keyword implies use of an 802.2 header but no SNAP header? On what types of interfaces is this type of encapsulation valid?

SAP encapsulation on IOS implies use of the 802.2 header immediately before the IPX packet. SAP and SNAP are valid on Ethernet, FDDI, and Token Ring. SAP also refers to the field in the 802.2 header that is used to identify IPX as the type of packet that follows the 802.2 header.

9 Name all the items that a SAP access list can examine to make a match.

Network

IPX address (network and node)

Subnets of the first two using a wildcard

Service type

Server name

10 True or false: If all IP or IPX access list statements in a particular list define the deny action, the default action is to permit all other packets.

False. The default action at the end of any IP or IPX access list is to deny all other packets.

11 In an IPX access list with five statements, a **no** version of the third statement is issued in configuration mode. Immediately following, another access list configuration command is added for the same access list. How many statements are in the list now, and in what position is the newly added statement?

Only one statement will remain in the list: the newly added statement. The **no access-list** x command deletes the entire access list, even if all the parameters in an individual command are typed in when issuing the **no** version of the command.

12 Name all the items that a standard IPX access list can examine to make a match.

Source network

Source IPX address (network and node)

Subset of node part of address (using mask)

Destination network

Destination IPX address (network and node)

Subset of node part of IPX address (using mask)

Answers to the Chapter 11 Q&A Section

1 How often does IPX RIP send routing updates, by default?

Every 60 seconds.

2 Describe the metric(s) used by IPX RIP in a Cisco router.

The primary metric is a counter of timer ticks. If two routes to the same network tie with the ticks metric, the hop count is considered. Ticks are increments of 1/18th of a second. The number of ticks is not measured but is set with defaults of 1 on LAN interfaces and 6 on WAN interfaces. The IPX **delay interface** subcommand overrides the defaults.

3 Does IPX RIP use split horizon?

Split horizon means that routes learned through updates received on interface *x* will not be advertised in routing updates sent out interface *x*. IPX RIP uses split horizon by default. SAP also uses split-horizon concepts.

4 True or false: RIP and SAP information is sent in the same packets. If true, can only one of the two be enabled in a router? If false, what commands enable each protocol globally in a router?

False. Only one command is used, and it enables both: **ipx routing**. Neither type of update is sent unless IPX also is enabled on the interface with the **ipx network** interface subcommand.

5 What does *GNS* stand for? Who creates GNS requests, and who creates GNS replies?

GNS stands for Get Nearest Server. Clients create the request, which is a broadcast looking for a nearby server. Servers and routers reply, based on their SAP table, with the IPX address of a server whose RIP metric is low.

6 How often does a router send SAP updates, by default?

Every 60 seconds.

7 If Serial0 has a **bandwidth 1544** interface subcommand and Serial1 has a **bandwidth 56** interface subcommand, what metric will IPX RIP associate with each interface?

IOS is unaffected by an interface's bandwidth when considering IPX RIP metrics; ticks will default to 6 for any serial interface, regardless of bandwidth setting.

8 What **show** commands list IPX RIP metric values in a Cisco router?

```
show ipx route
show ipx servers
```

This is a trick question. The services listed by the **show ipx servers** command also contain a reference to the RIP metrics; the information is handy when looking for good servers for a GNS reply.

9 How many bytes comprise an IPX address?

10 bytes. The network portion is 32 bits, and the node portion is 48 bits. The node part conveniently is the same size as a LAN MAC address.

10 What do *IPX* and *SPX* stand for?

Internetwork Packet Exchange and Sequenced Packet Exchange.

11 Define *encapsulation* in the context of Cisco routers and Novell IPX.

Data-link encapsulation describes the details of the data link header and trailer created by a router as the result of routing a packet out an interface. Novell allows several options on LANs. Encapsulation is used for any routed protocol on every router interface. Novell just happens to have many options that are still in use, particularly on Ethernet.

12 Give an example of an IPX network mask used when subnetting.

There is no such thing as subnetting with IPX. This is an example of a question meant to shake your confidence on the exam. Thoughts such as, "I've never read about subnetting IPX!" can destroy your concentration. Be prepared for unusual questions or answers such as this on the exam.

13 Describe the headers used for two types of Ethernet encapsulation when using IPX.

Ethernet_II uses Ethernet version 2 headers (destination and source address, and type field). Ethernet_802.3 uses an 802.3 header (destination and source address, and length field). Ethernet_802.2 uses an 802.3 header and an 802.2 header (802.2 adds DSAP, SSAP, and Control fields). Ethernet_SNAP uses an 802.3 header, an 802.2 header, and then a SNAP header (SNAP adds OUI and protocol fields). The names in this answer use Novell's names. The corresponding keywords in IOS are **arpa**, **novell-ether**, **SAP**, and **SNAP**, respectively. The Novell names refer to the last header before the IPX header. See Tables 11-4 and 11-5, respectively, for a reference for all LAN encapsulations.

14 Name the part of the NetWare protocol specifications that, like TCP, provides end-to-end guaranteed delivery of data.

Sequenced Packet Exchange (SPX).

15 Name the command that lists all the SAP entries in a Cisco router.

show ipx servers. Many people remember that the command uses either the **servers**, or **server**, or **service**, or **sap** keywords. The exam is likely to list those four keywords as the four answers; spend a little time memorizing the commands summarized at the beginning of each configuration section in most chapters of this book.

16 How many different values are possible for IPX network numbers?

2^{32}, or around four billion. Networks 0 and FFFFFFFF are reserved. The size of the network number is one big reason why there is no need for subnetting IPX networks.

17 Create a configuration enabling IPX on each interface, with RIP and SAP enabled on each as well, for a 2501 (two serial, one Ethernet) router. Use networks 100, 200, and 300 for interfaces S0, S1, and E0, respectively. Choose any node values.

```
ipx routing 0200.1111.1111
interface serial 0
ipx network 100
interface serial 1
ipx network 200
interface ethernet 0
ipx network 300
```

The node part of the address was supplied in the IPX routing command so that the IPX addresses are easily recognizable on the serial interfaces. This helps troubleshooting because it will be easier to remember the IPX addresses used when pinging.

18 In the previous question, what would be the IPX address of the serial 0 interface? If another user wanted to know but did not have the enable password, what command(s) might provide this IPX address?

```
100.0200.1111.1111
show ipx interface
```

If you left off the node parameter on the IPX routing command in the previous question, the IPX address would have a node number equal to the MAC address used on the Ethernet interface.

19 What **show** command lists the IPX address(es) of interfaces in a Cisco router?

show ipx interface. The other **show** commands list only the IPX network numbers, not the entire IPX addresses.

20 How many Novell encapsulation types are valid in the IOS for Ethernet interfaces? What about for FDDI and Token Ring?

There are four encapsulations for Ethernet, three encapsulations for FDDI, and two encapsulations for Token Ring. Tables 11-4 and 11-5, respectively, list the different encapsulations.

21 A router is attached to an Ethernet LAN. Some clients on the LAN use Novell's Ethernet_II encapsulation, and some use Ethernet_802.3. If the only subcommand on Ethernet0 reads **ipx network 1**, which of the clients are working? (All, Ethernet_II, or Ethernet_802.3?)

Just those with Ethernet_802.3 are working. The associated IOS keyword is **novell-ether**, and this is the default IPX encapsulation. This question is just trying to test your recall of the default encapsulation for Ethernet.

22 A router is attached to an Ethernet LAN. Some clients on the LAN use Novell's Ethernet_802.2 encapsulation, and some use Ethernet_SNAP. Create a configuration that allows both types of clients to send and receive packets through this router.

```
interface ethernet 0
ipx network 1 encapsulation sap
ipx network 2 encapsulation snap secondary
```

Subinterfaces also could have been used instead of secondary IPX networks.

23 True or false: Up to 64 IPX networks can be used on the same Ethernet by using the IPX secondary address feature. If true, describe the largest number that is practically needed. If false, what is the maximum number that is legal on an Ethernet?

False. Only one network per encapsulation is allowed. Because four Ethernet encapsulations can be used with IPX, four IPX networks are supported. Using the same logic, only three networks are allowed on FDDI, and two are allowed on Token Ring.

24 In the **ipx network 11** interface subcommand, does the IOS assume that 11 is binary, octal, decimal, or hexadecimal? What is the largest valid value that could be configured instead of 11?

All IPX network numbers are considered to be hexadecimal by IOS. The largest value is FFFFFFFE, with FFFFFFFF being reserved as the broadcast network.

25 What IOS IPX encapsulation keyword implies use of an 802.2 header but no SNAP header? On what types of interfaces is this type of encapsulation valid?

SAP encapsulation in IOS implies use of the 802.2 header immediately before the IPX packet. SAP and SNAP are valid on Ethernet, FDDI, and Token Ring. SAP also refers to the field in the 802.2 header that is used to identify IPX as the type of packet that follows the 802.2 header.

26 How would a user who does not have the enable password find out what access lists have been configured and where they are enabled?

The **show access-list** command lists all access lists. The **show ip interfaces** and **show ipx interfaces** commands identify interfaces on which the access lists are enabled.

27 Create a configuration to add a SAP access list to filter all print services (SAP 7) from being advertised out a router's serial 0 and serial1 interfaces.

```
access-list 1000 deny -1 7
access-list 1000 permit -1
interface serial 0
ipx output-sap-filter 1000
interface serial1
ipx output-sap-filter 1000
```

In the two **access-list 1000** commands, the **–1** represents the wildcard meaning "any network." SAP Type 7 is for print services; the first statement matches those services and denies those services. However, other proprietary print solutions could use a different SAP type. This access list matches only for the standard SAP type for printers.

28 Name all the items that a SAP access list can examine to make a match.

Network

IPX address (network and node)

Subnets of the first two using a wildcard

Service type

Server name

Many people would consider checking the network number and checking a full IPX address as the same item. These functions are listed separately here only to make sure that you recall that both variations are possible.

29 True or false: If all IP or IPX access list statements in a particular list define the deny action, the default action is to permit all other packets.

False. The default action at the end of any IP or IPX access list is to deny all other packets.

30 In an IPX access list with five statements, a **no** version of the third statement is issued in configuration mode. Immediately following, another access list configuration command is added for the same access list. How many statements are in the list now, and in what position is the newly added statement?

Only one statement will remain in the list: the newly added statement. The **no access-list** *x* command deletes the entire access list, even if all the parameters in an individual command are typed in when issuing the **no** version of the command.

31 Name all the items that a standard IPX access list can examine to make a match.

Source network

Source IPX address (network and node)

Subset of node part of address (using mask)

Destination network

Destination IPX address (network and node)

Subset of node part of IPX address (using mask)

Many people would consider checking the network number and checking a full IPX address as the same item. These functions are listed separately here only to make sure that you recall that both variations are possible. Also, the mask can be used only if the full IPX address is specified and masks out only parts of the node part of the address.

32 Name all the items that an extended IPX access list can examine to make a match.

Protocol

Source socket

Source network

Source IPX address (network and node)

Subset of entire address (using mask)

Destination socket

Destination network

Destination IPX address (network and node)

Subset of entire IPX address (using mask)

Many people would consider checking the network number and checking a full IPX address as the same item. These functions are listed separately here only to make sure that you recall that both variations are possible. Also, the mask can be used only if the full IPX address is specified and masks out only parts of the node part of the address.

33 In an extended named IPX access list with five statements, a **no** version of the second statement is issued in configuration mode. Immediately following, another access list configuration command is added for the same access list. How many statements are in the list now, and in what position is the newly added statement?

Five statements will remain in the list, with the newly added statement at the end of the list. The **no deny | permit. . .** command deletes only that single named access list subcommand in named lists. However, when the command is added again, it cannot be placed anywhere except at the end of the list.

34 Name all the items that a named extended IPX access list can examine to make a match.

Protocol

Source socket

Source network

Source IPX address (network and node)

Subset of entire address (using mask)

Destination socket

Destination network

Destination IPX address (network and node)

Subset of entire IPX address (using mask)

The same matching criteria are used for numbered extended IPX access lists as are used for named extended IPX access lists.

35 Configure a SAP numbered access list so that SAPs 4 through 7 are matched in network BEEF with a single command.

You cannot match more than one SAP with a single access list statement. To match four separate SAP values, four separate access list statements are required.

36 What command could someone who has only the Telnet password, not the enable password, use to find out what IPX access lists were enabled on which interfaces?

The **show ipx interfaces** command lists all interfaces and details about each interface, including the name and number of all standard, extended, and SAP access lists enabled on each interface.

37 What command would display the contents of only IPX access list 904?

Both the **show access-list 904** and the **show ipx access-list 904** commands would show the same contents. Both actually show the information in the same format.

APPENDIX **B**

Decimal to Hexadecimal and Binary Conversion Table

Decimal Value	Hexadecimal Value	Binary Value
0	00	0000 0000
1	01	0000 0001
2	02	0000 0010
3	03	0000 0011
4	04	0000 0100
5	05	0000 0101
6	06	0000 0110
7	07	0000 0111
8	08	0000 1000
9	09	0000 1001
10	0A	0000 1010
11	0B	0000 1011
12	0C	0000 1100
13	0D	0000 1101
14	0E	0000 1110
15	0F	0000 1111
16	10	0001 0000
17	11	0001 0001
18	12	0001 0010
19	13	0001 0011
20	14	0001 0100
21	15	0001 0101
22	16	0001 0110

continues

Decimal Value	Hexadecimal Value	Binary Value
23	17	0001 0111
24	18	0001 1000
25	19	0001 1001
26	1A	0001 1010
27	1B	0001 1011
28	1C	0001 1100
29	1D	0001 1101
30	1E	0001 1110
31	1F	0001 1111
32	20	0010 0000
33	21	0010 0001
34	22	0010 0010
35	23	0010 0011
36	24	0010 0100
37	25	0010 0101
38	26	0010 0110
39	27	0010 0111
40	28	0010 1000
41	29	0010 1001
42	2A	0010 1010
43	2B	0010 1011
44	2C	0010 1100
45	2D	0010 1101
46	2E	0010 1110
47	2F	0010 1111
48	30	0011 0000
49	31	0011 0001
50	32	0011 0010
51	33	0011 0011
52	34	0011 0100

Decimal Value	Hexadecimal Value	Binary Value
53	35	0011 0101
54	36	0011 0110
55	37	0011 0111
56	38	0011 1000
57	39	0011 1001
58	3A	0011 1010
59	3B	0011 1011
60	3C	0011 1100
61	3D	0011 1101
62	3E	0011 1110
63	3F	0011 1111
64	40	0100 0000
65	41	0100 0001
66	42	0100 0010
67	43	0100 0011
68	44	0100 0100
69	45	0100 0101
70	46	0100 0110
71	47	0100 0111
72	48	0100 1000
73	49	0100 1001
74	4A	0100 1010
75	4B	0100 1011
76	4C	0100 1100
77	4D	0100 1101
78	4E	0100 1110
79	4F	0100 1111
80	50	0101 0000
81	51	0101 0001
82	52	0101 0010

continues

Decimal Value	Hexadecimal Value	Binary Value
83	53	0101 0011
84	54	0101 0100
85	55	0101 0101
86	56	0101 0110
87	57	0101 0111
88	58	0101 1000
89	59	0101 1001
90	5A	0101 1010
91	5B	0101 1011
92	5C	0101 1100
93	5D	0101 1101
94	5E	0101 1110
95	5F	0101 1111
96	60	0110 0000
97	61	0110 0001
98	62	0110 0010
99	63	0110 0011
100	64	0110 0100
101	65	0110 0101
102	66	0110 0110
103	67	0110 0111
104	68	0110 1000
105	69	0110 1001
106	6A	0110 1010
107	6B	0110 1011
108	6C	0110 1100
109	6D	0110 1101
110	6E	0110 1110
111	6F	0110 1111
112	70	0111 0000

Decimal Value	Hexadecimal Value	Binary Value
113	71	0111 0001
114	72	0111 0010
115	73	0111 0011
116	74	0111 0100
117	75	0111 0101
118	76	0111 0110
119	77	0111 0111
120	78	0111 1000
121	79	0111 1001
122	7A	0111 1010
123	7B	0111 1011
124	7C	0111 1100
125	7D	0111 1101
126	7E	0111 1110
127	7F	0111 1111
128	80	1000 0000
129	81	1000 0001
130	82	1000 0010
131	83	1000 0011
132	84	1000 0100
133	85	1000 0101
134	86	1000 0110
135	87	1000 0111
136	88	1000 1000
137	89	1000 1001
138	8A	1000 1010
139	8B	1000 1011
140	8C	1000 1100
141	8D	1000 1101
142	8E	1000 1110

continues

Decimal Value	Hexadecimal Value	Binary Value
143	8F	1000 1111
144	90	1001 0000
145	91	1001 0001
146	92	1001 0010
147	93	1001 0011
148	94	1001 0100
149	95	1001 0101
150	96	1001 0110
151	97	1001 0111
152	98	1001 1000
153	99	1001 1001
154	9A	1001 1010
155	9B	1001 1011
156	9C	1001 1100
157	9D	1001 1101
158	9E	1001 1110
159	9F	1001 1111
160	A0	1010 0000
161	A1	1010 0001
162	A2	1010 0010
163	A3	1010 0011
164	A4	1010 0100
165	A5	1010 0101
166	A6	1010 0110
167	A7	1010 0111
168	A8	1010 1000
169	A9	1010 1001
170	AA	1010 1010
171	AB	1010 1011
172	AC	1010 1100

Decimal Value	Hexadecimal Value	Binary Value
173	AD	1010 1101
174	AE	1010 1110
175	AF	1010 1111
176	B0	1011 0000
177	B1	1011 0001
178	B2	1011 0010
179	B3	1011 0011
180	B4	1011 0100
181	B5	1011 0101
182	B6	1011 0110
183	B7	1011 0111
184	B8	1011 1000
185	B9	1011 1001
186	BA	1011 1010
187	BB	1011 1011
188	BC	1011 1100
189	BD	1011 1101
190	BE	1011 1110
191	BF	1011 1111
192	C0	1100 0000
193	C1	1100 0001
194	C2	1100 0010
195	C3	1100 0011
196	C4	1100 0100
197	C5	1100 0101
198	C6	1100 0110
199	C7	1100 0111
200	C8	1100 1000
201	C9	1100 1001
202	CA	1100 1010

continues

Decimal Value	Hexadecimal Value	Binary Value
203	CB	1100 1011
204	CC	1100 1100
205	CD	1100 1101
206	CE	1100 1110
207	CF	1100 1111
208	D0	1101 0000
209	D1	1101 0001
210	D2	1101 0010
211	D3	1101 0011
212	D4	1101 0100
213	D5	1101 0101
214	D6	1101 0110
215	D7	1101 0111
216	D8	1101 1000
217	D9	1101 1001
218	DA	1101 1010
219	DB	1101 1011
220	DC	1101 1100
221	DD	1101 1101
222	DE	1101 1110
223	DF	1101 1111
224	E0	1110 0000
225	E1	1110 0001
226	E2	1110 0010
227	E3	1110 0011
228	E4	1110 0100
229	E5	1110 0101
230	E6	1110 0110

Decimal Value	Hexadecimal Value	Binary Value
231	E7	1110 0111
232	E8	1110 1000
233	E9	1110 1001
234	EA	1110 1010
235	EB	1110 1011
236	EC	1110 1100
237	ED	1110 1101
238	EE	1110 1110
239	EF	1110 1111
240	F0	1111 0000
241	F1	1111 0001
242	F2	1111 0010
243	F3	1111 0011
244	F4	1111 0100
245	F5	1111 0101
246	F6	1111 0110
247	F7	1111 0111
248	F8	1111 1000
249	F9	1111 1001
250	FA	1111 1010
251	FB	1111 1011
252	FC	1111 1100
253	FD	1111 1101
254	FE	1111 1110
255	FF	1111 1111

APPENDIX **C**

Subnetting Practice: 25 Subnetting Questions

This appendix lists 25 separate questions, asking you to derive the subnet number, broadcast address, and range of valid IP addresses. In the solutions, the binary math is shown, as is the process that avoids binary math using the "subnet chart" described in Chapter 6, "TCP/IP and IP Routing." You might want to review Chapter 6's section on IP addressing before trying to answer these questions.

25 Subnetting Questions

Given each IP address and mask, supply the following information for each of these 25 examples:

- Size of the network part of the address
- Size of the subnet part of the address
- Size of the host part of the address
- The number of hosts per subnet
- The number of subnets in this network
- The subnet number
- The broadcast address
- The range of valid IP addresses in this network

Determine the information in the previous list for the following 25 IP addresses and masks:

1 10.200.10.18, mask 255.192.0.0

2 10.200.10.18, mask 255.224.0.0

3 10.100.18.18, mask 255.240.0.0

4 10.100.18.18, mask 255.248.0.0

5 10.150.200.200, mask 255.252.0.0

6 10.150.200.200, mask 255.254.0.0

7 10.220.100.18, mask 255.255.0.0

8 10.220.100.18, mask 255.255.128.0

9 172.31.100.100, mask 255.255.192.0

10 172.31.100.100, mask 255.255.224.0

11 172.31.200.10, mask 255.255.240.0

12 172.31.200.10, mask 255.255.248.0

13 172.31.50.50, mask 255.255.252.0

14 172.31.50.50, mask 255.255.254.0

15 172.31.140.14, mask 255.255.255.0

16 172.31.140.14, mask 255.255.255.128

17 192.168.15.150, mask 255.255.255.192

18 192.168.15.150, mask 255.255.255.224

19 192.168.100.100, mask 255.255.255.240

20 192.168.100.100, mask 255.255.255.248

21 192.168.15.230, mask 255.255.255.252

22 10.1.1.1, mask 255.248.0.0

23 172.16.1.200, mask 255.255.240.0

24 172.16.0.200, mask 255.255.255.192

25 1.1.1.1, mask 255.0.0.0

Suggestions on How to Attack the Problem

If you are ready to go ahead and start answering the questions, go ahead! If you want more explanation of how to attack such questions, refer back to the section on IP subnetting in Chapter 6. However, if you have already read Chapter 6, a reminder of the steps in the process to answer these questions, with a little binary math, is repeated here:

Step 1 Identify the structure of the IP address.

A Identify the size of the network part of the address, based on Class A, I, and C rules.

B Identify the size of the host part of the address, based on the number of binary 0s in the mask. If the mask is "tricky," use the chart of typical mask values to convert the mask to binary more quickly.

C The size of the subnet part is what's "left over"; mathematically, it is 32 – (network + host)

D Declare the number of subnets, which is $2^{\text{number-of-subnet-bits}} - 2$.

E Declare the number of hosts per subnet, which is $2^{\text{number-of-host-bits}} - 2$

Step 2 Create the chart that will be used in steps 3 and 4.

A Create a generic subnet chart.

B Write down the decimal IP address and subnet mask in the first two rows of the chart.

C If an easy mask is used, draw a vertical line between the 255s and the 0s in the mask, from top to bottom of the chart. If a hard mask is used, draw a box around the interesting octet.

D Copy the address octets to the left of the line or the box into the final four rows of the chart.

Step 3 Derive the subnet number and the first valid IP address.

A On the line where you are writing down the subnet number, write down 0s in the octets to the right of the line or the box.

B If the mask is hard and there is a box in the chart, use the magic number trick to find the decimal value of the subnet's interesting octet, and write it down. Remember, the magic number is found by subtracting the interesting (non-0 or 255) mask value from 256. The magic number multiple that's closest to but not larger than the IP address's interesting octet value is the subnet value in that octet.

C To derive the first valid IP address, copy the first three octets of the subnet number, and add 1 to the fourth octet of the subnet number. Write down this sum as the fourth octet.

Step 4 Derive the broadcast address and the last valid IP address for this subnet.

A Write down 255s in the broadcast address octets to the right of the line or the box.

B If the mask is hard and there is a box in the chart, use the magic number trick to find the value of the broadcast address's interesting octet.

C To derive the last valid IP address, copy the first three octets of the broadcast address and subtract 1 from the fourth octet of the broadcast address.

Question 1: Answer

The answers begin with the analysis of the three parts of the address, the number of hosts per subnet, and the number of subnets of this network using the stated mask. The binary math for subnet and broadcast address calculation follows. The answer finishes with the easier mental calculations using the subnet chart described in Chapter 6.

Table C-1 *Question 1: Size of Network, Subnet, Host, Number of Subnets, Number of Hosts*

Item	Example	Rules to Remember
Address	10.180.10.18	N/A
Mask	255.192.0.0	N/A
Number of network bits	8	Always defined by Class A, B, C
Number of host bits	22	Always defined as number of binary 0s in mask
Number of subnet bits	2	32 – (network size + host size)
Number of subnets	$2^2 - 2 = 2$	$2^{\text{number-of-subnet-bits}} - 2$
Number of hosts	$2^{22} - 2 = 4{,}194{,}302$	$2^{\text{number-of-host-bits}} - 2$

The binary calculations of the subnet number and broadcast address are in Table C-2. To calculate the two numbers, perform a Boolean AND on the address and mask. To find the broadcast address for this subnet, change all the host bits to binary 1s in the subnet number. The host bits are in **bold** print in the table.

Table C-2 *Question 1: Binary Calculation of Subnet and Broadcast Addresses*

Address	10.180.10.18	0000 1010 10**11 0100 0000 1010 0001 0010**
Mask	255.192.0.0	1111 1111 11**00 0000 0000 0000 0000 0000**
AND result (subnet number)	10.128.0.0	0000 1010 10**00 0000 0000 0000 0000 0000**
Change host to 1s (broadcast address)	10.191.255.255	0000 1010 10**11 1111 1111 1111 1111 1111**

To get the first valid IP address, just add 1 to the subnet number; to get the last valid IP address, just subtract 1 from the broadcast address. In this case:

10.128.0.1 through 10.191.255.254

10.128.0.0 + 1= 10.128.0.1

10.191.255.255 – 1= 10.191.255.254

Steps 2, 3, and 4 in the process use a table like Table C-3, which lists the way to get the same answers using the subnet chart and magic math described in Chapter 6. Figure C-1 at the end of this problem shows the fields in Table C-3 that are filled in at each step in the process. Remember, subtracting the interesting (non-0 or 255) mask value from 256 yields the magic number. The magic number multiple that's closest to but not larger than the IP address's interesting octet value is the subnet value in that octet.

Table C-3 *Question 1: Subnet, Broadcast, First and Last Addresses Calculated Using Subnet Chart*

	Octet 1	Octet 2	Octet 3	Octet 4	Comments
Address	10	180	10	18	N/A
Mask	255	192	0	0	N/A
Subnet number	10	128	0	0	Magic number = 256 – 192 = 64
First address	10	128	0	1	Add 1 to last octet of subnet
Broadcast	10	191	255	255	128 + 64 – 1 = 191
Last address	10	191	255	254	Subtract 1 from last octet

Subnet rule: Multiple of magic number closest to, but not more than, IP address value in interesting octet

Broadcast rule: Subnet + magic – 1

This subnetting scheme uses a hard mask because one of the octets is not a 0 or a 255. The second octet is "interesting" in this case. The key part of the trick to get the right answers is to calculate the magic number, which is 256 – 192 = 64 in this case (256 – mask's value in the interesting octet). The subnet number's value in the interesting octet (inside the box) is the multiple of the magic number that's not bigger than the original IP address's value in the interesting octet. In this case, 128 is the multiple of 64 that's closest to 180 but not bigger than 180. So, the second octet of the subnet number is 128.

The second tricky part of this process calculates the subnet broadcast address. The full process is described in Chapter 6, but the tricky part is, as usual, in the "interesting" octet. Take the subnet number's value in the interesting octet, add the magic number, and subtract 1. That's the broadcast address's value in the interesting octet. In this case, 128 + 64 – 1 = 191.

Finally, Figure C-1 shows Table C-3 with comments about when each part of the table was filled in, based on the steps in the process at the beginning of the chapter.

Figure C-1 *Steps 2, 3, and 4 for Question 1*

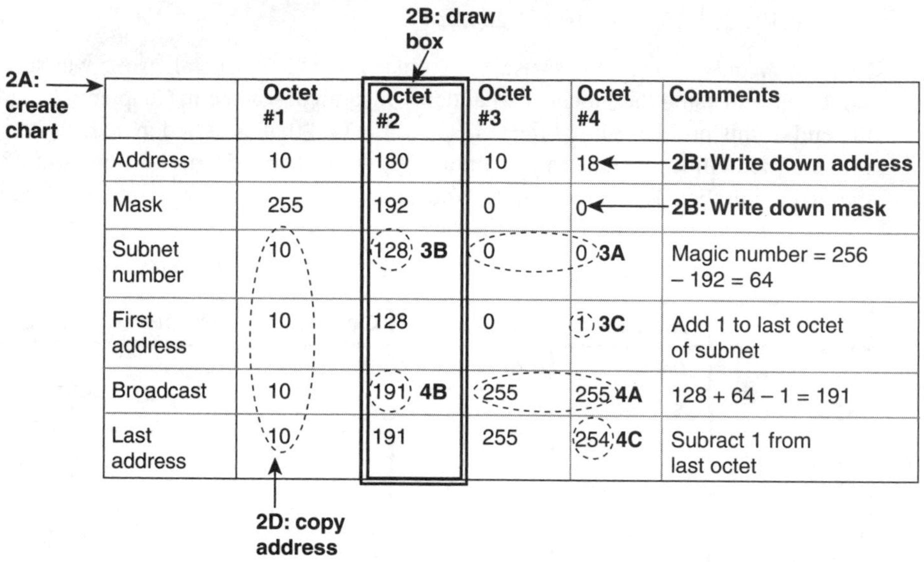

Question 2: Answer

Table C-4 *Question 2: Size of Network, Subnet, Host, Number of Subnets, Number of Hosts*

Step	Example	Rules to Remember
Address	10.200.10.18	N/A
Mask	255.224.0.0	N/A
Number of network bits	8	Always defined by Class A, B, C
Number of host bits	21	Always defined as number of binary 0s in mask
Number of subnet bits	3	32 – (network size + host size)
Number of subnets	$2^3 - 2 = 6$	$2^{\text{number-of-subnet-bits}} - 2$
Number of hosts	$2^{21} - 2 = 2{,}097{,}150$	$2^{\text{number-of-host-bits}} - 2$

Table C-5 presents the binary calculations of the subnet number and broadcast address. To calculate the subnet number, perform a Boolean AND of the address with the subnet mask. To find the broadcast address for this subnet, change all the host bits to binary 1s in the subnet number. The host bits are in **bold** print in the table.

Table C-5 *Question 2: Binary Calculation of Subnet and Broadcast Addresses*

Address	10.200.10.18	0000 1010 110**0 1000 0000 1010 0001 0010**
Mask	255.224.0.0	1111 1111 111**0 0000 0000 0000 0000 0000**
AND result (subnet number)	10.192.0.0	0000 1010 110**0 0000 0000 0000 0000 0000**
Change host to 1s (broadcast address)	10.223.255.255	0000 1010 110**1 1111 1111 1111 1111 1111**

Just add 1 to the subnet number to get the first valid IP address; just subtract 1 from the broadcast address to get the last valid IP address. In this case:

10.192.0.1 through 10.223.255.254

Table C-6 lists the way to get the same answers using the subnet chart and magic math described in Chapter 6. Remember, subtracting the interesting (non-0 or 255) mask value from 256 yields the magic number. The magic number multiple that's closest to but not larger than the IP address's interesting octet value is the subnet value in that octet.

Table C-6 *Question 2: Subnet, Broadcast, First and Last Addresses Calculated Using Subnet Chart*

	Octet 1	Octet 2	Octet 3	Octet 4	Comments
Address	10	200	10	18	N/A
Mask	255	224	0	0	N/A
Subnet number	10	192	0	0	Magic number = 256 – 224 = 32
First address	10	192	0	1	Add 1 to last octet of subnet
Broadcast	10	223	255	255	192 + 32 – 1 = 223
Last address	10	223	255	254	Subtract 1 from last octet

Subnet rule: Multiple of magic number closest to, but not more than, IP address value in interesting octet

Broadcast rule: Subnet + magic – 1

This subnetting scheme uses a hard mask because one of the octets is not a 0 or a 255. The second octet is "interesting" in this case. The key part of the trick to get the right answers is to calculate the magic number, which is 256 – 224 = 32 in this case (256 – mask's value in the interesting octet). The subnet number's value in the interesting octet (inside the box) is the multiple of the magic number that's not bigger than the original IP address's value in the interesting octet. In this case, 192 is the multiple of 32 that's closest to 200 but not bigger than 200. So, the second octet of the subnet number is 192.

The second tricky part of this process calculates the subnet broadcast address. The full process is described in Chapter 6, but the tricky part is, as usual, in the "interesting" octet. Take the subnet number's value in the interesting octet, add the magic number, and subtract 1. That's the broadcast address's value in the interesting octet. In this case, 192 + 32 – 1 = 223.

Question 3: Answer

Table C-7 *Question 3: Size of Network, Subnet, Host, Number of Subnets, Number of Hosts*

Step	Example	Rules to Remember
Address	10.100.18.18	N/A
Mask	255.240.0.0	N/A
Number of network bits	8	Always defined by Class A, B, C
Number of host bits	20	Always defined as number of binary 0s in mask
Number of subnet bits	4	32 – (network size + host size)
Number of subnets	$2^4 - 2 = 14$	$2^{\text{number-of-subnet-bits}} - 2$
Number of hosts	$2^{20} - 2 = 1{,}048{,}574$	$2^{\text{number-of-host-bits}} - 2$

The binary calculations of the subnet number and broadcast address are in Table C-8. To calculate the subnet number, perform a Boolean AND of the address with the subnet mask. To find the broadcast address for this subnet, change all the host bits to binary 1s in the subnet number. The host bits are in **bold** print in the table.

Table C-8 *Question 3: Binary Calculation of Subnet and Broadcast Addresses*

Address	10.100.18.18	0000 1010 0110 **0100 0001 00100001 0010**
Mask	255.240.0.0	1111 1111 1111 **0000 0000 0000 0000 0000**
AND result (subnet number)	10.96.0.0	0000 1010 0110 **0000 0000 0000 0000 0000**
Change host to 1s (broadcast address)	10.111.255.255	0000 1010 0110 **1111 1111 1111 1111 1111**

Just add 1 to the subnet number to get the first valid IP address; just subtract 1 from the broadcast address to get the last valid IP address. In this case:

10.96.0.1 through 10.111.255.254

Table C-9 lists the way to get the same answers using the subnet chart and magic math described in Chapter 6. Remember, subtracting the interesting (non-0 or 255) mask value from 256 yields the magic number. The magic number multiple that's closest to but not larger than the IP address's interesting octet value is the subnet value in that octet.

Table C-9 *Question 3: Subnet, Broadcast, First and Last Addresses Calculated Using Subnet Chart*

	Octet 1	Octet 2	Octet 3	Octet 4	Comments
Address	10	100	18	18	N/A
Mask	255	240	0	0	N/A
Subnet number	10	96	0	0	Magic number = 256 – 240 = 16
First address	10	96	0	1	Add 1 to last octet of subnet
Broadcast	10	111	255	255	96 + 16 – 1 = 111
Last address	10	111	255	254	Subtract 1 from last octet

Subnet rule: Multiple of magic number closest to, but not more than, IP address value in interesting octet

Broadcast rule: Subnet + magic – 1

This subnetting scheme uses a hard mask because one of the octets is not a 0 or a 255. The second octet is "interesting" in this case. The key part of the trick to get the right answers is to calculate the magic number, which is 256 – 240 = 16 in this case (256 – mask's value in the interesting octet). The subnet number's value in the interesting octet (inside the box) is the multiple of the magic number that's not bigger than the original IP address's value in the interesting octet. In this case, 96 is the multiple of 16 that's closest to 100 but not bigger than 100. So, the second octet of the subnet number is 96.

The second tricky part of this process calculates the subnet broadcast address. The full process is described in Chapter 6, but the tricky part is, as usual, in the "interesting" octet. Take the subnet number's value in the interesting octet, add the magic number, and subtract 1. That's the broadcast address's value in the interesting octet. In this case, 96 + 16 – 1 = 111.

Question 4: Answer

Table C-10 *Question 4: Size of Network, Subnet, Host, Number of Subnets, Number of Hosts*

Step	Example	Rules to Remember
Address	10.100.18.18	N/A
Mask	255.248.0.0	N/A
Number of network bits	8	Always defined by Class A, B, C
Number of host bits	19	Always defined as number of binary 0s in mask
Number of subnet bits	5	32 – (network size + host size)
Number of subnets	$2^5 - 2 = 30$	$2^{\text{number-of-subnet-bits}} - 2$
Number of hosts	$2^{19} - 2 = 524,286$	$2^{\text{number-of-host-bits}} - 2$

The binary calculations of the subnet number and broadcast address are in Table C-11. To calculate the subnet number, perform a Boolean AND of the address with the subnet mask. To find the broadcast address for this subnet, change all the host bits to binary 1s in the subnet number. The host bits are in **bold** print in the table.

Table C-11 *Question 4: Binary Calculation of Subnet and Broadcast Addresses*

Address	10.100.18.18	0000 1010 0110 0**100 0001 00100001 0010**
Mask	255.248.0.0	1111 1111 1111 1**000 0000 0000 0000 0000**
AND result (subnet number)	10.96.0.0	0000 1010 0110 0**000 0000 0000 0000 0000**
Change host to 1s (broadcast address)	10.103.255.255	0000 1010 0110 0**111 1111 1111 1111 1111**

Just add 1 to the subnet number to get the first valid IP address; just subtract 1 from the broadcast address to get the last valid IP address. In this case:

10.96.0.1 through 10.103.255.254

Table C-12 lists the way to get the same answers using the subnet chart and magic math described in Chapter 6. Remember, subtracting the interesting (non-0 or 255) mask value from 256 yields the magic number. The magic number multiple that's closest to but not larger than the IP address's interesting octet value is the subnet value in that octet.

Table C-12 *Question 4: Subnet, Broadcast, First and Last Addresses Calculated Using Subnet Chart*

	Octet 1	Octet 2	Octet 3	Octet 4	Comments
Address	10	100	18	18	N/A
Mask	255	248	0	0	N/A
Subnet number	10	96	0	0	Magic number = 256 – 248 = 8
First address	10	96	0	1	Add 1 to last octet of subnet
Broadcast	10	103	255	255	96 + 8 – 1 = 103
Last address	10	103	255	254	Subtract 1 from last octet

Subnet rule: Multiple of magic number closest to, but not more than, IP address value in interesting octet

Broadcast rule: Subnet + magic – 1

This subnetting scheme uses a hard mask because one of the octets is not a 0 or a 255. The second octet is "interesting" in this case. The key part of the trick to get the right answers is to calculate the magic number, which is 256 – 248 = 8 in this case (256 – mask's value in the interesting octet). The subnet number's value in the interesting octet (inside the box) is the multiple of the magic number that's not bigger than the original IP address's value in the interesting octet. In this case, 96 is the multiple of 8 that's closest to 100 but not bigger than 100. So, the second octet of the subnet number is 96.

The second tricky part of this process calculates the subnet broadcast address. The full process is described in Chapter 6, but the tricky part is, as usual, in the "interesting" octet. Take the subnet number's value in the interesting octet, add the magic number, and subtract 1. That's the broadcast address's value in the interesting octet. In this case, 96 + 8 – 1 = 103.

Question 5: Answer

Table C-13 *Question 5: Size of Network, Subnet, Host, Number of Subnets, Number of Hosts*

Step	Example	Rules to Remember
Address	10.150.200.200	N/A
Mask	255.252.0.0	N/A
Number of network bits	8	Always defined by Class A, B, C
Number of host bits	18	Always defined as number of binary 0s in mask
Number of subnet bits	6	32 – (network size + host size)
Number of subnets	$2^6 - 2 = 62$	$2^{\text{number-of-subnet-bits}} - 2$
Number of hosts	$2^{18} - 2 = 262{,}142$	$2^{\text{number-of-host-bits}} - 2$

The binary calculations of the subnet number and broadcast address are in Table C-14. To calculate the subnet number, perform a Boolean AND of the address with the subnet mask. To find the broadcast address for this subnet, change all the host bits to binary 1s in the subnet number. The host bits are in **bold** print in the table.

Table C-14 *Question 5: Binary Calculation of Subnet and Broadcast Addresses*

Address	10.150.200.200	0000 1010 1001 01**10 1100 1000 1100 1000**
Mask	255.252.0.0	1111 1111 1111 11**00 0000 0000 0000 0000**
AND result (subnet number)	10.148.0.0	0000 1010 0110 00**00 0000 0000 0000 0000**
Change host to 1s (broadcast address)	10.151.255.255	0000 1010 0110 01**11 1111 1111 1111 1111**

Just add 1 to the subnet number to get the first valid IP address; just subtract 1 from the broadcast address to get the last valid IP address. In this case:

10.148.0.1 through 10.151.255.254

Table C-15 lists the way to get the same answers using the subnet chart and magic math described in Chapter 6. Remember, subtracting the interesting (non-0 or 255) mask value from 256 yields the magic number. The magic number multiple that's closest to but not larger than the IP address's interesting octet value is the subnet value in that octet.

Table C-15 *Question 5: Subnet, Broadcast, First and Last Addresses Calculated Using Subnet Chart*

	Octet 1	Octet 2	Octet 3	Octet 4	Comments
Address	10	150	200	200	N/A
Mask	255	252	0	0	N/A
Subnet number	10	148	0	0	Magic number = 256 – 252 = 4
First address	10	148	0	1	Add 1 to last octet of subnet
Broadcast	10	151	255	255	148 + 4 – 1 = 151
Last address	10	151	255	254	Subtract 1 from last octet

Subnet rule: Multiple of magic number closest to, but not more than, IP address value in interesting octet

Broadcast rule: Subnet + magic – 1

This subnetting scheme uses a hard mask because one of the octets is not a 0 or a 255. The second octet is "interesting" in this case. The key part of the trick to get the right answers is to calculate the magic number, which is 256 – 252 = 4 in this case (256 – mask's value in the interesting octet). The subnet number's value in the interesting octet (inside the box) is the multiple of the magic number that's not bigger than the original IP address's value in the interesting octet. In this case, 148 is the multiple of 4 that's closest to 150 but not bigger than 150. So, the second octet of the subnet number is 148.

The second tricky part of this process calculates the subnet broadcast address. The full process is described in Chapter 6, but the tricky part is, as usual, in the "interesting" octet. Take the subnet number's value in the interesting octet, add the magic number, and subtract 1. That's the broadcast address's value in the interesting octet. In this case, 148 + 4 – 1 = 151.

Question 6: Answer

Table C-16 *Question 6: Size of Network, Subnet, Host, Number of Subnets, Number of Hosts*

Step	Example	Rules to Remember
Address	10.150.200.200	N/A
Mask	255.254.0.0	N/A
Number of network bits	8	Always defined by Class A, B, C
Number of host bits	17	Always defined as number of binary 0s in mask
Number of subnet bits	7	32 – (network size + host size)
Number of subnets	$2^7 - 2 = 126$	$2^{number-of-subnet-bits} - 2$
Number of hosts	$2^{17} - 2 = 131,070$	$2^{number-of-host-bits} - 2$

The binary calculations of the subnet number and broadcast address are in Table C-17. To calculate the subnet number, perform a Boolean AND of the address with the subnet mask. To find the broadcast address for this subnet, change all the host bits to binary 1s in the subnet number. The host bits are in **bold** print in the table.

Table C-17 *Question 6: Binary Calculation of Subnet and Broadcast Addresses*

Address	10.150.200.200	0000 1010 1001 011**0 1100 1000 1100 1000**
Mask	255.254.0.0	1111 1111 1111 111**0 0000 0000 0000 0000**
AND result (subnet number)	10.150.0.0	0000 1010 0110 001**0 0000 0000 0000 0000**
Change host to 1s (broadcast address)	10.151.255.255	0000 1010 0110 011**1 1111 1111 1111 1111**

Just add 1 to the subnet number to get the first valid IP address; just subtract 1 from the broadcast address to get the last valid IP address. In this case:

10.150.0.1 through 10.151.255.254

Table C-18 lists the way to get the same answers using the subnet chart and magic math described in Chapter 6. Remember, subtracting the interesting (non-0 or 255) mask value from 256 yields the magic number. The magic number multiple that's closest to but not larger than the IP address's interesting octet value is the subnet value in that octet.

Table C-18 *Question 6: Subnet, Broadcast, First and Last Addresses Calculated Using Subnet Chart*

	Octet 1	Octet 2	Octet 3	Octet 4
Address	10	150	200	200
Mask	255	254	0	0
Subnet number	10	150	0	0
First valid address	10	150	0	1
Broadcast	10	151	255	255
Last valid address	10	151	255	254

This subnetting scheme uses a hard mask because one of the octets is not a 0 or a 255. The second octet is "interesting" in this case. The key part of the trick to get the right answers is to calculate the magic number, which is 256 – 254 = 2 in this case (256 – mask's value in the interesting octet). The subnet number's value in the interesting octet (inside the box) is the multiple of the magic number that's not bigger than the original IP address's value in the interesting octet. In this case, 150 is the multiple of 2 that's closest to 150 but not bigger than 150. So, the second octet of the subnet number is 150.

The second tricky part of this process calculates the subnet broadcast address. The full process is described in Chapter 6, but the tricky part is, as usual, in the "interesting" octet. Take the subnet number's value in the interesting octet, add the magic number, and subtract 1. That's the broadcast address's value in the interesting octet. In this case, 150 + 2 – 1 = 151.

Question 7: Answer

Table C-19 *Question 7: Size of Network, Subnet, Host, Number of Subnets, Number of Hosts*

Step	Example	Rules to Remember
Address	10.220.100.18	N/A
Mask	255.255.0.0	N/A
Number of network bits	8	Always defined by Class A, B, C
Number of host bits	16	Always defined as number of binary 0s in mask
Number of subnet bits	8	32 – (network size + host size)
Number of subnets	$2^8 - 2 = 254$	$2^{\text{number-of-subnet-bits}} - 2$
Number of hosts	$2^{16} - 2 = 65{,}534$	$2^{\text{number-of-host-bits}} - 2$

The binary calculations of the subnet number and broadcast address are in Table C-20. To calculate the subnet number, perform a Boolean AND of the address with the subnet mask. To find the broadcast address for this subnet, change all the host bits to binary 1s in the subnet number. The host bits are in **bold** print in the table.

Table C-20 *Question 7: Binary Calculation of Subnet and Broadcast Addresses*

Address	10.220.100.18	0000 1010 1101 1100 **0110 0100 0001 0010**
Mask	255.255.0.0	1111 1111 1111 1111 **0000 0000 0000 0000**
AND result (subnet number)	10.220.0.0	0000 1010 1101 1100 **0000 0000 0000 0000**
Change host to 1s (broadcast address)	10.220.255.255	0000 1010 1101 1100 **1111 1111 1111 1111**

Just add 1 to the subnet number to get the first valid IP address; just subtract 1 from the broadcast address to get the last valid IP address. In this case:

10.220.0.1 through 10.220.255.254

Table C-21 lists the way to get the same answers using the subnet chart and magic math described in Chapter 6.

Table C-21 *Question 7: Subnet, Broadcast, First, and Last Addresses Calculated Using Subnet Chart*

	Octet 1	Octet 2	Octet 3	Octet 4
Address	10	220	100	18
Mask	255	255	0	0
Subnet number	10	220	0	0
First valid address	10	220	0	1
Broadcast	10	220	255	255
Last valid address	10	220	255	254

This subnetting scheme uses an easy mask because all of the octets are a 0 or a 255. No math tricks are needed at all!

Question 8: Answer

Table C-22 *Question 8: Size of Network, Subnet, Host, Number of Subnets, Number of Hosts*

Step	Example	Rules to Remember
Address	10.220.100.18	N/A
Mask	255.255.128.0	N/A
Number of network bits	8	Always defined by Class A, B, C
Number of host bits	15	Always defined as number of binary 0s in mask
Number of subnet bits	9	32 – (network size + host size)
Number of subnets	$2^9 - 2 = 510$	$2^{\text{number-of-subnet-bits}} - 2$
Number of hosts	$2^{15} - 2 = 32{,}766$	$2^{\text{number-of-host-bits}} - 2$

The binary calculations of the subnet number and broadcast address are in Table C-23. To calculate the subnet number, perform a Boolean AND of the address with the subnet mask. To find the broadcast address for this subnet, change all the host bits to binary 1s in the subnet number. The host bits are in **bold** print in the table.

Table C-23 *Question 8: Binary Calculation of Subnet and Broadcast Addresses*

Address	10.220.100.18	0000 1010 1101 1100 0**110 0100 0001 0010**
Mask	255.255.128.0	1111 1111 1111 1111 1**000 0000 0000 0000**
AND result (subnet number)	10.220.0.0	0000 1010 1101 1100 0**000 0000 0000 0000**
Change host to 1s (broadcast address)	10.220.127.255	0000 1010 1101 1100 0**111 1111 1111 1111**

Just add 1 to the subnet number to get the first valid IP address; just subtract 1 from the broadcast address to get the last valid IP address. In this case:

10.220.0.1 through 10.220.127.254

Table C-24 lists the way to get the same answers using the subnet chart and magic math described in Chapter 6. Remember, subtracting the interesting (non-0 or 255) mask value from 256 yields the magic number. The magic number multiple that's closest to but not larger than the IP address's interesting octet value is the subnet value in that octet.

Table C-24 *Question 8: Subnet, Broadcast, First and Last Addresses Calculated Using Subnet Chart*

	Octet 1	Octet 2	Octet 3	Octet 4
Address	10	220	100	18
Mask	255	255	128	0
Subnet number	10	220	0	0
First address	10	220	0	1
Broadcast	10	220	127	255

This subnetting scheme uses a hard mask because one of the octets is not a 0 or a 255. The third octet is "interesting" in this case. The key part of the trick to get the right answers is to calculate the magic number, which is 256 – 128 = 128 in this case (256 – mask's value in the interesting octet). The subnet number's value in the interesting octet (inside the box) is the multiple of the magic number that's not bigger than the original IP address's value in the interesting octet. In this case, 0 is the multiple of 128 that's closest to 100 but not bigger than 100. So, the third octet of the subnet number is 0.

The second tricky part of this process calculates the subnet broadcast address. The full process is described in Chapter 6, but the tricky part is, as usual, in the "interesting" octet. Take the subnet number's value in the interesting octet, add the magic number, and subtract 1. That's the broadcast address's value in the interesting octet. In this case, 0 + 128 – 1 = 127.

This example tends to confuse people because a mask with 128 in it gives you subnet numbers that just do not seem to look right. Table C-25 gives you the answers for the first several subnets, just to make sure that you are clear about the subnets when using this mask with a Class A network.

Table C-25 *Question 8: Subnet, Broadcast, First and Last Addresses Calculated Using Subnet Chart*

	Zero Subnet	First Valid Subnet	Second Valid Subnet	Third Valid Subnet
Subnet	10.0.0.0	10.0.128.0	10.1.0.0	10.1.128.0
First address	10.0.0.1	10.0.128.1	10.1.0.1	10.1.128.1
Last address	10.0.127.254	10.0.255.254	10.1.127.254	10.1.255.254
Broadcast	10.0.127.255	10.0.255.255	10.1.127.255	10.1.255.255

Question 9: Answer

Table C-26 *Question 9: Size of Network, Subnet, Host, Number of Subnets, Number of Hosts*

Step	Example	Rules to Remember
Address	172.31.100.100	N/A
Mask	255.255.192.0	N/A
Number of network bits	16	Always defined by Class A, B, C
Number of host bits	14	Always defined as number of binary 0s in mask
Number of subnet bits	2	32 – (network size + host size)
Number of subnets	$2^2 - 2 = 2$	$2^{\text{number-of-subnet-bits}} - 2$
Number of hosts	$2^{14} - 2 = 16,382$	$2^{\text{number-of-host-bits}} - 2$

The binary calculations of the subnet number and broadcast address are in Table C-27. To calculate the subnet number, perform a Boolean AND of the address with the subnet mask. To find the broadcast address for this subnet, change all the host bits to binary 1s in the subnet number. The host bits are in **bold** print in the table.

Table C-27 *Question 9: Binary Calculation of Subnet and Broadcast Addresses*

Address	172.31.100.100	1010 1100 0001 1111 01**10 0100 0110 0100**
Mask	255.255.192.0	1111 1111 1111 1111 11**00 0000 0000 0000**
AND result (subnet number)	172.31.64.0	1010 1100 0001 1111 01**00 0000 0000 0000**
Change host to 1s (broadcast address)	172.31.127.255	1010 1100 0001 1111 01**11 1111 1111 1111**

Just add 1 to the subnet number to get the first valid IP address; just subtract 1 from the broadcast address to get the last valid IP address. In this case:

172.31.64.1 through 172.31.127.254

Table C-28 lists the way to get the same answers using the subnet chart and magic math described in Chapter 6. Remember, subtracting the interesting (non-0 or 255) mask value from 256 yields the magic number. The magic number multiple that's closest to but not larger than the IP address's interesting octet value is the subnet value in that octet.

Table C-28 *Question 9: Subnet, Broadcast, First and Last Addresses Calculated Using Subnet Chart*

	Octet 1	Octet 2	Octet 3	Octet 4
Address	172	31	100	100
Mask	255	255	192	0
Subnet number	172	31	64	0
First valid address	172	31	64	1
Broadcast	172	31	127	255
Last valid address	172	31	127	254

This subnetting scheme uses a hard mask because one of the octets is not a 0 or a 255. The third octet is "interesting" in this case. The key part of the trick to get the right answers is to calculate the magic number, which is 256 – 192 = 64 in this case (256 – mask's value in the interesting octet). The subnet number's value in the interesting octet (inside the box) is the multiple of the magic number that's not bigger than the original IP address's value in the interesting octet. In this case, 64 is the multiple of 64 that's closest to 100 but not bigger than 100. So, the third octet of the subnet number is 64.

The second tricky part of this process calculates the subnet broadcast address. The full process is described in Chapter 6, but the tricky part is, as usual, in the "interesting" octet. Take the subnet number's value in the interesting octet, add the magic number, and subtract 1. That's the broadcast address's value in the interesting octet. In this case, 64 + 64 – 1 = 127.

Question 10: Answer

Table C-29 *Question 10: Size of Network, Subnet, Host, Number of Subnets, Number of Hosts*

Step	Example	Rules to Remember
Address	172.31.100.100	N/A
Mask	255.255.224.0	N/A
Number of network bits	16	Always defined by Class A, B, C
Number of host bits	13	Always defined as number of binary 0s in mask
Number of subnet bits	3	32 – (network size + host size)
Number of subnets	$2^3 - 2 = 6$	$2^{\text{number-of-subnet-bits}} - 2$
Number of hosts	$2^{13} - 2 = 8190$	$2^{\text{number-of-host-bits}} - 2$

The binary calculations of the subnet number and broadcast address are in Table C-30. To calculate the subnet number, perform a Boolean AND of the address with the subnet mask. To find the broadcast address for this subnet, change all the host bits to binary 1s in the subnet number. The host bits are in **bold** print in the table.

Table C-30 *Question 10: Binary Calculation of Subnet and Broadcast Addresses*

Address	172.31.100.100	1010 1100 0001 1111 011**0 0100 0110 0100**
Mask	255.255.224.0	1111 1111 1111 1111 111**0 0000 0000 0000**
AND result (subnet number)	172.31.96.0	1010 1100 0001 1111 011**0 0000 0000 0000**
Change host to 1s (broadcast address)	172.31.127.255	1010 1100 0001 1111 011**1 1111 1111 1111**

Just add 1 to the subnet number to get the first valid IP address; just subtract 1 from the broadcast address to get the last valid IP address. In this case:

172.31.96.1 through 172.31.127.254

Table C-31 lists the way to get the same answers using the subnet chart and magic math described in Chapter 6. Remember, subtracting the interesting (non-0 or 255) mask value from 256 yields the magic number. The magic number multiple that's closest to but not larger than the IP address's interesting octet value is the subnet value in that octet.

Table C-31 *Question 10: Subnet, Broadcast, First and Last Addresses Calculated Using Subnet Chart*

	Octet 1	Octet 2	Octet 3	Octet 4
Address	172	31	100	100
Mask	255	255	224	0
Subnet number	172	31	96	0
First valid address	172	31	96	1
Broadcast	172	31	127	255
Last valid address	172	31	127	254

This subnetting scheme uses a hard mask because one of the octets is not a 0 or a 255. The third octet is "interesting" in this case. The key part of the trick to get the right answers is to calculate the magic number, which is 256 – 224 = 32 in this case (256 – mask's value in the interesting octet). The subnet number's value in the interesting octet (inside the box) is the multiple of the magic number that's not bigger than the original IP address's value in the interesting octet. In this case, 96 is the multiple of 32 that's closest to 100 but not bigger than 100. So, the third octet of the subnet number is 96.

The second tricky part of this process calculates the subnet broadcast address. The full process is described in Chapter 6, but the tricky part is, as usual, in the "interesting" octet. Take the subnet number's value in the interesting octet, add the magic number, and subtract 1. That's the broadcast address's value in the interesting octet. In this case, 96 + 32 – 1 = 127.

Question 11: Answer

Table C-32 *Question 11: Size of Network, Subnet, Host, Number of Subnets, Number of Hosts*

Step	Example	Rules to Remember
Address	172.31.200.10	N/A
Mask	255.255.240.0	N/A
Number of network bits	16	Always defined by Class A, B, C
Number of host bits	12	Always defined as number of binary 0s in mask
Number of subnet bits	4	32 – (network size + host size)
Number of subnets	$2^4 - 2 = 14$	$2^{\text{number-of-subnet-bits}} - 2$
Number of hosts	$2^{12} - 2 = 4094$	$2^{\text{number-of-host-bits}} - 2$

Table C-33 shows the binary calculations of the subnet number and broadcast address. To calculate the subnet number, perform a Boolean AND of the address with the subnet mask. To find the broadcast address for this subnet, change all the host bits to binary 1s in the subnet number. The host bits are in **bold** print in the table.

Table C-33 *Question 11: Binary Calculation of Subnet and Broadcast Addresses*

Address	172.31.200.10	1010 1100 0001 1111 1100 **1000 0000 1010**
Mask	255.255.240.0	1111 1111 1111 1111 1111 **0000 0000 0000**
AND result (subnet number)	172.31.192.0	1010 1100 0001 1111 1100 **0000 0000 0000**
Change host to 1s (broadcast address)	172.31.207.255	1010 1100 0001 1111 1100 **1111 1111 1111**

Just add 1 to the subnet number to get the first valid IP address; just subtract 1 from the broadcast address to get the last valid IP address. In this case:

172.31.192.1 through 172.31.207.254

Table C-34 lists the way to get the same answers using the subnet chart and magic math described in Chapter 6. Remember, subtracting the interesting (non-0 or 255) mask value from 256 yields the magic number. The magic number multiple that's closest to but not larger than the IP address's interesting octet value is the subnet value in that octet.

Table C-34 *Question 13: Subnet, Broadcast, First and Last Addresses Calculated Using Subnet Chart*

	Octet 1	Octet 2	Octet 3	Octet 4
Address	172	31	200	10
Mask	255	255	240	0
Subnet number	172	31	192	0
First valid address	172	31	192	1
Broadcast	172	31	207	255
Last valid address	172	31	207	254

This subnetting scheme uses a hard mask because one of the octets is not a 0 or a 255. The third octet is "interesting" in this case. The key part of the trick to get the right answers is to calculate the magic number, which is 256 – 240 = 16 in this case (256 – mask's value in the interesting octet). The subnet number's value in the interesting octet (inside the box) is the multiple of the magic number that's not bigger than the original IP address's value in the interesting octet. In this case, 192 is the multiple of 16 that's closest to 200 but not bigger than 200. So, the third octet of the subnet number is 192.

The second tricky part of this process calculates the subnet broadcast address. The full process is described in Chapter 6, but the tricky part is, as usual, in the "interesting" octet. Take the subnet number's value in the interesting octet, add the magic number, and subtract 1. That's the broadcast address's value in the interesting octet. In this case, 192 + 16 – 1 = 207.

Question 12: Answer

Table C-35 *Question 12: Size of Network, Subnet, Host, Number of Subnets, Number of Hosts*

Step	Example	Rules to Remember
Address	172.31.200.10	N/A
Mask	255.255.248.0	N/A
Number of network bits	16	Always defined by Class A, B, C
Number of host bits	11	Always defined as number of binary 0s in mask
Number of subnet bits	5	32 – (network size + host size)

continues

Table C-35 *Question 12: Size of Network, Subnet, Host, Number of Subnets, Number of Hosts (Continued)*

Step	Example	Rules to Remember
Number of subnets	$2^5 - 2 = 30$	$2^{\text{number-of-subnet-bits}} - 2$
Number of hosts	$2^{11} - 2 = 2046$	$2^{\text{number-of-host-bits}} - 2$

Table C-36 shows the binary calculations of the subnet number and broadcast address. To calculate the subnet number, perform a Boolean AND of the address with the subnet mask. To find the broadcast address for this subnet, change all the host bits to binary 1s in the subnet number. The host bits are in **bold** print in the table.

Table C-36 *Question 12: Binary Calculation of Subnet and Broadcast Addresses*

Address	172.31.200.10	1010 1100 0001 1111 1100 1**000 0000 1010**
Mask	255.255.248.0	1111 1111 1111 1111 1111 1**000 0000 0000**
AND result (subnet number)	172.31.200.0	1010 1100 0001 1111 1100 1**000 0000 0000**
Change host to 1s (broadcast address)	172.31.207.255	1010 1100 0001 1111 1100 1**111 1111 1111**

Just add 1 to the subnet number to get the first valid IP address; just subtract 1 from the broadcast address to get the last valid IP address. In this case:

172.31.200.1 through 172.31.207.254

Table C-37 lists the way to get the same answers using the subnet chart and magic math described in Chapter 6. Remember, subtracting the interesting (non-0 or 255) mask value from 256 yields the magic number. The magic number multiple that's closest to but not larger than the IP address's interesting octet value is the subnet value in that octet.

Table C-37 *Question 12: Subnet, Broadcast, First and Last Addresses Calculated Using Subnet Chart*

	Octet 1	Octet 2	Octet 3	Octet 4
Address	172	31	200	10
Mask	255	255	248	0
Subnet number	172	31	200	0
First valid address	172	31	200	1
Broadcast	172	31	207	255
Last valid address	172	31	207	254

This subnetting scheme uses a hard mask because one of the octets is not a 0 or a 255. The third octet is "interesting" in this case. The key part of the trick to get the right answers is to calculate the magic number, which is 256 – 248 = 8 in this case (256 – mask's value in the interesting octet). The subnet number's value in the interesting octet (inside the box) is the multiple of the magic number that's not bigger than the original IP address's value in the interesting octet. In this case, 200 is the multiple of 8 that's closest to 200 but not bigger than 200. So, the third octet of the subnet number is 200.

The second tricky part of this process calculates the subnet broadcast address. The full process is described in Chapter 6, but the tricky part is, as usual, in the "interesting" octet. Take the subnet number's value in the interesting octet, add the magic number, and subtract 1. That's the broadcast address's value in the interesting octet. In this case, 200 + 8 – 1 = 207.

Question 13: Answer

Table C-38 *Question 13: Size of Network, Subnet, Host, Number of Subnets, Number of Hosts*

Step	Example	Rules to Remember
Address	172.31.50.50	N/A
Mask	255.255.252.0	N/A
Number of network bits	16	Always defined by Class A, B, C
Number of host bits	10	Always defined as number of binary 0s in mask
Number of subnet bits	6	32 – (network size + host size)
Number of subnets	$2^6 - 2 = 62$	$2^{number-of-subnet-bits} - 2$
Number of hosts	$2^{10} - 2 = 1022$	$2^{number-of-host-bits} - 2$

Table C-39 shows the binary calculations of the subnet number and broadcast address. To calculate the subnet number, perform a Boolean AND of the address with the subnet mask. To find the broadcast address for this subnet, change all the host bits to binary 1s in the subnet number. The host bits are in **bold** print in the table.

Table C-39 *Question 13: Binary Calculation of Subnet and Broadcast Addresses*

Address	172.31.50.50	1010 1100 0001 1111 0011 00**10 0011 0010**
Mask	255.255.252.0	1111 1111 1111 1111 1111 11**00 0000 0000**
AND result (subnet number)	172.31.48.0	1010 1100 0001 1111 0011 00**00 0000 0000**
Change host to 1s (broadcast address)	172.31.51.255	1010 1100 0001 1111 0011 00**11 1111 1111**

Just add 1 to the subnet number to get the first valid IP address; just subtract 1 from the broadcast address to get the last valid IP address. In this case:

172.31.48.1 through 172.31.51.254

Table C-40 lists the way to get the same answers using the subnet chart and magic math described in Chapter 6. Remember, subtracting the interesting (non-0 or 255) mask value from 256 yields the magic number. The magic number multiple that's closest to but not larger than the IP address's interesting octet value is the subnet value in that octet.

Table C-40 *Question 13: Subnet, Broadcast, First and Last Addresses Calculated Using Subnet Chart*

	Octet 1	Octet 2	Octet 3	Octet 4
Address	172	31	50	50
Mask	255	255	252	0
Subnet number	172	31	48	0
First valid address	172	31	48	1
Broadcast	172	31	51	255
Last valid address	172	31	51	254

This subnetting scheme uses a hard mask because one of the octets is not a 0 or a 255. The third octet is "interesting" in this case. The key part of the trick to get the right answers is to calculate the magic number, which is 256 – 252 = 4 in this case (256 – mask's value in the interesting octet). The subnet number's value in the interesting octet (inside the box) is the multiple of the magic number that's not bigger than the original IP address's value in the interesting octet. In this case, 48 is the multiple of 4 that's closest to 50 but not bigger than 50. So, the third octet of the subnet number is 48.

The second tricky part of this process calculates the subnet broadcast address. The full process is described in Chapter 6, but the tricky part is, as usual, in the "interesting" octet. Take the subnet number's value in the interesting octet, add the magic number, and subtract 1. That's the broadcast address's value in the interesting octet. In this case, 48 + 4 – 1 = 51.

Question 14: Answer

Table C-41 *Question 14: Size of Network, Subnet, Host, Number of Subnets, Number of Hosts*

Step	Example	Rules to Remember
Address	172.31.50.50	N/A
Mask	255.255.254.0	N/A
Number of network bits	16	Always defined by Class A, B, C
Number of host bits	9	Always defined as number of binary 0s in mask
Number of subnet bits	7	32 – (network size + host size)
Number of subnets	$2^7 - 2 = 126$	$2^{\text{number-of-subnet-bits}} - 2$
Number of hosts	$2^9 - 2 = 510$	$2^{\text{number-of-host-bits}} - 2$

Table C-42 shows the binary calculations of the subnet number and broadcast address. To calculate the subnet number, perform a Boolean AND of the address with the subnet mask. To find the broadcast address for this subnet, change all the host bits to binary 1s in the subnet number. The host bits are in **bold** print in the table.

Table C-42 *Question 14: Binary Calculation of Subnet and Broadcast Addresses*

Address	172.31.50.50	1010 1100 0001 1111 0011 001**0 0011 0010**
Mask	255.255.254.0	1111 1111 1111 1111 1111 111**0 0000 0000**
AND result (subnet number)	172.31.50.0	1010 1100 0001 1111 0011 001**0 0000 0000**
Change host to 1s (broadcast address)	172.31.51.255	1010 1100 0001 1111 0011 001**1 1111 1111**

Just add 1 to the subnet number to get the first valid IP address; just subtract 1 from the broadcast address to get the last valid IP address. In this case:

172.31.50.1 through 172.31.51.254

Table C-43 lists the way to get the same answers using the subnet chart and magic math described in Chapter 6. Remember, subtracting the interesting (non-0 or 255) mask value from 256 yields the magic number. The magic number multiple that's closest to but not larger than the IP address's interesting octet value is the subnet value in that octet.

Table C-43 *Question 14: Subnet, Broadcast, First and Last Addresses Calculated Using Subnet Chart*

	Octet 1	**Octet 2**	**Octet 3**	**Octet 4**
Address	172	31	50	50
Mask	255	255	254	0
Subnet number	172	31	50	0
First valid address	172	31	50	1
Broadcast	172	31	51	255
Last valid address	172	31	51	254

This subnetting scheme uses a hard mask because one of the octets is not a 0 or a 255. The third octet is "interesting" in this case. The key part of the trick to get the right answers is to calculate the magic number, which is 256 – 254 = 2 in this case (256 – mask's value in the interesting octet). The subnet number's value in the interesting octet (inside the box) is the multiple of the magic number that's not bigger than the original IP address's value in the interesting octet. In this case, 50 is the multiple of 2 that's closest to 50 but not bigger than 50. So, the third octet of the subnet number is 50.

The second tricky part of this process calculates the subnet broadcast address. The full process is described in Chapter 6, but the tricky part is, as usual, in the "interesting" octet. Take the subnet number's value in the interesting octet, add the magic number, and subtract 1. That's the broadcast address's value in the interesting octet. In this case, 50 + 2 – 1 = 51.

Question 15: Answer

Table C-44 *Question 15: Size of Network, Subnet, Host, Number of Subnets, Number of Hosts*

Step	**Example**	**Rules to Remember**
Address	172.31.140.14	N/A
Mask	255.255.255.0	N/A
Number of network bits	16	Always defined by Class A, B, C
Number of host bits	8	Always defined as number of binary 0s in mask
Number of subnet bits	8	32 – (network size + host size)
Number of subnets	$2^8 - 2 = 254$	$2^{\text{number-of-subnet-bits}} - 2$
Number of hosts	$2^8 - 2 = 254$	$2^{\text{number-of-host-bits}} - 2$

Table C-45 shows the binary calculations of the subnet number and broadcast address. To calculate the subnet number, perform a Boolean AND of the address with the subnet mask. To find the broadcast address for this subnet, change all the host bits to binary 1s in the subnet number. The host bits are in **bold** print in the table.

Table C-45 *Question 15: Binary Calculation of Subnet and Broadcast Addresses*

Address	172.31.140.14	1010 1100 0001 1111 1000 1100 **0000 1110**
Mask	255.255.255.0	1111 1111 1111 1111 1111 1111 **0000 0000**
AND result (subnet number)	172.31.140.0	1010 1100 0001 1111 1000 1100 **0000 0000**
Change host to 1s (broadcast address)	172.31.140.255	1010 1100 0001 1111 1000 1100 **1111 1111**

Just add 1 to the subnet number to get the first valid IP address; just subtract 1 from the broadcast address to get the last valid IP address. In this case:

172.31.140.1 through 172.31.140.254

Table C-46 lists the way to get the same answers using the subnet chart and magic math described in Chapter 6.

Table C-46 *Question 15: Subnet, Broadcast, First and Last Addresses Calculated Using Subnet Chart*

	Octet 1	Octet 2	Octet 3	Octet 4
Address	172	31	140	14
Mask	255	255	255	0
Subnet number	172	31	140	0
First valid address	172	31	140	1
Broadcast	172	31	140	255
Last valid address	172	31	140	254

This subnetting scheme uses an easy mask because all of the octets are a 0 or a 255. No math tricks are needed at all!

Question 16: Answer

Table C-47 *Question 16: Size of Network, Subnet, Host, Number of Subnets, Number of Hosts*

Step	Example	Rules to Remember
Address	172.31.140.14	N/A
Mask	255.255.255.128	N/A
Number of network bits	16	Always defined by Class A, B, C
Number of host bits	7	Always defined as number of binary 0s in mask
Number of subnet bits	9	32 – (network size + host size)
Number of subnets	$2^9 - 2 = 510$	$2^{\text{number-of-subnet-bits}} - 2$
Number of hosts	$2^7 - 2 = 126$	$2^{\text{number-of-host-bits}} - 2$

Table C-48 shows the binary calculations of the subnet number and broadcast address. To calculate the subnet number, perform a Boolean AND of the address with the subnet mask. To find the broadcast address for this subnet, change all the host bits to binary 1s in the subnet number. The host bits are in **bold** print in the table.

Table C-48 *Question 16: Binary Calculation of Subnet and Broadcast Addresses*

Address	172.31.140.14	1010 1100 0001 1111 1000 1100 0**000 1110**
Mask	255.255.255.128	1111 1111 1111 1111 1111 1111 1**000 0000**
AND result (subnet number)	172.31.140.0	1010 1100 0001 1111 1000 1100 0**000 0000**
Change host to 1s (broadcast address)	172.31.140.127	1010 1100 0001 1111 1000 1100 0**111 1111**

Just add 1 to the subnet number to get the first valid IP address; just subtract 1 from the broadcast address to get the last valid IP address. In this case:

172.31.140.1 through 172.31.140.126

Table C-49 lists the way to get the same answers using the subnet chart and magic math described in Chapter 6. Remember, subtracting the interesting (non-0 or 255) mask value from 256 yields the magic number. The magic number multiple that's closest to but not larger than the IP address's interesting octet value is the subnet value in that octet.

Table C-49 *Question 16: Subnet, Broadcast, First and Last Addresses Calculated Using Subnet Chart*

	Octet 1	Octet 2	Octet 3	Octet 4
Address	172	31	140	14
Mask	255	255	255	128
Subnet number	172	31	140	0
First valid address	172	31	140	1
Broadcast	172	31	140	127
Last valid address	172	31	140	126

This subnetting scheme uses a hard mask because one of the octets is not a 0 or a 255. The fourth octet is "interesting" in this case. The key part of the trick to get the right answers is to calculate the magic number, which is 256 – 128 = 128 in this case (256 – mask's value in the interesting octet). The subnet number's value in the interesting octet (inside the box) is the multiple of the magic number that's not bigger than the original IP address's value in the interesting octet. In this case, 0 is the multiple of 128 that's closest to 14 but not bigger than 14. So, the fourth octet of the subnet number is 0.

The second tricky part of this process calculates the subnet broadcast address. The full process is described in Chapter 6, but the tricky part is, as usual, in the "interesting" octet. Take the subnet number's value in the interesting octet, add the magic number, and subtract 1. That's the broadcast address's value in the interesting octet. In this case, 0 + 128 – 1 = 127.

Question 17: Answer

Table C-50 *Question 17: Size of Network, Subnet, Host, Number of Subnets, Number of Hosts*

Step	Example	Rules to Remember
Address	192.168.15.150	N/A
Mask	255.255.255.192	N/A
Number of network bits	24	Always defined by Class A, B, C
Number of host bits	6	Always defined as number of binary 0s in mask
Number of subnet bits	2	32 – (network size + host size)
Number of subnets	$2^2 - 2 = 2$	$2^{\text{number-of-subnet-bits}} - 2$
Number of hosts	$2^6 - 2 = 62$	$2^{\text{number-of-host-bits}} - 2$

Table C-51 shows the binary calculations of the subnet number and broadcast address. To calculate the subnet number, perform a Boolean AND of the address with the subnet mask. To find the broadcast address for this subnet, change all the host bits to binary 1s in the subnet number. The host bits are in **bold** print in the table.

Table C-51 *Question 17: Binary Calculation of Subnet and Broadcast Addresses*

Address	192.168.15.150	1100 0000 1010 1000 0000 1111 10**01 0110**
Mask	255.255.255.192	1111 1111 1111 1111 1111 1111 11**00 0000**
AND result (subnet number)	192.168.15.128	1100 0000 1010 1000 0000 1111 10**00 0000**
Change host to 1s (broadcast address)	192.168.15.191	1100 0000 1010 1000 0000 1111 10**11 1111**

Just add 1 to the subnet number to get the first valid IP address; just subtract 1 from the broadcast address to get the last valid IP address. In this case:

192.168.15.129 through 192.168.15.190

Table C-52 lists the way to get the same answers using the subnet chart and magic math described in Chapter 6. Remember, subtracting the interesting (non-0 or 255) mask value from 256 yields the magic number. The magic number multiple that's closest to but not larger than the IP address's interesting octet value is the subnet value in that octet.

Table C-52 *Question 17: Subnet, Broadcast, First and Last Addresses Calculated Using Subnet Chart*

	Octet 1	Octet 2	Octet 3	Octet 4
Address	192	168	15	150
Mask	255	255	255	192
Subnet number	192	168	15	128
First valid address	192	168	15	129
Broadcast	192	168	15	191
Last valid address	192	168	15	190

This subnetting scheme uses a hard mask because one of the octets is not a 0 or a 255. The fourth octet is "interesting" in this case. The key part of the trick to get the right answers is to calculate the magic number, which is 256 – 192 = 64 in this case (256 – mask's value in the interesting octet). The subnet number's value in the interesting octet (inside the box) is the multiple of the magic number that's not bigger than the original IP address's value in the interesting octet. In this case, 128 is the multiple of 64 that's closest to 150 but not bigger than 150. So, the fourth octet of the subnet number is 128.

The second tricky part of this process calculates the subnet broadcast address. The full process is described in Chapter 6, but the tricky part is, as usual, in the "interesting" octet. Take the subnet number's value in the interesting octet, add the magic number, and subtract 1. That's the broadcast address's value in the interesting octet. In this case, 128 + 64 – 1 = 191.

Question 18: Answer

Table C-53 *Question 18: Size of Network, Subnet, Host, Number of Subnets, Number of Hosts*

Step	Example	Rules to Remember
Address	192.168.15.150	N/A
Mask	255.255.255.224	N/A
Number of network bits	24	Always defined by Class A, B, C
Number of host bits	5	Always defined as number of binary 0s in mask
Number of subnet bits	3	32 – (network size + host size)
Number of subnets	$2^3 - 2 = 6$	$2^{\text{number-of-subnet-bits}} - 2$
Number of hosts	$2^5 - 2 = 30$	$2^{\text{number-of-host-bits}} - 2$

Table C-54 shows the binary calculations of the subnet number and broadcast address. To calculate the subnet number, perform a Boolean AND of the address with the subnet mask. To find the broadcast address for this subnet, change all the host bits to binary 1s in the subnet number. The host bits are in **bold** print in the table.

Table C-54 *Question 18: Binary Calculation of Subnet and Broadcast Addresses*

Address	192.168.15.150	1100 0000 1010 1000 0000 1111 100**1 0110**
Mask	255.255.255.224	1111 1111 1111 1111 1111 1111 111**0 0000**
AND result (subnet number)	192.168.15.128	1100 0000 1010 1000 0000 1111 100**0 0000**
Change host to 1s (broadcast address)	192.168.15.159	1100 0000 1010 1000 0000 1111 100**1 1111**

Just add 1 to the subnet number to get the first valid IP address; just subtract 1 from the broadcast address to get the last valid IP address. In this case:

192.168.15.129 through 192.168.15.158

Table C-55 lists the way to get the same answers using the subnet chart and magic math described in Chapter 6. Remember, subtracting the interesting (non-0 or 255) mask value from 256 yields the magic number. The magic number multiple that's closest to but not larger than the IP address's interesting octet value is the subnet value in that octet.

Table C-55 *Question 18: Subnet, Broadcast, First and Last Addresses Calculated Using Subnet Chart*

	Octet 1	Octet 2	Octet 3	Octet 4
Address	192	168	15	150
Mask	255	255	255	224
Subnet number	192	168	15	128
First valid address	192	168	15	129
Broadcast	192	168	15	159
Last valid address	192	168	15	158

This subnetting scheme uses a hard mask because one of the octets is not a 0 or a 255. The fourth octet is "interesting" in this case. The key part of the trick to get the right answers is to calculate the magic number, which is 256 – 224 = 32 in this case (256 – mask's value in the interesting octet). The subnet number's value in the interesting octet (inside the box) is the multiple of the magic number that's not bigger than the original IP address's value in the interesting octet. In this case, 128 is the multiple of 32 that's closest to 150 but not bigger than 150. So, the fourth octet of the subnet number is 128.

The second tricky part of this process calculates the subnet broadcast address. The full process is described in Chapter 6, but the tricky part is, as usual, in the "interesting" octet. Take the subnet number's value in the interesting octet, add the magic number, and subtract 1. That's the broadcast address's value in the interesting octet. In this case, 128 + 32 – 1 = 159.

Question 19: Answer

Table C-56 *Question 19: Size of Network, Subnet, Host, Number of Subnets, Number of Hosts*

Step	Example	Rules to Remember
Address	192.168.100.100	N/A
Mask	255.255.255.240	N/A
Number of network bits	24	Always defined by Class A, B, C
Number of host bits	4	Always defined as number of binary 0s in mask

Table C-56 *Question 19: Size of Network, Subnet, Host, Number of Subnets, Number of Hosts (Continued)*

Step	Example	Rules to Remember
Number of subnet bits	4	32 – (network size + host size)
Number of subnets	$2^4 - 2 = 14$	$2^{\text{number-of-subnet-bits}} - 2$
Number of hosts	$2^4 - 2 = 14$	$2^{\text{number-of-host-bits}} - 2$

Table C-57 shows the binary calculations of the subnet number and broadcast address. To calculate the subnet number, perform a Boolean AND of the address with the subnet mask. To find the broadcast address for this subnet, change all the host bits to binary 1s in the subnet number. The host bits are in **bold** print in the table.

Table C-57 *Question 19: Binary Calculation of Subnet and Broadcast Addresses*

Address	192.168.100.100	1100 0000 1010 1000 0110 0100 0110 **0100**
Mask	255.255.255.240	1111 1111 1111 1111 1111 1111 1111 **0000**
AND result (subnet number)	192.168.100.96	1100 0000 1010 1000 0110 0100 0110 **0000**
Change host to 1s (broadcast address)	192.168.100.111	1100 0000 1010 1000 0110 0100 0110 **1111**

Just add 1 to the subnet number to get the first valid IP address; just subtract 1 from the broadcast address to get the last valid IP address. In this case:

192.168.100.97 through 192.168.100.110

Table C-58 lists the way to get the same answers using the subnet chart and magic math described in Chapter 6. Remember, subtracting the interesting (non-0 or 255) mask value from 256 yields the magic number. The magic number multiple that's closest to but not larger than the IP address's interesting octet value is the subnet value in that octet.

Table C-58 *Question 19: Subnet, Broadcast, First and Last Addresses Calculated Using Subnet Chart*

	Octet 1	Octet 2	Octet 3	Octet 4
Address	192	168	100	100
Mask	255	255	255	240
Subnet number	192	168	100	96
First valid address	192	168	100	97
Broadcast	192	168	100	111
Last valid address	192	168	100	110

This subnetting scheme uses a hard mask because one of the octets is not a 0 or a 255. The fourth octet is "interesting" in this case. The key part of the trick to get the right answers is to calculate the magic number, which is 256 – 240 = 16 in this case (256 – mask's value in the interesting octet). The subnet number's value in the interesting octet (inside the box) is the multiple of the magic number that's not bigger than the original IP address's value in the interesting octet. In this case, 96 is the multiple of 16 that's closest to 100 but not bigger than 100. So, the fourth octet of the subnet number is 96.

The second tricky part of this process calculates the subnet broadcast address. The full process is described in Chapter 6, but the tricky part is, as usual, in the "interesting" octet. Take the subnet number's value in the interesting octet, add the magic number, and subtract 1. That's the broadcast address's value in the interesting octet. In this case, 96 + 16 – 1 = 111.

Question 20: Answer

Table C-59 *Question 20: Size of Network, Subnet, Host, Number of Subnets, Number of Hosts*

Step	Example	Rules to Remember
Address	192.168.100.100	N/A
Mask	255.255.255.248	N/A
Number of network bits	24	Always defined by Class A, B, C
Number of host bits	3	Always defined as number of binary 0s in mask
Number of subnet bits	5	32 – (network size + host size)
Number of subnets	$2^5 - 2 = 30$	$2^{\text{number-of-subnet-bits}} - 2$
Number of hosts	$2^3 - 2 = 6$	$2^{\text{number-of-host-bits}} - 2$

Table C-60 shows the binary calculations of the subnet number and broadcast address. To calculate the subnet number, perform a Boolean AND of the address with the subnet mask. To find the broadcast address for this subnet, change all the host bits to binary 1s in the subnet number. The host bits are in **bold** print in the table.

Table C-60 *Question 20: Binary Calculation of Subnet and Broadcast Addresses*

Address	192.168.100.100	1100 0000 1010 1000 0110 0100 0110 0**100**
Mask	255.255.255.248	1111 1111 1111 1111 1111 1111 1111 1**000**
AND result (subnet number)	192.168.100.96	1100 0000 1010 1000 0110 0100 0110 0**000**
Change host to 1s (broadcast address)	192.168.100.103	1100 0000 1010 1000 0110 0100 0110 0**111**

Just add 1 to the subnet number to get the first valid IP address; just subtract 1 from the broadcast address to get the last valid IP address. In this case:

192.168.100.97 through 192.168.100.102

Table C-61 lists the way to get the same answers using the subnet chart and magic math described in Chapter 6. Remember, subtracting the interesting (non-0 or 255) mask value from 256 yields the magic number. The magic number multiple that's closest to but not larger than the IP address's interesting octet value is the subnet value in that octet.

Table C-61 *Question 20: Subnet, Broadcast, First and Last Addresses Calculated Using Subnet Chart*

	Octet 1	Octet 2	Octet 3	Octet 4
Address	192	168	100	100
Mask	255	255	255	248
Subnet number	192	168	100	96
First valid address	192	168	100	97
Broadcast	192	168	100	103
Last valid address	192	168	100	102

This subnetting scheme uses a hard mask because one of the octets is not a 0 or a 255. The fourth octet is "interesting" in this case. The key part of the trick to get the right answers is to calculate the magic number, which is 256 – 248 = 8 in this case (256 – mask's value in the interesting octet). The subnet number's value in the interesting octet (inside the box) is the multiple of the magic number that's not bigger than the original IP address's value in the interesting octet. In this case, 96 is the multiple of 8 that's closest to 100 but not bigger than 100. So, the fourth octet of the subnet number is 96.

The second tricky part of this process calculates the subnet broadcast address. The full process is described in Chapter 6, but the tricky part is, as usual, in the "interesting" octet. Take the subnet number's value in the interesting octet, add the magic number, and subtract 1. That's the broadcast address's value in the interesting octet. In this case, 96 + 8 – 1 = 103.

Question 21: Answer

Table C-62 *Question 21: Size of Network, Subnet, Host, Number of Subnets, Number of Hosts*

Step	Example	Rules to Remember
Address	192.168.15.230	N/A
Mask	255.255.255.252	N/A
Number of network bits	24	Always defined by Class A, B, C
Number of host bits	2	Always defined as number of binary 0s in mask
Number of subnet bits	6	32 – (network size + host size)
Number of subnets	$2^6 - 2 = 62$	$2^{\text{number-of-subnet-bits}} - 2$
Number of hosts	$2^2 - 2 = 2$	$2^{\text{number-of-host-bits}} - 2$

Table C-63 shows the binary calculations of the subnet number and broadcast address. To calculate the subnet number, perform a Boolean AND of the address with the subnet mask. To find the broadcast address for this subnet, change all the host bits to binary 1s in the subnet number. The host bits are in **bold** print in the table.

Table C-63 *Question 21: Binary Calculation of Subnet and Broadcast Addresses*

Address	192.168.15.230	1100 0000 1010 1000 0000 1111 1110 01**10**
Mask	255.255.255.252	1111 1111 1111 1111 1111 1111 1111 11**00**
AND result (subnet number)	192.168.15.228	1100 0000 1010 1000 0000 1111 1110 01**00**
Change host to 1s (broadcast address)	192.168.15.231	1100 0000 1010 1000 0000 1111 1110 01**11**

Just add 1 to the subnet number to get the first valid IP address; just subtract 1 from the broadcast address to get the last valid IP address. In this case:

192.168.15.229 through 192.168.15.230

Table C-64 lists the way to get the same answers using the subnet chart and magic math described in Chapter 6. Remember, subtracting the interesting (non-0 or 255) mask value from 256 yields the magic number. The magic number multiple that's closest to but not larger than the IP address's interesting octet value is the subnet value in that octet.

Table C-64 *Question 21: Subnet, Broadcast, First and Last Addresses Calculated Using Subnet Chart*

	Octet 1	Octet 2	Octet 3	Octet 4
Address	192	168	15	230
Mask	255	255	255	252
Subnet number	192	168	15	228
First valid address	192	168	15	229
Broadcast	192	168	15	231
Last valid address	192	168	15	230

This subnetting scheme uses a hard mask because one of the octets is not a 0 or a 255. The fourth octet is "interesting" in this case. The key part of the trick to get the right answers is to calculate the magic number, which is 256 – 252 = 4 in this case (256 – mask's value in the interesting octet). The subnet number's value in the interesting octet (inside the box) is the multiple of the magic number that's not bigger than the original IP address's value in the interesting octet. In this case, 228 is the multiple of 4 that's closest to 230 but not bigger than 230. So, the fourth octet of the subnet number is 228.

The second tricky part of this process calculates the subnet broadcast address. The full process is described in Chapter 6, but the tricky part is, as usual, in the "interesting" octet. Take the subnet number's value in the interesting octet, add the magic number, and subtract 1. That's the broadcast address's value in the interesting octet. In this case, 228 + 4 – 1 = 231.

Question 22: Answer

Table C-65 *Question 22: Size of Network, Subnet, Host, Number of Subnets, Number of Hosts*

Step	Example	Rules to Remember
Address	10.1.1.1	N/A
Mask	255.248.0.0	N/A
Number of network bits	8	Always defined by Class A, B, C
Number of host bits	19	Always defined as number of binary 0s in mask

continues

Table C-65 *Question 22: Size of Network, Subnet, Host, Number of Subnets, Number of Hosts (Continued)*

Step	Example	Rules to Remember
Number of subnet bits	5	32 – (network size + host size)
Number of subnets	$2^5 - 2 = 30$	$2^{\text{number-of-subnet-bits}} - 2$
Number of hosts	$2^{19} - 2 = 524{,}286$	$2^{\text{number-of-host-bits}} - 2$

Table C-66 shows the binary calculations of the subnet number and broadcast address. To calculate the subnet number, perform a Boolean AND of the address with the subnet mask. To find the broadcast address for this subnet, change all the host bits to binary 1s in the subnet number. The host bits are in **bold** print in the table.

Table C-66 *Question 22: Binary Calculation of Subnet and Broadcast Addresses*

Address	10.1.1.1	0000 1010 0000 0**001 0000 0001 0000 0001**
Mask	255.248.0.0	1111 1111 1111 1**000 0000 0000 0000 0000**
AND result (subnet number)	10.0.0.0	0000 1010 0000 0**000 0000 0000 0000 0000**
Change host to 1s (broadcast address)	10.7.255.255	0000 1010 0000 0**111 1111 1111 1111 1111**

Just add 1 to the subnet number to get the first valid IP address; just subtract 1 from the broadcast address to get the last valid IP address. In this case:

10.0.0.1 through 10.7.255.254

Take a closer look at the subnet part of the subnet address, as is shown in bold here: 0000 1010 **0000 0**000 0000 0000 0000 0000. The subnet part of the address is all binary 0s, making this subnet a zero subnet. This subnet should be avoided unless you are running out of available subnets to use.

Table C-67 lists the way to get the same answers using the subnet chart and magic math described in Chapter 6. Remember, subtracting the interesting (non-0 or 255) mask value from 256 yields the magic number. The magic number multiple that's closest to but not larger than the IP address's interesting octet value is the subnet value in that octet.

Table C-67 *Question 22: Subnet, Broadcast, First and Last Addresses Calculated Using Subnet Chart*

	Octet 1	Octet 2	Octet 3	Octet 4
Address	10	1	1	1
Mask	255	248	0	0
Subnet number	10	0	0	0
First valid address	10	0	0	1
Broadcast	10	7	255	255
Last valid address	10	7	255	254

This subnetting scheme uses a hard mask because one of the octets is not a 0 or a 255. The second octet is "interesting" in this case. The key part of the trick to get the right answers is to calculate the magic number, which is 256 – 248 = 8 in this case (256 – mask's value in the interesting octet). The subnet number's value in the interesting octet (inside the box) is the multiple of the magic number that's not bigger than the original IP address's value in the interesting octet. In this case, 0 is the multiple of 8 that's closest to 1 but not bigger than 1. So, the second octet of the subnet number is 0.

The second tricky part of this process calculates the subnet broadcast address. The full process is described in Chapter 6, but the tricky part is, as usual, in the "interesting" octet. Take the subnet number's value in the interesting octet, add the magic number, and subtract 1. That's the broadcast address's value in the interesting octet. In this case, 0 + 8 – 1 = 7.

Question 23: Answer

Table C-68 *Question 23: Size of Network, Subnet, Host, Number of Subnets, Number of Hosts*

Step	Example	Rules to Remember
Address	172.16.1.200	N/A
Mask	255.255.240.0	N/A
Number of network bits	16	Always defined by Class A, B, C
Number of host bits	12	Always defined as number of binary 0s in mask

continues

Table C-68 *Question 23: Size of Network, Subnet, Host, Number of Subnets, Number of Hosts (Continued)*

Step	Example	Rules to Remember
Number of subnet bits	4	32 – (network size + host size)
Number of subnets	$2^4 - 2 = 14$	$2^{\text{number-of-subnet-bits}} - 2$
Number of hosts	$2^{12} - 2 = 4094$	$2^{\text{number-of-host-bits}} - 2$

Table C-69 shows the binary calculations of the subnet number and broadcast address. To calculate the subnet number, perform a Boolean AND of the address with the subnet mask. To find the broadcast address for this subnet, change all the host bits to binary 1s in the subnet number. The host bits are in **bold** print in the table.

Table C-69 *Question 23: Binary Calculation of Subnet and Broadcast Addresses*

Address	172.16.1.200	1010 1100 0001 0000 0000 **0001 1100 1000**
Mask	255.255.240.0	1111 1111 1111 1111 1111 **0000 0000 0000**
AND result (subnet number)	172.16.0.0	1010 1100 0001 0000 0000 **0000 0000 0000**
Change host to 1s (broadcast address)	172.16.15.255	1010 1100 0001 0000 0000 **1111 1111 1111**

Just add 1 to the subnet number to get the first valid IP address; just subtract 1 from the broadcast address to get the last valid IP address. In this case:

172.16.0.1 through 172.16.15.254

Take a closer look at the subnet part of the subnet address, as shown in bold here: 1010 1100 0001 0000 **0000** 0000 0000 0000. The subnet part of the address is all binary 0s, making this subnet a zero subnet. This subnet should be avoided unless you are running out of available subnets to use.

Table C-70 lists the way to get the same answers using the subnet chart and magic math described in Chapter 6. Remember, subtracting the interesting (non-0 or 255) mask value from 256 yields the magic number. The magic number multiple that's closest to but not larger than the IP address's interesting octet value is the subnet value in that octet.

Table C-70 *Question 23: Subnet, Broadcast, First and Last Addresses Calculated Using Subnet Chart*

	Octet 1	Octet 2	Octet 3	Octet 4
Address	172	16	1	200
Mask	255	255	240	0
Subnet number	172	16	0	0
First valid address	172	16	0	1
Broadcast	172	16	15	255
Last valid address	172	16	15	254

This subnetting scheme uses a hard mask because one of the octets is not a 0 or a 255. The third octet is "interesting" in this case. The key part of the trick to get the right answers is to calculate the magic number, which is 256 – 240 = 16 in this case (256 – mask's value in the interesting octet). The subnet number's value in the interesting octet (inside the box) is the multiple of the magic number that's not bigger than the original IP address's value in the interesting octet. In this case, 0 is the multiple of 16 that's closest to 1 but not bigger than 1. So, the third octet of the subnet number is 0.

The second tricky part of this process calculates the subnet broadcast address. The full process is described in Chapter 6, but the tricky part is, as usual, in the "interesting" octet. Take the subnet number's value in the interesting octet, add the magic number, and subtract 1. That's the broadcast address's value in the interesting octet. In this case, 0 + 16 – 1 = 15.

Question 24: Answer

Table C-71 *Question 24: Size of Network, Subnet, Host, Number of Subnets, Number of Hosts*

Step	Example	Rules to Remember
Address	172.16.0.200	N/A
Mask	255.255.255.192	N/A
Number of network bits	16	Always defined by Class A, B, C
Number of host bits	6	Always defined as number of binary 0s in mask
Number of subnet bits	10	32 – (network size + host size)
Number of subnets	$2^{10} - 2 = 1022$	$2^{\text{number-of-subnet-bits}} - 2$
Number of hosts	$2^6 - 2 = 62$	$2^{\text{number-of-host-bits}} - 2$

Table C-72 shows the binary calculations of the subnet number and broadcast address. To calculate the subnet number, perform a Boolean AND of the address with the subnet mask. To find the broadcast address for this subnet, change all the host bits to binary 1s in the subnet number. The host bits are in **bold** print in the table.

Table C-72 *Question 24: Binary Calculation of Subnet and Broadcast Addresses*

Address	172.16.0.200	1010 1100 0001 0000 0000 0000 11**00 1000**
Mask	255.255.255.192	1111 1111 1111 1111 1111 1111 11**00 0000**
AND result (subnet number)	172.16.0.192	1010 1100 0001 0000 0000 0000 11**00 0000**
Change host to 1s (broadcast address)	172.16.0.255	1010 1100 0001 0000 0000 0000 11**11 1111**

Just add 1 to the subnet number to get the first valid IP address; just subtract 1 from the broadcast address to get the last valid IP address. In this case:

172.16.0.193 through 172.16.0.254

Table C-73 lists the way to get the same answers using the subnet chart and magic math described in Chapter 6. Remember, subtracting the interesting (non-0 or 255) mask value from 256 yields the magic number. The magic number multiple that's closest to but not larger than the IP address's interesting octet value is the subnet value in that octet.

Table C-73 *Question 24: Subnet, Broadcast, First and Last Addresses Calculated Using Subnet Chart*

	Octet 1	Octet 2	Octet 3	Octet 4
Address	172	16	0	200
Mask	255	255	255	192
Subnet number	172	16	0	192
First valid address	172	16	0	193
Broadcast	172	16	0	255
Last valid address	172	16	0	254

This subnetting scheme uses a hard mask because one of the octets is not a 0 or a 255. The fourth octet is "interesting" in this case. The key part of the trick to get the right answers is to calculate the magic number, which is 256 – 192 = 64 in this case (256 – mask's value in the interesting octet). The subnet number's value in the interesting octet (inside the box) is the multiple of the magic number that's not bigger than the original IP address's value in the interesting octet. In this case, 192 is the multiple of 64 that's closest to 200 but not bigger than 200. So, the fourth octet of the subnet number is 192.

The second tricky part of this process calculates the subnet broadcast address. The full process is described in Chapter 6, but the tricky part is, as usual, in the "interesting" octet. Take the subnet number's value in the interesting octet, add the magic number, and subtract 1. That's the broadcast address's value in the interesting octet. In this case, 192 + 64 – 1 = 255.

You can easily forget that the subnet part of this address, when using this mask, actually covers all of the third octet as well as 2 bits of the fourth octet. For instance, the valid subnet numbers in order are listed here:

172.16.0.64
172.16.0.128
172.16.0.192
172.16.1.0
172.16.1.64
172.16.1.128
172.16.1.192
172.16.2.0
172.16.2.64
172.16.2.128
172.16.2.192
172.16.3.0
172.16.3.64
172.16.3.128
172.16.3.192

And so on.

Question 25: Answer

Congratulations, you made it through all the extra subnetting practice! Here's an easy one to complete your review—one with no subnetting at all!

Table C-74 *Question 25: Size of Network, Subnet, Host, Number of Subnets, Number of Hosts*

Step	Example	Rules to Remember
Address	1.1.1.1	N/A
Mask	255.0.0.0	N/A
Number of network bits	8	Always defined by Class A, B, C
Number of host bits	24	Always defined as number of binary 0s in mask
Number of subnet bits	0	32 – (network size + host size)
Number of subnets	0	$2^{\text{number-of-subnet-bits}} - 2$
Number of hosts	$2^{24} - 2 = 16,777,214$	$2^{\text{number-of-host-bits}} - 2$

Table C-75 shows the binary calculations of the subnet number and broadcast address. To calculate the subnet number, perform a Boolean AND of the address with the subnet mask. To find the broadcast address for this subnet, change all the host bits to binary 1s in the subnet number. The host bits are in **bold** print in the table.

Table C-75 *Question 25: Binary Calculation of Subnet and Broadcast Addresses*

Address	10.1.1.1	0000 1010 **0000 0001 0000 0001 0000 0001**
Mask	255.0.0.0	1111 1111 **0000 0000 0000 0000 0000 0000**
AND result (subnet number)	10.0.0.0	0000 1010 **0000 0000 0000 0000 0000 0000**
Change host to 1s (broadcast address)	10.255.255.255	0000 1010 **1111 1111 1111 1111 1111 1111**

Just add 1 to the subnet number to get the first valid IP address; just subtract 1 from the broadcast address to get the last valid IP address. In this case:

10.0.0.1 through 10.255.255.254

Table C-76 lists the way to get the same answers using the subnet chart and magic math described in Chapter 6.

Table C-76 *Question 25: Subnet, Broadcast, First and Last Addresses Calculated Using Subnet Chart*

	Octet 1	Octet 2	Octet 3	Octet 4
Address	10	1	1	1
Mask	255	0	0	0
Network number	10	0	0	0
First valid address	10	0	0	1
Broadcast	10	255	255	255
Last valid address	10	255	255	254

INDEX

Symbols

Numerics

A

B

C

D

E

F

G

H

I

J-K-L

M

N

O

P

Q-R

S

T

U

V

W

X-Y-Z

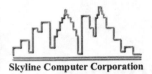

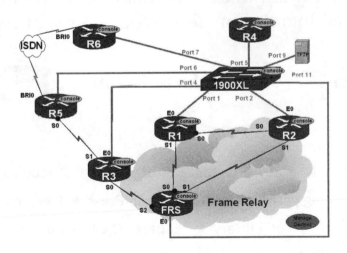

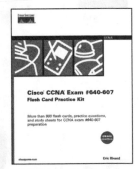